Corporate Financial Management

CORPORATE FINANCIAL MANAGEMENT

by RAYMOND P. KENT

Professor of Finance and Business Economics
University of Notre Dame

Revised Edition

1964

RICHARD D. IRWIN, INC.
HOMEWOOD, ILLINOIS

REVISED EDITION

First Printing, April, 1964

Second Printing, January, 1965

Third Printing, July, 1966

Library of Congress Catalogue Card No. 64–17244

PRINTED IN THE UNITED STATES OF AMERICA

To Claudia, Ray, Claudia Marie, and Bob

PREFACE

In revising this textbook, as in preparing the original edition, I have aimed at a combination of reasonably detailed descriptions of the principles, procedures, institutions, and instruments of the field of corporation finance with a closely integrated treatment of the techniques, formulas, and other tools and processes of problem solving and policy formulation, which is to say, decision making. Knowledge of facts and phenomena, though doubtless good for its own sake, is likely to be all the more significant and all the better appreciated if focused upon its usefulness in decision making. In acquiring this knowledge, the student should discover why there are problems that need solutions and alternative courses of action that require decisions, while advancing in his capacity to analyze the complexities of actual situations and circumstances to reach decisions of his own. On the other hand, a study of the tools and procedures of decision making, without a knowledge of the facts and phenomena about which decisions are to be made, would surely be pointless and futile.

Although it is necessarily my opinion that the sequence of topics in the textbook is a logical one for courses bearing such descriptive titles as "Corporation Finance" and "Business Finance," instructors who prefer a different order of course presentation should have no great difficulty in adapting the book to serve their requirements. Such adaptation should be especially easy for those who prefer to take up the means of financing rather early in the course and to leave asset management till later. This can be done by going directly from Chapter 6 to Chapter 12 or to Chapter 14, as one may choose. Since financial management is simultaneously asset management and liability-and-equity management, it would not seem to matter greatly which aspect of this dual focus is treated first. At any rate, the chapters on financing (Chapters 14 to 33) are quite comprehensible as a unit without an earlier investigation of asset management. Instructors will find, too, I think, that the book is adaptable for courses of either one or two semesters. It should not require an undue amount of hurrying to cover the whole book in a single semester, while a more intensive treatment of most of the topics covered will be possible in two-semester courses. In one-semester courses, some instructors may decide, of course, that some of the topics should be passed over lightly or omitted so that more time can be spent on others; and in two-semester offerings, some may decide that the textbook should be supplemented with readings, cases, or problems (in addition to those I have supplied), or some combination of these.

I must confess to a prejudice. I like to keep the word *capital* in harness. I do not think that it should be used to mean virtually everything that is entered on both sides of the balance sheet of a business enterprise, both individual items and collections of items. It surely cannot mean, all at once, cash, cash and other current assets, cash and other current assets minus current liabilities, fixed assets, all assets, the par or stated value of the owners' investment in stock, the owners' entire investment or equity, and the owners' equity plus all the liabilities. To avoid this kind of confusion, therefore, I have pretty well confined the term to the concept *working capital*, although I must admit that, in quite different senses but where the context is clear, I have some references to capital stock, capitalization (of expenditures), and recapitalization (certain reshufflings among liabilities and equity). Throughout, at any rate, I use the term *equity* for the stockholders' investment, the term *financial structure* (as in Chapters 14 and 15) for the whole array of liability and equity items often referred to elsewhere as "capital structure" and "capitalization," and the expressions *management of fixed assets* and *fixed asset budgeting* (Chapters 10 and 11 and Chapter 13 in part) for the kinds of topics that are generally treated by other writers under the head of "capital budgeting."

I am most pleased to have this opportunity to express my great appreciation to all those whose advice and criticism have served to make this book better than it otherwise would have been. As all the effort that went into the first edition continues to be reflected in this revised edition, I remain deeply indebted to all who helped me with the earlier work, especially Professor Hubert H. Frisinger of the University of Toledo, Professor LeClair H. Eells, for long a most esteemed colleague at the University of Notre Dame, Professor Stanley W. Preston of Louisiana State University, the late Professor Karl A. Boedecker of Michigan State University, Professor Sergei Dobrovolsky of Wayne State University, Professor Edward E. Edwards of Indiana University, and Professor Donald M. Halley of Tulane University. For further advice and criticism that have been most helpful to me as I planned and worked on this revised edition, I express sincere gratitude to Professor Eells, who is always most generous in giving me the rich benefits of his wide knowledge and long experience, Professor Harold W. Stevenson, of the University of Minnesota, for his detailed and incisive analysis of the original edition, Professor James O. Horrigan, another generous Notre Dame colleague, for his discerning comments and many useful suggestions, and the many professors at many colleges and universities who furnished briefer comments and suggestions based upon their experience in using the first edition. Finally, Claudia my wife has helped me in innumerable ways constantly and patiently—to her my debt is greatest of all.

RAYMOND P. KENT

Notre Dame, Indiana
October, 1963

TABLE OF CONTENTS

CHAPTER

PART III. ASSET MANAGEMENT

PART IV. BUDGETING AND CONTROL

PART V. FINANCIAL STRUCTURE

PART VI. FINANCING WITH COMMON STOCK

PART X.   FINANCING WITHOUT SECURITIES

INDEX

Part I

FINANCE AND THE
BUSINESS CORPORATION

chapter 1

THE FIELD OF CORPORATION FINANCE

INTRODUCTION

Like all other things that bear the label *finance* or *financial*, corporation finance has to do with money. As a field of study, it embraces all the theories, procedures, institutions, instruments, problems, and policies that are involved in the acquisition and use of money by business corporations.

Business corporations seek to acquire many kinds of assets, and the money holdings of the typical corporation at most times represent only a minor fraction of its total assets; nevertheless, the quest for land, buildings, machinery, equipment, inventories, and other kinds of assets usually starts out as a quest for money. Because money is the generally accepted medium of exchange, it is the one kind of asset that is readily convertible into all other kinds. Thus business corporations want to acquire money so that it can be used to buy productive facilities.

Business Corporations

Business corporations, with whose financial activities the study of corporation finance is concerned, constitute just one of several classes of corporations that operate in the United States—a very large class, but far from being all-inclusive. Such a corporation is a distinct entity or personality created by the federal or a state government as a means by which people can pool their resources to carry on some kind of business activity for the purpose of deriving profits in which they alone have the right to share.

It is the profit motive of the business corporation—or, perhaps one should say more accurately, the profit motive of its stockholders—that distinguishes it from other classes of corporations; and it is its status as a distinct entity or personality that distinguishes it from other forms of business enterprise.

Other Classes of Corporations

Stockholders make contributions to the assets of business corporations in the expectation of receiving dividends in proportion to the respective amounts of their contributions; and, as indicated, they do not expect any-

3

body who is not a stockholder to share in the dividends, no matter how worthy or needy he may be. Other kinds of corporations are operated in the expectation or hope that their income will exceed their expenses, but without expectation that any excess of income will be shared as dividends by any class or group, regardless of its responsibility for success or failure. Thus, *public corporations,* including chiefly incorporated city governments and school districts, will simply use excess revenues of a given year to pay off accumulated debts or to carry on their regular operations in the following year. One does not expect the excess to be distributed as dividends to the citizens who can be regarded as the stockholders or members of these municipal corporations.

A state government, deriving profits from the operations of an incorporated system of liquor stores in which it has sole ownership, or a city government, obtaining profits as owner of a separately incorporated waterworks or bus line—such enterprises being classified as *public proprietary corporations*—are expected to devote this income to police and fire protection, education, highway building and maintenance, and other public functions, or perhaps to the expansion of the proprietary enterprises themselves, but not, in any case, to pay pro rata cash dividends to the citizens of the state or the city.

Likewise, corporations organized for religious, educational, charitable, and scientific purposes are expected to devote directly to these purposes any income they currently receive in excess of current expenditures. The Red Cross does not distribute dividends to its members, that is, the people who make contributions to it, even though, in some years, it may have more revenue than it expends upon its great work of philanthropy. Corporations having objectives of the kinds just mentioned are classified as *private nonprofit corporations;* they are described as "private" to distinguish them from public (governmental) entities and enterprises, and as "nonprofit" because no net income or profit is payable to their members regardless of the size of the excess of current income over current expenditures.

Enterprises described as *cooperative corporations* have primary objectives such as helping their members to cut production or distribution costs by means of mass buying and selling or the joint use of certain kinds of facilities. Though such corporations may pay moderate dividends on the basis of stockholdings, most of their distributions of "profits" to members are generally made proportional to the total value of goods each member has brought from them, the quantity of his output he has sold through them, or the extent to which he has used their facilities. Accordingly, the distributions are chiefly rebates upon fees and charges paid by members, rather than shares in net income.

In our analysis of the materials of corporation finance, therefore, we will ignore the financial activities of public corporations, public proprietary corporations, private nonprofit corporations, and cooperative corporations. Some of these—particularly the public proprietary corporations and the cooperatives—may be business enterprises in every aspect but profit motive, and the others may be strongly advised to employ "sound business methods" in managing their affairs; nevertheless, their policies and procedures in matters of finance tend to be quite different from those of business corporations.

Special Position of Financial Institutions

In the study of corporation finance, it is also customary to ignore the activities of commercial banks, savings banks, and other financial institutions insofar as these activities have to do with their own procedures in acquiring money. Though most financial institutions are incorporated and have as their primary objective the earning of profits for the benefit of their stockholders, their distinctive arrangements for acquiring money give them a character decidedly different from that of manufacturing, mercantile, and other such subclasses of business corporations. The fact that our Federal Reserve and commercial banks have the capacity *to create money* puts them in a position quite unlike that of other business corporations. Likewise, the receiving of deposits makes the money-acquiring processes of some other classes of financial institutions far different from those of nonfinancial business corporations.

But the use to which money is put by financial institutions is a matter of very great interest in the study of corporation finance, for the reason that these institutions are the most important suppliers of money to non-financial business corporations. Hence we will give close attention to the activities of financial institutions, not primarily from the standpoint of how they run their affairs—this constituting much of the material of the separate field of study called *money and banking*—but with emphasis upon their service to all other kinds of business corporations in providing them with money in a wide variety of circumstances and on the basis of terms and conditions of great diversity.

Operating Areas of Business Corporations

The exclusion from our study of the financial activities of public, private nonprofit, and cooperative corporations, as well as the money-acquiring procedures of financial institutions, should not lead one to the conclusion that the field of corporation finance is a decidedly limited one. Quite the contrary. Materials of almost endless variety as they concern tens of thousands of operating corporations remain available for study, so that the student is faced with the task, not of seeking topics worthy of analysis, but of sifting through the abundant materials to discover those that are truly important.

We find, indeed, that corporation finance is concerned with the finance functions of almost 790,000 business corporations operating in all areas of manufacturing, mining and quarrying, and contract construction; providing transportation, communication, and other public utility services, including railroads, airlines, truck and bus lines, telephone companies, television and radio broadcasting companies, and electric power and gas companies; engaging in wholesale and retail trade, including incorporated food stores, department stores, restaurants, automobile agencies, and gasoline filling stations; and providing many kinds of professional and personal services, including incorporated engineering firms, employment agencies, hotels, motels, theaters, barber shops and beauty parlors, and laundries and dry-cleaning establishments. A breakdown of the number of corporations functioning in these areas as indicated by federal income tax returns filed for fiscal years ending between July 1, 1960, and June 30, 1961, is presented in Table 1–1.

TABLE 1–1
Number and Industrial Classification of Business Corporations, 1960–61[a]

Industrial Classification	Number
Agriculture, forestry, and fisheries	17,139
Mining and quarrying	13,017
Construction	72,332
Manufacturing	165,863
Public utilities	43,852
Trade	355,623
Services	121,024
Total	788,850

[a] Based on federal income tax returns filed by "active" corporations for fiscal years ending between July 1, 1960, and June 30, 1961. There were also 334,388 returns filed for this period by corporations engaged in finance, insurance, and real estate, and 17,337 returns of corporations the nature of whose business was not allocable. In addition, returns filed by "inactive" corporations—defined as those reporting no item of income or deduction—numbered 47,068.

Source: U.S. Treasury Department, Internal Revenue Service, *Statistics of Income, 1960–61—Preliminary: Corporation Income Tax Returns* (Washington, D.C.: U.S. Government Printing Office, 1962), pp. 1, 5.

Other Forms of Business Enterprise

The status of business corporations as distinct entities or personalities distinguishes them from other forms of business enterprise. As an entity or personality, a business corporation is a being quite separate from the persons who organize it, its stockholders, and its managers. If three men decide to establish a business enterprise and have it incorporated, a fourth "entity" or "person" comes into existence the moment the state issues a charter to them.[1] As a person created by the action of the state govern-

---

[1] The organizers of a corporation (or their attorneys) draw up articles of incorporation setting out details as to its structure and purposes. These are submitted to a designated state official, usually the secretary of state, who, if he finds them in proper order, authorizes the carrying on of business according to the terms of the articles *and* the state's corporation laws. This authorization may be said to be the corporation's charter. These matters are taken up in detail in Chapter 3. It should be mentioned that the federal government charters but few business corporations other than financial institutions such as national banks, federal savings and loan associations, and federal credit unions.

ment, the new corporation has power to buy and sell goods, to own land, buildings, machinery, and other equipment, to hire employees, to bring lawsuits, and so on, all in its own name as if it were itself a human being.

In contrast to this, a proprietorship is a business carried on by a single individual in his own name. A proprietor may give his enterprise a resounding title such as the "Imperial Manufacturing Company," but this action does not endow the enterprise with existence or being apart from his own. Similarly, three men who establish a general partnership are not confronted by a fourth being coming into existence by action of the state; as individual human beings, and in their own names, the partners buy and sell goods, hold land, buildings, and other property, hire labor, and engage in other kinds of activities. Other less common forms of business enterprise are also generally lacking in status as legal entities or personalities. Among these are business trusts, joint-stock companies, limited partnerships, mining partnerships, partnership associations, and joint ventures. In a few states, the business trust has gained a position comparable to the legal-entity status of a corporation; nevertheless, the remaining states generally refuse to recognize such an enterprise as a distinct person or entity. Thus, a business trust, enjoying what amounts to legal-entity status in one state, is likely to be treated as a partnership by other states into which it may wish to expand its business activities. In the case of business corporations, on the other hand, all states recognize and honor their status as legal entities without regard to the origin of their charters. New York, for example, treats as persons business corporations established in the other forty-nine states; likewise, each of the forty-nine treats as persons corporations chartered by New York.

Corporation Finance and Business Finance

Just as corporation finance, as a field of study, avoids treating the financial policies and activities of certain classes of corporations, such as public corporations and private nonprofit corporations, so also does it give no direct attention to the finance functions of the noncorporate forms of business enterprise as mentioned in the preceding paragraph. Here again, however, the student should avoid the conclusion that the field of corporation finance is an unduly restricted one. Much of the subject matter of corporation finance is directly and precisely applicable to the financial activities of all kinds of private profit-seeking enterprises, and not to that of business corporations only. Although, therefore, the term *business finance* is often used to describe a field of study somewhat broader than corporation finance, one should realize that a good knowledge of corporation finance provides a broad grasp of the theories that are applied, the procedures and instruments used, the institutions employed, the problems faced, and the varieties of policies that are adopted in connection with the finance functions of all forms of business enterprise.

The general scope of finance functions, the circular flow of cash, the adoption of sound asset-management policies, budgetary procedures, decisions as to what amounts of money can be safely borrowed, the selection of lending institutions to which applications for loans will be made, settling upon the kinds and terms of loans, deciding what proportion of profits can be safely withdrawn by owners for their personal use—these are but a few examples of the financial phenomena that are much the same for all kinds of business enterprises regardless of their form. Other similarities abound. A mortgage bond issue of a corporation closely compares with the mortgage debt of any other kind of borrower, and a promissory note given to a lender by a corporate borrower is likely to be indistinguishable in form from that given by, say, a proprietor or the members of a partnership. Again, the certificates of beneficial interest issued by business trusts are quite similar to stock certificates issued by corporations; indeed, certificates of beneficial interest are often referred to simply as "stock." In a word, then, corporation finance may be thought of as a subdivision of business finance, but it is a very large subdivision, encompassing much of the field of the latter.

THE MATERIALS OF CORPORATION FINANCE

Although the remainder of this textbook is dedicated to an analysis of the theories, procedures, institutions, instruments, problems, and policies of corporation finance, it should be advantageous to have a preliminary view of these materials. Such a preliminary view should help the student to see the interrelationships among the materials as they are taken up in connection with specific topics in subsequent chapters—to help him to see how the parts fit into the whole picture.

Theories or Principles

Because a business corporation is simultaneously a creature of the state and a private profit-seeking enterprise, it is surrounded, so to say, with both legal theories and economic and accounting theories. Some principles of corporation finance, therefore, are largely if not exclusively legal; others have their origin in economics and accounting; and still others blend ideas originating in the law, on the one hand, and in economics and accounting, on the other.

The legal theory that most strongly influences the financial policies and practices of business corporations has already been indicated, namely, that the corporation is a distinct entity having a life apart from the lives of its organizers, stockholders, managers, and other employees. Closely related to this are legal theories that a business corporation owns its own property; that only stockholders, as such, are the owners of a corporation; that the stockholders, though owning the corporation, do not own its assets; and that bondholders, as creditors, have no ownership rights. Upon other legal theories are based the respective managerial rights of stockholders and boards of directors, the ranking of rights between common stockholders and preferred stockholders, and the liability of stockholders who buy stock at a discount. Still other legal theories indicate the rights of creditors, how rights vary between secured and unsecured creditors, and the order in which creditors' claims will be met through the liquidation of a corporation's assets if it is unable to meet them in the ordinary course of business.

Most of the economic theories that find a place in the principles of corporation finance are inseparable from accounting theories—it is virtually impossible to say where one of these areas of thought leaves off and the other begins, as they apply to corporation finance. At any rate, it can be said that economic and accounting theories, in a kind of partnership, indicate what are reasonable proportions between stockholders' equity and debt in the financial structures of corporations, relate the value of corporations' assets to their earning power, and distinguish between the asset values of corporations as going concerns and the sum of the market values of the separate items that make up the assets. Other theories of this joint classification may justify write-ups and write-downs in asset values as carried on the books, indicate the appropriate ways to treat items of extraordinary expense and income, and serve as criteria for the proper management of the surplus accounts. Likewise, we encounter theories as to when and how expansion of the scale of business operations by the individual corporation is justified, as well as theories as to why corporations run into financial difficulties.

Both legal and economic and accounting theories are applicable to questions involving dividend payments. Legal theory indicates under what circumstances boards of directors may declare dividends without themselves incurring liability; and economic and accounting theory supplies the pros and cons of dividend declaration from the standpoint of expediency—from the standpoint, one might say, of trying to balance the long-run welfare of the corporation with the immediate interests of its stockholders. Again, both legal theory and economic and accounting theory come into play—and sometimes into conflict—in the determination of what outlays of cash are properly to be treated as current operating expenses and what are to be treated as acquisitions of assets to be charged off to expense over a period of years. The managers of a business corporation may be inclined to treat certain outlays as current expenses, but whether they may deduct such outlays from income in computing their federal income tax liability depends upon the legal theories of deductible expenses as incorporated in the federal tax legislation.

Procedures

Procedures employed in the performance of the finance functions of business corporations are, again, both legal and economic. Aside from promotional activities in planning new corporations, the legal procedures come first; it is necessary, first of all, to get the enterprise firmly established as a creature of the state. This requires the filing of articles of incorporation with the appropriate official of the state from which a charter is desired, as well as taking certain additional actions the law requires. Later on, other legal procedures may be necessary, as when the corporation wishes to change the provisions of its original articles, to qualify new security issues for sale within the state or in interstate commerce, or, perhaps, to merge with another corporation. At all times, certain other procedures will be governed, at least in part, by stipulations of pertinent laws, such as procedures for calling and holding stockholders' and directors' meetings, choosing directors, and counting votes.

Economic or business procedures in corporation finance include the forecasting of cash flows, controlling cash receipts and disbursements, safeguarding and temporarily investing cash balances, keeping records and making reports, offering new issues of securities to present stockholders, making arrangements with investment bankers for the underwriting of new securities issues, negotiating with commercial banks and other direct lenders, listing securities on the stock exchanges, and making provisions for the retirement of securities already outstanding. Many of these procedures require a high degree of managerial skill, while others, such as supervising cash receipts and disbursements, record keeping, handling transfers of stocks and bonds, and paying dividends on stock and interest and principal on bonds, tend to be quite mechanical.

Institutions

The principal institution dealt with in the study of corporation finance is obviously the business corporation itself. Other institutions are treated because they provide financial assistance to business corporations, supply certain kinds of clerical aids that relieve them of burdensome details, or have the authority to regulate some kinds of corporate financial activities.

Institutions that provide financial assistance to corporations are chiefly, of course, the various kinds of banking institutions. Some of these, such as the investment banking houses, serve corporations by helping them, as it were, to sell their securities to the public. Others grant loans to them direct; these include commercial banks, commercial finance companies, and sales finance companies. Still others, such as the stock exchanges and brokerage houses, contribute to the attractiveness of new security issues by providing market facilities for those already outstanding. Finally, "institutional investors" are important because they buy large quantities of corporate securities without necessarily entering into any kind of direct negotiations with the corporations that issue the securities. Institutional investors include life insurance companies, trust companies, the trust departments of commercial banks, investment companies, and pension and endowment funds.

Trust companies and the trust departments of commercial banks are significant for a second reason: they help corporations with the clerical details of managing their security issues. In this regard, they serve as transfer agents and registrars of stock issues, indenture trustees for bond issues, and paying agents for dividends and other kinds of cash distributions.

Institutions having the power to regulate specific phases of corporate financial activities are governmental agencies. Some of these, such as the Interstate Commerce Commission and many of the state public service commissions, have authority to approve or reject financing projects proposed by the corporations subject to their jurisdiction; others, including the federal Securities and Exchange Commission and the state securities commissions, have the authority to prevent the sale of security issues that have not been properly qualified for sale in accordance with the respective federal and state laws; and a final group, including trustees in bankruptcy, may entirely supplant corporation managements, at least temporarily, in the determination of financial policies.

Instruments

As corporation financial policy is strongly influenced by the provisions of certain kinds of laws, these laws must be allotted an important place as instruments for study. Laws having significant prescriptions with respect to corporation finance include the corporation codes of the various states on the basis of which corporations are formed, have their charters amended, merge or consolidate with other corporations, and are dissolved; laws that give government agencies authority to regulate the security issues of certain kinds of corporations, especially corporations providing transportation, communication, and other public utility services; those that require the registration of security issues, security dealers, and stock exchanges; those that provide for the reorganization of corporations; those that establish procedures for the recording of liens, the obtaining of judgments, and the initiating of foreclosure actions; and those that give the quality of negotiability to promissory notes, bonds, stock certificates, and certain other documents.

Many kinds of instruments are used in the issuance of stock and in the exercise of stockholders' rights. These include stock certificate books, stockholders' ledgers, stock-purchase warrants, registration statements, prospectuses, proxy statements, and proxy forms. Likewise, borrowing calls into use many different kinds of instruments, whether the borrowing is done through the sale of bond issues or by means of loans obtained direct from banking institutions. Such instruments include bond certificates, bond coupons, indentures, authentication forms, registration statements, prospectuses, promissory notes, underwriting contracts, and term-loan agreements.

Also highly significant in both the study and practice of corporation finance are cash and fixed asset budgets (and other kinds of budgets, as well) as instruments for forecasting cash flows, and balance sheets, statements of manufacturing costs, income statements, statements of sources and applications of funds, and other reports indicating the results of operations. All such budgets, statements, and reports are of great importance as "tools" of financial management.

Problems and Policies

The kinds of problems that are dealt with in corporation finance, as a field of study, are largely identical with those actually faced in the financial management of business corporations. They all involve a search for the best ways of applying theories or principles, with the help of existing institutions, and with the use of suitable instruments, to attain specific goals. As so described, they are necessarily of a bewildering variety and of many degrees of complexity. Only a small sampling of these problems need be mentioned here: setting maximum and minimum levels within which corporation managements will seek to maintain their cash holdings; deciding what to do with temporary excessive holdings of cash; deciding whether or not to sell on a credit or deferred-payment basis; selecting advantageous inventory valuation methods; choosing between the purchase and lease of plant and machinery; selecting favorable depreciation-charging methods; deciding whether in certain instances the cost of additional assets should be met by further investment by stockholders or through the expansion of debt; determining whether, in given circumstances, preferred stock should be issued rather than additional common stock; deciding to what extent earnings should be retained and to what extent used for cash dividends; finding a workable relationship between the respective amounts of long- and short-term debt; selecting channels through which securities will be sold or loans will be sought; fixing terms and features of security issues to enhance their marketability; adjusting asset values when they appear to be out of proper relationship with earning power; selecting appropriate policies for the retirement of debt; and meeting the extraordinary kinds of difficulties that are occasioned by recessions and depressions in general business activity.

Identity in the scope of the problems of corporation finance, as a field of study, and the problems of financial management in operating corporations does not necessarily mean that students of finance and corporation managers must agree upon solutions to specific problems. As a rule, corporation managers, in adopting policies—which are, after all, solutions to problems, as actually selected—strive toward the goal of maximizing the strength and profitability of their enterprises. But what appears to a corporation management to be a good policy may really be a bad one from the standpoint of the welfare of society as a whole. Accordingly, the student of finance must seek solutions and support policies that, at least, are not harmful to the general welfare, and that, desirably, make a positive contribution to it. He may find it imperative to condemn as un-

ethical or antisocial certain kinds of policies that some corporate managements adopt and implement. On the other hand, corporate managers who
are aware of their social responsibilities, and who are willing to give these
responsibilities proper weight in their decision making, can generally be
expected to adopt policies that can be fully approved by the impartial
student.

IMPORTANCE OF CORPORATION FINANCE

Dominance of the Corporation

The importance of corporation finance is proportional, one might say,
to the tremendous productivity of the very business corporations with
which it is concerned. Everyone is aware of the vast flow of goods that
comes annually from the factories, workshops, stores, and warehouses that
are owned and operated by corporations—a flow that contributes greatly
toward satisfying high standards of living and assuring national well-being
in a material sense. Such a flow of output must be financed: corporations
must raise money to add to their equipment, to meet their payrolls, and
to cover other costs incurred in preparing goods for the market. Men and
machines may stand idle, despite a strong market demand for the goods
they could produce, if the corporations that hire the men and own the
machines do not have enough money to put these factors of production to
work. "Bottlenecks" in the production stream due to a lack of adequate
means of financing are thus possible, in addition to those that exist because
of a lack of physical facilities and skilled manpower of particular kinds.

Of the total of approximately 4,800,000 private business enterprises in
operation in the United States, slightly fewer than one fourth are corporations.[2] But though corporations are far outnumbered by both proprietorships and partnerships in business as a whole, they outnumber proprietorships and partnerships in many areas of business, as in most sectors of
manufacturing, in railroad transportation, in communication services, and
in electric power and gas production and distribution. The dominance
of the corporation in manufacturing—in number of establishments, number of employees, size of payrolls, and value added in productive operations—is indicated by the data of the Bureau of the Census presented in
Table 1–2.

Even where outnumbered, moreover, corporations tend to dominate in
volume and value of output, number of employees, and size of payrolls,

---

[2] The Department of Congress estimated the number of business firms in operation on January 1, 1961, at 4,713,000. If we relate this figure to the number of
"active" corporations filing income tax returns for fiscal years ending between July
1, 1960, and June 30, 1961, as reported in Table 1–1, that is, 1,140,575, we get a proportion of corporations to the whole business population of 24.2 per cent. On January 1, 1963, according to a preliminary estimate of the Department of Commerce,
the total business population was 4,797,000 firms. See *Survey of Current Business,*
June, 1963, p. 2.

TABLE 1–2
Comparative Position of Corporations in Manufacturing in 1958
(Employees in thousands; dollar amounts in millions)

Forms of Enterprise	Number of Establish-ments	Number of Employees[a]	Salaries and Wages	Value Added in Production[a]
Corporations.............	162,749	14,229	$69,963	$133,755
Proprietorships..........	91,276	542	1,637	3,115
Partnerships.............	41,958	543	1,836	3,663
Other...................	2,199	77	314	738
Total...............	298,182	15,394	$73,750	$141,270

[a] Items do not add exactly to total because of rounding.

Source: U.S. Department of Commerce, Bureau of the Census, *United States Census of Manufactures, 1958*, Vol. I: *Summary Statistics* (Washington, D.C.: U.S. Government Printing Office, 1961), p. 3-2.

except in a few fields such as agriculture and some of the personal service areas. The field of retail trade, for example, is usually regarded as being one especially suitable for unincorporated enterprises; yet data for the year 1958, as presented in Table 1–3, indicate that corporations accounted

TABLE 1–3
Comparative Position of Corporations in Retail Trade in 1958
(Dollar amounts in millions)

Forms of Enterprise	Number of Establishments	Sales[a]	Salaries and Wages[a]
Proprietorships..........	1,240,171	$ 63,337	$ 5,221
Corporations.............	277,805	106,099	13,659
Partnerships.............	259,352	27,744	2,535
Cooperatives.............	5,964	1,306	104
Other...................	5,033	1,161	71
Total...............	1,788,325	$199,646	$21,589

[a] Items do not add exactly to total because of rounding.

Source: U.S. Department of Commerce, Bureau of the Census, *United States Census of Business, 1958*, Vol. I: *Retail Trade—Summary Statistics* (Washington, D.C.: U.S. Government Printing Office, 1961), p. 5-2.

for 53.1 per cent of the retail sales and 63.3 per cent of the total retail payroll of that year, even though they owned only 15.5 per cent of the retail outlets then in operation. It is noteworthy, moreover, that a larger number of corporations operate in the area of retail trade than in any other major field of business activity except that of real estate.[3]

The overall dominance of business corporations in productive operations is demonstrated by the size of their contribution to the national income, that is, total payments to the factors of production for their respective contributions to output. In 1962, the corporate share amounted to $244 billion out of total contributions of private businesses of $368 billion.[4] Despite their minority in numbers, therefore, business

---

[3] Of the corporations engaged in trade listed in Table 1–1 on page 6, 217,269 were classified as retail trade corporations. Active real estate corporations numbered 223,884.

[4] *Survey of Current Business*, July, 1963, p. 17.

corporations far exceed in production all other forms of private enterprise combined.

Large and Small Corporations

Almost all large business enterprises, regardless of their fields of operation, are incorporated, but this does not mean that corporation finance, as a field of study, has to do solely with "big business." Though some kinds of business activity are unquestionably concentrated in a few "giant" corporations, the average corporation, like the average proprietorship and the average partnership, is a relatively small undertaking. Referring to a further breakdown of the 1960–61 income tax data as presented in Table 1–4, we find that of a total of 1,140,575 corporations that filed tax re-

TABLE 1–4
Number, Assets, and Net Income of Business Corporations,
by Size of Total Assets, 1960–61[a]

Size of Total Assets (in thousands)	Number of Returns	Total Assets (in millions)[b]	Net Income (in millions)[b]
Under $25.................	325,250	$ 2,975	$ 204[c]
25 under 50..............	169,047	6,141	68[c]
50 under 100.............	190,316	13,694	380
100 under 250............	229,142	36,392	1,213
250 under 500............	105,174	36,622	1,223
500 under 1,000..........	54,991	38,203	1,384
1,000 under 2,500.........	34,173	52,627	2,024
2,500 under 5,000.........	13,810	48,318	1,708
5,000 under 10,000........	8,280	57,818	1,853
10,000 under 25,000.......	5,804	89,406	2,919
25,000 under 50,000.......	2,110	72,997	2,302
50,000 under 100,000......	1,145	79,745	3,083
100,000 under 250,000.....	766	119,391	4,671
250,000 or more..........	567	552,297	21,028
Total.................	1,140,575	$1,206,624	$43,515

[a] All active corporations filing federal income tax returns for fiscal years ending between July 1, 1960, and June 30, 1961. Unlike Table 1–1, therefore, this table includes data for corporations in finance, insurance, and real estate, and for those the nature of whose business was not allocable by industry.
[b] Items do not add exactly to total because of rounding.
[c] Net loss.

SOURCE: U.S. Treasury Department, Internal Revenue Service, *Statistics of Income, 1960–61—Preliminary: Corporation Income Tax Returns* (Washington, D.C.: U.S. Government Printing Office, 1962), p. 25.

turns, no fewer than 325,250 had total assets individually of less than $25,000. Two quick computations show, moreover, that 1,073,920 corporations had total assets individually of less than $1 million, and that all but 18,672 had total assets individually of less than $5 million. Thus, a very large majority of corporations are small or, at most, only moderately large. All of which, of course, does not gainsay the vast role of the giants. Of great significance is the fact that only 567 corporations in the top size group had asset holdings of $552,297 million out of a total for all corporations of $1,206,624 million, equal to 45.8 per cent, and net profits of $21,028 million out of a total of $43,515 million, equal to 48.3 per cent.

Most appropriately, therefore, corporation finance must be concerned with the finance functions of corporations of all sizes—large, intermediate, and small. That is the point of view of this textbook. Nevertheless, one must not assume that there are great differences in the character of the financial activities of corporations of the different size groups, aside from the amount of money involved in specific kinds of transactions. Most corporat ns start out as small enterprises, but from the beginning they face financial problems much like those simultaneously facing large corporations that have been operating for many years, and much like those that they themselves will continue to encounter as they grow older and larger. Although the amounts of money involved in corporate affairs may vary enormously depending upon the size of corporations, the character of financial problems tends to be much the same for all corporations regardless of size; they may thus be said to differ in degree but not in kind.

Questions

1. As a field of study, corporation finance embraces what kinds of subject matter? Is there any significant difference between corporation finance and business finance? Explain.

2. How are business corporations distinguished from public corporations, public proprietary corporations, private nonprofit corporations, and cooperative corporations? Which of the latter group most closely resemble business corporations? Explain.

3. Give examples by name of each of the five classes of corporations mentioned in the foregoing question.

4. Why are financial institutions treated in a special way in studies in corporation finance?

5. What is meant by the description of business corporations as "entities" or "personalities"? Does this description apply also to the other classes of corporations mentioned in Question 2? Does it apply to partnerships and proprietorships? Why or why not?

6. By means of examples, show the difference between legal theories applicable to corporation finance and economic and accounting theories.

7. Aside from the business corporation itself, what three classes of institutions are important in the study of corporation finance?

8. Discuss the reasonableness of the proposition that policies are "solutions to problems, as actually selected."

9. Why is the idea of "social responsibility" introduced in this chapter? Does it really belong here? Discuss.

10. What evidence is there for the claim that the business corporation is the dominant form of business organization in the United States?

Problems

1. In terms of value added by production, what do the data of Table 1–2 indicate about the size of the average manufacturing corporation by comparison with the average proprietorship and the average partnership engaged in manufacturing?

2. What, if anything, does Table 1–3 reveal about the level of wages and salaries paid by corporations in retail trade by comparison with levels paid by proprietorships and partnerships?

3. From the data of Table 1–4, compute to three decimal places the rates of net income earned in relation to total assets by corporations having assets between $50,000 and $100,000, between $500,000 and $1 million, between $5 million and $10 million, and between $50 million and $100 million. As indicated by these rates, does profitability vary directly or inversely with size, or is there, perhaps, no clear relationship of this kind?

chapter 2

THE BUSINESS CORPORATION

CHOICE OF THE FORM OF ORGANIZATION

People who establish business enterprises generally have full freedom in choosing the form of organization they will use, whether the proprietorship, the general partnership, the corporation, or one of the less common forms mentioned in the preceding chapter. Likewise, those who are already operating businesses of particular forms are usually quite free to change these forms. A proprietor may decide that it would be advantageous to take in several additional investors as partners; or the members of a partnership may conclude that the incorporation of their firm would be beneficial; or the stockholders of a corporation may decide that it would be helpful to reorganize as a partnership.

Why are decisions of these kinds made? Why is one form of organization selected in preference to others? The answer to these questions must surely be that enterprisers select the form of organization that they think will serve them best. They see certain advantages in the use of a given form of organization not present at all or to the same degree in other forms; likewise, they probably recognize certain disadvantages peculiar to it. The matter of selection is purely relative: the form of organization that will serve best in a given situation may be quite inappropriate under other circumstances.

Advantages and disadvantages in the use of specific forms of organization are largely financial in character—having to do with ease in acquiring money from owners and prospective owners, whether few or many, ease in borrowing, credit standing, expenses incurred in getting organized, the burden of taxation, and so on. The very selection of a form of organization puts it to use, as it were, as a financing instrument. Hence the business corporation which was described in the preceding chapter as the principal institution with which corporation finance deals might also have been described as, in and of itself, an important instrument of finance.

No attempt will be made in the following pages to present an exhaustive list of the advantages and disadvantages of each of the various forms of organization. Since our study is devoted to corporation finance, it should suffice to confine our attention to the advantages and disadvantages of the corporate form of organization. Reference will be made here and there to certain advantages and disadvantages of the proprietorship and the general partnership, but the objective of these references will be to point up the position of the corporation rather than to give a well-rounded account of the features of these other forms of enterprise. At the same time, reference to the limited partnership, the joint-stock company, the business trust, and other relatively rare forms of organization will generally be avoided, as such reference would probably be more confusing than enlightening; in any case, such forms are decidedly of limited importance in the totality of business.

ADVANTAGES OF THE CORPORATE FORM OF ORGANIZATION

Limited Liability of Stockholders

Nature of Limited Liability. The principle that a stockholder in a business corporation risks only the amount of money that he has actually invested in it, and not his entire wealth, is an outstanding reason for the attractiveness of the corporate form of organization. Innumerable investors who would be unwilling to participate as owners in partnerships tend to have an entirely different attitude toward the purchase of corporate stock. The "limited liability" of a corporation's stockholders, as contrasted with the unlimited liability of sole proprietors and members of general partnerships for the debts of their enterprises, is the thing that makes the difference. For example, a person may invest $2,000 in the stock of a corporation with this thought in mind: "I can afford to lose this sum"; but he might shy away from investing the same amount in a partnership, thinking: "If things go badly, I might lose every cent I have, including my home, as all my property could be seized in satisfaction of the debts of the partnership."

In a strict sense, the stockholders of a corporation are not liable at all for its debts. This fact follows from the position of a corporation as a legal entity. As an entity or person, the corporation makes its own contracts, including those whereby it incurs obligations to make payments, and it alone is responsible for fulfilling them. People who enter into contracts with corporations are expected to know the nature of this exclusive corporate responsibility. Such responsibility means that any and all of the corporation's assets may be seized to satisfy creditors' claims if they are not satisfied by cash payments in the ordinary course of business. Thus, assets contributed by the stockholders, as well as those which the creditors themselves have supplied, may be seized—it is in this sense, then, that the stockholders are said to be limitedly liable for a corporation's debts. They may not get back what they invested, since it may have to be used to pay off the creditors. But personal assets of the stockholders —property which they have not invested in the corporation—are generally quite beyond the reach of its creditors.

Such a limitation upon the liability of stockholders remains in effect regardless of the amount of losses creditors may suffer. A bankrupt corporation may have sufficient assets to pay off creditors' claims at a rate of only 20 or 30 cents on the dollar, yet the stockholders have no legal responsibility whatsoever to ease the creditors' losses. The stockholders may still be wealthy despite the loss of the full value of their investment in the corporation, and the creditors may be men of quite limited means; nevertheless, the doctrine of limited liability prevents the former from being burdened with an obligation to the latter.

Limited Liability in Large Corporations. Large enterprises, in particular, are likely to find the limited-liability feature of the corporate form of organization indispensable; in fact, one can say that, in most instances, enterprises have been able to grow to large and even giant sizes only because they were able to incorporate and thus to give their stockholders the protection of limited liability. Large incorporated enterprises are able to offer their stock issues to thousands of individual and institutional investors with full assurances that the buyer risks only the amount of his investment. Many investors thus approached are able to spare only a few hundred dollars, and many others, not more than a thousand or two; but, whether the amount available for investment is large or small, no investor is repelled by fear of loss of personal wealth *not invested* in the enterprise.

Indeed, any investor might be called foolhardy, regardless of the amount of his wealth and the prestige of the firm in which he invests, should he be willing to participate as an owner in a large enterprise without the protection of limited liability. Imagine one's becoming unlimitedly liable for all the debts of an enterprise of the size of the United States Steel Corporation or of the Westinghouse Electric Corporation on account of an investment in it of, say, $1,000!

Limited Liability in Small Corporations. Even for smaller enterprises, the limited-liability feature can be decidedly attractive. If the organizers of a relatively small enterprise anticipate a need of offering stock to many prospective buyers—expecting, probably, to get from each buyer only a moderate sum—they can hardly hope for success unless they are able to provide the protection of the limited-liability feature. A wealthy capitalist might be willing to back the venture by participating as an owner to the extent of a few thousand dollars, but he would be unlikely to participate should he have to assume full personal responsibility for its debts.

On the other hand, the limited-liability feature may not mean much to a small group who are pooling their own funds in a business venture and who have no expectation of making an outside appeal for proprietary funds. If they have little in the way of personal assets outside the business, they are likely to see little difference between limited and unlimited liability: they can hardly lose much beyond what they have actually invested. Or if they have a substantial amount of nonbusiness assets, they may decide that the best way to protect these assets is to transfer title to their wives, to their children, or perhaps to trust estates. Another consideration is that they may think it futile to try to escape unlimited liability by incorporating when creditors, by the terms of contracts, can in effect reestablish it. Thus, the principal stockholders of a small close[1] corporation may be told by a banker that he will grant it loans only if they cosign or endorse its promissory notes.

Divisibility of Ownership

Flexibility in Stock Issues. The stock of a business corporation may be described as *shares of ownership* in it. It is an instrument of marvelous flexibility. Stock issues can be tailored to provide attractions to prospective investors of varying means, interests, and temperaments. It can be given a value of many hundreds of dollars or of only a few cents—or, indeed, of a fraction of a cent. The organizers of a corporation who wish to raise, say, $100,000 by a sale of stock may decide upon an issue of 1,000 shares of $100 par value, of 10,000 shares of $10 par value, of 100,000 shares of $1.00 par value, or of 1,000,000 shares of a par value of 10 cents, depending upon the class of people to whom they will make their sales appeal.

So flexible, indeed, are stock issues, that the shares need not be given a value at all at the time they are authorized in a corporation's charter. Such no-par stock, as it is called, may be sold from time to time at varying prices depending upon the changing market situation. Again, flexibility is such that the features of issues can be readily changed; our states are most liberal in permitting changes. A corporation that originally provided for an issue of no-par stock may subsequently have its articles of incorporation amended to give the stock a par value; or if it originally issued stock of a par value of $10, it can have its articles changed to give the stock a value of $5.00; or if it originally provided for an issue of 10,000 shares of a given value, it can have the articles changed to permit it to issue an additional 10,000 or 20,000 shares of the same or a different par value.

Still further flexibility is imparted to stock in that it can be issued in different classes; in this way, holders of stock of the different classes can be given varying rights to dividends, participation in management, participation in assets in case of dissolution, and so on. Many corporations put

---

[1] A *close* corporation is one whose entire outstanding stock is owned by a single individual, the members of a family, or some other small group. The stock is "closely held," that is, it has but few owners. On the other hand, an *open* corporation is one whose stock is widely distributed, so that anybody who wants to buy some can usually find somebody else who is willing to sell. Sometimes open corporations are described as "public" corporations, but this use of the term is confusing, because city governments, other municipal corporations, and government proprietary corporations are also classified as public corporations.

out both common and preferred stocks. And if two classes of stock should be insufficient to tap the potential market, arrangements can be made for the issuance of two or more classes of common and two or more classes of preferred, each with different rankings according to the terms of the articles of incorporation.

Divisibility and Limited Liability. The extraordinary divisibility of stock, as an advantage of the corporate form of organization, must be recognized as being closely tied in with the limited-liability feature of corporate enterprise. Without this tie-in, divisibility might not be considered as an advantage at all. It would be rather ridiculous for a corporation to provide for the issuance of thousands of shares valued at a few cents or a few dollars each if there were no prospects that people would be willing to buy such small slices of ownership. The prospects would surely be quite slim if the prospective buyers could not be promised the protection of limited liability.

In this regard, it is pertinent to observe that, legally, ownership interests in a partnership are just as divisible as are those in corporations. There is nothing in the laws pertaining to partnerships to prevent the sale of ownership interests of 1/10,000 or 1/100,000; but, as a practical matter, people would not ordinarily be willing to buy such interests as they would at the same time assume full liability for partnership debts, nor would members of existing partnerships be willing to accord to people having minute interests the full power to enter into contracts on behalf of their partnerships—which is, indeed, one of the rights of any full-fledged partner.

Transferability of Shares

Corporations have a financing advantage over the proprietorship and partnership in that, through the sale of stock, they are often able to attract investors' funds on a temporary basis. Stock has no date of maturity which states when the principal or face value is repayable, but absence of a maturity date does not mean that the typical investor expects to hold stock for his entire lifetime and then bequeath it to his heirs. He may think of it simply as a short-term asset, to be disposed of when he needs money for some other purpose. The more strongly he has this attitude, the more willing is he likely to be to buy stock as a means of using his money temporarily to earn income. He buys today in the expectation of being able to sell next year, and he may actually be able to sell next year because somebody else may be willing to buy at that time in the expectation of being able to resell in, say, six months.[2]

---

[2] All this is not meant to imply that corporate stockholders can always sell their shares at what they would consider fair prices. It is often virtually impossible or at least extremely difficult to find buyers for shares in close corporations. Even for stockholdings in corporations whose shares are widely held, possibilities of getting a fair price depend upon whether or not the stocks are listed on prominent stock

Advantage accrues to the corporation because it gets its money in the original sale of its stock issues, *and its assets and life are not affected by subsequent transfers of that stock*, no matter what their number and frequency may be. The original buyer of the stock holds it for, perhaps, three years and then sells it, and the new owner holds it for three months, and the next buyer holds it for only three weeks. But the corporation is affected only by the first transaction, since it has no obligation to redeem the stock, that is, to use its assets to buy it back. Nobody disputes the right of the selling stockholder thus to sever his interests in the corporation. Nobody suggests that a lawsuit for damages should be brought because of his withdrawal. Nobody claims that the person who buys the stock someone else is selling has no right to become a stockholder.

The situation in a partnership is quite different from this. A person would not ordinarily become a member of a partnership on a temporary basis, for his withdrawal would cause a dissolution of the partnership! As the ownership interest of a withdrawing partner must generally be paid off out of partnership assets, this payment may make it impossible for the remaining partners to carry on. At the least, their business operations are likely to be seriously disrupted by a withdrawal. In some instances, it is true, an outsider might be willing to buy out the interest of the withdrawing partner, but finding such a person does not necessarily solve the problem. Brown may be willing to buy out Green's interest in the partnership of Grey, Black, and Green, but this requires more than an agreement between Brown and Green. According to the doctrine of *delectus personae*, people who form partnerships have the right to decide who their partners will be—partners cannot be forced upon them. Green cannot make Brown a partner simply by selling his interest to him. Brown must be accepted by Grey and Black; if they are not willing to accept him, and if Green still insists upon withdrawing, he must be paid off, presumably out of the partnership assets. If Grey and Black cannot be forced to accept Brown as a partner, neither can they force Green to remain as a partner when he no longer wishes to remain. Of course, if he has specifically agreed to maintain his position as a partner for a given period of years, and if he decides to withdraw before the expiration of that period, Grey and Black may have grounds for bringing against him a lawsuit for damages.

Independent Life of the Corporation

The corporation enjoys a most important advantage in having a life quite independent of those of its stockholders, directors, and officers. Because it is a distinct entity, it can go on living for as long as the state which creates it says it can; and as a being "invisible, intangible, and ex-

exchanges, the scope of investor interests in them, the tempo of business activity in the industries in which the corporations operate and in the economy as a whole, and other factors.

isting only in contemplation of law," [3] it need not have its life related in any way to the lives of human beings. The fact is that the organizers of business corporations can generally get perpetual charters simply for the asking. Only a few states do not issue perpetual charters, and even these few permit the stated term of life to be quite a long one; they provide also for easy amendment to charters so that a corporate life that is approaching expiration can be extended by an additional generous grant of years. Thus corporate longevity is always possible, either by way of perpetual life from the beginning, or by a ready process of rejuvenation.

By contrast, general partnerships are seriously limited in attractiveness since their continued existence is so closely dependent upon the lives of their owners as human beings. People may refuse to become partners in business concerns, despite high confidence in the integrity and abilities of the people with whom they would be associated, because they realize that any partnership may be suddenly terminated by the death, insanity, bankruptcy, or other legal incompetence of one or more of the partners, or simply because one of the partners decides that he must withdraw. At the very time that a partnership may be moving along most successfully, operations may be disrupted and the whole outlook changed because it becomes necessary to pay off the interest of a partner to his executor if he dies, to his commission or guardian if he goes insane, to the trustee if he goes bankrupt, or to the man himself if he wishes to withdraw. Prospective creditors, too, may be quite reluctant to grant loans or to sell on account to partnerships whose early demise, for reasons of the kinds indicated, they anticipate. Though they would have claims against the assets of the partnership superior to those of the owners, they might wish to avoid the delays and difficulties of estate settlement, court proceedings, and the like.

In the case of the corporation, a person may become a stockholder with full assurance that his coming will not disturb its operations in any way; that his going, if he decides to sell his stock later on, likewise will

---

[3] The corporation was so described by Chief Justice Marshall in his celebrated opinion in the Dartmouth College Case. His full statement was as follows: "A corporation is an artificial being, invisible, intangible, and existing only in contemplation of law. Being the mere creature of law, it possesses only those properties which the charter of its creation confers upon it, either expressly, or as incidental to its very existence. These are such as are supposed best calculated to effect the object for which it was created. Among the most important are immortality, and, if the expression may be allowed, individuality; properties by which a perpetual succession of many persons are considered as the same, and may act as a single individual. They enable a corporation to manage its own affairs, and to hold property without the perplexing intricacies, the hazardous and endless necessity, of perpetual conveyances for the purpose of transmitting it from hand to hand. It is chiefly for the purpose of clothing bodies of men, in succession, with these qualities and capacities, that corporations were invented, and are in use. By these means, a perpetual succession of individuals are capable of acting for the promotion of the particular object, like one immortal being."—*Dartmouth College* v. *Woodward*, 4 Wheaton 518 (1819).

cause no disturbance; and that the comings and goings of other stock-holders will similarly be free of unsettling effects. He knows that, should certain stockholders die, become insane or bankrupt, or suffer other legal disabilities, their stock would be taken over temporarily by executors, guardians, or trustees, and that, depending on circumstances, these new holders would sooner or later turn it over to heirs or sell it in the market —all these events having no effects upon the life of the corporation. He may expect, moreover, that banks and other lenders and suppliers of mer-chandise will be quite willing to extend credit to the corporation as they need not fear having their claims held up pending legal proceedings such as the settlement of decedents' estates and the handling of the affairs of bankrupts.

Independence of life is especially important for larger enterprises. In many of our largest corporations, hundreds of shares of stock are ex-changed between departing stockholders and arriving stockholders every business day; yet such transfers simply require, as one might say, a few clerical operations, and not a ripple in the life of the corporation and its current activities results. In small corporations, on the other hand, cer-tain transfers of stock may have profound effects upon business opera-tions, even though there is no legal impact upon the life of the corpora-tion. The death of a principal stockholder who has also been the president and general manager of a corporation may truly be as disrupt-ing to its operations as the death of a partner in the case of a partnership.

Satisfactory Credit Standing

Because the owners of proprietorships and partnerships are unlimitedly liable for the obligations of their enterprises, while the stockholders of corporations have only limited liability for corporate obligations, one might expect the proprietorships and partnerships to have high prefer-ence in obtaining loans, in buying goods on account, and in incurring debts in other ways. Nevertheless, the limited-liability feature of corpo-rations apparently does not detract from their position as debtors and prospective debtors; indeed, the access of corporations of given sizes to credit appears to be somewhat better than that of proprietorships and partnerships of comparable size groupings.

The following may be cited as probable reasons why the credit stand-ing of proprietorships and partnerships is not superior to that of corpora-tions: the fact that a very large proportion of the assets of proprietors and partners are their business assets, so that they have little outside their businesses to back up their "unlimited" liability; the conviction of many creditors that the seizure of personal assets, such as homes, household fur-niture, and the family automobile, is a poor means of enforcing business claims; and creditors' full awareness of the fact that proprietors and part-ners can put their nonbusiness assets in the names of their wives or chil-dren or set up trusts to hold them, thus effectively removing them from seizure for the satisfaction of business debts. On the other side of the picture, one reason why the credit standing of corporations may not be weakened because of limited liability is that prospective creditors have ways of nullifying it. For example, a commercial bank may agree to grant a loan to a corporation only on condition that its principal stockholder or stockholders consent to endorse the corporation's promissory note. In this way, should the corporation fail to meet its obligations, the private property of these stockholders would be subject to seizure to satisfy the bank's claims.

Representative Government

The operation of business corporations on the basis of a system of representative government has both advantageous and disadvantageous aspects. Representative government in the corporation means that the stockholders, even though they are the owners of the enterprise, do not determine operating policies, negotiate specific kinds of purchase and sales contracts, hire employees, and so on, but choose directors who have the power to do these things. The stockholders occupy a position somewhat like that of American citizens who elect representatives to Congress, to state legislatures, and to city councils—representatives who, rather than the citizens themselves, have the power to enact laws. But there the parallelism ends, for American citizens, as voters, also choose governmental executives, from the President down to township officials, whereas, in a business corporation, it is normally the function of directors to choose the executive officers.

At any rate, once directors and officers have been chosen, prospective creditors, in particular, can find clear lines of authority and can determine definitely whether or not certain officers have the power to negotiate specific kinds of contracts. For transactions between a corporation and a commercial bank, for example, the bank is likely to stipulate that before a deposit account is opened, checks are drawn, or loans are granted, the board of directors of the corporation must adopt and submit a resolution authorizing the opening of the account and specifically designating which of its officers have the right to sign checks, to borrow money in its name, and to pledge its property as collateral security for loans.

No one would question the right of a proprietor to borrow money or to buy on account in his own name for the benefit of his business, but in transactions with partnerships, creditors may get themselves into family quarrels which they would much rather avoid. The members of a partnership may agree among themselves that only Partner X has the right to buy materials and supplies, but Partner Y, thinking that quick action must be taken to get the advantage of some "bargain," may sign some purchase contracts in violation of the agreement. Partnership law holds that each partner is a principal in the sense of having capacity to enter into contracts binding the partnership as long as they are related to partnership business. Accordingly, Partner Y binds the partnership, and the supplier from whom he buys gets a valid claim; nevertheless, there may be many delays and difficulties as the latter tries to obtain payment, occasioned by the warring that may be going on among the partners as a result of Partner Y's failure to live up to his agreement.

It is possible that prospective investors will shy away from the corporation because of its representative form of government. Realizing that the corporate stockholder risks his money but gets only an indirect right to management—that is, by choosing directors who make the actual decisions—these investors may decide not to buy corporate stock. On the whole, however, we are so accustomed to representative government in political affairs that we are inclined to accept it in corporate affairs without hesitation. Indeed, a major criticism of the corporate form of organization from the standpoint of social welfare is that many stockholders fail to exercise the rights of participation in management that they *do* possess—that they ignore calls to stockholders' meetings, cast no ballots for directors, and pass up opportunities to vote on issues that the directors actually present to them for decision.

DISADVANTAGES OF THE CORPORATE FORM OF ORGANIZATION

Burdens upon Establishment

Often cited as a disadvantage of the corporate form of organization are the expenses and difficulties of getting started. But these are, at most, a minor disadvantage; certainly their financial burdens are of modest proportions. Seeing that the procedure of incorporation as set out in the state law is followed through carefully (so that the right of the enterprise to carry on business activities as a corporation and to enjoy the advantages of the legal-entity status will never be questioned) usually requires the services of competent attorneys. But the formation of any other kind of enterprise in which two or more persons are to be associated as owners, whether a general partnership, a limited partnership, a business trust, or some other form, should be guided just as carefully by competent attorneys. The establishment of a general partnership on the basis of an oral contract, or on the basis of a contract written by the partners themselves, is often a dangerous thing. As many as possible of the questions of rights and responsibilities that are likely to come up later should be anticipated, and governing provisions concerning them clearly written down. Foresight of this kind in the establishment of a partnership, no less than care required in the establishment of a corporation, generally calls for the assistance of legal counsel.

Aside from attorneys' fees, the most important items of expense ordinarily incurred in the establishment of a corporation are the fees and organization taxes that must be paid to the government of the state in which the corporation is chartered. In no state are these prohibitive; rarely, indeed, would the organizers of a business enterprise decide to forgo the advantages of the corporate form simply to avoid these costs. Filing fees, as a rule, do not exceed $50. In a few instances, the organization tax is also established as a set amount, as Arizona's $25, but most states provide for a variable tax related to the amount of stock that the new corporation is authorized to issue. Connecticut, for example, levies its organization tax at the rate of 1 cent per share of authorized capital stock, with a minimum tax of $50. In some states, the rate structure is regressive, that is, the rate is lower for certain larger batches of stock than for smaller amounts; such a rate structure in a given state serves as an invitation to larger corporations to make that state their home. Thus, the state of Delaware, which has been an extremely popular state for incorporations, has an organization tax on par-value stock of 10 cents for each $1,000 of stock up to $2 million, 5 cents for each $1,000 on amounts of stock between $2 million and $20 million, and 2 cents for each $1,000 on amounts over $20 million. A Delaware corporation having an authorized stock issue of $10 million would accordingly pay a tax of $600—certainly not a great burden for a corporation of that size.

Other special kinds of expenses incurred by corporations upon organization include the costs of forms used in applying for the charter, stock certificate books, minute books, and forms for the stockholders' ledger. But legal stationers carry materials of these kinds designed for general use, and their charges are quite moderate. Greater expense is incurred, of course, if the organizers of a corporation decide that they want something distinctive, as, for example, a specially engraved stock certificate form.

Government Regulation

More important than the expense and difficulty of getting started as a disadvantage of the corporate form of organization is the government regulation to which corporations are subjected. Here reference is made to special kinds of regulations which, as a rule, apply only to corporations, and not, of course, to those general kinds of regulations that apply to all kinds of business enterprises, or to all kinds in a given industry. The special regulations may be classified as follows: (1) those of the state of incorporation prescribing specific procedures for certain kinds of actions, (2) those pertaining to qualification to "do business" in states other than the state of incorporation, and (3) those requiring reports and authorizing investigations.

Prescribed Procedures. State laws require certain formalities in the procedures of the corporations they charter, especially for actions taken by the stockholders, the choice and service of directors, and changes in the scope of operations.

The state laws uniformly provide that there must be an annual meeting of the stockholders, and they go on to stipulate how and when notice of this meeting and of special meetings must be given, under what circumstances notice of meetings may be waived, what constitutes a quorum, what business may be taken up at a meeting with or without notice, how votes are to be counted, and so on. They require that a record of actions taken at stockholders' and directors' meetings—"minutes"—be kept. They usually designate the minimum number of directors a corporation may have, frequently set down certain qualifications for directors, and designate what the term of office of directors shall be. Likewise, they have provisions concerning the removal of incompetent directors, quorums for directors' meetings, and the filling of board vacancies between the annual meetings of the stockholders. Provisions such as these are not difficult to observe, of course, but they are restrictions upon freedom of action of a kind that the members of partnerships do not have to worry about. For the small close corporation in which the same few people are simultaneously stockholders, directors, and officers, such provisions are likely to be condemned as requiring "a lot of red tape."

If the directors of a business corporation want to change its name, its authorized stock issues, the duration of its life, the scope of its operations, or anything else provided for in its articles of incorporation, they cannot do so by simply voting the change and having the stockholders approve it. They must draw up articles of amendment, have the stockholders approve them, submit them to the secretary of state or other designated state official, pay filing fees—and additional taxes, if the authorized stock is being increased—obtain from the state official a certificate of amendment or some similar document, and file a copy of the articles of amendment with the county recorder. The members of a partnership, on the other hand, may take comparable actions entirely on their own volition, without need of any legal procedures as here described.

Entrance to Other States. Although a corporation is legally recognized as a person, it is not a citizen of the state in which it is incorporated or of the United States. It does not enjoy, therefore, the protection of the provisions of the Fourteenth Amendment to the Constitution which says: "No State shall make or enforce any law which shall abridge the privileges or immunities of citizens of the United States." [4] Accordingly, any state government may forbid corporations chartered by other states to do business within its borders, or it may place restrictions upon their activities such as it does not place upon corporations that it itself charters. Proprietors and the members of partnerships, on the other hand, cannot be so excluded or restricted; if they are "born or naturalized in the United States," they are citizens of the state in which they reside and of the United States, thus getting the protection of the provision quoted above.

In this regard, each of our state governments classifies corporations

---

[4] Section 1.

operating within its borders as *domestic, foreign,* and *alien* corporations. To it, a domestic corporation is one that it itself has chartered; a foreign corporation is one chartered by another state; and an alien corporation is one chartered by a foreign country. Thus, a Delaware corporation is a domestic corporation in the purview of the state of Delaware, but it is classified as a foreign corporation in each of the other states in which it operates. Likewise, a corporation chartered in Canada would be classified as an alien corporation in all our states. In certain circumstances, then, a state can exclude or restrict the activities of foreign and alien corporations as thus classified.

Nevertheless, the state governments may not restrict the operations of foreign and alien corporations in interstate and international commerce. Under the Constitution, Congress has the power to regulate interstate and international commerce, and it is a well-established doctrine that the states may not take any action that would place unreasonable burdens upon this commerce. Always an important question, therefore, is the distinction between intrastate and interstate commerce—between what constitutes "doing business" in a given state and what represents "doing business" across state lines. The distinction is by no means clear; but some rules have been enunciated by the courts for guidance. The following are samples of these rules: A corporation is said to be doing business in a foreign state if it owns real estate or maintains a sales office there, if it sells through agents who have power to enter into contracts without reference to the home office, if it sells things which must be installed by its employees, if it stores goods in warehouses in the foreign state preparatory to sale, or if it buys goods there and stores them temporarily pending shipment to the home state. If a corporation can avoid circumstances of these kinds in its transactions with firms and individuals in other states, its operations will generally qualify as interstate in character; as such, they will not be subject to the restrictive regulations of the other states.

Although state governments have the power to restrict, and even to exclude, the intrastate activities of foreign corporations, they rarely do so. Each state observes a policy of reciprocity, freely permitting foreign corporations to come in to do business in the expectation that other states will freely permit entrance to its chartered corporations. The expectation is fully justified, for the system of reciprocity is now nationwide in scope. Nevertheless, entrance to a foreign state is not without legal complexities, and the red tape involved is clearly burdensome to corporations. To obtain a license or "certificate of authority" to do business in the foreign state, a corporation must generally file with it a certified copy of its articles of incorporation and designate an agent resident within the state upon whom legal papers can be served—the state wants to be able to reach the corporation through the agent if it cannot do so directly. In connection with this filing requirement, a fee must be paid, and usually a tax also, the latter based more or less arbitrarily on the proportion of the corporation's assets to be employed in the foreign state, as determined by the use of a prescribed formula.[5]

The filing and tax-paying procedure must be followed through for each foreign state in which a corporation wishes to enter to do business. What is more, foreign states must usually be notified of important changes in a corporation's organization and scope of operations—changes such as those that necessitate the amendment of its articles of incorporation in the home state. For a corporation wanting to do business in many states, the obtaining of certificates of authority and the filing of notices of subsequent changes may be a considerable burden. Proprietorships and partnerships, to repeat, are subject to no such requirements.

The failure of a corporation to obtain a certificate of authority in a foreign state in which it does business means that it will have no standing in the courts of that state in bringing lawsuits, as for the enforcement of contracts. In some states, moreover, the corporation and its agents are subject to fines.

Reports and Investigations. Government regulation places a further burden upon corporations in requiring them to file annual reports and in making them subject to certain kinds of investigations. Each state usually requires annual reports of its own chartered corporations as well as of foreign corporations doing business within its borders. A corporation that operates in many states may have a sizable burden in turning out the required reports, because the prescribed content differs rather widely from state to state. As a rule, the individual report is not difficult to prepare, as the data required are not comprehensive; on the other hand, some states require the disclosure of information that the managers of business enterprises might prefer to keep secret. For many years, for example, the only definitive information that the public had about the assets and liabilities of the Ford Motor Company was that revealed in its annual report required by the Commonwealth of Massachusetts.

Investigations to which corporations are subject are chiefly examinations to determine whether taxes are being paid in the proper amounts. Tax collectors generally have powers to inquire into the affairs of all classes of taxpayers, but, because corporations must pay several special kinds of taxes, they are likely to be visited more often by tax investigators than are unincorporated enterprises and individuals. In some instances, moreover, a corporation's records may be subject to inspection to determine the payment or nonpayment of certain taxes not levied upon the corporation itself. This applies particularly to stock-transfer taxes im-

---

[5] Like organization taxes, entrance taxes levied upon foreign corporations are technically based upon capital stock—the proportion of a corporation's capital stock to be used in the foreign state. But corporations do not "use" their capital stock anywhere, since stock simply represents shares of ownership belonging to the stockholders. By most formulas, therefore, the amount of capital stock "used" in the respective states is determined on the basis of assets held or to be held therein in relation to total assets.

posed by the federal government and by a few of the states including New York. Tax investigators may want to look at the stock certificate books to see that the transfer stamps in the proper amounts have been appropriately attached.

Taxes upon Corporations

Although a few managers of business enterprises probably decide against incorporation because of the expenses and difficulties of starting, and many, to avoid the kinds of government regulation just described, most of those who decide against incorporation, it is surely safe to say, do so because they wish to avoid certain special kinds of taxes that are levied upon corporations by both the federal and state governments. Corporations must pay their share of taxes that are imposed on all persons, or on all businesses, or on all businesses that operate in particular industries, such as property taxes, manufacturers' excise taxes, retail sales taxes, business license taxes, and gross income taxes; but they are also singled out for additional levies that individuals and enterprises of other forms[6] are not called upon to pay. For annual franchise taxes on corporations imposed by the states, the additional tax burden varies from trifling to substantial amounts; but, large or small, it is an expense of operation that unincorporated businesses are not required to meet. For state-imposed corporation income taxes, the degree of burden depends upon whether or not the state also has a personal income tax and upon how corporate dividends are treated in personal tax returns. And for the federal corporation income tax—the heaviest, by far, of all corporation taxes—the degree of burden depends upon many things, including the size of the corporation's income, the size of stockholders' income from sources other than the corporation (this being important, of course, because, as everybody knows, the federal government also has a steeply graduated personal income tax), the extent to which stockholders can withdraw corporate income in the form of salaries, and the proportion of income they want the corporation to retain for expansion.

Always, therefore, to be considered most carefully in arriving at decisions whether or not to incorporate is an estimation of what incorporation would cost in the way of special taxes—in additions to the tax bill beyond what unincorporated businesses must pay. In some instances, the decision to incorporate is a foregone conclusion. This is true of enterprises having or expecting to have many owners (stockholders). These enterprises must be able to offer their owners the privilege of limited liability, regardless of the price in taxes they must pay for it. In other instances, the prospective tax bill clearly exceeds a reasonable price for the advantages of the corporate form, so that incorporation must be quickly ruled out

---

[6] Unless such enterprises are recognized as being so similar to corporations that they are treated as corporations for tax purposes. Thus, business trusts are required to pay federal corporation income taxes.

But, in between, there are many situations where it is most difficult to determine whether corporate tax bills plus the other disadvantages we have discussed outweigh or are outweighed by the advantages corporations enjoy. Obviously, such situations call for prolonged study before decisions are arrived at—study not only of the present circumstances, but also of prospects of future changes in tax legislation. Finally, there are situations—undoubtedly the most interesting of all—where owners of business enterprises can reduce their overall tax obligations by incorporating. For those who find themselves in this position, the special taxing of corporations turns out to be an advantage of the corporate form rather than a disadvantage!

State Taxation

Annual Franchise or Capital Stock Taxes. Approximately three fourths of the states impose upon corporations an annual tax related to stock issues variously called a franchise tax, a capital stock tax, a license fee, a privilege tax, or a corporation fee. This tax is levied upon both domestic and foreign corporations; it is usually based upon outstanding capital stock, although some states use as a base authorized capital stock, some use authorized or outstanding stock plus all or a portion of the surplus accounts, and at least one or two use stock plus surplus plus debt. The usual procedure is to tax only that proportion of capital stock that can be allocated to the individual taxing state, the allocation being made in terms of tangible property held in the state in relation to total tangible property, or, in some instances, in terms of both tangible property and gross sales within and without the state. Although a state may constitutionally tax the entire capital stock of domestic corporations, it usually chooses not to do so, in order not to make itself unattractive for incorporations; thus its procedure of allocation applies to both domestic and foreign corporations.

Pennsylvania's tax of one half of 1 per cent ($5.00 per $1,000) is applied to the actual cash value of capital stock "used in the state," that is, allocated as indicated above. Delaware—always to be mentioned in view of its popularity as a state of incorporation—has a series of flat charges graduated up to $55 for 10,000 shares of stock, with $27.50 the charge for each additional 10,000 shares; it also stipulates that the tax may not be less than $5.50 or more than $100,000. Michigan charges one half of 1 per cent on capital stock and surplus allocated to the state, with a minimum of $10. Colorado has a charge ranging from $10 on corporations with authorized capital stock up to $50,000 to $250 on those with authorized capital stock of $1 million or more; and Florida has a regressive schedule running from $20 on corporations with capital stock not exceeding $10,000 to $2,000 on those having capital stock of more than $2 million.

State Net Income Taxes. Some states levy upon corporations an annual net income tax in addition to an annual capital stock tax; some levy an annual net income tax in lieu of a capital stock tax; and some have neither of these two kinds of taxes. (The last-named group, however, usually has some modest fee, from $1 to $10, to be paid when the annual corporate report is filed.) In all, about three fourths of the states have corporation net income taxes in their tax structures.

Most states having corporation net income taxes levy a flat rate on the taxable income regardless of amount, the most common rate being 5 per cent. The lowest rate charged at the present time is Missouri's 2 per cent, and the highest Idaho's 10.5 per cent. A few states have progressive rate schedules, that is, the higher brackets of income are taxed at higher rates than are the lower brackets. Thus North Dakota has a rate schedule running from 3 per cent on the first $3,000 of income to 6 per cent on income in excess of $15,000.

According to accepted constitutional principles, a state may tax the entire net income of domestic corporations, but only that portion of the income of foreign corporations that is derived from doing business within its borders. However, only Alabama and Louisiana tax the entire net income of domestic corporations; other states choose not to do so lest they be bypassed by people seeking corporate charters. Taxing only income derived within the state, whether that of domestic or that of foreign corporations, requires some basis of allocation, and the states take care of this by setting up allocation formulas. The one most commonly used—often referred to as the "Massachusetts formula"—is this:

$$\frac{\dfrac{\text{Tangible property within the state}}{\text{Total tangible property}} + \dfrac{\text{Gross sales within the state}}{\text{Total gross sales}} + \dfrac{\text{Payroll within the state}}{\text{Total payroll}}}{3} = \begin{array}{l}\text{Proportion} \\ \text{of total} \\ \text{taxable by} \\ \text{the state}\end{array}$$

Thus, a corporation having one fourth of its property, one fifth of its gross sales, and one tenth of its payroll within a state using this formula would have $\frac{11}{60}$ of its net income subject to taxation by that state. Because of variations in the formulas used, the total net income upon which a corporation may be taxed in combination by all the states in which it does business may be more or less than the amount of its true net income. This fact indicates an important need of a uniform formula for use throughout the country.

Federal Corporation Income Tax

Relation to Individual Income Taxes. Because the federal government taxes corporate net income at the high rate of 30 per cent on the first $25,000 and at the much higher rate of 52 per cent on all amounts in excess of $25,000,[7] and because dividends paid by corporations are included in the income of the stockholders to be taxed again in the individual income tax structure (with only a moderate exclusion and a moderate tax credit[8]), incorporation would appear to be an extremely expensive way of carrying on business operations. The "double taxation" of corporate income—as corporate income and, again, as dividends distributed to stockholders—would seem to be an unconscionable burden. But the entire income of proprietors and partners from their businesses is taxed as individual income in the year derived, and the rates of the individual income tax run from 20 per cent on the first $4,000 of income to 91 per cent on that portion of income over $400,000.[9] Stockholders in corporations do not pay individual income taxes on that portion of corporation earnings *which the corporations do not pay out as dividends;* hence it may turn out to be advantageous to have business income taxed at the corporate rates if, by this means, the amount of income taxable as individual income can be substantially reduced.

Accordingly, the organizers of new business enterprises must carefully estimate the relative tax burdens that will fall upon the owners should they operate as proprietors or partners, on the one hand, or as corporate stockholders, on the other. Indeed, continuing analysis of relative tax burdens is appropriate for businesses already in operation, for changing circumstances may make it advantageous to incorporate proprietorships and partnerships, or, contrariwise, to surrender corporate charters and to continue business as proprietorships and partnerships. Estimates and analyses of these kinds are most difficult. Not only must there be comparisons on the basis of present corporate and individual tax rates, but consideration must be given to possible or probable rate changes in the future. Moreover, certain provisions of the income tax legislation complicate the analysis. Among these are provisions that permit corporations to deduct as expenses "reasonable" salaries paid to stockholders who are also officers or other employees, allow corporate deductions for payments of medical expenses and up to $100 a week for living expenses for employee-stock-

---

[7] Rates in effect in the year 1963.

[8] Dividends received up to $50 may be excluded from the taxpayer's taxable income. If both husband and wife receive dividends and if they file a joint tax return, up to $50 may be excluded for each, but one spouse cannot take the unused exclusion of the other. The "dividends received credit" permits a deduction from the tax obligation equal to 4 per cent of *taxable* dividends—that is, dividends not excluded under the $50 rule—provided that the credit does not exceed 4 per cent of taxable income. For example, a taxpayer reporting taxable dividends of $10,000 but with taxable income of only $9,000 (after taking allowable deductions and personal exemptions) would deduct from his tax bill $360, not $400.

[9] For married persons filing joint returns with their spouses. For single individuals and for married persons not filing joint returns, the range of rates is from 20 per cent on the first $2,000 of income to 91 per cent on income in excess of $200,000. For all classes of personal taxpayers, the total tax may not exceed 87 per cent of taxable income.

holders[10] absent from work because of sickness or injury (such payments not being includible in the stockholders' individual income subject to tax), and recognize certain kinds of payments as deductible expenses for corporations but not for other forms of business organizations.

Position of Stockholders Having Moderate Incomes. The payment of federal corporation income taxes almost always works to the disadvantage of stockholders who have moderate incomes. Let us suppose, for example, that a corporation's before-tax income attributable to the shares held by a small stockholder is $800, that it pays tax on this income of, let us say, $400,[11] and that it gives the remaining $400 to the stockholder as a dividend. Suppose, further, that the stockholder's income from other sources is $6,000, that his allowable deductions for certain kinds of expenses amount to $700, that he is married and has two children, and that he files an individual tax return jointly with his wife. At the rates in effect in the year 1963, his individual income tax would amount to $636[12] and this plus the $400 of tax paid by the corporation would, as it were, make his total tax bill $1,036. Were he, however, to receive $800 as a share in partnership profits, rather than as a dividend on corporate stock, his total tax bill would be only $740.[13]

Position of Stockholders Having Large Incomes. Stockholders who have relatively large incomes can be benefited or hurt by having income taxed as corporate income, depending upon the amounts of dividends their corporations distribute from the profits that remain after the payment of the tax. To illustrate, let us suppose that Mr. Green is one of three partners who are analyzing the pros and cons of incorporation. The partners have been sharing profits equally, and Green's share has been

---

[10] These deductions are allowed for such payments on behalf of any employee, but here, of course, attention is confined to employees who are also stockholders.

[11] It may be assumed that the corporation's net income is well above $25,000, so that its tax rate on total income approaches 52 per cent.

[12] In this and the following illustrations, allowance is made for the exclusion of $50 of dividends from taxable income and for the "dividends received credit" referred to in footnote 8 on page 35.

[13] The very important question of tax shifting and incidence is ignored in this illustration and in those that follow. One could argue that the corporation might have been able to raise the selling prices of its goods to cover all or a portion of its income tax liabilities. In that circumstance, its customers, rather than its stockholders, or in addition to its stockholders, would be bearing all or a portion of the corporate income tax levies. Assuming the complete shiftability of the tax, its repeal in a fully competitive situation should have resulted in a lowering of selling prices by the amount of the tax, so that the profit distributable to the stockholder of the illustration would still have been only $400. In that case, however, one could hardly say that the stockholder's "tax bill" included anything in addition to his individual tax of $636. But such an assumption would logically require one to consider also the possibilities of shifting the individual income tax on the partnership profits. Unfortunately, little is known conclusively of the extent to which taxes on the profits of corporations and other businesses are shifted; hence, business managers, in considering income taxation in relation to the merits and demerits of the corporate form, are likely to disregard the possibilities of shifting in making comparisons of the kinds illustrated in the text.

averaging $200,000 a year. He is married, has two children, and files individual income tax returns jointly with his wife who has no separate income. Assuming that he has $4,000 of allowable deductions and no income from other sources, and applying 1963 tax rates, his individual income tax comes to $129,072. The partners anticipate that, should they incorporate, the profits of the enterprise would continue to average $600,000, and they expect to allow themselves salaries of $20,000 each—salaries which they have every reason to believe the Internal Revenue Service would allow as a deductible expense to the corporation as "reasonable" compensation for their managerial services. The tax on the corporation's net profit of $540,000, after deduction of the salaries, would be $275,300, and Green's share of this, so to say, would be $91,767. His individual income tax on the salary, with allowance for the deductible expenses of $4,000 and personal exemptions for himself, his wife, and his children, would come to $3,200. Thus, his total tax bill, corporate and individual, would be $94,967, an amount $34,105 less than his tax bill as a partner. Such a prospective tax saving would appear to make incorporation highly desirable, but the full amount of the saving would be enjoyed only if the partners agreed that, as stockholders, their salaries of $20,000 would be quite enough for living expenses and that all other earnings after corporate taxes would be left with the corporation. Should they, at the other extreme, decide that they would want to take out as dividends all corporate earnings after taxes, they would quickly conclude that incorporation would be most undesirable, for their combined corporation and individual tax bill would be unconscionably high. Mr. Green's individual tax on his $20,000 salary and dividends of $88,233 (one third of the corporation's profit of $540,000 reduced by corporation income taxes of $275,300) would be $51,450. This sum plus his share of the corporate taxes of $91,767 would bring his total tax obligations to $143,217. Of course, the partners might agree that, as directors of the proposed corporation, they would allow themselves dividends which, at the maximum, would not make their tax liability greater than it would be if they were being taxed as partners. Dividends to Green of about $67,000 would make his total federal taxes approximately equal to the $129,072 personal tax paid on his $200,000 share of partnership income.

Further Considerations. One thing that Mr. Green, his partners, and all other people coping with comparable problems would want to be sure of is that they could justify as reasonable whatever salaries they wished to allow themselves as corporate employees. The Internal Revenue Service must be satisfied that salaries are in keeping with the value of services rendered; if not so satisfied, it may disallow all or part of them as a deductible corporation expense.

Another point that must be kept in mind by those who weigh the respective tax advantages and disadvantages of operating as proprietorships and partnerships, on the one hand, or as corporations, on the other, is that corporate managements must be in a position to defend themselves if accused by the Internal Revenue Service of retaining earnings to enable stockholders to avoid the individual income taxes they would have to pay if the earnings were distributed as dividends. Under Sections 531–537 of the Internal Revenue Code of 1954, a corporation is permitted to accumulate $100,000 of earnings without question, but further accumulations in any year become subject to a special additional tax of 27½ per cent on the first $100,000 and 38½ per cent on any amount over $100,000 if the Internal Revenue Service is able to prove that they are retained for the avoidance of individual income taxes.

A third consideration is that corporation dividends paid in any year are subject to individual income taxes even though they represent accumulations of past years. Accordingly, it would not be wise for Mr. Green and his fellow stockholders to forgo dividends for, say, five years, and then to take out in the sixth year all the earnings thus accumulated. In general, therefore, stockholders when forgoing dividends in favor of corporate expansion plan to make the plowing-under permanent. Usually they expect the value of their stock to rise in some close relationship to the accumulation of earnings. This enables them to have their reward, if they want it, by selling all or a portion of their stock and thereby realizing a "capital gain." The pleasant aspect of this procedure is that capital gains are taxed in the individual income tax structure at a maximum rate of 25 per cent,[14] rather than at the steeply progressive rates on "ordinary" income which, as was mentioned above, run as high as 91 per cent. Perhaps even better, stockholders may plan to leave the corporate earnings accumulate (and, of course, their potential capital gains) till the time of death. In this way, individual income taxes on retained corporate earnings, as well as capital gains taxes on increases in the value of stocks are completely avoided.

---

[14] The general rule is that only 50 per cent of net "long-term" capital gains (after the deduction of net short-term capital losses, if any) are recognized as taxable income, and that the taxpayer may choose to have this portion of the long-term gain taxable at the ordinary rates of the individual income tax or at the special capital gains rate of 50 per cent. If the latter is chosen, the maximum tax is obviously 25 per cent *of the gain itself* (.50 × .50). But the capital gains rate will not be chosen until the taxpayer's total income, including 50 per cent of the long-term capital gain, rises to the ordinary individual income tax brackets in which the rate of tax is more than 50 per cent. At the tax rates in effect in 1963, this meant that married persons filing joint returns would choose the special capital gains rate only when their taxable income, including 50 per cent of long-term gains, exceeded $36,000, and that single persons and married persons filing separate returns would so choose only when their taxable income exceeded $18,000. It is obvious, therefore, that the rate of 25 per cent was functioning as a maximum rate.

A "long-term" capital gain is one derived upon sales or exchanges of stocks, bonds, and other "capital assets," as defined in the law, held for periods of more than six months. Short-term gains, derived from sales or exchanges of "capital assets" held for six months or less, are taxed at the ordinary rates of the individual income tax to the extent that they are not offset by short-term capital losses and net long-term capital losses.

In a different direction, the partners would also want to consider the possible tax advantages of establishing several corporations to take over the partnership assets. If the partnership had been manufacturing several products, each in a separate plant, or if it had been operating a chain of retail stores, each plant or store might be separately incorporated. From the tax standpoint, the objective would be to establish such a number of corporations as would insure none having net taxable income in excess of $25,000. In this way, all the net income of the several corporations would be taxed at 30 per cent and none of it would get into the 52 per cent bracket as in the illustration. Aside from the tax aspects of the move, moreover, the partners might see a great advantage in limiting their risks of loss. Should one of the separate corporations fail, its creditors could seize its assets in satisfaction of their claims, but the assets of the remaining corporations would be beyond their reach. Another advantage might be that each plant or store could be more efficiently managed if it were owned and operated by a separate corporate entity. Thus, Harold Blancke, president of the Celanese Corporation of America, in announcing in July, 1959, the establishment of three new subsidiaries—the Celanese Fibers Company, the Celanese Chemical Company, and the Celanese Plastics Company—explained the move in this way: "The new companies, having more distinct and autonomous identities, will provide more independent management and greater organizational flexibility in support of the parent company's long-range program to develop new and expanded markets for Celanese products."[15]

Taxation of Unincorporated Firms as Corporations. In view of the fact that owners of unincorporated businesses may see tax advantages in incorporation, Congress added provisions to the Internal Revenue Code of 1954 to permit them to elect to have their business profits taxed as if they were corporate profits. The members of a partnership can choose to have the corporate income tax rates apply to their partnership profits in bulk; in this way, they pay individual income taxes only on whatever portion of partnership profits they withdraw for personal use, just as corporate stockholders pay individual taxes only on the portion of corporate profits they receive as dividends. Once such an election is made, however, it is irrevocable unless a shift in ownership interests of 20 per cent or more occurs.

The privilege of election is accorded to sole proprietorships and to other forms of unincorporated enterprises having not more than 50 members; but a person owning an interest of 10 per cent or more in a firm electing to be taxed as a corporation cannot simultaneously be an owner in another firm so electing. In most cases, money or other property invested by the owners must be a material income-producing factor in the business; however, exceptions are made for firms that derive 50 per cent or more

---

[15] *The New York Times,* July 16, 1959, p. 35.

of their income as dealers or brokers in real estate, securities, or commodities.

Regardless of the privileges of election, most owners of proprietorships and partnerships who see tax advantages in having their profits taxed as if they were corporate profits actually go through with the process of incorporation. They conclude that, if taxation is no bar to incorporation, they may as well gain limited liability and the other advantages of the corporate form of organization as discussed in this chapter. This was indicated in a report of the Treasury that, for tax years ending between July 1, 1959, and June 30, 1960, only 445 tax returns were received from unincorporated businesses choosing to be taxed as corporations, whereas the tax returns of "active" corporations for the same period numbered 1,074,120.[16]

Treatment of Small Corporations as Partnerships. While owners of unincorporated businesses apparently have little reason to elect to have their businesses taxed as corporations without actually incorporating, they might see considerable merit in incorporating if they could elect to have their corporations treated for tax purposes as if they were partnerships. They could thus gain the advantages of incorporation without subjecting themselves to the "double taxation" of corporate income as earned and as dividends when distributed. The privilege of making an election of the latter kind was accorded by Congress in 1958 to "small business corporations."

To qualify as a "small business corporation," a corporation must have only one class of stock (that is, only common stock), not more than ten individual stockholders (among whom estates may be included), and no stockholder who is a nonresident alien. It cannot qualify if more than 80 per cent of its gross receipts are derived from sources outside the United States, nor if its gross receipts from royalties, rents, dividends, interest, annuities, and gains from sales or exchanges of stock or securities exceed 20 per cent of its total gross receipts. All stockholders must consent to the election to have their corporation treated as a partnership for tax purposes. The election means that the stockholders must report in their individual income tax returns for each year their respective shares of corporate net income earned in that year, whether or not received as dividends. The corporation, accordingly, pays no tax on its income, regardless of the amounts distributed as dividends or retained.

An election can be revoked should the stockholders of a "small business corporation" find the special tax arrangement no longer advantageous. Like an election itself, a revocation requires the consent of all stockholders. If made in the first month of a taxable year, it can be applied to

---

[16] U.S. Treasury Department, Internal Revenue Service, *Statistics of Income, 1959–60: Corporation Income Tax Returns* (Washington, D.C.: U.S. Government Printing Office, 1962), pp. 5, 8.

that year; if made later, it becomes effective for the following taxable year. Revocation also occurs automatically if the enterprise no longer qualifies as a "small business corporation"—if it adds a stockholder who does not consent to the prior election, if it gets more than ten stockholders, if a nonresident alien becomes a stockholder, if more than 80 per cent of its gross receipts in any year are derived from foreign sources, and so on.

Future Taxes

In weighing the attractions and burdens of incorporation, organizers and owners of business enterprises are well advised to consider not only tax statutes currently in force but also the possibilities of changes therein. It has already been mentioned that possible changes in federal corporation income tax rates must be considered, but the same advice is applicable for all kinds of special taxes levied upon corporations. A consideration of equal importance is the likelihood that varieties of taxes not currently on the statute books will be imposed. Surmises here may be chiefly concerned with what Congress might decide to do, as federal taxes affecting business enterprise tend to be much heavier than those imposed by the states.

Forecasts may well be based upon what has happened in the past. Thus, it is pertinent to observe that wars almost invariably bring new taxes, as well as increases in the rates of old ones; and it is surely not by chance that corporations are often singled out to bear certain kinds of additional burdens. The levying of an excess-profits tax upon corporations can surely be anticipated for the period of any future war of considerable magnitude, in view of our adoption of such a tax in 1918, 1940, and 1950. In the matter of wartime levies, the federal capital stock tax adopted in 1917 and not repealed until 1925 also deserves mention. But circumstances unrelated to war sometimes give rise to new or refurbished taxes upon corporations. Among these we may recall the interrelated capital stock and declared-value excess-profits taxes in effect from 1934 to 1945, and the much-condemned undistributed-profits tax in effect from 1936 to 1938.

Questions

1. In what sense is it said that the stockholders of a business corporation are only limitedly liable for its debts? Is the corporation itself only limitedly liable? Explain.

2. What is the relationship between the doctrine of the corporation as a distinct legal entity and the doctrine of limited liability?

3. Why is the doctrine of limited liability likely to be less significant for small corporations than for large ones?

4. What is a close corporation? an open corporation? a public corporation?

5. In what respects is corporate stock "flexible" as a financing instrument? Cannot ownership interests in partnerships be made equally flexible and with equal advantage? Explain.

6. Of what advantage to corporations is the easy transferability of their shares? Are not shares of ownership in partnerships transferable with equal ease? Explain.

7. How does the "life" of a corporation differ from that of a partnership? In terms of life, which of these two forms of organization has the principal advantages?

8. How can one account for the fact that the credit standing of corporations does not seem to be weakened because of the limited liability of stockholders?

9. In what sense does the concept of "representative government" apply to the operations of business corporations? Is this advantageous for the stockholders? Discuss.

10. What are the principal burdens in establishing corporations? Would they be likely to dissuade most businessmen from seeking corporate charters? Why or why not?

11. To what extent can a corporation chartered in a given state operate in interstate commerce? To what extent can it "do business" in other states? Why is this distinction important for corporations but not for partnerships?

12. From the standpoint of any given state, what are domestic corporations? foreign corporations? alien corporations?

13. Aside from organization and entrance taxes, two other kinds of taxes are commonly imposed upon corporations by state governments. What are these? In general terms, how burdensome are they?

14. Assuming that the federal corporation income tax is not shifted, why is it likely to be especially burdensome to stockholders who have moderate incomes? Under what circumstances can it work to the advantage of stockholders who have large incomes?

15. Explain why each of the following is an important factor in determining the burden of the federal corporation income tax upon stockholders: the size of corporate income, the size of the stockholder's income from sources other than dividends, the amount of dividends distributed, salaries paid to stockholders as employees, and the special treatment of long-term capital gains in the federal tax laws.

16. If a "small business corporation" elects to have its income taxed by the federal government as if it were a partnership, how and when is the income actually taxed?

Problems

1. What organization tax would a Connecticut corporation pay on an authorized issue of 100,000 shares of stock of $10 par value? 100,000 shares of $50 par value? 100,000 no-par shares?

2. What organization tax would a Delaware corporation pay on an authorized issue of 30,000 shares of $20 par value? one million shares of $5.00 par value?

3. What annual franchise tax would a corporation pay to the state of Michigan on $4 million of capital stock and surplus allocated to that state?

4. What annual franchise tax would a corporation pay to the state of Del-

aware on allocated capital stock amounting to 50,000 shares of $5.00 par value? 800,000 shares of $1.00 par value?

5. State X levies an annual corporation income tax of 5 per cent on income allocated to it on the basis of the Massachusetts formula. In a certain year, the sales of Bonner & Elkin, Inc., in state X amounted to $6 million out of total sales of $30 million; its payroll in state X amounted to $1 million and its total payroll to $10 million; and the value of its tangible property located in state X amounted to $3 million while its total tangible property was valued at $12 million. Its total net income was $4 million. What was the amount of its income tax liability to state X?

6. At the federal corporation income tax rates in effect in the year 1963, as mentioned in this chapter, what would be the tax liability of a corporation with net taxable income of $20,000? $200,000? $2 million?

7. John Doe received $8,000 in dividends in a certain year in which his net taxable income under the federal individual income tax amounted to $21,000. Assuming that the dividend exclusion and the dividends received credit described in this chapter in footnote 8 were in effect, what would be the amount of Doe's dividends received credit? What would the amount of this credit be if Doe's net taxable income had been $7,000?

chapter 3

THE FORMATION OF
BUSINESS CORPORATIONS

It is easy to form a business corporation. The states are most generous in granting corporate charters; in their general incorporation statutes or codes, they have outlined simple procedures whereby charters can be obtained quickly and conveniently. In most states, the secretary of state or some subordinate official in his department has the authority to issue charters; but whoever the official is, or whatever the department in which he may be located, he is generally able to exercise his authority purely as a matter of clerical routine.

An attractive aspect of incorporation is that the secretaries of state or other officials do not have power to pass upon the merits of the business ventures for which charters are sought—the legislatures have not given these officials the right to sit in judgment upon the proposed incorporations that come before them. They do not reject applications on the grounds that the incorporators and proposed directors have had insufficient managerial experience, that they are starting out with too little money to accomplish what they propose to do, or that they wish to enter a field of enterprise in which competition is already much too keen. All that the officials are concerned with is to see that the requirements of the law are fulfilled and that the prescribed fees and taxes are paid. If these conditions are met, they have no choice but to issue the charters applied for. In our day, free enterprise thus means not only freedom to establish new enterprises and free access to markets, but also ready access to corporate charters.

Only when applicants for charters propose to carry on businesses which our states, under their police powers, choose to regulate closely in the public interest do the state officials with whom applications are filed have the authority to reject them. Such businesses usually include railroads, streetcar and bus lines, and certain other classes of enterprises in the transportation field, electric, gas, and water companies, commercial and savings banks, savings and loan associations, credit unions, and insurance companies. Applications for charters for businesses of these kinds customarily bypass the secretaries of state and go direct to other officials who already have regulatory jurisdiction in the respective fields, as the superintendents of banking, the secretaries of insurance, and the public service commissions.

PROCEDURE OF INCORPORATION

Taking Subscriptions to Stock

The first step in the establishment of a business corporation is the taking of subscriptions to the stock that it will issue. The states are extremely easygoing in their requirements here, ordinarily stipulating that subscriptions of $1,000 or $2,000 must be obtained before the application for a charter is filed, and that at least half the amount so stipulated must be paid in before the corporation begins business.

Nevertheless, the promoters of a new corporate organization are likely to pay little attention to the minimum subscription requirements of the state law. If, for example, they anticipate that their enterprise, to get started on a strong footing, will need a stockholders' investment of $100,000, they would be acting rather foolishly were they to proceed with the incorporation upon accumulating subscriptions of only $1,000 or $2,000. Indeed, many proposed ventures stop at this point. The refusal of relatives, friends, and acquaintances to subscribe a sufficient amount disillusions the promoters, and they reluctantly abandon their projects— and their dreams!

Adequate subscriptions to the stock of proposed corporations, on the other hand, may be obtained, as one might say, almost instantaneously. This is especially true of the incorporation of firms already well established as unincorporated businesses. Thus, the members of a partnership may reach a decision to incorporate with the dominant figure among them saying something like this: "We have made approximately equal contributions to the partnership's assets, and we have been sharing profits and losses equally. We will establish a corporation, have it take over the partnership assets at their present book values, and have it issue us equal blocks of stock of the same total value." In such circumstances, assuming the quick agreement of the other partners, the subscription books are opened and closed, as it were, simultaneously.

Subscribers' Meeting

When stock has been subscribed in an amount sufficient to promise success in getting a new corporate venture started, a meeting of the subscribers is held. The principal purpose of the meeting is to choose incorporators who will have the responsibility of carrying through the procedure of incorporation as prescribed by the state law. The incorporators draw up and sign the articles of incorporation (with the advice and aid of competent attorneys, it is to be expected), submit them to the secretary of state, pay the required fees and taxes, and take care of whatever other details the law may require.

The state laws generally provide that there must be not fewer than three incorporators, that they must be natural persons—which means that corporations, as *legal* persons, cannot serve as incorporators of other corporations—and that they must be at least 21 years of age. In most states, there is the further stipulation that some number or proportion of the incorporators must be citizens of the United States, and some go on to provide that some number or proportion must be residents of the state to which the application for a charter is being made.

Some states stipulate that the original board of directors shall be elected at the subscribers' meeting; in others, the choice of directors is deferred until a meeting of the stockholders to be held after the charter has been granted.

Very often the subscribers name themselves as the incorporators, and also, if it is appropriate to do so at the time of the subscribers' meeting, as the first board of directors. Because most corporations start as small ventures involving only a few persons, such persons, or most of them, can usually be expected to serve in all capacities, that is, first as subscribers and incorporators, and subsequently as stockholders, directors, and officers.

Articles of Incorporation

The document that most concerns the incorporators is known in some states as the "articles of incorporation" and in others as the "certificate of incorporation." Throughout this textbook, the former of these designations is used exclusively; hence the student should note that the "articles" discussed in the next few pages and referred to elsewhere may be a "certificate" in his home state or in some other state whose law he may examine.

The articles of incorporation are of major importance in the life of a business corporation. When the secretary of state accepts and approves the articles as having been properly prepared, the new corporate entity is authorized to carry on business in accordance with the terms of the self-same articles and in accordance with the terms of the state law under which they have been filed and approved. The state law gives every corporation established under it certain broad powers that need not be mentioned in the articles, and it likewise places upon it certain responsibilities and limitations whether or not they are mentioned in the articles. Thus it may be said that the powers, responsibilities, and restrictions provided for in the state law, coupled with the provisions contained in a corporation's articles, constitute its *charter*. When it is said, therefore, that a corporation may do this or that according to the terms of its "charter," what is meant is that the action is in accordance with either the provisions of the state law or those of its own articles.

The states require that certain details be specifically set out in the articles of incorporation (see Figure 3–1); other details, they provide, may be included or excluded at the discretion of the incorporators. Let us, first of all, consider what is required.

Name. The name of the proposed corporation must be stated in the articles. Many states prescribe that the name must include a word such as

FIGURE 3–1
Form of Articles of Incorporation (New Jersey)

FORM 2

(R. S. 14:2–3, 4)

CERTIFICATE OF INCORPORATION

OF THE

This is to Certify, That we ....

....

do hereby associate ourselves into a corporation, under and by virtue of Title 14 of the Revised Statutes, and do severally agree to take the number of shares of capital stock set opposite our respective names.

(a) The name of the corporation is

....

(b) The location of the principal office in this State is at No. .... Street, in the .... of .... County of ....

(c) The name of the agent therein and in charge thereof, upon whom process against this corporation may be served, is ....

(d) The objects for which this corporation is formed are ....

....

The corporation shall also have power to conduct its business in all its branches, have one or more offices, and unlimitedly to hold, purchase, mortgage and convey real and personal property in any State, Territory or colony of the United States and in any foreign country or place.

(e) The total authorized capital stock of this corporation is .... dollars, divided into .... shares of a par value of .... dollars each.

(f) The names and post-office address of the incorporators and the number of shares subscribed for by each, the aggregate of which ($ ....) is the amount of capital stock with which this company will commence business, are as follows:

Name.	Post-Office Address.	Number of Shares.

(g) The period of existence of this corporation is unlimited.

In Witness Whereof, we have hereunto set our hands and seals the .... day of .... A. D., One thousand nine hundred and ....

.... (L. S.)
.... (L. S.)
.... (L. S.)

Signed, sealed and delivered in the presence of

....

STATE OF

COUNTY OF .... } ss.

Be it Remembered, That on this .... day of ...., A. D. nineteen hundred and .... before me, a ...., personally appeared ....

whom I am satisfied are the persons named in and who executed the foregoing certificate, and I having first made known to them the contents thereof, they did each acknowledge that they signed, sealed and delivered the same as their voluntary act and deed, for the uses and purposes therein expressed.

corporation, incorporated, or *limited,* or an abbreviation of one of these words, so that everybody will know that the enterprise is a corporation and that its stockholders, therefore, have limited liability for its debts. Other states, however, are not so precise in their requirements, so that it may be impossible to determine from the names used by business enterprises organized in these states whether or not they are corporations. Another common prescription is that the name must not be identical with or confusingly similar to that of another domestic corporation already in operation or to that of a foreign corporation already authorized to do business in the state. Moreover, the name must not include words suggesting that the corporation has powers that it does not or cannot have. Thus, the "South Bend Banking Corporation" would not be an acceptable name for a manufacturing company.

There is much in a name. So the Securities and Exchange Commission found in its comprehensive special study of the securities markets published in 1963. Referring to the many "hot issues" of common stocks floated by corporations in certain "glamour industries" in the period 1959–61, the SEC reported:

> Some companies with prosaic names were rechristened in order to give the impression, correct or not, that they had some connection with electronics, in much the same way as Hollywood starlets are renamed and glamorized to satisfy the public's craving for romance. Monumental Engineering Corp. became Astrotherm Corp.; North Shore Name Plate Corp. became Anodyne Corp.; Iresco, Inc., became Aero Space Electronics, Inc.; Safety Tower Ladder Co., Inc., which manufactures safety belts and attachments, became Air Space Devices, Inc. A representative of American Orbitronics Corp. told prospective customers, "I'm told the name alone is worth $5 a share in this crazy market." [1]

Purposes. The incorporators must be especially careful in stating the "purposes" or "objects" of the proposed corporation. As a general rule, a corporation can undertake only such kinds of business activities as are specifically described in its articles as the "purposes" or "objects" for which it is formed. It is particularly important that narrow definitions of purposes be avoided; if not avoided, an enlargement of the corporation's scope of operations may necessitate the red tape of formally amending the articles (a procedure to be discussed later in this chapter).

The importance of the statement of "purposes" or "objects" was illustrated by recent changes made in the articles of incorporation of the Curtis Publishing Company, publisher of the *Saturday Evening Post,* the *Ladies' Home Journal,* and other popular magazines. Before the changes, its statement of purposes was this: "Manufacturing, printing, and publishing newspapers, periodicals, magazines and books and materials necessary

---

[1] Securities and Exchange Commission, *Report of Special Study of the Securities Markets,* House Doc. No. 95, Pt. 1, 88th Cong., 1st sess. (Washington, D.C.: U.S. Government Printing Office, 1963), p. 498.

therefor." In the amendment, however, several further sweeping statements of purposes were added, including the following:

(3) The prosecution and improvement of the business and arts of communication including the creation, construction, installation, servicing and operation of communications systems of every type and kind, throughout the world and interspace and the sending and receiving of communications of every nature and kind.

(4) The purchase, sale, leasing, merchandising and distribution of articles of commerce of every nature and kind.

(5) The creation, purchase, sale and dissemination of advertising material and services of every nature and kind.

* * * * *

(7) The development, exploitation, sale and leasing, of timber and mineral resources of every nature and kind.[2]

On the other hand, every kind of action that the corporation may or must take to achieve its stated purposes need not be listed in detail in the articles. Most kinds of actions will be readily recognized by courts as "incidental" to its stated purposes or "implied" by the very fact that the corporation is a business enterprise. When, for example, the stated purpose is to manufacture and sell certain kinds of appliances or "appliances of every nature and kind," it is not necessary for the incorporators to state in the articles that the corporation shall have as "purposes" the buying of raw materials, the hiring of labor, the placing of advertising in this or that medium, the borrowing of money from banks, the issuing of bonds, and so on.

A broad statement of purposes enables the stockholders, directors, and officers of a corporation to extend its scope of activities freely without fear that actions in new directions will be adjudged "*ultra vires*." Acts *ultra vires* are those outside the stated purposes of the corporation and beyond the powers incidental thereto. In some states, a corporation has no standing in the courts in trying to enforce contracts found to be *ultra vires*. The other parties to the contracts will not be required to fulfill their obligations if they can prove to the satisfaction of a court that the corporation, in entering the contracts, has attempted to do something beyond its powers. Yet the corporation itself is not likely to be permitted to avoid its obligations under existing contracts even if it can prove that it was acting beyond its powers in entering them. Moreover, stockholders may seek injunctions to prevent their corporations from carrying on what they regard as *ultra vires* functions, and they may sue directors personally for losses incurred because of alleged *ultra vires* acts. The attorney general of the state, too, may go to court to obtain injunctions to prevent corporate acts alleged to be *ultra vires*; indeed, he may initiate proceedings for the dissolution of corporations on the grounds that they persist in committing such acts. Such legal difficulties are likely to origi-

---

[2] *Notice of Annual Meeting and Proxy Statement*, March 8, 1963, pp. 6, 13.

nate, of course, only when the statement of purposes in the articles of incorporation is narrow or ambiguous. Although, therefore, directors may successfully defend themselves and their corporations in legal proceedings of the kinds referred to, it would surely be far better to avoid the threat of such litigation in the first place by a broad, clear statement of purposes.

Principal Office and Resident Agent. A state should be able at all times to reach its corporate creatures to serve legal papers, to assess taxes, to make inquiries, and to transact other kinds of public business; hence comes the requirement for a principal office within the state and a resident agent. In most instances, the incorporators designate as the principal office what will be that truly, and name the president of the proposed corporation as its resident agent.

However, the designation of *any* office and agent, as long as they are located within the state, will usually satisfy the legal stipulation. An attorney, for example, may be named as resident agent and his office designated as the corporation's "principal office." Such an arrangement is common when most of a corporation's plants and sales and administrative offices are (or are expected to be) located outside the state of incorporation. In states where personal property owned by corporations is taxed at the places where their "principal offices" are located, small cities and villages where tax rates are relatively low may be selected for the location of such offices. For example, the borough of Flemington, New Jersey, with a population of 3,232 reported in the 1960 census, is the location of the "principal office" of the $11.5 billion Standard Oil Company (New Jersey)!

Life. With few exceptions, our states authorize perpetual charters for corporations. Some provide that the life of every corporation chartered will be perpetual unless the incorporators state a specific term of years in the articles of incorporation; in these states, therefore, nothing need be said in the articles about the life or "duration" of the corporation if perpetual existence is wanted or is acceptable. In the few states that do not grant perpetual charters, a term of years must obviously be specified in the articles; and in all other states, of course, the articles must designate either perpetual life or a term of years, whichever may be desired.

In states where perpetual corporate life is generously made available, incorporators almost always accept it for their enterprises. Even if the purposes of the corporation are expected to be fulfilled in a few years, perpetual life is the source of no inconvenience. It is as easy to wind up the affairs and effect the dissolution of a corporation having perpetual life as to terminate the life of one having, according to the "duration" stated in its articles, only a few months or years remaining. Because incorporators tend always to anticipate that something will turn up to justify the continued operation of their corporations, even those that start out with short-term objectives, they wish to make unnecessary a later amendment of the articles to extend the corporate life.

Stock Issues. At the minimum, the corporation laws require the incorporators to state in the articles whether the corporation will issue only one class of stock or two or more classes, how many shares of the single class or of the several classes will be authorized, whether or not the stock will have a par value, what the par value will be, and the amount that must be paid in upon stock subscriptions before the corporation will commence business. For the amount that must be paid in before business starts, the laws, as indicated above, stipulate some modest minimum sum, such as $500 or $1,000.

As a general rule, if more than one class of stock is to be authorized, as common and preferred, or common and two or more classes of preferred, the incorporators have the choice of including in the articles all pertinent details of the "designations, preferences, privileges and voting powers of the shares of each class, and the restrictions or qualifications thereof,"[3] or of stating that the board of directors shall have power to fix these details from time to time before shares of the respective classes are issued. Likewise, the articles may provide for the issuance of a given class of stock in series, and the details may be included in the articles or a statement may be inserted saying that the board of directors shall have power to determine these details from time to time. For example, a corporation may have only one class of preferred stock, but it may reserve the right to issue blocks from time to time with differing dividend rates, voting powers, and other features.

If power to establish the details of different classes or series of stock is reserved to the board of directors, subsequent action by the directors in the exercise of this power must be taken by the adoption of formal resolutions. Copies of these resolutions must be filed with the secretary of state and usually with a designated county official in the county in which the corporation's principal office is located—that is, the "principal office" as designated in the articles. The idea is that a complete public record of the details of a corporation's stock should be available for examination by anyone interested in the corporation, such as persons who may wish to buy some of the stock and prospective creditors. The public record is also useful, of course, in the levying of taxes upon the corporation, especially the annual franchise tax if the state has one.

Directors and Incorporators. Provisions in the articles concerning the board of directors may generally be quite brief; in some states, indeed, nothing need be said in the articles about the board. About all that needs to be indicated in the states that require a statement is the number of directors the corporation will have or a permitted range in the number

---

[3] State of New York, *Stock Corporation Law*, sec. 5.

of directors, as not fewer than five nor more than ten. In almost all states, the minimum number permitted is three. Michigan is exceptional in allowing for a single director in any of the business corporations it charters.

Obviously, the names and addresses of the incorporators must be included in the articles, since it is they who are the applicants for the charter. In some states, each incorporator must indicate the number of shares of stock for which he has subscribed; in others, the law has no such requirement.

Other Provisions. So much for the provisions that the state laws, in one way or another, require to be included in the articles of incorporation. If the incorporators so choose, additional details about the organization and government of the corporation may be included, provided only that such details do not run counter to the provisions of the laws. For example, the law of New Jersey authorizes inclusion in the articles of—

. . . any provision, consistent with law, which the incorporators may choose to insert, for the management of the business and the conduct of the affairs of the corporation, and any provision creating, defining, limiting and regulating the powers of the corporation, its directors and stockholders or any class of stockholders.[4]

The common practice, nevertheless, is to keep out of the articles all kinds of provisions not specifically required. Additional details about organization and government can be much better placed in the bylaws of the corporation (to be described briefly below) where they can be amended from time to time as the changing circumstances of the corporation may require. Altering details set out in the articles generally requires the formal process of amendment, whereas changing the bylaws can be effected with much less formality and fuss.

Filing the Articles

After the articles of incorporation have been properly drawn, the requisite number of copies are filed with the secretary of state (or such other official as the state may have designated) and the prescribed fees and taxes are paid. When the secretary of state approves the articles as being in conformity with the state law, the existence of the corporation begins. The approval is indicated in various ways. In some states, the secretary simply notifies the incorporators of his approval; in others, he issues a "certificate of incorporation" which is a specific authorization to the corporation to carry on business in accordance with the provisions of its articles and the state law—in substance, this is the "charter" as that term was defined earlier in this chapter; and in still others, the secretary returns a copy of the articles duly certified.

A further filing requirement laid down in the state laws is that for placing a copy of the articles of incorporation on record in the office of a county official in the county in which is located the corporation's prin-

---

[4] State of New Jersey, *The General Corporation Law,* chap. 2, sec. 14:2–3.

cipal office, as designated in the articles. This official is variously the county clerk, the recorder of deeds, or the prothonotary.

Organization Meetings

Stockholders' Meeting. Following approval of a corporation's articles by the secretary of state, meetings of the stockholders and the original board of directors are generally in order; although, as is indicated in the second paragraph following, a meeting of the stockholders at this time may be unnecessary. If the stockholders have a meeting, it is ordinarily held for the purpose of drawing up and approving bylaws and electing the first board of directors. The bylaws may be described as a body of internal legislation for the government of the corporation. They must not have any provisions in conflict with the articles of incorporation or the state corporation laws, although they may limit the exercise of powers granted in the articles and laws; accordingly, they may be said to be supplementary to the laws and articles, containing details not prescribed in or forbidden by the laws, and not thought to be convenient for insertion in the articles.

Covered in the bylaws are the time and place of the annual meeting of the stockholders, the giving of notice of such meetings, what constitutes a quorum, who presides, method of voting, whether or not cumulative voting is permitted,[5] the use of proxies, and the calling of special meetings; the number, qualifications, and compensation of the directors, the time and place of directors' meetings, what number of directors constitutes a quorum, and the method of filling vacancies in the board; designa-

---

[5] Cumulative voting is designed to give "proportional representation" on the board of directors to whatever factions may exist among the stockholders, so that each faction will be in a position to promote its views and protect its interests. In cumulative voting, each stockholder has votes equal to the number of shares he owns times the number of directors to be elected, and he may cast this "cumulated" total for a single candidate or distribute it among two or more candidates. Suppose, for example, that the majority faction among the stockholders of a corporation holds 7,500 of its 10,000 shares and the minority faction the remaining 2,500 shares, and that nine directors are to be elected. In ordinary voting, the majority would cast 7,500 votes for its slate of nine candidates, and it would thus win all the places on the board since the minority could not cast more than 2,500 votes for any candidate. In cumulative voting, on the other hand, the minority with 22,500 votes could cast, say, 11,250 votes for each of two candidates, and the majority could not possibly defeat these two candidates and win all nine places on the board, no matter how it might divide up its 67,500 votes. In fact, 9,001 votes would be required to choose one director, as determined by the following formula:

$$\frac{\text{Total votes available (90,000)}}{\text{Number of directors to be elected (9)} + 1} + 1 = 9,001$$

Accordingly, the majority could be sure of seven places but not eight or nine, and the minority could be sure of two places but not three or four. Should the minority try to get more than its "proportional representation" by casting, say, 5,625 votes for each of four candidates, it would probably be frozen out completely, since the majority could cast 7,500 votes for each of nine candidates. For cumulative voting to be successful in providing proportional representation, therefore, each faction must know its strength and concentrate or spread its votes in keeping with this knowledge.

tion of the titles of the principal officers, as president, vice president, secretary, and treasurer, the general scope of their duties, their scale of compensation, and whether or not they are to be bonded; procedures for the issuance and transfer of stock and the keeping of records of the stockholders; provisions for the control of the corporation's cash and valuable papers, and for the safeguarding of its property of other kinds; limitations upon the amount of its indebtedness and upon the pledging of its property for the security of its obligations; and provisions designating the procedure for amending the bylaws.

In some states, the corporation laws confer upon the directors the power to adopt, amend, and repeal bylaws, unless the power is reserved to the stockholders in the articles of incorporation; and many others authorize a delegation of the power to the directors by specific provision in the articles of incorporation. Theoretically, the principal function of bylaws is to protect the interests of the stockholders as owners of a corporation; hence giving directors the right to adopt, amend, and repeal these rules of internal government is illogical. Because, however, bylaws adopted by directors are subject to amendment, repeal, or replacement by action of the stockholders taken at annual or special meetings, the stockholders continue to have the final authority. At any rate, if the directors have powers with respect to the bylaws, and if the stockholders are satisfied to let them exercise these powers, no questions pertaining to the bylaws need be taken up at the organization meeting of the stockholders. Indeed, the stockholders need have no organization meeting at all if the directors are to take care of the bylaws and if the first board itself was chosen by the subscribers at their earlier meeting.

Directors' Meeting. First in the order of business at the directors' organization meeting is the adoption of the bylaws if that job falls within their province. Next comes the choice of the officers and other key personnel, the fixing of lines of authority, the allocation of duties and responsibilities, and the setting of a scale of salaries if not already set out in the bylaws. Finally, the directors adopt an official seal which is to be placed upon reports to the state, stock certificates, and other documents requiring a seal. These actions must be taken to complete the organization of the corporation, and they constitute, as it were, the agenda of the organization meeting; however, the directors may continue, if they wish, with what could be called a regular business meeting. Indeed, they may be quite anxious to go ahead with the discussion and ratification of many pending contracts having to do with the actual launching of business operations.

General Corporate Powers

Important to the careers of business corporations are the general powers conferred upon them by the state corporation laws. These powers may be exercised even though not mentioned in the articles and regardless of what the stated purposes of the individual corporations may be. They tend toward uniformity from state to state, although one must always be on the lookout for exceptions. The general powers granted by the state of Delaware are as follows:

Every corporation created under the provisions of this chapter shall have power to—

(1) Have succession, by its corporate name, for the time stated in its certificate of incorporation, and when no period is limited, it shall be perpetual;

(2) Sue and be sued, complain and defend in any court of law or equity;

(3) Have a corporate seal, which may be altered at pleasure, and to use the same by causing it or a facsimile thereof to be impressed or affixed or reproduced or otherwise;

(4) Hold, purchase and convey real and personal estate, and to mortgage or lease any such real or personal estate with its franchises. The power to hold real and personal estate, except in the case of religious corporations, shall include the power to take the same by devise or bequest;

(5) Appoint such officers and agents as the business of the corporation requires and to allow them suitable compensation;

(6) Make by-laws not inconsistent with the Constitution or laws of the United States or of this State, fixing and altering the number of its directors for the management of its property, the regulation and government of its affairs and for the certification and transfer of its stock with penalties for the breach thereof not more than $20;

(7) Wind up and dissolve itself or to be wound up and dissolved in the manner provided for in this chapter;

(8) Conduct business in this State, other states, the District of Columbia, the territories and colonies of the United States and in foreign countries, and have one or more offices out of this State, and to hold, purchase, mortgage and convey real and personal property both within and without this State;

(9) Make donations for the public welfare or for charitable, scientific or educational purposes;

(10) Indemnify any and all of its directors or officers or former directors or officers or any person who may have served at its request as a director or officer of another corporation in which it owns shares of capital stock or of which it is a creditor against expenses actually and necessarily incurred by them in connection with the defense or any action, suit or proceeding in which they, or any of them, are made parties, or a party, by reason of being or having been directors or officers or a director or officer of the corporation, or of such other corporation, except in relation to matters as to which any such director or officer or former director or officer or person shall be adjudged in such action, suit or proceeding to be liable for negligence or misconduct in the performance of duty. Such indemnification shall not be deemed exclusive of any other rights to which those indemnified may be entitled, under any by-law, agreement, vote of stockholders, or otherwise.[6]

Beyond such a general grant of powers, the states provide that their corporations will have such additional powers as are necessary or convenient for the accomplishment of their stated purposes. For example, Illinois sets out this type of provision as follows: "To have and exercise all powers necessary or convenient to effect any or all of the purposes for which the corporation is formed."[7]

---

[6] State of Delaware, *General Corporation Law*, sec. 122.

[7] State of Illinois, *The Business Corporation Act*, sec. 5.

AMENDING THE ARTICLES

Avoidance of Amendments

Any lack of foresight on the part of the incorporators or their attorneys in drawing up articles of incorporation does not mean that a corporation will be straitjacketed throughout its life; as far as legal procedure goes, it is as easy to amend the articles as to have them approved in the first place. As a practical matter, however, it is usually much easier for a handful of incorporators to agree upon the details of the articles than to get the approval, later on, of the requisite number of stockholders for amendments. All the more is this likely to be true, of course, if, at the time amendments are proposed, there are many stockholders, and if the proposals for amendment are of a controversial nature. It behooves incorporators, therefore, to proceed with such care that they can be reasonably sure that amendments, aside from those involving stock authorizations, will not be necessary for many years.

Only in the matter of stock issues is it likely that amendment from time to time will be anticipated as a desirable step. Many of the states, as we have seen, base their organization taxes on the authorized stock issues, rather than on the amount of stock to be issued immediately. In such states, therefore, tax liabilities of this kind can be minimized by limiting the authorized stock issues to an amount not in excess of what will probably be issued in the first few years of operation.[8]

Amending Procedure

The ordinary procedure for amending the articles begins with the adoption by the board of directors of a resolution setting forth a careful statement of the proposed amendment. The resolution is then submitted to the stockholders for their approval. This may be done at the regular annual meeting of the stockholders or at a special meeting called at any time. Depending upon the state law and provisions in the articles themselves, an affirmative vote of stockholders owning a majority or two thirds or some other proportion of the stock "represented at the meeting and entitled to vote" is necessary for approval.

Upon approval by the stockholders, articles of amendment are drawn up and are submitted to the secretary of state in duplicate or triplicate, as the law may require, together with the inevitable filing fee, and with a payment for taxes if the amendment calls for an increase in the authorized stock. The secretary may issue a "certificate of amendment" or indicate his approval in whatever other way the law provides for; at any rate, approval by the secretary, as for the original articles, has the effect of putting into force the change desired. There is also a requirement for

---

[8] In various situations, however, stockholders' interests may be best served if boards of directors have substantial amounts of authorized stock available for immediate issuance without need of an approval vote of the stockholders. For a discussion of this matter, see below, pp. 475–76.

filing a copy of the articles of amendment with an official of the county in which the principal office of the corporation is situated.

CHOOSING THE STATE OF INCORPORATION

Location of Properties and Business Activities

Because most corporations are small at the time of their establishment, the great majority are incorporated in the states in which their promoters reside. The promoters expect to locate their plants, stores, or other properties entirely within the borders of their home states, and they anticipate that all or almost all their business activities, for many years or perhaps permanently, will be similarly confined. There may be little prospect of their "doing business" in other states. Almost as a matter of course, they plan from the beginning to send their "papers" to Springfield, Albany, Atlanta, Harrisburg, Sacramento, and so on, because they reside in the states whose capitals these cities are. In most instances, they probably do not even consider the fact that they could get a charter in another state as easily, or almost as easily, as in the home state. Those promoters of small, localized corporations who do consider this possibility are likely to reject it quickly, thinking of the additional red tape of having to obtain a certificate of authority from the state of residence, and of the continuing obligation to pay taxes and to file reports in both the chartering state and the state of residence.

"Shopping around" among several states to find the one which appears to offer most advantages for incorporation is thus likely to be of interest only to larger enterprises. The members of a partnership already doing business in many states would be likely to analyze most carefully the advantageous and disadvantageous aspects of these states should they decide to incorporate. They might even select a state in which very little of their business was being transacted, or none at all, should they be convinced of the preponderance of its advantages. Likewise, the managers of a corporation that has grown large and has extended its operations into several states may be more or less constantly on the lookout for advantages to be gained by giving up the corporation's charter in the state of original incorporation and obtaining a new one in another state. In the spring of 1963, for example, the management of the Elgin National Watch Company asked its stockholders to approve a switch in its incorporation from Illinois to Delaware principally to escape two provisions of Illinois law, one requiring that cumulative voting in the election of directors be permitted, and the other requiring the offering of new issues of stock first to the existing stockholders.[9] However, Elgin's management failed to get sufficient votes approving the proposed move.

---

[9] For an explanation of cumulative voting, see footnote 5 on page 53. A requirement that new issues of stock must be first offered to the existing stockholders is known as their "preemptive right." For a discussion of this right, see below, pp. 367–69.

Mergers and consolidations, too, present opportunities for renewed analysis of the merits and demerits of charters as granted by different states. If Corporation A chartered in Maryland and Corporation B chartered in Ohio—each doing business in several states—are to be combined, it may be decided that the most advantageous arrangement would be to have a new corporation, Corporation C, chartered in Delaware to take over A and B.

When circumstances appear to make "shopping around" advisable, advantages and disadvantages are usually thought of in terms of three things: (1) taxation, (2) the stability of the corporation laws, and (3) the liberality of these laws.

Taxation

The burden of special corporate taxes is of great importance in deciding whether or not a business should be incorporated. This we have already seen. It is of much less importance in choosing the state of incorporation, although still worthy of study. A major reason for this reduced importance is that the heaviest tax levies placed on corporations are those of the federal government, and such taxes are payable, of course, regardless of the state of incorporation—or even the country of incorporation.[10] Another reason is that the states that levy annual franchise and corporate income taxes impose them on foreign corporations as well as on domestic ones.

Nevertheless, some tax economies are possible by judicious choice of the state of incorporation. States that place relatively high organization taxes upon total authorized stock are likely to be avoided. Also likely to be quite unattractive are states that annually tax the entire net income of their domestic corporations. Finally, an analysis of the formulas by which states allocate their annual franchise and net income taxes may reveal that the selection of a particular state for incorporation may minimize the total burden of these taxes.

Stability of Corporation Laws

A corporate charter is of the nature of a contract between the corporation and the state that grants it. But the states reserve the right to change the terms of the contract unilaterally, that is, to change their corporation laws without asking their corporate creatures for permission to do so. The greater the possibility, therefore, that a state will change its

---

[10] Alien corporations pay federal corporation income taxes on that portion of their income that is derived within the United States, its territories, and dependencies. Certain credits against the tax liability are allowed for taxes paid to foreign governments, but such credits obviously do not reduce the total tax bill. Nevertheless, certain arrangements have been available from time to time whereby incorporation in foreign countries has been a means of considerable tax savings. Witness the use of "Bermuda corporations" and the registry of American-owned tankers under the flags of Liberia and Panama.

laws significantly from time to time, the less attractive it is as a source of charters. Especially do promoters think it wise to avoid states whose laws lack clearly stated provisions concerning one or more important aspects of corporate organization, government, and powers, as well as states whose laws have ambiguous or conflicting provisions.

A comprehensive body of court decisions in which the corporation laws have been thoroughly analyzed and interpreted may be also said to be a source of stability. It is always disturbing, and sometimes quite upsetting, to corporate policies to have a court declare a provision of the corporation laws void because of a conflict with the state constitution; and similarly upsetting may be a court decision that the legislature meant thus-and-so when it enacted a certain feature of the law while corporate managements had always thought that the legislature meant something quite different. A consistent line of many court decisions is likely to be found in a state that has already chartered many thousands of corporations, and this very fact surely contributes further to its popularity.

Liberality of Corporation Laws

Of outstanding importance to larger enterprises seeking the most favorable state for incorporation is the comparative liberality of the corporate laws of the various states. The more generous the grant of powers and privileges to corporations and the fewer the restrictions placed upon them, the greater is the liberality of the laws said to be. Few would question the common sense of promoters in seeking liberality as thus described!

Liberality for Directors. A phase of liberality that is especially sought is the concentration of corporate powers in the board of directors. Directors like to be in a position to make almost all kinds of decisions without having to go continually to the stockholders for a new grant of powers or for approval of actions they propose to take. Liberality of this kind is found in provisions of corporation laws that specifically place in the directors the power to adopt, amend, and repeal bylaws; permit them to change the number of directors and to fill vacancies occurring between annual meetings of the stockholders; and authorize staggered terms for the directors, with only one half, one third, or one fourth coming up for election each year, so that it is difficult for a faction among the stockholders opposed to the incumbent board to gain control. Liberal provisions are also found with respect to the capacity of directors to manage stock issues, to issue stock in exchange for property and services, and to declare dividends. Numbered among liberal provisions of these kinds are those permitting articles of incorporation to authorize the directors to put out additional batches of stock from time to time and to determine what classes of stock such issues will be, what rights and preferences they will have, and so on; giving directors wide discretion in the valuation of property and services for which stock is given, and relieving them of liability for overgenerous valuations except in cases of proven bad faith or fraud; permitting the directors to allocate to the surplus accounts portions of the proceeds of the sale of no-par stock; allowing the payment of dividends out of sources of surplus other than net profits on operations, such as premiums received in the original sale of stock and surplus put on the books as a result of write-ups in the value of assets; and permitting the payment of dividends out of current profits even though deficits of earlier years have not been made good. Liberality favoring the directors may also be said to exist in state laws that provide that holders of simple majorities of the stock may approve proposals of the directors requiring stockholder approval, rather than, say, majorities of two thirds or three fourths.

Other Liberal Features. Other features of corporation laws generally described as "liberal," though not directly involving the directors, include the following: permission to hold annual and special meetings of the stockholders outside the state of incorporation; the granting of wide powers to corporations to buy and sell property, their own stock previously issued, and the stocks of other corporations; permission to issue nonvoting stocks and stocks lacking the preemptive right (the latter being the ordinary right of stockholders to get the first chance to buy additional issues in proportion to their existing holdings); power to issue par-value stock at a discount without liability accruing to the subscribing stockholders or the directors for the amount of the discount; and annual-report requirements calling for minimal information.

In almost all states, recent trends in legislation having to do with the chartering and operations of corporations have been rather strongly in the direction of liberality. Thus, comparisons of state corporation laws on the basis of their degrees of liberality, though still of importance, are not nearly so important as in times past when some states were known as "charter-mongering states." Such states were so called because they had deliberately adopted liberal laws to attract incorporations at a time when the laws of other states were relatively strict. At the present time, one seldom hears references to "charter-mongering states"; one is more likely to hear allusions to a few states as being "strict," the implication being that all others are liberal in varying degrees.

Questions

1. Support or attack this proposition: Our states are reluctant to issue corporate charters, and applications are often rejected on the grounds that the applicants are not qualified to operate businesses in the the corporate form.

2. How much of the stock of a proposed corporation must be subscribed before it qualifies for a charter? How much must be paid in for stock before the corporation is qualified to begin business?

3. In the formation of a new corporation, what work is done by the incorporators? How are the incorporators chosen?

4. If only natural persons are qualified to serve as incorporators, how has it been possible for many corporations to establish subsidiary corporations?

5. What are the articles of incorporation of a corporation? What is the relationship between the articles and the corporation's charter?

6. In the preparation of the articles of incorporation for a new corporation, why is so much emphasis given to the statement of its "objects" or "purposes"?

7. What details about a corporation's authorized stock issues must be given in its articles of incorporation? about its life or "duration"?

8. What kinds of operating powers do corporations have even though not specifically stated in their articles of incorporation?

9. What kinds of rules or regulations are included in a corporation's bylaws? How are the powers to adopt, amend, and repeal bylaws shared between boards of directors and stockholders? Who has the final word?

10. What is the procedure for amending a corporation's articles of incorporation? For what reasons might corporations want to amend their articles?

11. As a criterion for determining from what states corporate charters will be sought, how important is location of properties and principal business activities? How important is taxation?

12. Give several examples of provisions that account for the description of some state corporation laws as "liberal."

Problem

The articles of incorporation of the Ace Construction Company provide that its board of directors shall have seven members to be elected annually and that cumulative voting is permitted in their election. The corporation has outstanding 100,000 shares of stock, and a minority group wants to be sure to get its "proportional representation" on the board by concentrating its votes cumulatively on the maximum number of candidates it is sure to elect. How many candidates should the group nominate if the members of the group own 16,000 shares? 37,000 shares?

Project

Obtain a copy of the "general corporation law" of your home state and compare its provisions, item by item, with the general description of the features of such laws in this chapter. For class discussion, note especially in what details the provisions of the law of your state differ from the description in this chapter. (In most states, the general corporation law is supplied in pamphlet form free of charge by the secretary of state. In some states, a small charge, such as one dollar, is made. At any rate, the student should find it enlightening to check general statements in reference to corporations as made throughout this textbook against the specific provision of the corporation law of his own state.)

Part II

FINANCE FUNCTIONS
AND CASH FLOWS

chapter 4

FINANCE FUNCTIONS

Although financial questions are importantly involved in decisions whether or not to incorporate, choices as to the states in which charters will be sought, decisions as to what stock issues articles of incorporation should provide for, and so on, it can be said that the responsibilities of corporate financial managers come into being only when the process of organization has been completed. Before that, decisions are in the hands of organizers and promoters who may or may not subsequently become the financial managers. It is the objective of the present chapter, therefore, to analyze in a broad way the duties and powers of corporate financial managers—as a preliminary, so to say, to the more detailed treatment in the remainder of this textbook. Our immediate task is twofold: (1) to examine what may be called the *finance functions* of business corporations (and really of all kinds of business enterprises), and (2) to study the lines of authority and responsibility in corporations for the fulfillment of these functions.

THE SCOPE OF THE FINANCE FUNCTIONS

It is often said that all the operations of business enterprises can be classified as falling within three areas: production, marketing, and finance. No great difficulty is ordinarily encountered in deciding what are production and marketing functions, but the scope of the finance functions cannot be so readily distinguished. The reason for this uncertainty about the scope of the finance functions is that it is quite impossible, in most instances, to divorce financial considerations from production and marketing goals, decisions, and operations. Almost all kinds of actions in the areas of production and marketing directly, or at least indirectly, involve the acquisition and use of money. The determination of factory employment policies clearly comes within the purview of production, but employment requires the payment of wages and salaries and social security taxes, and it is likely to call also for the provision of certain classes of "fringe benefits." Where, then, is the separation between the production function of setting employment policies and the finance function of providing means of meeting the costs of employment? All the more is the point of separation hard to find when it is realized that the finance function in the matter of employment is not simply one of looking for money once employment policies have been set; it is one of helping to decide what employment policies are feasible, given the financial position of the business enterprise and its access to additional sources of funds. The determination of advertising policies—deciding what products to advertise, settling upon the content of advertising material, selecting the mediums to be used, and so on—is surely a marketing function; but advertising requires outlays of cash and necessarily, therefore, involves finance. How can one say where the marketing function of establishing advertising policies ends and where begins the finance functions of determining what advertising budget is financially sound and of actually providing the money for it?

In truth, the questions raised have no clear-cut answers. The finance functions having to do with the acquisition and use of money are there, but their limits cannot be clearly marked out for the general run of businesses. The limits vary in inuumerable ways, depending upon the dissimilar positions of individual enterprises. A corporation that finds itself in a tight financial position, having limited cash resources and lmited access to additional cash, must surely give financial considerations dominant weight, that is, it must try to devise production and marketing policies in keeping with its strained circumstances. On the other hand, the managers of a corporation having access to a plentiful supply of cash can doubtless feel free to study a wide range of possibilities in deciding upon production and marketing policies, expecting to be able easily to devise financial policies to fit their production and marketing decisions.

Although it is difficult to set limits to the finance functions, the functions themselves can be readily classified and described. They are of two kinds, and they may be called, respectively, *executive* finance functions and *incidental* finance functions. Executive finance functions require great skill—a high order of administrative ability—in planning and execution; and the incidental functions have to do with routine work, chiefly clerical, that is necessary to carry into effect financial decisions at the executive level.

The executive finance functions are the following:

1. Establishing asset-management policies.
2. Determining the allocation of net profits.
3. Estimating cash flows and requirements.
4. Controlling the flow of cash.
5. Deciding upon needs and sources of new outside financing.
6. Carrying on negotiations for new outside financing.
7. Checking upon financial performance.

This listing is not necessarily in the order of priority—priority in the sense of importance, or priority in the sense of the timing of decisions. Each of the executive finance functions is important, and decisions and actions concerning most of them must be made more of less simultaneously. All are closely interrelated, so that a change in decisions in one category is likely to require changes in decisions in some or all the others. For example, cash flows cannot be estimated until asset-management and profit-allocation policies have been at least tentatively determined; yet the determination of these policies depends in a very important way upon estimates of the inflow of cash in the ordinary course of business, together with estimates of the amount of cash that can be raised through new outside financing. (As used in studies in corporation finance, the term *financing* means the acquisition of cash or other assets by incurring debts, by sales of additional stock, or by retaining net profits and the "cash throw-offs" from charges for depreciation, depletion, and amortization.[1] Incurring debts and selling additional stock to acquire assets are often described as means of "outside" or "external" financing; while retaining profits and cash throw-offs is described as "internal" financing.) In a similar way, decisions about the payment of cash dividends to the stockholders—a matter obviously having to do with the allocation of net profits—must be tied in with acceptable asset-management policies and properly related to estimates of cash flows and requirements and a consideration of sources of new outside financing.

The incidental finance functions are as follows:

1. Supervision of cash receipts and disbursements and the safeguarding of cash balances.
2. Custody and safeguarding of securities, insurance policies, and other valuable papers.
3. Taking care of the mechanical details of new outside financing.
4. Record keeping and reporting.

Executive Finance Functions

Establishing Asset-Management Policies. All finance functions are concerned with the management of cash—with the control, as it were, of the cash flows of the individual enterprise. Cash requirements can be estimated, and arrangements can be made to take care of them, only if the financial managers know quite definitely how cash will be used as it is acquired by the enterprise. Outstandingly this means that they must know how much cash will be "tied up" in the various kinds of noncash assets. Thus, the establishment of sound and consistent asset-management policies is an indispensable prerequisite to successful financial management.

The financial managers themselves must participate in determining asset-management policies. Their special knowledge of the cash-flow processes, the possibilities of slowdowns and speedups in the ordinary inflows and outflows of cash on account of changing business conditions, the sources of new financing, the prevailing terms and conditions of new financing, and so on, should be invaluable in asset planning. Were they

---

[1] Why cash throw-offs are recognized as sources of assets is explained in Chapter 6. See pp. 112–13.

to have no such authority, plans prepared by others for the acquisition of assets might often be quite unrealistic in view of the enterprise's financial position and prospects.

The relationship of asset-management policies to financial management can be readily understood if reference is made to the kinds of questions that must be answered before policy decisions are finally reached. Consider questions such as the following: What will be the inventory policy of the enterprise? Will it buy stocks of goods for resale, or will it be able to obtain them on a consignment basis? What are the minimum varieties and quantities of goods that it must have on hand at all times to serve its customers adequately? Will it buy goods in extraordinary quantities in anticipation of price increases? Will it attempt to sell slow-moving goods by substantial price cuts? Will it sell for cash or on account? If it sells on account, will it allow a cash discount for early payment? What rate of discount will it allow? If it needs additional facilities, will it buy these outright or seek to rent them? If it buys them outright, will it pay cash in full at once, or will it be able to arrange payment on an installment basis over a period of months or years? If it rents them, will it be required to make a large initial rental payment?

The determination of asset-management policies, it should be added, includes decision making about the kinds and coverages of insurance that an enterprise will carry—an area of decision making in which financial managers are ordinarily expected to be much more competent than production and marketing executives. The enterprise's stake in inventories, buildings, and other facilities is protected against losses due to fire, windstorm, and other hazards if insurance coverages of the proper kinds are obtained. But the enterprise is likewise protected against drains from its assets due to embezzlement, robbery, damages to be paid on account of injuries to its employees and the public, and so on, when it carries surety bonds upon employees who handle cash and securities, robbery insurance, workmen's compensation insurance, public liability insurance, and the like.

The role of financial managers in trying to reach answers to questions of the kinds listed above and in planning an adequate program of insurance coverages—their role, that is, in establishing asset-management policies—cannot ordinarily be an exclusive one. Production managers can be expected to insist upon their right to participate in making decisions concerning the carrying of inventories of raw materials and factory supplies, employment policies, and the purchase or renting of factory machinery and equipment; and marketing executives, likewise, in decisions involving the carrying of inventories of finished goods, advertising policies, and customer credit policies. Once again, therefore, we come to the conclusion that there is no exact way of determining where financial management leaves off and production and marketing management begins. The individual enterprise must seek, therefore, to establish lines of authority in such manner that every decision will be based upon a careful balancing of production, marketing, and finance considerations.

Determining the Allocation of Net Profits. The typical corporation may be said to have three choices in the allocation of whatever net profits it has after the payment of income taxes: to pay dividends to the stockholders as a return upon their investment, to make distributions to people other than the stockholders, as in employee profit-sharing plans, and to retain them for the expansion of assets. The second alternative is ordinarily made on a long-range basis, so that once an employee profit-sharing plan, for example, has been adopted as a "fringe benefit," it continues annually to be apportioned a percentage of the net profits as a matter of contract or as a matter of fixed policy. Whether or not, therefore, a corporation has an allocation of the second kind, its continuing free choices in the use of net profits generally involve only the other two alternatives, that is, the payment of dividends and the acquisition of additional assets.

It may appear that the latter of these alternatives is by far the more important since a corporation cannot continue to operate profitably without an adequate supply of productive assets, and since the stockholders' interests are necessarily served in assuring this capacity for continued profitable operation. Nevertheless, dividend policy cannot be based simply on a standing decision to distribute to the stockholders whatever cash is left after all likely and possible cash needs "in the business" have been allowed for; if that were the basis of policy, all too often no dividends would be paid, for corporate managements tend always to have in mind expansion plans sufficiently broad to absorb all cash that is likely to become available. On the contrary, corporate managements must realize that dividend policies have important bearings upon prospects of additional sales of stock as a means of raising cash, upon credit standing which determines capacity to buy on account and to borrow money, and, indeed, upon their own prospects of continuing to hold their jobs.

The determination of dividend policies is almost exclusively a finance function. Only because dividend payments reduce the amount of cash available for other purposes are production and marketing executives inclined to be interested; their interest, therefore, is likely to be much less keen than in the determination of asset-management policies. Accordingly, the financial managers are much more likely to have the final word in decisions upon dividends than in asset-management decisions.

Cash Requirements and Flows: Estimation and Control. A prime responsibility of financial management is to see that an adequate supply of cash is on hand at the proper times for the acquisition of assets and for making allocations of net profits, as in the payment of dividends and in making appropriations as for employee profit-sharing plans. (The meeting of all kinds of current operating expenses, it is important to emphasize, is simply a process of acquiring assets; likewise, the paying off of liabilities is ordinarily the discharge of obligations for assets already acquired. When, therefore, one speaks of a need of cash for the "acquisition of assets," one necessarily allows for the use of cash for the payment of operating expenses and meeting maturing liabilities.) A failure of the financial managers to provide cash in adequate amounts at the proper times must at least impede the smooth flow of operations, and, of course, it may result in grave embarrassment.

As a rule, the financial managers must look to the ordinary day-to-day operations of their corporations as the source of the principal volume of inflowing cash. For most businesses, this inflow comes from sales, either at the time of sale or at a later time if goods or services are sold on a deferred-payment basis. In most instances, likewise, cash requirements are closely related to the volume of sales. It is clear, then, that asset-management and profit-allocation policies must be closely tied in with the anticipated level of sales; and it is equally clear that the responsibility for providing cash in the proper amounts at the proper times requires forecasting. It is not enough to forecast the year's collections from sales, and the year's cash requirements on the basis of expected sales, for such a forecast would reveal little about the timing of cash inflows and outflows. Financial embarrassment might result from a lack of coordination in the inflows and outflows, even though, in annual totals, cash receipts might substantially exceed cash disbursements. Thus, forecasts must ordinarily be put on the basis of monthly expectations within the longer period of, say, a year; often, indeed, it is advantageous to use periods shorter than a month for the estimates, especially in forecasts for the immediate future. Needless to say, forecasts must make allowance for anticipated inflows of cash from sources other than sales, as well as for outflows other than those required for meeting the expected level of sales.

By means of forecasting, the financial managers ought to be able to judge rather closely how much cash will be coming in and going out from month to month, or perhaps from week to week. They will realize, of course, that much of the cash flows, since they depend upon the volume of operations, will not be strictly controllable by decisions that they may make. Nevertheless, they will know that the timing of the flows can be at least moderately altered by certain kinds of decisions, as by decisions to concentrate advertising campaigns or to offer goods at reduced prices in certain months, to modify inventory accumulation policies, or to change dividend payment practices as by paying dividends semiannually rather than quarterly. On the basis of the forecasts, too, the financial managers may anticipate a need of borrowing during some period in the course of the year when, as the forecasts indicate, cash inflows from ordinary operations will be quite insufficient to meet cash requirements, and they may, accordingly, take immediate steps to arrange for loans; or they may anticipate having excess supplies of cash in certain

periods, and they may make immediate plans for the temporary investment of these excess funds.

Deciding upon Needs and Sources of New Outside Financing. As was
just indicated, the financial managers, on the basis of their forecasts of the
volume of operations, may have to plan upon borrowing as a means of
supplementing cash flowing from these operations; as was indicated
earlier, such borrowing would be described as a means of "financing."
Two of the principal means of outside financing are the sale of additional
stock and all kinds of borrowing, including borrowing from commercial
banks and other financial institutions and the flotation of bond issues.

As was indicated, too, financing plans require foresight. On the basis
of their forecasts of the inflow and outflow of cash in the ordinary
course of operations, the financial managers should be able to judge rather
closely the time when additional funds from outside sources will be
needed, how long they will be needed, and from what sources the means
of repayment (in the case of borrowing) are to be derived. The financial
managers would hardly be acting competently if they woke up to a realization of a need of additional funds only when the cash account had been
almost exhausted.

Not only must the financial managers foresee financing requirements,
they must select the means of meeting them. In this regard, a distinction
must usually be made between short-term requirements that turn up again
and again year after year in much the same pattern and long-term requirements. The distinction is important for two reasons: (1) it tends to
indicate the nature of the requirements, and (2) it suggests what are
likely to be the best sources of the funds needed. Short-term requirements usually result from unevenness in the inflow and outflow of cash
on account of the very nature of business operations. Production requiring large outlays may be heavily concentrated in one period of the year,
whereas sales may be concentrated in a later period; thus, cash disbursements for production in the earlier period may require temporary borrowing, to be repaid out of the later cash inflows from sales. Financing
of this kind is often planned for on a continuing basis, as by making and
annually renewing arrangements for "lines of credit" at commercial banks
or with sales finance companies. Long-term requirements, on the other
hand, most commonly arise because of programs for substantial expansion
in the scope of operations. Additional plant, machinery and equipment,
and other facilities may be needed to meet an expected long-range expansion in sales, and, typically, cash inflows from ordinary operations are
quite inadequate to take care of both the expansion of facilities and continued outlays required for day-to-day activities. Commercial banks, sales
finance companies, and other lenders that supply short-term funds may
also be willing to provide some longer-term funds, and the financial managers may not need to go beyond them in getting the cash needed for
expansion; on the other hand, for various reasons, they may prefer to go

to the stockholders and ask them to buy additional stock, or to institutions such as investment banking houses and life insurance companies which concentrate upon providing long-term money.

Carrying on Negotiations for New Outside Financing. When decisions have been made that outside financing must be undertaken, the financial managers have the responsibility to arrange for it. As was said above, short-term financing requirements are often arranged for on a continuing basis, as in the establishment of lines of credit at commercial banks. (Commercial banks are distinguished from all other classes of financial institutions in that they alone receive deposits of the public subject to repayment on demand upon the written orders of the depositors. By its very nature, therefore, a commercial bank offers checking account facilities to its customers.[2]) A line of credit is a commitment of a lender to a borrower to advance funds up to designated amount at any time within a specified period that the borrower may want them. At the time that the line of credit is arranged, there is usually an agreement upon the maturity of the loans that may be granted and whether such loans are to be secured or unsecured. The interest rate the borrower is to pay may also be stipulated, although the determination of the interest rate may be deferred until the time that the funds are actually called for. Even a continuing arrangement of this kind, however, requires negotiations. As lines of credit are ordinarily "held open" for not more than a year, it is necessary to reopen negotiations annually for the renewal of the lines. To keep a line open, the borrower is generally required also to file periodic financial statements with the lender so that he may be assured that the credit standing of the borrower is not deteriorating in any significant way.[3]

When corporations need to borrow only sporadically for short-term purposes, they are unlikely to have lines of credit already set up. Accordingly, when loans are applied for, delays in getting the funds are to be expected on account of the compiling and analysis of credit information by prospective lenders. Thus, the beginning of negotiations well before money is actually needed is important; once again, therefore, foresight is to be emphasized.

Negotiations and the completion of arrangements for long-term financing usually require much more time than does the working out of

---

[2] For a brief statement upon the importance of the commercial banks in our economy, see below, pp. 784–85.

[3] It is customary to require balance sheets and income statements. The requirement may be for monthly, quarterly, semiannual, or annual statements, depending upon the size of the line of credit, the nature of the borrower's business, his usual practices in preparing statements, and other factors. Lenders frequently stipulate that, at least once a year, statements prepared by certified public accountants must be submitted. For a discussion of the nature of balance sheets, see below, pp. 89–90, and of income statements, pp. 97–98. For a further discussion of lines of credit as arranged with commercial banks, see pp. 788–91.

arrangements for short-term borrowing, so that advance planning is all the more important. Procedures for the issuance of additional stock and for the issuance of bonds, in particular, are generally complex and time consuming. The financial managers of a corporation do not decide upon a long-term financing project one week and carry it through the following week. Such a project may require several months for negotiations and for the working out of procedures in meticulous detail.

Checking upon Financial Performance. Much attention in financial management must be given to checking upon performance. Especially important is observing day-to-day cash inflows and outflows to see how close to the forecasts they are proceeding. Nobody expects the actual results of operations to be exactly as predicted, and the likelihood of moderate divergences between actual results and those forecast should have already been allowed for in any sound forecasting procedure. The occurrence of moderate divergences, therefore, should not be the source of any surprise nor of any need of a sudden change in plans. When, however, actual results turn out to be far different from what was anticipated, drastic changes in financial planning are likely to be necessary. The new situation must be anlayzed to determine what changes in the financial plans must be immediately instituted, and all estimates about future developments must be thoroughly recast.

Checking upon performance also requires a looking back to operating periods that have come to an end to evaluate the wisdom and efficiency of the financial planning of these periods. A time shortly after the end of the year when all results of operations are known is a good time for such an evaluation. A reconsideration of the *wisdom* of completed financial plans is especially important. While a net profit at approximately the level forecast may have been derived, such a reconsideration may indicate that the profit would have been substantially larger if certain policies had not been adopted at all or had been materially modified. Or it may indicate that certain outside means of financing actually selected were inferior to others that could have been chosen—that, for example, intermediate-term, rather than short-term loans, should have been sought. As for checking the efficiency of financial planning, perhaps cash inflows and outflows were nicely coordinated in the course of the year, but still not according to the pattern of expectations. Expenditures of certain kinds may have been much greater than had been anticipated, but no difficulties may have been encountered because cash inflows from sales were also much greater than anticipated; or it may be that, while some expenditures were much greater, others were much less than the forecasts indicated. Reasons for substantial variations of these kinds must be sought, and judgments must be arrived at as to whether or not the actual state of affairs could better have been anticipated had different forecasting principles and techniques been used. All of which means that analyses of what has happened (analyses *ex post*, they may be called if one wishes to use an elegant term) should be of great value in improving the standards, techniques, and procedures of financial control.

Incidental Finance Functions

The incidental finance functions follow from the exercise of the executive finance functions. They chiefly involve all the "paper work" that has to be done to provide the facts and materials for efficient financial control. They usually require a great amount of time, often much more than is required for the executive functions. Deciding upon a need of new financing and the form it should take, for example, may require only a few hours of discussion among the financial managers; but the clerical work involved in, say, an offering of additional stock to the present stockholders may require many days of work of numerous employees—work in preparing and sending out notices of the offering, filling in and sending out subscription warrants, keeping a record of these, receiving and recording subscriptions, and subsequently sending out and keeping a record of the stock certificates themselves. On the other hand, the incidental finance functions are, for the most part, of a routine, repetitive character, so that they require only a moderate amount of supervision by the financial managers. The financial managers need only to set up rules of procedure, select forms to be used, participate in establishing standards for the employment of competent personnel, and, once again, to check upon performance to see that the rules are observed and the forms properly used.

Supervision of Cash Transactions and Custody of Cash Balances. All assets of a business corporation must be protected in the most careful ways possible, but the protection of cash is almost invariably the particular responsibility of the financial managers. Protective provisions for cash receipts and balances include the careful selection of commercial banks as depositaries and filing with each a resolution of the board of directors stating specifically how the deposit account or accounts are to be handled —who may make deposits, how deposits are to be segregated (as when the corporation plans to have two or more accounts at the same bank, such as a general account and a payroll account), and what signature or combination of signatures are required upon checks drawn upon the accounts. They include measures for the safeguarding of coin, paper money, and checks coming into the corporation's possession and for the bonding of employees handling these items, requirements such as that all cash and cash items (chiefly checks) must be deposited in the bank or placed in its night depositary on the day received, and the placing of responsibility for the custody and replenishment of the "petty cash funds" that are set up for making small disbursements in paper money and coin. Protective provisions include other rules of "internal check," such as the rule that employees who handle cash and cash items must have no access whatsoever to the accounting records—a safeguard designed to reduce temptations toward embezzlement on the part of employees who might hope to cover up defalcations by fictitious entries on the books.

The protective supervision of cash disbursements goes somewhat beyond the measures for safeguarding cash already referred to. Here the basic idea is that each disbursement must be made only upon proper authorization, whether it is made by check drawn upon the bank or from the petty cash funds. Invoices and other bills must be carefully checked for prices, extensions, and footings; and, even more importantly, there must be assurance in every instance that materials and services billed for were actually received. A rule commonly applied is that officers who are given power to authorize payments should not also have the capacity to sign checks or to have custody of the petty cash funds. The rule of requiring two signatures upon each check, as that of the president or a vice president, in addition to that of the treasurer or an assistant treasurer, is also a means of safeguarding against improper payments. Still a third rule is that requiring the prompt entry of every payment in the accounting records, and the frequent auditing of these records to insure that payments are being made only in accordance with authorizations.

Custody and Safeguarding of Valuable Papers. The custody of all kinds of papers and documents evidencing the ownership of property and property rights of various kinds is also generally a responsibility of the financial managers, and protective rules for safeguarding these instruments must ordinarily be regarded as essential as for cash. The papers and documents include obligations of the United States Treasury, in which many corporations temporarily invest idle cash, as during slack periods or accumulated to meet liabilities coming due at specific times such as federal income tax payments; life insurance policies, where corporations observe the rather common custom of insuring the lives of principal officers, naming themselves, of course, as beneficiaries; other insurance policies covering the many kinds of hazards against which corporate managements decide protection is needed, as the risk of the destruction of buildings and equipment by fire, windstorms, and explosions, the risks of injuries to employees, and the risks of injuries to other persons or their property; promissory notes received from customers; securities of other enterprises, as stock in subsidiary corporations; deeds and certificates of title insurance; and stock certificate books and unissued bond certificates (if these are not in the possession of transfer agents and indenture trustees, respectively[4]).

Decisions to invest in treasury obligations or in the securities of other enterprises, to carry insurance of certain kinds and amounts, to accept promissory notes from customers under certain terms and conditions, and so on, fall within the province of the executive finance functions—obvi-

---

[4] For a discussion of the functions of transfer agents, see below, p. 362; of indenture trustees, pp. 626–30.

ously, these are asset-management decisions. Hence, the work of custody and safeguarding referred to is, once again, the "routine" kind of activity that originates in connections with or follows upon the exercise of the executive functions.

The examples given above of the rules and procedures that are adopted to protect cash should readily suggest the kinds of parallel actions that must be taken to safeguard valuable papers and documents. Suffice it to say that any lack of care in the adoption of protective measures or any lack of rigor in their enforcement reflects most unfavorably upon the competence of the financial managers.

Taking Care of Mechanical Details of Outside Financing. Deciding upon new outside financing, negotiating with prospective stock buyers or lenders, working out the details of loan contracts, the signing of contracts, arrangements, when required, for the pledge of property, and the signing of documents to effect the pledges—all these kinds of activities clearly come within the purview of the executive functions. But when actions such as these have been taken, much work often remains to be done, especially for the issuance of bonds or of additional stock. However, most of the additional work is of a routine, clerical character; it can be delegated to clerical employees, with a need only of proper direction and continued supervision to see that it is properly done.

Clerical work related to new stock issues has already been briefly described. That connected with bond issues includes the checking of bond forms for omissions, misstatements, and typographical errors as they are delivered for proofreading by the printer; the checking of the serial numbers of the bonds to be sure that they are all in order and all accounted for; and the examination of all bonds before delivery to be sure that they have the proper signatures and bear the corporate seal.

Much clerical work, moreover, is often required to keep up with stocks and bonds already outstanding. A principal source of such work is the need of making transfers. Mr. Black who has a certificate for 50 shares of stock wants to sell 20 of his shares to Mr. Brown. Black endorses the certificate to this effect and turns it in to the corporation; and the corporation must cancel it and issue two new certificates, one for 30 shares to Black and one for 20 shares to Brown. Likewise, bondholders may wish to sell bonds that are registered in their names on the books of the corporation, exchange coupon or bearer bonds for registered ones or vice versa, or exchange bonds of one denomination for others of a different denomination.

The clerical work involved in issuing stocks and bonds and in taking care of subsequent transactions in them often becomes so voluminous, especially in larger corporations, that trust companies and the trust departments of commercial banks are hired to "take over." The corporate financial managers expect it to be much more economical to hire out the work than to maintain a permanent staff of employees to do it; nevertheless, they continue to have responsibility to see that the trust institutions do the work competently.

Record Keeping and Reporting. If all the finance functions, as reviewed in the preceding pages, are to be fulfilled creditably, accurate accounting records must at all times be available to the financial managers, and accurate reports drawn from the records must be forthcoming at convenient intervals. Accounting records and reports, we are often told, are "tools" of management of outstanding importance. This does not necessarily mean that the financial officers must have direct responsibility for the keeping of records and the drawing off of reports. At the least, however, they must be in a position to insist upon the assembly and reporting of such kinds of information as they find indispensable for the fulfillment of their duties. They should have authority to prescribe new forms for records and reports, and especially to order extensions in the scope of the data to be assembled, if the accounting system already in use is deficient in these respects.

Actually, however, most corporations place the financial officers in a position where, as it were, they have only themselves to blame if records and reports are inadequate; they do this by assigning to them jurisdiction over the accounting department and its activities. The accounting department is most commonly found in the office of the treasurer or the controller—officers who ordinarily have at least moderate authority with respect to some or all the finance functions already analyzed. Indeed, in the absence of information to the contrary, one usually takes for granted, upon looking at the roster of officers of a given corporation, that either its treasurer or its controller (if it uses both these designations) must be its chief accounting officer, at the same time concluding that he probably has additional functions specifically in the area of finance.

The preparation and interpretation of reports drawn from the accounting records often require a high order of executive ability—in the sense, as always, of ability to make significant decisions. Although, therefore, the discussion in this section has been largely confined to operations of a clerical character, one must allow for the fact that the principal financial officers of a corporation may devote much time and exercise meticulous care in working over the details of reports of certain kinds. This is almost surely to be true of the federal income tax return, other statements and reports required by taxing authorities, reports to the regulatory authorities such as the Securities and Exchange Commission, and annual and other reports to the stockholders; but it is often true also of other varieties of financial reports aside from those designed solely for internal use.

THE FINANCIAL MANAGERS

In the foregoing description of the finance functions of business corporations, frequent references were made to the "financial managers." Who are these people? What positions do they hold in the typical business corporation? In truth, we cannot be very sure about the answers to these questions—we cannot point out an officer having a title such as "treasurer" and say that he is the principal financial officer, that his subordinates are thus and so, and that his powers and responsibilities include this and that. As we look closely at the setups of individual corporations, we find that, in some, the treasurer is indeed the principal financial officer with broad powers of decision making, but we also find that, in others, his functions would seem to make him only a "chief clerk," and that, in many others, his role fits in at various levels between these two extremes. The lines of authority concerning the finance functions are scattered around in American corporations in a bewildering variety of ways, and things are often not what they seem to be. Thus, the production manager of one corporation may be truly its chief financial officer in the sense that he generally has the final word when financial decisions are made; in another, it may be the sales manager; in another, the vice president for finance; in another, the chairman of the board of directors; in another, the chairman of the executive committee of the board of directors; and in many others, as one might well expect, the president.

One fact about which we can be reasonably sure is that most of the powers of financial management, as most of other corporate powers, reside in the board of directors. The corporation laws of the states are unanimous in saying so. Thus, the law of New York states: "The business of a corporation shall be managed by its board of directors";[5] and that of Illinois puts it this way: "The business and affairs of a corporation shall be managed by a board of directors." [6] We can also be reasonably sure that officers who have designations such as "treasurer" and "controller" will have responsibility for some of the finance functions, although not necessarily the more important ones. Beyond this, our area of certainty is, indeed, severely limited. Let us, however, look at the status of the financial managers in as orderly a fashion as the situation permits.

THE BOARD OF DIRECTORS

Limitations upon Directors' Powers

Although the powers of financial management of a corporation tend to be concentrated in its board of directors, powers held by the board are not absolute. They are limited by the provisions of corporation laws, the stipulations of the corporation's own bylaws, and legal rules of directors' responsibility.

Statutory Limitations. Most important among the limiting provisions of the corporation laws are those that give the stockholders the power to elect and remove directors. In a sense, then, the stockholders have the ultimate powers of management; if they are not satisfied with what the di-

---

[5] State of New York, *General Corporation Law*, sec. 27.
[6] State of Illinois, *The Business Corporation Act*, sec. 33.

rectors do, they can replace them with others who are more likely to perform according to their wishes. Ultimate control in the stockholders is often absolute in corporations having a limited number of stockholders, and especially in those having a handful who own a sufficient number of voting shares to give them a decisive voice. For a corporation with thousands of stockholders, on the other hand, the replacement of an inefficient or unpopular board may be long delayed. Though stockholders owning a majority of the voting shares may be quite dissatisfied with the policies of the incumbent board, they may not, individually, realize the extent to which their fellow stockholders share their dissatisfaction; thus they may make no effort to combine in an annual meeting to effect a change. In such circumstances, an inefficient or unpopular board may succeed in being virtually self-perpetuating.

Other statutory restrictions upon the powers of boards of directors include requirements for the submission of certain kinds of proposals to the stockholders for their approval. Here again, of course, the stockholders may be said to have the ultimate power of decision making. Typical among proposals that must be submitted for stockholder approval are those for the amendment of the articles of incorporation to permit additional issues of stock or to change the features of stock already outstanding, for amendments to the articles for other reasons, for the merger of the corporation with others, and for the sale of all or almost all of the assets.

Limitations in the Bylaws. In their right to adopt, amend, and repeal bylaws, the stockholders have a continuing means of limiting the exercise of power by the board of directors.[7] As examples, the directors may be restricted in their capacity to borrow money in the name of the corporation, to pledge its property as security for loans, and to fix the level of salaries to be paid to the officers. Directors' powers may also be limited somewhat by provisions of bylaws that stipulate in some detail the powers and duties of the president, vice president, and other officers. The directors might wish to delegate some of these stipulated powers to officers other than those designated. Nevertheless, this kind of limitation is not likely to be a serious handicap, as the directors generally have the right to choose officers and remove them at will; hence the officers can be moved around so that delegated powers of management will be where the directors want them to be.

Legal Rules of Directors' Responsibility. The exercise of managerial powers by the board of directors is also limited by the very nature of their position. Elected to protect and promote the interests of the stockholders, the directors accept a kind of fiduciary responsibility. Whatever their personal interests may be, they must always act in good faith to ad-

---

[7] It was explained in the preceding chapter that, although this right may be given to the board of directors by the state law or in the articles of incorporation, the stockholders retain power to alter or repeal bylaws adopted by the directors, as well as to adopt other bylaws of their own choosing.

vance the welfare of the corporation and its stockholders as they make all kinds of managerial decisions. They must not seek to advance their own interests to the detriment of those of the stockholders, as when making contracts with other firms in which they participate as owners. They must not spend the corporation's money or use its property wastefully, as in the payment of lavish salaries or fees to friends and relations who do little for the corporation to merit such payments. On behalf of the corporation and all its stockholders, any stockholder may bring lawsuits for damages against directors on grounds that they are dissipating the corporation's assets to advance their personal interests or that they are otherwise mismanaging its affairs. Additionally, he may ask the court to remove the accused directors.

Dominance of Directors

Although it is wise to take account of limitations upon the powers of boards of directors, we must recognize, nevertheless, that the board remains as the chief repository of corporate powers. Even when the directors must go to the stockholders for the approval of certain proposals, they usually have their way. They are able to present their proposals in the most favorable light, well buttressed with data and arguments carefully selected to prove their point, and the stockholders—especially where they are numbered in the hundreds or thousands—are not likely to be prepared to present a strong opposing collection of data and arguments. Very large numbers of the stockholders of larger corporations, in particular, are often described as being "apathetic" in the sense that they will readily assent to what the directors do and want to do as long as the corporation is making fair profits and they are receiving reasonable dividends.

Delegation of Powers

But saying that the board of directors is the chief repository of corporate powers does not mean that the board meticulously exercises all the powers with which it is endowed. As boards ordinarily meet not oftener than once a month, they must delegate to the officers quite extensive authority to make decisions concerning the multitude of transactions and problems that come up for consideration every day. Were it necessary for the officers to run to the board for advance approval of every proposed decision of significance, the corporation would be quickly reduced to a state of impotence. Some boards, it is true, try to keep close contact with the officers by setting up, from among their own members, one or more committees. Directors appointed to a specific committee are expected to develop a much more extensive knowledge of the matters with which it is concerned and competence in dealing with them than can the general run of directors; moreover, since a committee usually consists of only three or four directors, it can be much more quickly called together for consultation on pressing problems than can the whole board. If there is only one committee, it is usually called the "executive committee"; if there is more than one, there is still likely to be an executive committee, and others may be, for example, a finance committee, a production committee, a sales committee, and a personnel committee.

The usefulness of committees is customarily greatly enhanced by a rule that whatever a committee approves within its special jurisdiction will, as a matter of course, be ratified by the whole board at its next meeting. Thus, quick action can often be taken when the officers, in their individual capacities, are unwilling to take responsibility for making certain decisions or are lacking in delegated authority to make them. The use of committees, however, does not eliminate the need of delegating extensive decision-making authority to the officers; although committees may be more accessible to the officers than is the whole board, a need of the officers to consult frequently with the respective committees would seriously slow down the pace of corporate activity. Accordingly, only extraordinary matters, rather than those of daily routine, are reserved for submission to committees or to the board itself.

Basic Responsibilities

A board of directors must be careful to avoid extreme generosity in delegating authority, either to its own committees or to the officers. Overgenerous delegations of authority may be the grounds for stockholders' suits charging the directors with gross negligence or mismanagement—especially so, of course, if decisions made by committees and officers, however well-intentioned, result in losses. Too generous delegations to officers may be particularly dangerous, since the officers are not selected by the stockholders nor are they directly responsible to them, whereas the directors are so selected and are so responsible. Even committees composed of directors cannot be given sweeping powers without danger to the full board. It is a well-established principle of corporation law that directors hold and exercise power only collectively, that is, as a board. This means, in effect, that the individual director, as a director, enjoys managerial authority only when, at regular or special meetings, he participates with his fellow board members in arriving at decisions.

All of which indicates that the board of directors of a business corporation has certain basic responsibilities that cannot be delegated without danger of charges of gross negligence or mismanagement. These may be listed as follows:

1. The determination of major operating policies.
2. The approval or disapproval of extraordinary contracts.
3. The appointment of officers and the supervision of their work.
4. The determination of the time and amount of dividend payments.

Major Operating Policies. Major operating policies are those that are likely to have a very important bearing upon the corporation's success or failure. A decision to add an important line of new products, or to drop important items already being produced; to spend large sums of money for the "automation" of certain factory processes; to transform selling channels, as by closing retail outlets and substituting sales through jobbers and wholesalers; to adopt a comprehensive financial plan—that is to say, a budget[8]—for the coming year; to borrow money by the flotation of a bond issue; to call an outstanding bond issue for redemption; to effect a large-scale expansion of operations; to inaugurate a system of paid vacations for employees—each of these would surely be a policy of major importance the responsibility for which the directors could hardly avoid. On the other hand, the directors would not be likely to be accused of neglect of duty if they were to delegate rather complete power to the production manager to make from time to time such piecemeal changes in factory layout as he might find convenient; to the sales manager to drop wholesalers from the corporation's preferred list and to add others, as he might see fit; or to the advertising manager to vary the amounts of money to be spent upon each of the advertising mediums, while keeping within the limits of the total budgeted expenditure.

Extraordinary Contracts. In the course of any business day, the typical corporation enters into scores of contracts—and many corporations, into hundreds and thousands. Every time a sale or purchase is made, or an employee is hired, or a service is arranged for, a contract comes into being. It quickly becomes apparent, therefore, that the board of directors of a corporation could not possibly be responsible for the specific approval or disapproval of the mass of contracts it enters. Their responsibility extends only to contracts of extraordinary significance.

Should the directors decide, for example, that, to meet a growing demand for the corporation's products, the factory facilities must be expanded, they might delegate to certain officers the tasks of seeking a factory site, having specifications for the building, machinery, and equipment drawn up, and negotiating with landowners, building contractors, and machinery manufacturers on prices, terms of payment, delivery dates, and so on. But the directors would surely recognize it to be their duty to review the officers' findings, to consider alternative courses of action, to study the details of tentative contracts for the purchase of land, the erection of the building, and the purchase of the machinery and equipment, and, finally, to give specific approval to these contracts or to reject them.

Appointment and Supervision of Officers. Because the directors, by the very nature of the corporate setup, must delegate much authority to the officers, they have the duty of exercising reasonable skill and prudence in the selection of the officers and the supervision of their work. Officers are removable at will by the directors; hence, they can be held strictly

---

[8] For a discussion of budgets and budgetary principles and procedures, see below, pp. 244–87.

accountable for their stewardship. The directors would be hard put to find excuses were they to permit incompetent officers to remain long in their positions. Supervising the work of the officers requires much more than simply having them report back the results of extraordinary assignments, as in the foregoing illustration of planning for factory expansion; it requires continual evaluations of the performance of the officers in handling the ordinary day-to-day tasks of administration assigned to them. Helpful to such evaluations are requirements that the officers report frequently to the board upon their activities and decisions. Also helpful is a continuous audit of the books and records of the corporation—indicated by the rule of many corporations that the auditor always reports direct to the board—as are periodic audits made by firms of certified public accountants.

Dividend Policies. The authority of the directors to decide what dividends, if any, will be paid to the stockholders is sometimes described as an "inalienable right"; this means that the directors cannot give the power away, without grave danger of personal liability, even should they be willing to do so. The right surely cannot be delegated to any officer. Even the stockholders, who are the owners of the corporation, cannot determine dividend policies. They may place in the bylaws certain restrictions upon the payment of dividends, as by establishing upper limits, but they have no authority to order the payment of dividends of a given amount. Only by choosing directors who will surely accede to their wishes as to dividend payments can the stockholders be said to have power with respect to dividend policies.

Legal Qualifications

The corporation laws of the states are not at all strict in setting down legal qualifications for directors. One rule that is well-nigh universal is that a corporation must have not fewer than three directors. Approximately one third of the states stipulate that directors must be stockholders, but this is not a difficult requirement, as the ownership of one share usually suffices. Thus, the owner of all the stock of a corporation needs only to donate or sell a "qualifying share" to each of the people he wishes to elect as directors. Some of the states require that all or some proportion of the directors be residents. Such a requirement is not ordinarily a source of difficulty, although it can be for a corporation that has its principal operations concentrated in places distant from the state in which its charter was obtained.

The usual term of office for directors is one year, although many states permit the election of directors for longer terms on a staggered basis, with only one half, one third, or one fourth of the directors coming up for election each year. An advantage claimed for election on a staggered basis is that the "holdover" directors can keep to the operating policies already in effect while newly elected directors are getting their bearings;

but this mode of election turns out to be disadvantageous to the stock-holders when they wish to oust a board for the very reason that they do not like its existing operating policies.

Practical Situations

In the management of corporations, as in life generally, activities do not always proceed according to rules, and appearances are often deceiving. The corporation laws may be quite clear in granting broad powers to the directors, and legal rules of directors' responsibility may indicate a need of great caution in delegations of their powers; yet we must allow for the many instances in which powers actually reside where they do not seem to belong and responsibilities are taken lightly by those upon whom they are supposed to devolve.

Especially in small corporations are we often likely to find theory and practice rather far apart. A stockholder who owns, say, 90 per cent of the voting stock of a corporation of moderate size is likely to have no difficulty in getting the directors to adopt the major operating policies he proposes, to choose as officers the persons he recommends, to approve the contracts he thinks should be approved and to reject those he does not like, and even to declare the dividends that he thinks should be paid. Such a stockholder may issue numerous orders to the officers, and they are not likely to refuse to obey on the grounds that they are employees of the corporation and not his employees. Such a stockholder might choose not to be a member of the board of directors or to serve as an officer, yet all the corporate powers could surely be said to be his.

In the small corporation, too, informality is often the order of the day. All the stockholders may be simultaneously directors and officers. As they expect to elect themselves as directors year after year, they may decide that there is not much sense in having an annual meeting of the stockholders; and as they are engaged in active day-to-day management in their capacity as officers, they may see little of value in formal directors' meetings. Should a stockholder-director-officer run into a problem of unusual difficulty, he might buttonhole each of his colleagues, discuss the problem, get some advice, and make a decision—all without a specific counting of "yeas" and "nays" and the entry of a vote in the minute book.

FINANCIAL OFFICERS

The Treasurer

In almost every corporation, the treasurer, as may be inferred from his title, has significant functions as a finance officer; nevertheless, he may not be the corporation's chief finance officer in the sense of having final authority to make important decisions or of being most influential in advising the board of directors in its decision making. In many corporations of all sizes, but particularly in the smaller ones, he is an officer of this description; but, in many others, particularly in the very large ones, his position, power, and influence are clearly subordinated.

At the least, jurisdiction over the incidental finance functions tends to be concentrated in the treasurer. He ordinarily has custody of all the cash resources, owned securities, insurance policies, and other valuable papers; he is responsible for all cash receipts and for their prompt deposit in the banks with which the corporation has accounts; he supervises all cash disbursements, usually having the duty of signing (or cosigning with another officer) all checks that are issued; he takes care of the technical details of borrowing from banks and other lenders; and he has responsibility for obtaining surety bonds upon all employees whose positions warrant this kind of insurance protection.

Very often the treasurer is charged with the duty of preparing financial reports for the use of the directors and other officers, for submission to the stockholders, for supplying information to banks and other lenders, and for filing with governmental agencies. Closely related to this duty is that of preparing and filing tax returns with federal, state, and local taxing authorities. When responsibility for the preparation of reports and tax returns is placed in the treasurer, he is likely also to have jurisdiction over the accounting department; thus he may have responsibility for the assembly and maintenance of the records from which the reports and tax returns are derived. The preparation of budgets, whereby the scope of future operations is estimated and planned for, is often, too, a duty of the treasurer; in many cases, however, the treasurer's responsibility extends only to cash and fixed asset budgets,[9] and all other tasks of budgeting are assigned to other officers.

The treasurers of many corporations prepare and disburse what is called the "confidential payroll"; in some, all payroll administration is a function of the treasurer's office. A "confidential payroll" is so called because it comprises the salaries of the corporation's executives—information which, it is thought, ought not to be disclosed to payroll clerks and other employees of the payroll department. In many corporations, too, the treasurer is in charge of "credits and collections," that is, he decides which customers will be permitted to buy on account and the maximum credit each will be allowed, and he supervises collections from them.

The Controller

Many large corporations, and quite a few of medium size as well, have controllers in addition to treasurers. In almost all instances where there is both a treasurer and a controller, the latter assumes responsibility for all or almost all varieties of record keeping and for the preparation of financial statements and other reports based upon the records. He is thus

---

[9] Principles and procedures in the use of cash and fixed asset budgets are analyzed below, pp. 248–59, 282–87.

generally recognized as a corporation's chief accounting officer. His position as such makes it feasible for him, rather than the treasurer, to prepare tax returns and to work up the budget and to check performance in accordance with it. It is often regarded as appropriate, however, to leave with the treasurer responsibility for the preparation and supervision of the cash budget as well as for the budgeting of additions to long-term assets such as machinery and equipment. In many instances, payroll matters are transferred from the treasurer's department to that of the controller, and in some, the controller is given jurisdiction over credits and collections.

Many corporations give their controllers the authority to pass upon and approve all disbursements before payment is actually made by the treasurers. Such an arrangement may be simply one aspect of a system of "internal check" designed to safeguard a corporation's assets, and particularly its cash resources.

Other Finance Officers

If the treasurer of a corporation has only limited authority to make day-to-day financial decisions and only limited access to the board of directors to advise it with regard to financial matters of major importance, much broader capacities of these two kinds are almost surely to be found in an officer of superior rank. This officer is most likely to be the president. One ordinarily expects the president of a corporation to have broad powers of decision making, always subject, of course, to the policies laid down by the board of directors; and probably most corporation presidents feel that they have both the abilities and the duty to take the leading role in making decisions whether they have to do with production or marketing or finance.

It is by no means uncommon, however, for a corporation president to acknowledge that he is a "production man" or a "marketing man" and that, accordingly, he has little knowledge of the intricacies of finance or competence to grapple with them. Such a president may be quite satisfied to let the treasurer play the role of principal financial officer, or, perhaps, to assign it to the executive vice president or to a "vice president for finance."

Even a president, however, may not be the principal finance officer of a corporation, no matter how much he aspires to that position and how confident he may be of his capacities to deal with financial problems. Though he may appear to be the chief executive officer, his powers of decision making with respect to finance (and other matters, as well) may be much less than those of the chairman of the board of directors, the chairman of its executive committee, the chairman of its finance committee, or two or all three of these. In a word, the president may be an official subordinate to directors having chairmanships of the kinds indicated.

Questions

1. Why is it difficult to separate the finance functions of business enterprises from their production and marketing functions?

2. On what basis is a distinction made between executive finance functions and incidental finance functions?

3. What is the scope of "asset management" as a finance function? Why is the determination of insurance programs included within the scope of this function?

4. Is profit allocation so difficult and time consuming that it deserves classification as a separate finance function? Explain.

5. In the forecasting of cash flows, why does major emphasis fall upon the anticipated level of sales?

6. What is "financing"? What is the distinction between internal and external financing?

7. By what procedure do the financial managers of a business enterprise determine when and how much outside financing is needed? How do they determine whether this financing should be short-term or long-term?

8. What kinds of "negotiations" are necessary for outside financing? How much time do they require?

9. What is meant by "checking upon financial performance" as a finance function? Should not this be included among the incidental finance functions rather than with the executive functions? Discuss.

10. Support or attack this proposition: Since the incidental finance functions chiefly involve "paper work" that can be performed by clerical employees, the finance officers need to devote very little time and attention to them.

11. Give several examples of rules commonly observed for the safeguarding of cash balances. Mention several classes of "valuable papers" it is important to protect.

12. Briefly describe the four basic responsibilities of corporate boards of directors.

13. In what respects are the powers of boards of directors limited by state corporation laws? In what respects can they be limited by corporations' own bylaws?

14. To what extent, if at all, do boards of directors run into the danger of stockholders' lawsuits for damages when they delegate powers to make decisions to officers? to board committees? Discuss.

15. Why is it sometimes difficult to determine who are the principal finance officers of given business corporations?

chapter 5

THE FLOW OF CASH

To understand the nature of the problems involved in the determination of asset-management and dividend policies, and in the fulfillment of the other executive finance functions described in the preceding chapter, one must have a good knowledge of the processes whereby, in the typical business enterprise, cash is constantly being converted into various kinds of noncash assets and these, in turn, are constantly being reconverted into cash. An examination of these processes is the purpose of the present chapter and the following one.

CURRENT AND FIXED ASSETS

The conversion of cash into some kinds of noncash assets and their reconversion into cash take place in a short period of time. Assets that move in such a short cycle are called *current assets*. Current assets are said to comprise cash itself and all other kinds of assets that will be converted into it in the ordinary course of business within one year. Aside from cash, therefore, current assets generally include inventories of goods to be processed and sold, accounts receivable or claims upon customers for goods sold to them, other short-term receivables, short-term holdings of investment securities, and certain kinds of items called prepaid expenses and deferred charges.

But the conversion of cash into noncash assets and their reconversion may also be an intermediate- or long-term process. The longer cycle is said to involve *fixed assets*, including buildings, factory machinery and equipment, store and office fixtures, delivery equipment, mineral deposits, standing timber, patents, and franchises. In keeping with the definition of current assets in terms of a year, fixed assets may be described in a negative sense as those assets that will not be *completely* converted into cash in the ordinary course of business within one year. It is recognized that most kinds of fixed assets are gradually being converted into cash, but that, as indicated, the overall process of conversion requires more than a year; often, indeed, it requires a long period of years. The managers of a business enterprise may expect to sell for cash within three or four months all the goods held in their inventory at the beginning of that period, so that inventory is, without question, a current asset; but they may expect to "recover the cost" of their store fixtures only within a period of 20 years, so that this asset must be classified as fixed. The cost of fixed assets is "recovered" by means of charges for depreciation, depletion, and amortization, about which more will be said later in this chapter.

THE CIRCULATION OF CURRENT ASSETS

The constant movement of cash into noncash current assets and their reconversion into cash is often described as the "circular process"; accordingly, current assets are frequently called "circulating assets." To see how the circular process works, let us consider what goes on in a manufacturing firm. For this purpose, we may assume that a new corporation, the ABC Manufacturing Corporation, has just completed its organization and is getting ready for actual manufacturing operations.

Original Position

Transaction 1. To set the stage for these operations, let us further assume that stock of a par value of $450,000 was exchanged for fixed assets of various kinds and values, and that stock of a par value of $550,000 was sold for that amount of cash. Although this transaction does not involve the circulation of current assets, we may keep track of it by calling it Transaction 1.

With the stage thus set, we may wish to see what the position of the corporation is just before it launches its manufacturing operations. A picture of this position can best be shown by means of a *balance sheet*. With names and values assigned to the fixed assets acquired, such a balance sheet would be as follows:

Balance Sheet 1

ABC MANUFACTURING CORPORATION
Balance Sheet
Date

ASSETS			LIABILITIES AND EQUITY	
Current Assets:			*Stockholders' Equity:*	
Cash.............		$ 550,000	Common stock........	$1,000,000
Fixed Assets:				
Land..............	$ 25,000			
Building...........	120,000			
Machinery and				
equipment.......	280,000			
Delivery equipment	14,000			
Office fixtures......	11,000	450,000	Total Liabilities and	
Total Assets...		$1,000,000	Equity..........	$1,000,000

Balance sheets constitute a class of *financial statement* of outstanding importance and of widespread use throughout the business world. Such a statement is designed to reveal the "financial position" of an enterprise at the close of business on the day indicated in its heading. As the transactions of each day have the effect of changing a firm's financial position, one day's balance sheet is no longer "true" or "accurate" at the close of the following business day. A balance sheet is simple in conception: there is nothing mysterious about it. On one side are listed all the assets that an enterprise owns, with their assigned values, and on the other side are listed the sources of these assets in type and amount. The sources consist of *liabilities* or obligations to creditors and the *equity, net worth, capital,* or *interests* of the owners of the enterprise, as the book value of the owners' investment is variously called.[1] Every asset must have come from some source; hence, the total of assets and the total of liabilities and equity must always be equal. The balance sheet must always balance! In Balance Sheet 1 of the ABC Manufacturing Corporation, therefore, we see that the sale of common stock was the source of all the assets as listed there.

Cash to Inventories

Transaction 2. After acquiring the necessary fixed assets, the ABC Manufacturing Corporation spends $125,000 in buying raw materials, $10,000 for factory supplies, and $1,000 for office supplies. Thus, the process of circulation begins and the current asset position of the corporation is changed. The altered position can be shown in a new balance sheet as follows (with the fixed asset section and the liability side omitted, since the transaction does not affect them):

Balance Sheet 2 (in part)

Current Assets:

Cash................		$414,000
Inventories:		
Raw materials.....	$125,000	
Factory supplies....	10,000	
Office supplies......	1,000	136,000
Total Current Assets.........		$550,000

Transaction 3. Next, labor is hired to work upon the raw materials (direct labor) and other factory personnel is assigned to tasks not involving direct work upon these materials (supervision and indirect labor). Raw materials that cost $90,000 go immediately into the productive process, workers whose labor is classified as direct receive wages of $58,000, and supervisory and other factory workers are paid salaries and wages totaling $22,000. A total of $30,000 is paid in cash in meeting various factory "overhead" expenses, such as the cost of power, light, heat, and maintenance and repairs of the building and machinery, and factory supplies worth $750 are used up. Finally, a charge is made to factory expense for the estimated cost of the "wear and tear" upon the factory building

---

[1] Sometimes the term *liabilities* is used to include owners' equity as well as obligations to creditors; but confusion is avoided when its use is limited to the latter.

and equipment on account of operations to date—this charge for *depreciation*, as it is called, is $650 for the building and $3,400 for the machinery and equipment. All these developments produce changes in the financial position of the ABC Manufacturing Corporation, and this altered position can be shown in a new balance sheet as follows (with the cost of raw materials used and all other costs incurred to date reflected in an inventory of "goods in process"):

Balance Sheet 3

ABC MANUFACTURING CORPORATION
Balance Sheet
Date

ASSETS			LIABILITIES AND EQUITY	
Current Assets:			*Stockholders' Equity:*	
Cash.............		$ 304,000	Common stock........$1,000,000	
Inventories:				
Raw materials...$ 35,000				
Goods in process. 204,800				
Factory supplies. 9,250				
Office supplies.... 1,000		250,050		
Total Current Assets.......		$ 554,050		
Fixed Assets:				
Land.............		25,000		
Building..........$120,000				
Less: Allowance				
for depreciation 650		119,350		
Machinery and				
equipment.....$280,000				
Less: Allowance				
for depreciation 3,400		276,600		
Delivery equipment		14,000		
Office fixtures......		11,000		
Total Fixed Assets.....		$ 445,950		
Total Assets.....		$1,000,000	Total Liabilities and Equity.....$1,000,000	

Transaction 4. Of the total inventory of goods in process shown in the foregoing balance sheet, goods valued at $179,000 are completed in the following period. To bring these goods to a state of completion, direct labor is expended upon them at a cost of $80,000, and other expenses are allocated to them as follows: supervision and indirect labor, $30,000; out-of-pocket overhead expenses, $40,000; factory supplies used, $800; depreciation of building, $500; and depreciation of machinery and equipment, $2,000. Additional expenses are allocated to uncompleted goods in process as follows: direct labor, $8,000; supervision and indirect labor, $3,000; out-of-pocket overhead expenses, $4,000; factory supplies

used, $80; depreciation of building, $50; and depreciation of machinery and equipment, $200. All these operations produce further changes in the financial position of the ABC Manufacturing Corporation, and its new status is shown in a balance sheet as follows:

Balance Sheet 4

ABC MANUFACTURING CORPORATION
Balance Sheet
Date

ASSETS			LIABILITIES AND EQUITY	
Current Assets:			*Stockholders' Equity:*	
Cash..............		$ 139,000	Common stock........$1,000,000	
Inventories:				
Raw materials...$ 35,000				
Goods in process. 41,130				
Finished goods... 332,300				
Factory supplies.. 8,370				
Office supplies.... 1,000		417,800		
Total Current Assets.......		$ 556,800		
Fixed Assets:				
Land..............		25,000		
Building..........$120,000				
Less: Allowance for depreciation 1,200		118,800		
Machinery and equipment.....$280,000				
Less: Allowance for depreciation 5,600		274,400		
Delivery equipment		14,000		
Office fixtures......		11,000		
Total Fixed Assets.....		$ 443,200		
Total Assets.....		$1,000,000	Total Liabilities and Equity.....$1,000,000	

Although the foregoing balance sheet would reveal to the financial managers of the ABC Manufacturing Corporation how it stood upon the completion of the transactions described up to this point, they might well want to know how changes in the corporation's position were brought about—how, in other words, the corporation moved from the position revealed in Balance Sheet 1 to that revealed in Balance Sheet 4. To provide this information, the accountants would prepare a second kind of financial statement of great importance in the business world, namely, a statement of the cost of goods manufactured. Such a statement is designed to show the scope of manufacturing operations in dollar terms *over a period of time*, whereas, as we have seen, the balance sheet shows the financial position at the close of business on a designated day. As a summary of the manufacturing operations of the ABC Manufacturing Corporation, the statement would be as follows:

ABC MANUFACTURING CORPORATION
Statement of Cost of Goods Manufactured
For the Period—

Raw materials:		
Purchases..	$125,000	
Less: Inventory, end of period........................	35,000	$ 90,000
Direct labor..		146,000
Manufacturing expenses:		
Indirect labor and supervision.........................	$ 55,000	
Power, light, heat, etc..............................	74,000	
Factory supplies used................................	1,630	
Depreciation of factory building......................	1,200	
Depreciation of machinery and equipment..............	5,600	137,430
		$373,430
Less: Goods in process, end of period.................		41,130
Cost of Finished Goods Manufactured.................		$332,300

At a glance, therefore, the financial managers could see the value of raw materials acquired during the period, how much had been used, and how much remained unused at the end of the period; what had been the total costs of direct labor, other factory personnel, and the various kinds of out-of-pocket overhead expenses; the value of factory supplies used; what had been charged for depreciation of the factory building and equipment; and the respective values of the goods completed during the period and the goods remaining uncompleted at the end of the period.

Inventories to Receivables

Transaction 5. From its finished goods inventory, the ABC Manufacturing Corporation sells goods valued at $250,000. The selling price is $300,000, and the customers buy "on account," which means, of course, that they do not pay the purchase price immediately but merely incur an obligation to pay it within the period of credit allowed by the corporation. The full difference between the value of the goods sold and the selling price is not profit, for the ABC Manufacturing Corporation incurs various kinds of selling and administrative expenses in addition to its manufacturing expenses. Let us assume, therefore, that selling expenses, including salesmen's salaries, advertising, and out-of-pocket delivery expenses as for gasoline and truck maintenance and repair, amount to $14,000; and that administrative expenses, including salaries and wages, maintenance of office equipment, and light and heat, amount to $7,500. In addition, there should undoubtedly be charges to expense for the estimated depreciation of the delivery equipment and the office fixtures on account of their use up to date; these charges we may assume to be $1,100 and $275, respectively. Furthermore, the officers of the corporation anticipate that, in view of the collection experience of other firms in the same line of business, not all the claims upon customers will be collected in full. They estimate that such uncollectible accounts will amount to one half of 1 per cent of the sales figure; accordingly, they consider the amount of this estimate, $1,500, as an additional expense of operation—an expense generally labeled "bad debts." The officers also anticipate that their collections from customers will be somewhat reduced on account of discounts allowed for early payment. Such discounts, like the allowance for "bad debts," represent an offset to gross sales income; nevertheless, it is customary to take discounts up as an expense when payments less the discounts are received, rather than to charge an expense account in advance on the basis of an estimate of what discounts will be taken. A final assumption is that office supplies of a value of $225 have been used up in taking care of transactions to date.

Even, however, after all these expenses have been accounted for as deductions against the income from sales (in addition to the cost of finished goods sold), the balance is not clear profit for the corporation. Its liability for income taxes must also be taken into consideration. We may assume that the state or states in which the corporation derives its income have no income taxes, so that only the federal income tax applies here. On the basis, then, of the corporation's indicated net profit *before taxes* of $25,400, it would anticipate having to pay a federal income tax of $7,708.[2]

All these elements of Transaction 4 would place the ABC Manufacturing Corporation in a new financial position, as indicated in the balance sheet at the top of the next page.

Analysis of Balance Sheet 5. Balance Sheet 5, unlike the ones preceding it, shows an increase in total assets, as well as changes on the liability side. The increase in total assets is explained, of course, by the fact that the claims upon customers, recorded as accounts receivable, exceed by $25,400 the cost of goods sold and the expenses of selling and administration.

The sources of assets, as was said earlier, are shown on the liability side of a balance sheet. As we look at the asset side, we may say: "These are the things that the corporation owns." And as we look at the liability side, we may say: "It is from these sources that the assets came." In the case of the ABC Manufacturing Corporation, we could say that, of the total assets of $1,025,400 shown in Balance Sheet 5, the stockholders supplied assets of a value of $1,017,692, and that the federal government supplied assets of a value of $7,708! As the federal government could insist upon collecting its taxes on the profits of business enterprises as soon as derived, its willingness to wait for collection until some future tax payment date means that it temporarily leaves assets with the enterprises. So

---

[2] Applying the rates of tax in effect for the year 1963.

Balance Sheet 5

ABC MANUFACTURING CORPORATION
Balance Sheet
Date

ASSETS				LIABILITIES AND EQUITY			
Current Assets:				*Current Liabilities:*			
Cash.............		$ 117,500		Estimated liability for			
Accounts receivable	$300,000			federal income tax.....$		7,708	
Less: Reserve for							
bad debts.....	1,500	298,500		*Stockholders' Equity:*			
				Common			
Inventories:				stock.....$1,000,000			
Raw materials...$	35,000			Surplus..... 17,692		1,017,692	
Goods in process.	41,130						
Finished goods...	82,300						
Factory supplies..	8,370						
Office supplies....	775	167,575					
Total Current							
Assets.......		$ 583,575					
Fixed Assets:							
Land.............		25,000					
Building..........$120,000							
Less: Allowance							
for depreciation	1,200	118,800					
Machinery and							
equipment.....$280,000							
Less: Allowance							
for depreciation	5,600	274,400					
Delivery equipment $	14,000						
Less: Allowance							
for depreciation	1,100	12,900					
Office fixtures......$	11,000						
Less: Allowance							
for depreciation	275	10,725					
Total Fixed							
Assets.....		$ 441,825					
Total				Total Liabilities and			
Assets.....		$1,025,400		Equity..........$1,025,400			

it is with all kinds of liability and equity items: creditors and owners contribute to an enterprise assets that they leave for short or long periods. All the assets are contributed by somebody: this, to repeat, is the reason why balance sheets must always balance—why the total of the assets must always be equal to the total of the liabilities and equity.

Liabilities and the stockholders' equity can be looked upon, not only as sources of assets, but also as claims upon the assets. But the moment that we shift our point of view from liabilities and equity as sources to their role as claims, we hasten to emphasize the distinction between the claims of creditors and those of owners. One of the most important facts of business life is that creditors must generally be paid when obligations to them come due; if not, the debtor enterprise may quickly find itself in serious difficulties. On the other hand, owners, such as the stockholders of a corporation, are much more moderate in their demands for payment. Only if they vote the liquidation of their corporation do they expect— or, rather, hope—that their claims will be paid in full. Otherwise, they usually expect to enforce their claims only to the extent of getting a reasonable dividend from time to time, and are quite satisfied to leave in the corporation indefinitely the bulk of the assets they have contributed. Even in the matter of "enforcing" claims for dividends, indeed, their success, as we saw in the preceding chapter, depends upon decisions of the board of directors, rather than upon their own wishes.

Because creditors are so much more insistent upon the satisfaction of their claims than are the stockholders, it is usually found desirable to classify creditors' claims as to time of payment. The financial managers must be ever anxious to meet these claims as they fall due, but obviously their anxiety will tend to be much greater in connection with claims coming due in a few weeks or months than in connection with those whose due dates are much more remote. Accordingly, creditors' claims, like assets, are classified as *current* and *fixed,* the current liabilities being those payable in the ordinary course of business (almost invariably in cash) within one year, and fixed liabilities being those payable in the ordinary course of business beyond one year. In this way, the definitions of current and fixed liabilities parallel the definitions of current and fixed assets.

A final observation about the details of Balance Sheet 5: the student will notice that the net profit on sales after the deduction of the estimated liability for federal income taxes was placed in an account called "surplus" on the liability side under the equity heading. As shown in a corporation's balance sheet, every equity item stands for a contribution of the stockholders to the assets; hence, the entry in the surplus account in Balance Sheet 5 indicates that the stockholders of the ABC Manufacturing Corporation have increased their contribution to assets beyond the amount of their original investment in its common stock. The corporation earned a profit on the stockholders' investment, and that investment is therefore increased. The increase in the investment remains, of course, as long as it is not offset by the payment of dividends to the stockholders or by subsequent losses; as long as the profit is not disturbed, therefore, the surplus account must remain to show that the additional investment is there. Surplus is nothing more or less than this. It is not something put into a balance sheet to make it balance. All assets, liabilities, and equity items must be placed in the balance sheet if it is to balance, and surplus is simply one of the equity items. One must be especially careful not to confuse surplus and cash. Because surplus appears on the liability side of balance sheets, *it can never be cash,* nor can it be said to represent a certain amount of cash as shown on the asset side. Some corporations have large surplus accounts and little cash; others have large amounts of cash and little surplus. Thus we inevitably come back to saying that surplus simply represents a contribution by the stockholders to assets over and above the par or stated value of their stock. Since surplus is an equity item, it may also be described as a claim of the stockholders upon the assets; nevertheless, it is an undifferentiated claim—it is not a claim upon any specific asset. Indeed, this is the general status of all the liabilities and equity items shown in a balance sheet. The claims of creditors extend to *all* the assets indiscriminately, regardless of what they may have contributed individually,[3] and owners' interests or claims likewise extent to all the assets, regardless of what may have been done with their money as originally invested or as accumulated through profits.

Income Statement. Just as a statement of cost of goods manufactured was found useful in indicating how the ABC Manufacturing Corporation moved from its position as shown in Balance Sheet 1 to that shown in Balance Sheet 4, so also can an income statement—a third kind of financial statement of major importance—be used to reveal why the corporation's position shifted from that of Balance Sheet 4 to that of Balance Sheet 5. Such a statement (really, in this instance, a résumé of Transaction 5) would be drawn up as follows:

ABC MANUFACTURING CORPORATION
Income Statement
For the Period—

Sales		$300,000
Less: Cost of goods sold:		
Cost of finished goods manufactured	$332,300	
Less: Inventory, end of period	82,300	250,000
Gross profit on sales		$ 50,000
Less: Selling and administrative expenses:		
Salesmen's salaries, advertising, etc	$ 14,000	
Office wages, light and heat, etc	7,500	
Depreciation of delivery equipment	1,100	
Depreciation of office fixtures	275	
Office supplies used	225	
Bad debts	1,500	24,600
Net profit before federal income tax		$ 25,400
Less: Estimated liability for federal income tax		7,708
Net Profit to Surplus		$ 17,692

Thus, the financial managers would be able to see how the accounts receivable of $300,000 came into being; why, however, they are carried at less than the full amount of sales on account of the allowance for bad debts; why the inventories of finished goods and office supplies were reduced; why cash was reduced on account of the payment of expenses;

---

[3] It is possible, however, to give preferred claims against certain assets by specifically pledging them to secure obligations owing to one or more of the creditors.

why the values of the delivery equipment and office fixtures were written down; why a tax obligation was set up as a liability; and, finally, why there was an increase in the equity accounts equal to the net profit after the provision for federal income tax.

Receivables to Cash

Transaction 6. The completion of our illustration of the circulation of current assets requires only, as a final step, the collection of cash from customers as payments upon their obligations for goods purchased. Let us assume that the ABC Manufacturing Corporation allows 1 per cent discount on accounts paid within ten days of the date of invoices, and that most of the customers take advantage of this inducement toward prompt payment by remitting $217,800 to settle obligations totaling $220,000. On the asset side of the corporation's balance sheet, only the cash and accounts receivable accounts are affected by this transaction; and, on the liability side, the federal income tax obligation and the surplus account are affected by the sales discounts of $2,200 which, of course, must be accounted for as a further expense of operation. The new position of these affected accounts would be as follows:

Balance Sheet 6 (in part)

Current Assets:			*Current Liabilities:*	
Cash...............		$335,300	Estimated liability for	
Accounts receivable...$80,000			federal income tax.......$ 6,960	
Less: Reserve for			*Stockholders' Equity:*	
bad debts........ 1,500		78,500	Surplus.................. 16,240	

Continuity in the Circular Flow

For the sake of simplicity, the foregoing illustration was presented in steps to bring out the details of the movement of cash to inventories, inventories to receivables, and receivables back to cash. Actually, of course, businesses do not, as a rule, undertake one kind of operation in one time interval, another kind in a second time interval, and still another kind in a third. All the movements tend to be continuous and constantly overlapping. On any day, an enterprise is likely to be buying raw materials and supplies, using direct and indirect labor in the factory, meeting many kinds of cash expenses, completing goods that have been in process, putting additional raw materials into process, making sales, and collecting from customers on account of sales made earlier. As cash comes in from collections, it may be rather quickly spent in buying additional materials and supplies, in meeting the payroll, and in meeting other kinds of expenses. In terms of the illustration, the financial managers of the ABC Manufacturing Corporation might expect never again to have a cash balance equal to the $550,000 with which they began the circular process among the current assets. Thus, the estimation of cash requirements and the control of the flow of cash, as executive finance functions, are greatly complicated by the limitless variations that are possible in the timing of cash inflows and outflows.

For reasons of simplicity, also, the balance sheets, the statement of the cost of goods manufactured, and the income statement used in connection with the illustration were presented at points in the discussion where, it appeared, their significance would be most appreciated; whereas, in actual business practice, it is customary to have such statements prepared on the basis of an established time schedule, as monthly, quarterly, semiannually, or, at the very least, annually. The balance sheet of an operating business will show the effects of numerous transactions upon its financial position, rather than the effects of a handful of transactions, as in the illustrative balance sheets; and its statement of the cost of goods manufactured and income statement will report the volume of operations for a month or other specific period of time, rather than the scope of one or a few transactions, as in the illustration.

It should be mentioned also that many kinds of complications in addition to variations in the timing of cash inflows and outflows were ignored in the presentation of the illustration. But we shall consider some of the more important of these in the following chapter. For the moment, however, we may conclude our preliminary discussion of cash flows by analyzing what happens to fixed assets.

FIXED ASSETS AND THE FLOW OF CASH

Like noncash current assets, most of the fixed assets owned by business firms are involved in a process of conversion into cash. The reduction in the value of these assets that comes about through their use, "wear and tear," the "action of the elements," exhaustion, or the mere passage of time is periodically charged as an expense of operations. This expense, like all other expenses, the business enterprise expects to be able to cover in the selling prices of its goods or services; if the enterprise succeeds in covering it, it gets cash either immediately or at a later time (as it makes collections upon its accounts receivable) equal to the estimated reduction in value. How this works we have already seen in the effects of the depreciation charges of the ABC Manufacturing Corporation. Its illustrative balance sheets indicate how, at it were, fixed assets gradually become current assets. In comparing Balance Sheets 1 and 3, one sees in the latter a reduction in the total value of the fixed assets from $450,000 to $445,950 —a reduction equal to the depreciation charges of $4,050—and one sees an increase in the total amount of current assets of $4,050, an increase reflected in the inventory of goods in process on account of the taking up of depreciation as an expense.

The conversion of fixed assets into current assets, and ultimately into cash, is a relatively slow process; by definition, it requires more than a year. Otherwise, there would be no need of a separate classification of fixed assets. Obviously, however, the process is one of varying degrees of speed—or, perhaps one should say, of slowness. For some kinds of fixed assets, the process is a very slow one, indeed, as for factory and office buildings; for others, it is relatively rapid, as for delivery equipment and certain kinds of machines and machine tools. (Tools whose life does not extend beyond one year are customarily classified as "factory supplies" among the current assets rather than as "machinery and equipment" among the fixed assets.) Some kinds of fixed assets are not regarded as being "used up" at all; such assets do not participate in the process of conversion into cash. This is true chiefly of the land upon which factory and office buildings are erected, but it is also true of such fixed assets as stocks of subsidiary corporations held by their parents and franchises of perpetual duration.

Depending on the nature of different classes of assets, estimated reductions in their values, to be charged as current expenses of operation, are described as depreciation, depletion, and amortization.

Depreciation

Depreciation is a reduction in the value of fixed assets due to wear and tear in use and the action of the elements. Only physical assets, such as buildings, machinery and equipment, store fixtures, and office fixtures, can depreciate; considering the sense in which the term is used, it is impossible for intangible assets to depreciate.

Present-day charges for depreciation almost invariably include an allowance for what is called "ordinary obsolescence." An asset becomes obsolete when, because of technological developments or shifts in demand for products, it is no longer wise to continue it in use. Machines become obsolete—and some of them, rather quickly—because other machines which can do the job much more efficiently have been developed. A new machine may be expected to have a "useful life" of 20 years in the sense that it would continue in good working order throughout that period; but its owners, considering the speed at which technological changes are taking place in their industry, may estimate that after, say, ten years, it will have to be replaced by a much more efficient machine— one yet to be invented or developed. They would think of the machine as having *for them* a "useful life" of only ten years, rather than twenty, and they would want to recover its cost through depreciation charges in the shorter period.

In accounting for depreciation, then, the idea is to write down periodically the value of the depreciable asset during its "useful life"—as limited or reduced to allow for "ordinary obsolescence"—so that when the time comes for replacement the value remaining on the books will not exceed the scrap, secondhand, or trade-in value, as the case may be; and to charge these write-downs as current expenses of operations to be recovered in the selling prices of goods and services. Were a firm to ignore the steady decline in the value of its depreciable assets, and fail, therefore, to charge depreciation as an expense of operation, it would obviously be overstating its profits or understating its losses.

The charging of depreciation as a current expense to be recovered in the selling prices of goods and services has an effect as if the enterprise were gradually selling its fixed assets to the people who buy its products. When we buy an electric refrigerator, for example, we are not likely to think of ourselves as buying minute portions of the manufacturers' buildings, machinery and equipment, office fixtures, and other depreciable assets; but, in effect, we do buy minute amounts of these things when the price we pay is sufficient to cover depreciation charges in addition to all other costs. Thus, depreciable assets really move toward conversion into cash, but, as has been indicated, the movement is generally much slower than for noncash current assets.

Depletion

In careful usage, the term *depletion* is applied only to the exhaustion of natural resources. Depletion is the reduction in the value of land as coal or ore is mined, as oil is pumped, as timber is cut, and as other such exhaustive operations are performed. If a corporation were to invest $5 million in a tract of land containing an estimated five million tons of ore of a certain kind, the value of the land would obviously decline by one dollar with every ton of ore mined.[4] To operate profitably, the corporation would surely have to cover this cost of one dollar per unit, plus all its other expenses, and plus a markup in the selling price of its output.

In the development of "wasting assets"—a term often applied to natural resources subject to depletion—the output, in effect, becomes an inventory of the producing firm; once again, therefore, we have the gradual movement of a fixed asset into the current classification. And, of course, the inventory, in turn, continues the movement in the direction of cash as it is disposed of in sales to customers.

Amortization

Amortization is a loss in the value of fixed assets occurring by reason of the mere passing of time. It is an attribute of certain kinds of intangible fixed assets, such as patents, copyrights, and limited-term franchises. Whatever investment is made in intangible assets of these kinds must presumably be recovered during the period of their respective lives. As with depreciation and depletion, therefore, it is appropriate to make periodic charges to expense accounts so that the investment will be gradually recovered in the selling prices of the related goods or services.

If money invested in intangible assets of the kinds mentioned is to be fully recovered through sales, the periodic charge to amortization expense must be based upon a realistic estimate of the income-producing life of

---

[4] Assuming, of course, that the land would have no value for other purposes after all the ore had been removed.

the asset rather than upon a term arbitrarily fixed by legislation or by the decree of a governmental body. Should a corporation, for example, spend $500,000 in research and experimentation in the development of a new product for which it obtains a patent, it might be most unwise to write off only one seventeenth of this value each year simply because the federal government gives patent rights for 17 years. If it were reasonably estimated that the popularity of the patented article would not extend for more than four years, then it would be appropriate to write off $125,000 of the patent value each year.

Questions

1. What kinds of assets owned by a business enterprise are classified as current assets? as fixed assets? What is the principal test or rule for distinguishing between these two classes of assets?

2. Why are current assets described as "circulating assets"? Do fixed assets also "circulate"? Explain.

3. What are the two principal sources of a firm's assets? What is the relationship between total assets and total sources of assets?

4. In what sense can the sources of a firm's assets be said to be claims against its assets? Why are these claims said to be "undifferentiated"? Why is it important to distinguish between liabilities as claims and equity as claims?

5. What kinds of creditors' claims are classified as current liabilities? as fixed liabilities? For a given creditor's claim, could there ever be a shift in this classification? Explain.

6. What is a balance sheet? Why must a balance sheet always be in balance?

7. What is an income statement? What is the relationship, if any, between a firm's income statement and its balance sheet?

8. Support or attack this proposition: When a business firm incurs expenses, it is thereby acquiring assets.

9. What is the nature of "surplus" as it appears in a corporation's balance sheet? How is it related, if at all, to the corporation's cash balance? its total assets? its other equity accounts?

10. What is depreciation? Why is it treated as an expense? What is its relationship to obsolescence?

11. Explain the proposition that, in effect, firms gradually convert fixed assets into current assets through their depreciation charges.

12. What kinds of assets are subject to depletion and amortization? Could a given asset be subject to both depletion and amortization simultaneously? Why or why not?

Problem

The inventories of the Boner Manufacturing Co., Inc., at the beginning and end of October, 19xx, were as follows:

	Beginning	*End*
Raw materials	$123,000	$114,000
Goods in process	178,000	169,000
Finished goods	275,000	258,000
Factory supplies	3,410	3,060
Office supplies	630	730

The corporation's transactions during the month were as follows:

Sales....	$942,000
Purchases of raw materials....	206,000
Cost of labor:	
Factory direct labor....	240,000
Factory indirect labor and supervision....	93,000
Salesmen's and truck drivers' wages....	54,000
Administrative salaries....	60,000
Factory supplies purchased....	2,200
Office supplies purchased....	310
Other factory expenses....	105,000
Other selling expenses....	50,700
Other administrative expenses....	25,200

At the end of the month, charges for depreciation and bad debts were made as follows:

Depreciation—factory building....	$1,020
Depreciation—factory machinery and equipment....	3,100
Depreciation—delivery equipment....	1,800
Depreciation—office equipment....	295
Bad debts....	3,400

For the month of October, 19xx, prepare a statement of cost of goods manufactured and an income statement. Assume that the federal income tax rate applicable to the October net profit is 52 per cent.

chapter 6

FURTHER ASPECTS OF CASH FLOWS

In the illustration of the operations of the ABC Manufacturing Corporation presented in the preceding chapter, complicating details were avoided as far as possible, so that the main course of the circular flow of cash could be made to stand out clearly. It now becomes necessary to look at some of the circumstances in the actual operations of businesses that result in modifications of cash inflows and outflows—that make cash flows vary from a relatively simple course such as that of the illustration. An examination of these circumstances is important, because they are the sources of most of the problems with which the financial managers of business enterprises must cope in establishing asset-management policies and in working toward other kinds of decisions.

The continuous overlapping of activities requiring cash payments and those producing cash receipts was briefly considered in the preceding chapter; other kinds of circumstances giving rise to complications in cash flows may be grouped as follows: (1) the prepayment and deferment of income and expenses; (2) breaks in the circular flow through additions and withdrawals of cash; (3) differences in the scope of business activities; and (4) general business developments of a cyclical kind.

PREPAYMENTS AND DEFERMENTS

The cash requirements of a business enterprise are increased by the prepayment of expenses and by the deferment of the realization of income in cash; its cash requirements are reduced by the incurring of expenses on a deferred-payment basis and by the receipt of cash as advance realization of income. Prepayments and deferments that cause an increase in cash requirements may be said to slow down the flow of cash; and those that result in a decrease in cash requirements may be said to speed up the flow of cash. Were a firm to operate entirely on a cash basis, selling each day for cash all goods bought that day for resale, and meeting by immediate cash payments all operating expenses, including the cost of the goods purchased, it could manage a given volume of operations with a much smaller cash investment than could a second firm that carried a large inventory over from day to day and sold on account. The circular flow of cash would be completed daily for the first firm, but it would require a much longer period for the second firm.

Included in the illustration of the operations of the ABC Manufacturing Corporation of the preceding chapter were examples of the prepayment of expenses in its purchases of raw materials, factory supplies, and office supplies; an example of the deferment of the realization of income in its sales on account; and an example of the incurring of an expense on a deferred-payment basis in its liability for federal income tax. Examples such as these deserve further examination; moreover, we must look at some others to get a well-rounded picture of the effects of prepayments and deferments.

Investment in Inventories

When a manufacturing firm buys raw materials and pays for them before it sells the finished goods in which they are incorporated, it prepays expenses. The same is true of a mercantile firm that buys finished goods and pays for them some time before it sells them to its customers. Such prepayments, of course, are extremely common. Firms hold inventories for weeks and months awaiting sale—inventories for which full payment has been made. While the inventories are being held, they may properly be classified as current assets and be shown as such in balance sheets; but when they are sold, they are transferred to expense accounts, being treated in much the same way as other manufacturing, selling, and administrative expenses.

Cash is released from inventories as cash sales are made or as collections are made from accounts receivable, but the typical firm that deals in tangible products must be constantly replenishing its inventories. If the firm is to continue to serve its customers efficiently, it cannot permit its inventories to fall below some minimum limit. It must *permanently* "tie up" cash in inventories at this minimum level. At certain times in the course of the year, inventories may be much larger than the minimum required, but the additional cash absorbed in inventories is there only temporarily, as it is released when the inventories are sold down toward the minimum. Not so, however, with cash absorbed in inventories at the minimum level, for, by definition, its release would make it impossible for the firm to serve its customers efficiently.

If, for example, inventories worth not less than $100,000 must always be carried by a certain firm if it is to give its customers good service, its financial managers may as well decide that cash of that amount has been put permanently beyond reach—as being forever unavailable for other purposes. The composition of the inventories would change, probably daily, but the inventories, as a prepaid expense (or, alternatively, in the balance sheet sense, as a current asset) would permanently dam up $100,000 of cash.

Prepayment of Other Expenses

The prepayment of any expense has effects upon the circular flow of cash similar to those resulting from investment in inventories; it slows this flow, or, to put the proposition in its alternative form, it increases cash requirements. To see why this is so, we may analyze the transaction of the ABC Manufacturing Corporation in buying office supplies. The corporation immediately spent $1,000 for such supplies, yet it is reasonable to assume that they would not all be used up for several months. Suppose that supplies worth $100 were consumed in the first month. At the end of that month, then, the corporation would have a "prepaid expense" of $900, damming up, as it were $900 of cash. Had the corporation decided to buy, in the beginning, only enough supplies for the one month, its expenditure would have been only $100 instead of $1,000, and it would have had $900 of cash available for other uses. To put it differently, it could have managed to get along with $900 less of cash. Indeed, had it decided to operate its office on a hand-to-mouth basis, it might have needed only about $4.00, say, to buy each day the office supplies needed for that day! All of which does not mean that the managers of the ABC Manufacturing Corporation were unwise to invest $1,000 in office supplies, for the "tying up" of cash of this amount may have been justified by lower prices for quantity purchases, and, even more importantly, on grounds of convenience.

Premiums paid to insurance companies for protection against property losses on account of fire, windstorm, and other hazards represent another very common kind of prepaid expense. Such premiums are almost invariably payable in advance, and the insurance companies encourage prepayment for two, three, or more years by providing lower rates for longer-term policies than for one-year policies. Other examples of prepaid expenses are advances to employees against wages and salaries yet to be earned and advance payments to suppliers for merchandise to be delivered later.

Carrying Accounts Receivable

The realization of income in cash is obviously deferred when a firm sells goods to its customers "on account," that is, when it gives them a certain period of time beyond the date of sale in which to make payment. The firm's circular flow of cash is necessarily slowed, depending upon the length of the credit period allowed.

Alternatively, once again, we can say that the cash requirements of a firm selling on account are increased. In a manufacturing firm, for example, money is spent in buying materials and supplies, in paying labor, and in meeting other manufacturing, selling, and administrative expenses, but it is not recouped as soon as goods are sold. Cash must be available to make the necessary outlays, but it is not immediately forthcoming from customers to continue these outlays.

It may be objected, however, that any increase in cash requirements because of selling on account must be, in most instances, a short-run requirement, perhaps of not more than 30 or 60 days—perhaps of not more than ten days if cash discounts for early payment are allowed. But such an objection is not valid. The contrary is true: the carrying of accounts receivable, like the carrying of inventories, tends to absorb or tie up cash *permanently*. While it is true that individual accounts are paid off in short periods of time, these are constantly replaced by others as long as the firm continues to sell on account. Thus, there will be a permanent absorption of cash in accounts receivable related to the minimum amounts to which these accounts fall. As with inventories, the amount of cash absorbed in accounts receivable will often be well in excess of the minimum; but it can hardly be less than this if the firm is to continue to satisfy those customers who wish to buy on account and who can qualify on the basis of credit standing.

One should observe that the amount of cash absorbed in accounts receivable is not the amount of the receivables, but is "related" to it. This is so because claims upon customers include a firm's markups or profit margin—a factor that requires no outlay of cash by the firm. If, for example, a firm produces goods at a total cost of $25,000 and sells them on account for $30,000, cash absorbed in accounts receivable obviously amounts to the smaller of these figures.

Acquisition of Goods and Supplies on Account

While spending cash for inventories, the prepaying of other expenses, and the carrying of accounts receivable absorb cash—slow down its flow, as it were—obtaining goods and supplies on a deferred-payment basis conserves cash, or, in other words, reduces the need of it. The creditors who await payment for goods and supplies furnished serve as a new or additional source of assets, as is indicated by the appearance of the obligations owing to them as "accounts payable," classified as a current liability, in the balance sheet. It is true that the individual obligations that constitute these accounts must be paid within the allowed credit periods (and paid scrupulously if the debtor firm is to preserve a good credit rating), but these obligations tend to be constantly replaced by others as additional purchases on account are effected. For the typical business enterprise, therefore, "accounts payable" represent a permanent source of assets—a permanent means of reducing cash requirements—as measured by the minimum amount to which they fall over the years, and a temporary source, as measured by amounts in excess of the minimum.

For illustration, we may refer again to the transactions of the ABC Manufacturing Corporation. Had the corporation in Transaction 2, bought its raw materials and factory and office supplies on account, the current sections of Balance Sheet 2 would have appeared as follows:

Current Assets:			*Current Liabilities:*	
Cash................		$550,000	Accounts payable.........$136,000	
Inventories:				
Raw materials.......$125,000				
Factory supplies.....	10,000			
Office supplies.......	1,000	136,000		
Total Current				
Assets..........		$686,000		

Thus, the corporation would have had current assets of $136,000 in excess of the total disclosed in the original Balance Sheet 2; and, obviously, the trade creditors would have been the suppliers of these additional assets, a fact indicated by the entry for accounts payable on the liability side. (As was explained in the preceding chapter, one could also say that the trade creditors would have had a claim against the assets of the corporation to the amount of $136,000; but it is to be repeated that this would have been a claim against all the assets—an undifferentiated claim—and not simply a claim against the raw materials and supplies they actually would have sold to the corporation.)

By this point, the observing student may have concluded that the author has got himself into a tight spot: earlier he said that cash requirements are increased through investment in inventories, and now he says that cash requirements are reduced when goods and supplies are bought on account. But authors should always be able to get out of tight spots; in this instance, that apparently can be done by observing that the *net* effect upon cash requirements and cash flows depends upon the timing of the resale of inventoried goods and the timing of the payment to the trade creditors. When a business enterprise buys goods on account, it obviously does not thereby tie up any money in inventories; it is the creditors who supply the additional goods. The enterprise's cash requirements are not increased, and its flow of cash is not slowed in any way. But should it pay off the creditors before reselling the goods and collecting payment from the buyers, it would cause cash to be absorbed in the inventories. On the other hand, should it sell the inventoried goods for cash some days or weeks before the due dates of its obligations to the trade creditors, not only would it not tie up cash in inventories, but it would have the creditors, as it were, supplying it with cash that could be used for other purposes. For most businesses, however, the value of the inventories at any time usually exceeds the amount of trade accounts payable, so that the excess roughly measures in each case how much of a firm's cash has been absorbed in inventories.[1]

Accrued Wages

It is customary for most businesses to pay payrolls only every week or every two weeks, and sometimes, particularly salaries, only monthly. Moreover, payrolls are often deferred to give the payroll department adequate time to make them up, as when the payroll to be paid at the middle or end of this week covers wages earned last week. The employees of an enterprise, therefore, make a net contribution to its assets equal to the

---

[1] The measure is ordinarily an inexact one on account of differences in the methods of valuing inventories. If, for example, inventories appear in a balance sheet at values less than cost, the excess of these values over the amount of trade accounts payable shown in the same balance sheet obviously does not measure, in any accurate way, how much cash the inventories have absorbed. For a discussion of inventory valuation methods and their effects, see below, pp. 158–62.

amount of the unpaid wages: they provide the enterprise with asset-building services, as one might say, and they do not make immediate demands for payment. Such a contribution reduces the cash requirements of the employing firm. Furthermore, this reduction in cash requirements has elements of permanence. If the firm's unpaid wages never amount to less than a certain sum, the employees make a permanent contribution to its assets of that amount, releasing an equivalent amount of cash for other uses. And, of course, the employees make additional temporary contributions to assets to the extent that unpaid wages, from time to time, exceed the minimum.

To refer once again to the transactions of the ABC Manufacturing Corporation, as presented in the preceding chapter, let us suppose that $6,000 of the wages and salaries earned by its employees had not been paid at the time of the preparation of Balance Sheet 3. As a result, the corporation's assets at that time would have been $6,000 greater, the addition being attributable to the employees' contribution. Accordingly, the current sections of the balance sheet would have appeared as follows:

Current Assets:			*Current Liabilities:*	
Cash.................		$310,000	Accrued wages...........$6,000	
Inventories:				
Raw materials......	$ 35,000			
Goods in process....	204,800			
Factory supplies.....	9,250			
Office supplies.......	1,000	250,050		
Total Current Assets..........		$560,050		

Other Deferred Payments

Many other kinds of expenses that do not require immediate cash payments are incurred by business enterprises. The expenses go into the building of noncash assets, but, temporarily at least, the enterprises do not have to use cash equivalent to the value of these additions. Cash is conserved: at least temporarily, it can be used in other directions.

In addition to trade creditors and employees, therefore, electric power companies, water companies, telephone and telegraph companies, repairmen, firms that provide professional services, and many other service institutions contribute to the assets of the business enterprises to which they sell their services. Daily use is made of these services—and resulting accretions to the assets of the business enterprises, therefore, take place—but the suppliers of the services are generally willing to await payment for some days or even weeks after they have submitted their respective statements or bills.

In a similar way, governmental bodies, by deferring the collection of taxes, make temporary contributions to the noncash assets of the enterprises upon which the taxes are levied. Taxes add to assets no less than do all other kinds of expenses—in the sense that they are properly includible in the valuation of goods to be sold; yet such additions to noncash assets do not have to be matched with cash outlays until the tax payment dates arrive. In the preceding chapter, we saw how this works with the federal corporation income tax. It works in much the same way with other kinds of taxes, federal, state, and local. Thus, the liability for state and local property taxes may be said to come into existence on the date of assessment; but the state and local governments generally establish tax payment dates some months beyond the dates of assessment.

It is of interest to observe that governmental bodies provide business firms with an additional source of cash when they call upon them to act as tax collectors. Although tax monies acquired in this capacity do not constitute business expenses, their effects upon assets are much the same as if they were expenses. If, for example, a firm adds a federal excise tax or a state sales tax to the selling price of its goods, it is in a position to use for business purposes the tax monies collected from its customers until such time as they must be paid over to the taxing government. Likewise, a portion of the assets contributed by employees through their unpaid labor service comes to represent a government contribution through the deduction from payrolls of federal withholding and social security taxes. Thus, should a firm's unpaid payroll amount to $10,000, and should $800 of this represent personal income taxes of the employees withheld, and $225 represent deductions for social security taxes, the employees could be said to be making a contribution to the firm's assets of $8,975, and the federal government, a contribution of $1,025. Many managers of business enterprises, nevertheless, are not at all pleased to have tax collection duties thrust upon them. They generally feel that the expenses of bookkeeping and reporting far outweigh the advantages of the temporary use of tax funds.

Unearned Income

The receiving of cash income in advance of the sale of goods or the performance of services obviously reduces a need of cash from other sources; it may also be said to speed the flow of cash. Cash income is received in advance much more commonly by financial institutions and transportation firms than by enterprises engaged in manufacturing and selling tangible products. Examples include the receipt of premiums by insurance companies for protection of lives and property to be provided in the ensuing year or period of years, and the advance sale of tickets for passenger transportation by railroads, airlines, bus lines, and other transportation companies.

Sometimes customers of manufacturing companies make advance payments to cover at least part of the cost of goods to be produced for them, especially when the goods have to be specially designed. During World War II, many manufacturers, especially smaller ones, were able to produce war materials for the federal government only because its advance payments gave them the means to do so.

BREAKS IN THE CIRCULAR FLOW

When one speaks of the circular flow of current assets, one has in mind, as we have seen, the spending of cash for inventory and in meeting other varieties of operating expenses (all these being included in the value of goods offered for sale), the conversion of these goods into cash as sales are made or as collections are made upon accounts receivable, the respending of this cash for additional inventory and in meeting additional operating expenses, and so on continuously. But it is clear that the managers of business enterprises can decide, from time to time, to remove cash from the circular process, and that, likewise, they can decide, now and then, to pump additional cash into it. This is the meaning of "breaks" in the circular flow of current assets to be considered in this division of the chapter.

In corporations, the most common reasons for the removal of cash from the circular process are the payment of dividends to stockholders, the repayment of borrowings, and the purchase of fixed assets. Less common reasons include the use of cash to buy out other businesses and to pay off portions of the stockholders' investment, as in the retirement of preferred stock. The only significant reason for adding to the amount of cash in the circular process is to make possible an expansion in current operations—to enable the corporation to expand its inventories, meet a larger volume of operating expenses, and carry a larger quantity of accounts receivable. The cash added chiefly comes from borrowing and the sale of additional stock, although other sources may be occasionally available, as, for example, the sale of fixed assets or donations from stockholders. In many cases, of course, the drawing in of additional cash and its use occur, as it were, outside the circular process, as when a corporation borrows from one financial institution to repay loans owing to another, or floats a bond issue to raise money to expand its holdings of fixed assets.

If the amount of cash already in the circular process is in excess of what is needed to continue it, the financial managers obviously have no great problem in drawing off the excess and devoting it to other uses. Likewise, they have no serious problem if additional cash is needed to expand current operations and it is readily forthcoming from lenders or stockholders. On the other hand, a corporation's problems relative to "breaks" may be quite difficult—and even, at times, insolvable—when, for example, cash is sorely needed for the expansion of current operations and it cannot readily be obtained from lenders or from the sale of additional stock, or when there is an acute need to replace or add to fixed assets and cash cannot be withdrawn from the circular process or readily

obtained from outside. Whether or not such problems are easy or difficult depends largely upon two factors: (1) the corporation's profit or
loss experience, and (2) its rate of expansion. Let us see how these factors apply in a variety of situations.

Profitable Corporations Not Expanding

Corporations that consistently operate at a profit while having no occasion or intention to expand the scale of their operations must tend constantly to build up an excess supply of cash in their circular processes.
Without loss of efficiency or profit-making potentialities, this excess cash
can be readily withdrawn for the payment of dividends, for the repayment of debts, for the replacement of fixed assets, or for other purposes.
The tasks of their financial managers are likely to be not at all nerve
wracking.

With each complete movement of the circular flow, such a corporation will have a *cash throw-off* equal to the amount of its profit (before
the deduction of income taxes) plus the amount of its "bookkeeping
charges" for depreciation, depletion, and amortization. Assume that a
manufacturing corporation produces goods at a total cost of $448,000 and
sells them for $500,000. Included in the total cost of $448,000 are the
costs of raw materials, direct labor, manufacturing overhead, selling, and
administration of $410,000—for all of which cash outlays must be made
sooner or later, depending upon prepayments and deferments—depreciation charges of $35,000, and an allowance for bad debts of $3,000. If the
corporation collects from its customers $497,000 (indicating that its esti-
mate of bad debts was correct, and assuming that it allows its customers
no discounts for prompt payment), it will have $87,000 of cash in excess
of what it currently spent in producing the goods sold; or, to put the
matter in more significant terms, it will have $87,000 of cash in excess of
what it needs to maintain production at the existing level. Thus, the corporation's cash throw-off is $87,000, an amount equal to its profit of
$52,000 plus the depreciation charge of $35,000.

Of the cash throw-off of $87,000, the financial managers of this corpo-
ration would probably retain or invest in short-term securities $21,540 to
enable it to pay, when due, the federal income tax on its profit.[2] They
might also decide to invest temporarily in high-quality securities an
amount equal to the depreciation charge, $35,000, to accumulate a fund
to be used to replace the fixed assets at the expiration of their useful lives.
Indeed, they might decide to invest more than this, should they expect
the replacements to cost more than did the fixed assets already held. On
the other hand, should replacement requirements not be expected to materialize for several years, they might decide to use the money, in the
meantime, for other purposes, as for the repayment of debt. The balance

---

[2] Computed at the rates in effect in the year 1963. We may assume that the states
in which the corporation derives its income have no corporation income taxes.

of the cash throw-off—that portion not allocated for the payment of income taxes and for the replacement of fixed assets—would be freely disposable at the discretion of the financial managers. Probably a goodly amount would be allocated for the payment of dividends to the stockholders, and the remainder for such purposes as the repayment of debt or the retirement of preferred stock.

A pleasant aspect of the position of the corporation of the foregoing illustration—assuming its continued operation at the existing level and continued success in selling—is that a cash throw-off of approximately $87,000 would become available upon the completion of each round of the circular process. The exact amount of cash becoming available for withdrawal within any period would depend upon the effects of prepayments and deferments of income and expenses; nevertheless, it can be said that *eventually*, in connection with each circuit, approximately $87,000 of cash could be withdrawn without reducing the efficiency or profitability of the corporation's productive operations. Needless to say, the cash throw-off could vary, too, because of changes in the profit margins. For example, the corporation might not be able to increase its selling prices to absorb increases in costs; thus it might remain profitable, but at a reduced level. The financial managers might, therefore, have some rather difficult problems to cope with—but surely not nearly so difficult as those of corporations that operate in the red or that need to expand at a rapid rate.

Break-Even Corporations Not Expanding

Assuming no occasion or wish to expand the scale of operations, the financial managers of corporations that are able only to break even in their operations will be in a position to withdraw cash from the circular process. Although the gross income of a break-even corporation is, by definition, only sufficient to cover all its operating costs, including charges for depreciation, depletion, and amortization, it should have a cash throw-off with each circuit equal to these charges. These cash throw-offs would most likely be accumulated for the replacement of fixed assets, probably by means of temporary investment in high-quality securities. If, then, the cost of replacing the assets turned out to be no greater than their original cost, the corporation could continue to operate without financial embarrassment for a period of many years or even of many decades. The situation would not be a happy one for the stockholders, as the corporation would have no profits out of which dividends could be paid. Accordingly, they might decide to liquidate the corporation to recover as much as possible from their profitless investment; but, at any rate, the threat to its life would not come from an inability to meeting operating expenses or to pay off maturing liabilities.

Suppose, for example, that the corporation of the illustration given above were able to sell its output for only $448,000, of which it is able to collect only $445,000 because $3,000 of the accounts receivable turn out to be uncollectible. It could continue with the existing level of operations by the expenditure of $410,000 for materials, labor, and other out-of-pocket operating expenses, and it would have the remaining $35,000, equal to the charges for depreciation, available for withdrawal from the circular process.

Loss Corporations Not Expanding

Any corporation that is able to sell its goods at prices high enough to cover its out-of-pocket costs for materials, labor, and operating expenses plus some portion of its charges for depreciation, depletion, and amortization will have cash throw-offs equal to the amounts by which the latter charges are covered. If such a corporation has no occasion or wish to expand, it ought to be able to continue in operation without financial embarrassment, except embarrassment in the sense of not being able to pay dividends, until such time that the fixed assets must be replaced. Should the corporation of our illustration be able to sell its goods for only $425,000 and to collect only $422,000 from its customers, it would be covering its depreciation charges to the extent of $12,000, and this, of course, would be the amount of each cash throw-off. While such a sum would doubtless prove to be quite inadequate for the replacement of the fixed assets, it could be withdrawn, with each round of the circular process, without interfering with current operations at the existing level.

Instead of a cash throw-off, there is a cash deficit with each round of the circular process for any corporation that is unable to sell its goods at prices high enough to cover its out-of-pocket costs. Such a corporation is likely to quickly encounter serious financial difficulties. If it is to continue the current scale of operations, it must repeatedly pump money into the circular process—with each round, an amount approximately equal to the cash deficit; likewise, it must look outside for new sources of cash for the replacement of fixed assets when that becomes necessary. Its prospects must be poor, indeed, for lenders are not to be expected to risk their money on such a losing venture, nor are stockholders likely to be willing to add additional funds to an investment that has already become most unattractive to them.

Expanding Corporations

Profitable corporations that are rapidly expanding the scale of their operations are likely to find their cash throw-offs quite insufficient to meet all their requirements. The problem facing their financial managers is not one of deciding what to do with the throw-offs, but of finding ways to supplement them from outside sources. They might decide to trim dividends to the bone or to omit them entirely—not necessarily a wise decision—so that all or almost all the profits, after provision for income taxes, could be devoted to the expansion of current operations. Likewise, they would probably decide to devote to the same drive for expansion the portion of the cash throw-offs attributable to depreciation, depletion, and amortization charges—assuming, of course, no immediate need for the replacement of fixed assets.

In many instances, however, an expansion of current operations—an expansion in the volume of the circular flow, as we may also call it—is impossible unless there is also an expansion in the volume of fixed assets. Hence, the rapidly expanding corporation is most unlikely to be able to meet out of its cash throw-offs a need both to expand the size of the circular flow and the volume of its fixed assets. Accordingly, it will probably find it necessary to go to outside sources in a quest for funds. Its profit experience and its growth potentialities, of course, should make it attractive to lenders, and, if it has not been extremely niggardly in its dividend policies, to present and prospective stockholders as well.

Breaks in the circular flow in the case of break-even and loss corporations that wish to expand will surely involve additions to cash, rather than withdrawals, if additions can be arranged for. The financial managers of such corporations will doubtless look everywhere for new sources of cash, although they may not succeed in finding them. In most instances of this kind, the financial managers find themselves in a vicious circle. The very reason why their corporations have been operating at or below the break-even point is that they have not been able to reach a volume of production and sales that would put them in a profitable position; yet their very lack of profitability tends to make lenders look upon them as questionable risks, and to make stockholders and prospective stockholders shy away from buying additional issues of their stock. Expanding the scale of operations would make possible a spreading of fixed and semivariable overhead expenses over a larger quantity of produced goods, thereby reducing costs of production per unit of output; yet the money to make possible the expansion may be difficult to come by. Cash throw-offs, representing the portion of depreciation, depletion, and amortization charges that is covered by sales proceeds, may be quite inadequate to finance expansion of the scope that is needed—and especially so, of course, if the expansion requires both an increase in the size of the circular flow and additions to fixed assets.

THE SCOPE OF BUSINESS ACTIVITIES

Patterns of cash flow—and, therefore, of cash requirements—differ greatly among business enterprises according to the nature of their respective operations, the seasonality and secular trend of these operations, and the competitive situation in which each business finds itself.

Nature of Operations

For an understanding of variations in cash-flow patterns related to the nature of operations, let us compare the positions of manufacturing and mercantile firms.

Manufacturing Firms. As a rule, the circular processes of manufacturing enterprises are slower than those of firms engaged in mercantile operations or in providing services; hence, the cash requirements of manufacturing establishments are generally higher *for a given volume of total sales.* Manufacturing operations are time consuming—sometimes long drawn out, especially if goods in process must be aged—and selling the finished product may require as much time for a manufacturer as for a merchant. Thus, the circular flow of the manufacturer who sells on account spans, as it were, three time intervals—the time required for manufacturing, the time required for selling, and the time required for the collection of payments from customers; while that of a merchant who sells on account spans only the second and third of these intervals. To put the comparison on a different basis, one may say that the manufacturer who sells on account must invest in raw materials, goods-in-process, and

FIGURE 6–1

Cash Flows of a Manufacturing Firm

* Equal to the sum of net profit before income taxes and depreciation charges; available for income tax payments, dividends, expansion in the volume of the circular process, investment in fixed assets, repayment of debt, and so on.

finished goods inventories and in accounts receivable, whereas the merchant who sells on account has only to invest in finished goods and accounts receivable. Difference in the circular flows of manufacturing firms and mercantile firms, both types selling on account, can be seen by a comparison of Figures 6–1 and 6–2.

Among manufacturing enterprises themselves, important differences in the circular flow occur because of very wide variations in the time required to turn out finished products. The flow must necessarily be slow —cash requirements must be relatively high for a given volume of sales— when goods in process must be aged for months or even years, as in the tobacco and distilling businesses, or when much time is needed to complete all the multifarious details of turning out the completed product, as

FIGURE 6–2

Cash Flows of a Mercantile Firm

* Equal to the sum of net profit before income taxes and depreciation charges; available for income tax payments, dividends, expansion in the volume of the circular process, investment in fixed assets, repayment of debt, and so on.

in shipbuilding. On the other hand, manufacturers that are able to complete within a few hours or days the total productive process, because of assembly-line methods or because the productive process, by its very nature, is a simple one, may complete their circular flows much more rapidly than do the merchants to whom they sell their finished products.

Although it is the preponderant policy of American manufacturers to sell their goods on account, some are able to speed up the circular flow of their current assets by selling on a cash basis. Thus, our automobile producers have long been noted for their policy of selling only on the basis of immediate cash payment.

Mercantile Firms. As with manufacturers, wide variations in circular flows occur among mercantile establishments on account of the myriad varieties of the products they sell. Some kinds of goods, such as fresh fruits and vegetables, must be sold quickly if they are to be sold at all; others, such as most kinds of apparel, move less quickly but by no means slowly; and still others, such as household tools and many other kinds of hardware, move rather slowly. Much attention, therefore, is given to inventory "turnovers" as an indicator of the speed or slowness of circular flows in different kinds of mercantile establishments. Inventory turnover is computed by dividing the total cost of sales for a year or other period of time by the average inventory (at cost) held during the period. To effect a given volume of sales, therefore, a firm having an annual turnover of 2 must have a much larger average investment in inventories than one whose annual turnover is, say, 5. To put this proposition in alternative form, once again, the circular flow of the first firm must be much slower than that of the second.[3]

A significant way by which mercantile firms can control their cash flows, and thereby alter the amount of their cash requirements, is by choosing to sell or not to sell on account. As a rule, such firms have much more discretion in this matter than do manufacturers, as selling on account is not nearly so universal a policy in merchandising as in manufacturing. In some instances, it is true, a merchant might lose many of his customers were he to choose to sell only for cash, while his competitors were all selling on account. In many mercantile lines, however, it appears that the choice can be rather freely made. Witness the operation, side by side, of "independent" grocers who sell on account and chain stores that insist upon a cash-and-carry basis.

Seasonality and Secular Trend

Seasonality. Wide variations in the cash flows of business enterprises occur not only because of the almost limitless diversity of their products, they occur because of seasonal swings in production and selling. A firm that is able to produce or sell at close to a constant rate throughout the

---

[3] For a further discussion of inventory turnover and its significance, see below, pp. 153–57.

year will be likely, of course, to have a smoothly moving cash flow; its cash requirements will tend to be uniform from month to month. On the other hand, a firm whose operations are characterized by wide seasonal fluctuations will necessarily have a very jerky kind of circular flow; this will be evidenced by a large throw-off of cash at certain times, and, at others, a pressing need to pump into the circular process much additional cash.

Seasonality in business activity—and in cash flows and requirements—may result from the behavior of either supply or demand; although it is probably true that much more seasonality results from variations in demand than from variations in supply. Natural forces are often accountable for variations in supply. For example, processors of frozen foods and canners must concentrate their productive activities at the times when nature provides her harvests, and steel companies that are dependent upon the Mesabi Range must stock up their inventories of iron ore before the lake routes freeze over. Nature, likewise, has much to do with variations in demand, as one can readily see by considering the many kinds of goods that are sold in great quantities in wintertime but only in driblets, if at all, in the summertime, as well as the many kinds whose seasonal performance is the opposite of this. Custom, too, causes variations in demand. The custom of gift-giving at Christmastime results in December sales for many mercantile establishments far out of line with average monthly sales for the year.

Processors of frozen foods and canners must tie up extraordinary sums of money in their inventories at the time of harvests; their stock must be sufficient to meet demand until the time of the next "pack." They cannot escape the seasonal pattern in these operations, although they may try to even out their production by adding product lines with different seasonal patterns. Grocers who sell frozen foods, on the other hand, may not be much bothered by the seasonal pattern of the supply of such foods, since they can buy from month to month in accordance with seasonal changes in demand. Indeed, manufacturers are generally much more burdened by seasonal fluctuations in both supply and demand than are merchants; the former must ordinarily accept the burden of accumulating large inventories of seasonal goods for the very reason that the latter refuse to accept such burdens.

Secular Trend. The secular trend of an industry is its long-run tendency to expand, contract, or remain stable in volume of output, regardless of short-run fluctuations of a seasonal, cyclical, or random character. (Cyclical fluctuations will be discussed below; random fluctuations are short-lived changes in the volume of business activity due to such events as strikes, destructive storms, and temporary shortages of raw materials.) Industries that have an expanding secular trend are often described as "growth industries"; happily, we have many of them, including electric power and electronics, chemicals, synthetic fibers, plastics, aerospace research and development, and recreation equipment. Industries having a contracting secular trend are, fortunately, much fewer in number and importance; they include street railways, railroads in certain aspects of their operations, such as long-distance passenger traffic and track mileage, and some branches of the textile industry.

Growth industries tend to be chronically short of cash. Though they may be enormously profitable, profits after income taxes and dividends are likely to be most inadequate to meet the constantly recurring needs to add to both noncash current assets and fixed assets to take advantage of ever-expanding markets. Continually, therefore, must they be on the lookout for new outside sources of cash for the development of their productive facilities. In industries subject to secular decline, by contrast, the individual firms, especially if they continue to operate profitably despite decreasing volume, are likely to have substantial cash throw-offs that can be safely withdrawn from the circular process. Such firms can be expected to reject as most unwise all suggestions for the investment of available cash throw-offs in existing kinds of fixed facilities; however, investments in other kinds of facilities may be judged sound and desirable as when prospects are attractive for adding new expanding lines to take up the slack in the declining lines. In the absence of opportunities to take on new lines, the financial managers of firms in declining industries are most likely to use cash throw-offs in the payment of "liquidating dividends" to the stockholders as a procedure of gradually retiring their investment and gradually withdrawing from business operations.

Competitive Situation

On many occasions, the managers of business firms must adopt policies they do not like simply because their competitors have decided to adopt the same kinds of policies. A comfortably situated manufacturer or merchant may take on additional product lines or develop new service facilities in the expectation of gaining a competitive advantage. He may expect his competitors to imitate his innovation, but he may hope to have succeeded in weaning away some of their customers before they have developed comparable facilities. As indicated, the competing firms may dislike the innovation, but their managers may quickly decide that they have no choice but to follow along. These firms may not be nearly so comfortably fixed as the innovator—they may, indeed, be extremely short of cash. Thus, they may be forced to look for new sources of cash for a kind of expansion hitherto regarded as outside their "normal" area of operation.

Where competition is not keen, the financial managers of business enterprises may find it possible to conserve cash by changing operating policies long in effect. A manufacturer may drop product lines upon which he had been only breaking even, thereby making possible a reduction of his cash investment in inventories and, assuming that he sells on account, in accounts receivable. Or he may drop such lines in order to expand others upon which he has substantial margins of profit. Similarly, a merchant who has been selling on account may reduce his cash requirements—speed up the circular process—by making a decision to sell henceforth only on a basis of "cash on delivery."

BUSINESS CYCLE

The great majority of business firms experience alternative "waves" of expansion and contraction which we know as the "business cycle." Our business history clearly shows that such waves have been going on since early in the nineteenth century, and that each period of expansion or contraction and its succeeding period of movement in the opposite direction has lasted longer than one year but not more than twelve years. Thus, the business cycle is a kind of fluctuation in business activity different from seasonal fluctuations which recur annually according to a distinct pattern, and different from the secular trend which, as was indicated above, is a long-term tendency—usually in terms of decades—in a given direction. We speak, for example, of the severe contraction in business activity—the "depression"—of 1929–33, the postwar expansion period of 1946–48, the period of contraction or "recession" lasting from late 1948 to late 1949, the period of expansion or "prosperity" from then to the summer of 1953, the contraction or "recession" running from then to late summer in 1954, the subsequent expansion to the summer of 1957, the succeeding period of contraction ending in the spring of 1958, the expansive movement from then till the spring of 1960, the following contraction till February, 1961, and the expansion beginning then and still obtaining in the late fall of 1963.

Cyclical Patterns

Cyclical movements in total business activity pose many problems for the financial managers of business concerns. The managers of firms in "growth industries," continually on the lookout for cash to finance expansion, find their cash requirements even more pressing in periods of general business expansion; on the other hand, even they are likely to "enjoy"—that does not seem to be the proper word!—some respite from these pressures in times of general business contraction. Managers of firms in declining industries, by contrast, may be delighted with increasing sales in periods of cyclical expansion—they may begin to hope that their industry is no longer declining; but in periods of cyclical contraction, they may think that decline is ending in death as sales fall off to an extraordinary degree. In a similar way, a merchant whose sales have a distinct seasonal pattern may know that his December volume always tends to be about 80 per cent above average monthly sales; but in a period of general business expansion, the average may be in the vicinity of $2 million and the December sales, around $3.6 million, whereas in a period of contraction, the average may be approximately $1 million and the December volume, around $1.8 million. It would obviously be possible for him to make serious mistakes in accumulating inventory for the December market (and for other months as well, of course)—perhaps understocking in periods of cyclical expansion, so that customers must be turned away unsatisfied, and perhaps overstocking in periods of cyclical contraction, so that the cash flow would be slowed in an extraordinary way by the failure of much of the inventory to move.

While it is generally true that cash needs become most pressing for most kinds of businesses in periods of cyclical expansion, pressures of this kind are also often experienced in periods of contraction. Inventories become slow moving, yet the trade creditors who supplied them, the employees, and the suppliers of services must be paid. Whence does the money come to meet these obligations? Likewise, accounts receivable tend to become "slow." Even customers of hitherto high credit repute, finding themselves pinched, ask for extensions of the credit period, and delays in collections are experienced whether or not extensions are granted. In this way, forecasts of collections from accounts receivable as a means of meeting a firm's own obligations may turn out to be seriously in error.

Shifts in the Price Level

Often extremely important as sources of difficulty for the financial managers of business enterprises are the price changes that take place in the course of the business cycle. The tendency is for most kinds of prices to rise in periods of general business expansion, and to fall in periods of general business contraction. In some periods of expansion, the rise in prices is rapid and substantial—a development described as "inflation"— and in some periods of contraction, the fall in prices is likewise rapid and substantial—in which case, it is described as "deflation." Price developments of an inflationary or deflationary degree can be expected to pose problems of greater difficulty for financial managers than those engendered by price changes of a slower or more moderate kind.

Even if all prices were to change in equal proportions in the same direction in a given period, financial problems growing out of the price developments would not be eliminated. In a period of rising prices, for example, the typical firm needs more cash even if its volume of operations is no greater than before the price rise began. In such a period, the same volume of operations requires higher cash outlays for inventories, labor, and other kinds of services, and if goods are being sold on a credit basis, accounts receivable also absorb more cash. A need to replace fixed assets adds to the difficulties, since their cost at higher prices can not be met out of cash throw-offs resulting from depreciation charges upon the lower-cost assets to be replaced. On the other hand, equal proportional increases in prices of all classes would mean increases in the amount of profits; accordingly, the larger cash requirements for current assets, or for both current and fixed assets, might be met, at least in part, from this source.

Actually, of course, all kinds of prices do not change proportionally in a given direction in periods of general business expansion and contraction. Some prices do not change at all; some move in the same direction as the general movement, although not to the same degree, and often more slowly or more rapidly; and others even move in the direction opposite that of the general movement. Such a diversity of price changes has the effect of easing the financial problems of some business firms while intensifying those of others. A firm that is able to raise its selling prices by a greater amount than that by which its total costs increase in a period of rising prices tends to have its problems eased. Like any other firm, it must increase its cash outlays to maintain the same level of operations, but its increased margin of profit may yield sufficient additional cash for this purpose—perhaps more than a sufficient amount. On the other hand, a firm that is unable to increase its selling prices by an amount to match increases in its costs has its difficulties multiplied; it must step up its cash outlays to maintain a given volume of operations while, simultaneously, its cash throw-offs on account of profits are reduced.

Questions

1. Compare the cash needs of firms that must carry large inventories to serve their customers adequately with those of firms that can get along successfully with small inventories. For both classes of firms, does it make any difference whether goods are bought for cash or on account? Explain.

2. In what sense can it be said that firms tie up cash "permanently" in inventories and accounts receivable?

3. Even though a firm's operations are not expanding, its cash needs are likely to expand in periods of rising prices. Is this proposition true or false? Explain.

4. Explain how it is possible for "accounts payable" to trade suppliers to be a source of cash for operations beyond inventory acquisitions.

5. In what sense can it be said that a firm's employees make a "permanent" contribution to its assets and thereby reduce its need of cash?

6. Is it not rather farfetched to claim that governments, in the process of levying and collecting taxes, make contributions to the assets of business firms? Discuss.

7. Why is the cash required to carry accounts receivable "related" to the amount of the receivables rather than exactly equal to this amount?

8. What is the nature of cash throw-offs? What do they amount to for a firm that operates at a profit? for one that breaks even? for one that operates at a loss?

9. How often do cash throw-offs occur?

10. What kinds of financial difficulties, if any, are likely to be encountered by break-even corporations that have no need to expand operations? by those that do have such a need?

11. For equal volumes of sales, manufacturing companies generally have greater cash requirements than mercantile firms. Why?

12. Distinguish between supply and demand forces as causes of seasonality in business activity and cash flows. Why do these forces tend to affect manufacturers more severely than merchants?

13. What is the nature of secular trend in given lines of business activity? How does it influence the cash requirements of individual enterprises?

14. Explain why cash requirements are affected by the competitive situation in which businesses find themselves.

15. What is a business cycle? When does it occur? How long does it last? What effects does it have upon the cash needs of business firms?

Problems

1. During a certain year, the following changes occurred among the assets and liabilities of the Selma Processing Company:

Inventory (at cost)	+$18,000
Accounts receivable	− 28,000
Prepaid expenses	+ 3,000
Accounts payable	− 22,000
Accrued wages	+ 5,000
Accrued taxes	− 2,000
Fixed assets	+ 9,000

The increase in fixed assets resulted from acquisitions of machinery at a cost of $30,000 partially offset by depreciation charges of $21,000. For several years, the company has been selling its products at a uniform markup of 40 per cent, a markup sufficient to cover all its operating expenses including depreciation.

What amount of cash was absorbed or released as a result of the changes described?

2. For the Selma Processing Company of Problem 1, what amount of cash would have been absorbed or released if the changes in fixed assets were as described, but all other changes, in the amounts shown, were in the opposite directions?

Part III

ASSET
MANAGEMENT

chapter 7

THE MANAGEMENT OF CASH AND SHORT-TERM INVESTMENTS

Having in mind the processes by which cash flows in and out of individual business firms; how cash movements—and, therefore, cash requirements—are affected by prepayments and deferments of income and expenses, seasonal patterns of operation, the forces of secular growth and decline, competitive factors, and cyclical developments in general business activity; how cash requirements vary according to the nature of operations, as, for example, between manufacturing and mercantile enterprises; and how cash throw-offs become available, we are prepared to turn our attention to a detailed study of the use of cash in the acquisition and maintenance of the more important kinds of business assets. How cash is to be so used depends upon the asset-management policies that the directors and officers of individual enterprises decide upon. Hence, our investigation of the use of cash will be an investigation of asset-management policies, as presented in this chapter and the four chapters immediately following.

At the outset, it is well to repeat[1] that the payment of all kinds of business operating expenses is really a procedure of acquiring assets. This is clearly seen in factory operations where the costs of raw materials, direct labor, and overhead expenses find their way into the valuation of inventories of goods in process and finished goods. But it is no less true of selling and administrative expenses. Business firms expect to cover all such expenses in the selling prices of their products; hence they are, by implication, also included in the valuation of inventories of finished goods, whether such goods are produced by the firms themselves or are bought for resale. One should not lose sight of this essential fact even though, in accounting statements, selling and administrative expenses are not shown as being included in inventories or in accounts receivable. The making of payments for advertising, delivery costs, or office salaries is just as much an acquisition of assets as is the buying of factory, store, or office equipment. It follows, therefore, that business managers must be as careful in controlling expenses as they are in the formulation and execution of policies having to do with the acquisition and maintenance of things that are specifically labeled as "assets."

---

[1] See above, pp. 69–70.

ASSET MANAGEMENT IN GENERAL

Considering the diversity of the scope of operations among our millions of business firms, the many varieties of their seasonal patterns, the varied influences of secular growth and decline, the diverse effects of cyclical developments in general business activity, the wide differences in the degree of competition among firms and industries, and variations among firms in their access to new sources of cash, it is patently impossible to formulate a set of asset-management rules or policies that would be good for all businesses at all times. Indeed, a most reasonable conclusion is that asset-management policies that are good for a given firm at a given time may be quite bad for another at that time, as well as for the firm itself at other times when surrounding circumstances have changed.

Accordingly, our study of asset-management policies must be confined to an analysis of the principal theories that the financial manager should know about, and the principal problems he is likely to encounter, in arriving at decisions about the best uses of cash in investment in the various classes of assets. Our interest must be devoted basically to the kinds of materials, as it were, that the financial manager has to work with, rather than to an attempt to tell him what is the best thing he can do in given circumstances. We will find it especially desirable to give attention to alternative policies among which financial managers may choose; for policy determination is usually not a discovery of ideal solutions to problems, but one of compromise, as when we say that we can have more of one thing if we are satisfied to get along with less of another.

Conservation of Cash

Although it is impossible to formulate a set of asset-management policies of universal applicability, one policy or rule that appears to be unanimously accepted is that cash must be conserved. Few businesses, even the wealthiest, have sufficient cash to do all the things they wish to do. Financial managers, therefore, must be constantly on the lookout for ways to reduce cash requirements—to economize in its use. Whether it is better to buy or to rent equipment, to expand one class of assets rather than another, to use cash for expansion or to pay dividends—problems such as these arise because available cash is limited in amount and must be used, as it were, sparingly. Another way of looking at the rule of the conservation of cash is to say that, because cash is expensive, it ought to be acquired and used with caution. In the case of corporations, cash can be acquired from stockholders on a continuing basis ordinarily only if there are good prospects that they will be rewarded through the distribution of reasonable dividends. Cash can be acquired from lenders only on the basis of an obligation to pay interest and an obligation to repay the principal of loans. The interest is an additional expense of operation in any case; moreover, either the principal or the interest obligation can turn out to be a most expensive one, in the sense that it may threaten the very existence of the corporation should difficulty in meeting it result from an inept use of the cash.

Statistics of Corporate Assets

Before we take up a detailed analysis of what the financial managers of corporations may decide in the formulation of asset-management policies, we should find it worthwhile to look at what they have actually been doing. Their decisions are revealed (but in part only, of course) in the actual distributions of assets as disclosed in their balance sheets. Excellent statistics of corporate asset distributions, as compiled from balance sheets submitted with federal income tax returns, are published annually by the Internal Revenue Service of the Treasury Department. In Table 7–1 are presented data of this kind for fiscal years ending between July 1, 1960, and June 30, 1961, of broad industrial groupings of corporations (with some exceptions as noted in a footnote to the table) and their total.[2]

The relationships indicated by these figures can be taken as being reasonably definitive. Shifts in the position of particular assets in relation to one another and to the respective totals can be expected to take place from year to year; yet one has no reason to expect a pronounced shifting in any short period of years, except, perhaps, between periods of high prosperity and depression of considerable severity. But the data probably have serious shortcomings in strong tendencies to underemphasize the importance of inventories, and possibly also accounts receivable, and, accordingly, to overemphasize the importance of cash and investment in government securities. This probability follows from the choice of slack seasons for the ends of corporations' fiscal years—the very dates for which the balance sheets that accompany their income tax returns are compiled. Especially do corporations select times at which inventory taking and valuation will be least burdensome, and that generally means times when their inventories are at or close to their lowest levels. At such times, too, accounts receivable balances may be unusually low, because many collections from credit customers have already been made on account of the sales of preceding brisk periods.

However all this may be, the following relationships as indicated by the tabular data appear to be noteworthy: (1) a division between current and fixed assets in the total cross section of corporations only moderately

[2] One may consult the *Statistics of Income* reports of the Treasury for the data of subgroups within the broad classifications. For example, within the retail trade classification will be found separate data for corporations in each of the following business areas: foods; general merchandise; apparel and accessories; furniture, home furnishings and equipment; automotive dealers and gasoline stations; eating and drinking places; building materials, hardware, and farm equipment; and other retail stores.

TABLE 7-1
Classes of Assets of Business Corporations in 1960-61[a]
(Dollar amounts in millions)

CLASSES OF ASSETS	AGRICULTURE, FORESTRY, FISHERIES		MINING AND QUARRYING		CONSTRUCTION		MANUFACTURING	
	Amount	Per Cent	Amount	Per Cent	Amount	Per Cent	Amount	Per Cent
Cash..............	$ 255	6.3	$ 1,074	6.3	$ 1,625	10.5	$ 15,373	5.9
Notes and accounts receivable........	545	13.4	2,259	13.3	5,584	36.3	43,371	16.5
Inventories.........	472	11.6	921	5.4	1,643	10.7	55,760	21.3
Investments—government obligations..	45	1.1	923	5.4	298	1.9	12,873	4.9
Other current assets..	50	1.2	285	1.7	219	1.4	3,779	1.4
Other investments...	478	11.8	2,255	13.3	1,189	7.7	31,388	12.0
Depreciable assets....	1,265	31.1	6,547	38.6	2,545	16.6	85,594	32.6
Depletable assets....	36	.9	1,939	11.4	52	.3	4,095	1.6
Land..............	740	18.2	202	1.2	295	1.9	3,684	1.4
Intangible assets....	7	.2	249	1.5	12	.1	801	.3
Other assets........	171	4.2	294	1.7	1,904	12.4	5,551	2.1
Total Current Assets........	$1,367	33.6	$ 5,462	32.2	$ 9,369	61.0	$131,156	50.0
Total Fixed Assets........	2,697	66.4	11,486	67.8	5,997	39.0	131,113	50.0
Total Assets....	$4,063	100.0	$16,949	100.0	$15,367	100.0	$262,271	100.0
Number of income tax returns.......	17,139		13,017		72,332		165,863	

[a] Active corporations filing federal income tax returns for fiscal years ending between July 1, 1960, and June 30, 1961, excluding corporations engaged in trade not allocated to wholesale or retail; in finance, insurance, and real estate; and in miscellaneous operations not classified as to industry. Receivables as reduced by reserves for bad debts, and depreciable and depletable assets as reduced by allowances for depreciation and depletion, respectively. Total current and fixed assets as computed by the author, classifying the first five items as current assets and the remainder as fixed assets. In some instances, vertical items do not add exactly to totals because of rounding. Percentages supplied by the author.

favoring the latter; (2) the relatively large holdings of cash and government securities (mostly short-term, one presumes) by all industrial groups except public utilities; (3) the very high proportions of current assets in the construction, wholesale trade, and retail trade groups; (4) the very high proportion of fixed assets in the public utility group, as well as the relatively high proportion in mining and quarrying and among the service corporations; (5) the position of inventories as the largest current asset in the manufacturing and retail trade groups; (6) the extraordinarily high proportion of receivables to total assets in the construction industry, its extraordinarily low level among public utilities, and its substantial level in all other groups; and (7) the quite wide divergence of the asset distri-

TABLE 7–1 (Continued)

PUBLIC UTILITIES		WHOLESALE TRADE		RETAIL TRADE		SERVICES		ALL GROUPS[b]	
Amount	Per Cent	Amount	Per Cent	Amount	Per Cent	Amount	Per Cent	Amount	Per Cent
$ 3,632	2.5	$ 3,471	8.1	$ 4,643	10.2	$ 1,787	9.0	$ 31,860	5.8
5,757	4.0	14,928	34.8	10,312	22.7	3,449	17.4	86,205	15.6
3,093	2.1	12,203	28.5	15,128	33.3	856	4.3	90,076	16.3
3,098	2.1	778	1.8	434	1.0	384	1.9	18,833	3.4
2,332	1.6	708	1.7	718	1.6	418	2.1	8,509	1.5
7,214	5.0	4,783	11.2	3,058	6.7	2,449	12.3	52,814	9.6
115,915	80.1	4,453	10.4	8,621	19.0	8,243	41.5	233,183	42.3
134	.1	58	.1	33	.1	21	.1	6,368	1.2
885	.6	589	1.3	1,196	2.6	1,139	5.7	8,730	1.6
146	.1	52	.1	68	.1	134	.7	1,469	.3
2,569	1.8	834	1.9	1,269	2.8	972	4.9	13,564	2.5
$ 17,912	12.3	$32,088	74.9	$31,235	68.7	$ 6,894	34.7	$235,483	42.7
126,863	87.7	10,769	25.1	14,245	31.3	12,958	65.2	316,128	57.3
$144,774	100.0	$42,857	100.0	$45,481	100.0	$19,853	100.0	$551,615	100.0
43,852		117,437		217,269		121,024		767,933	

[b] With exceptions as indicated in preceding footnote.

SOURCE: U.S. Treasury Department, Internal Revenue Service, *Statistics of Income, 1960–61— Preliminary: Corporation Income Tax Returns* (Washington, D.C.: U.S. Government Printing Office, 1962), pp. 17–24.

bution pattern of public utilities from that of each of the other groups, as well as from that of the overall totals.

CASH

It might appear that a corporation's cash position must depend upon all its asset-management policies—that it must be the resultant of all the decisions concerning investment in noncash assets, borrowing, the payment of dividends, and so on. Nevertheless, certain policies with respect to cash balances themselves must be formulated—policies, one might say, not immediately related to other kinds of asset-management decisions. Such purely cash policies include all the rules established for the protection of cash while it is in a corporation's possession—rules of the kinds briefly discussed in Chapter 4—together with the standards set for minimum and maximum cash balances, precautions exercised to avoid the special federal tax on "unreasonable accumulations of surplus," and rules for the investment of cash temporarily in excess supply.

Minimum Balances

The financial managers of most corporations set a figure below which they do not want the cash balances to fall at any time except in periods of emergency. The idea is that, no matter how large cash outlays must be at certain times or in certain circumstances, except for emergencies, cash in excess of the established minimum should be available to meet these outlays, so that the minimum need not be encroached upon.

Emergencies. As indicated, the possibility of the occurrence of emergencies is a reason for setting a standard of minimum balances, although, as we shall see later, it is not the only reason. The most common kind of emergency planned for is an extraordinary slowing down of the cash inflow from normal sources in periods during which customary outlays must continue to be made. In a period of business recession, the sales volume may fall off both sharply and suddenly, and many accounts receivable, hitherto judged to be of high quality, may turn out to be "slow"; yet the corporation's obligations to make current cash payments may not be appreciably diminished. For minimum balance standards, therefore, financial managers often set levels of cash holdings that would enable their corporations to meet the normal outflow for a period of two or three weeks, or a month, or perhaps as long as two months, even should the normal inflow of cash from operations come to a complete halt.

Credit Standing with Trade Creditors. A second reason why financial managers decide to have at all times, except in emergencies, cash balances not less than stipulated sums is to maintain their corporations' credit standings with trade creditors. As a matter of course, a corporation will take advantage of opportunities to buy goods and supplies on account, but suppliers do not, as a matter of course, sell on account to every corporation that asks for such accommodations. The suppliers' decisions whether or not to sell on account will be based upon analyses of a prospective buyer's credit position; in other words, they will evaluate his position to determine whether or not he has or will have the capacity to pay within the allowed credit period. Because suppliers are almost always short-term creditors, they are inclined to concentrate attention upon the buyer's *working capital position.* Working capital is defined as the net difference between the total of a firm's current assets and the total of its current liabilities; its "working capital position" is, accordingly, the total array of the kinds and amounts of its current assets and the kinds and amounts of its current liabilities. This array is important to the trade supplier because the goods sold will be added to the buyer's current assets and his claim for payment will be added to the buyer's current liabilities.

In analyzing a prospective buyer's working capital position, the trade supplier will unquestionably give particular attention to cash holdings. Suppose, for example, that Corporations A and B have working capital positions as follows:

CORPORATION A

Current Assets:		*Current Liabilities:*	
Cash.....................	$ 5,000	Accounts payable............	$40,000
Accounts receivable.........	60,000	Accrued wages..............	5,000
Inventories................	75,000	Other accrued expenses.......	15,000
Total Current Assets....	$140,000	Total Current Liabilities	$60,000

CORPORATION B

Current Assets:		*Current Liabilities:*	
Cash.....................	$ 25,000	Accounts payable............	$40,000
Accounts receivable.........	40,000	Accrued wages..............	5,000
Inventories................	75,000	Other accrued expenses.......	15,000
Total Current Assets....	$140,000	Total Current Liabilities	$60,000

Suppose, further, that each of these corporations wishes to buy $20,000 worth of goods on account from a certain supplier. It might appear, at first glance, that both corporations are equally creditworthy: they have equal amounts of current assets and current liabilities, so that the dollar amounts of their working capital are likewise equal. But the supplier would not be satisfied with first glances. He would surely notice that Corporation A could pay off only 8⅓ per cent of its existing current liabilities out of its cash resources, and only 6¼ per cent should a liability to him of $20,000 be added; whereas Corporation B could pay off 41⅔ per cent of its existing current liabilities, and 31¼ per cent were a liability of $20,000 to be added. Though he might not reject A's application for credit, surely he would be much less inclined to grant it (aside from other considerations) than to grant that of B.

For the sole purpose of making their working capital positions look better, some corporations (as well as business enterprises of other legal forms) at times borrow money before submitting their balance sheets to prospective trade creditors. Any action that is specifically designed to improve the "look" of the working capital position for credit purposes, but not actually strengthening that position, is often described as "window dressing." A short-term loan does not increase the amount of a firm's working capital, since it adds equal amounts to current assets and current liabilities, but the augmentation of the cash account tends to make the firm's situation look more favorable. Had Corporation A of the foregoing illustration borrowed, say, $10,000 from a commercial bank, the current section of its balance sheet (disregarding whatever discount the bank might have charged) would have appeared as follows:

CORPORATION A

Current Assets:		*Current Liabilities:*	
Cash......................	$ 15,000	Accounts payable...........	$40,000
Accounts receivable.........	60,000	Notes payable..............	10,000
Inventories................	75,000	Accrued wages.............	5,000
Total Current Assets....	$150,000	Other accrued expenses.......	15,000
		Total Current Liabilities	$70,000

In this way, the corporation would have had cash equal to 21¾ per cent of its current liabilities even as increased by the obligation to the lending bank, and equal to 16⅔ per cent were a further liability of $20,000 to the supplier to be added.

Good Bank Relations. Maintaining good relations with the commercial banks from which they borrow is a third reason why business enterprises establish standards for minimum cash balances. Commercial bankers preach the doctrine that their lending capacity comes chiefly from the deposits left with them by customers, rather than from the capital accounts of their stockholders, and that firms that wish to borrow should contribute to this lending capacity by leaving substantial deposit balances with them. Bankers are especially devoted to this doctrine in times of "tight money," that is, when the volume of acceptable loan applications exceeds their capacity to lend. In such periods, they are likely to be generous in granting loans to firms that customarily maintain sizable deposit balances, and to be rather niggardly toward firms not so qualifying, assuming that they are willing to do anything at all for the latter class.

Often, too—particularly in periods of "tight money"—commercial banks stipulate in loan contracts that, *while the loan is outstanding,* the borrower must not let his deposit balance fall below some percentage of the loan, perhaps 10 or 15 per cent, or perhaps as much as 20 per cent. Such "compensatory balances" undoubtedly enable banks individually to grant larger volumes of loans than otherwise would be possible[3]—to take care of a larger number of their customers—and give them interest income at higher rates than the rates stated in the loan contracts. For the borrower, however, there are commensurate burdens in his inability to use the entire proceeds of the loan and in the payment of a higher rate of interest than the named rate on the portion of the proceeds that he is actually permitted to use. In setting standards for their cash balances, at any rate, the financial managers of business enterprises must obviously give attention to bankers' attitudes toward deposit balances, as indicated both in their preachments and in their actual demands for compensatory balances in connection with loan contracts.

---

[3] But the lending capacity of the commercial banking system as a whole is not thereby increased, since that depends upon the amount of the system's own cash (primary) reserves. Thus, the fact that an individual bank is able to increase its lending capacity by the enforcement of a compensatory-balance rule means that the lending capacity of other banks is held to a level below what it otherwise would tend to be.

Although the keeping of substantial cash balances with commercial banks to qualify for loans, or in relation to loans already obtained, appears to work a hardship upon firms that borrow, there is usually a savings factor to be considered. Most banks levy service charges upon each depositor measured in relation to the volume of clerical operations involved in handling his account. The charges are assessed at a few cents for each item handled—as for checks and other "cash items" deposited in an account, checks drawn upon the account, deposit slips, checks certified, and promissory notes taken for collection—and at quantity rates on the amount of paper money and coin deposited. But the banks generally reduce total service charges as thus computed by giving the customer a "credit" in proportion to his average deposit balance, the idea being that, because customers' deposits contribute to a bank's earning capacity, it can afford to allow them "free" services in proportion to these deposits. Accordingly, the financial managers of business firms may conclude that their deposit balances pay their way by reducing or eliminating bank service charges that otherwise would be assessed.

Minimum Standards in Periods of "Tight Money." In periods of "tight money," financial managers face strong temptations to relax whatever standards for minimum cash balances they have previously maintained. This is so, because such periods are generally characterized by high levels of business activity.[4] As their sales expand, many firms find that additional cash requirements tend to exceed by far the throw-offs becoming available through the circular process. As workers are added to the payroll, and as, perhaps, wage rates are increased, more money must be made available; inventories must be expanded, probably at higher prices; and more money must be tied up in accounts receivable. In such circumstances, every effort must be made to use cash as efficiently as possible, and the holding of idle balances, in keeping with an established standard, may not appear to be a very efficient way of doing things. Financial managers may even conclude that the prompt use of all their cash would preclude a need to borrow, so that they could afford to ignore bankers' preachments and compensatory balance rules. Borrowing at the high rates of interest that usually prevail in periods of "tight money" while holding idle cash balances, might look like an unsound policy.

Nevertheless, arguments for holding to the established cash standards appear to be much stronger than for relaxation; these include the need of maintaining credit standing with trade suppliers at a time when dependence upon them is presumably growing, the possibility of needing to borrow after cash balances have been exhausted and of finding nobody willing to lend, and, most important of all, the possibility that business activity will abruptly turn downward, perhaps causing the very kind of emergency for which minimum standards are primarily designed.

---

[4] Historically, the principal exceptions have been periods of "tight money" occasioned by financial crises in depressions, as in 1893, 1907, and 1932–33.

Maximum Balances

The financial managers of many establishments have no occasion to worry about setting upper limits to their cash balances. They are well pleased if they succeed in having only sufficient cash to meet requirements for current outlays plus the amounts of the minimums they have established. But many firms tend to accumulate cash far beyond what they need for current outlays and to satisfy minimum balance standards. For many, the accumulations are purely temporary ones, so that no difficult problem of cash management arises. This is particularly true of the accumulations that take place in the slack seasons of businesses whose operations fluctuate substantially each year according to seasonal patterns; all that is required is the holding of the excess cash or its temporary investment in high-quality, short-term securities until needed for the more active seasons. Other enterprises, however, tend to accumulate excess cash chronically; these are generally highly successful enterprises, large and small, that are not expanding at a fast pace, if they are expanding at all. Their cash throw-offs, after allowing for the continuance of the circular process, the replacement of fixed assets, the payment of income taxes, and the distribution of generous dividends to the stockholders, constantly tend to pile up funds well beyond the minimum standards. What should be done with these funds?

In seeking an answer to this question, the financial managers should not lose sight of the fact that cash is an expensive asset and that, as always, the rule of the conservation of cash should be applied. Idle funds are expensive in the sense that, if they cannot be used profitably in a given business, they are likely to be usable profitably elsewhere; hence income possibilities are probably being lost as long as the funds continue to be held idle. If there is every assurance that a corporation's working capital position would be quite strong without such funds, and if there is no reasonable opportunity to use them profitably in expanding operations, they should unquestionably be distributed to the stockholders. To give the stockholders the opportunity to dispose of the cash as they might choose would surely be more fitting than to have the directors substitute their own choice, as by investing the excess money in securities of unrelated corporations.

However, the financial managers of corporations that enjoy strong cash positions are inclined to be quite generous in their estimates of cash requirements. Minimum balances that might be needed for "emergencies" are likely to be very generously estimated, and the concept of "emergency" itself is likely to be expanded to cover many kinds of possibilities not ordinarily envisaged when that term is employed. Thus, the financial managers may think of the convenience of having large amounts of ready cash available should inventions and innovations make a transformation of operating facilities and procedures necessary, should opportunities arise for the buying out of competing firms upon favorable terms, or should a general business depression of unusual severity develop. It may be that the financial managers would be quite right in so thinking. At any rate, recent trends, as seen particularly in large corporations, have been in the direction of the accumulation of cash balances and holdings of short-term, high-quality investments well beyond what appears to be necessary for quite safe working capital positions.

The holding of cash and short-term investments in amounts in excess of reasonable requirements is often criticized as tending to weaken the sense of responsibility of business managers. If liberal dividends are already being paid to the stockholders, the managers may feel that their principal obligation to the stockholders has been fulfilled; accordingly, they may think themselves at liberty to use the remaining excess cash in trying out new projects. Their vigilance in seeking ways to cut costs may be greatly reduced. Indeed, they may be quite extravagant in replacing fixed assets having many years of useful life remaining, in furnishing their own office quarters, in wining and dining customers and prospective customers, and so on. On the other hand, net profit as *a rate of return on total assets* tends to be reduced if cash (or any other asset) is superabundant; hence the managers, realizing that their stewardship may be judged by a comparison of this rate of return with that of other corporations, may prefer to pass excess cash on to the stockholders rather than to use it extravagantly.

Cash Holdings and Special Taxation

Directly related to the determination of policies for maximum cash balances is a need to exercise precautions to avoid taxation according to the terms of Sections 531–537 of the Internal Revenue Code of 1954. As was pointed out in Chapter 2, this legislation places a special tax upon corporations found to be unreasonably accumulating surplus to enable stockholders to avoid high rates of personal income tax. The burden is upon the Internal Revenue Service to prove the unreasonable accumulation, but the holding of cash and short-term investments[5] far beyond the current or prospective needs of a corporation could well be taken as strong evidence of such an accumulation. A corporation that has large amounts of excess cash and only vague plans for future expansion would be likely to find itself in a vulnerable position.

One must remember, of course, that there is no typically close relationship between the size of the cash account and the size of the surplus account or accounts of a corporation. A corporation that has large

---

[5] Although we are interested here chiefly in excessive holdings of cash or its alternative, short-term, high-quality securities, heavy investment in stocks or long-term bonds unrelated to the investing corporation's purposes, as indicated in its articles of incorporation, might also be taken as evidence of unreasonable accumulation of surplus.

amounts of cash and little surplus cannot be reached by the provisions of Sections 531–537. Such a corporation might be one in a declining industry, the conditions of which were examined in Chapter 6. On the other hand, a corporation having what appears to be excess amounts of cash as well as a large surplus account may have real difficulty in trying to refute charges of unreasonably accumulating surplus.

Investment of Excess Cash

A most remarkable development of the past ten years, roughly speaking, has been the ever-increasing attention given by many corporate managements—especially the managements of large corporations—to the short-term investment of idle cash. The treasurers of this and that corporation have been hailed for their astuteness in controlling their corporations' "money position," as they have constantly sought to pick up a few dollars of interest income by investing idle cash for three or four days, or as they have chosen one kind of investment security rather than another to gain an interest-rate differential of perhaps one fourth of a percentage point. Although the amount of interest to be earned on each dollar of a weekend investment may seem to be infinitesimal, interest earned in a year can amount to a tidy supplement to income from sales if the investments of very short term involve many hundreds of thousands or millions of dollars and if the transactions can be repeated frequently in the course of the year. After all, each year has 52 weekends and some have 53! As a government securities dealer remarked: "Some financial men earn more by investing idle corporate cash over a weekend than some operating divisions can earn in a week." [6]

Corporate treasurers who think along the lines suggested in the preceding paragraph generally have the attitude that, while "minimum cash balances" must constantly be planned for, substantial portions of them from time to time can safely take forms other than cash itself. They are encouraged to invest portions of these balances even for a few days because of the widespread availability of short-term investment outlets of virtually riskless character—outlets to be discussed in the following pages.

Other corporate treasurers—perhaps they could be said to be more "conservative"—are inclined to argue that the bother of investing for a few days portions of what are supposed to be "minimum cash balances" is not compensated for by the interest earned. But they readily agree that there can be no excuse for the idleness of funds held in excess of minimum balances, such as for tax payments to be disbursed in a month or two, meeting a sinking-fund payment on a bond issue due in, say, two months, or other such outlays of some degree of remoteness. Similarly, almost all treasurers would surely agree that temporary investment is imperative for cash accumulated by seasonal enterprises during their slack periods, as

---

[6] *The New York Times*, June 15, 1963, p. 27.

well as for that being assembled by any enterprise for the future expansion of the scale of its operations. A corporation, for example, may sell additional stock or float a bond issue to finance the acquisition of additional fixed assets, but a considerable period of time may be expected to elapse between the date when the proceeds of the sale of the securities will be received and the date on which payment for the fixed assets must be made. The wisdom of bridging the two dates by the temporary investment of the cash could hardly be questioned.

SHORT-TERM INVESTMENTS

To put temporarily idle cash to work in earning interest, the financial managers of business corporations generally choose among short-term obligations of the federal Treasury, certain additional kinds of short-term "paper" of very high quality, time deposits in commercial banks, and, especially in smaller corporations, share accounts in savings and loan associations. They conclude that their choice must be in the direction of something that is "as good as cash" in the sense of safety, and, of course, having the additional advantage of providing a return. The watchword is that safety must never be sacrificed for income.

Credit and Money-Rate Risk

Safety in the short-term investment of funds means two things, namely, the avoidance of credit risks and the avoidance of what is called "money-rate risk" or "interest-rate risk." Credit risk is determined by the capacity of debtors to meet their obligations, while money-rate risk develops from fluctuations in the market prices of obligations due to changes in the structure of interest rates. Thus, we usually say that obligations of the Treasury are entirely free of credit risk, for nobody doubts the capacity of the federal government to pay off its obligations at their face value at maturity. But the market prices of treasury obligations fluctuate—a fact indicating that they are by no means free of money-rate risk. Fluctuations in the market prices of treasury obligations occur, not because of anything that the Treasury does or does not do; they fluctuate, as was indicated, simply because the structure of market rates of interest changes from time to time. Treasury bonds having several years to run to maturity and bearing interest at 3 per cent will surely fall below par value if market rates of interest upon securities of that quality and the same maturity go to 3½ per cent. If investors can buy at par a security of a certain quality and maturity paying 3½ per cent, they will not be willing to pay par value for one of the same quality and maturity paying only 3 per cent; thus the 3 per cent bond must fall below par value to a level at which the return on the two bonds is equalized![7]

---

[7] The equalization comes about because, though the investor would be paying less than par value for the 3 per cent bond, he would receive interest at 3 per cent on the par value, and the par value itself as principal at maturity.

If investment securities must be sold at prices less than the prices paid for them, due to a rise in market rates of interest between the dates of purchase and resale, the losses are as hard to take as would be those resulting from the inability of debtors to pay at maturity the full amounts of their obligations. For this reason, corporate managers, in seeking investment outlets for idle cash, must be as zealous to avoid money-rate risks as to avoid credit risks. They can avoid credit risks by buying only securities of the highest quality, as treasury obligations, but how can they avoid money-rate risks? The answer is that they can do so by concentrating in short-term obligations. Money-rate risk is a function of time to maturity—in other words, the longer the time to maturity the greater is this risk. Thus, should the applicable market rate of interest rise from 3 per cent to 3½ per cent, a 3 per cent obligation having three months to run to maturity would fall in market price only from par to 99.87, whereas one having 20 years to run would fall from par to 92.85.

Treasury Obligations

Treasury bills and certificates are the most popular mediums for the temporary investment of the excess cash of business corporations. Because these instruments are obligations of the federal government, they are devoid of credit risk, and because they invariably have maturities of not more than one year, money-rate risk is slight. In view of the large size of our national debt, these instruments are available in abundant quantities, and the typical corporation has little difficulty in buying a sufficient amount to satisfy its requirements. At the end of April, 1963, for example, $49.4 billion of bills were outstanding and $21.8 billion of certificates.[8] For the same date, the Treasury estimated holdings of bills by corporations other than the Federal Reserve banks and other financial institutions at $7,175 million, and their holdings of other federal obligations maturing within one year—probably consisting largely of certificates—at $1,484 million. By contrast, holdings of these corporations in treasury obligations maturing beyond one year were estimated at only $2,327 million.[9]

Bills. Two batches of bills are sold every week by the Treasury, being offered broadside to all who may wish to enter subscriptions by filing the prescribed form at the Federal Reserve banks. The usual maturity for one batch is 91 days, and for the other, 182 days. In the early summer of 1963, the weekly sales of 91-day bills amounted in par value to approximately $2.1 billion, and of the 182-day bills, to approximately $800 million. In ordinary circumstances, the proceeds of the bill sales of any week are simply used by the Treasury to pay off the issue of 91-day bills sold 13 weeks earlier and the issue of the 182-day bills sold 26 weeks earlier. In some periods, however, the Treasury gets "new money" by stepping up the amount of its weekly offerings, as it thereby takes in

[8] *Federal Reserve Bulletin,* June, 1963, p. 824.
[9] *Ibid.,* p. 825.

more than enough to pay off the earlier issues. For several years, the Treasury also offered quarterly issues of bills maturing in one year, but in August, 1963, it shifted to monthly offerings of one-year bills. In some years, too, the Treasury puts out special issues of "tax anticipation bills"; these issues run for periods of varying lengths, since they are slated to mature on or close to important tax payment dates such as the following March 15 or June 15. The Treasury's practice of issuing tax anticipation bills recognizes the popular corporation policy of early accumulation of cash to pay income taxes; hence it taps this tax money in advance, as it were, by means of its special offerings.

Business corporations, as well as other classes of buyers, can enter subscriptions for bills of the various issues with the Federal Reserve banks of their respective districts. Bills are sold to the highest bidders among those entering subscriptions, and are redeemed at maturity at par value. The bills do not bear interest on their face; hence the bid price indicates the interest rate on the basis of which the subscriber is willing to buy. For example, if a corporation bids 99.250 for a quantity of 91-day bills, it indicates that it expects to earn in the period of 91 days 75 cents on each sum of $99.25 of its investment, this amounting to a rate of interest of approximately 3 per cent per annum. To encourage the entry of subscriptions by corporations and other investors who do not want to make guesses as to what the level of acceptable bids will be, the Treasury provides that subscriptions up to $200,000 may be entered by prospective buyers without the designation of bid prices. Bills to cover such subscriptions are then supplied by the Treasury at a price equal to the average of the accepted bids.

Many corporations invest in bills as well as in other classes of treasury obligations without entering subscriptions at the Federal Reserve banks. There exists for all kinds of treasury marketable obligations a broad, well-organized market in which a large volume of transactions takes place daily. Accordingly, a corporation can buy already-outstanding treasury obligations directly or indirectly from dealers. The existence of excellent market facilities is, of course, an important reason why investment in treasury obligations is popular among corporations. A corporation need not hold such securities till maturity if it requires cash earlier; it can simply sell them to a dealer.

Certificates. Treasury certificates of indebtedness traditionally have had maturities ranging upward from six months and never longer than one year. Recently, however, the Treasury has been issuing certificates on a regular quarterly basis, with each issue running for a full year to maturity. Each issue of certificates bears interest at a rate designated by the Treasury at the time it is offered for subscription. As with bills, anyone can enter subscriptions for new certificates at the Federal Reserve bank of his district, as well as buy already-issued certificates through banks and other dealers in government securities.

Other Treasury Marketable Obligations. Two additional classes of marketable obligations are issued by the Treasury, namely, notes and bonds. Notes are intermediate-term obligations, generally having maturities between three and five years. Bonds are classified as long-term obligations, usually having maturities of more than ten years and as long as forty years, although a few issues of recent years have had maturities between five and ten years. Treasury notes and bonds that are closely approaching their maturity dates have the same qualities as bills and certificates, that is, a total lack of credit risk and only a slight degree of money-rate risk. Corporations, therefore, can invest in them as safely as in bills and certificates.

Corporations that are accumulating funds for intermediate- and long-term purposes, as for plant expansion to be undertaken several years hence, often invest such funds in treasury notes and bonds having maturities close to the time that the money will be needed for the expansion projects. As the Treasury will surely pay off these obligations at par at maturity, the corporations can ignore interim fluctuations in their market prices—fluctuations likely, of course, to be much wider than for bills and certificates.[10] On the other hand, a corporation would be ill-advised to invest cash needed in a few months in notes and bonds having several years to run to maturity, as declines in market value due to rising rates of interest might wipe out, or more than wipe out, the interest earned on such securities. On July 5, 1963, for example, notes of the Treasury's 1½ per cent issue due in October, 1965, were selling in the market at 96½, and bonds of the 2½ per cent issue due in December, 1968, were selling at 93⅝.[11]

Other Short-Term Investment "Paper"

Other instruments or "paper" both readily available and attractive for the short-term investment of excess corporate cash include obligations of state and local governments, maturing bonds of high-rated business corporations, promissory notes of finance companies and other business enterprises, and time certificates of deposit issued by commercial banks (to be discussed separately below). Additionally, some large corporations are in a position to lend excess funds to dealers in government securities.

Although many of the debt instruments of state and local governments of high credit rating have maturities too lengthy to preclude money-rate risk, many also are closely approaching their maturity dates—they are now short-term obligations regardless of their original maturities. That such issues are attractive to corporate treasurers was indicated in income tax returns filed with the Internal Revenue Service for fiscal years ending

---

[10] Technically, the accumulation of cash for an intermediate- or long-term objective takes the funds or the securities in which they may be invested out of the current asset classification. It is logical, therefore, to show the funds or securities, as the case may be, among the fixed assets in the corporation's balance sheet.

[11] Aubrey G. Lanston & Co., Inc., *Comparative Yields of United States Treasury Issues*, July 8, 1963, p. 2.

between July 1, 1960, and June 30, 1961, where nonfinancial corporations reported holdings of $1,765 million of state and local issues.[12] Always a special advantage of investment in such issues is the exemption of interest earned upon them from federal income taxes.

The rates of interest that can be earned by short-term investment in the maturing bonds of high-rated business corporations are often better than can be gained for equal periods of time on treasury obligations and obligations of state and local governments, even with the latters' tax-exemption feature. However, the available evidence does not indicate any widespread preference for the corporate issues for this or any other reason.

Much more popular with many corporate treasurers who are inclined to invest in business rather than government "paper" are the promissory notes sold broadside by sales and consumer finance companies and other enterprises as means of short-term borrowing.[13] The large finance companies sell the notes through their own facilities, but the smaller companies as well as enterprises in other industrial areas usually depend upon the services of specialized dealers who buy issues in bulk and then retail them to their customers. In a dealer's list of offerings, a corporate treasurer can usually find notes of qualities and maturities to meet his requirements, and he can get what he wants even more facilely in dealing with the large finance companies that market their own notes. Such a company will generally issue a note for any sum a corporation wants to advance temporarily, bearing interest at a publicly announced rate, and for any maturity requested from three days to nine months. Thus it offers an opportunity for precisely tailored investment, including weekend arrangements.

Short-term investments by way of loans to government securities dealers usually take the form of "repurchase agreements" whereby the dealer sells the corporation a block of government securities at a designated price, at the same time obligating himself to buy back the selfsame securities at an agreed-upon time at a slightly higher price. In effect, the transaction is a loan, with the government securities serving as collateral, and the differential in prices being the interest paid by the dealer and earned by the corporation.

Bank Time Deposits

Many corporations transfer temporarily idle cash balances from their demand deposit or checking accounts with the commercial banks to time

---

[12] U.S. Treasury Department, Internal Revenue Service, *Statistics of Income, 1960–61—Preliminary: Corporation Income Tax Returns* (Washington, D.C.: U.S. Government Printing Office, 1962), pp. 17, 23.

[13] Such promissory notes are generally known as "open-market commercial paper" or simply "commercial paper." In Chapter 32, their characteristics, marketing, and use are examined in greater detail from the standpoint of the issuers as borrowers. See pp. 800–801.

deposit accounts with the same institutions. This is done because the banks are forbidden by law to pay interest on checking accounts, while they do pay interest on time accounts. The banks may be asked to carry the time deposit balances as "open accounts" which are comparable to individuals' savings accounts although never technically classified as such; or they may be asked to issue certificates of deposit. A certificate of deposit (CD) is made payable "to the order of" the corporate depositor or to the "bearer"—whichever way the corporation wants it—and it stipulates that payment of the face amount plus interest at a designated rate shall be made by the bank on a specified day upon the surrender of the certificate.

As an outlet for idle corporate money, bank time deposits, especially in the form of CD's, have recently enjoyed a huge boost. For many years, smaller corporations and corporations of intermediate sizes had made extensive use of "open accounts" and CD's as means of earning a return on temporarily idle money, but the financial managers of large corporations showed relatively little interest in bank time accounts. Since 1961, however, the attitude of the latter has shifted markedly. Many metropolitan banks began in that year to urge their large corporate customers to put their idle funds in CD's, and certain securities dealers helped out by announcing that they would provide market facilities for buying and selling CD's. Still further help was given in two actions taken by the Board of Governors of the Federal Reserve System and the Federal Deposit Insurance Corporation—one effective January 1, 1962, and the second on July 17, 1963—authorizing member and insured banks to step up substantially the rates of interest payable on time accounts and certificates.[14]

With these developments, the financial managers of many large corporations have been finding from time to time that they can earn higher rates of interest on CD's maturing in 90 days or more than on treasury obligations and other investments of equal or shorter maturities, and they have channeled much idle money in this direction. As evidence of this, a special Federal Reserve survey among 410 large banks showed that outstanding CD's in denominations of $100,000 or more increased from $778 million at the end of 1960 to $5,584 million on December 5, 1962.[15] Even when expecting to need their money in, say, two or three months, corporations have frequently found it advantageous to take out CD's having maturities of six months and more. When wanting to recover their

---

[14] Since January 1, 1957, the maximum interest rates permitted on CD's and time deposits other than savings accounts had been as follows: on deposits payable in less than 90 days, 1 per cent; payable in 90 days to 6 months, 2½ per cent; and payable in 6 months or more, 3 per cent. After the second change had become effective on July 17, 1963, the permitted rate on CD's and time deposits payable in fewer than 90 days remained at 1 per cent, but the rate permitted on such instruments payable in 90 days or more was 4 per cent. See *Federal Reserve Bulletin,* July, 1963, p. 957.

[15] *Ibid.,* April, 1963, pp. 458–60.

money for operations, they have been able to sell their CD's to dealers at prices giving them rates of return materially higher than they would have got had they originally invested in CD's or other "paper" maturing in two or three months.

Although bank "open accounts" and CD's continue to be popular with smaller corporations, the developments since 1961, except for increases in interest rates as authorized and actually offered, have not added significantly to this popularity. The reason is that market transactions are largely restricted to CD's having face values of $1 million or more, although there is a fair volume of transactions in CD's down to $500,000 in value, and a few in instruments of values down to $100,000 or even less.

The compensatory-balance rules of commercial banks, related to outstanding loans as discussed earlier in this chapter, ordinarily are not satisfied by the holding of balances in time deposit "open accounts" and CD's. Nevertheless, the typical banker will surely recognize time balances as a source of funds for loans, and will, accordingly, take them into consideration in deciding how much he can "afford" to lend to his corporate customers. Likewise, it is not customary to give credit against service charges on the basis of balances held in "open accounts" and CD's, so that a corporation having only a moderate balance in its checking account may be required to pay service charges for the "activity" in that account, even though it is simultaneously carrying relatively large amounts as time balances.

Share Accounts in Savings and Loan Associations

Often the managers of smaller corporations prefer to "invest" temporarily idle cash in the shares of savings and loan associations. Such associations are chartered by both the federal and state governments. Their principal operations are the sale of their shares to accumulate funds and to lend these funds for the construction of residential property, the purchase of existing residential property, and the repair and modernization of such property.

Investment in the shares of savings and loan associations is attractive because the associations of a given locality generally pay higher rates of interest (usually called "dividends") on their share accounts than the commercial banks of the same locality pay on their time deposits. Moreover, most of the associations have their accounts insured by the Federal Savings and Loan Insurance Corporation to the amount of $10,000 individually—a kind of protection matching the insurance of deposit accounts up to $10,000 by the Federal Deposit Insurance Corporation provided by most commercial banks.

A disadvantageous aspect of share accounts is that the savings and loan associations do not have an absolute obligation to meet withdrawal demands at specified times or within given periods following the receipt of withdrawal requests. Payments need be made to meet withdrawal demands only as money becomes available, whereas, for commercial banks, failures to meet withdrawal demands according to the terms of contracts with depositors mark the defaulting banks as insolvent and therefore subject to reorganization or liquidation by the federal or state supervisory authorities. However, most savings and loan associations are subject to rules limiting their further lending as long as they have deficiencies in cash and other asset reserves, so that, in effect, they must use most of the money collected on outstanding loans and other inflowing funds to meet the withdrawal requests. In recent years, almost all of the savings and loan associations have maintained positions of sufficient liquidity to meet all withdrawal requests without delay. Accordingly, most holders of share accounts, including corporations, look upon their balances in these accounts as being as readily accessible as balances in time accounts with commercial banks.

Questions

1. Is not the incurring of operating expenses a source of liabilities and possible losses, rather than a procedure of acquiring assets, as is claimed in the text? Discuss.

2. Is it not an exaggeration to claim that the financial managers of great corporations such as General Motors seek to conserve cash—to economize in its use? Discuss.

3. Why is it likely that the published balance sheets of many corporations understate the importance of inventories and accounts receivable? If this is so, the importance of what kinds of assets is likely to be overstated?

4. In which industrial areas are current assets much larger in amount than fixed assets, and in which are fixed assets much larger in amount than current assets? In which areas are inventories especially large among the current assets? accounts receivable?

5. Discuss the relationship between a firm's cash balance and its credit standing with trade suppliers.

6. What is the relationship between a firm's cash holdings and its access to commercial bank loans and services?

7. What is working capital? To evaluate a firm's working capital position is it sufficient to determine the ratio of its current assets to its current liabilities? Why or why not?

8. Support or attack this proposition: The typical corporation should set a level above which it does not want its total holdings of cash and short-term high-quality investments to go.

9. If a firm has excess cash not to be needed for, say, a week, and if it uses it to buy short-term high-quality investment "paper," can this "paper" be reasonably regarded as part of the firm's cash balance? Discuss.

10. Why is investment in long-term treasury obligations, despite their high quality, undesirable for corporate funds that will be needed for operations within a few months?

11. What are the four classes of the Treasury's marketable obligations? How do they differ among one another?

12. Why might a corporate treasurer choose to invest temporarily idle

money in short-term obligations of state and local governments rather than in short-term treasury obligations?

13. How can one account for the recent surge in the popularity of certificates of deposit issued by commercial banks as means for investing corporate cash temporarily in excess supply?

14. How do share accounts in savings and loan associations compare with bank time deposits as investment outlets for excess corporate cash with respect to safety, ease of withdrawal, and rate of return?

Problems

1. If a treasury 4 per cent bond is selling in the market at 98, would a buyer who holds the bond to maturity earn more or less than 4 per cent on the amount of his investment? Explain. What, if anything, would the price of 98 indicate about the maturity of the bond? a price of 88?

2. If a person buys a treasury 3½ per cent bond at its current market price and holds it to maturity, he will earn 3¼ per cent a year. Is the market price above or below 100? Explain. From the figures given, can one say whether the market price is far above or far below 100 or only narrowly above or below? Explain.

3. A corporate treasurer bids 99.230 for $3 million of to-be-issued 91-day treasury bills. If the bid is accepted and if the corporation holds the bills to maturity, it will be earning a return at what annual rate of interest?

4. What interest income would a treasurer earn for his corporation by making a "weekend investment" of $5 million for four days in a finance company's commercial paper paying interest at 3 per cent per annum. (Make the computation on the basis of a 360-day year, that is, on the basis of "ordinary" interest.)

chapter 8

THE MANAGEMENT OF INVENTORIES

IMPORTANCE OF INVENTORIES

The statistics presented in the preceding chapter showed inventories to be outstandingly important among the assets of corporations engaged in manufacturing, wholesale trade, and retail trade, and of minor importance only for public utilities, service corporations, and corporations engaged in mining and quarrying. For the majority of American corporations, therefore, inventory management policies are of major significance; this is all the more emphasized by the fact that manufacturing and mercantile corporations constituted 65 per cent of the number, and held 64 per cent of the total assets, of the corporations whose balance sheets were summarized in Table 7–1 in the preceding chapter.

It is true, of course, that considerable variations in the importance of inventories in asset structures exist among manufacturing and mercantile corporations. This is revealed by the data of Table 8–1 in which inventory figures for the subgroups of manufacturing and retail trade corporations are presented as percentages of total assets. Noteworthy in the manufacturing classification is the extremely high percentage of inventory investment in relation to total assets in tobacco manufactures, and the quite high percentages in the subgroups designated "apparel and products made from fabrics" and "transportation equipment except motor vehicles," as well as the relatively low percentages in the subgroups designated "petroleum refining and related industries" and "printing, publishing, and allied industries." Noteworthy in the retail trade classification are the high percentages of inventory investment for corporations selling automobiles and gasoline, apparel and accessories, and building materials, hardware, and farm equipment, as contrasted with the low percentage for corporations operating eating and drinking places. In all instances, however, one should keep in mind the probable understatement of the average level of inventory investment; for, as was pointed out in the preceding chapter, many corporations close their fiscal years, and prepare their tax returns with accompanying balance sheets, in slack seasons when inventories can be expected to be at or near their lowest annual levels.

It is apparent, therefore, that for most manufacturing and mercantile corporations—and for many others as well—the formulation and execution

TABLE 8–1
Investment in Inventories in Relation to Total Assets in Manufacturing and Retail Trade, 1960–61
(Dollar amounts in millions)

Business Classification	Inventories	Total Assets	Ratio to Total Assets[a]
Manufacturing:			
Beverage industries..........................	$ 1,299	$ 5,373	24.2
Food and kindred products.....................	4,286	18,433	23.3
Tobacco manufactures.........................	2,553	3,463	73.7
Textile mill products........................	2,633	9,151	28.8
Apparel and products made from fabrics.........	1,698	4,623	36.8
Lumber and wood products, except furniture......	1,154	5,604	20.6
Furniture and fixtures........................	733	2,521	29.1
Paper and allied products.....................	1,491	10,555	14.1
Printing, publishing, and allied industries.........	1,051	8,825	11.9
Chemicals and allied products..	4,103	24,243	16.9
Petroleum refining and related industries..........	3,109	41,885	7.4
Rubber and miscellaneous plastic products........	1,361	5,163	26.4
Leather and leather products.	611	1,969	31.0
Stone, clay, and glass products.................	1,390	8,974	15.5
Primary metal industries......	5,386	26,763	20.1
Fabricated metal products (including ordnance), except machinery and transportation equipment...	3,251	12,227	26.6
Machinery, except electrical and transportation equipment....................................	6,108	21,088	29.0
Electrical machinery, equipment, and supplies.....	4,176	15,081	27.7
Transportation equipment, except motor vehicles..	3,489	9,572	36.5
Motor vehicles and motor vehicle equipment......	3,335	17,567	19.0
Professional, scientific, and controlling instruments; photographic and optical goods; watches and clocks....................................	1,356	4,863	27.9
Other manufacturing industries..................	1,187	4,329	27.4
Total Manufacturing[b]......................	$55,760	$262,271	21.3
Retail trade:			
Food..	$ 1,800	$ 5,696	31.6
General merchandise...........................	3,681	12,805	28.8
Apparel and accessories.......................	1,539	3,980	38.7
Furniture, home furnishings, and equipment.......	1,027	3,426	29.9
Automotive dealers and gasoline service stations...	3,577	7,772	46.0
Eating and drinking places.....................	143	1,984	7.2
Building materials, hardware, and farm equipment.	1,589	4,263	37.3
Other retail stores............................	1,773	5,554	31.9
Total Retail Trade[b].......................	$15,128	$ 45,481	33.3

[a] Ratios computed by the author.

[b] Items do not add exactly to totals because of rounding.

SOURCE: U.S. Treasury Department, Internal Revenue Service, *Statistics of Income, 1960–61—Preliminary: Corporation Income Tax Returns* (Washington, D.C.: U.S. Government Printing Office, 1962), pp. 18–22.

of sound inventory management policies must be a managerial responsibility of the highest rank. It is often said that more firms fail on account of inept inventory management than for any other reason. The managerial objective must be the avoidance of "overinvestment" and "underinvestment" in inventories—a proposition which appears to indicate that there must be some "right amount" of inventory investment for maximizing profits. But while it is easy to indicate the harmfulness of overinvestment and underinvestment, it is often most difficult to recognize overinvestment and underinvestment in actual situations. It is most difficult, in other words, for the managers of the individual enterprise to set an inventory volume that will surely be the "right amount."

Evils of Overinvestment

The most obvious evil that results from overinvestment in inventories is that the erring firm is likely to find itself short of cash for other purposes, as for the payment of maturing liabilities, the carrying of accounts receivable, and the expansion of fixed assets. Instead of generating its own funds for these purposes, as might be possible with a better-designed inventory program, such a firm is likely to find it necessary to increase its borrowings, thereby adding to its overhead expenses by way of interest costs.

Excessive quantities of goods in inventories require storage space. Facilities that could be better used for other purposes may have to be used for storage, or, indeed, additional facilities may have to be bought, erected, or rented. Costs of handling, inspection, and accounting are increased. Insurance charges and personal property taxes, since they are based upon the value of property, go up.

For some kinds of goods held in inventories, losses through shrinkage and spoilage may increase substantially; for others, there may be increased danger of theft; and for still others, goods may become obsolete on account of changes in customers' preferences. For almost all kinds of goods, there is the further danger of declines in supply prices; thus the overinvesting firm may find itself with a high-cost inventory at a time when its competitors are carrying on their operations with goods purchased more recently at lower prices.

Consequences of Underinvestment

A firm that is unduly niggardly in its inventory investment policy is likely to lose customers. Customers of a mercantile firm in this position may go elsewhere because they cannot find on its shelves a sufficient variety of goods of a given line to make a reasonable selection or because they are precluded from "one-stop shopping" for the reason that it does not carry a sufficient variety of lines. Customers of a manufacturing firm similarly situated may turn away because of what they consider unreasonable delays in the delivery of goods ordered.

Besides having difficulty in holding customers' goodwill, manufacturing firms with inadequate inventory investment are likely to be burdened with many unnecessary costs of operation. Shortages of raw materials may bring temporary shutdowns, with many kinds of overhead expenses continuing to accumulate during the periods of idleness. Labor costs, too, tend to mount, perhaps as a result of slowdowns whereby the workers try to stretch out the limited supplies of raw materials to make them last as long as possible, and perhaps through labor turnover as dissatisfied workers quit their jobs to seek employment elsewhere.

A firm with inadequate inventories, moreover, is at the mercy of rising prices. Lack of foresight in the accumulation of inventories in times of plentiful supply and relatively low prices may result in substantial increases in costs of goods manufactured or in costs of goods sold. It is hard enough to take increased supply prices due to rising costs incurred by the suppliers, but all the greater is the burden if unforseen shortages enable the suppliers to mark up their prices sharply. Even in the absence of price increases due to rising costs or shortages, hand-to-mouth stocking of inventories is often expensive in increased transportation costs. Firms faced with a lack of goods to maintain manufacturing or selling operations may see no alternative but to have new supplies delivered by faster, but more expensive, means of transportation, as by choosing express shipments in place of freight, or air freight in place of rail freight.

"Right Amount" of Inventory Investment

So great is the diversity among firms in the role of inventories in the earning of profits, and so complex are the circumstances that must bear upon the decisions of the individual firm, that one must quickly confess the impossibility of formulating a set of rules or standards whereby the "rightness" of the inventory policies of business enterprises can be determined. No two firms will be faced with an identical set of circumstances in consideration of which decisions must be made. What, therefore, is "right" for one firm may be wrong for another; and what is "right" for a given firm at a certain time will not necessarily continue to be right for it at another time. Nevertheless, certain observations about the determination of good inventory policies can be made.

In the first place, "overinvestment" and "underinvestment" in inventories cannot be recognized simply by their size. A firm having a very large inventory—much larger relatively than those of its competitors—will be in a most favorable position if supply prices are rising or if shortages in supply are developing; its managers, therefore, would deserve great praise as being wiser than those of the competing firms. Likewise, an extraordinarily small inventory at certain times may indicate great astuteness of financial managers in foreseeing the coming of a business recession with declining prices or a shift in consumer preferences to goods of other kinds.

Inventory policies must be expected to differ markedly among businesses according to the nature of their activities. Typically, for a given volume of sales, manufacturing concerns must have larger inventories than mercantile firms, since the former, in addition to holding finished goods for sale, must also have inventories of raw materials and goods in process.

Manufacturing firms that carry through time-consuming processes from remote raw material stages to highly complex finished goods stages will surely have much greater investment in inventories—given a certain volume of sales—than those that buy finished parts and simply assemble some final product. Mercantile firms that sell things that can be classified as daily necessities, such as many kinds of foods, will almost invariably have smaller inventories in relation to sales than those that sell articles that the average customer buys only once or twice in a lifetime, as many items of household furniture.

Location is also an important factor in the determination of sound inventory policies—location both as to sources of supply and as to sales outlets. For example, a firm that is dependent upon foreign sources of supply for its principal raw materials will ordinarily find it necessary to carry a much larger inventory in relation to sales than one whose suppliers are located in the same country. The same is true for an eastern firm whose chief sources of supply are located on the West Coast as compared with one whose suppliers are located in the same community. In a similar way, a firm that establishes branch warehouses at various points throughout the country may find it desirable to carry complete lines of goods at each of them; it will be likely, therefore, to have a total inventory much larger, in relation to sales, than a firm that makes all its deliveries from a single warehouse. For many firms, of course, location is shiftable, and shifting may result in large inventory economies. The *Wall Street Journal* reports a decided trend in recent years toward the "consolidation" of warehouse facilities, as in the Raytheon Company's substitution of a single "distribution center" for the eight warehouses it formerly operated, and the replacement of twelve warehouses by four "distribution centers" by the Whirlpool division of the Radio Corporation of America.[1]

Closely related to location as a determinant of inventory management policies is the speed of deliveries of goods both inward and outward. This depends upon the availability of the different kinds of transportation facilities, as well as upon the varying competence of the carriers that are available. Speed in delivery also depends upon the reliability of suppliers. Inventory trimming may be possible for a firm that can depend upon its suppliers to dispatch goods quickly upon receiving orders, whereas it is not likely to be feasible for one whose suppliers are erratic in their treatment of orders.

Other important factors that account for widely diverse inventory policies (although not always justifying diversity) are the great variations among businesses in the seasonality of their operations, both in sources of supply and in customer demand; judgments as to the future course of general business activity, as anticipations of cyclical expansion with rising prices or of cyclical contraction with falling prices; special situations aris-

---

[1] January 24, 1963, pp. 1, 6.

ing because of firms' positions in "growth" or "declining" industries; and peculiar competitive situations whereby, for example, firms must add certain lines of goods for no better reason than that their competitors have decided to add these lines. All these factors were discussed in Chapter 6 as causes of variations in cash flows; at this time, therefore, a further detailed analysis is unnecessary. Suffice it to say that, since inventories constitute the most important single asset of many manufacturing and most mercantile enterprises, modifications in cash flows brought about by the factors mentioned must largely involve the tying up of additional cash in expanded inventories or the release of cash as inventories are reduced.

INVENTORY TURNOVER

Although the formulation of a set of policies that ought to be "right" for the generality of businesses at all times may be impossible, a means of testing the reasonableness of inventory investment at a given level is available and widely used. This is the computation of inventory "turnovers." The computation of turnovers is, at best, a very rough method of testing, and serious errors can result if turnover figures are accorded greater weight in arriving at judgments than they deserve—if turnover ratios, in other words, are used routinely or mechanically in judging inventory investment policies without analyses of the complex circumstances that bear upon policy formulation in the individual firm. Nevertheless, turnover ratios have proved themselves to be of great worth in innumerable instances.

Computation of Turnovers

The inventory turnover of a firm for a given period of time can be computed by the solution of either of the following two formulas:

$$\text{Inventory turnover} = \frac{\text{Cost of goods sold}}{\text{Average inventory at cost}}$$

$$\text{Inventory turnover} = \frac{\text{Net sales}}{\text{Average inventory at selling prices}}$$

It is immaterial whether the one or the other of these formulas is used, as the result should be approximately the same for both. Most firms value their inventories on a cost basis—although, as we shall see in the subsequent discussion of inventory valuation, "cost" may actually be "cost or market, whichever is lower." Some firms, however, find the use of the second formula more convenient; department stores, for example, customarily value their inventories at selling prices, using the so-called "retail method" for this purpose.

For greatest accuracy in the computation of inventory turnovers, monthly inventories should ordinarily be used, this being especially desir-

able if the size of inventories fluctuates substantially in the course of the
year. "Average inventory" for a year, then, is the sum of the opening
inventory and the inventory at the end of every month, this total to be
divided by 13. Many firms, as we have seen, operate on the basis of a
"fiscal year" other than the "calendar year," for the very reason that they
want their yearly operations to conclude at a time when inventories are
at or near their lowest level. This arrangement makes possible appreciable
economies in the work of inventory taking and valuation. For a firm in
this position, however, a turnover ratio computed on the basis of the
average of opening and closing inventories would be much higher than
one computed on the basis of an average of monthly inventories; accordingly, it would be quite misleading.

Interpretation of Turnover Ratios

An inventory turnover ratio, standing by itself, means absolutely nothing. To say that the turnover of a particular firm is, say, 5 indicates
nothing as to the wisdom of its inventory management policies. To give
meaning to a turnover figure, one must compare it with other such figures.
Most fruitful are comparisons with a firm's turnover ratios computed for
other periods and comparisons with those of other firms operating in the
same area of business activity, that is to say, with the ratios of one's competitors. Should a firm's turnover ratio in the year just ended be 5, whereas
in the preceding year it was 5½, and in the year before that it was 6,
strong evidence of growing deficiencies in inventory management is
brought out—not conclusive evidence, by any means, but sufficient, certainly, to warrant a thoroughgoing analysis of the situation. Likewise,
should a firm's turnover ratio in the year just ended be 5, while those of
principal competitors were, say, 6, 6½, and 7, respectively, an investigation of the causes of what appears to be a record of poor performance
would surely be in order.

Out-of-Line Ratios on the Low Side. If a firm's inventory turnover
ratio declines from year to year, or if, for any year, its ratio is materially
less than those of competing enterprises, there is justification for suspicion
that serious mistakes have been made in inventory management. The likelihood of overinvestment in inventories is especially to be considered.
Thus, if the cost of goods sold of each of two firms is $500,000, and if one
has average inventories of $60,000 while the other has average inventories
of $80,000—their ratios being respectively, of course, 8⅓ and 6¼—the
evidence is strong that the second firm is carrying larger inventories than
it needs to carry to serve its customers properly.

Overinvestment here might mean simply that the second firm has over-
stocked goods of proper qualities and kinds that it will eventually sell at
satisfactory prices. Another possibility, however, is that the firm has been
caught with an unusual amount of slow-moving goods, so that it may not
have excessive quantities of other kinds of goods that move more speedily.

Still another possibility is that the inventory of the second firm includes large quantities of shopworn or obsolescent goods upon which its managers are reluctant to acknowledge losses, as would be done by a drastic cutting of selling prices to move them.

Out-of-Line Ratios on the High Side. Rising inventory turnover ratios and ratios higher than those of competing firms are usually accepted, at first glance, as being indicative of good inventory management. If, in a certain year, each of two corporations sells for $600,000 goods that cost $400,000, and if the first carries an average inventory of $80,000 while the second carries one of $100,000, the first corporation has a gross profit *as a rate of return* upon its average investment in inventory of 250 per cent, whereas the second has a rate of return of only 200 per cent. Should the two corporations incur about the same amount of operating expenses, as might well be expected, the first would likewise have a much more favorable rate of net profit (assuming, as seems reasonable, that the investment of the stockholders of the first corporation would be $20,000 less than that of the second). One can well understand, therefore, why managers of business firms tend to take pride in inventory ratios that are high in comparison with those of earlier years and with those of other firms. Indeed, the maximization of turnover is often considered to be the principal objective of inventory management policies.

Need of Caution in Analysis. Nevertheless, a comparison of turnover ratios can easily lead to unsound conclusions. Comparative ratios, standing alone, can never wisely be taken as proof that inventory management has been good or bad. When ratios are found to be out of line, praise for or blame upon the makers of policy must be withheld, as it were, until the reasons for the out-of-line result have been sought and found. For one thing, inventory ratios vary according to the methods of inventory valuation that are used—a topic to be discussed a little later in this chapter—and especially if the methods of valuation are changed. A relatively low ratio may result from the heavy stocking of inventory in anticipation of price increases—should the price increases actually come about, the managers would surely be deserving of praise rather than blame; or it may result from a "stabilization" of production, that is, the spreading out of productive operations over the year, as by a manufacturing firm whose sales are heavily concentrated in a few months.

On the other hand, a relatively high turnover ratio may not really be an indicator of favorable results and prospects. It may indicate a serious underinvestment in inventories. Surely there would be strong evidence of this if, while a firm's turnover rate is rising, its sales are falling off or are expanding at a slower rate than the rates of other firms. A loss of customers on account of inability to show them complete lines or to make prompt deliveries could hardly be regarded as a favorable development.

Stabilization of Production and Inventory Turnover. The need of exercising great care in the interpretation of comparative inventory turn-

over ratios can be emphasized by considering the position of a manufacturing corporation that wishes to stabilize its productive activities even
though its sales are largely concentrated in a few months of the year. Let
us assume that the corporation's sales in the months from January through
September (in terms of cost of goods sold) are uniform at $20,000 a
month, and that in October, November, and December, they reach the
high level of $80,000 a month. To serve its customers adequately, the
corporation must have at the beginning of each month from January to
September inventories of raw materials, goods in process, and finished
goods of $40,000, and at the beginning of October, November, and De-
cember, inventories of these three kinds totaling $100,000. Accordingly,
the corporation has the choice of limiting the scale of its manufacturing
operations in the period from the beginning of December to the end of
August, and then stepping it up mightily in September, October, and
November—or of trying to even out production throughout the year. If
it takes the former course, its inventory turnover ratio will be 7.8 (cost of
goods sold of $420,000 divided by average inventory of $53,846, the latter
figure being the sum of 10 inventories at $40,000 and 3 at $100,000 divided
by 13). If it takes the latter course, the ratio will be only approximately
3.6, as may be shown on the basis of the following table and computation:

Month	Production (At cost)	Cost of Goods Sold	Inventory at End of Month
			$ 55,000[a]
January	$ 35,000	$ 20,000	70,000
February	35,000	20,000	85,000
March	35,000	20,000	100,000
April	35,000	20,000	115,000
May	35,000	20,000	130,000
June	35,000	20,000	145,000
July	35,000	20,000	160,000
August	35,000	20,000	175,000
September	35,000	20,000	190,000
October	35,000	80,000	145,000
November	35,000	80,000	100,000
December	35,000	80,000	55,000
Total	$420,000	$420,000	$1,525,000
Average inventory			$ 117,308

$$\frac{\$420,000}{\$117,308} = 3.6 \text{ turnovers}$$

[a] Inventory at the end of the preceding year.

Were the corporation to shift from the first course in one year to the
second course in the following year, an injudicious observer might condemn the management for the sharp drop in its inventory turnover ratio
from 7.8 to 3.6. Would this condemnation have any merit? Definitely
not from the point of view of public welfare, for the stabilization of

employment in seasonal industries is an important social goal. From the standpoint of the profit-seeking interests of the stockholders, moreover, the condemnation would probably not be justified, for stabilization of production very often results in increased net profits, and not the contrary. It is true that the corporation would incur increased costs of carrying a much larger average inventory—costs of storage facilities, handling, accounting, insurance, personal property taxes, and possibly spoilage, shrinkage, and theft; and it might have to borrow money for investment in the inventories, thus incurring an additional interest expense. On the other hand, labor costs and overhead expenses per unit of output might well be materially reduced. With stabilized production, the corporation could offer full-time regular employment to all its personnel. It would thus be able to avoid the annual costs of recruiting and training a short-term labor force upon the approach of the peak period, and possibly payments for overtime during that period. A year-around labor force, furthermore, would probably be much more competent and loyal than that portion of one brought in only on a temporary basis. In the matter of overhead expenses, the corporation would no longer accumulate expenses in connection with idle facilities, as for insurance, maintenance, and property taxes. Indeed, with operations stabilized throughout the year, the corporation would almost surely be able to get along with a much smaller aggregate of facilities. Accordingly, the increased investment in inventories might be offset in whole or in part, or more than offset, by a reduction of investment in fixed assets.

INVENTORY VALUATION

Relation to Turnover Ratios

It was mentioned above that inventory turnover ratios vary according to the method of inventory valuation used, and especially if the valuation method is changed from one year to another. If, for example, a firm values its inventories at cost at a time when market prices are declining, it will have a lower turnover ratio than will a firm that, in the same circumstances, values its inventories at "market." (One should observe that "market" or "market price" in inventory valuation means the price at which goods in the inventory could be replaced at the time of inventory taking.)

Let us suppose that each of two firms, Corporations A and B, has an inventory of 30,000 units valued at $1.00 per unit at the beginning of a certain month, that in the course of the month each buys 50,000 units at a price of $1.00 per unit, and that at the end of the month each has 20,000 units remaining in its inventory. A values its inventory at cost, and B, at "cost or market, whichever is lower." Let us assume that, at the end of the month, "market" is 90 cents per unit. The computation of the respective turnovers, then, would be as follows:

	Corporation A	Corporation B
Cost of goods sold:		
Inventory, beginning of month...........	$30,000	$30,000
Purchases............................	50,000	50,000
Goods available for sale................	$80,000	$80,000
Less: Inventory, end of month.........	20,000	18,000
Cost of goods sold.................	$60,000	$62,000

Inventory turnovers—

$$\text{Corporation A:} \quad \frac{60,000}{\dfrac{30,000 + 20,000}{2}} = 2.40$$

$$\text{Corporation B:} \quad \frac{62,000}{\dfrac{30,000 + 18,000}{2}} = 2.58$$

Relation to Profits and Income Taxes

The effects of different methods of inventory valuation upon turnover ratios are significant, but much more important are their effects upon the amount of profits recognized and consequently upon the amount of income tax liabilities. These more important effects can be understood if we carry the foregoing illustration a step further. We may assume that the sales of 60,000 units of each of the corporations were made at a price of $1.40 a unit. Accordingly, Corporation A would recognize a gross profit on sales of $24,000, whereas Corporation B's gross profit on sales would be placed at $22,000. Assuming that the two corporations incurred the same amount of operating expenses, A would have a net profit $2,000 greater than that of B. Because the federal taxing authorities permit business firms to select whatever method of inventory valuation they wish (as long as it is "reasonable," it is used consistently from year to year, and it is changed, if at all, only with the permission of the Internal Revenue Service), A would have $2,000 more of taxable income than B. With federal corporation income tax rates prevailing at 30 per cent on the first $25,000 of taxable income, and 52 per cent on amounts in excess of $25,000, A's inventory valuation method would obviously be working to its disadvantage.

It is to be noted, too, that Corporation A, after the deduction of federal tax liabilities, would have more net profit available for dividends than would Corporation B. It might be pleasant for the directors of A to be able to report a higher net profit after taxes than its competitor; however, A's stockholders might expect to receive a larger amount of cash dividends. If, therefore, the directors of A were inclined to be generous in the distribution of dividends, they would face two cash drains in relation to the $2,000—one in the direction of the federal Treasury, and one in the direction of the stockholders in cash dividends.

Considerations in the Selection of Inventory Valuation Methods

As a rule, the financial managers of business enterprises seek a method of inventory valuation that will result in the lowest possible amounts of gross and net profits, and that will, at the same time, be acceptable to the federal taxing authorities as "reasonable" for the computation of income tax liabilities. This does not mean that the financial managers seek to understate their profits; rather, it means that they go along with the oft-stated principle of "conservative" accounting that all losses should be accounted for but that profits should not be taken up till actually earned. Indeed, at the time that a given method of inventory valuation is used, it is quite impossible to say whether it results in an understatement or overstatement of profits; a final conclusion about this can only be reached subsequently as the inventoried goods are sold. At the time of inventory taking, therefore, as much as can be said is that one method results in higher or lower profits *at that time* than do other methods.

Avoidance of Income Taxes. The avoidance of federal and state income taxes—especially the former, of course—is doubtless the principal reason why the financial managers of business enterprises seek the inventory valuation methods that will result in profit figures of the lowest possible levels. While it may appear that taxes avoided in one year will have to be paid in subsequent years, it does not always work out that way. If, for example, the long-term trend of prices is upward, as it has been in the United States since 1933, the use of the last-in, first-out method of inventory valuation (lifo) may well result in a net decrease in tax liabilities that will never be offset.

Furthermore, even if taxes avoided in one year must be made up in a subsequent year, corporate managers are generally pleased with the deferment. Cash "saved" from current tax payments can be used temporarily for expanded operations, and expanded operations will be likely to increase the corporations' capacity to pay taxes in future years. For a variety of reasons, corporate managers are doubtless inclined to think that improvements in their corporations' positions from year to year will make tax payments in future years less burdensome than they would be at the moment. And there is always the hope that tax rates in the future will be lower than at present.

Avoidance of Demands for Increased Dividends. A second reason for the choice of inventory valuation methods that result in the lowest possible profit figures is the avoidance of pressures upon corporate directors to raise the levels of cash dividends paid to the stockholders. In ordinary circumstances, the higher a corporation's profits the greater are the stockholders' expectations for generous dividends—expectations to which the directors must surely give consideration in almost any circumstances, but especially if they were voted their directorships by narrow margins. If the directors would prefer to use available cash to the greatest extent possible for expansion rather than for increases in cash dividends, it must seem wise to them to hold down, by whatever means possible, the amount of profits reported—means that include a careful choosing among inventory valuation methods.

Some justification for directors' attitudes toward tax and dividend payments, as just described, is found in the fact that a corporation's *cash position* is not improved by the use of an inventory valuation method that results in higher reported profits than do other methods, nor is that position impaired by the use of a method that results in lower reported profits. In the illustration given on pages 157–58, there was no indication that Corporation A had a cash throw-off exceeding that of Corporation B, even though it was reporting a net profit exceeding that of B by $2,000. Since all aspects of the operations of the two corporations, except their inventory valuation methods, were described as identical, it would be reasonable to assume that cash collections on account of sales, cash payments to trade suppliers, and cash payments to meet operating expenses were also identical. If this were so, Corporation A would be in no better position to pay income taxes and dividends than Corporation B.

Inventory Valuation Methods

The methods of inventory valuation most commonly used by American business enterprises are the following:

1. Specific identification.
2. First-in, first-out (fifo).
3. Last-in, first-out (lifo).
4. Average cost.

The specific identification method can be used conveniently when each item is clearly distinguishable as having been included in a particular purchase, as in the case of bulky items such as electric refrigerators, television sets, and suites of living room furniture. The other methods are used when various lots purchased from time to time are intermingled in such a way that the identity of each item, or bushel, or ton—whatever the measure may be—cannot be traced to a given purchase invoice.

In the use of the first-in, first-out method, the inventory at the end of a period is considered as having goods most recently purchased—an application of the idea that the older stock is moved first. In the use of the last-in, first-out method, the closing inventory is considered as having goods most remotely purchased—thus, in many instances, the closing inventory will be assumed to contain all or much of the goods contained in the opening inventory. In the use of the average cost method, the closing inventory is considered as having an array of items in proportion to those contained in the opening inventory and in each of the purchases made in the course of the year or other period.

For the computation of taxable profits, the federal income tax authorities permit the use of any of these methods, provided that the method chosen is used consistently from year to year. Except for the last-in, first-out method, moreover, the taxpayer may choose to value his closing inventory either at cost or at "cost or market, whichever is lower," provided, again, that he is consistent in using the one alternative or the other.

Application of Inventory Valuation Methods: Illustrations. Depending upon price changes currently going on, each of the methods of inventory valuation as well as each of the alternatives tends to give differing results. For a demonstration, a few simple figures will suffice. Suppose that a corporation had four items in its opening inventory valued at 65 cents each and that in the course of the year—a period of falling prices—it made purchases of individual items at prices in cents as follows:

64   62   59   58   56   53   51

We may further assume that the corporation has three items in its closing inventory, that the market (replacement) price at the time of inventory taking is 50 cents, and that, for the specific identification method, the items in the closing inventory are those of the third, fourth, and fifth purchases. The corporation's closing inventory, then, might have any one of the following values, depending upon the valuation method (or its alternative, if available) selected:

Valuation Method	Cost	Cost or Market, Whichever Is Lower
Specific identification................	$1.73	$1.50
First-in, first-out...................	1.60	1.50
Last-in, first-out...................	1.95	
Average cost......................	1.808	1.50

To see how the variations in inventory values might work out in a period of rising prices, let us assume that the market (replacement) price at the end of the year was 77 cents, and that, in the course of the year, individual purchases were made as follows:

67   68   70   72   73   74   76

Assuming all other facts to be the same as in the first illustration, the corporation's closing inventory valuation might be any one of the following amounts:

Valuation Method	Cost	Cost or Market, Whichever Is Lower
Specific identification................	$2.15	$2.15
First-in, first-out...................	2.23	2.23
Last-in, first-out...................	1.95	
Average cost......................	2.073	2.073

Effects of Use of Different Methods. When one reflects that differences in inventory values, as produced by the various methods of valuation, mean differences in cost of goods sold, gross and net profits, and income tax liabilities, one can see why care in the selection of the method to be used is important. It is true that, if prices move upward and downward more or less persistently within a given range, the advantage which a particular method gives in one year or in a series of years is likely to be offset by a disadvantage in another year or series of years. On the other hand, if price movements tend to persist in a given direction over a long period of time—something that has been characteristic of economic development in the United States—there is no doubt that a method can be selected that will give a corporation a long-term net advantage. The advantage of the use of the last-in, first-out method in a period of increasing prices has already been mentioned. Although the beginning of the long-term upward trend in prices that continues at the present time dates from 1933, it was not till 1939 that Congress specifically authorized the use of the last-in, first-out method. Since 1939, therefore, and particularly since the end of World War II, many business enterprises have received permission to switch to this method.

Aside from possibilities of cutting net income tax liabilities, the last-in, first-out method is said to give a "truer" picture of earning capacity than does, for example, the first-in, first-out method. In a period of rising prices, a corporation that uses the last-in, first-out method is likely to find its cost of goods sold rising at a rate close to the rate of rise in its sales income; this happens because it charges to cost of goods sold the prices paid for goods most recently purchased—purchased, that is, at the rising prices. On the other hand, a corporation using the first-in, first-out method is likely to find its cost of goods sold moving up at a rate more slowly than the rate of rise in sales income; this occurs because it charges to cost of sales goods purchased more remotely at lower prices. In a period of falling prices, likewise, the corporation that uses the last-in, first-out method again finds its cost of sales moving in close relationship with sales income, while the corporation that uses the first-in, first-out method appears to be selling earlier-purchased high-priced goods at lower selling prices.

Rising prices and an expansion in business activity generally go hand in hand, making it possible for most enterprises to show good profits without need of such additions as would tend to result from the use of a particular inventory valuation method; and falling prices and a contraction in general business activity generally go together, producing a situation in which it is highly advantageous to be able to show profits, even if the profits are attributable to the use of a given inventory valuation method. Thus, the last-in, first-out method seems to have superiority in both directions; in other words, it tends to "smooth out" profits during the swings of the business cycle, holding them down somewhat in years of business expansion, and preventing an exaggerated fall in years of business contraction.

INVENTORY ECONOMIES

Some business enterprises are able to economize in their investment in inventories by passing on to other firms some of the burdens of inventory accumulation. A lowering of its profit margin is the usual price that the economizing firm pays for the privilege of shifting burdens, since the firms that accept the burdens are willing to do so ordinarily only if they can do so profitably. However, a firm subject to strict limits upon its access to cash may regard this "price" as not too much to pay; without opportunities for the shifting of inventory burdens, it might not be able to remain in business at all. Procedures of shifting include the following: (1) obtaining goods on consignment, (2) the negotiation of exclusive sales contracts, and (3) the farming out of certain kinds of manufacturing operations.

It is obvious that shifting the burdens of carrying inventories is only one among many possibilities of cutting investment in inventories and the costs of handling and distribution. However, shifting is directly related to the financial capacities of firms to carry inventories and, therefore, to financial management, while other possibilities of economies, though important to finance, fall principally within the purview of production and sales management. Interest in achieving economies of the latter classification has been especially strong in recent years, with many corporate managements confessing their long neglect of soaring distribution costs while concentrating upon efforts to pare production costs. Evidence of strong interest in this avenue of inventory economies has been seen in the consolidation and automation of warehouses, closer inventory control through the use of electronic computers, the dropping of slow-moving goods from product lines, the elimination of numerous variants of basic "models" of given products (not the automobile industry, for this one!), and, among retailers, the development of cooperative buying.

Consignments

When a firm receives goods on consignment, it does not get title to them, and it ordinarily has no obligation to make payment until it has sold them and collected from its customers. The firm (consignee) acts simply in the capacity of an agent for the firm supplying the goods (consignor), and its compensation is really not a sales profit but a commission at a fixed rate on the selling price of the goods. The commission is likely to be less than would be the profit margin were it buying outright and selling from its own inventory—a fact illustrative of the "price" of burden shifting, as mentioned above. A moderate amount of cash is still needed by the consignee for what might be called "inventory investment," as he usually meets out-of-pocket costs of freight and drayage, other handling, and perhaps advertising. Such expenses are chargeable against the consignor, and are reimbursed, as it were, when payments are collected from customers. Assume, for example, that a consignee incurs $180 of expenses in acquiring and selling at $4,000 certain goods shipped to him on consignment. The consignor allows a commission of 20 per cent on the selling price. After collecting from his customers, therefore, the consignee would remit $3,020 to the consignor, that is, $4,000 less his commission of $800 and less $180 to cover his expenses.

Outstanding among enterprises that obtain a substantial portion of their wares on a consignment basis are firms in the retail jewelry trade. Considering the high unit value of many of these wares, as diamond rings and brooches, and considering the limited access to cash of small shop owners, many would be unable to carry reasonable selections were it necessary for them to buy their entire stocks outright.

Exclusive Sales Contracts

The carrying of inventories of finished goods pending sale is largely obviated by the negotiation of exclusive sales contracts whereby manufacturing firms agree to sell their entire output to other firms. As soon as goods have been completed, they can be delivered to the buying firm, and if the latter has agreed to pay promptly, cash is quickly released for reinvestment in productive operations. Inventories of raw materials and goods in process must still be carried by the selling firm, although in some instances the buying firm even undertakes to supply the raw materials.

Exclusive sales contracts are numerous; they are the tie that binds thousands of "supplier" firms to great manufacturing corporations, as in the automobile industry. Each supplier may make only one or a few parts to be incorporated in the final product of the large corporation, but the latter, in turn, may have hundreds of different kinds of parts and subassemblies coming in, as it were, from all directions.

Not only does the supplier firm economize in its need of cash for investment in finished goods inventories, it also eliminates almost all kinds of selling expenses. On the other hand, an exclusive sales contract ties the fortunes of the supplier very closely to those of the buying firm; if sales of the latter fall off, it has no choice but to reduce its purchases from the supplier, and the supplier, in turn, finds itself without a developed alternative market. Moreover, the managers of the buying firm, well aware as they must be of the dependence of the supplier, are likely to be shrewd bargainers in negotiations to fix the prices at which parts are to be delivered. They must be willing to allow the supplier firm a fair margin of profit if it is to be persuaded to continue the intercompany relationship; nevertheless, this margin may be considerably less than that of comparable firms selling in the open market.

Farming Out Manufacturing Operations

In many instances, the farming out of manufacturing operations is simply the "other side" of the exclusive sales contract. The supplying firm is able to economize in investment in finished goods inventories, but the large buying firm is able to reduce its investment in raw materials and goods in process—or, at least, to reduce the length of the period required for such investment. Aside from this, as indicated previously, the buying firm may be able to obtain parts and subassemblies at lower prices than would be charged in the open market.

But many firms, large and small, farm out manufacturing operations without thought of exclusive sales contracts. A substantial number of enterprises that are well known on account of the popularity of their branded "products" carry on no manufacturing operations whatsoever— the products are really those of unidentified manufacturers. Such enterprises engage other firms to carry through the complete manufacturing processes, providing them with detailed specifications, and sometimes lending them special kinds of dies, tools, and machines upon which the buying firms have patents. Some "brands" of great popularity are actually produced by several manufacturers, the product getting a single identity only when it receives the label of the buying firm. Hence, the latter is essentially a selling organization.

In other cases, firms that farm out manufacturing operations also reserve some manufacturing functions for themselves. Participation by such firms in manufacturing is subject to wide variations. At one extreme are firms that depend upon other manufacturers only to a small extent, so that their inventory economies tend to be quite small; and at the other extreme are firms that undertake only a relatively simple final assembly of parts and subassemblies manufactured elsewhere.

PURCHASE DISCOUNTS

A final topic for consideration in relation to inventory management policies is the proper treatment of discounts allowed for the prompt payment of invoices of raw materials, finished goods, and supplies. For example, a trade supplier may allow the buyer 30 days for the payment of a given invoice, but he may permit the buyer to take a discount of, say, 2 per cent if he pays within ten days. The "terms" of this transaction would be indicated thus: 2/10 n/30—the "n" standing for "net" or the full amount of the obligation.

The accounting aspect of the treatment of discounts is easily disposed of: when discounts are taken, it matters little whether they are handled as reductions from the prices of goods bought or are entered in the income statement as "other" or "miscellaneous" income. Slight are the effects of these alternative modes of treatment upon inventory turnover ratios and the amounts of gross and net profit.

Much more significant is the question of when business firms should take advantage of discounts offered by suppliers for prompt payment. If a firm has cash available for payment within the discount period, it obviously has the choice of so using it or of using it for some other business objective. Which use will be the most advantageous? If it does not have cash available, it may be in a position to borrow to meet the payment within the discount period—here the question of advantage turns upon the relationship between the rate of discount allowed and the rate of interest that the firm would have to pay upon the borrowed money. Customarily, discount rates, if stipulated at all, are set at levels to make them clearly attractive; hence, financial managers hold it to be a good rule that discounts should normally be taken, whether a firm's own funds or borrowed funds are to be used for this purpose. A related observation is, therefore, that a lack of cash and a lack of borrowing capacity to enable a firm to take advantage of desirable discounts is evidence of poor financial management!

Suppose, for example, that a firm has bought a shipment of goods for $10,000 on terms of 2/10 n/30, that it has no cash available for payment within 10 days, but that it expects to have $10,000 available at the end of the 30-day period. Should it simply forget about the discount? In ordinary circumstances, this would be unwise. Assume that on the tenth day the firm could obtain a bank loan of $9,800 repayable in 20 days with interest at 6 per cent per annum. By borrowing and making payment to the supplier on that day, the firm would be earning the discount of $200, and this, reduced by the interest of $32.67 payable to the bank, would give it a net saving of $167.33. For the 20-day period, the firm would be earning net interest at a rate of 30.7 per cent per annum on the prepayment of $9,800.

It is possible, however, for discount terms to be unattractive. If the terms of the invoice mentioned above were 1/10 n/120, the borrowing of $9,900 for 110 days at 6 per cent per annum would cost $181.50 in interest, while the discount to be earned would amount to only $100. In periods of "tight money," moreover, highly competent financial managers may decide to forgo quite generous purchase discounts in the belief that the limited supplies of cash, whether derived from operations or through borrowing, can be used more profitably in other directions. They might judge the scramble for hard-to-get cash to be the very reason for the offer of generous discount terms by their trade suppliers.

Aside from extraordinary situations, as in periods of "tight money," the repeated failure of firms to take advantage of attractive discounts is widely regarded as an unfavorable reflection upon their creditworthiness. Such a firm, therefore, both misses an income opportunity and suffers some impairment in its credit rating.

Questions

1. Does not the proposition that "more firms fail on account of inept inventory management than for any other reason" exaggerate the importance of inventories in business operations? Discuss.

2. If a firm has sufficient cash left to take care of all its operations comfortably, why could not its profits be maximized despite an overinvestment in inventories?

3. How can the financial managers of business concerns determine whether or not they are overinvesting in inventories? underinvesting?

4. State several reasons why a firm may have the "right amount" of inventory investment even though smaller inventories are carried by well-managed competing firms having comparable sales volumes.

5. How are inventory turnovers computed? What do such ratios reveal individually? in comparisons with other ratios of the same kind?

6. If a firm's inventory turnover ratios rise from year to year while its sales also steadily expand, does this indicate continued improvement in its inventory management? Explain.

7. What are the probable economies of stabilized production that might more than offset the increased costs of carrying larger average inventories? Why is stabilized production described as desirable from the standpoint of public welfare?

8. If a corporation has a choice between two values for its inventory at the end of an accounting period, why will it ordinarily select the lower of these values?

9. In the valuation of inventories "at cost or market, whichever is lower," what does "market" stand for? Is this the so-called "retail method" of valuing inventories? Explain.

10. Why is it claimed that the last-in, first-out method of inventory valuation gives a "truer" picture of operating results than other methods of valuation give?

11. Explain the differences between a consignment and a sale.

12. If one firm enters into a contract to sell its entire output to another, which of these firms gains the benefits of "inventory economies," or do both firms gain such benefits? Explain.

13. Is it always an indication of poor financial management when firms fail to pay trade suppliers early enough to take advantage of purchase discounts offered? Explain.

Problems

1. On January 1, 19xx, the inventory of the Excellent Sales Corporation amounted to $120,000 at cost, and on December 31, to $170,000. In the course of the year, the following additional estimates of its inventories, all at cost and all thought to be reasonably accurate, were made: March 31, $205,000; June 30, $220,000; and September 30, $260,000. Its cost of goods sold for the year was $1,080,000. Compute its inventory turnover (*a*) using the opening and closing inventories, and (*b*) using all quarterly inventories. Which turnover figure is the more realistic? Why?

2. Leeds & Cooke, Inc., deals exclusively in a certain product of which it had on hand at the beginning of the year 19xx 80,000 units valued at $6.00 a unit. During the year it bought additional quantities of the product in the following order at the prices indicated:

100,000 at $6.10
200,000 at $6.20
100,000 at $6.35

At the end of the year 110,000 units of the product remained unsold. The "market" at that time was $6.30. Net sales for the year amounted to $4,900,000.

Determine the corporation's gross profit on sales (that is, net sales less cost of goods sold) on the basis of each of the following methods of inventory valuation:

a) Average cost—at cost.
b) Average cost—at cost or market, whichever is lower.
c) First-in, first-out—at cost.
d) First-in, first-out—at cost or market, whichever is lower.
e) Last-in, first-out—at cost.

3. L. J. Knox & Company has received bills from suppliers totaling $75,000 upon which the terms are 1/10 n/30. It has insufficient cash to pay within ten days although it expects to have no difficulty in meeting the bills at the end of the 30-day period. However, it could obtain a 20-day loan from its commercial bank at a rate of interest of 5 per cent per annum.

Would it be wise for Knox to borrow in order to take advantage of the purchase discount offered? What would be its net saving in so doing? What would this net saving amount to as a per-annum rate of interest on the amount of its early payment to the trade suppliers?

chapter 9

THE MANAGEMENT OF
ACCOUNTS RECEIVABLE

CHOICE OF SELLING TERMS

Areas of Limited Choice

In many areas, business firms have little if any choice between selling for cash and selling on account. The policy of selling on account has become so firmly established in these areas that individual firms would place themselves in a position of severe competitive disadvantage were they to try to operate on a basis of cash selling. This is especially true in the majority of manufacturing industries, in the construction industry, and in wholesale trade, but it is also true in a goodly number of retail mercantile and service lines.

In fields of business enterprise in which selling on account is a firmly established practice, the individual firm must be in a position to tie up cash—much of it continuously, it is probable—in accounts receivable,[1] the amount depending, of course, upon the volume of its sales and the terms of the credits granted. If it has the opportunity to increase the volume of its sales, it will ordinarily need additional cash, not only for the expansion of its inventories, but also for carrying the expected expansion in the volume of its accounts receivable. Customers who increase the size of their orders and new customers will expect, as a matter of course, to be "carried" by the firm for the customary credit period. Inadequacy in the firm's access to cash, therefore, could be a serious obstacle to expanded sales and profits—much more so than for an enterprise that is in a position to sell for cash.

Areas of Broad Choice

In fields of business activity in which the terms of sale are not standardized, as in many retail lines, the individual firm must weigh the relative advantages of selling for cash and selling on account. In such fields, the firm that sells on account is often thought to have a competitive advantage, since it may well be in a position to attract customers who prefer to pay cash in addition to those who prefer to buy on a deferred-payment basis. But an advantage of this kind is by no means assured; more-

---

[1] Unless it chooses a means of economizing in investment in receivables, as discussed in the concluding section of this chapter. See pp. 186–90.

over, such an advantage may be offset in whole or in part, or more than offset, by the burdens of credit selling.

As for the burdens of selling on account, probably the most obvious one is the need of additional cash for investment in accounts receivable—a burden that is measurable in terms of the interest or dividends that must be paid to acquire the cash. Also to be regarded as burdens are the costs of credit administration, including all the expenses of making credit investigations, maintaining files and accounting records concerning credit customers, and handling delinquencies. A third kind of burden results from bad-debt losses whereby the firm fails to collect from given customers all or portions of amounts due.

If, to cover these additional costs, a firm sells at prices higher than are charged by its cash-selling competitors, it may drive away prospective cash customers; such people are likely to feel that they ought not to be made to bear costs of operation that are of no specific benefit to them. If, on the other hand, it sells at the same prices as its competitors, its expanded gross profits due to increased sales may be swallowed up, or more than swallowed up, by the burdens of credit selling referred to. In some cases, however, an expanded volume of sales at prices no higher than those of cash-selling competitors makes possible operating economies sufficient to cover all or a substantial proportion of the special costs of selling on account; thus, a firm that is able to develop such economies stands to gain material advantages by selling on account. In other instances, firms are able to add "finance charges" to the prices of goods sold to credit customers, so that their prices to cash customers need be no higher than those of competitors that sell only for cash. In retail trade, however, such an imposition of additional charges upon credit customers is generally feasible only when the period of deferred payment is a lengthy one, as when payments are to be made in installments during a period of a year or more.

All of which leads to the conclusion that, where a choice as to terms of sale is available, it is not likely to be a clear-cut one. It must depend upon a host of circumstances, each of which may be evaluated in different ways by different groups of business managers. In a given situation, the financial managers of some firms will be convinced that a policy of selling only for cash is bound to be the more profitable one, while the managers of others will be as strongly persuaded that the advantages of selling on account outweigh its disadvantages. This must be so, since we find some stores selling a given line of goods on a cash basis and others selling the same line on a credit basis operating in close proximity to one another.

Recent Developments

Whatever may be the choice in individual cases, postwar developments have been sharply toward increased selling on account. Evidence is strong that the financial managers of more and more businesses have been concluding that net profits can be expanded by the adoption of selling-on-account practices, the lengthening of credit periods, and the carrying of increased balances for individual customers. Typical of this evidence have been the "go-now-pay-later" arrangements for passenger transportation inaugurated by railroads and airlines and the proliferation of "credit cards" issued by oil companies, hotels, and other enterprises. In some cases, no doubt, the adoption or liberalization of credit policies has been a means of defending levels of profits already achieved, rather than a move for their expansion; in other words, firm that would have preferred to continue to sell for cash have thought it necessary, in order to hold their customers, to fall into line with credit-selling competitors.

For business as a whole, data published by the Securities and Exchange Commission may be cited to show the rapid postwar expansion in accounts receivable. Its estimates of the current assets of all business corporations other than banks, savings and loan associations, and insurance companies as of December 31, 1948, and December 31, 1962, are presented in Table 9–1. Here the increase in receivables in dollar amount and percentage stands out dramatically.

TABLE 9–1
Current Assets of Business Corporations, 1948 and 1962[a]
(Dollar amounts in billions)

CURRENT ASSETS	AMOUNTS HELD DECEMBER 31		INCREASES	
	1948	1962	Amount	Percentage
Cash............................	$ 25.3	$ 39.7	$ 14.4	56.9
U.S. government securities..........	14.8	19.8	5.0	33.8
Accounts and notes receivable.......	42.4	149.1	106.7	251.7
Inventories.......................	48.9	100.9	52.0	106.3
Other...........................	1.6	13.3	11.7	731.3
Total......................	$133.0	$322.8	$189.8	142.7

[a] Excluding banks, savings and loan associations, and insurance companies.
SOURCE: Estimates of the Securities and Exchange Commission, as reported in the *Federal Reserve Bulletin*, February, 1957, p.186; June, 1963, p. 832. (Amounts and percentages of increase supplied by the author.)

CREDIT ADMINISTRATION

Allocation of Authority

For firms that decide to sell on account, the establishment of policies and the devising of procedures for "credits and collections" are necessarily matters of great importance. Aside from whatever decisions in these matters boards of directors may choose to make, they are generally thought to fall within the jurisdiction of the principal financial officers of enterprises, whether financial vice presidents, treasurers, controllers, or whoever else they may be. As a recognized asset-management function of financial officers, indeed, the management of credits and collections is second only to the administration of cash and short-term investments. In the management of inventories and the various kinds of fixed assets, production and sales managers are often much more competent than the financial officers in shaping policies likely to prove most favorable. Accordingly, decisions about inventory and equipment requirements are often reached upon the insistence of production and sales managers that "we must do this" and "we must buy that," so that financial managers are left only with an assignment to "find the money." Most questions concerning accounts receivable, on the other hand, are not technical ones of production and selling; they are financial problems. Choosing which prospective customers will be allowed to buy on account is based upon credit investigations, and such investigations are largely analyses of the financial positions of the prospective customers, a kind of work for which the financial officers should be well prepared. Deciding whether cash discounts shall be allowed for early payment is essentially a financial problem of weighing the advantage of a speedier flow of funds—a net reduction in cash requirements—against the obvious disadvantage of the discounts themselves as a financial cost. Similarly, deciding whether certain delinquent customers shall be pressed for payment or whether extensions of the credit period will be readily granted is a matter of comparing financial burdens—the cost of carrying accounts for lengthy periods as against the possibility of losing the patronage of customers who are pressed for payment.

All this does not mean that the sales executives should have nothing to say about credit policies and practices. The sales executives can be expected to contribute highly significant information about the position and prospects of present and prospective customers—kinds of information and observations that tend to improve the quality of credit analyses; and they surely should be in a position to oppose the adoption of credit standards which they think would be unreasonably restrictive. Indeed, a conviction that financial officers tend to be overanxious about bad-debt losses has led a goodly minority of firms to place primary responsibility for credit administration in their sales managers. But the majority, though they may recognize tendencies toward undue strictness in their financial officers, appear to be convinced that the sales executives, in their anxiety to expand the volume of sales, tend to err even more seriously in the direction of laxity. The ideal solution here, as in most cases where conflicting interests must be reconciled, is doubtless the promotion of mutual respect and a spirit of cooperation; this should mean, in the matter of credit administration, a close and harmonious working relationship among the financial and sales managers.

Credit Terms

Where selling on account is an established policy in a given field of industry, the individual firm often has as little discretion in deciding upon the terms of its credit sales as it has, in the first place, in deciding whether or not to sell on account. The terms of credit, no less than the fact that credit will be granted, tend to become standardized. Any firm that might be tempted to liberalize its credit terms to attract customers from its competitors would probably reject the temptation rather quickly in the expectation that the competitors would promptly imitate its example, so that nobody would have a net gain in sales and all would be disadvantaged by the increased burdens in relation to their accounts receivable. Thus, the length of the credit period, the availability of cash discounts, the rate of such discounts, the period within which they may be taken, specially allowed deductions from customer remittances (as for local advertising of the seller's product to be undertaken by the customer)— existing practices concerning matters such as these must usually be accepted and applied as "standard." The determination of broad credit policies by the managers of the individual firm is, therefore, not likely to be a difficult chore.

Far different is the situation of the managers of firms operating in areas in which credit practices among competitors vary greatly. Such managers face the intricate problem of deciding precisely where they will put their firms—at one extreme with a rigorous cash-and-carry policy, at the other extreme with a policy of nothing-down-and-a-dollar-a-week, or, what is more likely in most instances, a point somewhere between these extremes. Because the range of possible selection is so wide, it must be difficult in virtually every case to determine what point or position is or would be the best one; and even after a position has been selected and maintained for a lengthy period, there are no easily applied criteria for judging if profits are maximized there. There is always the possibility that moving to a position of less or more liberal credit granting would result in a net addition to profits; yet a firm's managers will ordinarily be reluctant to change policies to test these other positions, because of the probable difficulty of retracing their steps should a change turn out to be a bad one, in the sense of reduced profits. For example, a firm might not add much to its sales volume by extending its credit period from 30 to 60 days, but a return to a 30-day basis might lose some customers who, before the change, were quite satisfied with that basis.

Choosing Credit Customers. A decision by a business enterprise to sell on account does not obligate it to accept as credit customers all who may wish to be so treated. Whether credit selling is an industry-wide practice or an independently determined policy, the individual firm must select its credit customers as carefully as it selects the varieties and qualities of the goods it includes in its inventories. Its objective must always be to choose customers from whom payment according to the terms of credit sales is reasonably assured, and to avoid those in relation to whom the risks of nonpayment are relatively high.

This does not mean that the typical firm that sells on account hopes to avoid bad-debt losses; its objective, rather, is *to minimize them in relation to its volume of sales.* The complete avoidance of bad-debt losses would ordinarily require a restriction of credit selling only to buyers of the strongest credit ratings; hence a substantial additional volume of sales to people not so highly rated—but most of whom, no doubt, would meet their obligations—would be sacrificed for the dubious record of having a perfect collection experience. If a firm can expand its net profits by $50,000 (before deductions for bad debts originating in the additional sales) by selling to a group of customers having credit standings substantially inferior to the best, and if it thereby incurs bad-debt losses of $30,000, the net result would surely indicate the wisdom of the sales expansion. A record of low bad-debt losses may thus be indicative of a too restrictive credit policy—of poor financial management, rather than the reverse.

The risks that a firm can afford to take in its selection of credit customers depend on such circumstances as its margin of profit and the phase of the business cycle in which the sales take place. Other things being equal, a bad-debt loss of $100,000 would be a much bigger blow to a firm whose markup measured in terms of selling prices is 20 per cent than to one with a markup of, say, 50 per cent. The loss would wipe out the gross profit on $500,000 of sales of the first firm, but that on only $200,000 of sales of the second. As for the business cycle, the probabilities of collecting payments from customers of relatively poor credit standing are generally much better in its expansion phase than in the contraction phase; hence, more liberal selling to these people may be hazarded in periods of expansion. During periods of general business contraction, on the other hand, increased caution in selling on account even to customers of hitherto excellent credit standing may be advisable—something that would be out of the question in the expansion phase of the cycle.

Credit Limits. Deciding which prospective customers will and will not be allowed to buy on credit requires something more than a mere placing of names in one category or the other. For each customer who is approved for credit, a maximum limit for the amount of his indebtedness at any time is usually also desirable. An analysis of the financial position of a customer may indicate that he should be able to meet obligations up to $10,000 without serious difficulty, but that he would be overextending himself should he take on an obligation to pay within a limited period of time, say, $12,000 or $14,000. For this customer, accordingly, the selling firm would be wise to set $10,000 as the maximum credit to be outstanding at any time.

For firms of the highest credit standing, sellers ordinarily set no limits —they are happy to sell on account as much as these firms are willing to take, always depending, however, on the sellers' own cash positions, that is, their capacity to carry the accounts. For other firms, the maximum limits are not necessarily the final word. When the seller, on the basis of repeated transactions, finds that the buyer meets his obligations within the prescribed limit faithfully and without apparent strain, he may move the limit upward by successive steps, perhaps rather substantially with each step. In other instances, though there may be no reason to lift limits on a permanent basis, special circumstances may justify going beyond them occasionally.

The setting of limits makes possible the handling of most sales on account on a routine basis. As long as a customer's orders are within his limit, and provided that his obligations already on the books are not past due, the orders can be filled without reference to the credit department for specific approvals. Only orders that go beyond the limits, or about which special problems are involved, need go to the credit manager and his staff for separate consideration.

Credit Periods. Among manufacturers and wholesalers, in particular, the time allowed to buyers to pay for goods purchased on account is usually tailored in relation to the period required for the buyers, in turn, to resell the goods and to collect payment for them. Thus, the buyer will not necessarily pay out of his existing means at the time of sale to him, but out of the proceeds of resales to his own customers. For this reason, credit terms upon interbusiness sales of goods of rapid turnover, such as foodstuffs, are usually much shorter than for goods of relatively slow turnover, such as electrical appliances and furniture; likewise, they are often shorter on sales to firms which themselves sell for cash than to firms that sell on a deferred-payment basis. In a similar way, credit sales of goods to be devoted to the buyer's own use, such as industrial equipment, often call for shorter terms than sales to buyers for resale.

As a rule, firms selling on account tend to be somewhat less strict in insisting upon payment within the prescribed credit period than with other conditions of the credits they grant. This does not mean that a well-managed firm will be lax in its collection policy; if it were, it could hardly be described as "well managed." What is meant is that such a firm is likely to take prompt action to collect past-due accounts if extensions, for good reasons, have not been requested; but that, on the other hand, it is likely to be rather generous in granting extensions when they are requested well in advance of due dates and the requests are well supported with evidence to justify them. At the very time of sale, moreover, such a firm will probably allow some customers terms longer than the usual ones, if the customers are able to advance good reasons for special treatment. Many firms, indeed, deliberately take on a limited number of customers who are known to be "slow pay"; they conclude that the additional profits to be made on sales to these people will exceed the additional costs of carrying the receivables for longer periods as well as expanded collection expenses.

Sales Discounts. In the preceding chapter, it was pointed out that buyers of goods should find it highly advantageous—except, possibly, in certain extraordinary situations, as in periods of "tight money"—to take cash discounts allowed for prompt payment. But if the taking of discounts is advantageous to buyers, the granting of such discounts must ordinarily be disadvantaegous to the sellers. If the buyer, in taking cash discounts, earns interest at a high rate—30.7 per cent per annum in the illustration of the preceding chapter—the seller necessarily pays interest at the same high rate on the money that his customers pay him, as it were, ahead of time. It is a reasonable proposition, therefore, that sellers generally ought not to allow cash discounts unless the competitive situation has made the giving of discounts a standard practice.

Where the seller has a choice in the matter, circumstances justifying cash discounts must be rare indeed. Allowing cash discounts should have little effect toward reducing bad debts. Customers who are able to pay within ten days to earn a discount will surely pay within 30 or 60 days or whatever the regular credit period may be, if they are not allowed a discount; and people whose accounts are destined to turn out to be uncollectible will rarely have more capacity to pay if a discount is allowed than if not allowed. And, in the matter of high interest rates, a firm that needs money within ten days from the date of certain sales ought to be able—in consideration of the good, collectible accounts on its books, if for no other reason—to find a financial institution willing to lend it the money at a rate per annum of, say, 5 or 6 per cent. Only in periods of "tight money" is it possible that such a financial institution may not be found.

Notes and Drafts. In a few lines of business, such as the wholesale jewelry trade, the buyer on credit is customarily required to give the seller a promissory note in which a promise to pay the amount of the invoice at a designated time is specifically written out with the signature of the buyer; in a few others, the seller draws a draft upon the buyer ordering him to pay the amount of the invoice at a designated time, and the buyer is required to write the word "accepted," the date of acceptance, and his signature upon the face of the instrument. In legal complexion, an accepted draft and a promissory note are much the same, for the acceptor of a draft, no less than the signer of a note, promises to make payment according to the terms of the instrument. For this reason, both notes and accepted drafts are usually shown among the current assets in the selling firm's balance sheet simply as "notes receivable," a designation which distinguishes them from the more common "accounts receivable," the designation for claims upon customers not evidenced by notes or drafts.

The use of notes and drafts, by contrast with the use of book accounts for recording customers' obligations, offers some advantages. For unpaid obligations that become the subjects of lawsuits, it may be somewhat easier for sellers, by producing customers' notes or accepted drafts, to prove their rights to payment than it would be to prove it by means of book entries, invoices, and other such documents. If a seller wants to borrow from a commercial bank or other lender on the security of his receivables, he will surely find it more convenient to discount his holdings of notes and accepted drafts or to transfer them to the lender as collateral than to sell or pledge accounts receivable. Moreover, some debtors seem to feel a stronger compulsion to pay written obligations than oral ones. All the more is this to be expected when the note or draft of a debtor is made payable at the bank with which he ordinarily does business, for the "dishonor" of a note or draft presented through the bank for payment would undoubtedly injure his credit standing, not only with the trade creditor, but with the bank itself.

Despite these advantages of the use of notes and drafts, the vast majority of American firms that sell on a credit basis are quite satisfied to sell on "open account," that is, by simply recording in ledger accounts customers' obligations to pay. Of course, they have, additionally, invoices, copies of bills of lading, and other kinds of documents to prove the existence of obligations should disputes arise as to their nature and amounts. In some cases, however, firms that do not use notes and drafts in the ordinary procedures of credit selling make use of them in handling delinquent accounts. A customer who does not pay within the allowed credit period may be granted an extension only if he agrees to sign a note specifically promising payment at the end of the extended period. The delinquent debtor may be required to make the note payable at his bank, but whether he is or is not so required, presentment of the note for payment through that bank is often thought a desirable procedure for putting additional pressure upon him. A delinquent debtor who refuses to sign notes, or who refuses to cooperate with his creditor in other ways, may be prodded, nevertheless, if the creditor chooses to draw a draft upon him for the amount of his unpaid obligation and have it presented to him for payment by the bank with which he keeps his deposit account and from which, perhaps, he obtains loans. Although the draft, being simply an order to pay, adds nothing to the creditor's right to payment, the debtor may fear a loss of credit standing in the eyes of his bank should he fail to honor it.

Credit Investigation

Classifying prospective customers as acceptable or nonacceptable as credit risks and determining credit limits for the acceptable ones require a painstaking collection and analysis of many kinds of pertinent information about each applicant. Credit investigation is expensive, but the firm that tries to economize in its outlays for this purpose is likely to have resulting bad-debt losses far exceeding what it saves through its efforts toward expense cutting. In small, isolated transactions, to be sure, the costs of thoroughgoing credit investigations could hardly be justified; hence, such sales must be made, if at all, on the basis of rather scanty credit information. But, for the general run of transactions, the assembly and analysis of comprehensive credit data, whatever it may cost, is indispensable.

Character, Capacity, and Capital. The objective of a credit investigation, it is often said, is a judgment of the character, capacity, and capital of the person or firm that applies for credit. On the basis of the judgment as to the "three C's of credit," applications will be granted or denied, or it may be that sale on "regular terms" will be denied, with the door left open for the working out of some kind of special terms.

Character pertains to the integrity of the customer—his moral qualities. Does he have the intention of fulfilling his obligation? Will he make every effort to meet the obligation according to its terms? Or will he try to delay payment even though he is well able to pay within the allowed credit period? Will he demand reductions in his obligation by dishonest claims that goods were received in poor condition or that they were not exactly what he ordered? *Capacity* has to do with managerial ability. Does the customer have the knowledge, skill, and experience to run his business properly? Specifically, can he, within a reasonable time and with a reasonable profit, resell the goods bought on account, so that he will have the means to make payment within the allowed credit period? *Capital* is concerned with the customer's financial position—the existing relationship of his assets and liabilities. Does he have the facilities necessary for the operation of a successful business? Are these facilities conveniently located and intelligently arranged so that they can be used with a minimum of operating costs? What liabilities does the customer already have—their nature, amount, and terms? Which of these liabilities will have priority of payment over the obligation to the selling firm? Will the addition of an obligation to the selling firm make the customer's liabilities unreasonably high in relation to his own investment in the business?

Sources of Credit Information. To answer questions of the kinds just suggested—and many others of similar import—information is drawn from many sources. With repeat customers, much useful information can be drawn from the selling firm's own ledgers and files. Here is a record of how the customer has behaved in the past—whether he has customarily made payment within the discount period or within the allowed credit period, or has permitted his account to become delinquent; whether he has shown restraint in making claims for damaged goods, or has been unreasonable in this regard; whether or not he has attempted to deduct cash discounts long after the expiration of the discount period; and whether he has been prompt or slothful in answering correspondence concerning credit problems.

Interviews with customers, both old and new, are usually considered an important means of acquiring credit data. The customer should know more about his business than anybody else, and the information that he supplies should be invaluable, assuming that he gives it both frankly and honestly. In many instances, however, only the salesmen of a credit-granting firm have personal contacts with the customer, and salesmen often resent being delegated the task of collecting credit information, feeling that it interferes with their primary goal of making sales. Many salesmen, indeed, are probably poorly equipped to judge what is or is not important from the standpoint of credit analysis—they may collect the wrong facts or put erroneous interpretations upon the right ones. Thus, there is every good reason—except for the additional expense involved—for credit managers or members of their staffs to visit customers to make their own judgments. "Field trips" of credit men among customers have been increasing in popularity: more and more widely is it being recognized that personal relationships originating in direct contacts of credit men with customers give both a much better understanding of mutual problems. Such an understanding often makes possible the working out of difficult situations on a much friendlier and mutually satisfactory basis than otherwise would be possible.

The customer also provides information about himself by supplying financial statements—a balance sheet, an income statement, and, for a corporation, a statement of surplus, and, desirably, a series of these over a period of years. Judgments about a customer's "capital" are largely based upon an analysis of such statements. Various ratios computed from these statements are compared with similar ratios computed from earlier statements and with representative ratios computed for other firms in the same industry (as published, for example, by Dun & Bradstreet and by some trade associations). Such comparisons often reveal much about the position and prospects of the customer's business.

Additional credit information is obtained by correspondence with other sellers-on-account and banks and by drawing upon the many facts and figures accumulated by credit-rating agencies and credit interchange bureaus. A new customer who wishes to buy on account will be asked to supply the names of several other firms from which he buys on that basis, as well as the name of the bank with which he does business; these will be asked by the selling firm for whatever information they can reveal about the applicant's creditworthiness. Firms and banks thus approached for credit information are inclined to be rather generous in providing it—as long as they can feel that they are not revealing something confidential—since they hope to be treated generously, in turn, when they take this route to obtain information about their customers and prospective customers. Generally regarded as essential for any firm selling a substantial volume of goods on account are subscriptions to the services of Dun & Bradstreet, which is a general credit-rating and credit-reporting agency, or of specialized agencies in certain business fields, such as the Jewelers Board of Trade and the Lumberman's Credit Association, Inc., and membership in local credit interchange bureaus affiliated with the National Association of Credit Management. Dun & Bradstreet provides its subscribers with its *Reference Book* in which credit ratings are given to a large majority of firms operating in all lines of business in the United States and Canada, and, upon specific request, it provides detailed reports upon the affairs of individual firms (the subscription price varying, of course, according to the number of such reports requested); and the specialized agencies supply similar services in their respective fields. Members of local credit interchange bureaus turn into them periodically information as to their experience with all their credit customers, and copies of these reports are filed with the central office of a national interchange system. From the central file, reports summarizing evaluations of individual firms, as filed by their trade creditors, can be drawn at the request of the member of the local interchange bureau.

Interpretation and Revision. Greater acumen and skill are required in analyzing credit data than in gathering it. The analyst must be able to pick out and assign appropriate weights to the facts that are most significant as indicators of a customer's position and prospects; this obviously means that he must have a sufficient sense of discrimination to recognize other facts as being relatively inconsequential. Especially must he avoid what may be called "mechanical interpretations" of a customer's position, as in the interpretation of ratios computed from the customer's financial statements. Ratios of a given magnitude must not be regarded as absolute indicators of the strength or weakness of the customer's credit standing; they can have meaning only when evaluated in the light of surrounding circumstances. A careful analysis of the particular circumstances of a customer's operations may result in a favorable judgment as to his credit-worthiness, despite an out-of-line situation in his ratios as compared with those of other firms or with his own in preceding years.

No less important than original evaluations of customers' credit positions is their continual re-evaluation, so that maximum limits can be increased as improvements are shown, or reduced or even canceled if deterioration is apparent. What may be a safe limit for a given customer in a period of expansion in general business activity may become quite unsafe in a period of general business contraction; and what may be a safe limit for a customer who is expanding his sales of a given type of goods may be quite unsafe if he is taking on new lines with which he has had little experience. In brief, credit administration requires constant vigilance to detect changes in circumstances and conditions that tend to make earlier evaluations of doubtful further usefulness.

Collection Policy

A thoroughgoing investigation of an applicant for credit and a continuing careful analysis of assembled data pertaining to him should have the very beneficial effect of keeping down the costs, difficulties, and possible loss of goodwill incident to efforts to collect payment on overdue accounts. Accordingly, a striving for economies in credit investigation and analysis may turn out to be shortsighted in that economies realized may be more than offset by additional costs incurred in prodding delinquent customers to meet their obligations, as well as by bad-debt losses. With competent credit management, expenses in collecting a substantial majority of a firm's accounts should be very small; this means that a goodly majority of the customers should be of such credit standing that they can be depended upon always, or almost always, to pay in strict accordance with the terms allowed them.

But rare is the firm selling on account that has no collection problems. An extremely low incidence of delinquencies, indeed, would doubtless be indicative, in most instances, of too strict credit standards—indicative of a neglect of sales possibilities upon which profits probably would considerably exceed additional collection expenses and bad-debt losses. Many firms, as has been noted, deliberately choose to sell to firms known to be "slow pay" as well as to classes of customers of inferior credit standing among whom, on the average, a certain incidence of bad debts is expected.

But if sales on account are made to customers of slow-pay reputation and to others of inferior credit ratings, efforts must be made to collect from *all* these people. All have obligations to pay, and the hope is that all will pay. The expectation of an *average* number of delinquencies or an *average* bad-debt loss does not mean that this customer or that one is to be excused as a matter of course if he fails to pay on time or if he indicates his intention of not paying at all. Thus, collection policies must be as carefully devised and administered as are those having to do with credit investigation and analysis. For the slow-pay people, the objective generally is to collect as quickly as possible but with as much finesse as possible so that their goodwill can be preserved; for those with whom the likelihood of payment decreases with each passing day—because of their deteriorating financial position, for example—the objective ordinarily is to collect as quickly as possible, regardless of the preservation of goodwill.

In trying to collect overdue accounts, credit managers make varied uses of collection letters, telephone calls, telegrams, collection drafts, the services of attorneys and collection agencies, and lawsuits for judgments against delinquent customers. However, we need not attempt to review here the substance, logic, and priorities of these procedures. Suffice it to say that, in most instances, the procedures can be made largely a matter of routine, but that, nevertheless, a study of the individual case often suggests departures from routine that can prove to be most beneficial.

Credit Insurance

Since the determination of a firm's insurance program is essentially a finance function, its financial managers are likely to be responsible for weighing the pros and cons of credit insurance as a means of reducing the risks of selling on account. Credit insurance is designed to give sellers protection against *abnormal* losses upon their accounts receivable. Hence the financial managers of a firm must consider, on the one hand, the possibilities of abnormal losses, and, on the other, the premiums charged for the protection that credit insurance provides. Where a firm has a few accounts much larger than the average of its accounts, where a relatively small firm has only a few large accounts the loss of any one of which would seriously threaten its solvency, where a firm's customers are largely concentrated in one locality or in an industry noted for rather violent cyclical fluctuations, where there is much uncertainty about the future course of general business activity—situations such as these are likely to make the protection of credit insurance attractive.

Credit insurance policies can be obtained either for general coverage of accounts receivable or for the coverage of specific accounts. For the firm that has a few accounts much larger than the average, therefore, specific coverage for these large accounts might be regarded as adequate.

In consideration of the premium charged, the insurance company agrees to bear (usually) 90 per cent of the loss on insured accounts in excess of what may be called the "normal" losses of the insuring firm. On the basis of the firm's loss experience of recent years, the "normal" loss ratio is stipulated, so that only losses on current sales exceeding this ratio make the protective provisions effective. As indicated, too, the insuring firm is usually a "coinsurer" to the extent of 10 per cent of even the abnormal losses; this means that it must absorb this portion of the abnormal losses in addition to whatever proportion is determined to be the "normal" losses.

Obtaining credit insurance does not eliminate the need of careful credit and collection administration. The insurance companies do not insure accounts whose credit ratings (as published by Dun & Bradstreet and other rating agencies) fall below certain stipulated levels, nor do they insure portions of accounts in excess of the maximum limits that they prescribe. Necessarily, therefore, the insuring firm continues to take the full risk on sales to customers whose credit ratings are below the stipulated levels, as well as on sales in excess of the maximum limits prescribed by the insurance companies for customers with acceptable ratings.

TESTING ACCOUNTS RECEIVABLE MANAGEMENT

As means of evaluating the results of a firm's accounts receivable management policies—and, therefore, of judging the soundness of the policies —its financial managers may compute several kinds of ratios and call for the preparation of several kinds of reports. A brief survey of the more significant of these ratios and reports is appropriate at this time.

Ratio of Accounts Receivable to Credit Sales

Probably most useful as a quick means of checking the effectiveness of credit and collection policies is the ratio of accounts receivable at the end of a month to the credit sales of that month. Suppose, for example, that a firm's accounts receivable at the end of a certain month amount to $80,000 and that its credit sales for the month were $50,000. The ratio is thus 1.6. Is this good or bad? The answer depends, of course, upon the credit terms stipulated by the firm. If the firm sells on the basis of net payment in 30 days, with no discount allowed for prompt payment, the ratio would indicate a substantial volume of delinquencies, for at least $30,000 of the account balances must have originated in sales of months preceding the present one.[2] If the firm allows a cash discount for payment within, say, ten days, with the net amount due in 30 days, the ratio would be indicative of a much worse delinquency situation, since many of the buyers in the present month must have already paid to take advantage of the discount. If, on the other hand, the firm's terms call for net payment in 60 days, with no cash discount allowed for earlier payment, the ratio would indicate the possibility that no accounts are delinquent, and that, indeed, quite a few of the customers have paid well before the expiration of the 60-day period.

As with almost any ratio, the usefulness of a ratio of accounts receivable to credit sales in enhanced if it can be compared with similar ratios of other firms and with the same type of ratio for the firm itself computed for other periods. Unfortunately, published statements of other firms usually do not give details as to monthly credit sales and monthly balances of accounts receivable, nor do credit-rating agencies and trade associations publish information of this kind. But a firm can certainly compare its own ratios as computed from month to month. Thus, in terms of the illustration just used, the situation is improving, whatever the credit terms of the firm may be, if in the preceding month the ratio was 1.7, and in the month before that, 1.9; likewise, it is deteriorating if in the preceding month the ratio was 1.4, and in the month before that, say, 1.2.

Aging Accounts Receivable

While the ratio of accounts receivable at the end of a month to the credit sales of that month serves as a quick means of testing, the financial managers of a business enterprise are likely to want details about the exact status of the accounts that are "current" (not past due) and those that are delinquent. For this purpose, a statement in which the accounts receivable are "aged" is most commonly used. A form of this statement, with a few illustrative entries, is presented as Figure 9–1.

Such a statement is especially useful in judging the effectiveness of credit and collection policies when it is compared with similar statements prepared for preceding months. For example, deterioration in the quality of the accounts receivable is indicated if the largest proportion of delinquencies reported this month are in the 31- to 60-day class, whereas last

---

[2] Allowance must be made, of course, for the varying lengths of months. Were the month of the illustration a February of 28 days, the situation would appear to be better than if it were March. If February, obligations upon sales made on January 30 and 31 would not yet be due, but if it were March, sales on the first day of that month should have already been paid for.

FIGURE 9–1
Form for Aging Accounts Receivable

JAMES BATES & CO., INC.
Age of Accounts Receivable
September 30, 19—

CUSTOMER	ADDRESS	TOTAL BALANCE	CURRENT	OVERDUE 1–30 Days	OVERDUE 31–60 Days	OVERDUE 61–90 Days	OVERDUE Over 90 Days
Ames Corporation.	Chicago, Ill.	$ 6,285.20	$ 6,285.20				
Anderson & White.	Denver, Colo.	1,812.45			$1,812.45		
Atlas Sales Co.....	Sioux City, Ia.	850.00	700.00	$ 150.00			
Ballinger Corp....	Dallas, Tex.	5,212.90	5,212.90				
Bond & Drexel....	Detroit, Mich.	1,281.50				$ 623.20	$ 658.30
Total........		$286,175.19	$245,112.20	$23,189.50	$9,175.12	$5,283.12	$3,415.25

month only a small proportion were in this class and in longer-term classes. Comparison with aging statements of the same month in preceding years is also desirable, as certain seasonal factors affecting many of the firm's customers may account for a rise in the amount and length of delinquencies in the same month or group of months year after year. If expansions in the amounts and lengths of delinquencies in preceding years according to a seasonal pattern did not result in an unusual amount of bad-debt losses, a rise this year need not occasion undue anxiety.

Delinquency Ratios

Monthly statements in which accounts receivable are aged provide data for the computation of various kinds of significant delinquency ratios. In terms of the totals presented in Figure 9–1, it is significant that total delinquencies at the end of September amounted to 14.3 per cent of accounts receivable at that time, and that, in turn, delinquencies of 1 to 30 days amounted to 8.1 per cent of accounts receivable, those of 31 to 60 days, to 3.2 per cent, those of 61 to 90 days, to 1.8 per cent, and those over 91 days, to 1.2 per cent. A comparison of ratios of this kind from month to month is often much more revealing of an improving or deteriorating situation than a comparison of the *amounts* of current balances and delinquencies, especially if the volume of credit sales and accounts receivable varies substantially throughout the year on account of seasonal factors. Suppose, for example, that the August aging statement of James Bates & Co., Inc. revealed a total of approximately $35,000 of balances 1 to 30 days past due. A comparison of that figure with the related figure of $23,189.50 in the September statement might be taken as evidence of improvement; but if total accounts receivable at the end of August had amounted to approximately $500,000, the ratio of delinquencies in the 1- to 30-day class in that month would have been in the vicinity of 7 per cent—obviously, a more favorable ratio than that of September.

Often useful also are ratios of delinquencies to the credit sales of the months in which, as it were, the delinquencies originated. Referring again to Figure 9–1, and assuming that James Bates & Co., Inc. sells on the basis of 30 days net, the balances 1 to 30 days past due must have originated in August, those 31 to 60 days past due, very largely in July, and so on. If, then, ratios of past-due balances to the credit sales of the originating months are found to be out of line with other similar ratios for other months or for the same months in other years, an investigation of the reasons for the deviations is immediately suggested.

Bad-Debt Ratios

Many business firms base judgments of the quality of their credit and collection policies, in part at least, upon ratios of bad-debt charge-offs of a given period to the credit sales of that period. But such ratios must be used with caution. Whether or not they are significant depends upon a firm's charge-off policy. If the firm delays for a year or more in writing off accounts eventually found to be uncollectible, the charge-offs of any year are obviously quite unrelated to the credit sales of that year. Similarly, it is patently illogical to relate to this year's credit sales an uncollectible account charged off, say, in April, but originating in a sale made in December of last year.

Even when charge-offs are properly related to the year or periods in which the uncollectible accounts originated, judicious interpretation is necessary. If the ratio of bad debts to the related credit sales increases from year to year, and sales are not expanding significantly, growing laxity in credit administration is strongly indicated; but if the increase in the ratio is accompanied by rapidly expanding sales, it may simply reflect a policy of extending credit to additional classes of lower-rated customers in the expectation that earnings from the additional sales will exceed the increased incidence of bad debts. In the latter case, therefore, the bad-debt ratio must be considered in relation to changes in net profits; only on the basis of such a consideration can the wisdom of the new policy be determined. Again, bad-debt ratios declining from period to period, with sales decreasing or, at least, not expanding significantly, may be indicative of an unwise tightening of credit standards and terms; while declining ratios from period to period with sales rapidly expanding would be good evidence of a high degree of administrative efficiency.

Usually to be recommended is the keeping of a record of credit orders declined on account of unsatisfactory ratings of the would-be buyers. Studied in relation to bad-debt ratios, such a record may suggest certain conclusions deserving further investigation. For example, low bad-debt ratios for periods in which many orders were declined would, again, be indicative of excessive strictness in credit standards and terms; and, on the other hand, high bad-debt ratios in periods in which there were many refusals to sell on account would be evidence of incompetence in credit administration.

Collection Reports

A further means of checking upon the quality of a firm's credit and collection policies is the preparation of periodic reports to show what percentage of customers' balances on the books at the beginning of each period is collected during the period. For a firm whose credit period does not exceed 30 days, a monthly report is likely to be most useful; for one whose credit period falls between 30 and 60 days, a bimonthly report, and so on. In such a report, it is usually desirable, for purposes of comparison, to show the percentage collections of one or more preceding periods or of the "year to date," as well as those of the same months or periods of the preceding year. Changes in collection percentage points from period to period may also be shown to emphasize the comparison. The accounts themselves can be classified in various ways, but a classification on the same basis as in the aging statement, as illustrated in Figure 9–2, is likely to be especially useful in tying together the two kinds of data.

FIGURE 9–2
Collection Report

JAMES BATES & Co., INC.
Collections as Percentages of Opening Balances
For the Month of October, 19—

CLASSIFICATION	CURRENT MONTH	PRECEDING MONTH	YEAR TO DATE (AVERAGE)	LAST YEAR		NET CHANGE— CURRENT MONTH LAST YEAR TO CURRENT MONTH THIS YEAR
				Same Month	Year to Date (Average)	
Current............	92.6	93.3	91.9	88.2	87.7	+4.4
Past due:						
1–30 days.........	86.5	87.7	88.0	84.5	85.4	+2.0
31–60 days........	63.8	67.9	65.2	59.3	61.3	+4.5
61–90 days........	54.2	61.2	56.5	52.2	53.2	+2.0
Over 90 days......	45.7	43.3	42.8	38.7	40.1	+7.0

ECONOMIZING INVESTMENT IN ACCOUNTS RECEIVABLE

In some lines of business, it is possible for firms to sell substantial volumes of goods on a credit basis and yet to invest little or none of their own cash in carrying accounts receivable. One way that this can be done is to have customers sign promissory notes evidencing their obligations to pay and then to sell these notes to financial institutions such as sales finance companies and commercial banks. A second way is to use the services of factors. Let us consider these procedures.

Sale of Customers' Notes

The procedure of taking and selling customers' notes is feasible chiefly in connection with sales of goods on an instalment payment basis. It is especially prominent, therefore, in the sale of consumer durable goods, such as automobiles, electrical appliances for the home, household furniture, jewelry, and furs. But it has also long been common in the sale of machinery and other productive equipment to farmers; and, in recent years, it has rapidly grown in popularity in the sale of machinery and equipment to manufacturing companies.

Conditional Sales Contracts. The instrument most commonly used in effecting instalment sales is the conditional sales contract. The instalment buyer of an automobile, for example, signs a contract in which he promises to pay a specific sum of money monthly for a stipulated period such as 24 or 30 months. The total of the instalment payments thus promised is equal to the selling price of the automobile plus certain insurance and "finance" charges and minus the down payment made at the time of purchase or the allowance for a used car traded in. The seller of the automobile—or his assignee if he sells the contract, as to a financial institution—retains title to it until full payment of the instalments has been made, and the contract provides that, upon such full payment, the instalment buyer becomes the owner. If the buyer defaults upon the contract, he forfeits all payments made up to that time, and the seller or his assignee has the right to repossess the car.

Arrangements with Financial Institutions. In buying an instalment sales contract from a dealer in automobiles or other durable goods, a sales finance company or commercial bank ordinarily pays him an amount equal or close to the unpaid balance of the selling price. Thus, with the down payment or the trade-in plus the payment received from the financial institution, the dealer is in a position much as if he had sold on a straight cash basis. In fact, he is exactly in this position, one might say, if he is able to sell the contract on a nonrecourse basis. This means that the financial institution gives up its right to proceed against the dealer to recover losses due to the instalment buyer's default; it bears the loss should its advance to the dealer exceed its collections from the buyer plus whatever it can recover by repossessing and reselling the automobile or other good. However, buying instalment contracts on a nonrecourse basis is not favored by the financial institutions; only a few of the smaller sales finance companies, it appears, are willing to operate on this basis.

Sometimes dealers sell their contracts on a full-recourse basis, whereby they are contingently liable for the instalment buyer's unpaid obligation; on such a basis, however, the dealer has the right to reposses the financed article and to recover by its resale as much of his loss as is possible. By far the most common procedure is for the dealer to sell his contracts on the basis of a "repurchase agreement." On this basis, the dealer agrees to buy back the financed article from the financial institution, for the amount of the instalment buyer's unpaid obligation, *if it is possible for the financial institution to repossess it.* If an automobile, for example, has been confiscated by a government agency because it had been used for illegal purposes, or if it is beyond repossession because the instalment buyer has "skipped" with it, the financial institution, rather than the dealer, bears such loss as is not covered by insurance.

Sale of Contracts versus Loans. It is not unreasonable to argue that a dealer who assigns instalment contracts on a recourse or repurchase basis is really selling his goods on account, that he continues to carry accounts receivable, and that he is actually borrowing from the sales finance company or the commercial bank to carry these accounts receivable. It can be argued, in other words, that the dealer simply borrows to carry accounts receivable just as he might borrow for any other purpose.

Nevertheless, there are substantial differences between the sale of instalment contracts and obtaining a loan, say, on the security of one's accounts receivable. On a loan, the dealer has a primary obligation to pay at a specific time; in a sale of contracts, he is only contingently obligated to pay, that is, only if the instalment buyer does not pay. Most instalment contracts are paid without a hitch, so that the dealer, one might say, has no further concern with these once they have been assigned to a financial institution. Even when defaults occur, the resale of the financed articles is often sufficient to meet the instalment buyers' unpaid obligations. Again, the financial institutions see to it that financed goods are well protected by insurance—the premiums being paid by the instalment buyers; accordingly, if an automobile, for example, is demolished in a collision, the loss falls chiefly upon the insurance company rather than upon the dealer. Still another common circumstance that eases a dealer's worries about his contingent liability is that most sales finance companies and commercial banks set aside individual "loss reserves" for the benefit of each dealer with whom they do business. To such a reserve is allocated a portion of the "finance charge" as collected by the financial institution upon the instalment contracts assigned by the dealer. Thus, a dealer's own cash is encroached upon by losses only when they exceed the amount accumulated in his loss reserve.

Factors' Services

Factors are specialized business organizations that are willing to assume full responsibility for the management of the accounts receivable of other enterprises. For their clients, as we may call those who use their services, they investigate the credit standings of prospective customers, approve sales to those of acceptable ratings, and undertake to make collections. In effect, they buy a client's accounts receivable as originating in approved sales, and upon these they take the full risks of nonpayment. A factoring organization that has agreed to handle a client's receivables obligates itself to pay on a computed "average due date" for all the accounts or invoices assigned to it within a given period such as a month. The payment is the amount of the accounts reduced by such cash discounts as the client allows (whether or not the client's customers actually take these discounts[3]), whatever allowances have been made for returned goods, other similar allowances, and the amount of the factor's commission or fee. The factor's obligation is binding whether or not it has collected from the client's customers. If the client so wishes, the factor will provide cash in advance of the average due date; in this circumstance, the client receives in cash the amount of the receivables less the amount of the deductions indicated above[4] and less an additional interest charge measured by the number of days for which the advance is made.

If a client chooses to wait for payment until the average due date, it does not economize in its investment in accounts receivable. For the period from the date of sale to the average due date, it obviously carries accounts much as it would were it not using the factor's services. Nevertheless, it relieves itself of all expenses of credit and collection administration; likewise, it avoids all risks of bad-debt losses, since the factor buys the accounts without recourse. A factor's charges for these kinds of services depend upon the types of goods the client sells, the volume of its sales, the average size of its invoices, and classes of its customers, their credit ratings, and other similar circumstances; they range from less than 1 per cent on the net amount of receivables to more than 2 per cent.[5]

However, the client can avoid investing cash in accounts receivable by indicating to the factor that it wants immediate payment as orders are approved by the factor and as the goods are billed and delivered. For advance payment of this kind, as was indicated above, the factor charges interest for the period from the date of the advance payment to the average due date. Rates of interest generally range between 6 and 7 per cent per annum. It should be observed that a client does not really obtain a loan from the factor by means of the arrangement just described; the client has no obligation to make any kind of repayment nor to "make good" on any accounts that turn out to be uncollectible. The interest is paid, therefore, simply as a means of having the advantage of present funds as against future funds, that is, as a means precisely of avoiding the investment of cash in accounts receivable.

Up to the early years of the present century, the services of factors were available almost exclusively to textile manufacturers, their sales

---

[3] This rule applies because, in computing average due dates, the factor uses the earliest dates provided for in the terms of the individual sales. Thus, a sale on April 12 on terms of 2/10 n/60 would be considered as due on April 22. By this arrangement, the factoring organization must use its own funds in making payment to the client if the client's customer does not pay within the ten-day period; but it is compensated, as it were, by taking the cash discount for itself.

[4] Since the amount of allowances for returned merchandise, damages in transit, and the like cannot be known when the advance is given, the factor ordinarily retains a "reserve" equal to 5 to 10 per cent of the face amount of the accounts. Any excess of the "reserve" over allowances as subsequently granted is later paid over to the client.

[5] Clyde William Phelps, *The Role of Factoring in Modern Business Finance* (Baltimore: Commercial Credit Co., 1956), pp. 52–53.

agents, and converters; but, since then, a substantial broadening of the scope of their operations has taken place. The expansion was directed, first, to apparel manufacturers and wholesalers, but, more recently, factors' services have been made available to enterprises quite unrelated to the textile and apparel industries, including manufacturers, wholesalers, and distributors of furniture, electrical appliances, hardware, chemicals, cosmetics, paint, and paper products.[6] Nevertheless, by far the greatest volume of accounts handled by factors continue to originate in the textile and apparel industries. It has been estimated that about $4 billion of sales are being factored annually in the United States.[7]

Questions

1. Compare the size and growth of the investment of corporations collectively in accounts receivable with their investment in inventories.

2. To what extent can it be said that business firms have a choice between selling for cash and selling on account?

3. Where corporations have clear choices in deciding upon terms of sale, what arguments can be advanced for selling only for cash?

4. Why is the "credits and collections" function of business enterprises usually assigned to finance officers rather than to sales executives?

5. Even though a firm finds it necessary to offer credit terms to its customers to meet competition, it still has many decisions to make. About what must these decisions be made?

6. An important goal of credit administration is to minimize bad-debt losses? Is this proposition true or false? Explain.

7. Discuss the pros and cons of allowing sales discounts as a means of prodding credit customers to make early payments.

8. For what reasons are promissory notes and commercial drafts sometimes used in connection with selling on credit?

9. On the basis of what kinds of factual information do credit managers judge the creditworthiness of customers and prospective customers? What are the principal sources of these facts?

10. Explain the meaning of "character, capacity, and capital" as criteria for credit judgments.

11. To what extent does credit insurance protect firms against bad-debt losses on their accounts receivable?

12. Show how ratios of accounts receivable to credit sales can be used as means of testing the quality of firms' credit management.

13. What is the procedure of "aging" accounts receivable? What is such an analysis supposed to reveal?

14. What is a conditional sales contract? What is done with such contracts by selling firms that want to economize in their investment in accounts receivable?

15. Explain the procedure by which and the terms on which factoring organizations take accounts receivable off the hands of selling firms.

[6] *Ibid.*, pp. 67–68.
[7] *Ibid.*, p. 66.

Problems

1. Over a three-year period, the credit sales and charge-offs of bad debts of the Mason Manufacturing Corporation were as follows:

Year	Credit Sales	Charge-offs
19xx	$3,500,000	$16,200
19yy	4,300,000	17,500
19zz	4,900,000	25,800

However, all the accounts charged off in each year originated in the credit sales of the preceding year. On sales of the year 19zz, it is estimated that charge-offs will amount to about $35,000.

Do these figures indicate an improvement or a deterioration in the corporation's credit management? Explain.

2. Analyses of the accounts receivable of Tad Wheeler & Co., Inc., showed the following percentages of receivables current and past due at the end of July, August, and September, 19xx:

	July	August	September
Current	86.2	87.5	89.6
Past due:			
1–30 days	8.5	5.2	3.3
31–60 days	2.9	6.1	1.6
61–90 days	1.3	.9	5.3
Over 90 days	1.1	.3	.2

What do these figures reveal about the effectiveness of the corporation's credit and collection policies?

chapter 10

THE MANAGEMENT OF FIXED ASSETS

Sometimes one encounters statements such as that current assets are the "lifeblood of industry"—statements that seem to imply that current assets are much more important in business operations than fixed assets. But trying to rank current and fixed assets in the order of importance is much like trying to decide which blade of a pair of scissors is the more important. In the typical business enterprise, current and fixed assets must be combined in appropriate proportions for effective and profitable operations; one class of assets is no more dispensable than the other. A retail establishment owning a large and well-selected inventory of goods would doubtless be most unhappily situated were it to lack facilities for the storage, display, and sale of these goods; while, on the other hand, a manufacturing concern would surely be similarly uncomfortable were it to have an excellent building and rows of machines well laid out but to lack raw materials and cash with which to pay wages and to meet other kinds of operating expenses. Only, therefore, in the sense that current assets include cash—with which anything marketable, including fixed assets, can be bought, provided one has enough of it—can it be said that such assets are more important for business purposes than are fixed assets.

When a distinction is made between the *ownership* of assets and their *use*, a further argument, it is true, can be advanced for giving current assets a superior ranking. The typical enterprise owns all the current assets it employs in its operations, but enterprises collectively use fixed assets worth many billions of dollars which they do not own. Opportunities for renting land, buildings, machinery, and other fixed assets abound, in contrast with opportunities for acquiring current assets on a nonownership basis, as, for example, obtaining inventories on consignment. Thus, the financial managers of a business firm must ordinarily estimate cash requirements on a basis of needing to buy inventories, to carry receivables, and to meet current operating expenses; but they may simultaneously plan to avoid large outlays of cash for fixed assets in the expectation of being able to rent such facilities.

Unfortunately, statistics of the value of fixed assets *used* by firms in the various industrial sectors are not available; hence it is impossible, in any exact way, to rank these sectors according to the preponderance of fixed or current assets in their complements of productive facilities. However, ownership data, such as were presented in Table 7–1 on pages 130–31, give us a fair idea of what the situation is. A study of the figures there presented for holdings of land and other fixed assets indicates the outstanding position of such assets in public utility operations, their quite substantial position in the operations of enterprises in agriculture, forestry, and fisheries, mining and quarrying, manufacturing, and service, and their more moderate—but by no means inconsequential—position in construction and in wholesale and retail trade.

However, as an indicator of the importance of fixed asset management in the affairs of business concerns, statistics of fixed asset acquisitions in a given period of time tend to be more significant than statistics of ownership at a specific time. Statistics of acquisitions are presented in Tables 10–1 and 10–2. Much has been heard of the great surge of business spend-

TABLE 10–1
Net Corporate Acquisitions of Assets, 1946–62[a]
(In billions of dollars)

Year	Plant and Equipment	Inventories	Receivables	Cash and U.S. Government Securities	Other Assets	Total[b]
1946	$ 12.5	$11.2	$ 4.8	$ −4.7	$ −.6	$ 23.2
1947	17.0	7.1	7.6	1.0	c	32.7
1948	18.8	4.2	4.1	1.0	.2	28.3
1949	16.3	−3.6	.6	3.2	c	16.5
1950	16.9	9.8	13.8	4.5	.3	45.3
1951	21.6	9.8	4.7	2.8	.6	39.5
1952	22.4	1.3	5.8	.1	.4	30.0
1953	23.9	1.8	1.1	1.8	c	28.6
1954	22.4	−1.6	2.2	c	.8	23.8
1955	24.2	6.7	11.9	5.0	2.8	50.6
1956	29.9	7.6	8.8	−4.3	3.0	45.0
1957	32.7	2.1	4.5	− .3	1.3	40.3
1958	26.4	−2.4	6.7	2.7	1.9	35.3
1959	27.7	6.6	10.9	2.9	4.1	52.1
1960	30.8	2.6	7.6	−3.1	3.1	41.1
1961	29.6	1.8	9.6	2.5	4.9	48.3
1962	32.0	3.8	11.3	1.2	5.3	53.6
Total	$405.1	$68.8	$116.0	$ 16.3	$28.1	$634.2
Percentages of grand total	63.9	10.8	18.3	2.6	4.4	100.0

[a] Excluding banks and insurance companies. No deductions against plant and equipment for depreciation charged during the period.
[b] In some instances, horizontal items do not add exactly to totals because of rounding.
[c] Less than $50 million.

Source: *Survey of Current Business*, October, 1958, p. 18; July, 1962, p. 24; July, 1963, p. 29. (Vertical totals and percentages supplied by the author.)

ing for facilities in the postwar period: its phenomenal character is surely proved by the figures of the two tables. In Table 10–1 are presented estimates of the U.S. Department of Commerce of corporate acquisitions of assets of the principal classes in the period 1946–62. Here the predominant position of plant and equipment acquisitions, by comparison with acquisitions of other classes of assets, stands out clearly—amounting to the

TABLE 10–2
Expenditures on New Plant and Equipment by U.S. Business, 1946–62
(In billions of dollars)

Year	Manufac-turing	Mining	Railroads	Other Trans-portation	Public Utilities	Commu-nica-tions	Commer-cial and Other[a]	Total[b]
1946..........	$ 6.8	$ .4	$ .6	$ .9	$ .8	$ .8	$ 4.5	$ 14.8
1947..........	8.7	.7	.9	1.3	1.5	1.4	6.1	20.6
1948..........	9.1	.9	1.3	1.3	2.5	1.7	5.2	22.1
1949..........	7.1	.8	1.4	.9	3.1	1.3	4.7	19.3
1950..........	7.5	.7	1.1	1.2	3.3	1.1	5.7	20.6
1951..........	10.9	.9	1.5	1.5	3.7	1.3	5.9	25.6
1952..........	11.6	1.0	1.4	1.5	3.9	1.5	5.6	26.5
1953..........	11.9	1.0	1.3	1.6	4.6	1.7	6.3	28.3
1954..........	11.0	1.0	.9	1.5	4.2	1.7	6.5	26.8
1955..........	11.4	1.0	.9	1.6	4.3	2.0	7.5	28.7
1956..........	15.0	1.2	1.2	1.7	4.9	2.7	8.4	35.1
1957..........	16.0	1.2	1.4	1.8	6.2	3.0	7.4	37.0
1958..........	11.4	.9	.8	1.5	6.1	2.6	7.2	30.5
1959..........	12.1	1.0	.9	2.0	5.7	2.7	8.2	32.5
1960..........	14.5	1.0	1.0	1.9	5.7	3.1	8.4	35.7
1961..........	13.7	1.0	.7	1.9	5.5	3.2	8.5	34.4
1962..........	14.7	1.1	.9	2.1	5.5	3.6	9.5	37.3
Total.....	$193.4	$15.8	$18.2	$26.2	$71.5	$35.4	$115.6	$475.8
Percentages of grand total..	40.7	3.3	3.8	5.5	15.0	7.4	24.3	100.0

a Including trade, service, finance, and construction.
b In some instances, horizontal items do not add exactly to totals because of rounding.
Source: U.S. Department of Commerce, Office of Business Economics, *U.S. Income and Output* (Washington, D.C.: U.S. Government Printing Office, 1958), p. 193; and *Survey of Current Business*, various issues.

almost unbelievable sum of $405.1 billion in the 17-year period, and equal to 63.9 per cent of total corporate acquisitions. This does not mean, of course, that a net expansion in the value of fixed asset holdings occurred at this level, since charges to depreciation during the period partially off-set the additions to book value on account of the acquisitions;[1] nevertheless, the fact remains that corporations poured $405.1 billion into new plant and equipment, while allocating to the expansion in receivables only a little more than one fourth as much, and to the expansion in inventories only about one sixth as much. That corporations were not alone in spending heavily for plant and equipment is shown by Table 10–2. Comparing the pertinent totals of the two tables, one sees that proprietorships, partnerships, and other noncorporate business enterprises spent close to $70 billion for plant and equipment in the 17-year period.[2] The industrial breakdown of Table 10–2 is additionally significant in showing the outstanding role of manufacturing, "commercial and other," and public utility enterprises in plant and equipment acquisitions.

[1] For the amount of corporate charges to depreciation in the postwar years, see Table 15–3 on page 326.
[2] The comparison is not exact, since Table 10–1 excludes and Table 10–2 includes outlays of banks and insurance companies for plant and equipment.

DETERMINANTS OF INVESTMENT IN FIXED ASSETS

According to economic theory, decisions of corporate managers and other businessmen to invest or not to invest in additional fixed assets have two determinants: (1) their estimates of the rates of return to be earned upon such additional investment, and (2) the prevailing structure of interest rates. If the managers of a corporation estimate that the purchase of a group of machines will yield an annual net return equal to 12 per cent of the amount invested, and if money for the acquisition of the machines can be borrowed at 5 per cent per annum, they will surely be strongly inclined to go ahead with the investment. They would proceed in the expectation of earning 7 per cent each year on the amount invested after paying interest on the borrowed money. Even if the corporation had available for investment in the machines money already accumulated, as from past profits, the managers would surely give no less attention to prevailing interest rates. They would have a choice between investing in the machines and lending the money out, as by buying bonds of other enterprises or of governmental bodies. Investing in the machines would mean a decision to forgo the interest that could be earned through the purchase of bonds. Accordingly, it would be quite reasonable to hold that the investment of the corporation's own money in the machines would involve an interest cost of 5 per cent, assuming that high-quality bonds paying interest at that rate were available in the market.

In a similar way, one would hardly expect the executives of a corporation to adopt a plan to buy or have built an additional factory building if they anticipated that, during the life of the building, the net annual return would amount to 4 per cent of the amount to be invested, and if money needed for the investment could be borrowed only at 5 per cent or more. Here, again, current rates of interest would be an important determinant of their decision, even if the corporation had an accumulation of cash that could readily be spared to pay for the building. If the corporate managers could invest this money in high-quality government bonds paying a return of 5 per cent, they would be most unlikely to choose to invest in the building—to give up the opportunity for a 5 per cent return for one of only 4 per cent.

Estimating Rates of Return

In weighing the pros and cons of additions to investment in buildings, machinery, equipment, rolling stock, and other fixed assets, the financial managers of business concerns are likely to think in the first instance of the expansion of the sales volume that the new investment will make possible, the prices at which they will be able to sell the enlarged volume of output, what the additional costs of materials and direct labor will be, what will be the additional overhead costs directly resulting from the use of the new facilities, and increases to be expected in other kinds of overhead expenses. In the first instance, therefore, the managers may arrive at certain conclusions as to the *amounts*, if any, by which they expect profits to expand through the use of new facilities. But, sooner or later, conclusions about dollar amounts of profits will surely be translated into conclusions about anticipated *rates* of return. Such a translation takes place when the cost of new facilities is taken into consideration. Quite pleasant may be a conclusion that during the life of a group of new machines annual profits would be expanded by $500,000; but the conclusion would be likely to be all the more pleasant—and all the more pro-motive of quick action—should the managers learn that the new machines would cost $2.5 million, as that figure would promise a relatively high rate of return; whereas the conclusion would quickly take on an unpleasant hue were they to be told that the cost of the new machines would be $25 million, as a very poor rate of return would thereby be indicated.

In working up estimates of rates of return, moreover, business managers must give due weight to the important fact that the amount of any invest-ment in fixed assets of the kinds mentioned in the preceding paragraph[3] will not remain constant. Over the life of new facilities, the investment will be periodically written down as depreciation is charged.[4] Hence, rates of return must be thought of in terms of the average investment in the assets during the period of their useful lives, and not simply in terms of the original amount invested. Referring to the foregoing illustration, the rate of return on the investment in the machines at an original cost of $2.5 million *would not be* 20 per cent per annum—it would be substan-tially higher than that, since the average investment in the machines over the period of their lives would be substantially less than $2.5 million.

In thinking of interest costs on money invested in fixed assets, similarly, the financial managers of business enterprises must expect them to fall periodically during the years in which the fixed assets are used. If invest-ment in such assets periodically declines through depreciation charges, money "tied up" in them should likewise be released. It is normally re-leased, of course, in the cash throw-offs resulting from the depreciation charges. Such cash throw-offs can be used for instalment repayments of money borrowed, thereby reducing the balances upon which interest must continue to be paid; or they can be used for other business purposes, if the money originally invested came from an enterprise's own accumula-tions.

Rough Method of Estimation. Further to clarify the role of rates of expected return and interest rates as determinants of investment decisions, as well as to indicate the relationships between these rates and dollar

---

[3] That is, excluding assets not subject to depreciation, depletion, and amortization.
[4] Although the discussion is restricted here to depreciable assets, the principles analyzed apply also to assets subject to depletion and amortization. See above, pp. 101–2; also see the preceding footnote.

amounts of anticipated changes in sales, costs, and profits, a somewhat detailed illustration should be helpful. We shall see how an identical investment decision might be reached, first, on the basis of a rough method of analysis, and, second, on the basis of a so-called "exact" or "scientific" method.

Let us suppose that the financial managers of a certain corporation are grappling with the question of whether or not they ought to endorse a recommendation of the production managers for the purchase of some additional machinery. The machines would cost $610,000, have estimated useful lives of five years, and have no residual or scrap value at the end of that period of time. Depreciation would be charged on the "straight-line" basis[5] at $122,000 a year. It would be necessary to borrow money to buy the machines, and a prospective lender has committed himself to advance the required funds at an annual rate of interest of 5 per cent; however, the financial managers would expect to be able to repay $122,000 of the principal of the loan annually out of the cash throw-offs occasioned by the depreciation charges. Accordingly, the interest would be payable, from year to year, only on the decreasing outstanding balances of the loan. Let us assume, finally, that the corporate managers anticipate that an increase in annual sales of $550,000 would be made possible by the acquisition of the machines, and that additional expenses for materials, labor, maintenance, power, all kinds of taxes, and other overhead items (except depreciation and interest) would be $372,000.

With all these facts properly rearranged, the computation of an expected rate of return by the rough method would proceed as follows:

Anticipated increase in sales (annually for five years). $550,000
Anticipated increase in expenses (excluding depreciation
   and interest). $372,000
Depreciation. 122,000   494,000
Estimated increase in net profit (before interest). . . . . $ 56,000

$$\text{Average investment} = \frac{\$610,000 + \$488,000 + \$366,000 + \$244,000 + \$122,000}{5}$$

$$= \$366,000$$

Estimated rate of return: $56,000 \div \$366,000 = 15.3\%$

As the corporation would pay interest at 5 per cent on $610,000 for the first year, on $488,000 for the second year, on $366,000 for the third year, and so on, its total interest payments for the five-year period would be the sum of $30,500, $24,400, $18,300, $12,200, and $6,100, or $91,500, and the average annual payment would be $18,300—an amount obviously equal to 5 per cent of the average investment of $366,000. Accordingly, the

---

[5] By this method, the annual depreciation charge is arrived at by the use of the following formula: $\dfrac{\text{Cost} - \text{Scrap value}}{\text{Years of useful life}}$ = Annual depreciation charge. For a discussion of this and other methods of charging depreciation, see below, pp. 224–27.

financial managers could anticipate an additional net profit after interest each year equal on the average to 10.3 per cent of the average amount invested in the machines; and this anticipation, presumably,[6] would lead them to approve the recommendation of the production managers for the acquisition of the machines.

Exact Method of Estimation. Businessmen who wish to be as precise as is mathematically possible in their estimates of rates of return to be earned upon investments in fixed assets can use a "scientific" method based upon compound discount formulas. In this procedure, the cost of the fixed assets is recognized as the *present value of a stream of future additions to income;* hence, the rate of return that will be earned is the rate of compound discount that, applied to these future additions to income, will exactly equate the sum of their present values to the cost of the assets. In terms of the foregoing illustration, the stream of future additions to income (before deductions for depreciation and interest) is made up of $178,000 to be received by the end of the first year, another $178,000 to be received by the end of the second, another $178,000, by the end of the third, and so on. At what rate must we discount each of these future additions to income to give them a combined present value of $610,000? Let us try 15 per cent, since the rough method of computation gave us an estimated rate of 15.3 per cent. We find that:

$178,000 discounted for one year at 15 per cent equals[7]............$154,783
$178,000 discounted for two years at 15 per cent equals............ 134,594
$178,000 discounted for three years at 15 per cent equals.......... 117,038
$178,000 discounted for four years at 15 per cent equals........... 101,772
$178,000 discounted for five years at 15 per cent equals........... 88,497

Total...$596,684

---

[6] One cannot be absolutely sure about such things, as there could be other uses to which the money could be put—uses which, as demonstrated by a similar kind of analysis, might promise rates of return after interest of more than 10.3 per cent. If that were so, and if the corporation's capacity to borrow, as well as to obtain additional funds by other means, were limited to $610,000 or thereabouts, one or more of the other projects, rather than the machine purchase proposal, would be likely to be adopted.

[7] This means that if $154,783 is invested for one year at 15 per cent, the principal of the investment plus interest of $23,217 will amount to $178,000 at the end of the year; if $134,594 is invested for two years at 15 per cent, compounded annually, the principal plus interest (of $43,406) will amount to $178,000 at the end of the second year; and so on. The present value of future amounts discounted at given rates can be found by the solution of the following formula: $P = A\left(\dfrac{1}{(1+i)^n}\right)$, where P is the present value, A is the future amount, i is the interest rate per period, and n is the number of periods. In terms of the illustration, the formula for the present value of the income to be derived in the fifth year would be: $P = 178,000\left(\dfrac{1}{(1.15)^5}\right)$. In many textbooks in the mathematics of finance and accounting, tables of the present value of $1.00 at various rates for various numbers of periods are given. When such tables are available, all one needs to do is to select the appropriate present value of $1.00 and multiply by the future amount involved, as the $178,000 of the illustration.

This result indicates that if $596,684 were the cost of the new machines, the rate of return would be exactly 15 per cent on the diminishing amount of the investment over the period of their useful lives. But, by the terms of our illustration, the sum of $610,000—and not $596,684—must be invested if the machines are to be acquired. This means, therefore, that the rate of return would actually be less than 15 per cent. Would it be as low as 14 per cent? Had we set out above to find the sum of the present values using a discount rate of 14 per cent, we would have had a result of $611,087, indicating that the rate of return would be more than 14 per cent. At what point the rate would fall between 14 per cent and 15 per cent could be determined approximately by a process of interpolation, as it is called. The difference of 1 percentage point accounts for a difference in present value of $14,403 (that is, $611,087 — $596,684); accordingly, the true rate of return must be approximately—

$$.14 + \left(\frac{611,087 - 610,000}{14,403} \times .01 \right) = .140755, \text{ or } 14.0755\%$$

By a further process of refinement—really a somewhat laborious procedure of trial and error—the rate would be found to be almost exactly 14.0743 per cent.

To grasp the logic of the theory of the compound discount procedure, we may carry the illustration a step further by setting up a table to show what the interest charges and the profits would be from year to year on the diminishing amount of the investment and what sums would be available for the instalment repayment of the loan. In keeping with the theory, the depreciation charges from year to year should equal the increasing amounts of the loan-repayment instalments—this representing an application of the sinking fund method of charging depreciation, as distinct from the straight-line and other methods. Such a table is the following:

Year	Amount of Investment (and Loan) Beginning of Year	Income before Interest and Depreciation	Interest at 5 Per Cent	Profit at 9.0743 Per Cent	Balance of Income for Repayment of Loan (Also the Depreciation Charge)
1......	$610,000.00	$178,000.00	$30,500.00	$55,353.23	$ 92,146.77
2......	517,853.23	178,000.00	25,892.66	46,991.53	105,115.81
3......	412,737.42	178,000.00	20,636.87	37,452.99	119,910.14
4......	292,827.28	178,000.00	14,641.36	26,572.00	136,786.64
5......	156,040.64	178,000.00	7,802.03	14,159.63	156,038.34

Thus the balance of income at the end of the fifth year would be sufficient[8] for the final instalment payment on the loan; and a depreciation charge of this amount would simultaneously have the effect of reducing the book value of the machines to zero.

---

[8] The small difference of $2.30 results from the fact that the computed rate of return of 14.0743 per cent does not represent a *perfect* refinement.

Business Attitudes in the Estimation of Rates of Return

Economic theorists hold that business managers will go ahead with plans for adding to their investment in fixed assets as long as the anticipated rates of return on the amounts to be invested are equal to or exceed the rates of interest that must be paid on borrowed money or that could be earned if their own money were invested elsewhere. But they add that businessmen's estimates of rates of return are subject to variations both sharp and sudden. At a given time, a businessman may be extremely optimistic forecasting the growth in demand for his product, and he may therefore think in terms of high rates of return upon additions to his productive facilities; but only a few days later, because of rumors that a substitute for the product has been developed in somebody's laboratory, he may have turned completely pessimistic, refusing to think further of expansion regardless of the attractiveness of the interest rate at which he could borrow the necessary money.

In most instances, undoubtedly, business executives are cautious in estimating rates of return to be expected upon further investment in fixed assets. The longer the life of contemplated acquisitions, the greater their caution is likely to be. Prospects for the next few years may, indeed, be rosy, and businesses may add short-lived fixed assets with considerable enthusiasm; but when it comes to buildings and other long-lived assets, serious misgivings about their usefulness beyond a short period of years are likely to be entertained. Extremely cautious is the business executive who, when contemplating the purchase of machines likely to have ten or more years of useful life, says: "I would invest gladly in this new equipment if I were sure of getting my money out of it in five years." Because of his fear that the equipment will be worthless at the end of five years, he obviously anticipates a relatively low rate of return upon new investment. In terms of the illustration given above, there may be excellent possibilities that additional sales each year would be $650,000 and additional costs other than depreciation and interest not more than the $372,000 actually estimated, or that, with additional sales at $550,000, additional costs would be only $300,000, but caution prompts the corporate managers to put down the figures that were actually used in the illustration.

As a rule, then, most businessmen do not anticipate extraordinarily high rates of return upon projects for the expansion of fixed assets. After a decision to proceed has been made, they may *hope* for such an outcome; but the decision itself is most likely to be based upon an analysis in which all adverse factors are carefully weighed, and not upon hopes. Accordingly, a low or moderate level of interest rates by no means assures a vast undertaking of investment projects. It certainly gives no such assurance in periods of general business contraction. In such periods, anticipated rates of return often fall to the vanishing point and continue on to negative levels, for the idleness of many existing productive facilities makes thoroughly unattractive most kinds of propositions for additions. Even in periods of general business expansion, though anticipated rates of return may hold to relatively high levels for a few months or years, sooner or later they tend to recede sharply, for further additions to productive facilities become less and less attractive when many additions have already been made.

Interest Rates and Investment Decisions

Considering the caution with which businessmen typically estimate rates of return to be earned upon further investment in fixed assets, the proposition that they will go ahead if anticipated rates of return are equal to or exceed prevailing rates of interest is not difficult to accept. All the more acceptable is this proposition when it is realized that true rates of interest are often much higher than quoted rates. We may hear, for example, that commercial banks are lending money to manufacturers at a rate of 5½ per cent per annum to buy machinery and equipment. But this does not mean that the banks have an unlimited capacity or willingness to lend for that purpose at that or any other rate. It surely does not mean that a bank would be willing to lend an unlimited amount at that rate to any one manufacturer! At the bank at which he ordinarily does business, a manufacturer might be able to borrow $100,000 at 5½ per cent for the purchase of machinery, but what would happen to his investment decision if he needed $500,000?

On the basis of most careful analysis, he might anticipate a rate of return of 15 per cent on an investment of $500,000 in additional machinery, but if lenders, on the basis of their own credit analysis, decided that loans to him in excess of $100,000 would be too risky, he would presumably find it necessary to abandon his plans for expansion. It might appear, therefore, that his investment decision was a negative one despite a great excess of the expected rate of return over "prevailing interest rates." Actually, however, the prevailing interest rate *for him* could surely be said to be much higher than 5½ per cent. In fact, he might be able to find a less conservative lender who would be willing to advance the full $500,000; but surely such a lender would demand interest payments at a rate much higher than 5½ per cent—probably at more than 15 per cent, as would be indicated by the very abandonment of the expansion project.

In periods of "tight money," even business firms of high credit standings may find it impossible to borrow all the money they want for their investment projects at rates of interest they would consider reasonable. In such periods, lenders simply lack a sufficient supply of funds to meet the demand at the going rate of interest, or, indeed, the demand as it would be at substantially higher rates; hence, they are inclined to ration their scarce loan funds among their regular customers, including those of high credit ratings, thus trying to retain the goodwill of as many of them as possible. The result is much the same as if they offered each customer a reasonable share of the scarce loan funds at a moderate rate, with a stipulation that any additional amount asked for would be advanced only at a very high rate of interest. Hence, the average true rates of interest "prevailing" upon loans of the larger amounts could be said to be much higher than the rates actually charged on the loans as rationed.

Choosing among Investment Projects

The foregoing discussion of the role of interest rates in investment decisions leads to the conclusion that the managers of most business enterprises—even those of high credit standing—must generally weigh with utmost care alternative ways of investing cash already acquired or available for acquisition. If it is true that loan funds available to it at reasonable rates of interest are limited in amount, presumably such funds as are borrowed or otherwise acquired should be devoted to investment outlets that promise to be more profitable than any others that might be selected. It is not enough for the financial managers to conclude that a given investment in fixed assets should be made, because, let us say, the necessary money can be obtained at a rate of 6 per cent and a rate of return of 10 per cent over the life of these assets can reasonably be anticipated. Perhaps the same amount of money devoted to an expansion of inventories and accounts receivable would produce a rate of return per year of 15 per cent. If, then, one project or the other has to be chosen, because sufficient cash cannot be made available for both simultaneously, the choice should undoubtedly fall to the second.

It might be objected, however, that expanding the sales volume would be quite impossible without an expansion in fixed assets, and that, likewise, a return of 10 per cent upon the projected investment in fixed assets could be anticipated only on the assumption that an expansion of investment in inventories and accounts receivable would also be possible. In other words, it might be argued that, since fixed assets, inventories, and accounts receivable are all used jointly in producing income, it is impossible to say what the rate of return on a given asset, standing separately, may be. But a counterargument can be offered. Suppose that the firm has been renting productive equipment and that, to increase output, it could rent additional equipment of similar kinds. The choice facing the financial managers, then, would be this: should they use the available money to buy equipment to replace what they had been renting, without, therefore, planning for an increased volume of sales, or should they rent additional equipment and use the money to expand inventories and accounts receivable in relation to an expanded sales volume? Thus, it would be possible to say that the first alternative would result in increased annual profits (before the deduction of interest) equal to 10 per cent of the average amount of the investment, and that the second alternative would produce an increase in profits amounting to a return of 15 per cent.

ECONOMIZING INVESTMENT IN FIXED ASSETS

When limitations upon the availability of cash make necessary a choice between current asset expansion and fixed asset expansion, it falls in most instances to the former. Such a preponderance of choices necessarily indicates businessmen's estimations of higher rates of return to be earned upon additions to current assets than upon additions to fixed assets. This attitude is strongly engendered, no doubt, by the abundance of opportunities to rent buildings, machinery, and other facilities, as contrasted with the dearth of opportunities of this kind in relation to current assets. For example, buildings and space in buildings are generally available for rent for a wide variety of uses in many localities, while relatively few trade suppliers are willing to provide inventory on a consignment basis. Moreover, the offering of great quantities of productive facilities of the fixed classification for rent means that rental charges tend to be held to moderate levels; while the refusal of most trade suppliers to deliver goods on consignment means that the few who are willing to do so can be strict in their terms.

Rental arrangements are, by far, the most common means of economizing investment in fixed assets—in avoiding absorptions of cash that, in the judgment of business managers, can be better used in inventory investment or in other directions. However, renting is not the whole story, for, as will be explained subsequently, stabilizing production, "farming out" manufacturing operations, and "contracting out" for peak production loads are additional means of economy in fixed asset investment.

Leases

Certain classes of property, if they are to be acquired at all, must be obtained on a lease basis; the owners refuse to sell. This is true of land sites in prominent locations in many of our principal cities. Such sites are often made available on leases running for fifty years or more, and the tenants put up imposing buildings, expecting to recover their value during the periods of the leases, since the contracts usually provide that "improvements" revert to the lessors at the expiration of the lease periods as originally set or as later extended.

Owners of patents on machinery have sometimes refused to sell the patented machines, making them available only on lease to other firms. For many years, for example, it was impossible to buy many kinds of shoe-manufacturing and shoe-repair equipment upon which the United Shoe Machinery Corporation held patents and certain kinds of office equipment and machines produced by the International Business Machines Corporation; but proceedings of the federal government resulted in court orders to these companies to offer their products for sale to those who prefer to buy rather than to rent. Other owners of patents refuse to sell the patents themselves but willingly license other firms to produce the patented products, the latter usually paying a royalty per unit of output. Such a royalty is a rental payment for the "use" of an intangible fixed asset, that is, the patent itself. As an example, many of the "wonder drugs" developed and patented by pharmaceutical firms in recent years have been produced and sold, with distinctive trade names, by other firms licensed by the discoverers.

By means of another kind of rental or royalty arrangement of outstanding importance, many enterprises in the extractive industries gain access to what may be called their "raw materials." Although some mining and lumber companies own their own lands, a large number much prefer to gain access to mineral deposits and standing timber on the basis of royalty contracts. The owners of land are asked to grant mining and cutting rights in consideration of a royalty to be paid at a stated rate per unit of output or as a percentage of the value of the output. Such contracts usually provide for a minimum payment to be made annually whether or not extractive operations proceed; in this way, the landowner is assured an annual income during the term of the contract, even though the lessee may decide to defer development until a later time. By means of such contracts, the investment of the mining and lumber companies in fixed assets can generally be limited to machinery and equipment needed to drill wells, to sink shafts, to fell trees, and so on.

On the other hand, certain kinds of property are rarely made available for rental, especially highly specialized kinds, such as factory buildings that require features, facilities, and layouts peculiarly designed for the manufacture of given lines of products but of little usefulness for other kinds of manufacturing operations. Owners of factory sites are unlikely to construct rental property of peculiar and intricate design for fear that, should the original tenant fail or abandon the lease for any other reason, it would be impossible to attract a new one.

In between, of course, there are innumerable classes of property available on either a sale or a lease basis, so that enterprises that could use such property conveniently have a "rent or buy" choice. Such obviously is the situation in many localities for office buildings, store buildings, and warehouses; but it is also widely true for various kinds of factory, store, and office machinery and equipment, delivery trucks, and even automobiles for the use of salesmen.

Popularity of Leases. Business firms whose access to cash is severely limited must of necessity, one might say, rent land and buildings and perhaps other kinds of property if they are to be able to carry an adequate amount of inventories and accounts receivable. Such is commonly the situation of enterprises newly or recently established. Only moderate amounts of money can be put into these enterprises by the owners, additional funds cannot be attracted as by offerings of stock to "outsiders," and the prospects of the enterprises, from a credit standpoint, are so uncertain that borrowing beyond modest limits is impossible.

Well-established firms, though they may not be so severely limited in the availability of cash, often also have occasions to weigh carefully the respective advantages and disadvantages of the ownership and the rental of land, buildings, and other fixed assets. As indicated by the illustration presented earlier in this chapter, they may decide that the rate of return to be earned on investment in inventories and accounts receivable is likely to be substantially higher than that to be expected on investment in, say, land and buildings; hence, they choose to rent land and buildings and to direct their cash resources, as it were, into inventory and accounts receivable. Although such firms might be in a position to finance all their present requirements for both fixed and current assets through borrowing or sales of additional stock, they might prefer to reserve these means of financing to take care of future current asset requirements expected to result from expansions in the volume of sales. Were they to issue stock or borrow at present to buy fixed assets, they might find it difficult later to put out still more stock or to increase their borrowings to carry larger inventories and larger amounts of accounts receivable without which expansions in the volume of sales could not be effected.

In many cases, too, the managers of business concerns conclude that they are well equipped and staffed to manufacture and sell, or simply to sell, certain kinds of products, but that they are not so well fixed for the management of real estate. They realize that landowners expect to earn net returns—perhaps substantial ones—out of the rentals they charge, but they conclude that the costs of ownership might turn out to be not much less than the rentals. Landowners are likely to be specialists in the management of real estate, knowing how to keep costs down—a fact to be reflected in the rents they charge; whereas the business firm, by inept real estate management or by taking upon itself the costs of hiring specialists of its own, may find ownership to be quite expensive. The fact, therefore, that landowners often enjoy substantial net incomes is no more a reason for a firm to decide to own its land and buildings than is the realization of profits by producers of raw materials a reason for a firm's decision to manufacture its own raw materials.

Even firms of the strongest credit standing—firms whose access to money, if not unlimited, is nevertheless very great—often find it wise to rent certain kinds of property rather than to own it. This is seen especially in the rental of office space in our principal cities. Many firms of this class decide that they must have their principal business offices in New York or Chicago or some other great city, but they are content to rent suites of offices, or perhaps whole floors or several floors, in buildings owned by others. From the standpoint of their access to cash, they could well afford to put up their own office buildings—as some, indeed, do—but their financial managers apparently conclude that the disadvantages of this would outweigh the advantages.

Construction for Tenants. The popularity of leases is enhanced by the fact that many owners of land can be prevailed upon to put up buildings designed to meet the requirements of given tenants. This arrangement is most common in the construction of store buildings for the occupancy of chain store organizations. Unlike many kinds of factories, the store buildings are not so highly specialized in design and layout that other merchants could not be attracted should the original tenants move out. Nevertheless, it is the contract with the original tenant that persuades the landowner to build. This contract generally assures the landowner of the recovery of his investment in the building as well as a reasonable annual income during the period of the original tenant's occupancy. On the basis of market research, the chain store organization picks out promising sites for new stores and agrees to sign leases of, perhaps, twenty years if the owners will put up buildings according to certain specifications. Loans for the construction can usually be obtained without difficulty from financial institutions, since principal and interest obligations to them will be more than covered by the rentals that the chain store organization agrees to pay. Similar leasing arrangements originate in the promotion of suburban "shopping centers," which have had a phenomenal growth since the close of World War II. In this kind of arrangement, the promoters themselves usually take the initiative. Having obtained options to buy likely sites for shopping centers, they approach chain store and other mercantile enterprises with propositions to build facilities according to their specifications on the promise of long-term leases.

A long-term lease, in consideration of which a landowner consents to construct a building for the use of the tenant, will usually provide that all costs of maintenance and repair, insurance, and property taxes are to be borne by the tenant; thus the rental payment itself becomes, in effect, a straight recovery by the landowner of the principal of his investment and net income. Needless to say, such a lease must be prepared with great care; it is important that the rights and responsibilities of both landowner and tenant be set out clearly and in detail so that disputes and possibly litigation because of omissions or ambiguities will be avoided. Long-term leases often give the tenant the option of having the term extended for an additional period of years upon the expiration of the original term. Such provisions customarily prescribe a sharply reduced rental for the additional period, since, by the end of the original term, the landowner will have recovered the full amount of his investment in the building.

Sale-and-Leaseback. Similar in form and results to the arrangements just described is sale-and-leaseback, a procedure that has had its development almost entirely since the close of World War II. By this arrangement, business firms already owning land and buildings sell them to life insurance companies, college endowment funds, or pension trust funds, and then lease them back for (usually) terms of twenty years or more. Firms that operate department stores, especially department store chains, have been especially prominent in working out arrangements of this kind. In these transactions, the life insurance companies and other investors gain an advantage in finding new outlets for investment funds, as do the mercantile establishments, in being able to devote to inventories, accounts receivable, and current operating expenses the funds released by the sale of their properties. A further advantage derived by the mercantile firms is the deductibility of all expenses in connection with the leases in the computation of federal income taxes. If a firm agrees to bear all expenses of insurance, property taxes, and maintenance, and to pay a rental over and above these costs, it may, as a rule, deduct all such items in determining its taxable income; if it were the owner of the property, it would still be permitted to deduct insurance, property taxes, and maintenance, but its deductible charge for depreciation would probably be much less than the amount of the rental. For a 20-year lease upon a building having an estimated useful life of 40 years, for example, the rental might be well over twice the allowable depreciation charge.

As with leases for which buildings are specially constructed for tenants, those originating in sale-and-leaseback arrangements usually give the tenants options to have the leases extended for additional periods or additional series of periods, for which the rental payments will be materially reduced. Since the investment institution is expected to recover the full amount of its investment with interest during the original period of a lease, some contracts have given the tenant at the expiration of this period the further option of buying back the property at what is often described as a "nominal" price. But the wisdom of such a provision is doubtful, since the Internal Revenue Service might hold the whole transaction to be an instalment sale of the property by the investment institution to the mercantile company. In so holding, it would probably limit the deductibility of the rental payments to amounts equal to the interest costs involved and what it would consider "reasonable" charges for depreciation.

Term of Leases. While leases that originate in arrangements of the kinds described in the foregoing paragraphs are invariably long-term, many storerooms, offices, and warehouses are rented for short periods—very frequently for periods not exceeding one year. As between long-term and short-term leases, advantages and disadvantages are pretty well mixed both for the landowner and the tenant.

For the landowner, a long-term lease is advantageous in assuring a steady return for a lengthy period of years, relieving him of worries about extended vacancies upon the departure of given tenants, and possibly, as indicated above, removing responsibilities for maintenance, insurance, property taxes, and so on—except for the responsibility, one might say, of making periodic inspections to see that the tenant is fulfilling his obligations in these directions. On the other hand, if the landowner contracts for a fixed rental, it may turn out within a few years to be unreasonably low because of a rise in property values in the neighborhood or a substantial increase in the general level of prices. For the tenant, a long-term lease is advantageous in establishing the right to continue operations at a given location for a lengthy period of years; additionally, should rents for property in the neighborhood generally rise during the term of the lease, he might have the advantage of occupying much cheaper quarters than his competitors. But the tenant is likely to be disadvantaged if he finds it impossible to develop a sales volume of the size originally anticipated—perhaps because of a deterioration of the neighborhood or the arrival upon the scene of one or more competing enterprises—or if the trend of rents turns out to be downward throughout the neighborhood during the period of the lease.

Short-term leases enable landowners to adjust their rents in step with changes in property values and price levels, as well as to get rid of tenants found to be unsatisfactory, but they burden them with more pressing responsibilities for the maintenance of their properties and, not infrequently, the task of seeking new tenants as others move out. For the tenant, in turn, short-term leases give freedom of movement when given locations prove to be unsatisfactory, as well as opportunity to press for reduced rentals when circumstances so warrant. In times of high-level business activity when buildings are relatively scarce, however, the short-term tenant, though fully satisfied with his rented facilities, may be forced to abandon them because of demands of the landowner for substantial increases in rental payments.

Rental Payments. Because short-term leases come up for renewal with relative frequency, they almost always provide for rental payments of fixed amounts. Many long-term leases likewise provide for fixed payments, but some stipulate varying payments, usually on the basis of the volume of sales. A lease that calls for variable payments ordinarily fixes a basic sum that is to be paid monthly, quarterly, or annually in good times and bad, with provision for an additional payment equal to a stipulated percentage of the sales volume. In this way, the landowner is assured a minimum income even in bad times—provided, of course, that the tenant remains solvent—and, in good times, he is in a position to share, as it were, in the good fortunes of his tenant. The tenant, too, is likely to be quite satisfied with such an arrangement: the burden of rental payments is reduced as sales go down, yet he is able to pay increased rents with ease when sales are booming.

Lease of Entire Assets. It is legally permissible for a business firm to lease all or almost all of its operating assets to another firm; thus, a tenant firm, at one stroke, so to say, may come into possession of a wide variety of assets, perhaps of great values, with no outlay of cash, and with only the obligation to be fully responsible for the maintenance of the assets as well as to pay a periodic rental. It is a principle of corporation law that a board of directors has no authority to lease the entire assets of the corporation they manage; hence, a lease of such scope must have the approval of the stockholders. Some state laws permit approval by a simple majority of the shares voted at a stockholders' meeting, provided that a quorum is represented, while others require larger majorities, such as two thirds or three fourths. On the other hand, the rule is that the directors of the corporation wishing to lease the entire assets of another enterprise can approve the lease without submitting it to the stockholders for their ratification.

In our day, the leasing of entire assets rarely occurs. Indeed, one can say that transactions of this kind have always been rare except in the railroad industry. In that industry, they have been of outstanding importance, many of the great railroad systems—of the East, especially—having been largely built up by the combination of large numbers of "leased lines." The Pennsylvania Railroad acquired most of its facilities west of Pittsburgh by leasing the entire assets of the old Pittsburgh, Fort Wayne, and Chicago, and the Pittsburgh, Cincinnati, Chicago, and St. Louis; while the New York Central assembled most of its facilities in the same region by leasing the operating properties of the Cleveland, Cincinnati, Chicago, and St. Louis (the "Big Four") and the Michigan Central.

The early leases of the entire assets of railroad companies, as negotiated chiefly in the last three decades of the nineteenth century, often ran for terms of 99 or 100 years, 250 years, 500 years, and up to 999 or 1,000 years. A few were perpetual. In view of such extremely long terms, a tenant company generally assumed all the current liabilities of a lessor, became guarantor of the principal and interest of the lessor's outstanding bonds, and took upon itself an obligation to pay a dividend at a stipulated rate upon the lessor's outstanding stock. The securities of the lessor, accordingly, came to be designated as "guaranteed bonds" and "guaranteed stock." Actually, then, the rental payments to be made by the tenant were the amounts needed to meet interest and principal requirements on the lessor's bonds and dividend requirements at the stipulated rate on its stock, with, perhaps, a small additional amount for the remaining operating expenses of the lessor. With such arrangements in force, a lessor company had, in effect, no remaining functions; it had to continue its existence as a party to the lease, but it tended to become a mere "shell"— a "set of books," as has often been said.

Although lessor companies are still the legal owners of a moderate proportion of the aggregate railroad properties operated by other companies, the Pennsylvania, the New York Central, and other system companies have long since bought controlling stock interests in most of the companies whose properties they originally acquired by lease. In many instances, the system companies, upon gaining control or sometime thereafter, merged the lessors with themselves, thus causing the lessors to pass out of existence as separate entities. In the remaining cases, the lessors

have been continued in existence, and operations have ostensibly continued on a lease basis, but the position of the lessors as subsidiary corporations—though still merely "sets of books"—has been more significant
than their position as owners of leased properties. Where lessor corporations have been continued in existence, their bonds have been for the
most part long since paid off, but those portions of their stock not held
by the system companies remain in the hands of investors as "guaranteed
stocks."

Instalment Buying of Machinery and Equipment. Sometimes it is
argued that the purchase by business enterprises of machinery and equipment on instalment payment contracts is much the same as leasing as a
means of economizing investment in fixed assets. As an instalment purchase requires a much smaller immediate outlay of cash than would a
cash purchase, there is no denying that, temporarily, the amount of cash
absorbed in fixed assets is reduced. Likewise, some instalment contracts,
notably equipment-trust contracts employed by our railroads to acquire
much of their rolling stock, specifically state that the periodic payments
are rents for the use of the equipment.

Nevertheless, there is a fundamental difference between a true lease
and an instalment payment contract. Under a true lease, the tenant is
not in a process of buying the property; regardless of the number and
amount of payments he has made, he is no closer to ownership than when
he made the first payment. Under an instalment payment contract, on
the other hand, the acquirer of the property is really buying it. As he is
ordinarily required to provide a substantial down payment, he makes an
immediate investment of appreciable size. Much more importantly, however, the contract stipulates that when he has made the final instalment
payment, title to the property will be transferred to him.

We may conclude, therefore, that the acquisition of machinery and
equipment on an instalment payment basis is not a means of economizing
investment in fixed assets—that it is, rather, a procedure of acquiring fixed
assets on a credit basis. It is much the same as when a firm borrows
money with which to buy fixed assets by a single payment. But borrowing money and obtaining goods on credit are means of financing, a subject with which we are not specifically concerned in this chapter. For
this reason, we may defer a consideration of instalment buying to a later
chapter.[9]

Stabilized Production

Economies in investment in fixed assets can usually be achieved by stabilizing or regularizing production, that is, by spreading it out as evenly
as possible throughout the year. This is an important fact for business
firms whose sales are heavily concentrated in one or two periods during

---

[9] See below, pp. 817–19.

the year. In Chapter 8, it was pointed out that the stabilization of production requires a much heavier investment in inventories than does production on a concentrated seasonal basis, and an illustration was presented to show why this is so; but it was there argued that reduced costs of training new employees, the greater efficiency of a satisfied work force, reduced investment in fixed assets, and other advantages might more than offset the disadvantage of the larger inventory investment.[10] In the present chapter, then, we have the occasion to stress reduction in investment in fixed assets as one such advantage.

A brief illustration should help. Let us suppose that a firm sells 20,000 units of output in each of the first nine months of the year, and 140,000 units in each of the last three months, and that $10 of investment in fixed assets is required for each unit of output per month. If the firm chooses to operate its productive facilities according to the seasonal pattern of its sales, and if it produces each month only a sufficient number of units to meet the sales of the following month, it will need an investment in fixed assets of $1.4 million. But if it decides to produce 50,000 units each month to meet its annual volume of sales of 600,000 units—stocking up excess units produced in the lean sales months to meet the large demand of the last three months of the year—it will need an investment in fixed assets of only $500,000. By way of the second alternative, the needed additional investment in inventories might offset or more than offset the economy in fixed asset investment, but that fact would not necessarily argue the undesirability of this alternative. The financial managers would have to take into consideration the relative costs of carrying fixed assets idle for much of the year—depreciation, maintenance, insurance, property taxes, and so on—and those of carrying what might be called idle inventory, with proper attention to advantages and disadvantages not directly related to investment, such as the reduction in labor turnover which stabilization would make possible.

It should be observed that stabilization of production is much more readily attainable by industries whose seasonality results from variations in demand for their products than by those where supply factors account for the seasonality. Where seasonality results from variations in the supply of raw materials, as, for example, in most branches of the canning industry, stabilized production is likely to be difficult to achieve, if not impossible. Indeed, industries whose raw materials are available only seasonally are likely to need disproportionately large investments in both fixed assets and inventories—adequate facilities to take care of the supplies quickly as they become available, as with perishable crops, and the finished goods themselves pending their gradual sale throughout the months until the next supply of raw materials becomes available. Nevertheless, a fair degree of stabilization is sometimes achieved by adding lines

---

[10] See above, pp. 155–57.

of products that can be turned out with the use of the same facilities that the original product lines require but in the latters' off seasons.

Farming Out Manufacturing Operations

Attention was also directed in Chapter 8 to the farming out of manufacturing operations as a means of economizing investment in inventories. Farming-out arrangements are also a means of economizing investment in fixed assets. The two kinds of economy tend always to go together. If a firm buys parts and subassemblies for its finished products, instead of producing them itself, it simultaneously avoids investment in inventories of raw materials needed for their production and in the machinery and other facilities that would otherwise be needed to turn them out.

The farming out of manufacturing operations is an extremely common procedure. The farming out is sometimes complete in the sense that selling firms perform no manufacturing functions whatsoever upon the products they sell under their own brands. Produced by manufacturing firms other than the sellers are many brands of notable reputation, such as the "Coldspot" line of home refrigeration equipment of Sears, Roebuck and the "Tru-Cold" line of Montgomery Ward. At the other extreme, the farming out may involve only some relatively insignificant parts of a firm's final product; and, in between, of course, dependence upon outside suppliers for parts and subassemblies is subject to a wide range of variations.

The farming out of manufacturing operations is often especially advisable for new firms. Such a firm would ordinarily have greater difficulty gathering all the money that would be needed for a complete array of productive equipment, and it must give important weight to the possibility that its products will not have the market appeal expected. A failure to develop an adequate market would be bad enough, but the situation would clearly be much worse if this failure had to be followed up with the liquidation of a large amount of fixed assets. On the other hand, a supplying firm with idle capacity could probably be readily engaged to manufacture products according to the specifications of the new firm; it would have the advantage of at least a temporary expansion in its operations, and it could hardly envisage grave consequences in the event of a subsequent loss of the manufacturing contract because of the inability of the new firm to develop a market. As new firms grow in experience and build a steady demand for their goods, they may find it advisable to absorb more and more of the manufacturing functions, but, with such experience and such a market situation, they would surely be in a much better position to do so than originally. They could probably devote a substantial proportion of their profits to investment in factory facilities, and their access to loan funds would surely be much better than it had been earlier. Nevertheless, many of our largest and most successful business organizations find reasons to continue farming-out arrangements indefinitely.

Contracting Out for Peak Loads

In some instances, manufacturing companies whose sales patterns are distinctly seasonal find it possible to depend upon other firms for assistance in taking care of peak requirements. Such a company may plan to carry on manufacturing operations at a stable pace throughout the year, producing enough monthly to meet sales requirements at the average level of the slack season, but contracting with other firms to supply it with the additional output needed to meet the peak demand. A successful program of this kind makes possible economies in investment in both fixed assets and inventories. In terms of the illustration presented on page 211, the manufacturing company might decide to produce 40,000 units monthly throughout the year; but production at that level would leave it with a deficiency of 120,000 units needed for its three peak months. Accordingly, it would contract with another firm to supply 40,000 units for each of the three months of high-level sales.

Questions

1. Compare the investment of business corporations in new plant and equipment in the period since 1946 with their additions to inventories and accounts receivable. Does the excess of the former indicate that business managers regard fixed assets as being more important than current assets? Discuss.

2. How do business managers estimate the rates of return to be earned on additional investments in fixed assets? What role does depreciation play in these estimates, if any?

3. Are prevailing interest rates important as an investment determinant only for business enterprises that would have to borrow to finance plant and equipment expansion? Explain.

4. In their estimates of probable net returns on new investment in fixed assets, to what extent, if at all, can business managers depend upon rates of interest reported as being charged by various classes of financial institutions?

5. Describe the "rough" method of estimating net rates of return on new investment in fixed assets.

6. Explain the idea of discounting as it is applied in the "exact" method of estimating rates of return on new investment in fixed assets.

7. In what ways do business managers show their caution in estimating rates of return to be earned by expanding plant and equipment?

8. How important is leasing as a means of economizing in investment in fixed assets? What classes of property are widely available for leasing and for use on a royalty basis?

9. For the tenant, what are the comparative advantages of short-term leases as against long-term leases?

10. Explain the procedure of sale-and-leaseback. What advantages does this arrangement have for the seller-tenant and for the buyer-lessor?

11. Why is the instalment buying of machinery and equipment excluded from the procedures of economizing in fixed asset investment? Is the exclusion logical? Why or why not?

12. If a firm subject to great seasonal fluctuations in the demand for its products decides to stabilize its productive operations, how will this decision be likely to affect its investment in fixed assets?

Problems

1. The managers of Boxon Corporation are considering the purchase of additional machinery and equipment that would cost $3 million. It is estimated that the new facilities would have a useful life of ten years and no scrap value. Depreciation would be taken on a straight-line basis. It is further estimated that the use of the new machinery and equipment would make possible an expansion in annual sales of $2,600,000, and that costs of production and other operating expenses, other than depreciation and interest, would increase by $2,200,000. It would be possible to borrow $3 million at a rate of interest of 5 per cent per annum, the loan to be repaid in annual instalments equal to the depreciation charges.

a) As determined by the "rough" method of computation, what annual rate of return on the new investment would be anticipated before the deduction of interest? after this deduction?

b) Would the managers of Boxon be likely to go ahead with the project? Why or why not?

c) How would you answer (*b*) if, all other figures remaining as given, the expected expansion in sales were $2,700,000?

d) How would you answer (*b*) if, all other figures remaining as given, the expected expansion in sales were $2,700,000 and the rate of interest to be paid on the borrowed money were 8 per cent?

2. The Fox-Kelly Corporation has just invested $662,425 in new machinery in the expectation that it will yield a return of 8 per cent before the deduction of interest during the four years of its expected useful life. The estimate was made by the "exact" or "scientific" method, with expanded sales income (after the deduction of expanded costs except interest and depreciation) in each of the four years expected to be $200,000, and with no scrap value anticipated for the machinery at the end of its useful life. Money to buy the machinery was borrowed at a rate of 5 per cent a year.

Assuming that depreciation is to be charged on the sinking fund basis, and that annual loan repayments equal to the depreciation charges will be made, prepare a table similar to that on page 199 to demonstrate the accuracy or inaccuracy of the 8 per cent estimate. (Show all results to the nearest dollar.)

chapter 11

FURTHER ASPECTS OF FIXED ASSET MANAGEMENT

The interests of financial managers in the management of fixed assets do not cease as soon as a given group or combination of such assets has been acquired. Financial problems with respect to fixed assets already owned continue as long as they are held. Some of these are routine in character, as, for example, providing cash on a continuing basis to keep the assets in a proper state of repair, to have them insured, and to pay property taxes upon them. Cash to meet expenses such as these, as for other operating costs, is expected to be derived in the regular course of business out of the proceeds of sales. Often, however, additional cash must be provided to increase the productive potential of existing fixed assets, that is, for "improvements and betterments." Expenditures for improvements and betterments, as, for example, the placing of partitions for the better utilization of office space or the addition of new kinds of appliances to machines to increase their capacities, do not simply conserve the existing values of assets; they increase these values.

The financial managers, moreover, must give careful thought to policies of charging depreciation to account for the gradual loss of value of fixed assets because of "wear and tear and the action of the elements." Even though a firm's depreciation charges do not require current cash outlays, they do have important bearings upon the profits it reports and the income taxes it must pay, and, in many cases also, upon its dividend policies, its credit standing, the attractiveness of its stock, its property tax liabilities, and its pricing policies.

DEPRECIATION POLICY

Objectives in Charging Depreciation

The periodic charging of depreciation may be said to have two objectives: (1) to recognize as a current cost of operation the "using up" of fixed assets in the normal course of business, and therefore to include this cost among the expenses of producing and selling, and (2) to retain in the business enterprise net asset values equal to the original values of the fixed assets. These two objectives are really so closely related as to be virtually identical; nevertheless, it may contribute to clarity to treat them separately.

Cost of Fixed Assets as Expense. In the illustrations presented in Chapter 5, we saw how depreciation charges are included among expenses of operation in the same way as are costs requiring current cash outlays. Indeed, total expenditures in the purchase of depreciable fixed assets could be immediately carried to expense accounts if their useful lives did not extend beyond one accounting period. Were a firm's accounting period, say, 20 years, and were it expected that all its original depreciable assets would wear out within that period, the firm could most conveniently charge the cost of the assets to an expense account and ignore the procedure of making a periodic charge for depreciation. Indeed, expenditures for "small tools" and other productive equipment expected to be short-lived are often treated exactly in this way. The cost of small tools, for example, is charged to an expense account, and, at the end of the accounting period, a deduction from this account is made for the value of tools still on hand, just as the inventory of office supplies at the end of the period is often deducted from the expense account for office supplies to arrive at the net expense for the period.

Only because what we call depreciable "fixed assets" are expected to have useful lives well beyond the ordinary accounting period of one year, therefore, are they treated differently from expenses. The services that are derived from direct and indirect labor and electric power are instantaneous; accordingly, there is no question that obligations incurred in obtaining these services are immediately chargeable as expenses of the current year. But the services to be derived from the use of a factory building may be expected to run for 40 years, so that it seems to be appropriate to set its cost up originally as an "asset," and then to allocate a portion of this cost on some reasonable basis to each of the years of service. Such an allocation is, of course, the depreciation charge. Were the full cost of the building to be charged to an expense account in the year of acquisition, the profits of that year would be greatly understated, and those of each of the remaining 39 years overstated. And if, on the other hand, the cost were set up in an asset account and no annual depreciation charge taken, profits would be overstated in the first 39 years, and greatly understated in the fortieth year, assuming that the valuelessness of the building were then recognized.

Retention of Net Asset Values. A second objective of charging depreciation, we say, is to retain in an enterprise net asset values equal to the original values of its fixed assets. How this works we saw in Chapter 6. In that chapter, we observed that the cash throw-off with each circular flow of current assets is equal to profits (before income taxes) plus depreciation; and we noted that the depreciation charge has the effect, as it were, of converting fixed assets into current assets. As the portion of the throw-off attributable to depreciation is not income, no part of it should be paid to the government as taxes nor to the stockholders as dividends. Hence, it is retained in the business. A further illustration may be provided to show what happens. Suppose that a corporation begins business with assets and stockholders' equity as follows:

ASSETS		LIABILITIES AND EQUITY	
Current assets	$500,000	Common stock	$900,000
Fixed assets	400,000		

Let us assume that the corporation's fixed assets are expected to have a useful life of ten years and that their residual, trade-in, or "scrap" value at the end of that period is expected to be $50,000. If, therefore, the corporation charges depreciation on the straight-line basis, the annual charge will be $35,000. The corporation has, let us say, annual sales of $600,000, and annual out-of-pocket costs of operation of $480,000. Accordingly, its annual profit before income taxes, but after deduction of the depreciation charge, is $85,000. After the payment of income taxes, the entire remaining profit, let us say, is distributed as dividends to the stockholders. But the cash throw-off is $120,000, not $85,000; hence, at the end of the first year (assuming no further acquisitions of fixed assets), the balance sheet should look like this:

ASSETS			LIABILITIES AND EQUITY	
Current assets		$535,000	Common stock	$900,000
Fixed assets	$400,000			
Less: Allowance for depreciation	35,000	365,000		

And at the end of the tenth year (with the same assumptions), it should appear as follows:

ASSETS			LIABILITIES AND EQUITY	
Current assets		$850,000	Common stock	$900,000
Fixed assets	$400,000			
Less: Allowance for depreciation	350,000	50,000		

Thus, by appropriate depreciation policy, the corporation will have conserved its assets; it will hold a total of assets at the end of the ten-year period equal to what it had in the beginning, although the composition of these assets will have changed.

Depreciation Charges and the Replacement of Fixed Assets

Nothing in the foregoing illustration indicates that the corporation would have sufficient *cash* to replace its fixed assets at the end of the ten-year period. It is true, of course, that the corporation might have set up a *replacement fund* by investing annually in high-quality securities $35,000, that is, an amount equal to the cash throw-off on account of the annual depreciation charge. In this way, it might have had available for replacement purposes at the end of the ten-year period $350,000 plus the earnings on the fund. But if the corporation had had opportunities to expand sales during this period, it might have decided to use the annual cash throw-off of $35,000 to increase its inventories and accounts receivable. In this way, it would have had no more cash on hand at the end of the period than at the beginning; and it would find it impossible to use inventories and accounts receivable as means of replacing the fixed assets. It would thus find it necessary to look elsewhere for a new source of cash to effect the replacement.

The important fact which the foregoing discussion is designed to emphasize is that the proper charging of depreciation, though it conserves a firm's assets, does not automatically provide means to replace assets of the fixed classification. If goods are sold at prices high enough to cover all expenses of operation, including depreciation charges, there will be a cash throw-off equal to the depreciation charges, but the financial managers may decide to use this cash in many different ways. Unless they specifically set it aside, as by investment in securities, their capacity to replace fixed assets when they have outlived their usefulness is by no means assured.

Replacement at Higher Prices. Thinking of depreciation charges as providing means to replace fixed assets, many business executives argue that, for income tax computations, they ought to be permitted to deduct depreciation charges based upon the replacement cost rather than the original cost of such assets. The idea is that, in or following periods of inflation, replacement assets of exactly the same qualities and capacities as the original ones will cost substantially more than did the original ones; thus depreciation charges based upon original cost must necessarily be inadequate for replacement. This plea has been much heard of in recent years, and understandably so, since the trend of prices has been generally upward—and somtimes sharply—since 1933.

Nevertheless, the federal income tax authorities persistently reject this kind of plea as being unrealistic. It is their contention that taxable profits represent the difference between income and the costs incurred in deriving that income, and they hold that costs are to be measurd by what has actually been spent in turning out products—not by what may have to be spent at some future time. The cost of labor is the bill for wages actually paid or accrued, and not what may have to be paid for wages next year; accordingly, the tax authorities argue, the proper depreciation charge is the portion of the original cost that can reasonably be allocated to the current year—and not an allocation based upon what may have to be paid for fixed assets at some future time.

Appropriations of Surplus for Replacement. Although the income tax regulations preclude, for tax purposes, the deduction of depreciation based upon the prospective replacement cost of fixed assets, the financial managers of a business firm may nevertheless think it expedient to set up a fund to provide for higher-cost replacements. To do this, they would doubtless place in the fund an amount equal to the cash throw-off from depreciation as actually charged, and add a further amount derived, it is likely, from the cash throw-off from profits. For the latter amount, they would restrict dividend payments to the stockholders, and "appropriate" for replacement purposes the profits thus withheld. In terms of the illustration given above, suppose that the corporation's managers expect the cost of replacing the fixed assets at the end of ten years to be $600,000. They want to accumulate the difference between this sum and the expected trade-in value of the existing fixed assets ($50,000), that is, $550,000, and they estimate that cash contributions to the replacement fund of $47,000 annually, with interest to be earned on fund investments, will give them the amount aimed at. Of the annual cash throw-off from profits, they could take $12,000, add it to the throw-off of $35,000 on account of depreciation, and invest the combined sum of $47,000 in the replacement fund. Income tax liabilities, of course, would not be reduced by this allocation of $12,000, but dividends to the stockholders would necessarily be curtailed by that amount. At the end of the first year, then, the balance sheet of the corporation would appear as follows:

ASSETS			LIABILITIES AND EQUITY	
Current assets......		$500,000	*Stockholders' Equity:*	
Fixed assets:			Common stock.............	$900,000
Machinery and			Surplus appropriated	
equipment......$400,000			for replacement of	
Less: Allowance			fixed assets.............	12,000
for depreciation. 35,000				
$365,000				
Replacement fund. 47,000	412,000			
Total Assets..		$912,000	Total Equity...........	$912,000

It should be observed that the withholding of profits from dividend payments, like the charging of depreciation, results in no automatic provision for the replacement of fixed assets. Just as the cash throw-off provided by depreciation charges can be invested in inventories or accounts receivable, so also can that thrown off by profits not paid out as dividends. If cash for the replacement of fixed assets must be on hand at a given time, it must be specifically put aside for that purpose—unless, of course, there are expectations that it can be drawn in from outside, as by borrowing or by the sale of additional stock. At any rate, cash thought to be "temporarily" invested in inventories and accounts receivable is likely to prove to be permanently thus invested—incapable of being pulled out at will for fixed asset purposes.

Application of Depreciation Theory

That properly allocated costs of depreciation, no less than the costs of labor, raw materials, and miscellaneous overhead items, ought to be recovered by a business establishment before profits are recognized is a theory beyond argument. But the application of the theory is not an easy matter. Difficulties abound even though one is willing to concede that, in keeping with the federal income tax regulations, depreciation should be based upon original cost.

Estimation of Useful Lives.   One difficulty is that of estimating the useful lives of the many different kinds of depreciable assets owned by operating businesses. The estimation of probable life is especially difficult in times of rapid technological development—something that seems to be a lasting and, for the most part, a highly desirable feature of present-day civilization. Certain kinds of machines owned by a business enterprise may still be in excellent operating condition but may be quite useless, because public fancy has swung away from the product they were designed to turn out, or because newly invented machines of greater efficiency can turn out the product at much lower cost. In estimating the useful lives of depreciable assets, business managers are expected to make allowance for "ordinary obsolescence"—the normal probability, one might say, that useful lives will end some years before physical deterioration would render the assets unfit for efficient use. The income tax regulations permit taxpayers to allow for such "ordinary obsolescence" in determining what their deductible charges for depreciation should be; but allowance for "extraordinary obsolescence" is permitted only when the taxpayer is able to prove to the satisfaction of the tax authorities that specific actual or impending events will have the effect of substantially shortening the lives of machines and other assets as originally estimated.

A demonstration of the great influence of estimates of useful lives upon the finances of business enterprises has recently been occurring. In the summer of 1962, the Treasury published new "guidelines" for making these estimates—in effect, authorizing the charging of depreciation on the basis of substantially shorter asset lives than had previously been permitted. As a result, many business managers immediately revised their estimates of useful lives downward, stepped up their depreciation charges, and thereby reduced their income tax liabilities, all this being revealed in tax returns. According to a survey reported by the Department of Commerce, corporations increased depreciation charges in 1962 by $2.4 billion on account of their adjustments to estimated asset lives, thereby reducing their tax bills by approximately $1,250 million.[1]

Estimation of Residual Values.   A second difficulty arises from the need of estimating what will be the residual, trade-in, or scrap value of depreciable assets at the end of their estimated useful lives. Errors in estimating this value are ordinarily not so far reaching in effect as are errors in estimating the duration of useful life, but they can be significant. In some cases, residual values are often substantial, as for trade-in allowances for delivery trucks; in others, they are less than nothing, as when the cost of removal of old buildings exceeds the value of materials that can be

---

[1] *Survey of Current Business*, July, 1963, p. 3.

salvaged. Technological developments can account for errors in estimating residual values, no less than in estimating useful lives. At the time of the acquisition of a particular kind of machine, for example, the managers of a firm may decide that it should have a good secondhand market eight years later when it will no longer be useful to the firm; but inventions and innovations in the meantime may have the effect of eliminating this secondhand market, causing the residual value to fall to a level barely better than scrap value.

Selection of Method. Still a third difficulty is that of selecting the best method of allocating over the years of estimated useful life the total amount to be charged off as depreciation. Should equal annual charges be made? Should more be charged in the early years than in later years, or the reverse of this? Should the depreciation charges be related directly to output—with high charges, therefore, in years of high-level production and much smaller ones in years of low-level activity?

Such questions are important. Differences in methods of charging depreciation will usually mean differences from year to year in the amount of profits recognized and the size of income tax and property tax liabilities, and they may also account for variations in dividends, the selling prices of products, property insurance coverage and premiums, in the market behavior of corporate stocks, and credit standing—matters to which we will give attention a little later. Although, therefore, total depreciation charges over the period of useful life may be identical regardless of the method used, any method will tend to produce operating results and financial positions from year to year different from those that other methods would produce.

Effects of Varying Estimates of Useful Life: Illustration. In order to understand more clearly the effects of differences in estimates of the useful lives of depreciable fixed assets, we should find it advantageous to employ an illustration. Let us assume that three corporations, A, B, and C, have approximately identical complements of depreciable fixed assets acquired at a cost of $1.2 million, and that each earns annually $500,000 before deductions for depreciation and federal income taxes. We may also assume that there are no applicable state income taxes. Two further assumptions are that the managers of all three corporations decide that the fixed assets will have no residual value at the expiration of their useful lives, and that they all choose to charge depreciation on the straight-line basis. But there agreement ends, for the managers have quite different opinions about the useful lives of the assets. The managers of Corporation A hit upon eight years, and accordingly set the annual depreciation charge at $150,000; the managers of Corporation B are more—should we say?—pessimistic, thinking in terms of a useful life of six years, and therefore setting the annual charge at $200,000; while those of Corporation C are decidedly optimistic, setting their sights upon a useful life of 12 years with an annual depreciation charge of $100,000. In any of the early years, then, the results of operations of the three corporations would be as follows:

	A	B	C
Net profits before depreciation and federal income taxes	$500,000	$500,000	$500,000
Less depreciation	150,000	200,000	100,000
Net profits before federal income taxes	$350,000	$300,000	$400,000
Less federal income taxes[a]	176,500	150,500	202,500
Net profits to surplus	$173,500	$149,500	$197,500

[a] Computed at the rates in effect in the year 1963.

Now, let us make the further important assumption that the lives of the depreciable assets of all three corporations will actually turn out to be eight years, and that they will have no residual value at the expiration of that period. Since Corporation A's estimate is the correct one (with the additional assumption that the straight-line method of charging depreciation is the most appropriate one for it), its annual depreciation charge, its determination of net profits, and its income tax payments must also be correct throughout the eight-year period. It is in a position to judge correctly the amount of property insurance it should carry from year to year, and it probably incurs property tax assessments in reasonable relation to the declining value of the assets. As the corporation's profits after income taxes are correctly reported, its directors presumably are not misled in making decisions about the distribution of dividends and the pricing of the corporation's products; and outsiders, it may also be presumed, are also saved from error in judging the creditworthiness of the corporation, as well as in judging the reasonableness of the market value of its stock.

For Corporation B, however, the overcharging of depreciation in the first six years of the lives of its depreciable assets results in distortions. Its directors may make unwise changes in operating policies—unwise because they are based upon faulty information. The apparent lower earning capacity of B, in comparison with A and C, may bring adverse judgments upon its directors and officers, and these may be reflected in declines in the market value of the corporation's stock and a lowering of its credit rating. The directors may decide to be less liberal than the directors of A in paying dividends—a decision which may also lead to a decline in the market value of its stock—and they may also decide, in an attempt to bring up the level of their net profits after income taxes, to raise the selling prices of their products. But the latter kind of action might only have the effect of driving customers to A and C. On the other hand, some of the distortions appear to work to B's benefit, namely, a lower level of income tax payments than A's, probably a lower level of property tax assessments, and lower insurance premiums if insurance is carried on the basis of the book values of the fixed assets. Nevertheless, the distortions do not work in the same direction for the full period of eight years; in the seventh and eighth years, their effects tend to be reversed. In those years, it is no longer permissible to deduct depreciation for income tax purposes, since the assets have been fully depreciated; hence, net profits both before and after income taxes, and the income taxes themselves, are higher than those of A. Such a result may have a favorable influence upon the market behavior of B's stock and upon its credit rating; and B's directors may be inclined to step up the level of dividend distributions, and perhaps to lower the selling prices of the corporation's products. On the other hand, the reduction of the book value of the fixed assets to zero would probably not preclude continued property tax assessments, nor, it is likely, a continued carrying of property insurance.

The position of Corporation C in the early years looks much better than that of either A or B. Although it must pay more federal income taxes than either of its fellows, its net profits after income taxes are still substantially better than theirs. Its directors may be rather generous in their dividend policies, and this may have a highly favorable effect upon the market value of its stock and its credit rating. It may have more property taxes to pay if assessors give close attention to book values, but this is problematical as assessors in many localities are notoriously inefficient. It may be tempted to lower the selling prices of its products, feeling that it can afford to do this in view of its superior profit record. But the apparent advantages cited here do not last forever. The sad day of awakening comes, shall we say, at the end of the eighth year when C's managers come to realize that they have a group of useless fixed assets still valued on the books at $400,000. Charging off this remaining book value as a loss, assuming that the assets are removed to make place for new ones, would reduce profits for the year to zero (loss of $400,000 added to the regular depreciation charge of $100,000 against net income from sales of $500,000), and this would surely make for gloomy prospects for dividends, as well as for the market value of the corporation's stock and its credit standing. The directors and officers of C might sincerely regret what now are recognized to have been overgenerous dividend payments of prior years, perhaps overpayments of property taxes and excessive property insurance coverage, and perhaps price cuts. In the eighth year, it is true, Corporation C apparently would have no federal income taxes to pay, but even about this we cannot be absolutely sure. The Internal Revenue Service might argue against the deductibility of all or a part of the loss of $400,000. The regulations say that profits and losses upon the sale or removal of fixed assets are recognized as the difference between the selling price of the assets and their cost as reduced by depreciation allowed or *allowable*. The Internal Revenue Service might contend that Corporation C did not take depreciation to the extent that it was "allowable."

Methods of Charging Depreciation: Illustration. In the foregoing illustration, our acceptance of $150,000 as the proper amount of the annual charge for depreciation was based upon the explicit assumption that the straight-line method of charging depreciation was the most appropriate one. But such an assumption, though it was useful for the purposes of the illustration, must not be regarded as of the nature of a rule. There are many good arguments in support of other methods of allocating depreciation charges. Thus, while we can continue to say that, with respect to the illustration, the proper amount of depreciation must *average* $150,000 annually during the eight years, we could hardly insist that it must be exactly that amount each year. The managers of Corporation A might have decided that charging varying amounts from year to year, though averaging $150,000, would represent a more appropriate way of handling the costs of the exhaustion of fixed assets. Had they, therefore, selected a different method, effects from year to year upon profits, income tax and property tax liabilities, property insurance coverage and premiums, dividend policies, market behavior of stock, credit rating, and pricing policies might have been somewhat different from those already described.

To see why some or all these effects would be expected to vary in relation to the method of depreciation used, let us determine what the annual depreciation charges of Corporation A would have been had it used any of three other popular methods, namely, the sum-of-the-years'-digits method, the fixed-percentage-of-diminishing-value method, and the production-units method. For the last-named method, we may assume that the productive capacity of the fixed assets for the entire period of their useful lives was estimated at 2,400,000 units of product, so that the charge per unit of output was put at 50 cents. Depreciation charges on the basis of each of the three methods would have been as follows (the straight-line charges also being shown for purposes of comparison):

YEAR	STRAIGHT-LINE METHOD 12½% PER YEAR	SUM-OF-THE-YEARS'-DIGITS METHOD	FIXED-PERCENT-AGE-OF-DIMIN-ISHING-VALUE METHOD (25%)	PRODUCTION-UNITS METHOD	
				Units Produced	Depreciation Charge
1.........	$ 150,000	$ 266,667	$ 300,000	200,000	$ 100,000
2.........	150,000	233,333	225,000	250,000	125,000
3.........	150,000	200,000	168,750	300,000	150,000
4.........	150,000	166,667	126,563	350,000	175,000
5.........	150,000	133,333	94,922	400,000	200,000
6.........	150,000	100,000	71,191	340,000	170,000
7.........	150,000	66,667	53,394	290,000	145,000
8.........	150,000	33,333	40,045	270,000	135,000
Total..	$1,200,000	$1,200,000	$1,079,865	2,400,000	$1,200,000

Although the first three of the four methods of charging depreciation illustrated here are doubtless the most popular in present-day use, the four do not exhaust the list of available procedures. For federal income tax accounting, the Internal Revenue Service permits the use of any "reasonable" method that is sanctioned by trade practices.

Computation. The mechanics of computing depreciation by the four methods used in the foregoing illustration deserve a few words of explanation. The annual charge by the straight-line procedure is found, of course, by subtracting the estimated residual value (if any) from the cost of the asset and dividing the remainder by the estimated number of years of useful life.

In applying the sum-of-the-years'-digits method, one adds 1, 2, 3, 4, and so on, for as many years as is the estimate of the asset's useful life; this total becomes the denominator of a fraction, the successive annual numerators of which are the digits themselves, beginning with the largest and running down to 1; and these successively smaller fractions are then multiplied, each in its annual turn, by the difference between original cost and residual value. Referring to the illustration, the sum of the digits 1 to 8 is 36; accordingly, depreciation for the first year was taken at $\frac{8}{36}$ of $1.2 million (no residual value having been assumed), for the second year, at $\frac{7}{36}$, for the third year, at $\frac{6}{36}$, and so on. It would be possible, obviously, to run the fractions in the opposite direction, using a depreciation rate of $\frac{1}{36}$ in the first year, $\frac{2}{36}$ in the second year, and so on; but there is little evidence that this variation is actually used by American businesses.

In the application of the fixed-percentage-of-diminishing-value method, the fixed percentage is applied to the original cost of the asset to find the depreciation charge for the first year; this amount of depreciation is subtracted from the cost to arrive at a new base to which the fixed percentage is applied to ascertain the depreciation charge for the second year; the base is then further reduced by the second depreciation charge, and, for the third year, the fixed percentage is applied against the new balance so found—and so on. For fixed assets that have estimated residual values, the fixed percentage to be used can be determined by mathematical formula; it is the percentage which, as applied over the years, will have the effect of reducing the original value to the residual value at the expiration of the period of useful life.[2] For assets having no estimated residual values, on the other hand, any relatively high fixed percentage could be used, for

---

[2] The formula is the following:

$$r = 1 - \sqrt[n]{\frac{\text{residual value}}{\text{cost}}}$$

where r is the fixed percentage, and n the number of years of useful life. For example, had a residual value of $150,000 been assumed in the illustration, we could have substituted in the formula as follows:

$$r = 1 - \sqrt[8]{\frac{150,000}{1,200,000}}$$

Solving the formula would have given us a fixed percentage of 22.8894 per cent.

even a rate of 99 per cent applied against the *diminishing values* would never bring book values down to zero. In the illustration, nevertheless, the fixed percentage was placed at 25 per cent as being wholly realistic, because federal income tax regulations limit the fixed percentage to a maximum of not more than twice what would be the straight-line depreciation rate. (The fixed percentage has generally been limited to 1½ times what would be the straight-line rate for property acquired before January 1, 1954, as well as for *used* property acquired since then.)

For the use of the production-units method, it is necessary to estimate the life of fixed assets, not in years, but in units of product they have the capacity to turn out before reaching a state of deterioration that would make their removal advisable. This estimate of total productive capacity is divided into the difference between cost and residual value to get a rate of depreciation per unit of output. Actual output in a year or other period of time is then multiplied by the computed rate to find the depreciation charge for that period. Sometimes this method is rearranged, as one might say, to make it a production-hours method. The procedure is the same, except that the original estimate of useful life is in terms of the probable total hours of operation (as of machines) rather than in terms of probable total product.

Comparison of Methods. The substantial differences in the amounts of depreciation chargeable from year to year on the basis of the four methods of our illustration indicate that the selection of methods is a matter of considerable importance. The financial managers of business concerns must study the pros and cons of each method. When they consider the probable effects of their selection of methods upon profits, income taxes, property taxes, pricing policies, and so on, they will doubtless conclude that decisions must be arrived at only after painstaking analysis.

A strong argument in favor of the sum-of-the-years'-digits and the fixed-percentage-of-diminishing-value methods is that heavy charges for depreciation should be concentrated in the early years of useful life because expenses for repairs and maintenance are likely to be relatively small in those years; in this way, the costs of using depreciable fixed assets tend, at least roughly, to be equalized annually over the course of their lives. Although the Internal Revenue Service had "recognized" the two methods for many years, new interest in them was generated by "liberalized" provisions of the Revenue Act of 1954 specifically authorizing their use for *new* tangible depreciable assets acquired after December 31, 1953. Observers have generally agreed that these provisions of the tax legislation of 1954 initiated a strong swing in the direction of the two methods. A disadvantage of the fixed-percentage-of-diminishing-value method is that it may result in total depreciation charges for the period of useful life somewhat less than determinable by other methods. The reason for this was indicated previously, namely, that the "fixed percentage" is limited by law to a maximum of twice what the rate of straight-line depreciation would be. But, in ordinary circumstances, the disadvantage is not likely to be a serious one. Referring again to our illustration, the fixed assets would still have a book value of $120,135 at the end of the eighth year, if they had been depreciated on the fixed-percentage basis; but were they really value-less at that time, the corporation would be able to deduct the write-off of $120,135 in determining the amount of its taxable income.

An important advantage claimed for the production-units or production-hours method is that depreciation charges vary from year to year accord-ing to the volume of operations: in periods of low income, these charges are low, and in periods of high income, they are relatively high. Such a result should be promotive of stability in annual profits. An objection to this method is that depreciation—certainly in the sense of "ordinary obso-lescence"—goes on as rapidly in periods of low production or idleness as in periods of high production. Moreover, the Internal Revenue Service has not shown much enthusiasm for this method, holding that it is impos-sible to arrive at reasonable estimates of the lifetime productive capacities of most kinds of fixed assets.

Undoubtedly the straight-line method continues to be a highly popular means of computing depreciation charges despite the concession of the Revenue Act of 1954 toward the sum-of-the-years'-digits and the fixed-percentage methods. The straight-line method has the outstanding merit of simplicity; it is easily understood and applied; and its use has generally been approved without question by the federal revenue authorities. Its principal weakness appears to be the placing of heavier burdens upon later years, in the sense that depreciation charges plus maintenance costs are almost sure to be heavier in those years than in the early years of useful life.

For one class of fixed assets, the financial managers of a business con-cern may judge one method of charging depreciation to be the best, and for other classes, other methods. They may pick and choose, perhaps coming to a decision to use two or three or even four or more methods, each for a different class of fixed assets. They may even adopt different methods for different asset units within a given class, as by using the straight-line method for some machines, and the fixed-percentage method for others. Under federal tax regulations, at any rate, the taxpayer is under no obligation to use a uniform method—the requirements are only that the results of the methods chosen, whether one or more, are reason-able in the sense of precluding excessive charges against income, and that permission be obtained in advance (in most instances) for changes from one method to another.

Preference for Rapid Depreciation

A large majority of business managers doubtless prefer to charge off the value of depreciable fixed assets, via the depreciation route, at a rapid pace. They are inclined to underestimate periods of useful life as well as residual values. They are likely to turn more and more to the sum-of-the-years'-digits and the fixed-percentage-of-diminishing-value methods further to "accelerate" their depreciation charges. Inclinations of these kinds are strongest, of course, in periods of prosperity and rising prices; but they do not seriously weaken in periods of less active business, as long as sales proceeds are sufficient to cover the depreciation charges together with all other expenses.

The fear that fixed assets will become obsolete much more quickly than the "ordinary obsolescence" component of depreciation charges allows for is probably the most compelling reason for preferences for speedy write-offs. In times of rapid technological advance, business managers in almost any field of industry can hardly escape fears that, within a short period of time, inventions and innovations of a revolutionary character will make obsolete their well-equipped and efficient factories. Constantly are they and we being told that the development of atomic power for peacetime use, the "automation" of industrial processes, and other innovations will work an industrial transformation of unprecedented scope.

The fact that expenses for repairs and maintenance are generally low in the early years of the lives of fixed assets and tend to mount substantially in later years is a second reason for the acceleration of depreciation charges. Overall annual costs in the use of fixed assets, it is held, can be pushed in the direction of uniformity by coupling relatively high depreciation charges with the low costs of repairs and maintenance in the early years, and by joining relatively low charges for depreciation to the much higher expenses for repairs and maintenance in the later years.

Rising prices also encourage rapid write-offs. In periods during which selling prices rise and depreciation and other fixed charges remain unchanged, profit margins generally expand. But business managers are inclined to look upon the expansion in profit margins as largely illusory. Anticipating much higher prices for the replacement of their depreciable assets, they are likely to conclude that depreciation charges based on original cost, unless accelerated in some way, give a distorted view of profitability.

A further reason for a preference for rapid write-offs of fixed asset values is the conviction of many business managers that highly desirable replacements are unlikely to be opposed by fellow managers if much of the value of the assets to be replaced has already been written off. To understand this proposition, we may refer to the illustration on page 224. Suppose that at the end of the fifth year the production managers of Corporation A strongly advise the replacement of the machinery on the grounds that much more efficient machines are now available and that, accordingly, the retention of the old machines will gravely weaken the corporation's competitive position. If the corporation had been using the straight-line method of charging depreciation, its write-offs to the end of the fifth year would have amounted to $750,000, but if, say, the sum-of-the-years'-digits method had been used, total write-offs would have amounted to $1 million. With the straight-line method in use, then, the replacement would mean a loss of $450,000 upon the old machines, but with the sum-of-the-years'-digits method, a loss of only $200,000 (disregarding the possibility of a residual value at the end of the fifth year, though none was anticipated for the end of the eighth year). Thus, the board of directors and top financial executives might be much more amenable to the recommendation of the production managers in the latter circumstances than in the former.

Preferences for rapid write-offs can be attributed, finally, to the high rates of federal corporation income taxes (as well as to the high personal income tax rates that apply to the profits derived by many owners of unincorporated businesses). High rates of income taxation undoubtedly promote a zealous and continuous effort on the part of taxpayers to try to take advantage of every possible deduction. Because depreciation charges are only estimated expenses, there is a "natural" tendency, one might say, to make the estimates as high as the Internal Revenue Service will allow. One can argue that the reduction in the tax bill this year on account of high depreciation charges will be offset by higher tax liabilities in later years when depreciation charges must necessarily be lower. But it is not easy to convince the business manager that things will work out that way. In rebuttal, he may say that tax rates in later years may be lower than they are at the present time; and he may add that, even if the rates are not reduced, the advantage of a tax saving this year of a given amount is by no means offset by additional tax liability of the same amount due some years hence, since, in the intervening period, he can use the amount of the saving in expanding the operations and the profits of his business.

REPLACEMENT POLICY

Replacements at Expiration of Useful Life

Even though the useful life and the residual values of fixed assets turn out to be pretty close to the original estimates, and cash is or can be made available for their replacement, the decision as to replacement requires as much care in investigation as does an original decision to invest. Replacement cannot be looked upon simply as a matter of routine. On the contrary, competent financial managers will consider all reasonable alternative uses of cash; they will be on the lookout for alternative uses that promise rates of return exceeding the rate that the replacement would probably provide.

In most cases, of course, it will be quickly apparent that no alternative uses could come close to the replacements in estimated levels of profitability—this conclusion appears to be a reasonable one, if we can assume that most original decisions to invest in fixed assets are wise ones! In other cases, however, changes in circumstances since the time of original investment make anticipated rates of return on certain alternative uses of cash much greater than to be expected through replacement. The anticipation of a rapidly expanding sales volume might lead to a decision to reserve for investment in inventories and accounts receivable cash that otherwise would be spent for fixed asset replacement, and, with it, therefore, a decision to rent fixed facilities instead of buying them. Likewise, a level of prices for replacements much higher than originally paid might lead to a decision that manufacturing operations hitherto undertaken by a firm would better be farmed out in the future to other enterprises.

Replacements to Increase Efficiency

Often financial managers run into special problems of replacement well before the expiration of the originally estimated useful lives of certain kinds of their fixed assets. Such problems are likely to be concerned especially with factory machinery and equipment, as when newly developed machines have productive features far superior to those of machines already in use. Suppose, for example, that a corporation owns a group of machines carried on its books at the depreciated value of $2 million. According to its original estimates, the machines were to have an additional useful life of five years and a residual value at the end of that period of $250,000. But now much more efficient machines appear on the market, and a replacement group could be bought by the corporation for $6 million. Having an estimated life of ten years and an estimated residual value of $400,000, the new machines will turn out exactly the same product as the old; but their greater efficiency means that, in their use, labor, maintenance, power, spoilage, and other costs per unit of output will be substantially less than in the use of the old machines. The appearance of the new machines has caused the secondhand value of the old to fall, say, to $800,000, and their prospective residual value at the end of five years, to $100,000. Thus the corporation's managers face a difficult decision. Assuming cash to be available, shall they buy a group of new machines to gain immediate advantage of the lower production costs they would make possible, at the same time accepting a loss of $1.2 million on the sale of the old machines, or shall they continue with the old machines to the end of the period of their useful lives? Taking the loss might wipe out the corporation's operating profits for the year, or even for a longer period of time, and this fact might lead the financial managers to decide rather quickly not to make the replacement.

A more intelligent approach would be to compare the probable annual costs of output with the old machines continued in use with estimations of the annual costs that would be incurred should the new machines be purchased. Assuming estimated annual manufacturing costs (other than depreciation and interest) to be $5.2 million and $4.5 million respectively, and assuming that interest is to be recognized as a cost at the rate of 6 per cent a year, a "rough" comparison could be worked out as follows:

	Old Machines Retained	*New Machines Acquired*
Manufacturing costs other than depreciation and interest...	$5,200,000	$4,500,000
Depreciation (on straight-line basis)—		
Old: $1,900,000÷5..................................	380,000	
New: $5,600,000÷10...............................		560,000
Interest on average investment in the machines—		
Old: $1,240,000×.06ᵃ................................	74,400	
New: $3,480,000×.06...............................		208,800
Estimated annual total costs of production................	$5,654,400	$5,268,800

ᵃ Placing the residual value at $100,000, so that the decline in investment (like depreciation) amounts to $380,000 each year.

The comparison would strongly indicate the advisability of acquiring the new machines, for the annual saving in costs of $385,600 would suffice to offset the loss on the sale of the old machines in a period of less than four years.[3]

In the opinion of many financial managers, depreciation and interest charges on old assets should be included in a comparison of the kind set out above on the basis of their current secondhand value rather than upon the basis of their book value. Their reasoning is that, when such second-hand value is less than book value, depreciation charges *in the past* (in the sense here, definitely, of obsolescence) have simply been understated, and that, therefore, the book value is quite fictitious. Being fictitious, it should be ignored in cost comparisons *for the future*. In an application of this doctrine, the comparison would work out as follows:

	Old Machines Retained	*New Machines Acquired*
Manufacturing costs other than depreciation and interest...	$5,200,000	$4,500,000
Depreciation (on straight-line basis)—		
Old: $700,000÷5..................................	140,000	
New: $5,600,000÷10...............................		560,000
Interest on average investment in the machines—		
Old: $520,000×.06................................	31,200	
New: $3,480,000×.06...............................		208,800
Estimated annual total costs of production................	$5,371,200	$5,268,800

Those who prefer this basis of comparison argue that the comparison it-self gives the final answer as to the desirability of replacement: regardless of what the loss might be upon the disposal of old facilities, if estimated annual costs with the use of new facilities are lower—even if only moder-

[3] A comparison on the basis of applying compound discount formulas to find depreciation and interest charges—that is, applying the procedure illustrated on page 198 —would give a net difference in annual total costs of $372,192, an amount still quite sufficient, of course, to prove the wisdom of acquiring the new machines.

ately—than estimated for the use of old facilities, the substitution should unquestionably be made.[4]

Disposal of Superfluous Fixed Assets

Sometimes corporation managers are reluctant to dispose of fixed assets that have reached the end of their useful lives. The market for a firm's products may have contracted, and it may therefore no longer need as many machines as before, but the superfluous machines may be kept in place indefinitely in the hope that the market may some day revive. Or a firm, while putting new machines into operation at the normal replacement time, may hold on to the old ones in the expectation of pressing them into service to help take care of rush orders and to maintain production should breakdowns in the newer facilities occur.

In some instances, subsequent events prove the soundness of decisions to retain old assets; but very often the retention turns out to be a continuous source of expense without commensurate advantages. The space occupied by the superfluous facilities could be better used for other purposes, and expenditures for property taxes, insurance, and maintenance simply encroach upon the income derived from the use of active facilities. Moreover, almost all secondhand values fall continually with the passing of time, so that the amount of cash to be derived from sale may be substantially reduced by delay. Accordingly, business firms are often advised to make periodic surveys of their fixed asset holdings to weed out items that have come to be burdens rather than blessings.

CAPITALIZATION POLICY

Capitalization versus Expense

In the establishment of policies for fixed asset management, standards must be set to distinguish between expenditures that add to the value of fixed assets and those that simply keep these assets in good operating condition. Whether an expenditure is to be "capitalized," that is, added to the value of the fixed asset, or charged to an expense account depends upon its effects on the life and efficiency of the asset. Thus we distinguish additions, replacements, and betterments, as adding to the value of assets, from expenditures for repairs and maintenance, as only sustaining the capacity of assets to remain in ordinary operation.

In the normal course of business activity, it is usually easy to recognize additions and replacements; rarely, therefore, are they confused with re-

---

[4] Many would prefer to reach a conclusion of this kind only when a significant saving in costs is demonstrated through the use of compound discount or other so-called "scientific" formulas. In the illustrative case, the compound discount method would reveal an annual saving of $87,316, appreciably less than the $102,400 found by the use of the "rough" method, but still quite large enough to argue the advisability of buying the new machines.

pairs and maintenance. Knocking out a wall of a factory building and joining thereto a new structure for additional operating space, and the installation of newly purchased machines in this space, obviously represent additions to plant and equipment. Likewise, one is not likely to question placing in the fixed asset accounts the purchase price of new machines installed as replacements for old ones (provided, of course, that the book value of the old machines is removed as they are traded in, sold in the secondhand market, or scrapped).

But betterments—or improvements, as they are also called—are often difficult to distinguish from repairs and maintenance. The customary standard for making the distinction is that betterments increase the productive capacity of fixed assets beyond their original capacity or extend their useful lives beyond the original estimates. Nevertheless, the standard is difficult to apply, chiefly because certain kinds of expenditures often have elements of both betterments and repairs and maintenance. The replacement of leaking iron pipe with new sections of the same kind of pipe is surely a repair, but if the replacement is made with copper pipe, an element of betterment is obviously added. Similarly, the rewiring of burned-out motors is surely to be treated as a repair, but a betterment is involved if worn-out motors attached to certain kinds of machines are replaced with motors of higher horsepower rating. Appropriately, in most cases of these kinds where betterments are involved, a portion of the expenditures should be added to the asset accounts and the remaining portion should be charged to expense.

Consequences of Errors in Capitalization

If expenditures for additions, replacements, and betterments are charged immediately to expense accounts, the consequences are much the same as result from the overcharging of depreciation; and if expenditures that should be charged as repairs and maintenance are added to asset accounts, the consequences are similar to those that result from the undercharging of depreciation. In the long run, things will tend to come out even. In the first case, expenses will be overstated in the current year, but understated in subsequent years as there will be no charges for depreciation upon the additions, replacements, and betterments; and in the second case, expenses will be understated in the first year, but in subsequent years the expenditures that should have been taken up as repairs and maintenance will be gradually charged off by way of depreciation deductions.

But the consequences may be bad precisely because expenses—whether repairs and maintenance or depreciation—are not properly allocated to the years to which they belong, and even though, in the long run, total charges to expense accounts may be the same as if no errors had been made. In a year in which expenses are overstated, as by charging additions, replacements, and betterments to expense accounts, profits are reduced and the directors may decide to reduce dividend payments; one or both of these results may cause a decline in the market value of the corporation's stock as well as some deterioration in its credit rating. The lowered rate of return on stockholders' investment may tempt the managers of the corporation to raise the selling prices of its products, but this action may injure it competitively. On the other hand, there may be some consolation in lowered income tax and property tax liabilities. It is true that such advantages and disadvantages are likely to be reversed in later years as a result of a counterbalancing understatement of expenses; but this does not necessarily mean that the errors in capitalization policy would have no lasting harmful effects. The financial managers would be basing their decisions throughout upon distorted data, and the possibilities are great that some of these decisions would thus be rendered unwise.

Tendencies toward Undercapitalization

The possibilities of serious distortions in the asset and income positions of corporations as a result of errors (whether deliberate or inadvertent) in the treatment of addition, replacements, betterments, repairs, and maintenance are substantially reduced by the vigilance of the federal income tax authorities. They can be expected to assess corporations for additional taxes when their returns indicate that expenditures that should have been added to assets were, instead, deducted as expenses—or when this information is subsequently revealed in tax audits of the corporations' books. If it is subjected to an additional assessment in this way, a corporation will surely take immediate steps to correct its own books, that is, by capitalizing the expenditures, so that, in subsequent years, it will be permitted to write them off by way of depreciation charges.

But there are many situations, especially in the matter of betterments, as we have seen, where it is difficult to say precisely how much should be added to asset accounts and how much charged to expense accounts. In such doubtful situations, most corporate managements undoubtedly favor charging expense for the maximum amount that will be permitted by the tax authorities. Allowable deductions are zealously sought in periods of high tax rates; at present federal income tax rates on corporations, any deduction produces a "tax saving" equal to 52 per cent of the deduction, assuming the corporation to have remaining taxable income in excess of $25,000. Although a deduction this year for expenditures related to fixed assets means smaller deductions or none at all in future years, it may be that tax rates will be lower later on. Regardless of possibilities of a lowering of rates, moreover, most corporate taxpayers are quite happy to defer tax payments, even though the total amounts to be paid over the years are not thereby reduced. They have a good theoretical reason for so choosing, since the present (discounted) value of a future tax payment is less than an immediate payment of the same amount.

Other reasons for favoring the immediate deduction of expenditures related to fixed assets to the maximum extent permitted by the federal tax authorities are similar to the reasons discussed previously for favoring "accelerated" depreciation. Accordingly, a brief restatement at this point should suffice. In periods of rising prices, corporate managers are inclined to look upon increases in their profit margins as being largely illusory. The margins will come down again, they expect, when it becomes necessary to replace low-cost fixed assets with high-cost ones; hence, it is realistic, at once, to seek deductible expenditures that will hold down the profit figures. All the more is this reasonable, they are likely to conclude, because holding down the level of reported profits does not reduce the amount of cash throw-offs. Fear of extraordinary obsolescence—fear, that is, that depreciation charges with their allowance only for "ordinary" obsolescence are inadequate—also seems to make wise additional deductions, wherever they can be found, to supplement the depreciation charges. Replacement of fixed assets before the expiration of their useful lives, as originally estimated, is also less likely to be impeded if the fixed asset accounts have not been substantially increased by outlays for betterments—if, in other words, it has been possible to charge at least a portion of such outlays to expense accounts at the time incurred. Finally, the expectation of increased expenses for the repair and maintenance of fixed assets as they grow older may seem to justify charging off as current expenses as many outlays as the law and regulations can be stretched to allow, even though some of these may have the complexion of betterments.

TESTING FIXED ASSET INVESTMENT POLICIES

Ratio of Fixed Assets to Net Sales

It has often been said that the ownership of expensive fixed assets is, in itself, of no advantage to business enterprises. Only if a reasonable rate of return is earned upon the expensive fixed assets is the ownership justified. A firm that is able to develop a sales volume of $1.2 million while employing fixed assets worth $300,000 (together with current assets, of course) would normally be expected to be more profitable than one in the same line of business having a sales volume of approximately the same figure but using fixed assets worth $400,000.

In the light of this kind of reasoning, ratios of fixed assets to net sales are often computed as means of testing the soundness of fixed asset investment policies. Such a ratio is found by dividing the average investment in fixed assets by the net sales for the year. The sum of the investment as revealed in the accounting records at the beginning and end of the year divided by 2 usually suffices for the figure for average investment. However, it is customary to exclude fixed assets not used in the ordinary course of business, as, for example, a factory building that a manufacturing corporation rents to another manufacturer. Investment in fixed assets, it should be added, is the original value less all depreciation charged against the assets from the time of acquisition.

As thus computed, the ratio of fixed assets to sales indicates how many dollars or cents have been invested in fixed assets to produce one dollar of sales. In terms of the figures cited above, the first firm has an investment in fixed assets of 25 cents for each dollar of sales, whereas the second has an investment of 33⅓ cents. Fixed asset ratios of this kind show wide variations from industry to industry. In the railroad and public utility industries, a dollar or more of fixed assets is generally needed for each dollar of sales, and, on the other hand, in most retail trade lines, investment in fixed assets ordinarily amounts to only a minor fraction of the sales volume. In the heavy-goods manufacturing industries—basic iron and steel, machinery manufacture, the manufacture of transportation equipment, and so on—the ratio of fixed assets to sales tends to be relatively high in comparison with that of enterprises engaged in light manufacturing operations.

As with other ratios, ratios of fixed assets to net sales have little significance individually; only when they can be used for comparisons in like situations are they useful for testing purposes. But even comparisons in like situations must be interpreted with caution. The fact that a given firm's ratio is out of line with what it was in earlier years or with what is being currently shown by competing firms is ordinarily to be taken as proof of nothing; it simply indicates that an investigation ought to be made to account for the difference, with praise or blame to be withheld pending the results of the investigation. A competing firm may have a lower ratio because it rents much of its equipment. The firm making the analysis may have an extraordinarily high ratio on account of the installation of new kinds of laborsaving equipment; but the equipment, by making possible a substantial reduction in costs, may give it a strong position in meeting competition. In a similar way, ratios may differ from firm to firm because of differences in methods of charging depreciation; and for the individual firm, they may decline from year to year for no other reason than that annual depreciation charges constantly reduce the book value of fixed asset investment.

Ratio of Fixed Assets to Net Profits

Since the computation of ratios in relation to fixed assets is designed to test the profitability of investment in these assets, it appears that a ratio of such assets to net profits (before the deduction of income taxes) is a better testing device than the ratio to net sales. A ratio of fixed assets to sales ignores operating costs, but a ratio of fixed assets to net profits necessarily allows for differences in costs, since net profits are found by subtracting operating costs from sales income. If certain assets are excluded from the computation because they are not used in the ordinary course of business, logic requires that the net income derived from them be excluded from the figure for net profits. The profitability of these assets in relation to the net income they produce can then, of course, be separately judged.

The firm that installed new kinds of laborsaving machinery may have fixed assets of, say, $500,000 and annual sales of $1 million whereas its principal competitor, lacking such machinery, may have an equal sales volume but total fixed assets of only $250,000. The undiscriminating analyst might hastily conclude that the first firm had "overinvested" in fixed assets since it has 50 cents in fixed assets for every dollar of sales, while its competitor has an investment in fixed assets of only 25 cents per dollar of sales. But if the first firm's total operating expenses amount to $800,000 while those of the second amount to $950,000—the former figure being much lower than the latter chiefly because of reduced labor costs—the first firm would appear to have invested wisely. The comparative ratios of fixed assets to net profits, $2.50 and $5.00, respectively, would thus tend to lead more directly to a sound conclusion than would a comparison of ratios of fixed assets to sales.

Ratios of Operating Assets to Net Sales and Net Profits

As a testing device, the ratio of total operating assets—that is, the total of both current and fixed assets used in the ordinary course of business—to net sales has been preferred by many analysts to the fixed-assets-to-sales ratio. The operating-asset ratio is said to be superior because it indicates the efficiency with which a firm uses all its assets in generating a given sales volume, and not simply fixed assets alone. But there appears to be no good argument for the exclusive use of one type of ratio or the other; both types can easily be computed, and perhaps one will reveal information worthy of further analysis that the other does not reveal.

A ratio of operating assets to net sales suffers from the same defect as the fixed-asset-to-sales ratio, since it ignores varying levels of operating expenses. For this reason, a ratio of operating assets to net profits should be more reliable as a testing device than a ratio to net sales.

Questions

1. What justification is there for saying that the cost of fixed assets is a business operating expense? If there is justification, does it apply to all classes of fixed assets? Explain.

2. Why does the charging of depreciation have the effect of retaining in an enterprise net asset values equal to the original values of its depreciable fixed assets? Is this always the result? Why or why not?

3. Support or attack this proposition: A firm that charges depreciation in reasonable amounts during the useful lives of its fixed assets will have no financial difficulty in replacing them at the appropriate time.

4. Under what circumstances might it be advisable to "appropriate" surplus for the replacement of fixed assets? What would be the effect of the "appropriation"?

5. What are the principal sources of difficulty in determining how much depreciation a firm should charge?

6. What is harmful about overcharging depreciation in the early years of useful life? Will not this be balanced by lower charges in later years? Explain.

7. Explain the techniques of computing depreciation by each of the following methods: straight-line, sum-of-the-years'-digits, fixed-percentage-of-diminishing-value, and production-units.

8. Why are income tax considerations important in the selection of methods of charging depreciation? In this regard, what was the significance of the Treasury's new "guidelines" published in 1962?

9. Why do business managers generally favor rapid write-offs of the value of their fixed assets by way of depreciation charges?

10. If an original investment in fixed assets was wise, a reinvestment at the expiration of their useful lives must also be wise. Do you agree? Why or why not?

11. Explain the "rough" mathematical procedure by which business managers might decide the advisability of replacing existing machines having many remaining years of useful life with new machines of greater efficiency.

12. Why is the distinction between repairs and maintenance and additions and betterments important in fixed asset management?

13. What is supposed to be revealed by computing ratios of fixed assets to sales, fixed assets to net profits, and operating assets to net profits? What are the weaknesses of these ratios?

Problems

1. When buying a group of machines at a cost of $1,800,000, the managers of the Taylor Steel Company estimated that they would have a useful life of eight years and a scrap value of $200,000. They decided to charge depreciation on the sum-of-the-years'-digits basis. As it turned out, the machines had a useful life of only six years and a scrap value of only $100,000.

Assuming that the federal income tax rate of 52 per cent was applicable to the income against which depreciation was charged, and that it would still have been applicable had depreciation been charged on a six-year basis, draw up a table to show how the corporation's tax obligations and net income after tax were distorted during the six years because of the errors in estimating useful life and scrap value.

2. The financial managers of Belton, Inc., want to minimize its federal corporation income tax obligations for the next few years. They have just bought some factory machinery at a cost of $800,000, and, according to the Treasury's guidelines, the machinery may be depreciated over a period of five years. It is estimated that the scrap value will be $50,000. To achieve their objective, should they use the sum-of-the-years'-digits or the fixed-percentage-of-diminishing-value method (the latter at 40 per cent—twice what the straight-line rate would be)? Assume that income differentials due to differences in depreciation charges would involve the 52 per cent federal tax rate.

3. The Lee Plastics Co., Inc., is considering the desirability of replacing some of its machinery with new machines that incorporate important cost-saving improvements. The costs of producing the corporation's output with the existing machines, excluding depreciation and allowances for interest, have averaged $7 million a year, and it is estimated that these costs for output of the same volume would be cut to $6,500,000 should the new machines be acquired. The old machines are carried on the books at a depreciated value of $3,200,000, and their remaining useful life is estimated at six years. Originally, they were expected to have a residual value of $400,000, but the appearance of the new machines on the market has reduced their immediate resale or trade-in value to $1 million and their expected residual value at the end of six years to $80,000.

The new machines would cost $8 million and would have estimated useful lives of ten years and an estimated residual value of $600,000.

Should the corporation proceed with the replacement? Prepare analyses as on pages 230–32 to support your position. Assume that depreciation would be charged on the new machines, as on the old, on the straight-line basis, and that an interest rate of 6 per cent should be used where appropriate.

Part IV

BUDGETING
AND CONTROL

chapter 12

FORECASTING CASH FLOWS

For the successful management of the finances of a business enterprise, something is needed in addition to a thorough knowledge of the circular flow of cash and of the kinds of conditions and circumstances that affect it, as discussed in Chapters 5–7, the arrival at sound decisions as to asset-management policies, as discussed in Chapters 8–11, and, of course, a high order of managerial competence. A fourth ingredient must be added. This ingredient may be described as *financial forecasting*. The financial managers of an enterprise must be in a position at all times to anticipate with reasonable closeness how much cash will flow in from month to month within a period of moderate length, such as a year, and what the cash requirements will be from month to month within the same period. Careful forecasts of cash flows make possible the avoidance of many difficulties and, indeed, serious financial embarrassment. Probable sources of difficulty can often be skirted or completely eliminated by appropriate prompt adjustments in operating policies. Forecasts indicate the limits within which the financial managers must make their decisions for the forecast period.

The determination of asset-management policies, financial forecasting, and advance decisions to borrow or to sell additional stock, to repay debt or to retire stock, and to pay dividends at specific times—all these are phases of *financial planning*, without which no business can be operated efficiently. These phases of planning are obviously quite closely inter-related. If a forecast indicates, for example, that a shortage of cash will develop at a certain time within the coming year, immediate plans may be made to borrow or to sell additional stock to supplement the regular cash inflow from operations. If prospects are slim for thus supplementing the cash flow, certain changes in asset-management policies may be decided upon well in advance so that the threatened shortage of cash will not occur. Thus, the introduction of a new line of products or the purchase of additional factory facilities, as originally planned for within the coming year, may have to be deferred to a later period. Again, a financial forecast may indicate that it would be quite convenient to distribute a cash dividend at certain times but not at others, or that any distribution of cash dividends within the year would subject the cash account to a dangerous strain.

Most important among the instruments used in financial forecasting are *budgets*. Many kinds of budgets may be prepared by the individual firm, but those of particular interest to its financial managers are cash and fixed asset budgets. In the discussion of this chapter and the following one, therefore, major attention will be directed to these two classes of budgets; nevertheless, it should be helpful to begin the discussion with a broad view of budgets, budgetary systems, and budgetary control.

BUDGETS IN GENERAL

Nature of Budgets

As used by business enterprises, a budget is a detailed estimate in numerical terms of the scale of operations in some phase of activity in some future period. Budgets are always forecasts of future activity, as contrasted with statements of manufacturing costs, income statements, and other similar statements which are reports upon what has happened in the past. Budgets are detailed. All kinds of anticipated transactions within the area of business activity surveyed must be separately accounted for, and, as a rule, the volume of each kind of transaction for each month or for some other series of short periods within the longer forecast period must be separately estimated. Budgets are prepared in numerical terms, although not necessarily in terms of dollars and cents. Manufacturing expense and selling expense budgets will surely be in terms of dollars and cents, but sales and production budgets, for example, may be in terms of units of production, and direct labor budgets, in terms of hours of employment.

Budget Periods and Breakdowns

In business budgets, the forecast period is most commonly one year, with a monthly breakdown within that period. In some instances, the budget is made, as it were, continuous; this is done by extending the forecast by one month as the end of each month of actual operations approaches. After a start has been made with a year's forecast, estimates for January of next year are added toward the end of January of this year, estimates for February of next year toward the end of February of this year, and so on; in this way, a forecast for a full year is always available. In other instances, monthly breakdowns are made for only three to six months, with quarterly figures for the remainder of the year; and in still others, the breakdowns are in terms of weekly, biweekly, or ten-day periods for the months immediately ahead or possibly for the entire year. Obviously, many other variations are possible.

Some budgets are made on a long-range basis. Especially do business managers think it important to have a "long view" of requirements for additional buildings, machinery and equipment, and other fixed facilities.

Expenditures for research represent another area for which long-term forecasts are often thought desirable. For phases of activity such as these, budgets for five or ten years or even for longer periods are commonly prepared. Accordingly, business managers are often able to discuss their "long-range expansion plans" with a surprising amount of detail about when and how various steps are to be taken.

Budgets as Instruments of Control

Although budgets were introduced above as devices for business planning, they must be recognized as being, in addition, important instruments of control. If properly prepared, they are estimates of what is reasonably attainable—not of what could be attained in the best possible circumstances. It is expected that strong efforts will be exerted to reach projected goals, but there is no expectation that superhuman powers will be available and that all contingencies will turn out favorably. Budgets are sound only if possibilities of unfavorable developments in general business activity and in the affairs of the firm itself, as well as expectations of favorable developments, are given proper weight.

If, therefore, budgets are forecasts of attainable results, responsibility for their achievement can be assigned to the production, sales, and financial executives. All the more is this true if, as is customary, these executives are given a large share of authority in deciding what the budgets are to contain with respect to the operations over which they have jurisdiction. In conferences at various managerial levels, the original estimates of what is reasonably attainable may be changed, but ordinarily only after the executives have agreed on the soundness of the substitute figures. Accordingly, it is only after the operating executives have had their say, as it were, that the budgets are approved by the board of directors as a plan of operation for the forecast period. Depending upon their individual jurisdictions, therefore, the operating executives can be called upon to give an account of their stewardship if the volume of sales turns out to be substantially less than budgeted, if production fails to keep pace with the volume called for in the budget, if direct labor hours substantially exceed the number forecast for the budgeted volume of output, if selling expenses are markedly greater than the budget figure for a certain level of activity, or if, at certain times within the forecast year, cash is not available to meet obligations as they come due.

Control through the use of budgets is often said to be based upon analyses of variances. When actual results of operations are reasonably close to the budget estimates, the presumption is strong that managerial authority is being exercised efficiently. Although there is no reason for complacency, in the sense of neglecting to seek means of further improvement, the outcome can hardly be other than praiseworthy. On the other hand, a substantial falling short of actual results from those projected always justifies a search for causes followed by a fixing of responsibility, unless, perhaps, the variances are found to have resulted from outside developments that could not have been foreseen.

Fixed and Variable Budgets

In the preparation of budgets, a single set of figures may be selected in the expectation that operations during the forecast period will be carried on at a given percentage of the firm's capacity. Budgets so prepared are described as *fixed budgets.* They have the advantages of simplicity and relative ease in assembly, but, due to unforeseeable developments, the actual scale of operations may turn out to be materially different from what was forecast. In such circumstances, the budgets quickly lose effectiveness as instruments of control, and the operating executives, who are supposed to be achieving results as budgeted, lose their bearings. If, for example, the volume of sales in terms of units falls 10 per cent below the budget figures, this does not mean that manufacturing overhead expenses, selling expenses, and other classes of expenses will likewise be down by 10 per cent; in consideration of the influence of fixed and semi-variable costs,[1] such a result is not to be expected. During the forecast period, frequent revisions of the whole range of budget figures might be necessary; but this would prove that the budget itself had been, in the first place, a poor tool for planning.

To avoid difficulties of the kinds referred to, many firms prefer to use *variable budgets* whereby separate sets of estimate, each for a different level of operations, are prepared. The primary set is based upon the volume of sales actually expected in the forecast period, but also formulated at once are other sets based on sales volumes of other levels—5 per cent above the primary estimates, 10 per cent above, 5 per cent below, 10 per cent below, and so on. If, then, sales start out as anticipated, budgetary control will be based upon the primary set of estimates, but if, a few months later, sales soar to a level 10 per cent above anticipations, the alternative budget already prepared for that level will become effective.

Budget Systems

It is probably safe to say that virtually every business manager, no matter how small his enterprise, does something in the way of budgeting —certainly in the sense of forecasting, if not in the sense of control. He may put no figures on paper in an orderly way, but surely he reflects from time to time about what sales he is likely to make in the next few weeks or months, what volume of goods he will need to purchase or produce, how many employees he must have, how much cash he will be collecting from his customers, what his total outlays will be, and so on. Such a reflective procedure may be derided as "hit or miss"—one likely to lead

---

[1] See below, pp. 252–53.

to serious errors in decision making—but at least it is indicative of the fact that budgeting, in a broad sense, is a practice well-nigh universal.

As one moves from the hit-or-miss procedures of forecasting toward the most formal and elaborate budgetary systems, one encounters systems of many different scopes. Some firms are quite satisfied to confine their formal budgeting to the use of cash budgets. Some prepare fixed asset budgets in addition to cash budgets. Some tend to concentrate their attention upon sales and production budgets; and some give primary attention to the various kinds of expense budgets. Many business managers, particularly those in control of firms of small and medium sizes, shy away from the installation of formal budget systems to avoid the extra administrative costs involved, but they forget that intelligent planning and control by means of budgets should be a means of avoiding many costly mistakes.

A complete budget system includes a specific budget for each significant phase of operations and a "master budget" in which the key figures from the specific budgets are brought together. For a manufacturing corporation, the specific budgets ordinarily include the following: (1) a sales budget containing a monthly breakdown of expected sales in terms of units of the various kinds of products, unit prices, gross sales (units times prices), and perhaps further breakdowns as for geographical areas in which it is expected sales will be made; (2) a production budget indicating what scale of manufacturing operations must be undertaken from month to month to meet the anticipated sales volume; (3) a materials budget showing what raw materials must go into production monthly; (4) a direct labor budget indicating the number of hours of employment, the wage rates, and the total wages of employees needed to turn out the products; (5) manufacturing expense, selling expense, and administrative expense budgets setting forth all the costs, other than material and direct labor costs, expected to be incurred in producing and selling output and in the general administration of the enterprise; and (6) budgets for miscellaneous income and expenses.

Related to these are: (1) inventory budgets, setting out details about what kinds and quantities of raw materials must be on hand from month to month, the indicated size of monthly goods-in-process inventories, and the quantities and kinds of goods to be carried from month to month in the finished goods inventories; (2) an accounts receivable budget showing estimates of monthly debits to customers' accounts for credit sales, estimated monthly collections, and estimated monthly balances of uncollected accounts; (3) an accounts payable budget having comparable details; (4) budgets for monthly accruals of income and expenses; (5) a fixed asset budget indicating anticipated additions to machinery, equipment, and other fixed assets, as well as expected sales and junking of fixed facilities that will reach the end of their useful lives during the forecast period; and (6) the cash budget summarizing all the effects upon cash flows and balances expected to result from the scale of operations indicated in the other budgets.

Supplementary budgets can be used to set out details that are avoided in the principal budgets to which they are related; for example, monthly advertising expenses can be carried as single figures in the selling expense budget, but a supplementary advertising budget can indicate what proportions of the appropriations for advertising are to be spent upon the various media.

CASH BUDGETS

Scope of a Cash Budget

A cash budget is a detailed estimate for some future period of time of cash inflows from all sources, cash disbursements for all purposes, and the resulting cash balances. As in the construction of most of the other kinds of budgets, the usual forecast period of a cash budget is one year. For this period, a breakdown is provided in terms of weeks, months, or other brief segments. Always possible, of course, are modifications in budgetary procedures. When the outlook is very uncertain, the financial managers of an enterprise may have to be satisfied with a projection for only six months or, perhaps, for as little as three months. Likewise, when approaching periods in which cash is expected to be unusually "tight," the financial managers may want breakdowns on a weekly basis—or even on a daily basis—though they may ordinarily be satisfied with monthly breakdowns.

Cash Budgets and Income Statements

Considering the foregoing definition of a cash budget, one should readily conclude that it is not an income statement projected for a forthcoming period. On the basis of the information contained in sales, materials, direct labor, and other operating budgets, it is true, income statements for future periods can be projected; such *pro forma* statements, as they are called, are often prepared, and they have significant uses. But they have little to do with the control of cash. The purpose of a projected income statement is to account for all sources of income to be tapped and for all classes of expenses to be incurred in a given period, *whether or not the income will be realized in cash in the period and whether or not the expenses will be matched by cash payments.* The purpose of a cash budget, on the other hand, is to account for all expected inflows of cash, whether to be derived from income sources of the period or of other periods or from nonincome sources, such as borrowing and stock sales; and to account for all expected outflows of cash, whether payments of expenses accrued in prior periods, those of the forecast period, or those (prepayments) of subsequent periods, or whether payments not immediately related to expenses, as those for the purchase of fixed assets or for dividend distributions to the stockholders. Thus, a firm that projects for the coming year a net profit before income taxes of, say, $800,000, may simultaneously anticipate in its cash budget a net increase in cash of $1 million, or perhaps one of only $400,000 or $500,000, or perhaps a net decrease in cash of, say, $200,000.

How transactions affect cash budgets and *pro forma* income statements in different ways is indicated in the following table. The sampling of transactions included should suffice to show why the results of operations as projected for a given period in an income statement can be far different from the projected net change in cash holdings expected to result from the cash transactions of the same period.

Transactions Anticipated in Forecast Period	In Pro Forma Income Statement	In Cash Budget
Collections upon accounts receivable of past periods......	Excluded	Included
Collections upon current sales to customers.............	Included	Included
Current sales, payment to be made in subsequent periods.	Included	Excluded
Payment of current expenses..........................	Included	Included
Incurring of expenses chargeable to forecast period but to be paid subsequently..............................	Included	Excluded
Prepayment of expenses chargeable to subsequent periods	Excluded	Included
Depreciation charges.................................	Included	Excluded
Purchase of new fixed assets for cash..................	Excluded	Included
Purchase of new fixed assets, payment to be made in subsequent periods.....................................	Excluded	Excluded
Sale of old fixed assets for cash at price less than remaining book value.....................................	Loss included	Total sales price included
Borrowing from banks................................	Excluded	Included
Repayment of bank loans.............................	Excluded	Included
Payment of cash dividends to stockholders.............	Usually included	Included

Construction of Cash Budgets

For a firm having a complete system of budgetary control, the preparation of a cash budget is a relatively simple matter. Most of the information needed for it is contained in budgets that precede it in formulation. It is necessary only to transfer to the cash budget the details of monthly cash receipts as indicated in sales, accounts receivable, and miscellaneous-income budgets; and details of monthly cash expenditures as found in the materials and direct-labor budgets, the various overhead- and miscellaneous-expense budgets, and the fixed asset budget. In some instances, of course, information contained in sales and other operating budgets must be adjusted for the cash budget, as when sales figures given in terms of units of product are translated into dollar and cents estimates by the application of probable selling prices. Moreover, details of probable borrowing and repayment of loans, sales and retirements of stock, and payments of cash dividends must be inserted in the cash budget independently, so to say, of the other budgets.

Even when a firm is satisfied to confine its system of budgetary control to cash and fixed asset budgets, most of the information that would be contained in the kinds of operating budgets referred to above must, nevertheless, be assembled. Estimates of sales, collections, production, direct labor hours, and so on, must be as carefully made and broken down for weekly, monthly, or other periods as if full-fledged budgets for the various phases of operations were to be used. A failure to assemble careful estimates of any kind of transaction likely to cause significant amounts of cash to flow in or out would obviously detract from the reliability and usefulness of the cash budget itself.

Sales and Collections. Like budgeting in general, cash budgeting begins with the forecasting of sales; for the typical business, the whole scale of operations of all varieties must be planned in relation to the expected sales volume. But projected sales figures, even if in terms of dollars and cents, cannot be taken directly into the cash budget. The important question is what cash collections will be made on account of sales. In the first place, therefore, it is necessary to have separate estimates of cash sales and credit sales. Secondly, "returns and allowances" must be estimated, with separate figures for those to be credited to customers' accounts and those to be met by cash refunds. Thirdly, the amount of cash discounts that customers will probably take must be judged. Finally, with these estimates available, the actual volume of collections from credit customers must be estimated. This must take into account customers' debit balances on the books at the beginning of the forecast period as well as those to be created by credit sales during the period. The allowed credit period and the likelihood of prompt payment through the allowance of cash discounts are of outstanding importance, of course, as determinants of month-to-month collections, but their influence upon the timing of collections can ordinarily be gaged on the basis of customers' payment behavior in the past. Necessarily, however, due weight must be given to new circumstances that may tend to cause future alterations in this behavior.

Other Cash Income. For most businesses engaged in selling tangible products or services, cash receipts in the ordinary course of business from sources other than sales are of minor or negligible importance; nevertheless, if such sources obtain, estimates of how much cash they will bring in must be included in the cash budget. The problem of estimation is usually not a difficult one. Rentals, interest on short-term investments, and dividends on holdings of stock of other unaffiliated enterprises ought generally to be easily estimable. But some items may be quite difficult to estimate. For example, probable cash receipts from royalties may be an elusive figure, as when a firm has licensed others to manufacture a product under its patents with royalties to be measured in proportion to the output of the licensees. Although discounts on purchases are often treated as "other income" in income statements, the preferable procedure in cash budgets is to classify them as deductions from the cash that must be paid in the forecast period for materials and supplies.

In the preparation of cash budgets by corporations that own subsidiaries, little attention is ordinarily given to the cash dividends that the subsidiaries are likely to pay to the parent corporation in the course of the forecast period. Instead, the cash inflows and outflows of the subsidiaries are estimated as carefully as for the parent company itself, and these, with proper adjustments for intercorporate cash transactions, are consolidated with those of the parent. In this way, the cash prospects of the whole family of corporations, parent and subsidiaries, can be seen in a single consolidated budget.

Cash Payments for Raw Materials or Finished Goods. Estimates of the amount and timing of payments for raw materials or finished goods during a forecast period are, as a rule, closely related to the sales estimates, but the relationship is not necessarily a precise one. A decision to carry larger inventories, whether of raw materials, goods in process, or finished goods, would obviously call for purchases beyond what would be required to meet estimated sales; while a decision to cut inventories would make it possible to meet a portion of estimated sales out of inventory already held, thereby bringing purchase requirements for the forecast period below what they otherwise would be. At any rate, when production schedules and buying programs have been established—on the basis, one might say, of sales estimates and separate inventory policy decisions—the timing of purchases and of payments therefor are not likely to be difficult to estimate.

In estimating month-to-month payments for raw materials and finished goods, the financial officers of an enterprise must give due weight to circumstances similar to those to be weighed in estimating cash collections from sales: they must distinguish between cash purchases and purchases on account, estimate probable "returns and allowances," consider the credit terms of the various suppliers from whom goods will be purchased, and anticipate prompt payment to take advantage of whatever cash discounts may be allowed. Likewise, they must anticipate paying suppliers on obligations standing on the books at the beginning of the forecast period, as well as the nonpayment of obligations that will originate during the period but will not reach their due or discount dates by its end.

Direct Labor. Business enterprises that pay direct labor on piece-rate bases can estimate their direct labor wage bill by simply applying the piece rates to the units of output called for in the production budget, at the same time taking into account prospective additional wage costs in the form of social security taxes, paid holidays and vacations, payments into company pension funds, payments for overtime work, and such bonuses as may be prescribed by incentive systems in operation. Enterprises that pay hourly rates must estimate the number of direct labor hours of workers of various skills that will be required to turn out the units of product as scheduled in the production budget, multiply the hours so found by the respective hourly rates, and add in supplemental wage costs of the kinds referred to above.

In making their estimates, enterprises of both classes must weigh all possibilities of changes during the forecast period in wage rates, payroll tax rates, and the scale of payments for "fringe benefits." Not to be overlooked, also, is the fact that accrued wages on the books at the beginning of the forecast period will require early payments in cash, and that accrued wages on the books at the end of the period will not require cash payments until the following period.

Overhead Expenses. In considering problems of estimating what cash payments will have to be made in a forecast period in meeting manufacturing, selling, and administrative expenses, one might hastily conclude that the least difficulty ought to be encountered with respect to "fixed" expenses, such as property taxes, property insurance, some of the executive salaries, and certain kinds of charges for maintenance. By definition, such expenses can be expected to hold at a specific level whether the scale of operations is high or low or somewhere in between. But fixity in an expense item does not mean that it will not change from this year to next year; it simply implies that if a change takes place, the new level will prevail regardless of the scale of operations next year. Local governments may raise their property tax rates, and insurance companies, their rates for property insurance. Or the forecasting firm may be planning additions to fixed assets which will hardly escape the watchful eye of the property tax assessor and upon which the firm will surely want to carry insurance. One must conclude, therefore, that great care must be used in forecasting payments to meet "fixed" overhead expenses—that difficulties in estimation can no more be avoided here than in forecasting variable and semivariable expenses.

As for variable expenses, ease in forecasting is suggested by the fact that such expenses, by definition, are expected to vary in proportion to production or sales. If a firm's unit sales next year are expected to be 10 per cent less than this year, its packaging costs and salesmen's commissions, as well as some kinds of its delivery expenses, may also be expected to fall by approximately 10 per cent. But difficulties cannot be wholly avoided; there are possibilities of future changes in prices and costs. If the selling prices of the firm's products are to be lowered with no change in the salesmen's commission rate, or if the commission rate is to be reduced, the fall in total commissions can hardly be expected to be proportional to the fall in unit sales; or if the prices of supplies used in packaging the products are expected to fall, total costs of this kind can be expected to be down by more than 10 per cent.

Difficulties in estimating semivariable expenses come, as it were, from two directions: the different kinds of expenses of this group tend to have disproportional patterns of variation in relation to the scale of operations, and changes in prices and rates affect them no less than fixed and variable expenses. A forecast of a lowered sales volume may be coupled with budgetary provisions for a substantial increase in outlays for advertising, the impliction being that, without increased spending for advertising, the decline in sales volume would be expected to be much more severe. At the same time, the total increase in the advertising budget might be required not only because of the decision for a more extended coverage, but also because of expected increases in rates for, say, newspaper and magazine space. In a similar way, a reduction in production of 5 per cent might be projected without any cut in the estimated compensation for the factory superintendent and foremen, while a projected cut of 10 per cent might be coupled with an estimated reduction in factory supervisory expenses of more than that proportion, in the expectation of lowered salary rates and the laying off of one or more of the foremen.

Prepayments and accruals, it should be apparent, also complicate the estimation of cash outlays for meeting overhead expenses in a forecast period. In one year, payments for property insurance may be negligible, because policies prepaid in prior years are still in force; but payments for this purpose in another year may be substantial because most of the policies then come up for renewal. Estimates of cash payments for office supplies in the forecast year may be quite small in consideration of the large quantity expected to be on hand, and already paid for, at the beginning of the year, while cash disbursements for factory supplies may be placed at a relatively high figure because of an expected low inventory at the beginning of the year. In a comparable way, a large expense for an extraordinary advertising campaign projected for the late months of the forecast year may not show up in the cash budget, as payment is expected to be deferred until the following year.

Other Expenses. In their income statements, many concerns present a grouping of expense items separate from (and following) their classifications of manufacturing, selling, and administrative expenses. Such a grouping is variously labeled as "other," "miscellaneous," "financial," or "nonoperating" expenses, and it includes such items as interest expense, sales discounts, and expenses incurred in the maintenance of properties not employed in the ordinary operations of the business.

For cash budgeting, of course, cash outlays in connection with "other" expenses must be as carefully estimated as are those directly related to manufacturing, selling, and administration. With sales discounts, however, we have already seen that the better budgetary practice is to regard them as deductions from cash to be collected from customers, rather than as disbursements. Only in relatively rare instances do customers remit in full and then ask for refunds for the discounts they forgot to take. Cash requirements for interest on debts already outstanding or to be contracted in the forecast year are ordinarily quite easy to estimate. All one needs to know is the amount of debt, the portion of the year it will be outstanding, and the rate or rates of interest already stipulated or expected to be stipulated.

ILLUSTRATIVE CASH BUDGET

The usefulness of cash budgets as instruments of financial planning and control can be demonstrated by the presentation and analysis of an illustrative budget of a manufacturing corporation. We may assume that in the fall of the year 19xx the managers of the Carver Manufacturing Corporation tackle the job of preparing the cash budget for the following year, that is, for the year 19yy. On the basis of developments in the year 19xx to date, they expect the financial position of the corporation at the end of that year to be as indicated in the *pro forma* balance sheet presented in Figure 12-1.

Assumptions

Aside from their assumptions about the financial position of the corporation at the end of the year 19xx, as indicated in the *pro forma* statement, the financial managers of the corporation have the following additional facts and estimates (among others) to take into consideration in the preparation of the cash budget:

1. It is expected that operations in the year 19yy will be at approximately 90 per cent of capacity.

2. The corporation has a distinct seasonal pattern in its sales, the lows occurring in January, February, and March, followed by a rapid expansion to peak levels in August, September, and October, and sharp falloffs characterizing November and December.

3. The corporation sells to a few customers on a cash basis, but most of its sales are on account. Its terms for credit sales call for net payment in 30 days, and no cash discounts are allowed for earlier payment. Accordingly, collections on accounts receivable in any month very largely flow from the sales of the preceding month.

4. Despite the seasonal pattern of its sales, the corporation tries to regularize production. It builds up its inventories in months of slack sales to be able to meet the requirements of the peak months.

5. The corporation has a seasonal problem also in its purchases of raw materials. The price situation makes a concentration of raw material buying in the period from December through April highly advantageous. The corporation ordinarily continues to buy raw materials throughout the year, but in much smaller quantities in the other seven months.

6. In view of the seasonal pattern of its sales, the corporation steps up its expenditures for advertising and other promotional efforts in April, May, and June. (This indicates that the corporation is willing to accept the seasonal pattern of its sales. Were it to conclude that the seasonal pattern could be changed by its own efforts, it would be likely to concentrate its selling efforts in or before the off-season months.)

FIGURE 12–1

Carver Manufacturing Corporation
Balance Sheet
Projected for December 31, 19xx

ASSETS

Current Assets:

Cash..		$ 415,000	
Short-term treasury obligations...............		350,000	
Accounts receivable.........................	$195,000		
Less: Reserve for bad debts................	8,000	187,000	
Accrued interest receivable....................		2,250	
Inventories:			
Raw materials.............................	$110,000		
Goods in process..........................	92,000		
Finished goods............................	158,000	360,000	
Prepaid expenses.............................		56,000	
Total Current Assets....................			$1,370,250

Fixed Assets:

Land.......................................		$ 38,000	
Factory building............................	$200,000		
Less: Allowance for depreciation...........	75,000	125,000	
Machinery and equipment....................	$900,000		
Less: Allowance for depreciation...........	240,000	660,000	
Delivery equipment.........................	$ 12,000		
Less: Allowance for depreciation...........	4,000	8,000	
Office equipment...........................	$ 10,000		
Less: Allowance for depreciation...........	4,000	6,000	
Total Fixed Assets.....................		837,000	
Total Assets.........................		$2,207,250	

LIABILITIES AND EQUITY

Current Liabilities:

Accounts payable.....................................	$ 65,500	
Accrued wages.......................................	30,000	
Accrued expenses....................................	46,000	
Accrued taxes.......................................	42,000	
Total Current Liabilities...........................		$ 183,500

Stockholders' Equity:

Capital stock.........	$1,600,000	
Earned surplus......................................	423,750	
Total Equity....................................		2,023,750
Total Liabilities and Equity.....................		$2,207,250

7. The corporation's standard for minimum cash balances is $280,000.

8. Accounting for the treasury securities shown in the *pro forma* balance sheet were purchases of $200,000 at the end of September, and $150,000 at the end of October, 19xx. In those months, cash was in excess supply, but it was recognized that the excess was only a temporary

one; accordingly, the investment in short-term obligations was made in anticipation of a high level of cash needs in the early months of the year 19yy. (For the sake of simplicity, it is assumed that the securities were bought at par on the date of issue and that they pay interest at the rate of 3 per cent per annum.)

9. The accrued taxes entered in the *pro forma* balance sheet are the estimated unpaid balance of federal income taxes projected for the year 19xx—a balance payable in equal instalments on March 15 and June 15, 19yy.

10. For several years, the corporation has been paying cash dividends to its stockholders in January, April, July, and October, each equal to 1¼ per cent of the par value of its outstanding common stock, $1,600,000.

Carver's Cash Budget

On the basis of anticipations of position at the beginning of the year 19yy, as indicated in the *pro forma* balance sheet, the additional facts and estimates just outlined, and all the various kinds of information to be drawn from sales, accounts receivable, raw materials, production, and other budgets, the financial managers of the Carver Manufacturing Corporation, we may assume, draw up a cash budget for the year 19yy of the form and content of the accompanying illustration (Figure 12–2). This indicates what they anticipate in the way of cash inflows and outflows, as well as monthly cash balances, if the enterprise operates, as expected, at close to 90 per cent of capacity. Should their budgetary system be "variable," they would draw up comparable cash budgets for operations at other levels related to capacity, as 80 per cent, 85 per cent, and 95 per cent.

A few of the items included in the receipts and payments sections of the illustrative budget require explanation:

1. It is expected that a portion of the factory building, not needed for the productive operations of the corporation, will be rented to another manufacturer beginning in April at an annual rental of $20,000 payable quarterly in advance (line 4).

2. In anticipation of a substantial increase in the scale of operations in the year 19zz, the corporation plans to buy additional machinery at a cost of $150,000 in November, 19yy (line 24).

3. The income tax payments indicated for September and December of $18,000 each are anticipated payments on account of a declaration of estimated tax liabilities to be made for the year 19yy—in keeping with the "pay-as-you-go" tax assessment of corporations as provided for in the Internal Revenue Code of 1954. The amount of these anticipated payments were determined, we may assume, on the basis of the expected net profits of the Carver Manufacturing Corporation for the year 19yy as found in a *pro forma* income statement (to be presented and discussed in the following chapter).

FIGURE 12-2

Carver Manufacturing Corporation
Cash Budget
For the Year 19yy

Line		January	February	March	April	May	June	July	August	September	October	November	December	Total
1	Cash receipts from operations:													
2	Cash sales.........	$ 20,000	$ 15,000	$ 10,000	$ 20,000	$ 30,000	$ 30,000	$ 25,000	$ 35,000	$ 50,000	$ 40,000	$ 25,000	$ 15,000	$ 315,000
3	Collections—accounts receivable.	180,000	120,000	100,000	110,000	190,000	240,000	305,000	315,000	460,000	420,000	395,000	250,000	3,085,000
4	Rental income.........			5,000			5,000			5,000			5,000	20,000
5	Total.........	$ 200,000	$135,000	$ 115,000	$ 130,000	$220,000	$ 275,000	$330,000	$ 350,000	$515,000	$460,000	$420,000	$270,000	$3,420,000
6	Additional sources of cash:													
7	Sale of treasury obligations......		$200,000	$ 150,000										$ 350,000
8	Interest on treasury obligations..		2,000	1,500										3,500
9	Short-term loans.........				$ 180,000	$ 90,000								270,000
10	Total.........		$202,000	$ 151,500	$ 180,000	$ 90,000								$ 623,500
11	Total Cash Receipts.........	$ 200,000	$337,000	$ 266,500	$ 310,000	$310,000	$ 275,000	$330,000	$ 350,000	$515,000	$460,000	$420,000	$270,000	$4,043,500
12	Cash payments for operations:													
13	Raw materials.........	$ 89,000	$ 85,000	$ 79,000	$ 72,000	$ 65,000	$ 37,000	$ 28,000	$ 15,000	$ 11,000	$ 14,000	$ 17,000	$ 21,000	$ 533,000
14	Direct labor.........	80,000	74,000	82,000	78,000	81,000	77,000	78,000	81,000	75,000	79,000	74,000	71,000	930,000
15	Manufacturing expense.........	50,000	48,000	51,000	49,000	50,000	48,000	49,000	50,000	48,000	51,000	47,000	46,000	587,000
16	Selling expense.........	40,000	39,000	46,000	64,000	58,000	65,000	46,000	48,000	44,000	42,000	40,000	37,000	569,000
17	Administrative expense.........	36,000	37,000	40,000	37,000	38,000	43,000	37,000	34,000	36,000	40,000	37,000	49,000	469,000
18	Federal income tax.........			21,000			21,000			18,000			18,000	78,000
19	Total.........	$ 295,000	$283,000	$ 319,000	$ 300,000	$292,000	$ 291,000	$238,000	$ 228,000	$232,000	$226,000	$220,000	$242,000	$3,166,000
20	Additional cash payments:													
21	Dividends.........	$ 20,000			$ 20,000			$ 20,000			$ 20,000			$ 80,000
22	Discount on loans.........				3,000	$ 1,500								4,500
23	Repayment of loans.........								$ 180,000	$ 90,000				270,000
24	Purchase of fixed assets.........											$150,000		150,000
25	Purchase of treasury obligations..									200,000	200,000			400,000
26	Total.........	20,000			$ 23,000	$ 1,500		$ 20,000	$ 180,000	$290,000	$220,000	$150,000		$ 904,500
27	Total Cash Payments.........	$ 315,000	$283,000	$ 319,000	$ 323,000	$293,500	$ 291,000	$258,000	$ 408,000	$522,000	$446,000	$370,000	$242,000	$4,070,500
28	Net cash receipts or payments (−)	$ −115,000	$ 54,000	$ −52,500	$ −13,000	$ 16,500	$ −16,000	$ 72,000	$ −58,000	$ −7,000	$ 14,000	$ 50,000	$ 28,000	$ −27,000
29	Cash balance—beginning of month	415,000	300,000	354,000	301,500	288,500	305,000	289,000	361,000	303,000	296,000	310,000	360,000	415,000
30	Cash balance—end of month.....	$ 300,000	$354,000	$ 301,500	$ 288,500	$305,000	$ 289,000	$361,000	$ 303,000	$296,000	$310,000	$360,000	$388,000	$ 388,000

Analysis

In setting up their cash budget for the year 19yy, the financial managers of Carver would doubtless first fill in the details of lines 2–5 and
13–19 to reflect cash flows and balances expected to result from ordinary
operations. The planned expenditure of $150,000 for machinery in No-
vember would next be entered (line 24) as something definitely programmed and for which financing would appear to be assured. Then the
dividend payments (line 21) would probably be entered on a tentative
basis. Although such payments would be at the discretion of the board
of directors, to be finally decided upon at its meetings during the course
of the year, the prospective profit for the year 19yy (as revealed in the
pro forma income statement presented in the following chapter) would
seem to justify dividends at a rate at least as high as had been paid for
several years. Moreover, the board's approval of the cash budget containing the tentative dividend figures would surely indicate its intention
to continue dividends at the existing rate.

A preliminary computation of monthly cash balances on the basis of
all the items of cash inflow and outflow referred to in the preceding paragraph would indicate that, for the year as a whole, the cash situation
would be satisfactory—that, without regard to the later entries for the
purchase and sale of securities and borrowing and the repayment of loans,
the cash balance at the end of the year would be larger by $24,000 than
at the beginning. But it would be quickly observed that the seasonal pattern of the corporation's sales and collections and of its raw material buying would bring the cash balance at the end of February far below the
minimum standard of $280,000 and would cause quite serious cash deficits
in the period from March through August. Hence, the additional entries
on lines 7–9. These entries indicate how Carver's financial managers plan
to meet the extraordinary cash drains that will begin in February. In the
fall of 19xx, they invested excess cash in short-term obligations of the
federal Treasury, and lines 7 and 8 show that they plan to liquidate these
securities in February and March. Presumably, also, they have established a line of credit at a commercial bank, as is indicated by the entries
for short-term loans on line 9 for April and May (with entries for the
anticipated discount on the loans separately entered on line 22). It is
worth mentioning here, in passing, that the willingness of the commercial
bank to grant the loans would surely be strengthened by a demonstration of the corporation's capacity to repay—a demonstration for which
the cash budget itself would serve excellently.

With the very large cash requirements of the early months planned
for, Carver's financial managers would observe that, beginning in August,
cash inflows from sales and collections far exceeding outflows for ordinary operations would cause the cash balance to mount well above the

minimum standard. For this reason, they plan to repay the bank loans in August and September, as indicated by the entries on line 23, and to invest in short-term treasury securities the additional excess cash expected to be available in September and October, as shown on line 25.

Since the corporation tends to run toward cash shortages early in the year, and, indeed, must borrow to avoid what would be quite serious shortages, one might suggest a deferment of the dividend payments to stockholders till later in the year when plenty of cash is expected to be available. Such a deferment would reduce the borrowing requirements of the corporation by $60,000, yet, in the closing months of the year, the stockholders could still be given a dividend of $80,000 if that continued to be the overall level chosen by the directors. Nevertheless, there is no compelling reason why a corporation that is in debt, or that must go into debt following the payment of a cash dividend, should avoid dividend distributions. If that were the rule, a great number of corporations that now pay regular quarterly dividends would never pay dividends at all! The presence or absence of debt is only one factor to be considered by a board of directors in deciding about dividend payments. Other factors are of equal or greater importance—these will be taken up for study in Chapter 25.[2] With respect to our illustration, then, we may conclude that the directors of the Carver Manufacturing Corporation, because they anticipate profits for the year well above the dividends entered in the cash budget, and because they see certain advantages in regular quarterly payments, are quite content to plan for dividend payments even in months when cash requirements for operations are especially heavy.

Questions

1. What kinds of anticipations are included in the scope of financial forecasting?

2. Is not financial forecasting likely to be suject to such a wide margin of error as to be of little real value? Discuss.

3. What is the relationship between financial forecasting and budgeting?

4. What is a budget? a cash budget? a fixed asset budget?

5. Budgets are prepared for periods of what length? How detailed can they reasonably be?

6. If budgets are simply forecasts, what justification can there be for also describing them as instruments of control?

7. What is the difference between a fixed budget and a variable budget? Which is likely to be the more useful? Why?

8. Give several examples of anticipated transactions that would require differing treatment in cash budgets and projected income statements.

9. What is the relationship, if any, of a cash budget to a sales budget? to a production budget? to a budget for direct labor?

---

[2] See especially pp. 597–603.

10. What special difficulties are encountered in trying to forecast the cash payments to be made in meeting overhead expenses?

11. In estimating borrowing requirements and dividend-paying capacity for the coming year, would the financial managers of a business firm get any help from a cash budget? Explain.

Problem

To show the effects of the following transaction of the Lennox Products Company upon its cash flows for the year 19yy and upon its net income after income taxes, prepare a table with the following columnar headings for amounts:

Cash		Net Income	
Inflow	Outflow	Decrease	Increase

Compute the net increase or decrease in the corporation's cash balance and the amount of its net income after federal income taxes resulting from all these transactions combined.

Cash sales for the year......................................	$ 820,000
Credit sales for the year.....................................	14,650,000
Collections on credit sales for the year........................	13,710,000
Collections on credit sales for 19xx...........................	1,065,000
Purchases of raw materials and supplies on account............	6,289,000
Payments to suppliers on forgoing............................	5,467,000
Payments to suppliers on goods bought in 19xx.................	975,000
Advance payments to suppliers on goods to be delivered in 19zz..	50,000
Inventory of raw materials and supplies, 1/1/19yy..............	468,000
Inventory of raw materials and supplies, 12/31/19yy...........	535,000
Wage and salary charges for the year.........................	4,145,000
Accrued payroll of 12/31/19xx paid in 19yy....................	95,000
Other payroll payments in 19yy...............................	4,010,000
Accrued expenses of 12/31/19xx paid in 19yy..................	300,000
Other operating expense payments in 19yy.....................	2,310,000
Accrued expenses, 12/31/19yy to be paid in 19zz..............	285,000
Federal income tax paid in 19yy on 19xx income................	550,000
Federal income tax paid in 19yy on estimated 19yy income......	425,000
Estimated unpaid federal income tax, 12/31/19yy..............	525,260
Purchase of machinery on the instalment plan:	
Cost...	4,000,000
Downpayment..	800,000
Instalment payments in 19yy...............................	420,000
Sale of discarded equipment for cash:	
Selling price...	40,000
Book value..	90,000
Depreciation charges in 19yy.................................	620,000
Dividends declared in 19xx, paid in 19yy......................	200,000
Dividends declared and paid in 19yy..........................	250,000
Dividends declared in 19yy to be paid in 19zz.................	300,000

(Further reference to this problem and its solution is made in the problem at the end of the following chapter.)

chapter 13

CONTROLLING THE FLOW OF CASH

CASH BUDGETS AS CONTROL INSTRUMENTS

The usefulness of cash budgets as instruments of control should be quite apparent on the basis of the illustrative budget and its analysis as presented in the closing pages of the preceding chapter. This usefulness can be all the more appreciated if one reflects upon the difficulties that the financial managers of the Carver Manufacturing Corporation might encounter in the year 19yy were they to lack a forecast of expected cash flows and advance plans for adjustment to distortions in the flows. They could be certain that the cash account could be replenished by the sale of the short-term treasury obligations; but control of the corporation's cash position beyond that would presumably be on a makeshift basis.

Assuming that cash flows on account of ordinary operations turn out to be pretty close to the illustrative figures, and that the short-term treasury obligations are actually sold in February and March, the financial managers would find cash beginning to fall well below the minimum standard in April. They might decide that it would be appropriate to borrow, but the amount to be borrowed and the probable time when repayment could be made would be matters of great uncertainty. If they had not already established a line of credit at a commercial bank, they might not be able to borrow at all. At least, there would be delays for the bank's credit investigation before the loan would be granted. Later in the year, as cash became more plentiful, the financial managers might decide that they could start to repay the bank loans, but they would be uncertain about the speed at which repayment could be made. After the loans had been repaid, and cash continued to pile up, there would be further uncertainty about how quickly the excess cash ought to be invested in short-term securities. The question whether already available cash should be used to pay for the machinery bought in November, or whether some other source of cash should be tapped for this purpose, would, likewise, have to be decided on a makeshift basis. Meanwhile, the payment of quarterly dividends of $20,000 could hardly be judged as being reasonable or unreasonable, since an overall picture upon which to base a judgment would be lacking.

Further Control Aspects in Terms of the Illustration

The problems of cash control faced by the financial officers of our illustrative corporation can be described as relatively easy ones. They could have been made more difficult by the use of a different set of illustrative figures or by changes in the assumptions upon which the illustration was built. But whether problems are easy or difficult, the forecast of what is likely to happen to cash movements must surely be regarded as essential for *sound* solutions. How a cash budget can serve as a basis for different sets of decisions in keeping with different sets of anticipations may, accordingly, be described in terms of the illustrative cash budget of the Carver Manufacturing Corporation. Although we need not attempt to exhaust the possibilities, we can see how, as it were, the details of lines 7–9 and 21–25 of the illustrative budget could be changed if circumstances were somewhat different from those originally assumed.

Alternatives in a Tight-Money Situation. Suppose, for example, that the commercial bank had notified the officers of the corporation that, because of extreme tightness in its lending capacity, it would have to reduce Carver's line of credit to, say, $150,000. The unavailability of approximately $120,000 that the bank would, in ordinary circumstances, be expected to supply would obviously be a matter of only temporary embarrassment, and would occur only in the year 19yy and not in every year; accordingly, the finding of a temporary or short-run solution for the problem would appear to be a reasonable objective. The embarrassment would be temporary, of course, since the cash budget indicates that whatever amount the corporation must borrow can be paid back in August and September, and that cash tends to pile up excessively in the later months of the year.

It might be decided that the circumstances were sufficiently of an "emergency" character to justify permitting cash balances to fall below the minimum standard of $280,000. A survey of the end-of-the-month cash balances shown on line 30 of the illustrative budget indicates that the cut in the bank's line of credit could be balanced, as it were, should the corporation be satisfied to let its cash balance fall as low as approximately $170,000. But justification for this move would by no means be clear; perhaps this "emergency" would not be important enough to excuse a weakening of the cash position. The tight-money situation that prompted the bank to cut the line of credit might be expected to affect the corporation's customers also, causing them to slow down in meeting their obligations. To conserve their own cash, moreover, the customers might postpone purchases; thus the corporation's sales and collections, though not ultimately reduced from the total expected volume, might come in months later than originally anticipated. The delay in cash inflows would surely mean a reduction in the corporation's cash balances below $170,000. A further consideration is that periods of tight money often precede periods of general business recession the "emergency" character of which—with reduced sales and delays in collections—can hardly be doubted.

Accordingly, Carver's financial managers might decide that, though the minimum balance standard of $280,000 could be breached, this concession ought not to be relied upon to make up the entire deficiency of $120,000 in bank loans. Perhaps a drop of $40,000 or $50,000 below the minimum standard should be the limit of the breach. Accordingly, other means of conserving cash or supplementing its inflow would have to be sought. In a close corporation, one or more of the stockholders might be willing to advance funds on a loan basis for a few months, but this would not be a likely solution for a large corporation with a wide scattering of stockholders unless one or a few had quite large interests. Another possible partial solution would be the deferment of dividends till late in the year; this would have the effect of conserving $60,000 of cash during the tight period, and, with the temporary lowering of the minimum balance standard, it might be expected to be sufficient to meet the difficulty. Another possibility would be to buy raw materials less aggressively in the early months of the year, although some penalty might have to be paid in higher prices later on. Again, purchase discounts could be forgone so that the corporation could hold on to its cash to the end of the credit periods stipulated by sellers of raw materials.

On the other hand, Carver's financial managers would not be likely to give much thought to more far-reaching solutions to what would be, or would appear to be, a temporary problem. They might be able to speed up the inflow of cash by granting discounts to their customers for early payment; but such a change in credit terms could not easily be limited to a few months only—once the customers had been allowed discounts, they would be likely to anticipate their continued availability. Likewise, the corporation might be in a position to borrow on a long-term basis as by a bond issue, but this would not appear to be a sound way of curing a cash deficiency of a few months in one year. The same could be said for an additional issue of stock. Although the stockholders might be willing to buy additional stock, it would seem to be wiser to defer the use of this source of long-term money for some as-yet-unforeseen long-term purpose, rather than to use it now for a purpose extremely short-term in character.

Long-Term Funds for Equipment. In the original illustration of the Carver Manufacturing Corporation in the preceding chapter, a decision was made to use available cash to buy some new machines in November at a cost of $150,000. But with a change in assumptions, the decision might have gone in a different direction. Suppose that the expenditure was expected to be only the first of a series of heavy outlays to prepare the corporation for a substantial expansion in the level of its output. In that situation, a search for new intermediate- or long-term funds would seem

to be in order. Though the corporation could spend $150,000 for equipment without seriously weakening its working capital position, it obviously could not continue to make a series of outlays of large amounts
without danger. Accordingly, the financial managers, considering the
overall expansion programmed in their fixed asset budget, might immediately decide to sell additional stock or to float a bond issue to meet the
total cost of the machines plus all the other equipment expected to be acquired over a period of several years. However, it would apparently be
reasonable to use present cash to the extent of $150,000 to take care of the
first step in the expansion program, and later on to put out additional
stock or a bond issue of sufficient size both to finance further fixed asset
acquisitions and to replenish the $150,000 of cash taken from working
capital.

All the more would a stock or bond issue appear to be advisable for
financing the acquisiton of equipment when additional cash requirements
for the circular process are taken into consideration. A sizable expansion
in the level of operations ordinarily requires not only additional fixed assets but also more current assets as well—additional cash is needed for
minimum balances, for absorption in inventories and accounts receivable,
and for meeting day-to-day operating expenses. It might be expected that
some of these additional requirements would be offset by increased buying of raw materials on account and increases in unpaid payrolls and unpaid (accrued) expenses of other kinds, but such sources of additional
current assets could hardly be expected to carry the whole load. Accordingly, the need of additional cash for the circular process, as well as for
the purchase of fixed assets, would have to be kept in mind. In the original Carver case, had the expansion program not been expected to go
beyond the expenditure of $150,000 for machines, the decision to use
available cash to meet the expenditure might have been predicated upon
an assurance that the corporation's line of credit at the bank could be increased to meet increased cash requirements for current purposes. If,
however, a quite costly expansion program were envisaged—with an expectation, therefore, that much cash would be needed both for the purchase of fixed assets and for the circular process—the financial managers
of Carver might decide that they would not be able, or would not want,
to rely upon the bank for all the additional cash expected to be needed for
the latter purpose. Hence, they would probably decide that a portion of
the additional cash requirements for current asset expansion, as well as all
the cash needed for fixed asset expansion, should be acquired on an intermediate- or long-term basis. Were this their decision, they would make
their stock or bond issue big enough to cover both kinds of requirements.

Changing Circumstances during the Budget Period

The foregoing discussion was designed to indicate the usefulness of cash
budgets as tools of financial planning regardless, one might say, of the

nature of business conditions anticipated. We started out with a given set of circumstances as anticipated and described what the decisions of the financial managers might be in the light of these anticipations; then we varied the anticipated circumstances somewhat to show how the variations would be likely to require decisions of different kinds. But cash budgets are also useful as guides in meeting unexpected changes in circumstances that occur during the periods for which they are forecasts.

The most far-reaching change in circumstance that is likely to occur during a budget period, and to make actual operating results quite different from what were anticipated, is an expansion or contraction in general business activity. Such a development may cause sales to rise well above or to fall well below the level that was forecast. In the Carver case, operations at 90 per cent of capacity were anticipated for the year 19yy, but what if they had risen to 100 per cent or fallen to 80 per cent? Difficulties could hardly be avoided, but in a good budget system--one of "variable" budgets, as described in the preceding chapter—they would have been anticipated and prospective solutions already worked out. The 80 per cent budget or the 100 per cent budget would become the financial plan for the year, and the 90 per cent one would be discarded even though major attention originally centered upon it.

But competent planners ought not to be so wide of the mark that sales would start out at a level requiring operations at 80 per cent or 100 per cent of capacity when they expected sales that would require a level of operations midway between these levels. What is more likely to happen, therefore, is that sales will proceed for a while as anticipated and then veer off, perhaps sharply, in one direction or the other. In other words, a rise or fall in business activity occurring near the beginning of the budget year ought, as a rule, to have been anticipated and planned for; but the forecasters might readily be excused for not having foreseen such a development taking place in, say, July or August. Unquestionably, there are difficulties in switching in midstream, so to say, from a 90 per cent budget to one at 80 per cent or 100 per cent—and all the more so if a gradual shift, perhaps over a period of two or three months, is appropriate. But the difficulties should be minor compared with what they would likely be were no budgets available. If a plan is available for meeting whatever financial problems a *full year* at a level of 80 per cent or 100 per cent of capacity would be expected to create, it should also be highly useful in indicating what should be done if operations for only three or four months are at one of those levels.

Sometimes, of course, things happen that have not been anticipated in any of the budgets, regardless of the number of levels of operation planned for. For example, suppose that in August the Carver Manufacturing Corporation were offered at a most attractive price a batch of raw materials equal to the volume that it would ordinarily buy in the months from December through April. Were we to assume its cash position in

August to be at least roughly as indicated in the illustrative budget of the preceding chapter, and the raw materials to cost $360,000, important changes in the plans as set out in the budget would have to be made to take advantage of the offer. But the budget would enable Carver's managers to recognize rather quickly where the changes could be made, and it would assure them, as it were, of the wisdom of the changes. The bank could be asked to extend the maturities of its loans with a demonstration by means of the budget that the delay in payment would be one of only a few months; and the plan of investing in short-term securities in September and October would surely be revised, since the objective of much of this planned investment would have already been realized.

PERIODIC REPORTS FOR CONTROL

As operations move into and through the year or other period of time covered by a cash budget, the financial officers must be supplied with periodic reports to enable them to check the budgeted figures against actual developments. The essential purpose of this requirement is to indicate if and when and to what degree financial plans must be switched.

Daily Cash Reports

The preparation of daily cash reports is probably the most convenient means of maintaining a running comparison of actual cash flows with budget projections. Although cash budgets are not set up on a daily basis, and although the actual cash receipts and payments of any one day are not likely to be of any great significance, the observance of cash receipts and disbursements in the reports of several consecutive days will indicate whether the rate of flow is or is not proceeding as expected. Moreover, the balance figures in the daily reports will indicate whether or not net inflows or outflows of the year to date have been close to the expected level. Such figures indicate, too, of course, when borrowing under already-arranged bank lines of credit should be effected, as well as when superabundant cash should be used to repay bank loans or to buy short-term investment securities.

A daily cash report is ordinarily a simple document. Aside from the heading and date, many such reports contain nothing more than the opening cash balance of the day, the cash receipts and disbursements of the day, and the closing balance. Some are expanded to give broad classes of receipts and payments, as in Figure 13–1 which is a format that the Carver Manufacturing Corporation might want to use. Sometimes still more elaborate reports are used, as by the addition of columns to a form such as Figure 13–1 for the "month to date" and the "year to date" for the entry of the opening balances of the month and year, the cumulative amounts of receipts and disbursements by major classes, and the closing balances. However, it is probably better to reserve such details for monthly cash reports.

FIGURE 13–1
Carver Manufacturing Corporation
Daily Cash Report
January 2, 19yy

Opening balance..		$415,000
Receipts:		
Cash sales..	$ 1,100	
Collections—accounts receivable..........................	4,100	
Other—		
Total Receipts.....................................	$ 5,200	
Payments:		
Operations...	9,600	
Other—		
Dividends..	20,000	
Total Payments....................................	$29,600	
Excess of receipts/*payments*...............................		24,400
Closing Balance..		$390,600

Monthly Cash Reports

Monthly cash reports are designed to bring together for comparison and analysis the major details of actual cash flows for the individual month and for the year to date and those of the budget for the same periods. Such a report indicates to what extent cash receipts for the month and for the year to date have exceeded or fallen short of projected receipts, and to what extent actual cash payments have exceeded or fallen short of projected payments. What is more, the specific items of receipts and payments in which principal variances have occurred stand out, as it were, for special study.

A type of monthly report that would tie in with the budget system of the Carver Manufacturing Corporation is presented as Figure 13–2; it has been filled in with assumed receipts and payments for the month of February 19yy, and for the two months ending February 28. The report shows that in February receipts fell short of expectations by $8,000, and that payments exceeded expectations by $13,400, for a total deficiency in actual net receipts, by comparison with the budgeted figures, of $21,400. On the other hand, net receipts in January must have been higher than expected, since the year-to-date columns indicate that the cumulative deficiency for the two months amounts to only $3,100. The specific variances item by item, as revealed in the report, should be even more important than their totals in indicating to Carver's financial managers when and in what direction, if at all, changes in financial planning should be effected.

Other Reports

While daily and monthly cash reports identical with or comparable to the kinds illustrated are the principal means of checking cash flows to in-

FIGURE 13-2
Carver Manufacturing Corporation
Monthly Cash Budget Report
For the Month of February, 19yy

	This Month			Year to Date		
	Actual	Budget	Excess of Actual	Actual	Budget	Excess of Actual
Cash receipts:						
Cash sales..............	$ 15,600	$ 15,000	$ 600	$ 39,200	$ 35,000	$4,200
Collections—accounts receivable.............	111,400	120,000	8,600	298,400	300,000	1,600
Rental income...........						
Sale of investments.......	200,000	200,000		200,000	200,000	
Interest income..........	2,000	2,000		2,000	2,000	
Short-term loans.........						
Long-term loans.........						
Other...................						
Total..............	$329,000	$337,000	$ 8,000	$539,600	$537,000	$2,600
Cash payments:						
Raw materials...........	$ 87,200	$ 85,000	$ 2,200	$179,100	$174,000	$5,100
Direct labor.............	76,200	74,000	2,200	156,500	154,000	2,500
Manufacturing expense...	52,800	48,000	4,800	96,700	98,000	1,300
Selling expense..........	41,600	39,000	2,600	77,000	79,000	2,000
Administrative expense...	38,600	37,000	1,600	74,400	73,000	1,400
Federal income tax.......						
Interest expense..........						
Dividends...............					20,000	20,000
Fixed assets.............						
Repayment of loans......						
Investment in securities...						
Other—.................						
Total..............	$296,400	$283,000	$13,400	$603,700	$598,000	$5,700
Excess of actual receipts/ payments over budget...			$21,400			$3,100

sure the constant availability of adequate cash, it should not be inferred that they are the only classes of cash reports prepared by business firms. But other classes are generally concerned with the safeguarding of cash, rather than with its availability; these include statements for the reconciliation of deposit balances as reported by banks with the cash balances shown in the accounting records, and reports on disbursements from, and balances in, petty cash funds.

Moreover, one should not infer that financial managers, in attempting to control the flow of cash, make decisions solely on the basis of cash reports. A judgment about a firm's cash position at a given time can be sound only if the person making the judgment knows what are its volume of accounts receivable, inventory position, obligations owing to trade creditors, accrued payroll, unpaid obligations for all kinds of accumulated expenses, and so on. In other words, he must know what the prospects are for cash inflows and outflows in the immediate future—not only on the basis of what was budgeted several months earlier, but on the basis of *what has actually happened* in the immediate past to sales and purchases on account, the incurring of expenses on a deferred-payment basis, and so on. Accordingly, the financial managers must, as a rule, give as close attention to periodic reports of accounts receivable, inventories, accounts payable, payrolls, and the like, as they give to daily and monthly cash reports.

OPERATING STATEMENTS AS TOOLS OF CONTROL

Well-designed budget systems usually include a forecasting of the results of operations for the coming year in terms of income and expenses and net profit or loss; and well-designed accounting systems always provide for operating statements to show what the results of operations have actually been. Forecasts are made at least for the full year, but often also for monthly, quarterly, or semiannual periods; while accounting statements that show the actual results of operations are a "must" for the full year, but most useful, too, when also prepared for monthly, quarterly, or semiannual periods. Operating statements of both the forecast and actual-results varieties are of major importance as tools of cash control, as the following discussion will show.

Projected Operating Statements and Changes in Plans

The primary financial objective of business operations is the earning of profits, and not simply insuring that the enterprise will have at all times enough cash to meet its maturing obligations. A cash budget drawn up by a corporation on the basis of preliminary operating plans for the coming year may show that its cash balance at the end of the year would be larger than the opening balance; but a projected or *pro forma* income statement may indicate that, if the preliminary plans of operation are carried into effect, the result will be a net loss. The prospects of a net loss on operations, as pictured in the *pro forma* statement, might lead to decisions for comprehensive changes in operating plans—changes aimed toward reducing expenses and increasing income or toward finding new sources of income. But such changes would doubtless require major alterations in the cash budget, probably introducing cash management problems of a much more difficult kind than had been anticipated in relation to the original plans.

All of which does not imply that prospective profits can always be increased or losses eliminated by changes in operating plans. In many cases, an analysis of projected operating statements will, indeed, reveal defects in preliminary plans that can be corrected; but in many others, the results estimated in projected statements will be quickly recognized as the best that can be hoped for. At any rate, the thing to be emphasized is that a favorable cash outlook is not enough—it must always be related to the outlook for profits and losses. In some instances, the profit prospects can be substantially improved without giving rise to insuperable difficulties in cash management; in others, projected cash flows and positions preclude material changes in operating plans, even though the changes would improve profit prospects; and in still others, a compromise may appear to be the best solution—one recognizing that moderate changes in operating plans are compatible with the cash outlook.

Illustration. The reason why changes in cash balances as projected in cash budgets may differ widely from anticipated profits and losses was indicated in the preceding chapter in the discussion of differences in the contents of cash budgets and income statements.[1] For a further consideration of this matter and its significance, we may again refer to the affairs of the Carver Manufacturing Corporation. With its cash budget for the year 19yy before us (as presented on page 257 in the preceding chapter), let us examine its projected statement of cost of goods manufactured and income statement for the same year. We may assume that these two statements were set up as in Figures 13-3 and 13-4.

As we see at once, the projected increase in cash and its "equivalent" (in this instance, short-term marketable treasury securities) is far different from the anticipated net profit on operations after allowance for federal income taxes. The cash budget reveals an expected decrease in cash from $415,000 to $388,000, but an increase in holdings of short-term securities from $150,000 to $200,000, making for a net increase in cash and equiva-

FIGURE 13-3
Carver Manufacturing Corporation
Statement of Cost of Goods Manufactured
Projected for the Year Ending December 31, 19yy

Raw materials:		
Inventory, January 1	$110,000	
Purchases	552,000	
	$662,000	
Less: Inventory, December 31	145,000	$ 517,000
Direct labor		937,000
Manufacturing expense:		
Depreciation—factory building	$ 5,000	
Depreciation—machinery and equipment	60,000	
All other	623,500	688,500
		$2,142,500
Add: Goods in process, January 1		92,000
		$2,234,500
Less: Goods in process, December 31		109,000
Cost of Goods Manufactured		$2,125,500

[1] See above, pp. 248-49.

FIGURE 13–4
Carver Manufacturing Corporation
Income Statement
Projected for the Year Ending December 31, 19yy

Gross sales..		$3,467,000
Less: Returns and allowances..........................		69,000
Net sales...		$3,398,000
Cost of goods sold:		
Finished goods inventory, January 1...................	$ 158,000	
Cost of goods manufactured..........................	2,125,500	
	$2,283,500	
Less: Finished goods inventory, December 31..........	227,000	2,056,500
Gross profit on sales....................................		$1,341,500
Selling and administrative expenses:		
Depreciation—delivery equipment.....................	$ 2,000	
Depreciation—office equipment.......................	500	
Bad debts...	13,600	
Other selling expenses..............................	551,000	
Other administrative expenses.......................	463,000	1,030,100
Net profit on sales.....................................		$ 311,400
Other expense:		
Interest expense....................................		4,500
		$ 306,900
Other income:		
Rental income......................................	$ 16,667	
Interest income.....................................	3,750	
Purchase discounts..................................	6,100	26,517
		$ 333,417
Estimated liability for federal income tax.................		167,877
Net Profit..		$ 165,540

lent of $23,000. But the *pro forma* income statement, as supported by the statement of manufacturing costs, projects a net profit of $165,540 after the deduction of $167,877 for estimated federal income taxes. If the net profit will be approximately $165,540, why will cash and its equivalent increase by only $23,000? The answer must be that some of the expense and income items entered in the operating statements are not reflected in the cash budget because of prepayments and deferments, and that some of the cash receipts and disbursements entered in the cash budget (in this instance, cash disbusements only) are not reflected in the operating statements. Outstanding among these differences are the expenditure of $150,000 for new machines shown as a payment in the cash budget but not taken up anywhere in the operating statements; the total charges for depreciation of $67,500 in the operating statements not requiring a cash disbursement and not therefore shown in the cash budget; the big deduction in the income statement of $167,877 for estimated federal income taxes, whereas only $78,000 for income tax payments is entered among the disbursements in the cash budget; and the payment of cash dividends of $80,000 to the stockholders shown as such in the cash budget but ignored in the operating statements.[2]

Cash Budget Items Based upon Projected Operating Statements

Apart from serving as a means of coordinating, as it were, the profit- and cash-control objectives of business enterprises, projected operating statements yield certain kinds of information essential for sound cash budget policies. For the Carver Manufacturing Corporation, the entries for federal income tax payments in September and December, 19yy, in the cash budget could only be based upon the total tax liability as computed in the projected income statement on the estimated net profit for the year. (Under the Internal Revenue Code, any corporation that expects to have a net profit of more than $100,000 in the current year is required to file by the fifteenth day of the ninth month of that year a declaration of estimated tax, and to pay by that day a first instalment of the estimated tax, as well as to pay a second instalment by the fifteenth day of the twelfth month of the year.) Again, the expectation that Carver's directors will vote the regular quarterly dividend of $20,000, as shown in the cash budget, would presumably have for its basis the level of anticipated net profit after income taxes, as revealed in the *pro forma* income statement. And, finally, the decision to use cash already on hand in the amount of $150,000 to pay for the machines to be bought in November, as indicated in the cash budget, would be likely to be predicated also on the profit expectation as arrived at in the income statement. The payment of $150,000 would not be a drain from the circular process—from working capital, that is—since all of it could be considered as coming from the cash throw-off on account of depreciation and profits "plowed under" after provision for federal income tax and the payment of dividends.

One should not conclude, however, that information about cash receipts from sales and cash expenditures for operating expenses would be drawn from projected statements of manufacturing costs and income statements for inclusion, after proper adjustment, in the cash budget. As was indicated in the preceding chapter, this sort of information is drawn from separate budgets for sales, accounts receivable, production, direct labor, inventories, manufacturing expenses, and so on. These detailed budgets provide the data for the construction of both the cash budget and the *pro forma* operating statements; and only certain special items of information that appear in the *pro forma* statements, as applied in the manner described in the preceding paragraph, lay the foundation for additional entries in the cash budget.

---

[2] A "statement of sources and application of funds" may be used to show the complete relationship between changes in cash and equivalent, on the one hand, and profits, tax liabilities and payments, prepayments and deferments, and other items, on the other. Such a statement is illustrated and discussed below. See pp. 279–82.

Current Operating Statements

As tools of cash control, current operating statements of actual results, as distinct from projected ones, supplement daily and monthly cash reports, as do reports of sales, inventories, accounts receivable, accounts payable, and accrued expenses. They are clearly supplementary because, in most instances, results shown in current operating statements substantially different from those forecast will have already been reflected in the daily and monthly cash reports. If, from time to time, the volume of sales or of manufacturing operations get out of line from the levels forecast, the inflows and outflows of cash are likely to vary commensurately.

It is possible, however, for the cash flows to be proceeding much as was expected while out-of-line situations of harmful character are developing elsewhere. For example, raw materials may be purchased in the usual quantities at the prices anticipated, and payments made to the suppliers at the appropriate times, but extraordinary amounts of spoilage in manufacturing operations may occur. This fact might be observed by a careful examination of periodic inventory reports or of specific spoilage reports, but it would surely be "dramatized" by the higher-than-expected manufacturing costs shown in a current statement of such costs and by the lower-than-expected profit as disclosed in a current income statement.

BALANCE SHEETS AS TOOLS OF CONTROL

It is most advantageous for the financial managers of a business enterprise to have available for analysis forecasts of the financial position of their enterprise for various dates in the approaching year, as well as to have periodic reports on the actual financial position as the year progresses. Hence, projected or *pro forma* balance sheets are important as tools of planning, and current balance sheets, important as instruments of continuing control.

Projected Balance Sheets

Although the expected level of cash at the end of each month or quarter in the coming year can be picked up from the cash budget, the amount of accounts receivable, from the receivables budget, the amount of inventories, from the inventory budgets, the amount of current obligations, from accounts payable, payroll, and accrued expense budgets, and so on, it is most convenient to bring these items together in one place as soon as the detailed budgets have been completed. This is done by the preparation of projected monthly or quarterly balance sheets. A projected balance sheet makes it possible to judge to what extent an enterprise's financial position will be strengthened or weakened as a result of its planned activities up to the date for which it is prepared.

Often projected balance sheets reveal errors in planning or expectations not readily discoverable elsewhere. Because a projected balance sheet brings together all prospective assets and liabilities as of a given date, unsatisfactory groupings and relationships among groups can be readily seen. While working upon the detailed separate budgets for the coming year, the financial managers of a corporation might make unrelated decisions for substantial spending in April for machinery and equipment and a substantial outlay to meet an instalment on a long-term loan, and for large purchases of raw materials on account in May. No bar to these transactions in the two months might be indicated by the entry of the proposed cash disbursements in the cash budget; but a *pro forma* balance sheet for April 30 of the coming year might show that the corporation's working capital position would be gravely weakened by the proposed April transactions. Projected balance sheets for later months might reveal that the weakness in working capital would be temporary, but the financial managers would realize that it would be showing up starkly at the very time that the suppliers of raw materials would be asked to grant extraordinary credits. Rather than holding to plans that could lead to the embarrassment of having their requests for credit refused, the financial managers would surely be inclined to rearrange the timing of the three transactions.

In a similar way, corporate financial managers know that their reported balance sheets are analyzed by prospective lenders, stockholders, bondholders, prospective investors in their stocks and bonds, and others who have financial interests of one kind or another. Accordingly, they have good reason to switch to new plans if the effects of earlier tentative decisions, as reflected in *pro forma* balance sheets, would be likely to be judged adversely by competent analysts. The contents of an actual balance sheet to be published some months hence must be expected to be quite close to the projected one—otherwise, forecasting would be nonsensical. If, therefore, the projected statement looks weak, plans must be changed so that the balance sheet of actual position *will not look so* when the time for its publication comes.

Because analysts tend to place great weight upon various ratios computed from balance sheet data, the financial managers of businesses should find it advisable to compute the same kinds of ratios with respect to the figures assembled in their projected balance sheets. This should enable them to see in what direction the judgments of the analysts are likely to go, and to prompt them to change plans should it appear that the judgments are likely to be adverse. Of significance, therefore, are ratios of the kinds discussed in earlier chapters—cash to current liabilities, accounts receivable to credit sales, cost of goods sold to average inventories, fixed assets to sales, operating assets to sales, and so on. Many other ratios can be computed, but we need not survey the list, nor need we rehash the significance, merits, and demerits of those considered earlier. But we should find it advantageous to give further consideration to the analysis of working capital position, since balance sheet analysts always emphasize that aspect of financial standing. The matter of working capital position was briefly discussed in Chapter 7, but there attention was given chiefly to the relationship of cash to current liabilities.

Working Capital Ratio. Although one may know very little about balance sheet analysis, one is likely to know that the working capital ratio is the most widely used of all analytical devices based on the balance sheet, that it is the ratio of total current assets to total current liabilities, and that a widely respected rule of thumb is that the ratio should be no weaker than 2 to 1.

The great popularity of the working capital ratio reflects the fact that almost everybody who has occasion to analyze balance sheets, whether he is primarily interested in the short-term or the long-term outlook, knows that the outlook for any period of time can only be bleak for firms that are not currently *solvent,* that is, in a position apparently to meet obligations currently coming due and expected to come due in the near future. Cash need not be already available to meet all the current liabilities shown in a balance sheet; but there should be good prospects of an adequate short-term inflow, indicated by holdings of accounts receivable and inventories. For most kinds of enterprises, therefore, working capital analysis is an examination of the relationship between cash (and "equivalent," that is, short-term treasury obligations and other short-term high-quality investments), accounts receivable, and inventories on the one hand, and the array of current liabilities on the other.

It might appear that if the total of cash, accounts receivable, and inventories is equal to the total of current liabilities, solvency is assured, so that to look for a ratio in the vicinity of 2 to 1 is to expect too much. But creditors want a margin of protection. There may be delays in collecting upon accounts receivable, and even greater delays in converting inventories into accounts receivable and, in turn, collecting upon these accounts; but due dates of liabilities come along without interruption, unless further deferments are specially arranged for. Looking at the situation from another angle, it may be said that short-term creditors think it would be most unreasonable for them to be the sole suppliers of a firm's current assets. When, therefore, they insist upon a ratio such as 2 to 1, they say in effect that at least half of the current assets should be supplied by the stockholders; however, they may be satisfied if some or even all of this half is provided by long-term creditors, such as bondholders.

Nevertheless, a working capital ratio such as 2 to 1 should not be regarded as something sacred. In some lines of business, firms tend consistently to have ratios weaker than this without adverse judgment; and in many others, stronger ratios are commonplace and often come to be generally expected. The intelligent analyst knows, moreover, that the ratio of the individual firm will vary from month to month or from quarter to quarter, sometimes quite materially, according to changing circumstances having no great bearing upon solvency. He will keep in mind, too, the possibility of "window dressing"[3] as a procedure to improve the appearance of working capital positions.

In sum, the financial managers of business enterprises want working capital positions as indicated in projected balance sheets to be in line with what is expected in their respective fields of business activity. Although an unfavorable projection is only an expectation, they would not want to aim for a situation they would not want to come about. All the more is this true if they expect to publish or to supply to creditors actual balance sheets for the dates for which the projections are made—hence, the desirability of changing plans to make the projected balance sheets, and, it is presumed, the actual balance sheets later on, look as favorable as possible.

Acid Test. A second testing device for working capital position is known as the "acid test" or the "quick ratio." It is the ratio of cash (and "equivalent") and receivables, reduced by the reserve for bad debts, to the total of current liabilities. The application of the acid test to the working capital position of a firm is predicated on the obvious fact that inventories are a step further removed from cash than are accounts receivable, and upon the idea, therefore, that short-term creditors ought to be able to expect payment from existing cash balances and collections from accounts receivable, and not have to depend upon the liquidation of inventories. Hence 1 to 1 is often said to be a desirable standard for the acid test.

But, as with the working capital ratio itself, an acid-test "standard" such as 1 to 1 ought not to be worshipped as something sacred. Much depends upon circumstances. A seasonal business that seeks to stabilize production will tend to have a weak acid-test ratio during its period of slack sales, but, probably, a powerful one in its period of heavy selling. The earlier weak position, therefore, would have to be judged in relation to the market prospects for the firm's products in the later period.

In the use of projected balance sheets as tools of planning, at any rate, financial managers must surely keep in mind the widespread application of the acid test, and take steps to adjust policies should projections indicate that at certain times in the coming year this ratio, in the absence of the adjustments, would look quite unfavorable to prospective creditors and other analysts.

Illustration. To illustrate the use of working capital and acid-test ratios, we may refer once again to the affairs of the Carver Manufacturing Corporation. Its expected financial position at the end of the year 19xx was indicated in the balance sheet presented near the end of the preceding chapter on page 255. In the matter of working capital, its projected situation would appear to be a most favorable one. The projected working capital ratio is 7.5 to 1 (total current assets of $1,370,250 to total current liabilities of $183,500), and the acid test, 5.2 to 1 (total current assets of

---
[3] See above, pp. 133–34.

$954,250, after excluding inventories and prepaid expenses, to current liabilities of $183,500)—both far above the rule-of-thumb standards, and presumably quite satisfactory on any other basis, considering all that we now know of the activities of our illustrative corporation.

But Carver's managers would be especially interested in what their financial and working capital positions are likely to be at the end of March, 19yy, since they expect to go to the bank to borrow money in April, and at the end of April, since they expect to return to the bank for another loan in May. They want to be able to present favorable current balance sheets to the bankers at the appropriate times. For our purposes, however, it should suffice to consider only the projected situation at the end of March. Let us assume, then, that the *pro forma* balance sheet drawn up for that date is that presented in Figure 13-5.

Thus, the working capital ratio at the end of March is expected to be slightly stronger than at the end of December, at 7.6 to 1 (total current assets of $1,273,350 to total current liabilities of $163,380); but the acid-test ratio is expected to be down from 5.2 to 1 to 2.5 to 1 (total cash and net receivables of $420,600 to total current liabilities of $163,380). Nevertheless, Carver's officers would not be likely to regard the indicated "deterioration" in the acid-test ratio a serious matter. The ratio remains well above the rule-of-thumb standard, and the decline in the three-month period is defensible as something to be expected in a period of heavy inventory stocking by a seasonal enterprise having a policy of stabilizing production.

Current Balance Sheets

As actual operations produce changes in the financial position of a business enterprise during the course of a year or other period of time, the net effects of these changes can be seen in balance sheets prepared from time to time. Just as planned programs of operation can be approved when projected balance sheets indicate that they will result in the maintenance of a favorable financial condition, so also can such programs continue to merit approval when current balance sheets indicate that a satisfactory financial position continues to be maintained; and just as changes in plans may be decided upon because projected balance sheets disclose that, without the changes, an unsatisfactory financial position would result, so also may plans be changed in "midstream," as it were, when current balance sheets indicate that operations to date have resulted in a deteriorating financial position.

Thus, current balance sheets serve as important instruments of continuing control. Their significance as instruments of control tends to be somewhat greater, of course, if they are to be supplied to prospective creditors or otherwise published; but a lack of pressure for disclosure should hardly be expected to reduce their significance in any material way. For example, the financial managers of a corporation that publishes a balance

FIGURE 13–5
Carver Manufacturing Corporation
Balance Sheet
Projected for March 31, 19yy

ASSETS

Current Assets:

Cash...		$ 301,500
Accounts receivable.........................	$128,300	
Less: Reserve for bad debts.................	9,200	119,100
Inventories:		
Raw materials.............................	$216,000	
Goods in process.........................	132,000	
Finished goods............................	444,000	792,000
Prepaid expenses............................		60,750
Total Current Assets.....................		$1,273,350

Fixed Assets:

Land...		$ 38,000
Factory building............................	$200,000	
Less: Allowance for depreciation...........	76,250	123,750
Machinery and equipment....................	$900,000	
Less: Allowance for depreciation...........	255,000	645,000
Delivery equipment.........................	$ 12,000	
Less: Allowance for depreciation...........	4,500	7,500
Office equipment............................	$ 10,000	
Less: Allowance for depreciation...........	4,125	5,875
Total Fixed Assets......................		820,125
Total Assets...........................		$2,093,475

LIABILITIES AND EQUITY

Current Liabilities:

Accounts payable....................................	$ 49,880	
Accrued wages......................................	32,250	
Accrued expenses...................................	60,250	
Accrued taxes......................................	21,000	
Total Current Liabilities.........................		$ 163,380

Deferred Credit:

Rent received in advance.............................		5,000

Stockholders' Equity:

Capital stock..	$1,600,000	
Earned surplus......................................	325,095	
Total Equity.......................................		1,925,095
Total Liabilities and Equity......................		$2,093,475

sheet and operating statements only annually must know that developments revealed in monthly and quarterly statements, though these are prepared only for internal use, must eventually be reflected in the annual published reports.

STATEMENTS OF SOURCES AND APPLICATIONS OF FUNDS

Often useful as an additional tool of financial management are *statements of sources and applications of funds*. Such a statement is essentially an explanation of changes in financial position as revealed in successive balance sheets. It can be used for projections to show why the financial position of an enterprise at the end of given future periods is expected to be different from that at earlier dates; and it may be used currently to explain what has actually caused changes in financial position between balance sheet dates.

The format of statements of sources and applications of funds differs widely, depending upon the kinds of changes in financial position that the analyst wishes to emphasize. Since, however, our interest is primarily in cash control, we may confine our attention to an illustrative statement designed to account for changes in cash balances between two balance sheet dates. We return, as it were, to the question raised earlier in this chapter as to why changes in holdings of cash and its equivalent may differ greatly from the amounts of profits or losses reported in operating statements. In the earlier discussion, the principal reasons for differences in the projections of the Carver Manufacturing Corporation for the year 19yy were stated, but now it is desirable to account for all reasons for differences, both major and minor—in other words, to show precisely how the total difference between changes in cash balances and the amount of profits is expected to come about in the year 19yy. We already have on page 255 of the preceding chapter the projected balance sheet for December 31, 19xx, and we now need such a statement for December 31, 19yy. In Figure 13–6, therefore, an assumed statement for the latter date is presented, and, for convenience in comparison, the earlier statement is repeated.

Our explanation, then, would take the form of a statement of sources and applications of funds set up as in Figure 13–7.

Analysis

The statement shows that the amount of cash and equivalent, in the absence of "applications," would be expected to increase by the full amount of the net profit before allowance for federal income taxes and by much more besides, for a total of $459,250. The increments of cash beyond the amount of the profit would be expected to come from the cash throw-off occasioned by depreciation charges to the amount of $67,500; through a "conservation" of cash totaling $39,400 by the acquisition of raw materials, supplies, and services on account, as indicated by the entries for accounts payable, accrued wages, and accrued expenses; because credit customers are expected to pay $15,600 in excess of the amount of sales to them in the year, as indicated by the entry for the decrease in accounts

FIGURE 13–6

Carver Manufacturing Corporation
Balance Sheets
Projected for December 31, 19xx and 19yy

	19xx		*19yy*	
ASSETS				
Current Assets:				
Cash..........................		$ 415,000		$ 388,000
Short-term treasury obligations...		350,000		400,000
Accounts receivable.............	$ 195,000		$ 186,400	
Less: Reserve for bad debts.....	8,000	187,000	15,000	171,400
Accrued interest receivable......		2,250		2,500
Inventories:				
Raw materials...............	$ 110,000		$ 145,000	
Goods in process.............	92,000		109,000	
Finished goods...............	158,000	360,000	227,000	481,000
Prepaid expenses...............		56,000		63,000
Total Current Assets........		$1,370,250		$1,505,900
Fixed Assets:				
Land.........................		38,000		38,000
Factory building...............	$ 200,000		$ 200,000	
Less: Allowance for depreciation	75,000	125,000	80,000	120,000
Machinery and equipment.......	$ 900,000		$1,050,000	
Less: Allowance for depreciation	240,000	660,000	300,000	750,000
Delivery equipment.............	$ 12,000		$ 12,000	
Less: Allowance for depreciation	4,000	8,000	6,000	6,000
Office equipment...............	$ 10,000		$ 10,000	
Less: Allowance for depreciation	4,000	6,000	4,500	5,500
Total Fixed Assets..........		$ 837,000		$ 919,500
Total Assets.............		$2,207,250		$2,425,400
LIABILITIES AND EQUITY				
Current Liabilities:				
Accounts payable...............	$ 65,500		$ 78,400	
Accrued wages.................	30,000		36,000	
Accrued expenses...............	46,000		66,500	
Accrued taxes..................	42,000		131,877	
Total Current Liabilities....		$ 183,500		$ 312,777
Deferred Credit:				
Rent received in advance........				3,333
Stockholders' Equity:				
Capital stock..................	$1,600,000		$1,600,000	
Earned surplus.................	423,750		509,290	
Total Equity...............		2,023,750		2,109,290
Total Liabilities and Equity		$2,207,250		$2,425,400

FIGURE 13–7

Carver Manufacturing Corporation
Statement of Sources and Applications of Funds
Projected for the Year 19yy

Cash and equivalent, January 1, 19yy.............................$765,000
   (Cash, $415,000, short-term treasury obligations, $350,000)

Add sources of cash:

Net profit before deduction of federal income tax...............	$333,417
Cash throw-off from depreciation..............................	67,500
Increase in accounts payable.................................	12,900
Increase in accrued wages...................................	6,000
Increase in accrued expenses.................................	20,500
Decrease in accounts receivable..............................	15,600
Rent received in advance....................................	3,333
	$459,250

Deduct applications of cash:

Payment of dividends to stockholders.........................	$ 80,000
Payment of federal income taxes.............................	78,000
Purchase of machinery......................................	150,000
Increase in inventories.....................................	121,000
Increase in prepaid expenses................................	7,000
Increase in accrued interest receivable.......................	250
	$436,250

Net increase in cash and equivalent............................$ 23,000

Cash and equivalent, December 31, 19yy........................$788,000
   (Cash, $388,000, short-term treasury obligations, $400,000)

receivable; and because of the anticipated prepayment by Carver's tenant of $3,333 of rent.

But cash and equivalent are not expected to increase by $459,250, or by any sum near that figure, on account of anticipated uses or "applications" of cash during the coming year. It is anticipated that $80,000 will be paid to the stockholders as dividends, that $78,000 will be paid to the federal Treasury on account of income taxes, and that $150,000 of cash will be used in buying additional machinery. It is anticipated, moreover, that $121,000 of cash will be devoted to expanding inventories, and that payments of $7,000 will be made in the year 19yy for expense items chargeable to later years, and therefore not to be deducted in computing the profit for 19yy. And, finally, it is anticipated that interest income in the amount of $250, though to be included in profit in the year 19yy, will not have been realized in cash by the end of that year.

Thus, projected "applications" come to a total of $436,250, and the deduction of this amount from the expected total of the "sources" leaves a net projected increase in cash and equivalant of only $23,000.

Suggested Uses

Although the preparation of statements of sources and applications of funds appears to be fully justified by their function as a managerial tool, some corporation executives, writers on finance, and accountants recommend putting them to other uses. It is their contention that stockholders, employees and their unions, solicitors of funds for charitable purposes, and others often misjudge corporations' capacities to pay dividends and wages, to give donations, and to make other kinds of cash outlays, because they look only at reported figures of corporate profits. Since, therefore, statements of sources and applications of funds—of the form used in our illustration—clearly show that profits and cash availability are not necessarily closely related, the recommendation is that such statements be included as a matter of course with annual reports to stockholders, among the documents to be considered in wage-bargaining negotiations, and wherever else publicity is given to the size of profits.

FIXED ASSET BUDGETS

It was stated in the preceding chapter that the financial managers of business enterprises are particularly concerned with cash and fixed asset budgets. Much space was subsequently allotted in that chapter and in the present one to a discussion of cash budget principles and procedures; it remains for us, therefore, to give attention to fixed asset budgets. However, because of the lengthy examination of fixed asset management in Chapters 10 and 11—an examination encompassing many topics closely related to decision making about fixed asset acquisitions—an adequate treatment of budgeting for fixed assets will require at this time much less space than has been given to budgeting for cash.

Scope of Fixed Asset Budgets

From the standpoint of the periods for which plans are made, fixed asset budgets are said to be of two kinds: annual budgets and long-term budgets. Annual fixed asset budgets are comparable to budgets for raw materials, direct labor, and the various classes of overhead expenses in that they set out for the coming year the anticipated costs to be incurred from month to month in the purchase of fixed assets. Like budgets of the kinds mentioned, therefore, they serve as a source from which details about expected monthly cash expenditures are drawn for inclusion in cash budgets. The use of annual fixed asset budgets tends to be confined to relatively large enterprises that have great aggregations of fixed assets of many kinds, among which replacements must constantly be made, and to which additions are constantly required. Smaller concerns, as well as larger ones with limited amounts and varieties of fixed assets, can usually get along without annual fixed asset budgets; their long-term budgets provide details of projected fixed asset expenditures of the approaching year sufficient for the requirements of their cash budgets.

A long-term fixed asset budget is a projection of expected expenditures for fixed assets for a period of years. Very often, the period covered is describable more properly as "intermediate" rather than as "long," since it may be as short as three years, and only occasionally does it exceed ten years. It is probable that five years is the most common planning period. Long-term fixed asset budgets are useful for enterprises of all sizes, small and large, and they are of special importance to financial managers, since long-range financing plans must be closely related to them. Since it may be assumed that, typically, the details of annual fixed asset budgets, where used, are picked up from the long-term ones, we may well confine our attention in the following paragraphs to the latter.

Basis of Long-Term Fixed Asset Budgets

As in the preparation of the many kinds of annual budgets, the setting up of a long-term fixed asset budget begins with a forecast of sales. The longer the period of years for which a sales forecast can reasonably be made, the longer is the period that can be covered by a fixed asset budget. A firm that has experienced an expansion in its sales volume at a steady rate over a period of many years—even though interrupted at times by recessions in general business activity—has a basis for a rather confident prediction of the pace at which it will have to expand output and the pace at which, therefore, it will have to augment its productive facilities in the next few years. This has generally been the situation for many firms engaged in the basic steel and aluminum industries, those that provide certain kinds of public utility services, such as water, electricity, and air transportation, and many that produce certain kinds of consumer goods, such as automobiles and some varieties of foodstuffs. On the contrary, the sales outlook for firms in some industries is often so cloudy that little can be done in the way of planning long-range expenditures for fixed assets. This appears to be especially true of most branches of the textile industry at the present time.

In the preparation of annual operating budgets, as we saw in the preceding chapter, the sales forecast is followed up by the preparation of detailed budgets of the expected costs of production, selling, and administration. Something of the same kind must be done for the projection of fixed asset acquisitions. Although forecasts of operating costs for several years can hardly be expected to be as accurate as short-run projections, or even as accurate as the longer-run projections of sales, reliable estimations of future operating costs must be made available, for otherwise the merits of proposals for acquisitions of fixed assets could hardly be soundly evaluated. It is said, indeed, that *every* proposed addition to fixed assets that will require the expenditure of more than a modest sum of money must be shown to be necessary to maintain or expand a firm's profitability. Such a demonstration cannot be made solely in terms of projected sales. Without related cost estimates, sales projections must obviously be of little value. Attention must surely be given to the fixed costs that the very acquisitions and uses of new fixed assets will entail, that is, depreciation, maintenance and repairs, property taxes, and insurance; but deserving equal attention are the economies that the new facilities are expected to make possible, such as reduced need of labor and reduced spoilage of materials.

Contents of Long-Term Fixed Asset Budgets

For a large number of firms, plans for expenditures found in long-term fixed asset budgets are quite closely, if not exclusively, confined to replacements of existing fixed assets. If a firm's sales volume has not been expanding, and is not expected to expand, it is not likely to be planning to buy additional facilities. The principal problem of fixed asset budgeting for such firms is, therefore, one of estimating the useful lives of present facilities—a problem quite closely related, obviously, to the depreciation question. Regardless of depreciation policy, however, the possibility of "extraordinary obsolescence" often deserves special emphasis. In other words, due weight must be given to the possibility that the useful lives of fixed assets will be substantially shorter than the Internal Revenue Service allows for in its regulations on "allowable" depreciation. And, always, of course, there is the additional problem of the wisdom of replacing facilities at all—the problem of purchase versus rental, as considered in Chapter 10.

The long-term fixed asset budgets of business enterprises that anticipate continued growth in sales must include estimated expenditures both for replacement and for the addition of facilities. Their problems of forecasting expenditures for replacement are necessarily much the same as for firms that do not expect to expand, as mentioned in the preceding paragraph. As for additions to facilities, the content of budgets depends upon the expected direction and rate of growth. Firms that expect simply to expand the output of their existing lines need ordinarily plan only for buying facilities of the kinds they already have. Their officers should already be thoroughly familiar with the capacities of such facilities, their costs, both present and prospective, and the competence and dependability of the various suppliers. On the other hand, firms that expect their growth to come chiefly from new product lines are likely to have their estimates of expenditures clouded somewhat by uncertainties about what kinds of new facilities should be selected, what combinations would make for greatest efficiency, and what would be the best timing for the acquisitions.

Because expansion programs often require lengthy periods for their completion, long-term fixed asset budgets must be as accurate as possible in indicating the pace at which, month by month, payments must be made from start to completion. A fixed asset budget would be of little value if a figure such as $5 million were entered for a given year as the estimated total cost of a building program to be started in that year, and if expectations were that completion of the program would require two or three years. Nor would the spreading of the proposed expenditure evenly on a monthly basis over the whole construction period be of much help, since payments for construction are generally contracted for, not according to any plan of even spacing, but according to the various stages of completion.

Long-term fixed asset budgets must also include estimates of cash proceeds or trade-in values of facilities to be disposed of during the forecast period. The sale of unused present facilities in the secondhand market, or their sale as "scrap," may be expected to produce a cash inflow during the forecast period that will offset in part contemplated expenditures for new facilities—perhaps only in a moderate way, but still significantly— and, of course, allowances for trade-ins in connection with the purchase of new facilities likewise reduce the net outlays that will be required.

Finally, long-term fixed asset budgets (and annual ones, as well) do not include estimated expenditures for the maintenance and repair of fixed assets and for "small tools" and other kinds of short-lived equipment. Although difficulties in distinguishing between repairs and maintenance, on the one hand, and betterments or improvements, on the other, are numerous (as was pointed out in Chapter 11), it is always advisable that the distinction be drawn as closely as possible, so that expenditures that can reasonably be classed as betterments can be included in the fixed asset budget, while those for repairs and maintenance can be relegated to the ordinary annual expense budgets. In the matter of short-lived equipment such as small tools, the "fixed asset" designation may be given to the inventory of the quantity on hand as carried in the balance sheet, but the usual practice is to treat, much the same as any other operating expense, the cost of such equipment used up in a year or other short period. Hence, the estimated costs of replenishing short-lived equipment are customarily carried in the regular expense budgets.

Significance of Long-Term Fixed Asset Budgets

Financial managers realize that without long-range fixed asset budgets, financial planning can fall into serious error. If proposals for fixed asset expenditure are taken up one by one, and only for the year ahead, with approvals and rejections determined on the merits of each proposal standing by itself, financing capacity may be exhausted before the most important proposals—to be reached only in later years—come up for consideration. On the other hand, all the preliminary studies and analyses that are necessary for deciding what is to go into a long-term fixed asset budget almost guarantee that each spending proposal will be evaluated, not simply on its own merits, but in relation to the merits of all others. In the purchase of fixed assets, as in so many other phases of its activities, a business enterprise does not have sufficient access to cash to do all the things that it would like to do, and even though every proposal may promise significant benefits, the enterprise must often limit its choices— presumably to the proposals that promise the greatest benefits.

The long-term budgeting of fixed asset acquisitions makes possible a proper timing of whatever preliminary steps must be taken to get projects under way, as well as the timing of the actual commencement of the projects. A new factory building requires a desirable site, architectural plans, and the working out of arrangements with building contractors. The design and manufacture of new machines often, too, require much time, so that it is highly advantageous to be able to order them well before the time when they will be needed. Delays in taking actions of the kinds indicated can result in substantial increases in financial burdens, including higher costs for the facilities themselves, higher interest rates on money borrowed, and the loss of potential sales because of temporary inadequacies in productive capacity due to delayed construction or delivery of new facilities.

Long-term budgeting for fixed assets can also eliminate repeated heavy costs of arranging and rearranging factory, store, and office layouts. Plans made from year to year confined to machinery acquisitions of the following year, for example, can result in poor placement of the successive acquisitions. Each year's additions might not seem to justify a rearrangement of factory layout, but fitting them in to the existing layout could mean a considerable loss of efficiency; and a continued process of "fitting in" might result in general disorganization after a few years. On the other hand, should the layout be adjusted in the first year to make for the most efficient use of that year's acquisitions, costly additional adjustments might have to be made in each of the following years in aiming at the goal of maximum efficiency. But if all the acquisitions to take place over a period of, say, five years were planned for originally in a long-term budget, a single rearrangement of layout could probably also be planned at once, allowing space, as it were, for the successive additions. The financial managers might decide, indeed, that it would be cheaper to acquire immediately many of the facilities expected to be needed over a five-year period than to obtain them, portion by portion, annually—cheaper in precluding repeated serious disruptions in production for installation.

Finally deserving mention among the advantages of long-term budgeting for fixed assets is the possibility of concentrating expenditures in periods in which the prices of such assets are relatively low. The heavy demand for productive facilities in periods of high prosperity tends to drive up their prices and to make for delays in deliveries. Hence, it would appear to be wise for the individual firm to try to concentrate its spending for fixed assets to periods of general business contraction when prices tend to fall and building contractors, machinery manufacturers, and others have idle capacity. It requires courage to go ahead with expansion projects at times when a firm itself has idle capacity, but if its managers have confidence in their own long-range sales forecast—and, therefore, in their long-range projections of fixed asset needs—they have good reason to accelerate spending for such assets. Not least among the merits of such a procedure is the contribution that it is likely to make to social welfare. By reducing demand for productive facilities in times of prosperity and increasing it in times of business slump, the individual firm makes a contribution toward stability in the whole economy.

Questions

1. If a firm's sales fall off sharply as a result of a general business recession, does not this development make its cash budget quite useless? Explain.

2. What kind of information is presented in daily and monthly cash reports? How do these reports tie in with cash budgetary control?

3. To what extent, if at all, are projected income statements and balance sheets sources of details to be incorporated in cash budgets?

4. Give several examples of possible disclosures in projected income statements and balance sheets that would not be apparent in cash budgets.

5. What is a working capital ratio? a "quick" ratio? What are such ratios supposed to reveal about a firm's financial position? Of what significance are they in forecasting?

6. As "rules of thumb," what working capital and "quick" ratios are generally recognized as indicative of satisfactory financial position? Is there any logic in these "rules of thumb"? Why or why not?

7. What is a statement of sources and applications of funds? As shown in such a statement, what are the principal sources of funds? the principal applications?

8. How is the use of statements of sources and applications of funds related to cash budgeting?

9. In fixed asset budgeting, expenditures for which of the following purposes are budgeted: additions, betterments, replacements, small tools, maintenance and repairs? If you exclude any of these purposes, explain why.

10. Why are reasonably dependable sales forecasts important for fixed asset budgeting?

11. If cash, sales, production, and other such budgets are usually forecasts for not more than a year, how can financial managers justify attempts to forecast fixed asset requirements for periods of five or ten years?

Problem

Using the solution to the problem presented at the end of Chapter 12, prepare an income statement for the Lennox Products Company for the year 19yy, and a statement of sources and applications of funds (of the form of Figure 13–7 in this chapter) to account for the net increase or decrease in its cash balance as a result of the year's transactions. For the latter statement, assume that cash and equivalent (short-term investments of high quality) amounted to $445,000 at the beginning of the year 19yy.

Part V

FINANCIAL STRUCTURE

chapter 14

SIMPLE COMMON STOCK STRUCTURES

Financial management is as much concerned with the control of liabilities and stockholders' equity as it is with the control of assets. Since liabilities and stockholders' equity are sources of assets, these two aspects of financial management are inextricably interrelated. Decisions must be made about the kinds and amounts of assets that must be acquired and maintained; but such decisions require complementary ones about the sources from which the assets will be sought. Success in management requires not only a judicious selection and administration of assets; it requires a judicious selection of sources. A corporation that appears to have the right kinds and amounts of assets may run, nevertheless, into serious financial difficulties in periods of general business contraction, because it has depended too heavily upon creditors to supply the assets. It may find itself "top heavy" with debt. On the other hand, a corporation that has made serious errors in the acquisition and administration of assets may be saved from bankruptcy if its liability management has been wise. A corporation may suffer losses year after year because of poor asset management and yet survive long enough for the correction of its mistakes, if creditors' claims have been held to a manageable minimum, and if, therefore, most of the assets have been supplied by stockholders. For stockholders, as a rule, are much more willing than are creditors to await the correction of mistakes.

The liabilities and stockholders' equity of a business corporation, as the sources of its assets, constitute its "financial structure"; accordingly, the management of liabilities and stockholders' equity is the building of financial structures. The objective of sound liability and equity management is to erect and maintain forms of financial structure—various combinations of amounts and types of liabilities and equity items—best suited to the circumstances of individual corporations. In working toward this objective, decisions are required, in the first place, upon what proportion of the assets can appropriately be sought from creditors, and what remaining proportion, therefore, must be obtained from stockholders. For assets to be sought from creditors, further decisions are necessary as to what proportions of these should be sought, respectively, for short, intermediate, and long terms, and as to what classes of creditors (trade suppliers, commercial banks, other kinds of lenders, and so on) appeals should be made.

Other decisions are required as to whether owners' contributions to assets —the *equity* contributions—are to be sought from stockholders of only one class or of two or more classes, as buyers of common stock and buyers of preferred stock. And, finally, decisions are needed about the extent to which equity contributions by way of the accumulation of profits can or should be depended upon.

Another way of looking at liability and equity management is to say that it is concerned with "financing"—a term that was defined in Chapter 4.[1] When decisions have been made about the sources from which assets will be sought, financing comes into the picture as the actual procedure whereby the sources are reached and tapped. Some selected sources may turn out to be sterile, so that financing, if it is to be carried through successfully, must go off in a different direction. At any rate, decisions about sources, whether first choices or alternative ones, and the actual tapping of these sources in "financing" determine the shape of financial structures. If less desirable sources must be reached because more desirable ones are not fruitful, the presumption is that the resulting financial structures, at least in the minds of the financial managers, are not so "good" as the more desirable choices would have made them.

In first taking up the matter of liability and equity management, we need a general view of the principles that govern the building of sound financial structures. A survey of principles is, therefore, the primary objective of this chapter and the following one. Having a general knowledge of principles, we can then proceed safely, beginning with Chapter 16, to discuss in detail how common stock, preferred stock, accumulated profits, bonds, and other instruments are fitted into, arranged, and rearranged in financial structures—how, in other words, these are used as means of financing. An immediate examination of numerous details concerning instruments of finance and their uses, without a set of unifying principles for guidance, might appear to be quite aimless. That is a kind of danger we may hope to avoid.

SCOPE OF SIMPLE COMMON STOCK STRUCTURES

The form of financial structure most favored by the managers of American business corporations is the "simple common stock structure." Such a preference is proved by the fact that a very large proportion of corporations have this type of structure. Its popularity is further indicated by its frequent description as the "ideal" form for industrial corporations—the broad class that includes all those in manufacturing, mining and quarrying, construction, wholesale and retail trade, and the service industries. (For a sampling of large corporations that have simple common stock structures, see Table 14–1.) Doubtless, however, this

---

[1] See above, p. 67.

TABLE 14–1

Some Large Corporations Having Simple Common Stock Structures[a]

(Amounts in millions of dollars)

Corporation	Total Assets	Common Stock	Earned Surplus	Capital Surplus	Other Surplus Accounts
Great Atlantic & Pacific Tea Company.....	768	24	167	345	—
International Nickel Company of Canada, Ltd..................................	760	73	478	61	—
North American Aviation, Inc.............	663	8	179	52	—
Weyerhaeuser Company	618	221	293	15	20
J. C. Penney Company	553	39	308	—	—
Phelps-Dodge Corporation...............	446	127	276[b]	—	—
United Fruit Company...................	338	192	107[b]	—	—
Libbey-Owens-Ford Glass Company........	240	52	157	8	—
Pullman, Incorporated...................	231	91	54	31	—
Freeport Sulphur Company...............	182	76	66	8	—
Otis Elevator Company..................	177	26	111	4	—
Zenith Radio Corporation................	144	9	98	1	—
Baldwin-Lima-Hamilton Company........	131	57	30	27	—

[a] As of December 31, 1962, except for J. C. Penney Company, January 31, 1963, and Great Atlantic & Pacific Tea Company, February 23, 1963.

[b] Classes of surplus not differentiated.

SOURCE: Moody's Investors Service, *Industrial Manual, 1963.*

proposition is somewhat exaggerated, as what is "ideal" for the individual corporation depends most importantly upon its peculiar circumstances; and the exaggeration is clearly demonstrated by the experience of many highly successful industrial corporations that have from time to time, or apparently permanently, departed from the simple common stock form of structure. Nevertheless, high esteem for the simple common stock structure can scarcely be denied.

Nature of Simple Common Stock Structures

A corporation is said to have a simple common stock structure when all its assets, other than those supplied by short-term creditors, have been contributed by its common stockholders. In a negative sense, it may be said that such a corporation does not use as means of financing preferred stock, bonds, intermediate- or long-term bank loans, or other forms of intermediate- or long-term debt.

The contribution of the common stockholders to assets can be made by various routes, and not simply in the original purchase of stock. The aggregate of their contributions will ordinarily be indicated in the balance sheet, therefore, by one or more surplus accounts in addition to the common stock account itself. But let us look at this matter in some detail.

Contributions of the Common Stockholders

For most corporations, the contributions of common stockholders to assets go at least moderately beyond the par or stated value of the stock they have acquired, as indicated by the amounts appearing on their books or in their balance sheets as "capital stock" or "common stock"; for many, indeed, the contributions far exceed the par or stated value.

Premiums and Donations. For one thing, buyers of common stock, at the time of its original issue by the corporation, may pay more for it than the par or stated value. They may pay an amount equal to a substantial multiple of the par or stated value, as is indicated in Table 14–2,

TABLE 14–2
Some Recent Public Offerings of Common Stock

Corporation	Month of Offering	No. of Shares	Par Value	Offering Price
Precision Instrument Company......	April, 1962	125,000	No par	$13.00
Thermogas Company...............	Aug., 1962	500,000	$1.00	10.00
Stowe-Woodward, Inc..............	Sept., 1962	237,140	$5.00	10.00
L. L. Ridgeway Enterprises, Inc.....	Oct., 1962	170,000	$1.00	9.00
Tyson Foods, Inc..................	April, 1963	100,000	$2.00	10.50
Portland General Electric Company..	April, 1963	725,302	$3.75	25.75
Cosmodyne Corporation............	May, 1963	150,000	No par	17.00
Capital Cities Broadcasting Corporation....................	June, 1963	250,000	$1.00	22.75
Continental Telephone Company....	July, 1963	400,000	$1.00	11.00

SOURCE: *The Wall Street Journal.*

which lists some recent offerings of common stock to the general public. Note particularly the frequency of extremely wide spreads between par values and offering prices. The excess payments by investors in common stocks may be carried in surplus accounts called "premium on common stock" or, as is the more popular practice, in accounts labeled "capital surplus"; but, regardless of the label, the obvious fact is that the account represents an additional contribution to assets by the common stock buyers.

Again, common stockholders may donate cash or other property to their corporations. Such action by stockholders is by no means uncommon; it is likely to be encountered especially in "family corporations" where, for example, a man may make a contribution with full assurance that it can benefit only himself, his wife, and his children because they are the only stockholders. The value of the property donated may be shown on the books and in the balance sheet as "donated surplus," or, like the premium mentioned above, it may be included in "capital surplus." Whatever it is called, however, it obviously represents a stockholder contribution to assets.

Accumulated Profits. By far, however, the greatest contribution that is made to assets by the generality of common stockholders beyond the par or stated value of their stock comes from the accumulation of profits. In the years since the close of World War II, as is indicated in Table 14–3, American corporations collectively have distributed dividends to their stockholders equal to only about 52 per cent of their profits after taxes; thus profits "plowed under" have been an enormous source of additional net assets[2] to these corporations.

Although it is sometimes said that corporate profits, whether distributed or not, "belong" to the stockholders, the fact of the matter is, of course, that the expanded net assets which retained profits represent, like all corporate assets, belong to the corporations themselves as distinct en-

TABLE 14–3
Corporate Profits and Dividends, 1946–62
(Dollar amounts in billions)

Year	Profits after Income Taxes[a]	Dividends	Retained Profits	Percentage Retained
1946......	$13.4	$ 5.8	$ 7.7	57.5
1947......	18.2	6.5	11.7	64.3
1948......	20.5	7.2	13.3	64.9
1949......	16.0	7.5	8.5	53.1
1950......	22.8	9.2	13.6	59.6
1951......	19.7	9.0	10.7	54.3
1952......	17.2	9.0	8.3	48.3
1953......	18.1	9.2	8.9	49.2
1954......	16.8	9.8	7.0	41.7
1955......	23.0	11.2	11.8	51.3
1956......	23.5	12.1	11.3	48.1
1957......	22.3	12.6	9.7	43.5
1958......	18.8	12.4	6.4	34.0
1959......	24.5	13.7	10.8	44.1
1960......	23.0	14.4	8.6	37.4
1961......	23.3	15.0	8.3	35.6
1962......	26.3	15.9	10.3	39.2

[a] In some instances, dividends and retained profits do not add exactly to "profits after income taxes" because of rounding.

Sources: U.S. Department of Commerce, Office of Business Economics, *U.S. Income and Output* (Washington, D.C.: U.S. Government Printing Office, 1958), pp. 205–7; and *Federal Reserve Bulletin*, June, 1963, p. 832.

tities. Nevertheless, retained profits most certainly give the stockholders an additional "claim" against the assets—a claim over and above that measured by the par of stated value of their stock. Any claim to assets is simultaneously a source of assets; accordingly, the stockholders are unquestionably the contributors of the additional net assets acquired by way of retained profits.

In their books and balance sheets, corporations customarily show stockholders' claims on account of accumulated retained profits as "earned surplus" or simply as "surplus." The simple designation *surplus* is often used especially when there are no other surplus accounts, the implication being that surplus necessarily means accumulated profits unless

---

[2] The term *net assets* means the difference between total assets and the total of obligations to creditors. Accordingly, net assets are always increased through the retention of profits, whether the profits are the means of actually acquiring additional assets or the means of paying off debts.

there is a designation to the contrary. However, many corporations use the designation *earned surplus* even when there are no other surplus accounts.

Surplus Reserves. Sometimes accumulated retained profits are disguised, as it were, under titles such as "reserve for working capital," "reserve for contingencies," and "reserve for plant expansion." A transfer is made from the earned surplus account to one or more of these "surplus reserves," as they are called; but the transfer obviously has no effect upon the actual amount of accumulated profits. It likewise has no effect upon the stockholders' claims upon assets, or, to put the same idea in different words, the contribution to assets that they have actually made.

The principal reason for the setting up of surplus reserves is to indicate to stockholders that the directors have no intention of using these portions of accumulated profits as a basis for dividend payments. In ordering a transfer from earned surplus to a reserve for working capital, for example, the directors say in effect: we cannot pay dividends of this amount because cash must be retained for current operations. Likewise, a transfer to a reserve for plant expansion is intended to mean this: we cannot pay dividends of this amount because we must use some of our available cash for further investment in facilities.

Size of Surplus Accounts. In summary, then, a corporation that is described as having a simple common stock structure may have one or many accounts indicating that the common stockholders have made contributions to assets slightly, moderately, or vastly in excess of the contribution shown in the common stock account itself. It is a remarkable fact, indeed, that American business corporations collectively have much larger totals in their surplus accounts than in their common stock accounts. This situation is also true of most classes of corporations, classified as to industry, as indicated in Table 14–4. The very high levels of surplus by comparison with the levels of common stock in construction, manufacturing, and wholesale and retail trade, and in the service industries are especially noteworthy.

The fact that preferred stock and fixed liabilities (intermediate- and long-term debt) are shown in the financial structures of all classes of corporations listed in Table 14–4 should not be taken as a contradiction of the statement made previously that a large majority of American corporations have simple common stock structures. While it is true that most corporations in the public utility area have preferred stock or long-term debt or both in their financial structures, it is no less true that the typical industrial corporation does not use these instruments of financing. Another point to be noted in connection with the tabular data is that preferred stockholders sometimes make contributions to assets beyond the par or stated value of their stock, as by buying the stock at premium prices or by making donations. Likewise, such a contribution may be said to be made when corporations have profits sufficient to pay prescribed

TABLE 14–4
Financial Structures of Nonfinancial Business Corporations, 1960–61[a]
(In percentages of total liabilities and equity)

Area of Operations	Number of Tax Returns	Current Liabilities	Fixed Liabilities	Preferred Stock	Common Stock	Surplus
Agriculture, forestry, and fisheries........	17,139	24.2	23.0	1.8	29.4	21.6
Mining and quarrying..	13,017	16.0	21.0	1.6	16.5	44.9
Construction..........	72,332	42.7	22.6	1.0	12.8	20.9
Manufacturing........	165,863	19.5	16.1	2.4	17.0	45.0
Public utilities........	43,852	10.2	41.3	4.2	20.9	23.4
Transportation.....	*33,491*	*12.4*	*35.6*	*1.6*	*17.0*	*33.4*
Communication......	*5,431*	*10.5*	*33.2*	*1.2*	*31.7*	*23.4*
Electric and gas......	*1,299*	*8.3*	*49.6*	*7.5*	*18.7*	*15.9*
Wholesale trade.......	117,437	39.2	13.3	1.9	15.4	30.2
Retail trade..........	217,269	31.0	15.9	2.0	18.1	33.0
Services..............	121,024	27.7	33.7	1.4	15.1	22.1

[a] "Active" corporations filing federal income tax returns for fiscal years ending between July 1, 1960, and June 30, 1961.

SOURCE: Computed from U.S. Treasury Department, Internal Revenue Service, *Statistics of Income, 1960–61—Preliminary: Corporation Income Tax Returns* (Washington, D.C.: U.S. Government Printing Office, 1962), pp. 17–18, 20–21, 24.

dividends on the preferred but choose to retain the profits instead of paying the dividends. Contributions to assets by preferred stockholders by way of surplus accounts, however, do not necessarily give them claims against assets of equal amount. That depends upon the terms of the contracts between corporations and their preferred stockholders. Thus, the original sale of preferred stock at a premium does not, of itself, entitle the preferred stockholder to a premium if the stock is subsequently called for redemption.[3]

Short-Term Debts

Although a corporation that maintains a simple common stock structure has as its only long-term source of assets the contributions made by its common stockholders—whatever avenues these may take—it may depend rather heavily upon "outside" sources of short-term financing. It is likely to welcome opportunities to buy goods and services on account, and it would hardly pay its employees from day to day, so that it will ordinarily have a continuous liability for accrued payroll. It will surely refrain from paying taxes until approximately their due dates, so that it will usually be carrying a liability for accrued taxes; and it may depend upon commercial banks or other financial institutions for short-term working capital loans, especially if its operations are subject to rather substantial seasonal fluctuations. If such a corporation has little or nothing in the way of fixed assets, the owners of its common stock may be the suppliers of hardly more than half of the total (current) assets; they

[3] The scope of preferred stockholders' claims against corporate assets is discussed below, pp. 528–30.

would hardly provide much less than half, in view of the devotion of trade suppliers, bankers, and other short-term creditors to the 2 to 1 standard for working capital, as discussed in the preceding chapter. On the other hand, if such a corporation has a large volume of fixed assets, a proportion of total assets much greater than 50 per cent will necessarily have been contributed by the common stockholders—all the fixed assets, as it were, plus, it is to be expected, at least half of the amount of the current assets.

ADVANTAGES OF SIMPLE COMMON STOCK STRUCTURES

The advantages and disadvantages of simple common stock structures (as well as of other forms of financial structure to be discussed in the next chapter) may best be considered from the standpoint of existing common stockholders. The boards of directors and executive officers of most business corporations are often said to be "common-stock-minded," by which is meant that they seek in every possible way to advance the interests of the common stockholders. This does not mean that the welfare of employees, customers, creditors, and others is neglected, for neglect of this kind could be expected in most circumstances to work out to the quite serious disadvantage of the common stockholders. What is meant, therefore, is that where a choice among alternative policies can be made, those that promise rather clear advantages for the common stockholders will almost invariably be selected in preference to those whose prospective advantages to the common stockholders are less significant or less certain. Since common stockholders usually have the exclusive or predominant voice in the election of directors, and since the directors, in turn, choose the executive officers, concern for the welfare of common stockholders is not difficult to understand.

From the standpoint of the welfare of common stockholders, then, a simple common stock structure promises advantages of the following kinds: (1) protection of the corporation's solvency, (2) maintenance of a good credit standing, (3) reservation of financing capacity for times of pressing need, and (4) avoidance of restrictions upon managerial discretion. Although these advantages tend to overlap somewhat, we should find it enlightening to examine them individually.

Protection of Solvency

However strong the profit motives of corporations may be, they can never wisely be permitted to take precedence over safety. Safety means solvency—the capacity of the corporation to meet its obligations as they come due. Tens of thousands of corporations, launched with enthusiasm, with many having great promise, have failed because their managers neglected to protect their solvency.

Solvency is promoted by simple common stock structures, because common stockholders themselves ordinarily have no legal rights to demand cash payments from their corporations. The corporation has no obligation to pay cash dividends, nor does it have, at any time, an obligation to redeem the stock at its par or stated value. Thus, all the assets that common stockholders contribute to their corporations are held, as it were, without offsetting claims that must be paid in cash at stipulated times. If cash is in short supply, therefore, it can be conserved to pay current operating expenses and to meet current liabilities.

This advantage is especially important in times of severe contractions in general business activity when the inflow of cash from operations tends to be seriously reduced. Corporations that have cumulative preferred stock issues in their financial structures often decide, despite financial strain, to continue the payment of current dividends, but they thereby weaken their capacity later on to pay interest and principal on their debts. And corporations that have bond issues or other forms of intermediate- or long-term debt (fixed liabilities) *must* pay interest and maturing instalments of the principal in bad times as well as in good if they are to remain safely in operation.

The consequences of the nonpayment of debts are usually disastrous for common stockholders. By legal processes, all the assets may be seized and sold by creditors for the satisfaction of their claims; and because the sale takes place in demoralized markets, often nothing at all is left for the common stockholders. Frequently, indeed, the sale yields much less than is necessary to satisfy the creditors' claims. Or the nonpayment may lead to an expensive, time-consuming procedure of reorganization in the course of which the claims of the common stockholders are likely to be drastically cut down or even entirely eliminated. No corporation avoids long-term debt more sedulously than E. I. duPont de Nemours & Company which has stated its financial policy as follows:

> Two basic principles govern DuPont financial policy. First and most elementary, is to stay out of debt . . . Despite all temptations, the company has no funded indebtedness.
>
> The second principle . . . is to save part of what is earned as seed money for future development. Funds for expansion, insofar as possible, come from internal sources—reinvested earnings plus set-asides from depreciation reserves.[4]

Nevertheless, simple common stock structures do not guarantee solvency. Many corporations with financial structures of this kind have failed. Current liabilities must still be paid. But it is clear that the chances of survival must be much greater for corporations whose assets have been supplied preponderantly by common stockholders, to whom

---

[4] *DuPont: The Autobiography of an American Enterprise*, published by the company at Wilmington, Delaware, 1952, p. 131.

no current payments need be made, than for those in like operating circumstances that have depended upon long-term creditors for much of their assets—creditors to whom interest and principal payments must continue to be made.

Maintenance of a Good Credit Standing

As a rule, corporations that have simple common stock structures have higher credit ratings than do those of comparable size, scope of operations, and managerial competence that have preferred stock or bonds or other forms of fixed liabilities in their financial structures. Trade suppliers, bankers approached for short-term loans, and other prospective short-term creditors expect their corporate debtors to conserve cash in difficult times by suspending the payment of dividends on common stock; but they know that interest payments and contractual payments on the principal of intermediate- and long-term debt cannot be suspended without grave danger to their own claims. They may suspect, moreover, that corporations having preferred stocks in their structures will try to maintain dividend payments on these, thereby using cash that might better be conserved for meeting their claims. Directors might feel that the nonpayment of preferred dividends would reflect unfavorably upon the credit standing of their corporations, since it would be a confession of cash shortage; yet the payment, as indicated, might offend creditors and prospective creditors. Thus, some weakening of credit standing apparently results from the very existence of preferred stock in financial structures, whether or not dividends are being currently paid upon it.

Even in good times, the credit standing of corporations having preferred stocks or fixed debts or both in their financial structures is likely to be somewhat inferior to that of corporations of comparable position that have simple common stock structures. Although both classes of corporations may meet their obligations to short-term creditors with ease in good times, prospective creditors can be expected to keep in mind what might happen to their claims should business conditions deteriorate suddenly. Such a consideration must generally lead them to prefer the corporations with the simpler structures.

Reservation of Financing Capacity

Corporations that maintain simple common stock structures are ordinarily in a much better position to tap additional sources of assets than are those of comparable circumstances that have already tapped several sources. Sometimes, therefore, the former may be able to take advantage of expansion opportunities not readily accessible to the latter. For one thing, additional sales of common stock at good prices should be somewhat easier for the corporations with the simple structures. In times of prosperity, when investor interest in almost all kinds of common stocks is high, the common stocks of these corporations are likely to be more attractive than those of corporations having more complex structures. Prospective buyers are well aware of the prior claims of the latters' long-term debt and preferred stocks to interest and dividend payments, as well as to principal payments, that is, their prior claims to assets.

Even in times of contractions in general business activity, the corporation that has a simple common stock structure is likely to find itself favorably situated to undertake further financing, should it wish to do so. In such a period, it might want to take advantage of reduced costs of construction and relatively low prices of machinery and equipment. The market for additional common stock at a good price might, indeed, be quite poor; but its prospects for selling on favorable terms a new issue of preferred stock would surely be much better than for corporations already having preferred stock or bonds or both outstanding; and its prospects for selling a bond issue on attractive terms would likely be far superior to those of corporations of comparable size, scope of operations, and managerial competence already having preferred stock or bonds or both in their financial structures.

The reservation of financing capacity is sometimes said to be a retention of the "best security" for later issue. In this sense, the "best security" is understood to be that which will continue to be attractive to investors even in bad times. In periods of depression, investor interest in common stocks, and in most new issues of preferred stock as well, is almost surely to be at a low ebb; but, unless the financial markets are completely demoralized, as in depressions of greater severity, it is likely to be sustained in bonds for whose safety ample assurances can be given. Although using a bond issue to finance expansion would ordinarily be looked upon as anything but the "best" for a corporation whose management is devoted to a simple common stock structure, such financing might still be acceptable on a temporary basis. The corporate managers might anticipate a sale of common stock later on when buoyancy had been restored to the market, the proceeds of the sale to be used to retire the bond issue. Or they might make the bonds convertible into common stock at the option of the holder in the expectation that, when good levels of common stock prices had been restored in the market, wholesale conversions would take place.

Avoidance of Restrictions on Managerial Discretion

When corporations issue preferred stocks or incur long-term debts, as by selling bonds or borrowing directly from banks and other lenders, they must generally agree to some limitations on their freedom of action. These limitations come into force through various kinds of "protective provisions" that buyers of security issues and lenders require to be included in their contracts. Typical of such protective provisions are limits placed upon dividend payments to common stockholders, the payment of salaries and bonuses to executive officers, sales of fixed assets, additional borrowing, the pledging (or the further pledging) of assets, merging or consolidating with other corporations, the retirement of preferred stock (as for the protection specifically of bondholders), and the purchase by the corporations of shares of their own outstanding common stock; as well as stipulations that working capital ratios will not be permitted to fall below stated levels, that properties will be kept in proper repair, that adequate insurance coverages will be provided, and that taxes will be paid at the proper times.

Many such limitations, it is true, are not grievously burdensome; they may require nothing more than sound financial policy would seem to demand, even in the absence of preferred stock issues or long-term debt. It is true, too, that if the management of a corporation wants to do something that is subject to contractual restrictions, it can ask for a waiver of the restrictions, as by a vote of preferred stockholders or by the specific consent of direct lenders or, in the case of bond issues, of indenture trustees. Nevertheless, corporations with simple common stock structures generally avoid all or most restrictions of the kinds described, as it is not customary for short-term creditors to insist upon comparable contractual provisions. Accordingly, they are free to adopt policies on their merits, without fearing that the results might be interpreted as violative of contractual restrictions; nor need they seek the permission of somebody else for actions they propose to undertake. By contrast, the managers of corporations subject to contractual limitations may at times forgo attractive courses of action because of apparent conflicts with the limitations. They may request waivers, only to have their pleas rejected; or, because they fear rejections, they may decide not to seek concessions.

DISADVANTAGES OF SIMPLE COMMON STOCK STRUCTURES

While the advantages of simple common stock structures from the standpoint of the interests of existing common stockholders are rather definite, the disadvantages tend to be possibilities only. Much depends upon the situation of the individual corporation. What may be a clear-cut disadvantage for some corporations may have elements of advantage to others; or—what is more likely—one or more of the disadvantages that could be suffered by some corporations may be easily avoidable by others. But we may best look at these crosscurrents, as it were, as we consider each of the possible sources of disadvantage.

With this proviso in mind, then, we may list these possible sources as follows: (1) neglect of opportunities to "trade on the equity"—to obtain assets on a basis of relatively "cheap" interest or dividend payments; (2) greater expense of common stock flotations by comparison with sales of preferred stock and the negotiation of long-term debt; (3) danger of loss of control; (4) danger of "dilution" of the claims of existing common stockholders to future profits; and (5) danger of "dilution" of their claims to assets.

Neglect of Opportunities to "Trade on the Equity"

As a rule, a successful corporation can sell preferred stock on the promise of a rate of dividends substantially less than its current or expected rate of profits on the investment of its common stockholders. Ordinarily, too, it can obtain funds by way of bond issues or other means of long-term borrowing at rates of interest somewhat below the dividend rate it would have to promise on a preferred stock issue. The cheapness of borrowed money is enhanced, moreover, by the deductibility of interest payments as an expense in income tax computations. Dividend payments on preferred and common stocks are not thus deductible.[5] Accordingly, the use of "cheap" funds can give a common stock "leverage" —they can act as a fulcrum, so to say, in raising the profit rate on common stock to a level higher than could be reached without their use. It follows, therefore, that dependence upon relatively "expensive" common stock funds as the sole long-term source of assets *may* represent an unreasonably conservative and unimaginative financial policy.

A corporation that includes fixed debt in its financial structure is said to "trade on the equity." The investment of the common stockholders provides protection for the creditors. As the common stockholders' claim upon assets is a residual one, unpaid creditors can seize all assets—those contributed by the stockholders as well as those contributed by themselves, as it were—to satisfy their claims. Thus, the corporation, in seeking to attract funds from creditors, "trades" on the protection given by the common stockholders, and it expects to get the creditors' funds more cheaply than it gets common stock funds precisely because of the "cushion" of protection provided to the former by the latter.

The concept of trading on the equity is also applicable to issues of preferred stock. Many authorities, however, hesitate to apply the term to arrangements whereby cheaper preferred stock funds are employed to augment the rate of profit on common stock. The reason for this hesitation is that contributions to assets by preferred stockholders, no less than those of common stockholders, are *equity* contributions. The pre-

---

[5] An exception to this rule is the deductibility of a percentage of dividends paid on the preferred stocks of certain classes of public utilities. The percentage deductible is determined by a formula in the Internal Revenue Code based upon the tax rates currently in effect. If the tax rates are changed, therefore, the percentage changes also. As determined in relation to the corporate tax rates in effect in the year 1963, the proportion of public utility preferred dividends that are deductible in computing taxable income is 26.923 per cent; however, the deduction may not exceed 26.923 per cent of taxable income itself (as computed before any dividends-paid deduction). Some additional exceptions to the general rule of the nondeductibility of dividends are provided for personal holding companies and certain classes of financial institutions, but these exceptions have no bearing on the discussion in this chapter.

ferred stockholders of a corporation are owners, and not creditors; hence, it tends to be confusing to say that a corporation is trading on the equity when it issues preferred stock. When, however, preferred stock is given a claim upon assets superior to that of common stock, as is customary, the contributions of common stockholders to assets unquestionably provide a "cushion" of protection for preferred stockholders. The protective aspect should encourage investment in preferred stock, yet the buyers of preferred ought not to expect a rate of return as high as on common stock which has the greater risks.

Use of Bonds. For illustration, let us assume that two corporations, A and B, are identical in their circumstances except that A has common stock and surplus as its only long-term sources of assets, whereas B has a bond issue in addition to common stock and surplus. Each corporation, let us say, has assets valued at $10 million and current liabilities of $2 million. B's bond issue amounts to $3 million; it bears interest at the rate of 5 per cent. Accordingly, B's common stock and surplus amount to $5 million, while the equity of the common stockholders of A amounts to $8 million. Now, let us assume that in a certain year each corporation has a profit of $2.4 million before the deduction of federal income taxes, and, for B, before the deduction of bond interest. It may also be assumed that there are no state net income taxes. With these assumptions, the results of operations of the two corporations may be compared as follows:

	Corporation A	Corporation B
Profits as indicated	$2,400,000	$2,400,000
Less bond interest		150,000
		$2,250,000
Less federal income tax[6]	1,242,500	1,164,500
Net profit to surplus	$1,157,500	$1,085,500
Rate of profit on common stockholders' equity	14.47%	21.71%

Thus, the cheapness of bondholders' funds to B, on account of both the relative lowness of the rate of interest and the deductibility of the interest as an expense, enables it to earn a much higher rate of profit on the contribution of its common stockholders than is earned by A.

Use of Preferred Stock. Were B to have outstanding a preferred stock issue of $3 million, rather than a bond issue of that size, and were the dividend rate on the preferred stock 6 per cent, the results of its operations would be comparable with those of A as follows:

---

[6] In this and subsequent illustrations, the federal income tax is computed at the rates in effect in the year 1963 that is, at 30 per cent on the first $25,000 of income and at 52 per cent on all income in excess of that figure.

	Corporation A	Corporation B
Profits as indicated......................	$2,400,000	$2,400,000
Less federal income tax..................	1,242,500	1,242,500
	$1,157,500	$1,157,500
Less preferred dividends.................		180,000
Net profit to surplus.....................	. 1,157,500	$ 977,500
Rate of profit on common stockholders' equity..............................	14.47%	19.55%

B's common stockholders would still have a substantial advantage over A's, although not so great as by the inclusion of the bond issue in its financial structure. The reduction in the margin of their advantage would result, of course, from both the higher rate of return on the preferred stock and the nondeductibility of the preferred dividends as an expense for income tax determination.

Adverse Aspects of Trading on the Equity. But all is not necessarily sweetness and light in the matter of trading on the equity. The practice can turn out to be a very unhappy one for the common stockholders, as it certainly does in periods of low profits and losses. Referring to our first illustration above, suppose that in a year of depressed business activity, the profits of Corporations A and B (with financial structures as previously described) amount to only $200,000. Their positions could then be compared as follows:

	Corporation A	Corporation B
Profits as indicated......................	$200,000	$200,000
Less bond interest.....................		150,000
		$ 50,000
Less federal income tax..................	98,500	20,500
Net profit to surplus.....................	$101,500	$ 29,500
Rate of profit on common stockholders' equity..............................	1.27%	.59%

While a rate of return of only 1.27 per cent would not give the common stockholders of A anything to be particularly happy about, at least they could have the satisfaction of knowing that it was more than twice that of B.

Were B to have outstanding $3 million of 6 per cent preferred stock, as in the second illustration above, the margin of advantage to A's common stockholders would be even greater. In that situation, B's income tax liability would be equal to that of A at $98,500, leaving it with profit after tax of $101,500. If, then, it decided to pay the preferred dividend of $180,000, it would have to charge $78,500 against accumulated surplus, leaving its common stockholders with a *negative* rate of profit of 1.57 per cent.

Even more discouraging—and dangerous—for the corporation that trades on the equity are profits before the deduction of bond interest falling short of the amount of this interest, as well as losses before this deduction. Assume, for example, that in a certain year of depression, profits for A and B before income tax deductions (and before the interest deduction for B) amount to $20,000. The comparison would work out as follows:

	Corporation A	*Corporation B*
Profits as indicated......................	$20,000	$ 20,000
Less bond interest......................		150,000
		−$130,000
Less federal income tax..................	6,000	
Net profit or loss (−) to surplus............	$14,000	−$130,000
Rate of profit or loss (−) on common stockholders' equity..................	.18%	−2.60%

Under our federal income tax laws, however, B would be permitted to carry back its loss of $130,000 and write it off, as it were, against its taxable profits of the three preceding years, or, if the profits of those years were insufficient to absorb it, to carry the unabsorbed portion forward as a write-off against the profits of the following five years. If it had had taxable profits of, say, $500,000 in the third preceding year, the effect of the carry-back would be to reduce the taxable profits of that year to $370,000, so that it would have a claim for a tax refund of $67,000 (52 per cent of $130,000). Actually, of course, the refund would not reduce B's loss or rate of loss in the current year; for tax purposes only, the loss, so to say, would be simply transferred to another year.

However that may be, B's tax refund would undoubtedly be a most welcome means for the replenishment of its working capital, drained through the payment of the bond interest. But if, for several years running, B's profits were substantially less than the bond interest, or if it incurred losses before the deduction of that interest, it might soon exhaust its capacity to claim tax refunds. There would then be no replenishments of working capital from this source, even partial ones, and B might be pushed closer and closer to a default upon its bond interest obligations. All the greater would the danger of default be if B were under contractual obligation to allocate cash each year to pay off some of the principal of the bonds, as would be likely.

Such dangers of default in times of losses and low profits explain why many corporate managements are satisfied to forgo the apparent advantages of trading on the equity. If they forgo the possibilities of raising the rate of profit on common stockholders' equity through "leverage," they also avoid the dangers of default in times of business depression. For them, forgone possibilities of enhanced rates of profit are not too great a price to pay for assurances of solvency, better credit ratings, and the other advantages of the simple common stock structure.

Greater Cost of Common Stock Flotations

In addition to moderate interest and dividend rates and the deductibility of interest in determining taxable income, as sources of "cheapness" in financing with preferred stock and bonds, the lower costs of "floating" preferred stocks and bonds as compared with the costs of selling common stock issues are generally a further source of economy. As a rule, a greater proportion of the gross proceeds of common stock issues is absorbed by the expenses of selling than with preferred stock issues, and, in turn, a greater proportion of the gross proceeds of preferred stock issues is thus absorbed than with bonds. The principal item of selling expense is the compensation paid to investment bankers for their services in finding buyers for corporate securities. Difficulty in finding buyers generally increases with the riskiness of securities. Moreover, if the investment bankers *underwrite* securities issues, that is, guarantee their sale at specific prices, their own risk increases with the riskiness of the issues. On either or both these counts, therefore, they expect their compensation to be graduated accordingly. Other expenses of selling include federal and state issuance taxes,[7] attorneys' and accountants' fees, registration fees, and the costs of printing and engraving.

Thus, a manufacturing corporation might expect to incur expenses of about $480,000 in selling a common stock issue of gross proceeds of $7.5 million; about $300,000 in selling a preferred stock issue of the same gross proceeds; and about $260,000 in selling a bond issue of equal gross amount. Such figures are suggested by the costs of the securities flotations registered with the Securities and Exchange Commission in the years 1951, 1953, and 1955, as reproduced in Table 14–5. The average levels of cost indicated in the table were those of registered securities "publicly offered" through investment bankers, that is, offered broadside to many investors, and did not include those "privately placed," that is, sold in bulk to one or a few investors, such as life insurance companies. The costs of private placements are usually considerably less than those of public offerings. Because, however, only a relatively few common stock issues are privately placed, whereas many bond issues are so sold, selling cost differentials unfavorable to common stock are accentuated.

It is clear, therefore, that high flotation costs for common stock might prompt some corporate managements to abandon their simple common stock structures. Were they to anticipate repeated trips to the market to obtain "new money," they might decide that economies in flotation costs together with the benefits of trading on the equity would justify a switch to preferred stock or bonds. On the other hand, flotation-cost levels and differentials are of little or no significance to corporations that are able to

---

[7] The state taxes are chiefly of the kinds described in Chapter 2. See above, pp. 27–28. Details as to the federal issuance tax are presented below, pp. 479–81.

TABLE 14–5
Cost of Flotation of Publicly Offered Security Issues Registered with the SEC and Sold through Investment Bankers, 1951, 1953, and 1955[a]
(As percentages of proceeds of public sale)

SIZE OF ISSUE (MILLIONS OF DOLLARS)	Manufacturing	Electric, Gas, and Water	Communication	Mining	Other	ALL INDUSTRIES
Bonds:						
Under 0.5.........	.....	.....	.....	.....	.....	.....
0.5– 0.9..........	12.12	.....	.....	.....	10.54	11.49
1.0– 1.9..........	9.03	5.00	4.70	.....	6.94	8.17
2.0– 4.9..........	6.16	2.23	.....	.....	6.26	3.78
5.0– 9.9..........	3.47	1.52	.....	4.40	3.35	1.83
10.0–19.9.........	2.34	1.28	1.25	2.64	1.97	1.52
20.0–49.9.........	1.71	1.20	1.04	.....	1.74	1.33
50.0 and over......	1.30	1.15	1.03	.....	1.15	1.19
Total[b]..........	2.67	1.33	1.01	3.52	1.80	1.49
Preferred Stock:						
Under 0.5.........	.....	.....	.....	.....	.....	.....
0.5– 0.9..........	18.38	10.67	7.44	.....	11.57	12.63
1.0– 1.9..........	11.15	6.13	6.41	.....	12.68	8.07
2.0– 4.9..........	5.11	3.76	5.43	.....	7.34	4.88
5.0– 9.9..........	3.97	3.42	4.92	.....	3.63	3.72
10.0–19.9.........	2.62	2.84	4.15	.....	2.78	2.92
20.0–49.9.........	3.65	3.10	.....	.....	.....	3.20
50.0 and over......	2.51	.....	.....	.....	.....	2.51
Total[b]..........	5.22	3.12	6.54	.....	6.80	4.34
Common Stock:						
Under 0.5.........	19.69	.....	.....	33.42	14.76	27.15
0.5– 0.9..........	13.68	12.23	8.19	32.96	21.43	21.76
1.0– 1.9..........	12.84	6.52	5.98	22.18	11.53	13.58
2.0– 4.9..........	8.61	5.42	5.76	17.71	12.88	9.97
5.0– 9.9..........	6.38	4.53	6.68	12.33	14.28	6.17
10.0–19.9.........	4.88	2.95	5.08	11.50	6.60	4.66
20.0–49.9.........	5.48	4.20	.....	15.63	.....	5.37
50.0 and over......	.....	.....	.....	.....	.....	.....
Total[b]..........	10.06	4.55	6.07	20.00	12.26	10.28

[a] Including 265 issues of bonds with gross proceeds of $5.9 billion, 120 issues of preferred stock amounting to $850 million, and 230 issues of common stock with proceeds of almost $1 billion. The median size of issues was $15 million for bonds, $4 million for preferred stock, and $2 million for common stock. Issues ranged in size from $100,000 to $300 million.

[b] Median percentages.

SOURCE: Securities and Exchange Commission, *Cost of Flotation of Corporate Securities, 1951–1955* (Washington, D.C.: U.S. Government Printing Office, 1957), pp. 9, 38–40.

finance expansion, whether moderate or extensive, with the cash throw-offs from retained profits, as well as those having only a few stockholders who are both willing and financially able to buy whatever additional issues of common stock are deemed necessary.

Danger of Loss of Control

The simple common stock form of financial structure could hardly look very attractive to an individual stockholder or closely knit group in control of a corporation if its continuance threatened to undermine that position of control. Control in this sense means, of course, the capacity to choose all or a majority of the board of directors, and thus, as it were, to determine all operating policies, distributions of dividends, the allocations of executive offices, and the scales of compensation for those offices. For many persons and groups in control of corporations, the possible consequences of loss of control are truly horrible to contemplate—the rejection of operating policies that may have been developed carefully and lovingly over the years, the withholding of badly needed dividends, and the loss of the presidency, vice presidency, or other high office with its emoluments.

Accordingly, controlling stockholders whose margin of control is small will almost certainly vote to abandon the simple common stock structure if retained profits are insufficient to finance needed expansion and if they lack the means to buy additional common stock in proportion to their present holdings. A controlling group having 51 per cent of the common stock of a corporation, and facing the bitter opposition of another group that held the remaining 49 per cent, would unquestionably consider it suicidal to vote for an additional issue unless it were in a position to subscribe to at least 51 per cent of it. However, a controlling group holding, say, 80 per cent of the outstanding common stock of a corporation might vote an additional issue to be sold to the minority or to "outsiders" as long as the sale would not reduce their own proportion of ownership below 51 per cent.

Moreover, the holding of 20 or 30 per cent of the common stock of a corporation, or even a smaller percentage, may be sufficient to give a group of stockholders control, provided that the remainder of the stock is quite widely distributed among hundreds or thousands of owners. Such a group having, say, 30 per cent of the outstanding common stock might, therefore, vote an additional issue in the expectation that, though it itself would not subscribe, its reduced percentage of ownership of, say, 20 per cent would still be ample to insure control. Nevertheless, the danger of loss of control would obviously be present here. In not a few situations of this kind, "opposition groups" have quietly bought up a sufficient amount of the scattered stock, and have just as quietly persuaded a sufficient number of the corporation's small stockholders to vote with them, to enable them to oust groups that had previously felt quite secure in their positions of control.

In some very large corporations all of whose stock is very widely distributed, the boards of directors have come to occupy positions usually described as "self-perpetuating." Only gross mismanagement or other developments of a most extraordinary character would be likely to cause the scattered stockholders to unite to oust such a board. The members of these boards often own but little stock in the corporations they control. In considering proposals for new issues, therefore, they are likely to be quite unconcerned about their own wish or financial capacity to subscribe.

Indeed, it is not unreasonable for them to conclude that additional issues, by promoting an even wider distribution of the stock, will further entrench them in their positions of control.

Dilution of Claims to Future Profits

Selling additional common stock to raise money for expansion might be objectionable to the existing common stockholders of a corporation because they fear a dilution of their claims to future profits. Additional assets might be needed to enable the corporation to hold its competitive position, yet these stockholders might expect the rate of earnings on the additions to be less than that already being earned. Their expectation would be that, should additional shares be sold and should they themselves not subscribe, earning power would be transferred from them to the buyers of the new issues. The matter of control, as discussed above, might be of no consequence to these stockholders, but they would still have reason to object to financing by further common stock sales.

For illustration, let us suppose that a corporation has outstanding 100,000 shares of common stock of $40 par value and that it has surplus accounts representing accumulated profits of $3 million. Its profits after income taxes have averaged 14 per cent of the common stockholders' investment. Several directors now propose the sale of 50,000 additional shares at a price equal to the book value per share of the old stock, that is, $70,[8] and they claim that a return of 20 per cent could be earned on the additional assets the sale would provide. But most of the present stockholders, not expecting to subscribe to any of the additional stock, object to the proposed issue on the grounds that the rate of return on the new assets would not be more than 8 per cent. They expect the outcome to be as follows:

Assumed continued profit on the old investment of $7,000,000
    at 14%. . . . . $ 980,000
Assumed profit on the new investment of $3,500,000[9] at 8%.   280,000

    Total Expected Profit. $1,260,000

Expected new rate of profit—
  $1,260,000 ÷ $10,500,000. . . . .   12%

Since each share of old stock would have rights to dividends no better than each share of the new, the present stockholders anticipate that the rate of profit attributable to their investment would be reduced from 14 per cent to 12 per cent. Or, to state their expectation in an alternative

---

[8] In a simple common stock structure, the book value is the sum of the par or stated value of the stock and all the surplus accounts divided by the number of shares outstanding.

[9] For the sake of avoiding complexities at this point, the probable substantial costs of selling the additional stock are ignored.

way, they fear that the new stockholders would be very generously treated by being accorded a rate of profit of 12 per cent even though their investment would earn only 8 per cent.

Dilution of Claims against Assets

If it is proposed that additional common stock be issued at a price below the book value of existing stock, and if present common stockholders are unable or unwilling to subscribe, they have an additional reason to worry about the possibilities of dilution—in this instance, dilution of their claims against the assets of the corporation. A new share of common stock, regardless of what is paid for it, has a claim against assets equal to that of an old share.[10] Therefore, a sale of new stock at a price below the book value of the old results in a transfer of claims against assets from the old to the new.

To see how this works, let us assume the same facts as in the foregoing illustration, except that the proposal calls for the sale of the 50,000 shares of additional stock at a price of $58 a share. The existing stockholders might find the proposal seriously disadvantageous to them in a manner demonstrable as follows:

```
Book value of old stock:
    Common stock (par or stated value)........................$4,000,000
    Surplus................................................... 3,000,000
        Total.................................................$7,000,000

Book value per share—
    $7,000,000 ÷ 100,000 shares...............................    $70

Book value after sale of new stock:
    Common stock..............................................$6,000,000
    Earned surplus............................................ 3,000,000
    Capital (or paid-in) surplus..............................   900,000
        Total.................................................$9,900,000

Book value per share—
    $9,900,000 ÷ 150,000 shares...............................    $66
```

The stockholders might oppose the proposed issue on the grounds that, for each share held, they would be losing a claim against assets of $4.00; and they might argue the unfairness of "contributing" a claim of $8.00 to each share of new stock, since it would immediately have a book value of $66 though only $58 would be paid for it.

Proponents of additional issues, as in the foregoing case, might argue that the book value of common stock, as a measure of the claims of stockholders against assets, is really not very significant and that, therefore, "dilution" is nothing to worry about. They might argue that common

---

[10] A possible exception occurs if the new stock is sold at a discount. For a discussion of this matter, see below, pp. 373–74.

stockholders' claims against assets are likely to be asserted only in the
event of dissolution, that dissolution is rarely voted by the stockholders
of successful corporations, and that the dissolution of unsuccessful ones
usually occurs when there is little left against which their stockholders can
assert claims. Nevertheless, dilution can be hurtful. Two possibilities may
be mentioned.[11] A corporation, though successful, may have reason to
curtail the scope of its operations. It would then presumably have the
means to pay "dividends in partial liquidation" to the stockholders, and
these would be a settlement of claims as evidenced by the stock and
surplus accounts. Again, after a corporation has completed a sale of additional stock, such as that proposed in the illustration, it may have the
opportunity to sell out at a handsome price to another corporation. But
the benefits of the attractive price would be shared pro rata by the
former's stockholders, old and new, regardless of differences between the
former book value of old stock and the selling price of new.

FEASIBILITY OF SIMPLE COMMON STOCK STRUCTURES

Decisions for or against simple common stock structures cannot always
be reached solely by weighing apparent advantages and disadvantages, no
matter how carefully the weighing may be done. In some situations, this
kind of financial structure is, as it were, forced upon corporations; and in
others, it is departures from the simple common stock form that are
forced. In a word, the feasibility of the simple structure is by no means
identical with its desirability.

Two important determinants of feasibility were indicated in the forgoing discussion of the possible disadvantages of simple structures: (1)
size of profits, and (2) the interests of present common stockholders in
control. It is obvious that if the profits that a corporation can earn and
retain are sufficient to finance all desirable expansion, its problems of
maintaining the simple form of structure are minimized. Controlling interests are not disturbed; there are no high differential costs of common
stock sales to be concerned about; and the stockholders need have no fears
about the dilution of their claims to assets and future profits. It is likewise clear than an important obstacle to the simple form of structure is
removed if the positions of control of given groups of stockholders or
directors would not be threatened through additional common stock sales,
because they would subscribe pro rata for additional shares, because they
could afford a drop in their percentage of ownership, or because a very
wide distribution of stock ownership is already, so to say, the source of
their power.

Other important determinants of feasibility are age, expansion requirements, stability of profits, government regulation of rates and security issues, and market conditions. These deserve analysis.

---

[11] Further attention is given to this matter in Chapter 16. See pp. 354–58.

Newly Established Corporations

Youth is a most significant circumstance making for simple common stock structures. Most corporations start as small business organizations, the personal ventures, one might say, of single individuals or small groups. Until they have established a record of several years of successful operations, "outsiders" are strongly disinclined to be interested in them as investors, either as buyers of such securities as they might want to issue or as grantors of intermediate- or long-term loans. Hence, the predominant source of assets for a new corporation at its commencement and for the first few years of its operation must generally be the organizers themselves —the money they can put up originally or subsequently for its common stock and the profits, if any, they can retain for operations.

Even a new corporation, however, is not likely to be cut off completely from "outside" sources of assets; but such sources are almost surely to be short term in character. Limited amounts of raw materials or finished goods may be obtainable on account from trade suppliers; labor can ordinarily be hired on the basis of some deferment of wage payments, as a week or two weeks; certain kinds of services may be forthcoming on a deferred-payment basis; and, in some cases, indeed, commercial bankers who have confidence in the managerial abilities of the organizers may be prevailed upon to grant moderate amounts of short-term loans for working capital purposes. Nevertheless, longer-term sources of assets, aside from the organizers' own investment, are likely to be unavailable.

Expansion Requirements

Necessary and Optional Expansion. For corporations that survive their periods of infancy, expansion requirements are outstandingly important in determining the feasibility of continuing with simple common stock structures. Here we may distinguish between what may be called *necessary* expansion, on the one hand, and *optional* expansion, on the other. A corporation may have survived the trying years of infancy, but its situation as a maturing enterprise may be quite weak from the standpoint of profitability. Because of inadequacies in its facilities, it may only be able to break even or to garner nominal profits. The correction of these inadequacies could be said, therefore, to be *necessary* for its continued existence. But the addition of facilities to correct the inadequacies obviously could not be financed out of profits, and the poor profits record might likewise preclude further sales of common stock. Should the corporation have an opportunity to borrow on a long-term basis, it could be expected, accordingly, to depart from the simple common stock structure without much hesitation.

Another corporation may enjoy a wide range of expansion choices. It may be carrying on operations quite profitably at a given level, but its managers may believe that profits could be increased substantially through investment in additional assets. Nevertheless, they would be under no compulsion to expand. If convinced of the superiority of the simple common stock structure, they might decide to enlarge the scale of operations only to the extent that the expansion could be financed through the retention of profits and additional sales of common stock.

Rate of Expansion. Whether or not simple common stock structures can be maintained depends not only upon the amount of money needed for given expansion programs but also upon the time when it is needed, that is, upon the speed with which the expansion must be effected. A corporation that envisages substantial growth, but at a slow, steady pace over a long period of years, may have no difficulty in meeting outlays for expansion out of retained profits and the proceeds of occasional sales of additional amounts of common stock; while one that must spend large amounts of money within a short period of time may find these means of financing quite insufficient.

A corporation might find itself in the latter kind of position because its competitors are adding many new facilities, perhaps to take advantage of technological developments that promise a substantial lowering of costs of production, or perhaps to make possible the manufacture of complementary products to improve service to their customers. If the corporation is to remain strong, therefore, it must quickly follow the competitors' lead. Although it may have been financing moderate growth by means of retained profits, it would be likely to find this means inadequate to finance the new requirements for rapid expansion. If, at the same time, the market for additional issues of common stock were not favorable, it might promptly decide that the better part of valor would be to give up the advantages of a simple common stock structure and issue preferred stock or contract long-term debt.

Rising Prices. The amount of money needed for expansion tends to rise, of course, with rising prices. A corporation that is planning to double its facilities over a period of years must make allowance for the possibility or probability that the costs of the additions will be rising as the expansion takes place. If, on the basis of present prices, the cost of the additional facilities is estimated at $5 million, but if it is anticipated that, due to rising prices, actual outlays will average, say, 15 per cent above present prices, then obviously an additional means of financing in the amount of $750,000 must be planned for. It is conceivable that the corporation's financial managers might conclude that, though $5 million could be provided out of retained profits and sales of common stock, the further requirement of $750,000 could not be so financed. They might, therefore, plan to tap the preferred stock or bond market for this additional amount.

Even corporations that are not planning expansion in the sense of adding to the volume of their assets face a problem of "expansion" in periods of rising prices. Simply to carry unchanged quantities of goods in their inventories and to carry the same volume of accounts receivable (in the sense of *quantity* of goods sold on account), they must expand the amount of their investment; and likewise if they must replace fixed assets when prices have risen. Thus, difficulty in maintaining simple common stock structures may ensue. Although profits tend to expand as rapidly as prices —and, for many corporations, more rapidly—stockholders may expect higher rates of dividends in view of the decline in the purchasing power of the dividend dollar. Moreover, any increase in capacity to use retained profits as a means of financing may be more than offset by inability to increase materially the amount of assets short-term creditors are willing to supply. Periods of rising prices are often periods of "tight money" in which short-term creditors are under great pressure to increase restrictions upon credit extensions and terms.

Stability of Profits

As a rule, records of stable profits through the upswings and downswings of the business cycle weaken the attractions of simple common stock structures; in other words, they make the advantages of trading on the equity all the more attractive. Corporations well established as producers or sellers of products of stable demand, such as many kinds of processed foodstuffs, petroleum products, tobacco, and electric power, need to be much less hesitant to depart from the simple common stock structure than do those whose products are subject to erratic demand, such as most kinds of "heavy goods," including automobiles, other transportation equipment, factory machinery and equipment, and farm machinery. The latter are much more likely than the former to place great emphasis upon the dangers of trading on the equity.

Suppose, for example, that two corporations of comparable size, A and B, have profit records over an eight-year period as set down below (with negative figures indicating losses), and that these records are typical of their business cycle experience:[12]

Year	Corporation A	Corporation B
1	$ 500,000	$ 800,000
2	520,000	900,000
3	550,000	1,000,000
4	570,000	1,200,000
5	520,000	900,000
6	470,000	−100,000
7	430,000	−400,000
8	440,000	−300,000
Total	$4,000,000	$4,000,000
Average	$ 500,000	$ 500,000

---

[12] This is not meant to imply that eight years is the ordinary duration of cycles in general business activity, whether measured from peak to peak or from trough to trough. While business cycle authorities do estimate that "major" cycles in the United States have averaged between eight and nine years, they also point out that actual cycles have varied in duration from but little more than one year to as much as eleven years.

We may assume that both corporations have had simple common stock structures, and that the respective amounts of their stockholders' investments have been just about identical. Accordingly, the *average* rate of return for the two groups of stockholders in the eight-year period has also been approximately equal. Such an equality in the average rate of return might suggest that trading on the equity should be no more dangerous for B than for A. Were B to have a bond issue outstanding, why could it not set aside cash in the good years to insure its capacity to meet its obligations in the lean years?

To ask such a question is to suggest where lie the dangers of trading on the equity. The extraordinary profits of the good years might prompt the directors of B to be overgenerous in their dividend declarations, especially so if dividends had been suspended in a preceding period of losses. But an even greater danger is that the cash throw-off from profits in the good years would be used in large part immediately for the expansion of inventories, accounts receivable, and fixed facilities, so that this drain, plus that for dividends—even if dividends were held to moderate levels—would lead to severe cash shortages in the poor years of a kind to threaten solvency. Once again, the lack of a direct relationship between the size of the cash account and the size of surplus accounts must be stressed. Many corporations with comparatively large surplus accounts have defaulted upon their obligations in times of business depressions. Using only the figures presented above, and assuming that B paid dividends of only $300,000 each year for the first five years, it would reach the first loss year (the sixth year of the table) with a surplus of $3.3 million; but if it had spent for noncash assets the cash throw-offs from the accumulated profits, its financial position in the last three years of the eight-year period could be dangerously weak. By contrast, A would continue to have substantial cash throw-offs from its profits of the sixth, seventh, and eighth years. Were it, therefore, to have bonds or other forms of long-term debt in its financial structure, they should offer no serious threats to its solvency.

Government Regulation of Rates and Security Issues

Rate Regulation. In one important area of business enterprise, that of public utility corporations, government regulation of the rates that may be charged for services to the public militates against the maintenance of simple common stock structures. Rate regulation is made applicable principally to electric power, gas, and water companies, to railroads, airlines, bus lines, and other enterprises in the field of transportation, and to telephone and telegraph companies. It is imposed by both the federal and state governments, depending upon the area served by the individual utility—by the federal government, through the Federal Power Commission, the Interstate Commerce Commission, the Civil Aeronautics Board, and the Federal Communications Commission; and by the state governments, through agencies of various titles but generally known collectively as the "public service commissions."

The principal objective of public utility rate regulation is to insure a level of rates that will be "fair" both to the public and to the utilities themselves. Fairness is expected to be achieved by permitting service rates that will enable the utility, with good management, to earn a "reasonable" rate of return upon the value of the assets it employs in providing its services. Problems of extraordinary complexity are involved in determining what assets are to be included in the rate base, and especially in determining what valuations are appropriate for these assets. For the moment, however, it is sufficient to note that, whatever may be the final judgments about includible assets and their values, the "reasonable" rate of return itself is usually fixed within a range from 5 to 8 per cent.

If, therefore, all or almost all of the assets of a public utility corporation are supplied by the common stockholders, if it is allowed to charge service rates designed to give it a rate of return on these assets of, say, 6 per cent, and if it actually succeeds in earning this rate of return, the profit rate on the stockholders' investment is likewise limited to 6 per cent. But such a profit rate may be insufficient to attract common stock funds, as profit rates in unregulated industries may actually be, or may have good prospects of being, substantially higher than that. Accordingly, to be in a position to compete effectively for common stock funds, the utility must arrange its financial structure to be able to hold out good prospects of a rate of return higher than 6 per cent. In a word, it finds it highly important to give its common stock leverage by trading on the equity. If it earns 6 per cent on its assets, but acquires a substantial proportion of them by selling preferred stock that carries a dividend rate of, say, 5 per cent or bonds that bear interest at a rate of, say, 4 per cent, or by selling both preferred stock and bonds, then it succeeds in boosting the rate of return upon its common stock.

Nevertheless, public utility corporations, no less than those engaged in other areas of enterprise, may overdo trading on the equity. Many have done so, especially in the field of transportation, as has been evidenced by repeated waves of railroad bankruptcies and by the chronic difficulties of many street railway, interurban railway, and bus line systems. Service rate regulation aimed at allowing a reasonable rate of return on assets does not guarantee that the utility will actually earn that rate. Many transportation corporations have fallen far short, with difficulties in meeting obligations on bonds and other forms of long-term debt ensuing. With the railroads and electric railways, especially, excessive trading on the equity had been developed long before rate regulation had become effective, so that regulation could hardly be blamed for their difficulties in meeting obligations. Moreover, allowing railroads, electric railways, and bus lines to increase their charges to the public has often resulted simply in driving traffic to competing means of transportation. A recognition of the more circumscribed role that changing economic and technological conditions were forcing upon them led many railroad managements to use much of the cash throw-offs from their extraordinary profits of the period of World War II to reduce their long-term debt; in this way, they evidenced a lessened devotion to trading on the equity as a financial policy.

Regulation of Security Issues. In most instances, federal and state agencies that are empowered to regulate the rates that public utilities may charge for their services also have the authority to approve or disapprove the issuance of additional securities by the utilities as means of financing. A utility may be steered in the direction of greater "simplicity" in its financial structure by official disapprovals of its proposals to issue preferred stock or to contract additional amounts of long-term debt. It is not that the regulatory agencies frown upon trading on the equity, or that they are inclined to insist upon a decisive movement in the direction of simple common stock structures. They recognize the importance of giving common stock leverage so that it will be attractive to investors. But they insist upon a reasonable relationship between the investment of common stockholders and those of preferred stockholders and long-term creditors, while emphasizing also that such reasonable relationships are different for different kinds of utilities, depending largely upon their present and prospective earnings capacities. Thus, the Securities and Exchange Commission, which has regulatory jurisdiction over the security issues of public utility systems registered with it under the Public Utility Holding Company Act of 1935, has said:

> That the achievement and preservation of sound capitalization ratios are essential to the financial health of the public utility industry has been recognized not only by the Commission and some other regulatory bodies, but also by informed writers on the subject. Most of these authorities are generally agreed on the necessity for an adequate "cushion" of common stock equity to withstand the shock of a severe decline in earnings, and for not too excessive an amount of debt, notwithstanding the apparent cheapness of bond money versus common stock money and the deductibility for tax purposes of interest expense. Quite a number urge that a company should not use up all of its bonding credit, but rather should reserve a substantial portion of it for such time when it may become difficult to sell common stock.[13]

At times, accordingly, regulatory commissions reject proposals for bond issues on the grounds that market conditions are favorable for sales of additional common stock, and reject proposals for the retirement of preferred stock on the grounds that the money can be better used for the retirement of long-term debt. "Simplification" in financial structures has also been advanced by insistence by many regulatory commissions that the individual utility limit the varieties of its security issues. The utility is

---

[13] Securities and Exchange Commission, *Annual Report*, 1956, p. 161.

told that it will be permitted to issue only one kind of preferred stock and only one kind of bonds (in addition to one kind of common stock, of course), and that, accordingly, it must plan its long-range financing on such a basis. Or if the utility already has a badly "splintered" financial structure, it is advised to draw its long-term financing plans with the objective of "consolidating" its many varieties of preferred stocks and bonds into one or two new issues of uniform character.

Market Conditions

Sometimes the market for common stock is so highly favorable that corporate managements decide upon additional issues almost as a matter of course. If money is needed for expansion, taking advantage of the high prices at which common stock can be sold appears unquestionably to be the best way of getting it; and this may be so even though, under other circumstances, the attractions of trading on the equity would be quite compelling. Thus, by force of circumstances, one might say, corporations may continue with simple common stock structures without any strong convictions upon the part of their managements about the superiority of this form.

At other times, the market for common stock is so depressed that corporate managements quickly conclude that it would be a very poor source of needed funds. The sale of additional common stock at low prices, it is decided, would most unreasonably dilute the interests of present stockholders—especially, as we have seen, their claims against assets, their rights to vote, and their claims upon future profits. But the markets for preferred stock or bonds or both are not necessarily depressed simultaneously with that for common stock; when they are not depressed, therefore, decisions to tap them, rather than to sell common stock, are surely, in many cases, to be expected.

At all times, the availability of funds in the hands of different classes of investors is an important determinant of the amounts that business corporations can succeed in drawing from given markets. A "favorable" common stock market most surely does not mean that any one corporation can sell an unlimited amount of additional common stock at a good price, or, indeed, at any price. How much it can sell depends upon the amount of investment funds held by individuals and institutions that are ordinarily interested in buying common stock, as well as upon the amount of such funds that other corporations are seeking to draw from the market. Especially significant in this regard are provisions of law and stipulations in contracts that forbid or closely limit investment in common stocks by many of our most important classes of financial institutions. Commercial banks are generally forbidden to invest in common stocks other than the stocks of their subsidiaries; and, in most states, investment in common stocks by life insurance companies and mutual savings banks is subject to strict standards and limits. In a similar way, trust agreements and wills sometimes restrict investment in common stocks by trustees of personal estates and pension and endowment funds, and sometimes such restrictions are imposed by law and court decrees. Hence, it is entirely possible for financial institutions to have an abundance of funds available for investment in bonds while, simultaneously, the money holdings of investors interested in common stock issues are quite limited. Accordingly, the managements of given business corporations may decide that, though the common stock market is "favorable" for a limited amount of money, their great needs require that they go elsewhere to reach the much larger supply of funds in the hands of individuals and financial institutions that are not buying common stocks.

Questions

1. What is the composition of a corporation's financial structure? Is care in the management of financial structure as important as in the management of assets? Why or why not?

2. In simple common stock structures, what place is there, if any, for surplus? short-term debt? long-term debt?

3. In simple common stock structures, what is the minimum proportion of total assets likely to be contributed by the common stockholders? Explain.

4. According to the statistics taken from corporate income tax returns for fiscal years 1960–61, in which industrial area or areas were current liabilities the principal source of assets? fixed liabilities? preferred stock? common stock? surplus? common stock and surplus combined?

5. How does a corporation's simple common stock structure contribute to its solvency? to its good credit standing?

6. What is trading on the equity? Explain why it can be both advantageous and dangerous to common stockholders.

7. Compare the advantages and disadvantages of trading on the equity with bonds with the pros and cons of doing so with preferred stock.

8. To what extent, if at all, are the dangers of trading on the equity reduced by the provisions of the Internal Revenue Code permitting the carry-back and carry-over of net operating losses?

9. Compare the costs of selling new issues of common stock, preferred stock, and bonds. Of what do these costs chiefly consist?

10. Explain how sales of additional common stock by a corporation may dilute the claims of its existing common stockholders (*a*) to future profits, and (*b*) against assets.

11. To what extent is the financial structure of a corporation likely to be influenced by the interests of its existing common stockholders in control?

12. How is the financial structure of a corporation likely to be influenced by the size of its profits? the stability of its profits?

13. What influence upon corporate financial structures is exerted by the age of corporations? the rapidity of their growth?

14. What kinds of effects upon financial structures may result from government regulation of (*a*) corporations as issuers of securities, and (*b*) financial institutions as investors in securities?

15. How may changing conditions in the securities markets influence the form of corporate financial structure?

Problems

1. Assuming the levels of flotation costs to be equal to the percentages shown in Table 14–5, what would be the amount of these costs to a manufacturing corporation in selling a bond issue at a public offering price of $1,-500,000? a preferred stock issue of the same size? a common stock issue of this size?

2. With the same assumption as in Problem 1, what would be the respective amounts of flotation costs to an electric power company of the three kinds of security issues if the public offering price were $25 million?

3. In a certain year, Baxter & Sloan, Inc., had a net profit of $3,200,000 before the deduction of federal income taxes.

a) Assuming that the corporation had no preferred stock or bonds in its financial structure, that the common stockholders' equity amounted to $14 million, and that federal income tax rates were 30 per cent on the first $25,000 of taxable income and 52 per cent on the balance, what rate of profit did it earn on the stockholders' equity?

b) What would have been the rate of profit on Baxter & Sloan's common stockholders' equity had the equity amounted to $8 million and had the corporation had outstanding $6 million of 6 per cent preferred stock upon which the dividend of $360,000 was paid in the course of the year? (Assume that the net profit amounted to $3,200,000 before the deduction of both the federal income taxes and the preferred dividends.)

c) What would have been the rate of profit on Baxter & Sloan's common stockholders' equity had the equity amounted to $8 million and had the corporation had outstanding $6 million of 6 per cent bonds upon which the interest obligation of $360,000 was paid in the course of the year? (Assume that the net profit amounted to $3,200,000 before the deduction of both the federal income taxes and the bond interest.)

4. With the assumption that Baxter & Sloan's net profit before income taxes (and before deduction for preferred dividends or bond interest, where applicable) amounted to only $380,000, and with all other facts as stated in parts (*a*), (*b*), and (*c*) of Problem 3 unchanged, what would have been the rate of profit on the common stockholders' equity in each instance?

5. The Lane Supply Corporation has outstanding 500,000 shares of common stock of $5.00 par value and its surplus amounts to $1,500,000. On the average, it has been earning an after-tax profit equal to 14 per cent of the stockholders' equity. It now sells to outsiders 250,000 additional shares of common stock at a price of $12 a share. On the assets acquired with the proceeds of this issue. however, the corporation succeeds in earning an after-tax profit of only 9 per cent.

a) To what extent, if at all, was the claim of the old stockholders to corporate earnings diluted by the sale of the new stock?

b) How was their per-share claim to assets affected by the transaction?

c) Considering the effects determined in (*a*) and (*b*), did the sale of the new stock work to the advantage of the old stockholders or to their disadvantage?

chapter 15

FINANCIAL STRUCTURES WITH PREFERRED STOCK AND LONG-TERM DEBT

The analysis of the preceding chapter indicates that corporate managements are impelled to add preferred stocks or long-term debt or both to their financial structures for a variety of reasons. Many are unquestionably persuaded to move in that direction by the attractions of trading on the equity—by convictions, as it were, that good prospects for enhanced rates of profit on the investment of common stockholders more than offset mild increases in the danger of insolvency, moderate weakening of credit standing and access to funds in time of pressing need, and the acceptance of some restrictions on managerial discretion. All the more is this kind of decision likely to be made by corporations that have records of and prospects for stable profits; and still more surely by utility corporations on account of rate regulation, especially when they, too, enjoy a reasonable degree of stability in their profit-making capacities.

Fear of loss of control such as would or could result from additional common stock sales is undoubtedly another very common reason for decisions to add preferred stocks[1] or fixed debt or both to financial structures. Also important is the unavailability of sufficient common stock funds to finance needed expansion, either because of the youth of corporations or because of temporary disdain of the investing public for new common stock issues regardless of the ages and financial prestige of the issuers. Much less important, on the other hand, are fears of dilution in the claim of common stockholders to future profits and assets. And, finally, a combination of reasons often accounts for corporate decisions to depart from the simple common stock form of financial structure.

EXTENT OF FINANCING WITH PREFERRED STOCK AND LONG-TERM DEBT

The relative positions of preferred stock and long-term debt (fixed liabilities) in the financial structures of business corporations in various fields of industry were indicated in Table 14–4 presented on page 297 of

---

[1] Control through the ownership of common stock is not ordinarily endangered in any immediate way by the sale of preferred stock. Preferred stock can usually be made nonvoting except on proposals that would weaken the priority of its claims and in certain contingencies, as the nonpayment of dividends for a year or more. See below, pp. 530–32.

the preceding chapter. But it is of interest to see, not only relative positions at a given time, but also the extent of the use of the respective means of financing from year to year.

Preferred Stock

The dollar amounts of preferred stock sales in each year since 1946, as reported by the Securities and Exchange Commission, are set out in Table 15–1, with the figures for common stock sales for the same period also

TABLE 15–1

New Issues of Preferred and Common Stock Offered for Cash, 1946–62[a]
(In millions of dollars)

Year	Preferred Stock	Common Stock
1946	$ 1,126	$ 891
1947	761	778
1948	492	614
1949	425	736
1950	631	811
1951	838	1,212
1952	564	1,369
1953	489	1,326
1954	816	1,213
1955	635	2,185
1956	636	2,301
1957	411	2,516
1958	571	1,334
1959	531	2,027
1960	409	1,664
1961	449	3,273
1962	436	1,318
Total	$10,220	$25,568

[a] Gross proceeds of both registered and unregistered issues offered publicly or by private placement for cash sale, but excluding issues of $100,000 or less, intercorporate transactions, issues of investment companies, and issues to be sold over an extended period of time, such as offerings under employee-purchase plans.

SOURCE: Securities and Exchange Commission, *Annual Reports* and *Statistical Bulletin*, various issues.

shown for comparison. Total sales of preferred stock for the entire period from 1946 through 1962 amounted to $10,220 million, while the total for common stock in the same period was $25,568 million. Such totals, however, do not mean that there were additions of equal amounts to net corporate assets financed by the two stock sources, since substantial amounts of stock are retired every year. Unfortunately, the available statistics do not show how much of each kind of stock is retired from year to year. However, for a coverage somewhat different from that of the table, SEC figures show that retirements of the two kinds of stock combined in the period 1946–62 amounted to approximately 32.8 per cent of the combined amount of new issues in the same period.[2]

---

[2] Computed from data published by the Securities and Exchange Commission in *Net Changes in Corporate Securities Outstanding*, mimeographed release, April 1, 1961, and in its *Statistical Bulletin*, June, 1963, p. 16.

Bonds

Statistics of new corporate bond issues, retirements of old ones, and the resulting net changes in amounts outstanding, as compiled by the SEC for the period 1946–62, are presented in Table 15–2. The enormous total

TABLE 15–2
Corporate Bond Financing, 1946–62[a]
(In millions of dollars)

Year	New Issues	Retirements	Net Increase[b]
1946	4,721	$ 3,625	$ 1,096
1947	5,015	2,011	3,004
1948	5,938	1,283	4,655
1949	4,867	1,583	3,284
1950	4,803	2,802	2,004
1951	5,682	2,107	3,575
1952	7,344	2,403	4,940
1953	6,651	1,896	4,755
1954	7,832	4,033	3,799
1955	7,571	3,383	4,188
1956	7,934	3,203	4,731
1957	9,638	2,584	7,053
1958	9,673	3,817	5,856
1959	7,125	3,049	4,076
1960	8,044	3,010	5,034
1961	9,205	4,090	5,114
1962	8,593	3,566	5,028
Total	$120,639	$48,445	$72,192

[a] The SEC explains that these data are not exactly comparable with those of stock sales as presented in Table 15–1 because of adjustments described as follows: "The following types of sales, not included in the basic figures, are added: Sales to the general public of securities held by affiliated companies or by Government agencies, sales of securities sold privately to foreigners, and sales by investment companies. Among other adjustments, a deduction is made from the original data of sales of securities of foreign companies in the United States, and an adjustment is made to deduct from the total offerings the amount of issues which, although they were offered for sale, were not actually sold."

[b] Because of rounding, "net increase" in some instances is not the exact difference between "new issues" and "retirements."

Source: Securities and Exchange Commission, *Net Change in Corporate Securities Outstanding*, mimeographed release, April 1, 1961; and *Statistical Bulletin*, June, 1963, p. 16.

of $120,639 million of new bond financing in the 17 years covered by the table might lead one to suspect that, in a collective sense, American corporations have generally been largely neglecting stock as a source of assets in favor of a heavy dependence on bonds. But bonds are debts that must be paid off periodically or at their maturity dates. Thus, when large amounts of bonds have been issued in past years, every current year must witness substantial retirements of the earlier issues as long as corporations remain solvent. Many new issues of bonds, therefore, are "refunding" issues, all or most of their proceeds being earmarked to pay off maturing earlier issues. Nevertheless, the net increase in bonds outstanding of $72,192 million in the 17-year period, by comparison with the net increase in stock issues in the same period, has been truly remarkable. Evidently, therefore, corporate managements have been much impressed with the advantages of bond financing, as indicated in the preceding chapter and as further developed later in this one.

All Sources of Assets

The statistics of changes in the outstanding volume of bonds do not give a complete picture of the amount of year-by-year financing on the basis of long-term debt; there are other forms of long-term corporate debt, such as "term loans" granted by commercial banks and mortgage loans granted by other classes of financial institutions. Likewise, figures for changes in the amount of outstanding stock do not give us a complete account of year-to-year contributions to corporate assets by stockholders, for, as we saw in the last chapter, retained earnings represent a most important additional contribution made by them. What is more, changes in the relative positions of stockholders and long-term creditors as sources of corporate assets are still not clearly to be seen unless the roles of short-term creditors and cash throw-offs from depreciation as "sources of funds" are introduced for comparison. Fortunately, therefore, we are able to refer to a comprehensive accounting for all sources of corporate funds for the period 1946–62 as published by the Office of Business Economics of the Department of Commerce and as reproduced (and rearranged) here in Table 15–3.[3] The details for each year and the totals are net figures—not, for example, the total sales of bonds, but total sales less retirements, and not total short-term borrowing from banks, but new loans less the repayment of others. Thus, a negative figure indicates repayments or retirements greater than new amounts acquired from a given source—its reduction as a source of assets by means of funds derived from other sources.

Especially notable among the disclosures of Table 15–3 is the standout performance of depreciation throw-offs as a source of corporate funds in the postwar years—not only its total, but also its tremendous rate of expansion in this period.[4] The role of stockholders as contributors to assets is seen to be much more important than is indicated when the respective volumes of stock and bond issues are simply compared. The contribution of stockholders in the 17-year period through stock buying and the retention of earnings combined equaled 29.1 per cent of total sources of funds, while that of bondholders and other long-term creditors amounted

---

[3] The Department of Commerce reports yearly discrepancies ranging from $300 million to $5 billion between the total estimated sources of funds as presented in Table 15–3 and the total estimated uses of funds, that is, net asset acquisitions. Although such discrepancies need not disturb us, since they are not of unreasonable size considering the complexity of the data and their magnitude, they do call attention to the fact that the data on sources of funds are not claimed to be exact summations.

[4] How depreciation charges serve as a source of funds was explained above, pp. 112–13.

TABLE 15–3
Sources of Corporate Funds, 1946–62[a]
(In billions of dollars)

YEAR	STOCKHOLDERS Stock Sales	STOCKHOLDERS Retained Earnings[b]	STOCKHOLDERS Total	DEPRECIATION	LONG-TERM CREDITORS Bond Sales	LONG-TERM CREDITORS Other	LONG-TERM CREDITORS Total	SHORT-TERM SOURCES Bank Loans	SHORT-TERM SOURCES Trade Payables	SHORT-TERM SOURCES Federal Income Tax Liabilities	SHORT-TERM SOURCES Other	SHORT-TERM SOURCES Total	GRAND TOTAL[c]
1946	$ 1.3	$ 7.2	$ 8.5	$ 4.2	$ 1.1	$ 1.8	$ 2.9	$ 2.1	$ 3.7	$ −1.6	$ 2.1	$ 6.3	$ 21.9
1947	1.4	11.4	12.8	5.2	3.0	1.9	4.9	1.4	4.5	2.1	1.5	9.5	32.4
1948	1.2	12.6	13.8	6.2	4.7	1.3	6.0	.5	1.3	.9	.4	3.1	29.1
1949	1.6	7.8	9.4	7.1	3.3	−.6	2.7	−1.7	−.3	−2.2	.5	−3.7	15.5
1950	1.7	13.0	14.7	7.8	2.0	.5	2.5	2.1	8.8	7.3	1.0	19.2	44.2
1951	2.7	10.0	12.7	9.0	3.6	1.5	5.1	3.9	2.7	4.3	1.9	12.8	39.6
1952	3.0	7.4	10.4	10.4	4.9	1.5	6.4	1.6	2.7	−3.1	2.4	3.6	30.8
1953	2.3	7.9	10.2	11.8	4.8	.5	5.3	−.1	.4	.6	2.2	3.1	30.4
1954	2.1	6.3	8.4	13.5	3.8	.5	4.3	−1.1	−.2	−3.1	.4	−4.0	22.2
1955	2.7	10.9	13.6	15.7	4.2	1.7	5.9	3.7	5.5	3.8	2.1	15.1	50.3
1956	3.2	10.5	13.7	17.3	4.7	3.2	7.9	2.2	5.5	−1.7	3.0	9.0	47.9
1957	3.5	8.9	12.4	19.1	7.0	1.4	8.4	.3	2.4	−2.2	2.1	2.6	42.5
1958	3.6	5.7	9.3	20.3	5.9	1.4	7.3	−.4	3.8	−2.5	1.7	2.6	39.4
1959	3.7	9.5	13.2	21.6	4.1	1.8	5.9	5.4	5.3	2.1	3.7	16.5	57.1
1960	3.0	6.2	9.2	22.9	5.0	1.7	6.7	1.3	4.5	−1.6	3.2	7.4	46.2
1961	4.5	5.6	10.1	24.0	5.1	1.6	6.7	.4	6.1	.6	1.8	8.9	49.7
1962	2.1	7.0	9.1	27.8	5.0	3.1	8.1	3.0	5.5	.9	3.2	12.6	57.8
Total......	$43.6	$147.9	$191.5	$243.9	$72.2	$24.8	$97.0	$24.6	$62.2	$ 4.6	$33.2	$124.6	$657.0
Percentage of grand total......	6.6	22.5	29.1	37.1	11.0	3.8	14.8	3.7	9.5	.7	5.1	19.0	100.0

[a] Excluding banks and insurance companies.
[b] Including depletion.
[c] In some instances, items do not add exactly to horizontal subtotals and grand totals because of rounding.

SOURCE: Survey of Current Business, October, 1958, p. 18; July, 1962, p. 24; and July, 1963, p. 29. (Vertical totals and percentages supplied by the author.)

to only approximately half that amount, at 14.8 per cent. Nevertheless, the latter figure remains quite impressive, though still less than the combined total of all short-term sources of funds at 19.0 per cent.

It is often instructive to take notice of changes in the direction of corporate financing on the basis of comprehensive data such as those of Table 15–3. For example, a comparison of the four major sources of financing in the first six years of the 17-year period of the survey with the most recent six years, as percentages, gives the following results:

	Stockholders	Long-Term Creditors	Short-Term Creditors	Depreciation
1946–51........	39.4	13.2	25.8	21.6
1957-62........	21.6	14.7	17.3	46.4

The enormous increase in cash throw-offs from depreciation as a source of corporate funds, related to the very sharp drop in the proportion contributed by stockholders, explains in part the "profits squeeze" about which so much has been said in recent years. Reported corporate profits have been substantially reduced by stepped-up charges for depreciation made possible, in part, by more liberal rules of the Treasury for charging depreciation in the determination of taxable income. If a larger portion of the sales dollar is regarded as covering depreciation costs, less necessarily remains as profit. It is worth adding that, because the immediate postwar period was one of extraordinary demand for peacetime goods, as people tried to make up the huge backlog of depression and wartime deficiencies, the profit rates—and, therefore, corporate capacities to retain earnings—were pushed to extraordinary heights.

Of significance, too, is the contrast in the patterns of corporate financing between years of general business expansion and years of contraction or recession. In the postwar period, the calendar years 1949 and 1960, and the years ending June 30, 1954 and 1958 were recession years, while the calendar years 1948, 1950, 1959, 1961, and 1962, and the years endings June 30, 1953, 1955, and 1957 were, in general, periods of expanding business activity. Such a comparison can be made as in Table 15–4 by a rearrangement of the sources-of-funds data of Table 15–3 and additional figures for the years ending June 30 also drawn from the reports of the Office of Business Economics of the Department of Commerce.

CHOICE OF PREFERRED STOCK

From the standpoint of the interests of the common stockholders of a business corporation, the advantages of raising funds by means of preferred stock issues rather than by contracting long-term debt are closely comparable to the advantages of the simple common stock structure itself, as discussed in the preceding chapter. Such a parallelism is to be expected, since preferred stock is an equity security. Although its ownership rights are usually made to differ in various ways from those of com-

TABLE 15–4
Corporate Financing in Four Postwar Cycles[a]
(In billions of dollars)

	Year Ending Dec. 31....			Year Ending June 30....			Year Ending June 30....			Year Ending Dec. 31....		
	1948	1949	1950	1953	1954	1955	1957	1958	1959	1960	1961	1962
Stockholders:												
Stock sales............	$ 1.2	$ 1.6	$ 1.7	$ 2.8	$ 2.4	$ 1.8	$ 4.0	$ 3.1	$ 3.7	$ 3.0	$ 4.5	$ 2.1
Retained earnings[b]....	12.6	7.8	13.0	8.3	6.2	8.7	9.9	5.6	9.5	6.2	5.6	7.0
Total...........	$13.8	$ 9.4	$14.7	$11.1	$ 8.6	$10.5	$13.9	$ 8.7	$13.2	$ 9.2	$10.1	$ 9.1
Depreciation............	6.2	7.1	7.8	11.0	12.6	14.6	18.7	20.6	21.6	22.9	24.0	27.8
Long-term debt.........	6.0	2.7	2.5	6.0	4.1	5.2	8.4	8.4	5.9	6.7	6.7	8.1
Short-term debt.........	3.1	-3.7	19.2	6.5	-6.2	6.8	5.5	-8.3	16.5	7.4	8.9	12.6
Grand Total........	$29.1	$15.5	$44.2	$34.6	$19.1	$37.1	$46.5	$29.4	$57.2	$46.2	$49.7	$57.8

[a] Excluding banks and insurance companies.
[b] Including depletion.

SOURCE: *Survey of Current Business*, October, 1958, p. 20; July, 1962, p. 24; and July, 1963, p. 29.

mon stock, the preferred stockholders participate as owners of the corporation, nevertheless. Since preferred stock represents ownership, therefore, its issuance by a corporation is not so radical a departure from the simple common stock structure as is the incurring of long-term debt. All the more is this true by reason of the fact that the preferred stock issues of corporations are generally held to amounts far less than the amounts of their outstanding common stock issues. That this is generally so is indicated in Table 15–5 in which are listed some of our leading corporations that have preferred stocks but no long-term debt in their financial structures.

TABLE 15–5
Some Large Corporations Having Preferred Stock but No Long-Term Debt in Their Financial Structures[a]
(Shares in thousands; dollar amounts in millions)

CORPORATION	TOTAL ASSETS	SHARES OUT-STANDING		TOTAL STATED VALUES		ALL SURPLUS ACCOUNTS
		Preferred	Common	Preferred	Common	
E. I. duPont de Nemours & Company..	$2,861	2,389	45,983	$239	$230	$2,156
Eastman Kodak Company............	1,023	82	38,382	4	384	430
International Paper Company........	1,009	162	42,684	16	107	762
Montgomery Ward & Company......	767	202	12,566	20	197	424
American Smelting, Refining and Mining Company................	477	500	5,464	50	124	219
United States Gypsum Company.....	368	78	8,040	8	32	287
Hercules Powder Company.........	317	235	18,092	10	19	203
Rohm & Haas Company............	231	62	4,834	6	24	169
Armstrong Cork Company..........	222	162	5,167	17	5	168
Beatrice Foods Company...........	149	77	4,937	45	8	77

[a] As of December 31, 1962, except Montgomery Ward & Company, January 30, 1963.
SOURCE: Moody's Investors Service, *Industrial Manuals.*

Reasons for choices in favor of preferred stock, accordingly, may be discussed under heads similar to those presented in the preceding chapter in the analysis of the advantages of simple common stock structures, namely, (1) protection of solvency, (2) maintenance of credit standing, (3) reservation of further financing capacity, and (4) avoidance of restrictions upon managerial discretion. The disadvantages of choosing preferred stock, on the other hand, hardly require specific detailed treatment, as they should be sufficiently indicated in the discussion of the disadvantages of simple common stock structures in the preceding chapter, as well as in the discussion of the advantages of long-term debt financing presented later in this chapter.

Solvency

The solvency of business corporations is endangered much less by the issuance of preferred stock than by the contraction of long-term debt. As with common stock, dividends on preferred are payable at the discretion of boards of directors. Directors may decide, for a year or two or for a long series of years, that available cash must be conserved for current operations and for the payment of debts rather than used for dividend payments. The nonpayment of dividends gives preferred stockholders no legal right of action, as by seeking judgments and seizing assets to satisfy them, or by initiating bankruptcy proceedings. Likewise, preferred stock has no maturity date at which the principal (par or stated value) becomes due and payable.

Nevertheless, the presence of preferred stock in financial structures often has some effect toward increasing the danger of insolvency. The danger does not originate in bad times when the supply of cash may be short and liabilities pressing, for in such periods boards of directors will surely not hesitate to decide against the payment of preferred dividends, as well as against retirements of the preferred stock itself. Rather, the danger is likely to originate when business activity is falling off but before serious strains are felt. Boards of directors may be inclined to continue dividends on the preferred to preserve its attractiveness to investors, but subsequent events may prove that the cash so used would have been better conserved for other purposes. In their preferred stock contracts, moreover, many corporations agree to use cash equal to stipulated percentages of their profits for the retirement of the stock. Cash drains in this direction, added to all the others to which corporations are subject, may leave all too little to enable them to weather periods of business adversity without serious strain.

Credit Standing

Because the claims of preferred stockholders against the assets of a corporation are inferior to those of all classes of creditors, the presence of preferred stock in a financial structure has a tendency to enhance the corporation's credit standing. The assets contributed by preferred stockholders, no less than those contributed by common stockholders, provide a "cushion" of protection for creditors. This means, of course, that all such assets, in addition to what they themselves have contributed, may be seized by the creditors by legal action if their claims are not met according to contractual terms in the normal course of business.

The creditors, however, have reason to be all the more pleased when additional assets that might have been contributed by buyers of preferred stock are contributed, instead, by common stockholders. This is the basis for the conclusion stated in the preceding chapter that, other things being equal, the credit standing of a corporation with a simple common stock structure is likely to be superior to that of a comparable one with both common and preferred stocks outstanding. Creditors are likely to anticipate that, in periods of declining business activity, preferred dividends will be continued after dividends on common have been suspended. Moreover, they are likely to give weight to the possibility that the use of cash by corporations for the retirement of preferred stock may leave them somewhat short when their own claims come due.

Further Financing Capacity

Although the credit standing of a corporation that has issued preferred stock will probably be somewhat inferior to that of another that, in like circumstances, maintains a simple common stock structure, the degree of inferiority is not likely to be great. Certainly, its credit standing will tend to be substantially superior to that of a comparable corporation that has already included long-term debt in its financial structure. The latter kind of difference in credit position is likely to be especially significant at times when markets for common and preferred stocks are unfavorable. At such times, prospective lenders are reluctant to advance funds to corporations that are already "saddled with debt." Though such a corporation may be in a position to give them claims against assets equal, dollar for dollar, with the claims of existing creditors, this may be insufficient inducement. And if the corporation can only give them claims subordinate to those of present creditors, all the greater will their reluctance probably be. On the other hand, a corporation with preferred stock but without long-term debt can offer prospective creditors a superior claimants' position; it is likely to be in a position, indeed, to give them priority over existing short-term creditors, as by arranging for them a mortgage lien upon its properties.

However, one possible element of weakness in the position of the corporation with preferred stock but without existing long-term debt must be mentioned. This is the provision found in many preferred stock contracts requiring the consent of the owners of a substantial proportion of the preferred stock, such as two thirds or three fourths, for any long-term financing that would give rise to claims having priority over their own. A corporation might be unable to get this consent, even though it had found investors willing to lend funds on a long-term basis.

Avoidance of Restrictions on Management

Of the kinds of restrictions upon managerial discretion mentioned in the preceding chapter, those contained in preferred stock contracts generally circumscribe freedom of action much less than do those of contracts upon the basis of which long-term debt is incurred. Buyers of preferred stock know that, by its very nature, it must be less safe than are or would be the bonds of the same issuer, and they realize that no list of restrictions upon management, however long, could have the effect of giving it a degree of safety equal to that of bonds. They insist upon restrictions, it is true, but because they are promised a rate of return higher than that which is or would be promised to bondholders, they are willing to be moderate in limiting managerial discretion.

Also favoring preferred stock in this regard is the fact that waivers of contractual restrictions can usually be more easily obtained from preferred stockholders than from bondholders. A corporation knows who its preferred stockholders are and where they can be reached. It can call them together for a meeting, explain as persuasively as possible the reasons for the request for a waiver, and ask for approval as a "vote of confidence." On the other hand, it is not likely to know who all the holders of its bonds are, although it may know some of them. It may be able to reach all of them through various kinds of public notices, but considerable difficulty is involved.

CHOICE OF LONG-TERM DEBT

Impressive though the foregoing list of advantages of preferred stock issues may be, there is much to be said for the attractiveness of long-term borrowing as an alternative. The attractiveness of long-term debt appears to have been amply proved by American corporations that have resorted to it in the postwar period, as shown in the figures of sources of corporate funds presented earlier in this chapter in Table 15–3. It appears to be proved by the great number of our leading corporations that have substantial volumes of long-term debt but no preferred stock in their financial structures. A sampling of these corporations may be found in Table 15–6.

TABLE 15–6
Some Large Corporations Having Long-Term Debt but No Preferred Stock in Their Financial Structures[a]
(Amounts in millions of dollars)

Corporation	Total Assets	Long-Term Debt	Common Stock	All Surplus Accounts
Standard Oil Company (New Jersey)	$11,488	$830	$1,516	$6,094
Gulf Oil Corporation	4,244	259	826	2,387
Texaco, Inc.	4,166	319	1,609	1,672
Socony Mobil Oil Company	4,136	243	732	2,232
Standard Oil Company (Indiana)	3,109	391	901	1,552
Pennsylvania Railroad Company	2,846	749	135	1,617
General Electric Company	2,820	222	422	2,815
Sears, Roebuck & Company	2,792	350	227	1,473
Southern Pacific Company	2,519	697	425	1,162
New York Central Railroad Company	2,382	680	7	1,227
International Business Machines Corporation	1,985	425	715	665
Commonwealth Edison Company	1,837	842	506	256

[a] As of December 31, 1962, except Sears, Roebuck & Company, January 31, 1963.
SOURCE: Moody's Investors Service, *Manuals.*

Three advantages of long-term borrowing, by contrast with the sale of preferred stock, have to do with comparative costs: (1) lower rates payable for the use of investors' or lenders' funds, (2) lower costs in acquiring the funds, and (3) the deductibility of interest in computing income tax liabilities. Two other advantages are also worthy of consideration:

(4) avoidance of sharing of control, and (5) avoidance of dilution in common stockholders' claims to assets.

Lower Rates for the Use of Funds

Corporations that choose to abandon the simple common stock form of financial structure and find, at the same time, that they have reasonable access to both the preferred stock and long-term debt markets must be greatly impressed by the fact that, as a rule, they can borrow at a rate of interest materially below the dividend rate they would have to promise on preferred stock. If they expect levels of profits to be high enough and stable enough to justify trading on the equity, they may see no particular threat to solvency or credit standing in long-term borrowing. Accordingly, they may decide to reach for the maximum advantage of trading on the equity, that is, by financing at the lower long-term debt rate rather than at the preferred stock rate.

The size of the differentials between interest rates on long-term debt and dividend rates on preferred stock varies at any time according to the investment rating—essentially, the credit standing—of the individual corporation. Moreover, the differentials for all groups expand and contract from time to time, although not necessarily uniformly, depending upon the demands for long-term funds via the preferred stock market and the bond market respectively, as well as upon the supply of investment money in the hands of preferred stock buyers and bond buyers respectively and their attitudes toward the assumption of risks in investment. Regardless of the frequency of shifts and the absolute levels of interest and preferred dividend rates, however, the differential between them for corporations of a given investment rating seldom is less than one half of a percentage point. In planning to issue preferred stock, therefore, even corporations of the highest prestige must ordinarily anticipate having to name a dividend rate at least one half of a percentage point higher than the interest rate they would expect to pay were they issuing bonds instead.

While a differential of one half of a percentage point or thereabouts in favor of bond issues might appear to be insufficient inducement to give up the advantages of preferred stock issues as discussed above, it must be emphasized that, in long-term financing, the differential is multiplied over and over again. A corporation that puts out a preferred stock issue of $20 million having a dividend rate of 5 per cent will have *each year* a financial cost $100,000 in excess of that of another corporation that puts out a bond issue of the same face amount having an interest rate of 4½ per cent.

Lower Costs in Acquiring Funds

Corporations that are in a position to sell either long-term debt instruments or preferred stocks generally find that the flotation costs favor the former by a substantial margin. Long-term borrowing, therefore, has a cost advantage in addition to that measured by the spread between dividend and interest rates, as just described.

Some expenses of flotation of preferred stock issues tend to be less than those incurred in the flotation of bond issues of comparable size and of comparable issuers; these include transfer agency fees (as against trustees' fees for bond issues), printing and engraving expenses, and legal fees. But most of the other kinds of expenses of preferred stock issues are close to or higher than for debt issues. Differentials unfavorable to preferred stock are especially pronounced in the compensation paid to investment bankers—by far the most sizable item of expense in flotations for which their services are employed. The size of these differentials is indicated in Table 17–2 presented in Chapter 17 on page 385, and their effects upon total flotation costs were already indicated in Table 14–5 presented on page 308 of the preceding chapter. Investment bankers ordinarily demand a higher rate of compensation upon preferred stock transactions than upon bond transactions because they anticipate greater difficulties in selling the preferred stock; if they *underwrite* (which is, to repeat, a guaranteeing of sale at a specific price), they demand a higher reward as compensation for the greater risks of not being able to "unload" preferred stocks at the prices guaranteed.

Income Tax Treatment of Bond Interest

Strong is the belief that the deductibility of interest paid for borrowed money in determining federal income tax liabilities, as against the nondeductibility of dividend payments on common and preferred stock, has been an extremely important reason for the heavy volume of long-term corporate debt financing in the period since the close of World War II. At any rate, there is no denying that the volume of such financing by comparison with sales of preferred and common stocks has been much greater than in any earlier period of equal length, and, likewise, that the rates of the federal corporation income tax have been higher than in any earlier peacetime period.

The illustrations presented in the preceding chapter in the discussion of trading on the equity indicated the nature of the deductibility advantage. Nevertheless, a further illustration at this point should be useful. For this purpose, let us assume that a certain corporation, to raise $10 million of additional funds, has the choice of putting out a bond issue or a preferred stock issue. Since our objective is to see the tax advantage of the bond issue, we may ignore differences in probable flotation costs and we may further assume that, regardless of the corporation's choice, the rate of return it would have to promise investors is 5 per cent. A final assumption is that the corporation expects to earn an average annual profit of $2 million before the deduction of bond interest or preferred dividends, as the case may be, and before the deduction of the federal income tax. Accordingly, the tax advantage of the bond issue would be demonstrable as follows:

	Bond Alternative	*Preferred Stock Alternative*
Profit as indicated............................	$2,000,000	$2,000,000
Less: Bond interest......................	500,000	—
Taxable profit............................	$1,500,000	$2,000,000
Less: Federal income tax................	774,500	1,034,500
	$ 725,500	$ 965,500
Less: Preferred stock dividends..........	—	500,000
Profit available for common dividends and retention............................	$ 725,500	$ 465,500

The bond route would thus be expected to result in a tax saving of $260,000 (the difference between $1,034,500 and $774,500, or, alternatively, between $725,500 and $465,500). A pleasant aspect of this would be, of course, that such a tax saving would be expected year after year as long as the full amount of the bonds was outstanding. The managers of the corporation would surely feel that, since the annual tax saving would amount to 2.6 per cent of the face amount of the bonds, the cost of the funds supplied by the bondholders would actually be, not 5 per cent, but only 2.4 per cent. They might expect to say, as is so often said, that "Uncle Sam" would be bearing approximately half the interest cost on the bonds. On the other hand, they would realize that, should their choice go to preferred stock, the cost of the funds acquired would stand at 5 per cent—"Uncle Sam" having no part in this.

Avoidance of Sharing of Control

Long-term lenders to corporations are creditors; as such, they get no rights to participate in management, as that expression is generally understood. They may demand that certain kinds of restrictions upon managerial discretion be placed in their contracts, but they do not ask for the privilege of participating in decision making outside the scope of the restrictions. They do not vote in the annual election of directors nor upon questions that corporations are required by law to submit to their stockholders.

By contrast, preferred stockholders participate directly in management in various ways. Hence, groups of common stockholders that have narrow margins of control in given corporations may vote against preferred issues and in favor of debt issues for fear that the former might seriously weaken their positions. Under the laws of two states—Illinois and Mississippi—preferred stockholders have equal voting power, share for share, with the common stockholders. In either of these states, therefore, a

group having 51 per cent of the outstanding common stock of a corporation would be most unlikely to approve a preferred stock issue if they
expected that purchases by an opposing group would give it more than
50 per cent of the combined total of the existing common and the new
preferred. In other states, the general rule is that preferred stock may be
deprived of the ordinary power to vote for directors and upon questions
that the law requires to be submitted to the stockholders; nevertheless,
certain "contingent" and "vetoing" voting powers are usually retained by
the preferred stockholders. This reservation of limited voting powers is
customarily insisted upon by investment bankers as a means of making
preferred stocks attractive to investors, as well as by institutional investors
if they undertake to buy whole issues or large parts of issues for their
own portfolios. Illustrative of contingent voting powers is a provision
that preferred stockholders shall have the right to vote in the election of
directors if dividends on the preferred have not been paid for a designated
period of time such as a year. An example of vetoing powers—one mentioned earlier—is a provision requiring the approval of two thirds or three
fourths or some other proportion of the preferred stock for a subsequent
issues of bonds.[5] Thus, a controlling group of common stockholders
might shy away from a "nonvoting" preferred stock for fear that, at
some future time, their control might be lost through the ballots of preferred stockholders exercising contingent voting powers because of, say,
the nonpayment of dividends.

Avoidance of Dilution of Common Stockholders' Claims to Assets

In the matter of payments, bondholders and other long-term creditors
of a corporation are likely to be quite satisfied if it pays interest periodically at the stipulated rate and the principal or face amount of the obligations at maturity. Should the corporation wish to retire debt before
maturity, as by calling bonds for redemption, it may be required to pay
a bonus or premium over and above the face amount plus whatever interest may have accumulated. But the bonus or premium usually amounts
to not more than 2 or 3 per cent of the principal—sometimes it goes as
high as 6 per cent, but rarely beyond that—and it is likely to be considered by the debtor corporation simply as an additional interest cost. It
may be so treated for federal income tax purposes, so that deductible expenses are increased and tax liabilities are reduced if such a premium is
paid.

Buyers of preferred stock, on the other hand, are inclined to be much
more generous to themselves in stipulating what redemption prices for
their stockholdings they will agree to. Investment bankers and institutional investors often demand that such prices be fixed at premiums of 6

---

[5] The treatment here is not intended to be complete. The voting rights of preferred stockholders are analyzed at greater length in Chapter 22. See pp. 530–32.

or 7 per cent of the par or stated value of the stock, and sometimes at even higher percentages. Insistence by investors upon such premiums is justified on the grounds that corporations are likely to decide upon redemption when their financial positions are of the strongest—at the very time, therefore, when preferred stockholders are likely to be most anxious to retain their holdings. Along the same line, it is argued that when the outlook is poor, corporations can hardly be expected to be sufficiently well fixed financially to retire preferred stock; but that would be precisely the time when redemption would be most enthusiastically welcomed by preferred stockholders.

Because common stockholders and their representatives on a board of directors, in considering further financing, often anticipate that the good fortunes of the corporation will make possible the retirement of whatever new securities are to be issued, they may tend to veer away from preferred stock on account of redemption premium demands. They may conclude that the claim of the common stockholders to assets would be threatened with unfair dilution were a generous redemption price to be included in the preferred stock contract. For illustration, assume that a corporation has outstanding 100,000 shares of common stock of $100 par value, and that it has accumulated a surplus of $4 million. The claim of the common stockholders to assets is, therefore, $140 a share. Now comes a proposal that the corporation issue 20,000 shares of preferred stock. An investment banker is willing to buy this stock at the par value of, say, $100 a share, but he insists that the redemption price be placed at $115. Were the financing to be carried through on this basis, the buyers of the preferred stock could be said to have a claim against assets at the level of the redemption price. Although the claim, as originally established, would not be enforceable at any specific date, it would become so should the corporation at some time decide to redeem. The premium claim of the preferred stockholders of $15 a share, or $300,000 in total, would be granted at the expense of the common stockholders, for their claims against assets would be reduced from $140 to $137 per share.

Although dilution of common stockholders' claims to assets, as illustrated, is not likely to be considered a grave disadvantage of preferred stock issues—certainly not so great a disadvantage as the nondeductibility of preferred dividends for income tax purposes—it can at times be a strong argument against preferred stock financing. Should a corporation anticipate, for example, that it might want to retire a preferred stock issue as early as five years after the date of issuance, and should a prospective purchaser of the issue, such as an investment banker, demand a redemption premium of 15 per cent, the corporation might decide that preferred stock financing would be much too expensive. Were the dividend rate to be, say, 5 per cent, the corporate managers would not be unreasonable in fearing that the annual cost of preferred stock funds would actually prove to be much closer to 8 per cent.

INCLUSION OF BOTH PREFERRED STOCK
AND LONG-TERM DEBT

Many corporations, as a matter of continuing policy, include both preferred stock and long-term debt in their financial structures. The policy is especially prominent among public utilities, but it is by no means uncommon in many other areas of business enterprise. In only a few areas, indeed, is it impossible to find at least a few corporations that have adopted such a policy. Table 15–7 presents a listing of a few of our

TABLE 15–7
Some Large Corporations Having Both Long-Term Debt and Preferred Stock in Their Financial Structures[a]
(Amounts in millions of dollars)

Corporation	Total Assets	Long-Term Debt	Preferred Stock	Common Stock	All Surplus Accounts
General Motors Corporation...............	$9,169	$344	$284	$477	$5,891
United States Steel Corporation............	4,983	833	360	902	2,047
Bethlehem Steel Corporation...............	2,212	135	93	557	990
Atchison, Topeka & Santa Fe Railway Company..............................	1,633	203	124	243	955
Public Service Electric & Gas Company.....	1,552	751	125	333	170
International Harvester Company..........	1,527	139	82	565	404
Southern California Edison Company.......	1,524	708	130	264	237
Aluminum Company of America............	1,378	359	66	21	724
Procter & Gamble Company..............	1,090	87	2	42	687
Radio Corporation of America..............	1,059	255	15	35	440
Reynolds Metals Company................	992	374	95	109	256
American Tobacco Company..............	839	90	53	163	369
American Airlines, Inc...................	666	339	7	8	137

[a] As of December 31, 1962, except Procter & Gamble Company, June 30, 1962, and International Harvester Company, October 31, 1962.

SOURCE: Moody's Investors Service, *Manuals.*

leading corporations that have financial structures with both preferred stock and long-term debt.

In some cases, the inclusion of both preferred stock and long-term debt in financial structures is the result of deliberate choice upon the part of corporate managements; and, in others, it is the result of investor attitudes and conditions in the markets for long-term funds. Managements that have decided to depart from simple common stock structures may find that they have access to sufficient additional funds either by way of preferred stock sales or long-term borrowing, but a consideration of relative advantages and disadvantages may prompt them to choose a combination of these sources. On the other hand, managements may have strong preferences for one means of financing or the other, but they may find that, by the exclusive use of the means of their choice, they cannot acquire on reasonable terms as much money as they want. In a word, investors will not buy as much preferred stock as they would like to issue, or long-term lenders will not advance as much money as they would like to borrow.

Managerial Choices

A corporate management may decide that, though all needed funds could be raised without difficulty by means of preferred stock issues, exclusive dependence on this means of financing would not not be wise. Fears that issues of preferred stock beyond a certain level would endanger its own position of control might be a reason for such a decision—a danger might be seen in the contingent voting powers that would have to be given to the preferred stockholders. Or it might be felt that too great a dilution of the common stockholders' claim to assets could result from exclusive dependence upon preferred stock in the new financing. Some dilution on account of high redemption prices might be tolerable, but the management might decide to limit it by limiting the amount of the preferred stock issue itself. Even more importantly, relatively high dividend rates and the nondeductibility of dividends for tax purposes are often of great weight in decisions not to depend solely on preferred stock issues as sources of additional funds.

Likewise, the managers of a corporation that could borrow sufficient long-term funds to meet its expansion requirements fully may decide against relying exclusively on this source. They might conclude that, though solvency would not be endangered by partial financing with long-term debt, they would be taking undue risks were they to use this source solely. Or they might conclude that exclusive dependence upon long-term debt for present financing would leave the corporation with no borrowing capacity in the future—in times of emergency, in particular, when the markets for common and preferred stocks would likely be quite unfavorable. For such reasons, then, come managers' decision to include preferred stock, as well as long-term debt, in financial structures.

Investor Attitudes and Market Conditions

Availability of Investors' Funds. An important reason why corporations cannot sell as much preferred stock as they might want to sell is that the demand for preferred at most times is much weaker than is that for common stocks and bonds. In periods of depression, new issues of preferred stocks are often unsalable at anything close to fair prices; and even in times of prosperity, the preferred stock market generally does not become so buoyant as the markets for common stock and bonds. The simple fact is that investors collectively are much less interested in investing in preferred stocks than in the other two major classes of securities. Individual investors who are willing to take risks are inclined to accept the greater risks of common stock in the hope of deriving greater rewards than can be expected upon investment in preferred stocks; if they seek safety, they are inclined to want a full measure of it, as in debt instruments, rather than to take an in-between position, as in preferred stocks. Moreover, some of our most important classes of institutional investors are strictly limited by legal regulations in the amount of their preferred stock investment. Commercial banks are generally precluded entirely from preferred stock investment; and life insurance companies, mutual savings banks, and trustees who manage certain kinds of trusts must keep preferred stock holdings to small proportions of their total portfolios.

The interest of investors in bonds and other forms of long-term debt, on the other hand, tends to be perennial. Except in times of severest depression, substantial amounts of funds avaliable for investment in long-term debt instruments are likely to be found in the hands of investors. In life insurance companies, for example, collections of premiums and income earned on existing investments often exceed payments on policies and operating expenses even in times of serious business setbacks, and the excess receipts must be promptly invested to provide the further income needed to fulfill accumulating policy obligations. Yet, in times of high prosperity, when the market for common stock is booming, and that for preferred stock is quite favorable, the interests of life insurance companies in further investment in bonds do not wane, on account of the legal limitations upon their investment in stock.

Earnings Standards. The availability of large sums of money in the hands of individual and institutional investors never means that the individual corporation can get as much as it wants, whether by the issuance of preferred stock or the issuance of bonds. In deciding whether or not to buy new offerings of securities, investors judge quality and therefore attractiveness by applying various kinds of tests. Among the most important of these tests are earnings standards. Potential investors in a preferred stock want to know how much earnings the corporation will have available for dividends. They are especially concerned with what future earnings will be, but very often they must judge this by what earnings have been in the recent past. Thus, a popular test for preferred stock investment is that average earnings after the deduction of income taxes in a short period of years immediately preceding the year of the proposed issue—preferably including years both of depression and prosperity—should have been equal to two or three times the amount of annual dividends promised. In their analysis of the investment qualities of proposed issues of bonds, individual and institutional investors generally place even greater emphasis upon "earnings available for bond interest" in the past few years. Since, however, interest on bonds is a deductible expense for income tax purposes, bond buyers stress the ratio of average earnings *before* income taxes to the amount of bond interest to be paid, but they insist upon a much higher earnings-to-interest ratio than is expected for the earnings-to-dividends ratio by buyers of preferred stock. While, therefore, preferred stock buyers may insist upon average earnings *after* income taxes equal to two or three times preferred dividends, prospective long-term creditors usually demand average earnings *before* income taxes equal to three to seven times bond interest requirements.

To see how earnings standards function as determinants of the amounts of preferred stock and bonds corporations may be able to sell on reasonable terms, let us assume that a certain corporation wants to raise about $20 million, and that it is pondering the question whether it should offer preferred stock or bonds or both. It would have to set a dividend rate of 6 per cent on whatever amount of preferred stock it might decide to offer, and an interest rate of 5 per cent on bonds. Its average annual profit before the deduction of income taxes has been $3 million, and after this deduction, $1,445,500. It recognizes that earnings tests that investors are applying to proposed issues of preferred stocks and bonds are, respectively, two times and six times.[6] It is apparent, then, that the corporation (aside from other considerations) ought to be able to offer successfully either approximately $12 million of 6 per cent preferred stock ($1,445,500 ÷ .12) or $10 million of 5 per cent bonds ($3,000,000 ÷ .30). Apparently, therefore, the corporation could not raise the $20 million by sole dependence upon either preferred stock or bonds. Strange though it might seem, however, both of the earnings tests could be met were the corporation to offer $10 million of bonds and an equal amount of preferred stock. This conclusion can be demonstrated as follows:

Average earnings available for bond interest (equal to six times
    annual bond interest of $500,000 on $10,000,000 of bonds)....$3,000,000
Deduct bond interest.................................... 500,000
                                                     $2,500,000
Deduct federal income tax............................... 1,294,500
Average earnings available for preferred dividends (equal to approximately twice annual dividend requirements of $600,000
    on $10,000,000 of preferred stock).......................$1,205,500

The foregoing illustration may suggest that investors in preferred stocks and bonds are unreasonably cautious. Perhaps they are. But corporate managers, in planning new issues of securities, must make allowance for investors' caution, whether or not they think it unreasonable. It would be useless for them to argue that the new financing should substantially expand the corporation's earning capacity—that, therefore, earnings tests of two or three times preferred dividends or six or seven times bond interest based on *past* earnings demand too great a margin of pro-

---

[6] Such recognition is not likely to be subject to any wide margin of error. As soon as a corporation begins to negotiate with investment bankers or other prospective buyers of its securities, it is told that the preferred stock contract or the bond indenture *must* contain limitations upon total issues in terms of standards of earnings and of relationships of assets to liabilities and net worth such as are discussed here and in subsequent paragraphs of the text. These limitations in preferred stock contracts and bond indentures are generally known as "protective provisions." As found in preferred stock contracts, they are discussed below, pp. 533–38, and in bond indentures, pp. 666–68.

tection. If this is the degree of protection that investors look for, they can hardly be expected to buy corporate offerings of preferred stocks and bonds that fall short of their standards.

Standards for Relationships of Assets to Liabilities and Equity. Even the meeting of investors' earnings tests, conservative though they may seem to be, does not necessarily give a corporation clear sailing in offering new issues of preferred stock or bonds. Prospective investors can be expected to apply other kinds of tests, especially tests involving relationships of assets to liabilities and stockholders' equity in total or the equity of the common stockholders in particular—relationships as they would be *after* the proposed financing had been completed. Investors want to be sure that the individual corporation will not be depending too heavily upon the kind of security they buy as a source of its assets.

Standards applied by investors in preferred stocks are generally not so uniform as are those applied by buyers of bonds. For issues of industrial corporations, for example, some groups of investors are likely to be satisfied if the amount of preferred stock to be outstanding will not exceed the amount of common stock and surplus; while others are inclined to be more restrictive in their demands, as in asking that the amount of preferred stock plus all debt, current and fixed, not exceed 50 per cent of the total assets.

The various classes of investors in bonds are usually quite consistent in fixing limits beyond which, in their opinion, corporations in the different fields of business should not go in incurring debt. Their quality standards relate *total* debt, on the one hand, to current assets, total assets, or total tangible assets,[7] on the other, as well as total debt to the total equities of the stockholders. The investors often expect both of these types of standards to be satisfied simultaneously.

For the bonds of industrial corporations, for example, a widely accepted standard is that total long-term debt should not exceed the amount of working capital, and another is that total debt of all kinds should not exceed the amount of the stockholders' equity. To see how these standards would be applied both separately and simultaneously, let us assume that a certain corporation, if successful in proposed financing whatever direction it might take, would have assets and current liabilities as follows:

ASSETS		LIABILITIES AND EQUITY	
Current assets	$6,000,000	Current liabilities	$2,500,000
Fixed assets	7,000,000	Bonds	To be determined
		Common and preferred stock and surplus	Amount needed to balance

The application of the working capital test—that the amount of long-

---

[7] That is, total assets less intangibles such as goodwill and stockholdings in subsidiaries.

term debt should not exceed working capital—would mean a limitation of the bond issue to $3.5 million. With a bond issue at that level, stockholders' equity would have to amount to $7 million to provide the total complement of assets of $13 million. Thus, the second test—that total debt of all kinds should not exceed equity—would be easily satisfied.

Suppose, however, that the corporation's assets and current liability position after the financing were expected to be as follows:

ASSETS		LIABILITIES AND EQUITY	
Current assets.....$7,000,000		Current liabilities.......	$2,500,000
Fixed assets....... 6,000,000		Bonds................	To be determined
		Common and preferred	
		stock and surplus.....Amount needed to balance	

Now the working capital standard would permit a bond issue of $4.5 million, but this amount would be excessive by the equity standard. With total assets of $13 million and a bond issue of $4.5 million, total stockholders' equity would be only $6 million, and this would be less than the total amount of debt. Accordingly, investors in bonds whose judgment was based upon a simultaneous application of the two standards would probably be unwilling to buy unless the bond issue were limited to $4 million and equity increased, as by a new preferred or common stock issue, to $6.5 million.

Questions

1. How has the postwar volume of financing with common and preferred stocks compared with the volume of bond financing? How has the volume of stock retirements compared with the volume of bond retirements?

2. In relation to one another, how has each of the following ranked as sources of corporate funds in the postwar period: stockholders' investment, depreciation, long-term debt, and short-term debt?

3. In what directions and to what extent, if at all, do the patterns of corporate financing vary between periods of business recession and periods of expansion?

4. Why is depreciation classified as a source of corporate funds?

5. How can there be any danger to solvency as a result of including preferred stock in corporate financial structures?

6. How is the addition of preferred stock to a corporation's financial structure likely to affect its credit standing? its further access to long-term funds?

7. For the raising of long-term funds, why do income tax considerations often influence corporate managements toward bond financing in place of financing with preferred stocks?

8. Aside from income tax considerations, why does bond financing tend to be "cheaper" than preferred stock financing?

9. In imposing restrictions upon corporate managements, how do bond contracts compare with preferred stock contracts?

10. If their common stockholders fear loss of control, are corporations more likely to favor bond issues for long-term financing or preferred stock issues? Explain.

11. For choices between bonds and preferred stocks for long-term financing, of what importance are the premiums to be paid upon redemption?

12. For what reasons do corporate managements often decide to include both preferred stock and bonds in their financial structures?

13. Explain how investors' attitudes influence decisions of corporate managements toward bonds, preferred stock, or both for long-term financing.

14. What is the nature of the "earnings standards" commonly applied by investors in evaluating the investment merits of corporate securities? Explain how such standards are applied in judging preferred stock and bond issues.

Problems

1. A corporation has outstanding 600,000 shares of common stock. It has had average annual earnings of $2 million before the deduction of federal income taxes. Its management decides that earnings before income taxes could be increased by $800,000 were the corporation to spend $3 million upon additional facilities. The money could be raised by selling an issue of preferred stock with a dividend rate of 6 per cent or a bond issue with an interest rate of 5½ per cent. Assuming that the profit expectation of the management would be exactly realized, and disregarding the costs of selling the security issues, what would be the net profit after federal income taxes per share of common stock if the financing were done by means of (*a*) the preferred stock issue, and (*b*) the bond issue. (For this and the following problem, assume that the federal income tax rates are 30 per cent on the first $25,000 of taxable income and 52 per cent on the balance.)

2. A corporation's average net profit before deduction of federal income taxes in the past three years has been $3,600,000. To finance a program of expansion, it wants to raise as much as possible by a bond issue, a preferred stock issue, or a combination of the two. It is told by investment bankers that it would have to designate a 5 per cent interest rate on a bond issue and a 5½ per cent dividend rate on a preferred stock issue. The bankers say that such rates would attract many investors provided that the corporation did not attempt to market excessive issues—excessive in the sense of failing to satisfy the investors' "earnings standards."

a) Assuming that investors in the corporation's bonds would expect its recent before-tax earnings to be equal to three times the interest requirement, what is the maximum amount of bonds for which it would be likely to find a ready market?

b) Assuming that investors in the corporation's preferred stock would expect its recent after-tax earnings to be equal to two times the dividend requirement, what is the maximum dollar amount of preferred shares for which it would be likely to find buyers?

c) Assuming investors' standards to be as stated in (*a*) and (*b*), what are the maximum amounts of bonds and preferred stock in combination for which the corporation would be likely to find buyers?

Part VI

FINANCING WITH COMMON STOCK

chapter 16

COMMON STOCK AS A
SOURCE OF ASSETS

Common stock is of outstanding importance as a source of corporate assets. For the thousands of new business corporations that are formed every year, it tends to be almost an exclusive original source of assets; and for most of these corporations that survive, its predominant role is maintained for many years. Only with the development of good earnings capacities—usually a slow process—is it possible for retained profits as shown in surplus accounts to rival, and then perhaps to outrank, common stock as a source of assets; and only with the building of good credit reputations—usually a slow process, also—is it possible for debt, as a source of assets, to compete, as it were, with common stock. For some corporations, common stock always remains as the most important source of assets, regardless of the duration of their lives.

As a source of assets, indeed, the role of common stock can hardly be thought of as being measured only by the amount of cash or the value of other assets turned into corporations in exchange for it. It is not unreasonable to regard it also as the source of assets acquired by way of retained profits. In consideration of the risks they assume, the owners of common stock are claimants against all corporate profits that remain after income taxes and responsibilities to preferred stockholders have been met. To the extent, therefore, that common stockholders receive dividends that fall short of these profits, they make further contributions to corporate assets.

Why are millions of investors willing to make asset contributions to corporations through the purchase and ownership of common stock? To put the question in alternative form, why do corporations find common stock a financing instrument of extraordinary usefulness? The objective of the present chapter is to provide an answer to these questions. The answer must focus upon the rights or privileges that corporations afford to their common stockholders. These rights are attractive, although the degree of attractiveness differs from corporation to corporation. The rights *must* be attractive; otherwise, we have no explanation why people give huge sums of money, great aggregations of assets of other kinds, and innumerable hours of service in exchange for common stock.

COMMON STOCK AS A CONTRACT

In Chapter 2, stock was described as shares of ownership in a corporation; but it may also be defined as a contract between a corporation and its stockholders. The stockholders of a corporation are truly its owners, but ownership does not make them identical with it, as in a partnership. The corporation remains apart from its stockholders as a distinct legal entity; as a separate personality, it has the capacity to enter into contracts with people who want to become its stockholders. It does enter such contracts when it issues stock.

Nature of the Contract

To be binding, a contract must have "consideration," that is, mutual promises or obligations of the parties to do or not to do something that legally can be done. With corporate stock, consideration is provided by the corporation in giving the stockholder a "bundle of rights" which it promises to respect at all times, and by the stockholder, in his promise to pay the agreed-upon price for the stock. It is, of course, the "bundle of rights" that attracts buyers of stock, and it is the buyers' promises to pay that are sources of corporate assets.

The terms and conditions of stock as a contract are ordinarily not found in any one place. They are determined, in the first place, by the provisions of the laws of the state in which the corporation is chartered. Such laws stipulate what rights *must* be given to the stockholders, what rights *may* be given, and how certain rights may be limited. Thus, the stockholders obtain the rights conferred by law, whether or not the corporation's articles of incorporation and bylaws have anything to say about them. Secondly, the corporation's articles of incorporation contain other details of the contract—granting rights of some kinds, and withholding others, as may be permitted by the state laws. In the third place, the corporation's bylaws may contain other provisions concerning stockholders' rights, ordinarily not granting any not contained in the state laws or in the articles, and certainly not contradicting the laws and articles in modifying rights granted in those places, but setting details as to how the rights are to be exercised, as, for example, how the stockholders are to choose the directors at annual meetings and how they may have their stock transferred should they want to sell all or part of it. And, finally, further features of the contract are likely to be found in resolutions adopted by the corporation's board of directors, particularly designations as to the price prospective stockholders must pay for the stock, whether in cash, other property, or services.

Common and Preferred Stock

Establishing the fact that stock is a contract does not contradict the definition of stock as shares of ownership: it simply gives a legal complexion to the definition. In buying stock of a corporation, a person becomes one of its owners, but his rights as an owner are not necessarily the same as the rights he enjoys in the ownership of a house or an automobile; they depend upon the terms of his contract with the corporation. The rights of stockholders of a given class sometimes differ from state to state on account of dissimilar provisions of state laws; and, even within a single state, they may differ among corporations as they apply in different ways permissive provisions of the state laws. Within the single corporation, furthermore, very important differences in ownership rights may be provided for contractually with stockholders of distinct classes.

It is a basic principle of corporation law, nevertheless, that every business corporation must issue and have outstanding at all times a kind of stock that carries the full rights of ownership, as those full rights are recognized in the law of the state and in the decisions of its courts. Whatever this stock may be called by the individual corporation, it is known definitively as *common* stock. The corporation may have one or more additional classes of stock in which the rights of ownership are limited in various ways—generally known as *preferred* stock—or it may not have such additional classes, but, in any event, it cannot dispense with common stock. We readily conclude, therefore, that if a corporation has only one kind of stock outstanding, such stock must be common stock; and, this being true, it necessarily follows that common stock; and, this being true, it necessarily follows that common stock is the first stock a corporation issues and the last it retires.

In passing, we may note that many corporations that have only one kind of stock outstanding refer to it simply as "capital stock." Since any single issue of stock must be common stock, these corporations take it for granted that everybody must know that their "captial stock" is truly common stock. Sometimes, too, corporations use the word *capital* in the designation of two or more classes of stock, as "common capital stock" and "preferred capital stock." Although such terminology is justifiable, since the words *stock* and *capital stock* may best be regarded as synonyms, the simpler designations "common stock" and "preferred stock" are more popular.

Classification of Common Stockholders' Rights

From the standpoint of the attractiveness of common stock to investors—and therefore of its usefulness to corporations as a means of financing—the full rights of common stockholders may be classified in two groups: (1) those rights, three in number, in which attractiveness chiefly resides; and (2) a further group, five in number, whose principal function, as one might say, is to protect the rights of the first group.

The rights of the first group are the following: (1) to share in such dividends as may be distributed, (2) to have a claim against assets, and (3) to participate in management. Those of the second group are as follows: (1) to have a stock certificate as evidence of ownership, (2) to sell or otherwise dispose of the stock, (3) to subscribe to additional issues of stock in proportion to existing holdings, (4) to inspect the books of the corporation, and (5) to take action in the courts to put a stop to or to prevent corporate activities alleged to be illegal, or *ultra vires*, or mismanagerial.

RIGHTS TO DIVIDENDS, ASSETS, AND MANAGEMENT

A large majority of investors in common stock, both individual and institutional, are undoubtedly motivated primarily by expectations of receiving dividends at a rate in excess of the rate of return expected from investment in preferred stock or bonds or, indeed, from any other use of their money. But their motivation tends always to be a mixed one. Investors in common stock know that it is a policy of most corporations to retain substantial proportions of their net profits to finance expansion; but they know also that a retention of profits adds to their claims against assets, and they expect these added claims to be reflected in increases in the market value of the common shares they hold. To put the matter in another way, they expect retained profits to add to corporate profit-making capacities—a development that should enhance the attractiveness of the common stock in the market. They buy, therefore, both for dividend income and for "appreciation" in market value.

For other investors, the feature of common stock that is primarily attractive is the right it accords to the stockholder to participate in management. These investors want to gain or retain control in the corporations whose common stock they buy; they regard the advantages of exercising control of greater importance than rights to share in dividends and to have claims against assets. It is not that such investors have no interests in dividends and claims against assets, but, rather, that their interests in these directions are clearly subordinate to their interests in control.

Interrelationship of Rights to Dividends and Assets

The proposition that rights to share in dividends and claims to assets are intermingled, so to say, as attractions to investors in common stock may be further developed by means of an illustration. Let us suppose that a certain corporation has outstanding 100,000 shares of common stock of $50 par value upon which it is able to earn an annual profit of 10 per cent after the deduction of income taxes. We may assume that the market value of the stock is also $50. Up to the present time, the corporation has not accumulated a surplus, as it has been paying out dividends equal to the full amount of its net profits. Now, however, it decides to cut its dividend rate to 5 per cent and to use the balance of its annual net profit to finance a program of expansion. It expects to be able to earn 10 per cent after taxes on the retained profits. If, then, this expectation were fulfilled, the results of its new policy in a five-year period would be as follows (with the net profit for the sixth year entered for later reference):

Year	Net Profit after Income Taxes	Dividends	Retained Profit	Surplus Accumulation
1......	$500,000	$250,000	$250,000	$ 250,000
2......	525,000	250,000	275,000	525,000
3......	552,500	250,000	302,500	827,500
4......	582,750	250,000	332,750	1,160,250
5......	616,025	250,000	366,025	1,526,275
6......	652,628			

In the five-year period, the reduced level of dividends would result in an increase in the book value of the common stock—its claim against assets per share—from $50 to $65.26. If, moreover, the expansion program had been completed by the end of the fifth year, and if, accordingly, a decision were made to distribute dividends equal to all the profits of the sixth year, the dividend rate would be 13.05 per cent of the par value of the stock ($652,628 ÷ $5,000,000). Had the market value of the stock been $50 when dividends were being paid at a rate of 10 per cent, prospects for future dividends at 13.05 per cent of par value, evaluated jointly with the higher level of the claims of the common stock against assets, would surely tend to push the market value well above $50. Considering all the forces that play upon the stock market, and all its vagaries, we can hardly say what the new market price would be; but we can say that, considering the affairs of our corporation solely, it ought to be in the vicinity of $65.

The illustration clearly indicates the reason why, for many investors in common stock, possibilities of appreciation strongly rival in attractiveness prospects of dividend payments at given levels—why such investors are not repulsed, so to say, because of corporate policies of retaining substantial proportions of current profits. Had the corporation of the illustration forgone its expansion program and continued to pay dividends during the five-year period at 10 per cent of par value, they would have amounted in total to $25 a share. With the expansion program in effect, the dividends would be cut to a five-year total of $12.50, but were it possible to sell the stock at $65 a share at the end of the fifth year, a person who had bought it at $50 at the beginning of the five-year period would have additional income of $15 for a total of $27.50. The difference of $2.50 in stockholder income as between the two alternatives would be due to the compounding of earnings upon the retained profits; this would appear to be a distinct advantage of the second route.[1] But likely to be much more important for large stockholders with high levels of income

---

[1] If, however, the stockholder were able to reinvest at 10 per cent compounded annually half of the amount of dividends received by way of the first alternative, his total income per share for the five-year period would likewise be $27.50.

is the fact that the $12.50 profit on the sale of the stock would be treated as a "long-term capital gain" in federal income tax determination. As such a capital gain, it would be subject to a tax rate not exceeding 25 per cent, rather than to the steeply progressive rates of the individual income tax to which dividends are subject.[2]

Right to Share in Dividends

Although the foregoing demonstration indicates the difficulty of putting the attractiveness of the common stockholder's right to share in dividends and the attractiveness of his claim against assets in separate compartments, it is still desirable to treat certain aspects of these two rights separately.

At the very least, it is to be observed that, for many small investors, dividend prospects represent the principal criterion for or against buying given common stocks. Market appreciation, leading to capital gains, will surely be welcomed by such investors; but rarely will they consider it a reasonable substitute for dividends at a good level. Income tax rates in the higher brackets do not bother them, and matters of management and control are likely to be of slight interest. Accordingly, a corporation that has been rather niggardly in its dividend policy would probably be unsuccessful should it try to sell additional common stock to such small investors.

Directors' Discretion in Paying Dividends. Although of outstanding importance in making common stock attractive to investors, the right of common stockholders to share in dividends is a limited one. Regardless of the size of a corporation's current profit and its accumulation of profits in past periods, actual distributions of dividends depend upon decisions of its board of directors. Corporation laws are quite clear in giving the directors the power to decide how profits can be best used to promote corporate objectives—whether they should be retained in whole or in part for corporate purposes or used as the basis for dividend distributions.

A decision of the directors of a corporation to distribute dividends to the common stockholders is formalized by the adoption of a resolution stating the amount to be paid, the date of payment, and the date as of which a list of the stockholders who are to receive the dividends will be taken from the stock records. If no such resolution is adopted, the stockholders ought not to expect to receive dividends. Dividend payments

---

[2] For the rules governing the taxation of capital gains, see footnote 14 on page 38. The advantage of the capital gains rate in comparison with the rates applicable to dividends as ordinary income is moderately offset by the provision of the law that no tax is to be paid on the first $50 of dividends and that a "dividends-received credit" equal to 4 per cent of taxable dividends (but not exceeding 4 per cent of net taxable income) may be deducted from the tax bill. These concessions, however, are likely to be of minor significance to taxpayers in the higher income tax brackets.

require formal action, whereas the payment of interest on bonds, like the payment of any other kind of expense, is a matter of routine operations. Even a handful of stockholders in a close family corporation cannot legally help themselves to cash, whether or not in some uniform percentage of their stockholdings. If they want to withdraw cash beyond whatever salaries they allow themselves, they must declare a dividend by formal resolution, taking this action in their capacity as members of the board of directors to which doubtless they will have elected themselves.

Stockholders' Actions to Force Dividends. If the stockholders are dissatisfied with the proportion of profits that the board of directors is willing to allocate for dividends, their normal recourse is to elect a different, more generous group of directors. Like many "remedies" for injustices, however, this one may actually be of little applicability. If all the directors are chosen by a small group of stockholders who own a narrow majority of the common stock, and if this group much prefers appreciation in book and market values to dividends-in-hand, it does not help the minority much to be told that they ought to elect a different array of directors.

Occasionally, however, a court of equity, upon appeal by unhappy stockholders of a corporation, will order its directors to make a dividend distribution. Courts of equity are most reluctant to substitute their judgment for that of boards of directors; they are inclined to believe that the directors, being on the firing line, are in a better position to know how the long-range interests of their corporations can best be promoted. Nevertheless, such a court can sometimes be convinced that directors have ulterior motives for their refusal to distribute dividends. The appealing stockholders may be able to convince the court, for example, that the nonpayment of dividends over a lengthy period of years has been designed to freeze them out—to force them, as it were, to sell their stock at sacrifice prices, so that it could be bought up by the directors themselves or by controlling stockholders who might not be directors. A court thus persuaded would be likely to issue an order to the directors to make a substantial distribution. Failure of the directors to heed such an order would make them subject to punishment for contempt of court.

The most celebrated case of this kind originated in 1916 when John and Horace Dodge brought proceedings against the Ford Motor Company to force more liberal dividend payments. Henry Ford had announced that annual dividends would be limited to 60 per cent of the par value of the company's outstanding stock, but the par value of its stock at that time amounted to only $2 million, while its surplus had grown to $112 million, its profit for 1916 was expected to amount to almost $60 million, and it had over $52 million of cash on hand. A business corporation, the court said, "is organized and carried on primarily for the profit of the stockholders. The powers of the directors are to be employed for that end . . ."; and it decreed that the company should distribute an additional dividend of $19 million, at the same time enjoining it from unreasonably withholding dividends in the future.[3]

Dividends as Pro Rata Distributions. Another matter worthy of mention at this time[4] is that dividends on common stock are always pro rata distributions. The right of each common stockholder to receive dividends as declared by a corporation's board of directors is equal, share for share, with that of every other common stockholder. Were a corporation to sell an original issue of common stock of a par value of $20 at, say, $40 a share, and a later issue at, say, $25 or $75, the two batches would be indistinguishable in their right to dividends. On a share for which he paid the corporation only $25, a stockholder would get a dividend, if declared, equal to that payable on a share for which another stockholder paid $40; and likewise as between shares for which the selling prices may have been $40 and $75, respectively.

In a similar way, changes in the prices at which stock transactions take place among investors in the market have no effect on rights to dividends. A and B may have originally bought their stock from a corporation at $50 a share, but A subsequently sells his holdings to C at $125 a share. C's right to dividends for each share is exactly the same as B's.

Claim against Assets

Considered by itself, rather than in combination with the right to share in dividends, the common stockholder's claim against assets may appear not to be worth much. Such an inference appears especially to be supported when the claim against assets is described, as it often is, as a claim "in dissolution." The managements of successful corporations rarely set target dates for dissolution, and the dissolution of unsuccessful ones ordinarily occurs under such circumstances that little is left for the satisfaction of the claims of common stockholders, as those claims are measured in the stock and surplus accounts.

Nevertheless, dissolution ought not to be emphasized. The claim of the common stockholders against assets is a continuous one, and often of much greater significance during the lives of corporations than at the time of their deaths. It is true that common stock has no date of maturity at which it will be retired at book value in the ordinary course of operations, and that it is not redeemable at any time or at specified times at the option of the stockholder. It is true, likewise, that the claim of the common stockholder against assets is a "residual" one, in the sense that it ranks last in the scale of priorities—in the sense that, if all claims are to be

[3] *Dodge* v. *Ford Motor Company,* 204 Michigan 459 (1919). For an interesting account of the background, development, and aftermath of this case, including the subsequent action of Ford in buying up all outstanding minority stock of the company, see Keith Sward, *The Legend of Henry Ford* (New York: Rinehart & Co., Inc., 1948), pp. 66–74.

[4] Dividends and dividend policies are further discussed at length in Chapters 24 and 25. See especially pp. 587–90, 597–603.

settled as far as assets will permit, those of creditors and (usually) preferred stockholders must be satisfied in full, and only what is left can be
allocated to the claims of common stockholders. Despite these facts,
however, the attractiveness of common stock to investors is undoubtedly
greatly enhanced by its claim to assets. Let us consider why this is so.

Accumulation of Wealth in Corporations. For wealthy and well-to-
do common stockholders, in particular, the building up of corporate
assets through the retention of profits is a highly popular means of amass-
ing further wealth, just as would be the expansion of the assets of proprietorships and partnerships of which they might be owners. If their
stock ownership gives them control, they have good reason to feel that
the corporate assets are always at their disposal—that their wealth as
stored up in the corporations can be withdrawn at any time should they
want to use it elsewhere. The declaration of dividends equal to the total
of accumulated surplus could be the means of withdrawing a substantial
proportion of the assets; and, were that not enough, they could sell their
stock if it were possible to get a price close to its remaining book value,
or, if prices offered were not satisfactory, vote to dissolve. It is well to
keep in mind that a large majority of corporations are small and medium
in size and are controlled by one or a few stockholders. Such corporations, therefore, can serve ideally as storehouses of wealth.

Even with larger corporations in which the wealthy or well-to-do
common stockholder does not have control, and does not expect to gain
it through further stock buying, their service as storehouses of accumulating wealth can be most attractive. As long as the market value of his
common stock goes up in some reasonable relationship to the amount of
profits retained, such a stockholder can feel that his claim to assets can
be "cashed" at any time by a sale of the stock in the market. On the
other hand, he would surely allow for the probability that, in times of
general business slump, weakness in the common stock market as a whole
would temporarily make disadvantageous the "cashing" of his claim to
assets.

Actually, many wealthy and well-to-do investors store wealth through
common stock investment with no thought of withdrawing it or "cashing" it during their lifetimes. Having plenty of income to maintain high
planes of living, they look upon their accumulating claims against corporate assets as a good means of providing estates to be left at the time
of death to their spouses, children, or other heirs. The workings of the
federal personal income tax laws tend to encourage this kind of estate
planning. As was indicated earlier in this chapter, the taxpayer may
choose to have net profits derived from sales of common stock held for
more than six months taxed as capital gains, rather than as "ordinary"
income at the steeply progressive rates applicable thereto. But if the
stock is not sold at all during one's lifetime, whatever appreciation in its
market value may have taken place between the date of purchase and

the date of one's death is not taxed *as income* at all. The value of the stock at the date of death (or its value one year thereafter, at the option of the executor or administrator) is subject to the federal estate tax, but this fact does not gainsay the nontaxability of the appreciation as income.

Mergers and Consolidations. Another way that the claims of common stockholders against the assets of their corporations can be "cashed" without the liquidation of assets and the paying off of all creditors and other prior claimants is by the transfer of these assets, and the assumption of the corporate debts, by other corporations. When such a wholesale transfer is made to another corporation which thereafter remains in operation, the transaction is known as a *merger;* and when two or more corporations make such a transfer to a newly formed corporation, it is described as a *consolidation.* Hundreds of mergers and consolidations occur every year in the United States, more abundantly, of course, in periods of high-level business activity, but in sizable numbers also in periods of recession and depression. The chances are good, therefore, that the typical successful corporation will be approached from time to time by other corporations with what are thought to be attractive propositions to combine.

In working out the details of a proposal of merger or consolidation, provision is usually made for the paying off of current liabilities of the corporation to be absorbed, for the "assumption" of its long-term debts by the absorbing corporation, that is, the transfer of liability for these debts, and for an exchange of its stock at a given ratio for that of the absorbing corporation. The common stockholders of the corporation to be absorbed are not likely to vote in favor of the merger or consolidation if they think the proposed exchange ratio is unfavorable to them. If they vote in favor in the thought that the exchange offer is reasonably generous, they may plan to sell the stock to be received from the absorbing corporation, thereby "cashing" their existing claims against corporate assets; or, of course, they may plan to hold the exchange stock as a way to continue to store wealth.

A proposal of merger or consolidation can be especially attractive to the stockholders of a closely held corporation who have already been rather anxious to "cash" their claims against its assets. The fact that the stock had been closely held would probably mean that no market interest in it had been established; thus selling to the general run of stock buyers at a reasonable price would be difficult if not impossible. If, then, the stock offered in a merger proposal had a broad, active market, the stockholders' claim against assets could be quickly "cashed" as soon as the exchange of stocks had taken place.

When mergers and consolidations are effected according to the procedures of state laws for "statutory fusions," as they often are, the corporations whose assets have been absorbed and whose liabilities have been assumed by other corporations are dissolved by the very operation of the laws. But dissolution by this route, as has been amply indicated in the foregoing discussion, does not mean a settlement of the claims of common stockholders on a "residual" basis. The market value of the stock of the absorbing corporation received by the common stockholders of the absorbed corporations may be much greater than the existing book and market values of the stock given up. Hence, they may have their claims satisfied generously, while the bondholders of the absorbed corporation simply get claims of unchanged amounts as "assumed" creditors of the absorbing corporation. It is entirely possible for an absorbing corporation, running into financial troubles subsequent to a merger or consolidation, to default upon the bonds of an absorbed corporation it has assumed. The ultimate fate of the owners of these bonds could therefore turn out to be a rather sad one, whereas that of the common stockholders of the absorbed corporation, long since paid off, as it were, by an exchange of stock, could have been most pleasant. Such happenings have been common in the history of American corporate enterprise.

Holding Company Absorptions. A realization by common stockholders of their claim against the assets of their corporation may occur by a combination arrangement even simpler than the merger or consolidation. One corporation may want to obtain control of the assets of a second corporation, but with the expectation of keeping it in operation as a separate legal entity. In other words, it plans to occupy a position as parent or holding company to the acquired corporation. (The usual distinction is that a parent company carries on its own productive operations while holding controlling stock interests in one or more subsidiaries; while a holding company is nonoperating in the sense of turning out products, functioning simply as owner and controller of subsidiaries.)

A common procedure is for the holding company (let us call it that) to go to the stockholders of the corporation it wants to acquire and offer them some of its own stock in exchange for their holdings. As with mergers and consolidations, the offer must be reasonably generous to assure sufficient acceptance to give the holding company the control it seeks. The stockholders who accept the offer may thus be enabled, through an immediate sale of the exchange stock, to "cash" on a favorable basis their claim against assets. The creditors of the corporation being acquired have no such opportunity. As this corporation remains in existence as an entity distinct from the holding company, it continues to be responsible for its debts according to their original terms. It could run into difficulties and default upon its obligations. In such circumstances the holding company might suffer the loss of its investment in the subsidiary, but the latter's original common stockholders would be in the clear, assuming that they had sold their allotments of holding company stock while its market price was still good.

Partial Liquidating Dividends. Finally to be mentioned as a way that common stockholders' claims against assets may be realized without corporate dissolution is the distribution of dividends in partial liquidation. Sometimes corporations find it advisable to curtail the scope of their operations but without going out of business. They may find, for example, that some of their lines are unprofitable, while others are highly profitable; and they may decide, accordingly, to discontinue the former and to concentrate upon the latter. But the change in scope of operations may mean that their assets are far beyond what they now need. Hence, they sell the superfluous assets and distribute the proceeds to the common stockholders as liquidating dividends. Dividends of this kind are usually classed as "liquidating dividends," even though there may be sufficient balances in the surplus accounts against which they can be charged. The designation is an appropriate one, since the dividends are obviously not distributions in the ordinary course of business. At any rate, they do constitute a realization by common stockholders upon their claims against assets without dissolution.

It is of interest to point out, moreover, that liquidating dividends may ordinarily be charged against the common stock account, if sufficient surplus is not available. This could be done by reducing the par or stated value of the outstanding stock, or by having the common stockholders surrender equal proportional amounts of their holdings. Actions such as these normally require amendment to the articles of incorporation, but, as we saw in Chapter 3, amendment is neither a difficult nor an expensive procedure. However, charges against the common stock account for liquidating dividends must not be carried to a point where existing creditors would be endangered. A common legal rule is that both directors and stockholders are personally liable to creditors (the directors, totally; the stockholders, pro rata) for assets distributed as liquidating dividends that should have been retained to meet obligations to them.

Right to Participate in Management

As was indicated in Chapter 3, in connection with the discussion of the managerial powers and responsibilities of boards of directors, the right of stockholders to participate in management extends in three directions: (1) to elect the board of directors; (2) to adopt, amend, and repeal by-laws; and (3) to pass directly upon matters of great importance to their welfare, such as proposals for merger or consolidation with other corporations, the sale of entire assets, and dissolution. For preferred stockholders, managerial powers of these kinds may ordinarily be restricted in various ways, but never for the common stockholders. Some corporations, it is true, have outstanding two or more "classes" of what they call common stock, in all but one of which the voting powers of the stockholders may be restricted. Of a given corporation, for example, the Class A Common may have few or no voting powers while the Class B Common will have such powers in full. In all such instances, therefore, the Class B Common is the true common stock, while the Class A Common is really of the nature of a preferred stock—it is most likely to be a *weak* preferred, as is often said.

For buyers of common stock who are interested in the control of corporations, the capacity to choose all, or at least a majority, of the members of the boards of directors is the matter of outstanding importance. In some instances, control may be sought to assure the approval of proposals for merger, consolidation, or sales of entire assets. Thus, a group having large minority holdings of the common stock of a corporation may want to buy up additional shares to get the decisive voice in voting upon a proposed merger it strongly favors. In rarer instances, control may be sought so that liquidation and dissolution can be voted. Some financiers—"promoters-in-reverse," they might be called—are constantly on the lookout for corporations that are "worth more dead than alive." The market price of a corporation's stock may be very low because it has been piling up losses year after year, yet the corporation may own quite valuable assets. The promoters-in-reverse, therefore, plan to gain control at limited cost by quietly buying up small parcels of stock here and there, perhaps over an extended period of time, then to vote dissolution, and to win, it is expected, handsome liquidating dividends after the sale of the high-quality assets. But we need say no more about procedures such as this; since our interest is in common stock as a financing device, we must concentrate upon the attractiveness of new issues, rather than upon motives for buying stock already outstanding. Finally, in regard to managerial powers of common stockholders, capacity to adopt, amend, and repeal bylaws, standing by itself, can be dismissed as a most unlikely objective for common stock purchases for control.

When people buy common stock primarily to gain or insure their capacity to choose all or a majority of corporate directors, rather than because of the attractions of rights to dividends and claims against assets, their objectives may be of many kinds. Among these, the following appear to be especially worthy of brief analysis: (1) the gaining of executive positions, (2) capacity to "throw business" to other enterprises, and (3) capacity to determine operating policies. Once control of a corporation has been gained by a given group of common stockholders, such objectives are presumably achievable whether they elect themselves to the board of directors or choose "dummies" who can be relied upon to do their bidding.

Gaining of Executive Positions. In corporations of small and medium sizes, it would seem that the chief "plums" to be striven for, in most instances, are the executive offices and the salaries that go with them, and not rights to dividends and claims against assets. Most corporations, it is worth repeating, are of these sizes. In such a corporation, the stockholders are generally few in number, they elect themselves to the board

of directors, and, as directors, they appoint themselves as officers. To
avoid the federal corporation income tax, they are likely to establish salary scales for themselves at levels designed to drain off virtually all the
earnings left after the payment of operating expenses—certainly at the
maximum level that the Commissioner of Internal Revenue is likely to
permit; hence they need have no great interest in dividends. Nor are they
likely to be thinking about realizing claims to assets through dissolution,
mergers with other corporations, and exchanges of stock with holding
companies; for any such move could be expected to deprive them of their
executive offices with the precuniary rewards thereof.

    Capacity to "Throw Business." Not necessarily overshadowing in-
terests in dividends and assets, but of great importance in its own right
as an attraction of common stock ownership, is the possibility of influ-
encing corporate buying and selling policies to the personal benefit of
the stockholder. The ownership of controlling interests, of course, in-
sures a capacity to determine buying and selling policies; but often, also,
the ownership of sizable blocks of common stock by minority stockholders serve to make them quite "influential." To keep such a minority
stockholder "on our side," the controlling group, especially if its margin
of control is a narrow one, may be quite willing to throw business in directions that will make him happy.

    Vast amounts of corporate business flow in peculiar directions as de-
termined by the personal interests of directors and "influential" stockholders. Corporation A buys large quantities of raw materials from Corporation B, rather than from any of a dozen other potential suppliers,
because two directors of A have large stockholdings in B; Corporation
B, in turn, buys much of its raw materials from Corporation C, because
a third director of A is the principal stockholder in C; Corporation C
ships its products by Railroad X rather than by Railroad Y, because three
other directors of Corporation A are stockholders and directors of Railroad X; and Railroad X turns some of its legal business over to the law
firm of M, N, O & O, because the two O's are, respectively, a son and a
grandson of still another director of Corporation A. Such an illustration
is by no means farfetched; indeed, considering the bewildering ramifica-
tions of "vested interests" that actually prevail in American business society, it is a highly simplified version.

    All this does not mean that, typically, directors deliberately reject their
responsibilities to the general run of stockholders of the corporations
they manage in order to advance their own personal interests, the interests
of a few "influential" stockholders, or those of relatives, friends, and
business associates elsewhere. Some do. But it is often possible to "throw
business" in one direction or another without disadvantage to the corporation whose business it is. In terms of the illustration, Corporation B's
product may be as good as that of the other potential suppliers, and its
price no higher than theirs, so that Corporation A's action in making B

the exclusive supplier would apparently work no harm to A's stock-holders.

Capacity to Determine Operating Policies. Although buying and selling policies designed to "throw business" here and there, as just discussed, are operating policies, the objective of controlling operating policies, as a reason for common stock buying, is often of quite different character from that of serving the personal interests of influential people, whoever they may be. For example, minority holders of common stock and "outsiders" often become convinced that the existing managements of certain corporations are woefully incompetent—that expansion opportunities of most promising kinds are being ignored, that costs of operations, especially administrative expenses, have become unconscionable, and so on. They conclude, therefore, that if they could gain control and put their quite different policies into effect, the welfare of the corporations and all their stockholders would be immeasurably enhanced.

Such persons may be avid buyers of whatever new issues of common stock the criticized corporations offer for sale, provided that their purchases would give them control or, at least, move them much closer to it. Toward the same objective, of course, substantial purchases of common stock, already outstanding, may be made in the market. Often, however, people who want to challenge the position and competence of an existing management, do not expect to be able, personally, to get enough of the stock to insure control; but they hope that their substantial voting power will be augmented by the votes of thousands of small stockholders whom they expect to persuade to join with them in their move to replace the management. Such expectations, and the efforts to fulfill them, sometimes lead to "proxy fights" of great intensity and widespread interest. The management and the challengers exert every effort to line up the general run of stockholders on their respective sides; and sometimes the outcome is not known till the votes are actually counted at the stockholders' meeting. Some of the "proxy fights" of the spring and early summer of 1963 may be cited as examples. These included partially successful efforts of "dissident" stockholders of the Chicago and Eastern Illinois Railroad Company and of the Campbell Machine Company; the unsuccessful campaigns of "dissident" stockholders of the Brown Company, the New England pulp and paper manufacturer, Arden Farms Company, Acme Steel Company, and Lincoln Printing Company; and a fight for control of the American Smelting, Refining, and Mining Company, the doubtful outcome of which led to litigation to determine who won.

PROTECTIVE RIGHTS

The rights of common stockholders in business corporations included in the second grouping presented on page 350 were described as protective rights. They have little capacity in themselves to attract the funds of

investors; nevertheless, they are of great importance in assuring investors
that their rights to dividends, to assets, and to voting power will be safe-
guarded at all times.

Right to Have a Stock Certificate

At the very minimum, the individual common stockholder must be in a
position to be able to prove his ownership of common shares—to prove, as
it were, his entitlement to all other rights. It is not enough for him to be
told that the corporation will have a record of his ownership. Errors can
occur in record keeping, and the fraudulent manipulation of records is by
no means impossible or unheard of. Accordingly, corporation laws invariably stipulate that the common stockholder (and the preferred stockholder, too) must be given a certificate as evidence of his ownership.

In quality, common stock certificates vary from elaborately engraved
forms specially prepared for the sole use of the given corporation, to
cheap printed ones that can be bought from legal stationers and in which
the name of the corporation as well as other pertinent details can be typed
or written in. In content, they all tend toward a uniform simplicity, containing the name of the corporation, the state of incorporation, the total
authorized issue of common stock, the par or stated value, if any, or a
designation that the stock has no par value, a serial number, the name of
the stockholder to whom the certificate is being issued, the number of
shares it represents, the fact that these are common shares, the date of issue, the signatures of the president and treasurer or secretary (or of certain other officials who may sign alternatively), and the corporate seal
(see Figure 16–1).

A corporation must, of course, keep a record of the stock certificates it
issues: it must know the names and addresses of, and the number of shares
held by, each of its common stockholders, so that dividend checks, notices
of annual and special meetings, proxy forms for voting at meetings, and
other official communications will reach the right people. For this purpose, a *stockholders' ledger* or *stock transfer book* is used; in this record,
each stockholder has an "account" in which he is credited with all shares
he acquires and debited for all shares he transfers to others. Most corporations find it convenient to record transfers of stock as a routine function
in the treasurer's office; but larger ones that have thousands of stockholders and numerous daily transfers usually prefer to turn over the job
of record keeping to trust companies and the trust departments of commercial banks which, among other things, offer specialized services as
transfer agents. Many large corporations employ these institutions also as
registrars for their stock. The function of a registrar is to see that no
error is made in issuing stock—that the total of shares represented by certificates does not exceed the authorized issue, that the individual certificate
is for the correct number of shares, that it bears the correct name of the
stockholder, and so on. Because of the registrar's verification function,

FIGURE 16-1—Common Stock Certificate

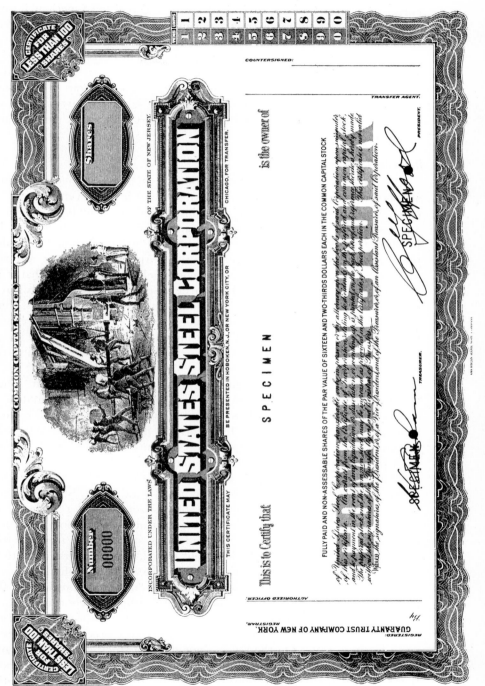

corporations that hire out both the transfer and registry functions invariably select as a registrar a trust company or trust department different from that selected as transfer agent. As the transfer agent can be counted upon for a high level of accuracy, the independent check of a second institution as registrar makes for great certainty that errors will be avoided in the issuance of certificates. Transfer agents and registrars countersign the certificates they process, and these countersignatures carry strong assurances to the individual stockholder that his certificate is genuine and was properly issued.

Right to Transfer the Stock

Were the prospective investor in common stock to be given no assurances that he could sell it or otherwise dispose of it whenever he might so choose, he probably would decide against buying it. Rights to dividends and assets and voting rights may look attractive at a given time, but the intelligent investor always wants to be able to "get out" should his judgment about the future prospects of the corporation become adverse. Many people are willing to buy common stock in the thought that it is, for them, a short-term investment—to be disposed of, accordingly, in a few weeks or months, so that their funds can be used elsewhere. Thus, the right to transfer is universally recognized as a basic protective provision for the common stockholder. It includes the right to sell the stock, to give it away, to bequeath it to one's heirs, and to pledge it, as in providing collateral for loans.

Nevertheless, restrictions upon transferability are not uncommon. They occur most often in close corporations. The handful of stockholders in such a corporation may want to exclude "outsiders" from stock ownership more or less permanently. In the articles of incorporation or bylaws, therefore, they may include a provision that any stockholder who wants to dispose of his holdings must first offer them to the corporation. The price at which the offer is to be made may be stipulated, or some other means of arriving at a reasonable price may be indicated. Such a restriction upon transfer is probably enforceable, especially so if a statement of the restriction is placed upon the stock certificates. Even more assurance of enforceability can apparently be had if the stockholders merely agree among themselves that, should any want to sell, they will first offer their stock to the corporation or, perhaps, to the remaining stockholders, as on a pro rata basis. It is to be expected that courts would recognize the mutual promises as sufficient consideration for a binding contract.

Mechanics of Transfer. The typical corporation, however, places no obstacles in the way of stock transfers. Indeed, the process of transfer is eased in every way. On the reverse side of most stock certificates a convenient assignment form is provided (see Figure 16–2). To sell his stock, therefore, the owner needs only to fill in this form, designating who the buyer is and who is given the seller's "power of attorney" to have the

FIGURE 16-2
Transfer Form on Back of Stock Certificate

UNITED STATES STEEL CORPORATION

EXTRACT FROM CERTIFICATE OF INCORPORATION TO WHICH REFERENCE IS MADE ON THE FACE HEREOF.

The holders of the preferred stock shall be entitled to receive when and as declared, from the surplus or net profits of the corporation, yearly dividends at the rate of seven per centum per annum, and no more, payable quarterly on dates to be fixed by the by-laws. The dividends on the preferred stock shall be cumulative, and shall be payable before any dividend on the common stock shall be paid or set apart: so that, if in any year dividends amounting to seven per cent. shall not have been paid thereon, the deficiency shall be payable before any dividends shall be paid upon, or set apart for the common stock.

Whenever all cumulative dividends on the preferred stock for all previous years shall have been declared and shall have become payable, and the accrued quarterly installments for the current year shall have been declared, and the company shall have paid such cumulative divi-

dends for previous years and such accrued quarterly installments, or shall have set aside from its surplus or net profits a sum sufficient for the payment thereof, the Board of Directors may declare dividends on the common stock, payable then or thereafter, out of any remaining surplus or net profits.

In the event of any liquidation or dissolution or winding up (whether voluntary or involuntary) of the corporation, the holders of the preferred stock shall be entitled to be paid in full both the par amount of their shares, and the unpaid dividends accrued thereon before any amount shall be paid to the holders of the common stock; and after the payment to the holders of the preferred stock of its par value, and the unpaid accrued dividends thereon, the remaining assets and funds shall be divided and paid to the holders of the common stock according to their respective shares.

For value Received _____ hereby sell, assign, and transfer unto

_____

PLEASE PRINT OR TYPEWRITE NAME AND ADDRESS OF ASSIGNEE

_____

_____

_____ *Shares*

of the Capital Stock represented by the within Certificate, and do hereby irrevocably constitute and appoint

_____ *Attorney*

to transfer the said stock on the Books of the within named Corporation with full power of substitution in the premises.

Dated _____ 19___

In Presence of

_____

NOTICE THE SIGNATURE TO THIS ASSIGNMENT MUST CORRESPOND WITH THE NAME AS WRITTEN UPON THE FACE OF THE CERTIFICATE, IN EVERY PARTICULAR, WITHOUT ALTERATION OR ENLARGEMENT, OR ANY CHANGE WHATEVER.

THIS SPACE MUST NOT BE COVERED IN ANY WAY

stock transferred on the books of the corporation. If he so wishes, in fact, the seller can simply sign the assignment form "in blank," leaving it for the buyer or a subsequent holder to fill in the other details. Likewise, an assignment form separate from the stock certificate may be used—filled in fully or signed in blank; this is known as a "stock power." At any rate, the buyer or his agent, such as a broker, sends the endorsed stock certificate, or the stock certificate with the "stock power," to the corporation or its transfer agent, if it employs one. The certificate is canceled, and a new one is issued in the name of the buyer. At the same time, of course, the transaction is recorded in the stock transfer book, so that the change in ownership will be a matter of record.

If a stockholder wants to sell only a portion of the shares represented by a certificate, he indicates that fact in the assignment form, and the certificate and form are sent to the corporation or its transfer agent. The certificate is canceled but, in this instance, two new ones are issued—one to the buyer for the number of shares bought, and the other to the seller for the number of shares retained.

Stock Certificates as Negotiable Instruments. Contributing to the ease of stock transfers is the fact that all our states and the District of Columbia have adopted legislation to make stock certificates negotiable instruments. Giving stock certificates the quality of negotiability means that, as the lawyers say, innocent purchasers for value ordinarily get good title to the stock represented by certificates even though the original owners or subsequent holders did not have good title. Suppose that a stock certificate made out in the name of A and endorsed by him in blank is stolen by B and sold by B to C. C gets good title, assuming that he had no knowledge of the theft, and regardless of the fact that B, the thief, had no title at all. C is "innocent" in his lack of knowledge of the theft, and he is a "purchaser for value" in that he paid cash to B. If C were to know of the theft, or were he to receive the stock certificate as a gift from B, he would not get good title; but were he, in turn, to transfer the certificate to D, who could qualify as an innocent purchaser for value, the latter would get good title. On the other hand, were B to steal an unendorsed stock certificate made out in the name of A and then forge A's signature in the assignment form, neither C, in the first instance, nor D, in the second, would get good title. The innocent purchaser for value is not protected against forgery.

The negotiability of stock certificates makes it possible for them to pass from hand to hand without worries on the part of purchasers for value about the goodness of title of sellers and other earlier holders. As long as the purchaser for value is satisfied as to the genuineness of the endorsement of the person whose name appears on the face of the stock certificate, he need have no fears about the goodness of his own title. Accordingly, a given stock certificate having the endorsement of the original owner in blank can be sold over and over again until some buyer decides to send it in to the corporation or its transfer agent to be exchanged for a new certificate in his own name.

Right to Subscribe to Additional Issues of Stock

The common stockholder's rights to dividends, assets, and voting power can be weakened or diluted if his corporation sells additional common stock to other investors. A person who owns 1,000 shares of the common stock of a corporation that has a total of 10,000 shares outstanding and no preferred stock gets one tenth of all dividends that are declared, has one tenth of the total voting power, and has a claim against assets equal to one tenth of total stockholder claims; but should his corporation sell 5,000 additional shares to other buyers, these rights would be reduced to one fifteenth. Hence comes the doctrine of the common stockholder's "preemptive right," as it is called: that, before additional common stock is offered to anybody else, he should have the privilege of subscribing in the proportion of his present holdings to the total already outstanding. In terms of the illustration, were the holder of 1,000 shares privileged to buy one tenth of the additional issue, or 500 shares, he would be enabled to protect and maintain his one tenth interest. The logic of the preemptive right requires that when stock is offered to existing stockholders at a given price, and they do not buy, it will not be offered to others at a lower price; if the price is to be lowered, it must first be reoffered to the stockholders at the reduced price.

The logic of the preemptive right also requires that present common stockholders be given the first opportunity to subscribe on a pro rata basis to issues of preferred stocks and bonds that are convertible into common stock or that have attached to them warrants that empower their holders to buy common stock at stipulated prices. The dilution of the common stockholder's claims through the exercise of convertibility rights or warrants given to outsiders could be as serious as dilution resulting from "outside" sales of common stock itself. Since, indeed, preferred stock is usually given claims to earnings and assets having a priority over those of common stock, it is not unreasonable to argue that the common stockholder should have the preemptive right to subscribe pro rata to new issues of preferred, whether or not it is convertible into common. All the stronger is this argument if the preferred stock carries voting power.

Present Status of the Preemptive Right. The foregoing description of the preemptive right has been set down in tentative terms—in terms of logic, of arguments, and of what could or should be—rather than by means of positive statements, because, speaking broadly, the preemptive right is the weakest of the rights of common stockholders. Long recognized in its full scope in the common law—that is, the body of legal rules and principles built up over the centuries in the decisions of judges in Anglo-Saxon countries—it has been whittled away in recent decades by many state legislatures. The corporation laws of a few states now stipulate that the common stocks of corporations chartered therein do not have the preemptive right unless it is specifically provided for in the individual corporation's articles of incorporation or bylaws; and a larger number provide that, though the right is given in the first instance, it can be removed or limited by provisions in articles or bylaws.

At the present time, therefore, whether or not a common stock has the preemptive right—and how extensive it is—depends variously on the provisions of the state laws and each corporation's own articles and bylaws. Where it continues to be in effect, it usually extends to new issues of securities convertible into common stock or having warrants attached for the purchase of common stock, as well as to additional direct issues of common itself. It usually extends, too, to new offerings of preferred stock having voting power, although there is a tendency to make it inapplicable to new issues of nonvoting preferreds. (For a description of the preemptive rights of the common stocks of a few leading corporations selected at random, see Table 16–1.)

TABLE 16–1
Preemptive Rights of the Common Stocks of a Few Leading Corporations

Corporation	*Preemptive Rights Provided*
Allied Chemical Corporation	Full
Aluminum Company of America	None
American Telephone and Telegraph Company	Full, but with exceptions recognized in New York law
American Tobacco Company	Only such as are provided for in New Jersey law
Anaconda Company	Full
Borden Company	None
Chesapeake & Ohio Railway Company	Full, except when waived by 2/3 vote
Detroit Edison Company	To the extent provided for in New York law
General Electric Company	Full
Great Atlantic & Pacific Tea Company	Full
Liggett & Myers Tobacco Company	Only such as are provided for in New Jersey law
National Dairy Products Corporation	Full except for stock reserved for sale to employees
J. C. enney Company	None
Pennsylvania Railroad Company	Full
Reynolds Metals Company	None
Southern California Edison Company	None

SOURCE: Moody's Investors Service, *Manuals.*

Common stockholders are often in a position to demand the benefits of the preemptive right even though it is denied in the articles or bylaws. The holders of a majority of the common shares of a corporation can, of course, put through an amendment to the articles or bylaws, if only that is necessary. But probably more significant is the fact that additional issues of stock usually require amendment to the articles—a step that must have the approval of the stockholders. In proposing additional issues, therefore, the directors may feel compelled to give the present stockholders the first opportunity to buy, fearing a rejection of their proposals should they attempt to ignore stockholder preferences in this matter.

Exemptions from the Preemptive Right. Even where the preemptive right continues in effect, certain kinds of stock transactions are generally held to be exempt from it, namely, (1) continuing sales of original issues, (2) direct exchanges of stock for assets other than cash, and (3) sales of treasury stock.

The first of these exemptions means that a buyer of stock does not get an immediate right to subscribe to a pro rata share of the remaining portion of the original issues. Assume that a newly formed corporation proposes to issue 100,000 shares of common stock to complete its organization and the acquisition of operating assets. When, say, 60,000 shares have been sold, an original buyer of 6,000 shares cannot assert a right to have the first opportunity to buy one tenth of the remaining 40,000 shares slated for sale.

The second exception allows for the possibility that corporations may be able to acquire desirable parcels of property in direct exchanges for common stock, even though sales of the stock at fair prices to raise cash to buy the property might be impossible. The owners of the desired properties could be quite willing to part with them in exchange for stock, while other investors, including existing stockholders, might have little interest in acquiring additional shares. The opportunity to acquire the properties might be lost if the stock had first to be offered to the present stockholders; the delay might be fatal, or the refusal of the stockholders to buy might lead the property owners to change their minds about the attractiveness of the stock.

Treasury stock is a corporation's own stock, once issued and fully paid for, but subsequently reacquired by the corporation, as by gift or by purchase in the market. Resales of treasury stock are exempt from the preemptive right, because the right pertains to the first offering of *new* stock. If the right obtains, it will have been applied when the stock, now reacquired, was first sold.

Right to Inspect the Corporation's Books

The right of the common stockholder to inspect the books of his corporation, though important for his protection, is subject to rather strict limitations. It is designed essentially for two purposes: (1) to enable him to know who his fellow stockholders are, and (2) to enable him to check upon the performance of the corporation's management.

Access to Fellow Stockholders. Since the individual common stockholder shares his ownership jointly with all other common stockholders, he should have a means of finding out who these people are, how many shares they own, and what their addresses are. He may want to communicate with his fellow owners to line up votes for a slate of candidates whom he plans to nominate for directorships, to persuade them to join him in supporting or opposing some proposed amendment to the articles or bylaws, or for some other reason quite in keeping with his interests as an owner. He might think the present management of the corporation incompetent, but his efforts toward replacing it would be seriously impeded could he not easily reach his fellow stockholders. The criticized management could hardly be expected to help him, but at least it could not conceal information as to stockholdings. Thus, the corporation laws generally provide that the stockholders' ledger or stock transfer book must be open for inspection by stockholders at the office of the corporation or its transfer agent, usually for at least two or three hours during each business day.

In the usual circumstances, personal inspection of the stock records by individual stockholders is avoided by a willingness of the corporation, upon proper request, to supply lists of stockholders, their addresses, and the number of their shares. If, however, the stockholder has reason to feel that a list is inaccurate, he may insist upon actual inspection of the records. If the privilege of inspection is denied him, he may appeal to the courts for a writ directing the corporation to open the records to him. On the other hand, corporations not infrequently deny access to the stock records and refuse to supply lists of stockholders on the grounds that the stockholder has no good reason, *as a stockholder*, for wanting this information. They may claim, for example, that the stockholder plans to use or sell the list of his fellow stockholders as a "sucker list" for promotions of other enterprises or for appeals of "charities" of dubious reputation. If satisfied with such allegations, a court would doubtless turn down the stockholder's appeal for a writ.

Checking upon Performance of Management. To check upon the performance of a corporation's management, the common stockholder needs to know many details about the corporation's income, expenses, assets, and liabilities. But many details of this kind could be used to the detriment of the corporation. Accordingly, a distinction must somehow be made between what the stockholder is entitled to know to protect his interests and what he could use, or pass on to others to use, in ways harmful to the corporation. The typical corporation management is likely to feel, therefore, that the kind of information contained in balance sheets, income statements, and statements of surplus, as supplied in annual and other reports to stockholders, is about as much as can be safely revealed. They will probably give the stockholder access to the accounting records for interim information of the same kinds as are included in the published reports, but rarely will they be willing to go beyond this limit. For example, managements will generally admit that the stockholder has a right to know what are the amounts of accounts receivable and payable, how much has been borrowed from banks, what is the book value of the different kinds of fixed assets, what total sales, total expenses, and net profits before and after taxes amount to, and so on; but they are likely to deny his right to know the names, addresses, and current balances of specific customers and suppliers, the names of the banks from which money has been borrowed, the unit costs of manufacture of individual products, and so on. They are likely to hold that information of the latter kinds could be of inestimable advantage to competitors.

If, then, the stockholder demands detailed information different from the kinds usually included in published statements, it is likely to be refused him without hesitation. His only redress would be to appeal to the courts for an order directing the corporation to give him the desired information or access to the records where it could be found. But the court would give the management an opportunity to explain its stand. It would then be up to the court to weigh the merits of the stockholder's demands as against the reasons advanced by the management for its refusal to accede.

Right to Prevent Wrongful Corporate Actions

As losses resulting from the wrongful actions of a corporation injure its stockholders individually as well as collectively, each has standing in the courts to bring proceedings to prevent such actions as well as to secure redress if losses have already been caused. Wrongful actions include those that are illegal and *ultra vires*, all modes of conduct classified broadly as "mismanagement," and acts designed unfairly to advance the interests of given groups of common stockholders at the expense of other groups. Actually, of course, the term *mismanagement* pretty well covers all the kinds of injurious actions against which the stockholder has the right to protect himself by appeal to the courts.

Agreements aimed at illegal ends are, of course, unenforceable. Likewise, certain corporate acts, such as making contributions to political parties, are expressly forbidden by law. Thus, if a corporation spends money for an illegal purpose, it stands to lose all such funds, together with whatever fines may be imposed upon it.

Acts *ultra vires* are chiefly contracts that are outside the scope of the powers of a corporation, as provided for in the state law and in its articles of incorporation. Courts have sometimes held such contracts to be unenforceable by the corporation, but enforceable by other parties. Upon contracts that are favorable to it, the corporation may have difficulty getting the other parties to fulfill their obligations; but upon those that are to its disadvantage, it may be compelled to perform. But stockholder suits to prevent *ultra vires* actions, or to secure redress for losses due to them, are rare. So broadly are articles of incorporation drawn nowadays in their statement of corporate purposes, that courts are unlikely to find any course of (legal) action outside their scope.

Considered as a separate category, mismanagement includes gross negligence upon the part of the directors in fulfilling their responsibilities, their delegation of extraordinary powers to executive officers without proper safeguards, and their authorizing or permitting corporate funds to be spent lavishly for purposes not clearly beneficial to the corporation. As to the last-named item, even contributions to charitable and educational institutions may be condemned as a misuse of corporate funds. However, many states have amended their corporation laws specifically to authorize contributions of these kinds.

Finally, actions designed to promote the interests of given groups of stockholders at the expense of other groups usually originate in efforts of majorities to take advantage of minorities. An example of this kind of action would be the sale of some of the choicest assets of one corporation at a ridiculously low price to a second, because the controlling stockholders of the first are the sole stockholders of the second.

Although the individual stockholder may be convinced that his corporation is being mismanaged, he is likely to be slow in seeking legal remedies. If he is successful in taking legal action, the court is to be expected to assess the corporation for his expenses in bringing the suit; but if he is unsuccessful, he must generally meet the expenses of litigation out of his own pocket. Meanwhile, the managers of the corporation, in defending it or themselves, can freely use its funds in hiring expensive legal talent and in meeting other costs; usually, indeed, they are not personally assessed for the costs of the litigation, even when decisions go against them. Moreover, the individual stockholder, in bringing suit, does so on behalf of all the stockholders, and not solely for his own benefit. Other stockholders may applaud his action, but they tend to display little enthusiasm in offering to share the expenses and other burdens of his suit.

Stockholders' suits against directors for damages alleged to have been already incurred through mismanagement are much more common than suits to prevent wrongful actions. It should be easier to prove mismanagement after severe losses have occurred than to prove that certain policies or procedures will lead to such losses. In the former instance, the losses are, as it were, factual evidence in support of the stockholder's claim; while in the latter, he has no comparable factual support. What is more, fellow stockholders are much more likely to give aid to efforts to secure damages than to support mere allegations that serious losses threaten because of alleged mismanagement. Not to be disregarded, too, is the fact that some suits against directors for damages are brought by stockholders for their nuisance value. The suing stockholders do not expect the suits to reach the trial stage. They hope to be "bought off." And directors, though quite confident about the adequacy of their defense, may be strongly tempted to "buy off" the suing stockholders. The cost of this means of settlement may appear quite small in comparison with the expenses, the time lost, the unfavorable publicity, and other frustrations of extended litigation.

OBLIGATIONS OF THE COMMON STOCKHOLDER

In buying common stock from a corporation—in acquiring, as it were, all the rights described in the preceding pages—the investor generally incurs only one obligation: to pay the price agreed upon. If he subscribes at $100 a share, and pays in $40, he remains under obligation to pay in the remaining $60 according to the terms of the subscription contract. If he fails to pay, his stock, under the rule in most states, is offered at auction for whatever it will bring. If this is more than $60, the excess up to $40 is ordinarily returnable to him; and if less, he can be sued for the deficiency.

However, it is possible for the obligation of the subscriber to common stock to amount to more than the agreed-upon price. This is usually so when a stock having a par value is sold for less than that value. In a few states, such as New York and Pennsylvania, moreover, the stockholders, even though they have paid the agreed-upon price or the par value, as the case may be, may still be obligated to make additional pro rata payments if needed (as in the event of insolvency) to meet unpaid liabilities for wages.

Discount Rule

The par value of a common stock is simply an arbitrary price tag placed upon it in the articles of incorporation or, if the state law so permits, in the bylaws or resolutions of the board of directors. The organizers of corporations (or, subsequently, the directors, where permitted) can choose whatever par value or price tag they wish, or, under the laws of all states except Nevada, they may choose not to use an absolute price tag at all—in which case, the stock is said to be no-par stock. Thus, if a par value is to be used by a given corporation for a total issue of, say, $100,000, the state is generally quite unconcerned whether this is to be made up of 100 shares of $1,000 par value or 100,000 shares of $1.00 par value or some other combination of number and value.

Once a par value has been selected, however, it becomes a matter of considerable importance to the corporation and the stockholder. The general rule is that if a par-value stock is sold at a price below the par, the subscribing stockholder remains liable to creditors of the corporation for the difference between the price actually paid and the par value, that is, for the amount of the discount. The law assumes, as it were, that trade suppliers, banks, and others who extend credit to corporations do so in the belief that their claims are protected by assets contributed by the common stockholders in an amount equal at least to the par value of the outstanding stock. In effect, then, they are held to be deceived if the contribution of the common stockholders has actually been less than this, unless they are specifically informed about the true state of affairs before their credits are granted. Hence also comes the rule that directors make themselves liable to creditors to the extent that they deliberately cause "impairments" of the common stock, that is, cause its book value to fall below its par value.[5] Such an action could be, for example, the declaration of cash dividends in excess of the amount of accumulated profits.

It is to be emphasized that the liability of the common stockholder who buys stock at a discount is only a contingent obligation—and an obligation, not to the corporation, but to its creditors. So long as the stockholder has paid the price agreed upon, the corporation has no further claim upon him. If, accordingly, the corporation remains solvent at all times, the discount rule remains of little importance. The liability of the stockholder on account of the discount may thus be said to materialize only when the corporation defaults upon its obligations to creditors.

As a practical matter, moreover, the discount rule tends to be limited in its applicability only to sales of stock for cash. The corporation laws provide that the judgment of boards of directors about the value of property and services received in exchange for common stock is conclusive, unless fraud can be proved. For example, it would be difficult for creditors to prove that a factory building for which common stock of a par value of $75,000 had been given was really worth only about $50,000.

Likewise, commissions paid to investment bankers and other expenses incurred in selling common stock for cash are commonly held to be outside the scope of the discount rule. If an issue of common stock of $1 million is offered to the public at par value, but the corporation realizes only $850,000 because commissions and other flotation costs amount to $150,000, the individual buyer, as a rule, escapes discount liability. He actually pays the par value even though the corporation realizes only 85 per cent of that value.

No-Par Stock

Although the respective merits of par-value and no-par stock may best be reserved for examination in a subsequent chapter,[6] the general inapplicability of the discount rule to no-par stock may be briefly treated here. The prime reason for the early popularity of no-par stock, once it had been authorized by the states, was precisely because it served as a means of escaping the discount rule.

Even upon a no-par stock, of course, a price tag must be put when the time comes for its sale. Generally, however, corporate directors are empowered to decide how much of the proceeds of sale is to be carried to the common stock account and how much is to be treated as paid-in surplus; moreover, they can vary these proportions in successive sales. One corporation may sell an issue of no-par common at $40 a share and carry the whole proceeds to its common stock account; while another,

---

[5] This rule does not apply, however, when the impairment is simply a matter of bookkeeping, as when directors decide that asset values are overstated and order their write-down on the books.

[6] See below, pp. 477–81.

selling at the same price, may carry $25 to the common stock account and $15 to a paid-in or capital surplus account. Later, the former might sell a second batch at $55, carrying $30 to the stock account and $25 to a surplus account; and the latter, on selling a second batch at $30, might allocate $20 to the stock account and $10 to a surplus account. In none of these transactions, obviously, would there be a basis for claims that the stock was being sold at a discount.

It is a widely held rule, however, that once a given portion of the proceeds of the sale of no-par stock is allocated to the common stock account, it then becomes "stated capital" upon which creditors are justified in relying for protection. Though beyond the scope of the discount rule, "stated capital" is subject, therefore, to the rule as to impairments. Accordingly, corporate directors become liable to creditors to the extent that "stated capital" is deliberately impaired by actions voted by them, as by the payment of cash dividends in excess of the amount of available surplus.

Subsequent Holders of Common Stock

When people buy common stock from other holders, rather than direct from the corporation, they become entitled to all the rights of common stockholders as soon as the transfer has been recorded in the stock records of the corporation. Their obligation to pay is one in favor of the seller, and not in favor of the corporation or its creditors. If the seller endorses a stock certificate made out in his name and transfers it to the buyer before receiving payment, he has a right of action against the buyer to force payment, but this does not affect the corporation. As soon as the buyer effects the transfer of ownership in its records, it recognizes his rights as a stockholder, regardless of his unpaid obligation to the seller or litigation to enforce that obligation. Likewise, the price agreed upon between buyer and seller is entirely outside the scope of the discount rule. If the stock was fully paid for at the time of original issue, the discount rule has no further application to it; in subsequent transactions, it can be sold at only a minor fraction of the original price, or, indeed, it can be given away, without question of contingent liability to creditors of the corporation.

Suppose, however, that a par-value stock is originally sold at a discount, that the original buyer resells to somebody else, and that the corporation later becomes insolvent. Who is liable to the creditors for the amount of the discount? On account of the diversity of laws and court decisions, the answer cannot be a simple one, but some general observations can be expressed. A few states, such as Indiana, specifically permit the sale of stock at a discount even when the sale is made for cash; in these jurisdictions, therefore, the discount rule is not applicable to either original or subsequent buyers. Elsewhere the rule appears to be that a subsequent holder of stock (that is, anybody other than an original buyer from the corporation) escapes liability for the discount if he buys the stock in good faith and without knowledge of the fact that it was originally sold at a discount. Under this rule, and on the basis of the doctrine of implied warranty, the original buyer from the corporation appears to continue to be liable for the amount of the discount. Some states provide that, if stock is sold at a discount, the stock certificates must clearly indicate the amount by which it is subject to assessment. As such a notation on a stock certificate would certainly be sufficient notice to subsequent holders, it would have the effect of relieving the original owner from liability. Many states stipulate that stock certificates must not be issued unless the stock is "full paid and nonassessable," and stock certificates issued by corporations chartered in these states almost invariably bear a notation that the stock is, indeed, full paid and nonassessable. Such a notation apparently suffices to relieve subsequent holders of liability even if, at the time of purchase, they actually know that full payment had not been made for the stock when the certificate was originally issued. Presumably, also, it relieves original buyers from liability, once they resell the stock. But directors who approve the issuance of certificates bearing the full-paid-and-nonassessable notation apparently continue to be liable to corporate creditors indefinitely, if, in fact, full payment was not received. Some states, however, put a time limit on the applicability of the discount rule. As an example, Delaware stipulates that all liabilities for discounts expire six years from the date of issuance of certificates. Within such a period of time, it appears, creditors are expected to be able to discover whether or not stock was fully paid for at the time of its issuance.

Risks of Common Stockownership

Although we thus give much attention to the legal obligation of the common stock buyer to pay the full agreed-upon price, as well as to the applicability of the discount rule, we ought not to neglect certain economic aspects of the common stockholder's obligation. From the economic standpoint, the obligation of the common stockholder is to bear the risks of corporate enterprise—risks as measured by the full amount of his investment, both original investment and subsequent additions to its accumulated through the retention of profits. As a reward for this risk bearing, the stockholder enjoys the rights described in this chapter.

In the abstract, the rights of common stockholders look most attractive, but in the concrete, as they apply to the affairs of individual corporations, they may turn out to be of much less value than was anticipated or even quite valueless. In providing useful services or in turning out useful products, a corporation may be quite successful from the social point of view, but its stock may decline to negligible value because operating costs year after year absorb all its income. This is risk bearing. Or the stockholder may be entirely dispossessed, having all his high-sounding rights taken from him, if the corporation defaults upon its obligations to creditors, and if the seizure and sale of its assets yield not more than enough to satisfy their claims. This, too, is risk bearing.

Rights attract and risks repel investors. For the individual corporation, therefore, success in using common stock as a means of acquiring assets must depend upon the respective weights investors place upon the attractiveness of the rights of ownership, on the one hand, and upon the risks of ownership, on the other.

Questions

1. How can the description of stock as shares of ownership in a corporation be reconciled with its description as a contract between the corporation and the stockholder?

2. What is the "consideration" for the contract between a corporation and its stockholder? Where are the terms and conditions of the contract found?

3. What is capital stock? preferred stock? treasury stock?

4. Why is it said that the common stockholder's claims to dividends and assets are closely interrelated?

5. With what degree of certainty can the common stockholder of a highly profitable corporation expect to receive dividends? Explain. If the amount of dividends is not to his liking, what can he do to improve the situation?

6. Why is the common stockholder's claim to assets of particular interest to wealthy investors? How is taxation related to this interest?

7. What is meant by the description of the common stockholder's claim to assets as a residual one? Under what circumstances can it prove not to be residual?

8. What is included in the common stockholder's right to participate in management? Why is this right much more important to some investors than the right to share in dividends and assets?

9. Is the ownership of a stock certificate really the ownership of stock? Explain. What is meant by the negotiability of stock certificates? Of what importance is it?

10. Support or attack this proposition: The common stockholder's right to sell his stock cannot be restricted in any way.

11. What is the common stockholder's "preemptive right"? To what kinds of transactions is it ordinarily inapplicable? Allowing for these exceptions, how strong is the right?

12. For what reasons might the managers of a corporation deny the right of given stockholders to inspect its books?

13. Describe the kinds of "wrongful" acts of corporate managements against which the common stockholder can protect himself by legal action.

14. In return for the "bundle of rights" given by a corporation to the common stockholder, what is his legal obligation to it? Does he also have any other kind of obligation? Discuss.

15. When a par-value common stock is sold at a discount, what is the liability, if any, of the original buyer? subsequent buyers? the directors of the corporation? In whose favor does this liability run?

16. To what extent does the discount rule apply to no-par stock? the impairment rule?

Problem

By its articles of incorporation, the Abner Black Co., Inc., is authorized to issue 500,000 shares of common stock of $5.00 par value and 50,000 shares of 6 per cent preferred stock of $20 par value. Nothing further is said about the common stock in the articles or in the corporation's bylaws. In these circumstances—

a) To escape the application of the discount rule, what is the minimum price at which each share of the common stock can be sold to the public?

b) If the corporation sells some of the common stock to investment bankers at $4.50 a share and if the bankers resell to the public at $5.00, is liability to creditors for discount incurred by the bankers, the public buyers, neither, or both?

c) If the corporation's directors authorize the issuance of 50,000 shares of the common stock in payment for a factory building that changed hands three years ago at a price of $200,000, is the stock being "sold" at a discount?

d) If an investor subscribes to some common shares at a price of $15 a share, can he fulfill his contract by paying in $5.00 a share, while refusing to pay the balance on the grounds that it is illegal for the corporation to sell at a price in excess of the par value?

e) To what annual rate of cash dividends is the owner of shares of the common stock entitled?

f) What minimum proportion of the corporation's annual after-tax profit would the directors be required by law to pay out as cash dividends to the common stockholders?

g) Does the common stockholder have voting power in the election of directors? in passing upon proposed changes in the corporation's articles of incorporation?

h) Would the common stockholder be required to give up his stock if the corporation wanted to call it for redemption?

chapter 17

SALES OF COMMON STOCK TO THE GENERAL PUBLIC

In using common stock as a means of acquiring assets, a business corporation may choose among several routes. These routes may be classified as follows:

1. Public offering for cash:
   a) Offering to the general public.
   b) Offering limited, in the first instance, to the corporation's existing common stockholders.
2. Private placement for cash.
3. Direct exchange for property other than cash or for services.
4. Offering for cash to specified classes of investors other than common stockholders, such as promoters, officers, employees, preferred stockholders, and bondholders.
5. Offering in exchange for the corporation's own preferred stock or bonds.
6. Miscellaneous procedures.

A very large proportion of the common stock sold annually for cash by American business corporations is disposed of by "public offerings," a method of selling that includes offerings to the general public, to the corporations' existing security holders (except for close corporations whose security holders are few in number), and to other special groups such as their employees. Offerings of common stock to existing "security holders" are almost entirely tenders to the people who are already their common stockholders. For immediate offerings for cash, as distinct from selling over a lengthy period of time (as when options to buy stock are given to corporate officers), offerings to the general public are much more important than offerings to existing security holders (common stockholders), and the latter, in turn, far more important than offerings to other special groups. In the year ended June 30, 1962, of total common stock issues of $1,979 million registered with the Securities and Exchange Commission for immediate offering for cash, issues of $1,327 million equal to 67.0 per cent of the total were slated for disposal to the general public, $607 million or 30.7 per cent for disposal to security holders, and only $45 million or 2.3 per cent for sale to other special groups.[1]

In seeking to sell a new issue of common stock to the general public

---

[1] Securities and Exchange Commission, *Annual Report,* 1962, p. 172.

or to its existing common stockholders, a corporation may undertake to do the selling job entirely on its own—thereby making a "direct offering" —or it may employ the services of investment bankers who are specialists in the merchandising of securities. Direct offerings of common stock are much more popular in sales to existing stockholders than in sales to the general public, as is shown in Table 17–1. The 1959–61 data of the table

TABLE 17–1
Selling Channels for Stock Issues Registered with the SEC, 1959–61[a]
(Amounts in millions of dollars)

	1959	1960	1961	Total Amount	Per Cent
Offered to stockholders:					
Through investment bankers	$ 457	$ 158	$ 319	$ 934	10.5
Direct	81	224	1,143	1,448	16.2
Total	$ 539	$ 381	$1,461	$2,381	26.7
Offered to others:[b]					
Through investment bankers	$2,212	$1,636	$2,408	$6,256	70.2
Direct	83	121	74	277	3.1
Total	$2,295	$1,757	$2,482	$6,533	73.3
Grand Total	$2,833	$2,138	$3,943	$8,914	100.0

[a] Issues of both common and preferred stocks offered for cash sale, excluding issues of investment companies and offerings under employee stock-purchase plans. In some instances, items do not add exactly to totals because of rounding. Horizontal totals and percentages supplied by the author.

[b] Chiefly, of course, the general public.

SOURCE: Securities and Exchange Commission, *Report of Special Study of the Securities Markets*, House Doc. No. 95, Pt. 1, 88th Cong., 1st sess. (Washington, D.C.: U.S. Government Printing Office, 1963), p. 604.

were derived from a special study of the securities markets published by the SEC in 1963. Although the SEC's report did not account for direct offerings and investment-banker offerings of preferred stocks and common stocks separately, other SEC figures indicate that sales of common stock amounted to 91.4 per cent of the combined total of $8,914 million of registered issues offered for cash in the three-year period.[2]

The private placement of a security issue is its sale in bulk to one or a small group of individual or institutional investors, such as individual capitalists, life insurance companies, pension and retirement funds, and religious, educational, and charitable organizations for their endowment funds. But while private placements, especially with life insurance companies, are of outstanding importance in sales of bonds, they are of quite limited significance in the sale of common stock.

Much common stock is given in direct exchange for property other than cash and for services. In the incorporation of businesses formerly carried on as proprietorships and partnerships, for example, the usual procedure is for the newly established corporations to "buy out" the

---

[2] Derived from Securities and Exchange Commission, *Report of Special Study of the Securities Markets*, House Doc. No. 95, Pt. 1, 88th Cong., 1st sess. (Washington, D.C.: U.S. Government Printing Office, 1963), p. 600.

former proprietary interests by giving common stock in exchange. In this way, assets of many kinds and values (probably including, in the typical case, some cash) are acquired, as it were, by direct exchange. Similarly, mergers and consolidations are frequently completed by exchanges of the common stocks of the surviving or new corporations for those of the corporations being absorbed. In this way, all the net assets of the absorbed corporations are "financed," so to say, by means of the common stocks given by the surviving or new corporations. As for services, common stock is often given to promoters for their work in establishing new corporations and in arranging mergers and consolidations, to investment bankers for their work in raising funds, and to corporate officers as supplements to their cash salaries.

Corporations often make standing offers to certain persons or groups of persons entitling them to buy at designated prices stipulated numbers of shares at given times or from time to time. A right to buy on the basis of such a standing offer is described as a *stock option*. Options are frequently given to promoters, investment bankers, and corporate officers and other employees. Similar rights to buy are sometimes attached to preferred stocks and bonds as a means of improving their attractiveness; often these are described as "stock-purchase warrants" rather than as "options."

Offerings of common stock made by corporations in exchange for their own preferred stocks or bonds are usually made at the time these securities are issued. From the beginning, the preferred stocks or bonds are convertible into common stock at stipulated ratios at the option of their holders. By this arrangement, assets are acquired in the first instance through the sale of the preferred stocks or bonds; but if conversion is later effected, common stock is substituted, as it were, as the source of assets—much as if the assets had been acquired in the first place by the sale of common stock.

Finally, miscellaneous uses of common stock include its very popular use for dividends as well as its quite rare distribution as "bonus stock" to buyers of preferred stock and bonds.

We shall find it convenient to devote the remainder of the chapter to the procedure of selling common stock for cash to the general public. Chapter 18 will be devoted to offerings to existing common stockholders, and Chapter 19 to the remaining uses of common stock, as indicated in the foregoing outline and discussion. The final two chapters on the use of common stock as a financing instrument, Chapters 20 and 21, will take up the major problems that arise in the management of common stock issues.

THE ROLE OF INVESTMENT BANKERS

As the data of Table 17–1 reveal, business corporations customarily employ the services of investment bankers when they decide to sell common stock for cash to the general public. The managers of the typical corporation doubtless feel that, though investment bankers' commissions will take a substantial slice of the proceeds of their common stock issue, their own efforts to sell "direct" would be even more costly. The managers of a manufacturing corporation, for example, may be thoroughly competent in technical matters pertaining to the fabrication and sale of their products, while they may know very little about the state of the securities markets and the names, finances, and interests of likely buyers of common stock. On the other hand, the investment bankers, as specialists in the buying and selling of securities, can be expected to know when and where and how it is best to bring out new common stock issues, as well as who among their customers are likely to be most interested in subscribing to them.

It must be recognized, nevertheless, that hundreds of individual issues of common stock, not accounted for in the statistics of the Securities and Exchange Commission because of their small size or because they need not be registered with it, are sold annually in the United States "direct" by promoters of new corporations and by small corporations already in operation. But the people reached in such direct selling usually constitute an extremely small segment of the "general public," being, as is most likely, relatives, friends, business associates or acquaintances, and well-to-do fellow townspeople of the promoters or the managers of operating corporations. However, there is little to be said about the doorbell ringing, the buttonholing, and the sometimes tearful pleading, and other procedures that go with the direct selling of small common stock issues. Accordingly, we may confine our attention to the more formal procedures of selling with the assistance of investment bankers. To be kept in mind, however, is the fact that legal regulations pertaining to common stock sales, as discussed later, are as applicable to direct sales as to sales through investment bankers.

Nature of Investment Banking

Investment bankers are essentially merchants in securities. They buy entire issues of new securities and retail them in smaller lots to their customers. They undertake to guarantee the success of offerings of new issues of securities by corporations to their existing stockholders. They serve as agents of issuers in seeking institutional investors who may be willing to buy entire issues or large portions of them; as agents, too, they agree to exert their "best efforts" to help corporations dispose of security issues to the public. They effect what are called "secondary distributions" of securities by buying large blocks already held by individual and institutional investors and retailing them among their customers. Upon the orders of their customers, they act as brokers in buying and selling already-outstanding securities through the facilities of the stock exchanges. And in the over-the-counter market—that is, all market facilities for trading in securities other than the stock exchanges—they likewise buy and sell already-outstanding securities, either as brokers on a commission basis, or as dealers buying and selling in their own names in the expectation of making profits through differences in buying and selling prices.

In all these kinds of operations, the investment bankers function as *middlemen*, channeling funds from those who are willing to put their money into long-term securities to those who have such securities to dispose of.[3]

Underwriting

From the standpoint of corporations that want to obtain long-term funds, the first two functions of investment bankers as stated in the foregoing list are of paramount importance. If a corporation can get reputable investment bankers to agree to buy an entire issue of its securities, or to guarantee the success of an offering of new securities to its present common stockholders, it is assured of receiving cash in the amount agreed upon in its contract with them. There is no such assurance when investment bankers simply agree to serve as agents or "finders" in looking for institutional investors that may be willing to buy, or, likewise as agents, to exert their "best efforts" in trying to sell to the general public.

Thus, it may be said that corporations are best served by the investment bankers when the latter are willing to act as "underwriters." As the term is used in investment banking, underwriting is a guaranteeing of the sale of a security issue within a specified period of time at a stipulated price. If 100,000 shares of a corporation's common stock is underwritten by investment bankers "at 85," they guarantee that the corporation will receive by a stated date, after the deduction of the bankers' compensation but before the deduction of other selling expenses, $8.5 million. If the stock is to be offered to the general public, the investment bankers make good on their guaranty *by actually buying* the stock in bulk "at 85," expecting to resell it among their customers in small parcels at a higher "public offering price." If the stock is being offered to the corporation's existing stockholders, the investment bankers "stand by" with an *obligation to buy* at the agreed-upon price whatever portion of the issue the corporation does not succeed in selling to the stockholders or to others to whom the stockholders may assign their subscription rights.

As underwriting is risky, investment bankers are cautious in coming to decisions whether or not to make underwriting commitments. An obvious risk is that the bankers may have to resell at a price lower than

---

[3] On the basis of the size of their own stockholders' or partners' equities, as reported at various times in the year 1962, the ten leading investment banking houses are the following: Merrill Lynch, Pierce, Fenner & Smith, Inc.; Equitable Securities Corporation; Allen & Company; Bache & Company; Eastman Dillon, Union Securities & Company; Francis I. DuPont & Company; Lehman Brothers; Blyth & Company, Inc.; First Boston Corporation; and Wertheim & Company.

that guaranteed to the corporation or, possibly, at a price not sufficiently higher than the guaranteed price to cover their own costs of handling the security issue. While the issuer of underwritten securities must bear all the expenses directly incurred in preparing them for the market, the bankers still have to meet their own ordinary operating expenses, including, most importantly, the salaries of their staffs. Another kind of risk grows out of the fact that investment bankers usually undertake to "make a market" for securities they have underwritten. This means that, after the securities have been sold to investors, the bankers continue to quote prices at which they are willing to buy them back. Should many investors in an issue change their minds as to its investment merits and decide to unload their purchases quickly, the bankers would find their inventories of reacquired securities mounting dangerously. A third kind of risk is that the investment bankers always stand in danger of losing the confidence and goodwill of their customers when securities they have underwritten and sold to these customers turn out to be disappointing in performance.

Cost of Underwriting

As a risk-bearer, the investment banker expects to be suitably compensated. Difficulties in finding buyers of securities, dangers of sudden unfavorable turns in market conditions while securities are being offered, and the possibilities of subsequent poor performance, all tend to vary in direct relation to the type of security. Thus, as is indicated in Table 17–2, the compensation paid to investment bankers—known variously as "commission," "discount," and "spread"—is generally much higher for underwritings of common stock than for underwritings of preferred stock and bonds.[4]

The risks incurred by investment bankers also tend to vary in relation to the size of issues, the size of the issuing corporations, the industries in which they are engaged, their profit and dividend records, their credit reputations, the state of the market from time to time, and other factors. It is impossible to say precisely, or even approximately, what weight is given to each of these factors in the determination of the bankers' commission in given underwritings. The data of Table 17–2 clearly show that commissions as percentages are generally much higher for small issues. As for the industries of issuers, it is noteworthy that bankers' corporations having poorer records of earnings and dividends and poorer credit reputations than many of the larger corporations that put out large issues. As for the industries of issuers, it is noteworthy that bankers' compensation for public utility issues runs substantially lower in all but one of the size groupings than for issues of manufacturing corporations,

---

[4] See also Table 14–5 on page 308 for a comparison for the same years of total costs of flotation of bonds, preferred stock, and common stock.

TABLE 17–2

Underwriting Commissions upon Publicly Offered Security Issues Registered with the SEC and Sold through Investment Bankers, 1951, 1953, and 1955[a]

(As percentages of proceeds of public sale)

Size of Issue (Millions of Dollars)	Industry of Issuer					All Industries
	Manufacturing	Electric, Gas, and Water	Communication	Mining	Other	
Bonds:						
Under 0.5.........	....	....	....	....	....	....
0.5– 0.9..........	7.42	....	....	....	7.69	7.53
1.0– 1.9..........	6.50	3.00	2.50	....	5.25	5.80
2.0– 4.9..........	4.61	1.04	....	....	4.34	2.37
5.0– 9.9..........	2.58	.73	....	3.04	2.50	1.01
10.0–19.9..........	1.70	.62	.72	1.88	1.44	.88
20.0–49.9..........	1.30	.68	.57	....	1.34	.85
50.0 and over......	1.02	.64	.66	....	.91	.88
Total[b]..........	1.73	.66	.61	2.46	1.25	.80
Preferred Stock:						
Under 0.5.........	....	....	....	....	....	....
0.5– 0.9..........	11.70	8.00	5.17	....	8.32	8.67
1.0– 1.9..........	8.69	4.46	4.44	....	10.00	5.98
2.0– 4.9..........	4.06	2.67	4.31	....	6.43	3.83
5.0– 9.9..........	3.28	2.57	4.40	....	2.71	2.93
10.0–19.9..........	2.20	2.28	3.56	....	2.23	2.40
20.0–49.9..........	3.23	2.76	....	....	....	2.84
50.0 and over......	2.12	....	....	....	....	2.12
Total[b]..........	4.05	2.25	4.85	....	5.80	3.34
Common Stock:						
Under 0.5.........	15.70	....	....	25.50	11.76	20.99
0.5– 0.9..........	10.63	7.96	5.95	26.52	16.32	17.12
1.0– 1.9..........	10.57	5.08	4.95	18.96	9.20	11.27
2.0– 4.9..........	7.29	4.32	4.90	15.23	11.16	8.47
5.0– 9.9..........	5.61	3.84	5.81	10.38	11.76	5.31
10.0–19.9..........	4.40	2.52	4.52	11.11	6.15	4.20
20.0–49.9..........	5.08	3.85	....	15.00	....	4.98
50.0 and over......	....	....	....	....	....	....
Total[b]..........	8.00	3.78	5.00	16.67	9.82	8.75

[a] Including 265 issues of bonds with gross proceeds of $5.9 billion, 120 issues of preferred stock amounting to $850 million, and 230 issues of common stock with proceeds of almost $1 billion. The median size of issues was $15 million for bonds, $4 million for preferred stock, and $2 million for common stock. Issues ranged in size from $100,000 to $300 million.

[b] Median percentages.

Source: Securities and Exchange Commission, *Cost of Flotation of Corporate Securities, 1951-1955* (Washington, D.C.: U.S. Government Printing Office, 1957), pp. 9, 38–40.

and that commissions for issues of mining companies run far higher than for any other industrial class.

Some of the findings of the SEC in a later study of cash commissions paid to investment bankers for their services in marketing common stock issues are presented in Table 17–3. A comparison of the commission rates of 1960–61 with those of 1949 and 1953 reveals sharp increases in the

TABLE 17–3
Investment Bankers' Cash Compensation on Publicly Offered
Common Stock Issues, 1949, 1953, 1960, and 1961[a]
(As percentages of gross proceeds[b])

Size of Issue (*Thousands of dollars*)	*1949*	*1953*	*1960*	*1961*
300 and under	10.9	11.6	15.0	15.2
Over 300	6.4	5.8	9.4	9.6
301 to 499	11.3	14.3	15.4	11.8
500 to 999	8.4	10.9	11.5	11.8
1,000 to 2,999	9.4	8.5	9.1	9.2
3,000 to 4,999	6.4	6.4	6.6	7.2
5,000 to 9,999	6.5	3.6	6.2	5.7
10,000 and over	4.6	4.2	4.4	3.2

ᵃ Issues registered with the SEC and publicly offered issues exempt from registration under its Regulation A (see below, pp. 402-3) offered for cash sale through investment bankers, including offerings to issuing corporations' existing stockholders.

ᵇ Median percentages in the broad classes of the first two lines of the table; all other items as unweighted averages.

SOURCE: Securities and Exchange Commission, *Report of Special Study of the Securities Markets*, House Doc. No. 95, Pt. 1, 88th Cong., 1st sess. (Washington, D.C.: U.S. Government Printing Office, 1963), p. 616.

price of the bankers' services for both the issues of $300,000 and under and the issues of more than $300,000. Although the nature of the figures makes it somewhat difficult to pinpoint where among the larger issues the weight of the increased commissions chiefly fell, it is clear that the percentage increase in commission rates upon the larger issues collectively was greater than upon the issues of $300,000 and less. One of the most remarkable revelations of the SEC's later study, moreover, was that the bankers in 1960 and 1961 received noncash compensation in addition to cash commissions on a much larger proportion of common stock flotations than in 1949 and 1953. For flotations of over $300,000, supplementary noncash compensation was given to the bankers in only 1 per cent of the offerings in 1949 and in only 11.8 per cent in 1953, but in 34.7 per cent in 1960 and in 41.6 per cent in 1961. For flotations of $300,000 and under, the respective percentages for the four years were 13.1, 21.4, 46.0, and 70.8.[5] The noncash compensation consisted of "cheap stock" and options giving the bankers the right to buy given numbers of shares at set prices. The "cheap stock" designation was given by the SEC to shares, additional to the shares in the public offerings, sold to the bankers at prices below the prices at which the public offerings were being made. The SEC made no attempt to put a dollar value upon the noncash compensation, but it did observe that cash commission rates were generally higher for flotations in which additional noncash compensation was provided than for flotations without additional compensation. This is brought out in Table 17–4 which also provides a comparison among cash commission rates as paid by corporate issuers of common stock classified by industry.

―――――――――
[5] Securities and Exchange Commission, *Report of Special Study*, p. 619.

TABLE 17–4

Investment Bankers' Cash Compensation on Publicly Offered Common Stock Issues, by Industry of Issuer and Type of Compensation Arrangement, 1949, 1953, 1960, and 1961[a]

(As median percentages of gross proceeds[b])

	1949		1953		1960		1961	
	Cash Only	Cash Plus	Cash Only	Cash Plus	Cash Only	Cash Plus	Cash Only	Cash Plus
Issues of $300,000 and under:								
Manufacturing....	4.7	16.5	6.7	20.0	11.2	19.0	10.2	16.2
Extractive........	18.0	27.0	20.0	32.0	11.5	....	32.7	....
Public utilities....	3.9	....	7.0	23.4	8.2	....	10.8	....
Other...........	12.9	42.5	11.6	....	12.8	18.0	15.1	16.6
All industries...	7.8	25.5	10.0	30.0	12.4	18.3	11.6	16.4
Issues of over $300,000:								
Manufacturing....	6.5	....	8.0	21.3	7.7	12.3	8.2	11.7
Extractive........	14.0	28.0	10.8	18.2	17.0	7.8	14.6	15.0
Public utilities....	6.0	....	2.8	....	4.0	....	3.7	15.0
Other...........	7.5	....	9.3	11.1	8.4	13.6	8.5	12.6
All industries...	6.2	28.0	4.8	15.8	7.9	12.7	8.0	12.3

[a] Issues registered with the SEC and publicly offered issues exempt from registration under its Regulation A offered for cash sale through investment bankers, including offerings to issuing corporations' existing stockholders.

[b] Items in "cash only" column are percentage cash commissions to investment bankers in flotations for which they received no other compensation; and items in "cash plus" column are percentage *cash* commissions in flotations for which the bankers received additional noncash compensation.

SOURCE: Securities and Exchange Commission, *Report of Special Study of the Securities Markets,* House Doc. No. 95, Pt. 1, 88th Cong., 1st sess. (Washington, D.C.: U.S. Government Printing Office, 1963), p. 618.

Availability of Underwriting Services

The statistics of investment bankers' commissions and noncash compensation for underwriting common stock issues indicate a risk evaluation by the bankers that is unfavorable to small corporations. This may be due as much to a lack of competition for small issues among the bankers as to weaknesses in the issues themselves. The larger investment banking houses are inclined to have but little interest in small issues. They often have lower limits, such as a million dollars, below which they are unwilling to go except in unusual circumstances. At the same time, the thousands of smaller firms of securities dealers scattered throughout the country generally look upon underwriting as a minor phase of their operations. They derive most of their income as brokers and dealers in buying and selling securities already outstanding. While many of them are likely to be interested in attractive underwriting propositions, they are inclined to proceed cautiously and only upon assurances of rather generous compensation. For them, therefore, underwriting tends to be an occasional operation rather than a matter of strong, sustained interest.

Accordingly, most small corporations and many of intermediate sizes have reasons to fear disappointment in seeking underwriting for new common stock issues. New corporations, smaller corporations that have been unable to establish good records of earnings, and others that, though moderately successful, have relatively weak growth prospects, all are likely to arouse little interest among reputable investment bankers.[6] Hundreds of common stock underwriting proposals that come to them are rejected by the bankers. In many other cases, the managers of small corporations are told frankly that the underwriting commission would have to be set at so high a level as to make common stock financing by offering to the general public a poor means of acquiring funds. In many instances, too, requests for underwriting are withdrawn by corporation managers when they learn how high the flotation costs, especially the underwriting commissions, would be. However, requests for underwriting that would ordinarily be rejected or withdrawn at one time may be accepted on relatively favorable terms at other times. Changes in investor attitudes toward particular industries account for switches in the attitudes of the bankers. Witness the successive flurries in recent years of common stock flotations, including many small offerings, in uranium mining and prospecting, electronics and electrical equipment, solid-fuels and other aerospace research and development, vending machines, scientific instruments, printing and publishing, and boats and other sporting goods.

A conclusion that the smaller corporations may find it difficult or impossible to get new issues of their common stock underwritten does not necessarily imply that large corporations have clear sailing when they seek underwriting services. At least, however, large corporations can generally expect the bankers to give their proposals most careful consid-

---

[6] All of which does not gainsay the fact that, in a booming market, small corporations are likely to find many new investment banking "houses" that are eager to take on their proposed issues. See Securities and Exchange Commission, *Report of Special Study*, pp. 15–19, 261–68, 493–94. The SEC found: "To a large extent, broker-dealers who managed the underwriting of unseasoned issues of common stock in 1961 were relative newcomers to the field. More than half (271) of these underwriters had been organized less than 6 years before the offering, while over one-fourth (146) were formed in either the year preceding or the year in which the offering was made. . . . Yet many of the new underwriters were managed by individuals who themselves were new to the securities industry. In only about 25 percent of the 271 new broker-dealer firms did a majority of the principals (i.e., partners, officers, or directors) have 5 or more years' experience. When the very new firms that were formed in 1960 or 1961 are considered as a separate group, the lack of background in the securities field becomes even more striking. . . . The more recently created underwriters operated with only modest amounts of capital. Ninety-five (or 35 percent) of the 271 new firms had net capital of less than $10,000 in 1961, and only 1 percent ranked among the relatively big underwriters with net capital of $500,000 or more. This tendency toward smallness is even more manifest among the 146 new firms formed in 1960 or 1961. Sixty-six of these firms (or 45 percent) had net capital of less than $10,000 and none was in the large-sized category." At an earlier place in its report, the SEC noted: "Another group of specialists are those who do not purport to be financial planners but who concentrate on the sale to the public of stock of promotional or unseasoned companies. The merchandise they offer and the selling methods they use preclude concern on their part for the interests of their individual customers. Despite the intricate and specialized nature of their merchandise, they apply to the sale of securities the merchandising methods more suitable for selling vacuum cleaners or used cars."

eration. The larger underwriting houses want to avoid rejecting meritorious proposals since they depend upon underwriting spreads for a substantial share of their total income. Underwriting is for them a major operating area, and opportunities to underwrite attractive issues are zealously sought.

"Best-Efforts Selling"

Sometimes investment banking houses, though unwilling to underwrite certain issues of common stock, are willing to serve as agents in seeking buyers for them. The agency arrangement is known as "best-efforts selling." The bankers ask for a commission only upon whatever shares they succeed in selling, yet, because their very refusal to underwrite indicates expectations of extraordinary difficulties in selling, the commission rate is usually higher than for underwritten offerings. In its studies of public offerings of common stock in 1961, the SEC found the median commission rate for best-efforts selling to be 15.0 per cent on issues of more than $300,000 and 12.9 per cent on issues of $300,000 and under on contracts without additional noncash compensation, while the comparable rates for underwritten issues were 8.0 per cent and 11.2 per cent, respectively. For contracts with additional noncash compensation, the median cash commission rates for best-efforts selling were 15.0 per cent on issues over $300,000 and 17.5 per cent on issues of $300,000 and under, compared with cash commission rates on underwritten flotations of 11.6 per cent and 13.3 per cent, respectively.[7] Because, indeed, bankers generally fear that poorly performing securities sold on a best-efforts basis will reflect upon them as unfavorably as poorly performing underwritten issues, the larger, stronger houses are generally content to leave best-efforts selling to the smaller houses.

Although best-efforts arrangements for common stock issues may be the best deals that given corporations, especially smaller ones, can get, they may not be good enough; the corporate managements may decide that they must try other alternatives for needed financing. A principal drawback is the incurring of all the expenses of preparing an issue for sale without any assurances of sale; if the flotation is unsuccessful, the venture may leave the corporation with less cash than it had at the start. Because any security issue is usually designed to produce cash needed for a specific project, the possibility that sales may fall short even moderately, as by one third or one fourth of the issue, tends to cast doubt on the feasibility of the best-efforts arrangement. What is more, some of the state securities laws—the "blue-sky laws," to be discussed a little later— provide that the proceeds of best-efforts sales are to be put in escrow, and are to be returned to investors, less the selling commission, unless all or almost all the issue is sold.

---

[7] Securities and Exchange Commission, *Report of Special Study*, p. 618.

UNDERWRITING PROCEDURE

The first step in the procedure of underwriting a common stock issue is ordinarily the presentation of a proposal by the financial officers of a corporation to the investment banking house of their choice.[8] Sometimes the procedure is, as it were, reversed. Alert investment banking houses are constantly on the lookout for attractive financing opportunities, and they often take the initiative in suggesting to corporate managements how their financial structures could be better ordered by the replacement of existing classes of liabilities or stock issues by new issues of stocks or bonds, or in suggesting to close corporations that the time has arrived for them to "go public." A corporation "goes public" when, for the first time, it makes an offering to the general public of a new issue of its own securities, ordinarily common stock, or its principal stockholders make such an offering of some of their holdings.[9]

When the proposal comes from a corporation, the bankers subject it, so to say, to a preliminary investigation. If this turns out favorably, they launch a much more extensive investigation. And if this, too, is favorable, they are prepared to push ahead with all the other steps that are necessary to bring the financing to completion—steps to be discussed in detail in the following pages.

To be kept in mind in the course of this discussion is the fact that the procedures of underwriting common stock issues are closely paralleled by those in the underwriting of preferred stocks and bonds. Thus, the description of procedures in the present chapter should make unnecessary further extended treatment in later chapters where financing with preferred stock and bonds is taken up.

Preliminary Investigation

The principal financial officer of a corporation, on taking a common stock financing proposal to an investment banking house, can expect to be accorded "red-carpet service." Cordial relations presumably exist already if the house has in the past successfully handled financing for the

---

[8] An alternative procedure is to make a public announcement of the details of the issue and invite investment bankers and anybody else who may be interested to submit bids for it. Railroads and certain classes of public utilities are required by government regulation to offer most kinds of their securities for "competitive bidding." Because, however, many more bond issues than stock issues have been offered by the competitive bidding route, a discussion of the matter is deferred to Chapter 29 where procedures in the sale of bonds are analyzed. See pp. 718–24.

[9] For a description of some kinds of efforts of investment bankers to drum up business in the period 1959–61, see Securities and Exchange Commission, *Report of Special Study*, pp. 495–500. The author advises the student to continue his reading in the SEC's report, especially pages 512–16, to see that the underwriting procedure is not always quite so thorough and orderly as described in the following pages of this textbook.

corporation; but the reception of the financial officer is likely to be no less cordial even if he is approaching the house for the first time.

If the contact is a first approach, the bankers will ask about the corporation's history, products, and activities, and especially about the nature and scope of the plans for financing. The financial officer will be asked to supply recent financial statements and other compilations of data—but, in general, only materials already available or collectible at no great expense. The bankers want such information only for the purposes of a preliminary analysis, the results of which will indicate whether or not a more time-consuming and costly detailed investigation would be justifiable. With assurances from the financial officer that the data called for will be quickly supplied, the bankers, in turn, are able to give him assurances that the preliminary investigation will be carried through promptly and that a decision as to whether or not they are willing to proceed further in the direction of underwriting will be quickly forthcoming.

The preliminary investigation is carried on by the *buying department* of the investment banking house. For its study, it has the information supplied by the financial officer during his interview and the additional data supplied by him subsequently in documentary form, together with such further information about the corporation and its affairs that the bankers' *research department* is able to assemble from published sources.

On the basis of the earlier discussion of the risks of investment banking, one may readily conclude that many proposals for security flotations do not survive the preliminary investigation. But for those that do survive, detailed investigations become the next order of business.

Detailed Investigation

Although no contract, written or oral, is entered into before investment bankers launch detailed investigations of proposed security issues, there are certain "understandings" between bankers and prospective issuers that are generally recognized and observed. The corporation is expected throughout the period of investigation to give it unstinted cooperation in supplying a mass of information about itself, including, probably, some of a secret character that it would be most unwilling to disclose to anybody else, in having experts of various kinds prepare special reports, and in patiently bearing the expenses of these operations. It is also understood that the corporation will not take its proposal to any other investment banking house while the investigation is under way, and that it will not deny the investigating house the role of "originator" of the security issue should it be willing to go ahead with the underwriting.

Reports of experts include, at the minimum, financial statements certified by public accountants and opinions of attorneys on the corporation's legal status, the scope of its corporate powers, its capacity to issue additional common stock, and the nature of current or pending litigation, if any, in which it may be involved. Other kinds of reports that may be called for, depending upon circumstances, are those of management engineers analyzing the corporation's administrative setup, its factory facilities and their layout, the nature and composition of its products, its sources of raw materials and other supplies, and its labor relations; those of appraisers establishing current values of its physical plant; and those of market analysts upon the corporation's product distribution facilities and channels, its relationships with wholesalers, jobbers, and others, and its advertising policies.

Having reports prepared by experts is costly for the corporation, as is also the time that its own officers and employees must give in providing information both to the bankers and to the experts and in cooperating in other ways. Moreover, the corporation is billed for expenses specially incurred by the investment bankers in connection with the investigation, although not for the bankers' regular operating expenses, as for the wages and salaries of its staff members. But the managers of the corporation are likely to conclude philosophically that most of the materials assembled will be needed anyway for the preparation of a registration statement and prospectus—documents to be discussed a little later. They also know that the collected data will be useful in presenting the underwriting proposition to other investment banking houses should the house making the investigation decide against underwriting.

Underwriting Decision

If the investment banking house finds that the results of its detailed investigation are favorable to its corporate client, and if it continues to be satisfied with the market situation in general, it is ready to commit itself to serve as the originator and as a principal underwriter of the proposed common stock issue. Such a commitment is ordinarily made in a letter written by the bankers to the corporation, following a "negotiation conference" at which the bankers and the corporate officials agree upon all the details of the proposed issue and of their own relationship that can be definitely established by that time. The letter sets forth all these details as constituting the "understanding" between the bankers and the corporation. While the corporate officers will have been given some assurances about the probable gross proceeds of the issue, the letter is most unlikely to contain any statement about the price at which the bankers will eventually underwrite it. As further time-consuming steps must be taken before the offering is actually made to the public, and as drastic changes could take place in the market situation in the interim, it would be much too risky for the bankers to make a firm price commitment at this stage of the proceedings. On the other hand, they may be willing to come to an immediate agreement upon the underwriting commission and to include this as a specific detail in their letter.

Investment bankers often recommend means of financing other than the means proposed to them. For a given corporation, they may be willing to underwrite one kind of security issue, perhaps bonds, but not another kind, perhaps common stock. When corporate managements have strong convictions about the form their financing should take, no agreement may be possible if these convictions conflict with the judgments of the investment bankers and if the corporate officers are unwilling to switch their plans. Often, however, financial officers of corporations go to investment bankers with no strong choices as to the means of financing to be used; they expect the bankers, on the basis of their expert knowledge of sources of funds and market conditions, to advise them how best to proceed. Not infrequently, too, as detailed investigations proceed, both the bankers and their corporate clients come to a conclusion that financing plans different from those originally tentatively agreed upon should be substituted as having greater promise of success.

Preparation by the Corporation

A corporation whose common stock financing proposal has been accepted by an investment banking house has certain functions to perform in getting its new issue prepared for the public offering. Most obviously, it must have unissued stock available for the offering. As it would be unlikely to have such a quantity already authorized, it must have its articles of incorporation amended to provide for the additional shares. This action requires an approving vote of the existing common stockholders. Moreover, should the existing stock have the preemptive right, the stockholders must be asked to waive that right with respect to the new issue, or, alternatively, to approve a further amendment to the articles of incorporation to rescind the right as it would apply to the proposed issue as well as to future ones.

Investment bankers sometimes stipulate that they will underwrite only if certain features of authorized common stock—that already outstanding and that to be issued—are changed. Such changes almost invariably require the approval of the existing common stockholders. Thus, a change from an established par value to no par or one in the opposite direction may be prescribed. Or a change from a high to a low par value may be requested—a move normally effected, with respect to shares already outstanding, by the issuance of two or more shares of the lower par value for one share of the existing higher par, as, for example, five $20 shares for one of $100. The investment bankers ask for such changes in the expectation that the stock will thus be made more attractive to the classes of investors to whom it is to be offered.

Further preparatory work is required of the corporation, in close cooperation with the investment bankers, in drawing up a registration statement and prospectus to qualify the common stock issue for public sale in accordance with the requirements of the federal Securities Act of

1933, as well as in taking steps to qualify the issue for sale in various states according to the provisions of their "blue-sky laws."

Registration under the Federal Securities Act

The objective of the federal Securities Act is to protect investors in new security issues offered for sale in interstate commerce from misrepresentation, deceit, and other fraud, and, for every issue so offered, to provide them with all "material facts" presumably necessary for intelligent investment decisions. The use of the mails and other instrumentalities of interstate commerce is denied to issuers of securities unless they file registration statements with the Securities and Exchange Commission, the registration statements are permitted by that agency to become "effective," and approved prospectuses are made available to the people to whom the securities are offered for sale. Use of the mails and other instrumentalities of interstate commerce in ways contrary to the prescribed procedures is a criminal offense, punishable by fine, imprisonment, or both, and it also gives rise to certain kinds of civil liabilities.

Securities and Exchange Commission. Responsibility for the enforcement of the Securities Act of 1933 was originally entrusted by Congress to the Federal Trade Commission, but in 1934 it was transferred to the Securities and Exchange Commission, a new agency established by the Securities Exchange Act adopted in that year. Under the 1934 legislation, as its title implies, SEC was given authority to regulate the activities of national securities exchanges, the conduct of members of these exchanges, and certain kinds of financial activities of corporations whose securities are traded on the exchanges, in addition to the powers respecting new security issues as transferred from the Federal Trade Commission. Later legislation has given the SEC much additional authority, including powers to regulate the structure and financing activities of public utility holding company systems, the operations of securities dealers and brokers in the over-the-counter market, and the activities of investment companies and investment advisers, as well as certain advisory powers related to proceedings in bankruptcy.

The SEC is composed of five members who are appointed by the President with the advice and consent of the Senate. The term of office is five years, but members may be reappointed. To contribute to continuity of policy, the terms of members are "staggered," one member's term expiring each year. Not more than three members may be of the same political party.

The SEC's headquarters are in Washington. However, to speed up its work as well as to provide convenient facilities for people who have business with it, the SEC operates nine regional offices and eight branch offices in various parts of the country.

Registration Statements. Registration statements required under the Securities Act of 1933 are generally long and complex documents. Such a statement must be signed by the corporation, its principal executive officers, including its principal financial and accounting officers, and a majority of its board of directors. All these signers are subject to criminal and civil penalties for wilful omissions and misstatements of material facts; and such liability extends also to the nonsigning directors, experts who participated in preparing the registration statement, and all underwriting investment bankers. Although all these persons, except the corporation itself, can probably escape liability by demonstrating that they were "reasonably prudent" in their contributions (or in certain other ways), they are likely to feel that the best way to escape liability is to be clear and honest in the first place—to avoid concealments of what might be adjudged material facts and to state straightforwardly what are obviously material facts. Hence, they are inclined to err in the direction of excessive description and to include facts of no great importance, rather than to err in the direction of brevity.

The SEC describes the content of a registration statement as follows:

> In general the registration statement of an issuer other than a foreign government must describe such matters as the names of persons who participate in the direction, management, or control of the issuer's business; their security holdings and remuneration and options or bonus and profit-sharing privileges alloted to them; the character and size of the business enterprise, its capital structure, past history and earnings, and its financial statements, certified by independent accountants; underwriters' commissions; payments to promoters made within 2 years or intended to be made; acquisitions of property not in the ordinary course of business, and the interest of directors, officers, and principal stockholders therein; pending or threatened legal proceedings; and the purpose to which the proceeds of the offering are to be applied.[10]

However, one might say that the SEC itself tends to err in the direction of brevity in this descriptive outline. It should be added, at least, that the registration statement must contain copies of the corporation's articles of incorporation, its bylaws, its contract with the underwriters of the security issue, and other "material" contracts not negotiated in the ordinary course of business. Moreover, a considerable amount of detail is required for many of the items contained in the SEC's descriptive statement. On the other hand, the SEC must be praised for its continued efforts to show how factual data can be presented in registration statements more simply than has been customary without loss of disclosure value.

At the time of filing a registration statement, the registering corporation must pay a fee equal to .01 per cent of the "maximum aggregate price at which the securities are proposed to be offered." For an issue of, say, 300,000 shares of common stock whose price to the public is expected not to exceed $30 a share, the fee would thus be $900—an additional item of expense, but surely one of the least burdensome of flotation costs.

---

[10] Securities and Exchange Commission, *Annual Report*, 1961, p. 25.

The Securities Act provides for a "waiting period" of 20 days from the date of the filing of a registration statement until it becomes "effective," that is, until the securities may be offered for sale. The waiting period gives the SEC's staff time to examine the registration statement to determine if, indeed, it does appear to be a straightforward disclosure of all material facts, if copies of all prescribed documents have been included, and if the prospectus is an adequate summary. The SEC has authority to permit registration statements to become effective after waiting periods of less than 20 days. It has been especially liberal in advancing effective dates when it has appeared that early offerings would materially enhance selling prospects. In every such case, of course, the SEC must be satisfied as to the completeness of the registration statement, either as originally filed, or as amended in accordance with its instructions.

Prospectuses. A prospectus is a part of a registration statement, and, at the same time, a comprehensive summary of it. It is expected to cover all the material facts contained in the main body of the registration statement, but in briefer form. Financial statements included in the prospectus must be as complete as in the principal registration statement presentation, although supporting schedules may generally be abbreviated or omitted. Copies of articles of incorporation, bylaws, and other documents may usually be omitted from the prospectus, although, of course, it may include excerpts when apparently necessary to clarify certain material facts. Despite the idea of the prospectus as a summary, however, it, too, tends to be a long document. Prospectuses of twenty, thirty, or more printed pages are quite common. (For an illustrative cover page of a prospectus, see Figure 17–1.)

The reason why prospectuses are required is that few prospective investors in securities are expected to examine the registration statements themselves. After filing, the complete registration statements are available for examination in the reading rooms of the SEC, and photostatic copies can be obtained at a moderate cost. But if a new security issue is to be offered to thousands of investors, it is hardly to be expected that more than a handful will want to see the full registration statement. The more convenient prospectus can be mailed or handed to the prospective investor when he is asked to buy. Indeed, it *must* be tendered to people who are asked to buy. Thus, one will notice in newspaper advertising of new security issues subject to the registration requirements of the Securities Act a statement identical with or similar to the following (see Figure 17–2):

This announcement is not an offer to sell or a solicitation of an offer to buy these securities. The offering is made only by the Prospectus.

Injunctive Proceedings. Were a corporation and its investment bankers to attempt to sell a new issue of securities in interstate commerce with-

FIGURE 17–1
Cover Page of a Prospectus

PROSPECTUS

150,000 Shares

DUCOMMUN METALS & SUPPLY CO.

COMMON STOCK
Par Value $2 Per Share

THESE SECURITIES HAVE NOT BEEN APPROVED OR DISAPPROVED BY THE SECURITIES AND EXCHANGE COMMISSION NOR HAS THE COMMISSION PASSED UPON THE ACCURACY OR ADEQUACY OF THIS PROSPECTUS. ANY REPRESENTATION TO THE CONTRARY IS A CRIMINAL OFFENSE.

From January 1, 1958 to March 9, 1959 inclusive the Common Stock was quoted in the Los Angeles over-the-counter market at prices ranging from a low of 13⅝ bid, 14⅛ asked, to a high of 22¾ bid, 23¾ asked. These prices are adjusted for the 50% stock dividend paid on February 19, 1959. The closing quotation on March 9, 1959 was 22½ bid, 23½ asked.

	Price to Public	Underwriting Discounts and Commissions(1)	Proceeds to Company(2)
Per Share	$23.00	$1.61	$21.39
Total	$3,450,000	$241,500	$3,208,500

(1) The Company has agreed to indemnify the Underwriters against certain civil liabilities, including liabilities under the Securities Act of 1933.

(2) Before deducting expenses payable by the Company estimated at $39,000.

IN CONNECTION WITH THIS OFFERING, THE UNDERWRITERS MAY OVERALLOT OR EFFECT TRANSACTIONS WHICH STABILIZE OR MAINTAIN THE MARKET PRICE OF THE COMMON STOCK OF THE COMPANY AT A LEVEL ABOVE THAT WHICH MIGHT OTHERWISE PREVAIL IN THE OPEN MARKET. SUCH STABILIZING, IF COMMENCED, MAY BE DISCONTINUED AT ANY TIME.

Among the Underwriters named herein is:

BLYTH & CO., INC.

The date of this Prospectus is March 10, 1959.

out registering it with the SEC; were they to register it but attempt to sell before the registration statement had become effective; were they to offer it for sale after the effective date without making copies of the prospectus available to investors solicited; or were they to make false and misleading statements about the securities in letters, newspaper advertising, and other advertising media—were they to do any of these things, the SEC could be expected to appeal to the federal courts for an injunction to put a stop to such violations of the legislation. The continuance of violations after the issuance of an injunction would be punishable as being in "con-

FIGURE 17–2
Newspaper Advertisement of a New Common Stock Issue

This is not an offer of these securities for sale. The offer is made only by the Prospectus.

NEW ISSUE

100,000 Shares

Polarad Electronics Corporation

Common Stock

($1 Par Value)

5,000 of the Shares are initially being offered to employees
upon the terms set forth in the Prospectus.

Price $19 per Share

---

*Copies of the Prospectus may be obtained from only such of the underwriters,
including the undersigned, as may lawfully offer these securities in this State.*

Kidder, Peabody & Co.

Paine, Webber, Jackson & Curtis   Dean Witter & Co.

Clark, Dodge & Co.   Dominick & Dominick   W. C. Langley & Co.

Carl M. Loeb, Rhoades & Co.   Model, Roland & Stone   R. W. Pressprich & Co.

Shearson, Hammill & Co.   Shields & Company   Tucker, Anthony & R. L. Day

June 18, 1959.

---

tempt of court." In addition, the SEC would surely certify its charges of violations of the Securities Act to the Department of Justice for action in accordance with the criminal provisions of the legislation.

In its annual report for the year ending June 30, 1961, the SEC, in describing its moves for injunctions, stated that "28 such injunctions were obtained and 9 cases were pending at the end of the year." Illustrative of the bases of its actions for injunctions is the following explanation of its move in one case:

... the Commission charged the company and certain of its officers, directors and employees with violating the registration provisions of the act. The complaint alleged that the defendants were engaged in selling education programs designed to educate a person while he sleeps, and had sold "inactive distributorships" to certain investors for a stipulated sum in return for which the investor was to receive a percentage of the profits realized by the defendants' sale of its programs. The Commission contended that the defendants' "inactive distributorships" were investment contracts. A permanent injunction was entered by consent.[11]

Apart from criminal penalties, corporations and investment bankers who are found guilty of selling securities in violation of the Securities Act incur civil penalties. The legislation gives the buyer a right of action (within certain time limits) to recover the purchase price, or if he has resold at a loss, to recover the amount of the loss.

Stop-Order Proceedings. After a registration statement has been filed with it, the SEC may issue a stop order, rather than seek an injunction, to bring to a halt actions deemed to be in violation of the Securities Act. A stop order results in an indefinite suspension of the "effectiveness" of the registration statement, whether or not the effective date has been reached or passed. The SEC gives wide publicity to its stop orders to warn investors of the likelihood of fraud in the security offerings involved. To continue to sell a security issue when a stop order is in force against it is a criminal violation of the Securities Act; and rights of investors to recover the purchase price or to sue for losses are fully available.

The stop-order procedure is also used by the SEC when its staff comes to the conclusion that registrants have deliberately omitted material facts in registration statements or have tried to garble some of those included. Such strong evidence of intentions to deceive or misrepresent is regarded as justifying—and, indeed, demanding—a warning to the investing public.

An example should be of interest. With respect to a registration statement filed by the Consolidated Development Corporation for the issuance of 448,000 shares of common stock having a par value of 20 cents, the SEC explained its stop-order action in this way:

> The Commission found the registration statement to be materially deficient in failing to set forth clearly that the registrant had been financially unsuccessful in its petroleum operations and was in serious financial condition; that, as a result of recent Cuban governmental acts and its lack of success in the oil business, the registrant had suspended its oil exploration activities in Cuba and was faced with the possibility of having to write off all of its Cuban properties and equipment, leaving it with practically none of the assets shown on the balance sheet filed with the registration statement.
>
> The information in the registration statement regarding registrant's proposed real estate operations was also materially inadequate and misleading in many respects. Among other things, the registration statement failed to disclose the funds necessary for drainage of the Florida land proposed to be acquired, the competitive real estate developments in the area, that no funds were available for acquiring or developing Florida real estate, and registrant had no specific plans for raising such funds.
>
> The registration statement failed to disclose that if the proceeds from the offering did not exceed $100,000 the entire amount thereof might go to the

---

[11] Securities and Exchange Commission, *Annual Report*, 1961, pp. 46, 48–49.

underwriter in payment of advances to the registrant, so that the financing might be solely for the benefit of the underwriter and failed to set forth material facts regarding the issuance and distribution of registrant's outstanding securities, particularly 2 million shares of its common stock.[12]

Letter-of-Comment Procedure. In most instances, however, corporations and their investment bankers are quite conscientious in wanting to fulfill all the requirements of the Securities Act; accordingly, they try to make their registration statements and related prospectuses as foolproof as possible at the time of original filing.

Even in this circumstance, however, the staff of the SEC may find some minor defects—unclear statements, inadequate cross-references, and the like—that ought to be corrected before the effective dates. But minor defects do not require drastic action. The SEC's customary procedure is simply to send the registrant a "letter of comment" noting the deficiencies and prescribing that they be corrected by means of amendments. In themselves, corrective amendments to a registration statement do not cause a postponement of its effective date; hence the SEC asks the registrant to file immediately an amendment to defer the effective date. This does not mean that the effective date actually will be deferred, but the SEC wants to be in a position to defer should the corrective amendments not be filed within a reasonable time. Were the corporation to refuse to file an amendment to defer the effective date, or were it to indicate is some other way its intention not to amend the registration statement as advised in the letter of comment, the SEC would be likely to issue a stop order.

One kind of amendment that the SEC ordinarily accepts as a matter of routine without deferring effective dates is the so-called "price amendment." By such an amendment, the registrant inserts the price at which the registered securities will be sold to the underwriting investment bankers and that at which the bankers will reoffer them to the public. Because changes in market conditions from day to day can materially affect the prospects of a successful sale *at a predetermined price*, the SEC recognizes that prices can best be set just before the public offering is to be made. At the time of the original filing, therefore, registrants omit the price data from their registration statements, and customarily add the price amendment the day preceding the effective date.

SEC's Responsibility. The SEC does not guarantee the completeness or accuracy of the registration statements that it permits to become effective. In view of the experience and competence of the SEC's staff, however, there is reasonable assurance, for both the issuer and the investor, that a registration statement that has become effective is complete and accurate. Nevertheless, as will be explained below, security buyers can still avail themselves of civil remedies on the grounds of omissions or mis-

---

[12] *Ibid.*, p. 31.

statements of material facts in the registration statement or prospectus. Moreover, criminal prosecution is still possible after effective dates on the basis of allegations that material omissions or misstatements, though they slipped by the SEC, were wilful.

Under no circumstance does the SEC pass upon the investment merits of the security issues registered with it. In permitting a registration statement to become effective, *it does not approve the securities:* it simply indicates that, as far as it can judge, the disclosure requirements and other applicable provisions of the Securities Act have been satisfied. Thus, the SEC has no duty—indeed, it has no power—to prevent registration statements covering highly speculative securities from becoming effective, as long as it is convinced that the requirements of the legislation and its own rules have been met. The spirit of the regulatory legislation is that if people are willing to invest in ventures to prospect for gold in the Middle West or to attempt to convert carbon into uranium, they should be permitted to do so, provided that the disclosures of registration statements and prospectuses for these ventures enable them to know what they are doing. In keeping with this principle, the SEC requires that every prospectus carry on its first page in boldface type the following statement:

These securities have not been approved or disapproved by the Securities and Exchange Commission. [Name of issuer] has registered the securities by filing certain information with the Commission. The Commission has not passed on the merit of any securities registered with it. It is a criminal offense to represent that the Commission has approved these securities or has made any finding that the statements in this prospectus or in the registration statement are correct.

Civil Remedies. In adopting the Securities Act of 1933, Congress relied upon the alertness of investors, as well as upon the efficiency of the SEC,[13] to root out fraudulent practices in the interstate sales of new issues of securities. It did this by giving investors rights to sue issuers, underwriters, and other responsible parties for reason of violations of the legislation. But this feature of the legislation has not been of great significance. Relatively few suits against issuers and underwriters have been brought by investors, and, in the suits that have been brought, judgments for the plaintiffs have been less common than judgments for the defendants.

Earlier in this chapter it was mentioned that the original buyer of a security may sue the issuer and underwriters for the return of the purchase price or for the recovery of losses (should he have resold the security) if the issuer fails to file a registration statement, if the security was sold before the effective date of the registration statement or without tendering a prospectus, or if false or misleading statements as to material facts were employed in advertising the security. A similar remedy is

---

[13] Originally, of course, the Federal Trade Commission.

available to the original buyer on grounds of misstatements or omissions of material facts in the prospectus even though it was filed with a registration statement that was permitted to become effective.

Both the original buyer and subsequent holders of a security are authorized to sue the issuer, underwriters, signers of the registration statement, nonsigning directors, and experts on grounds of omissions or misstatements of material facts in the registration statement. Here the suit is for the recovery of losses as measured by the difference between the purchase price and the value of the security at the time of bringing suit or at the time of resale, as the case may be. However, the issuer and other defendants can escape liability to the extent that they are able to prove that the decline in value resulted from causes not related to the omissions or misstatements of material facts. Moreover, all defendants except the issuer can escape liability if able to prove that, after "reasonable investigation," they had "reasonable grounds" for believing that there were no omissions or misstatements of material facts in the registration statement, or, specifically, in those portions for which they were individually responsible. Still further, if the issuer has published an income statement for a period of at least a year beginning after the effective date of the registration statement, the plaintiff cannot recover unless he can prove that, in buying the security, he *relied upon* incomplete or misleading statements in the registration statement. And finally in this regard, it is to be mentioned that in all suits in which omissions or misstatements of material facts are alleged—whether in registration statements, prospectuses, letters, or other advertising material—defendants can avoid liability if able to prove that the plaintiff had knowledge of the omissions or misstatements at the time he bought.

Such limitations upon security buyers' rights of recovery undoubtedly explain, in large measure, the scarcity of their lawsuits within the scope of the Securities Act. Supplementing these limitations, indeed, are others restricting the time periods within which suits may be brought. Without getting into minute technicalities, we may observe that, generally, suits must be brought within one year of the discovery of omissions, misstatements, or violations, and, in any event, not after three years from the date of public offering or sale.

Exemptions under Regulation A. To reduce the costs of security flotations for small enterprises, Congress permits the SEC to exempt individual issuer's flotations aggregating in any year not more than $300,000. The SEC provides for such exemptions in its Regulation A.

The general rule of Regulation A is that any corporation or other issuer that proposes to sell securities of not more than $300,000 aggregate value in any year need not file a comprehensive registration statement if it files a "notification" with the SEC giving basic information about itself and the proposed issue. The notification must include certain exhibits, such as copies of agreements with underwriters and financial statements (which, however, need not be certified), and an "offering circular" containing "what may be called 'bare bones' facts concerning the company and the securities to be offered."[14] Even the offering circular may be dispensed with for issues of less than $50,000, except for newly established enterprises and those that have not had a net profit in at least one of their two preceding fiscal years. The waiting period for offerings under Regulation A is only ten days, and this period may be further shortened at the SEC's discretion.

In view of its interests in protecting the investing public from fraud, the SEC does not grant exemptions under Regulation A as a matter of routine. It has expressed its attitude as follows:

> Regulation A is designed to assist legitimate small business and new ventures in bringing to market a small issue of securities. Regulation A was not designed as a shield for the perpetration of fraud on the investing public. One problem in this area is to detect as quickly as possible those filings which are schemes to obtain "front money" to line the pockets of the promoters rather than to obtain funds for the conduct of bona fide business. Another problem is to detect those offerings under the regulation which are sold without use of the required offering circular, but rather are sold by false and misleading sales talk by high pressure salesmen often operating out of "boiler-rooms."[15]

Other Exemptions. Other exemptions from registration requirements are provided for in the Securities Act. A blanket exemption is given to all issues of our federal, state, and local governments, although not to those of foreign governments. Securities issued by organizations that are supervised and regulated by government agencies other than the SEC are generally exempt; these include issues of national and state banks, federal and state savings and loan associations, life insurance companies, and railroads. Also exempt are securities issued by enterprises in receivership or bankruptcy, such as receivers' and trustees' certificates, and by enterprises in the process of reorganization, provided that the issues are authorized by courts or other governmental agencies. Securities of nonprofit organizations and issues of promissory notes having maturities of not more than nine months are also given exemptions.

Since the jurisdiction of the federal government in the regulation of security transactions presumably extends only to those in interstate and foreign commerce, a further exemption is given to issues sold entirely within the borders of the individual states by enterprises incorporated or established and doing business therein. Public protection is not needed when whole security issues are sold in bulk to one or a very few investors, such as life insurance companies, as it is assumed that these buyers will have sufficient expertness in investment to protect themselves; hence an exemption is provided for "private placements" of this character. Still another exemption is given for exchanges of securities between corporations

---

[14] Securities and Exchange Commission, *Annual Report*, 1956, p. 30.
[15] *Ibid.*, p. 57.

and their own existing security holders, provided that no commission or other payment is made directly or indirectly in soliciting exchanges. This exemption applies, for example, when holders of a corporation's convertible bonds surrender them in exchange for shares of its common stock.

Finally, the provisions of the Securities Act are not intended to apply to resales of securities by investors except, of course, by underwriters and dealers. An investor who buys 100 shares of a new issue of stock for his own portfolio and, later on, sells the stock to another investor remains entirely outside the reach of the Securities Act. However, the provisions of the legislation do apply when the controlling stockholder of a corporation seeks, through underwriters, to dispose of his holdings; such a "secondary distribution" must be registered with the SEC in the same way as new issues.

Qualification under State Blue-Sky Laws

In addition to the federal government, all the states except Nevada have enacted laws to regulate sales of securities within their respective borders. In fact, the state legislation generally antedated that of the federal government by many years, beginning with that of Kansas in 1911. The state protective laws are commonly known as "blue-sky laws." The origins of this colorful designation are somewhat obscure, but its meaning was well expressed by the Supreme Court in a 1917 case when it said that the laws were aimed at "speculative schemes which have no more basis than so many feet of blue sky." [16] Though the states were early on the scene with the regulation of security selling, their laws tended to be ineffective. It was especially difficult, and often impossible, for the state regulatory authorities to prevent or proceed against frauds attempted or perpetrated in interstate transactions. Hence the need of federal regulation.

The adoption of the federal Securities Act, however, did not make the state blue-sky laws inoperative; accordingly, security issues, whether or not registration with the SEC is necessary, must generally be qualified with the securities commissions of the states in which they are to be offered for sale. A few of the states do exempt from their registration requirements issues registered with the SEC; and these and other states provide exemptions for certain reasons of other kinds. Registration, moreover, is not required in the four states that have so-called "fraud laws"—New York, New Jersey, Delaware, and Maryland; in these states, injunctive and punitive proceedings initiated by the attorneys general, rather than registration, are depended upon to curb fraudulent security offerings.

Despite the exceptions, however, an offering of new securities will ordinarily require registration in a substantial number of states, assuming that underwriting bankers plan to seek buyers over a wide area. Such

---

[16] *Hall* v. *Geiger-Jones Co.*, 242 U.S. 539 (1917).

registration entails additional expenses, not only in filing fees, but also in terms of the services of officers, attorneys, and others in preparing the necessary forms.

It is entirely possible for one or more of the state securities commissions to refuse consent for the sale of a new security issue even though the SEC permits its registration statement under the federal Securities Act to become effective. In many states, indeed, the protective function of the securities commission is broader than that of the SEC. Many commissions may deny permission for the sale of securities they consider to be too speculative or the terms of which they regard as unfair to prospective buyers. A state commission's refusal of permission to sell applies, of course, only to the state where it has jurisdiction.

Formation of Underwriting Syndicate

Investment banking houses that serve corporations as "originators" of their new issues of common stock or other securities are willing to take sole responsibility for the underwriting only when the issues are relatively small. Taking sole responsibility for underwriting a large issue would be much too hazardous for the typical originator. The limited proprietary interests of its partners or stockholders could be gravely impaired or even wiped out by losses should an unfavorable turn in the market make it necessary for it to cut the "public offering price" to a level well below the price guaranteed to the issuing corporation. For a large issue, therefore, the originator invites other investment banking firms to join with it in an "underwriting syndicate" or "purchase group." They agree to share the underwriting spread with the bankers who accept their invitation, but they willingly pay this price because the accepting bankers also share in the risks of underwriting. What is more, a house that invites other houses to join the syndicates it forms expects to receive invitations when the latter, in turn, take the lead in setting up syndicates.

It is the work of the *syndicate department* of an investment banking house that is serving as the originator of an issue to line up other houses as additional underwriters. While the registration statement is being prepared, the syndicate department decides how many other houses to invite, which houses these should be, and what portion of the issue should be offered to each. The location of the banking houses, their financial capacities, their prestige, their selling facilities, and other factors are considered in deciding upon the makeup of the syndicate. Some syndicates are quite large; for example, 347 investment banking houses joined the syndicate for the underwriting of the largest debt issue ever offered by a business corporation in the United States—the $350 million debenture bond issue of Sears, Roebuck & Company in September, 1958; 256 houses participated in the underwriting of 2.9 million shares of common stock of Universal Oil Processes, Inc., offered to the public in February, 1959; and a 138-member syndicate underwrote the $250 million 36-year debenture bond issue of the American Telephone and Telegraph Company offered in July, 1963.

Customarily it is on the day preceding that on which the registration statement is to be filed with the SEC that the originator wires or telephones its invitations. It gives a description of the proposed security issue and its estimate of what the public offering price and the price to the bankers will be, and it states the number of shares the invited house is being asked to underwrite. Following the filing of the registration statement, a copy of it or of the prospectus is sent to each invited house, together with copies of proposed contracts to cover the underwriting. The contracts include one to govern the operations of the syndicate, a purchase contract to be entered into with the corporation issuing the securities, and a selling-group contract or agreement. They are understood to be subject to later amendment. Each invited house is expected, within a day or two, to notify the originator of its acceptance or rejection of the invitation. Although no contract among the acceptors is signed at this time, any accepting house that later withdrew for anything but a grave reason would suffer serious damage to its reputation.

The originator of a security issue is not likely to offer any other prospective underwriter an allotment in excess of the amount that it itself is willing to underwrite. For an issue of 300,000 shares of common stock, for example, it might decide to take responsibility as underwriter for 30,000 shares, and it might offer a block or blocks of the same size to another large house or two. Most of the invited houses, however, would be offered smaller allotments, but, in any case, a sufficient number of invitations would be sent out to give strong assurances that the full issue of 300,000 shares would be subscribed. This would probably mean an offer to other underwriters of more than 270,000 shares (exclusive of the originator's own allotment) to allow for the possibility that some will not accept the number of shares offered or even none at all. If, then, acceptances should amount to more than 270,000 shares, the originator would have the right to scale these down.

Formation of Selling Group

Investment banking houses that join an underwriting syndicate usually expect to sell direct to their customers a portion of the securities they underwrite, but, because they are anxious to dispose of the issue as quickly as possible after the effective date of its registration statement, they generally depend upon other securities dealers to help them with the selling job. For this purpose, it is customary for the originating house to assemble a "selling group" of "selected dealers." In consultation with the other houses that have accepted invitations to join the syndicate, the syndicate department of the originating house decides what dealer firms are to be invited to join the selling group. It is likewise the privilege of the originating house, as manager of the underwriting syndicate, to decide what portion of the issue will be reserved for offering to the selling group. The originator is also privileged to reserve a portion of the issue for offering to institutional investors—although this reservation is likely to be quite small or nil for common stock issues. The portion of the issue that is not reserved for the selling group (and, possibly, for institutional investors) will then be "taken down" by the underwriters for their own direct selling.

The inducement to dealers to join a selling group is a "price concession" allowed by the underwriters. This means that the dealers are offered the security at a price below the public offering price, so that, when they resell to their customers at the latter price, the differential is their (gross) profit.

Some difficulty in the formation of selling groups results from the provisions of the Securities Act that forbid offerings of securities without supplying prospectuses giving the information the legislation requires. An exception is made in the law for offerings by originators to prospective underwriters in the setting up of syndicates, but there is no such exception for offerings to prospective members of selling groups. But the "selected dealers" can be apprised of the fact that an offering of a given security is to be made to them when its registration statement will have become effective, and detailed information about the security can be supplied them by means of a "red-herring prospectus."

Thus, the syndicate department of the originator, after drawing up its list of selected dealers, provides them with the "red-herring prospectus" well before the effective date. Except for details as to price, such a prospectus usually contains all the information that the final prospectus will have—information as corrected to remedy deficiencies found by the staff of the SEC—but it bears a notice in red ink along the margin of the cover page that it is not an offer to sell or the solicitation of an offer to buy any security, that it is not a final prospectus, that the registration statement has not become effective, and that no offer to sell can be made or offer to buy accepted until the effective date. The red ink explains the popular designation for the "red-herring prospectus"; somewhat more elegant is its official designation as a "preliminary prospectus." Each dealer is also supplied by the originator with a copy of the proposed selling agreement, the signing of which later on will bind him to buy whatever number of shares he then agrees to accept.

Final Arrangements

Shortly before the effective date of the registration statement, the issuing corporation comes to a final agreement with the originator on the price at which its new issue of securities will be sold to the underwriters and the price at which they will be reoffered to the public. The originator then notifies the other prospective underwriters of these terms, and, assuming the terms to be acceptable, all sign in person or by proxy the "agreement among underwriters." Following this, the originator, for itself and as representative of the other underwriters, signs the "purchase contract" with the corporation. It is then necessary to file the "price amendment" to the registration statement and to dispatch numerous copies of the final prospectus—now including, of course, the price data—to the other underwriters and to the selected dealers to be available for delivery to prospective investors on and after the effective date.

On the effective date, the originator, as manager of the syndicate, makes its definitive offer by telegram to the prospective members of the selling group, that is, the selected dealers. It may simply ask them to offer subscriptions for whatever amounts of the security issue they want to take; or it may offer designated amounts, asking them to accept. The price of these offerings is, of course, the public offering price less the "price concession." When a dealer is offered a definite amount of a security, he is usually privileged to offer to subscribe to an additional amount, with the understanding that the added subscription may be accepted in whole or in part or fully rejected at the discretion of the originator.

The dealer is expected to wire promptly his subscription or a notice of his intention not to subscribe—ordinarily by noon on the effective date. If he subscribes, he confirms the subscription by signing the selling agreement and sending it to the originator.

All is thus cleared for a concerted effort by all the underwriters and selected dealers to sell the security issue beginning at the time designated by the originator for the public offering. In most instances, the time set is the opening of business on the day following the effective date. The originator offers its "take down" to its own customers and other portions of the issue to institutional investors, if some have been reserved for them; the other underwriters try to market their respective "take downs" with their own customers; and the members of the selling group approach theirs. In all these offerings, it is to be presumed that, in keeping with the requirements of the Securities Act, copies of the final prospectus are tendered to all individual and institutional investors contacted.

Purchase Contract

Since a purchase contract, as referred to previously, establishes the rights and obligations of the corporate issuer of securities and those of the investment bankers who serve as underwriters, it deserves a brief description.

Of particular significance among the provisions of the typical purchase contract are the following items: a description of the securities involved in the transaction; various "warranties" of the issuer, such as that the registration statement and prospectus will contain, at the effective date, no omissions or misstatements of material fact, and that it will use the proceeds of the issue fully for the purpose indicated in the registration statement; the specific agreement of the issuer to sell the issue to the bankers at the designated price; the "closing date" upon which the securities are to be delivered to the bankers and payment made by them; the commitment of the bankers actually to make a public offering at the public offering price within a designated period; the right of the bankers to sell at a price concession to the selected dealers; provisions about the issuer's responsibility for flotation expenses; the issuer's obligation to make available sufficient quantities of the preliminary and final prospectuses; and the obligation of the issuer to indemnify the bankers for liabilities they may incur because of omissions or misstatements in the registration statement and prospectus for which the issuer was responsible, and the obligation of the bankers similarly to indemnify the issuer for liabilities arising from omissions or misstatements for which they were responsible.

The typical purchase contract also contains certain "market-out" provisos. They permit the bankers to cancel their commitment to underwrite should there occur before the date of the public offering—or even, in some circumstances, before the closing date—certain kinds of events such as serious adverse changes in the financial condition of the issuer or in the market situation, the filing of certain kinds of lawsuits against the issuer, the outbreak of war, and the suspension of stock market or bank operations. The inclusion of market-out clauses in the purchase contract might appear to rob the security issuer of even minimum assurances of getting for his issue the price agreed upon or, indeed, any other price—it might seem to make underwriting anything but a guaranty of sale. Actually, however, investment bankers have taken advantage of market-out escape hatches in only a few instances. They doubtless realize that a frequent invoking of these clauses would gravely impair the attractiveness of their services. Accordingly, issuers who sign purchase contracts can still generally feel that the bankers' commitment is "firm" in every respect.

Closing Date

As set in the purchase contract, the closing date is the day upon which settlement is to be made between the security issuer and the underwriters. Most commonly, it occurs from seven to ten days after the date of the public offering. Each underwriting house delivers to the originator, as manager of the syndicate, its check for the portion of the issue it was allotted, and the originating house delivers to the issuer all checks thus received together with its own. The issuer, in turn, delivers to the originator the securities themselves. It is then the task of the originator to parcel out the securities among the underwriters, the selected dealers of the selling group, and institutional investors according to their respective commitments. Needless to say, the underwriters must make payment for their individual allotments whether or not the securities have as yet been resold to investors or payment has been received, since this responsibility is the very essence of underwriting.

Financial Outcome

In the foregoing lengthy description of the procedure of underwriting new issues of securities to be sold in interstate commerce, many references have been made to public offering prices, prices to the investment bankers, underwriting commissions, the sharing of commissions between originators and other underwriters, and price concessions made to the selected dealers of selling groups. An illustration will clarify the relationships among these price items. Such an illustration should show, indeed, how financial considerations lead issuing corporations, originators, other underwriters, and dealers to pool their talents, as it were, for the success of given security flotations.

Let us suppose that a certain manufacturing corporation is having 300,000 shares of new common stock underwritten by a syndicate of investment bankers at a price of $26.40 a share. It is agreed that the public offering price will be $28, so that the contemplated underwriting commission is $1.60 a share.[17] The bankers therefore undertake to pay the corporation on the closing date $7,920,000, and we may assume that they do succeed in reselling the stock directly and through selected dealers for total proceeds of $8,400,000. The total commission of $480,000 would be, accordingly, the major cost of the flotation to the corporation. In addition, expenses in getting the issue ready for the public offering, including fees for lawyers, accountants, engineers, other experts, and the stock-transfer agent, federal stamp taxes, state capital stock taxes, printing and engraving, and the SEC registry fee, would probably run in the vicinity of $70,000 or $80,000, further reducing the proceeds to the corporation (using the smaller of these estimates) to $7,850,000. Also to be considered would be the value of the time of officers and other employees of the corporation that had to be devoted to their work with the originator in preparing the registration statement and prospectus and in taking care of the numerous other preparatory tasks; however, we need not attempt to put this value in terms of dollars, as that would largely be a matter of guessing.

As for the distribution of the commission, the agreement among underwriters would probably allocate to the originator about 10 per cent, or $48,000 (that is, 16 cents a share), as compensation for all its work of preparation and as manager of the syndicate and selling group, and about 30 per cent to the underwriters for their risk-bearing service. The latter allocation would mean a risk-bearing compensation of 48 cents a share, less a moderate deduction for the expenses of the syndicate. Were the originating house to be underwriting, say, 30,000 shares, it would have additional compensation (before the expense deduction) of $14,400. All this

---

[17] This figure and those given subsequently for its distribution among the bankers, as well as that for other flotation costs, are suggested by the actual results of recent common stock offerings of comparable size floated by manufacturing companies.

would leave 60 per cent of the commission, or 96 cents a share, as the "price concession" to the selected dealers of the selling group, out of which they would have to meet their own selling expenses. As the originator would be likely to sell some of its block of 30,000 shares direct to its own customers, it would have still further compensation from this source. Were its "take down" 16,000 shares, for example, this additional compensation would amount to $15,360, giving it a total gross profit of $77,760 in its threefold capacity as originator, underwriter, and retailer. Similarly, an underwriter of 20,000 shares with a "take down" of 12,000 shares would have combined compensation of $21,120 ($9,600 plus $11,520), while the gross profit of a selected dealer taking 2,000 shares at $27.04 and reselling them to his customers at $28 would be $1,920.

A Final Observation

It might occur to the student that many corporate managements would be frightened away from efforts to sell new security issues by public offerings in interstate commerce, considering all the complexities of the procedures and of the regulatory legislation as described in the foregoing pages. It is true that before 1933 a public offering in interstate commerce was a much simpler matter, and that, after the adoption of the Securities Act of that year, both corporations and investment bankers proceeded warily. By now, however, the provisions of the legislation are well understood, and those who set out in good faith to meet its requirements have no reason to anticipate great difficulties in procedure or the incurring of quite unexpected statutory penalties or civil liabilities. Much work has to be done in preparing registration statements and prospectuses, in qualifying under blue-sky laws, and in the formation of underwriting syndicates and selling groups, but all this is largely a matter of routine to the investment bankers. Moreover, firms of lawyers that specialize in the legal aspects of security selling can be consulted by the bankers when they run into special problems.

Accordingly, the big question for corporate managements is not whether their financing projects would survive the complexities of the laws and procedures, but whether they can find investment bankers who would be willing to underwrite on reasonable terms. Complex procedures add to the costs of flotation, but it is the whole list of costs, rather than the procedures themselves, that are likely to constitute a stumbling block.

Questions

1. Distinguish between public offerings and direct offerings of new security issues and between public offerings and private placements. Which of these are important in the sale of common stock?

2. Why is it said that corporations are best served by investment bankers when the latter are willing to act as underwriters?

3. What kinds of risks are incurred by investment bankers when they underwrite security issues?

4. What kinds of conditions determine the size of investment bankers' cash commissions for underwriting new security issues? How high do these commissions run? How frequently do the bankers also get noncash compensation? Of what does it consist?

5. What are the respective objectives of investment bankers' "preliminary" and "detailed" investigations of proposed security issues? What is included in a detailed investigation?

6. What are the important steps that a corporation must take in getting a new common stock issue ready for an offering to the general public?

7. What are the objectives of the federal Securities Act of 1933? How are these objectives furthered by requirements for registration statements and prospectuses?

8. What kind of information must a corporation supply in its registration statement for a new security issue? What is the relationship between a registration statement and a prospectus?

9. To what use *must* prospectuses be put in the selling of securities registered effectively with the Securities and Exchange Commission? Why does the law contain this requirement?

10. For what reasons does the SEC seek injunctions? issue stop orders? issue letters of comment?

11. What responsibility does the SEC have to prevent the sale of fraudulent securities? highly speculative securities?

12. What remedies does an investor have if he feels that he has been defrauded through violations of the federal Securities Act?

13. Under the federal Securities Act, what special treatment is provided for security issues of not more than $300,000? Is the SEC required to give this special treatment to all such issues? Explain.

14. What is a "blue-sky law"? Why were such laws not very effective in protecting investors before 1933? Are they effective today? Explain.

15. How and for what reason does the originator of a large security issue form an underwriting syndicate? a selling group?

16. What inducements do investment banking houses have for joining underwriting syndicates and selling groups?

Problem

A syndicate of investment bankers has agreed to underwrite the sale of 200,000 shares of common stock of a corporation at $18.50 a share. The stock, which has a par value of $5.00, is to be reoffered by the bankers to the public at $21 a share. Among themselves, the underwriters agree that the originating investment banking house will be allowed 25 cents a share for its preparatory work and for managing the syndicate and selling group, and that the price concession to the "selected dealers" of the selling group will be $1.60 a share.

a) Leaving out of consideration flotation expenses chargeable to it, the corporation would be entitled to what total payment from the bankers if they succeeded in selling all shares at $21 each? if they had to cut the public offering price moderately and succeeded in selling at an average price of only $20? if they had to cut the public offering price severely and succeeded in selling at an average price of only $17.50?

b) Assuming a successful sale of all shares at $21, what would be the total compensation of the originating house if it underwrote 40,000 shares and "took down" 18,000 shares for retail sales to its own customers? What would be the total compensation of another underwriting house if it underwrote 20,000 shares and "took down" 12,000 shares for its own retail selling?

chapter 18

SALES OF COMMON STOCK TO EXISTING STOCKHOLDERS

For many corporations, sales of common stock to their own common stockholders are much more important as a means of acquiring cash than sales to the general public, but for many others, sales to the general public predominate.[1] Regardless of this mixed situation, however, sales to the general public were given priority of treatment in the preceding chapter because the basic pattern of investment banking procedures and government regulation of selling could be most conveniently explained in relation to such sales. With the basic pattern in mind, therefore, it will be necessary in the present and succeeding chapters to take note only of variations in procedure and regulation.

The strong preference of many corporate managements for offerings of additional common stock to their existing common stockholders grows out of a conviction that these people constitute the best market. The very fact that a certain group of investors have already bought and continue to hold the common stock of a given corporation indicates that they are likely to be more interested in buying additional shares than the wide range of investors who, up to date, have not been sufficiently interested to buy, or, at any rate, to buy and hold.

SCOPE AND PROCEDURES OF RIGHTS OFFERINGS

An offering of common stock by a corporation to people who are already its common stockholders is known as a "rights offering," and the stockholders are said to obtain the stock by "privileged subscriptions." Having a sufficient amount of unissued[2] stock available for the purpose, the board of directors of the corporation adopts a resolution to set out the terms and conditions of the offering. The resolution states the number of shares to be offered, the price per share at which the offer is made, the "record date" at the close of business on which the names of the stockholders entitled to buy will be determined, the date and hour at which the subscription books will be closed—the "expiration date"—and the man-

---

[1] For Securities and Exchange Commission data indicating the importance of sales to existing stockholders compared with sales to the general public and "others," see Table 17–1 and the related discussion in the preceding chapter, pp. 379–81.

[2] It would be possible to make an offering of treasury stock, but this rarely happens.

ner in which payment is to be made for shares subscribed. Immediately after the record date, the corporation or its stock-transfer agent, if it employs one, fills in and sends a *subscription warrant* to each stockholder whose name appeared in the stock records at the close of business on that day. (See Figure 18–1 for a reproduction of the warrant used by the

FIGURE 18–1
Face and Back of a Subscription Warrant

Florida Power Corporation in its rights offering of May, 1959.) The stockholder then has the period up to the time set for the closing of the subscription books to decide whether or not he wants to subscribe. If his decision is affirmative, he endorses the subscription warrant to that effect and sends it, together with the requisite cash payment, to the corporation or its subscription agent. On the other hand, if he does not want to subscribe, he is ordinarily permitted to sell or give away his subscription privilege by endorsing the subscription warrant to somebody else. (The endorsement forms are also illustrated in Figure 18–1.) The latter may then subscribe by sending in the warrant with cash. Whether it is the existing common stockholders or the transferees of their warrants who subscribe, the final step is simply for the corporation or its stock-transfer agent to fill in and deliver the new stock certificates.

The procedure of common stock financing as just outlined is described as a "rights offering" because, in the terminology of the securities markets, the stockholder is said to get "rights" to subscribe to the new stock. He gets as many rights as the number of shares already held, and, in the usual circumstances, a new share costs, so to say, a certain number of rights plus cash in the amount of the offering price. Suppose, for example, that a corporation that has 200,000 shares of common stock outstanding is making a rights offering of 40,000 shares at a price of $60 a share. Its subscription warrants would represent, therefore, 200,000 rights, so that five rights plus $60 would be required for the purchase of one new share. A stockholder who held 100 shares would receive a subscription warrant for 100 rights, entitling him to buy 20 new shares at a total cost of $1,200.

For illustration, the details of some recent rights offerings of common stock, including that of the Florida Power Corporation, are presented in Table 18–1.

Number of Shares to Be Offered

In deciding how large a rights offering can be, the board of directors of a corporation must proceed cautiously. As a rule, the wider the distribution of existing stockholdings, the larger the amount of stock that can be sold in a rights offering. But even with a wide distribution of existing stockholders, the directors can all too easily fall into the error of making the offering too large in relation to the amount of stock already outstanding. They are going to make an abrupt demand upon each of their stockholders to increase his investment in the corporation, and they must realize that the offering of large amounts of stock may make this demand unconscionable. In any event, they want to avoid the acute embarrassment of making a rights offering only to have it rejected by most of the stockholders.

Distribution of Existing Stockholdings. Given two corporations of equal size, a narrow distribution of the stock of one would mean that the average holdings of its stockholders must be large, and a broad distribution of the stock of the other would mean small average holdings. If, then, each corporation were putting up an identical amount of additional stock in a rights offering, the large stockholders of the first would be asked to make a quite large additional investment by comparison with that asked of the stockholders of the second. To illustrate, let us say that A and B each have 100,000 shares of common stock outstanding and that each plans to make a rights offering of 20,000 shares at $60 a share. A has 40 stockholders with average holdings, therefore, of 2,500 shares; while B has 1,000 stockholders whose average holdings amount to 100 shares. On the average, accordingly, each stockholder of A is asked to

TABLE 18–1
Some Rights Offerings of Common Stock, 1958–63

Corporation	No. of Shares	Record Date	Expiration Date	Rights Required per Share	Offering Price	Stock Exchange Market Prices[a]	
						Record Date	Expiration Date
P. Lorillard Company	364,670	11/25/58	12/9/58	8	$ 68	$ 84⅞	$ 83¼
Florida Power Corporation	703,485	5/14/59	6/3/59	12	25	28¼	27⅜
Virginia Electric & Power Company	710,000	6/2/59	6/18/59	20	33	36	33¾
American Telephone & Telegraph Company	11,191,112	2/23/61	4/14/61	20	86	114¼	128¾
Southwestern Public Service Company	442,362	3/6/62	3/21/62	20	30	34⅞	34¼
Potomac Electric Power Company	536,221	3/7/62	3/21/62	15	39	43⅜	45
Oklahoma Gas & Electric Company	328,912	3/8/62	3/27/62	20	38	45½	44¼
National Cash Register Company	319,090	3/27/62	4/11/62	25	100	116¾	102¼
Public Service Company of Colorado	1,242,822	9/6/62	9/24/62	10	23½	26⅜	25¼
Interstate Power Company	132,294	5/22/63	6/7/63	26	24¾	27½	26⅝
Burroughs Corporation	742,144	7/19/63	8/5/63	9	23¾	27⅞	26¾

[a] Closing market prices on the days indicated.

buy 500 additional shares at a total cost of $30,000, whereas each of B's stockholders is offered only 20 shares at a total cost of $1,200. The chances ought to be good that the typical stockholder of B would have a balance of $1,200 or more in a savings account or other savings medium —a balance which he might be willing to use to buy stock. But would the chances be as good that the typical stockholder of A would have $30,000 of readily available cash, or, if available, that he would be willing to use it to buy the offered stock? It is often argued that large stock-holders are much more likely to have their investment programs well planned than are small stockholders—to be much more reluctant, there-fore, to make switches in their portfolios simply because corporations in which they are common stockholders decide to make rights offerings.

Size in Relation to Existing Shares. With other conditions favorable, the probabilities of success for a rights offering are likely to be greater the smaller its size. If the corporations of the illustration given above were offering only 10,000 shares at $60 to 40 and 1,000 stockholders, respectively, the small stockholders of Corporation B would surely be all the more able to find and all the more willing to invest $600, and even the large stockholders of Corporation A might be willing to change their investment plans to the extent of $15,000, though reluctant to do so to the extent of $30,000. On the other hand, were the offerings 40,000 new shares, many of the small stockholders of B might be caught with sav-ings balances considerably less than $2,400, and the large stockholders of A, if expected to balk when asked for $30,000, would surely balk all the more upon being requested to add $60,000 to their common stock in-vestment.

So clear is the relationship between the size of rights offerings and the probabilities of their success that corporate financial managers often spread out their demands upon the stockholders. Having decided that additional common stock is the appropriate medium for raising large sums of money—large in relation to the book and market values of com-mon stock already outstanding—they plan a series of rights offerings, perhaps on an annual basis, rather than attempt a single large offering. Again in terms of the illustration, the small stockholder would surely be more able and willing to add $600 to his investment in each of four years than to invest $2,400 at one shot; and, with the large stockholder, the chances ought to be much better to persuade him to add $15,000 an-nually than to persuade him to invest $60,000 at any one time.

Offering Price

The price at which new common stock is tendered to the existing stockholders in rights offerings is almost invariably set substantially below the market price of shares already outstanding. In its studies of the costs of corporate security flotations in the year 1955, for example, the SEC found that the offering prices in 80 per cent of the 57 common stock rights offerings registered with it were more than 5 per cent below the respective market prices, and, in 50 per cent of the issues, more than 10 per cent below the market prices.[3]

It might appear that a corporation's common stockholders should want to buy their pro rata allotments of additional common shares even should they have to pay at the level of the existing market price. This willingness should be prompted, as it were, by anxiety to protect from dilution their claims to voting power and to corporate assets and earnings. As the consequences of dilution were discussed in Chapters 14 and 15, and the importance of the claims to voting power and to corporate assets and earnings was further discussed in Chapter 16, we need no further emphasis upon the matter of dilution at this time. Suffice it to recall that, as an example, a stockholder who owns 5,000 shares out of a total of 100,000 has his ownership interests or claims reduced from 5 per cent to 4 per cent if the corporation issues 25,000 additional shares and he buys none of these.

Nevertheless, the financial managers of a corporation whose stock is widely held and continually traded in the market can hardly hope for success in a rights offering unless they offer the new stock to their existing stockholders at what appears to be a "bargain," that is, at a price materially below the prevailing market price. Were they to offer the new stock at the market price, the typical stockholder, even if keenly concerned about maintaining his proportional ownership interests, would be likely to feel no great compulsion to buy direct from the corporation. He could buy in the market as readily. Moreover, he could time his market purchases to suit his own convenience, rather than to buy precisely within the subscription period set arbitrarily by the corporation. Even were the offering price and the market price to be identical at the time of the directors' resolution, moreover, the identity would not necessarily be preserved to the end of the subscription period. Indeed, the rights offering itself, by its promise of adding to the supply of stock, would tend to cause the market price to fall. If it did fall, therefore, the stockholder could buy more cheaply in the market than direct from the corporation![4] A further reason for setting the offering price below the market price is to induce nonsubscribing stockholders to sell their subscription rights to other investors who will subscribe. But these stockholders will have no significant inducement to transfer their subscription rights unless the rights have a market value—a market value which, as a rule, can exist only if the offering price of the new stock is less than its market value.

---

[3] Securities and Exchange Commission, *Cost of Flotation of Corporate Securities, 1951–1955* (Washington, D.C.: U.S. Government Printing Office, 1957), p. 23.

[4] In all such price comparisons, however, one must remember that the typical investor must pay a brokerage commission when buying in the market, whereas he pays no commission when buying direct from the corporation.

Stockholders' Attitudes. A rights offering can be successful, generally speaking, only if a large proportion of the new stock is actually subscribed by existing stockholders. This conclusion was implied in the earlier discussion of the breadth of the distribution of stock already outstanding and the relationship between its quantity and the size of the new issue. The corporate managers hope, indeed, that "outsiders" will participate in the buying through the exercise of rights sold by nonsubscribing stockholders; but they know that the market for both stock and rights will react most unfavorably and doom the offering should a large percentage of the stockholders try to sell their rights. Much depends, therefore, upon the "loyalty" of the existing stockholders.

In view of what was said in Chapters 14 to 16 about the claims of common stockholders to voting power, it is reasonable to say that loyalty is forced, as it were, upon stockholders who have narrow margins of control, as well as upon those who seek to wrest control from intrenched groups. Indeed, groups that have narrow margins of control can surely be expected to vote against additional issues of voting stock unless they are in a position to buy their pro rata allotments; while strong minority groups that are contending for control will surely feel strong compulsion to subscribe to additional issues allotted to them, for a failure to subscribe would be tantamount to giving up the fight.

In most large corporations, and in many smaller ones as well, a very large majority of the stockholders have virtually no interest in control. Yet great numbers of these stockholders are often enthusiastic about buying additional common stock offered by their corporations. Their loyalty to a given corporation is not forced in any way: they have been pleased with its policies. If earnings have been good and dividends liberal, the opportunity to make additional investments would seem to be, indeed, a privilege to be highly appreciated. These stockholders expect earnings to expand at least in proportion to their increased investment, and the going dividend rate, or even a higher one, to be maintained on the combined stock, old and new. To such stockholders, it would be unconscionable for the corporate management to offer new stock for sale without giving them the first "crack" at it. Perhaps these stockholders have been watching for a drop of a few points in the market price of the stock, expecting to buy additional shares should the drop take place, but being disappointed repeatedly as the buying of other investors has kept the market price up. Now comes the corporation itself with an offer of shares at a price materially below the market price—truly a remarkable opportunity!

Rights offerings can be just about as attractive in corporations whose dividend policies have been relatively niggardly, provided that their earnings have been good, prospects for future earnings are likewise, and the market has behaved accordingly. Many well-to-do stockholders are quite satisfied to take small dividends, or to forgo them entirely, as long as the market price of the stock—except, of course, for temporary fluctuations—

rises in reasonable relationship to the amount of retained profits. These stockholders are quite happy to accumulate wealth in the form, as it were, of corporate assets, while avoiding the high federal income taxes they would have to pay on current dividends, and possibly anticipating cashing their earnings later on as capital gains subject to a limited rate of tax.

An incidental advantage of modest significance in buying stock by privileged subscriptions is that brokerage commissions are avoided— charges that must be paid by the buyer when already-issued stock is bought from other investors in the market.

Market Behavior of Stock and Rights. An explanation is appropriate for the proposition stated above that, should a large percentage of the stockholders of a corporation try to sell their rights, the market for both stock and rights would react unfavorably. The principal determinant of the market value of rights, as will be explained below, is the difference between the market price at a given time of stock already outstanding and the offering price of the new shares. Since the market values of stock and rights are thus tied together, any change in one of these values in a given direction will be accompanied or followed by a commensurate change in the other in the same direction.

If, therefore, many stockholders offer their rights for sale, their action will tend to cause the market price of rights to fall, and this, in turn, will exert a depressive force on the market price of the stock itself. Outsiders who are interested in buying in the market either stock or rights will hold off their purchases expecting to be able to buy at lower prices later on. An initial decline in the market prices of stock and rights, by narrowing the "bargain" aspect of the rights offering, may prompt the sale of rights by other stockholders who had planned to enter their privileged subscriptions. These and still other stockholders, worried by the price decline in the stock or about the prospects of dilution, may decide to sell their existing stockholdings as well as the rights. Speculators would see in the declining prices favorable opportunities to sell both stock and rights short, expecting to be able to cover their short positions later by buying at still lower prices, and their sales would add to the market supplies. The cumulative effects of continued transactions of these kinds, then, might well be to depress the market price of the stock to the level of the offering price. At that level, the rights would be virtually valueless,[5] and neither present stockholders nor outsiders would have much inducement to enter subscriptions to the new shares.

Assignability of Rights. It would thus be most hazardous for the

---

[5] The rights might still have a slight value because brokerage commissions must be paid on stock bought in the market but not on that bought direct from the corporation. On the other hand, commissions must also be paid on the buying and selling of rights. If, moreover, the stock were listed on a stock exchange, brokerage commissions would have no influence upon the transactions of members of the exchange for their own accounts, since they pay no commissions on these transactions; yet some of these members might be leading speculators in the stock and rights.

financial managers of a corporation to make a rights offering without strong faith in their stockholders' loyalty—strong expectations, one might say, that a large proportion of the stockholders will enter subscriptions.[6] Nevertheless, the managers of corporations that have thousands of stockholders can hardly expect to get unanimous acceptance of their offers. A goodly number of stockholders in such a corporation may not have sufficient cash available to buy their allotments, and they may be unwilling to borrow or sell other assets. Stockholders who have what they think are well-balanced investment portfolios may decide that the additional stock would not fit in. A not inconsiderable number of others, probably small stockholders in particular, may think of the rights as a kind of dividend, giving little or no thought to subscribing. And at least a small percentage could be expected to toss their subscription warrants into the wastebasket—the depositary of all kinds of communications from the corporation except for dividend checks.

But in making a rights offering, as in the adoption of any other kind of financing program, the hope of the financial managers is that all or almost all of the securities offered will be sold. The offering is expected to yield cash of a given amount for a purpose such as the acquisition of additional fixed assets, so that spending plans will be frustrated if most of the rights that are not exercised by the stockholders are not exercised by somebody else. Hence come the ideas of making the rights assignable and of promoting assignment, as it were, by giving them a market value. A market value is given them, as we already know, by setting the offering price of the new stock substantially below the market price of the outstanding stock. This action, therefore, contributes simultaneously to the goal of attracting stockholders' subscriptions and that of encouraging nonsubscribing stockholders to sell their rights so that other investors will subscribe.

Value of Rights. To the stockholder who is eager, or at least willing, to subscribe to his allotment of new stock—as well as to the wastebasket tosser—the market value of rights presumably has relatively little significance. But it is a matter of great importance to the stockholder who looks upon his rights as a dividend, as well as to any of his fellows who decide that they cannot or ought not subscribe. It is likewise of great importance to corporate financial managers who hope, as we have seen, that rights not exercised by stockholders will be sold by them so that other investors will exercise them.

But what should a right be worth in the market? Obviously, its value should be related to the size of the "bargain" being offered by the corporation. But if two or more rights are required to buy one new share,

---

[6] Without prospects of strong stockholder support for the offering, investment bankers would not be likely to consent to underwrite. Thus, the hazard could not be shifted to them. Banker participation in rights offerings is discussed later in this chapter. See pp. 431–35.

only a portion of the "bargain" is attributable to each right. What is more, the time element must be taken into consideration. In the period between the announcement of the rights offering and the record date, the "bargain" itself is not the difference between the market price of old stock and the offering price of new. The reason is that in this period— the "rights-on" period, it is called—the market price of a share of stock *includes the value of the right that still attaches to that share.* Anybody who buys a share of stock in time to get his name on the corporation's books by the record date really buys both a share and a right; hence, the value of the share alone must be what he pays minus the value of the attached right. All this is indicated in the following formula for the determination of the value of a right in the rights-on period:

$$\frac{(M - v) - O}{n} = v$$

where M is the market value of a share of the existing stock, O is the offering price for a new share, n is the number of rights required for the purchase of a new share, and v is the value of a right. The formula can be simplified as follows:

multiplying by n,	$M - v - O = vn$	
transposing,	$M - O = vn + v$	
factoring,	$M - O = v(n + 1)$	
dividing by $(n + 1)$,	$\dfrac{M - O}{n + 1} = v$	

For illustration, let us assume that a corporation that has outstanding 100,000 shares of common stock of $50 par value is making a rights offering of 20,000 additional shares at an offering price of $60 a share. It therefore issues 100,000 rights, and five rights and $60 are required for the purchase of one new share. At a time in the rights-on period when the market value of old stock is, say, $69 a share, the value of a right, as determined by substitution in the formula, would be as follows:

$$\frac{\$69 - \$60}{5 + 1} = \$1.50$$

When it is too late for the buyer of old shares to get his name on the corporation's books by the record date, no part of what he pays can be attributed to the value of rights, since he gets no rights. He buys "ex rights." The "bargain" being offered by the corporation is measurable in the ex-rights period, therefore, by the exact difference between the market price of old stock and the offering price of new; and the value of a right is this difference divided by the number of rights required to buy one new share. Thus, the formula for the determination of the value of a right in the ex-rights period is simply the following (the symbols having the same meaning as in the formula given previously):

$$\frac{M - O}{n} = v$$

But if a buyer gets both a share and a right in the rights-on period, and only the share itself in the ex-rights period, he ought not to be willing to pay as much for the share as for the share-plus-right. On the basis of the nature of the transaction itself—leaving out of consideration all other kinds of influences upon his decision to buy—the price he should be willing to pay in the ex-rights period is precisely the price acceptable in the rights-on period reduced by the value of the right that he does not get. Thus, we say that, abstracting from all other influences that affect price, the market price of a share should fall by the value of a right at the time that a stock "goes ex rights." In terms of the illustration just given, the value of a right would still be $1.50 after the stock had gone ex rights were the market price of the stock to fall as expected from $69 to $67.50. This result can be demonstrated by substituting in the formula of the ex-rights period as follows:

$$\frac{\$67.50 - \$60}{5} = \$1.50$$

Fluctuations in Market Prices. The foregoing illustrations and related discussion are not meant to imply that the value of a right during the whole period from the date of the directors' resolution setting up a rights offering to the date of the closing of the subscription books remains unchanged, that the market price of stock always falls by exactly the value of a right when the old stock goes ex rights, or that the market prices at which rights are actually bought and sold are precisely what the formulas indicate they should be.

The market price of a stock is affected through the period of a rights offering, not only by the special influences of the offering itself, but by all the other influences that normally play upon the market—by all the forces, one might say, that affect investors' attitudes toward the corporation specifically and toward common stocks in general. Ordinarily, therefore, the market price will be subject to at least as many fluctuations during the period of the rights offering as would be likely to occur in a period of equal length in which no rights offering was being made. All that the formulas indicate, therefore, is the approximate price at which rights ought to be selling on a given day or during a given hour if the market price of the stock and the offering price of new shares are thus-and-so. If the market price of the old stock fluctuates from hour to hour, then the market price of rights should do the same. In the rights offering of the Florida Power Corporation in May, 1959, for example, the market price of the stock on May 21 (in the ex-rights period) ranged from 27¾ to 28⅜ a share while the market price of rights varied from ⁷⁄₃₂ to ¼.

Moreover, while there is a normal expectation that the market price of old stock will fall by approximately the value of a right when it goes ex rights, other influences quite unrelated to the rights offering may counterbalance this tendency to fall. Indeed, they may be powerful enough to force the price up, or they may work in such manner as to extend the scope of the fall.

Finally, the prices at which rights are actually sold at given times may be somewhat different from what the formulas indicate they should be. Given the market price at which old stock is sold at a certain hour on a certain day, the appropriate formula may indicate that the value of a right is, say, $1.50; but we may learn that some rights were actually sold at that hour at $1\frac{3}{8}$ or $1\frac{9}{16}$. The market is imperfect, and buyers and sellers do not always know all that is going on around them. But speculators especially can be expected to be quick in noticing out-of-line relationships between market prices of old stock and of the rights, and to buy or sell to take advantage of the situation. Their transactions—a kind of "arbitrage," as it is called—should have corrective effects upon the market price discrepancy.

Selling of Rights. With the foregoing discussion of the technical aspects of rights values in mind, we should be able to understand more clearly the hope of corporate managers that nonsubscribing stockholders will sell their rights to other investors. In terms of the illustrations, why should not the owner of 100 shares who does not want to subscribe sell his rights for $150 or thereabouts? The alternative is to see the rights vanish into thin air at the expiration of the subscription period. He may hold, of course, till close to the end of the subscription period in hopes that the value of the stock—and, therefore, the value of the rights—will rise; but, if he is wise, he will not permit the rights to expire without selling. The opportunity to sell explains why some stockholders look upon rights as a kind of "dividend."

In this regard, one should notice the strong element of compulsion that is implicit in a rights offering. Although the existing common stockholder is said to be "privileged" to buy a certain number of additional shares, he is forced, in effect, to do one of two things, namely, to increase his investment in the corporation, or to sell a part of his ownership interests by selling the rights. Regardless of what he does, the sale of the new stock will dilute the claims of each existing share to voting power and to corporate assets and earnings. If he sells the rights allotted to him, he should know that he thereby parts with a portion of his ownership interests. And should he want to maintain the present proportion of his claims, he should know that he *must* subscribe to the shares allotted to him, or, alternatively, to buy an equal number in the market. The third possible alternative—to do nothing—is not a reasonable one at all. If the stockholder does nothing with respect to the rights, his existing holdings are diluted anyway; hence he suffers this dilution without the compensation he could get by selling the rights. Thus, we can readily conclude that the wastebasket tosser is not very smart in the ways of investment.

That a sale of rights is a sale of ownership interests is given recognition in the federal income tax regulations. The full proceeds of such a sale are not taxable as income; in fact, it is possible that no part of the proceeds will be taxable. The regulations provide that the original cost of the stock held by the stockholder is to be allocated between the stock and the rights, in proportion to their respective market values at the time of the sale of the rights, and that only the difference between the selling price of the rights and the cost allocated to them is to be reported as taxable income. To illustrate, assume that a stockholder owns five shares which he bought some years ago at $40 a share, that he receives five rights entitling him to buy one new share, and that he sells the five rights for $7.50 at a time in the ex rights period when the market price of the stock is $67.50. The "cost basis" of the rights is found by the following formula:

$$\frac{\text{Market value of rights}}{\substack{\text{Combined market value} \\ \text{of stock and rights}}} \times \text{Cost of stock} = \text{Cost basis for rights}$$

Substituting, we get:

$$\frac{\$7.50}{\$337.50 + \$7.50} \times \$200 = \$4.35$$

Accordingly, only the difference between $7.50 and $4.35 or $3.15 is recognized as taxable income. In a subsequent sale of stock, its "cost basis" would be $195.65, that is, the original cost of $200 reduced by the "cost basis" of $4.35 attributed to the rights.

Buying of Rights. But the existence of a market value for rights requires buyers as well as sellers. If there is obvious inducement to stockholders to sell their rights should they not want to subscribe, what inducement is there for buyers? Continuing with the illustrative figures we have been using, we may put the question this way: To acquire a share of stock, why would anyone be willing to buy five rights at $1.50 each and to pay the corporation $60, for a total cost of $67.50, when he could buy in the market at the same total cost per share?

One reason for buying was indicated at an earlier point in our discussion, namely, that from time to time during the subscription period the market value of rights may fall somewhat short of the values computed by the formulas. Although market forces are constantly tending to correct discrepancies between rights values and stock values, the adjustment is not automatic; hence "bargains" for outsiders, as distinct from the "bargain" for stockholders to which frequent reference has been made, may turn up. They would presumably hurry to buy if rights were selling at 1¼ or 1⅜ at a time when, as a formula computation would show, the market value ought to be $1.50 or $1.60.

But even when the rights value in the market is equal to, or even slightly above, the formula value, there are reasons for a demand for rights. One is a saving in commissions. Were he to buy a share of stock in the market at $67.50, the investor would have to pay his broker a commission on the full amount; but were he to buy five rights at $1.50 each, he would pay a commission on only the total price of $7.50. In using the rights to get a share from the corporation, he would pay no commission on the $60 purchase price payable to it. Another saving is in stock-transfer taxes. These would be fully assessed on the market purchase of stock, but not in the purchase of rights nor in the buying of stock direct from the issuing corporation.

Often of much more importance than these reasons for buying rights are the profit expectations of speculators. Speculation in rights is much cheaper in terms of the amount of money that must be invested than speculation in the stock itself. This means that potential profits upon advances in market value, as percentages of the amount invested, are much more promising for rights speculations than for stock speculations. In terms of the rights offering that we have been using for illustration, a rise in the market value of an outstanding share from $67.50 to $70 in the ex rights period should be accompanied by a rise in the market value of a right from $1.50 to $2.00. Thus, a speculation in five rights at $7.50 would give the same (gross) profit of $2.50 as a speculation in a share of stock at $67.50. But a profit of $2.50 on an investment of $7.50 represents a rate of return of 33⅓ per cent; while an equal profit on an investment of $67.50 amounts to a rate of return of only about 3.7 per cent. Although corporations generally prefer to see their stock, old and new, go into the hands of long-term investors, they have no compelling reason to be unhappy about the temporary support given by speculators to their rights offerings. When speculators buy rights and exercise them for a quick profit, the corporation does succeed in getting its money; and the people who, in turn, buy from the speculators may be long-term investors.

Setting the Offering Price. Although the financial managers of a corporation are likely to be fully aware of the reasons why the offering price in a rights offering should be set materially below the market value of outstanding stock, this awareness does not give them a means of deciding exactly what the offering price should be. They want the offering price to remain well below the market price throughout the period of the offering, and they know that the offering itself, as a source of new supply, will have tendencies to depress the market price. However, they must also consider the possibility that the market price of outstanding stock will rise during the period of the rights offering. If the corporation appears to have good prospects for expanding its profits handsomely through an expansion of facilities, the very announcement of the rights offering as a means of financing the expansion may be so well received by the stockholders and other investors as to lead to spirited buying of both stock and rights.

The kind of dilemma that is faced by corporate managers in fixing an offering price may be illustrated. Suppose that a certain corporation wants to raise by a rights offering a net amount of approximately $4 million. It is anticipated that the flotation costs will be about 5 per cent of the gross proceeds. The present market price of outstanding stock is $80, and the financial managers ponder the question whether they should offer 60,000 new shares at $70 a share or 56,000 shares at $75. They themselves might contemplate not buying any of the additional stock; hence they would want to limit dilution of their present ownership interests. Or, regardless of their own position, they might want to limit dilution to protect the interests of all nonsubscribing stockholders. In either case, a wish to limit dilution would support a decision in favor of the smaller number of shares at the higher price. Also supporting such a decision would be the usual expectation of stockholders that the dividend rate in effect before the rights offering *will not be reduced* after the completion of the financing. With approximately the same amount of money to be made available by either route, it ought obviously to be easier to maintain a given dividend rate on 56,000 additional shares than on 60,000. On the other hand, it would be clear that, should the financing tend to move unfavorably, a drop in the market price from $80 to $75 would be much more likely to occur than a drop from $80 to $70. There is, of course, no single correct answer to a problem of this kind. Even success in the financing does not prove that the offering price selected was the best of all that could have been selected. Perhaps a higher price, giving the corporation more funds for the number of shares issued, would have been no less successful.

Rights Offerings versus Underwritten Offerings to the Public. The foregoing illustration of the financial managers' dilemma gives us the opportunity to make a rather significant comparison of the *financial* attractiveness of a rights offering with that of an offering to the general public underwritten by investment bankers, as discussed in the preceding chapter.

For an offering to the general public, the corporate managers would expect to incur flotation costs higher than for the rights offering—equal, let us say, to 8 per cent of the gross proceeds. But they would expect the bankers to agree to a price for the public sale quite close to the prevailing market price. If, therefore, 54,000 shares were taken by the bankers for public sale at $80 a share, the net proceeds to the corporation, despite the higher level of flotation costs, would be approximately the same as in a rights offering of 60,000 shares at $70 or one of 56,000 shares at $75. The higher flotation costs of the offering to the general public—representing preponderantly, of course, compensation to the bankers—

would thus not, of itself, make this procedure of sale unattractive. This is so because the excess costs of flotation would be less than the loss of proceeds in a rights offering on account of the lower selling price.

Such a conclusion, however, does not gainsay our earlier one that, for the new issues of common stock of many corporations, their existing common stockholders constitute the best market. Nor does it call into question directors' decisions that existing stockholders should be enabled to protect their ownership interests through rights offerings, even though that means of selling, in given cases and for given numbers of shares, may yield smaller net proceeds than would offerings to the general public.

Other Features of Rights Offerings

Record Date. The record date for a rights offering is customarily set from ten days to two weeks from the date on which the directors adopt their resolution to make the offering. People who have bought stock without having it transferred to their names on the corporation's books are thus given time in which to make this transfer, so that they will get the subscription warrants to which they are entitled. Likewise, as we have seen, people who buy outstanding stock after the date of the resolution are able to know whether or not they can get their names on the books in time to get subscription warrants—to know, in other words, whether they are buying "rights-on" or "ex rights."

For a stock traded on a stock exchange, the governing "record date" is usually *not* the date set by the corporate directors. The New York Stock Exchange, for example, provides that stock sold through its facilities must be delivered on or before the fourth full business day after the date of sale. According to its rules, therefore, a listed stock in connection with which rights have been declared goes ex rights at the close of business on the fourth full business day *before* the record date set by the corporate directors. Were the corporation's record date Friday, August 12, the stock would sell on the exchange on a rights-on basis on Monday, August 8, but on an ex-rights basis on Tuesday, August 9.

Subscription Warrants. After the record date, the corporation or its stock-transfer agent sends a subscription warrant to each stockholder whose name appeared on the stock records at the close of business on that day. Such a warrant is a formal certificate stating that the person named in it is entitled to buy a given number of shares of common stock at the designated offering price; it states how many rights the certificate represents and the number required for the purchase of a new share, the time limit for subscriptions, the place or places where warrants are to be surrendered and payment made, and the means of payment that will be accepted. If instalment payment is permitted, that provision will also necessarily be included. On either the front or back of the subscription warrant, two forms are ordinarily provided: the subscription form itself, to be filled in by the stockholder or buyer of rights if he wants to buy some or all the shares allotted; and an assignment form, to be filled in or endorsed in blank before transfer if he chooses to sell the rights.

The filling in and sending out of subscription warrants, together with copies of the prospectus and a covering letter, is a voluminous—and expensive—operation for large corporations that have thousands of stockholders. Such a corporation customarily hires a trust company or the trust department of a commercial bank to do this work. Likewise, the same trust company or department, and perhaps one or two others, is hired to serve as "subscription agent" to handle incoming warrants and payments.

Closing of Subscription Books. The date for the closing of the subscription books is usually set not less than two weeks beyond the record date, often at three or four weeks, and sometimes as long as eight weeks. It is the common practice for the directors, in their resolution and in the subscription warrants themselves, to state precisely the hour beyond which subscriptions will not be accepted, as 3 P.M., Eastern Standard Time. Warrants not received by the corporation or its subscription agents by this time are void, and the rights they represent worthless.

Manner of Payment. Because of the abrupt way in which corporations, by rights offerings, ask their stockholders to buy additional stock, the directors sometimes permit payment in instalments. Instalment arrangements usually call for a down payment of a stipulated proportion of the offering price, to be made when the warrants are sent in, with the balance to be paid in quarterly or semiannual instalments over a period of not more than a year.

Rights Offerings and the Preemptive Right

A final point to be made in this division of the chapter is that, despite the prominence of the word *right,* there is no necessary connection between rights offerings and the preemptive right of common stockholders to buy new common stock issues, as discussed in Chapter 16. If the preemptive right obtains—it is rather a weak one, as we have seen[7]—it exists continuously, whereas the "rights" of a rights offering are short-lived. The preemptive right may never be applied if a corporation has no occasion to put out additional amounts of common stock, or it may be waived by the stockholders with respect to given issues. If it is applied, the stockholders do, indeed, get "rights" according to the procedure described in this chapter; but they may also get such "rights" even though the preemptive right is not in force—because the directors of their corporation decide that they are the best market for new offerings. The common stock of the Dow Chemical Company, for example, has no preemptive rights, yet its common stockholders have been given subscription

---

[7] See pp. 367–69.

privileges repeatedly—in 1940, 1941, 1943 (to preferred stock), 1949, 1950, 1951, and 1952.

The idea here is that many new issues of common stock are offered to existing stockholders because directors think that they are more likely than other people to buy whether or not the preemptive right is applicable. Where directors are convinced that the stockholders are not likely to want to subscribe, they can be expected to ask the stockholders to approve the offering of new issues elsewhere, as to the general public, whether or not this requires a waiver of the preemptive right.

REGULATION OF RIGHTS OFFERINGS

Under the Securities Act of 1933, a rights offering to stockholders is a "public offering" and is fully subject to registration requirements unless it qualifies for one of the exemptions provided for in the legislation.[8] As a rule, then, all the work of preparing a registration statement and the related prospectus must be undertaken, and copies of the prospectus must be made available, after the effective date, to all stockholders and others to whom the new stock is offered for sale. Indeed, the directors of the corporation may not make the rights offering to the stockholders until the registration statement has become effective. Thus, the adoption of the directors' resolution, to which frequent reference has been made in this chapter, takes place after the registration statement and prospectus have been filed with the SEC and the prescribed "waiting period"—as, possibly, shortened by the SEC—has expired.

Although the state blue-sky laws are generally more liberal than the federal Securities Act in providing exemptions for rights offerings, such an offering by a large corporation to many stockholders ordinarily requires qualification in as least a few states. This, then, is another kind of preparatory work that must be taken care of.

BANKER PARTICIPATION IN RIGHTS OFFERINGS

How the work of preparing registration statements and prospectuses for rights offerings and of qualifying them under state blue-sky laws is shared, if it is to be shared, depends on whether or not issuing corporations call upon investment bankers to assist in the flotations. If called upon, the investment bankers aid in the preparatory work in much the same manner as described in the preceding chapter for offerings to the general public; if they are not called upon, all the work of preparation remains, of course, with the corporation.

But a much more important consideration in deciding whether or not to seek the aid of investment bankers is the outlook for success in the flotation. If a corporate management has great confidence that the stock-

---

[8] For the scope of these exemptions, see pp. 402–4.

holders will respond most favorably to a rights offering, it may decide to bypass the bankers; but if it is somewhat worried about the outcome, it will probably ask them to help out. For rights offerings of both common and preferred stocks (but consisting very largely of common stock) registered with the SEC for immediate cash sale to stockholders in the years 1959–61, the dollar proportion having participations of investment bankers amounted to 39.2 per cent. Data for offerings exempt from registration requirements under the SEC's Regulation A in the same three-year period indicate that the bankers participate in a substantially smaller proportion of small offerings to stockholders.[9]

When called upon to assist with a rights offering, the investment bankers may likewise be more or less confident about the outcome. If confident, they are likely to underwrite the flotation on what is called a "standby" basis, but if they lack confidence, they may participate only as selling agents in a so-called "dealer-manager arrangement." Also, of course, they may choose not to participate at all—rejecting a plea for assistance, even as they reject many proposals for the underwriting of security offerings to the general public.

The response of investment bankers to a request for their participation depends, of course, upon what they find in an investigation of the corporation's affairs. If a preliminary investigation indicates the probability that underwriting would be feasible, it is followed by a detailed investigation as for prospective underwritings of offerings to the general public. If, on the other hand, there is early agreement on a dealer-management arrangement, further investigation by the bankers is likely to be much less extensive.

Standby Contracts

In a standby contract, the investment bankers, as underwriters, guarantee the success of a rights offering. They guarantee that the corporation will receive, at the minimum, an amount equal to the number of shares being offered times the offering price, minus the commission allowed them; and, in so guaranteeing, they obligate themselves to take off the hands of the corporation the shares not subscribed by stockholders or by buyers of rights.

Compensation for the Bankers. In the typical underwritten rights offering, the principal service supplied by the investment bankers is that of risk bearing. In agreeing to underwrite, they have an expectation that most of the offering will be taken by stockholders and buyers of rights, but it is always possible for things to turn out badly—hence the risk. On account of differences in timing, in fact, the risk in a rights offering tends to be greater than in the underwriting of an offering to the general public.

_____
[9] Securities and Exchange Commission, *Report of Special Study of the Securities Markets*, House Doc. No. 95, Pt. 1, 88th Cong., 1st sess. (Washington, D.C.: U.S. Government Printing Office, 1963), p. 604.

In the latter, the bankers begin to sell immediately after the registration statement has become effective; but in a rights offering, they have an additional "waiting period," as it were, to the end of the subscription period. On the other hand, if most of the stock of a rights offering is taken by stockholders and buyers of rights, as the bankers expect, their selling job will be light. On the basis of considerations of these kinds, therefore, the compensation to be paid to the bankers is generally fixed at a flat rate on the total amount of the issue, this being essentially a reward for risk bearing, and there is a provision for additional compensation per share for whatever shares remain unsold at the end of the subscription period. An illustration should help. Suppose that, on an offering to stockholders at 70, the bankers are allowed a commission of 1 per cent on the entire issue and an additional commission of 3 per cent on shares taken over at the end of the subscription period. The bankers would get 70 cents for each share subscribed by stockholders and buyers of rights, so that the proceeds to the corporation on these shares, disregarding other expenses of flotation, would be $69.30 each. Unsubscribed shares would then be taken over by the bankers at $67.20 ($70 reduced by the total commission of 4 per cent allowed on these shares). But their earning of $2.80 on each of these shares would still depend upon their finding buyers at 70 or better. If they had to sell at prices less than 70, they would obviously be giving up some of the 4 per cent commission; and, indeed, if they had to sell at prices below 67.2, they would be taking a loss, comparable with the losses that are always possible in other underwriting procedures.

In some standby contracts, the bankers are allowed the additional commission, not only on shares taken over at the end of the subscription period, but also for shares to which they subscribe through the exercise of rights. They are thus encouraged to buy rights during the subscription period, thereby adding a source of demand that tends to support their market value. In some contracts, too, additional compensation of a different kind is allowed the bankers for contacting stockholders, encouraging them to subscribe, and handling their subscriptions. However, all items of compensation in connection with a given rights offering ordinarily add up to a total substantially below what would be the underwriting spread were the same issue to be offered to the general public.

Many underwriting contracts for rights offerings provide that, if the bankers are able to sell the leftover shares at a markup in excess of the commission rate designated in the contract, a refund of all or a portion of the excess is due the corporation. If the unsubscribed shares of the foregoing illustration, taken over by the bankers at 67.2 were resold to the public at 73, the "excess" would obviously be $3.00 a share. Depending upon the terms of the standby contract, then, some portion or all of the three dollars would be payable to the corporation. It is for this reason that the bankers' guaranty was described above as a "minimum" one. Refunds of excess proceeds, however, are likely to occur only when the number of shares taken over by the bankers is quite small. A large number would mean that many stockholders must have decided not to subscribe and that relatively few investors must have bought rights in order to subscribe. Accordingly, the value of rights must have been driven down to zero or close thereto, and the market price of the stock itself must have fallen close to the corporation's offering price or even below. In such circumstances, the bankers would doubtless consider themselves lucky if able to sell at the offering price the shares taken over.

Illustration. In the rights offering of the Florida Power Corporation of May, 1959, to which several references have been made in this chapter, the underwriters were allowed 15 cents a share on the entire issue. They were to receive an additional 48 cents a share for unsubscribed shares taken over at the end of the subscription period as well as for shares subscribed by them through their own purchase and exercise of rights, provided that all shares thus acquired amounted to more than 15 per cent of the total offering.

As it turned out, however, the provision for additional compensation remained inoperative because purchases by the underwriters through the exercise of rights amounted to only 10,800 shares and of unsubscribed shares to 15,528, the total of these two items amounting to only about 3.7 per cent of the total offering of 703,485 shares. The underwriters resold the 10,800 shares at 28⅜ a share, and reoffered the 15,528 shares at 27⅜, in both instances allowing a price concession of 45 cents a share to the members of a selling group. The contract obligated the bankers to pay the corporation 50 per cent of the excess of their selling price of unsubscribed shares, as reduced by the price concession, over the subscription price.[10]

Syndicates and Selling Groups. For large rights offerings, as for large offerings to the public, originating investment banking houses invariably invite other houses to join underwriting syndicates. The originating house regards the risk as being too great for it to bear alone; it is therefore willing to share the underwriting commission with invited houses that agree to share the risk. For large offerings, likewise, the originator usually lines up a selling group to retail some portion of the take-over of unsubscribed shares and the shares it may buy through the exercise of rights. In many cases, however—as for the Florida Power Corporation—the members of the selling group may have very little to do.

Dealer-Manager Arrangements

In a dealer-manager arrangement for a rights offering, the investment banking house that agrees to serve as "manager" helps the corporation to prepare its issue for the market and then to sell it. These functions include assistance in the preparation of the registration statement and pro-

---

[10] Prospectus of May 14, 1959, and Supplement of June 4, 1959.

spectus and in qualifying the stock issue under applicable blue-sky laws, and the formation of a group of dealers to solicit subscriptions by stockholders and assignees of their warrants. The dealer group is comparable to a selling group formed for the underwriting of an offering to the general public, but since the dealers act as agents, as does the manager, they make no commitments to buy some of the stock as would the members of a selling group.

A dealer-manager agreement specifies what compensation the manager is to receive for his advisory, preparatory, and managerial services, and the rate per share to be paid to him and the dealers for the subscriptions they obtain.

Questions

1. Why is an offering of additional shares of common stock to a corporation's existing stockholders called a "rights offering"? Is such an offering directly related to the stockholders' preemptive right? Explain.

2. In connection with a rights offering, what is a privileged subscription? a subscription warrant?

3. In relation to the number of shares of common stock already outstanding, how many rights does a corporation issue in making a rights offering? How many rights are required for the purchase of a new share?

4. Why are the distribution of existing stockholdings and the number of new shares offered important as determinants of the success of rights offerings?

5. In making a rights offering, why does a corporation usually set the offering price at a level substantially below the current market price of its stock?

6. Why is loyalty of the existing stockholders of great importance for the success of rights offerings?

7. How is the theoretical value of a right computed in the rights-on period? in the ex-rights period? Why does the computation differ for these two periods? Will the market value of a right always be equal to the theoretical value? Explain.

8. Why is there said to be a strong element of compulsion in a rights offering?

9. Why do "outsiders" buy rights in the market when they can as conveniently buy the stock itself?

10. Explain the nature of the problem faced by corporate managers in deciding at what level to set the offering price of a rights offering.

11. In a rights offering, what is the significance of the record date? the expiration date? If the outstanding stock is listed on a stock exchange, what bearing does this have on the record date?

12. Discuss this proposition: Because the common stockholders of a corporation should already know a great deal about it, registration of a rights offering under the federal Securities Act ought not to be required.

13. In a standby contract for a rights offering, what responsibility do investment bankers accept? Do they have anything to do before the expiration date? Explain. How is their compensation determined?

14. What do investment bankers undertake to do in a dealer-manager arrangement for a rights offering?

Problems

1. A corporation that has outstanding 400,000 shares of common stock of $5.00 par value is making an offering of 50,000 additional shares to its common stockholders at a price of $52 a share.

a) How many "rights" does it issue?

b) How many shares of the new stock is the holder of 200 shares of old stock "privileged" to buy? How much would these shares cost him?

c) Near what prices would rights be likely to be selling at a given time in the (1) rights-on period and (2) in the ex-rights period, if the market price of old stock were 56½?

d) If in the rights-on period rights first sold for $1.25 each and then fell to 75 cents, from what level to what level did the price of old stock probably move simultaneously?

2. Several years ago, John Doe bought 400 shares of the common stock of a certain corporation at a price of $35 a share. This year he received from the corporation 400 rights entitling him to buy 40 additional shares at a price of $50 a share. Instead of buying, however, he sold the rights for $200 at a time when the corporation's outstanding stock was selling in the market at 55½. Under the federal income tax regulations, what taxable income, if any, did Doe derive from this transaction?

chapter 19

OTHER PROCEDURES OF COMMON STOCK FINANCING

Reserved for discussion in this chapter are all significant means for the acquisition of corporate assets through the issuance of common stock other than sales to the general public and sales to existing stockholders. As was indicated in Chapter 17, these additional means include the following: direct exchanges of common stock for property other than cash and for services, offerings for cash to specified classes of investors other than existing common stockholders and the general public, private placements for cash, offerings in exchange for outstanding preferred stock and to cancel outstanding bonds, and one or two procedures that can best be classified simply as "miscellaneous."

DIRECT EXCHANGES FOR PROPERTY

Quite large amounts of land, buildings, machinery and equipment, inventories, accounts receivable, and other assets are acquired annually by business corporations in the United States in direct exchanges for shares of their common stock. In many instances, the acquisition of assets by direct exchanges is, so to say, a matter of form only, as in the incorporation of businesses formerly conducted as proprietorships and partnerships. In many others, direct exchanges for property are an outstanding means of growth for individual corporate entities; this is often so in mergers and consolidations and in the acquisition of subsidiaries by holding companies. In rarer instances, they are the means whereby corporations, large and small, come into possession of individual parcels of property.

Incorporation of Proprietorships and Partnerships

The acquisition of all the operating assets of a proprietorship or partnership by a newly formed corporation in exchange for some or all of its authorized common stock is describable as a matter of form only, since the character and scope of the enterprise, except as to its legal complexion, is unlikely to be changed by the transaction in any material way. The legal form is changed, the corporation, as an entity, now owns the assets, and the former proprietor or partners now as stockholder or stockholders own the corporation and not the assets; but policies, procedures, the owners' attitudes, and their participation in management are likely to be much the same as before.

Basically, therefore, the means of financing the corporate assets continues to be the cash invested in the proprietorship or partnership by the owners, whether derived from their original resources, accumulated through the retention of profits, or borrowed. Nevertheless, from the standpoint of *corporate* financing, it is technically true to say that the means used in acquiring assets is the direct exchange of common stock for them.

Mergers, Consolidations, and Holding Company Acquisitions

The acquisition by given corporations of all or substantially all of the operating assets of other corporations has long been a favored method of corporate growth. A corporation that wants to expand the scope of its existing kinds of operations, or to diversify its lines, has the choice of building or buying new facilities or of trying to acquire those held by other enterprises. The latter procedure has much to recommend it. It makes possible what may be called instantaneous growth, whereas the building or buying of new facilities is a slower process; it limits competition, since new productive facilities are not added to existing ones; and it eliminates uncertainties about the cost of facilities and their capacities to do particular kinds of jobs.

Exchanges of Common Stocks. Especially significant from the standpoint of finance is that the acquisition of the operating assets of other enterprises can often be arranged by a simple exchange of common stocks. "The most widely used method of financing acquisitions," says the Federal Trade Commission, "is that of exchanging the stock of the acquiring firm for the stock of the acquired firm or firms." [1] In a merger proposition, Corporation A offers a certain number of shares of its common stock in exchange for the common stock of Corporation B; if the stockholders of B accept the offer, the stock of A is distributed to them in the ratio agreed upon, the assets of B become the property of A, and B is dissolved. In a proposal for consolidation, a newly formed corporation, Corporation C, offers some of its common stock in exchange for that of A, and another block of shares in exchange for that of B; if the stockholders of A and B accept the offer, they receive C's stock in the agreed-upon ratio, the assets of their corporations are transferred to C, and their corporations are dissolved. In the holding company arrangement, Corporation A offers some of its common stock in exchange for some or all of that of Corporation B (presumably for at least enough to give it control); if the offer is accepted, the exchange is made, and A then holds the stock in B, continuing it in existence as its subsidiary.

In each of these transactions, it is clear, common stock is the financing

---

[1] Federal Trade Commission, *Report on Corporate Mergers and Acquisitions* (Washington, D.C.: U.S. Government Printing Office, 1955), p. 9.

medium—the acquiring corporation becomes the owner of aggregations of assets (or, for the holding company, gets control) by simply giving some of its common stock in direct exchange.

Advantages of Exchanges of Common Stock. But would it not be as feasible for Corporation A (whether the surviving corporation of a merger, the new corporation of a consolidation, or a holding company) to sell a new issue of its common stock to the general public or to its existing stockholders, and then to go to Corporation B or to B's stockholders with an offer to buy it or them out for cash? Many combinations are, indeed, effected as cash transactions; nevertheless, the use of cash can be much less attractive than direct exchange offers. If B were a large corporation, the large amount of new common stock that A would have to sell to raise the cash necessary for a buying-out transaction might not be salable at a reasonable price. An attempt to sell this amount might cause a sharp drop in the market price of A's stock already outstanding, while an offer of the same amount in exchange for B's stock would be unlikely to produce such a market reaction. Indeed, the prospects of a combination favorable to A, to be effected by an exchange of stock, might result in a rise in the market value of its outstanding shares. Moreover, A might expect to be able to carry through the exchange transaction without having it underwritten by investment bankers, anticipating, therefore, the avoidance of an underwriting commission such as it would expect to pay were the stock to be offered in a public sale. It might plan to hire investment bankers to solicit the stockholders of B to accept the exchange offer, but it would expect the cost of this service to be much less than an underwriting spread. Still another advantage to A would be the avoidance of upward pressure on the market price of B's stock. Were A to proceed quietly to buy up B's stock in the market, its very buying would tend to drive up the market price, making successive purchases more and more costly; and were it to go to B's stockholders individually with cash offers, the word of its activities would soon get around, and it could expect many to hold out for fancy prices.

A final advantage to A would be that many, and perhaps most, of B's stockholders would be likely to prefer stock to cash. The prospect of becoming stockholders in the merged or consolidated enterprise or in the holding company, as the case might be, could be much more attractive to them than that of getting cash for which they would have to find new investment outlets. Strongly contributing to such a preference is the fact that direct exchanges of common stock can generally be arranged on a tax-free basis under the terms of the federal income tax regulations. Thus if A were to pay cash for B's assets in an amount in excess of their book values (or other "cost bases" as prescribed in the tax regulations), the excess would be taxable income to it. Upon the distribution of this cash as a liquidating dividend by B to its stockholders, moreover, the latter would be individually subject to a capital gains tax on the amount by which the dividend exceeded the price they originally paid for their stock. On the other hand, a direct exchange arranged on a tax-free basis would result in no immediate tax liability either to Corporation B or to its stockholders.

Treatment of Debt and Preferred Stocks. All this does not mean that mergers, consolidations, and holding company acquisitions can usually be carried through without some outlay of cash. Although it is a common practice for acquiring corporations to assume the debts of acquired corporations (or simply to let them stand, as in holding company acquisitions of new subsidiaries), there may be good reasons to pay off some of these debts, particularly some or all of the current liabilities and perhaps small bond issues. If an acquired corporation has preferred stock outstanding, it must be taken care of separately. If callable, it may be paid off in cash at its redemption value; or, whether or not callable, preferred stock in the acquiring corporation, or even some of its common stock, may be offered in exchange for it.

In exchange offers, however, individual preferred stockholders have the right to refuse what is offered and to demand redemption of their stock in cash at a fair value—a value to be determined by negotiation, by an appropriate court to which an appeal is made, or by appraisers appointed by such a court. The right of the individual preferred stockholder to demand payment of the fair value in cash can be exerted even though a very large proportion of his fellow preferred stockholders approve an exchange offer. Indeed, common stockholders have a similar right of dissent—a right to demand cash even though a large majority of other common stockholders assent to an exchange offer. Thus, cash must be provided to pay off dissenting stockholders, whether preferred or common.

The fact is that many proposals for mergers, consolidations, and holding company acquisitions fall through simply because there are too many dissenters, for the managers of the acquiring corporations see that much of the advantage of direct exchange will be lost. In making exchange offers, therefore, financial managers of acquiring corporations often stipulate that the offers will be binding only if accepted by stockholders owning 85 or 90 per cent or some other high percentage of the outstanding common stock of the corporations to be acquired. Sometimes, indeed, such stipulations for high percentages of acceptances are extended to preferred stock as well. Stipulations of the kinds described are often made even though the state law may provide that the merger or other combination requires the approval of holders of only a simple majority or two thirds of the stock "entitled to vote" on the proposal.

Recent Developments. The number of mergers, consolidations, and holding company acquisitions in the period since the close of World War II has been phenomenal. Records accumulated by the Federal Trade

Commission disclose that in the 11-year period 1951–61, the 500 largest manufacturing corporations absorbed a total of 3,404 other firms, and the 50 largest merchandising corporations a total of 332 other firms. The largest 50 corporations in manufacturing accounted for 471 of the absorptions, the largest 100 for 884, and the largest 250 for 2,263; and the largest ten merchandising firms accounted for 85 and the largest 20 for 162. By industry, the greatest numbers of absorptions occurred in dairy products with 462; paper and allied products, 213; industrial chemicals, 204; grocery stores, 195; petroleum refining, 193; aerospace equipment, 170; and electrical equipment, 160. By numbers of mergers, the largest acquirers were the Beatrice Foods Company, in dairy products, with 183; the Borden Company, also in dairy products, 121; the American Marietta Company (now Martin-Marietta Corporation), chiefly in paints and varnishes, 73; Foremost Dairies, Inc., dairy products, 64; Textron, Inc., chiefly in aerospace equipment, 63; National Dairy Products Corporation, dairy products, 55; General Telephone and Electronics Company, communication equipment, 38; Genesco, Inc., footwear, 35; H. K. Porter Co., Inc., electrical equipment, 33; and the St. Regis Paper Company, paper and allied products, 33.[2]

Illustrative of the use of common stock in mergers were four acquisitions by Litton Industries, Inc., in 1962. A diversified company, with particular concentration in the manufacture of office machines, Litton was reported by the Federal Trade Commission as having acquired 27 other firms in the period of its study just referred to, 1951–61. In 1962, it issued 57,144 common shares in acquiring the Ingalls Shipbuilding Corporation; 136,000 shares in buying out the Poly-Scientific Corporation; 40,000 shares in acquiring the McKiernan-Terry Corporation; and 80,975 shares (plus $3,025,000 of debenture bonds) in taking over Emertron, Inc.

Individual Parcels of Property

In direct exchanges of common stock in connection with incorporations of proprietorships and partnerships and mergers, consolidations, and holding company acquisitions, corporations generally obtain conglomerations of assets of many kinds and values. Occasionally, however, corporations are able to obtain individual parcels of desirable property by giving some shares of their common stock in exchange. The owners of a factory site or a store building, for example, may be willing to part with it for stock, or perhaps partially for stock and partially for cash. Where it is possible to qualify such a transaction as a tax-free exchange in accordance

---

[2] House Select Committee on Small Business, *Staff Report on Mergers and Superconcentration,* 87th Cong., 2d sess. (Washington, D.C.: U.S. Government Printing Office, 1962), pp. 23–25, 46–47. This publication presents a complete listing of the acquiring and acquired firms together with details of official antitrust actions and decisions.

with the federal income tax regulations, the inducement to sell for stock can, indeed, be much stronger than one to sell for cash.

Temptation toward Generosity

When a corporation buys assets by paying cash for them, the amount of cash available for other purposes is immediately reduced; and because the "conservation of cash" is an ever-present objective of sound financial management, the corporate managers are likely to bargain closely. When, however, it buys by giving common stock in exchange, the temptation is strong to be relatively liberal in the amount of stock offered. The amount of stock that can be issued is without limit, for the articles of incorporation can be readily amended to provide for additional amounts if the quantity already authorized but unissued is insufficient for the offer. The only costs involved are the state capital stock taxes, the federal issuance tax, and minor printing and clerical expenses. In propositions for mergers, consolidations, and holding company acquisitions, moreover, generous offers should insure close to unanimous acceptance, thus reducing the amount of cash needed to pay off dissenters.

Getting something of value for pieces of paper (stock certificates) which a corporation can issue in unlimited amounts might appear to justify generosity of a very great degree; nevertheless, corporate managers have every reason to be just about as cautious in their bargaining when offering common stock as when offering cash. Too generous exchanges of common stock for property will seriously dilute the ownership interests of existing stockholders, and may give rise to great difficulties in future financing.

Dilution of Ownership Interests. How a dilution of the ownership interests of existing stockholders may occur as a result of a too-liberal issue of common stock may be illustrated in terms of a merger. Let us look simply at possibilities of dilution in stockholder claims upon earnings. Suppose that Corporation A has outstanding 500,000 shares of common stock of a book value of $50 a share upon which it has been earning a return after taxes of 12 per cent, that is, $3 million in total, or $6.00 a share. It wants to acquire the operating assets of Corporation B. The latter has outstanding 100,000 shares of common stock of a book value of $25 a share, and it has been earning a return after taxes of 20 per cent, that is, $500,000 in total, or $5.00 a share. In their anxiety to acquire the high earning power of B, and in the expectation that, through various economies of integration, the earnings of the merged companies will be substantially greater than the sum of their separate earnings, the managers of A offer one share of its stock in exchange for each share of B's. The offer is accepted unanimously by B's stockholders, and the stock of A issued to them is entered upon its books at $50 a share. This means, of course, that the value of the assets taken over from B is "written up" on A's books by the amount of $2.5 million. Accordingly, A now has outstanding 600,000 shares of a book value of $50 a share.

Now suppose that the expectations of A's managers are fulfilled: the earnings of A, as the surviving corporation of the merger, rise to $4.2 million. This amounts to $7.00 a share, so that all stockholders of A, the original ones and those who were formerly stockholders of B, are benefited. All presumably would praise A's managers for their wisdom in having pushed the merger. But suppose that the earnings of A amount to only $3.5 million, an amount equal to the sum of the formerly separate profits of A and B. This amounts to $5.83 ⅓ a share. The result is favorable to the former stockholders of B, since their earnings per share rise from $5.00 to $5.83 ⅓, but this occurs at the expense of the original stockholders of A, for their earnings per share fall from $6.00 to $5.83 ⅓.

Difficulties in Future Financing. The proposition that too generous exchanges of common stock for property may set the stage for difficulties in future financing can be illustrated in terms of the incorporation of a partnership. Since such an incorporation is likely to involve only a few people, it might appear inconsequential how much stock they decide to have their corporation issue to themselves in exchange for the partnership assets. Not so, however, should the corporation have occasion later to go to the market to raise additional funds. Let us assume that the net value of the assets of the partnership have been carried on its books at $300,000, but that the partners decide to carry them over to the corporation's books at a value of $500,000. The corporation issues them 50,000 shares of common stock of $10 par value. As it turns out, the profits of the corporation after taxes average $30,000 annually. Needing more cash, the corporate managers investigate the possibilities of selling some additional common stock to outside investors. But investment bankers and other potential investors are not likely to be interested. The rate of the corporation's earnings is only 6 per cent on the book value of its common stock investment, and that is hardly high enough to induce outsiders to part with their money. An offer of the additional common stock at a price substantially below $10 a share would promise a rate of return substantially higher than 6 per cent, but investors could be expected still to refuse to come in, upon consideration of the contingent liabilities incident to buying a par-value stock at a discount.[3]

It is likely, too, that an attempt to sell preferred stock would also fail. People interested in such investment would fear that profits would be unduly drained to maintain dividends at a given rate on the excessive amount of common stock, leaving insufficient cash and surplus for the continuance of preferred dividends in bad times. Similar fears of excessive cash drain by way of dividend payments on the common stock would probably, likewise, repel prospective investors in any bond issue that the corporation might try to sell. In any case, prospective investors in either preferred stock or bonds would be likely to be quite suspicious of the integrity and competence of the managers of a corporation (the former partners, we

---

[3] See above, pp. 373–74.

may assume) who had deliberately "watered" the common stock at the time of original issuance, that is, given it a value far in excess of the reasonable value of the assets received in exchange for it.

Justification for Some Generosity. The foregoing illustrations do not necessarily lead to the conclusion that the market value of common stock offered in direct exchanges for assets should never exceed what would be the prices of the assets in cash transactions. A more realistic conclusion is that there must be a material advantage to justify what may appear to be an "excessive" offer of common stock. Suppose, for example, that the owners of a store building that is outstandingly attractive to a certain corporation are willing to sell it for $1.9 million. This is recognized by the corporate managers as a fair price, but, in the course of negotiations, they learn that the owners would be willing to give the building in exchange for common stock of the corporation having a value of $2 million as measured by the current market price of outstanding shares. They estimate that the flotation costs of selling that much stock in a public offering would amount to around $200,000; hence they come quickly to the conclusion that getting the building for stock worth $2 million would be a much better "buy" than getting it for $1.9 million in cash.

Registration and Qualification

Transactions whereby common stock is given for isolated parcels of property and in connection with the incorporation of proprietorships and partnerships are generally classified as private; as such, they are exempted from the registration requirements of the federal Securities Act and the qualification requirements of the state blue-sky laws. Exemption is also the rule for common stock offers related to proposed mergers, consolidations, and holding company acquisitions where there are only a few stockholders in the corporations to be acquired. When, however, a large number of stockholders of other corporations are to be approached with an exchange offer, the offer becomes "public" and is, accordingly, subject to the registration requirements of the Securities Act and, in some of the states, to the qualification provisions of the blue-sky laws.

In the matter of the Securities Act, the distinction between a "few" and a "large number" of people to whom any offering of any kind of security is made is not clearly drawn. In close decisions, indeed, the test for a "public offering" tends to be more qualitative than quantitative. The investment community has generally accepted as a rule of thumb the proposition that an offering to fewer than 25 persons is private while an offering to 25 or more is public. Yet it is also a widely accepted proposition that what is public and private depends greatly upon the knowledge and investment acumen of the people to whom the offers are made. It might be expected, therefore, that an offering to 35 or 40 persons who know a great deal about the offering corporation's affairs might get by as a private transaction, while an offering to 15 or 20 persons who know little about the offeror and investment in general might be judged by the SEC to be public.

DIRECT EXCHANGES FOR SERVICES

Common stock is often given as full or partial compensation for services received by business corporations. Especially notable in this regard is the giving of common stock to promoters for their services in organizing new corporations or in arranging combinations among existing ones, to investment bankers for their services in floating new security issues, and to executive officers for their services as managers.

Compensation for Promoters

A promoter is a person who discovers what he thinks to be a favorable opportunity for a new business enterprise or for a combination of existing enterprises, and who, to exploit the discovery, takes steps to assemble and organize facilities, materials, men, and money. In the sense of this definition, most promoters obviously are individuals who set out to establish single businesses which they expect to manage indefinitely as sole owners, or, in combination with others, as partners or as corporate stockholder-managers. But there are also "outside" promoters who are interested in establishing new businesses, not in the expectation of remaining with them long as owners or managers, but in the expectation of profiting from their very work of assembling and organizing facilities, materials, men and money. The latter class includes "professional" promoters who constantly seek opportunities for new enterprises and combinations and take care, so to say, of the developmental tasks of bringing them into being, as well as others who engage only occasionally in promotional activities. The occasional promoters include, in turn, individual capitalists, investment bankers, officers of existing corporations, commercial bankers, engineers, and lawyers.

What amounts of common stock are taken by promoters who expect indefinitely to run the business corporations they establish is a matter that need not detain us. The considerations are much the same as in the incorporation of partnerships, as discussed above. Especially must such promoters keep in mind the possible difficulties in future financing should they give themselves common stock of a book value far in excess of the reasonable value of the specific assets they invest—an excess presumably to compensate themselves for their promotional services.

In a different category, the "outside" promoter has every reason to expect fair compensation for his services. He spends a considerable amount of his own money in seeking investors willing to supply funds to the proposed enterprise, looking for and interviewing prospective managerial and technical personnel, working out tentative contracts with suppliers, perhaps taking options upon factory or store sites or buildings, and so on. At the least, therefore, he expects reimbursement for such outlays, but, in addition, he demands a substantial reward for his intangible contribution in setting the stage, as it were, for a going concern. But the big problem is to determine what this contribution is worth. Should the enterprise turn out to be eminently successful, a high value of the contribution would be proved; but should it fail after a short term of operations, the promoter's contribution would be shown to be worthless. But the outcome can be known only with the passing years, while the promoter's compensation must be fixed at once if the enterprise is to be launched at all.

What the promoter gets, therefore, is likely to depend very largely upon how effective he is in persuading prospective investors and prospective managerial personnel of the soundness and the good profit-making potential of the projected enterprise. If these people are anxious to go ahead, they will surely be inclined to reward him generously; but if only lukewarm, they may feel that all he deserves is reimbursement for his out-of-pocket expenses. In any event, the more willing he is to take common stock as compensation, the more generously is he likely to be treated. New enterprises usually have great difficulties in raising enough cash for all their spending requirements; accordingly, opportunities to gain the benefits of promoters' services in direct exchange for common stock are likely to be much appreciated.

Compensation for Investment Bankers

Sometimes investment bankers are willing to take common stock as partial compensation for their services in underwriting securities issues or in selling them on best-efforts terms, especially when the issues themselves are common stocks. Such an arrangement is rare in flotations handled by the larger investment banking houses, but is frequently met in underwritings by smaller houses. Thus, it tends to be limited to flotations handled for corporations of small and medium sizes.

In a transaction of this kind, the cash commission is still likely to be substantial as a percentage of the gross proceeds, but the banker demands a portion of the common stock issue as additional compensation. Even though corporate managers may feel that these demands are exorbitant, they may acquiesce if a lack of adequate cash threatens the very survival of their enterprise, and if they do not have access to alternative sources of supply. The banker, in turn, may sell his allotment along with the balance of the issue, thus realizing the additional compensation in cash immediately, or hold it for his own account as a continuing investment.

In its special study of the securities markets published in 1963, the SEC found that, in addition to cash compensation, stock or options to buy stock were given to investment bankers in 34.7 per cent of the common stock issues of more than $300,000 registered in 1960 for cash sale through bankers, and in 41.6 per cent of those registered for cash sale through bankers in 1961, as well as for 46.0 per cent of issues of $300,000 or less in 1960 and 70.8 per cent of issues of this size offered for cash sale through bankers in 1961. The SEC noted that income tax considerations often prompt investment bankers to make some payment for stock or options to try to qualify their acquisitions as "investments" rather than as "compensation." It also pointed out that, in some instances, the investment bankers got stock or options in connection with "interim financing" preceding the making of public offerings. Referring to stock acquired by underwriters in some of the 22 common stock offerings for cash in the period 1959–61 which it selected for intensive study, it said:

> It is not unusual for an underwriting firm to purchase a substantial block of stock from the issuer or the selling stockholders prior to or simultaneous with the offering, at prices significantly below the offering price. In connection with the Arco offering of 170,000 shares at a price of $5 per share, Kletz, who managed the underwriting, purchased 10,000 additional shares at 50 cents per share. In the Gremar offering of 100,000 shares at $4.25 a share, Blauner, the managing underwriter, purchased 7,500 shares for [*sic*—read "from"] the president and sole stockholder at a price of $1 per share. In 4 others of the 22 new issues, the managing underwriters purchased cheap stock, which was placed either in account of the firm or principals of the firm and their associates. In all six cases in which cheap stock was purchased, the purchase price was less than 50 percent of the offering price and in two cases it was less than 10 percent.

On the other hand, the SEC noted the stated policy of some investment banking houses not to accept "cheap stock" or options as compensation for their services, adding: "By and large, these were the larger and older firms, which had comparatively rigorous standards as to the kind of issues which they would handle." [4]

Compensation for Managerial Services

Shares of common stock have often been given in generous quantities as supplemental compensation or bonuses to the top executives of many of our larger corporations. However, the practice has become much less common than it used to be; by reason of tax-saving possibilities, it has been largely supplanted by the giving of stock options to executives. But such companies as General Motors, DuPont, General Electric, Federated Department Stores, and Container Corporation still have provisions for stock bonuses in addition to stock option plans. For example, General Motors reports that 3,849,775 shares were awarded to executives in the period 1959–61. In its system, bonuses may be distributed either in cash or in common stock as decided by its Salary and Bonus Committee which is composed of five directors who themselves are not eligible for bonus payments.

Competition among corporations for executive talent of high quality tends to be extremely keen continuously, for, as is often said, such talent

---

[4] Securities and Exchange Commission, *Report of Special Study of the Securities Markets*, House Doc. No. 95, Pt. 1, 88th Cong., 1st sess. (Washington, D.C.: U.S. Government Printing Office, 1963), pp. 506–8, 510–11, 619.

is all too rare. It is not surprising, therefore, that bidding for top-quality executives often gets quickly into high figures. Such heady bidding convinces most boards of directors that they must be satisfied with somewhat less talented executives; but some hope to remain in the running by offering common stock or stock options in addition to cash. The board of a given corporation may decide that a cash salary of $300,000 for a most desirable president would put too great a strain upon the corporation's cash resources, but that a salary of $200,000 in cash plus common stock worth $100,000 could be safely managed.

As in direct exchanges of common stock for noncash property, corporations are subject to temptations toward generosity when they find it possible to use common stock to buy high-quality executive services. There is a temptation to think of the issuance of common stock as costless, except for issuance taxes and a few other minor expenses—as it certainly is from the standpoint of cash drain, but as it certainly is not from the standpoint of the interests of existing stockholders and the possibilities of success in future financing. Insufficient weight may be given to the fact that the issuance of common stock to executives dilutes the ownership interests of other stockholders, as well as to the probability that the threat of continued dilution will weaken the attractiveness of the common stock in future public offerings.

All this does not mean that it is bad policy to pay executives partially in common stock. Whether the policy is good or bad depends upon the circumstances of the individual corporation. If a man is really worth a given amount of cash plus a given array of claims to voting power, dividends, and assets, as represented by a certain amount of common stock—determined, let us say, by competition for him in the market—that is what he should get. But corporations often do a poor job in defending human valuations of this kind when they explain to other stockholders, labor leaders, congressional committees, and the public at large that stock is given to executives to induce them to exert their best efforts in the corporations' behalf. They thereby imply that the executives are worth only the cash portion of their salaries, but that this portion would be insufficient to induce them to exert their best efforts. Moreover, generous cash-and-stock salary and bonus payments—or, for that matter, generous salaries in cash exclusively—always justify suspicions of bad policy when they are determined by the very executives who receive them, as when they constitute a majority of the board of directors and when the board, because of a wide scattering of stockholdings, is self-perpetuating.

Registration and Qualification

The giving of common stock for the services of promoters and executives is ordinarily a private transaction not subject to the registration requirements of the federal Securities Act or to the qualification requirements of the state blue-sky laws. On the other hand, if common stock given to investment bankers is to be reoffered by them in interstate commerce to many buyers, registration according to the terms of the Securities Act is required; likewise, the qualification provisions of the blue-sky laws generally apply. When, however, the common stock received by investment bankers as compensation is simply a portion of an issue for which they are making a public offering, the registration and qualification of the whole issue automatically, so to say, take care of the portion allotted to them.

OFFERINGS BY OPTIONS

As a means of providing partial or supplemental compensation to investment bankers and executive personnel, the issuance of *stock options* is much more popular than the giving of common stock itself. Promoters, too, are often rewarded with options, in lieu of common stock or in addition to it; and options often make possible arrangements of greatest convenience with individual capitalists and institutional investors that are willing to advance substantial amounts of money on what is essentially an equity basis.

Nature of Options

A stock option is a contract whereby a corporation agrees to sell a specified number of shares of its common stock to a designated person or institution at a stated price. Usually the contract stipulates a time period, such as two, five, or ten years, within which the option must be exercised; it states that, at the end of the indicated time period, the option becomes void. Options are usually nontransferable, so that only the person or institution named in the contract can exercise the right to buy.

Disadvantageous Aspects of Options

Stock options are an uncertain means of financing. If the market price of a stock rises to and continues at levels above the price designated in the options, the option holders will surely buy, but just when they will buy—how long they will hold out for still better market prices—is problematical. Corporations that are growing rapidly and that, accordingly, tend to suffer a chronic shortage of cash welcome the additional amounts that flow in through the exercise of options; but those whose cash resources are already adequate may be able to use the inflowing cash only uneconomically. If, for example, a corporation of the latter class retires bonds with cash received through the exercise of options, it loses the advantages of trading on the equity. If the existing stock had been earning a return of, say, 12 per cent, and the bonds carried an interest rate of 5 per cent, the issuance of the new stock would mean a dilution of the earning power of the old. There is also uncertainty in the possibility that the market price of outstanding stock may never rise above the option price, so that the options prove to be no source of cash at all.

Dilution of the ownership interests of existing stockholders always stands as a probable disadvantage of the use of stock options, not only in the sense of using cash uneconomically as illustrated above, but in the more general sense of weakening claims to voting power, assets, and earnings. For illustration, assume that the option price of a stock is $50 a share and that the market price goes to $80. The market evaluates the claims attaching to each share at $80, and the existing stockholder has reason to feel that his ownership interests per share are worth that much. But along come the option holders with their privilege of buying equal shares in ownership interests for only $50, and sales to them obviously reduce the per-share interests of the other stockholders—a reduction which, if not offset by other market forces, should be matched by a decline in the market value of the stock.

The issuance of stock options may also have unfavorable repercussions upon common stock financing through other channels. A corporation that has been generous in issuing options is likely to find its existing stockholders and the investing public as a whole much less interested in buying new offerings than they might otherwise be. As many of these people understand the theory of dilution, they can be expected to make their investment decisions accordingly. Why, they may ask themselves, should they buy new stock at $70 or $80 a share when sizable sales to option holders at $50 and resales by them will exert significant downward pressures upon the market price? That investors should know about the danger of dilution through the exercise of options is indicated in the requirements of the federal Securities Act. Registration statements and prospectuses filed in accordance with that legislation must state what options the corporation has already issued or is to issue in connection with the security for which the registration is made, their terms, and the names and addresses of all persons who have received or are to receive more than 10 per cent of the total.

Popularity of Options

Considering the potential disadvantages to corporations in the use of options, one may wonder why they have been so popular. A reason applicable in some cases is undoubtedly the idea that the giving of options is a costless procedure—but the earlier discussion of the giving of stock itself for services has indicated how erroneous this notion can be. Another reason is compulsion of a sort. Corporate managements find themselves in weak bargaining positions, and they give options to get what they want though they would much prefer not to do so. This must be true in many instances where options are given to promoters and investment bankers. Still another reason, apparent in at least a small minority of situations, is self-serving, as when corporate officers who are directors having *de facto* independence of the stockholders authorize the issuance of options to themselves ostensibly as partial compensation for their services. But surely the most important reason must be a conviction of corporate managements that they are getting full value for the options—that the disadvantages of options are fairly balanced by the worth of the money and services acquired.

Options as Compensation

Compensation for Promoters and Bankers. Sometimes stock options are the sole reward received by promoters for their services in developing new enterprises and combinations; but, more commonly, they are received in addition to cash—cash in an amount at least sufficient to reimburse the promoters for their out-of-pocket expenses—or in addition to some shares of the common stock itself, or in addition to both cash and some common stock. When stock options are given to investment bankers for their services in connection with the flotation of securities, almost invariably they are supplemental to cash commissions or spreads. In some cases, the bargaining position of promoters and bankers is so strong that they demand and get stock options sufficient to enable them to buy control in the corporations involved. If the ventures turn out successfully, they can exercise the options and get control; and if the ventures are failures, they simply allow the options to expire.

In the statistics of "noncash compensation" reported by the SEC in its special study of the securities markets published in 1963, no distinction was made between the sale of "cheap stock" to investment bankers and their taking of options. However, for the 22 issues of common stock offered for cash sale in the period 1959–61 that the SEC selected for intensive study, it found that "the managing underwriter or persons connected with it" obtained options in ten. In only one of these ten instances, however, were the options exercisable at a price below the public offering price. The SEC described this case as follows:

This was the Custom Components offering of 165,000 shares at an offering price of $3. In this instance, the principal stockholder of the issuer granted to the managing underwriter, Manufacturers Securities Corp., warrants to purchase up to 16,500 shares at a price of $1 per share. The grant of the warrants was conditioned upon a successful offering, 1,000 warrants being granted for every 10,000 shares sold by the underwriter. For these warrants, the underwriter paid 1 mill each, or a total of $16.50.

The report of the SEC then continued as follows:

Although there was only one example among the 22 issues, the granting of warrants to the underwriter exercisable below the offering price was not at all uncommon during 1959–61. For example, in the offering of 150,000 shares of the common stock of Admiral Plastics Corp. on January 11, 1960, at $4, the managing underwriters received options to purchase 10,000 shares at 75 cents per share. Similarly, the managing underwriter of Astrex, Inc., which offered 100,000 shares to the public on September 20, 1960, at $4, received warrants to purchase 12,500 shares at a price of $2.25 per share. The study of underwriters' compensation conducted by the New York Stock Exchange revealed that out of 186 issues in 1960 that were reviewed, 36 (or 19.5 percent) involved warrants exercisable below the offering price, and of the 342 offerings in 1961, 61 (or 17.8 percent) involved warrants of this type. The percentage for the first quarter of 1962 dropped steeply to 1.7 percent.[5]

Compensation for Executives. The granting of stock options to corporate executives as supplements to their cash salaries has had a phenomenal development in recent years. Hundreds of corporations have fallen quickly into line in setting up programs for the awarding of option privileges to their officers and other "key employees"—a fact indicated by total registrations of $1,011 million of securities with the SEC in 1962 for delivery against employee stock options.[6] A very great proportion of the large corporations listed in Tables 14–1, 15–5, 15–6, and 15–7 presented in Chapters 14 and 15 reported stock-option programs in effect at the balance sheet dates indicated in those tables. For example, DuPont reported that it was reserving 1,621,237 shares for delivery upon executive options; United States Steel, 705,070 shares; Standard Oil (New Jersey), 1,009,955 shares; Union Carbide, 559,397 shares; and Gulf Oil, 746,001 shares. The General Electric Company has reported that of a total of 3,581,539 shares made available to its officers and "key employees" in the ten-year period 1953–62, options for 2,486,954 shares had been exercised by the end of 1962.[7] Although, for the individual corporation, the shares offered for purchase on option typically amount to only a very small fraction of total shares outstanding, generosity in granting options to executives sometimes seems to get out of hand, so that dangers of dilution are multiplied. The SEC has cited two instances as follows:

. . .Seventeen of the 22 issuers instituted stock-option plans shortly before or at the time of their public offerings. A comparison of the number of shares of outstanding stock of some of the issuers with the number of shares subject to option reflects the importance of the stock-option plans. For example, Geophysics' stock-option plans covered 143,209 shares, or over 35 percent of its outstanding stock, and Universal Electronics Laboratories Corp's. stock-option plan covered 60,000 shares, or 31 percent of its outstanding stock.[8]

Given the idea that stock bonuses, options, or something else must be given as supplements to cash salaries in the fierce competition for executives of top quality, it is not difficult to understand why there has been such a big swing to options. The reason stands out clearly: the treatment of options and the gains from their exercise in the federal income tax regulations. If options are properly qualified as "restricted options" according to the terms of the Internal Revenue Code, the executive has no

---

[5] *Ibid.*, p. 507.

[6] Securities and Exchange Commission, *Statistical Bulletin*, July, 1963, p. 15. Since the registrations were for delivery against *stock* options, one can be sure that the "securities" registered were exclusively or almost exclusively common stocks.

[7] General Electric Company, *Annual Report*, 1962, p. 27.

[8] Securities and Exchange Commission, *Report of Special Study*, p. 492.

income to report upon receiving options, and, what is much more important, he can easily manage to have the tax upon any subsequent gain—derived through the exercise of the options and the sale of the stock—limited at the maximum to the long-term capital gains rate of 25 per cent. By contrast, if he receives shares of common stock itself as supplementary compensation, he must report them as taxable income at their "fair market value"—income taxable at the steeply progressive rates applicable to "ordinary" income.

Illustration. Suppose, for example, that Jones, a man of great executive abilities, has the pleasant task of deciding which of two liberal offers for his services would be most rewarding in the long run. Corporation A offers him a cash salary of $200,000 and shares of common stock having a "fair market value" of $100,000; and Corporation B offers a cash salary of the same amount plus options to buy 4,000 shares of its common stock at $38 a share. The present market value of B's stock is $40 a share. At the moment, then, the additional compensation that B is offering appears to be worth only about $8,000. But prospects are excellent that within a few years the market value of B's stock will rise to at least 48. Jones would thus have good reasons to anticipate being able to derive a long-term capital gain of $40,000 by buying 4,000 shares at 38 for a total of $152,000 through the exercise of the options, holding the stock for more than six months, and then selling it at 48 for a total of $192,000. Should Jones, therefore, be quite satisfied as to the gain prospect, he would surely strongly favor B's offer. Assuming that he is married, has three dependent children, has no other income, and has deductible expenses of $20,000, his personal income tax (computed at the rates in effect in 1963) on a salary of $200,000 together with shares of stock having a market value of $100,000 would be $203,170, leaving him with income after tax of $96,830. In relation to B's offer, the tax on the $200,000 salary (the options not being taxable when received) would be $114,720, leaving him with income after tax of $85,280. But if later he actually derived a profit of $40,000, the tax upon it at the long-term capital gains rate of 25 per cent would be, of course, only $10,000, leaving him with $30,000 to be added to the $85,280 cleared earlier.[9]

Qualifications for Restricted Options. For a corporation to be in a position to make its offer attractive, and for the executive to be certain that his gains will be taxable only as long-term capital gains, both the corporation and the executive must be careful that all option transactions satisfy the rules laid down for "restricted stock options" in the Internal Revenue Code. These rules are as follows: (1) the option must be granted

---

[9] How advantageous the option route can be was indicated in a proxy statement of Magnavox Company in which its president was reported to have exercised options to buy 138,915 shares at $4.43 a share on February 22, 1962, a day on which the closing price on the New York Stock Exchange was $40.25! *The Wall Street Journal,* April 18, 1963, p. 15.

in connection with the optionee's employment; (2) the option price must be not less than 95 per cent of the fair market price of the stock at the time the option is granted; (3) the option must be exercised while the optionee is still in the employ of the corporation granting it or within three months after he leaves its employ; (4) the stock obtained through the exercise of the option must be held for more than six months, and the time of sale must be at least two years from the date upon which the option was granted;[10] (5) the option must be exercised within ten years from the date it was granted; (6) the option must be nontransferable during the optionee's lifetime; and (7) the optionee and his family, at the time the option is granted, must not own more than 10 per cent of the voting power of all classes of the corporation's stock. Rule 7, however, does not apply if the option price is at least 110 per cent of the fair market price of the stock at the time the option is granted and if the option is exercised within five years.

   Evaluation of Option Granting to Executives.   What was said earlier on the appropriateness of corporate policies of giving common stock as partial compensation to executives is clearly applicable to the giving of stock options. The possibilities of dilution and of difficulties in future common stock financing should surely be carefully weighed by boards of directors in considering the grant of options. But if access at a price to claims to voting power, dividends, and assets, in addition to cash compensation, is not beyond the worth of the services of particular executives, there certainly is every justification for giving it. Nevertheless, justification is hardly proved by claims that stock options will prod executives to exert their best efforts so as to cause the market price of the stock to rise and thus to increase the value of the options.

Options for Individual and Institutional Investors

   Newly established corporations, operating corporations of small and medium sizes, and others that have little or no access to the general markets for outside equity funds are sometimes able to acquire such funds direct from individual and institutional investors through arrangements in which stock options play a significant role. The individual and institutional investors include wealthy capitalists, partners and members of investment banking houses, officers of corporations other than those actually seeking the funds, trustees of family estates, pension funds, investment companies, so-called "venture capital" firms, investment banking houses that may be interested in investing for their own accounts rather than for resale as in normal underwriting procedures, and nonfinancial business corporations that hold cash in excess of what they need for their own

---

[10] To illustrate, profit on stock sold on August 1, 1964, would qualify as a long-term capital gain if the stock was bought through the exercise of options on or before January 31, 1964, *and if* the options were originally granted on or before August 1, 1962.

customary operations. The list of investors is rather long, but the total amounts of money they are willing and able to make available on an equity basis are quite small in relation to the volume of requests they are likely to get from the classes of corporations mentioned. Hence the much-heard plaint of a chronic shortage of outside equity funds for "small business."

When individual and institutional investors advance equity funds, they seek every possible tax saving. The investor wants his rewards to be taxable chiefly as long-term capital gains rather than as ordinary income. His advances to a corporation, therefore, might be made entirely in the form of loans; but he would receive from the corporation, not only its notes or bonds as evidence of its obligation to pay, but also options for the purchase of common stock. Because he would probably want to be in a position to take control of the corporation to protect his investment, he would be likely to demand options for sufficient shares to give control, and at a total price not exceeding the amount of the loans. Then should things go badly, he could demand the repayment of the loans, taking as much on them as the corporation would be able to pay, thereby minimizing his losses; should he think the prospects good but not with the existing management, he could simultaneously call the loans and exercise the options, paying for the stock with the loan repayments, and substitute his own management; and should all go well, he could exercise the options, with or without calling the loans, hold the stock for more than six months, and then sell for a profit that would be taxable as a long-term capital gain.[11]

One might inquire why the investor would not, in the first place, take a sufficient amount of common stock to give him control—why, when advancing what would really be equity funds despite the loan technique, he would not take an equity security. The fact is that individual and institutional investors, in making advances of equity funds to the classes of corporations we are considering, often do take common stock, or preferred stock plus common stock options, or preferred stock convertible at the investor's option into common stock. As a rule, the capital gains goal can be thus achieved as well as in the manner described. But the loan-and-stock-option procedure has at least two advantages over the immediate taking of equity securities. One of these advantages is obvious: should the investor want to pull out because things are going badly, his claim for loan repayment would rank ahead of the claims of stockholders, that is, the original owners of the corporation to which he granted the loans. The other is that interest paid to him by the corporation on his loans—which, incidentally, would be likely to be charged at a moderate rate, such as 5 or 6 per cent—would be deductible by the corporation as an

---

[11] An alternative procedure would be for the investor to have the corporation issue him bonds convertible into common stock at his option. This would give him about the same degree of flexibility as the stock option arrangement.

expense in its income tax return, whereas dividends paid on stock that he might have taken would not be deductible.[12]

OFFERINGS BY STOCK-PURCHASE WARRANTS

Quite similar to stock options in character, but differing in use, are stock-purchase warrants. Like an option, a stock-purchase warrant is a contract whereby a corporation agrees to sell a designated number of shares of its common stock at a stipulated price to the person or institution to which it is issued, and, sometimes, to anybody else to whom the original holder may assign it. Thus, three kinds of contracts for the delivery of common stock at stated prices are recognized: (1) subscription warrants whereby existing stockholders are privileged to buy on a pro rata basis, as analyzed in the preceding chapter; (2) stock options, as discussed in the preceding division of this chapter; and (3) stock-purchase warrants, to be discussed in this division. In practice, the three designations are sometimes used interchangeably; nevertheless, restricting the use of each term to a specific class of transactions, as indicated above, should doubtless aid understanding.

Warrants for Preferred Stockholders and Bondholders

Sometimes corporations attach stock-purchase warrants to their issues of preferred stock or bonds or both to enhance the salability of these kinds of securities. Weaknesses in a corporation's credit standing or earnings record may preclude a sale of preferred stock or bonds on what it would consider satisfactory terms; accordingly, it casts about to find a "sweetener" or two to add to its proposed issue. Stock-purchase warrants serve as such a "sweetener." The prospective buyer of preferred stock is offered not only a dividend at a given rate and the other ordinary rights of preferred stockholders, but also the right to buy at a stated price a certain number of shares of common stock; or a similar right to buy is offered to the prospective buyer of bonds in addition to a promise of interest at a designated rate and the repayment of principal at a specific time. Stock-purchase warrants are said to give the preferred stockholder or bondholder a speculative interest in the progress of a corporation over and above his ordinary interests; thus, it is thought that many investors who would not buy for the "ordinary interests" alone may be persuaded to buy the "package" of combined interests.

The price at which common stock is offered in stock-purchase warrants is usually well above the market price prevailing at the time the warrants are issued. If a corporation is unable to sell preferred stock or bonds without adding "sweeteners," the market price of its common stock is almost surely to be depressed, and it would not want to sell common

---

[12] See *Financing Small Business: Report to the Committees on Banking and Currency and the Select Committees on Small Business by the Federal Reserve System* (85th Cong., 2d sess.), Parts 1 and 2 (Washington, D.C.: U.S. Government Printing Office, 1958), pp. 525–38, 541–47, especially pp. 543–44.

at the depressed level. Whether or not, therefore, it will ever sell any common stock through the exercise of the stock-purchase warrants depends upon the subsequent behavior of the market price of the stock. There is some danger that, because it faces difficulty in selling the preferred stock or bonds, it will be overgenerous in the terms of its stock-purchase warrants, so that, if the market price of the common does rise substantially and the warrant are exercised, the ownership of other common stockholders will be unreasonably diluted. To provide some protection on this score, warrants often set a scale of rising prices at which, from period to period, the common stock can be bought—as, for example, at one level during the first five years from the date of the issuance of the preferred stock or bonds, at a higher level during the next five years, and so on. On the other side, however, it can be argued that if a corporation is enabled to carry on in a difficult situation by means of money supplied by buyers of preferred stock or bonds, and if it is quite successful in carrying on, these selfsame buyers deserve to be amply rewarded.[13]

Other Uses of Warrants

Issued to Institutional Investors. Corporations frequently issue stock-purchase warrants to institutional investors, especially life insurance companies, as partial compensation for long-term loans arranged for privately. In addition to interest received on the corporations' notes, therefore, the institutional investors get speculative interests with possibilities of further profits.

Inducements in Merger Proposals. Occasionally, corporations that want to absorb other enterprises in mergers offer warrants as part of the inducement to securities holders in the latter to accept the merger proposals. For example, the Symington-Wayne Corporation, in its annual report for 1962, stated that it had outstanding warrants to buy 263,963 shares of its common stock. These warrants were issued in 1958 when what was then the Symington-Gould Corporation absorbed the Wayne Pump Company. For each of their shares, the common stockholders of Wayne Pump were offered 2½ common shares in Symington-Wayne (the name being changed in connection with the merger) and a warrant to buy one share of its common stock at $10 to March 31, 1963, and at $15 thereafter to March 31, 1968.

Warrants as "Dividends." Occasionally, too, corporations distribute stock-purchase warrants as "dividends" to their common stockholders. But these are hardly dividends in any real sense of the word.[14] It is rather difficult to say what a corporation accomplishes by such a distribution,

---

[13] For a further discussion of the use of stock-purchase warrants in connection with preferred stock issues, see pp. 546–48, and in connection with bond issues, pp. 711–13.

[14] At any rate, the author finds no justification for including such distributions in his classification of dividends in a later chapter. See pp. 587–88.

although one can see possibilities of some benefit to the stockholder. If the corporation really wants to sell additional stock to its existing stockholders, it can do so at any time by making a rights offering. But "dividends" in warrants may contribute to stockholder happiness at the expense of speculators. If speculators bid up the price of warrants in the market, if the stockholders sell their warrants, and if the warrants are never exercised because the stock price does not go high enough to make this advantageous, the stockholders succeed in getting some of the speculators' cash "for free," as it were. But if the warrants are exercised by the speculators, what the stockholders got in selling them turns out to be compensation for the dilution in ownership interests that they suffer.

By way of examples, the Essex Chemical Company distributed a warrant "dividend" to its common stockholders in the spring of 1963, and in August the Consolidated Oil & Gas Corporation announced a similar distribution. For each five shares held, the Essex stockholder got the privilege of buying one new share at $4.50 in the period from April 30, 1963, to April 29, 1966. The Consolidated Oil stockholder was to get the right to buy one new share for each 25 shares held.

Warrants in Reorganizations. As the term is used in finance, a corporate *reorganization* is a comprehensive recasting of the financial structure of a corporation, necessitated by actual or threatened insolvency, and designed to rehabilitate it so that it can continue operating. In a reorganization, creditors and stockholders are subject to strong pressure to yield some of their rights, for the alternative is the liquidation of assets and the paying off of claims in the order of priority. Most reorganizations of corporations that have more than a few creditors and stockholders are reorganizations in bankruptcy, effected in accordance with the provisions of the federal bankruptcy statutes. The general rule in reorganizations in bankruptcy is that the acceptance of a plan of reorganization by the holders of two thirds of the claims of any class of creditors makes it binding on all the creditors of that class, provided that the plan is also approved by the court having jurisdiction; and that, with similar court approval, the acceptance of a plan by holders of one half of the shares of any class of stock makes it binding upon all the stockholders of that class. Accordingly, some creditors and stockholders who might prefer liquidation may be compelled by law, as it were, to go the other way and yield some of their rights.

In a reorganization, then, the goal is to reshuffle the claims of creditors and stockholders in such a way that the rehabilitated corporation will be able to continue operations without further imminent danger of insolvency and, indeed, with a fair credit standing. Important to this goal is the scaling down or elimination of the claims of creditors and stockholders to periodic payments of interest and dividends, as well as claims to the principal of obligations, as with short-term creditors and bondholders, or unpaid accumulated dividends, as with preferred stockholders. Accordingly, plans of reorganization call for such adjustments as the reduction of the rate of interest on bonds, making some or all of this interest contingent upon earnings, reducing the principal of one or more classes of debts, requiring creditors of one or more classes to take preferred or common stock in exchange for their claims, having preferred stockholders give up their claims to unpaid accumulated dividends, having them give up their cumulative preferred for noncumulative preferred or common, and requiring common stockholders to give up their holdings for a much smaller number of shares. The strongest claimants, such as mortgage bondholders, and other secured creditors, are called upon to make the least sacrifice, if any, and the "residual" claimants, the common stockholders, the greatest sacrifice. Indeed, such a treatment of claims may be said to be required by the "absolute priority rule," which has, in effect, been established for corporate reorganizations by the Supreme Court. By this rule, the respective classes of stockholders, as junior claimants, can be permitted to participate in a reorganized corporation only if the rights of the senior claimants, in the order of their priority, are fully taken care of.

All of which leads up to the use of stock-purchase warrants. Warrants are occasionally given in corporate reorganizations fully or partially to replace claims that must be given up. These claims may appear to be worthless on the basis of the present liquidating values of the assets, but not necessarily on the basis of what the value of the assets might prove to be should the reorganization be successful with the earning power of the corporation restored. By means of stock-purchase warrants, a stake in this potentiality of restored earning power can be given. If earnings are restored, and the market price of the common stock rises accordingly, the holders of warrants can buy in on favorable terms; if these developments do not take place, the worthlessness of the holders' original claims is definitely established.

Decisions about the classes of claimants who are to get warrants, if any, depend upon the severity of the situation facing the corporation that seeks to reorganize. In a less severe case, unsecured creditors may get preferred stock, the preferred stockholders may get common stock, and the common stockholders may have to be satisfied with warrants. In a more severe one, the unsecured creditors may get common stock, and both the preferred and common stockholders may only receive warrants, with the preferred getting a more generous allotment than the common. In situations of even greater severity, it should be added, the common stockholders, or both the preferred and common stockholders, may receive nothing. (This was the fate of all stockholders in the bankruptcies of the Davega Stores Corporation and Dejay Stores, Inc., both of which were terminated in 1963. Dejay had only common stock outstanding, but Davega had both common and preferred.) In some reorganizations, warrants have been given in partial satisfaction of claims; for example, preferred stockholders have received some common stock plus warrants to buy some additional shares of common.

EMPLOYEE STOCK-OWNERSHIP PROGRAMS

Apart from the stock given to corporate executives as bonuses and the very large amounts offered to them on the basis of restricted options, substantial volumes of common stock are sold direct to employees outside the executive classes, as well as indirectly, so to say, for the benefit of both executives and the rank and file of employees.

Direct offerings of common stock are made by many corporations to the general run of their employees not ranked as executives in "stock-purchase plans" and "savings plans." In both kinds of plans, stock is usually made available in stated amounts at prices below the going market prices. But in a stock-purchase plan, the corporation's only contribution in addition to the "bargain" price is its absorption of the administrative expenses of managing the program; while in a savings plan, it contributes stock or cash to supplement the employee contributions in addition to "picking up the tab" for administrative expenses.

Indirect sales of stock for the benefit of employees occur in profit-sharing and pension plans. A limited number of corporations have profit-sharing plans to which they contribute shares of their common stock or in which their cash contributions are invested in their own common stock; and many have pension plans in some of which the cash they contribute is partially invested in their own common stock. Some of the profit-sharing plans in which common stock is held provide for distribution to the eligible employees annually, and some prescribe a "holding period" of several years before distribution is made. Other profit-sharing plans are really pension plans, with distribution to begin for each employee at the time of his retirement, and, of course, other kinds of pension plans also provide for distributions beginning at the time of retirement, usually monthly cash payments to supplement benefits due under the federal Old Age and Survivors Insurance System. The book value of corporations' own common stock held by their pension funds at the end of 1962, including pension funds of the profit-sharing variety, was reported at $1,167 million out of a total book value of common stock holdings of $13,920 million, with the respective market values at $2,531 million and $18,725 million.[15]

Although some of the common stock sold to employees, contributed

---

[15] This refers to assets held by "trusteed" pension funds as distinct from "insured" funds. For insured funds, corporate cash contributions are turned over to and invested by life insurance companies which contract to pay the pensions much as they pay benefits on other kinds of insurance and annuity contracts. For the report on trusteed funds, see Securities and Exchange Commission, *Statistical Bulletin*, June, 1963, pp. 26–33.

to their savings funds, and acquired for pension funds is bought in the open market, most of it is hitherto unissued stock. Accordingly, the sales of unissued stock are a means of corporate financing as well as a means of providing "fringe benefits" to employees.

The terms upon which common stock is offered in employee stock-purchase and savings plans are generally tailored to qualify the offerings as restricted stock options, so that the tax concessions of the Internal Revenue Code, as described earlier in this chapter, can be gained. Likewise, the pension programs are patterned to make them "qualified plans" eligible for other kinds of tax concessions under the Code.

Development of Stock-Purchase and Savings Plans

Although the beginnings of employee stock-ownership plans are dated from the plan set up in 1901 by the newly formed United States Steel Corporation, the most enthusiastic early development came in the 1920's, particularly in the later years of that decade, in line, one might say, with the stock market boom of that period. Employee plans were widely hailed as the dawning of a new day in labor-management relationships: the employee was to become a capitalist, to be sympathetic toward the problems of management, and, presumably, to tone down his demands as a laborer. It should have been apparent, however, that the ownership of one or two or three thousand dollars' worth of stock, paying dividends of, perhaps, 6 per cent, could hardly cause many employees to neglect their interests as workers in favor of their interests as capitalists. At any rate, the stock market crash of 1929 put an end to many of the more grandiose expectations of the plans, as well as to many of the plans themselves.

A rather strong revival of interest in employee stock-ownership plans has taken place in the period since the close of World War II, especially since about 1950. As in the 1920's, the sustained upward push of stock prices has undoubtedly been a contributing factor. While most of the early plans, including those that mushroomed in the 1920's, were straight employee-purchase plans, many of the new postwar plans have been of the "savings" or "thrift" variety. In a study made in 1961, the New York Stock Exchange found that 114 of its listed corporations had purchase plans in which 530,000 employees were participating; 80 firms had savings plans with participation by 753,000 employees; and 39 corporations had profit-sharing plans in which 260,000 employees were participating. In all, about one fifth of the listed corporations had an employee-ownership plan of one of these three types, and, by industry, the leaders were public utility corporations and producers of petroleum and natural gas. It was found that in some of the savings plans, the employee contributions were invested solely in U.S. savings bonds; in some, partially in savings bonds and partially in the corporations' common stocks; and in others, entirely in the corporations' common stocks.[16] In virtually all savings plans, however, the corporation's contribution is made in its common stock or in cash to be invested in its common stock.

Features of Employee Stock-Ownership Plans

Stock-Purchase Plans. Taking a crosscut view, the principal features of employee stock-purchase plans are the following: (1) From time to time, perhaps annually, the corporation makes an offering of a specific number of shares to its employees. (2) The employee must have some minimum period of service to the corporation, such as six months or a year, to be eligible to subscribe. (3) Each employee is limited in the number of shares of each offering to which he may subscribe, the limitations being based upon criteria such as wage and salary levels, years of employment, and type of work done, or a combination of criteria. In many plans, subscriptions may not exceed 10 per cent of the employee's annual salary or wages. Often, senior executives and other "key employees" to whom ordinary stock options are given are not eligible, and in some the eligible employee may not subscribe to a new offering if he has not completed payment upon an earlier subscription. (4) The price at which the stock is offered is usually below the market price when the offering is made, but not below 85 per cent of the market price, so that the tax concession of the Internal Revenue Code will not be lost.[16a] (5) Payment is normally to be made in instalments by payroll deduction. In some plans, the employee may add cash payments from other sources. (6) The payment is to be completed within a period generally varying between six months and two years. (7) While the employee's payment is being accumulated, the corporation normally pays interest upon the balances in his "account." (8) The employee may cancel his purchase commitment at any time. He is entitled to the balance in his account, including interest as credited, and he may take this in cash or use it to buy outright the smaller number of shares it will cover. A cancellation of the commitment and the settlement are usually handled in the same way for an employee who quits or is fired. (9) Stock certificates are delivered to the employee only when he has paid his subscription in full.

Savings Plans. The features of savings plans differ in important details from those of stock-purchase plans, because of some differences in

---

[16] New York Stock Exchange, *The Exchange*, September, 1961, pp. 17–18.

[16a] It was indicated previously that, for restricted stock options, the offering price must be at least 95 per cent of the market value of the stock at the time it is offered in order to qualify subsequent gains on sale as long-term capital gains. However, offerings of stock to executives and other employees can still qualify as restricted options under the Internal Revenue Code if the offering price is between 85 per cent and 95 per cent of the stock's market value at the time an offer is made. But if the offering price falls within this range, subsequent gains on sale are treated as ordinary income up to the amount of the difference between the offering price and the market value at the time of the offer, and only the gains in excess of this amount are treated as long-term capital gains.

goals, but especially because the corporations make substantial contributions to the accumulations of the savings plans. Again, let us have a cross-section view, as follows: (1) The corporation announces that, for the year, it will accept employee contributions to the savings fund up to a stated total amount, and that it itself will add to the fund amounts equal to 20, 25, or 50 per cent or some other percentage of the employee contributions. Proposed employee contributions are scaled down if they exceed the total stipulated by the corporation. (2) To be eligible, the employee must have some minimum period of service with the corporation—usually a longer period than for participation in a stock-purchase plan. (3) How much the individual employee may contribute is governed by criteria similar to the criteria in stock-purchase plans. As in the purchase plans, too, a common rule is that an employee's participation may not exceed 10 per cent of his annual wages or salary. (4) The employee's contribution is made only by payroll deductions. (5) All the employee contributions, as soon as the payroll deductions are made, are collectively invested in U.S. savings bonds, the corporation's common stock, a combination of savings bonds and the corporation's stock such as 50-50, or, in a few instances, in a variety of stocks and bonds. Because of the immediate investment of the payroll deductions, the question of the corporation's paying interest on balances in employee accounts does not arise. On the other hand, the employee is entitled to interest and dividends received on the securities held for his account. (6) The corporation's contribution is made in shares of its own common stock. (7) Employees who wish to withdraw from the savings plan or who sever their employment, whether voluntarily or involuntarily, take out of the fund whatever securities their own contributions have bought, usually with no sharing or reduced sharing in the corporation's contribution. (8) For those who stay, there is a "holding period" of several years, at the expiration of which a distribution of the securities acquired, including the stock contributed by the corporation, is made. Thus, the securities acquired five years ago may be distributed at the end of this year, those acquired four years ago, at the end of next year, and so on.

Illustrations. To illustrate some of the features presented in the forgoing outlines, details about a few stock-purchase and savings plans at present in operation should be of interest.

In the stock-purchase plan of the American Telephone and Telegraph Company, the eligibility of employees to participate is based on their rates of pay. Nobody may subscribe to more than 300 shares in any offering, nor may he participate simultaneously in two or more offerings. The price at which stock is offered is 85 per cent of the market price on the last business day of the purchase period but not more than 85 per cent of the market price on the day on which the offering was announced. (This provision obviously protects the employee against a rise in price during the payment period, at the same time giving him the benefit of a fall.) Payment is made by payroll deductions over a period of two years, and the corporation credits interest to employee accounts at the rate of 3 per cent compounded semiannually.

In the savings plan of the Scott Paper Company for 1963, total employee contributions were limited to $2,500,000, and individual contributions to 10 per cent of weekly wages for 42 consecutive workweeks. The corporation committed itself to make contributions equal to 20 per cent of the employee contributions, less withholding tax deductions, and to raise these contributions to 25 per cent less such deductions should its profit reach a stipulated level. The contributions of both the corporation and the employees were to be invested exclusively in its common stock.

In the "Savings and Security Program" of the General Electric Company, begun in 1959, each employee's contribution is limited to 6 per cent of his salary or wages. Each dollar of the employees' contributions is matched by a corporate contribution of 50 cents, the aggregate being invested in a combination of U.S. savings bonds and the corporation's common stock. As the program's "holding period" is three years, its first payout was made early in 1963; this included savings bonds having a maturity value of $30 million and 540,000 shares of stock having a market value of about $43 million.

In the savings plan of the E. I. duPont de Nemours & Company, employees must have two years of service with the company to qualify. Their contributions are invested solely in U.S. savings bonds, and the corporation adds shares of its common stock equal in value to 25 per cent of the employee contributions. DuPont's holding period is four years.

Evaluation from the Corporate Standpoint

Motives for the installation and continuation of employee stock-purchase and savings plans appear to be mixed between financial and labor-management relationship goals. In most plans, employee contributions do serve as a source of cash by way of common stock sales, but the typical corporation could obtain an equal amount of cash more quickly by selling common stock to its stockholders or to the public. Thus, the only purely financial advantage of sales to employees are the avoidance of underwriting costs and the gaining of a somewhat wider diversification in ownership. But labor relations objectives also have financial aspects. It is claimed that the employee-stockholder is likely to be more efficient and more reluctant to quit his job than the worker who is not a stockholder. Increased efficiency and a reduction in labor turnover mean a reduction in costs—obviously a financial advantage. Likewise, employee stock-purchase and savings plans are said to encourage thrift which, in turn, makes for labor stability and satisfaction.

From the corporate standpoint, a disadvantage alleged for the savings plans is that employees' virtues cannot be measured by their capacities to save. The benefits of the corporations' contributions are denied to employees who are unable to save on account of extraordinary personal financial burdens, even though they may be good or even outstanding performers on the job. For both kinds of plans, to the extent that they involve spending employees' money for common stock, a possible major disadvantage is that the stock will not do well in earnings, dividends, and market price, with a resulting blow to morale. Disgruntled employee-stockholders would doubtless suffer a loss of efficiency, perhaps feel impelled to look for jobs elsewhere, and surely conclude that their thrift had been directed into wrong channels. In this regard, the claim is sometimes made that it is fundamentally unfair for a corporation to encourage its employees to invest in its own stock, since both their jobs and what is likely to be a substantial portion of their savings depend upon the fortunes of the single enterprise. The very business conditions that may force a corporation to lay off workers are likely to cause a sharp drop in the market price of its stock. Thus, at the time that the worker needs to draw upon his savings, he finds them evaporating.

Registration and Qualification

An offering of common stock in an employee stock-purchase or savings plan to a large number of employees located in two or more states is a "public offering" within the meaning of the federal Securities Act. Accordingly, it requires the formal process of preparing and filing a registration statement, the making of such amendments as the SEC prescribes, waiting for the effective date, and providing prospectuses to the employees to whom the offering is made. In some states, moreover, offerings to substantial numbers of employees require qualification under the blue-sky laws.

Likely to be exempt from the prescriptions of both federal and state laws, on the other hand, are small offerings (except for the notification requirement of the SEC's Regulation A) and offerings by corporations that have only a few employees.

PRIVATE PLACEMENTS OF COMMON STOCK

As defined in Chapter 17, a private placement of a security issue is a sale of the issue in bulk to one or a small group of individual or institutional investors. Of the total amount of common stock issued annually by business corporations in the United States, only a small percentage is sold by private placement. For the year 1961, for example, the SEC reported that of total common stock issues of $3,273 million and preferred stock issues of $449 million offered for cash sale for the account of the issuers (excluding issues of investment companies and stock offered under employee-ownership plans), only $279 million of common and preferred issues combined were privately placed.[17] Because, however, the SEC data

---

[17] Securities and Exchange Commission, *Annual Report*, 1962, p. 185; and *Statistical Bulletin*, July, 1963, p. 11.

only covered issues of more than $100,000, it is reasonable to assume that a goodly additional volume of stocks in issues of $100,000 or less was privately placed in that year. Nevertheless, our discussion of private placement must be quite brief at this point, since its principal application is in the sale of bonds.[18]

Occasions for Private Placements of Common Stock

Corporations of substantial size that have established good records of profits and that have good growth prospects occasionally find wealthy individual capitalists, trustees of family estates or of pension funds, or other individual or institutional investors who offer to buy the entire amount of new issues of stock. Such corporations could doubtless sell the stock to their existing stockholders or to the general public without difficulty, but sometimes they accept the offers of bulk purchases because they feel that they can get a better price that way, or, what comes to the same thing, that the expenses of flotation will be much less.

More commonly, however, private placements of common stock are made by newly established corporations, small ones that have been in operation for some years, and others that have little or no access to alternative sources of equity funds. These private placements represent, therefore, simply a variant in arrangements between corporations and individual and institutional investors, as discussed earlier in this chapter in relation to the use of stock options. In that discussion, it was pointed out that, while some such investors advance equity funds ostensibly on a loan basis and take stock options, others are content to take common stock at once in exchange for their funds. The immediate taking of common stock, then, is a private placement.

Direct Placement and Finders

The financial managers of a corporation that wants to sell an issue of common stock in bulk to one or a few individual or institutional investors may themselves set out to look for such investors, or they may employ the services of middlemen who are expected to know where equity funds can be found. The middlemen, who are called "finders," include investment bankers, lawyers, management consultants, and tax accountants. For their services, they expect to receive a "finder's fee." Corporate managers may themselves seek investors in the hope of avoiding the finder's fee; or, on the other hand, they may be quite willing to pay a finder's fee in the expectation that the finder will be able to obtain equity funds more readily and on better term than they could. Corporations that have access to alternative markets for funds can generally expect to be more successful in reaching willing investors without the assistance of finders than can those whose access to alternative sources is severely limited or nonexistent.

---

[18] See below, pp. 728–34.

In a study of securities flotations in the years 1951, 1953, and 1955, the SEC found that 70.3 per cent of the number and 75 per cent of the amount of both common and preferred stock issues privately placed were sold with the assistance of finders, and that finders' fees on these issues (average fees in various groupings) ranged from .62 per cent to 4.15 per cent—the size of the fees, as percentages, generally running inversely to the size of the issues.[19] It is a reasonable presumption that, for issues of a given size and quality of issuer, finders' fees on common stock issues would run substantially higher than on preferred stock issues, and that those on common stock issues of small corporations that were not included in the SEC's survey would run substantially higher than on the included issues. Thus, the Federal Reserve System received reports of finders' fees running from 5 to 10 per cent of the proceeds of equity advances of a common stock character.[20]

Exemption from Registration

Since the individual and institutional investors who buy common stock by way of private placements are presumed to be sufficiently knowledgeable and intelligent to make careful investigations of the affairs of corporations seeking their funds, private placements are exempt from the registration requirements of the federal securities legislation. Once in a while, however, the question arises as to when a private placement becomes, in effect, a public offering. The applicability of the Securities Act is supposed to be determined by the number of prospective investors to whom a security *is offered*—not the number who actually *buy*. An issue of a corporation's common stock might be offered in bulk by its officers or by a finder to many wealthy individuals or institutions, one after another, as, one after another, they reject the offer. Sometimes, too, investors form groups to advance funds to given corporations, each agreeing to contribute a specific amount or percentage of the total to be advanced.

But, as was indicated earlier in this chapter, the law and regulations draw no sharp lines between public offerings and private placements in terms of the number of people to whom securities are offered, whether simultaneously or successively. Moreover, it is well to recall that knowledge of offerers' affairs and investment acumen are tests for determining the public or private character of transactions at least as important as the number of persons involved.

EXCHANGES FOR PREFERRED STOCK AND DEBT

Common stock often serves as a means of financing in an indirect fashion: it is substituted, on a voluntary basis, for preferred stock or

---

[19] Securities and Exchange Commission, *Cost of Flotation of Corporate Securities, 1951–1955* (Washington, D.C.: U.S. Government Printing Office, 1957), pp. 63, 64.

[20] *Financing Small Business: Report to the Committees on Banking and Currency and the Select Committees on Small Business by the Federal Reserve System*, p. 530.

bonds that corporations had previously issued or for other debts they had previously contracted. Preferred stockholders, bondholders, or other creditors may be willing to give up their existing claims for claims as common stockholders; if they do consent to the exchange, the preferred stock or debt, though it was the original source of given batches of assets, is replaced in this function by common stock. A recasting of the financial structure of a corporation by voluntary exchanges of this kind is described as a *recapitalization*, in contrast with a reorganization in which, as was pointed out earlier in this chapter, a strong element of compulsion is present.

Exchange offers of common stock for preferred stock or debt are most commonly made at the time the preferred stock is issued or the debt is contracted. From the moment of its issuance, a preferred stock or a bond may be "convertible." The preferred stock or bond contract stipulates that the holder may, at any time or within a designated period of time, exchange his shares of preferred or his bond for a specific number of shares of common stock. A share of preferred stock, for example, may be exchangeable for two or three or five shares of common stock, and a bond of $1,000 par value may be exchangeable for common stock at a price of $25 a share—which would mean, of course, for 40 shares of common. But there is nothing to prevent a corporation's going to its preferred stockholders, bondholders, or other creditors and making a common stock exchange offer, even though it did not contract for "convertibility" in the first place. Such latter-day offers occur in goodly numbers, although not nearly so frequently as do offers from the beginning.

Convertible Preferred Stocks and Bonds

When a corporation, at the time of issuance, makes a preferred stock or bond issue convertible into common stock, it does so either because it thinks that the convertibility feature will enhance salability or because it actually wants the conversion to take place. The two motives may be mixed, but, in the individual case, the one or the other tends by far to predominate.

Adding the convertibility feature to enhance the salability of a preferred stock or bond issue is to give it a "sweetener." Beyond the ordinary rights of preferred stock or bonds, the prospective buyer is offered a speculative interest that, like any speculation, may or may not turn out to be valuable—much as he is offered a speculative interest when stock-purchase warrants are attached to preferred stock or bonds. If the corporation's earnings advance markedly and the dividends on its common stock are generous, the buyer may switch his limited-return preferred stock or bonds to enjoy the higher return being paid on the common stock; or if earnings so advance but dividends on common are continued at a modest level, with, however, its market price advancing materially in keeping with the high level of retained earnings, he may make the conversion with the intention of selling the common stock for a capital gain. If neither of these developments takes place, he may continue to hold the preferred shares or bonds with their superior claims upon earnings and assets. Here, as in the use of stock-purchase warrants in similar circumstances, issuing corporations, in view of their anxiety to sell, may err in the direction of generosity in setting the terms for conversion.

Many of the corporations that make their preferred stock and bond issues convertible to improve their appeal to prospective buyers are weak enterprises, but those that add the convertibility feature in the hope and expectation that conversion will take place are likely to be quite strong. In most cases, the latter would prefer to issue common stock in the first place, but, in view of temporary weaknesses in the common stock market, they choose not to sell common at a price that would unreasonably dilute the ownership interests of existing stockholders. If they need money at once, and if the market for preferred stock or bonds of the quality they can issue continues favorable, they offer one or the other with the conversion feature. They are confident that when strength returns to the common stock market conversion will take place; hence, they are likely to look upon the preferred stock or bonds simply as a means of "interim" financing.[21]

Later Offers of Conversion

When a corporation makes an offer of common stock in exchange for its outstanding preferred stock or bonds in respect to which the conversion feature was not originally included, it may be in a position to redeem the securities whether or not their holders accept the exchange offer, or it may be faced with financial difficulties of considerable severity.

Although exchange offers of this kind by corporations in strong positions are rather rare, they can be advantageous. Suppose that a corporation intends to retire its outstanding preferred stock or bonds, having the right to do this by simply calling the securities for redemption. Its managers know that it can make a public offering of common stock on favorable terms and use the proceeds for the redemption. But, to reduce flotation costs, especially underwriting commissions, they decide to go direct to the preferred stockholders or bondholders with an exchange offer; in so doing, they inform the security holders that securities not offered for exchange are to be presented for redemption on or before a designated day. To the extent, then, that the offer is accepted, the common stock flotation for cash can be reduced.

---

[21] Convertibility as a feature of preferred stock issues is further discussed below, pp. 541–46, and as a feature of bond issues, pp. 705–11.

Small corporations in financial difficulties are much more likely than large ones in similar straits to go to bondholders and other creditors with proposals for exchanges of common stock in whole or in part for their claims as creditors. Such a proposal may be made to only one or two of the larger creditors in the expectation that, should they accept, the remainder of the debt could be met without difficulty. Large creditors of small corporations may accept offers of this kind in the hope of realizing a larger proportion of their claims in the long run as common stockholders than could be realized by immediate legal proceedings to enforce payment. Such an acceptance would be all the more likely should the amount of stock offered to the large creditor or creditors be a substantial proportion of the total to be outstanding, or should they be otherwise assured of a substantial voice in management. A large corporation, on the other hand, would probably have to approach a goodly number of creditors to reach a sufficient aggregate of claims to make its effort worthwhile. If it had already defaulted on some or all these claims, or had to confess the probability of default, it would have reason to fear that one or more of the creditors would file a petition for its reorganization or dissolution in bankruptcy.

In the making of latter-day offers of common stock in exchange for preferred stock, large corporations have generally played a more prominent role than have small ones; but this may be only because more publicity has been given to the offers of the former. At any rate, offers of this kind are most commonly made when unpaid dividends on cumulative preferred stock have reached substantial levels. For example, a corporation that has not paid for six years its prescribed dividend of, say, 5 per cent a year on its preferred stock may hope to work out an "adjustment" with the preferred stockholders. Unless it is willing to go through a lengthy and expensive process of reorganization, the only ways it can get rid of the arrearages is by paying them in cash or by *getting the preferred stockholders to consent* to waive their accumulated dividend claims in whole or in part. Accordingly, it may offer a certain number of shares of common stock in full settlement of the arrearages, or it may offer a certain amount of cash plus shares of common stock. It may, indeed, go further than this in the hope of getting rid of some or all of the preferred stock itself, as by offering a larger number of shares of common stock in exchange for all the rights of the preferred stockholders, that is, for the preferred stock itself along with the claims to unpaid dividends.[22]

STOCK DIVIDENDS AND BONUS STOCK

Two further uses of common stock deserve only brief treatment in this chapter, namely, its use for stock dividends and its use as bonus stock. Stock dividends can be treated briefly, because a more lengthy discussion

---

[22] A further discussion of procedures aimed at "adjusting" the claims of preferred stockholders will be found on pp. 568–75.

can best be reserved for Chapter 25 wherein dividend policies are examined in detail; and bonus stock, because it is of little importance.

Stock Dividends

Although the typical common stockholder is primarily interested in the amount of cash dividends he receives or can expect to receive, boards of directors are frequently of the conviction that the interests of the common stockholders can be better served if all or very large proportions of the cash throw-offs from profits are retained to finance expansion or for other corporate purposes. But many boards feel that the common stockholder should get "something" currently as a reward for his investment despite an apparent need to retain all or a large percentage of profits. Hence, the device of the stock dividend:[23] the "something" that the stockholder gets is simply some additional shares of common stock, and, of course, he gets this, like any dividend, on a pro rata basis. If, indeed, the stockholder needs or wants cash, he can sell the shares he receives as a dividend; although he would thereby reduce his ownership in the corporation, as when he sells stock rights,[24] that fact may not worry him much.

Common stock that is distributed as a dividend appears not to be a source of assets, and one could argue that it ought not to be classified as a means of financing. There is much truth in this contention, for the assets acquired through retained profits are there whether or not stock dividends are distributed. In at least one significant sense, however, calling common stock distributed as dividends a means of financing can be justified. It is this: stock dividends can reasonably be said to be the source of such cash as boards of directors would be constrained to pay out as cash dividends (or as additional cash dividends) to satisfy the "clamor" of stockholders were they not distributing the stock dividends. In other words, to the extent that stockholders are content with stock dividends, cash that otherwise would be paid out to them can be retained.

Bonus Stock

In earlier days, a practice of some popularity was the offering of shares of common stock as a "bonus" to buyers of preferred stock and bonds, particularly the former. Bonus stock was used as a "sweetener" to improve the attractiveness of issues of preferred stock and bonds of relatively poor investment qualities. When, however, the bonus stock had a par value, there was always danger that the recipient would be held liable to corporate creditors for this value; since it was apparently given free, the creditors could argue that it had actually been sold at a discount of 100

---

[23] This is not to imply that the only reason for the distribution of stock dividends is to give common stockholders a reward in lieu of cash dividends in whole or in part. Other reasons for stock dividends are discussed below, pp. 608–13.
[24] See above, pp. 425–26.

per cent. To clear the way for the use of bonus stock without this danger was, indeed, an important reason for the advocacy of state legislation to permit the issuance of common stock without par value.

The giving of speculative interests to preferred stockholders and bondholders by convertibility provisions and by the attachment of stock-purchase warrants has displaced, except in rare instances, the use of common stock itself as bonus stock.

Questions

1. For acquisitions of corporate properties in mergers and consolidations, why is the direct exchange of common stock for common stock often favored by the acquiring corporations? by the stockholders of the acquired corporations?

2. How important has the merger movement been in the postwar period? In this movement, how important have been direct exchanges of common stocks?

3. Why is there said to be temptations toward generosity when common stock is given in exchange for noncash assets? What harm can come from such generosity? To whom? Is there any justification at all for this kind of generosity? Explain.

4. When common stock is given in exchange for property in mergers or otherwise, how can one judge whether or not the transaction is a "public offering" requiring registration?

5. What are the functions of promoters of business enterprises? In corporate promotions, what logic is there for giving common stock to the promoters as compensation for their services?

6. Support or attack this proposition: As compensation for underwriting new security issues, it is unethical for investment bankers to take "cheap" stock and stock options in addition to cash compensation.

7. As means of providing noncash compensation to corporate executives, why has there been a big shift in recent years from stock bonuses to stock options?

8. Why are stock options described as an "uncertain" means of financing?

9. In giving stock options as compensation to executives, why do corporations generally make sure that they qualify as "restricted" under the Internal Revenue Code?

10. Describe the loan-and-option device sometimes arranged with wealthy investors who provide what are essentially equity funds to small corporations. Why is such an arrangement favored by these investors?

11. Briefly explain the several uses to which stock-purchase warrants have been put.

12. Explain the distinction between employee stock-purchase plans and employee savings plans. How does corporate participation generally differ as between these two types of programs?

13. On what grounds are employee stock-purchase and savings programs sometimes adversely criticized? Is such criticism justified? Discuss.

14. In comparison with public offerings of common stocks, how important are private placements? What is the role of "finders" in private placements?

15. When issuing preferred stocks and bonds, why do some corporations

make these securities convertible into common stock? Do the same reasons apply when they make later offers of conversion? Explain.

Problems

1. Walker, Inc., wants to acquire the Caldwell Manufacturing Company by merger through an exchange of shares of common stock. Walker already has outstanding 500,000 shares of $10 par value, and it has balances in its surplus accounts totaling $8 million. In the past five years, during which its earnings have steadily expanded, its average after-tax profit has been $2,600,000. Caldwell has outstanding 300,000 shares of stock of $25 par value, and balances in its surplus accounts amount to $1,500,000. In the past five years, its earnings have been quite stable, with average after-tax profit amounting to $900,000. Neither corporation has preferred stock or bonds or other long-term debt in its financial structure.

One director of Walker observes that since the book value of its common stock amounts to $26 a share, and the book value of Caldwell's common stock is $30, a 1-for-1 exchange offer should be about right. He adds that absolute precision would require an offer of 15 shares of Walker's stock for 13 shares of Caldwell's.

Another of Walker's directors argues that it would be much more appropriate to make the exchange offer on the basis of the earning power of the two common stocks. He says that an offer on the basis of book values is really based on asset values carried on the books, that such values can be quite unrealistic, and that, in any case, there is no advantage in owning expensive assets unless they have commensurate earning power.

a) Which of these two directors is sounder in his reasoning?

b) If you agree with the first director, would you favor the 1-for-1 offer or the 15-for-13 offer?

c) If you agree with the second, what would be an appropriate exchange offer?

(This problem is carried a step further in Problem 1 at the end of the following chapter.)

2. A newly established corporation is authorized to issue 100,000 shares of common stock of $1.00 par value. It issues 40,000 shares to the organizers for the assets which they had held in a partnership. Additional money is needed for operations, and a private capitalist agrees to provide $55,000, taking in return the corporation's promissory note for $55,000 payable on demand and bearing interest at 6 per cent, together with options to buy 55,000 shares of common stock at $1.00 a share. Why would the capitalist prefer to take the note and options rather than 55,000 shares of common stock at once?

chapter 20

SOME PROBLEMS OF
COMMON STOCK MANAGEMENT

Although many of the important problems of common stock management were analyzed in the three preceding chapters, a few remain for study in this chapter and the following one. Some of these were implied in the earlier discussion, but they deserve more detailed treatment. In the present chapter, then, the following topics will be examined: determination of appropriate amounts of authorized common stock, original selection of pars and no pars, reasons for subsequent changes in pars and no pars, and the role of treasury stock. This will leave for study in the following chapter the pros and cons of listing common stock on the stock exchanges.

AUTHORIZED ISSUES OF COMMON STOCK

In Chapter 3 the point was made that corporations can easily increase their authorized issues of stock, whether common or preferred, by a simple procedure of filing amendments to their articles of incorporation. It was also said that authorizations of stock far beyond what a corporation is likely to issue within a few years is unnecessarily expensive, because many state organization taxes and some annual capital stock taxes are levied on amounts authorized, regardless of the number of shares that are actually sold or otherwise disposed of. In August, 1963, for example, the stockholders of Sterling Precision Corporation voted sharp reductions in authorized stock issues precisely to reduce its payments of annual capital stock taxes. With 3,594,428 common shares and 433,353 preferred shares outstanding, the corporation reduced authorized common stock from twenty to ten million shares, and authorized preferred from five to one million.[1]

But shortages in the supply of authorized but unissued stock can be a source of difficulties. They obviously can cause acute embarrassment to a corporation if they make it quite difficult or impossible for it to fulfill contracts to deliver stock; and they can so tie the hands of its board of directors as to preclude favorable opportunities for direct exchanges of stock for assets and services. Liberal authorized issues and liberal waivers of preemptive rights can be provided for quite simply by the few organizers of a corporation, whereas getting approvals of the requisite

---

[1] *The Wall Street Journal*, August 5, 1963, p. 2.

majorities of stockholders, when a corporation has grown large and its stockholders quite numerous, may be both difficult and expensive. In some cases, of course, it is impossible to get a sufficient number of stockholders to approve increased authorizations, or, if this approval is obtained, to get also a waiver of the stockholders' preemptive right to the added shares. Getting approvals is expensive if special meetings of the stockholders must be called, and special "literature" must be prepared to set out the merits of the proposals.

Contract Requirements

Corporations with excess cash sometimes buy shares of their common stock in the market to be held for future delivery against options given to executives or for resale in employee stock-purchase programs. But for most corporations, such a procedure would eliminate a major advantage of offers by options and offers to employees in stock-purchase plans— the advantage of using these as means of financing, of raising new money. For these corporations, it would likewise be unrealistic to issue stock options to promoters and investment bankers, to attach stock-purchase warrants to preferred stocks or bonds, to make such securities convertible into common stock, and to give stock-purchase warrants to institutional investors in connection with long-term borrowing, without having authorized but unissued stock available for delivery if and when called for by the contract holders. None of the possible alternatives to holding unissued stock for this purpose would make much sense. Stockholders might be expected to approve amendments to articles of incorporation to increase authorized issues to meet stock-delivery demands when made by contract holders; but the stockholders would be under no legal compulsion to give this approval. Shares could be bought in the market immediately to be held against future stock-delivery demands, but this would make the contracts (except for convertible preferred stocks and bonds) sources of cash drain rather than means of financing. For the convertible securities, the cash received in their sale would be largely used up in the purchase of shares to take care of possible conversions. Finally, even more serious cash drains could result if it were planned to buy shares in the market only when contract holders called for delivery. If, for example, a corporation had to buy shares in the market at a price of $30 a share to meet the demand of a holder of a $1,000 bond convertible into 40 shares, it would, in effect, be paying $1,200 to settle a debt of $1,000.

Authorized Stock at Directors' Disposal

When the stockholders of a corporation have a high degree of confidence in the acumen of its board of directors and its devotion to their welfare—when, in other words, they are confident that the board will not fritter away their ownership rights through excessive dilution—they have good reason to put at its disposal a rather generous amount of authorized common stock and to free this stock from the preemptive right. The directors will have "elbow room" to take quick advantage of opportunities to acquire assets and services in direct exchange for stock. Oftentimes particular parcels of property, all the assets of smaller concerns, or the services of an especially desirable executive can be acquired on highly favorable terms only if offers can be made promptly and without question about the acquiring corporation's capacity to deliver. Offers of common stock for the assets of another corporation or of stock or stock options as supplements to the proposed cash salary of a man of high executive qualities "provided that our stockholders agree to the issue" may not be enough. Even when owners of desirable properties and great executive skills appear to be willing to wait to see what the stockholders will do, the delay may prove to be fatal. During the waiting period, the owners of the properties and skills may have a change of heart, or, what is more probable, they may receive more favorable offers from other quarters.

Another reason for placing unissued stock at the unhampered disposal of the directors is to enable them to declare and distribute stock dividends. Because most stockholders are extremely pleased to get stock dividends, they can generally be counted upon to vote approval for new authorizations for this purpose. But as dividend policies are at the discretion of the directors, presumably this discretion should extend to distributions of dividend stock without a need of repeated referral of the matter to the stockholders for their vote.

That common stockholders are by no means averse to putting large amounts of unissued common stock at the disposal of boards of directors is indicated in the sampling of large corporations of Table 20–1. One will notice that the unissued stock of the Aluminum Company of

TABLE 20–1
Authorized and Unissued Stock of Some Large Corporations[a]

Corporation	Total Shares Authorized	Authorized Shares Unissued
American Telephone and Telegraph Company	300,000,000	56,898,870
Standard Oil Company (New Jersey)	250,000,000	33,467,339
General Motors Corporation	500,000,000	213,860,875
United States Steel Corporation	90,000,000	35,885,558
Gulf Oil Corporation	150,000,000	45,998,704
Pennsylvania Railroad Company	17,400,000	3,947,912
E. I. duPont de Nemours & Company	60,000,000	14,016,892
New York Central Railroad Company	10,000,000	3,454,548
Aluminum Company of America	50,000,000	28,630,413
General Electric Company	105,000,000	15,111,034
Union Carbide Corporation	36,000,000	5,479,263
International Business Machines Corporation	29,812,500	2,134,178
Eastman Kodak Company	90,000,000	51,617,754

[a] As of December 31, 1962, except for Pennsylvania Railroad Company and New York Central Railroad Company, December 31, 1961.

Source: Moody's Investors Service, *Manuals*.

America and Eastman Kodak Company exceeds the amounts outstanding.

THE QUESTION OF PAR AND NO-PAR VALUES

In the second and third decades of the present century, a controversy raged in American financial circles about the merits and demerits of provisions of state corporation codes that required the stock of business corporations to have par values. In the early part of this period, the par value of the stock of the great majority of corporations was $100, and, in truth, some of the state codes stipulated that par value could not be less than this figure. Critics of the par-value requirements emphasized the difficulties they engendered in corporate financing, and demanded the enactment of amendments to the laws to permit the issuance of no-par stock. Their campaigns were extraordinarily successful, for, beginning with New York in 1912, all the states except Nebraska adopted legislation to permit no-par issues.

But the sale of no-par stock at a wide range of prices generally below $100 tended to take away from that figure any remaining glory that it may have had for par-value issues. States that enacted no-par provisions saw no reason to continue to require values of not less than $100 for par stocks, if they had previously had such stipulations; and they amended their laws to permit lower par values, some of them setting the minimum at a figure such as $1.00, and some setting no minimum at all. Corporations that continued to prefer par values increasingly experimented with pars of $1.00, $5.00, $10.00, and other figures much below $100, whether or not they had previously been restricted by law. In fact, with the passing of time, and especially in the period since the 1930's, many corporate managements have become convinced that the setting of low par values for stocks is a means of getting all the advantages claimed for the no-par device together with the additional advantage of avoiding some of the tax discriminations to which no-par stock is sometimes subject. In the past two decades, accordingly, a strong trend from high pars and no pars toward low pars has been apparent, just as, in the 1920's especially, a strong movement from par-value stocks to no-par issues developed. Illustrative of these two trends was the action of the General Electric Company in changing from a par value of $100 to no par in 1926, and then switching from no par to a par of $5.00 in 1954; that of the Eastman Kodak Company in changing from $100 to no par in 1922 and from no par to a par of $10 in 1947; and that of Crucible Steel Company in going from $100 to no par in 1940 and then to a par of $25 in 1951.

Typical of present-day low pars are those of the Aluminum Company of America, the Great Atlantic & Pacific Tea Company, and Lockheed Aircraft Corporation, all at $1.00; General Motors, $1.66⅔; Ford Motor Company, $2.50; Sears, Roebuck, $3.00; National Dairy Products and Sinclair Oil, $5.00; the Borden Company, $7.50; Cities Service, $10; Texaco, Inc., $12.50; Socony Mobil, $15; United States Steel, $16⅔; and

Standard Oil (Indiana), $25. However, many corporations continue with no-par common stocks, including International Harvester, Montgomery Ward, Douglas Aircraft, Inland Steel, Kennecott Copper, and Union Carbide.

At the present time, therefore, the organizers of new corporations are likely to decide without much hesitation to issue stocks of low or no-par values. Why this is so may be best discussed in terms of the advantages and disadvantages attributed to no-par stock—this to be followed by an examination of the more recent claims as to the superiority of low par values over no pars.

Advantages of No-Par Stock

Ease in Further Financing. The principal advantage claimed for no-par stock is that it makes for ease in further common stock financing even though the market price of stock already outstanding has fallen. If a corporation originally sold an issue of common stock at its par value of $50 a share, and if the market price of this stock is now $40, it cannot sell an additional issue at $50. Nobody will pay that price to the corporation when he can buy in the market at $40; nor can investors safely buy the new issue at $40, for the discount rule would apply. The investors, as well as directors who did not have their dissents entered in the minutes, would be contingently liable to creditors for the amount of the discount. Were the stock no par, however, the second issue could readily be offered at $40—or at a lower price, as in a direct offering to existing stockholders—without question as to further liability.

Source of Paid-in Surplus. Closely related to the foregoing is the contention that the sale of no-par stock makes it possible for corporations to begin business with paid-in surpluses. The no-par provisions of state statutes generally permit the corporate directors to decide what portion of the proceeds of stock sales is to be carried to the capital stock account as "stated capital" and what portion is to be designated paid-in surplus. Many new corporations, it is said, must expect to incur net losses in the first few years of operations—until, that is, they get firmly established—and it is most desirable to have surpluses against which the losses can be charged. If surplus is not available to absorb losses, they result in "impairments" of the capital stock itself—the appearance of *deficits* on the books and in the financial statements—something that is hardly helpful in buying on credit, getting bank loans, or making further sales of securities. With a par-value stock, on the other hand, the very designation of a permanent price tag or par value, especially if a high one, may militate against sales of the stock at prices in excess of par, making the acquisition of a paid-in surplus at the start much less probable than in the use of no-par stock.

Avoidance of Subterfuges. Also related to the principal advantage claimed for no-par stock is the avoidance of subterfuges that used to be commonly employed in connection with par-value issues to try to avoid contingent liabilities for discount. In the incorporation of partnerships, for example, it was a common practice to issue stock of a total par value substantially in excess of the reasonable value of assets taken over. In the individual case, the former partners would agree among themselves to donate back to the corporation a goodly proportion of the stock thus received for the partnership assets. To raise cash, then, this donated stock could be sold at whatever price it would bring, supposedly without making directors and buyers liable to creditors for the amount of any discount.

But it is obvious that discount liabilities could not be removed with certainty by transactions of this kind; for creditors might sue on the grounds that the partnership assets plus the cash received in the sale of the donated stock still did not constitute full payment for the stock at its par value—that a fraud had been worked upon them. With no-par stock, on the other hand, there need be no occasion for worries about discounts: the partners could take as many shares for their assets as they thought reasonable, decide what value to put upon these for entry in the capital stock and paid-in surplus accounts, and then sell additional shares at whatever price could be obtained for them.

Promoting Investor Understanding. A fourth advantage claimed for no-par designations is that they minimize misunderstandings on the part of investors. Poorly informed investors may be misled by par values, thinking that shares must truly be worth the price tags placed upon them. To be offered a share at $50 when it is designated in the articles of incorporation of a corporation to be worth that much is not the same thing as to be offered at $50 a share to which no specific value is ascribed in the articles. In the latter circumstance, the would-be investor, even if poorly informed, would surely ask himself whether the share was really worth the offering price, and take steps to find out by analyzing the corporation's position and prospects. That, at any rate, is the nature of the claim that is made for no-par stock. If the claim is valid, the advantage *to the corporation* is clear, for it wants to have loyal, satisfied stockholders— stockholders who will be inclined to buy its products and to invest in more of its securities and to advise others to do likewise.

Disadvantages of No-Par Stock

Discriminatory Taxation. The most obvious disadvantage in the use of no-par stock is found in discriminatory tax burdens that it must sometimes bear. Although not of great weight, differentials in tax liabilities unfavorable to no-par shares can still be of material significance. Such differentials obtain in some of the state organization and entrance taxes and in a few of the state annual capital stock or franchise taxes.

In New York, the rate of the organization tax on corporations with par-value stock is one twentieth of 1 per cent, and on those with no-par stock, 5 cents a share. Accordingly, a newly organized corporation with authorized common stock of 100,000 shares of $50 par value would pay an organization tax of $2,500, while the comparable tax bill for a corporation with 100,000 authorized shares of no-par stock, destined to be sold at $20 a share, would be $5,000. If the same corporations were organized in New Jersey where the tax rate is 20 cents per $1,000 of par-value stock and 1 cent a share on no-par stock, each would pay an organization tax of $1,000, even though the par-value stock of the one might be sold for $5 million or more and the no-par stock of the other for only $2 million. Again, were they chartered in Maine, the corporation with par-value stock would pay an annual franchise tax of $300, while the corporation with no-par stock would pay $550. In their organization taxes, some states discriminate against no-par stock by basing the taxes on the dollar amounts of authorized stock while assigning an arbitrary value such as $10, $50, or $100 to each no-par share authorized, regardless of the price at which it may be sold.

Dangers of Dilution. A second disadvantage attributed to no-par stock is the possibility of serious dilution of the ownership interests of existing stockholders through successive issues of the stock. Boards of directors, it is said, are likely to be more liberal in giving no-par shares for services, for specific parcels of property, and for all the operating assets of other firms, as in mergers, than when giving par-value shares. If, for example, directors want to acquire property reasonably worth $100,000 in exchange for stock having a par value of $50, they are unlikely to offer much more than 2,000 shares. But no price tag stands in the way of a more liberal offer of no-par shares. Although already-outstanding no-par shares might have a book or market value of $50, that would not preclude the offering of, say, 2,500 such shares for the property. It would be as easy to enter 2,500 shares on the books at a "stated value" of $40 as to enter 2,000 shares with a "stated value" of $50.

Attractiveness of Low Par Values

The reason for the recent strong trend toward using low par values for common stocks can be readily adduced from the foregoing discussion of the advantages and disadvantages of no-par stocks. It appears that all the advantages claimed for no pars can be claimed also for low pars, while the latter also avoid the kinds of tax discriminations that sometimes burden no pars.

If a corporation sets the par value of its common stock at $1.00 and sells the original issue at $20 a share, and if the market value falls below this level, it can offer further issues at $16, $12, $8, and at still lower prices down to $1.00 without worry about the discount rule. The sale of the original issue, furthermore, would provide a paid-in surplus equal to $19 a share—a surplus against which such losses as might occur in the first few years of operation could be charged. No subterfuge, such as the donated stock procedure, would be needed to get these results. More-over, the prospective investor, on being offered $1.00 shares at $20, would have just about as much reason to make a careful investigation as when offered no-par shares. Finally, the shares of low par value, depending upon the state of incorporation, might turn up favorable tax discrimina-tion. In New York, a corporation authorized to issue 100,000 shares of stock of $1.00 par value would pay an organization tax of $50, whereas one with the same number of no-par shares, as indicated earlier, would pay $5,000, even though each stock might be sold at, say, $20 a share. In Maryland, where the tax law assigns a value of $20 to no-par stock, the corporation with 100,000 shares of $1.00 par value would pay an organi-zation tax of $20 while the no-par corporation with an equal number of shares would pay $300; and in New Hampshire, where an arbitrary value of $50 is assigned to no-par stock, the respective bills for organization taxes would be $150 and $2,750.

CHANGES IN PAR, NO-PAR, AND STATED VALUES

The fact that a corporation starts out with a specific par or no-par designation for its common stock does not mean that it must hold to this designation for the whole of its operating life. This provision of its articles of incorporation, like so many others, can be changed by subse-quent amendment provided that the amendment has the approval of whatever proportion of stockholdings the state law or the articles them-selves prescribe.

Effecting changes in par and no-par designations is an extremely com-mon procedure. When brought about by the voluntary approval of stockholders of solvent corporations, such changes come under the head of "recapitalizations"; when forced upon stockholders as in bankruptcy proceedings, they come within the scope of "reorganizations." The changes may be said to be of two classes: (1) those in which the desig-nations are changed without simultaneous changes in the number of shares, and (2) those in which the designations and number of shares are changed at the same time. Reasons for the selection of one procedure rather than the other will be brought out in the following discussion of the scope of the two kinds of changes. However, the discussion will be limited to recapitalizations, as the fate of common stock in reorganiza-tions was sufficiently indicated in the preceding chapter.

Changes without Variations in Number of Shares

The managements of corporations, with the approval of their stock-holders, often decide to reduce the par value of their common stock from high to low figures, to switch from pars to no pars, and to switch from no pars to low pars without, at the same time, changing the number of shares to be outstanding. The objective sought may be one or a combina-tion of the following: (1) to gain the advantages of no pars and low pars as discussed in the preceding division of this chapter, (2) to eliminate deficits already on the books or expected to occur, and (3) to make possible write-downs or write-offs of asset values.

Gaining Advantages of No Pars and Low Pars. The most obvious reason for changes in pars and no pars is to enable corporations to gain the advantages of no pars and low pars as already discussed. A great number of corporations have made switches precisely for this reason—so much so that the "trends" to no pars and low pars, as referred to earlier, have been even more significant on account of switches by long-established corporations than on account of the selection of no pars and low pars by new ones.

Suppose, for example, that a corporation's financial position is as indicated in the following condensed balance sheet:

Assets.....................$10,000,000	Liabilities.................$4,000,000
	Common stock.............. 5,000,000
	Earned surplus............. 1,000,000

The common stock consists of 100,000 shares of $50 par value, and its book value is obviously $60 a share. The corporation's earnings after taxes have been averaging around $200,000, or $2.00 a common share. The corporation wants to sell some additional stock to take advantage of highly favorable opportunities for expansion, but the market value of its stock, in view of its limited earning power, is now only $30. Clearly, new stock cannot be sold at $50, nor can the corporation, because of the discount rule, expect to find many buyers at a price in the vicinity of $30. Accordingly, a decision is made to reduce the par value from $50 to $5 a share—an action which is reflected in a revised balance sheet as follows:

Assets.....................$10,000,000	Liabilities.................$4,000,000
	Common stock.............. 500,000
	Capital surplus............. 4,500,000
	Earned surplus............. 1,000,000

As the action does not change the book value or the earnings record per share, it should have no immediate material effects upon the market value of the stock. Now, however, the corporation is in a position to offer the additional stock at a price around $30 a share—or, in fact, at any price down to $5.00—without worry about the discount rule.

In a similar way, a corporation in the position of the one just described might decide to switch from its par value of $50 to the no-par designation, perhaps feeling that tax discriminations against no-par stock are of no importance, considering its location and the states in which it does business. Such a switch, in truth, would allow for somewhat more flexibility than in the illustrated switch from a par of $50 to one of $5.00. In changing to no par, the corporation could leave its common stock account undisturbed, allowing the shares already outstanding to remain temporarily at a stated value of $50 a share. Or it could reduce the stated value to $25, carrying $2.5 million to capital surplus, or to $15, with $3.5 million going to capital surplus, or to some other level. If it then sold new stock at, say, $28, the directors would be in a position to decide what percentage of this amount should go to the capital stock account as stated capital and what percentage to a paid-in or capital surplus account. Likewise, if it appeared to be necessary for it later to accept a price even below $5.00 a share for another issue of common stock, it could go ahead with the financing without hesitation, whereas the corporation of the preceding paragraph, to effect the same kind of transaction, would find it necessary again to amend its articles. (It should be noted that the sale of additional no-par stock at $28 would necessarily reduce the stated value of the original shares, assuming it to have been left temporarily at $50. If, to illustrate, 50,000 shares were sold at $28 and the directors decided to allocate $20 of the proceeds to the capital stock account, that account would amount to $6 million—the original $5 million plus the $1 million thus allocated. Since old stock of a given class is indistinguishable from new in the rights it accords to stockholders, the stated value of each share, old and new, would now be $40, that is, $6,000,000 ÷ 150,000 shares outstanding.)

Almost needless to add is the fact that many corporations have made and are continuing to make switches from no pars to pars, especially low ones, specifically to gain the tax advantages indicated in our earlier discussion. Decisions as to whether the selected pars should be equal to or less than the stated values of no pars replaced vary according to the levels of these stated values and the outlook of the corporations individually. A corporation that switches from a no par with stated value of $25 is likely to choose a much lower par value; while one switching from a no par with a stated value of $5.00 may be quite satisfied to continue with the same figure as its par value.

Elimination of Deficits. The elimination of deficits, whether already incurred or in prospect, has been an important reason for the scaling down of par and stated values of corporate common stocks. A deficit is a debit or "red" balance in the earned surplus account; unless it is offset by credit balances in one or more capital surplus accounts, it signifies that the capital stock has been impaired. When shown in the balance sheet in the manner generally preferred by reputable accountants, the impairment is indicated by the deduction of the deficit from the stock accounts "on the liability side." Operating losses in excess of earned surplus earlier accumulated are the principal source of deficits; but they may also occur because of embezzlements, destruction of property by storms, floods, and other acts of God, and losses on sales of obsolete fixed assets carried on the books at substantial values.

Corporate managements do not like to show deficits in their balance sheets. It is not good for credit standing and for sales of additional securities. Nor is it good for one's reputation with employees, customers.

and the public generally. Hence, anxiety to get rid of deficits as quickly as possible is quite understandable. The most pleasant way to do this is to have earnings mount up rapidly, but this solution to the problem is not easy to come by, since it must depend upon many circumstances beyond the control of the managers. Were it not so, the deficits would not have appeared in the first place. Accordingly, "adjusting" the par or stated value of the common stock often suggests itself as the next best procedure, even though it is well understood that eliminating deficits by "adjustments" does not change the fact that losses have occurred and that they remain in the corporations' records.

For illustration, let us assume that the financial position of a certain corporation is as indicated in the following condensed balance sheet:

Assets	$9,000,000	Liabilities		$4,000,000
		Common stock	$6,000,000	
		Less: Deficit	1,000,000	5,000,000

It may be assumed that the common stock account represents 150,000 shares of $40 par value. For the elimination of the deficit, a reduction in the par value to $33.33⅓ a share would clearly suffice; but the corporation's managers would probably want to have some additional capital surplus to absorb further losses should they occur. Thus, the par value might be reduced to, say, $30, thereby making possible both the elimination of the deficit and the provision of a capital surplus of $500,000. In view of the trend toward low par values, however, the managers would be even more likely to recommend to the stockholders for their approval a reduction of the par value to some low figure such as $1.00 or $5.00.

The setting up of a balance in a capital surplus account in the way illustrated would not justify the payment of dividends chargeable against that account. Such a dividend payment would constitute a deliberate impairment of the capital stock; it would be potentially a means of defrauding existing creditors. Any competent court could be expected to hold that the dividend was being charged against the capital stock account despite the initial transfer from the capital stock account to the capital surplus account. In most jurisdictions, on the other hand, a transfer from the capital stock account to surplus accounts to eliminate a deficit, in the manner illustrated, would enable the corporation to pay dividends either on common or preferred stock or on both in an amount not exceeding current and future net profits. For example, if the corporation of the foregoing illustration were to have in the present year a net profit of $100,000, it could not pay any cash dividends whatsoever, according to the rule in most states, had it not reduced the par value of its common stock to eliminate the deficit. The profit would simply reduce the deficit to $900,000, and a dividend payment would add to this deficit, thus further impairing the stock. But had it eliminated the deficit by reducing the par value of its stock, cash dividends not exceeding $100,000 could be paid, as it would have an earned surplus of that amount against which the dividends could be legitimately charged.

A "recapitalization" of the kind described here was effected by the J. I. Case Company in April, 1962, when its stockholders approved a write-down from $12.50 to $1.00 in the par value of its 2,863,193 shares of outstanding common stock. The total write-down amounted, therefore, to $32,926,720. Of this, $26,814,519 was credited to the earned surplus account to eliminate an accumulated deficit of that amount, and the balance of $6,112,201 was credited to capital surplus.

Adjustments in par and stated values to "eliminate deficits" can be made, as it were, ahead of time, so that the deficits will never appear on the books and in balance sheets. Assume that a corporation has outstanding 200,000 shares of no-par common stock of a stated value of $20. It has an earned surplus of $75,000, but it expects to incur a loss of $300,000 in the current year. Accordingly, it takes action immediately to reduce the stated value of its no-par stock to, say, $5.00 a share, thus providing a capital surplus of $3 million. Should, then, a loss of $300,000 actually take place, $75,000 could be charged against earned surplus, and the remainder against the capital surplus, so that no deficit would appear.

Write-downs and Write-offs of Asset Values. Corporate managements often recognize that some of their assets are carried on the books at valuations unreasonably high in relation to the contribution to earnings made by these assets. But write-downs and write-offs of asset values by realistic amounts, they know, would result in deficits because of the meagerness of the surplus accounts to which the reductions would have to be charged. Overvaluations are most commonly recognized in fixed assets, both tangible and intangible, but sometimes in inventories, and even in other current assets as well. A corporation may have spent a lot of money in buying a patent covering a particular product or in developing a product for which it succeeds in getting a patent, only to find that high costs of production would require a selling price that would put the product beyond the reach of most potential buyers. Or it may have bought out a competing concern, paying much more than the fair value of its net tangible assets, the excess payment representing compensation for "goodwill," that is, for the superior earning capacity of the purchased concern as derived from a large body of loyal customers. It carries the excess payment as "goodwill" on its books but, alas! it has not succeeded in bringing over many of these customers of the purchased concern. Or, again, it may be carrying plant and equipment on the books at what are known to be unrealistic valuations, because of consistent undercharging of depreciation over the years.

Overvaluations of the kinds described usually mean that earnings records show up poorly. The earnings of a corporation having over-

valued assets may be satisfactory in relation to a *reasonable* valuation of
its assets, but they are poor when measured in terms of the book value
of assets, the par or stated value of the capital stock, and the book
amount of the total equity accounts. Yet these are criteria by which
credit grantors decide whether or not to grant loans or other credits,
and security buyers decide whether or not to buy a corporation's stocks
and bonds. Overvaluations, in a word, tend to weaken a corporation's
credit standing and its access to the securities markets for long-term
funds.

But there is a remedy. An immediate improvement in a corporation's
appearance to prospective creditors and security buyers and to the public
in general can usually be gained by write-downs and write-offs of asset
values to be charged against surplus—surplus provided, in part at least, by
reductions in the par or stated value of outstanding common stock. To
see how an "adjustment" of this kind can be made to work out, let us
consider the situation of a corporation whose financial position is indicated by the following condensed balance sheet:

Current assets.....................$4,500,000	Liabilities..........$3,750,000
Fixed assets:	Common stock....... 6,000,000
Plant and equipment....$3,500,000	Earned surplus....... 250,000
Patents.............. 800,000	
Goodwill............. 1,200,000 5,500,000	

We may assume that the corporation's common stock consists of 200,000
shares of a par value of $30 a share, and that its net profits have been
averaging around $300,000 annually. Thus, the profits have amounted
to a return of 3 per cent on total assets, 5 per cent on the stock itself,
and 4.8 per cent on the total equity accounts as shown in the balance
sheet, all these being rather weak rates of return. But the managers of the
corporation recognize that the patents and goodwill are valueless and that
plant and equipment, because of inadequate depreciation charges in past
years, are overvalued by $1 million. With the approval of the stock-
holders, a decision is made to write off the patents and goodwill and to
reduce the book value of plant and equipment to $2.5 million, as well as
to reduce the par value of the stock from $30 to $15 a share to provide
sufficient surplus to absorb the reductions in asset values. Since the write-
offs and write-down amount to $3 million, this amount is exactly bal-
anced by the transfer to be made from the common stock to the capital
surplus account. Nevertheless, it is decided that the surplus of $250,000
that remains will be carried as capital surplus rather than as earned surplus. Since the underdepreciation of plant and equipment and the over-
valuation of patents have resulted in overstatements of profits in preceding years, earned surplus is also overstated, and the recognition of past
errors in accounting must result in its elimination. Accordingly, the corporation's balance sheet, after all changes have been entered upon its
books, would appear as follows:

Current assets..............	$4,500,000	Liabilities................	$3,750,000
Plant and equipment.........	2,500,000	Common stock.............	3,000,000
		Capital surplus............	250,000

Immediately, therefore, the corporation's record is made to look better. On the basis of the figures of the revised balance sheet, its average earnings of $300,000 a year have amounted to 4.29 per cent on its assets, 10 per cent on its common stock, and 9.23 per cent on its total equity accounts. Moreover, the changes effected might bring about an improvement in future earnings figures. The amortization of patents would be eliminated as an annual charge although book charges for depreciation, in view of the undercharging of depreciation in prior years, would be likely to be higher. If, then, the elimination of patent amortization should exceed the increased charges for depreciation, and if the corporation should maintain the same scale of operations and the same selling prices for its products, it would have a larger margin of profit. Or, with lowered costs, the corporation might reduce its selling prices to capture a larger share of the market, thereby seeking a larger profit by way of a larger volume of sales.

Changes with Variations in Number of Shares

Changes in the par or stated values of common stock with simultaneous changes in the number of shares to be outstanding usually take the form of what are called *split-ups* and *reverse splits*. A corporation that has outstanding 200,000 shares of $100 par value may decide upon a 5 for 1 split-up, substituting one million shares of $20 par value; or one having outstanding two million no-par shares of a stated value of $1.00 may effect a 1 for 10 reverse split, substituting 200,000 no-par shares of a stated value of $10. These examples illustrate what may be labeled simple split-ups and reverse splits whereby the number of shares is changed in inverse proportion to the change in par or stated value, but no switch is made from par to no par or vice versa, no change is made in the total dollar amount of the common stock account, and no surplus account is affected. Not infrequently, however, corporations provide simultaneously for switches between par and no-par values when effecting split-ups and reverse splits. For example, a corporation with 200,000 common shares of $50 par value might, in a 4 for 1 split-up, substitute 800,000 no-par shares of a stated value of $12.50 each. Much more rarely, split-ups and reverse splits are accompanied by other adjustments in the common stock account to provide a capital surplus, as, for example, the split-up of 200,000 shares of stock of $50 par value for one million shares of $8.00 par value, with, accordingly, a capital surplus of $2 million resulting. In the following discussion of split-ups and reverse splits, however, only the simple variety will be considered, as the reasons for the other kinds of adjustments that might be used in combination have already been analyzed at length.

Split-ups to Promote Wide Distribution. The most important reason for split-ups is to lower the market value of outstanding common stock— a reason indicated by the concentration of a large majority of split-ups in periods of stock market boom. The rise in the market price of a corporation's stock in such a period may put it, in the judgment of the corporation's managers, beyond the reach of the great mass of potential investors. It is generally taken for granted that the typical investor would much rather buy, say, five shares of a given stock at $30 a share than one share at $150, even though the one share at $150 would give him the same proportional ownership rights as would five shares at $30. The typical investor has the conviction, it is claimed, that the $30 share is more likely to rise to, say, $40 in market value than is the $150 share to rise in an equal proportion, that is, to go to $200. Studies of the market behavior of stocks after split-ups tend to support this kind of expectation, although the evidence, considering the complex of forces always bearing upon the stock market, is by no means conclusive. At any rate, the decision of a corporation whose common stock is selling at $150 to split it up 5 for 1 would be in harmony with prevailing thinking. Such harmony in thinking has been amply demonstrated by the very large number of split-ups that have been effected in the long period of sustained business growth and price advances in the stock market since the end of World War II. A sampling of recent split-ups is presented in Table 20–2. Columns are added in the table to show the immediate mar-

TABLE 20–2
Some Common Stock Split-ups, 1959–63

| | | | CLOSING MARKET PRICES | |
CORPORATION	BASIS	DATE OF DIRECTORS' RESOLUTION	Day Preceding Resolution	Day of Resolution
Colgate-Palmolive Company............	3 for 1	2/17/59	94⅛	95⅜
Atlantic City Electric Company........	3 for 2	7/21/59	46	46¼
International Paper Company..........	3 for 1	10/11/60	88⅞	91½
R. J. Reynolds Tobacco Company......	2 for 1	7/13/61	130¼	129
Scott Paper Company.................	3 for 1	10/17/61	125	131½
Republic Aviation Corporation........	2 for 1	10/31/61	48⅜	50⅜
Hoover Ball & Bearing Company.......	2 for 1	3/31/63	46½	47
Electric Storage Battery Company......	3 for 2	8/7/63	54½	57⅞
Tonka Toys, Inc.....................	3 for 2	8/8/63	29[a]	28¾[a]
New York & Honduras Rosario Mining Company.........................	3 for 1	9/11/63	68½	69½
Jamaica Water Company..............	3 for 1	10/3/63	78[a]	77½[a]

[a] Bid prices in the over-the-counter market.

ket reaction to the announcements of the split-ups.

But this, in turn, raises the question why many corporate managements are anxious to bring down the market prices of their stocks within a range presumably favored by the great mass of investors. Widespread ownership—"wide distribution" is the popular term—is apparently desired.

Why? One reason is the enhancement of prospects for success in further offerings of common stock to existing stockholders: in Chapter 18 it was indicated that small stockholders are likely to be more willing to buy their allotted shares in new offerings than are large ones. Likewise, widespread ownership should mean general investor interest in any securities the corporation might want to offer and by whatever means—offerings of common stock through investment bankers to the general public, as well as offerings of preferred stocks and bonds. For corporations that produce consumer goods, in particular, widespread ownership of their stock is usually thought to be highly desirable. Consumers should surely be inclined to favor the products of the corporations in which they own stock. Especially if, in their minds, the choice between these products and those of competing concerns is a narrow one, the fact of their stockholding should weigh their buying decisions in the "right" direction. Finally, a reason for the favoring of wide distribution is fear of loss of control by corporate managements in shaky positions. A minority faction seeking to gain control might be expected to have much greater difficulty in trying to buy sufficient shares from numerous owners of small holdings, or to line up their votes, than it would have were it necessary only to approach a few large stockholders.

Split-ups Preparatory to New Offerings. Split-ups are often useful, not only to promote general investor interest in a corporation's securities, as indicated above, but also as a step immediately aimed at easing the sale of new offerings. Suppose, for example, that $150 is the market price of the stock of a corporation that is planning a new offering to its stockholders. The corporation's managers are reasonably confident that the contemplated flotation would be successful at an offering price of, say, $135 but, for the kinds of reasons already stated, they would be all the more confident were it possible to make the offering at a price in the vicinity of $25. A split-up of 5 for 1, therefore, would pave the way for the latter choice. The split-up would be expected to bring the market price down to approximately $30. Accordingly, an offering of five times as many shares as originally contemplated at a price of, say, $27, could be made in the expectation that, if successful, it would yield the same gross proceeds as expected of the offering originally planned.

Split-ups for Secondary Distributions. Sometimes split-ups are preliminary steps to sales of all or substantial portions of the holdings of large stockholders—a kind of operation described as a "secondary distribution." For illustration, let us say that a large stockholder wants to sell out his holdings of a stock quoted in the market at 200. In view of the limited number of investors who are interested in high-priced stocks, he fears that his attempt to "unload" will force down the market price sharply. To reach a much larger number of potential investors, therefore, he persuades the corporation—his vote alone may be sufficient—to effect a 10 for 1 split. He is then able to offer the stock at a price around 20—surely with much less danger of a sharp drop in market value. In such a secondary distribution, the corporation itself receives no money; nevertheless, because wider distribution is promoted, this can be beneficial for its own financing or for other reasons.

A rather spectacular split-up of this kind was effected in December, 1958, by the Great Atlantic & Pacific Tea Company to prepare the way for the disposal of some of the stock interests of members of the Hartford family. The existing common was split 10 for 1, an additional non-voting common was replaced by voting common also on a basis of 10 for 1, and the existing preferred was exchanged for voting common, three shares of the latter being given for each share of the preferred. Later, in March, 1959, Hartford interests offered for sale to the public 1.8 million shares of the voting common (the sole remaining class of stock).

Split-ups in Planning Combinations. Corporations not infrequently split up their common stock to make it more attractive to the stockholders of other corporations which they hope to absorb. Split-ups can be most helpful in advancing merger proposals and holding company acquisitions. Corporation A wants to absorb Corporation B in a merger or to gain control of it and continue it in operation as a subsidiary; in keeping with the usual attitude, it hopes that the combination can be effected very largely on the basis of an exchange of some of its stock for that of B. Careful studies of B's asset values and especially of its earnings record and prospects lead A's managers to the conclusion that they could afford to offer one share of its stock for six shares of B's. But immediately it is felt that the very exchange ratio mentioned might make the proposal *sound* unattractive to B's stockholders. A 1 for 1 exchange would surely sound much better, and it could be easily managed. Let A simply split up its stock on a 6 for 1 basis and then make its offer at 1 for 1—a more pleasant offer, presumably, although not essentially different from the one originally contemplated.

Split-ups and Bargaining Position. A final reason for split-ups is to make earnings records look much poorer than they actually are or have been. This may seem a strange objective in view of the emphasis placed by credit grantors, investors, and security analysts upon "earnings per share of common" and "earnings on stockholders' investment." But employees, labor union officials, tax assessors, potential competitors, and customers may also be inclined to give much attention to these measures of profitability. While, therefore, a corporation wants to look quite affluent to people of the first group mentioned, it probably prefers to be looked upon by those of the second group as having a "tough struggle." Too much affluence is all too likely to lead to demands for higher wages, higher assessments for property taxes, greater reluctance of income tax agents to allow deductions in tax computations for disputed items of expense, dissatisfaction on the part of customers who may feel that high profit rates must mean that the prices of the corporation's products are unreasonable, and incursions into the corporation's field of operations by other firms.

Sometimes, of course, the stand taken by employees, tax collectors, customers, and others is fully or partially justified; but, at other times, it is clearly built upon false premises, often related to some simple measure of profitability such as "earnings per share of common," and with other financial facts ignored. To the untutored or the careless investigator, a corporation that has "earnings per share of common" of $20 may appear to be ten times as profitable as one whose "earnings per share of common" amount to only $2.00, whereas the fact may be that the second is much more profitable than the first in percentage rates of return on total assets or on total stockholders' investment. At any rate, split-ups can be used as a means of defense against attacks based upon isolated measures of profitability such as "earnings per share of common." Obviously, "earnings per share of common" can readily be reduced from $20 to $2.00 by simply splitting up the common on a 10 for 1 basis.

Reverse Splits. Reverse splits—or *split-downs,* as they are sometimes called—are much less common than split-ups; as one would expect, they are chiefly a phenomenon of periods of business depression and depressed stock market prices.

If a high price for a share of stock, such as $150 or $200, tends to take the stock out of the investment range of the great mass of investors, an extremely low price, such as 50 or 75 cents, or even a dollar or two, tends to do exactly the same. The stock gets into the company of "cats and dogs" or "penny stocks" where it has attractions only for the wilder groups of speculators and those who lack investment acumen. Witness the flood of uranium stocks in recent years offered at 1 cent, 5 cents, and 10 cents a share. Moreover, the cats-and-dogs area is the happy hunting ground of fraudulent promoters who defy the securities laws to try to make a quick dollar. Accordingly, reverse splits effected by reputable corporations are chiefly designed to get their stocks out of association with the motley array of cats and dogs and up to a more dignified level. As an example, the Parvin-Dohrman Company (formerly the Starrett Corporation) effected as of June 1, 1963, a reverse split of 1 for 5 in both its common and preferred stocks, the objective being, according to its president, "to increase the company's prestige which has suffered because of the low class image connected with a $2.50 stock." [2] The closing price of the common stock on the American Stock Exchange on Friday, May 31, was, indeed, 2½, but at the close on Monday, June 3, the price was 12½!

A reverse split has the secondary effect of raising the level of profits per share—assuming that the corporation is not operating in the red. In

---

[2] *The Wall Street Journal,* May 31, 1963, p. 14.

time of business slump, this is likely to be regarded by corporate managers as desirable for its own sake; like increases in market price, it should be good for credit standing and investor interest. A report of earnings at $1.00 a share of common stock after a 1 for 10 reverse split is likely to sound much better than would one of 10 cents a share without the reverse split.

TRANSACTIONS IN TREASURY STOCK

Treasury stock, as we know, is a corporation's own common stock[3] originally issued as full paid and nonassessable and reacquired by the corporation by gift or purchase or in some other way. We have already seen that corporations sometimes buy their own common stock in the market for resale to employees under the terms of their employee stock-purchase plans, as well as to make deliveries to executives upon the surrender of stock options. We have also considered donations of common stock for resale made by stockholders to whom entire original issues have been given, as in exchanges for partnership assets—a practice much more common in earlier days of high par values than now. But a few aspects of treasury stock remain for examination: certain legal and accounting considerations, and the scope of certain kinds of transactions other than those already discussed. For the transactions, we shall find it convenient to classify some as "legitimate" and others as "questionable."

Legal and Accounting Aspects of Treasury Stock

Legal Rules. In their corporation laws, all states permit the corporations they charter to acquire treasury stock by purchase, gift, or in other ways, and to sell it, pledge it, or otherwise dispose of it. But it is not required that treasury stock be held for subsequent disposal. It can be canceled by means of an amendment to the articles of incorporation reducing the authorized issue by the amount of the treasury stock. A cancellation might be decided upon to reduce the burden of annual capital stock or franchise taxes.

Subject to some exceptions to be mentioned later, the principal limitation found in state laws is that a corporation's expenditures in acquiring treasury stock must not exceed the amount of its earned surplus. The corporation's directors have the power to declare and distribute cash dividends in an amount equal to the earned surplus; hence, they presumably do no injury to creditors if they choose to use cash to buy treasury

---

[3] Corporations may, of course, reacquire some of their own preferred stock that was fully paid and made nonassessable at the time of issuance. Such reacquired stock could reasonably be called "preferred treasury stock" or "treasury preferred stock." Ordinarily, however, when the term *treasury stock* is used without modification, it is understood to be common stock. A reason for this is that corporations generally cancel reacquired preferred stock, whereas they often have no intention to cancel when reacquiring common stock.

stock, paying not more than the balance in earned surplus after cash dividends, if any, have been deducted.

Other general rules found in the state laws and in court decisions include the following: that treasury stock cannot be voted by the directors or by anybody else, that it does not share in dividends, that it may be disposed of by the directors without the consent of the stockholders unless the articles of incorporation require this consent, and that it is not subject to the stockholders' preemptive right.

Accounting Treatment. As for the accounting aspects of treasury stock, two rules most emphasized by reputable accountants are that treasury stock should be carried as a deduction from the common stock account rather than as an asset, and that gain recognized *on the acquisition of the stock* should be carried as capital surplus or, even better, as a surplus account specifically titled to show its source. Suppose, for example, that the financial position of a certain corporation is as indicated in the following condensed balance sheet:

Assets...............$10,000,000	Liabilities.....................		$4,000,000
	Common stock.................		5,000,000
	Earned surplus................		1,000,000

The common stock, let us say, consists of 100,000 shares of $50 par value. Now assume that 10,000 shares of the corporation's stock are donated to it by one or more of its stockholders. The preferred way of showing the effects of this transaction would be as follows:

Assets...............$10,000,000	Liabilities...........		$4,000,000
	Common stock......$5,000,000		
	Less: Treasury stock..........	500,000	4,500,000
	Earned surplus.......		1,000,000
	Donated surplus (or Surplus from donation of treasury stock).........		500,000

Or assume that the corporation, instead of receiving a donation of stock, buys 10,000 shares in the market at $40 a share. Preferably the result would be shown as follows:

Assets................$9,600,000	Liabilities...........		$4,000,000
	Common stock......$5,000,000		
	Less: Treasury stock..........	500,000	4,500,000
	Earned surplus.......		1,000,000
	Surplus from purchase of treasury stock		100,000

The latter illustration demonstrates the reason for the rule limiting purchases of treasury stock to the amount of earned surplus. On the basis of the balance in its earned surplus account, the corporation, before buying the treasury stock, was in a position to pay cash dividends of $1 million; but after the spending of $400,000 in the treasury stock purchase, further purchases or the distribution of cash dividends for any amount in excess of $600,000 would unfairly threaten the safety of creditors. As a matter of fact, many accountants would insist that the balance sheet clearly show the reduction in the corporation's capacities to pay dividends and to buy treasury stock; this would be accomplished by reducing the earned surplus account to $600,000 and showing the $400,000 removed from it in a separate account with a descriptive title such as "surplus appropriated for treasury stock purchase." It may be observed, too, that by no stretch of the imagination could the "surplus from purchase of treasury stock" of $100,000 be said to add anything to the corporation's dividend-paying capacity.

Legitimate Transactions in Treasury Stock

Certain kinds of transactions in treasury stock are described here as "legitimate" in the sense that they clearly benefit corporations and their stockholders and, at the same time, do not weaken in any significant way the position of creditors.

For Options and Employee Stock-Purchase Plans. Purchases of outstanding stock to make delivery on stock options held by executives and for the purposes of employee stock-purchase plans generally fall in the category of legitimate transactions. New money is not raised when treasury stock is so used, except to the extent that selling prices to executives and employees exceed the prices at which treasury stock is bought. For at least a few corporations, however, acquiring additional cash is not an important objective of stock-option arrangements and employee purchase plans. When, therefore, a corporation does not need additional money, a delivery of unissued stock would seem to be less desirable than a purchase and delivery of treasury stock.

For Merger Transactions. Much the same can be said for the use of treasury stock in acquisitions of enterprises in mergers and other forms of combination. In the drive for diversification that has been pronounced in recent years, many corporations have accumulated large amounts of cash earmarked for absorbing other firms. Often, however, the stockholders and managements of firms singled out for absorption refuse to sell for cash, on account of the tax liabilities on the capital gains that would result. They would much prefer to sell out on a basis of exchanges of common stocks, since such exchanges can usually be worked out as tax-free arrangements. If, therefore, the acquiring firm already has cash to pay for an acquisition, it might prefer to buy up its own common stock in the market to make the exchange than to offer unissued stock. Indeed, many corporations have bought up some of their own common stock ahead of time, as it were—simply to have it available for exchanges should attractive merger opportunities turn up. In November, 1962, for example, the Standard Pressed Steel Company revealed that it had recently bought 25,400 shares of its common stock in the market and that it planned to continue to buy "for use in possible future acquisitions"; and in August, 1963, the Skelly Oil Company invited its common stockholders to tender to it up to 300,000 shares at prices not exceeding $70, the stock to be held "for use in acquisitions and its management stock-option plan." [4]

Donations. Also within the category of legitimacy are many transactions whereby corporations' own common stock is donated to them. A corporation may be sorely in need of working capital at a time when the possibilities of selling new securities or borrowing direct from financial institutions are quite slim; accordingly, one or a few of its stockholders, or perhaps all the stockholders on a pro rata basis, may donate a portion of their shares to the corporation in the belief that the corporation, and the remaining portion of their investment in it, can be saved by the resale of these shares. Donations for this purpose are more likely in family corporations, but they have sometimes been made even to large corporations having wide common stock distributions. Donations of common stock may also be a means of eliminating deficits from corporate books, as an alternative to reductions in par or stated values of all such stock outstanding. Upon receiving a donation of some of its common stock, a corporation is justified in carrying a credit to a surplus account equal to the par or stated value of the donated stock; if, then, the earned surplus account has a debit balance, this can be directly offset by the credit for donated stock.

Settlement of Claims. Sometimes corporations receive their own stock in settlement of obligations due them. A debtor who is unable to pay in cash may offer his holdings of the stock of the creditor corporation. Or the debtor, having pledged his stock for the satisfaction of his obligation, may forfeit it upon default. Again, upon a debtor's default, a corporation may sue and obtain judgment, thereafter seizing the debtor's holdings of its own stock in satisfaction of the judgment. Acquisitions of treasury stock in these ways appear to be quite legitimate; indeed, the state laws generally indicate specific approval by exempting such acquisitions from the rule limiting total acquisitions to the amount of earned surplus.

Use by Close Corporations. Another type of transaction that leads to acquisitions of treasury stock on what appears to be a legitimate basis is the buying back by close corporations of shares held by stockholders who wish to sever their connections. The few stockholders of such a corporation may agree that their *esprit de corps* and, with that, the corporation's profitability, would be ruined by the admission of outsiders as stockholders; in keeping with this conviction, they may enter into a contract

---

[4] *The Wall Street Journal,* November 9, 1962, p. 19; and August 9, 1963, p. 12.

among themselves to give the corporation the first chance to buy their stockholdings should they want to depart. A departure, therefore, would be the occasion for a treasury stock acquisition by the corporation.

Questionable Transactions in Treasury Stock

Certain kinds of treasury stock transactions are described in these pages as "questionable" because they can prove to be harmful to corporations and all their stockholders, to particular groups of stockholders, or to their creditors.

Purchases for Retirement. A most interesting question of legitimacy arises when corporate boards of directors decide to use excess cash to buy up outstanding common stock for retirement. It is a question for which, in truth, there is no clear-cut answer, but some of the pros and cons may be mentioned.

A corporation may have curtailed the scope of its operations, and prospects for re-expansion may be nil; at the same time, the directors may want to avoid the distribution of redundant cash by way of extraordinary dividends because substantial amounts of these dividends would be subject to income taxes when received by the stockholders. The buying up of stock in the market might thus appear to be an easy solution to the problem. The directors could argue that stockholders who offer their shares in the market are the very ones who want to give up their ownership interests—that, accordingly, the buying up of these shares would be preferable to reducing the interests of all stockholders indiscriminately, as by the distribution of dividends "in partial liquidation." If the shares could be bought in the market at less than their book value, the directors could also argue that the corporation's purchases would give the remaining stockholders increased per-share claims against assets. On the other hand, if more than book value had to be paid for the treasury stock, the remaining stockholders would seem to have a good reason to complain about the resulting reduction in the book value of their own shares. Even more gravely would they be injured if, subsequent to the purchase and retirement of the treasury stock, the affairs of the corporation were to go badly and operating losses make serious inroads upon the assets. The corporation could be condemned as having given preferential treatment of an extreme kind to the stockholders from whom the treasury stock had been bought.

Doubts about the legitimacy of purchases by corporations of their own common stocks for retirement can always be resolved, of course, by submitting the question to the stockholders themselves. This was done by the Richmond, Fredericksburg & Potomac Railroad Company when, in August, 1962, it asked its stockholders to tender to it their common or preferred shares so that it could use up $3 million of cash for which it had "no need." The secretary-treasurer said that investment of the money in short-term securities would yield a lower rate of return than the dividend rates the company was paying on its stocks, so that it would "save money" by buying back stock.[5]

Slack Season Investment. More clearly worthy of adverse criticism is a use of excess cash for dealings in treasury stock on a temporary basis. In the off-season of a corporation whose pattern of operations is highly seasonal, the directors might decide that the best way to "invest" excess cash till needed for the active season would be to buy some of the corporation's own common stock available in the market. The intention clearly would not be to retire the stock, but to resell it at or before the time cash would be needed for operations. The directors might try to justify the treasury stock transactions on the grounds that the dividends "saved" on the stock while held in the treasury would be much greater than the interest that could be earned by temporary investment in, say, short-term government securities. Moreover, the directors might be inclined to feel that, by "playing the market" astutely, they would be able to sell at a net gain. It is clear, at any rate, that a temporary investment of excess cash in treasury stock could hardly be other than speculative. Even if the possibility of capital gains were given no great weight in the directors' decision, it is obvious that the net saving as between dividend and interest rates could be more than offset by losses on resale. Stockholders, therefore, would have a sound basis for arguing that the risks of stock market speculation ought not to be added to the unavoidable risks of day-to-day operations.

Supporting Market Prices. Most questionable of all, in the realm of treasury stock transactions, are purchases made to arrest declines in the market values of stocks. To justify action of this kind, corporate managements have advanced the argument that sharp and rapid declines in the market prices of stock are injurious to credit standing and prospects for future financing, and some have even claimed that corporations have a duty to see that their stockholders get a "reasonable value" for their stock if they wish to sell; but such arguments are quite unconvincing. Corporations have no duty to selling stockholders to take extraordinary measures to protect the market value of their shares, and their buying has generally been of little help in saving credit standing and prospects for future financing when prices have been under the pressure of floods of selling orders. As a matter of fact, the very use of cash for stock purchases to stem price declines is likely to be much more injurious to credit standing and future prospects of all kinds, including survival, than are the price declines themselves.

In the second quarter of 1962 in which a very sharp drop in stock prices in all markets took place, many corporations bought up extraordinary amounts of their common stock. According to a report of the New York Stock Exchange, these corporations included McCrory Corporation

---

[5] *Ibid.*, August 8, 1962, p. 4.

which bought 195,100 shares during the quarter; Allied Supermarkets, Inc., 247,200 shares; Schering Corporation, 50,000 shares; Consolidation Coal Company, 140,857 shares; Gulf Oil Corporation, 225,000 shares; and Skelly Oil Company, 152,375 shares. In all instances, however, it was denied that purchases had been made to support market prices. Instead, the general attitude was that the period was a very favorable time to acquire treasury stock for possible future acquisitions and for delivery against stock options. For McCrory, raising "earnings per share" of the stock that remained outstanding was given as a reason for buying.[6]

Questions

1. Lacking sufficient unissued common stock, corporations could use what other means to make deliveries upon stock options, stock-purchase warrants, and convertible preferred stocks and bonds turned in for conversion? Why would these other means be likely to be unsatisfactory?

2. Aside from its use for deliveries upon options, warrants, and other such contracts, placing unissued common stock at the directors' disposal might be advantageous for the stockholders in what kinds of transactions?

3. What are the possible disadvantages to corporations and their stockholders in having large amounts of authorized but unissued stock available?

4. In the second and third decades of the present century, why did many corporate managements campaign for legislation to permit the issuance of no-par common stock?

5. How can one account for the great spurt in recent years in the popularity of common stocks of low par values?

6. What kinds of taxes sometimes discriminate against no-par stock? Are stocks of low par values subject to the same kind of discrimination? Explain.

7. From the standpoint of issuing corporations, compare no-par stocks with stocks of low par values in their attractiveness for (*a*) avoiding the discount rule, and (*b*) enabling the corporations to have paid-in surpluses.

8. Explain how deficits in corporations' surplus accounts can be eliminated by changes in the par or stated values of their common stocks. Do such changes eliminate the losses that caused the deficits? Do they affect the corporations' dividend-paying capacities? Explain.

9. Why might it be advisable to accompany a write-down in a corporation's asset values with a change in the par or stated value of its common stock?

10. Why is a stock split-up supposed to promote a wider distribution of the stock? Why is wide distribution desired?

11. Under what circumstances might a split-up of a corporation's common stock be advantageous in preparation for merger negotiations with another corporation?

12. Why is it said that a corporation might improve its "bargaining position" by splitting its common stock? In bargaining with whom might this improvement be realized?

13. Distinguish between unissued stock and treasury stock. Is it possible for a corporation to make a profit through transactions in treasury stock? Explain.

---

[6] *Ibid.*, July 20, 1962, p. 2.

14. To what extent, if at all, are corporations legally restricted in reacquiring their own common stock?

15. Discuss the reasonableness of a corporation's buying its own common stock in the market (*a*) to make delivery on stock options, (*b*) to be held for offering in merger proposals, (*c*) to use up excess cash with the intention of retiring the stock purchased, (*d*) to invest cash temporarily in excess supply for seasonal reasons, and (*e*) to try to check a decline in the market value of the stock.

Problems

1. Referring to Problem 1 at the end of the preceding chapter, how might a split-up of the common stock of Walker, Inc., have helped it to avoid difficulties in its merger negotiations with Caldwell Manufacturing Company? Assuming a decision by Walker's directors to make an offer based closely upon the relative earning power of the stocks of the two corporations, a split-up of what proportions would probably have been most advantageous? Why?

2. A corporation has outstanding 300,000 shares of common stock of $40 par value. It has operated for several years at a loss and has a deficit of $5 million in its earned surplus account.

a) How could it "manipulate" its equity accounts to eliminate the deficit and, at the same time, provide a surplus credit balance of, say, $1 million?

b) Could the directors legally declare cash dividends against the surplus credit balance established in (*a*)? Explain.

c) If in the year after the "manipulation" the corporation had an operating profit of $600,000, could cash dividends up to this amount be legally paid? Explain.

d) Would the "manipulation" require the approval of the stockholders? Would it require an amendment to the articles of incorporation?

3. S. S. Drake & Co., Inc., has outstanding 200,000 shares of common stock of $25 par value and an earned surplus of $40,000. Over a period of eight years, its average after-tax profit per share has been only 20 cents. As a result, the market price of its stock has been depressed for most of this period, not having risen above 4¼ within the period, and now standing at 3⅜. The president of the corporation believes that its earning capacity can be substantially improved if it can get some additional long-term money for needed machinery and working capital. He sees little prospect of getting this money by issuing preferred stock or by borrowing, but he thinks that there must be some way to make an additional issue of common stock look attractive to potential investors. Knowing that you are a student of corporation finance, he asks you for advice. What do you say?

chapter 21

THE LISTING OF COMMON STOCK
ON STOCK EXCHANGES

The listing of a common stock or other security may be defined as the provision of facilities by a stock exchange to its members, upon the basis of an agreement with the issuer, for trading in the security. A corporation that wants to have its common stock listed makes application to the stock exchange of its choice, as well as to the Securities and Exchange Commission if the exchange is registered as a "national securities exchange," as are all but four of our exchanges. Both the exchange and the SEC investigate the affairs of the applying corporation, the former with particular attention to the prospective trading interests of its members, and the latter with special concern for the protection of the investing public. If both the exchange and the SEC approve the application, the common stock becomes "listed." The exchange then designates a "post" on its floor where its members can meet to effect buying and selling transactions in the stock.

Whether or not to list common stock on one or more of our stock exchanges is a problem that faces the managements of only a small minority of American business corporations. On the basis of the exchanges' own admission standards, most corporations do not qualify for the listing of their common stocks; and a goodly number of those that could qualify find one or more reasons for not making applications for listing. As of December 31, 1961, according to a report of the SEC, only 3,041 issues of common stock in total were listed on all exchanges (avoiding duplications on account of "dual listings" of given common stocks on two or more exchanges).[1]

The fact that a corporation does not have its common stock and other securities issues listed on a stock exchange does not mean that there is no market for them. In almost all instances, the holder of an unlisted security who wants to sell can find one or more dealers who will either buy the security from him or undertake to find a buyer. Such transactions are said to take place in the over-the-counter market, the location of which is principally the hundreds of offices of securities dealers throughout the country, rather than a single site, as for a stock exchange. Indeed, the volume of transactions in the over-the-counter market in many unlisted securities far exceeds the volume on the stock exchanges in "inactive" and

---

[1] Securities and Exchange Commission, *Annual Report*, 1962, p. 43.

"less active" listed securities. Moreover, the over-the-counter market accounts for a substantial volume of transactions in listed securities, especially transactions in which large institutional investors are buyers or sellers. To buy large blocks of given stocks, institutional investors often find the total cost lower in the over-the-counter market than would be the price plus commissions they would have to pay if buying through stock exchange members; and to sell large blocks, they often find better offers in the over-the-counter market than would be the price less commissions for stock exchange transactions.

Nevertheless, the question of listing is important, as it must be considered at one time or another by most of the larger corporations of the country. Somewhere along the line, the management of a corporation that is reaching substantial size is likely to come to a realization that it could qualify for listing—and this brings up the question whether or not listing would be advantageous. Accordingly, the principal aim of the present chapter is to analyze the pros and cons of listing, as they are likely to be seen from the standpoint of corporate managements. First, however, it is desirable to survey some general aspects of the listing question.

GENERAL ASPECTS OF LISTING

Business corporations do not raise new money for their operations by the sale of common stock (or other securities) through the facilities of the stock exchanges. They do not deliver batches of new common stock to an exchange and expect its members to sell it to their customers. If they want to use common stock as a means of financing, they offer it to the public direct or through investment bankers, offer it to their existing stockholders with or without the aid of investment bankers, or use one or more of the additional selling procedures described in Chapter 19.

Only after a common stock has been rather widely distributed by one or more of these means, as well as by subsequent transactions among holders, is an exchange likely to consider accepting it for listing. Most members of an exchange—that is, the owners of "seats" who alone have the privilege of buying and selling through its facilities—make a large part of their income from commissions derived in handling buying and selling orders for their customers. Hence, in general, they want the exchange to list for trading only securities that are distributed widely enough to promise numerous transactions.

In having its common stock listed on an exchange, therefore, a corporation obtains market facilities, not for its own selling, but for selling by its stockholders and for buying by those who want to become stockholders. Through investment bankers, a corporation may have sold its common stock to A, B, C, and thousands of other investors; but now that the stock has been listed, A may hire a member of the exchange to sell his shares through its facilities, C may hire another member to buy some additional shares, and later C may resell to D, D to E, and so on.

The Exchanges

Although eighteen stock exchanges are currently in operation in the United States,[2] stock exchange transactions are heavily concentrated on the New York Stock Exchange. In the year 1962, it accounted for 71.3 per cent of the number and 86.5 per cent of the market value of shares of stock, both common and preferred, sold on all exchanges (see Table 21–1). Of the 3,041 issues of common stock listed on all exchanges on December 31, 1961, 1,541 issues were carried on the "Big Board." The American Stock Exchange, also located in New York City, had 1,001 stocks posted for trading at the end of 1961. In 1962, it accounted for 20 per cent of

TABLE 21–1
Sales of Stock on Stock Exchange in 1962
(Amounts in thousands)

	Market Value	Number of Shares
Registered exchanges:		
American	$ 3,648,312	332,618
Boston	252,353	5,332
Cincinnati	38,448	781
Detroit	230,012	6,221
Midwest	1,511,815	39,999
National	509	225
New York	47,340,720	1,186,513
Pacific Coast	1,096,032	49,923
Philadelphia-Baltimore-Washington	577,149	14,817
Pittsburgh	30,972	773
Salt Lake	1,733	10,572
San Francisco Mining	1,319	11,399
Spokane	2,702	4,383
Total	$54,732,076	1,663,557[a]
Exempted exchanges:		
Colorado Springs	$ 75	414
Honolulu	19,860	837
Richmond	640	11
Wheeling	376	14
Total	$ 20,951	1,276

[a] Items do not add exactly to this total because of rounding.

SOURCE: Securities and Exchange Commission, *Statistical Bulletin*, February, 1963, p. 12.

the number and 6.7 per cent of the market value of shares sold on all exchanges, leaving only 8.7 per cent of the number and 6.8 per cent of the market value of shares traded for the remaining sixteen exchanges.

---

[2] These are the stock exchanges of Boston, Cincinnati, Detroit, New York, Pitts- burgh, Salt Lake City, Spokane, Colorado Springs, Honolulu, Richmond, and Wheel- ing, the American and National (both of New York City), the Chicago Board of Trade, the Midwest (of Chicago), the Pacific Coast (of Los Angeles and San Fran- cisco), the Philadelphia-Baltimore-Washington, and the San Francisco Mining Ex- change. The newest of the stock exchanges, the National, began operations in March, 1962, but so far the number of its listings and its sales volume have been quite modest.

Stocks listed on the New York and American exchanges are generally of nationwide and often international interest, while many of those listed solely on the other exchanges are of interest especially to the people living in the respective regions they serve. However, quite a few important corporations of nationwide interest are listed on the "regional" exchanges—especially on the Midwest Stock Exchange of Chicago and the Pacific Coast Stock Exchange which maintains trading facilities in both Los Angeles and San Francisco. These are sometimes sole listings, a given stock not being traded on any other exchange, and more often dual listings, with the stock also being listed on one or more additional exchanges —most likely, the New York or the American. For some examples of single and dual listings, see Table 21–2.

TABLE 21–2
A Sample of Stock Exchange Listings and Admissions to Unlisted
Trading of Common Stocks, December 31, 1962[a]

Corporation	*Listed on*	*Admitted to Unlisted Trading on*
American Tobacco Company......................	New York	Boston Detroit Pacific
Consolidated Paper Company.....................	Detroit	
Crown Zellerbach Corporation.....................	New York Pacific	Philadelphia
Douglas Aircraft Company, Inc...................	New York Pacific	Boston Detroit
Firestone Tire & Rubber Company.................	New York Boston	Midwest Pacific
General Electric Company.......................	New York Boston	Detroit Midwest Pacific Philadelphia Pittsburgh
General Motors Corporation.....................	New York Detroit Midwest Pacific Philadelphia	Boston Cincinnati Pittsburgh
Holly Oil Company.............................	Colorado Springs Pacific	
Kaiser Industries Corporation.....................	American Pacific	Boston Philadelphia Pittsburgh
Northeast Airlines, Inc..........................	American	
Todd Shipyards Corporation.....................		American
Webcor, Inc....................................	Midwest	
Zion's Cooperative Mercantile Institution............		Salt Lake

[a] The Philadelphia-Baltimore-Washington Stock Exchange is entered as "Philadelphia," and the Pacific Coast Stock Exchange as "Pacific."

SOURCE: Moody's Investors Service, *Manuals.*

Listings with the New York or American exchange are likely to be sought especially by large corporations that have wide distributions of their common stocks, recurring needs of additional funds to be sought from many sources scattered over a wide area, and market outlets for their products throughout the country and perhaps abroad—assuming that they want to list at all. Such corporations are likely to have a decided preference for the New York Stock Exchange in view of its unequaled prestige. They sometimes also seek dual listings with one or more of the regional exchanges. On the other hand, corporations whose operating facilities, markets, and prospective sources of long-term equity funds are largely confined to given areas of the country may be quite satisfied to have their common stocks listed solely on one of the regional exchanges—again, if there is a wish to list at all.

In the matter of pros and cons, therefore, the managers of a corporation whose interests are largely concentrated regionally are likely to feel that all the advantages of listing can be had by listing on an exchange specifically serving its region—that, indeed, the disadvantages of listing on the New York or American exchange or on another outside its region would tend to outweigh the advantages. On the other hand, the managers of a corporation having broad, national interests are likely to decide that the maximum advantages of listing can be had only by listing with the New York Stock Exchange or possibly, as a second choice, with the American, and that, accordingly, disadvantages would tend to outweigh advantages if only a third choice were available, that is, one of the regional exchanges.

Government Regulation

Regulation of Exchanges and Their Members. The Securities Exchange Act of 1934 denies the use of the mails and other instrumentalities of interstate commerce to stock exchanges unless they register with the SEC or unless that agency exempts them from registration. Fourteen of our eighteen exchanges are registered with the SEC as "national securities exchanges" [3] and the remaining four have been exempted from registration. [4] Registered exchanges *and their members* must abide by many rules set down in the Securities Exchange Act and by many regulations of the SEC issued under authority of that legislation—rules and regulations specifically designed to protect investors.

Regulation of Listed Corporations. But the Securities Exchange Act and the rules of the SEC issued in accordance therewith do not stop with the regulation of the practices of the exchanges and their members; they reach out to the corporations whose securities are listed. In studying the

---

[3] The word *national* should not mislead one. The registered exchanges are "national" for purposes of the legislation and regulations, but, as brought out in the forgoing discussion, most of them are "regional" in the scope of their listings.

[4] As indicated in Table 21–1, the exempted exchanges are the Colorado Springs, Honolulu, Richmond, and Wheeling exchanges.

pros and cons of listing, therefore, a corporate management must give weight on one side or the other to the necessity of submitting to federal regulation as a consequence of listing. (This would not apply, of course, to a listing on an exempt exchange; but the very fact of exemption indicates the relative unimportance of the operations of the exempt exchanges. Hence, the typical management will be considering applying to a registered exchange, if it goes into the matter at all.) The corporate managers may conclude that federal regulation of the operations of the exchanges and their members is all to the good—that the common stock of the corporation should be all the more attractive to existing stockholders and to prospective buyers in view of the government's protective role. But they may be inclined to balk somewhat because the government insists that investor protection requires the imposition of certain kinds of controls upon the corporation's own practices. They may grudgingly admit that protective regulations as applied to a listed corporation, no less than those applied to the exchanges and exchange members, should promote investment in its securities; but they may think this advantage too costly in terms of the burdens of compliance.

However that may be, a corporation that wants to have its common stock (or other security) listed must file with the exchange and the SEC an application containing a vast array of information about its history, its properties, the scope of its operations, its management, its financial structure, and other "material facts"—information of the kinds presumably necessary, as in registration statements under the Securities Act, for intelligent investment decisions. Indeed, the contents of applications for listing and those of registration statements for new securities issues are closely comparable—to be expected, of course, since both have been prescribed by the SEC for the identical purpose of investor protection. Listed corporations must also file with the exchange and the SEC annual and semiannual financial reports to bring up to date, as it were, the financial data originally filed in the application; and monthly reports, if certain extraordinary developments occur, such as changes in controlling interests, material changes in the volume of outstanding stocks and bonds, important acquisitions and dispositions of assets, and the initiation or termination of important legal proceedings. Furthermore, directors and officers of corporations that have stocks listed on registered exchanges, as well as owners of more than 10 per cent of any class of a listed stock, must file statements of their holdings with the SEC and keep these up to date by making further reports in any months in which changes in holdings take place. All the information supplied in applications, annual and semiannual financial reports, special reports, and reports of stockholdings becomes, as it were, public property; the documents can be examined at the respective exchanges or in the offices of the SEC, and, of course, many significant items are published by newspapers and other purveyors of financial information. Much more extensive details about the affairs of the typical listed corporation can be readily picked up by the prospective investor than about those of the typical unlisted one.[5]

Of the additional rules that are imposed upon listed corporations for investor protection, only three need be mentioned here. One has to do with the solicitation of stockholders' proxies for voting at annual and special meetings. Whether a solicitation is being made by a corporate management or by somebody else, as by a group seeking to oust the existing management, the proxy form must be drawn in accordance with SEC prescriptions, and, when sent to the stockholders, it must be accompanied by a proxy statement declaring who is making the solicitation and who is bearing the cost, giving details as to the issues to be raised at the meeting, and supplying certain facts of other kinds as prescribed by the SEC's rules. When the solicitors know in advance that certain proposals are to be presented at a meeting, they must design the proxy form in such manner that the stockholder can indicate his vote for or against the proposals. Copies of proposed proxy forms and statements must be filed with the SEC at least ten days before distribution to the stockholders; if the SEC finds them defective under its rules, it notifies the solicitors so that corrections can be made before the distribution.

A second rule is that the directors and officers of a corporation whose stock is listed on a registered exchange, as well as stockholders who own directly or indirectly more than 10 per cent of any class of its stock, are forbidden to sell the stock short.

A third rule is that a listed corporation, by lawsuit brought by itself or by any stockholder, may recover from its directors and officers and from owners of more than 10 per cent of any class of its stock any profits made by them in transactions in its stock held for periods of less than six months.

SEC Action. Indicative of the SEC's role in protecting investors was its action in August, 1960, to revoke the registration (listing) of the common stock of the Cornucopia Gold Mines which had been carried on the American Stock Exchange. Among the reasons stated for this action were the following:

The Commission found the registrant's 1957 annual report to be false and misleading in a number of respects. The financial statements which purported to be certified by independent certified public accountants were, in fact, prepared and certified by an individual accountant who had made no audit of, nor had he even seen, the registrant's books and records. The statements he certified were copied, with some figure and wording changes, from statements prepared by another accountant. The financial statements furnished were false and misleading in a number of respects including, among other things, inclusion as cash at December 31, 1957, of the proceeds of a loan of $125,000

---

[5] Such a situation will no longer obtain for unlisted corporations whose stock is rather widely held if a recommendation for new legislation made by the SEC in April, 1963, is adopted by Congress. The SEC proposed that regulations identical with or quite similar to those applicable to listed corporations, as outlined in these paragraphs, be made applicable immediately to unlisted corporations having 750 or more stockholders and eventually to those having 300 or more stockholders.

made on January 20, 1958, the failure to reveal certain contingent liabilities, and to set forth the basis for determining the amounts at which buildings and equipment were listed as assets.

The annual report was also deficient in failing to indicate important changes in the business of the registrant and in stating that certain individuals had been directors of the registrant when, in fact, they had never consented to act as such and were not aware that they had been "elected" to that office.

The Commission also found that the registrant had failed to file current reports pursuant to section 13 of the act to report the acquisition of certain subsidiaries, to describe certain legal proceedings with respect to one of its subsidiaries and to reflect a change in control of the registrant. . . .

The Commission further found that the preliminary proxy material filed by the registrant with respect to a proposed meeting of stockholders in July 1958 contained false and misleading statements and omitted necessary information. . . .[6]

Listing Standards

For the admission of its common stock to a stock exchange, a corporation must generally be able to offer something more than proof of a reasonably wide distribution of the stock and a willingness to abide by the rules and regulations of the SEC and of the exchange itself. The exchanges do not want to list corporations that are obviously being mismanaged; those whose financial structures are so complex that it is difficult to know what are the respective rights of the various classes of security holders; or those that consistently operate in the red so that they are obviously moving fast toward bankruptcy. The listing of the common stocks of such corporations could only detract from the prestige of an exchange—and exchanges are most anxious to preserve their good names, considering the fact that, even when they conduct their affairs in a most careful way, they are often subjected to unfair criticism by the uninformed.

More positively, the exchanges want the listings of well-managed corporations that have established solid places for themselves in their respective industries, that have good records of earnings, and that have good promise of continued growth and prosperity. In this regard, the New York Stock Exchange describes its standards of eligiblity as follows:

. . . It is not only size, but vigor, repute, and performance which mark a company as one which will both well serve and be well served by the New York Stock Exchange.

In reviewing the qualifications of a company for initial listing, the Exchange seeks to deal with each case on its merits. It takes into account not only earnings records, but the degree of national interest in the enterprise, its place and stability within its industry, and the prospects for its industry's growth. . . .[7]

In relating these standards to listing applications for common stocks, the New York Stock Exchange employs certain tests which it describes as a "general guideline." According to these tests, the applicant must have annual earning power of at least $1.2 million after taxes and at least

---

[6] Securities and Exchange Commission, *Annual Report*, 1961, pp. 62–63.
[7] New York Stock Exchange, *A Listing on the New York Stock Exchange*, p. 2.

$2 million before taxes, and its publicly held common shares must have an aggregate market value of at least $10 million.[8] At least 600,000 shares of the common stock, aside from family and other concentrated holdings, must be distributed among not fewer than 1,500 holders of "round lots," that is, lots of at least 100 shares individually.

It is the policy of the New York Stock Exchange to consider the advisability of delisting any corporation's common stock when the aggregate market value of the outstanding shares or the value of the corporation's net tangible assets applicable to these shares falls below $4 million, and its average net earnings for the preceding three years falls below $400,000; or when the number of round-lot stockholders falls to fewer than 600; or when the stock outstanding, exclusive of family and other concentrated holdings, amounts to 250,000 or fewer shares or has a market value of $2 million or less.

To have its common stock listed on the American Stock Exchange, a corporation must have, as a rule, net tangible assets of at least $1 million, net earnings of at least $150,000 after income taxes in its most recent fiscal year, average net earnings in the preceding three years of at least $100,000, not fewer than 200,000 shares outstanding, and not fewer than 750 stockholders of whom at least 500 must hold 100 shares or more.[9] It may order the delisting of a corporation's common stock if the corporation has had no earnings for three years, the market value of the total stock issue falls below $1 million, fewer than 70,000 shares are in the hands of the public, or the stock is owned by fewer than 250 stockholders. Applying these criteria, the American took steps in August, 1963, to delist the common and preferred stocks and the convertible debenture bonds of Davega Stores Corporation and the common stock of Dejay Stores, Inc., trading in all of which had been previously suspended on account of bankruptcy proceedings; the common stock of National Brewing Company, because its publicly held shares had fallen below 70,000; and the common stock of North Rankin Nickel Mines, Ltd., because it had not had a profit in three years.[10]

Unlisted Trading

A moderate number of corporations have gained the benefits of listing without accepting its burdens. Before the adoption of the Securities Exchange Act of 1934, many of the exchanges—not including, however, the New York Stock Exchange—posted stocks for trading on their floors

---

[8] The market value of a whole issue of common stock is found by multiplying the number of shares outstanding by the closing price at which shares were sold on any given day. It is recognized, of course, that if any large proportion of outstanding shares were offered in the market in any short period of time, the market price would be likely to fall quite sharply. For this reason, "aggregate market value," though it may be used as a means of measurement, tends to be rather fictitious.

[9] American Stock Exchange, *Advantages of Listing*, pp. 8–9.

[10] *The Wall Street Journal*, August 2, 1963, p. 12.

even though the corporate issuers of these stocks had made no applications for listing and no commitments to pay fees, to provide financial reports or other information, or to do anything else. The members of the exchanges wanted facilities to deal in these stocks, the corporations had no means or wish to control how or where their already-outstanding stocks would be traded, and the exchanges went ahead to provide facilities for "unlisted trading." The Securities Exchange Act provided for the continuance of unlisted trading privileges on registered exchanges for securities already having such privileges prior to March 1, 1934, without at the same time imposing requirements upon the corporate issuers for financial statements and other disclosures of information. At the end of June, 1962, common and preferred issues not listed on any exchange but having unlisted trading privileges under this concession on one or more of the exchanges numbered 187.[11]

Under the legislation of 1934, the SEC may permit exchanges to admit for "unlisted trading" securities that are formally listed on other exchanges. On June 30, 1962, there were 1,532 such "admissions" of both common and preferred stocks in effect, the figure not being adjusted for duplications.[12] Here, of course, the issuing corporation does not escape regulation, nor the burdens of listing pertaining to the exchange or exchanges upon which its stock is listed. However, having the stock admitted to "unlisted trading" on another exchange provides an additional market without added burdens.[13]

ADVANTAGES OF LISTING

From the standpoint of corporate welfare, the advantages of having common stocks listed on the stock exchanges are likely to be thought of as including chiefly the following: (1) wider distribution of the stock, (2) aid in selling additional issues of the stock, (3) aid in selling other securities, (4) improved credit standing, and (5) advertising of products. Such a classification undoubtedly overlaps, for, as was pointed out in the preceding chapter, wide distribution is not so much an advantage in itself as it is a source of other advantages such as aid in selling additional stock or other securities and the promotion of the sale of products. To be kept in mind, moreover, is the idea that the advantages of listing are importantly influenced and conditioned by the scope of operations of the particular exchange upon which a stock is or is to be listed, whether national or regional, and—with the possible exception of the last-named advantage—by investor appreciation of the protective function of the federal regulations.

---

[11] Securities and Exchange Commission, *Annual Report*, 1962, p. 51.
[12] *Ibid.*, p. 52.
[13] Another provision of the Securities Exchange Act authorizes the SEC to permit exchanges to accept securities for unlisted trading if financial and other information about the issuers comparable to that required for formal listings is available. But this provision has been little used.

Wider Distribution of the Stock

It may seem strange to say that exchanges are not interested in listing common stocks unless they are widely distributed, but that an advantage of listing is to get wider distribution. But there is no conflict in the two propositions: a common stock, already widely held, tends to get even more widely scattered as a result of transactions in it effected through the market machinery of a stock exchange. Some investors refuse to buy unlisted stocks; many are much more reluctant to buy these than listed ones.

Regardless of intentions to hold stocks for long periods, virtually all investors want market facilities that insure quick sale at fair prices—changing conditions, they know, may make changes in investment plans imperative. Exchanges provide good market facilities. Buying and selling orders pour in to members from all parts of the country, or from all parts of a given region, and prices determined by these concentrated forces of supply and demand are likely to be fairer than those negotiated in random transactions in dealers' offices. The fact that the members of exchanges must obey an extensive body of rules promulgated by the exchanges themselves and by the SEC for the protection of their customers; that the scales of their commission rates are widely publicized; that the prices at which transactions actually take place are quickly reported and widely disseminated; that some members provide special facilities for odd-lot transactions, that is, for purchases and sales of fewer than 100 shares; that listed securities are usually more acceptable as collateral for loans than are comparable unlisted ones—all these factors tend to enhance the attractiveness of listed stocks.

Aid in Selling Additional Common Stock

The belief of corporate managements that listing aids the sale of common stock is indicated by the fact that in advertising new issues of such stock, as yet unlisted, they sometimes promise that an application for listing will be made to this or that exchange. Once a stock has been listed, moreover, additional shares, when sold, are included in the listing as a matter of course; thus, prospective buyers have this assurance of the availability of market facilities.

Because the market prices of listed stocks are the resultant of numerous buying and selling orders coming in from all directions, they tend to be highly reliable as guides to corporations and investment bankers in fixing the prices at which additional issues are to be offered—much more so than are price quotations given by dealers for stocks traded in the over-the-counter market. Indeed, since listing appears to increase demand by attracting investors who would not otherwise buy, the price of a stock as listed should be somewhat higher than it would be were it unlisted. It is likely, therefore, that the price at which additional shares of a listed stock are offered can be somewhat higher than it could be if the stock were unlisted. Moreover, investment bankers may pare their under-writing commissions in favor of flotations of additional shares of listed stocks, anticipating less selling effort than would be required if the already-outstanding stock were unlisted. Either or both these factors may mean, therefore, greater net proceeds to the issuing corporation.

Of even more direct aid to corporations in selling additional shares of listed stocks is the practice of the exchanges, for offerings to existing stockholders, of providing facilities for the buying and selling of rights. The stockholder who does not want to subscribe knows that he can sell his rights just about as readily as he could sell his shares themselves, and the publicity given to rights values through market transactions gives him a constant reminder to sell before the end of the subscription period. Likewise, the ready availability of rights on the exchange at well-publi-cized prices tends to attract buyers of rights—both those who want to subscribe and those who choose to speculate.

Aid in Selling Other Securities

All the publicity given to listed common stocks in daily newspapers, financial journals, investment newsletters, and the publications of invest-ment information services tends to be helpful to the sale, not only of addi-tional issues of the common stocks of listed corporations, but also their issues of preferred stocks and bonds. Whether or not the corporations promise to apply for the listing of the preferred stocks and bonds, in-vestor interest in these kinds of issues is, as it were, ready-made. Al-though published information about the finances of listed corporations usually emphasizes the position of their common stocks, the same infor-mation is obviously useful to prospective investors in judging the invest-ment qualities of their offerings of other types of securities.

In view of the "ready-made" interest of investors in the preferred stock and bond issues of listed corporations, investment bankers, in under-writing these issues, may expect a relatively easy selling job, and may demand, accordingly, somewhat lower commissions than they would ask of unlisted corporations. Facilities provided by the exchanges for trading in rights may also contribute to ease in selling new issues of preferred stocks and bonds of listed corporations. When such securities are made convertible into common stock, very often existing common stockholders are given the first opportunity to subscribe; hence, subscription rights become available for trading in the same manner as for new offerings of common stock by this route.

Improved Credit Standing

Aside from improving prospects of attracting buyers of bonds, a cor-poration, by having its common stock listed, tends to enhance its credit standing with other prospective creditors—especially if the exchange upon which the stock is listed itself has prestige. A wide distribution of a corporation's common stock and developed investor interest in other classes of its securities, as promoted by listing, should give prospective short- and intermediate-term creditors some confidence that obligations to them could be liquidated, if necessary, by the flotation of equity securities or long-term bonds. Contributing additionally to creditor confidence should be the management standards that exchanges expect listed corporations to maintain. Likewise, creditors may have more confidence in financial data filed with the exchanges and the SEC—considering the penalties for omissions and misstatements—than they would have in credit data supplied by the corporations to them direct.

Advertising of Products

The point was made in the preceding chapter that corporations, especially those producing consumer goods, favor wide distributions of their common stocks in the belief that stockholders will be inclined to prefer their products to those of competitors. But listing also appears to have some value in advertising products to people who do not become stockholders. Many people look at stock market quotations even though they have little interest in buying stocks, but the names of listed corporations thereby become familiar to them. Familiarity with the names of listed corporations is also promoted by the many news items that are published concerning them—a frequency of publication promoted, in turn, by constant disclosures of new information as required by federal reporting requirements. In shopping, therefore, people who are not stockholders may be strongly inclined to buy products of corporations whose names are familiar to them rather than the products of unknown enterprises.

DISADVANTAGES OF LISTING

As was indicated earlier, many corporations do not apply to the exchanges to have their common stocks listed even though it is apparent that they could easily qualify. The managements of these corporations are undoubtedly impressed with the advantages of listing as just discussed, but they must conclude that one or more of the disadvantages of listing outweigh the advantages. As they see them, the disadvantages are likely to encompass the following: (1) disclosure of "confidential" information about corporate affairs, (2) some loss by management of its freedom of action, (3) restrictions upon activities of insiders, (4) dangers in market price fluctuations, and (5) the burden of additional expenses. In some cases, what is looked upon as a disadvantage of listing to the corporation may be, more clearly, a disadvantage to its existing management or to controlling or other important stockholders. Such a distinction appears to be particularly applicable to the third of the disadvantages as listed here. But corporations, though legal entities, are owned and managed by human beings; it is they who weigh the pros and cons of listing—without, we may be sure, much drawing of fine lines between their own interests and those of their corporations.

Most of these disadvantages would vanish or, at least, become much less weighty for unlisted corporations with rather wide distributions of stock should they be made subject to federal regulations similar to those now applicable to listed corporations. As was indicated in footnote 5 on page 506, a recommendation to Congress for such an extension of regulations was made by the SEC in April, 1963. In testimony before a Senate subcommittee considering the SEC's proposal, Keith Funston, president of the New York Stock Exchange, stated that as many as 200 additional listings on that exchange might result from the enactment of the proposal.[14]

Disclosure of Information

Probably the most potent disadvantage that eligible corporations see in listing is the broad scope of the disclosure requirements of the exchanges and the SEC. Their managers are often inclined to argue that these demand details that should be recognized as "confidential." Details about sales and operating expenses, it is said, can be highly useful to competitors, especially when the competitors are smaller concerns that do not have their stocks listed and are not, therefore, subject to comparable disclosure requirements. Details about salaries paid and stock options given to principal executive officers, it is further claimed, put ammunition into the hands of employees and particularly the representatives of labor unions in collective bargaining. And directors, officers, and principal stockholders object to reporting their stockholdings and the scope of their stock transactions as effected from time to time.

Corporations that make public offerings of new securities in interstate commerce have less reason to object to the disclosure requirements related to listing than do those that make no such offerings. Information supplied in registration statements under the federal Securities Act is much the same as that required of listed corporations. Even so, the supplying of information under the Securities Act is a once-for-all action for a given issue (unless sales are to continue for a lengthy period, so that supplemental information must be filed from time to time), whereas that required of a listed corporation must be, so to say, constantly kept up to date.

Some Loss of Freedom of Action

Some loss of freedom of action must be accepted by corporations that list their securities on registered stock exchanges. The exchanges themselves have certain restrictions applicable to the characteristics of stock issues that may be listed. For example, the New York Stock Exchange will not list nonvoting common stocks—a restriction aimed at "classified" common stocks, as when a corporation has both a nonvoting Class A

---

[14] *The New York Times*, June 22, 1963, p. 26.

common and a voting Class B common in its financial structure. That exchange also stipulates that nonvoting preferred stockholders must have power to choose at least two directors when six quarterly dividends on the preferred have not been paid.

Also tending to limit freedom of action are the requirements for supplying stockholders with detailed information in proxy statements when corporate managements solicit proxies for voting at annual and special meetings. Especially significant is the stipulation that the proxy form itself must permit the stockholders to designate whether he wishes to vote yes or no on specific issues. Many managements doubtless prefer simple notices of meetings and simple proxy forms by which stockholders can assign their voting rights to the managements' nominees without knowing anything about proposals to be brought up and without opportunity to signify how their votes are to be cast.

Rules of the exchanges and the SEC on the prompt filing of details about important asset acquisitions and dispositions, legal proceedings, changes in liabilities as when bonds are sold privately to one or a few institutional investors, dividend declarations, and so on can also be obnoxious to some corporations. Early publication of information of this kind may be thought to be inimical to the best interests of the corporation— or, perhaps more often, to the best interests of insiders.

Restrictions upon Insiders

That directors, officers, and principal stockholders of corporations can be in a position to "make a killing" if they can keep secret certain kinds of corporate actions decided upon or actually taken is a proposition that few will question. They may have every reason to expect later revelations of these actions to result in substantial increases or decreases in the market prices of their corporations' stocks. In the individual case, therefore, the insiders' secret knowledge should enable them to make handsome trading profits by buying for a rise or selling short for a fall.

But such opportunities for insiders *of listed corporations* tend to be precluded by requirements for the prompt disclosure of important developments—the very kinds of developments that may lead to substantial changes in market prices; by the prohibition on short selling; and by the provision that listed corporations may recover profits made on sales of stock held for less than six months by directors, officers, and owners of more than 10 per cent of any class of stock.

Dangers in Market Price Fluctuations

The managements of listed corporations may be quite unhappy about the market performance of their stocks in periods of general business recession and depression. Though the individual corporation may continue to operate at a comfortable percentage of capacity and though its prospects for the future may be good, the market price of its stock may be driven down simply as a result of the widespread weakness in buying interests and the unloading of shares by poorly informed stockholders. The corporation's management might devoutly wish that much less publicity were given to the market quotations on its shares, as would be likely were they traded in the over-the-counter market rather than on a stock exchange. Such a managerial wish would be all the stronger, of course, were the corporation contemplating a new issue of securities, whether stocks or bonds. In any case, the management might expect some of the corporation's present and prospective creditors, such as trade suppliers and short-term lenders, to be much disturbed by the unfavorable market price performance.

Even in periods of prosperity, moreover, given listed stocks are sometimes subjected to "raids" by speculators. Professional speculators may buy the stock of a given corporation in expectation of a substantial improvement in its earnings. Their buying causes the price to rise, and then the "lambs"—less well-informed or even ignorant speculators—come in, their buying causing the price to rise to unreasonable heights. The professionals then sell to "cash their profits," and the resulting fall in price alarms the "lambs" and prompts them to sell also. The professionals may add price-depressing weight on the supply side by selling short. The result is that the price falls to a level far below what is reasonable in relation to the corporation's earnings prospects, and it is then time for the professionals to buy both to cover their short sales and to take a long position for an expected rise. The procedure may be repeated over and over again, and the stock itself may come to be regarded as highly speculative—something not very helpful for additional sales of securities or credit standing.

Another aspect of danger in market price fluctuations is that corporate managements may give entirely too much attention to them, neglecting the long-run interests of their corporations in so doing. They may deliberately adopt policies expected to have favorable market effects, and zealously avoid others expected to bring unfavorable market reactions. Such a choice of policies may be prompted by hopes of personal gain upon the managers' own speculative stock transactions (to be completed in periods longer than six months) or by expectations of improved marketability of new flotations or of better credit standing. But, as indicated, the choice may be contrary to the long-run interests of the corporation. Thus a write-down in the book values of outmoded fixed assets or slow-moving inventories, or the omission of dividends when cash is in short supply, may be highly desirable from the standpoint of a corporation's continued good health—but not desirable if the primary goal is to prevent even temporary declines in the market value of its stock.

Burdens of Additional Expenses

Corporations that have their securities listed on stock exchanges incur certain kinds of expenses that unlisted corporations may escape wholly or partially. Most important among these expenses are the costs of assembling and carefully reporting all the information required for listing applications, annual and semiannual reports, special reports, and proxy statements. Much of this work must be undertaken or at least supervised by a firm's higher-salaried personnel, and often outside experts, such as attorneys and certified public accountants, must be hired to assist. Unlisted corporations that choose to be liberal in providing information to their stockholders and the public incur comparable expenses, except for applications for listing—but not so those that choose to be illiberal.

Fees must be paid by corporations to the exchanges on which their securities are listed. For stocks listed on the New York Stock Exchange, an initial fee must be paid at the rate of 1 cent a share on the first 1 million shares, one half of a cent a share on the next million, one fourth of a cent a share on the next million, and one eighth of a cent a share on all shares over 3 million; together with an annual fee of $100 per 100,000 shares for the first 2 million shares, and $50 per 100,000 shares in excess of 2 million. The minimum initial fee is $2,000, and the minimum annual fee, $1,000. The annual fee is paid for only 15 years, provided, of course, that the stock remains listed that long.[15] For its initial fee, the American Stock Exchange charges 1 cent a share on the first 250,000 shares and one fourth of a cent a share for shares in excess of 250,000, with a maximum charge of $5,000. Its annual fee is $250.[16]

A third kind of expense in connection with listing—though not necessarily escaped, even in part, by unlisted corporations—has to do with stock certificates. The exchanges insist upon high-quality engraving for certificates to reduce the dangers of counterfeiting, constant provision of an adequate supply of certificates for transfers, and convenient transfer facilities. The last-named requirement usually necessitates the hiring of separate banks or trust companies to serve respectively as stock-transfer agents and registrars.

Questions

1. How can a single stock exchange be simultaneously a "national securities exchange" and a "regional exchange"?

2. What is meant by the "listing" of a stock on a stock exchange? a dual listing? unlisted trading?

3. What facilities are available for the buying and selling of securities not traded on stock exchanges? Where are they located?

4. Must all transactions in a listed stock be executed on the "floor" of the exchange on which it is listed? Explain.

5. Explain the proposition that corporations do not raise new money by the sale of securities through the stock exchanges. Can it be said that listing aids in the raising of new money? Why or why not?

6. In any typical discussion of stock exchanges, why are the operations

---

[15] New York Stock Exchange, *op. cit.*, p. 18.
[16] American Stock Exchange, *op. cit.*, pp. 10–11.

of the New York and American exchanges emphasized? What must a corporation do to have its common stock listed on either of these exchanges?

7. Why should the regulation of stock exchanges by the federal government promote a wide distribution of listed stocks?

8. What kinds of federal regulations must be observed by corporations that have their common stocks listed on stock exchanges registered with the SEC?

9. Explain whether or not a stock exchange can delist a corporation's common stock against the wishes of the corporation.

10. Why should the listing of a corporation's common stock aid it in selling preferred stock or bonds?

11. How is the credit standing of a corporation likely to be affected by having its common stock listed on a stock exchange?

12. Support or attack this proposition: As recommended by the SEC, the disclosure requirements that apply to listed corporations should be made applicable also to unlisted corporations having 750 or more stockholders.

13. In what respects are the activities of the "insiders" of listed corporations restricted by federal law? Who are these "insiders"?

14. How might speculative "raids" upon a corporation's listed common stock adversely affect the corporation itself?

Problems

1. What initial fee would a corporation have to pay the New York Stock Exchange for listing its 2,500,000 shares of common stock of $10 par value? What annual fee (for 15 years) would it have to pay?

2. What initial fee would the corporation of the foregoing problem have to pay if it were having its common stock listed on the American Stock Exchange rather than the New York Stock Exchange?

of the New York and American exchanges explained? What other considerations lead to having the common stock listed on other bond exchanges?

7. Why should the regulation of stock exchanges by the federal government become a part of the distribution of listed stocks?

8. Why is the listing of securities on the American Stock Exchange not their chief concern, while the issues with competitive distribution are?

9. To what extent are the relations between the organized security markets about against the volume of the corporations?

10. Why should the listing of securities on a common stock at a particular preferred stock account?

11. How is the credit standing of a corporation likely to be affected by having its common stock listed on the stock exchange?

12. Suppose an actual firm stands. As an example such as the SEC, the distinction with between a bond trading and their reputations should be made in relation also to...

13. To what degree are the restrictions as to the inclusion of bond corporations there are chiefly federal law. Why, then, are such...

14. How might the regulation of public issues corporations of a bond common stock and an adjustment affect corporate structure?

Problems

1. Why might the world of a corporation between the New York Stock Exchange and listing on a national stock? Common stock at $40 per share. What is annual ...

2. What should be considered the depository value the security problem may be priced at cost to the corporation as to attract funds in bond exchange rather than the New York Stock Exchange?

Part VII

FINANCING WITH
PREFERRED STOCK

chapter 22

CHARACTERISTICS OF PREFERRED STOCK

The recommendations of boards of directors to common stockholders for the approval of preferred stock issues presumably follow exhaustive studies of the pros and cons of further financing with common stock and financing with long-term debt—pros and cons of the kinds discussed in Chapters 14 and 15. Financing with preferred stock is selected because it appears to offer greater net advantages than are offered by each of the two principal alternatives. There may be danger of loss of control to existing controlling groups in further issues of common stock, the market for common stock may be poor while that for preferred issues is good, the issuance of bonds might too seriously endanger solvency in view of unstable earnings records, there may be a need of preserving future financing capacity—these are the kinds of considerations that lead to decisions for preferred stock financing.

Obviously, however, decisions in favor of preferred stock depend not only upon the pros and cons of alternative means of financing, they depend also upon the kinds of features that must be included in preferred stock contracts. If buyers of preferred stock demand no great concessions, then that means of financing is made all the more attractive; but if prospective buyers demand quite extensive concessions, preliminary choices for preferred upon the part of corporate managements may be judged to be poor ones after all. Corporate boards of directors, being generally common stock minded—and needing, in any event, the approval of common stockholders for preferred issues—are doubtless inclined to pare the rights of preferred stockholders to the greatest possible extent; but investment bankers and other important buyers of preferred stock, usually being astute also, are unwilling to advance their funds unless the features of preferred stock contracts are to their liking. Thus, what goes in and what is kept out of preferred stock contracts are arrived at through a process of bargaining.

In the great majority of cases, certain minimum features will be demanded by prospective buyers: that the stock have preferences to dividends and assets, that the preference to dividends be cumulative, and that special kinds of "protective provisions" be included; and certain minimum features will be insisted upon by the issuing corporations: that the stock be nonparticipating, that it be callable for redemption, that its voting powers be limited, and that it be deprived of preemptive rights. Such a combination of features demanded and conceded is often described as "conventional"—a combination, in other words, that one would expect to find in most preferred stocks outstanding at the present time. Other features depend more directly upon the bargaining process—upon, therefore, the financial position and prospects of the individual corporation, as well as upon the investment enthusiasm of prospective buyers. A strong corporation is unlikely to find it necessary to make many additional concessions, whereas a weak one may have to be quite generous in its efforts to attract buyers; and, again, any corporation is likely to be asked to make fewer concessions in periods of prosperity and buoyant security markets than would be demanded of it in periods of business and financial strain.

The hows and whys of the various kinds of features that get into preferred stock contracts may be conveniently treated under four heads: (1) modifications in the seven basic rights of stockholders as owners, as discussed in Chapter 16; (2) additional protective provisions for the benefit of the preferred stockholders; (3) special rights reserved to the corporation; and (4) special features to enhance attractiveness.

MODIFICATIONS IN BASIC OWNERSHIP RIGHTS

Like common stock, preferred stock is a contract between its owners and the issuing corporation. The corporation gives the buyers of preferred stock certain rights as to dividends, assets, and management and in other matters, and the buyers, in turn, obligate themselves to pay the price agreed upon, whether in cash, other assets, or services. It is a generally accepted legal doctrine that the rights of preferred stockholders *are exactly the same as those of common stockholders* unless the preferred stock contract specifically provides to the contrary. Thus, the description of an authorized issue of stock simply as "preferred" in a corporation's articles of incorporation, *without any designation of a dividend rate*, does not make it differ from the same corporation's common stock, unless the law, or the articles in keeping with the law, permits the board of directors to set the terms of the preferred contract, or unless the law itself has certain stipulations of its own differentiating preferred stock from common. (In the latter regard, it is always to be remembered that the terms of stock contracts necessarily include whatever stipulations the state law prescribes, whether or not these stipulations are repeated in the articles, corporate bylaws, or directors' resolutions.)

In general, then, preferred stockholders have the seven basic rights of stock ownership described in Chapter 16 unless they are modified in the preferred stock contract. Accordingly it is important that we analyze the kinds of modifications that are commonly introduced. (In connection with the following discussion of preferences to dividends and assets, some attention should be given to Table 22–1 in which the dividend and

TABLE 22–1
Dividend and Asset Preference Features of Some Prominent Preferred Stocks

Corporation	No. of Shares Outstanding December 31, 1962	Par Value	Dividend Rate	Cumulative Feature	Participating Feature	Preference to Assets in Dissolution[a] Voluntary	Preference to Assets in Dissolution[a] Involuntary
Aluminum Company of America........	659,909	$100	3¾%	Yes	No	Redemption call prices	$100
Bethlehem Steel Corporation..........	933,887	$100	7%	Yes	No	$100	$100
E. I. duPont de Nemours & Company:							
$4.50 series..................	1,688,850	No par	$4.50	Yes	No	$115	$100
$3.50 series..................	700,000	No par	$3.50	Yes	No	$107	$100
Eastman Kodak Company............	82,158	$50	$3.60	Yes	No	$100	$50
General Motors Corporation:							
$5.00 series..................	1,835,644	No par	$5.00	Yes	No	$100	$100
$3.75 series..................	1,000,000	No par	$3.75	Yes	No	$100	$100
International Paper Company..........	162,340	No par	$4.00	Yes	No	Redemption call prices	$100
Montgomery Ward & Company........	201,554	No par	$7.00	Yes	No	$100	$100
New England Power Company.........	100,000	$100	4.56%	Yes	No	Redemption call prices	$100
SCM Corporation.................	240,044	$50	5½%	Yes	No	Redemption call prices	$50
United States Steel Corporation......	3,602,811	$100	7%	Yes	No	$100	$100

[a] In all instances including accumulated unpaid dividends.

Source: Moody's Investors Service, *Manuals*.

asset preference features of a few preferred issues of prominent corporations are set out.)

Preference to Dividends

Almost all preferred stock offered in the ordinary course of business for cash or in exchange for other assets or services is given a preference to dividends at a designated rate. This preference is ordinarily the strong selling point for preferred issues: fundamentally, it is the feature that makes such stock *preferred*. The preference means that dividends at the designated rate must be paid before any dividends whatsoever may be paid on the common stock—unless, of course, the preferred stockholders are willing to waive their prior claim. So strong is the tradition of the preference to dividends that a stock simply described in a corporation's articles as, say, a "5% preferred stock of $100 par value," with nothing else said about it except for the number of shares authorized, would universally be recognized as having a preference to dividends of $5.00 a share annually. In disputes, the courts could be counted upon so to hold.

If a corporation has only sufficient profits to pay dividends on its preferred stock and does pay them, why the stock is "preferred" is clearly to be seen: the preferred stockholders get their dividends and the common stockholders get none. But one may wonder about the "preferred" designation in a corporation that has lavish earnings and pays dividends on its common stock at a level per share several times that of the preferred dividends. Nevertheless, the preferred stock of the second corporation would be much more attractive to investors than that of the first. The slim earnings of the first might be further reduced, necessitating a suspension of payment of preferred dividends, whereas the great volume of earnings of the second would give strong assurance of the continuance of its preferred dividends.

Dividend Rates and Frequencies. The rate of dividends on a no-par preferred stock is always stated as a certain number of dollars or cents a share annually, while that on a par-value preferred may be stated either in this way or in terms of a percentage. Thus, we may encounter a $2.00 dividend par or no-par preferred or a 5 per cent preferred, the former indicating that the dividend is to be $2.00 a share each year, whatever the par or stated value may be, and the latter indicating that the annual amount of dividends is to be equal to 5 per cent of the par value, whatever it may be.

Almost invariably, corporations make their preferred dividends payable quarterly. Accordingly, the holder of a $2.00 dividend preferred expects to receive 50 cents a share quarterly, while the holder of a 5 per cent preferred having a par value of $100 expects to get $1.25 a share quarterly. It follows that a corporation that is up to date in the payment of quarterly dividends on its preferred stock may immediately pay dividends on its common stock. It is under no obligation to hold up dividends on the common until it has paid the full-year rate or amount on the preferred.

Cumulative Feature. In all but a few instances, the preferred stockholder's preference to dividends is made *cumulative*. This means that if the preferred dividends at the designated rate are not paid at the time specified, they must be paid subsequently before any dividends may be paid on the common stock—unless, again, the preferred stockholders are willing to waive their prior claims. Without a waiver, a corporation that fails in a given year to pay its designated preferred dividend of, say, $5.00 a share cannot pay any dividends on its common stock until it has made up this "arrearage" of $5.00 a share on its preferred stock together with the additional preferred dividend requirements as they continue to accumulate, presumably quarterly. If the quarterly dates for the payment of preferred dividends are March 1, June 1, and so on, the corporation could make up the arrearage, say, in the middle of January, and immediately pay dividends on its common stock. But if it should make no distribution till March 1 or shortly thereafter, it would have to pay $6.25 a share on the preferred stock before making a payment on the common; if on or after June 1 but before September 1, $7.50 a share on the preferred before any payment on the common, and so on. Similarly, missing dividends on the preferred for two years would require a payment to the preferred stockholders of $10 a share plus current quarterly dividends of the third year before any dividend distributions on the common stock could be made.

Like the preference-to-dividends feature itself, the cumulative feature is universally recognized as an attribute of preferred stock unless it is specifically removed by contract. Were a corporation to call a stock issue "preferred" and give it a specific dividend rate without saying anything about cumulation, the courts, if called upon to decide, would surely hold it to be cumulative.

Noncumulative Preferred. A limited number of noncumulative preferred stock issues are outstanding in the United States at the present time, and some of them have high investment ratings on account of the excellent records of earnings of their issuers and the scrupulous payment of dividends. The noncumulative feature means that dividends on the preferred missed in any year or series of years need not be made up in subsequent years before the payment of dividends on common stock. Even if profits are sufficient to pay preferred dividends, the preferred stockholders get no holdover claim if the directors decide in good faith that expansion requirements or other legitimate corporate objectives demand that the profits be retained. Such is the doctrine that was established by the Supreme Court in the celebrated Wabash Railway Case of 1930.[1]

---

[1] *Wabash Railway Co.* v. *Barclay*, 280 U.S. 197 (1930).

Unless, therefore, a noncumulative preferred has stood the test of time, it is likely to have very little investment appeal. That being so, corporations, in bringing out *new* issues of preferred stock, are hardly likely to be tempted to try to make them noncumulative. Most noncumulative preferreds have originated and continue to originate in reorganizations of corporations that have fallen into severe financial difficulties—in reorganizations where, so to say, they have been or are forced upon security holders of weak bargaining positions.

As originating in reorganizations, noncumulative preferreds have been especially prominent in the railroad industry. Railroads having such preferreds outstanding at the present time include the Atchison, Topeka, and Santa Fe, the Milwaukee, the Norfolk and Western, the Southern, the Union Pacific, and the Western Maryland. The Santa Fe's 5 per cent noncumulative preferred paid dividends regularly from 1900 through 1932, 4 per cent in 1933, 5.8 per cent in 1934,[2] 5 per cent in 1935 through 1937, 2½ per cent in 1938, and 3½ per cent in 1939, and from 1940 to the present time it has paid the dividend regularly. The Union Pacific's 4 per cent issue of $10 par value originated in its reorganization of 1897. It paid dividends of 1½ per cent in 1898 and 3½ per cent in 1899; since then, its dividends have been met regularly.

Participation in Further Dividends. Some preferred stocks are described as "participating," their contracts providing for some sharing in dividend distributions beyond the designated rate to which they are basically entitled. However, the general rule is that, unless the contract specifically provides for participation, the preferred stockholders have no claim to dividends beyond the designated rate, no matter how great a corporation's profits may be, and no matter how generous the dividends paid upon its common stock.

Corporations whose proposed issues of preferred stock are likely to have no great investment appeal sometimes add a participation feature as a "sweetener." Accordingly, further consideration of this feature may best be deferred to the last division of this chapter where the matter of adding attractions to preferred issues is taken up.

Dividend Position of Preferred Stockholders. The holders of a corporation's preferred stock get their dividends only if declared by its board of directors. The corporation has no obligation to pay dividends, as it has obligations to pay its debts. The dividend commitment is not a debt; it becomes a debt only after the act of declaration. In fact, the corporation cannot legally pay prescribed dividends on its preferred stock if the surplus available for dividend distributions, as determined in accordance with the rules of the state law, is insufficient to cover them. The directors would make themselves contingently liable to creditors for the amount by which the dividends exceeded the available surplus.

---

[2] The dividend in excess of 5 per cent was accounted for by a difference between the railroad's fiscal year and the calendar year.

Still more important is the fact that the directors of a corporation are under no obligation to declare and pay preferred dividends even if sufficient surplus is available. Dividend distributions to preferred stockholders, as to common stockholders, are at the discretion of the directors. They may decide that the payment of a preferred dividend is practically impossible because of a shortage of cash, though legally permissible because of the existence of a sufficient balance in the surplus accounts. Or, with liberal amounts of cash available, they may decide that the welfare of the corporation—and presumably, therefore, of all its stockholders, both common and preferred—would be better served by using the cash to finance expansion projects rather than to distribute it as dividends. Or they may decide simply to hold the cash for contingencies, as when the business outlook is cloudy. Only in relatively rare circumstances can preferred stockholders get the assistance of courts to force the payment of dividends. They can probably get such assistance if able to prove to the satisfaction of the court that the withholding of dividends is tainted with fraud—designed, for example, to force them to sell their stockholdings at sacrifice prices.

Thus, one should notice that descriptions of the dividend preference and dividend cumulation features of preferred stocks always include, if complete, two provisos, namely, that dividends are payable *before any dividends may be paid on the common stock*, and that they are payable *unless the preferred stockholders waive their rights to them*. These provisos indicate that the preferred stockholders may not get all the dividends they expected to get or in the form expected. Indeed, they may get none indefinitely, especially if the corporation whose preferred stock they own operates at a loss year after year or if its earnings are of negligible size. The first proviso does not say categorically that preferred dividends *must* be paid—it only indicates a condition that must be satisfied before common dividends may be paid. However, preferred stockholders who do not receive dividends year after year are not likely to find much consolation in the fact that common stockholders also are not getting dividends. The second proviso indicates a possibility that preferred stockholders may give up their rights to unpaid dividends. They have often done so, especially when dividends have not been paid for several years and the accumulated arrearages have amounted to substantial sums. In some cases, they accept offers of corporate managements of additional shares of preferred, some shares of common, or something else in exchange for their dividend claims. In some cases, they are in effect forced to agree to some such exchange as in procedures of corporate reorganization.

Much of the foregoing discussion of the preferred stockholder's claims to dividends indicates that they are quite weak, but this point must not be overemphasized. A great number of corporations make quarterly dividend payments on their preferred stocks without fail; and many additional ones, though they may pass one or more quarterly payments now and then, make these up subsequently without hesitation. Even when faced with arrearages equal to 30, 40, or 50 per cent or more of the par or stated value of their preferred stocks, a goodly number, with improvements in earnings and cash positions, have set to work to clear them up by cash payment, and many have succeeded in doing so. Most corporate managements, it is reasonable to think, feel duty bound to respect the dividend rights of their preferred stockholders and to meet them if at all feasible. But a conscientious attitude of this kind is not the only reason for faithfulness in dividend payments. As unpaid preferred dividends stand in the way of dividends on the common, they can hardly be appealing to boards of directors that are common stock minded. Probably even more important is the fact that possibilities of additional flotations of either common or preferred on fair terms are greatly reduced as long as there are arrearages on the existing preferred. And probably most important of all is the blow to a corporation's credit standing that comes with the nonpayment of preferred dividends. Though prospective buyers of its bonds, bank lenders, trade creditors, and others know that the non-payment of preferred dividends does not mean insolvency, their attention is strongly directed to the weaknesses in the corporation's earnings or cash position or both that must have occasioned the nonpayment.

Preference to Assets

A large majority of preferred stock contracts give the preferred stock-holders a priority over common stockholders in claims upon corporate assets in the event of dissolution. The basic priority or preference is stated as a specific dollar amount per share. A stock of $100 par value is likely to have a basic preference to assets of $100; a stock of $5.00 par value originally sold at $100, a preference also of $100; and a no-par stock originally sold at $10, a preference of $10. Often the preference is larger in voluntary dissolutions than in involuntary ones. For example, with the $4.50 preferred of DuPont listed in Table 21–1, it will be noticed that if the corporation dissolves involuntarily, as for insolvency, the claim per preferred share shall be $100; but that if it dissolves voluntarily, the claim per share shall be $115. Thus, as it were, the preferred stockholder is to be given a premium when the corporation dissolves without being under pressure to do so.

In addition to the basic preference just described, preferred stock contracts usually give preferred stockholders an additional prior claim for unpaid cumulative dividends of earlier years as well as for dividends "accrued" in the current year up to the time of the approval of the dissolution move. All the preferred stocks listed in Table 21–1, it will be noticed, have this additional claim. This is a significant claim, since it is not determinable on the basis of earnings that might be or might have been available for the payment of preferred dividends. To illustrate, assume that a corporation paid no dividends on its 5 per cent preferred stock of $100 par value for six years prior to dissolution because it operated at a loss in each of those years. It is dissolving voluntarily—not yet having become insolvent—and its contract gives the preferred stock a basic preference in case of voluntary dissolution of $110 a share as well as the additional claim to unpaid cumulative dividends. Accordingly, the preferred stockholders would be entitled to receive a total of $140 a share before any payment in liquidation could be made to the common stockholders.

Legal Aspects. The common-law rule is that, in the event of dissolution, common and preferred stocks have equal claims to assets, share for share. This rule could work a grave hardship on a corporation's preferred stock if, for example, it had originally been sold for $100 a share, and its common stock, at $10 a share; or the hardship could be shifted the other way were these original selling prices reversed. But, as was indicated in the preceding paragraphs, a prior claim for the preferred stock is usually contracted for. At any rate, it is important to emphasize that the preferred gets only such prior claims as are specifically stated in the contract; otherwise, the common-law rule applies. On the other hand, when a prior claim is given the preferred stock, it is usually interpreted legally as *limiting* the preferred stockholder's right of recovery. In a word, when the prior claim has been satisfied, he has no further right to share in assets, regardless of the amount that the common stockholders may receive.

In the absence of contractual provisions, the only prior claim in dissolution that preferred stockholders might succeed in asserting is one for unpaid dividends to the extent that earned surplus is available. Even this claim, however, is a doubtful one in the light of the Wabash Railway decision. Accordingly, an attempt to enforce it would doubtless require a lawsuit.

Practical Aspects. The preferred stockholder's prior claim to assets, as contractually provided for, may appear to be of little value because wealthy corporations rarely dissolve and poor ones that do dissolve have little or nothing left for any class of stockholders after the settlement of creditors' claims. Though preferred stockholders usually have claims prior to those of common stockholders, they still rank as claimants behind all classes of creditors; and, all too often, the liquidation of assets of dissolving corporations brings in much less than is needed to meet creditors' claims.

However that may be, the preference to assets held by preferred stockholders, as for the "residual claims" of common stockholders, is often of importance when danger of dissolution on account of financial difficulties is exceedingly remote. When a corporation is approached with a proposition of merger or consolidation, considerable weight is likely to be given to its preferred stock's claims against assets. Promoters of combinations of these kinds usually seek to carry them through as far as possible on the basis of simple exchanges of securities. They want to avoid a need to pay off in cash a large number of dissenting stockholders. Thus, an asset preference feature, among others, is likely to give the preferred stockholders of the corporation approached a strong position to demand generous treatment. They know that they can dissent and demand payment in cash, in the expectation that a court or an appraisal committee appointed by a court, in deciding how much they ought to be paid, will likewise give considerable weight to the asset preference feature. Indeed, if they do dissent and are paid the full amount of their claims, these claims are immediately satisfied, while the claims of the prior-ranking bondholders may be simply assumed, without the bondholders' consent, by the surviving or new corporation.

Voting Powers

The common-law rule is that preferred stock is indistinguishable from common stock in the scope of its voting powers; for the election of directors and on all questions requiring stockholder approval, it has one vote per share, the same as common stock. However, all states except Illinois and Mississippi permit the corporations they charter to modify these basic voting powers in various ways.

Many corporations make no attempt to limit the voting powers of their preferred stocks even though the laws of the states in which they are chartered would permit them to do so. Of the preferred stocks listed in Table 22–1, those of Bethlehem Steel, Montgomery Ward, and New England Power have one vote per share. Some corporations, indeed, give their preferred stocks greater voting rights per share than they give their common stocks. As examples, the United States Steel preferred has six votes and the Eastman Kodak issue 25 votes per share, while the common stocks of these two corporations have only one vote for each share. The total number of shares of preferred stock that any corporation issues is usually much smaller than the total number of its common shares, so that the giving of full voting powers or even multiple votes to the preferred may not be of much concern to the common stockholders. The controlling interests may have such a large percentage of the common stock that there is little danger of loss of control even should all preferred shares be voted in opposition; or both the common and preferred stocks may be so widely distributed that control does not depend in any essential way upon stock ownership.

Even when preferred stocks have regular or ordinary rights to vote in the election of directors and in passing upon matters that are subject to stockholder approval, they are often given certain special voting powers in addition; and even more often are these special voting powers given to preferred stocks that have been denied the ordinary voting rights. The special powers are generally described as "vetoing" and "contingent" voting rights.

Vetoing Voting Powers. The approval of holders of two thirds or three fourths of preferred shares is often required for mergers, consolidations, sales of entire assets, and voluntary dissolution. Upon proposals aimed in these directions, the preferred *votes as a class*—in other words, the holders of a little more than one third or one fourth of the preferred shares may *veto* proposals even though only a majority vote of the common stock may be necessary to approve them and even though the common stockholders may vote very heavily in favor. Frequently, however, the preferred stock has such a veto power only if it *would be adversely affected* by the merger or other proposed action.

Aside from questions of merger, consolidation, sale of entire assets, and dissolution, many preferred stocks are given power to veto corporate actions that would materially affect their prior claims to dividends and assets. In virtually all preferreds, the approval of the holders of two thirds or three fourths of the preferred shares is required to change the stock's par or stated value, to change from par to no par or vice versa, to change the dividend rate, and, indeed, to alter other terms of the contract. Without a reservation of voting power in this area, preferred stock would hardly be salable. But the veto power is often extended to include proposals for further issues of the same kind of preferred; for issues of any other class of preferred that would have equal ranking in claims to dividends and assets; for issues of any other class that would have claims to dividends or assets or both prior to those of the existing preferred—what is often called a "prior-preference preferred"; for issues of bonds; and for the mortgaging of corporate properties whether or not in connection with bond issues.

Some examples may be cited: In the two issues of preferred of General Motors listed in Table 22–1, approval of holders of 75 per cent of the preferred is required for the issuance of prior preferreds and the mortgaging of the corporation's properties, but not for the issuance of bonds or of preferreds of equal rank with the existing preferreds. International Paper must have the approval of holders of 66⅔ per cent of its outstanding preferred for issues of additional preferred of the same class or of equal or prior ranking, but it need have no such approval for issues of bonds and the mortgaging of its properties. And Montgomery Ward must gain the approval of holders of a majority of its preferred shares for increasing the authorized amount of the preferred or for issuing other stock of prior or equal ranking, and approval of holders of 75 per cent for mortgaging its properties, subject to some exceptions.

On the other hand, no vetoing power is ordinarily given to preferred stock with respect to further issues of common stock or to issues of a preferred whose claims to dividends and assets would be inferior to its own claims—what is often called a "second preferred"; such issues, it is thought, tend to strengthen the claims of the existing preferred rather than to weaken them.

Contingent Voting Powers.   In the great majority of instances, the contingency to which the "contingent" voting powers of preferred stocks are related is the nonpayment of dividends. Whether or not they share with common stocks ordinary voting powers in the election of directors, many preferreds give their holders special rights in the choice of directors if a certain number of *quarterly* dividends upon them—usually two to six—have not been paid. The preferred, voting as a class separately from the common, is privileged to elect some number of directors or some proportion of the total board—usually a minority of the board members, but not infrequently a majority especially in the preferreds of public utility corporations. For example, holders of the $4\frac{1}{2}$ per cent cumulative preferred stock of the Celanese Corporation get the right to choose one fourth of the directors, but not fewer than two, if four quarterly dividends are in arrears; the holders of the 4.8 per cent cumulative second preferred of the Carrier Corporation, while having ordinary voting power, also have the right to choose two additional directors if six quarterly dividends are in arrears; and the Crown Cork and Seal Company, Inc., provides in the contract for its $2.00 dividend no-par preferred that the holders shall be privileged to choose one half of the board members if six quarterly dividends have not been paid.

The theory of contingent voting powers is that the preferred stockholders must have specific representation upon the board of directors to look after their interests, the implication being that the nonpayment of dividends may indicate some neglect of those interests by board members who have been too common stock minded. Logically, therefore, the special powers of the preferred stockholders to choose directors customarily expire if and when the arrearages in dividends have been cleared up.

In some contracts, contingent voting powers in the choice of directors, comparable to those just described, are available to the preferred stockholders should the corporations fail to meet prescribed redemption fund contributions or violate other contract terms, as designated.

Preemptive Rights

Already the weakest of the seven basic rights of ownership as they pertain to common stock, the preemptive right is even weaker in preferred stocks. In most preferred stock contracts, it is taken away completely. As most preferreds have no claims upon earnings beyond the established dividend rates, no claims upon assets beyond the amounts fixed in the contracts, and, for the election of directors, only contingent voting powers, it is commonly held that they need no preemptive rights for protection. Indeed, it is often argued that to give preferred stockholders subscription rights to new issues of common stock would work an injustice upon the existing common stockholders. Were the preferred stockholders to exercise subscription rights to common, they would get some ordinary voting power whereas before they had none, and new and different claims to earnings and assets—all at the expense of the common stockholders. Were they to sell their subscription rights, the proceeds would be, in effect, an unmerited cash contribution to them made possible by the dilution of the interests of the common stockholders. On the other hand, a good case can be made for giving preemptive rights to preferred with respect to common if the preferred has ordinary voting rights, if it participates in dividend distributions beyond its stipulated rate, or if it has claims upon assets in dissolution beyond a fixed amount or no preference to assets at all. Sometimes the preemptive right is given for reasons such as these, but, more often, it is not.

As for new issues of preferred of the same class or of prior-preference preferreds, the usual justification for denying the preemptive right to the existing preferred is its possession of the vetoing power. If the holders of an existing preferred conclude that a proposed new issue would weaken their voting powers (if they have these) and their claims to dividends and assets, they can simply vote down the proposal. Or they can approve on condition that the new stock be first offered to them—in which event, they could be said to have the preemptive right *de facto* although not by the terms of their contract with the corporation.

Other Basic Rights

In designing their preferred stock issues, corporations usually have no reason to disturb the four remaining basic rights of stockownership, as discussed in Chapter 16 in connection with common stock. They recognize that the preferred stockholder should have a stock certificate, as illustrated in Figure 22–1, to be able to prove his ownership; they willingly accord him the same privileges of inspection of books and records as they grant to the common stockholders; and they certainly would not want to suggest any limitation upon his right to go to court to protect the corporation and his own interests from actions alleged to be illegal, *ultra vires*, or mismanagerial. Once in a while, a preferred stock contract includes some kind of limitation on resale, or the preferred stockholders themselves agree to limit resale; but such restrictions do not differ essentially from the similar ones sometimes found in connection with common stocks.[3]

PROTECTIVE PROVISIONS FOR PREFERRED STOCK

Investors in preferred stocks, including investment bankers who expect to hold only temporarily as underwriters, want all reasonable assurances that their preferences to dividends and assets will be continuously protected. They realize that, as owners, they cannot get absolute assurances, but they may want some protection beyond vetoing and contingent

---

[3] See above, p. 364.

FIGURE 22–1
Preferred Stock Certificate

voting powers, the right to inspect corporate books and records, and the right to appeal to the courts to put a stop to activities claimed to be illegal, *ultra vires*, or mismanagerial, as well as to try to force the payment of dividends alleged to be unjustly withheld. They often demand that the contracts include one or more additional provisions for their protection.

Additional protective provisions are generally of three kinds: (1) restrictions upon the payment of dividends on common stock, (2) limitations upon further issues of the same class of preferred stock, and (3) requirements for the gradual retirement of the preferred stock itself. Some preferred stock contracts contain no protective provisions of these additional kinds; some contain only one or two of the three varieties; and some contain all three.

Restrictions upon Dividends on Common Stock

Protective provisions that impose restrictions upon the payment of dividends on common stock are designed to preserve the capacity of corporations to continue uninterrupted dividends on the preferred at the prescribed rates. If in prosperous years a corporation, after having taken care of its preferred dividend requirements, distributes common dividends equal to most of the remaining profits, it may, in lean years, have insufficient cash or earned surplus or both to continue dividends on the preferred.

Restrictions upon dividends on common stock are of several kinds, and two or more are sometimes included in the individual preferred stock contract. Two examples may be cited: In the contract covering the 4 per cent cumulative preferred stock of the Owens-Illinois Glass Company, it is provided that cash dividends may not be paid on the common stock if total common and preferred dividends paid after October 4, 1956, would exceed $53 million plus net earnings after December 31, 1956. As of December 31, 1962, the company reported that this provision made approximately $73 million of its surplus unavailable for cash dividends on the common. For the 6 per cent cumulative preferred of the Ethyl Corporation, the provision is simply that dividends on "junior" stock, that is, common stock and any preferred having claims to earnings inferior to the claims of the cumulative preferred, must not exceed 75 per cent of net earnings after April 1, 1956.

Limitations upon Further Issues

We have seen that preferred stockholders are usually given the power to approve or disapprove further issues of the same class of stock and issues that would have prior preferences. Often, however, corporations expect to put out additional batches of preferred stocks of a given class from time to time over the years. This is especially true of certain classes of public utility corporations for which permanent preferred stock financing is considered normal and justifiable. A corporation with such expectations does not want to have its financial planning clouded by possibilities of vetoes of existing preferred stockholders; if it starts out with 100,000 preferred shares, expecting eventually to have 500,000 or more outstanding, vetoes could seriously cripple its expansion program. In its preferred stock contract, accordingly, it will reserve the right to sell additional preferred shares of the same class from time to time without having to get the approval of the existing preferred stockholders.

But investors in preferred stock will not accept such a reservation without appropriate protective provisions. These are generally of two kinds: limitations of total preferred issues in relation to assets or common stock or both, and limitations in relation to profits. Both kinds of limitations are ordinarily employed simultaneously. For example, the contract for the 3¾ per cent preferred stock, Series A, of the United States Plywood Corporation provides that the corporation may issue additional preferred having equal ranking with the existing preferred without the consent of the holders of the latter provided: (1) that its net income for 12 consecutive months within the preceding 15 months and its average net income for the preceding three years plus bond interest charges have equaled three times its bond interest and preferred dividend requirements, and (2) that its tangible net assets, after any additional issue of preferred, will be equal to two times the sum of the following: its long-term debt, the total claims of the preferred to assets in case of involuntary dissolution, and the portion of its consolidated stock and surplus accounts applicable to unowned common stock of its domestic subsidiaries.

Requirements for Gradual Retirement

Especially in industrial corporations, preferred stock financing is often looked upon as a temporary expedient—to be used, for example, when the common stock market is depressed and that for preferred stocks is still favorable. This view is in line with the doctrine that the simple common stock structure is the "ideal" one for industrials. To the extent, therefore, that the doctrine is accepted by corporate managements and by the investment community, it is appropriate to include in contracts for preferred stock provisions for its gradual retirement. Many industrial corporations do include such provisions.

Protective Aspect of Retirement. Such provisions are looked upon as protective for preferred stockholders, as the position of remaining stockholders is presumably enhanced as more and more shares are retired. If a corporation has been able to pay dividends on an original issue of 10,000 shares, it should be all the more able to pay when the number of outstanding shares has been reduced to, say, 6,000. Moreover, the very action of the corporation in periodically acquiring shares for redemption tends to support the market value of unredeemed shares.

Redemption Funds. Retirement provisions usually prescribe the setting up of a "redemption fund" or "sinking fund" by periodical contributions of cash equal to a stipulated proportion of current profits, or current profits after the deduction of dividends on the preferred. If there are no profits, no contributions need be made, although often there is a supplementary requirement for some minimum contribution in fixed dollar amount or equal to the call price of a fixed percentage of the outstanding preferred shares. Fairly often, indeed, the prescribed contribution is set at such a fixed dollar amount or percentage, rather than as a percentage of current profits. A few examples may be cited. The contract of H. K. Porter Co., Inc., covering its 5½ per cent "cumulative sinking fund preferred" requires allocations to the redemption fund of 10 per cent of annual net earnings after tax deductions; however, this percentage requirement is reduced proportionally if the outstanding preferred is less than the total authorized issue. The Schering Corporation's contract for its 5 per cent cumulative issue stipulates that, beginning in 1968, the corporation shall redeem annually an amount equal to 3 per cent of the maximum amount that has been outstanding at any time. The Owens-Illinois Glass Company is required to devote $2 million annually to the retirement of its 4 per cent cumulative preferred, provided that it is able to buy it in at a price not in excess of the par value of $100. Its redemption fund contributions are freed for ordinary corporate use after one year to the extent that it has been impossible to repurchase at par or less.

Retirement Procedures. Preferred stock contracts generally require corporations to use at once the money set aside in their redemption or sinking funds. The money is to be paid out in actually redeeming preferred shares at a price not in excess of the "call price," that is, the redemption price as set in the contract. The favored way is to buy up shares in the market, since the sellers obviously want to give up their ownership. If stock can be bought in the market at prices below the call price, so much the better. But the corporation's very buying tends to drive up the market price; moreover, the fact that a preferred stock is callable for redemption at a specified price tends to have some influence in sustaining its market price. Many state laws forbid corporations to pay in the market prices higher than the call price, and many preferred stock contracts so provide also. If sufficient stock is not available in the market to exhaust the redemption or sinking fund, or if the market price exceeds the call price, the corporation may use either of two rights which it almost always reserves—a right to draw lots to determine whose shares shall be called for redemption and a right to make pro rata calls on all shareholders. Sometimes corporations "invite tenders" by notifying all preferred stockholders that money is available for redemption and asking them to signify their willingness to sell and the price they would be willing to take. The tenders (offers) are accepted beginning with the lowest price stipulated and continuing up the line till the available funds have been used up. Tenders at prices in excess of the call price are summarily rejected.

Legal Limitations upon Retirement. An interesting legal question arises when a corporation has a contractual obligation to provide retirement of a fixed dollar amount or a fixed percentage of outstanding preferred stock and yet has no earned surplus. In our discussion of common stock, we saw that money spent to acquire treasury stock is legally limited to the amount of earned surplus. Does the same rule apply to the retirement of preferred stock? In some states, such as California, it does. In such states, the law must be obeyed—the contractual provisions fail, because there can be no binding obligation to do something that is illegal. In many states, however, the laws are much more generous toward the retirement of preferred stock than toward the purchase of common treasury stock. The statutes of these states permit the direct reduction of the preferred stock account itself by amounts equal to the par or stated value of redeemed preferred stock, provided that the value of remaining assets is at least equal to outside liabilities and remaining stated capital. To retire preferred stock in these states, therefore, corporations need only sufficient earned surplus for the charging off of retirement premiums; indeed, they need no earned surplus at all if they can acquire the stock for retirement at prices no greater than par or stated value.

SPECIAL RIGHTS RESERVED TO THE CORPORATION

In issuing preferred stock, almost all corporations reserve the right to call it in for redemption; and some also reserve the right to issue additional shares of a given class without having to get the consent of the existing shareholders of that class. These two special rights were introduced in the forgoing discussion of preferred stock protective provisions, but they deserve further brief treatment.

Right to Call for Redemption

The reservation by corporations of the right to call their preferred stocks for redemption is a special privilege because, by nature, preferred stock is a permanent kind of security. Rights of ownership generally have no maturity; hence preferred stockholders, as owners, give up something of great significance when they accord their corporations the power to cause their ownership to cease—the power, as it were, to set a maturity, as is done when a call for redemption is made.

Scope of Call Privileges. Corporations that obligate themselves unconditionally to redeem certain portions of their preferred stocks annually must of necessity reserve the call privilege. Almost invariably, however, they reserve the right to call all the stock for redemption whenever they so choose, and not simply the amount needed to use up the cash allocated to their redemption funds. The broader call privilege may never be used, but the corporations want to be free to use it should circumstances so warrant.

The broader privilege is wanted, indeed, by almost all corporations, whether or not they have redemption fund provisions in their contracts. Thus "callability" can be said to be a conventional feature of present-day issues of preferred stocks. In corporations without redemption fund provisions, the expectation ordinarily is that the call privilege will be exercised, if at all, only when a decision has been made to call all shares for redemption simultaneously. A corporation may issue preferred stock as a temporary substitute for common stock financing, and, from the beginning, it may expect to retire the preferred from the proceeds of common stock sales when the market for common has improved. Or the accumulation of retained earnings may make possible the retirement of whole issues of preferred originally designed as temporary means of financing. Or, again, the retirement of whole preferred stock issues may be decided upon to get rid of unduly oppressive protective provisions that had to be accepted at the time of original sale. Funds for some such retirements may, indeed, be supplied from sales of new preferred stocks having protective provisions of a much less restrictive character. Nevertheless, corporations that expect to call their entire preferred stock issues at one stroke, if they call at all, do not lose sight of the fact that partial redemptions may turn out to be advantageous; hence they reserve the right to make partial calls, both by lot and on a pro rata basis, as well as to buy in the market and to invite tenders.

Call Prices. Call prices are usually set at par value (or at stated value for no-par preferreds) and "accrued dividends" for calls in connection with redemption fund provisions, while they are frequently set at premium levels for calls beyond the scope of such provisions. The theory appears to be that because redemption fund calls are for the protection of the preferred stockholder, he has no fair claim to a bonus upon redemption; but that because calls not related to redemption fund operations are for the particular benefit of the corporation—in rearranging its financial structure—the preferred stockholder should receive some compensation for being forcibly deprived of his investment. For example, the H. K. Porter preferred, referred to earlier, is callable for its redemption fund at the par value of $100, but otherwise at 103. Call prices outside the scope of redemption funds are sometimes set at figures such as H. K. Porter's 103, and sometimes they are scaled downward with the passing years. The latter arrangement is exemplified in the preferred stock of the New England Power Company, listed in Table 22–1, for which the call price is 106.81 to the end of 1967, thereafter 105.90 to the end of 1972, then 104.99 to the end of 1977, and thereafter 104.08, the lowest level to which it falls.

Issuance of Additional Shares

Corporations that plan to continue to expand their preferred stock issues want to avoid having to obtain the consent of the holders of two thirds or three fourths or some other relatively high percentage of the already-outstanding preferred shares every time that new shares are to be offered for sale. The protective provisions they must add to their contracts to compensate for this privilege, they are likely to feel, will tie their hands less tightly than would an obligation to obtain repeated consents. If they did not have the privilege, if permission to put out additional shares of the same class of preferred stock were refused by the existing preferred stockholders, and if they wanted, nevertheless, to employ preferred stock financing, all they could do would be to issue a "second preferred" whose claims to dividends and assets would necessarily be inferior to those of the existing preferred and whose attractiveness to investors would accordingly be much weaker.

Where the privilege is reserved, it can be used to greatest advantage if the board of directors is empowered to set varying contractual terms for the successive issues, such as different dividend rates, claims to assets upon dissolution, and call prices. In this way, advantage can be taken of growing strength in the preferred stock market generally or in the investment appeal of the corporation's preferred specifically. If, for example, the original issue of a preferred stock of $100 par value carried a dividend rate of 5 per cent, a call price of 110, and a claim to assets in voluntary dissolution of 105, a second issue might be salable later with a dividend rate of 4½ per cent, a call price of 105, and a claim to assets of 103. Likewise, preferred stock financing can be continued even if the market situation deteriorates. In terms of the foregoing illustration, a third issue might be put out with a dividend rate of 5½ per cent, a call price of 115, and a claim to assets in voluntary dissolution of 108.

The three separate issues illustrated would be said to rank *pari passu* in their claims to dividends and assets; that is, they would have equal *priority* of claims, although obviously not equal amounts of claims. Thus, the corporation would pay a quarterly dividend of $1.25 a share on the first issue, $1.125 on the second, and $1.375 on the third, or it might omit all three simultaneously; on the basis of its contract, it could not pay one of these dividends and not the other two, or any two but not the

TABLE 22–2
Preferred Stock Flotations of Duquesne Light Company

Year Issued	No. of Shares	Dividend Rate or Amount	Call Prices and Claims to Assets in Voluntary Dissolution[a]
1950 (August)....	550,000	4%	$53.00–$51.50
1950 (September).	150,000	3.75%	51.50– 51.00
1952............	140,000	4.15%	52.48– 51.73
1953............	100,000	4.20%	53.46– 51.71
1954............	120,000	4.10%	53.25– 51.75
1955............	160,000	$2.10	53.34– 51.84

[a] Call prices commence at the maximums shown and then fall from time to time till they reach the minimums. The prevailing call price at any time is simultaneously the liquidation value in the event of voluntary dissolution.

third. To indicate the equal priority but unequal claims of successive issues of preferred stock, corporations often designate them as Series A, Series B, and so on.

Illustrating differences in terms of the separate series of a given authorized issue of preferred stock are the flotations of the Duquesne Light Company as listed in Table 22–2. Duquesne's total authorized issue is 1,250,000 shares, all of $50 par value.

SPECIAL FEATURES TO ENHANCE ATTRACTIVENESS

In the discussion of miscellaneous methods of common stock financing in Chapter 19, it was pointed out that common stock is sometimes issued in exchange for preferred stock, as when holders of the latter exercise the privilege of "conversion" granted to them in preferred stock contracts. It was also pointed out that common stock is sometimes sold through the exercise of stock-purchase warrants attached to preferred stocks. Both the conversion privilege and the attachment of stock-purchase warrants are generally recognized as means of strengthening the sales appeal of preferred stocks. Another means of trying to spur sales, much less commonly used than conversion privileges and warrants, is the addition of so-called participation features to preferred stocks.

Convertibility

In making their preferred stocks convertible into common stock, some corporations signify, as it were, that they would much rather be issuing common stock in the first place. Money is needed quickly, but temporary weaknesses in the common stock market or in the attractiveness of their own common stocks make new offers of common inadvisable. Accordingly, convertible preferred is issued with confidence that in the not-too-distant future the holders of this preferred will find it to their material advantage to make the conversion and will actually make it. In their long-range prospects, such corporations are likely to be relatively strong enterprises.

Suppose, for example, that a corporation wants to raise approximately $3 million. It would like to sell additional common stock, but its common is now selling in the market at only 33. Investment bankers are willing to underwrite a new issue at 30, so that it would be necessary to issue 100,000 shares to produce the sum of money wanted. But the bankers are also willing to underwrite a preferred issue at $49 a share. Indeed, the bankers indicate that if the preferred shares were made convertible into common on a 1 for 1 basis, they would boost the underwriting price to $50—they anticipate that investors would be willing to pay approximately a dollar for the added conversion privilege. As giving the conversion privilege is entirely in line with the corporation's goal of ultimate common stock financing, it readily agrees to offer 60,000 shares of convertible preferred. Subsequently, the market price of the corporation's common rises to 60, and by the time that level has been reached all the preferred stockholders have converted. Thus, the corporation succeeds, in effect, in selling 60,000 shares of common at $50 a share,[4] whereas the sale price would have been only $30 had the corporation sold common originally.

In other corporations that provide for convertibility, the conversion feature is included, it is clear, simply to make possible the sale of preferreds that otherwise would be extremely difficult to sell. These corporations may have only scant anticipations that the market prices of their common stocks will ever rise to a level to promote conversion. They may not want to issue additional common stock by the conversion route or otherwise. But they are extremely anxious to sell preferred stock, and they hope that the conversion privilege will be a sufficient "sweetener" to attract buyers.

Conversion Terms. The terms of conversion are set in such a way that the immediate surrender of preferred stock in exchange for common is out of the question. In the foregoing illustration, had the corporation made each share of its preferred stock convertible into 1⅔ shares of common, it might just as well have issued the common right away and be done with it. Thus, what the preferred stockholder gets in the conversion privilege is a speculative interest in the corporation's earnings and dividend policies and in the market behavior of its common stock.

The essential element in the conversion terms is, of course, the *conversion ratio* or *price*, by which is indicated how many shares of common may be obtained for one share of preferred. Examples of conversion ratios have already been given: 1 for 1 and 1 for 1⅔. Others may be found in Table 22–3 in which are described the conversion features of a few preferred stocks at present outstanding. Ratios are necessarily used when no-par stocks are involved, although they are often used also for par-value stocks. When a conversion price is used, it indicates how much of the par value of a preferred share must be spent, so to say, to buy a common share. For the Reynolds Metals Company, as an example, a preferred share of $100 par value will exchange for 1⅓ shares of common since the conversion price of a common share is set at $75.

Devices to Force Conversion. From the standpoint of corporations that want conversion to take place, a difficulty of the conversion feature is that owners of convertible preferred may be quite satisfied to hold it indefinitely, even though conversion *and sale* would be profitable, and perhaps highly profitable. Accordingly, such corporations usually modify the conversion privilege in such manner that, with favorable market conditions, conversion can be forced. Suppose that each share of a corporation's preferred is convertible into two shares of its common. The preferred was issued at $50 a share at a time when the common was

---

[4] Leaving out of consideration the difference between actual preferred dividends and what the dividends on common might have been up to the time of conversion.

TABLE 22–3

Conversion Features of Some Preferred Stocks

Corporation	Description of Stock	No. of Shares[a]	Par Value	Expiration of Conversion Period	Conversion Price or Ratio
Carrier Corporation...........	4.8% cumulative second preferred	142,176	$50	February 1, 1967 (issued in July, 1957)	$63.50
Flintkote Company...........	4½% convertible second preferred	72,965	$100	No limit	3.2 common shares[b]
	4½% Series A convertible second preferred	120,225	$100	No limit	$37.334[c]
General Precision Equipment Corporation...........	$1.60 cumulative convertible preferred	59,011	No par	No limit	⅔ common share
National Distillers & Chemical Corporation...........	4½% cumulative convertible preferred	202,150	$50	May 1, 1965 (issued in June, 1961)	$38.88 to 4/30/62 $40.74 to 5/1/65
Reynolds Metals Company...........	4½% convertible second preferred	616,087	$100	No limit	$50[d]
Schering Corporation...........	5% cumulative convertible preferred	278,983	$30	September 1, 1967 (issued in September, 1957)	¾ common share to 9/1/62; ⁶⁄₁₁ common share to 9/1/67
SCM Corporation...........	5½% cumulative convertible preferred	240,044	$50	No limit	$16.50

[a] Outstanding December 31, 1962, except October 31, 1962, for Carrier Corporation.
[b] Increased from 2.1 common shares on account of 50 per cent stock dividend on common in April, 1959.
[c] Reduced from $56 on account of stock dividend referred to in preceding footnote.
[d] Reduced from $75 on account of 3 for 2 split-up of common stock in October, 1959.

SOURCE: Moody's Investors Service, *Manuals.*

selling at 18. Although the corporation has been quite profitable since issuing the preferred, it has been retaining most of its profits for expansion, so that dividends on common per share have been just about half the per-share level on preferred. Thus, the preferred stockholder has had no reason to convert to common to get larger dividends. However, the corporation's good earnings record and its excellent prospects have pushed the market price of its common stock to 40. But even this development gives the preferred stockholder no reason to convert unless he wants to take his capital gain and cease to be a stockholder. He can continue his speculative "ride" by simply holding the preferred stock, for its market price should have risen and should continue to behave in close relationship with the market price of the common. If the market price of the common is 40, and if one share of preferred is convertible into two shares of common, then the market price of preferred should be in the vicinity of 80; and if the common should go to 50, the preferred should go to 100.[5]

One device for forcing conversions is simply to limit the duration of the conversion privilege, as in the Carrier, National Distillers, and Schering preferreds listed in Table 22-3. Most commonly in the use of this device, the conversion privilege is available to the preferred stockholder for only five to ten years from the dates of issuance. If the common stock of the forgoing illustration is selling at 40 and the preferred at 80, and if the conversion privilege is just about to expire, the preferred stockholder must act quickly to protect the benefits that have accumulated for him. He knows that the market price of the preferred will fall back to the vicinity of 50 upon the expiration of the conversion privilege. He may convert and hold the common stock in expectation of further market appreciation; he may convert and sell the common stock to take his capital gain; or he may take his capital gain by selling the preferred

---

[5] Some discrepancy in the relationship of the market price of a preferred stock to that of the common stock into which it is convertible is possible on account of commissions payable on stock transactions and stock-transfer taxes. But underpricings of the preferred by amounts larger than accounted for by commissions and taxes tend quickly to be eliminated as a result of transactions described as "arbitrage." Arbitrage is a simultaneous buying and selling of some thing or things to earn a profit made possible by price discrepancies. Leaving commissions and taxes out of consideration, a price of 78 for the preferred stock of the illustration at a time when the common was selling at 40 would cause arbitragers to rush to buy preferred and to sell common. Each share of preferred bought would be converted into two shares of common for delivery on the sales contracts, and the profit on the simultaneous transactions would obviously be $2.00 per share of preferred. But the rush of buying orders for preferred would drive up its price, perhaps to 79; and the rush of selling orders would drive down the price of common, perhaps to 39½. If this were the outcome further arbitraging would not be profitable.

As for discrepancies on account of commissions and stock-transfer taxes, it should be mentioned that members of a given stock exchange pay no commissions on transactions that they themselves put through on its "floor." Thus the size of market price discrepancies that will occasion arbitrage is considerably narrowed when the convertible preferred and the related common are listed upon an exchange whose members are constantly on the lookout for opportunities for arbitrage, as they can certainly be expected to be.

stock itself. If he sells the preferred stock, the buyer will surely convert it. Regardless of who actually effects the conversion, therefore, the corporation's goal is achieved.

Another forcing device is the setting of a scale of conversion prices or ratios that, with the passing of time, are less and less favorable to the preferred stockholder. The longer he holds his preferred stock the fewer the number of common shares he will get when and if he does convert. Examples of this are found in Table 22–3 in the National Distillers and Schering convertible preferreds. In the case of Schering, if the preferred stockholder converted before September 1, 1962, he got $\frac{3}{5}$ of a share of common in exchange for each share of his preferred, but if he waited till after that date, he could get only $\frac{6}{11}$ of a share of common. Where stipulations of this kind obtain, there is often a rush for conversion near the end of each successive period. Whether or not this will happen continues to depend, nevertheless, upon the amount of dividends being paid on the common and the behavior of its market price.

A third device for forcing conversions, assuming market conditions to be favorable, is to call convertible preferreds for redemption. As was indicated earlier in this chapter, corporations almost always reserve the right to call their preferreds for redemption at any time in whole or in part. In contracts for convertible preferreds, however, they provide that, should the stock be called for redemption, the holder may elect to surrender his shares *for conversion* rather than for redemption up to the date set for redemption or up to a time shortly before this date. If, then, the market price of the convertible preferred of the illustration is 80, and the call price is 55, a call for redemption will surely result in a flood of conversions.

Antidilution Provisions. The conversion privilege would be of little or no value to investors were it possible for corporations to weaken or virtually annihilate it by split-ups of their common stock or by the distribution of stock dividends to their common stockholders. If, therefore, the conversion feature is to be made attractive to prospective investors in preferred stock, it must generally be buttressed with appropriate "antidilution" provisions.

Assume, for example, that a corporation's preferred stock is convertible into common at a ratio of 1 for 2. The market price of the preferred is 100, and that of the common, 44. But the price of the common has been advancing rapidly and prospects are that it will go well beyond 50. The preferred stockholders, therefore, have reason to begin to anticipate speculative profits; but, at this very time, a decision is made to split up the common stock on a 2 for 1 basis. An effect of the split-up would be a drop in the market price of common to a level around 22, and the preferred stockholders could give up their pleasant anticipations of profits were they not protected by an appropriate antidilution provision—one that, in this instance, would automatically cause a conversion ratio of 1 for 4 to supersede the original one of 1 for 2.

As stock dividends given to common stockholders have effects similar to those of split-ups, investors in convertible preferreds have every grounds to insist upon protection against dilution from this source. Suppose that a corporation has outstanding 400,000 shares of common stock of $20 par value, that it has an earned surplus of $7 million, and that its preferred stock is convertible into common at the ratio of one share of preferred for two of common. The corporation declares and distributes a 50 per cent stock dividend on the common, each common stockholder getting, of course, one additional share for each two shares held. Whereas the corporation formerly had 400,000 shares of common outstanding with a book value of $37.50 a share, it now has 600,000 shares with a book value of $25 each. Moreover, the market value of common should decline in like proportion, since the arbitrary change in the number of common shares outstanding does not increase the corporation's earning power. But the holders of convertible preferred ought not to be penalized by the stock dividend; accordingly, the workings of a proper antidilution clause would cause the automatic substitution of a new conversion ratio of 1 for 3.

Examples of the operation of antidilution provisions are indicated in footnotes in Table 22–3 in relation to the Flintkote and Reynolds Metals convertible preferreds.

Use of Stock-Purchase Warrants

By attaching to their preferred stocks warrants to buy common stock, corporations generally expect results quite similar to those they seek when adding the convertibility feature. Corporations that would prefer to sell common stock in the first place, but that do not do so because of unfavorable market conditions, may anticipate calling the preferred stock for redemption when the funds to make this possible are obtained from later sales of common stock through the exercise of warrants. In some instances, corporations stipulate that their preferred stocks are receivable at par or stated value in payment for common stock purchased with warrants, thereby largely wiping out the distinction between the stock-purchase and convertibility devices. On the other hand, corporations of relatively weak position that are inclined to think of warrants and convertibility purely as promotional features for the sale of preferred are likely to conclude that either of these devices can be made about as attractive as the other.

It appears that equality of attractiveness can easily be provided for. If the market price of a corporation's common stock is 18, it would not seem to matter whether it issues at 50 a preferred each share of which is made convertible into two shares of common, or, at the same price, a preferred having attached to each share warrants to buy two shares of common at 25. Should the market price of the common go to, say, 40, the convertible preferred share could be exchanged for two shares of common and the latter sold at a profit of $30; or, in the case of the attached warrants, two common shares could be bought at $50 and resold for $80, also at a profit of $30.

But there is a difference. The investor in convertible preferred, upon converting and selling the common stock received in exchange, gets his profit but ceases to be a stockholder; whereas the investor in preferred with warrants continues to be a preferred stockholder after exercising the warrants and selling the common stock thus obtained. Any investor might anticipate a desire to stay as a preferred stockholder; hence, at the time of the original offer of a preferred stock, he might be more attracted by warrants than by a convertibility privilege. Another apparent advantage of warrants results from the fact that they are usually made "detachable." This means that the preferred stockholder can sell them without in any way disturbing his position as such a stockholder. If common stock is purchasable by warrants at 25 at a time when its market price is 40, then the market price of a warrant for one share should be close to 15. Thus, it should be possible for the preferred stockholder to take his speculative profit without first having to put up the money to buy the common stock from the corporation.

On the other side of the picture, however, warrants may promise poorer prospects for sharing in generous dividends on common stock than does convertibility. Suppose, for example, that the dividend rate on the preferred stock referred to in the illustration above is 5 per cent, or $2.50 a share annually. With improvement in earnings, the corporation later establishes regular dividend payments at 8 per cent on the stated value of its common stock of $25, that is, $2.00 a share annually. The holder of a convertible preferred share may exchange it for two shares of common upon which he would earn $4.00 a year, equal to 8 per cent of his original investment of $50. But the holder of a preferred share with warrants, after buying two shares of common at $25, would have an investment of $100 in the corporation, upon which he would get $2.50 in preferred dividends and $4.00 in common dividends, equal to an average return of only 6.5 per cent.

Wherever the weight of advantage to preferred stockholders may appear to lie, corporations themselves cast their vote, so to say, in favor of convertibility. The convertibility feature is much more commonly employed than is the warrant feature.

Little needs to be said about the terms for the exercise of stock-purchase warrants; they closely parallel in purpose and effect those provided for in connection with convertibility. The number of common shares that the preferred stockholders may buy for each preferred share held and the price to be paid for the common must of necessity be clearly established. Especially with corporations that are anxious to sell common stock, the period in which the warrants may be exercised is usually limited, as to five or ten years, in order to "force" exercise of the warrants; and, for the same reason, a scale of successively higher prices of the common is often designated for subperiods within the longer period.

Likewise, the privilege of buying with warrants must normally be protected with antidilution clauses. Illustrations of both a time limit on the exercise of warrants and the workings of antidilution provisions are found in the contract of the Dorsey Corporation covering its 6 per cent preferred (32,500 shares of $50 par value) offered at $50 a share in April, 1959. Each preferred share was given two warrants, each for the purchase of one share of common at $12, and April 30, 1969, was set as the expiration date for the warrants. On account of certain transactions within the scope of the contract's antidilution provisions, Dorsey announced in November, 1960, a reduction in the warrant price of common to $10.176 a share, and again in May, 1963, a further reduction to $10.05 a share.

Participation Rights

Arrangements for Participation. A preferred stock is said to be "participating" if it has rights established by contract to share in dividend distributions beyond the amount of its stated preferential dividend rate. Participation arrangements of three types are recognized: full participation, immediate participation, and special participation.

In full participation, the preferred shares equally with the common in all distributions after the preferred has been allotted its regular dividend and the common a dividend of the same rate or dollar amount. Note that a very great difference in a preferred's participation can result depending upon whether the "equal" sharing is in terms of dollar amounts or in terms of a percentage of par or stated value. To illustrate, let us assume that a corporation has outstanding 100,000 shares of common stock of $10 par value and 20,000 shares of 5 per cent preferred stock of $25 par value. The directors decide to distribute total dividends of $300,000. Should the preferred fully participate with common in terms of dollar amount per share, the dividend would be $2.50 ($300,000 ÷ 120,000 shares) on each share of preferred and on each share of common; but this would amount to a 10 per cent return on the par value of the preferred and to a 25 per cent return on the par value of the common. Should, however, the full participation be in terms of a rate of return on par value, each share of common and preferred would receive a dividend equal to 20 per cent of its par value ($300,000 ÷ $1,500,000 total par value), or $5.00 for each preferred share and $2.00 for each share of common.

In immediate participation, the preferred begins to share in additional distributions as soon as it has been allotted its preferential rate. In terms of the foregoing illustration, the preferred would get its dividend of $1.25 a share, and then participate in the entire remaining $275,000 to be distributed. If the contract provided for immediate participation on a basis of a dollar amount per share, the preferred would get an additional dividend of approximately $2.292 ($275,000 ÷ 120,000 shares), and the common, a total dividend of $2.292 a share; if it provided for participation on a percentage basis, the preferred would get an additional dividend of $4.58⅓, and the common, a total dividend of $1.83⅓ (each of these at the rate of 18⅓ per cent of par value).

Special participation comprises all kinds of arrangements other than full and immediate participation. In the most common special arrangement, the preferred is alloted one, two, or three percentage points beyond its preferential rate. If the preferred of the foregoing illustration were participating to the extent of 2 per cent of par value, its maximum capacity to share in dividend distributions would be 7 per cent of par value. In the distribution of $300,000, therefore, it would receive $1.75 a share, and the common, $2.65 a share—the latter being equal, of course, to 26.5 per cent of the par value of the common.

Use of Participation Features. The more generous participation arrangements—full, immediate, and generous varieties of the special class—are pretty well confined to family and other closely held corporations. A father who sets up his son in an incorporated business may take preferred stock for his investment, being satisfied to let the son have the common stock; but it may be agreed that the son will take most of his compensation as a salary, and that most of the profits, if and when distributed, will go to the father. Thus, the preferred stock could be given a very liberal participation feature.

For corporations that offer their preferred stock widely to many investors, however, the usual participation feature, if one is included at all, is the allotting of nothing more than two or three extra percentage points to the preferred. A limited participation right is more likely to appeal to the mass of investors than a more generous one. They know that the boards of directors of most corporations are common stock minded—that while directors may not hesitate unduly before paying dividends equal to 7 per cent of the par value of preferreds where the preferential rate is, say, 5 per cent, they are likely to be most unwilling to pay dividends on preferreds equal to 10, 12, or 15 per cent of their par values. In other words, investors expect corporations to call preferred stocks for redemption to get rid of generous participation features when earnings are high and high rates of dividends *could* be paid.

As a device for enhancing the salability of preferred stocks, even special participation features of the limited variety are much less popular than convertibility and warrant features. Relatively strong corporations tend to shy away from participation arrangements. Their managers are likely to take the position that if the preferred stockholder is to share in extraordinary earnings, he should do so by becoming a common stockholder, either by way of conversion or the exercise of stock-purchase warrants, rather than to enjoy this sharing while maintaining his preferential standing as a preferred stockholder. And weaker corporations, accordingly, have reason to fear that the very inclusion of participating features will unduly call attention to their weakness.

Some Outstanding Participating Preferreds. Some details about the features of a few outstanding participating preferreds and their recent dividend records through 1962 should be of interest.

The participation feature has been very valuable to the holders of the 6 and 7 per cent "guaranteed" stocks of the Richmond, Fredericksburg & Potomac Railroad Company, both of $25 par value. These stocks have preference over the common stock to dividends at the "guaranteed" rates, but they get dividends per share equal to the per-share distributions on the common stock if the latter exceed dividends at the "guaranteed" rates. The dividend record of the period 1950–62 indicates the value of the participation. In this period, the annual dividends on the two preferred stocks averaged about $4.42 equal to a rate of 17.7 per cent on the par value.

Not nearly so valuable but still advantageous to the preferred stockholders is the participation feature of the $3.00 dividend no-par preferred of Arden Farms Company. It is preferred over common for its dividend of $3.00 a share, and it gets additional dividends equal to 25 per cent of any dividends declared on the common, with a participation limit of $1.00 a share. In the period 1944–62, its "participation" amounted to approximately 25 cents a year.

The 5 per cent preferred stock of $100 par value of the Chicago, Milwaukee, St. Paul and Pacific Railroad Company is peculiar, not only in having a right of participation, but also in its cumulation feature. Although this preferred is basically noncumulative, no dividends may be paid on the company's common stock unless dividends for the current and two preceding years on the preferred have been paid or provided for. As for participation, it shares dividends equally with the common stock up to $1.00 after the latter has received a dividend of $3.50. The Milwaukee's preferred paid dividends of $5.00 in 1946, $7.50 in 1947, $4.00 in 1948 and 1949, $7.00 in 1950, and $5.00 regularly from 1951 through 1962.

The participation feature of the 5 per cent convertible preferred of $100 par value of the Chicago and North Western Railway Company is offset by a provision making preferred dividends cumulative only to the extent that they are covered by earnings. Beyond dividends at its 5 per cent rate, this stock is entitled to participate equally with common in additional dividends up to $1.00 after the common has received $5.00 a share. But the recent record of this participating preferred has not been pleasant for the preferred stockholders. It paid regular dividends of $5.00 a year in the period 1945–48, nothing in 1949, $5.15 in 1950, nothing in 1951, $2.55, $3.25, and $3.30, respectively, in the years 1952–54, and nothing in the whole period 1955–62.

Questions

1. In the absence of specific contractual provisions, in what ways does a corporation's preferred stock differ from its common stock?

2. From the investor's standpoint, is any corporation's preferred stock always *better* than its common stock? Discuss.

3. What is meant by the description of a preferred stock as "cumulative"? Who decides whether or not a given preferred stock is cumulative?

4. Does a corporation really have an *obligation* to pay dividends on its preferred stock at the rate stated in its contract? Does it have an *obligation* to pay subsequently cumulative preferred dividends not paid in the current year? Explain.

5. Why can boards of directors, even though common stock minded, be generally depended upon to declare and distribute dividends on preferred stock when cash and surplus are available?

6. What is the scope of the "preference to assets" usually given to preferred stockholders? Of what significance is this preference?

7. What kinds of corporate actions are often made subject to "vetoing" voting powers held by preferred stockholders? What is the logic of giving such voting powers to preferred stockholders?

8. What is the reason for giving preferred stockholders "contingent" voting powers? What is the scope of these powers?

9. If a corporation is paying dividends regularly to its preferred stockholders, what justification could they have for wanting to limit the amount of dividends it pays on its common stock?

10. When a corporation reserves the right to sell additional issues of a given class of preferred stock, how is it likely to be limited, nevertheless, in the total amount that it may issue? Must it give the additional issues the same terms, such as the dividend rate, as given to the original issue?

11. When a corporation is required by contract to set up a redemption fund for its preferred stock, how and when is the money actually used for redemption?

12. Under what circumstances might the redemption of a corporation's preferred stock, as required by its contract, be illegal?

13. What is indicated by each of the following designations for preferred stocks: prior-preference preferred, second preferred, Series B preferred?

14. Both strong and weak corporations often make their preferred stocks convertible into common stock. How would the motives of these two classes of corporations be likely to differ?

15. What means are frequently employed by corporations to "force" the conversion of their convertible preferreds into common?

16. How are "antidilution provisions" supposed to protect holders of convertible preferred stocks? Are they really effective in this protective role? Explain.

17. What is distinctive about so-called participating preferred stocks? Why is a moderate participation feature likely to be more attractive to investors than a liberal one?

Problems

1. The preferred stock contract of the Mason Manufacturing Corporation provides for the payment of quarterly dividends on March 1, June 1, September 1, and December 1 on a cumulative basis at the annual rate of 6 per cent. Up to the year 19xx, it paid the quarterly dividends regularly, but in 19xx it paid only 1 per cent on March 1 and another 1 per cent on June 1.

a) In the following year, 19yy, what rate of dividends would it have to pay on the preferred stock on March 1 to be free to pay dividends on its common stock on that date or shortly thereafter?

b) If it paid no preferred dividends till September 1, 19yy, what rate would it have to pay on that date to be free to pay dividends on its common stock?

c) If it paid no preferred dividends till June 1, 19zz, would a payment on that date of a dividend of 13 per cent free it to pay a dividend on its common stock?

2. The Jellico Products Company has outstanding two issues of preferred stock: its Series A issue of 60,000 shares of $100 par value having a dividend rate of 4½ per cent; and its Series B issue of 50,000 shares of $100 par value having a dividend rate of 5 per cent. Its contract with the preferred stockholders permits it to put out further issues of equal ranking without their consent provided that two conditions are satisfied: (1) that average earnings available for preferred dividends in the preceding two years must have equaled twice the dividend requirement on all preferred to be outstanding; and (2) that total outstanding preferred plus long-term debt must not exceed 50 per cent of the corporation's assets (including assets to be acquired by issuing preferred stock) as reduced by its current liabilities.

Jellico wants to issue as many shares of Class C preferred stock as the forgoing limitations will permit. Such stock will have a par value of $100 and a dividend rate of 5½ per cent. It may be assumed that the proceeds of sale realized by the corporation will be equal to the par value.

How many Series C shares may Jellico issue, assuming that its earnings available for preferred dividends in the preceding two years averaged $1,440,000, and that its most recent balance sheet, in summary form, was as follows:

Current assets.............	$22,000,000	Current liabilities.........	$10,000,000
Fixed assets...............	29,000,000	Bonds payable.............	8,000,000
		Preferred stock............	11,000,000
		Common stock............	15,000,000
		Earned surplus............	7,000,000
	$51,000,000		$51,000,000

3. Each share of the preferred stock of Stein & Co., Inc., of $60 par value is convertible into three shares of its common stock within five years from the date of issue, and into 2½ shares of common within a second five-year period. The contract for the preferred contains standard antidilution provisions. Within the first five-year period, the corporation distributed a 50 per cent stock dividend to its common stockholders, and later effected a 3 for 2 split-up of the common stock.

Through the application of the antidilution provisions, what would be the new conversion ratios for the two five-year periods (*a*) as a result of the stock dividend, and (*b*) as a result of the split-up? (*c*) What were the original conversion *prices?* What were the conversion prices after the stock dividend? after the split-up?

chapter 23

SALE AND MANAGEMENT OF PREFERRED STOCK ISSUES

SELLING CHANNELS

Importance of Public Offerings and Private Placements

Statistics published by the SEC for the year ended June 30, 1962, indicate that public offerings of new preferred stock issues have a pattern similar to the pattern of public offerings of common stock. Of total new preferred stock issues of $252 million registered for immediate offering for cash, $150 million, or 59.5 per cent, was slated for sales to the general public, $96 million, or 38.4 per cent, for sales to the issuing corporations' existing security holders, and only $5 million, or 2.1 per cent, for sales to "other special groups." [1] The comparable percentages for common stock offerings, as presented in Chapter 17, were 67.1, 30.7, and 2.3, respectively.

On the other hand, while a very small proportion of the total value of common stock issues is privately placed with institutional investors, individual capitalists, and other "private" buyers, a substantial proportion of new issues of preferred stocks are so sold. For the calendar year 1962, the SEC reported offerings of new preferred stock issues of more than $100,000 individually totaling $436 million and registrations for public offering of $315 million,[2] so that the difference of $121 million is at least a rough indicator of the proportion of total issues that are sold as private placements.

Limited Significance of Other Selling Channels

All the miscellaneous channels for security selling, as surveyed in Chapter 19 in connection with sales of common stock, are generally much less important for preferred stock than for common stock. Of the miscellaneous channels, the most significant for preferred stock is probably that of direct exchange in mergers, consolidations, and holding company acquisitions. Corporations that want to absorb or gain control of other corporations very often offer to the latters' preferred stockholders a kind of preferred stock similar to or identical in features with what they already

---

[1] Securities and Exchange Commission, *Annual Report*, 1962, p. 172. Percentages supplied by the author.

[2] Securities and Exchange Commission, *Statistical Bulletin*, July, 1963, pp. 11, 16.

hold. In some instances, too, preferred stocks, especially convertible issues, are offered to the common stockholders of corporations to be acquired. Frequently such offers are accepted, so that the preferred stock that is accepted may be said to be the means of financing important asset acquisitions by the absorbing corporations and holding companies.

Also of some importance among the miscellaneous channels of preferred stock distribution is its exchange for the claims of certain classes of creditors in final settlements in corporate reorganizations. Holders of second and subsequent mortgages, debenture bondholders, and unsecured short-term creditors may realize that only a small percentage of their claims against a bankrupt corporation would be satisfied were its assets to be sold; and they may be persuaded, however reluctantly, that the corporation as reorganized could hardly survive for very long should their claims be simply postponed. Accordingly, they may agree to give up their claims as creditors in whole or in part and to take preferred stock in exchange. Though, therefore, the reorganized corporation does not "acquire" assets by such an issue of preferred stock, the issue surely enables it to retain assets already acquired.

In the incorporation of businesses formerly conducted as proprietorships and partnerships, preferred stock is sometimes given in part for proprietary interests. A limited partner, for example, may be willing to go along with the incorporation only if he is given preferred, rather than common, stock. Sometimes, too, holders of specific parcels of property, such as store and factory buildings, are willing to part with them in exchange for preferred stock, or perhaps for a combination of preferred and common.

But rare are the transactions in which preferred stock is given for the services of promoters, investment bankers, and corporate executives; and even more rarely are options to buy preferred given to these people. Sometimes it has been used in employee stock-ownership plans, particularly in those of public utility corporations, but emphasis in the general run of such plans has been on common stock. While preferred stock is frequently convertible into common stock, and sometimes has warrants attached for the purchase of common stock, it is most unusual for another kind of security, such as bonds, to be convertible into preferred or to have warrants attached for the purchase of preferred. Finally, the distribution of preferred as dividends or as bonuses in connection with the sale of other types of securities is likewise a rarity.

In the subsequent discussion of the selling of preferred stock, therefore, we will be justified in confining our attention to the three principal channels of distribution as indicated by the statistics cited. Even for these three channels, moreover, no useful purpose would be served in repeating all the mass of details about preparation for sale and the actual selling covered in Chapters 17–19 in the discussion of common stock flotations.

The preparation of preferred stock issues for sale and the procedures of selling them in the three channels follow quite closely the patterns of common stock financing. Our interest, therefore, should be largely directed to an analysis of the differing significance of each of the three channels as between preferred stock and common stock flotations. Nevertheless, the student should not forget that public offerings of preferred stock in interstate commerce require all the detailed work incident to complying with the provisions of the federal Securities Act as to registration statements and prospectuses, except, of course, that offerings of not more than $300,000 in any year may get by with the much less rigorous notification requirements. Also to be kept in mind are the additional government regulations embodied in the state blue-sky laws—regulations that are generally applicable to new offerings of preferred stock whether or not sold in interstate commerce. Finally to be kept in mind is the fact that employing the services of investment bankers also requires a great deal of preparatory work upon the part of both the issuing corporations and the bankers themselves.

Offerings to the General Public and to Security Holders

Differences in Investor Interests. A much larger proportion of preferred stock issues than of common issues are sold by offerings to the general public than to existing security holders because of the very nature of the investment interests of the two classes of potential buyers. By no means are all investors in the general public interested in preferred stock investment, but, except in times of severe depression, there is usually a sufficient number to enable worthy corporations to float preferred issues successfully. When, therefore, corporate managers—and investment bankers as their advisers—conclude that interest in preferred issues is much stronger among the general public than among existing security holders, it is more reasonable for them to choose to make offerings to the general public. On the other hand, managers and bankers know that many common stockholders are continuously concerned about preserving their shares in voting power, their claims to earnings, or their claims to assets, or any two or all three of these; hence, when financing is to be done by way of further common stock issues, they are inclined to offer them first to the present common stockholders.

Interests of Common Stockholders. The common stockholders of a corporation may have little interest in its proposed preferred issue, so that they would be a poor market for it. The very fact that they are already common stockholders indicates that they are willing to take risks; accordingly, they may find the relative safety of preferred stock of little attraction. But more than this, they may not want to buy the preferred because they see in it no threat to their ownership interests as common stockholders. If the proposed preferred is to have voting power, they may not be interested in control; if it is to be nonvoting, and they do have an interest in control, they may not be worried about its contingent voting rights. Similarly, the preferred's preference to dividends may not bother them, especially if it is nonparticipating, as it is likely to be. And they may pay little attention to its preference to assets, thinking of this, as so many people do, in terms of a dissolution the possibilities of which they consider to be exceedingly remote. If, therefore, they have the preemptive right to preferred issues, they may readily waive it so that an offering to the general public may be made. They would be less likely to waive the right in connection with further issues of common.

But the fact that substantial amounts of preferred stock, as indicated by the data cited earlier, are sold to existing security holders suggests that not all groups of common stockholders are uninterested in their corporations' preferred issues. Interest is certainly promoted by making preferred convertible into common or by attaching to it warrants to buy common; for here is a circumstance where buying is necessary for the protection of all the rights of common stockholders. (See Table 23–1 for some recent rights offerings of convertible preferred stocks to common stockholders.) Purchases of preferred by common stockholders are surely promoted also when the preferred is given ordinary voting power and when there is much anxiety about control—all the more, of course, the greater the actual jockeying among factions to gain or retain control. And, finally, giving preferred participation rights, especially if they are generous ones, should exert considerable pressure upon common stockholders to invest in preferred.

Interests of Other Security Holders. It is to be noted, moreover, that the existing "security holders" to whom new issues of preferred stock are sold are not distinguished as to class in the statistical reports. While the "security holders" to whom new issues of common stock are offered are almost invariably the existing common stockholders, it is not necessarily they to whom new issues of preferred are offered. A corporation's existing preferred stockholders may be enthusiastic about buying additional preferred shares. Although probably not having the preemptive right, they may still be the most likely class of investors; and the offering can be made to them if the common stockholders also do not have the preemptive right or are willing to waive it. On the other hand, corporations can hardly expect many of their bondholders or creditors of other classes to be much interested in buying new issues of their preferred stocks; rarely, therefore, are offerings made to creditor groups.

Private Placements of Preferred Stock

Private placements of preferred stocks occur more frequently than such placements of common stock chiefly because of legal prescriptions applicable to the investment policies of institutional investors. A few states, for example, permit life insurance companies to invest in preferred stock but

TABLE 23-1

Some Recent Rights Offerings of Preferred Stock to Common Stockholders

Corporation	Description of Stock	No. of Shares	Par Value	Subscription Price	Rights Needed to Buy One Share	Conversion Price or Ratio
Consolidated Edison Company........	4.12% convertible preference, Series A	946,454	$100	100	17	$80
Crucible Steel Company........	5¼% cumulative convertible	99,885	$100	100	38	$29
General Precision Equipment Company....	$2.98 cumulative convertible	105,928[a]	No par	50	11	1¼ common shares
Northwest Airlines, Inc........	Cumulative, 5¼% convertible series	457,873	$25	25	3	$26
Public Service Company of Indiana, Inc....	4.80% cumulative convertible	242,826	$100	100	20	2.5 common shares
SCM Corporation........	5½% cumulative convertible	240,044	$50	50	8	$17
Tropical Gas Company, Inc........	6% cumulative convertible	25,674	$100	100	27	$20
Washington Gas Light Company........	Serial preferred, $4.60 convertible series	100,386	No par	100	14	$52.50

[a] Offered in part also to holders of the corporation's $1.60 cumulative convertible preferred.

SOURCE: Moody's Investors Service, Manuals.

forbid investment in common stock; and many while permitting both kinds of investment, allow for much more liberal investment in preferred than in common.

Another important reason is that institutional investors, as a class, tend toward conservatism in their investment policies, even though this conservatism is not forced upon some of them by legal restrictions. For example, trustees who are free to invest trust estates according to what is called the prudent-man rule may feel that it is, indeed, prudent to invest portions of the estates in carefully selected preferred stocks, but that any substantial investment in common stocks would be judged imprudent should losses occur and should they be called to an accounting by action taken by the beneficiaries of the trust estates.

It was pointed out in Chapter 19 that convertible preferred stock issues, or such issues together with common stock options, are sometimes taken by individual capitalists who are willing to advance substantial amounts of equity funds to small and medium-sized corporations. Such capitalists, it was said, generally want to take their income from these ventures as capital gains rather than as ordinary income. Thus, they may be satisfied with moderate dividends on preferred stocks, expecting to convert to common stock or to exercise the options to buy it should they want to take control, or, upon the successful outcome of the ventures, should they want to sell the common to realize their capital gain.

PROBLEMS OF PREFERRED STOCK MANAGEMENT

Most of the problems encountered in the management of preferred stock issues closely parallel those of common stock management, as discussed in Chapters 20 and 21. Such a parallelism is to be expected, since both kinds of securities represent ownership or equity interests. Decisions must be made whether the directors should have at their disposal authorized but unissued preferred, and how much; whether preferred should have a par value, and, if so, at what level, or whether it should be no par; whether the corporation should deal in its own preferred stock in the market; and whether it should have the preferred listed on one or more of the stock exchanges. Generally, however, problems of these kinds, as they pertain to preferred stocks, are much more easily solved than when they pertain to common stocks. For preferred stocks, solutions tend to fall into the category of customary procedures, which is to say, they tend to be uniform from corporation to corporation.

Certain problems encountered in common stock management are rarely found in the control of preferred stock issues—questions of changing from par to no par, from no par to par, and from high pars to low pars, writedowns in par or stated values, split-ups, and reverse splits. As a rule, original decisions as to pars and number of shares stand as long as given preferred stock issues are outstanding. For example, the holders of preferred stocks—except in closely held corporations where almost anything can happen—can rarely be expected to consent to write-downs in the par or stated values of their stocks to eliminate deficits or to permit write-downs in asset values; as long as corporations are solvent, they expect the common stockholders to bear such burdens.

On the other hand, because preferred stock is not the same as common stock, it has certain management problems peculiarly its own. Two kinds stand out: the elimination or replacement of preferred issues themselves, and the elimination of dividend arrearages.

In the remainder of the present chapter, therefore, we shall look briefly at what may be called the "routine" problems of preferred stock management closely resembling the comparable problems of common stock management, and then at greater length at the two special kinds of problems just mentioned.

ROUTINE PROBLEMS

Authorized Issues

The possibility that the common stockholders of a corporation will refuse to approve from time to time new issues of preferred is rarely a good reason for placing at the disposal of the directors substantial amounts of authorized but unissued preferred.[3] If a proposed issue of preferred is to have voting power or if it is to be convertible or to have stock-purchase warrants attached, the common stockholders may insist that it first be offered to them; or they may make no such demand should they feel that the preferred will not significantly affect their own ownership interests. In either case, however, they are likely to approve the proposed issue without much delay. A deferring of requests for approval until such time that preferred is actually to be issued means, therefore, that state taxes on authorized but unissued stock can be avoided.

But requirements for the approval of existing *preferred* stockholders for additional issues of preferred may change the outlook. Sound financial programming may be hamstrung if further offerings of preferred of the kind already outstanding or of kinds that would have prior preferences must have the consent of the holders of a substantial majority of the existing preferred. In the absence of such a consent, further financing with preferred would require the replacement of the entire existing issue—something that could be quite costly in flotation expenses. Prospects, therefore, that a corporation will want to put out additional preferred from time to time over a period of years should presumably be matched with an original authorization to take care of these successive issues. At any time, accordingly, the existing preferred stockholders would not have the power to veto further sales from the authorized issue—their veto power would only reach issues going beyond the original authorization.

---

[3] For the considerations involving common stock in this regard, see above, pp. 475–76.

When, however, additional issues of preferred are not subject to the veto power of existing preferred stockholders, but only depend upon the satisfaction of protective provisions in the existing contract, such as those in terms of earnings, the ratio of preferred to assets, and its ratio to common, no need for authorized but unissued preferred stock obtains. If the protective provisions can be satisfied, consent of the common stockholders for the additional issues, when needed, will presumably be readily forthcoming. Here, of course, it is generally important to give the directors standing authority to serialize the successive issues, so that different dividend rates, call prices, and preferences to assets can be set in accordance with changing conditions in the preferred stock market.

Par and No Par

Although preferred stocks have generally shared with common stocks the earlier trend from par values to no pars and the later trend from high pars and no pars to low pars—and for the same reasons as with common[4]— this movement in the new directions has been slower than has that of common. Many preferred stocks of $100 par value remain oustanding, and a goodly number of new issues with pars at that figure come to the market each year. A reason for this is that corporations, when devising preferred stock issues for a receptive market, have no difficulty in selling them at or above a par value such as $100. If the dividend rate and other terms as originally decided upon are found upon investigation to preclude sale at par value, an increase in the proposed dividend rate and perhaps improvements in other terms can generally be expected to remedy the situation. Likewise, corporate managements do not ordinarily envisage pricing difficulties in selling successive issues of given preferreds. If an outstanding preferred is selling at 95 whereas its par value is 100, a second issue—Series B—can be given a better dividend rate and perhaps better terms of other kinds to insure its sale at 100 or better.

Preferred Treasury Stock

While many corporations never deal in their common stocks once they have been issued, most of those that issue preferreds typically regard it as highly probable that they will have occasion to buy back all or portions of their preferred issues. Such an expectation goes hand in hand with contractual agreements to set up redemption or sinking funds for retirement; but it is also strongly indicated by the customary reservation of rights to call preferred for redemption, regardless of redemption fund provisions.

Usually, however, the status of reacquired preferred stock as "treasury stock" is short-lived. Investors in a preferred stock would see little protection in a redemption fund requirement if the corporation could reissue at will preferred shares acquired in fulfillment of the requirement; hence,

---

[4] See above, pp. 477–81.

they generally insist upon a provision that reacquired stock must be promptly canceled. Even in the absence of redemption fund provisions, moreover, corporations do not ordinarily plan to resell when they buy up their preferred stocks in the market or call them for redemption. Their intention is to move toward the simple common stock form of financial structure or to replace the existing preferreds with new preferreds having materially different features or with long-term debt. Accordingly, immediate steps to cancel the reacquired preferred are usually taken as a matter of course.

In rare circumstances, it is true, corporations do reacquire their preferred stocks with the intention of reselling them. The most likely occasion for this is the disposal of preferred shares donated to provide working capital—something that is much more likely to happen in family and other closely held corporations than in those of wide stock distributions.

As was pointed out in the preceding chapter, state laws are generally more liberal in permitting reacquisitions of preferred stocks than common stocks. The general rule is that the cost of common treasury stock must not exceed the amount of earned surplus, whereas the cost of reacquired preferred stock may ordinarily be charged against the preferred stock account itself as long as this charge does not exceed par or stated value. Such a difference in legal stipulations gives corporation managements a comparatively wide degree of freedom in buying and calling preferred for cancellation—and, indeed, in acquiring for resale, should that kind of transaction be favored.

Listing

The question of listing a preferred stock on one or more of the stock exchanges seldom arises independently of that of listing the common stock of the same corporation. Rare is the corporation that would want to list its preferred but not its common, both being widely distributed. And rare, too, is the corporation whose common stock is closely held but whose preferred shares would nevertheless qualify for listing on the basis of their number and wide distribution.

Corporations that have their common stocks listed on a given exchange ordinarily apply to the same exchange to have their preferreds listed. If advantages are gained by the listing of common, presumably advantages of the same kinds, although probably of less significance, can be had by the addition of preferreds to the list. The exchanges themselves encourage the listing of preferreds by making listing requirements for them much milder in terms of number of shares and distribution than for common stocks.

CHANGES IN TERMS AND REPLACEMENT OF PREFERRED STOCK

Oftentimes corporate managements are unhappy because they have preferred stock issues outstanding or are dissatisfied with some of the terms of these issues. The stocks may have been sold when the corporations were under considerable financial pressure, were not well known, had limited earning power, or were subject to other unfavorable circumstances. Improvements in their situations, therefore, may prompt action to get rid of the sources of dissatisfaction.

The very presence of preferred stocks of any description in their financial structures is sometimes a source of dissatisfaction to corporate managements. They would much rather have the simple common stock form of structure or, perhaps, bonds instead of preferred stock—the latter chiefly to get the advantages of interest rates lower than preferred dividend rates and the deductibility of interest in the determination of taxable income. But the solution here does not appear to be a difficult one: common stock or bonds can be sold and the proceeds used to retire the preferred stock. Many such "refinancing" operations take place, particularly the replacement of preferred stocks carrying high dividend rates with bonds. In the summer of 1963, for example, Burlington Industries, Inc., sold $25 million of subordinated debenture bonds to institutional investors and used the proceeds to retire *four* issues of outstanding preferred stock as follows: 83,420 shares of 4 per cent preferred at a redemption price of $104; 96,000 shares of 4.2 per cent preferred at $101; 29,220 shares of 3 ½ per cent preferred at the par value of $100; and 32,245 shares of 4½ per cent second preference stock also at $100. Earlier in 1963, the International Harvester Company took steps to retire 408,362 shares of its outstanding 7 per cent noncallable preferred stock of $100 par value (half of the total outstanding shares) by offering for each share $175 face amount of 4⅝ per cent subordinated debenture bonds maturing in 1988. Holders of the preferred stock who wanted to make the exchange were asked to "tender" their shares to the corporation. Although the annual interest on $175 of bonds would amount to approximately $8.09, as against the $7.00 dividend on a share of stock, a substantial saving was envisaged on account of the deductibility of the interest for income tax purposes.

At any rate, the problem posed requires no further discussion in this chapter, as any such discussion would necessarily be repetitious of materials covered elsewhere. The advantages and disadvantages of common stock structures and of preferred stock financing as against bond financing were discussed in Chapters 14 and 15, the procedures of common stock financing, in Chapters 18–20, and the procedures of bond financing are scheduled for discussion in Chapter 29.

Our immediate attention, then, may be confined to situations where corporate managements are quite satisfied to have preferred stocks in their financial structures but are unhappy about the status of their existing preferreds. Dividend rates considered to be excessive are an outstanding source of dissatisfaction. A corporation that put out its preferred under relatively unfavorable circumstances may have had to designate a cumulative dividend rate of, say, 6 or 7 per cent. But now, with improvements in its financial position and increased demand for preferred stocks among investors generally, its managers are confident that a dividend rate of 4½ or 5 per cent would suffice to attract buyers of a new preferred issue. What to do?

But managerial dissatisfaction with the terms of existing preferred stock issues may have for its source terms of the contracts other than dividend rates. A corporation may want to issue additional preferred of the same class as that already outstanding, but its proposals to do so may have been vetoed by the existing preferred stockholders; or it may have found that additional issues are precluded by what it considers to be unduly oppressive protective provisions in its existing contract. Another corporation, originally planning to work toward a simple common stock structure, may now be quite satisfied to have preferred stock permanently in its financial structure; accordingly, it finds the redemption fund provisions of its existing contract distasteful. Another decides that restrictions upon common stock dividends in the existing contract are unreasonable. Another concludes that managerial discretion is seriously hampered by requirements in the existing contract about the maintenance of certain balance sheet ratios. Another wants to get rid of a participation feature. And in another, intense jockeying for control makes the present management, holding on by a narrow margin, extremely anxious to eliminate the conversion feature in the outstanding preferred. What to do?

Sale of New Preferred Stock

An obvious way for a corporation to eliminate sources of dissatisfaction of the kinds mentioned is to issue a new preferred stock and to use the proceeds of its sale to retire the outstanding issue having the obnoxious features. With the existing issue still outstanding, restrictive provisions in its contract might preclude the new issue, or its owners might be expected to vote against the new issue. But obstacles of this kind can easily be overcome. Assuming the outstanding stock to be callable, as, of course, it would be likely to be, the corporation could call it for redemption, borrow money from a bank to redeem it, and then use the proceeds of the new issue to repay the bank loan. With the old preferred eliminated, only the approval of the common stockholders would be required for the new offering of preferred. As an example, the Northwest Natural Gas Company, in July, 1963, arranged the sale of 60,000 shares of 4.68 per cent preferred stock of $100 par value to 16 institutional investors, and in the same month called for redemption at $107 a share the 60,000 shares of its outstanding 5.72 per cent preferred stock also of $100 par value.

Replacement to Reduce the Dividend Rate. When the objective in issuing a new preferred is to get the advantage of a lower dividend rate, a corporate management must be quite careful in estimating the costs of flotation, the cost of retirement in terms of the call-price premium, and the interest to be paid on the interim financing with bank loans. If it is not careful, it may find that it has gone to a great deal of trouble to no material advantage; in truth, the net result may be disadvantageous. The fact that a new preferred can be sold on the basis of a dividend rate of 5 per cent, whereas the dividend rate on the existing preferred is 6 per cent, does not mean that the corporation will have its annual bill for dividends cut by an amount equal to 1 per cent of the par or stated value of the existing issue.

For illustration, assume that a certain corporation has outstanding 100,000 shares of 6 per cent cumulative preferred of $50 par value. The stock is callable at 56, so that a total of $5,600,000 would be needed to pay off the stockholders. In addition, it would be necessary to borrow to effect the retirement pending the sale of the new stock, and it is estimated that the loan funds would be needed for two months. A bank is willing to lend $5,600,000 for that period at an interest rate of 4½ per cent per annum, or for a total interest charge of $42,000. However, the interest charge would be deductible against ordinary income in the determination of the corporation's income tax liability; assuming the corporation to be well into the 52 per cent bracket of the income tax, the charge would be offset by a tax saving of $21,840. This means that the corporation could use $21,840 of the cash throw-off from its earnings for preferred stock redemption or bank loan repayment, thus decreasing the amount needed from the new preferred stock issue for these purposes. Accordingly, the net amount needed to retire the preferred stock and to repay the bank would be $5,620,160 ($5,600,000 + $42,000 − $21,840). How much of the new preferred stock would have to be sold to provide cash in the amount of $5,620,160 would depend upon the deal that could be made with investment bankers. The bankers assure the corporate management that they could sell approximately 120,000 shares of 5 per cent preferred at $50 a share, the proposed par value of the new issue. They estimate that flotation costs, including expenses of registration and their own underwriting commission, at 4 per cent of the gross proceeds of the issue. The refinancing should thus require the issuance of new preferred in the total amount (rounded) of $5,854,000 ($5,620,160 ÷ .96). Dividends on the old stock amounted to $300,000 a year, and on the new they would amount to $292,700. Thus, what would appear to be a reduction in dividend requirements of $50,000 a year, were one simply to apply the two dividend rates to the par value of the old stock, would turn out to be a true reduction of only $7,300.

Obviously, the corporation of the illustration would fare badly were it required to offer in the new preferred a dividend rate of 5¼ or 5½ per cent; its dividend requirements would be increased as a result of the refinancing. Even with the new rate at 5 per cent as given in the illustration, the small annual "saving" in dividends of $7,300 could hardly be attractive to a common-stock-minded board of directors. Were the contract for the new preferred to set down substantial call-price premiums and were there some likelihood that it would sooner or later be called for redemption, the "saving" would appear to be a mere pittance. In terms of par value, moreover, the prospect of having $5,854,000 of new preferred to redeem, in place of $5 million of old, would further reduce the significance of the saving. Even should the directors be planning to keep the new preferred outstanding "permanently," the fact that the refinancing would add $854,000 to the preferred stockholders' claims to assets in the event of reorganization or dissolution could hardly be palatable.

Replacement to Eliminate Unsatisfactory Features. When corporate managements plan new issues of preferred stocks to get rid of undesirable features in existing issues, they must estimate the costs of elimination as carefully as when estimating the probable level of savings through dividend-rate reductions. Assuming that no change is to take place in the dividend rate, these costs are clearly as indicated previously: premiums paid in calling the old preferred, flotation expenses of the new, interest payments for interim financing less the related tax saving, and the *annual* dividend differential on the increased amount of preferred stock to be outstanding. In the illustration, the first three of these items totaled $854,000 and the annual dividend differential would be $51,240 (that is, dividends at 6 per cent on $5,854,000 of stock by comparison with dividends at the same rate on the existing $5 million of preferred stock). Would this be too much to pay for the elimination of severe restrictions upon additional issues under an existing contract, redemption fund requirements, the convertibility feature, or some other obnoxious feature or combination of features? It might or might not be in given circumstances, but nobody would deny that the cost should be known before action is taken.

The costs of eliminating unsatisfactory provisions in preferred stock contracts may be reduced, of course, by some adjustment downward in the dividend rate in the new issue—perhaps by something less than the full percentage point of the illustration. However, no such downward adjustment may be possible; in fact, the costs of eliminating unsatisfactory provisions may be increased by an upward adjustment in the dividend rate. What the corporation wants in its new preferred is to have weaker or fewer protective provisions than in the old, or it wants to take away such attractive features as ordinary voting power, convertibility, or participation. Though, therefore, its financial position and the market situation may have improved since the old preferred was issued, this improvement, as an influence upon dividend rates, may be offset or more than offset by weaknesses for the investor in the new contract as compared with the old.

Changes by Vote of the Preferred Stockholders

A second way for the reduction of dividend rates or the removal of objectionable features of existing preferreds is simply to get the preferred stockholders to approve the change. The state laws provide that the holders of a majority, two thirds, three fourths, or some other proportion of the outstanding preferred shares (most commonly, two thirds) may approve changes in the terms of preferred stock contracts, including dividend rates; and the general rule is that when holders of the prescribed proportion of shares approve, the changes are binding upon all the preferred shareholders. By this procedure, therefore, the same preferred stock remains outstanding with all features unchanged except those the alteration of which has been specifically approved.

But a corporation is unlikely to get the approval of its preferred stockholders for a lower dividend rate or other contractual changes unfavorable to them unless it is willing simultaneously to offer material concessions elsewhere in the contract. At a stockholders' meeting in April, 1963, for example, the holders of the prior preferred stock of the Curtis Publishing Company rejected a proposal to eliminate a contractual provision requiring approval of two thirds of this stock for mortgaging the corporation's property or adding to its long-term debt. The preferred stockholders objected that they would be giving up some of their rights while getting nothing in return.

However, the corporation may be inclined to offer no concessions. Its managers may be confident that a new preferred with the features wanted, and without new kinds of concessions, could easily be sold in the market; hence their position may be that the preferred stockholders should also be sufficiently aware of market conditions to accept the proposed change without demur. Nevertheless, the preferred stockholders would know that redemption of the preferred would be the alternative to their vote of approval. Without attractive concessions, therefore, they would surely be inclined to vote negatively, to take the redemption price with its premium (as would probably have been provided for), and then to decide whether or not to reinvest in whatever security the corporation might bring out as a replacement. Indeed, the corporation would have some basis for making concessions, since an approval vote by the stockholders would save it the premiums upon redemption, flotation costs of a new security, and interest costs (after the tax saving) for any necessary interim financing. Concessions to avoid these costs would appear to be especially advisable, of course, if the corporation were not contemplating expanding the amount of its prefered stock. If, however, the very changes proposed were designed to set the stage for much larger issues of such stock, the long-run burden of concessions needed to get an approval vote might be regarded as prohibitive.

Exchanges of New Preferred for Old

When the managers of a corporation come to the conclusion that they would have to offer concessions of certain kinds to preferred stockholders to get their approval for changes in the preferred stock contract, they may decide that the better procedure would be simply to devise a new issue and to offer it in exchange for the present one. Apart from the proposed changes and the concessions to be offered, there may be many minor points in the existing contract that have been ambiguous, difficult to apply, or otherwise awkward. The opportunity to "start from scratch" in writing a new contract may be quite appealing. Moreover, the expenses involved in an exchange procedure, if successful, may turn out to be not much more than would be incurred in taking a vote. An advantage of the exchange procedure—but applicable also to approvals of changes by vote— is that the filing of a registration statement with the SEC is not required provided that "no commission or other remuneration is paid or given directly or indirectly for soliciting such exchange." [5] Usually, also qualification under state blue-sky laws is unnecessary. A disadvantage is that, except in extraordinary cases, some of the preferred stockholders can be expected to refuse to make the exchange. Accordingly, the corporation must have cash available or means of acquiring it to redeem the stock of these holdouts at the call price.

Over the years, exchange offers have been fairly numerous—sometimes offers solely of new preferreds for old, and sometimes offers of new preferreds plus something else for older issues. In 1956, the Curtis Publishing Company received 265,149 shares of its outstanding $4.00-dividend no-par prior-preference preferred stock in acceptance of an exchange offer it had made. For each share of the prior-preference stock, it had offered $40 par value of 30-year 6 per cent subordinated income debenture bonds and one share of new $1.60-dividend no-par prior-preference preferred stock. It was with both these stocks—the unexchanged shares of the older $4.00-dividend stock as well as the newer $1.60-dividend stock—that Curtis was having troubles in the spring of 1963, as referred to earlier. In the spring of 1959, the Eastman Kodak Company offered two shares of a new $3.60 cumulative preferred of $50 par value for each share of its outstanding 6 per cent cumulative preferred of $100 par value. Shares of the older stock not offered for the exchange were then retired in May at $180 a share. In 1963, the American Sugar Refining Company offered new preferred shares and subordinated debenture bonds in exchange for its outstanding 7 per cent preferred of $25 par value. To accomplish its objective, it took a roundabout course. It established the American Sugar Company as a new wholly owned subsidiary, and then proceeded to have the new corporation absorb it as well as the Spreckels Company in which Refining had a 92 per cent ownership interest. Accordingly, the securities offered to Refining's preferred stockholders were issues of American Sugar Company, the surviving corporation. The offer was one share of new 5.44 per cent pre-

---

[5] Sec. 3(a)(9) of the federal Securities Act.

ferred of $12.50 par value and $25 of 5.3 per cent subordinated debenture bonds due in 1993 for each share of Refining's outstanding 7 per cent preferred.

ELIMINATION OF DIVIDEND ARREARAGES

General Aspects of the Problem

If corporate managements are sometimes unhappy because dividend rates in their preferred stock contracts are higher than they would have to name in new issues, or because other contractual provisions seem to be unreasonably burdensome, they have all the more cause for unhappiness when they contemplate dividend arrearages upon their preferreds. Arrearages equal to 5 or 10 per cent of the par or stated value of outstanding preferred stock may not be particularly worrisome, especially if general business conditions and the affairs of the individual corporation are showing marked improvement. But arrearages of 20, 25, or 30 per cent and of higher percentages are definitely a source of much corporate unhappiness, even when business conditions and the operating results of the individual corporation are improving.

Consequences of Large Arrearages. Although large dividend arrearages never in themselves threaten insolvency, they are quite burdensome. Access to new funds is sharply restricted. The possibility of selling new common or preferred stock at anything close to reasonable terms, as those terms are judged by the corporate managements, is exceedingly remote. Potential investors in bonds, too, are likely to shy away. Though they would have claims prior to those of the preferred stockholders, the very arrearages call attention to the corporation's poor earnings record, its weak cash position, or both. For the same reason, short-term lenders and trade suppliers may be niggardly in extending credit. All potential creditors may fear that, when cash does become available to the corporation in fair amounts, too much of it will be drained in efforts to clean up the arrearages.

Payment in Cash. Thus, corporations have good reason to try to avoid arrearages in the first place, and to try to get clear of them once they have accumulated. The hard route is to pay off the arrearages in cash. It has been taken valiantly by numerous corporations, some of them meeting in this way arrearages as high as 30, 40, and 50 per cent, and, in some instances, much greater arrearages. In the year 1958, for example, the Alleghany Corporation paid $149.87½ a share in clearing up a 27-year accumulation on its 5½ per cent preferred. The Maine Central Railroad, too, has been most valiant in trying to catch up with arrearages by cash payment. In the period 1920–24, it accumulated arrearages of $15 a share on its 5 per cent preferred stock, but it was able to eliminate these by extra payments in 1925 and 1926. Then, it omitted preferred dividends for the whole period from 1932 through 1949, building up arrearages of

$90 a share. Since then it has persistently chopped away at the arrearages by extra cash payments in most years, succeeding in bringing them down to a level of $25 a share by September, 1963.

But the cash-payment route is, indeed, a hard one, principally because, though current earnings may be good, it can ordinarily be expected to require a considerable period of time—the greater the arrearages the longer, of course, the period of time. During this period, the corporation's access to new funds and its credit standing, though steadily improving, may continue to suffer to an extent as seriously to circumscribe its activities. Prospective creditors, as was said previously, may be concerned about the very drain of cash in settling the arrearages.

The cash-payment route must surely impress the common stockholders as being a hard one. Already without dividends for at least the period of years during which the arrearages were accumulating, they must contemplate a further dreary series of dividendless years while the arrearages are being made up. Not only have they been starved for dividends and can they expect further starvation of this kind, but also have they seen the market price of their stock fall to low levels—where they can expect it to remain for a considerable stretch into the future. How nice it would be, therefore, if all the arrearages could be wiped out at one stroke by means of some kind of deal with the preferred stockholders!

Possibility of Settlement Deals. Because corporate managements are vitally concerned with access to funds and credit standing, and because, be it repeated, they are usually common stock minded, possibilities of working out deals with preferred stockholders to eliminate dividend arrearages have strong appeal. Over the years, hundreds of deals have been devised and offered, and a large number of them have been accepted. In offering deals, corporate managements tend to have a strong bargaining position, since the preferred stockholders, too, have been starved for dividends, they, too, have probably seen the market value of their stock sink well below par or stated value, and they know that boards of directors can continue the policy of nonpayment even if earnings are good. This does not mean, however, that deals always or usually work to the disadvantage of the preferred stockholders. Some do have such results, but, in many instances, preferred stockholders who agree to "adjustments" gain more in the long run than do dissenters who eventually receive their back dividends in full.

Position of Dissenters. In the matter of dissenters, only a minority of states stipulate that the acceptance of deals for the settlement of claims to dividend arrearages by some designated proportion of preferred stockholders shall be binding upon all. While, therefore, the dividend rate, the call price, and other terms of preferred stock contracts can generally be changed for all preferred stockholders by a vote of holders to two thirds, three fourths, or some other proportion of the preferred stock, the most common rule that applies to arrearage deals is that only the preferred stockholders who vote in favor are bound to the settlement thus agreed upon.

In any of the minority states, therefore, the managers of a corporation know that if they can get a favorable vote of the holders of the prescribed majority of the preferred stock, their offer of a settlement deal will be completely successful. In making the offer, they would be likely to stipulate that, unless an approval vote of the prescribed size is obtained, the offer will not be binding upon the corporation itself. The completion of a deal with the holders of a minority or even a small majority of the outstanding preferred shares could hardly be regarded by them as a sound solution to their problem: they would continue to face the question of what to do with the arrearage claims of the large number of stockholders who refused to vote approval.

In a state wherein the dissenting preferred stockholder is not bound by the approval vote of fellow stockholders, a corporation that wants to offer a settlement deal has equal reason to avoid binding itself unless a large percentage of the shares are voted in favor of the offer. Were the corporation not to stipulate what favorable vote is necessary to make its offer effective, the acceptance of the offer by holders of 30 or 40 per cent of the shares would be binding both upon these stockholders and upon itself; but this would leave 60 or 70 per cent of the dividend arrearages unaffected—and that could hardly be hailed as a reasonable solution to the corporation's difficulties. Usually, indeed, corporations stipulate that their offers will not be effective unless quite high percentages of the shares are voted in favor—85 to 90 per cent or more.

Attitude of Common Stockholders. As a group, common stockholders, too, have a right of dissent: proposed deals may fail to get the support of the holders of requisite majorities of the common shares. Most kinds of deals offered for the settlement of arrearages require amendments to the articles of incorporation, and this requires the consent of the common stockholders. Usually, however, favorable action by the common stockholders can be counted upon, since a basic objective of settlement deals is to clear the way for early resumption of dividends on the common stock. Only when proposed offers to the preferred, as devised by corporate managements, are thought by the common stockholders to be much more generous than necessary to secure acceptance are they likely to vote them down.

Replacement of Preferred Stock and Its Arrearages

Offers of Prior-Preference Stock. A popular method of clearing up large arrearages of preferred stock dividends is to offer new "prior-preference preferreds" in exchange for existing preferreds together with the claims for back dividends accumulated thereon. Suppose, for example, that arrearages on an existing preferred amount to 40 per cent of its par value. The corporation might ask its preferred stockholders to take 1.4

shares of the new prior-preference preferred in exchange for each share of their present holdings including the accumulated dividend claims. The new stock would have the prior-preference designation or a similar one because the corporation would want to give it claims to dividends and assets having priority over those of the existing preferred. To issue such a new preferred, the corporation would doubtless need the approval of the holders of two thirds or some other proportion of the existing preferred shares; but if holders of this proportion were to find the exchange offer attractive, they would surely also vote in favor of the new issue. Thus, the corporation would expect to get acceptance of the exchange offer and approval of the new issue, as it were, simultaneously.

In making offers of prior-preference preferreds in exchange for existing preferreds with their arrearages, corporate managements often stress the point that current earnings are large enough to enable them to begin the payment of dividends on the new stock at once; at the same time, they confess great uncertainty as to when it will be feasible to make an attack upon the arrearages on the existing stock should it not be exchanged. The implied threat not to resume dividends on the existing stock, coupled with what almost amounts to a promise to pay dividends immediately on the proposed prior-preference stock, is usually all that is needed to convince the dividend-starved preferred stockholders that they should make the exchange. Indeed, the implied threat and promise appear to be potent enough sometimes to enable corporations to designate dividend rates in the prior-preference preferreds lower than those of the existing issues.

Joint Offers of Prior-Preference and Common Stocks. Sometimes corporations offer prior-preference stock in exchange for existing preferred shares on a share-for-share basis, adding offers of common shares to take care of the dividend arrearages. In some proposed deals of this kind, cash to meet a limited amount of the arrearages, with common shares for the balance, is offered. Obviously, a wide range of proposals of this variety is possible in terms of the number of common shares solely or in terms of common shares plus cash.

Exclusive Offers of Common Stock. In a few instances, corporations offer common shares exclusively in exchange for the preferred and its arrearages. To get acceptance for such an offer, however, a corporation may have to give the preferred stockholders so many shares of common as to displace the existing common stockholders in position of control. The arrangement, then, tends to be a drastic one; by it, the common stockholders, since they must vote approval, acknowledge that their stock is of little value from the standpoint of earnings and dividend prospects as long as the preferred stock is outstanding. It must appear to them that they could hardly expect a dividend for themselves even were the preferred stockholders to give up all claims to the arrearages and simply demand current dividends.

Offers of Bonds. In some instances, offers of bonds are made as full or partial settlement for the claims of preferred stockholders, including their claims to dividends in arrears. The replacement of preferred stocks with their contingent claims to earnings and assets by bonds with fixed claims to interest and principal would hardly appear to be a good way to improve access to markets for new funds and to strengthen credit standing; but so-called "income bonds" may serve rather conveniently as a replacement security. A distinctive feature of income bonds is that the interest is payable only to the extent that it is covered by earnings—it is not a "fixed charge" as for ordinary bonds; hence, the failure to pay interest because earnings are not available, like a failure to pay dividends on preferred stock, does not mean that the corporation can be declared insolvent. A strong point favoring the replacement of preferred stocks with income bonds is that interest paid on the latter is deductible for income tax purposes, whereas, as we know, preferred dividends are not deductible.[6]

Compensation for Arrearages Only

Corporations sometimes ask their preferred stockholders to give up their rights to dividend arrearages for something offered in exchange without offering or requesting any other change in the stockholders' position. They are satisfied to let the preferred stock stand as is, provided only that a settlement for the arrearages can be worked out. The preferred stockholders may be told that dividends at the contractual rate can be resumed immediately if only the arrearages can be cleared out, but that, if they are not cleared out, it is difficult to see when cash payments to meet them can be made. To dividend-starved preferred stockholders, such a declaration, as was indicated above, tends to have compelling force.

Offers of Additional Shares of the Same Stock. What is offered as compensation is often preferred shares of exactly the same kind as that upon which the arrearages have accumulated. The amount of the offer, in terms of par or stated value, is related to, although not necessarily identical with, the amount of the arrearages. If, for example, arrearages amount to 40 per cent of the par value of the preferred, the offer may be three, four, or five tenths of an additional share for each share held. The acceptance of such a proposal might appear to promise little help toward a solution of the corporation's problem, since its bill for dividends would be increased. But such proposals are ordinarily made only after earnings have improved and when they are continuing to improve, so that the corporate managements expect to be able to pay dividends on a larger amount of preferred stock if they do not have to drain earnings in making up the arrearages.

---

[6] For a discussion of the distinctive features of income bonds, see pp. 641–42.

To illustrate, assume that the par value of a corporation's 5 per cent preferred stock is $5 million, that arrearages amount to 40 per cent of this value, and that current earnings available for dividends amount to $650,000. If the corporation undertook to pay off the arrearages, and if earnings continued to amount to $650,000 annually, five years would be required for it to become current in its preferred dividend payments, that is, to pay off the arrearages as well as to meet the additional dividend requirements of that period. During much of this five-year period, access of the corporation to new funds and its credit standing, though doubtless improving, would continue to be clouded, and the common stockholders, of course, could not hope for dividends. But if, on the other hand, the preferred stockholders accepted additional preferred—four tenths of a share for each share held, let us say—as compensation for surrendered rights to the arrearages, the outlook for the corporation and for both the common and preferred stockholders would immediately brighten. The annual dividend requirements on total preferred would rise from $250,000 to $350,000, but the remaining $300,000 of current earnings would be available annually for dividends on the common. Not that the board of directors would necessarily distribute this entire amount as common dividends, but its very availability should greatly improve the investment status of the common stock. Thus, the market value of the common should recover sharply, and the credit position of the corporation should look much stronger.

Offers of Common Stock. In some instances, the compensation offered for the surrender of claims to dividends in arrears is a stipulated number of shares of common stock. If a corporation is currently earning reasonable profits, its managers can say to the preferred stockholders that the elimination of the arrearages will clear the way for an immediate resumption of dividends on both the preferred and common. The foregoing illustration demonstrates why such a claim or prediction could be an honest one. At any rate, the preferred stockholders might accept the offer of common in the expectation of receiving dividends upon it in addition to restored dividends on the preferred at the designated contractual rate.

Other Types of Offers. Sometimes prior-preference preferred stock is offered for the arrearages only, rather than for both the existing stock and its arrearages.

In some cases, changes in existing preferred stock contracts favorable to the preferred stockholders are offered as compensation for a yielding of claims to arrearages. A corporation may make an offer to increase the preferred dividend rate, to make the stock convertible, to give it a participation feature or warrants for the purchase of common stock, or to introduce provisions for a redemption fund. Sometimes contractual changes are offered as sole compensation for the yielding of claims to back dividends, and sometimes as inducements in addition to some cash or shares of the same preferred, a prior-preference preferred, or common. For example, the preferred stockholders of the foregoing illustration might not ask for additional shares were they to be offered an increase from 5 to 7 per cent in the dividend rate upon their existing holdings. The amount of their prospective dividends would thus be made the same as by the stock-for-compensation route of the illustration. At the same time, the avoidance of the additional issue of stock could be of material advantage to the corporation in future financing.

Cash is frequently used as a supplemental means of persuading preferred stockholders to give up their claims to back dividends. Cash may be offered to take care of arrearages of, perhaps, one year, with the balance of the arrearages to be compensated for by additional stock or contract changes or both.

Illustrative Settlement Deals. Several recent offers of deals for the settlement of dividend arrearages may be cited for illustration.

In 1961, holders of 208,871 shares of the $20 par $1.25-dividend preferred stock of Atlas General Industries, Inc., agreed to take $^{36}/_{100}$ of a share of its common stock in lieu of their arrearage claims of $5.62 a share. The arrearages had accumulated since 1957 on account of dividend-payment restrictions in the corporation's bond indentures. Holders of 8,546 of the preferred shares refused to give up their arrearage claims, and Atlas paid these in cash.

In August, 1962, the Virginia-Carolina Chemical Corporation announced an offer of the following for each share of $100 par value preferred stock having arrearage claims of $96 a share: one share of common stock, 1.3 shares of 5 per cent prior-preferred stock of $50 par value, and one share of 5 per cent convertible preferred of $50 par value, convertible into 1.1 shares of common. In the proxy statement in which the offer was announced, it was "anticipated" that dividends on the new preferred would start in the quarter ending December 31, 1962, and that annual dividends would be paid on the common stock.[7]

Also in August, 1962, Browser, Inc., made the following offer for each share of its 4.8 per cent preferred stock of $25 par value with its arrearage claims of $14.40: $3.50 in cash payable in two instalments, one share of new 5 per cent preferred of $28 par value, and three fourths of a share of new Class B nonvoting common stock which would share equally with the regular common in dividends.

In April, 1963, the Coplay Cement Manufacturing Company got its preferred stockholders to approve an exchange offer by which ten shares of new 6 per cent preferred stock of $20 par value were tendered for each outstanding share of 6 per cent preferred of $100 par value with arrearage claims of $125.50.

At a meeting held in July, 1963, the preferred stockholders of the

---

[7] *The Wall Street Journal*, August 27, 1962, p. 9.

United Piece Dye Works voted to give up their $4.25-dividend preferred shares of $75 par value with arrearage claims of $23.31¼ a share for a new noncumulative $5.50-dividend preferred of the same par value. The contractual provisions of the new preferred were exactly the same as in the old except for the change in dividend rate and the noncumulative feature.

Questions

1. For immediate offerings for cash, how do the selling channels for new preferred stock issues compare with those for new issues of common stock?

2. In exchange for what kinds of securities of a corporation to be absorbed in a merger, might an offering of preferred stock of the absorbing corporation be attractive?

3. To what extent, if at all, are sales of new issues of preferred stock subject to regulation under the federal Securities Act?

4. Why are private placements of preferred stock issues more popular than such placements of new issues of common stocks?

5. Why is the designation of par and no-par values for preferred stock issues of much less importance than for common stock issues?

6. What costs are likely to be involved in replacing an outstanding preferred stock issue through the sale of a new preferred to get a lower dividend rate?

7. From the legal standpoint, what terms of preferred stock contracts can be changed by consent of the preferred stockholders? What are the rights of dissenters? For a given corporation, what is the likelihood of its getting such a consent?

8. Under what circumstances, if any, can a corporation force preferred stockholders to take new preferred stock in exchange for their existing holdings?

9. Why is it generally advisable for corporations to try to avoid arrearages in preferred dividends as well as to clear up as quickly as possible arrearages that have accumulated?

10. Why are corporations likely to be in rather strong bargaining positions when they offer "deals" to preferred stockholders to clear up preferred dividend arrearages?

11. What are the rights of dissenting preferred stockholders who refuse to agree to "deals" for the settlement of preferred dividend arrearages?

12. Why may offers of prior-preference preferred stock be especially attractive to preferred stockholders in getting them to give up claims to dividends in arrears?

13. In what ways is common stock sometimes used in offers to preferred stockholders for the settlement of preferred dividend arrearages?

Problems

1. Although the International Harvester Company, as stated on page 562 of this chapter, expected to cut down its cost of funds by substituting subordinated debenture bonds for half of its outstanding noncallable preferred stock, it was actually proposing to replace a $100 equity claim against assets for each preferred share with a $175 creditor's claim. For the 408,362 shares

of preferred it sought to retire, it therefore proposed to add a total of $30,627,150 to claims having prior ranking to the common stock.

a) Would not this disadvantage of the transaction more than offset the expected reduction in the cost of funds to the corporation? Explain in figures why you do or do not think so. In any computation involving tax saving, assume that the applicable federal income tax rate is 52 per cent.

b) If Congress were to reduce federal corporation income tax rates, would your opinion differ? In what way?

2. The Kelsey-Jordan Company has outstanding 100,000 shares of 6 per cent preferred stock of $100 par value callable for redemption at 105. It now has an opportunity to sell 100,000 shares of 5 per cent preferred at a public offering price of 100, the par value. Its expenses of flotation, including the investment bankers' commission, would be about $300,000. It already has cash available to meet these flotation expenses as well as to pay the premium on the outstanding preferred should it be called for redemption. Aside from possibilities of investing in government securities or securities of other corporations, its best alternative "internal" uses of this cash would be simply to redeem a portion of the outstanding preferred or to retire some of its outstanding 5 per cent bonds which it could call for redemption at 100.

Estimate what advantage there would be for the corporation's common stockholders in making the switch in preferred stocks and when this advantage would begin to be enjoyed.

Part VIII

FINANCING WITH
RETAINED EARNINGS

chapter 24

THE NATURE OF EARNINGS AND DIVIDENDS

IMPORTANCE OF EARNINGS AS A SOURCE OF ASSETS

For a very great number of American business corporations, retained earnings or profits constitute the most important source of assets; for almost all business corporations that are profitable, they represent a significant source of assets, if not the most important.

Corporations of small and middle sizes often have little or no access to outside sources of long-term funds, and their stockholders have but small amounts of free cash for buying additional stock. To finance expansion, therefore, these corporations, though they may be able to get fair amounts of short-term credits, must depend chiefly upon the retention of earnings. The managements of many corporations, both small and large, choose not to tap outside sources of long-term funds even when readily available; they choose the simple common stock form of financial structure, decide that they do not want to offer additional common stock to outsiders, and expect, therefore, to be quite liberal in retaining earnings as a means of financing growth. And the managements of most others, though they may tap many financial markets in their search for funds, generally decide that these sources must be substantially supplemented with generous amounts of retained earnings.

Data introduced in earlier chapters of this textbook indicate the great dependence of business corporations collectively upon retained earnings as a means of financing. Table 14–3 on page 295 shows for the postwar period the large amounts of earnings retained in relation to total earnings after the payment of income taxes. The fact that retained earnings in the first six years of this period substantially exceeded dividend payments is especially noteworthy. The importance of the postwar retention of earnings by comparison with all other sources of corporate funds in the same period is indicated in Table 15–3 on page 326, where it is shown that retained earnings supplied 22.5 per cent of all funds acquired by corporations (not including banks and insurance companies) in the period 1946–62. By contrast, stock sales supplied only 6.6 per cent of new funds; bond sales, 11.0 per cent; and short-term sources, 19.0 per cent.

The significance of retained earnings is indicated, of course, not only by what they amount to from year to year, but also by total accumulations over the years. Earnings accumulations are generally shown in surplus accounts, although, to be sure, such accounts often carry credits from sources other than earnings. At least roughly,[1] therefore, the data of Table 14–4 on page 297 demonstrate the outstanding role of earnings accumulations in most areas of American corporate business. Especially noteworthy among the revelations of these data are the following: the fact that surplus substantially outranks combined common and preferred stocks in the financial structures of enterprises in all areas except the agriculture-forestry-fisheries and the communications and electric and gas utilities areas; the extremely high proportions of surplus in financial structures in mining and quarrying, manufacturing, and retail trade; and the absence of an insignificant role for surplus in any area—even in communications and electric and gas utilities where its role is smaller than in any other business area, it is a more important source of assets than either current liabilities or preferred stock.

PROBLEMS OF EARNINGS AND THEIR ALLOCATION

From the standpoint of the typical corporate management, the most important problem relating to earnings is that of finding ways of expanding them. Rare is the management that is thoroughly satisfied with the level of earnings that has been achieved. On the contrary, most managements are constantly on the lookout for ways to expand sales and to cut costs so as to increase the margin of profits. Various aspects of this striving for increased earnings were discussed in the chapters on the management of assets—Chapters 7–11—as well as in the discussion of the pros and cons of the different kinds of financial structures in Chapters 14–15; and certain further considerations pertaining to corporate expansion will be examined briefly in the following chapter. But the problem of boosting earnings impinges upon every phase of business management, so that its treatment in a textbook in corporate financial management must necessarily leave many things unsaid.

Clearly a financing question is that of determining what earnings amount to. If a corporation borrows money, the sum involved is known precisely, but there is no such precision in accounting for earnings. One of the major responsibilities of corporate boards of directors is to decide what is to be done with earnings, but to fulfill this responsibility they must know, at least approximately, what results of transactions can be properly treated as earnings and what results should be excluded. Moreover, they must surely know that there is no precise relationship between the amount of earnings reported *for specific periods* and the availability of additional cash *at specific times*. When one speaks of the allocation of

---

[1] Another reason for roughness originates in the distribution of stock dividends. Balances in surplus accounts tend always to understate earnings accumulations because transfers are made from the surplus accounts to the capital stock accounts when stock dividends are declared and distributed.

earnings, one is inclined to think of allocations of cash, but these two concepts are by no means identical. Boards of directors have responsibility to decide what portion of the earnings will serve as a basis for dividend distributions, but they must know that such decisions are not entirely free ones. They must abide by legal prescriptions and limitations. These, then, are the topics for discussion in the remainder of the present chapter. With knowledge of the nature of earnings, their relationship to cash, and legal provisions as to dividend payments, the boards of directors are in a position to tackle the problem of the actual allocation of earnings—a problem to which the following chapter will be devoted.

MEANING AND DETERMINATION OF EARNINGS

The question *"What are earnings?"* may appear to be a witless one. One has only to look at corporate income statements to see what earnings are. In such a statement, the various sources of income—sales, commissions, interest, dividends, and so on—are listed by name and amount; the various kinds of expenses—cost of goods, wages and salaries, cost of supplies, property taxes, depreciation, and so on—are similarly listed; the net difference between the sums of income and expense items respectively is set out as "net income before income taxes" or "net earnings before income taxes" or "net profit before income taxes"; and then income taxes are deducted to give a final figure for "net income" or "net earnings" or "net profit." Some income statements, it is true, are more elaborate than others —some differentiating between operating and nonoperating income and expenses, and some adding still a third classification such as "nonrecurring" income and expenses. Some show a further deduction from "net earnings" for dividends paid, so that the final figure is for "net earnings retained" or "net earnings reinvested in the business." But, elaborate or not, every income statement seems to show much the same kind of thing, and there appears to be nothing mysterious about the result.

Earnings as Estimates

In every income statement, nevertheless, there is much uncertainty, if not mystery; this is true even though the statement has been prepared by highly competent accountants who observe generally accepted accounting principles. The final figure for "net earnings" is always an estimate— whether or not it is a "true" or close one will ordinarily be determinable only in subsequent years.

For corporations that sell on account, the figure for sales income is really only an estimate, its accuracy depending upon the charge for "bad debts." More important for the typical corporation is the fact that the cost of goods sold is an estimate, its accuracy depending upon the skill with which inventories are valued. The depreciation charge—a very important expense item for many corporations—depends for its accuracy upon the wisdom with which useful lives and scrap values are judged, but even more upon what the tax authorities will allow as a deduction in income tax computations. Having similar degrees of uncertainty, as one might say, are depletion charges against wasting assets and amortization charges against intangibles. More modest variations in "net earnings" can also result from differing valuations of supplies inventories.

Also contributing to a lack of precision in determining what "net earnings" amount to are differences in the treatment of certain kinds of expenditures. A corporation spends considerable sums of money in renovating its factory buildings, and it regards these expenditures as a cost of "repairs" and charges them currently as an expense. Another making similar expenditures classifies the results as "improvements" or "betterments," and adds the outlays to the asset account. By comparison with the second corporation, the first overstates its expenses in the current year but will understate them in subsequent years as it will have no depreciation charges against the outlays; but by comparison with the first corporation, the second is in error for the opposite reasons.

Earnings Excluded from Income Statements

Sometimes there is uncertainty about the amount of corporate net earnings, because certain items are not shown in income statements. Accountants differ in their opinions as to how certain kinds of "extraordinary" transactions should be treated. Although the weight of opinion favors showing as much as possible in income statements, almost all accountants make some allowance for direct credits to and charges against surplus accounts.

Examples of "earnings" that are often credited directly to surplus accounts are profits derived in the sale of treasury stock and discounts in the retirement of outstanding securities. A corporation that makes such direct credits to surplus is likely also to make direct charges against surplus accounts for losses on treasury stock transactions and for premiums paid in the retirement of its own securities. Such transactions are sometimes said to involve "capital" rather than "income"—hence the argument that they should not be shown in income statements. But if a corporation sells donated stock, it acquires new funds equal to the proceeds no less than when it derives funds through what are called "ordinary" earnings. Similarly, a corporation derives new funds if it resells treasury stock at a higher price than its buying price, or suffers a loss of funds if it resells at a lower price. Much the same can be said for discounts and premiums in the retirement of its own outstanding securities. An opportunity to retire a $1,000 bond by buying it in the market at 95 would seem to be equally advantageous with an opportunity to earn a profit of $50 in an ordinary sales transaction.

Some additional kinds of income and expense items, though shown in income statements by most accountants, are handled by others as direct credits and charges against surplus accounts. These include profits and losses on the sale of tangible assets not currently used in operations, as land that has been held as a possible future factory or store building site, and profits and losses on the sale of investment securities where the investment was not made in the ordinary course of business.

Position of the Directors

When, therefore, boards of directors take up the matter of deciding what portion of "earnings" should be retained and what portion distributed as dividends, their viewpoint must not be too closely circumscribed by figures appearing in income statements. While they may have great confidence in their accountants, they must realize that the statement figures are tentative and may be incomplete. Indeed, a realization that figures for "net earnings" are estimates is likely to prompt the typical board to be somewhat cautious in dividend declarations. Even when inclined not to retain any portion of current earnings for corporate purposes, a board might nevertheless decide to retain some simply to be able to offset revisions downward in the earnings estimate, should such revisions later appear to be advisable. In this way, earned surplus would be available to absorb write-downs in inventory values, charge-offs of accounts receivable in amounts exceeding the existing reserve for bad debts, losses on the disposal of fixed assets upon which adequate depreciation had not been charged, and so on.

The fact that a substantial amount of "earnings" had been carried directly to surplus accounts, on the other hand, might prompt a corporate board of directors to be much more liberal in dividend distributions than the earnings figure in the current income statement might seem to warrant. In a given case, for example, most of the funds currently needed for expansion might have been supplied by large profits derived in the sale of holdings of extraneous investment securities. Accordingly, the directors might decide upon a much larger dividend distribution than would have been advisable in the absence of such a special source of funds.

RELATIONSHIP OF NET EARNINGS TO CASH

When one hears or reads of decisions as to the "distribution of net earnings" made by the directors of corporations, one may be inclined to think of the net earnings as being a sum of cash that can be retained or paid out in the form of dividends. The corporations report their net earnings as excesses of income over expenses, and income may be thought of as being received in cash, and expenses as being paid in cash—hence the temptation to regard net earnings as a net increase in cash balances. A relationship does, indeed, exist between the amount of earnings and changes in cash holdings, but it is not necessarily a close one. This fact must ever be kept in mind by corporate directors—their decisions as to the "distribution of net earnings" must always be made with an eye upon the cash account as well as upon the figures for current net earnings and for accumulated earnings as carried in the surplus accounts.

Accrual System of Accounting

An important reason why earnings at a given level are not necessarily accompanied by an increase in cash of the same amount is because most corporations maintain their accounting systems on what is called the accrual basis. This means, in brief, that income is taken up in the period in which it is earned, whether or not it is realized in cash in that period, and that expenses are charged to the period to which they belong, whether or not they are met by cash payments in that period.

How the accrual system works—why it does not match cash inflows and outflows with credits to income and expense charges—was demonstrated in the discussion and illustrations of cash flows presented in Chapters 5 and 6. At this time, therefore, we need not review these matters in detail. Reference to a few aspects of the workings of the accrual system should suffice. Within a given period, some goods may be bought and then resold at a profit, but, though income is "taken up" as having resulted from these transactions, cash is actually reduced if payment has been made to the suppliers but payment from the corporation's customers has not been received. Or cash is increased by an amount exceeding the income taken up if payment has been received from the customers but the payment to the suppliers has not been made. Wages and salaries earned by employees in the last few days of an accounting period are entered as an expense of the period, but cash is not spent immediately if the payday for these days of service comes in the following period. Substantial amounts of goods and supplies may be bought and paid for in a given period, but, if they are still on hand at the end of the period, they are not chargeable as expenses in the income statement of the period. Similarly, services may be paid for in advance, as in the immediate payment of the full premiums on three-year and five-year insurance policies. Likewise, cash may be received in one period for goods to be delivered or services to be performed in a later period, so that the cash balance is augmented though there is no matching item of income in the income statement.

Effect of Book Charges

The fact that the depreciation, depletion, and amortization of fixed assets are universally recognized as expenses, and are entered as such in income statements, though there are no current matching outlays of cash, is really an additional aspect of the accrual system of accounting. Cash is spent when the fixed assets are acquired, but expense is recognized only as they are "used up," and this may take place over a long period of years. Thus, the original cash outlays are not shown in income statements, but so shown are the annual charges for depreciation, depletion, and amortization though no related cash disbursements are being made.

The relationship between charges of these kinds and cash flows was indicated in Chapters 5 and 6 in the discussion of the influence of depreciation charges specifically.[2] Again, therefore, it should not be necessary to review the matter at length. But two facts should be kept in mind. One is that charges for depreciation, depletion, and amortization (particularly depreciation charges for the great mass of corporations) are usually quite substantial as sources of differences between reported net earnings and changes in cash balances. The other is that depreciation, depletion, and amortization charges, regarded by themselves, have the effect of causing reported net earnings to be less than net cash inflows. The latter point, of course, simply recalls to mind the proposition of Chapter 6 that there is a "cash throw-off" approximating these charges provided that they and all other expenses are covered in the selling prices of goods or services. Likewise, it gives us the opportunity to lay renewed emphasis upon depreciation charges, in particular, as an enormously important source of corporate funds in the postwar period, as shown in Table 15–3 on page 326.

Direct Charges and Credits to Surplus

The earlier discussion in this chapter of direct charges and credits to surplus accounts was introduced to show that the "net earnings" as determined in a corporation's income statement may not allow for all its gains and losses in a given period. In the present analysis of the relationship of net earnings to cash, therefore, it is necessary only to point out that net inflows of cash may be more than reported net earnings on account of cash receipts credited directly to surplus accounts, and that they may be less on account of cash payments charged directly to these accounts.

Timing of Cash Flows and the Recognition of Net Earnings

Relationship of Earnings to Changes in Cash Balances. Probably the most important thing that can be said about the relationship of net earnings and cash is that, no matter how close the amount of net cash inflows and the amount of net earnings, the timing of increases in cash balances *on account of earnings* is rarely the timing of the recognition of earnings. Cash collected by a corporation from its customers in March could be said to be in part profit and in part a return on the costs of the goods sold and on the overhead expenses of selling; but how much is the one or the other cannot be known until after the books have been closed at the end of the following December! The cash balance goes up in March, but it can go down again—perhaps far down—long before the end of December, and not necessarily according to any pattern of relationship with the net earnings or losses to be reported for the year in an income statement.

In the course of a year, therefore, a corporation may have available to it a net new supply of cash approximately equal to the net earnings as determined at the end of the year plus the cash throw-off resulting from

---

[2] See above, pp. 90–91, 112–15.

charges for depreciation, depletion, and amortization. But, as was indicated, it does not follow that the cash balance *at the end of the year* must be greater than the balance at the beginning of the year by the amount of this net new supply. It is entirely possible that the net new supply, and perhaps more, will have been spent in the course of the year for additional fixed assets or inventories or for the redemption of preferred stock or bonds; thus the closing balance may be no greater, or perhaps it will be less, than the opening balance. Were the directors of the corporation, therefore, to make a decision as to the payment of cash dividends solely on the basis of reported net earnings, they could be gravely misled. They could be misled even though making proper allowance for the possibility of error in estimating earnings, as well as for direct charges and credits to surplus accounts. Solvency might be endangered by a drain of cash for dividends capping other drains that had taken place in the course of the year. In a word, earnings may be available for dividends, but cash may not be!

Earnings Allocation Decisions and Budgets. All this suggests that, in the well-managed corporation, decisions about the retention and distribution of earnings are likely to be made well ahead of the beginning of the year in which they are expected to be derived. In our examination of budgetary principles and procedures in Chapters 12 and 13, we saw the need of cash budgets in which, so to say, all the varied activities of enterprises in buying, selling, paying wages and salaries, meeting other expenses, and so on, are translated into cash inflows and outflows. We saw that income from sales may be reflected in increases in accounts receivable rather than in expanded cash balances, and that, though earnings are being derived, cash balances may not rise because inventories are being expanded or the net amount of accounts payable is being reduced. We saw, too, that estimated monthly cash balances are a basis for decision making about borrowing and the repayment of debt, the sale and retirement of securities, expenditure for new fixed assets, and the payment of cash dividends.

Thus it is that, in the workings of a budgetary system, and particularly in the use of cash budgets, decisions about the distribution of earnings are a matter of forecasting, and not of looking back after the results of operations are known. In effect, the financial managers say that at such-and-such a time they expect to have a given amount of cash, and that they will do thus-and-so with it. All the demands for cash will be evaluated, as it were, simultaneously, and decisions will be made as to how much cash should be absorbed in increased receivables and expanded inventories, how much spent in reducing accounts payable, how much borrowed and when and how repaid, how much spent for new facilities, and how much distributed as cash dividends. Cash expected to be derived from earnings must be lumped with that expected to come in from other sources in determining what the corporation can and cannot do in its overall financial planning. Actual developments may turn out to be different from what were forecast, and budgets may have to be revised as the year progresses. But changes in spending plans on account of such developments must still be based upon a simultaneous reconsideration of all cash sources and demands if decisions are to be sound.

Borrowing to Pay Dividends. Sometimes the question is raised as to whether it is sound policy for a corporation to borrow money to pay cash dividends to its stockholders. But if dividend payment is a matter of financial planning—a matter of "simultaneous decision making," as just discussed—the question tends to be pointless. The financial managers of a corporation may anticipate that earnings in the coming year will justify the payment of quarterly dividends at a given rate, but the cash budget may indicate that at one or more of the quarterly dates sufficient cash will not be available. Accordingly, they may plan to borrow. But it would be pointless to say that they were going to borrow in order to pay dividends. Since the anticipated shortage of cash would be expected to result from all kinds of spending, it would be more appropriate to say that the borrowing would partially finance the whole combination of outlays, rather than dividends specifically. Were this not so, any corporation that paid cash dividends while having liabilities for borrowed money on its books could be said to be paying the dividends with borrowed money; for, obviously, an alternative use of the dividend monies would be the repayment of the loans.

THE LEGALITY OF DIVIDENDS

Chiefly for the purpose of protecting creditors, our states place limitations upon the payment of dividends by the corporations they charter. Having granted the stockholders of these corporations the privilege of limited liability for corporate debts, they take the reasonable position that distributions of corporate assets by the dividend route must be limited so that debt-paying capacity will be preserved. In some cases, protection is extended to preferred stockholders, as by provisions that dividends must not reduce assets below the amount of outside liabilities, the par or stated value of the common stock, and the total *preference to assets* of the preferred stock.

Nature of Dividends

Definition. Before we discuss the legal rules of dividend payments, it would be well to investigate the nature of dividends. A dividend is a pro rata distribution of cash, other assets, promises to pay, or additional stock to the stockholders of a corporation chargeable against its surplus accounts or (for certain liquidating dividends only) against its capital stock accounts. To say that a dividend is a pro rata distribution means that all shares of outstanding stock, or all shares of a given class, participate equally in whatever is distributed.

Kinds of Dividends. By far the majority of corporate dividends are cash distributions, and they accordingly garner most attention of boards of directors, stockholders, other investors, lenders, and the rule-making authorities of state governments.

Once in a while, corporations have reason to distribute some asset other than cash. Such *asset* or *property dividends*, as they are called, have most commonly consisted of stocks or bonds held by the dividend-paying corporations in other corporations. Distributions of this kind have been made, for example, in the process of simplifying holding company structures under the terms of the federal Public Utility Holding Company Act of 1935, as well as when, as a result of antitrust proceedings, corporations have been ordered to divest themselves of interests in other corporations. Illustrative of the latter was the Supreme Court decision in 1961 finding that an illegal combination in restraint of trade resulted from the holding of 63 million shares of General Motors common stock by E. I. duPont de Nemours & Company. In keeping with the decision, the federal district court ordered DuPont to divest itself of the General Motors stock starting not later than July 30, 1962, and completing the disposal not later than February 28, 1972. DuPont decided to pass the stock on to its own stockholders, and in July, 1962, it made a first distribution of 36 per cent of the stock, its stockholders getting for each share of DuPont held a dividend of one-half share of General Motors. Even in the absence of legal compulsion, directors sometimes decide to "spin off" one or more of their corporations' subsidiaries. For example, the directors of the Interstate Engineering Corporation decided in June, 1963, to pass on to the stockholders the stock of its subsidiary the Interstate Electronics Corporation. For each share held in the parent company, the stockholder received as a dividend one share of the subsidiary's common stock.

In relatively rare instances, corporations distribute dividends in the form of promissory notes. These promises to pay or *scrip dividends* are simply a means of deferring the actual distributions of cash; when the notes mature, the cash is distributed.

In the area of rather frequent occurrence and high popularity are *stock dividends* which, indeed, are next to cash dividends in the order of frequency. As the term is used in finance, a stock dividend is *always* a distribution of additional shares of a corporation's own stock to its existing stockholders; accordingly, the term must be carefully distinguished from the term *dividend on stock* which can be used broadly to describe distributions of cash or anything else. By definition, a stock dividend could consist of common shares given to either common or preferred stockholders, or preferred shares given to either of these two classes of stockholders; but, in fact, the vast majority of stock dividends consist of common shares given to common stockholders.

What Is Distributed? Great emphasis must be placed upon the fact that dividends are not distributions of profits or surplus. These things cannot be distributed. Surplus is only a book account designed to show the claims of stockholders against corporate assets over and above the par or stated value of their stock. The very presence of a credit balance in surplus indicates that the stockholders already have this claim against assets; thus it is meaningless to say that a dividend represents a distribution of surplus--of the claim—to them. The claim can be reduced by distributions of dividends in the form of cash or other assets; it can be changed in character by dividends in the form of promises to pay; or it can be changed in form only by distributions of stock dividends; but it is the cash, other assets, scrip, or additional shares of stock that are distributed, and not the surplus. Thus it can be said that a dividend is chargeable against surplus or earnings or profits, or that is based upon surplus or earnings or profits. However, one need not raise an outcry against people who say that this or that corporation "distributed $50,000 of its surplus as a dividend," or that another "paid a dividend of $75,000 out of its earnings"; one has only to understand that what these people mean is that cash dividends of these amounts, chargeable against surplus, were paid.

Dividends as Liabilities. When the board of directors of a solvent corporation declares a cash dividend, the amount declared becomes an obligation to pay. It is proper, therefore, to debit the surplus account at once and to include the dividend among the current liabilities—assuming the usual practice of setting the payment date not more than a few weeks beyond the declaration date. Were the directors to try to rescind the dividend, the stockholders would have a right of action to force payment—the same as other creditors to whom payments due might be refused. However, the decision to rescind would probably be upheld if the directors were able to prove that the dividend payment would violate restrictive provisions of the state law of the kinds shortly to be discussed. There can be no legal compulsion to do something that is illegal. The same rule would appear to apply to asset and scrip dividends.

For stock dividends, on the other hand, the weight of legal opinion is that the directors are free to rescind them at any time before the actual distribution is made. Accounting for this difference in viewpoint is the fact that the distribution of a stock dividend causes no changes in total or individual stockholder claims against earnings and assets and to voting power; hence, nondistribution, it is argued, works no hardship upon them.

Basic Rules

The states have adopted three kinds of basic rules to govern dividend distributions: (1) the surplus rule: that dividends may be paid only to the extent that surplus is available; (2) the impairment rule: that dividends may not be paid if the capital has been impaired or if the payment will cause an impairment; and (3) the insolvency rule: that dividends may not be paid if the corporation is insolvent or if the payment will cause it to be insolvent. Some states have only one of these rules, some have two, and some have elements of all three.

It will be immediately noticed that the surplus and impairment rules are much the same. "Capital" for the impairment rule is usually understood to be the par or stated value of the corporation's stock, whether common only, or common and preferred. Thus, to say that a dividend may not impair the capital is much the same as saying that a surplus must be available. In some cases, however, courts have interpreted "capital" to mean amounts actually received in the sale of stock, whether more or less than par or stated value. With such an interpretation, a dividend charged against premiums paid in the purchase of stock (paid-in surplus) would appear to be illegal in a state having the impairment rule, but legal in one having the surplus rule.

Even the insolvency rule, though it sounds quite different from the other two, may not differ significantly from them in application. The insolvency rule is usually applied in the so-called "equity" sense, that is, in terms of ability to pay debts.[3] A dividend may not be paid if the corporation is unable to pay its debts as they come due or if the dividend will put it in that position. But in a state in which the surplus rule applies, were a corporation to pay a dividend in an amount not exceeding its surplus and then be unable to pay its maturing debts, the courts might well hold the dividend to be illegal. Courts are not bound by surplus figures entered upon corporations' books or shown in their balance sheets; they can take the nonpayment of debts as proof that assets are overvalued and that the surplus figures are therefore fictitious. In a state having the impairment rule, decisions of courts might follow the same line of reasoning. Though a dividend might appear *on the books* not to impair capital, because of the availability of balances in surplus accounts, a court might look upon the inability to pay debts as proof that an impairment had, indeed, taken place—that, again, assets must be overvalued and a genuine surplus nonexistent.

Legal Actions

Tendencies toward uniformity of results in the application of the three kinds of basic dividend rules should be expected because of their identical objective of protecting creditors. If, upon the nonpayment of obligations due them, the creditors of a corporation take legal action to prevent the distribution of a dividend that has been declared, the court will surely issue an injunction to stop the dividend payment, regardless of what the basic dividend rule of the state may be. The court would doubtless look upon the proposed dividend as being of a fraudulent character. Similarly, were a corporation to default upon maturing obligations shortly after having distributed a cash dividend to its stockholders, lawsuits brought

---

[3] In the *bankruptcy* sense, by contrast, insolvency is understood to mean that the reasonable value of the assets of an enterprise is less than the total amount of its obligations to creditors.

by the creditors for the recovery of the dividend could be expected to be successful for the same reason. The court might hold that the corporation's surplus was fictitious or that the dividend did, indeed, impair the corporation's capital, but, basically, its attitude would probably be that the dividend was fraudulent because of proved insolvency. On the other hand, if a corporation pays its debts when due, no creditor is likely to contest dividend declarations and payments on any grounds, whether lack of surplus, impairment of capital, or insolvency.

Thus it is that the applicability of basic dividend rules, as for other kinds of legal prescriptions, depends primarily upon court interpretations of the law and evaluations of the individual corporation's situation in the course of legal actions brought by persons who feel that their rights are being injured. The rules protect the creditors, but this protection demands action by them to safeguard their rights. The directors of a well-managed corporation are unlikely to adopt any dividend policy that would endanger its solvency, regardless of the state's rule and the likelihood of action upon the part of creditors. But a likelihood of action by the creditors would probably be the controlling consideration to be weighed by the directors of another corporation who are anxious to pay a dividend despite doubts as to its legality.

The actions that creditors can take are of two kinds: proceedings in equity for injunctions to prevent the distribution of declared dividends alleged to be illegal, and lawsuits for the recovery of cash or other assets allegedly distributed illegally. Preventive actions in equity are likely to be more helpful to creditors than lawsuits to recover assets already distributed. If a corporation can be barred from paying a cash dividend, the money remains available for the settlement of creditors' claims; but if it has already distributed the dividend, getting the money back can be a difficult matter. As for recovery, the general rule is that directors are liable to creditors for the amount of dividends illegally distributed. In some states, they are also subject to criminal penalties. However, a dissenting director can ordinarily escape all responsibility, civil and criminal, if he has his negative vote entered in the minutes. In some states, indeed, even the directors who voted what is later determined to be an illegal dividend can escape liability if able to prove that they acted in good faith, as by relying upon profits or surplus figures contained in statements certified by reputable accountants. As for stockholders, the legal principle appears to be that they can be forced to return illegal dividends if the distribution has caused the corporation to be insolvent. But the right of creditors to recover from stockholders tends to be even less certain than the right to recover from directors. Some states provide, for example, that illegal dividends cannot be recovered from stockholders who have received them in good faith. At any rate, even if directors, or directors and stockholders, are not provided with ready-made defenses, recovery can be expensive in terms of attorneys' fees, court costs, and delays; and even when judgments are obtained, the directors or stockholders may have no assets that can be seized for their satisfaction.

Dividends Based upon Capital Surplus

Looking at the matter broadly, one can say that, as a rule, any kind of surplus that a corporation has on its books can serve as a basis for cash dividends. Under the surplus rule, surplus obviously exists; under the capital impairment rule, distributions chargeable against any surplus account do not appear to impair capital; and under the insolvency rule, a dividend is not illegal, regardless of the account against which it is charged, if the corporation is not insolvent at the time of its declaration or is not made insolvent by its payment. Ordinarily, therefore, surplus arising from such varied sources as the following can serve as the basis for dividends: premiums received in the sale of par-value stocks, portions of the proceeds of no-par stocks allocated by the directors to paid-in or capital surplus accounts, receipts from of the sale of donated stock, profits upon dealings in treasury stock, profits on the sale of nonoperating assets that may have been credited to capital surplus, write-ups in asset values, and write-downs in the par or stated value of outstanding stock.

Dividends from Asset Write-ups. Always a doubtful basis for dividend payments, nevertheless, is surplus created by simply writing up the book values of assets. The directors of a corporation may claim that the assets have been undervalued (and earnings and surplus, therefore, understated) through the overcharging of depreciation and bad debts, the undervaluing of inventories, and earlier write-offs of assets still having recognizable values. The substantiation of such a claim would appear to justify the write-up and therefore the payment of a dividend based upon it. But if the write-up is defended on the grounds that rising replacement costs justify it, or that the value of assets held in combination by a "going concern" is greater than the sum of the values of the separate items of property regarded individually, a dividend based upon it would surely be subject to criticism. Such criticism would be in line with the generally accepted accounting doctrine that gains should be recognized only when realized through actual transactions.

Dividends from Write-downs of Stock Values. Under both the surplus and impairment rules, it appears that dividends paid on the basis of surplus created through write-downs in the par or stated value of outstanding stock could be legal or illegal, depending upon circumstances. Existing creditors could certainly claim that an impairment results from such a dividend even if not from the write-down itself, and, under the surplus rule, they could claim the surplus to be fictitious. People who became creditors after the write-down, however, would have no standing to make similar claims; this would be so even if they became creditors before the payment of the dividend. The formal action of the corporation in amending its articles to provide for the write-down would be notice to them that its "capital" had been reduced.

When corporations write down the par or stated values of their stock to eliminate deficits and then pay dividends chargeable against subsequent earnings, there ordinarily need be no misgivings as to legality. Under the impairment rule, impairments that result from operating losses give rise to no liability on the part of directors or stockholders; these are not deliberate impairments. But dividends may not be paid so long as the impairment stands; hence, subsequent earnings must be used, so to say, first to correct the impairment, and then, if there is an excess, dividends may be paid. If, however, a corporation, through a write-down in par or stated value, shows to all the world that its capital has been reduced as a result of losses, it clears the way for the payment of legal dividends chargeable against any subsequent earnings. Under the surplus rule, likewise, a corporation may not pay a dividend unless there is a sufficient net credit balance in one or more surplus accounts; hence a net debit balance—a deficit—must be more than cleared up by subsequent earnings before dividend-paying capacity is revived. But if the corporation eliminates the debit balance by a write-down in par or stated value—by an acknowledgment, once again, that its capital has been impaired by losses —any subsequent earnings immediately form a credit balance against which it would appear dividends could legally be charged.

Prescriptions of State Laws. Some states have specific prescriptions in their laws with respect to the payment of dividends from sources other than earnings. Maine and Indiana, for example, authorize dividends chargeable against paid-in surplus and surplus created by reductions in the par or stated value of outstanding stock. But most of the prescriptions are restrictive. Illinois provides that paid-in surplus and surplus originating from donations of stock may be used only for dividends on preferred stock; moreover, it prescribes that the preferred stockholders must be told of the sources when these sources are used. Illinois also stipulates that surplus created through write-ups in asset values may be used only for stock dividends. Other states, including California, Pennsylvania, Michigan, and Ohio, have comparable restrictions. Several states, in addition to Illinois, require notification to the stockholders when dividends are paid from sources other than earnings. Notification of this sort is always strongly advisable, whether or not required by state law. Lawsuits for damages have been brought by stockholders against directors on the grounds that the latters' "misrepresentations" of earnings led them to pay excessive prices for stock—"misrepresentations" in that dividends from sources other than earnings were not so described by the directors.

Dividends Chargeable against Current Profits

A few of the states permit the payment of dividends "out of net profits or surplus"—a stipulation understood to mean that dividends may be paid on the basis of current profits even though they are insufficient to eliminate deficits standing in the surplus accounts. Delaware, for example, provides that dividends may be paid out of profits of the current and the preceding year even though capital has been impaired through earlier losses; however, such dividends must not reduce the value of net assets (that is, assets less outside liabilities) below the total preference to assets of outstanding preferred stock. Thus, a Delaware corporation could pay dividends chargeable against the profits of the current and preceding years though losses had reduced the book value of common stock to a negligible amount. Comparable provisions are found in the laws of California, Minnesota, and New Jersey.

Liquidating Dividends

The legal rules as to dividend payments already discussed have to do with distributions in the "ordinary course of business." But, in addition, corporations may make distributions of cash or other assets to their stockholders chargeable against the capital stock accounts themselves when these assets are no longer needed for corporate purposes. Such distributions may be made in partial or complete liquidation.

A complete liquidation generally requires a formal process of dissolution the steps of which are prescribed in detail in the state laws. The directors adopt a resolution which must be approved by the holders of such share majorities as the laws stipulate. Usually, an approving vote of a simple majority of the shares suffices if the dissolving corporation is insolvent, while larger majorities are required if it is solvent. Upon approval, formal articles of dissolution are prepared and submitted to the secretary of state. Thereupon the assets are distributed as the law prescribes—always with safeguards to insure that the creditors are paid in full before any distribution is made to the stockholders. After the creditors have been satisfied, "dividends" may be distributed from time to time to the stockholders as portions of the assets are successively turned into cash.

Sometimes, however, corporations curtail their activities without intending to go out of business. Such curtailments will ordinarily result in excesses of assets, yet the corporations may have no balances in surplus accounts against which ordinary dividends could be charged. Accordingly, dividends in partial liquidation chargeable against the stock accounts themselves are permitted, always with the proviso that distributions to the stockholders do not endanger the claims of creditors. Strictly speaking, the retirement of preferred stock is a kind of partial liquidation, although, as we have seen, it may not presage any significant curtailment of operations. But cash paid to preferred stockholders for their holdings is rarely described as a liquidating dividend.

Actions taken recently by two corporations may be cited as illustrative of liquidating distributions. In July, 1962, the Pioneer Steamship Company, after selling four of its seven vessels, distributed a liquidating dividend of $60 a share to its common stockholders; and in April, 1963, after virtually completing the disposal of its remaining assets, it announced a further distribution of $20.28 a share. The latter announcement stipulated that the dividend would be paid upon the "permanent surrender" of the stock certificates by the stockholders. In July, 1963, the directors of the Murray Corporation of America approved a proposal to distribute to its common stockholders a dividend of $14 a share from "excess" cash accumulated through the disposal of some of its assets (chiefly its Triplex Screw division sold in May, 1962, and its Easy Appliance division sold in January, 1963). However, the distribution of the dividend was deferred pending a ruling of the Internal Revenue Service whether it would be taxed as ordinary dividend income to the stockholders or on a capital-gains-and-losses basis.

Restrictions upon Dividends in Contracts

Provisions of contracts, as well as state laws, often restrict corporate dividend-paying capacities. Contractual stipulations have a legal complexion, of course, in that courts can be called upon to enforce the terms of valid contracts and to assess damages for their violation.

In Chapter 22, we saw that restrictions upon the payment of dividends on common stock are a popular kind of "protective provision" as found in preferred stock contracts. Similar restrictions are customarily placed in bond contracts or indentures; sometimes, indeed, such contracts require that portions of earnings be specifically "set aside" and labeled as not being available for dividends, as in sinking fund reserves. Restrictions upon dividend payments are often prescribed also in contracts covering "term loans" granted by banks and other financial institutions, that is, loans having original maturities of more than one year. Lenders want to be sure that cash needed for working capital and eventually for the repayment of the loans is not too generously drained by dividend payments.

Questions

1. As a source of corporate assets in the postwar years, how have retained earnings compared with stock sales, bond sales, and the expansion of short-term debt?

2. Are not retained earnings, regardless of their amount, only a temporary source of corporate assets? Explain.

3. Defend or attack this proposition: The "net earnings" reported by business corporations are only estimates.

4. For the typical corporation, why is the amount of net earnings it re-

ports for a year unlikely to have any close relationship to its cash holdings at a given time, as at the end of the year?

5. What effects do depreciation charges have upon corporations' net earnings? upon their cash balances?

6. Is there any close relationship between a corporation's net earnings and its capacity to distribute dividends? to distribute *cash* dividends? Explain.

7. Under what circumstances might corporations be justified in borrowing in order to distribute cash dividends to their stockholders?

8. What is a dividend? Distinguish between a dividend on stock and a stock dividend. What is a liquidating dividend?

9. After declaring a dividend, can a board of directors legally revoke the declaration? Explain.

10. Distinguish among the surplus, impairment, and insolvency rules pertaining to the legality of dividend payments. Show that the three rules mean much the same thing.

11. With respect to alleged illegal dividends, what actions can creditors take for their own protection? What is the liability of directors who distribute illegal dividends and of the stockholders who receive them?

12. Looking at the matter broadly, to what extent, if at all, may cash dividends chargeable against each of the following sources be legally paid: (*a*) premiums received on stock sales, (*b*) portions of the proceeds of no-par stock credited to paid-in surplus accounts, (*c*) profits on the sale of treasury stock, (*d*) profits on the sale of nonoperating assets, (*e*) current profits that are insufficient to eliminate earlier deficits, (*f*) write-ups in asset values, and (*g*) write-downs in the par or stated value of outstanding stock?

13. Is it ever permissible in any state for a corporation to distribute cash dividends even though it has a net deficit in its surplus accounts? Explain.

Problem

The chairman of the board of directors of Allison & Steele, Inc., asks your opinion whether surplus derived from the following sources (after the deduction of income taxes, where applicable) could *safely* be the basis of cash dividends—safely in the sense of avoiding possible liability of the directors to creditors for illegal dividends:

a) Profit on reacquisition of treasury stock—$50,000. The corporation bought 10,000 shares of its common stock in the market at 15. In the original financing of the corporation, the common stock had been sold at its par value of $20 a share.

b) Profit on retirement of bonds—$1,000. During the year the corporation bought up in the market $20,000 face amount of its bonds at an average price of 95. The bonds were originally sold at par and were made callable for redemption at 103.

c) Profit from appreciation of land value—$60,000. On the basis of the selling prices of several parcels of land in the vicinity of the corporation's office building, the directors decided that the building site, carried on the books at original cost, was undervalued by $60,000. They therefore ordered a write-up of this amount.

d) Profit from sale of nonoperating assets—$40,000. A warehouse not used in the corporation's operations but previously rented to another firm was sold for $160,000. The warehouse had been carried on the corporation's books at the depreciated value of $120,000, although it had originally cost $250,000.

chapter 25

EARNINGS RETENTION AND DIVIDEND POLICIES

CRITERIA FOR POLICY

In decision making by boards of directors as to the retention of earnings and their use as the basis of dividend distributions, three important factors are involved: (1) liquidity needs, (2) cash requirements for growth, and (3) the position of the stockholders. Let us consider these in the order indicated.

Liquidity Needs

A fundamental proposition that few will dispute is that a corporation must not endanger its solvency through the distribution of cash dividends to its stockholders, whether preferred or common. Regardless of the size of its surplus accounts and the amount of its current earnings as reported in the income statement, if holdings of cash and short-term high-quality securities have been seriously depleted through the expansion of inventories and receivables, the purchase of fixed assets, the payment of debt, or for any other reason, the corporation's directors would obviously be unwise to drain these holdings further by paying cash dividends.

It is true that, in some cases, directors may decide that depletions of cash and other liquid resources are only temporary—that normal inflows will soon restore the liquid resources to a safe position for dividend payment; hence, they may see justification for short-term borrowing as a means of financing immediate dividend distribution. Even here, however, there is danger, for expectations of normal inflows may not be fulfilled. General business conditions, or conditions in the industrial areas in which a corporation's customers operate, may deteriorate rather abruptly, with the result that inventories become slow moving and some of the receivables difficult to collect.

In part, at least, liquidity needs explain why many corporations discontinue the payment of cash dividends in periods of business recessions and depressions, particularly prolonged ones. Although balances in surplus accounts may be substantial, they may largely represent investments in fixed assets, inventories, and receivables or reduced volumes of outside liabilities; if so, they are not matched by holdings of liquid assets. Holdings of cash and other liquid resources may not be unduly weak, but managers may decide to preserve them against possible drains through operating losses or to meet liabilities coming to maturity, and even to add to them the cash throw-off from current earnings, if there are any, and from depreciation charges, if these are being covered in whole or in part by current sales.

Cash Requirements for Growth

Multiplicity of Growth Opportunities. It is probably safe to say that a vast majority of corporate managers more or less constantly see important prospects for profit enhancement through expansions of facilities and scopes of operations. How sales can be expanded by larger expenditures for advertising, the hiring of more salesmen, the invasion of broader territories, the setting up of branch warehouses and display rooms, the opening of retail outlets; how they can be stabilized by adding new product lines; how costs can be cut by the acquisition of more suitable quarters, changes in location, the installation of laborsaving devices, large-scale purchasing of materials and supplies, the hiring of more specialized technical personnel; how many of these things can be done at a stroke, as it were, through the absorption of other enterprises in mergers or consolidations or as subsidiaries; how many can be done eventually if not immediately through greater expenditures for research—these are the visions of business managers. The list tends to be endless. The adoption of given programs suggests other steps that ought to be taken to get the full benefits; and the successful completion of given projects often opens new avenues for development not previously thought of.

A constant procession of what appear to be favorable opportunities to expand sales and cut costs must strongly tempt corporate managements to be very generous in their earnings retention policies or, looking at the matter from the other side, to be quite illiberal in the distribution of cash dividends. Money is needed to take advantage of the opportunities, money is provided by earnings, and decisions to use this money for expansion, rather than to look elsewhere for financing, may appear to be thoroughly sound. Cash obtainable elsewhere is costly, in the sense both of flotation expenses and periodic outlays in the form of interest and dividends, whereas that provided by earnings retention, already in hand, may seem to be costless. To distribute generous amounts of cash as dividends and then to try to get an equal amount back by the sale of new securities may seem to some corporate managers to be not only a costly procedure but a needless one. If all the earnings can be profitably used to finance expansion projects, why not devote them to this purpose and forgo dividends as long as may be necessary?

Growth in Relation to Stockholder Interests. It immediately becomes apparent, however, that an affirmative answer to this question would mean, for many corporations, no prospects for dividends indefinitely. If new opportunities for expanding sales and cutting costs constantly open up, there must be no limit to the amount of earnings that could be profitably retained and reinvested. Then comes the question: Why does a corporation expand its facilities in order to increase its earning power? And the answer seems to be that it does this for the benefit of its stockholders. But benefits for stockholders are subject to various kinds of evaluations, and corporate managers surely have some responsibility to avoid narrow evaluations entirely their own. It is surely their duty to distinguish their personal interests in expansion—possibly their desire for increased power and prestige and for higher levels of compensation—from those of the stockholders.

The principal benefit of stockownership that millions of stockholders look to is periodic cash income in the form of dividends. They may justly feel that, when earnings are good, to be denied cash dividends or to be allowed only niggardly ones is a policy contrary to their best interests. They may be compelled to cut their expenditures for consumption if they do not get the cash dividends their corporations are apparently able to pay, considering the level of their earnings—and this is a sacrifice they may not wish to make. Or they may feel that they should have the right to choose how income earned on their stock investments should be reinvested, rather than to have boards of directors make this decision for them.

As we shall see in the subsequent discussion of the position of stockholders, directors' policies of no dividends or niggardly ones are sometimes thoroughly in accord with the wishes of stockholders; but, much more frequently, such a policy is quite out of line with stockholders' evaluations of their own interests. At any rate, it is surely clear that the power of directors to determine policies as to earnings retention and distribution is by no means easy to exercise justly; it is, indeed, most difficult to weigh with maximum justice to the stockholders themselves their short-run interests, to be served by cash dividends, as against their long-run interests, to be promoted by earnings retention. That the boards of directors of many of our leading corporations—generally recognized, of course, to be people of high competence—are inclined to give at least as much attention to stockholders' short-term interests as to their long-term ones is indicated by the maintenance of regular cash dividend payments over the years, regardless of the pressures of expansion requirements; their overall distributions of 50 or 60 per cent or more of the earnings despite the same pressures; and their extreme reluctance to suspend cash dividend payments in periods of general business contraction when, they have reason to believe, the stockholders will have all the more need of cash income.

Liberality of Dividends and Future Financing. Aside from the question of justice to the short-run interests of stockholders, corporate managements generally realize that policies of relatively liberal cash dividends —where, of course, earnings justify them—are likely to be a fine advertisement for further financing ventures. The common stocks of corporations that pay relatively generous dividends usually sell at substantially higher prices than those of corporations whose earnings are comparable but whose dividend policies are illiberal. Thus, a corporation that has a liberal policy, if it is able to get premium prices for additional shares it sells, recoups in effect some of the dividends it has paid; in other words, it would need to sell fewer shares to bring in a given sum of money than would a comparable corporation whose dividend policy had been illiberal. Likewise, investors in preferred stocks are easily attracted to a corporation that has a long record of dividend payments upon its common stock; if the corporation has been able to pay dividends on the common year after year, a reasonable expectation would be that it should have no difficulty in paying dividends on a stock having a prior claim to earnings. Even buyers of bonds and other classes of lenders are inclined to look with great favor upon corporations with good dividend-paying records. The draining of cash periodically for dividends might appear to be an unfavorable factor, but a regular payment of dividends indicates a continued availability of cash—cash that could be diverted to the payment of debt interest and principal, should the need arise. On the other hand, a policy of not paying dividends tends to give rise to fears of the unavailability of cash for debt service—fears that too much of it will be tied up in buildings, machinery, and other illiquid assets.

Position of the Stockholders

The problem of what to do with earnings is eased for the boards of directors of many corporations because they are the sole stockholders; what they decide as directors is necessarily in full accord with their interests as stockholders. The problem is more difficult when stockholders are widely scattered and the directors' holdings amount to only a minor fraction of total shares outstanding. The problem tends to be most difficult when directors own controlling interests but the remainder of the stock is widely scattered.

Corporations Closely Held by Wealthy Stockholders. A few wealthy persons who are the sole stockholders in a highly profitable corporation, whatever its size, would be likely to regard with considerable loathing the prospect of receiving sizable cash dividends. Already perched in the higher brackets of the federal personal income tax on account of income derived from other sources, and having the means of meeting their consumption expenditures amply assured, they could hardly want further amounts of income that would be taxable at the regular rates. For them, therefore, a policy of a generous or complete retention of the earnings of the corporation would be uniquely attractive. They would expect expansion, financed with retained earnings, to result in increases in the value of their stock. If, therefore, they wanted later to realize the rewards of their corporation's profitability, they could do so by selling some or all the stock, having the increment in value taxed as a capital gain at the relatively moderate rate of 25 per cent. In fact, they might contemplate holding on to the stock with its increment till the time of their deaths, so that their shares in corporate profits would never be taxed *as income* to them or to their heirs.

For such a corporation, then, the major problem as to the disposal of earnings is likely to be, not deciding what proportion should be distributed as dividends, but finding opportunities for the investment of retained earnings reasonably related to corporate purposes in order that the special federal surtax on unreasonable accumulations of surplus can be avoided.[1]

Corporations Closely Held by Others. Tens of thousands of corporations are closely held by individuals whose livelihood depends largely or exclusively upon what income they can draw from these corporations. After withdrawals to take care of the stockholders' consumption needs have been allowed for, the problem of what to do with the remaining earnings is usually a slight one; the remainder, if it amounts to anything at all, is negligible. Indeed, corporations of this description are not likely to report much in the way of profits. If the stockholders hold positions as officers, as is probable, money needed for their livelihood will be withdrawn as salaries to the extent likely to be deemed "reasonable" by the Internal Revenue Service. In this way, corporate income taxes are avoided. But the point is that, whether withdrawals are salaries or dividends, not much is left after living expenses have been provided for.

Corporations with Wide Distributions of Stock. In a corporation whose stock is so widely distributed that no holder or closely knit group of holders has a controlling interest, the board of directors tends to be self-perpetuating. Although the directors themselves may own but little stock, they control the voting machinery, and they can ordinarily be confident that the stockholders will not band together to oust them unless a large number become convinced that their interests are being gravely neglected.

In corporate situations of this kind, the personal interests of the directors often conflict, in part at least, with those of the stockholders. Expansion promises greater prestige and power, and, for the directors who are also officers, a means of justifying larger salaries and bonus and stock-option arrangements. Accordingly, a policy of liberal retention of earnings to finance expansion is likely to be quite attractive.

But the directors do not want to lose their jobs, and they have reason to fear that a niggardly dividend policy is the very kind of thing that will convince many stockholders of the grave neglect of their interests. Thus, a subordination of the personal interests of the directors to those of the stockholders may seem to make good sense. Moreover, the di-

---

[1] See above, p. 38.

rectors have responsibility to serve the interests of the stockholders rather than their own, and justice in caring for stockholder interests would seem to require a relatively liberal cash dividend policy. A wide scattering of stockholdings means numerous small owners whose short-run interests in dividends are likely to outrank by far their long-run interests in appreciation.

Beyond this, a relatively liberal dividend policy appears to be in order —always assuming a good level of earnings—if the directors anticipate that expansion requirements will demand funds in excess of earnings, even if all should be retained. The consequence of a liberal policy, as was explained previously, should be relative ease in floating new security issues, whether common stock, preferred stock, or bonds. Even should the directors anticipate that total expansion could be financed by the retention of all earnings for a limited period of, say, five or six years, they would have to give due weight to the possibilities that actual requirements would prove to be much greater than anticipated. After the limited period of earnings retention, therefore, they might have to go to the market under relatively unfavorable circumstances, and especially so if they wanted to sell additional common stock.

Corporations with Mixed Stockholder Situations. Probably the most difficult problem of what to do with earnings is faced by the directors of corporations that are controlled by small groups of wealthy stockholders but that have the remainder of their stock widely distributed in the hands of small investors. The wide distribution of the noncontrolling stock would indicate a past policy of rather generous dividend distributions; otherwise, the small investors would not have bought. But a board of directors can change from a generous dividend policy even though it has been in effect for many years. Would it be justified in doing so?

Hardly can it be denied that, in a situation of this kind, a serious conflict exists between the interests of the controlling stockholders and those of the small stockholders. The conflict cannot be shrugged off, nor can it be easily resolved by appeals to justice. The controlling stockholders can claim the justice of their wish to avoid high tax rates on dividends they do not need; and the small stockholders can demand justice in the treatment of their need of current income. Probably about as much as can be said is that a "golden mean" should be sought. It would be easy to condemn a policy of nonpayment or one of very low payment as being utterly selfish on the part of the controlling interest; but, on the other hand, dissatisfaction with distributions falling short of very large proportions of earnings would reflect an extremely selfish stand of the small stockholders. Perhaps the "golden mean" would be distributions materially less generous than those of corporations whose stock is all widely held.

Here, again, prospective needs of further security flotations could be an important consideration in dividend policy determination. Should financing beyond the amount of retained earnings be anticipated—allowing for the possibility of retaining all earnings—and should the controlling interests not want to provide the additional funds expected to be needed, a more generous dividend policy would appear to be advisable. The corporation would want to have a receptive public for its new security offerings, and it could work toward this goal in no better way than to cultivate its existing "public"—its small stockholders.

Conclusions

In deciding whether to retain earnings or distribute dividends, boards of directors must study simultaneously, as it were, the three factors we have been examining individually. Their decisions are not always sound. Not infrequently the decisions are selfish in the sense of unreasonably favoring the directors' own interests or those of controlling groups of stockholders. But this does not mean that illiberal dividend policies are necessarily selfish ones. Quite different policies can be both wise and unselfish for different corporations even though, at first glance at least, their dividend-paying capacities appear to be much the same.

Thus, one corporation that has earnings at a given level may be quite generous in paying cash dividends because it is in a declining industry and earnings retention to finance growth is out of the question, while another with the same level of earnings may distribute quite modest cash dividends because it is in a rapidly growing industry and because its access to the market for funds, for reasons of its immaturity, is not strong. In a period of depression, one corporation, despite current losses, may dip into its surplus to pay dividends because its cash position is strong, and another, though it has a large surplus, may quickly suspend dividend payments because its cash holdings are scanty. One corporation may diligently search for new avenues along which to expand so that earnings can be withheld from its stockholders, all of whom are wealthy, while another may cancel certain expansion projects because its directors feel that the thousands of its small stockholders need dividends as current income.

REGULARITY OF CASH DIVIDENDS

It is one thing for the board of directors of a corporation to decide upon the distribution of cash dividends equal to 40, 50, or 60 per cent or some other percentage of earnings as a continuing policy; it is another for them to decide upon the timing of the distributions. If it is decided that the distribution pattern shall closely match that of current earnings, a high degree of irregularity in dividend payments can result. This would be necessarily so in corporations with highly unstable earnings—the "prince and pauper industries," including most of the so-called "heavy-goods industries"; but it would be at least moderately so additionally in many industries whose earnings are usually said to be stable, such as producers of processed foods, tobacco, and electric power. Even industries such as these often have substantial cyclical fluctuations in earnings.

But it may be decided that the rate of dividends shall be uniform or "regular" from year to year, regardless of the irregularity of the earnings pattern. In good years, an extraordinary amount of earnings can be retained to serve as the basis for dividends at an unchanged rate in poor years. Suppose, for illustration, that a certain corporation with 100,000 shares of common stock outstanding has earnings after taxes in an eight-year period as indicated in Table 25–1. It is the directors' policy to distribute dividends equal to 60 per cent of earnings. If the distribution were matched annually to current earnings, the rate of dividends per share ("earnings pattern policy") would be as shown in the third data column of the table. But if, at the beginning of the period, the directors were to anticipate earnings of the amounts shown, and were to decide upon a uniform rate of dividends throughout the eight-year period, the result would be as shown in the last two columns ("regular policy").

TABLE 25–1
Illustration of Dividend Payment Patterns

Year	Earnings after Taxes	Earnings Allocated to Dividends	Earnings Pattern Policy—Dividends per Share	Regular Policy	
				Earnings Retained for Future Dividends (Cumulative)	Dividends per Share
1.........	$1,500,000	$ 900,000	$ 9.00	$ 600,000	$ 3.00
2.........	1,200,000	720,000	7.20	1,020,000	3.00
3.........	600,000	360,000	3.60	1,080,000	3.00
4.........	200,000	120,000	1.20	900,000	3.00
5.........	−300,000	0	0	600,000	3.00
6.........	−150,000	0	0	300,000	3.00
7.........	250,000[a]	0[a]	0	0	3.00
8.........	700,000[b]	300,000[b]	3.00	0	3.00
Total..	$4,000,000	$2,400,000	$24.00		$24.00
Annual average..	$ 500,000	$ 300,000	$ 3.00		$ 3.00

[a] No allocation to dividends because of application of earnings against deficits of years 5 and 6.
[b] Remaining deficits of years 5 and 6 of $200,000 reduce allocable earnings of year 8 to $500,000, of which 60 per cent, as allocated to dividends, is $300,000.

In the March, 1963, issue of *Investment Facts* published by the New York Stock Exchange, it was reported that 447 of its listed common stocks had paid quarterly cash dividends uninterruptedly for periods ranging from 20 to 99 years. Seventy-two had paid quarterly cash dividends for 50 to 99 years, 88 for 35 to 50 years, 150 for 25 to 35 years, and 137 for 20 to 25 years. With the longest dividend-paying records were the American News Company, beginning in 1864; Pullman Incorporated, 1867; American Telephone and Telegraph Company, 1882; Washington Gas Light Company, 1885; New England Telephone and

Telegraph Company, 1886; Commonwealth Edison Company, 1890; Singer Manufacturing Company, 1890; Boston Edison Company, 1892; and the Consolidated Edison Company, 1892.

Advantages of Regularity

For the welfare of business corporations themselves, a policy of regularity in the payment of cash dividends to common stockholders tends to be highly beneficial. Stockholder loyalty is developed. Investors who are interested in income buy the stock and hold it for long periods, while speculators who are interested in short-run trading profits are not so likely to be attracted. Investors appreciate not only the steady income but also the relatively stable market prices that dividend regularity promotes; they have less reason to fear extraordinary sacrifices should they find it necessary to sell in periods of low or negative corporate earnings. But the very tendencies toward stability in market price tend to preclude extraordinary short-run gains for speculators. In terms of the illustration, the market price of the stock would tend to fluctuate over a broad range, as do the earnings and dividends, were the "earnings pattern policy" to be in effect; but with the "regular policy" in effect, the depressive force of the deteriorating earnings situation through the fifth year would tend to be strongly counteracted by the uninterrupted payment of dividends at the established rate. Indeed, chances would be good that stockholder loyalty would be much greater with a regular dividend rate of, say, $2.50 a share than with earnings pattern dividends averaging out, as in the illustration, at $3.00.

Stockholder loyalty means wide interest among the stockholders in buying such additional issues of common stock and of securities convertible into it as a corporation may decide to issue. Offerings by the rights procedure are likely to go extremely well. Loyal stockholders are likely to carry their message of satisfaction to other investors, urging or encouraging them to buy. Moreover, loyal stockholders are surely inclined to buy the corporation's products, and to urge others to buy, if within the range of their usual kinds of purchases.

A policy of regular cash dividends on common stock, especially if long maintained, attracts investors other than the present holders of a corporation's securities. Much publicity is given by brokers and dealers and by the stock exchanges to long unbroken records of dividend payments; the brokers and dealers always seem to regard such a record as the strongest kind of selling point in negotiations with their customers. The corporations with the long dividend payment records find themselves in the "100-year club" or the "50-year club" or the "20-year club" or whatever other "clubs" they may fit into. All this means immeasurable advantage in investor interest not only in selling additional common stock but also in selling preferred stock and bonds. Wise investors pride themselves on making investment decisions based on future prospects, rather than on the basis of what has happened in the past, but they can hardly fail to be influenced by distinguished records of regular dividend payments upon common stock. The very fact that a corporation has been able to pay regular dividends on its common stock for a considerable period of years is the basis of a strong presumption that it ought to have little difficulty in paying dividends on new preferred, and even less in meeting debt service on bonds. Even state government authorities who have regulatory jurisdiction over certain kinds of financial institutions seem to entertain such a presumption. In the "legal lists" which, in some states, prescribe the kinds and qualities of securities that may be bought for investment by trustees, mutual savings banks, and life insurance companies, a not unusual qualification for *bond* purchases, for example, is that the issuing corporation must have paid dividends *on its common stock* in each of the preceding five years. Having a corporation's securities satisfy the standards of the "legal lists" is important in gaining access to the great investment resources of the kinds of institutional investors named.

Disadvantage of Regularity

A disadvantage of a policy of regular cash dividends on common stock is the danger that it will be overdone. The rate of dividends selected may be too high. Though earnings for a considerable period of years may be carefully estimated, such a forecast, for the very reason that it is long-range, may prove to be much too optimistic. If, therefore, the board of directors originally fixes the dividend rate in the expectation of devoting, say, 60 per cent of average earnings to dividends, it may find with the passing years that the continuance of this rate requires the paying out of 70 or 80 per cent or a still higher percentage of average earnings. The high payout percentage may not embarrass the corporation for lack of cash, but earnings as a means of financing expansion become much less important than had been anticipated. Because the original anticipations of the directors come thus to be frustrated, the temptation must be strong to cut the regular dividend rate. But this would not be a happy solution—it would surely be a blow to the stockholders' loyalty as their income was reduced and the market price of their stock fell, and it would give rise to uncertainties about future policy, thus weakening the market for new securities of whatever kind the corporation might want to offer.

A greater danger than the selection of too high a rate for regular dividends is that a policy of regular dividends will be continued long after it should have been abandoned. Reluctance to depart from the "100-year club" or the "50-year club" may lead directors to continue cash dividends that definitely threaten solvency. Changing conditions in an industry may have brought earnings to a low level with little prospect of their substantial revival, yet the decision is that the dividend record must be maintained. Or, in a period of depression, though the surplus account of a corporation may be large, its cash balance may be small, yet comes the decision that cash must be further drained to maintain the record. Provisions of "legal lists" as to dividend payments, as illustrated previously, add to reluctance to break established records. If a bond is "legal" for investment by certain classes of institutional investors only if the corporation that issued it has paid cash dividends in each year for, say, five years, nonpayment in any year means that the bond is off the "legal list" for at least the ensuing five years.

FIGURE 25–1

Report of Dividends Declared from the *New York Times*

Dividends Announced

	STOCK		
Company.	Rate.	Pe-riod.	Pay-able.	of Record
Pall Corp (x)			
Star Market Co. ......2 pct	..	11- 1	10-15
(x) Thre-for-two stock split subject to approval.			
Increased			
Byers (AM) Co..... 7½c pct	Q	11- 1	10-10
Smith-Douglass 35c	Q	11-20	10-23
Extra			
Byers (AM) Co. 20c	..	11-	10-10
Reduced			
Pioneer Finance 5c	..	10-15	10- 4
Regular			
Air Products & Chem.... 5c	Q	10-21	10- 7
Behlen Mfg. 20c	Q	11- 1	10-15
De Vilbiss Co 40c	Q	10-21	10-10
Energy Fund $1.03	..	10-25	9-26
Gamble-Skogmo 30c	Q	10-31	10-17
Genl Mills 30c	Q	11- 1	10-10
Inter-Cty Title Guar&Mtge 30c	V	11- 8	10-18
Jane Colby 10c	Q	11- 1	10-10
Jefferson Construction .. 5c	Q	11-15	10-21
Jergens (Andrew) Co....20c	Q	10-31	10-15
Jergens (Andrew) Co ...20c	Q	1-31	1-10
Lucky Stores 20c	Q	11-15	10-25
Macoid Industries 5c	Q	10-30	10-14
Medical Sec Fund.......3c	..	10-28	10-14
Prtr(HK)Co 5½pct pf $1.37½	Q	10-31	10-11
Prtr(HK)CO 4¼pct pf $1.06¼	Q	10-31	10-11
Ramada Inns 20c	Q	12-31	12-20
Red Owl Stores 22½c	Q	11- 1	10-18
Schultz Sav-O Stores.....5c	Q	11- 1	10-21
Seligman & Latz.........20c	Q	10-30	10-11
Seligman & Latz B....6 2/3c	Q	10-30	10-11
Seligman & Latz pf.......$1	Q	10-30	10-11
Standard Products........15c	Q	10-22	10-10
Star Market 15c	Q	12-15	12- 1
Union Oil Calif..........50c	Q	11- 0	10-10
Winfield Growth Ind Fd..3c	..	10-31	10-16
(a)—Subject to approval.			
A—Annually. B—Bi-monthly. M—Monthly. S—Semi-annually. Q—Quarterly. V—Same amount paid on previous quarter.			

DIVIDEND MEETINGS TODAY

Atlas Brass Foundry	Natl Marine Terml pfd
Augusta Newspapers	Pan Amer Wrld Airwy
Automobile Banking	Real Est Invst Tr Am
Century Accept	Westgate-California

Extra and Special Dividends

The danger that too high a rate for regular dividends will be set is reduced by the boards of directors of many corporations by the choice of quite conservative rates when they first adopt a policy of regularity. If forecasts indicate that the distribution of a given percentage of earnings over a period of years would make possible a regular dividend rate on par or stated value of 6 per cent, perhaps a start will be made with a rate of 4 per cent. Should earnings fall short of expectations by as much as one third—a rather wide margin of error, obviously—the regular dividends could be continued at 4 per cent without difficulty; but should they be as high as, or higher than, forecast, additional distributions could be made from time to time as "extra dividends." (In this regard, see Figure 25–1.)

Although the payment of "extra dividends" introduces an element of irregularity in a program of regular payments, it is a highly popular device for experimentation, so to say, in dividend-paying capacity. In declaring an extra dividend, a board of directors informs its stockholders in effect that there is present justification for paying a dividend in excess of the regular one, but that there is no assurance that the higher level of payment can be or will be continued. If, then, earnings available for dividends continue to run well above the regular requirement, and if, accordingly, extra dividends have been distributed over a series of years, the directors may think it safe to step up the regular rate. They would then discontinue extra dividends until such time that excess earnings again suggested a need of experimenting toward a still higher regular rate. If, on the other hand, earnings continued only sporadically to be enough for extra dividends, a policy of sporadic extra dividends, without thought of raising the regular rate, could be continued indefinitely. And if but small amounts of excess earnings should become available after one or two extra dividends had been paid, the nonpayment of further extras would require no apology, no basis having been given to the stockholders to expect their continuance.

Because, however, stockholders may have some temptation to look upon extra dividends as paving the way for higher regular rates, corporate directors sometimes label as "special dividends," rather than as extras, distributions that are not likely to be repeated. Such a distinction in terminology appears to be particularly desirable when the distribution is based upon profits not derived in the ordinary course of operations. For example, a profit gained upon a sale of stock held by a corporation in a subsidiary might serve as the basis of a "special" dividend as distinguished from an "extra" one.

STOCK DIVIDENDS

Stock dividends are a strange breed. They are second in popularity to cash dividends from the standpoint of both the frequency of their distribution by corporations and the satisfaction with which they are received by stockholders; yet they appear to give the stockholder nothing. For illustration, assume that a certain corporation has outstanding 100,000 shares of common stock of $50 par value, that it has no preferred stock, and that it has an accumulated earned surplus balance of $3 million. A stockholder who owns 10,000 shares has one tenth of the total voting power, one tenth of the total claims to earnings, and one tenth of total ownership claims to assets as measured by the total book value of his holdings of $800,000. Now assume that the corporation distributes a stock dividend of 20 per cent or 20,000 shares, and that the stockholder referred to gets 2,000 of these shares. A transfer of $1 million is made from the earned surplus account to the common stock account. The stockholder now has 12,000 shares of a total of 120,000, and, accordingly, he still has one tenth of the total voting power and one tenth of total ownership claims to earnings and assets. Moreover, his claim to assets remains at $800,000 (12,000 shares at $50 par value plus a one tenth interest in the remaining surplus of $2 million).

What, then, is accomplished by a transaction of this kind? The answer depends upon its objectives. The objectives are chiefly of two types of quite distinct character: (1) to reduce the market value of the stock or the earnings and dividends per share, and (2) to substitute for or supplement cash dividends. These two types of objectives deserve separate examination. In relation to this examination, the data of stock and cash dividends distributed on the common stocks of thirteen corporations in the period 1958–62 as presented in Table 25–2 should prove helpful, and the following discussion should enable one to recognize which of the two types of objectives, if either, the thirteen corporations were pursuing in their declarations of stock dividends. The expressing "if either" in the foregoing sentence indicates the possibility of a third type of objective. For example, the objective of the Northern Pacific Railway Company in distributing its stock dividend of 20 per cent in 1958 was widely judged to be to bring the total of its outstanding shares closer to the share level of the Great Northern Railway Company with which a merger was being discussed.

Adjustments in Market Value or Per-Share Earnings and Dividends

Comparison with Split-ups. Because objectives of the first type closely parallel those of stock split-ups which were extensively discussed in Chapter 20, they require only brief treatment. With respect to adjustments in market value, one will recall that action to get the market price of a stock down from a very high level to a level more attractive to most classes of investors is undertaken to promote wide distribution, to prepare for new offerings of additional stock for cash, to prepare for offerings of stock to the stockholders of other corporations in connection with proposed mergers, consolidations, and holding company acquisitions, and to aid large stockholders to dispose of some or all of their holdings. If the market price of a stock is $150, a stock dividend of 200 per cent should have about the same effect as a 3 for 1 split-up in bringing the price down to the vicinity of $50.

With respect to adjustments in per-share earnings and dividends, one will remember the fears of corporate managements that high ratios will invite competition, lead to unreasonable wage and salary demands by labor unions, result in unfair treatment by tax assessors, and engender customer dissatisfaction because of suspicions that the high ratios result from exorbitant selling prices. If a certain corporation's "earnings per share" have been $25 and its "dividends per share," $15, these can be reduced to $5.00 and $3.00 respectively (assuming no changes in the levels of earnings and dividends) by either the distribution of a stock dividend of 400 per cent or a split-up of 5 for 1. Needless to say, a given stock dividend may have for its objectives reductions in market value, per-share earnings, and per-share dividends, all three.

Infrequency of Stock Dividends for Adjustment. Stock dividends designed for the class of objectives discussed here are usually quite large—50 per cent, 100 per cent, 200 per cent, and so on. The very nature of the objective requires that they be quite large. Because of their size, however, the individual corporation rarely has occasion to repeat such a dividend in any short period of years. Once the market price of a stock

TABLE 25–2
Cash and Stock Dividend Records of Thirteen Common Stocks, 1958–62

Corporation	Par Value of Stock	Cash Dividends					Stock Dividends, Per Cent				
		1958	1959	1960	1961	1962	1958	1959	1960	1961	1962
Bethlehem Steel Corporation	$8.00	$2.40	$2.40	$2.40	$2.40	$2.17½					
Boston Edison Company	$10.00	2.80	2.85	3.00	3.00	2.23½ᵃ		2	2	3	3
Carnation Company	$5.50	1.50	1.50	1.50	1.70	1.85	2	6	6		
Colorado Fuel & Iron Company	$5.00	.50					2				
Douglas Aircraft Co., Inc.	No par	2.50	1.00				3	100			
Eastman Kodak Company	$10.00	2.85	2.01ᵇ	2.04	2.25	2.30					
Jantzen, Inc.	$1.00	.80	.80	.80	.80	.80	4	6⅔	5	4	3
Liberty Fabrics of New York, Inc.	$1.00							10	10	5	5
Marathon Oil Company	No par	1.60	1.60	1.60	1.60	1.60					
Northern Pacific Railway Company	$5.00	2.00	2.00	2.20	2.20	2.35				2	2
Peabody Coal Company	$5.00	.40	.40	.40	.46	.54	20				
Sun Oil Company	No par	1.00	1.00	1.00	1.00	1.00	3	5	6	6	5
White Motor Company	$1.00	3.00	2.31¼ᶜ	2.00	2.00	2.00	100	5			

ᵃ Before 2½ for 1 split-up, $1.57½; after, 66 cents.

ᵇ Before 100 per cent stock dividend, 90 cents; after, $1.11.

ᶜ Before 100 per cent stock dividend, 87½ cents; after, $1.43¾.

Source: Moody's Investors Service, Manuals.

or the per-share figures related to it have been substantially reduced, it ordinarily takes a considerable period of years before a further adjustment of the same kind becomes advisable. This period may be shortened, of course, for corporations with profit prospects that build up most extraordinarily year after year; but, on the other hand, it may stretch out indefinitely for corporations whose profit potentials decline after one or two such adjustments have been made.

The performance of two corporations may be cited as illustrating what has just been said. The United Engineering & Foundry Company distributed a stock dividend of 100 per cent in 1911, one of 50 per cent in 1923, and one of 200 per cent in 1952; and the Island Creek Coal Company, after distributing a 400 per cent stock dividend in 1927, has made no further stock-dividend distributions except one of 2½ per cent in 1955.

Relation to Cash Dividends. Large dividends to reduce market prices and per-share earnings and dividends are rarely distributed in lieu of cash dividends. The likely situation is that cash dividends have already been quite large—the very thing that has caused the market price of the stock to soar to a level out of the investment range of large numbers of investors. The surplus upon which the large stock dividend is based will have been accumulated in spite of the payment of handsome cash dividends. In the minds of the directors, it will already represent additional permanent investment by the stockholders; hence they would have no expectation of its use as a basis for cash dividends. By the same token, they would hardly object to the proposition that the stockholders should have additional shares, to be provided by the stock dividend, as evidence of this additional permanent investment.

When a corporation distributes a large stock dividend for adjustment purposes, it usually reduces the cash dividend rate, so that total cash dividends will be no greater than before, or not much greater. If, for example, it has been paying cash dividends at 15 per cent on a par-value stock, it may reduce the rate to 5 or 6 per cent should it distribute a 200 per cent stock dividend; and if it has been paying, say, $3.00 a share on a no-par stock, it may, under the same circumstances, reduce the rate to $1.00 or $1.25 a share. As the accumulated surplus upon which the stock dividend is based has already been contributing to earnings, its mere transfer in part to the common stock account incident to the stock dividend adds nothing to earning power. If, therefore, the cash dividend *rate* already in effect was reasonable, all circumstances considered, the stock dividend gives no basis for a sharp increase in the *amount* of cash distributions. In this regard, one should notice in Table 25–2 that the distribution of 100 per cent stock dividends by the Eastman Kodak Company and the White Motor Company was followed by reductions in the rates of cash dividends paid—although, to be sure, in neither instance, was the cash dividend rate cut in half.

Relation to Surplus. While stock dividends and split-ups can be used with equal effectiveness for adjustments purposes, the results are different in terms of surplus. A stock dividend of 200 per cent, as we have seen, tends to have the same effects on market price and earnings and dividends per share as a 3 for 1 split-up; but the former requires a transfer equal to the par of stated value of the stock dividend from the surplus account or accounts to the common stock account, whereas the latter requires no such transfer. Thus, a corporation that has been extremely liberal in paying cash dividends, so that it has little remaining surplus, is necessarily limited to the split-up device; whereas one that has accumulated a large surplus has a choice between the two devices.

Substituting for and Supplementing Cash Dividends

Size and Frequency. The use of stock dividends for objectives of the second type is ordinarily easy to recognize because the dividend rate is so much smaller than when the objectives are of the adjustment kind. The directors of a corporation might decide that earnings would justify a cash dividend equal to 6 per cent of par or stated value, but because of a concurrent decision that all earnings must be retained for corporate purposes, they might substitute a stock dividend of 6 per cent; or they might decide that cash equal to only 3 per cent of par or stated value could be spared for dividend purposes, and they might therefore add a stock dividend also of 3 per cent.

Moreover, stock dividends of the second type, unlike those of the first, are often repeated periodically, sometimes for lengthy periods of years— in some instances, indeed, coming to be looked upon as "regular." A corporation's directors, having decided in one year that a stock dividend must be substituted for a cash dividend, are likely to make the same kind of substitution in subsequent years if they continue to decide that cash cannot be paid.

Directors' and Stockholders' Attitudes. Stock dividends of the second class, therefore, are generally voted by corporate directors to give the stockholders "something" as a current reward for their investment when earnings justify a reward but pressing needs to retain cash for corporate purposes obtain. In some cases, directors might prefer not to distribute dividends of any kind, but decide upon stock dividends so that records of long-continued dividends of one kind or another will not be broken. However, a more likely reason for declaring stock dividends when directors would prefer to distribute nothing is the belief that stock dividends will prevent stockholder "clamor" for cash distributions—or for larger cash distributions if modest ones are already being made. The thought is that stockholders—even widely scattered ones—will be quite critical of management if they see in corporate reports pleasant figures for profits and if they then must wait in vain for "something" as their share in these profits.

The fact is that great numbers of stockholders are often quite content to receive stock dividends in full or partial substitution for the cash dividends that corporate earnings would seem to justify. They are content provided that the directors of their corporations do not overdo the stock dividend policy as by trying to continue it indefinitely. The typical stockholder in a large corporation whose stock is widely distributed is not much interested in voting power and in his claim, as owner, to corporate assets. He is interested in current income, and this he can get in cash by simply selling the shares he receives as dividends. The amount of cash he gets may vary from year to year as the market price of the stock fluctuates, but as long as the market price prevails at good levels, he may feel that he has no reason to complain. His proportionate claim to future earnings is diluted by the sale of the dividend stock, but this fact ought not to disturb him if the *rate of dividends*, as paid in stock or in stock and cash, is not reduced. Nor should the rate be reduced. According to generally accepted doctrine, the distribution of stock dividends in lieu of cash does not justify reducing the dividend rate, even though maintaining the rate means a continued increase in dividend requirements as more and more dividend stock is issued. That earnings must be retained for corporate purposes is the justification for distributions of stock dividends in lieu of cash; but the retention, in turn, can be justified in most cases only if it expands earning capacity. The expansion in earning capacity, accordingly, should enable the corporation to meet the higher dividend requirements without difficulty.

Another reason for stockholder satisfaction with stock dividends is applicable chiefly to people of large incomes and extensive stockholdings. This reason is that, as a rule, profits from the sale of stock received as dividends can be reported as capital gains rather than as ordinary income. The maximum capital gains rate on stock or other property held for more than six months is a straight 50 per cent,[2] whereas tax rates on ordinary personal income are graduated to a high of 91 per cent. Thus, a stockholder whose income from sources other than dividends gets into brackets taxable at rates well over 50 per cent has reason to welcome stock dividends in lieu of cash—and, obviously, the greater the rate applicable to the top bracket of his income the greater the reason for this welcome. A modest offsetting factor is that, with cash dividends, the first $50 of dividends is excluded from taxable income, and that a credit equal to 4 per cent of taxable dividends (but not more than 4 per cent of total taxable income) may be deducted from the total tax bill; but this factor clearly is of little importance to people of large incomes.

Tax Treatment of Stock Dividends. On the basis of decisions of the

---

[2] It will be recalled that only 50 per cent of the amount of long-term capital gains is recognized as taxable income, so that the maximum tax rate on the full gain is really only 25 per cent (.50 × .50). One will recall, too, that if the taxpayer chooses to have his long-term capital gains taxed as ordinary income, he likewise includes only 50 per cent of the amount of these gains.

Supreme Court dating from 1920, stock dividends that did not change the stockholder's ownership interests were recognized as not constituting taxable income. Common shares given to common stockholders as dividends were declared to be nontaxable as income, whereas preferred shares given as dividends to common stockholders were held to be taxable. However, the Internal Revenue Code of 1954 extended the exemption of stock dividends by making all kinds or classes nontaxable as income when received, with two exceptions. The exceptions are unusual kinds of distributions: (1) when preferred stockholders are given stock in lieu of cash dividends for the current or preceding year, and (2) when the stockholder takes stock though he has the choice of taking cash or some other kind of property—such a distribution is known as an "optional dividend."

Most stock dividends consist of common shares given to common stockholders. Under the present regulations, these are clearly nontaxable as income when received, but subsequent sales of such shares generally result in taxable capital gains or deductible capital losses. Assume that a stockholder owns 1,000 common shares that he bought some years ago at a price of $40 a share. This year he receives a stock dividend of 50 shares. He now has 1,050 shares that cost him $40,000; therefore, $38.10 ($40,000 ÷ 1,050) is the "basis price" for the determination of capital gains or losses on sales of any of the shares. Should he sell the dividend stock at $50 a share, he would have a gain of $595 that would be taxable at the most at 25 per cent. If, in the following year, he received a further stock dividend of 60 shares, the new "basis price" would be computed as follows: $40,000 less $1,905 (the portion of the original cost attributed to the 50 shares sold earlier) divided by 1,060 (the number of shares now held). The new "basis price" would thus be $35.94.

ENTITLEMENT TO DIVIDENDS

Who is entitled to a dividend that a board of directors has declared? More specifically, the question may be put this way: If a stockholder sells his stock between the date on which a dividend is declared and the date on which it is payable, does he get the dividend or does the buyer?

Rights of Buyers and Sellers

The answer depends upon the content of the directors' resolution declaring the dividend and, if the stock is listed on a stock exchange, the rules of the exchange. In their resolution declaring a dividend, it is customary for directors to set a "record date" a week or two beyond the date of the resolution and a "payment date" another week or two beyond the record date. Stockholders whose names are on the books at the close of business on the record date are entitled to receive the dividend. Thus, anybody who has bought the stock and has not had it transferred to his own name must effect the transfer by the record date if he is to get the dividend allotted to his shares. It is clear, likewise, that anybody who buys the stock after the date of declaration but in time to get his name on the stockholders' ledger or stock-transfer book by the record date will also participate in the dividend, but that he will not participate if his purchase is made without enough time for the recording of the transfer by the record date. Sellers and buyers may agree among themselves, of course, as to who is to receive a dividend, regardless of the date of sale, but the general rule is that a corporation discharges its responsibility by making the distribution to the "stockholders of record" on the designated date without having to give attention to such private agreements. If the directors, in declaring a dividend, do not set a record date, the rule is that the date of declaration is itself the record date.

Stock Exchange Rules

The stock exchanges have their own rules as to the entitlement to dividends of buyers and sellers of stocks sold through their facilities. The "settlement" policy of the New York Stock Exchange, for example, is that each transaction must be settled by the delivery of securities and cash by the fourth full business day following the day of the transaction; hence, its rule as to entitlement to dividends is that the buyer gets the dividend if he buys at any time up to the close of business on the fourth full business day preceding the record date, but that the seller gets it if the transaction takes place thereafter. If Friday, August 22, is the record date, the buyer gets the dividend if he buys on Monday, August 18, since the stock will be delivered by the seller's broker on Friday and the transfer can be recorded on that day; but he does not get it if he buys on Tuesday, August 19, since delivery will not be made till Monday, August 25. When the buyer is entitled to the dividend, the stock is said to sell *dividend-on* or *cum-dividend*—the price he pays covers both the share and the dividend that has been declared upon it. When the buyer does not get entitlement to the dividend, the stock is described as selling *ex-dividend*—the price covers the value of the share only. If not affected by immediate influences other than the dividend, the price of the stock at the opening of trading on the third full business day preceding the record date—when it "goes ex-dividend"—can be expected to be lower than the closing price of the preceding day by the amount of the dividend.

Payment Procedure

The secretary of the corporation makes up a list of the stockholders as of the close of business on the record date, their respective shareholdings, and the amount of dividend to which each is entitled. This list is turned over to the treasurer who makes out and mails the dividend checks. Usually the checks are mailed ahead of the payment date so that they will reach the stockholders on that date. Where corporations employ stock-transfer agents, the work both of compiling the list of stockholders and of preparing and mailing the dividend checks is customarily turned over to them.

Questions

1. Defend or attack this proposition: As long as a corporation has unpaid debts, even though they are not yet due, it should not pay cash dividends.

2. Why is there likely to be some conflict between a corporation's need of cash for expansion and its stockholders' wish to receive cash dividends? How can the conflict be resolved, if at all?

3. Under what circumstances may a corporation ease its problem of financing expansion by being liberal in cash dividend distributions to its stockholders?

4. Why are dividend payment decisions likely to be especially difficult for corporations that are controlled by a few wealthy stockholders but that have the remainder of their stock widely distributed?

5. Distinguish between an earnings pattern policy and a policy of regularity in the payment of cash dividends. For the typical corporation, which policy is likely to be the more advantageous? Why?

6. What bearing does a policy of regular cash dividends on common stock have upon sales of additional common? sales of preferred stock? sales of bonds?

7. What are the possible dangers of a policy of regularity in the payment of cash dividends?

8. What do the directors of a corporation imply when they label a dividend as an "extra" dividend? as a "special" dividend?

9. Why are stock dividends described as a "strange breed"? Why are they so popular with stockholders despite this strangeness?

10. How do the objectives of boards of directors usually differ when they declare large stock dividends of, say, 50 or 100 per cent, and small stock dividends of, perhaps, 3 or 4 per cent?

11. Is there any justification for reducing the regular rate of cash dividends after the distribution of a large stock dividend? a small stock dividend? Explain.

12. In its effects, how does a large stock dividend resemble and differ from a split-up?

13. When a common stockholder receives additional common shares as a dividend, must he pay federal income tax on the dividend? When? How much of the dividend is recognized as income?

14. If a stockholder sells his stock between the date of a dividend declaration and the date of its payment, who is entitled to the dividend, if anybody? Explain.

Problems

1. The United Mills Corporation began the year 19xx with a balance in its common stock account of $10 million (representing a million shares of $10 par value) and an earned surplus balance of $6 million. Early in the year it effected a 4 for 1 split-up of its common stock, reducing the par value to $2.50, and later in the year it distributed a 20 per cent stock dividend.

What effect did these transactions have upon the number of outstanding common shares, their total par value, and the balance in the corporation's earned surplus account?

2. In the year 19xx, John Doe bought 400 shares of the common stock of the United Mills Corporation after the split-up referred to in Problem 1 but before the distribution of the stock dividend. He paid $30 a share. Several months after he received his stock dividend of 80 shares, he sold them at $38 a share.

a) Under federal tax regulations, what was his taxable income upon receiving the 80 shares? upon selling them?

b) In the following year, 19yy, Doe received an additional 80 shares of United Mills stock as a dividend, later selling 50 of these shares at $29 a share. What was his taxable income upon receiving the second 80 shares? upon selling the 50 shares?

Part IX

FINANCING
WITH BONDS

chapter 26

THE NATURE OF BONDS

BONDS AND NOTES

A corporate bond may be described as an unconditional promise of a corporation in writing under seal to pay a specific sum of money to the bearer or to the registered holder at a designated time. Technically, it is the seal that distinguishes corporate bonds from other kinds of corporate promises to pay. Under the common law, a seal made a contract binding upon the person using it with his signature whether or not other parties to the contract could prove that they had provided "consideration"; but state statutes have generally demoted seals to a position of insignificance, so that, at the present time, the person who signs under seal can, as a rule, deny his obligations on the grounds that the party or parties to whom the promise was made gave or promised nothing of value in return.

As a practical matter, therefore, bonds are distinguished from other kinds of corporate promises to pay chiefly by reason of the following features: (1) they are long-term obligations; (2) they are simultaneously promises to pay the face amount or "principal" at a designated date of maturity and to pay interest at a specified rate periodically; (3) they are units of a large number of instruments of identical terms (except, sometimes, the maturity) issued simultaneously; (4) they are issued according to the terms of a separate comprehensive contract, called an *indenture,* to which reference is made in the bond itself; (5) the separate comprehensive contract is entered into between the corporation and a third party, the *trustee,* to whom reference is also made in the bond; and (6) a certification by the trustee appears on the bond to indicate that it is one of the units covered by the indenture.

Bond Certificates

Simply by inspection, a bond or bond certificate, as illustrated in Figure 26–1, is readily distinguishable from any other form of corporate promise to pay. For one thing, a bond is usually labeled as such in its heading. For another, it is usually carefully engraved upon paper of special quality to discourage attempts at counterfeiting. Again, it usually contains a goodly amount of detail following the specific promise to pay: a recital of the fact that it is one of a group issued according to the terms

FIGURE 26-1—Bond Certificate

STANDARD OIL COMPANY

(AN INDIANA CORPORATION)

Nº M 00000

Nº M 00000

THIRTY YEAR 3⅜% DEBENTURE, DUE OCTOBER 1, 1962

(CONVERTIBLE ON OR BEFORE OCTOBER 1, 1956 UNLESS PREVIOUSLY REDEEMED)

ONE THOUSAND DOLLARS $1000

TRUSTEE'S CERTIFICATE OF AUTHENTICATION

This is one of the Debentures described in the within mentioned Indenture.

CONTINENTAL ILLINOIS NATIONAL BANK AND TRUST COMPANY OF CHICAGO, AS TRUSTEE

By

AUTHORIZED OFFICER

Standard Oil Company

By

Robert ⟨SPECIMEN⟩ Wilson

CHAIRMAN OF THE BOARD

SPECIMEN

PRESIDENT

SPECIMEN

ASST. TREASURER

of an indenture entered into on a stated date between the corporation and such-and-such bank or trust company as trustee; a declaration of the bondholder's right to have the bond in coupon or registered form and to switch from one form to the other; a statement of the corporation's right to call the bond for redemption; a description of the corporation's obligation, if any, to provide for bond retirement through sinking fund contributions; a statement of any special privileges the bondholder may have, as to convert the bond into common stock; a statement to the effect that provisions of the indenture, except as to the payment of interest and principal, may be modified with the approval of the holders of a stipulated proportion of the bonds (usually 66⅔ or 75 per cent); a denial of liability upon the part of the stockholders, directors, and officers of the corporation for its obligation represented by the bond; and a statement that the bond is not valid unless it bears a certification or "authentication" by the trustee. Finally, the seal of the corporation continues to be an identifying feature, despite its slight legal importance in most jurisdictions.

By contrast, short-term promissory notes, for example, are often quite simple documents, containing nothing more than the bare recital of the promise to pay with the corporation's signature and those of one or two of its officers. Even when note forms are complex, as judgment notes and so-called "collateral notes" such as one signs when borrowing money for stock market transactions, the details included are generally quite different from those of bond certificates, and there is no reference to an indenture or a trustee.

Corporate Issues of Long-Term Notes

Often corporations put out what appear to be bond issues, but the separate certificates are labeled "notes" rather than "bonds." A newspaper advertisement of a public offering of one corporation's issue of 20-year "bonds" may appear in close proximity to a notice of the sale of another corporation's issue of 20-year "notes." Almost always, however, one will observe that the designation *notes* is reserved for sales of long-term debt issues in bulk to one or a few institutional investors—in other words, for private placements.

A reason for the popularity of the designation *notes* for private placements is that, very often, the separate certificates or instruments are, indeed, rather simple note forms rather than elaborately engraved certificates. Another reason is that, sometimes, no trustees are employed in long-term debt transactions via the private-placement route. But these are differences in form rather than in substance. For long-term note issues sold to institutional investors, it is customary to draw up long and detailed contracts governing all the terms of the issuing corporations' obligations, whether or not they are called indentures, and whether or not trustees are appointed. Thus, a corporation's obligations on "notes" sold to institutional investors will generally be much the same as its obligations on "bonds" sold to the general public. It is to be kept in mind, therefore, that virtually all that is said in these pages about bonds, indentures, pledges of assets, sinking funds, protective provisions, and so on applies as well to "notes" sold to institutional investors as to "bonds" sold to the public.

Another Matter of Terminology: Debentures

Even with respect to long-term debt instruments that are offered publicly, one may notice that often these instruments are described as "debentures" rather than as "bonds." On July 23, 1963, for example, a syndicate of investment bankers advertised for public subscription $25 million of "4½% Sinking Fund Debentures" of the Burroughs Corporation. In the reports of government agencies, too, one may notice that long-term corporate debt instruments are often described as "bonds, notes, and debentures."

Really, however, the term *debenture* is simply a short form of the more formal term *debenture bond.* As we shall see, debenture bonds are distinguished from other classes of bonds by the fact that the issuing corporations pledge no assets for their saftey. For this reason, some people reserve the term *bond* for issues for which there are pledges of assets, and use the unadorned term *debenture* for those for which pledges are lacking. But "debentures" or "debenture bonds" that are publicly offered are issued according to the terms of detailed contracts or indentures entered into with trustees, so that, aside from the matter of pledged assets, there is no essential difference between them and instruments that are invariably called bonds. Again it may be said, therefore, that descriptive materials in these pages pertaining to "bonds" apply fully to so-called "debentures" save where distinctions are clearly indicated.

THE INDENTURE AND THE TRUSTEE

The Indenture

The whole array of terms and conditions on the basis of which bonds are issued is contained in the indenture. Some of these terms and conditions are set out completely in the bond certificates themselves, but most are mentioned only briefly there, if at all, with reference to the indenture for the full statement. The certificate may state, for example, that the bond is secured by a pledge of property, but the description of the property pledged is to be found in the indenture—where, in truth, it may require many pages as for a large corporation that pledges widely scattered plant properties of diverse kinds. In the indenture of 1952 covering the 3⅛ per cent first-mortgage bonds of the National Steel Corporation due in 1982, the description of the property pledged requires 49 large printed pages!

The indenture is ordinarily the complete contract. Should there be discrepancies between what is said in the bond certificates and what is said in the indenture, a court might have to be called upon to decide which statement should be binding. Customarily, however, greatest care is exercised to insure that there will be no discrepancies. Nor is there likely to be any question as to which indenture applies to which bond issue, as when a corporation has two or more bond issues outstanding simultaneously. Cross-references between certificates and indentures are precise in terms of descriptive titles of the bonds, dates of the indentures, and who are the trustees (the trustee of one bond issue will not ordinarily serve as trustee for another of the same corporation to be outstanding simultaneously). What is more, each indenture contains the complete forms of the bond certificate and the coupon for interest payments that are to be issued under it. The wording of the forms as contained in the indenture are followed with scrupulous accuracy when the certificates and coupons are actually engraved and printed.

Indentures are lengthy documents, often running to a hundred or more printed pages. Descriptions of pledged property, as was indicated previously, may require many pages; but, even when no property is pledged, a great mass of detail must be covered. The objective is to have everything stated so clearly that there will be no occasion for subsequent disputes and litigation over the nature of the rights and privileges of, and limitations upon, the bondholders, the rights and obligations of the corporation, and the duties and powers of the trustee. Because an indenture is a long-term contract, the objective is to anticipate how the corporation and its obligations and the trustee and its relationship to the corporation may be affected by many different kinds of events, and to incorporate provisions for adjustment to these events—how the bonded debt is to be treated should the corporation be involved in a merger or consolidation, how the conversion privilege, if it is given, is to be modified should the corporation effect a split-up in its stock, how "supplemental indentures" may be used for further issues of bonds of the same kind, how a "successor trustee" is to be appointed if the original one becomes disqualified or wishes to resign, and so on.

No attempt need be made here to outline in detail the contents of typical bond indentures. Without an immediate explanation of the items, a mere listing would be of little value. We can, as it were, pick up the contents of indentures as we go along, for all features of bonds as discussed in this and subsequent chapters necessarily constitute the substance of indentures.

But a concluding remark: One should know that, in practice, indentures for bond issues are given several names, especially bond indentures, mortgage indentures, trust indentures, trust agreements, and deeds of trust. The names are not fully interchangeable; for example, the contract for a bond issue for which there is no pledge of property would not be called a "mortgage indenture" or a "deed of trust"; nevertheless, it could be called, with equal propriety, a "bond indenture," a "trust indenture," or a "trust agreement."

The Trustee

Upon issuing bonds, a corporation becomes indebted to the people who buy them, but its obligation is governed by the indenture—a contract entered into by the corporation with a trustee. Because the bondholders are likely to be widely scattered, and because, in any case, they are likely to hold individually only small portions of the total debt, the trustee is appointed to safeguard their interests, as well as to represent them collectively in any necessary dealings with the corporation. Accordingly, the bondholders are said to be the "beneficiaries" of the relationship between the corporation and the trustee.

Because trust companies and the trust departments of commercial banks, particularly those of the larger cities, have long specialized in serving as indenture trustees, corporations when issuing bonds are inclined to turn to them as a matter of course. Sometimes investment bankers who are to underwrite a bond issue have something to say as to who the trustee shall be, but usually there is not much room for dispute as the fees and capabilities of the larger trust companies and departments are close to uniformity. Individuals may be selected as trustees, but, if they are appointed, their role is ordinarily that of co-trustees with trust companies or departments, with the latter delegated to do most of the work.

For indentures that must be qualified under the federal Trust Indenture Act of 1939 (to be discussed further a little later), the appointment of a bank or trust company as trustee is required, although it is permissible to have one or more individuals as co-trustees. The bank or trust company appointed—described as a "corporate trustee"—must have capital stock and surplus of not less than $150,000 and be subject to supervision by federal or state authorities.

While the role of an indenture trustee as a "protector" of the bondholders is always stressed, the fact that its services are of great convenience to the corporation ought not to be overlooked. It should be helpful to look at these two aspects of its work separately.

Convenience

If property is pledged for the security of the bondholders, it is easy to make the pledge to the trustee as a single entity; it would be most difficult to try to make pledges individually to hundreds or thousands of bondholders. After a pledge has been made to the trustee, the corporation may want from time to time to sell parcels of the pledged property that have lost their usefulness and to substitute new parcels. Although such a substitution should be advantageous for the bondholders, it would be most difficult to effect were it necessary for the corporation to reach and get the consent of every one of the bondholders. A much more convenient procedure is to provide in the indenture that the trustee shall have the right to approve substitutions. In issuing bonds, many corporations agree to make periodical contributions of cash to sinking funds to be used for the retirement of the bonds. It is easy to make these contributions in lump sum to a trustee who then has the responsibility to use the money as the indenture stipulates. Were the corporation not to use the services of the trustee in this connection, disgruntled bondholders might constantly accuse it of improper or unfair management of its sinking fund.

Also for convenience, the corporation can arrange with the trustee for various kinds of useful services of a routine character, thereby relieving itself of clerical burdens—although, of course, for a fee. It may pay interest on an entire bond issue by writing a single check payable to the trustee, depending upon the latter to make the piecemeal distribution to the bondholders. In a similar way, it may proceed to retire a portion of its bond issue by turning over to the trustee funds equal to the total call price of all bonds called for redemption, letting it parcel these out as the bonds are actually surrendered.

Protection of the Bondholders

The devotion of trustees to their duty of protecting the interests of bondholders is always expected to take precedence over serving the convenience of corporations. That is why they are "trustees" rather than "agents"—for trusteeship always implies a high degree of responsibility for the welfare of "beneficiaries."

Authentication. A primary protective duty is to see that the bond buyers get genuine bonds of the form provided for in the indenture and that the corporation does not put out more bonds than have been authorized. Before the delivery of bonds to investment bankers or other buyers, therefore, they are dispatched to the trustee for its certification or "authentication." The trustee checks the wording of the bond, the interest coupons, and the authentication form to be sure that they are in exact conformity with the wording of these instruments as set out in the indenture itself; it checks all bond serial numbers to be sure that they are in proper sequence and that there are no duplications; and it determines that the proper number of coupons with the correct interest payment dates are attached to each bond. When satisfied, it signs the authentication form which appears upon the face of the bond certificate. The form is ordinarily a simple statement such as the following:

Trustee's Certificate

This is one of the Bonds described in the within-mentioned Indenture.

FIRST NATIONAL BANK AND TRUST CO.,
As Trustee

By _____

Authorized Officer

Checking Compliance with Obligations. Like authentication, some of the other protective duties of the trustee are relatively easy to fulfill. If property is to be pledged, it is pledged to the trustee—hence it is readily apparent when and if this obligation is met. Whether or not property is pledged, the corporation agrees to provide adequate insurance coverages, for the interests of the bondholders would be gravely weakened were the corporate properties to be destroyed as by fire without insurance compensation. But the trustee can easily check upon insurance coverages. The corporation agrees to pay all its taxes promptly, since taxing authorities can be expected to obtain tax liens against properties for the amount of unpaid taxes and penalties—liens which generally have a priority of claim over bonds and other ordinary debt. However, checking to see whether or not the corporation is paying its taxes currently is not a difficult task for the trustee. The corporation agrees to keep its properties in good operating condition—compliance here may be a little more difficult to check upon, but surely a lot less difficult for a single trustee than it would be for hundreds or thousands of scattered bondholders if, individually, they had to check upon the fulfillment of this "covenant."

Problem of More Positive Protective Action. But protection of bondholders surely requires much more than simple checking procedures of the kinds mentioned. Suppose, indeed, that the trustee does find that the corporation is not providing adequate insurance, that it is not paying its taxes when due, and that it is not keeping its properties in a proper state of repair. These are defaults[1]—violations of the corporation's obligations or, to use the term just introduced, its "covenants." The defaults may be even more serious—the nonpayment of stipulated sinking fund contributions or the nonpayment of interest. To protect his interests following such defaults, the holder of a bond of $1,000 could hardly do much; were he to institute legal actions on his own, the value of his bond would soon be exhausted by the expenses involved. Hence the idea is that he should be able to look to the trustee for appropriate action, since the trustee's major role is that of protector.

In times past, nevertheless, trustees were often not very enthusiastic about taking action after defaults. In accepting appointments as trustees, they anticipated no vigorous protective action; they indicated this by insisting upon the inclusion of "exculpatory clauses" in indentures. The purpose of these clauses was specifically to relieve them of liability to their beneficiaries, that is, the bondholders, for failure to take protective actions. In fairness to them, it must be said that their fees as trustees were moderate and that they generally had no assurances of reimbursement for

---

[1] Technically, such violations become "events of default" when a written notice has been given to the corporation calling attention to them and demanding their correction, and the corporation has failed to make the correction within the period stipulated in the indenture, usually 90 days. The written notice may be given by the trustee or by holders of not less than a stipulated proportion of the bonds, usually 25 per cent.

money spent in taking protective actions. Accordingly, they were usually satisfied to wait till bondholders banded together to request action—at which time they could demand assurances that whatever expenses might be involved would be reimbursed.

In these circumstances, bondholders simply were not getting the protection that the trustee arrangement was theoretically supposed to give them. On the basis of its own investigations and those of the SEC in the 1930's, Congress took steps to remedy the situation by the adoption of the Trust Indenture Act of 1939. The legislation applies to bond issues for which registration statements must be filed under the Securities Act of 1933 and to those issued in interstate commerce in exchange for other securities of the issuers in recapitalizations—reshufflings of financial structures—and reorganizations (such exchanges in many instances not requiring registration under the Securities Act).

Provisions of the Trust Indenture Act. The Trust Indenture Act outlaws exculpatory clauses, requires the inclusion in every indenture of certain kinds of protective provisions, and imposes upon trustees a positive protective role. If there is danger that a trustee may neglect the interests of bondholders because it has other interests in or connections with the corporation or the underwriters of the bonds—if, in other words, there is a "conflict of interests"—it must resign as trustee, eliminate the conflict, or notify the bondholders of the conflict so that they may exercise their powers to terminate the trusteeship. The first step, and probably the third, would lead to the naming of a new or "successor" trustee. The corporation is required to provide various kinds of information to the trustee, and the trustee, in turn, must make an annual report to the bondholders accounting for any advances it may have made to the corporation, corporate monies it is possession, substitutions in pledged property it may have allowed, and the amounts of additional bonds it may have authenticated for issue. From time to time, lists of known bondholders must be supplied by the corporation to the trustee, and the trustee is required to make such lists available, upon request, to individual bondholders; this should enable bondholders to reach others should there be a wish to propose some kind of concerted action.

However, the most important prod to positive protective action contained in the Trust Indenture Act is the proviso that, upon the occurrence of defaults, the trustee must exercise its powers with the degree of care and skill that a prudent man would exercise in a similar situation. The "prudent-man rule" is vague—perhaps necessarily so, since it is designed to be applicable in a great variety of circumstances; nevertheless, it appears to be a great advance beyond exculpatory clauses. At the least, the trustee is on notice that a do-nothing policy following defaults may result in lawsuits brought by bondholders charging its negligence and demanding damages for losses incurred on account of the alleged negligence. A court might decide, for example, that a trustee was prudent in letting ride a corporate default in tax payments when prospects were good that the default would be corrected within a few months; but it might decide that another trustee, by letting ride a default in required sinking fund contributions, imprudently permitted an incompetent management to continue to dissipate corporate assets. Even in the matter of the defaulted tax payments, the first trustee could hardly expect to be adjudged prudent were it not to notify the bondholders of the default. In fact, a specific provision of the Trust Indenture Act is that the trustee must give bondholders notice of any default within 90 days of its occurrence.

DETERMINATION OF BOND FEATURES

As soon as a corporate management begins to plan a bond issue, it initiates, as it were, a process of bargaining. For a time, the bargaining may be entirely internal as the members of the management "team" discuss what they can afford to give, and what they hope to get, as features of the proposed bond issue. They will expect, as a matter of course, to make certain kinds of concessions and to gain certain ones—these are the "standard" features of bond indentures. They may readily admit that certain additional concessions will have to be made because of weaknesses in the corporation's financial position or the state of the securities markets; but, in general, they will want to give as little as possible and to gain as much as possible. But prospective buyers, such as investment bankers and institutional investors, are likely to be astute; they will have an attitude of much the same kind. When, therefore, an approach is made to the prospective buyers, the bargaining will quickly become a serious matter of give and take, with ground yielded or a concession made here to gain an advantage there. Sometimes managements are thoroughly disillusioned at the outset in finding that prospective investors demand much greater concessions than had been anticipated; in many such cases, plans for bond financing are dropped. At other times, the surprise is the other way around—it is found that prospective investors are avid for new bond issues and willing, therefore, to buy upon terms quite favorable to the issuers. In the great majority of successful offerings, at any rate, a considerable amount of "horse trading" will have occurred during the bargaining.

For an analysis of the features of bond issues about which bargaining revolves, we may keep in mind the following classification: (1) principal, interest, and maturity; (2) security; (3) guaranties; (4) protective provisions for the bondholders; (5) privileges wanted by the corporation; and (6) special inducements to be offered by the corporation. Unfortunately, however, an examination of these features cannot be made to follow the classification in any precise way. The reason for this is that all the features are closely interrelated. The pledging of a corporation's operating properties may have a significant influence upon the interest rate, and even upon the maturity of the bond issue. At the same time, the pledge is obviously a protective provision for the bondholders; yet it could also be considered a special selling feature offered by the corporation. And when a corporation pledges operating property, it is sure to demand certain privileges of possession and use of that property.

Although the overlap can thus be seen to be pervasive, it should be convenient to keep as close to the classification outline as possible. The remainder of the present chapter, therefore, will concentrate upon principal, form, interest, and maturity; in the following chapter, the main focus of attention will be security and guaranties; and in Chapter 28, what is left of items 4, 5, and 6 will be taken up for study.

PRINCIPAL AND FORM

Denominations

Not much argument is likely to arise about the principal or face value of proposed bonds—two designations used interchangeably for the dollar denomination. It is "standard" practice for corporations to issue bonds in units of $1,000 and to make principal and interest payable in "lawful money of the United States." Rather frequently, however, bonds are issued not only in $1,000, but also in $5,000, denominations. Occasionally, corporations put out so-called "baby bonds" of $500, $100, and even smaller denominations to try to reach investors unlikely to have as much as $1,000 available for investment. But most corporations apparently conclude that the advantage of reaching such investors would be more than offset by expenses of engraving and printing, making exchanges, and other tasks of issue and management.

Coupon and Registered Bonds

Coupon Bonds. A very large proportion of bonds outstanding at the present time are "coupon bonds." In the bond certificate itself, the corporation promises payment of the principal to the "bearer" at maturity, and attached to it are individual coupons for each interest-payment date between the date of issue and the date of maturity. As it is "standard" practice to make bond interest payable semiannually, a typical 20-year bond will have 40 coupons attached at the time it is issued. Each coupon, as illustrated in Figure 26–2, is of the nature of a promissory note payable to the "bearer" on the date inscribed upon it.

As each interest-payment date approaches, the bondholder clips the appropriate coupon so that it can be sent in for the interest due. Normally, he turns the coupon over to a commercial bank "for collection," depending upon it to take care of the clerical chores of picking up the payment. The bank, in turn, sends it direct to the trustee or indirectly through a "correspondent bank." The corporation will have issued to the trustee a single check for the total amount of interest on all coupons

FIGURE 26–2—Bond Coupons

now coming due, and the trustee parcels out this money as it makes payment upon the coupons coming in, as it were, from all directions. In a similar way, it is up to the bondholder, shortly before the maturity of the bond, to get it and the final coupon to the trustees to claim his principal and final interest payments. It is up to him, too, to get to the trustee the bond with all unmatured coupons should he happen to notice a newspaper advertisement of the corporation informing him that his bond has been called for redemption.

Since both the bond and coupons are bearer instruments, their ownership can be transferred by mere delivery. There is no need of notification to the corporation or a transfer agent, nor is there a cancellation of the old certificate and the issuance of a new one to the buyer, as with the transfer of ownership of stock certificates.

Registered Bonds. Customarily, however, corporations have been willing to issue "registered bonds" in place of coupon bonds when investors have so requested. Some corporations have provided registration "as to principal" only, but most have been willing to supply "fully registered" bonds, that is, registered as to both principal and interest. A bond registered as to principal bears the owner's name upon its face, for it is "to the order of" this person that the corporation promises to make the principal payment at maturity. The corporation or the trustee keeps a record of the owners of these registered bonds, and the record must be changed, as for stock certificates, when a sale or other transfer takes place. The original owner endorses the bond certificate in blank or to the order of the buyer or other transferee, and the latter sends it in for cancellation, getting a new registered bond payable to his order or a coupon bond, depending upon which form he asks for.

If the bond is registered as to principal only, coupons in bearer form for all interest-payment dates are attached; but if the bond is fully registered, the corporation, or more likely the trustee as its agent, pays the interest by check to the registered owner—in the same manner, obviously, that cash dividends are distributed to stockholders.

Some Excitement about Registered Bonds. Although the differences between coupon and registered bonds might seem to be a minor matter, considerable excitement developed in the summer of 1963 when, in June, the Firestone Tire & Rubber Company sold a $75 million issue of debenture bonds, all of which were to be fully registered unless buyers specifically asked for the coupon form; and when, in August, the United Aircraft Corporation floated a bond issue of approximately $43 million and designated that all the bonds would be fully registered, thus denying the buyer any choice of taking coupon bonds. In some quarters, these two issues were hailed as the beginning of a "trend" or even a "revolution," and the American Bankers Association in particular stepped up a campaign to promote a further switching in new corporate issues from the coupon to the registered form.

There are many good arguments for avoiding new issues of coupon bonds in favor of registered bonds. For both large and small investors, whether individuals or institutions, the principal argument is safety. Since a corporation has no record of the owners of its coupon bonds, it is very difficult if not impossible for owners of bonds and coupons that have been lost, stolen, or destroyed as by fire to prove ownership and to get replacements. Because, moreover, bonds and coupons are negotiable instruments, even proof of (previous) ownership is of no avail toward gaining repossession of lost or stolen bonds and coupons that get into the hands of people who qualify as innocent third parties—"innocent holders for value," as the lawyers say.[2] On the other hand, a person can get good title to a registered bond only if the original owner endorses it; and if a registered bond is stolen, destroyed, or lost, the registered owner can usually get a replacement from the corporation with little difficulty and only slight cost.[3]

Another argument for registered bonds, from the standpoint of small investors especially, is that the corporation or trustee can notify them by letter should their bonds be called for redemption. Holders of coupon bonds, on the other hand, may lose interest income by retaining them beyond their redemption dates, having failed to see newspaper advertisements announcing the redemption.

For institutional investors that hold large volumes of bonds in their investment portfolios, and for banks and trust companies that hold large volumes for the investment and safekeeping accounts of their customers, additional advantages claimed for registered bonds are principally economies in the time required to clip and handle coupons, and economies in the storage space needed for the bonds. It is estimated that about 300 million coupons are clipped and "processed" annually in the United States, and the United States Trust Company estimates that this requires 113,200 man-days of labor at a cost of $1,800,000.[4] As for storage space, one argument is that coupons make bonds bulky, and another is that registered bonds can be issued quite conveniently in large denominations —a single registered bond of, say, $1 million can replace 1,000 coupon bonds of $1,000 denomination or 200 of $5,000 denomination.

For the corporate issuer of bonds, the principal advantages claimed for fully registered issues are the elimination of the costs of engraving and printing coupons, reducing the cost of printing bond certificates, avoiding the substantial expense of newspaper advertising of calls for

---

[2] For an earlier brief treatment of the quality of negotiability, introduced in the analysis of stock certificates, see pp. 366–67.

[3] The corporation would be likely to require an indemnity bond to protect itself should the bonds alleged to be stolen, lost, or destroyed turn up properly endorsed in legitimate hands. But insurance companies supply indemnity bonds at moderate cost to people who have good reputations.

[4] *The Wall Street Journal*, July 9, 1963, p. 6.

redemption, and, especially, its knowing at all times who its bondholders are and having the means, therefore, to reach them direct should it have any problems to take up with them, such as proposals to amend the indenture. It is generally admitted, however, that these advantages to the corporation would be offset somewhat by increased costs of record keeping.

Bond Price Quotations

While the standard principal of corporation bonds is $1,000, bond prices are quoted in terms of $100 of face value. If a corporation sells a bond issue to investment bankers "at 98," it receives $980 for each $1,000 bond; similarly, if a person buys a bond whose selling price is quoted at 103, he pays $1,030.

Bonds are usually sold at a designated price "plus accrued interest." If the interest payment dates on a bond quoted at 103 are January 1 and July 1, and if the buyer buys on January 16, he pays $1,030 plus interest for 15 days on the principal of $1,000 at the rate designated in the bond itself. But on July 1 he receives interest for a full six-month period, so that his net interest income represents, as it should, earnings for the actual period of ownership from January 16 to July 1. Similarly, a corporation, in originally issuing bonds on January 16, with January 1 and July 1 designated as interest payment dates, receives the selling price and accrued interest for 15 days; but on July 1 it has a full six-month interest payment to make.

When a corporation has failed to meet its interest obligation on any due date, or when it has announced that it cannot meet an approaching interest obligation, market prices for its bonds will ordinarily be quoted "flat." This means that buyers pay the prices at which bonds are offered without any additions for accrued interest. Because of uncertainty about the size of interest payments, if any, on "income bonds"—to be discussed in the next section—they are usually also bought and sold in the market on a "flat" basis.

INTEREST

Interest is the price paid for the use of loanable funds. When a corporation borrows by selling a bond issue, it contracts to pay this price periodically at a designated rate over a long period of time. Whether it can afford to pay the price demanded by prospective buyers depends, as we saw in Chapter 10, upon the rate of earnings expected from the use of the proceeds in operations. If the interest rate that can be agreed upon is substantially less than the anticipated rate of earnings, then surely the corporation will want to go ahead with the bond flotation; but if it is higher, proceeding with the bond issue would surely appear to be a foolish venture.

Determinants of Interest Rates

All the bargaining that goes on in connection with proposed bond issues tends to focus upon the interest rate; it is not something to be considered as if it were an independent feature. If the corporation is willing to grant certain kinds of special concessions to the bond buyers, it will expect to be able to shade the interest rate downward; but if it wants to reserve certain special rights to itself, it may have to pay for these through an upward shading in the interest rate. Thus, many of the major features of the indenture will directly influence the level of the interest rate as agreed upon—if, indeed, agreement is finally reached.

But the "shading" of an interest rate upward or downward requires a starting point. The bargaining does not wander over a wide range of possible interest rates; it tends quickly to be confined to a narrow range based upon two considerations: the state of the market for long-term obligations, and the credit standing of the corporation that proposes to put out a new bond issue.

State of the Market. An analysis of the state of the market usually begins by reference to the current "yields" upon the long-term obligations of the U.S. Treasury. If these are relatively high, the market is "tight," that is, the supply of funds investors are willing to commit to long-term debt instruments is moderate in relation to the demand for such funds. Accordingly, any corporation, regardless of its credit standing, must expect to set a relatively high interest rate on any new bond issue it proposes to sell. If, however, the current "yields" on long-term treasury obligations are relatively low, the supply of funds available for long-term investment in bonds and other obligations is plentiful in relation to demand, and the market is therefore "easy." Regardless of its credit standing, a corporation planning to put out a new bond issue will expect to obtain its funds at a rate of interest substantially less than it would have to name in a "tight" situation.

The state of the market for long-term treasury obligations is determinable at all times, and not simply at times when the Treasury is offering new long-term issues. This is the significance of "yields." The yield of a bond is the *true* or *effective* rate of interest that the buyer will earn from the time of purchase till maturity if he buys at a given price. It is determined by the price, the rate of interest that the issuer of the bond has promised to pay (the *nominal* rate), and the time to maturity. It changes with every change in market price. If a treasury obligation due in 20 years and bearing interest at 4 per cent can be bought at par, the yield is also 4 per cent—the nominal and effective rates are identical. But if the 20-year 4 per cent bond is selling in the market at 95, investors are obviously demanding a rate of return of more than 4 per cent. They want $20 interest each six months upon an investment of $950, and they also want $1,000 at maturity even though they invest only $950 now.

Actually, as bond tables reveal,[5] the investor would be earning about 4.38 per cent upon his investment of $950: this would be the effective rate or yield. The market would be relatively "tight" by comparison with its state when the bond sold at par. Similarly, if the investor were willing to pay 105 for the bond, he would be accepting a yield of only 3.65 per cent, and the market would be relatively "easy." If the bond had only ten years to run till maturity, a price of 95 would mean a yield of 4.63 per cent, and a price of 105, a yield of 3.41 per cent; and if the bond with 20 years to run had a nominal rate of 3 per cent instead of 4 per cent, a price of 95 would give a yield of 3.35 per cent, and a price of 105, a yield of 2.68 per cent.

Credit Standing of the Issuer. Not only are the yields of long-term treasury obligations useful in determining whether interest rates on new issues of corporation bonds must be high or may be low because of conditions of tightness and ease in the market, they are useful when judgments are made about the specific levels at which interest rates on new bond issues should be set for given corporations in view of their very different credit standings. The yields on treasury obligations are "basic" because of their risklessness in the credit sense. No investor doubts that the Treasury will meet its interest and principal obligations on time and in full. The federal government has broad taxing powers with which it can *compel* people to pay into the Treasury a sufficient amount of money to enable it to meet all its obligations, and should its finances really get into a chaotic state, it could use its sovereign money-creating powers and simply print new money to pay interest and principal upon its obligations. No corporation can claim risklessness of this

---

[5] When a person buys a bond at a given price, he pays for two things: the amount of money he is to receive at maturity *discounted* at the effective rate of interest for the number of semiannual periods from the time of purchase till maturity, and the series of semiannual interest payments he is to receive *discounted* at the effective rate on a semiannual basis for the respective periods from the time of purchase to the time that each is due. By formula, the discounted or present value of the principal-at-maturity is $P = A(1 + i)^{-n}$, where P is the present value, A is the maturity value, i is the effective rate of interest, and n is the number of semiannual periods; and the present value of the series of interest payments—the present value of an *annuity* of equal periodic payments, as the mathematicians call it—is $P = R \dfrac{1 - (1 + i)^{-n}}{i}$, where P, i, and n have the same meanings as in the first formula, and R is the amount of the periodic interest payment. Combining these formulas and substituting figures from the illustration in the text, we get—

$$950 = 1,000(1 + i)^{-40} + 20 \frac{1 - (1 + i)^{-40}}{i}.$$

Fortunately, "bond tables" prepared by mathematicians give us solutions to such equations for many interest rates and a wide range of maturities. Glances at such tables, or simple interpolations in them, will reveal answers to questions such as these: what effective rate is earned, given a certain price, nominal rate, and maturity; what the price must be if one wants to earn a certain effective rate, given the nominal rate and the maturity; and what the nominal rate must be, given the price, the maturity, and the effective rate the investor wants to earn or the corporation is willing to pay.

degree. But some can claim a very high degree of risklessness when bargaining with investment bankers or other prospective buyers of proposed new bond issues. Their credit standings, as judged by their financial structures, their records of meeting obligations in the past, their earnings and dividend records, their prospective future earnings, investor evaluations of the competence of their managements, and other factors, are extremely good. These corporations can argue, therefore, that interest rates to be set upon their new issues of bonds need not be much higher than the yields upon treasury obligations of comparable maturities —that differentials of one third, one half, or two thirds of a percentage point ought to suffice to attract buyers. The managements of other corporations of somewhat weaker credit positions may concede at the outset of bargaining negotiations that the differential could hardly be less than 1 or 1½ percentage points; and the managers of still weaker corporations may readily agree that the differential could hardly be less than 2 or even 3 percentage points. Bargaining at a time of ease in the market for long-term funds when the yield on 20-year treasury bonds is, say, 3 per cent, a strong corporation might expect to sell a 20-year issue at an interest rate of 3¼ or 3⅜ per cent; but if the market were tight and the yield on the treasury bonds were 4½ per cent, bargaining on the corporation's issue might start in the vicinity of 5 per cent. Similarly, rate discussions concerning a proposed bond issue of a corporation of serious credit weaknesses might start at 5 or 5½ per cent in a period of ease and at 6½ or 7 per cent in a period of tightness.

When a corporation negotiates with investment bankers to have its bond issue underwritten, it must expect its true interest cost to be somewhat higher than the yield that the ulimate investor is willing to accept. Without question, its flotation costs, including most importantly the bankers' commission, increase the "price" it must pay for borrowed money. A bond issue bearing interest at 5 per cent to be offered to the public at par will obviously cost the corporation more than 5 per cent annually if it is underwritten by the investment bankers "at 98." Moreover, a tentative agreement about the interest rate and the "price to the bankers" reached early in the negotiations remains subject to adjustment till shortly before the effective date of the registration statement required by the federal Securities Act.[6]

Other Aspects of Interest Rates

As a rule, any corporation must expect to pay a higher rate of interest on a bond issue than would be asked of it on short-term bank loans or on other forms of short-term borrowing. For lengthy periods before the early 1930's, short-term rates for given classes of borrowers were higher than long-term rates for the same classes; during these periods, therefore,

---

[6] This timing of the final agreement was mentioned in Chapter 17 in connection with the pricing of underwritten stock issues. See p. 407.

a rate advantage could be enjoyed in long-term borrowing. But since the early 1930's, long-term rates for specific classes of borrowers have persisted at higher levels than comparable short-term rates—except for brief intervals, the yield curve, as we say, has been continuously upsweeping. An upsweeping yield curve indicates that corporations and other borrowers can economize in interest payments by borrowing for short terms even though the money is to be used for long-term purposes. If money is needed for 20 years, why not borrow for one year at the lower rate, borrow elsewhere for another year at the end of the first to repay the original loan, and so continue throughout the 20-year period? But corporate managements do not see it this way. For one thing, short-term borrowing for long-term purposes would weaken their working capital ratios, probably endangering their access to trade credit, inventory loans, and the like. Another consideration is the danger of insolvency—the danger of not being able to refinance the loans on schedule annually, as in periods of tight money. Finally, there is the possibility that the whole schedule of interest rates will rise; though the yield curve might still be upsweeping after two or three years, the short-term rate for a given borrower at that time might be higher than the rate for a bond issue would have been originally.

An upsweeping yield curve or pattern of interest rates means that, for given classes of borrowers, higher and higher rates must be designated the longer the maturities of their obligations. A corporation of a certain credit ranking can expect to pay a higher interest rate on a ten-year bond issue than on one for five years, a higher rate on a 20-year issue than on one for 15 years, and so on. This suggests a more practical means of economizing than annual borrowings and repayments. Corporations can save interest expenses from year to year while given bond issues are outstanding by not overestimating the periods for which long-term funds will be needed. Often corporations have put out bond issues running for 20 years and longer only to find that they could devote a sufficient amount of the cash throw-offs from depreciation and earnings to retire the bonds in much shorter periods. Had they made the maturities of the bond issues 10, 12, or 15 years in the first place, therefore, their annual interest charges while the bonds were outstanding would have been less.

The practical aspect of this for the generality of corporations was indicated by a strong trend toward shorter maturities for many years up to the early 1950's, followed by a moderate movement in the opposite direction. In the early years of the present century, maturities of 40 and 50 years and longer were common, but nowadays new bond issues with maturities beyond 30 years are exceptional. Often, indeed, corporations put out bond issues of 15- and 20-year maturities even when the proceeds are to be used to acquire assets expected to have lives much longer than that. The individual corporation expects to pay off a portion of such an issue during the initial period, and then to float a new issue to obtain funds to pay off the balance at its maturity, that is, as we say, to "refund" the balance.

When yield curves are upsweeping, a further means of economizing in interest payments is to issue bonds having staggered maturities. Such "serial bonds," as they are called, will be examined a little later in the discussion of bond maturities.

Importance of Timing

Because a bond interest rate, once set, must be paid during the entire life of the bonds, regardless of what may happen to market rates of interest during that period, and because the whole schedule of market rates fluctuates upward and downward with changes in the overall demand for and supply of long-term funds, care in the timing of bond issues is important. Suppose, for example, that a corporation puts out a 20-year bond issue bearing an interest rate of 4 per cent, and that, within a year or two, the market rate for bonds of similar quality goes to 5 per cent and stays in that vicinity for a lengthy period. The corporation's managers would have good reason to be pleased with their timing. The corporation would continue to pay 4 per cent on its outstanding bonds, while other corporations of comparable credit standing would have to pay 5 per cent on theirs were they to be borrowing in the later period. The differential of 1 percentage point could represent quite a handsome saving; for example, it would amount to $200,000 a year if the corporation's bond issue amounted to $20 million. On the other hand, the corporation's managers would have reason to regret their poor timing were they to put out the bond issue at 4 per cent and then find market rates for bonds of the same quality and maturity falling to 3½ per cent within a period of a few months. Better forecasting, they might conclude, should have indicated the desirability of a deferment of the financing or, perhaps, the desirability of short-term interim financing to be repaid out of the proceeds of a deferred bond issue.

A difficulty of timing is that long-term interest rates—and, in truth, the whole schedule of interest rates—tend to be relatively low in periods of business recession and depression, and to be relatively high in periods of prosperity and boom. In the periods of recession and depression, however, expansion projects are neither pressing nor attractive for most businesses, and, of course, their very lack of demand for funds is a principal reason why interest rates fall. Thus, advantage of the low rates cannot be gained by most corporations. Some, however, borrow "new money" for expansion projects despite the cloudy outlook; and a larger number sell "refunding" issues—they borrow at the low rates and use the proceeds to retire earlier issues bearing higher interest rates. In periods of business expansion, the renewed attractiveness of facility acquisition projects prompts corporations to hurry into the market to get long-term funds, but their very demand causes interest rates to rise. Probably most managements take the attitude that, though they missed the opportunity to borrow at the lowest rates, they had better go ahead with the financing before rates move to still higher levels. Some, however, decide that a rise in rates is temporary; at such times, accordingly, we hear that the financing of this or that corporation has been postponed. And, of course, in many cases a rise in rates brings them to a level above anticipated rates of return on expansion projects, so that common sense demands that the projects be postponed or abandoned.

Interest Rates and Bond Prices

From what was said a little earlier about nominal and effective rates of interest on bond issues, one should see that a corporation can agree to pay a certain effective rate without actually naming this rate in its bond certificates and indenture. On a 15-year issue, for example, it could set a 5 per cent rate, but, by selling the bonds at 94.94, actually provide the investor a yield of 5½ per cent. Other combinations of prices and nominal rates could similarly be chosen to give an effective rate of 5½ per cent on a 15-year issue, such as a nominal rate of 4½ per cent and a price of 89.88, a rate of 5¼ per cent and a price of 97.47, a rate of 5¾ per cent and a price of 102.53, and a rate of 6 per cent and a price of 105.06.

All this suggests that careful pricing may give some advantage in selling even though it is not designed to alter the effective rate and has no such result. Offering bonds at prices below par, in particular, tends to enhance their attractiveness to certain classes of investors. Small investors sometimes feel that they are getting a bargain in being able to buy "at a discount." But more important is the fact that large investors who report their income for tax purposes on a cash basis may report as a long-term capital gain, rather than as ordinary income, the difference between the price paid and the price at which a bond is redeemed (provided that it has been held by the taxpayer for more than six months).

Income Bonds

Outstanding at the present time are a few issues of bonds upon which the interest obligation need not be met currently if earnings are insufficient to cover it. These issues are known as "income bonds," although the word *income* does not necessarily appear in their titles. For example, the 4 per cent "adjustment" bonds of the Atchison, Topeka & Santa Fe Railway Company, due in 1995, are of the income variety.

Features of Income Bonds. Since interest is payable currently on income bonds only if earned, a failure to pay for lack of earnings is not a default—it does not give the bondholders and their trustee the right to take action to force payment, as by seeking judgment or forcing a reorganization in bankruptcy. As a rule, last year's earnings determine how much interest is to be paid this year. The indentures for income bonds set down in considerable detail rules for determining what amounts of earnings are available for bond interest. Whatever earnings are determined to be available by the application of these rules *must* be used in meeting the interest obligation up to the full amount of the coupon rate. If the earnings are sufficient to meet only a part of the obligation, they must be so used. Some indentures provide, however, that interest need be paid only in "round amounts," such as even ¼ or ½ percentage points or multiples thereof.

In some indentures, interest unpaid for lack of earnings cumulates fully and must be paid when earnings become available or, if the insufficiency of earnings continues, at maturity when the principal comes due. But a corporation that, for lack of earnings, has a big accumulation of interest to pay at maturity may find it impossible to pay either the accumulation or the principal. In other indentures, interest accumulates for only three years or thereabouts; if, therefore, earnings still do not materialize, the interest payment obligation goes into suspension, as it were, although the three-year accumulation or whatever it may be is still added to the principal as an absolute obligation at maturity.

It is stipulated in some indentures that interest may be paid upon the bonds at the discretion of corporate directors even though sufficient earnings are not available; and in some it is provided that certain events will make the interest obligation a fixed one, as in other classes of bonds, or that the corporate directors may simply make a decision to fix the interest obligation.

Finally, income bonds, like other bonds, have fixed dates of maturity—the obligation of a corporation to pay principal (and unpaid cumulative interest) at that time is not subject to deferment, regardless of the state of earnings.

Reasons for Use. Prominent among the reasons for the use of income bonds has been to speed the process of corporate reorganizations, particularly of railroad companies. Several of the issues now outstanding originated in the railroad reorganizations of the 1890's and the 1930's. In a reorganization, a major objective is to cut down substantially upon the fixed charges to which the rehabilitated enterprise will be subject. It presumably got into difficulties because of the disproportion between its debt burdens and its earning capacity; hence, it would benefit little if it emerged from reorganization with the same debt burdens. One way to cut down upon these burdens is to make what was formerly a fixed interest obligation a contingent one. Thus, income bonds have been, as it were, forced upon bondholders and other creditors having weak claims—upon the holders of the bankrupt enterprises' "junior obligations."

More recently, some interest in income bonds has developed among the managers of solvent corporations as having important possibilities as substitutes for preferred stock. Several corporations have offered income bonds to their preferred stockholders in exchange for their shares, and a few have sold issues of income bonds and used the proceeds to retire their outstanding preferred stocks. Some details of a sampling of these issues, as well as of the older reorganization issues, are presented in Table 26–1. It will be noticed that Armour & Company offered a very large issue of income bonds in 1954 in exchange for its outstanding $6.00 cumulative preferred stock. In fact, it has been more enthusiastic about income bonds than most other companies, having sold an earlier issue of 3½ per cent income bonds to a group of insurance companies in 1947. Of this earlier issue, which comes due in 1972, the amount outstanding on January 15, 1963, was $10,120,000. In view of their not unfavorable experience with income bonds in reorganizations, railroads have shown considerable interest in using income issues in less trying circumstances, especially for the replacement of preferred stocks. Recent issues of railroad income bonds—all turned out in the late 1950's—include those of the Gulf, Mobile & Ohio, the Missouri-Kansas-Texas, the Monon, the St. Louis-San Francisco, and the Virginian. The offer of the Gulf, Mobile & Ohio of income bonds in exchange for its preferred stock, originally made in 1957, has been left open on a continuing basis to the present time. Outside the railroad industry, however, no strong move in the direction of income bonds is apparent.

Income Bonds and Preferred Stocks. The big argument in support of the replacement of preferred stocks with income bonds, or the issuance of income bonds in the first place in lieu of preferred stocks, is the deductibility of bond interest for income tax purposes. Whenever a corporation meets its interest payments on income bonds, whether currently or after a delay, its interest costs are cut approximately in half by the tax saving; it gains no such benefit when it pays dividends on preferred stock. At the same time, its solvency is not endangered by the nonpayment of interest currently, just as it is not endangered by the nonpayment of dividends on preferred stock. And it is argued that people who are willing to invest in preferred stocks should be all the more willing to invest in income bonds, especially if, in the latter, the interest is fully cumulative. Their claim to interest is stronger than would be their claim to dividends as preferred stockholders: the interest must be paid if earned, whereas preferred dividends need not be paid, regardless of the size of earnings. Unpaid interest must be paid at maturity if not before; while the corporation has no obligation to pay preferred dividends at any time. Finally, the principal of income bonds comes due at a fixed maturity, while preferred stock has no maturity.

But an equally big argument against new financing with income bonds by solvent corporations is simply lack of investor appreciation of their alleged merits. People buy income bonds that have stood the test of time, but they appear to have little enthusiasm for new issues. If corporations of unimpeachable credit standing were to decide in large numbers to put

TABLE 26–1
Some Outstanding Issues of Income Bonds

Corporation and Bond Description	Amount Outstanding[a]	Year Issued	Purpose of Issue	Fraction Payable	Cumulation	Record of Payments[b]
American Steel & Pump Corporation, income 4s, Series A, due 1994..........	$ 2,566,000	1954	To pay off notes and for working capital	To extent earned	Fully from 4/1/56	1956–58—4% 1959—1% 1960—7% 1961–62—4%
Armour & Company, cumulative income subordinated debenture 5s, due 1984......	56,055,720	1954	Offered in exchange for $6.00 cumulative preferred	To extent earned	Fully	1955—4.05% 1956—5.95% 1957–62—5%
Atchison, Topeka & Santa Fe Railway Company, adjustment gold 4s, due 1995....	40,153,000	1895	Reorganization	To extent earned	Fully from 7/1/1900	Regularly except for 6-month delay in 1938
Chicago Great Western Railway Co., general income 4½s, due 2038..........	2,741,580	1938	Reorganization	To extent earned	13½%	Regularly
Chicago Railway Equipment Company, cumulative income subordinate debenture 6 2/3s, due 1986[c]........	2,225,100	1956	To retire 7% preferred stock	To extent earned	Fully	Regularly
Gulf, Mobile & Ohio Railroad Co., general mortgage income 5s, Series A, due 2015....	5,974,600	1940	Reorganization	¼%	15%	Regularly
Trans World Airlines, Inc., subordinated income debenture 6½s, due 1978..........	107,023,614	1961	To pay off interim notes issued to buy aircraft	To extent earned—need not pay if less than ¼%	Fully	1961—3.124%[d] 1962—nil

[a] As of December 31, 1962, except Atchison, December 31, 1961; American Steel & Pump, November 30, 1962; and Armour, January 15, 1963.

[b] Through 1962. An interest rate following two or more years means annual payment at this rate.

[c] Assumed in 1961 by American Seal-Kap Corporation in merger.

[d] Interest payment for approximately six months.

SOURCE: Moody's Investors Service, *Manuals*.

out income bonds, doubtless investor interest would increase enormously. But such corporations, if they want bonds in their financial structures to gain tax advantages or for other reasons, are not likely to hesitate to put out bonds with the time-honored fixed obligation to pay interest every six months. As long, therefore, as corporations of this description avoid income bonds, there is a suspicion that corporations that do issue such bonds must have serious misgivings as to their capacity to pay interest regularly.

MATURITY

Single Maturities

In the typical corporate bond issue sold at a given time, all the bonds have a single maturity date. Such an arrangement is reasonable for corporations that plan to trade on the equity indefinitely, expecting to put out new issues to raise money to pay off old ones as the latter come to maturity. This has been the traditional policy of public utility and railroad companies, although a recent trend in the policy of some of these enterprises is to plan for at least partial retirement during the life of their issues. In some instances, the policy of partial retirement has been adopted voluntarily, and, in others, as a result of the prodding of government regulatory commissions. Most industrial corporations, on the other hand, plan for a continuous procedure of retiring their bonded debt so that all but minor fractions will have been redeemed by final maturity dates. They agree to include in their indentures sinking fund provisions calling for periodical contributions aimed at this objective. A common sinking fund arrangement, for example, requires annual or semiannual allocations of cash for bond redemption such that equal portions of the issue will be retired in each of these periods and all by the final maturity. Thus, the sinking fund provisions for a 20-year issue would require an annual cash allocation sufficient to retire 5 per cent of the whole issue, or a semiannual allocation sufficient to retire 2½ per cent of the whole issue. The fulfillment of such a sinking fund requirement would mean, therefore, that only 5 per cent or 2½ per cent would still be unredeemed at the maturity date.

A policy of gradual redemption of a bond issue during the period of its life is in keeping with the doctrine that the simple common stock form of financial structure is the most desirable one for industrial corporations. According to this point of view, long-term borrowing is a substitute for financing with common stock or earnings, necessitated by unfavorable conditions in the market for common stocks or by temporary weaknesses in corporate earnings positions; thus it follows that a program of substantial periodic reductions in the debt is appropriate. The fact that facilities acquired with the proceeds of bond issues depreciate supports this view, especially from the standpoint of investors. As the assets wear out through use and the action of the elements, the argument runs, the debt through which they were acquired should be continually reduced.

For single-maturity bond issues registered with the SEC for public offering in the period 1950–61, the most popular maturity was 30 years. As shown in a study published by the Federal Reserve Bank of Philadelphia, this maturity accounted for 26.4 per cent of the dollar volume of such registrations. Second in popularity was 25 years accounting for 19.7 per cent of the registrations, followed by 20 years with 17.5 per cent, 15 years with 7.2 per cent, 12 years with 6 per cent, and 35 years with 3.2 per cent. Issues with maturities exceeding 25 years were largely those of public utility corporations supplying electric, gas, and sanitary services.[7]

Serial Maturities

If a corporation plans to retire equal portions of a bond issue annually or semiannually during its life, so that only a small fraction of the total, such as 5 per cent, will be left for redemption at maturity, why does it not set different maturity dates for different portions of the issue? For a 20-year issue, why not give 5 per cent of the bonds a one-year maturity, another 5 per cent, a two-year maturity, and so on up to a final 5 per cent having a 20-year maturity? As was mentioned earlier in this chapter, bonds having their maturities arranged like this are known as "serial bonds."

Advantages of Serial Issues. It was also stated earlier that, in periods of upsweeping yield curves, an advantage of serial issues is a reduction in interest expense. With all the bonds of a 20-year issue dated to mature in 20 years, all must be given a relatively high long-term rate; but with some dated to mature in one year, some in two years, and so on, a graduated scale of rates up to the top long-term rate could be provided.

Another advantage would appear to be a widening of the investment attractiveness of the bonds. Many investors do not want 20-year bonds; some want only short-term outlets for their funds, some want intermediate-term outlets up to five years, some are satisfied to go to ten years, and others to 15 years. Bonds having serial maturities, then, could appeal to each of these groups of investors.

A third advantage is that premiums need not be paid upon the redemption of serial bonds, whereas the payment of premiums is not uncommon in the periodic redemption of most of the bonds of single-maturity issues. If an investor really wants a long-term outlet for his funds, he may hesitate to buy a *callable* 20-year bond, since the call feature indicates that he may be able to retain the bond only for a much shorter period; hence comes the idea that the corporation may be able to overcome this hesitation by promising to pay a premium on redemption

---

[7] Federal Reserve Bank of Philadelphia, *Business Review*, February, 1963, pp. 14–17.

before maturity to compensate the investor for the trouble of having to find a new outlet for his funds. But if a person buys a serial bond coming due in two years, that must be precisely when he wants the principal returned to him; hence, he deserves no special compensation when it is returned at that time.

Use of Serial Issues. To gain these advantages, many corporations do put out serial issues, although the practice is not nearly so widespread as one might expect. Virtually all the issues of railroad companies to finance the acquisition of locomotives and cars (issues called "equipment-trust certificates" for special reasons to be examined in the next chapter) are serial issues, and a large number of the issues of "notes" sold by industrial companies by private placement also have serial maturities. But the use of serial issues elsewhere in corporate financing is slight, although of outstanding importance in the financing of state and local governments.

Patterns of maturities for serial bonds often vary from issue to issue. While railroads usually set semiannual or annual maturities for equal portions of their issues beginning six months or a year after the date of issue, maturity patterns of the privately placed serial issues of industrial corporations are subject to wide variations. Sometimes the earliest maturities are set two or three years after the date of issue, and sometimes unequal amounts are scheduled to mature on the different dates, usually, when this is the case, the larger amounts in later years. To illustrate a pattern of uniform maturities, the Series No. 21 equipment-trust issue of $8,100,000 of the Southern Pacific Company offered in June, 1963, may be cited. Its contract called for equal annual redemptions of $540,000 of certificates. The certificates were offered to the public at various prices to give yields as follows:

Maturity	Yield	Maturity	Yield
May 1, 1964	3.50	May 1, 1970	4.05
May 1, 1965	3.70	May 1, 1971	4.10
May 1, 1966	3.80	May 1, 1972–73	4.15
May 1, 1967	3.90	May 1, 1974–76	4.20
May 1, 1968	3.95	May 1, 1977–78	4.25
May 1, 1969	4.00		

Disadvantages of Serial Issues. The principal reason why business corporations, particularly industrials, have not made greater use of serial maturities in their publicly offered bonds, despite their obvious advantages, appears to be the fear of defaults. A default upon any maturity of a serial issue is a grave occurrence; if not corrected quickly, it is likely to require the slow and costly procedure of reorganization in bankruptcy, with a complete or partial loss of ownership interests by the stockholders. But the failure of a corporation to make a sinking fund payment as prescribed in an indenture for a single-maturity bond issue, while also a serious default, is not likely to have such dire consequences —at least, not so quickly. Bondholders and their trustees are inclined to look rather tolerantly upon sinking fund defaults, tending to be generous in allowing time for their correction.

Another reason for the limited use of serial issues, especially by industrial corporations, is custom. Traditionally, bond issues have been long-term obligations—not a mixture of short-, intermediate-, and long-term obligations. This tradition was long buttressed by the fact that, before the 1930's, long-term interest rates were often below short-term rates for lengthy periods of time, so that the use of the serial device would have meant increased interest costs, rather than reduced ones, as in periods of upsweeping yield curves.

Difficulties in quoting prices and in effecting transactions in serial bonds subsequent to their issue constitute a further disadvantage of serial issues. It is customary to give an entire serial issue a single nominal rate of interest (4 per cent in the Southern Pacific issue just cited) but to vary the selling prices of the several maturities to give varying effective rates according to the pattern of prevailing yield curves. If the prevailing yield curves are upsweeping, the earliest maturity will be given the highest price, the final maturity the lowest price, and the intervening maturities prices scaled downward between these extremes. Through the life of the issue, therefore, each maturity will ordinarily continue to require price quotations different from those of all other maturities. Moreover, buyers and sellers of serial bonds do not simply want to buy and sell bonds of the Blank Corporation—a given buyer wants to acquire an eight-year maturity, and a given seller has a 12-year maturity to offer for sale. For this reason, the market for certain maturities may be quite thin, even though overall supply and demand may be substantial; this makes for difficulty in bringing buyers and sellers together at prices they regard as reasonable. Because of quotation and transactions difficulties of these kinds, some of the stock exchanges, including the New York Stock Exchange, refuse to list serial bonds.

Questions

1. Of the six features of bonds mentioned early in this chapter, which would probably be lacking in a corporation's long-term promissory notes? in its "debentures"?

2. In general terms, state what goes into a bond indenture. Why is it convenient to have such a document separate from the bond certificates?

3. In what ways does the trustee of a bond issue protect the interests of the bondholders? How is this protective role treated in the federal Trust Indenture Act of 1939?

4. Aside from its protective role, the trustee of a bond issue ordinarily provides what services to the corporate issuer of the bonds?

5. What is a coupon bond? How does the bondholder collect interest on such a bond? What are the mechanics of transferring it, if he wants to sell?

6. How does the bondholder collect interest on a bond registered as to principal? registered as to both principal and interest? What are the mechanics of transferring bonds of these two registered classes?

7. What have been the principal arguments supporting the recent "trend" toward the replacement of coupon bonds with registered bonds?

8. When bonds are bought and sold between interest-payment dates, how does interest enter into such transactions, if at all?

9. As a determinant of the interest corporations must pay on new bond issues, how is the "state of the market" measured or evaluated?

10. How is it possible to determine the "market rate" on treasury long-term obligations in periods when the Treasury is not selling any new long-term obligations?

11. Why can some corporations sell new bond issues with interest rates only a little above the yield on treasury long-term obligations, while others must promise interest payments at much higher rates?

12. At times when short-term interest rates are much lower than long-term rates, would it not be advisable for corporations to borrow on a short-term basis even for long-term purposes? Explain. Would not serial bond issues be useful in holding down the total cost of borrowing? Explain.

13. If a corporation sells a 5 per cent bond issue to investment bankers at 97, why is its cost of borrowing said to be more than 5 per cent?

14. How do the interest-payment provisions of "income bonds" differ from those of bonds not so described? To what two uses have income bonds been chiefly put? Why have they not been more popular?

15. What advantages are claimed for serial bonds? To what extent are they used in corporate financing? Why are they not used more extensively?

Problem

Since all the Southern Pacific equipment-trust certificates described on page 647 of this chapter bore interest at the uniform nominal rate of 4 per cent, which of the maturities must have been offered to the public at par, at prices above par, and at prices below par? For which maturity must the offering price have been the highest? for which the lowest? What must have been the shape of the prevailing "yield curve" at the time these certificates were offered for sale?

chapter 27

SECURITY FOR BOND ISSUES

In the bargaining between corporations that want to issue bonds and investment bankers, institutional investors, and other prospective buyers of the bonds, the question of "security" is a matter of great importance. A corporation provides "security" for a bond issue by pledging some of its assets, very carefully designated, for the safety of the bondholders. All classes of bonds for which there are pledges of assets of one kind or another are known collectively as *secured bonds,* while those that lack pledges are described as *debenture bonds.*

With secured bonds, title to the pledged assets may be transferred to the trustee, or the trustee may simply be given a lien upon them. Whatever the procedure, the theory of security is that, should the corporation default upon its obligations to the bondholders, the trustee may sell (or seize and sell) the pledged assets and use the proceeds to pay off the bondholders' claims to interest and principal. Only after the bondholders' claims have been fully satisfied can these proceeds be used to meet the claims of other creditors. It is possible, however, for certain claims against the corporation to rank ahead of those of holders of bonds for which security has been provided—claims given preference in federal and state bankruptcy laws and state insolvency laws, such as those for unpaid taxes and wages and for the expenses of administration during the period of bankruptcy. On the other hand, the seizure and sale of pledged assets, if insufficient to meet the bondholders' full claims, does not relieve the corporation of liability for the unsatisfied portion. It had promised to pay full principal and interest, and not simply the amount recoverable through the sale of pledged assets.

GENERAL ASPECTS OF SECURITY

Influence upon Indenture Terms and Provisions

Whether or not security is provided for a bond issue usually has important influence upon many of the terms and conditions set forth in the indenture. Often the provision of security means that bond buyers will be willing to take a rate of interest lower than they would otherwise demand. Sometimes, in fact, they would not buy the bonds, whatever the rate of interest, were security not to be provided. In many cases, too, the question of security has important bearings upon what the maturity of the bonds shall be. Security or the lack of it significantly influences the kinds of protective provisions an indenture shall have, the rights that a corporation will want to reserve to itself, and what special inducements it may offer to promote sales. As was mentioned in the preceding chapter, security is itself a protective provision, and it may also be regarded as a special kind of feature to promote sale. But the influence of security upon indenture provisions is so pervasive that it hardly lends itself to treatment simply as a protective provision or as a selling feature; hence, the separate, detailed treatment planned for this chapter.

But a word of caution: the influence of security must not be exaggerated. Bond buyers want payment of interest and principal in the regular course of business by solvent corporations. In deciding whether or not to buy, therefore, they are likely to give much more attention to a corporation's present and prospective working capital position and to its earning power than to the character and value of assets pledged. They realize that the terms *safety* and *security* do not necessarily mean the same thing—that the debenture bonds of a corporation of strong financial position and excellent earning capacity are likely to be much "safer" than the secured bonds of another whose financial position and earning capacity are considerably weaker. They know, too, that after default there are likely to be long and troublesome delays in realizing upon pledged assets even though ultimately their claims may be fully satisfied. And they also recognize the possibility that, after long and troublesome delays, they may incur losses because the cash realized in liquidating pledged assets may prove to be much less than the value of the assets as originally pledged or as reduced by ordinary depreciation.

Attitudes of Corporate Managements

The typical corporate management, in bargaining about a bond issue, would doubtless prefer to avoid a pledge of assets. But managerial reluctance, of whatever degree, is not insuperable; this is proved by the existence of hundreds of secured bond issues in the United States at the present time. Corporate managements are surely inclined to yield when salability of issues is found finally to depend upon their willingness to pledge assets; and they are often persuaded to pledge assets as a means of obtaining concessions, such as lower interest rates or less oppressive sinking fund requirements. Custom, too, is an important factor in determining whether or not given kinds of bond issues, as well as varying kinds as sold in given industries, will be secured. Railroads of the highest credit standing provide security for their equipment-financing issues no less than do those of much weaker credit positions. Likewise, a tradition of providing security is much stronger in the railroad and public utility industries than among manufacturing and merchandising corporations.

At any rate, competent corporate managements can hardly be expected to pledge assets without a careful weighing of the pros and cons. Any pledge restricts freedom of action. Certain kinds of actions with respect to pledged property may be forbidden in the indenture, and permission of the trustee may be required for others. Restrictions upon further issues of secured bonds may be accepted as entirely reasonable at the time an indenture is drawn up, only to prove quite unrealistic with changing circumstances in later years. A pledge of assets, too, tends to weaken further debt-incurring capacity. Prospective unsecured creditors, such as commercial banks, trade suppliers, and investors in debenture bonds, are likely to conclude that, to satisfy their own claims in case of default, little would be available from assets pledged to secured bondholders; hence, they are likely to be less liberal in extending loans or credits and more rigorous in setting terms and conditions for their advances than they would be were there no pledges.

WHAT IS PLEDGED

Mortgages on Real Property

Land, buildings, machinery and equipment, and other things more or less inseparably attached to land and buildings (in the sense of not ordinarily being movable) are the kinds of property most commonly pledged as security for bond issues. Property of this description is known at law as *real property* or *realty*, and it is pledged by means of *real mortgages*. The popular usage, however, is to designate simply as *mortgage bonds*, rather than as "real mortgage bonds," issues secured by real property.

(In connection with the following discussion of mortgage bonds, reference to Table 27–1 should be helpful. In the table are presented some details about a sampling of outstanding mortgage issues, including details of types of indentures, the after-acquired property clause, and limitations on further issues—topics to be taken up a little later in this chapter.)

Priority of Mortgage Claims. A corporation may pledge all or almost all of its real property as security for a single bond issue, or separate parcels for separate bond issues; moreover, it may pledge a portion of its properties for a bond issue and other portions as security for loans negotiated with banks or other financial institutions. When the property pledged on a bond issue has not already been pledged to secure other obligations, the bondholders are said to have a "first mortgage" or a "first lien"—terms which simply indicate that there is no prior mortgage claim.

However, it is possible for a corporation to pledge the same property successively on two or more bond issues or loan contracts, so that lenders

TABLE 27-1
Some Outstanding Issues of Mortgage Bonds

Corporation and Bond Description	Year Issued	Amount Outstanding[a]	Type of Indenture	After-Acquired Clause	Limitations on Further Issues
Commonwealth Edison Company, first mortgage, Series L through U, rates, 3-4⅝%, due 1977-90	1944-60	$590,000,000	Open	Yes	Permitted to ⅔ of lesser of cost or fair value of property acquired after 12/31/44; available earnings in 12 out of 15 preceding months must equal 2½ times interest requirements on all bonds to be outstanding.
Cudahy Packing Company, first sinking fund 2⅝s, Series C, due 1967	1947	6,549,000	Limited open $30,000,000	Yes	Permitted to 60% of lesser of cost or fair value of property acquired after 10/31/43; earnings for not less than 2 nor more than 5 years shall have averaged 2½ times interest requirements on all bonds to be outstanding. Limitations on cash dividends only.
Jones & Laughlin Steel Corporation, first mortgage			Open	Yes	
Series A, 2¾s, due 1967	1947	32,500,000			
Series B, 3s, due 1975	1950	18,958,000			
Series C, 5s, due 1983	1958-59	40,000,000			
Series D, 4⅜s, due 1987	1962	50,000,000			
Louisville & Nashville Railroad Co, first and refunding mortgage, Series F through I, rates, 2⅞-3¾%, due 2003	1944-54	150,115,000	Open	All property acquired with proceeds of these bonds	Total bonds and prior liens not to exceed 3 times capital stock; no maturities before 4/1/2003 or after 4/1/2121.
Northern States Power Company (Minn.), first mortgage, in series, rates, 2¾-5%, due 1974-92	1944-62	295,529,000	Open	Yes	Permitted to 60% of lesser of cost or fair value of property acquired; earnings in 12 consecutive months out of preceding 15 equal to 2 times interest requirements on bonds to be outstanding.
Pittsburgh Steel Company, first mortgage 5s, due 1975	1955	25,750,000	Limited open $50,000,000	Yes	Consent of holders of ⅔ of present series required for further issues.

[a] As of December 31, 1962, except Louisville & Nashville Railroad, December 31, 1961.

SOURCE: Moody's Investors Service, *Manuals*.

on a second pledge would be said to have a second mortgage or lien, those on a third pledge of the same property, a third mortgage or lien, and so on. In the event of a sale of pledged property after a default, the proceeds are used first to meet the full claims of the holders of the first mortgage, and then, to the extent possible, to meet the full claims of the holders of the second mortgage, and so on. If the proceeds are only enough or are less than enough to meet the full claims of the holders of the first mortgage, the "security" of the second and subsequent mortgages is proved to be worthless. If a corporation that has, say, three successive mortgages on the same property pays off the obligation for which the first was given, the mortgage previously in the second position becomes a first mortgage, and that previously in the third position becomes a second mortgage.

First mortgages are often described as "senior" or "underlying" liens, and second and subsequent mortgages, as "junior" or "overlying" liens. The "underlying" and "overlying" designations are used especially in reference to the financing of railroads.

Value of Property Pledged. Prospective investors in mortgage bonds (and in other classes of secured bonds, as well) can generally be expected to insist that the value of property pledged be substantially in excess of the face amount of the bonds to be issued. These investors know that prices obtainable in the market for property seized and offered for sale to satisfy debts are likely to be much less than the "going-concern" values of the same property as carried on the books—that, indeed, defaults are most likely to occur in periods of general business depression when markets will probably be weak. On the other hand, allowance is usually made for the adaptability of the pledged property for alternative uses. When highly specialized property is pledged, bond buyers may insist that the bond issue be limited in amount to 50 per cent of the value of the property; but when the property is highly adaptable, they may be willing to agree to an issue equal to 75 or 80 per cent of its value. The most common limits to the size of bond issues in relation to the value of pledged property appear to be 60 and 66⅔ per cent.

Such limits apply also, of course, when the same property is pledged successively for two or more bond issues. Were a corporation, for example, to pledge property worth $20 million for a bond issue of $5 million, it might not have much difficulty in selling a second-mortgage issue of $4 million, and even an additional third-mortgage issue of $3 million. But were the first-mortgage issue $12 million, it is likely that the repledging of the same property for a subsequent issue would add little to its attractiveness. This would not mean that the second issue could not be sold, but that investors would be likely to regard a proposed second-mortgage issue as of the same standing as a debenture issue.

How Pledges Are Made. In pledging real property for the security of a bond issue, a corporation may transfer its title to the trustee or simply give the trustee a lien upon it, depending upon the law of the state in which the mortgage is executed. In the "title-theory states," a corporate mortgage, like any other mortgage, is a conveyance of title, and it reads much as if it were a deed. However, it contains a *defeasance* or *defeating clause* that says in effect that the transfer of title shall be void if the corporation fulfills its obligations as set out in the indenture. In a title-theory state, it might seem that, upon default, the trustee, having title, could immediately sell the pledged properties for the benefit of the bondholders; nevertheless, the title-theory states prescribe certain kinds of *foreclosure* proceedings that the trustee (or other mortgagee) must take to make the transfer of title "absolute." In the "lien-theory states," the giving of a mortgage by a corporation places in the hands of the trustee a prior claim to the property for the satisfaction of the bondholders' claims, but title remains with the corporation. In the event of default, the trustee, to get title, must likewise follow through with a "foreclosure" procedure. Accordingly, the requirements for foreclosure in both classes of states, as well as defeasance clauses in mortgages in the title-theory states, tend to give mortgages much the same complexion regardless of the individual state's "theory."

Possession and Use. Although the term *mortgage* means literally a "dead pledge," real property mortgaged in a bond indenture actually remains very much alive. Indenture provisions invariably stipulate that the corporation shall have "possession and use" of the pledged property as long as it does not default upon its obligations. Even after default, possession and use continue until foreclosure actions have been completed, if, indeed, the trustee chooses to take such actions. It is important for the bondholders that the corporation's earning power be not impeded by restrictions upon the regular productive use of the mortgaged property, so that making the property a "dead pledge" would clearly be contrary to their own interests.

However, possession and use do not require freedom to sell pledged properties piecemeal or in bulk or to combine them with those of other corporations as in mergers and consolidations. Hence, restrictions upon actions of these kinds are commonly found in indentures. Piecemeal sales are usually permitted so that a corporation can get rid of items of property that are no longer useful to it. But permission of the trustee is normally required, and there is usually a stipulation that property purchased in replacement will be pledged under the existing indenture or that the cash proceeds of piecemeal sales will be used for bond retirement if replacement is not contemplated. Bulk sales of all or most of the mortgaged property and combinations by way of mergers and consolidations are sometimes forbidden, but, much more often, the indenture simply provides that such transactions can be effected only if the buying or successor corporation accepts responsibility for all the indenture obligations of the corporation that issued the bonds.

Pledges of Personal Property

At law, all kinds of movable property, tangible and intangible, are classified as *personal property* or *personalty*. The classification includes many kinds of (movable) factory, store, and office equipment, "rolling stock," such as locomotives, cars, trucks, busses, and airplanes; and inventories, accounts receivable, cash, stocks, and bonds. Any such property may be pledged as security for bond issues by means of *chattel mortgages*, the term *chattel* being simply a synonym for the term *personal property*.

Actually, however, personal property ordinarily classified in business practice as "current assets," such as inventories and accounts receivable, is rarely pledged for bond issues. These kinds of personal property are too volatile to serve conveniently as pledges for long-term obligations, although they are frequently pledged as security for short-term loans obtained from commercial banks and other lenders. When movable factory, store, and office equipment is pledged, it is generally included with real property in issues of ordinary "mortgage bonds," although, to be sure, separate parcels are often pledged individually for specific loans, ordinarily intermediate in term.

Thus, we have left rolling stock and stocks and bonds as kinds of personal property that appear to be independently available for pledge purposes in connection with bond issues. The fact is that these two kinds of personal property do serve as security for almost all secured bond issues that lack pledges of real property. Accordingly, we may give our attention specifically to what are called, in the case of rolling stock, *equipment obligations*, and in the case of pledged stocks and bonds, *collateral-trust bonds*.

Equipment Obligations. Some railroads and other transportation companies, especially airlines, obtain part of the purchase price of their rolling stock by selling bond issues for which this equipment is pledged by means of chattel mortgages. Such mortgages are customarily called "equipment mortgages" to distinguish them from mortgages by which real property is pledged.

For the acquisition of rolling stock by railroads, however, the most common arrangement by far is the issuance of "equipment-trust certificates." The arrangement is known as the "Philadelphia Plan." Let us assume that a railroad wants to buy a group of locomotives which will cost $6 million. It gives its specifications to the manufacturing company. When the locomotives have been built, they are delivered to the railroad, but title to them goes to a commercial bank or trust company chosen to serve in the capacity of trustee. The railroad enters into a *lease* contract with the trustee, agreeing to rent the equipment and to pay an advance rental and periodical rents sufficient in total to meet principal and interest requirements on the equipment-trust certificates that are to be issued.

The advance rental or "down payment" usually ranges from 10 to 25 per cent of the cost of the equipment; in this case, let us say that it is 20 per cent, or $1,200,000. Accordingly, an issue of equipment-trust certificates is sold to raise the balance of the purchase price, $4,800,000. The proceeds of the sale of the certificates and the advance rental payment of the railroad are used, of course, to pay off the manufacturing company.

The equipment-trust certificates are obligations neither of the railroad nor of the trustee; rather, they represent participations in the ownership of the locomotives. They thus resemble stock. Indeed, the return on such instruments is often described as a "dividend" rather than as "interest." But, unlike stock, they have maturity dates. As in the Southern Pacific issue referred to in the preceding chapter, the invariable procedure is to provide serial maturities—ordinarily with equal amounts to be retired semiannually or annually over a period that most commonly ranges between 10 and 15 years. For our illustrative issue, certificates of $160,000 would be set to mature semiannually if semiannual redemption over a 15-year period were provided for. Unlike most stocks, too, equipment-trust certificates have guaranties. Our railroad would endorse the certificates with a guaranty of the payment of interest (dividends) periodically and the face amounts at their respective maturities. This kind of endorsement coupled with the obligations under the lease justifies the classification of equipment-trust certificates as bonds rather than as stocks. Railroad corporations include them among their long-term debt, and investors think of them essentially as debt instruments rather than as participations in ownership.

When our railroad company had made its rental payments faithfully over the 15-year period of the lease, the trustee would transfer to it the title to the locomotives. It would then have paid for them in full. Were it to default along the way, the trustee, as owner, could seize the locomotives and sell or rent them to another line. No time-consuming foreclosure procedures, as for pledged property, would be necessary. Moreover, the trustee should have no difficulty in finding a buyer or renter whose payments would be sufficient to take care of the certificates still outstanding. As 20 years or more is the expected useful life of locomotives, the rapid pace of certificate retirement by comparison with the pace of depreciation, together with the railroad's advance rental or down payment, generally assures an ample margin between the declining book (and market) value of the equipment and the volume of certificates still outstanding. In terms of our illustration, the book value at the time of the issuance of the certificates was $6 million, the cost of the locomotives, but the debt was only $4,800,000; thus there was a margin of safety of $1,200,000 provided by the advance rental. Allowing for depreciation on a 20-year straight-line basis, the book value at the end of one year would be $5,700,000, but the debt, after the retirement of the first two maturities, would be down to $4,480,000; five years after issue, the book value would be $4,500,000, but the debt would have been reduced to $3,200,000; and ten years after issue, while the book value of the locomotives would be $3,000,000, the remaining debt would be only $1,600,000. It appears, therefore, that the margin of protection should be ample throughout the life of the certificates.

The principal reason why railroads have favored financing with equipment-trust certificates rather than with equipment mortgages is the presence of "after-acquired property clauses" in existing indentures for outstanding mortgage bonds. As we shall see in a later discussion, such a clause automatically extends the lien of an existing mortgage to newly acquired property. In using the Philadelphia Plan, however, the railroad does not take title to new locomotives and cars until they have been fully paid for; therefore, during the period of payment—the period of the lease —the equipment is held, as it were, out of the reach of the after-acquired property clause. The buyers of equipment-trust certificates can be given the protection of what amounts to a first lien, whereas the lien could be no better than a second or a subsequent one were the railroad to take title immediately and issue equipment-mortgage bonds. A weak railroad already "mortgaged to the hilt" would probably not be able to sell equipment-mortgage bonds at all, or only on terms severely unfavorable to itself, but its equipment-trust certificates may well be grabbed up by investors of the most conservative classes—precisely because of the first-lien feature and the other protective aspects that have been described.

Collateral-Trust Bonds. Collateral-trust bonds, secured by pledges of stocks or bonds or both, used to be an extremely important kind of financing instrument, especially in the public utility and railroad fields; among other things, they served as a most useful building block in the erection of massive, many-tiered holding company "empires" in these two fields. Would-be empire builders might start out by establishing Corporation A to fill the role of a pure public utility holding company. They would have it sell nonvoting preferred stock and probably a minority portion of its common stock to the public, keeping a majority of the common shares for themselves. With the proceeds of sales of stock, Corporation A would buy up a controlling common stock interest in Corporation B, an operating public utility company. Then A would put out an issue of collateral-trust bonds, with the stock of B as the collateral, and use the proceeds to buy a controlling common stock interest in Corporation C, another operating company. Then C's stock could be put up as security for a second collateral-trust issue, the proceeds to be used to buy up common stock of another operating company. Along about this time, the promoters of A—the empire builders—might decide to set up a second-degree holding company, let us say, Corporation X. They would have X sell an issue of nonvoting preferred stock and some of its common stock to the public, but the majority portion of X's common stock they would issue to themselves in exchange for their holdings of A's common stock.

In this way, X would have cash from the sales of its own stock to be spent in buying up controlling interests in other companies, perhaps, like A, first-degree holding companies; and, of course, it would have A's stock available as collateral for an issue of collateral-trust bonds to raise additional cash for the same purpose.

This kind of thing could go on and on. In the 1920's, it did go on and on—not necessarily precisely according to the pattern just outlined, but certainly according to patterns not far different. In the old Associated Gas & Electric Company "empire," for example, there were twelve layers or tiers of holding companies! But many of these pyramids got into financial difficulties in the depression of the 1930's, and some even earlier than that, discrediting their builders as well as their means of financing, including collateral-trust bonds. And opportunities for further pyramid building or rebuilding, regardless of the methods of financing, appear to have vanished forever, because of the strict regulation of railroad holding companies by the Interstate Commerce Commission under the Emergency Transportation Act of 1933 and of public utility holding companies by the Securities and Exchange Commission under the Public Utility Holding Company Act of 1935, as well as the strict disclosure requirements of the Securities Act of 1933.

All of which does not deny that there have been and are less spectacular uses of collateral-trust bonds. Some corporations do own controlling common stock interests in other corporations; if, wishing to borrow by means of bond issues, they must provide security, they have every reason to offer to pledge these common stock interests. Other corporations own stocks and bonds without having controlling interests in the issuers of these securities, and they, too, may legitimately pledge these as collateral for their own issues. Some corporations have financed the operations of their subsidiaries by buying the latters' mortgage bond issues and using these as security for their own collateral-trust issues. They have done this when able to get better terms on single large issues of collateral-trust bonds than would have been available to the subsidiaries were their small issues of mortgage bonds to be offered to the public individually. Some corporations have financed their own operations by putting out collateral-trust bonds with some of their own mortgage bonds pledged as security— when the former could be sold on better terms or on a basis more attractive to investors than could the latter. Moreover, stocks and bonds are not infrequently pledged in given indentures as important additions to pledged real property, as is indicated by bond titles such as "first-mortgage and collateral-trust bonds."

Nevertheless, collateral-trust bonds, as a distinct type of debt instrument, have been relegated to a minor role in the financing of industrial corporations, public utilities, and railroads. Of the scattering of issues at present outstanding, a sampling with some descriptive facts is presented in Table 27–2.

TABLE 27–2

Some Outstanding Issues of Collateral-Trust Bonds

Corporation and Bond Description	Year Issued	Amount Outstanding[a]	Property Pledged
Chicago Great Western Railway Company, collateral-trust 3⅞s, due in 1969................	1954	$ 2,441,000	$8,750,000 of railroad's own first 4s, Series A, due 1988; may be withdrawn to the extent they exceed 175% of collateral-trust bonds.
Louisville & Nashville Railroad Company, collateral-trust 4⅞s, due 1987................	1962	25,000,000	Chiefly $30 million of L. & N. Series K first and refunding mortgage 5s of 2003; 83.29% of capital stock of Louisville, Henderson & St. Louis Railway Company; and 49.46% of capital stock of Nashville and Decatur Railroad Company.
New York Central Railroad Company, collateral-trust 6s, due 1980................	1955	25,190,500	For each $100 of collateral-trust bonds, $150 of Central's refunding and improvement 5s, Series C, due 2013, and 1 share ($100 par value) of Boston & Albany Railroad Company.
Collateral-trust 5¼s, due 1980................	1955	209,800	For each $100 of collateral-trust bonds, $100 of Central's bonds as described above and 1 share of Pittsfield & North Adams Railroad Corporation.
Northeastern Water Company, sinking fund collateral-trust 5½s, due 1986[b]................	1961	15,000,000	Entire capital stock of 22 subsidiaries, and 1,962,700 shares of American Water Works, Inc.
Northern Pacific Railway Company, collateral-trust 4s, due 1984................	1954	40,501,000	Initially, $78 million of railroad's own refunding and improvement 4s, Series E, due 2047, with withdrawal rights as collateral-trust bonds are redeemed; also right to substitute other bonds with at least equal liens.

[a] As of December 31, 1961, except Louisville & Nashville and Northeastern Water, December 31, 1962.
[b] Assumed by American Water Works, Inc., by merger in 1962.
SOURCE: Moody's Investors Service, *Manuals*.

General or Blanket Mortgages

Particularly common in railroad and public utility financing is the practice of pledging in single indentures "everything in sight" except current assets. For a given bond issue, the corporation may pledge all its real property, all its movable equipment including rolling stock, its patents and franchises, and its holdings of stocks and bonds (except short-term government obligations in which cash is temporarily invested when in surplus supply). Though bond issues of this description have real mortgage, equipment-mortgage, and collateral-trust features simultaneously, they are usually classified simply as "mortgage bonds," for the good reason that the value of pledged realty usually far exceeds the value of pledged personal property. In popular parlance, however, such bonds are often said to be secured by "general" or "blanket" mortgages to distinguish them from issues having simple real or chattel mortgages.

But one must not read too much meaning into a word such as *general*, especially if one is looking at the titles of older railroad issues. A goodly number of these continue to be outstanding, although many railroads have made great progress in the last three decades in simplifying their debt structures. At any rate, a bond issue of a public utility described as a general mortgage is very likely to have a first lien on all its operating properties and intangibles as mentioned in the preceding paragraph, but an older railroad issue so described could well have quite a different kind of standing.

In the heyday of railroad finance, fancy titles for bond issues were selected unconscionably, and, as a rule, it was *de rigueur* to get the word *first* in somehow so that unwary investors would have visions of a first lien. Thus, a "first general mortgage" might actually represent quite inferior liens. A railroad might have pledged Parcel A of its properties on two successive "divisional" bond issues; Parcel B, on three; and Parcel C, on two. Yet its management would feel free to call a later bond issue for which all three parcels were pledged a "first general mortgage," because this would be the first time that the properties "in general" had been pledged upon a single issue. Obviously, therefore, the word *first* modified "general" and not "mortgage," for the new bonds would have only third liens on Parcels A and C, and a fourth lien on Parcel B. Similarly, Railroad X may have pledged all its properties on two successive bond issues, and Railroad Y, also on two. The two railroads having been subsequently merged, a new bond issue might be planned. Would it be called a "third-mortgage" issue? Decidedly not. Much better sounding would be a title such as *first consolidated mortgage*. But we need not look at all such attractive titles. Two more examples should suffice. The title *first refunding mortgage* indicated that at least part of the proceeds of the bond issue was to be used to retire one or more earlier issues, but the investor could have been in serious error were he to conclude that, as a result of the retirement, he would have a first lien on the railroad's property. In the title *first and general mortgage,* the "first and" indicated that a first lien on some part of the railroad's property was being given to the buyers of the bond issue; but this parcel might be of minor importance and value, while the "general" portion of the mortgage might represent second, third, or subsequent liens on the rest of the railroad's property.

SIGNIFICANCE OF SECURITY

In the course of the preceding discussion, repeated references were made to the sale of pledged property for the satisfaction of bondholders' claims, but the point was also made that, except for equipment-trust certificates, "long and troublesome delays" are likely to occur in connection with the enforcement of these claims. The delays are chiefly occasioned by efforts of defaulting corporations to work out means of settlement that will preclude the seizure and sale of their assets, the most significant means of settlement being the procedures of reorganization according to the terms of the federal bankruptcy laws.

To understand the significance of security for bondholders, therefore, it is desirable to consider, first, how bondholders' claims of various priorities are met if assets are actually liquidated, and, secondly, what influence these priorities have in procedures for reorganization.

Satisfaction of Claims by Liquidation

The extent to which bondholders are protected by "security" when the assets of an insolvent corporation are actually sold to satisfy creditors' claims may best be seen in a series of illustrations. For this purpose, let us assume that at the time of its default a certain corporation had current assets valued on its books at $20 million and fixed assets valued at $25 million, and that, at the time of final settlement, its debts were as follows:

Current liabilities...	$12,000,000
First-mortgage bonds......................................	10,000,000
Second-mortgage bonds....................................	5,000,000
Debenture bonds..	4,000,000

For the sake of simplicity, we may assume that none of the current liabilities have preferences in liquidation as provided for in the bankruptcy laws and that none have been secured by pledges of assets—that all, therefore, have equal standing as unsecured claims. For convenience, also, let us assume that the amount shown for each of the four classes of liabilities includes all unpaid interest to the date of settlement; in this regard, it is to be remembered that interest claims rank with claims to principal, both being equally secured or unsecured, as the case may be. Finally, let us assume that all the fixed assets were pledged for the security of the first-mortgage bonds, and then repledged under the indenture for the second-mortgage bonds.

First Illustration. For a first illustration, let us say that the current assets realize in liquidation $18 million, and the fixed assets, $7 million. The latter amount would be devoted to meeting the claims of the first-mortgage bondholders, and their unsatisfied claims of $3 million would be added as an unsecured claim against the balance of the assets. (The corporation promised to pay them $10 million; it did not promise to pay them only what could be realized out of the pledged assets; hence, the unsatisfied portion of their claims remains as a corporate obligation.) The holders of the second-mortgage bonds would get nothing out of the proceeds of the sale of the pledged assets, so that their entire claims of $5 million would simply be added to all others against the unpledged assets. Accordingly, the total claims against the $18 million realized from the liquidation of the current assets would amount to $24 million (first-mortgage bonds, $3 million; second-mortgage bonds, $5 million; debenture bonds, $4 million; and current debts, $12 million). Thus, all classes of creditors except the first-mortgage bondholders would receive 75 cents on each dollar of their claims. For each dollar of first-mortgage claims, the bondholder would receive 70 cents from the liquidation of the pledged assets plus 75 per cent of his remaining claim of 30 cents, or 22.5 cents, for a total of 92.5 cents.

Second Illustration. For a second illustration, let us say that the current assets are liquidated for $15 million, and the fixed assets, for $13 million. Out of the latter amount, the claims of the first-mortgage bondholders could be completely satisfied, so that they would receive 100 cents on the dollar. In addition, $3 million of the claims of the second-mortgage bondholders could be met out of the sales proceeds of the pledged assets, leaving them with unsecured claims of $2 million against the balance of the assets. Thus, there would be total claims of $18 million against the cash realized from the liquidation of the current assets, so that a settlement at 83⅓ cents on the dollar could be made. For each dollar of his claims, a second-mortgage bondholder would receive 60 cents from the liquidation of the pledged assets and 33⅓ cents on the balance of his claim of 40 cents. Thus, recovery per dollar of claims would be as follows: first-mortgage bondholders, 100 cents; second-mortgage bond-holders, 93⅓ cents; and other creditors, 83⅓ cents.

Third Illustration. To make our concluding illustration extreme—but still realistic in terms of what could happen in a period of severe depression—let us assume that the current assets realize only $9 million, and the fixed assets, only $4 million. The latter amount would go entirely to the first-mortgage bondholders, leaving them with unsatisfied claims of $6 million to be added to those of the other creditors. The claims of the holders of the second-mortgage bonds would shift entirely to the "general" or "unsecured" classification, bringing the total to $27 million. Accordingly, the $9 million realized from the liquidation of current assets would permit a settlement at the rate of 33⅓ cents on the dollar. Thus, the recovery of the first-mortgage bondholders, per dollar of claims, would amount to almost twice that of the creditors of all other classes; it would be 60 cents on the dollar—40 cents from the pledged assets plus 20 cents from the unpledged ones.

Conclusions. Certain general conclusions as to how owners of bonds fare in liquidations can be drawn from the foregoing illustrations: (1) Except when pledged assets are absolutely worthless, holders of first-mortgage bonds always get a better settlement than do other classes of creditors (disregarding creditors whose claims are "preferred" in the bankruptcy statutes, as well as those to whom other assets may have been pledged, as short-term lenders having liens on inventories). (2) Nevertheless, first-mortgage bondholders may suffer severe losses, as in the third example—security does not give complete assurance against loss. (3) Depending upon the liquidating values of pledged assets, holders of bonds with second and subsequent liens may or may not benefit from these liens. (4) Holders of debenture bonds have claims no stronger than those of other unsecured creditors.

Claims in Reorganizations

For the reason that many corporations that default upon their obligations take quick steps to prevent the seizure and sale of their properties by creditors and their trustees, the consideration just given to the satisfaction of claims in liquidation might appear to be of theoretical interest only. Not so, however. It is true that corporations that get into severe financial difficulties are inclined to hurry to the federal courts to start proceedings for reorganization in bankruptcy, and that creditors and their trustees are held off from seizure and sale to give the courts time to study proposed plans of reorganization. It is true, also, that other corporations that find themselves in financial trouble, especially smaller ones, try to work out with their creditors informal arrangements for postponing settlement and even for the scaling down of their obligations—often with the implied threat likewise to petition for reorganization in bankruptcy, should the creditors be reluctant to bargain.

But the federal courts can hardly be expected to approve plans of reorganization unless these plans treat fairly all classes of creditors according to the priority of their respective claims. In judging fair treatment, the courts are likely to give considerable weight to the liquidation value of assets—to what each class of creditors would receive were the corporation to be dissolved rather than to be reorganized. These conclusions appear to follow from the decision of the Supreme Court in *Case* v. *Los Angeles Lumber Products Co.*,[1] in which it established what is called the absolute-priority doctrine for reorganizations. In an approved plan of reorganization, therefore, first-mortgage bonds, because of their prior claim to pledged assets, may remain "undisturbed," which is to say, having

---

[1] 308 U.S. 106 (1939).

claims of the same scope in the corporation as reorganized as they had previously. But other creditors, in view of the relative weakness of their claims, may be less generously treated. The holders of second-mortgage bonds may be offered debenture bonds in the reorganized corporation, or possibly such bonds for part of their claims, and preferred or common stock for the balance; and the holders of debenture bonds and other unsecured creditors may be offered some combination of new bonds and preferred or common stock, or possibly preferred or common stock solely. If new bonds are given to second-mortgage bondholders and to debenture bondholders and other unsecured creditors, some or all of them may be of the "income" variety, with interest to be payable for a period of years or indefinitely only if earned. In this way, therefore, what each class of creditors gets in a reorganization by comparison with what other classes get is likely to match rather closely the proportion of cash it would probably get were the corporation to be liquidated and dissolved.

In reorganization proceedings, the liquidation value of assets and the respective priorities of creditor classes are important for another reason. Although such proceedings temporarily hold off creditors and their trustees from the seizure and sale of assets, the court must be satisfied that the adoption of a proposed plan of reorganization will restore the corporation to good financial health and enable it to stay well (solvent) for a lengthy period. In numerous instances, this is not the finding of the court, so that proceedings for reorganization are switched to proceedings for liquidation and dissolution—whereby, in effect, seizure and sale actually do take place.

Moreover, liquidation values of assets and rankings of creditors' claims are immediately of controlling importance in many business failures. Often the financial difficulties of corporations, especially those of small and medium sizes, are so grave that no effort is made to reorganize; liquidation and dissolution, whether in bankruptcy or by way of less formal procedures, are decided upon at the outset.

OPEN-END AND CLOSED INDENTURES

Many corporations, when they first borrow by means of secured bond issues, have only moderate amounts of assets available for pledging and have only moderate needs of funds, but they anticipate further needs of long-term funds as they grow and acquire additional properties. Sometimes they pledge the original assets for bond issues of small size, and then, with each major addition to assets, have new indentures drawn up pledging the new properties for separate bond issues. Each such indenture is a *closed* one: all the bonds that it authorizes are immediately sold, so that later issues are necessarily outside its scope. But the procedure of using successive closed indentures soon results in a complex financial structure. There is a separate trustee for each indenture, and the individual indentures, being agreed upon at different times and under varying circumstances, are likely to differ from one another in restrictions, concessions, and other provisions. The procedure tends to be unduly expensive, and compliance with many different indenture conditions quite burdensome.

A better procedure would appear to be to have the original indenture permit the issuance of additional bonds from time to time subject to strict limitations. Such an indenture may be an *open-end* one wherein no specific dollar amount is stated as the authorized bond issue; or it may be a *limited open-end* one wherein a maximum dollar amount is stated, but an amount much greater than that of the original issue. (See Table 27–1 for examples of these two types.) Under an open-end indenture of either variety, the successive batches of bonds have equal rank; all the assets as successively pledged secure all the bonds equally, regardless of when they may have been issued. A first group of bondholders has no greater claim on the assets first pledged than have buyers of bonds issued later under the open-end indenture; nor do buyers of later issues have greater claims on assets pledged after the original pledge than has the first group. However, a limited open-end indenture becomes "closed" when the maximum stipulated amount of bonds has been issued.

But investors in bonds issued under open-end indentures demand safeguards. Early buyers of bonds, knowing that investors in subsequent batches will have equal rank with them, fear excessive total issues. The safety of their bonds could be dissipated by the corporation's lack of restraint in selling further batches. Although, therefore, they may agree to no dollar limit or to a high dollar limit in the indenture, they will surely insist that limits be set in other ways. On the other hand, they are ordinarily willing to concede that differences in circumstances at the times various batches of bonds are sold may justify differences in interest rates, maturities, and call prices.

Earnings Limitations

Many open-end indentures, such as those of Commonwealth Edison, Cudahy, and Northern States Power, as indicated in Table 27–1, contain restrictions upon further issues of bonds in terms of earnings available for bond interest. The most common kind of earnings limitation provides that additional bonds may be issued only to the extent that earnings actually available for bond interest in some past period equaled some multiple of the interest requirement on the total amount of bonds *to be outstanding* after the new issue. The multiple generally ranges from 2 to 4, and the test period is usually a rather short one immediately preceding the date of the proposed new issue. In the Commonwealth Edison indenture, for example, the stipulation is that earnings available for bond interest in 12 of the preceding 15 months must have equaled $2\frac{1}{2}$ times the interest requirement. Sometimes alternative test periods are designated; for example, it may be stipulated that the corporation may issue additional bonds if earnings available for bond interest in ten of the preceding 12 months *or* on the average in the preceding three years were equal to three times the interest requirement.

Property Limitations

Further issues of bonds under open-end indentures are often restricted, not only in terms of earnings available for bond interest, but also in terms of the value of property pledged. The most popular kind of restriction on pledged property simply stipulates that additional issues of bonds under the indenture must not exceed some percentage, such as 60 or 70 per cent, of the cost or "fair value" of additional property pledged, whichever of these measures of value is less. For example, a corporation whose indenture has a 70 per cent restriction may put out an original bond issue of $7 million upon pledging assets worth $10 million. If, later, it wanted to buy additional facilities at a cost of $4 million, it could meet part of the purchase price by issuing bonds of a face value of $2.8 million. The total pledged assets of $14 million would then protect total outstanding bonds of $9.8 million: the older bonds would have equal ranking with the later issue in claims against the new assets, and, likewise, the later issue would have equal ranking with the original one in claims against the assets originally pledged.

Property limitations sometimes take other forms of which the following are examples: (1) The total of outstanding bonds shall not exceed working capital or some percentage of it. (2) The total shall not exceed the par or stated value of outstanding stock, both common and preferred, or some percentage or multiple of this figure (as in the Louisville & Nashville Railroad issue). (3) The total shall not exceed the book value of stock and surplus, or some percentage or multiple. (4) *Total debt* shall not exceed 33⅓ per cent, 40 per cent, or some other percentage of total tangible assets. In some indentures, these kinds of restrictions—one or more—are used in addition to the kind of property limitation described in the preceding paragraph; and in others, they are used in lieu of it. It will be noticed that a restriction of the fourth type, as listed here, has the effect of limiting the amount of debt of all kinds and maturities, and not simply the amount of secured bonds.

Separate Application of Earnings and Property Limitations

Where indentures contain both earnings and property limitations on further issues, as is the common practice, the usual rule is that the stricter standard governs. To see how this works, let us return to the illustration in which the application of a 70 per cent property limitation was demonstrated. Let us assume that the indenture also provides that additional bonds may be issued only if earnings available for bond interest in a designated test period were equal to three times the interest requirement on total bonds to be outstanding. Assume that the original bonds bear interest at 5 per cent, that the same rate would be paid on the additional bonds that the corporation proposes to issue, and that test-period earnings available for bond interest amounted to $1,350,000. Although, therefore, the property restriction would permit the issuance of $2.8 million of bonds, as we have already seen, the application of the earnings restriction would cut this figure to $2 million. Three times the interest requirement of $350,000 on the bonds already outstanding is $1,050,000. This amount subtracted from $1,350,000 leaves $300,000 which is three times the amount of interest that the corporation is permitted to pay on additional bonds. The actual amount of interest permitted would be $100,000, and, at a rate of 5 per cent, this would allow for only $2 million of bonds ($100,000 ÷ .05).

Variations in Terms

Original investors in bonds to be issued under an open-end indenture are likely to be quite willing to give the corporation latitude in fixing for later issues interest rates, maturities, and call prices for redemption different from those of the original issue. The very authorization of further issues argues that the corporation should be empowered to tailor its successive offerings in keeping with changing conditions in the market for long-term funds.

Under a single open-end indenture, accordingly, a corporation might sell a first issue having an interest rate of 4½ per cent, a 20-year maturity, and call prices ranging downward from 103; a second issue with an interest rate of 4 per cent, a 15-year maturity, and call prices graduated downward from 102; and a third issue having an interest rate of 5 per cent, a 25-year maturity, and call prices ranging downward from 105. For separate issues with varying terms under a single indenture, a corporation is likely to use "series" labels. Thus, the 4½ per cent bonds would be labeled Series A, the 4 per cent issue, Series B, and so on. In the Commonwealth Edison mortgage issues, for example, it will be observed that separate "series" (L through U) were sold in the period between 1944 and 1960, and that interest rates on these varied between 3 per cent and 4⅝ per cent.

Restrictions in Closed Indentures

Except for priorities of claims, as for taxes and wages, allowed for in the bankruptcy statutes, buyers of bonds issued under a closed indenture have no cause to fear that other creditors will get claims upon the pledged property prior or equal to their own. Without their consent, the corporation cannot give such prior or equal claims. Nor are they asked to permit variations in terms in later issues, since, by definition, there are to be no later issues under a closed indenture. Nevertheless, the owners of a corporation's closed-indenture bonds have reason to be concerned about the total amount and kinds of debts that it may contract. The corporation's default upon subsequently issued debenture bonds or upon bank loans or, in truth, upon its obligations to trade creditors would be anything but pleasant for the secured bondholders. Despite the priority of their position, they could anticipate a long period of reorganization or liquidation during which interest would not be paid on their bonds and in which both the accumulated interest and the principal would be in jeopardy.

To reduce dangers of default in any direction, therefore, prospective buyers of secured bonds issued under closed indentures do not hesitate to demand indenture restrictions upon the total debt or the total long-term debt that the corporate issuers may contract. Such restrictions are commonly in the form of one or more of the broad types of property limitations referred to previously, that is, limitations of total debt or of total long-term debt in relation to working capital, total tangible assets, capital stock, or capital stock and surplus.

AFTER-ACQUIRED PROPERTY CLAUSES

A danger that buyers of mortgage bonds want to guard against is the possibility that debtor corporations will shift the bulk of their operations to new properties and will pledge these new properties for bond issues under separate indentures. A corporation that has been operating in the North, for example, may build new facilities in the South and rapidly concentrate more and more of its operations at the new location, perhaps eventually discontinuing production in the North. Such a shift would not reduce in any way the corporation's obligations under the original mortgage indenture; but, *in case of insolvency*, the lien on the original properties would be likely to be of little value. Thus, the position of the bondholders for whose safety these properties had been pledged could hardly be much better than that of unsecured creditors.

Accordingly, investors in mortgage bonds usually insist upon the inclusion in indentures of "after-acquired property clauses." Such a clause obligates the corporation to pledge under the indenture all property "hereafter acquired" of a character identical with or similar to that already pledged. To fail to pledge newly acquired property of this description would be a violation of a covenant no less than the nonpayment of interest or principal; upon such an occurrence, the trustee could take legal action to safeguard the bondholders' position.

Application in Open-End Indentures

After-acquired property clauses, one might say, go hand in hand with open-end indentures (including limited open-end ones in which the maximum dollar figure is set quite high). As the use of an open-end indenture envisages the sale from time to time of additional bonds to finance property acquisitions, and as its property limitation is likely to stipulate what amount of bonds in relation to the value of added pledged property may be issued, it is not likely to be a hardship *to be required* to pledge the newly acquired property. Such a requirement could be a hardship, however, if the earnings and property restrictions in the existing indenture were unduly severe.

Application in Closed Indentures

Not infrequently, after-acquired property clauses find their way into closed indentures, although their presence there may appear to be quite illogical. Newly acquired property must be pledged under the existing indenture, but additional bonds having the same rank as the existing ones cannot be issued. If the new property is pledged for a separate bond issue, only a second lien can be given.

Sometimes corporate managements, particularly those of manufacturing enterprises, accept after-acquired property clauses for their closed indentures, because they have few prospects of acquiring additional properties of a value that would justify further bond sales. Sometimes they accept such clauses because they look upon the bond financing as a temporary departure from the simple common stock form of financial structure which they plan to restore as quickly as possible: they expect to have the bonds retired before occasion arises for substantial additional acquisitions of property. In some cases, no doubt, the after-acquired property clause is forced upon corporations in weak bargaining positions, and even though their managements anticipate that it will be the source of difficulties in future financing. And it appears that, at least in a few cases, the after-acquired property clause is accepted by corporate managements, as it were, inadvertently—without their realizing its consequences for future financing.

Avoidance of After-Acquired Property Clauses

Many writers upon corporation finance give much attention to ways whereby corporations may acquire property, or its use, without making it subject to the liens of existing indentures containing after-acquired property clauses. But investment bankers, institutional investors, and other bond buyers know of these means of "avoidance" no less than do corporate managements and their attorneys. When prospective investors, therefore, anticipate that specific means of avoidance, if employed, would be harmful to them, they insist that the indentures contain covenants expressly precluding their use. But when, on the other hand, no harm is expected to result from the employment of certain means of avoidance, the investors may be willing specifically to allow them by indenture provisions or they may be satisfied to consent by silence—to have the indentures say nothing about them.

One means of avoidance is to lease property rather than to buy it outright, as in the Philadelphia Plan in acquiring railroad rolling stock. Another is to establish subsidiaries and have them acquire the new property. Another is to give to the sellers of newly acquired property "purchase-money mortgages" for the noncash part of the purchase price. The liens of such mortgage obligations are held by the courts to have priority over the liens of bonds whose indentures have after-acquired property clauses. A fourth means is for the corporation to have its properties absorbed by another in a merger or consolidation, for the general rule is that after-acquired property clauses in indentures of absorbed corporations cease to operate. A final and quite obvious way is to call for redemption the bonds that have an after-acquired property clause that is proving to be obnoxious.

For protection against methods of avoidance that could prove harmful to their interests, bond buyers often insist upon indenture prohibitions or restrictions upon mergers, consolidations, the establishment and operations of subsidiaries, and certain kinds of leasing arrangements. Thus, a corporation may be required to stipulate in its indenture that it will not allow itself to be absorbed by another in a merger or consolidation unless the absorbing corporation will specifically agree to make subsequently acquired property (and perhaps even its existing property) subject to the lien of the existing indenture. On the other hand, bond buyers are usually willing to permit, or at least to have the indentures remain silent about, the leasing of equipment according to the Philadelphia Plan and the use of purchase-money mortgages. Acquiescence in the equipment-leasing arrangement is prompted by the very need of the corporation, say, a railroad, to have ready access to an adequate supply of locomotives and cars, the relative cheapness of financing by the equipment-trust procedure, and the fact that the existing bonds will get a first lien on the equipment when the corporation pays off the equipment-trust certificates and takes title to it. It is prompted in acquisitions involving purchase-money mortgages because the existing bonds get immediately a second lien on the property so acquired—property that the corporation otherwise might not want to acquire at all.

DEBENTURE BONDS

Although security for bond issues is the topic for discussion in this chapter, it is well to look at the other side of the picture—to consider the characteristics of debenture bonds which, as we know, are unsecured. Such a consideration should be worthwhile both because debentures issues are of great importance in their own right, in terms of number and size of issues, and because it should throw further light upon the significance of security.

It was said earlier that safety and security do not necessarily mean the same thing. In the liquidation of a corporation after a default, the holders of its debenture bonds can hardly expect to realize as much on their claims as will holders of its mortgage bonds and other secured creditors; and in a reorganization, the debenture bondholders must ordinarily expect to make greater sacrifices than will secured bondholders and other

secured creditors. In these respects, the secured bonds *of a given corporation* can almost always be said to be safer than the debenture bonds
of the same corporation. But the capacity of corporations to avoid
defaults—which, after all, is the final criterion of safety—obviously does
not depend upon whether or not their bonds are secured. It depends
upon their financial position in general and their earning power. Thus,
the debenture bonds of corporations of strong financial position and high
earning capacity almost invariably rank higher from the standpoint of
safety than do the secured bonds of corporations of weaker financial
position and more limited earning power. Moreover, the holders of debenture bonds are not without claims to assets. Like any other class of
creditors, they have legal rights to take action to seize assets for the satisfaction of their claims if unpaid when due. For this reason, the debenture
bondholders of a corporation that has no obligations for which it has
pledged assets may feel that their claim to assets is almost as good as it
would be were their bonds to have a mortgage lien—*almost* as good, because other unsecured creditors would have equal pro rata claims. But
even the "almost" would deserve little emphasis were the amount of other
unsecured claims quite small in comparison with the amount of the
debenture bonds.

Postwar Issues of Debenture Bonds

Truly amazing has been the volume of postwar financing that has been
effected with debenture bonds. Hundreds of corporations that confined
their long-term borrowing in the 1920's to mortgage issues—or that
would doubtless have put out mortgage issues had they been borrowing
for long terms in that decade—have found the postwar market strongly
receptive to their debentures. In the 1920's, substantial numbers of industrial and public utility corporations were successful in financing with
debenture issues, and, indeed, a kind of tradition developed that this
kind of financing is peculiarly suitable for industrials. But in the postwar years, though industrial corporations have been far in the lead in the
parade of debenture issuers, this parade has been greatly swelled by many
additional public utility corporations and even to a considerable extent
by railroad companies with which the tradition of long-term borrowing
only on secured issues has been strongest.

Not only the total amount of postwar debenture financing, but also
the size of individual issues or series of issues has often been startling.
The following are samples of the larger issues: Allied Chemical, $200
million; the Aluminum Company of America, four issues totaling $475
million; American Telephone and Telegraph, 24 issues for a total of approximately $7,277 million, including eight issues of convertible deben-
tures totaling approximately $3,967 million offered to the corporation's
common stockholders; Columbia Gas System, 21 issues for a total of
approximately $875 million; Commonwealth Edison, five series for a

total of $268 million; Continental Oil, $100 million; General Motors, $300 million; Northern Natural Gas, 15 series for a total of $382 million (including, incidentally, $72 million in four issues of serial bonds); Pacific Telephone and Telegraph (a subsidiary of American), 13 series aggregating $902 million; Sears, Roebuck, $350 million; Socony Mobil Oil, $200 million; Standard Oil of Indiana, $200 million; Standard Oil of New Jersey, two issues totaling $235 million; United States Steel, two issues for a total of $540 million; and Westinghouse Electric, two issues totaling $321 million.

For reference in relation to the following discussion, some of the features of two of these issues, as well as of some smaller ones, are described in Table 27–3.

Issuers of Debentures

So high is the esteem in which some corporations are held by the investment community that they are able to issue debenture bonds on terms as favorable to themselves as would be obtainable on secured bonds. For such corporations, the issuance of debenture bonds, rather than secured ones, is, as it were, a mark of distinction. Though these corporations may have vast aggregations of pledgeable assets, they are quite pleased to take the debenture route and thus avoid all the complexities that secured issues involve.

At the other extreme are corporations that, to borrow on a long-term basis, have no choice but to sell debenture issues—they have no assets that could be conveniently used for pledge purposes. Such is often the situation with merchandising corporations that rent all or most of their operating facilities.

In between are large numbers of corporations that might be able to get better terms with secured bond issues than with debenture issues but that, nevertheless, prefer the latter. This kind of choice is made by many manufacturing corporations. The managements of these corporations are often convinced that their access to short-term credit would be too greatly restricted should they pledge their fixed assets on bond issues; they want to avoid such a restriction because they are accustomed to depend heavily upon trade suppliers and banks as sources of current assets. Public utility corporations frequently put out debenture issues because of decisions that their existing mortgage debt is as large as it should be. Although they may have additional pledgeable assets, and although their open-end indentures would permit new series of mortgage bonds, they decide that proposed long-term borrowing, though justifiable under existing circumstances, does not fit in with their long-range standards for trading on the equity. Hence, they choose debenture issues as a kind of temporary financing, quite often setting the stage to eliminate them painlessly by making them convertible at the holder's option into common stock.

TABLE 27-3

Some Outstanding Issues of Debenture Bonds

Corporation and Bond Description	Year Issued	Amount Outstanding[a]	Equal and Ratable Clause	Limitations on Further Long-Term Debt
Canada Dry Corporation, sinking fund debenture 4s, due 1976	1956	$ 9,695,000	Applies, except for liens on property acquired of not more than 2/3 of cost or fair value	No added long-term debt if, thereafter, tangible assets minus current liabilities are not 250% of total long-term debt; if current assets are not equal to current liabilities plus greater of long-term debt or $12,000,000; and if annual average net earnings for 3 years preceding did not equal at least 450% of total interest on long-term debt (excluding subordinated debt) and average annual rentals on long-term leases.
Caterpillar Tractor Company, sinking fund debenture 4⅛s, due 1977	1957	61,750,000	Applies	No added long-term debt if, thereafter, tangible assets less current liabilities are less than 2½ times total long-term debt. Same rule applies to added investments in foreign subsidiaries.
Glidden Company, sinking fund debenture 4⅜s, due 1983	1958	30,000,000	Applies, except for purchase-money liens up to 2/3 of lesser of cost or fair value of property acquired	No added long-term debt unless, thereafter, total does not exceed 35% of net tangible assets.
Phillip Morris Incorporated, sinking fund debenture 4⅞s, due 1979	1959	40,000,000	Applies, except for purchase-money mortgages and existing liens on property acquired	No added long-term debt unless, thereafter, tangible assets less current liabilities equal at least 2 times total long-term debt.

Scovill Manufacturing Company, debenture 4¾s, due 1982.............	1957	8,709,000	Applies	No limitations.
Seaboard Air Line Railroad Company, sinking fund debenture 3⅞s, due 1977.........	1952	13,953,000	Applies	No added long-term debt unless available earnings in 12 out of 15 consecutive calendar months next preceding equal 3 times annual fixed charges on all long-term debt to be outstanding.
Sears, Roebuck & Company, sinking fund debenture 4⅜s, due 1983.............	1958	350,000,000	Company and subsidiaries may not pledge unencumbered assets	Limitations upon repurchases of stock by company and subsidiaries, leases of property, and so on. See also statement in preceding column.
Socony Mobil Oil Company, debenture 4⅛s, due 1993.............	1963	200,000,000	Applies, with some exceptions	Limitations on sale and leaseback of property of corporation and subsidiaries.

[a] As of December 31, 1962, except Seaboard, December 31, 1961; Sears, Roebuck, January 31, 1963; and Socony Mobil, April 30, 1963.

SOURCE: Moody's Investors Service, *Manuals*.

Protective Provisions for Debentures

Theoretically, a corporation can issue as many debenture bonds as people are willing to buy. If an original indenture is closed, a whole succession of additional indentures can be drawn up for further issues, and, because nothing is pledged, the buyer of a bond anywhere along the line has claims of equal standing with those of any other buyer, though the latter may have bought many years earlier. But original buyers of debenture bonds know of this theoretical possibility, and they are usually wise enough to insist upon indenture restrictions upon further indebtedness closely comparable with those contained in indentures for secured issues.

One danger that buyers of debenture bonds want especially to guard against is a weakening of their claims against corporate assets by pledges of these assets to *other* creditors after the debenture bonds have been sold. Accordingly, indentures for debenture issues commonly provide that if secured bonds are subsequently issued the existing debentures will be secured "equally and ratably." A corporation that first issues, say, $10 million of debenture bonds, and later sells $20 million of mortgage bonds, would thus really have a total issue of $30 million of mortgage bonds, and no longer any debentures, although the latter would probably still be alluded to by that designation. Often, too, indentures for debenture issues contain restrictions upon any other pledging of property, its leasing to other concerns, and sale-and-leaseback arrangements, usually, however, with an exception allowing for pledges upon bank loans and other short-term advances not exceeding in maturity some limited period such as one year.

Buyers of debenture bonds also want to have protection against the dangers of excessive unsecured debt whose claims would rank equally with theirs. The most popular way of getting this protection is to insist upon indenture restrictions limiting further issues of all classes of long-term obligations. Sometimes the restrictions are extended to further short-term as well as long-term indebtedness. As indicated in Table 27–3, restrictions upon further issues of bonds are often set down in terms of property and earnings limitations quite similar to those found in mortgage indentures. Thus, the indenture for the debenture issue of the Canada Dry Corporation provides that additional long-term or funded debt may not be contracted unless, thereafter, the total long-term debt does not exceed 40 per cent of the total tangible assets as reduced by current liabilities, and that it plus the current liabilities (or the current liabilities plus $12 million, if greater) does not exceed the amount of current assets; and unless earnings on the average in the preceding three years have been equal to at least 4½ times interest requirements on total long-term debt, excluding that subordinated, and average rentals on long-term leases.

As Table 27–3 reveals, some indentures contain a property limitation or an earnings limitation but not both simultaneously, and some contain neither of these kinds of restrictions upon the incurring of further debt.

Subordinated Debentures

Subordinated debenture bonds are so called because the indentures on the basis of which they are issued make their claims against assets in case of corporate dissolution or reorganization inferior to those of designated kinds of "senior debt." Whereas an ordinary debenture bond has claims inferior to those of a mortgage bond of the same corporation because of the pledge of assets given to the latter, the inferiority in the position of the subordinated debenture comes about because it is specifically provided for in its own indenture. The senior debt to which the claims of debenture holders are made inferior usually comprises all liabilities for borrowed money, whether short-term or long-term, and whether already contracted or contracted after the subordinated debentures have been issued. It includes, therefore, bonds of other classes, including ordinary debentures, and bank loans, whether secured or unsecured, but not accounts payable to trade creditors, accrued expenses, and dividends payable.

Although bonds with subordinated claims had sometimes been issued in corporate reorganizations long before the late 1930's it was not till then that the use of subordinated debentures as ordinary financing instruments began its development. They were introduced as such by sales finance and consumer finance companies—organizations whose principal function is to grant loans to individuals for consumption purposes. In the postwar period, the finance companies have expanded their use of subordinated debentures, but in recent years their issues have been swamped, so to say, in a great flood that has come from industrial corporations, particularly manufacturing enterprises. If the postwar development of financing with ordinary debentures has been amazing, the multiplication of issues of subordinated debentures has been all the more so. Hundreds of corporations have put out such issues, and their popularity appears to grow from year to year. Some facts about a small sampling of these issues are presented in Table 27–4.

Reasons for Use. For issuing corporations, the principal reason why subordinated debentures have grown so rapidly in popularity is that they serve excellently as a substitute for common and preferred stocks in providing protection for creditors. Their sale provides cash directly but also sets the stage for additional borrowing. This is so because the subordination of the claims of subordinated debentures extends not only to senior debt existing at the time of their sale *but also to that contracted thereafter.* Like sale of stock, therefore, a sale of subordinated debentures, by expanding a corporation's assets and presumably its earning power, should encourage other lenders to supply funds to the corpora-

TABLE 27-4
Some Outstanding Issues of Subordinated Debenture Bonds

Corporation and Bond Description	Year Issued	Amount Outstanding[a]	Limitations on Further Long-Term Debt
Boeing Airplane Company, convertible subordinated debenture 4⅛s, due 1980.	1958	$ 30,531,000	No added long-term debt of corporation and subsidiaries (other than convertible subordinated debentures) unless consolidated net assets equal at least 225% of consolidated long-term debt.
Burroughs Corporation, convertible subordinate debenture 4⅛s, due 1981.	1956	29,867,900	No added long-term debt unless, thereafter, tangible assets less current liabilities equal at least 200% of long-term debt.
J. I. Case Company, convertible subordinated debenture 5½s, due 1983.	1958	20,130,100	No added long-term debt unless, thereafter, consolidated net tangible assets equal at least 225% of long-term debt.
Collins Radio Company, convertible subordinated debenture 4¾s, due 1980.	1960	12,000,000	No added long-term debt of corporation or any subsidiary unless, thereafter, consolidated tangible assets (except subsidiaries' real estate) less consolidated current liabilities equal at least 175 per cent of consolidated funded debt.
Hunt Foods & Industries, Inc., subordinated debenture 4⅜s, due 1986.	1961	38,760,500	No limitations.
National Alfalfa Dehydrating & Milling Company, subordinated debenture 5s, due 1975.	1957	1,469,150	No new liens without securing these debentures equally and ratably (with some exceptions).
Phillips Petroleum Company, convertible subordinated debenture 4¼s, due 1987.	1957	171,117,000	No limitations.

[a] April 30, 1962, for National Alfalfa; June 30, 1962, Hunt Foods; July 31, 1962, Collins Radio; others, December 31, 1962.

SOURCE: Moody's Investors Service, *Manuals.*

tion. As with investors in stock, the buyers of subordinated debentures supply assets that serve as a "cushion" of protection for all other classes of creditors; and they contribute earning power to which, as it were, they give other creditors claims superior to their own.

An illustration will clarify the protective role of subordinated debentures for holders of corporate obligations designated "senior." Assume that the assets of a failed corporation are liquidated for $8,550,000 and that creditor claims at the time of final settlement are as follows (including interest where allowable and disregarding the possibility of preferred claims under the bankruptcy statutes):

Debenture bonds...	$ 4,000,000
Subordinated debenture bonds...............................	2,400,000
Unsecured short-term bank loans............................	2,000,000
Other unsecured short-term obligations......................	3,000,000
Total..	$11,400,000

Both the debenture bonds and the short-term bank loans qualify as "senior debt" as that category is defined in the indenture for the subordinated debentures. The cash realized in liquidation is sufficient to pay 75 cents on each dollar of all classes of claims, but most of the $1,800,000 first tentatively allocated to the subordinated debenture bondholders does not stay with them. At 75 cents on the dollar, the debenture bonds have an unsatisfied claim of $1,000,000, and the bank lenders, an unsatisfied claim of $500,000. Accordingly, to satisfy these claimants, in whose favor the claims of the subordinated debentures have been waived, a transfer of $1,500,000 is made to them from the $1,800,000 first assigned to the subordinated debentures. As a result, the "ordinary" debenture bonds and the bank loans are paid off in full; the holders of the subordinated debentures receive only $300,000 in settlement of their total claims of $2,400,000, or 12.5 cents on the dollar; and the "other" short-term creditors receive an unadjusted 75 cents on the dollar for a total of $2,250,000.

In issuing subordinated debentures, many corporations indicate their expectation that the debentures will serve only temporarily as a substitute for common stock financing. They indicate this expectation by making the debentures convertible into common stock at the option of the holders, and by setting conversion prices not very far above the current market prices of their common stocks. Why, then, does not a corporation sell common stock in the first place and be done with it? The answer in part is that, later in making conversions, it really gets a better price for the common stock than it would have got had it sold common at the time of offering the debentures. Another facet of the answer is that flotation costs upon the issue of subordinated debentures are likely to be considerably less than would be those of a common stock flotation. As long as the debentures remain outstanding, moreover, the interest rate paid upon them may be less than the dividend rate being paid on the common stock; hence, like any debt issue, they provide the advantages—and give rise to the dangers—of trading on the equity. Whatever the relationship between the interest rate and the dividend rate, indeed, there is always the consideration that interest is deductible for income tax purposes while dividends are not.

Appeal to Investors. But a security cannot be sold simply because it has features to the liking of many potential issuers; investors, too, must find it to their liking. It might seem strange that individuals and institutions would be willing to buy a *bond* that is expressly given an inferior status in its claims to principal and interest in the event of reorganization or dissolution. Why do they buy? The answer must be primarily that the interest rate is attractive and that the buyers do not expect the issuers' reorganization or dissolution.

If relatively conservative investors would be willing to buy a corporation's preferred stock issue, all the more should they feel safe in buying its subordinated debentures. They would buy the preferred stock in the expectation that the corporation would be able to meet all its maturing debts, that dividends at the prescribed rate, though payable at the discretion of the board of directors, would actually be earned and paid, and that any redemption fund provisions for the retirement of the stock would be fulfilled. In buying subordinated debentures, similarly, investors expect the corporation to have no difficulties in meeting its obligations upon them as well as upon all debts designated as "senior." The corporation's obligation to pay interest and principal is absolute; as long as it is able to pay, the "inferiority" of the bondholder's position is not at all apparent. Moreover, the indenture of a subordinated issue, like that for any other kind of bonds, will surely have various kinds of safeguards for the bondholders.

As for the interest rate, it is likely to be somewhat higher than the corporation would have to pay were it selling an issue of ordinary debentures, but not so high as the probable dividend rate were it selling preferred stock. Thus, the investor is allowed some compensation for the additional risks he accepts, but not so much as he could doubtless demand were he to accept the greater risks of ownership by becoming a preferred stockholder.

Making subordinated debentures convertible into common stock and offering a large proportion of these convertible issues direct to the issuers' existing common stockholders add greatly to their investment appeal. If satisfied with a corporation's earnings record, dividends, and prospects, its common stockholders are likely to be most interested in acquiring additional shares and willing to buy bonds as an indirect way of getting access to them. They could go into the market to buy additional shares at once, but they may be somewhat cautious about extending their common stock commitments. By buying the debentures, they can hold the relatively secure position of bondholders until the market price of the stock has risen well above the conversion price—or indefinitely should it never reach that level, or, indeed, should it fall.[2] At any rate, accustomed as common stockholders are to their quite risky position as residual claimants against assets, they may give little thought to the "inferior" position of subordinated debentures.

GUARANTEED BONDS

A bond is said to be guaranteed when one or more individuals or corporations other than the issuer guarantee the payment of interest, or principal, or both. Most guaranties extend to both principal and interest. According to accepted terminology, a corporation never guarantees its own bonds; it has the unquestioned obligation to pay interest and principal, but this is not described as a guaranty. Even with equipment-trust certificates which bear the guaranty of the railroad in whose behalf they are issued, the issuer, as we have seen, is the trustee rather than the railroad.

Some guaranties for bond issues are made at the time of the original sale of the bonds, and others come into being only after the bond issues have been outstanding for some time. The whys and hows that explain this difference in timing we may proceed to examine.

Guaranties from the Beginning

When one or more individuals or corporations other than the issuer guarantee the payment of interest and principal upon a bond issue at the time of its origin, the objective is almost always to make the bonds more attractive to investors than they otherwise would be. The credit position of the issuer is likely to be relatively weak, and, without the guaranty, the bonds might not be salable at anything close to what the issuer and guarantor would regard as fair terms, if salable at all. Therefore, the guaranty is expected to be of decisive importance in "toning up" the investment appeal of the bonds.

Guaranties by Individuals. Bond issues guaranteed by individuals are almost always of small size. They are generally the issues of small, closely held corporations, and the guarantors are usually one or more of the principal stockholders. Such bond issues, moreover, are much more often sold by private placement with institutional investors than by public offerings. The high flotation costs of public offerings and the lack of interest of investment bankers in small issues tend to preclude public offerings.

Suppose, for example, that the president of a relatively small corporation goes to a life insurance company looking for funds. His corporation needs approximately $100,000, and he proposes that the insurance company buy a new bond issue of that face amount. But the insurance

---

[2] For a general discussion of convertibility as a feature of bond issues, see pp. 705–11, and the offering of new bond issues to existing stockholders, pp. 724–28.

company learns that the president owns 85 per cent of the stock of the corporation and that he is quite wealthy. As any loan to the corporation will principally benefit this man, the insurance company is likely to stipulate that it will buy the bonds, if at all, only if he will guarantee them.

Guaranties for Subsidiaries. Corporations sometimes guarantee the payment of interest and principal upon the bonds of their subsidiaries. If a proposed bond issue of a subsidiary is being offered to institutional investors, they are likely to have exactly the same attitude as in the foregoing case—that the financing of the subsidiary must be for the benefit of the parent corporation principally or exclusively (depending upon what proportion of the subsidiary's stock it owns), and that, therefore, the parent should be willing to "stand back of" the subsidiary's bonds. If, on the other hand, the bonds are to be offered to the public, the parent, without any pressure from investment bankers or anybody else, might add its guaranty as a means of getting a lower interest cost. Should its credit rating be higher than that of its subsidiary, and its affairs better known to the investment community, as would be likely, the interest rate differential between guaranteed and nonguaranteed bonds could be substantial. Any saving of interest expense to the subsidiary would be of direct benefit to itself.

Joint Guaranties in the Railroad Industry. Many guaranteed bond issues have originated in the railroad industry in connection with the building of bridges, terminal properties, and beltline facilities for the interchange of cars in and around our larger cities. The distinctive feature of these issues is that they have simultaneously the joint and several guaranties of two or more railroads. Assume, for example, that three railroads decide that they should have a new "union station" in a given city. They establish a new corporation to construct and operate the station, apportioning its stock among themselves. However, they want to obtain most of the money for construction from a bond issue to be sold by the joint subsidiary—the terminal corporation. But they know that the newly established terminal corporation can hardly have much of an investment rating, and that the mortgaging of the union station can hardly add much to the attractiveness of the proposed bonds—what could the bondholders do with the station if they had to foreclose upon it? To make the bonds salable upon reasonable terms, therefore, they add their guaranties. At the same time, they enter into contracts with the terminal subsidiary to use its facilities on a rental basis. Each railroad agrees to pay an annual rental in proportion to its prospective use of the facilities, and the rents in total are set at a level to cover interest and sinking fund requirements on the bonds and to meet maintenance expenses.

Upon bonds for which there are two or more guarantors—"joint bonds," as they are usually called—the standard practice is for each guarantor to accept liability for the full principal and interest. This is what is meant by the "several" of a joint-and-several guaranty. After a default, therefore, the bondholders or their trustee could bring suit against any one of the guarantors for full payment. Upon payment, this guarantor would then have a right of action against the other guarantors according to the proportions of their "joint" obligations. A joint bond issue guaranteed by a strong railroad and by two weak ones, therefore, would have its investment appeal primarily in the guaranty of the strong road.

Recent flotations of joint bonds have included three issues of the Chicago Union Station Company, sold in May, 1963—a 4⅛ per cent first-mortgage issue of $29 million maturing in 1988; a 3⅞ per cent debenture issue of $10 million maturing serially between June 1, 1964, and June 1, 1968; and a 4⅜ per cent debenture issue of $10 million with serial maturities running from 1969 to 1973. The three issues were guaranteed by the four railroads that own all the common stock of the terminal company and use its facilities, the Burlington, the Milwaukee, the Pennsylvania, and the Philadelphia, Baltimore & Washington.[3]

Later Guaranties

The guaranteeing of bond issues after they have been outstanding for some time has been a practice very largely confined to the railroad industry, and, even in that industry, it is now a matter chiefly of historical importance. In the discussion of leases in Chapter 10, it was pointed out that many of our large railroad systems, particularly those of the East, were largely built up by the leasing of the entire operating properties of many smaller companies. When approached with propositions for the leasing of their facilities, the smaller companies, as a rule, had bonds outstanding, so that acceptance of responsibility for these issues by the system companies became, as it were, a normal feature of the lease contracts. Whether or not formal guaranties were expressly given by the system companies, they obligated themselves to pay annual rentals sufficient to take care of the interest and principal requirements of the lessors' bonds, as well as to pay dividends at stipulated rates on their outstanding stock.

Questions

1. From the investor's standpoint, is a corporation's secured bond issue always safer than its debenture bond issue would be? Is the secured bond

---

[3] The interest of the Philadelphia, Baltimore & Washington Railroad Company in Chicago and its terminal facilities originated in 1956 when it absorbed the Pittsburgh, Cincinnati, Chicago & St. Louis Railroad Company in a merger. Although the Pennsylvania has a controlling stock interest in the Philadelphia, Baltimore & Washington, it operates the latter on the basis of a 999-year lease negotiated in 1918. Before the 1956 merger, the Pennsylvania owned almost all the outstanding common stock of the Pittsburgh, Cincinnati, Chicago & St. Louis though operating it also on a lease basis.

issue of any corporation always safer than the debenture bond issue of any other corporation? Explain.

2. Why do corporate managements consent to the pledging of assets for the security of bond issues? Would they generally prefer not to pledge assets? Why or why not?

3. With respect to priorities of claims, what is indicated by designations of bonds as follows: first mortgage, second mortgage, first consolidated mortgage, and first general mortgage?

4. In reference to the mortgaging of real property, what is the distinction between "title theory" and "lien theory"? Of what significance is this distinction?

5. Explain the procedure of the "Philadelphia Plan" by which railroad companies acquire and pay for locomotives and cars.

6. If equipment-trust certificates represent participations in ownership, why are they also classified as debt instruments?

7. Why are collateral-trust bonds so called? Could a single issue of bonds be simultaneously a mortgage and a collateral-trust issue? Explain.

8. Why is security for bond issues important for bondholders' safety even though defaulting corporations often seek to reorganize in bankruptcy?

9. What is the distinction between an open-end and a closed indenture? With which of these types of indentures, if either, does the after-acquired property clause fit in rather conveniently? Explain.

10. Explain how earnings and property limitations are applied to regulate the volume of bonds that may be issued under open-end indentures.

11. Do the successive issues of bonds under an open-end indenture differ from one another in priority of claims? Is the issuing corporation usually permitted to make them different in other ways? Explain.

12. Support or attack this proposition: Since corporations can "avoid" the after-acquired property clause as found in their indentures, this clause is of little value in protecting bondholders.

13. Why have debenture bonds grown so greatly in popularity with both issuing corporations and investors in the postwar period? What is the principal distinguishing characteristic of these bonds?

14. Some indentures provide that debenture bonds will, in certain circumstances, become secured bonds. What are these circumstances? What would be the ranking of the debenture bondholders' claim upon the pledged assets?

15. Why should a corporation's sale of an issue of subordinated debenture bonds *increase* its capacity to borrow from other sources?

16. Would a given corporation's preferred stock be likely to be safer than its subordinated debenture bonds, or vice versa? Defend your choice.

17. What is distinctive about a "guaranteed" bond issue? a "joint" bond issue?

Problems

1. The Oxford Corporation has outstanding $8 million of first-mortgage bonds bearing interest at 5 per cent issued according to the terms of an open-end indenture. It now wants to buy additional land and buildings which will cost $6 million, and it wants to finance this acquisition, as fas as possible, by the sale of additional bonds under the existing indenture. Investment bankers are willing to underwrite the additional bonds provided that the interest rate is set at 5½ per cent. The indenture stipulates that bonds may be issued

from time to time provided that additional issues do not exceed 66⅔ per cent of the value of additional property pledged, and provided that average earnings available for bond interest in the three preceding years have been equal to three times the interest requirement on both the bonds already outstanding and the additional bonds to be issued. Average earnings available for bond interest in the past three years have been $1,840,000.

Within the bounds of the indenture limitations, what additional face amount of bonds may the corporation issue?

2. The Yankton Tool Company, Inc., is nearing the end of a process of liquidation and dissolution in bankruptcy. Its fixed assets, which had been pledged as security for a first-mortgage bond issue, were sold for $5,200,000; its inventories, which had been pledged as security for short-term loans obtained from the First National Bank, were sold for $3 million; and its remaining current assets realized $3,920,000 in cash upon their liquidation. At the time of final settlement, all claims against the corporation, including accumulated interest, where allowable, were as follows:

First-mortgage bonds	$ 7,000,000
Debenture bonds	3,000,000
First National Bank	2,800,000
Other short-term creditors	5,500,000
Preferred stock (at par value, and not, therefore, including $3 million of cumulative dividends in arrears)	6,000,000
Common stock (at par value)	12,000,000

No dividends had been paid on the common stock for 13 years. Before that, for a period of ten years, the corporation had paid "regular" dividends of 6 per cent on the common stock.

Indicate what amounts of the cash realized in liquidation would go to the various classes of claimants. What percentage of its claims would each of these classes recover?

3. A corporation has outstanding a debenture bond issue of $10 million, the indenture for which provides that if the corporation subsequently issues mortgage bonds, the debenture bonds will be secured "equally and ratably." The corporation now wants to put out an open-end mortgage issue, and it plans to pledge its real property valued at $30 million. At the insistence of investment bankers, the corporation includes in its mortgage indenture a "property limitation" providing that bonds secured by the mortgage shall not exceed 75 per cent of the value of the pledged property.

What maximum amount of new bonds can the corporation issue without violating the terms of its indentures?

4. The Whittier Corporation is being liquidated in bankruptcy. In liquidation, its assets realize $10,200,000 in cash. This sum is to be distributed among the creditors whose claims at the time of final settlement are as follows:

Short-term bank loans	$2,500,000
Other current liabilities	5,000,000
Debenture bonds	3,500,000
Subordinated debenture bonds	6,000,000

None of the corporation's assets had been pledged as security for any of its debts, but the indenture for the subordinated debenture bonds makes the claim of these bonds subordinate to "senior debt" consisting of the short-term bank loans and the ordinary debenture bonds.

State what portion of the $10,200,000 would be paid to each of the four classes of creditors, and the percentage of its claims each class would recover.

chapter 28

OTHER FEATURES OF BOND ISSUES

FURTHER PROTECTIVE PROVISIONS

As creditors, investors in bonds demand many kinds of safeguards to protect their claims to interest and principal. In the preceding two chapters, many of these safeguards were examined. We saw that corporate issuers of bonds must include in their indentures various promises, such as their "covenants" to keep their properties in good operating condition, to provide adequate insurance coverage, and to pay all taxes when due, and that they appoint trustees whose principal function it is to look after the interests of the bondholders. We saw that they agree to limit further issues of bonds and, quite often, the incurring of additional debt of all kinds. Many corporations, we saw also, provide pledges of assets for the protection of bondholders, and some obtain for their issues guaranties of other corporations or individuals. It was disclosed, too, that corporations often protect their bondholders by agreeing to pledge for their safety not only existing properties but after-acquired property as well. For debentures, it was brought out that corporations agree not to issue secured bonds unless the debentures are given equal security.

Mention was made in Chapter 26 of the protective aspect of sinking funds set up by corporate debtors for the retirement of their single-maturity bonds. But this is a topic that deserves further examination. Three additional kinds of indenture provisions for the protection of bondholders likewise await analysis: (1) limitations upon dividend payments while bonds are outstanding, (2) other restrictions upon cash payments, and (3) authorizations for legal actions upon default.

Related to the discussion of sinking funds immediately following, as well as to the later discussion of callability features of bond issues, are the data of Table 28–1. Consultation of the table from time to time as the two topics are treated should be helpful to understanding.

Sinking Funds

The typical buyer of corporate bonds thinks that the issuers should be making provisions to pay them off during the course of their lives, and not cast about for means of doing so only as they approach maturity. Especially when the proceeds of bond issues are invested in assets subject to depreciation, depletion, or amortization does it seem reasonable that periodical reductions in the bonded debt should take place as the assets decline in value. The safety of the bondholders would appear to be progressively undermined were such a decline in asset values to take place while the full amount of original issues of bonds continued to be outstanding.

A mandatory periodical allocation of cash to a sinking fund for the redemption of portions of a bond issue obviously gives absolute and final protection to those bondholders whose bonds are thus redeemed; but it also strengthens the position of the remaining bondholders. When sinking fund requirements are placed in indentures, it is anticipated that payments into the sinking fund will be made possible by the cash throw-offs from depreciation, depletion, and amortization charges and from earnings. If, therefore, such throw-offs have enabled a corporation to retire in ten years 40 per cent of a 25-year bond issue, it should be all the more able to meet its remaining sinking fund obligations, as well as its interest obligations, upon the greatly reduced and steadily declining amount of bonds in the remaining 15 years. Moreover, the remaining bondholders should have the advantage of a steady demand for bonds for sinking fund redemption; this demand for bonds should support their market price, so that possibilities of loss on sale, should the bondholder wish to sell, ought to be greatly reduced.

Objectives. The objective of most mandatory sinking fund arrangements is to protect the bondholder by steady substantial reductions in the volume of outstanding bonds. In many cases, the protection demanded and given is provision for the elimination of almost the entire bond issue by sinking fund payments during its life, so that only a small fraction of the original amount is expected to remain to be redeemed at the final maturity. This is obviously the goal of the mandatory sinking fund contributions relating to the bond issues of Armco Steel, Glidden, Jones & Laughlin, Phillips Petroleum, and Westinghouse Electric as listed in Table 28–1. Protection of this degree is very commonly provided for in the indentures of industrial corporations—this in keeping with the idea that long-term borrowing by such corporations should be regarded as only temporary departures from financial structures of the simple common stock form. But some managers of industrial corporations, especially those of stable earning power, think otherwise when bargaining over sinking fund provisions, and their attitude is generally shared by managers of public utilities and railroads. This attitude is that sinking fund payments should be designed to extinguish only part of a given bond issue during its life, with the balance to be paid off at its maturity out of the proceeds of a new flotation at that time. As such managers look with favor upon a policy of continuous trading upon the equity, they can see no grounds for unseemly haste in trying to eliminate long-term debt. Why, they may ask, should a corporation try to retire

TABLE 28–1
Sinking Fund and Callability Features of Some Bond Issues

CORPORATION AND BOND DESCRIPTION	MANDATORY SINKING FUND CONTRIBUTIONS		OPTIONAL CONTRIBUTIONS ALLOWED	SINKING FUND CALL PRICES	NONSINKING FUND CALL PRICES	LIMITATIONS ON NON-SINKING FUND CALLS
	Year to Begin	Annual Amount[a]				
American Telephone and Telegraph Co., debentures (18 series) rates, 2¾–5%, issued 1940–62, due 1970–96, outstanding, end of 1962, $3,540,000,000.......	....	None	....	....	For example, 4⅝s of 1994, issued in 1962: to 1968—106.267 1969—105.98 1970—105.70 falling to 1994—100	For example, same series; not redeemable before 2/1/67
Armco Steel Corporation, sinking fund debenture 4.35s, issued 1959, due 1984, outstanding, end of 1962, $75,000,000...	1963	1963–66: 1,875,000 1967–83: 3,750,000	Up to mandatory amounts	100	1960—104.50 1961—104.30 1962—104.10 falling to 1983—100	Not redeemable before 4/1/64 with money borrowed at less than 4.35%
Commonwealth Edison Company, first mortgage, Series L through U, rates 3–4⅝%, issued 1944–60, due 1977–90, outstanding, end of 1962, $590,000,000...	1945	Renewal fund: cash equal to depreciation provision less cost or fair value of year's property additions, whichever less. Available for property additions or bond retirement	....	As in next column when "renewal fund" is used for bond retirement	Series U, 1960–90: 1961—104.63 1962—104.47 1963—104.31 falling to 1990—100	None
Glidden Company, debenture 4⅜s, issued 1958, due 1983, outstanding, end of 1962, $30,000,000..............	1964	1,500,000	Up to 1,500,000	100	to 1960–61—103¾ 1962–63—103½ 1964–65—103¼ falling to 1983—100	Not redeemable before 11/1/63 with money borrowed at less than 4.82%
Jones & Laughlin Steel Corporation, first mortgage, Series A, 2¾s, issued 1947, due 1967, outstanding, end of 1962, $32,500,000.........	1953	1953–57: 2,500,000 1958–62: 3,000,000 1963–66: 3,500,000	Up to mandatory amounts	100	to 1952—102 1953–54—101¾ 1955—101½ falling to 1965—100	None

Bond	Year	Sinking fund requirement	Additional (optional)	Sinking fund redemption price	Regular redemption price	Restrictions
Phillips Petroleum Company, convertible subordinated debenture 4¼s, issued 1957, due 1987, outstanding, end of 1962, $171,117,600..........	1968	1968-77, 3%, and 1978-86, 7% of amount outstanding 2/15/67. Bonds converted after 2/15/67 may be applied to sinking fund	None	100	to 1962—104¼ 1963—104⅛ 1964—103⅞ falling to 1987—100	None
Seaboard Air Line Railroad Company, first mortgage, Series B, 3s, issued 1950, due 1980, outstanding, end of 1961, $26,454,000..........	1952	If available from preceding year's income, amount to retire 1% of amount of Series B issued, and sinking fund deficiencies from prior years	None	1953-54—101⅞ 1955-57—101¼ 1958-60—101⅛ falling to 1977—100	1951-52—103⅜ 1953-54—103 1955-57—102¾ falling to 1977—100	None
Standard Oil Company (Indiana), sinking fund debenture 4⅛s, issued 1958, due 1983, outstanding, end of 1962, $200,000,000..........	1964	6,500,000	Up to 6,500,000	100	to 1960—104 1961—103¾ 1962—103½ falling to 1983—100	Not redeemable before 10/1/63 with money borrowed at less than 4.57%
United Biscuit Company, debenture 3⅜s, issued 1952, due 1977, outstanding, end of 1962, $7,990,000..........	1957	335,000	Up to 335,000	100	1953—105½ 1954—105⅜ 1955—105¼ falling to 1977—100	None
Westinghouse Electric Corporation, debenture 3⅛s, issued 1951, due 1981, outstanding, end of 1962, $285,000,000..........	1962	5% of total debentures issued ($300,000,000)	Up to 15% of total debentures issued	100	to 1957—103 1958—102¾ 1959—102½ falling to 1981—100	Callable only in amounts of not less than $25,000,000

a "Sufficient to retire" amount of bonds listed.

SOURCE: Moody's Investors Service. *Manuals*.

by periodic payments in 20 years the whole of a bond issue whose proceeds have been invested in assets expected to have useful lives of 40 or 50 years?

Some sinking fund arrangements have, as it were, a second kind of objective as a means of providing bondholder protection, namely, to preserve the values of pledged properties so that the margin of security for the outstanding bonds is maintained even though relatively few are redeemed until the final maturity. Such arrangements are found almost exclusively in the indentures covering secured bonds of public utilities as in the Commonwealth Edison issues. They provide that, at the discretion of the corporation, cash contributed to its sinking fund as prescribed in the indenture may be spent for improvements and additions to fixed facilities rather than for bond retirement. Whether or not the indenture has the after-acquired property clause—as it is likely to have—the improvements and additions must be pledged; moreover, no additional bonds may be sold in relation to the value of these improvements and additions, as might otherwise be permitted in an open-end indenture. Because a sinking fund is designed to "sink" or eliminate a debt, it is sometimes suggested that the term *improvement fund* would be a better title for a fund set up on the basis described. Nevertheless, the idea is that if prescribed cash allocations are not spent for improvements, they must be spent for bond redemption, as for any ordinary sinking fund. Some public utilities, indeed, provide for some "sinking" of the debt as a contractual obligation even though a substantial proportion of the sinking fund contributions may be spent for improvements. In the indentures of such utilities, it is typically provided that the periodical contribution to the sinking fund shall be thus-and-so, that this contribution shall be used for bond retirement unless spent for improvements and additions, but that, in any case, not less than a stipulated moderate portion will be used for retirement.

Contributions. A popular type of mandatory sinking fund provision is that the corporation will allocate annually or semiannually for bond retirement an amount of cash sufficient to redeem equal face amounts or equal percentages of the total quantity of bonds issued or of the total quantity outstanding at a given time. The Glidden, Standard Oil, and United Biscuit entries in Table 28–1 typify mandatory contributions to provide for redemptions of equal dollar amounts of bonds, and the Westinghouse Electric entry, redemptions of equal percentages. A percentage stipulation with respect to bonds outstanding at a given time is especially convenient for convertible issues, as in the case of Phillips Petroleum. At the time that sinking fund payments are scheduled to begin, the volume of outstanding bonds may have already been substantially reduced through conversions; hence, it is reasonable that the mandatory contributions should be adjusted accordingly.

Another popular arrangement for mandatory sinking fund contributions is to have them increase from year to year or at one time or several times during the lives of bond issues, as typified in the Armco Steel, Jones & Laughlin, and Phillips Petroleum indentures. In support of this arrangement is the argument that the corporation ought to be given a period of years to develop the income potential of the facilities acquired with the proceeds of the bond issue before having to make substantial contributions for its retirement. The same argument, of course, supports a delay of a few years before the start of mandatory sinking fund contributions—a common feature of recent indentures, as indicated in Table 28–1.

Sometimes it is argued that sinking fund contributions should be large in the early years and smaller in later years, because expenditures for repairs and maintenance are almost surely to vary in the opposite direction. With sinking fund contributions arranged in this way, annual outlays for redemptions and for repairs and maintenance in combination should tend to be equalized. There must, however, be some weakness in the argument, as the pattern of contributions suggested does not appear to be very popular.

In a goodly number of indentures, as in that of the Seaboard Air Line Railroad, the size of the required sinking fund contribution is related to the amount of net profit after the deduction of income taxes. Sometimes, in such indentures, minimum and maximum limits are placed on the contributions. It may be provided, for example, that the annual sinking fund contribution shall be an amount sufficient to retire bonds of $100,000 par value plus an amount equal to 10 per cent of net profit in excess of $500,000, but in no case shall it exceed an amount sufficient to retire bonds of $300,000 par value. Annual redemption of $100,000 of bonds would, therefore, be the minimum requirement, and the redemption of $300,000 the maximum, the actual level, whether at one of these extremes or in between, depending upon the amount of profit in excess of $500,000. Sometimes it is provided that when actual contributions fall below the maximum, the deficiency must be made up in later years if the margin of profit so permits. Relating sinking fund contributions to the size of profits may prove to be a better procedure *from the standpoint of the welfare of bondholders* than setting fixed contributions to be met in fair weather and foul. Fixed requirements can straitjacket a corporation to the detriment of the bondholders; in other words, demands of bondholders for protection by way of sinking funds can be overdone. If operating losses drain a corporation's working capital, its bondholders may be imperiled when a further sizable drain from working capital to a sinking fund must be made.

A final point on mandatory sinking fund contributions is that indentures for convertible bonds usually provide for a reduction in any year's sinking fund contribution by the amount of bonds that have been surrendered in exchange for common stock in that year up to the time that

the sinking fund contribution is due. As the convertibility feature of
bond issues will be discussed later in this chapter, it suffices here to observe that actual conversion serves the same purpose that sinking funds
are designed to serve—that of eliminating bonded debt. Accordingly, the
greater the number of bonds that take the conversion route, the less
necessary is dependence upon the operations of sinking funds.

   Use of Sinking Fund Cash. In times past, it was a common practice
of corporations to invest their cash contributions to sinking funds in government bonds and in corporate bonds other than their own. The interest earned upon such investments was used to buy additional bonds of
the same description, the idea being that the whole accumulation of investment securities, when sold at the maturity of the bond issue for
which the sinking fund was established, would provide sufficient cash for
its redemption. Often, however, the proceeds of sale were found to fall
far short of amounts needed to retire maturing bonds. Interest had not
been earned upon the sinking fund investments at the rate anticipated,
or the market for the sinking fund investments turned out to be poor
when the time for sale arrived. Even high-quality bonds might be down in
market value simply because market rates of interest had risen since the
time of their purchase. In many instances, the bonds selected for sinking
fund investment simply proved not to be of the high quality that trustees
had judged them to be.

   The multiplication of difficulties of these kinds led to a recasting of
sinking fund management. Why not invest sinking fund contributions
in the bonds whose redemption was being provided for? A corporation
could hardly go wrong in buying back its own obligations in preference
to those of other issuers whose market performance might turn out to
be bad. For a time, however, the older idea of accumulation continued
to prevail. When a corporation or its trustee invested sinking fund cash
in the corporation's own bonds, these were "held alive" in the sinking
fund, and the corporation continued to pay interest upon them. The
interest payments supplemented the regular sinking fund contributions
as means to buy back additional bonds. But the payment of interest into
a sinking fund was obviously nothing more than a stepping up of the
cash contribution, and it was clear that the same result could be obtained
more simply by setting the periodical sinking fund requirement at a
higher level in the first place. Hence, the idea of accumulation has likewise become outmoded, although, once in a while, one still hears of
sinking funds in which bonds are "held alive."

   The general rule at the present time, therefore, is that money allocated
by corporations to sinking funds is used directly to redeem the bonds
for which the sinking funds are established, that it is used *immediately*
for this purpose, and that, once reacquired bonds get into the hands of
the trustee, they are immediately canceled.

   The corporation itself is usually privileged to proceed direct in redeeming its bonds, using for this purpose, as it were, cash that it would otherwise have to turn over to the trustee. As a rule, sinking fund contributions may be made in cash or in the very bonds scheduled for retirement. If the market prices of a corporation's bonds fall below the call price from time to time during the year, the corporation may buy up enough to satisfy the sinking fund requirement; indeed, if it has plenty of cash available, and the market price is well below the call price, it may buy up enough bonds to take care of its sinking fund obligations for two or more years. At the time that its sinking fund contribution is due, then, it simply turns bonds over to the trustee rather than cash. Likewise, the corporation may make a partial contribution in bonds, as, for example, $125,000 in bonds and a sum of cash sufficient to retire another $75,000 face amount where the indenture requirement is for the annual redemption of a face amount of $200,000. Sometimes, as in Figure 28–1, corporations publish notices to bondholders that they have cash available for bond retirement, inviting those who want to sell to submit "tenders" at the prices they are willing to take. If a bond is selling in the market at 98, a corporation's buying will tend to drive up the price; but if all bondholders are approached for "tenders" simultaneously, many may be influenced by the market quotation of 98 to offer to sell at that price or at other prices not much higher.

FIGURE 28–1

Invitation for Tenders

PITTSBURGH, CINCINNATI, CHICAGO & ST. LOUIS RAILWAY COMPANY CONSOLIDATED MORTGAGE BONDS, SERIES "J"

In accordance with Sinking Fund Provisions of Mortgage covering issue of above Bonds, the undersigned invites tenders of Bonds for sale and delivery as of October 1, 1963, at a price not exceeding par and accrued interest, to extent of $989,146.67. Offerings will be accepted on the most advantageous basis to the Company, taking in consideration price, rate of interest and maturity.

Sealed tenders must be in the office of W. R. Gerstnecker, Treasurer, Pennsylvania Railroad Company, 380 Seventh Avenue, New York, N. Y., before three o'clock P. M., September 30, 1963, and must state Series Letter and numbers of Bonds offered. W. R. Gerstnecker, Treasurer, P.B. & W.R.R. Co.

Sinking Fund Calls. In most indentures of recent origin, sinking fund calls are prescribed somewhat as follows: Some 40 or 50 days before the sinking fund payment date, the corporation notifies the trustee how much of its obligation will be met in cash and how much in bonds that it has bought or perhaps got back through conversion. If the obligation is to be met wholly or partially in cash, the trustee immediately draws lots to determine whose bonds are to be called for redemption—a sufficient number, of course, to exhaust the cash contribution. Holders of called registered bonds are notified by mail individually, and advertisements listing the serial numbers of called coupon bonds, as in Figure 28–2, are published in newspapers. All holders of called bonds are thus informed of the time and place of redemption—the time usually being the day following that on which the corporation is obligated to make its sinking fund payment, as November 1 when the sinking fund payment date is October 31. By this procedure, therefore, the trustee does not

FIGURE 28–2
Sinking Fund Call Advertisement

To the Holders of
Alabama Gas Corporation
**First Mortgage Bonds, 5⅛ % Series E
Due 1984, Due August 1, 1984**

Notice is hereby given that, pursuant to the provisions of Section 5 of Article II of the Fifteenth Supplemental Indenture dated as of August 1, 1959, supplemental to First Mortgage and Deed of Trust dated as of April 1, 1941, as supplemented, amended and restated in a Ninth Supplemental Indenture dated as of April 1, 1949, between Alabama Gas Corporation and Chemical Bank & Trust Company (now Chemical Bank New York Trust Company), as Trustee, the undersigned, as Trustee, has drawn by lot, for redemption on September 15, 1963, out of moneys in the Sinking Fund applicable to such redemption $100,000 principal amount of the above-described Bonds bearing the following numbers:

Coupon bonds of $1,000 principal amount each bearing the distinguishing prefix "M":

4	286	756	2148	2630	3089	3480
21	343	806	2185	2678	3152	3524
50	363	855	2253	2717	3180	3559
70	397	1786	2302	2775	3221	3602
104	425	1818	2353	2796	3255	3616
141	466	1868	2402	2836	3284	3657
163	516	1933	2440	2859	3321	3709
166	561	1972	2474	2883	3378	3760
190	618	2018	2492	2925	3391	3849
219	686	2059	2543	3002	3421	
264	750	2102	2570	3052	3452	

Portions of registered bonds as follows:

Number	Portion being redeemed
RE 2	$ 3,000
RE 5	1,000
RE 27	20,000
RE 28	1,000

On September 15, 1963, there will become and be due and payable upon each coupon bond, and upon the portions of the registered bonds, so designated for redemption, the principal amount thereof, together with accrued interest thereon to said date, and a premium of 0.97% of such principal amount (being the price at which such Bonds are redeemable for the Sinking Fund on said date) upon presentation and surrender thereof at the Corporate Trust Department of the Trustee, 20 Pine Street, New York 15, N. Y.

From and after September 15, 1963, interest will cease to accrue on the coupon bonds and the portions of the registered bonds so designated for redemption.

CHEMICAL BANK NEW YORK TRUST COMPANY, *as Trustee.*

Dated: August 16, 1963.

---

buy in the market or "invite tenders," regardless of how low the market price may be; its function in redemption is simply to draw lots, to make the call, and then to pay off the called bonds at the call price with the money supplied by the corporation.

(In older indentures, the trustee was often given a choice of drawing lots, buying bonds in the market, or itself "inviting tenders," or it could be directed by the corporation to take one of these routes. As many of the older indentures are still in effect, one may occasionally see invitations for tenders published in the names of trustees.)

Holders of bonds that are called for redemption are hardly in a position to resist the call. No matter how much an investor may cherish the investment qualities of a called bond, he knows that he can never get more for it than the call price plus interest to the redemption date. In the redemption notice, he will have been told that no interest will accrue after that date. He can hold on to the bond if he wants to, and the trustee will continue to hold for him the cash allocated for its retirement, but holding would surely be a witless act since he would no longer earn interest. Only in exceptional circumstances, on the other hand, are people likely to continue to hold called coupon bonds inadvertently—not having seen or been told of the newspaper advertisements of the redemption call. Such a bondholder, in sending in to the trustee the interest coupon for the six months ending with the redemption date, would receive a return notice from the trustee that he should have sent in the bond itself with the interest coupon still attached.

Call Prices. Although bondholders as a class usually demand protection through the periodic scaling down of corporate bonded debt by the operation of sinking funds, they are not likely to be enthusiastic individually at the prospect of having their holdings called for redemption.

An investor who wants a long-term outlet for his funds has reasons to be displeased if his bondholdings are called well before the final maturity, and the earlier in the life of an issue that his holdings are called the greater is his dissatisfaction likely to be.

Even more important from the standpoint of corporations that are anxious to obtain long-term funds by the sale of bond issues is the possibility that people who are interested in long-term investment simply will not buy because of their expectation that redemption calls will deprive them of their purchases long before they want to give them up. How, then, can a corporation give the protection of a sinking fund and yet garner the funds of prospective investors who fear early calls for redemption?

In times past, the answer to this question was generally that the bondholder should be given a premium to compensate him for his disappointment in having his bond called early in its life, and that the earlier the call the larger the premium should be. Illustrative of this answer are the scales of sinking fund call prices for the Commonwealth Edison, Seaboard Air Line Railroad, and United Biscuit bonds as entered in Table 28–1. But the trend has been strongly in the direction of making the sinking fund call price the par value of the bonds—a trend indicated by all the other entries in Table 28–1 except for that of American Telephone and Telegraph which has no mandatory sinking fund requirements at all for its massive total of $3,540 million of debentures. However, the newer policy does not lose sight of the fact that the bondholder may be disappointed if his bond is called for early redemption, and that he may not buy in the first place for fear of such calls. But the problem seems to be met by simply deferring for a period of years the start of sinking fund contributions and therefore of the sinking fund calls themselves.

Restrictions upon the Payment of Cash Dividends

Basis of Restrictions. Always of concern to investors in bonds is the possibility that the corporate issuers of the bonds, if not restrained in some way, will be too generous in the payment of cash dividends to their common stockholders. The danger envisaged is not so much that the draining of cash for dividend payments will leave too little for bond interest and sinking fund requirements, as that the double drain for dividends and bond servicing will leave too little cash for ordinary operations —that, in other words, operations will be crippled by inadequacies in working capital. As a rule, therefore, bond buyers insist that certain restrictions upon dividend payments be included in indentures. Quite often the restrictions are so stated that, given certain circumstances, dividends on preferred stock as well as on common will be precluded.

Restrictions in Terms of Surplus and Working Capital. A popular kind of restriction is that, while the bonds are outstanding, dividends shall not be paid "out of" surplus accumulated before a stated date; this means, of course, that the dividends shall not be so large as to reduce surplus below the balance obtaining at the stipulated date. This date is usually that of the bond issue or one within the preceding year or two. An alternative way of putting this restriction is to stipulate that the amount of dividends shall not exceed profits derived since the stated date. Rather often, however, a portion of the earned surplus extant at the stated date, specified as a dollar amount, is made available for cash dividends; for example, it may be provided that dividends may not exceed the sum of net earnings after a given date and $10 million. Sometimes the restriction is that dividends must not reduce earned surplus below a stated dollar amount, or, alternatively, that they must not reduce "net tangible assets" (defined as total tangible assets less all debt including the bonds) below a given figure.

Restrictions in terms of working capital are also popular, as, for example, that the amount of working capital or the working capital ratio must not be reduced below a stated level through the payment of dividends. Another working capital provision commonly found in indentures is that dividend payments must not cause the amount of bonds outstanding to exceed the amount of working capital or some percentage of it.

Examples of these kinds of restrictions are presented in Figure 28–3.

Other Restrictions upon Cash Payments

In the absence of indenture restrictions, boards of directors could undermine the position of bondholders by draining corporate assets in reacquiring outstanding stock issues. The directors of a corporation might decide to call a preferred stock issue for redemption or to buy in common shares to be held as treasury stock, only to find, perhaps not long after, that the corporation lacks sufficient cash to meet its mandatory sinking fund payments as provided for in its bond indenture. In this way, the former owners of the stock redeemed or reacquired as treasury stock, instead of being kept in their customary position as inferior claimants to corporate assets, would actually have been treated as if their claims had priority over those of the bondholders. But prospective buyers of bonds know of such possibilities and accordingly often insist upon indenture restrictions upon drains of cash for stock retirement.

Sometimes there is an absolute prohibition upon the purchase by the corporation of shares of its outstanding common and preferred stock and upon calls of the preferred stock for redemption. When, however, an outstanding preferred stock has a provision for a redemption fund, calls of the stock for redemption in accordance with this provision are permitted. It is usual, also, to provide that if new stock issues are sold after the date of the bond issue, an amount equal to the proceeds of the stock sales may be used subsequently for stock retirement even while the bonds remain outstanding. Quite frequently, as seen in Figure 28–3, restrictions upon dividend payments and upon stock retirements are telescoped to

FIGURE 28-3

A Sample of Cash Dividend Restrictions in Bond Indentures

Air Reduction Company, Inc.

Sinking fund debenture 2¾s, issued in 1947, due in 1967. Amount outstanding, December 31, 1962, $3,100,000.

The corporation may not pay dividends (except stock dividends), make distributions on, or purchase or retire, stock unless thereafter the aggregate of all such payments after December 31, 1943, does not exceed the sum of $3,500,000, the proceeds of stock sales, and consolidated net income; and unless consolidated net working capital is not less than $20,000,000.

Cary Chemicals, Inc.

First lien 6s, issued in 1956, due in 1976. Amount outstanding, November 30, 1962, $1,713,500.

The corporation may pay no cash dividends in excess of 75 per cent of consolidated net income after September 30, 1957. The corporation agrees to keep its current assets equal to (1) $750,000 plus (cumulatively) 12½% of each year's net income, or (2) $1,250,000, whichever is less.

International Minerals & Chemical Corporation

Subordinated convertible debenture 3.65s, issued in 1952, due in 1977. Amount outstanding, June 30, 1962, $14,949,000.

The corporation may not pay cash dividends on its common stock or purchase any of its stock unless, after giving effect thereto, consolidated earned surplus exceeds $20,000,000.

National Dairy Products Corporation

Debenture 3⅛s, issued in 1951, due in 1976. Amount outstanding, December 31, 1962, $23,986,000.

The corporation may pay no cash dividends or acquire stock unless thereafter consolidated net tangible assets are at least $150,000,000, less the amount, if any, by which consolidated funded debt is less than $110,000,000.

Scovill Manufacturing Company

Debenture 4¾s, issued in 1957, due in 1982. Amount outstanding, December 31, 1962, $8,709,000.

The corporation may not pay cash dividends on its common stock or purchase its preferred or common stock, except for preferred stock sinking fund requirements, for an aggregate in excess of net income after December 31, 1956, the sum of $5,000,000, and proceeds of sales of stock after March 1, 1957.

Westinghouse Electric Corporation

Debenture 2⅝s, issued in 1946, due in 1971. Amount outstanding, December 31, 1962, $20,854,000.

The corporation may not pay dividends (except stock dividends) or make any other distribution on common stock unless thereafter consolidated current assets are at least equal to consolidated total liabilities.

SOURCE: Moody's Investors Service, *Industrials Manual*, 1963 give the directors a choice: cash may be used for stock retirement to the extent that actual dividends fall short of amounts permitted by the indentures.

Some indentures place limits upon corporate investment in subsidiaries set up to operate in foreign countries. The danger aimed at is that assets of foreign subsidiaries may be beyond the reach of the bondholders should the corporations default, their availability depending upon the laws and attitudes of the foreign governments—that, indeed, the seizure of the assets by governments turned hostile could be the cause of defaults.

In indentures covering bond issues sold in bulk to institutional investors, additional kinds of restrictions upon cash payments are often found. Quite common are limitations upon the payment of salaries and bonuses to executive officers. Often, too, permission of the institutional investor must be obtained for expenditures for new fixed assets beyond certain moderate limits, for the repayment before maturity of indebtedness other than the bonds, and for investment in subsidiaries, whether domestic or foreign.

Legal Remedies

Although bondholders as creditors, and trustees in their role as protectors of bondholders' interests, would have full power to take legal actions to enforce their rights in the absence of permissive provisions in indentures, the fact is that indentures usually specifically authorize various kinds of legal actions. They define what are "events of default" and then go on to say what the trustees and bondholders may do for the latters' protection upon the occurrence of such events.

Events of Default. The typical indenture designates as an event of default the nonpayment of any mandatory sinking fund contribution at the time due, the nonpayment of any principal obligation at the due date, and the nonpayment of interest after the elapse of a certain number of "days of grace" from the due date. The number of days of grace allowed before a nonpayment of interest becomes an event of default is usually 30, 60, or 90. No days of grace are ordinarily allowed for defaulted sinking fund and principal payments. For principal payments, courts have held that allowing days of grace destroys the negotiability of bonds.

Other failures of a corporation to fulfill its covenants become events of default when the corporation has been notified of such failures, has been asked to correct them, and has not corrected them within a stipulated period, usually 60 or 90 days. The notice of failure to fulfill covenants and the demand for correction may be given by the trustee or by the owners of a stipulated proportion of the outstanding bonds, usually 25 per cent. If, therefore, the corporation fails to pay its taxes when due or to keep its properties in a good state of repair, the matter may be called to its attention by the trustee or by the requisite proportion of the bondholders, with demand that the payment be made or the repairs effected.

If the corporation gets involved in certain kinds of legal processes and does not extricate itself from these within a short period, such as 60, 75, or 90 days, the result is also an event of default. Such involvements include its filing of a petition in a federal court for reorganization or dissolution in bankruptcy, confessing in writing that it is unable to pay its debts as they mature, asking that a receiver be appointed, making an assignment of assets for the benefit of some or all of its creditors, and consenting to the filing of a petition by creditors for the appointment of a receiver or for reorganization or dissolution in bankruptcy. They include also court orders or decrees finding the corporation to be insolvent, appointing a receiver, and approving as properly filed a petition for reorganization or dissolution in bankruptcy.

Finally, the typical indenture provides that an event of default occurs if the corporation fails to meet some debt other than the bonds covered by the indenture, if the maturity of this debt is "accelerated" because of this failure, and if the matter is not cleared up within, say, ten days after written demand for its correction has been made by the trustee or by holders of at least 25 per cent of the outstanding bonds. Suppose, for example, that a corporation has outstanding a mortgage bond issue and a debenture bond issue, the indenture for each of which has the provision just described. If, then, the corporation suffers an event of default upon the debenture issue, if as a result the maturity of the debenture issue is accelerated, and if the corporation, after notice, fails to pay off the debenture bonds or have the acceleration rescinded within the allowed period of grace, the result is *an event of default upon the mortgage issue.* ("Acceleration" is explained in the second succeeding paragraph.)

Remedies Available to the Trustee. The typical bond indenture contains a sweeping authorization of legal action upon the part of the trustee such as the following:

In case of an event of default hereunder, the Trustee may in its discretion proceed to protect and enforce the rights vested in it by this Indenture by such appropriate judicial proceedings as the Trustee shall deem most effectual to protect and enforce any of such rights, either by suit in equity or by action at law or by proceeding in bankruptcy or otherwise, whether for the specific enforcement of any covenant or agreement contained in this Indenture or in aid of the exercise of any power granted in this Indenture, or to enforce any other legal or equitable right vested in the Trustee by this Indenture or by law.

If an event of default seriously threatens the interests of the bondholders, and if it is one that the corporation is unlikely to be able to clear up within a reasonable time, the trustee may decide to accelerate the maturity of the bond issue as a preliminary to further legal action. The acceleration clause of the indenture will authorize the trustee to declare the entire principal amount of the bond issue "immediately due and payable." Assume, for example, that a corporation defaults in an interest payment upon its 20-year bond issue at the end of the fifth year. At the same time, the corporation is failing to meet maturing obligations owing to other creditors, and these creditors are hastening to the courts with suits to obtain judgment against it. In these circumstances, the trustee would be in a ridiculous position if it could sue only for the defaulted interest. The other creditors, if successful in their judgment suits, would be able to seize the corporation's best assets (if not pledged for the bond issue, of course) leaving little to meet the corporation's future obligations upon the bonds. Indentures, therefore, not only provide for acceleration, but also set forth as an additional covenant the corporation's obligation to pay the full principal upon acceleration. Nonpayment thus becomes an additional event of default—one that, since it concerns the payment of principal, permits no days of grace.

After acceleration, the trustee may sue the corporation for the payment of the full principal and accumulated interest; if property has been pledged for the bond issue, it may institute proceedings for the foreclosure of this property and its public sale, the proceeds to be used as far as possible to pay off the bondholders' claims. However, the trustee may decide that the bondholders would fare better if the corporation's properties were kept intact and a plan of reorganization worked out. If so, it would be likely to file with the federal district court a petition for the corporation's reorganization in bankruptcy. An advantage of this move would be its effect of holding in abeyance legal actions of other creditors to seize the corporation's assets.

For less serious defaults, the trustee may show forbearance. Should extreme tightness in the corporation's cash position prevent its paying some of its taxes on their due dates, though permitting it to meet all the rest of its obligations under the indenture and to other creditors, the trustee might let the default "ride" in the expectation that later cash inflows would suffice to clear up the delinquencies. In a period of business slump, it would be likely to ignore inadequacies in the corporation's expenditures for the maintenance of its plant and equipment. On the other hand, should the corporation have sufficient cash to meet all its obligations and simply be negligent in doing so, the trustee might take proceedings in equity asking for a writ directed to the corporation commanding it to fulfill these obligations.

Remedies Available to the Bondholders. In the typical bond indenture, the bondholders are not bereft of rights to take action to protect their interests even though this is supposed to be principally the job of the trustee. For one thing, they are usually privileged to accelerate the maturity of the bond issue when defaults have occurred. This action can be taken by written notice to both the corporation and the trustee, provided, usually, that holders of at least 25 per cent of the outstanding bonds concur.

As a rule, bondholders may take direct legal action against the corporation to enforce their claims if the trustee fails to take such action after a proper request. The trustee must have been notified in writing of an event of default by one or more of the bondholders; holders of some proportion of the outstanding bonds—usually 25 per cent—must have submitted a written request for action with an offer to indemnify the trustee for expenses to be incurred; and the trustee must have neglected to take action for some period of time—usually 60 days—after receiving the written request. The typical indenture stipulates that when a group of bondholders take direct action, they must do so for the benefit of all the bondholders, and not simply for themselves. Nevertheless, an exception is made for the right of the individual bondholder to sue in his own name and for his own benefit to recover defaulted interest and principal payments.

In the typical indenture, too, it is stipulated that holders of a majority of the outstanding bonds may direct the "time, method, and place" of actions to be taken by the trustee. However, this provision is usually weakened by the further stipulation that the trustee may decline to act as directed if, in good faith, it feels that the action would be contrary to the interests of bondholders not taking part in the move.

RIGHTS RESERVED BY CORPORATIONS

When corporations pledge their operating properties as security for bond issues, they demand the right to retain possession of the properties and to use them in the ordinary course of business. They reserve the right to sell pledged property no longer useful to them, agreeing, however, to substitute other properties of at least equal value or to turn the cash proceeds of sale over to the trustee for bond retirement. They often reserve the right to issue additional bonds according to the terms of existing indentures and to set varying interest rates, call prices, and maturities for these additional bonds, subjecting themselves, however, to limitations in terms of earnings and property in the exercise of this privilege. These matters we examined in the preceding chapter. In the foregoing division of this chapter, we saw that corporations usually ask for "days of grace" for the correction of certain kinds of defaults before trustees may take action of a decisive character to protect the bondholders.

What other kinds of rights do corporations insist upon reserving to themselves in their indentures? Two kinds deserve analysis: (1) the right to call bonds for redemption, and (2) the right to have the terms of indentures modified provided that holders of certain proportions of the outstanding bonds consent.

Callability

The right of corporations to call their bonds for redemption goes hand in hand with the present-day theory of sinking fund management. As we have seen, this theory is that cash contributed to sinking funds should be used at once to retire the bonds for which the sinking funds are set up. It is envisaged that bonds may not be available in the market at reasonable prices to use up the sinking fund contributions; accordingly, the right of the corporation to force surrender, as it were, at predetermined call prices appears to be entirely logical. Hence comes the indenture provision for the drawing of lots by the trustee to determine whose bonds shall be called and the stipulation that interest upon called bonds that are not surrendered will not accrue after the call date.

Most corporate issuers of bonds, however, demand and get call privileges much broader than those directly related to sinking fund requirements. Their financial managers hope that good fortune will enable them to retire bonds more rapidly than the sinking fund provisions require. They surely think it possible that long-term interest rates may fall during the lives of their bond issues, so that their replacement with new bonds bearing lower rates of interest would be advantageous. Fearing that certain terms of indentures will turn out to be too restrictive, they may want to be in a position to remove these restrictions by calling all outstanding bonds. If they are issuing bonds reluctantly in the first place because of devotion to the simple common stock form of financial structure, they may hope to be able to replace all the bonds by common stock sales when the market situation for common stock improves.

Call privileges beyond what are needed in connection with mandatory sinking fund contributions are generally of two kinds: (1) those related to *optional* sinking fund payments, and (2) those related to redemption outside the scope of sinking fund operations. The sinking fund provisions of many indentures state that the corporation shall make an annual or semiannual contribution sufficient to retire a given face amount of bonds, and that it may, at its option, make an additional contribution on any sinking fund payment date. It is usually stipulated that the optional contribution cannot exceed the mandatory one, and that the right to make optional contributions does not cumulate—that optional contributions missed cannot be made up by later ones beyond the stipulated limit. (The reason for these limitations is that, as noted later, call prices for sinking fund redemptions are almost always less than for those outside the scope of sinking fund operations.) Obviously, however, the combination of mandatory and optional sinking fund calls still envisages only gradual retirement; it does not permit the complete elimination of large amounts of remaining bonds at one stroke. Hence, the typical corporation asks for and gets the additional privilege of making calls for redemption unrelated to its mandatory and optional sinking fund contributions. The additional privilege is usually stated sweepingly as the right to call any quantity of bonds for redemption at any time, but one or more provisos that tone down the scope of this right often follow its broad declaration. Even corporations that have no sinking fund provisions in their indentures, or whose indentures permit the spending of sinking fund money for improvements, generally demand a broad call privilege of this kind.

Any limitation upon the broad call privilege is usually designed to assure investors that they will not be quickly deprived of their bondholdings. It may be provided, for example, that the privilege may not be used within the first five or ten years from the date of the bond issue. A variation of this proviso, found in many recent indentures, is that money borrowed at a rate of interest lower than that carried by the bond issue may not be used in the exercise of the broad call privilege within the first five years or thereabouts. This variation is designed to preclude for the stated period of years calls prompted solely by the corporation's desire to reduce its interest costs. In this regard, see the last column of Table 28–1 presented earlier in this chapter on pages 688–89.

In Table 28–1 may be found, also, scales of redemption prices of several outstanding bond issues. One will note that, until maturity or a date close to it in all instances, except for the "renewal fund" of Commonwealth Edison, the call prices for redemptions outside the scope of sinking fund operations are higher than those for sinking fund redemptions. The trend toward making par value the sinking fund call price, regardless of the time of sinking fund calls, has not carried over to nonsinking fund calls. Thus, the corporation suffers a penalty for redeeming by means of nonsinking fund calls. The idea seems to be that because sinking fund redemptions are demanded by bondholders for their own protection, they deserve no bonus or premium when their bonds are actually called through sinking fund operations; but because nonsinking fund redemptions are undertaken purely to serve the corporation's own financial objectives, the bondholder should be compensated for the part that he is called upon to play, however unwittingly. Note, however, that optional sinking fund contributions almost always get by with the same call prices as the mandatory ones, even though they, too, appear to serve the corporation's objectives much more closely than those of the bondholders.

Modification of Indenture Terms

As was pointed out previously, the financial managers of a corporation may want to reserve a broad call privilege as a means of eliminating a bond issue should its indenture terms prove to be too restrictive. It would let them call for redemption all the bonds with the obnoxious features and put out a new issue with terms more to their liking. But complete replacement or refunding is likely to be expensive, especially in underwriting commissions and costs of preparing a registration statement and prospectus. Moreover, the obnoxious features may prove to be most burdensome at a time when market conditions are quite unfavorable for new bond flotations. Accordingly, an alternative way for getting rid of unduly burdensome features of an indenture is usually provided for in the indenture itself.

The alternative way is to get the bondholders to consent to the desired change in indenture terms or features. The typical indenture provides that any of its terms and conditions, *except the interest rate, the principal obligation, and the due dates of interest and principal,* can be modified with the consent of holders of 66⅔ per cent, 75 per cent, or some other large proportion of the outstanding bonds.[1]

Since the exceptions specifically provide that the corporation's obligations as to principal and interest are not to be reduced or deferred by any modifications agreed upon, courts generally hold that consent of the proportion stipulated makes a change binding upon all bondholders—upon those who dissent as well as upon those who approve. With the hope of getting a sufficient number of bondholders to approve, therefore, a corporation may propose that its sinking fund obligations be reduced or rearranged; that it be permitted to issue new bonds having a prior lien over the existing ones or to incur debt beyond the limits set in the indenture; that requirements in the indenture for maintaining a given amount of working capital or a given working capital ratio be modified; that restrictions upon dividend payments be relaxed; or, for a debenture issue, that it be permitted to sell an issue of mortgage bonds without giving the debentures equal security.

Necessarily, of course, the financial managers must explain clearly to the bondholders why the change is desired—how it will benefit the corporation and, perhaps, strengthen the bondholders' own position, or at least not weaken it. On the other hand, should it be clear that the bondholders' interests would be affected adversely, the corporation may have to offer them something in compensation, such as a moderate increase in the interest rate. If sufficient assents are obtained, the corporation gets rid of the obnoxious feature or gets permission for what it wants to do rather painlessly; if not, it may decide upon a new issue whose proceeds are to be used to retire the existing one, or it may decide, in view of the costs of refunding, to try to go along with the existing indenture with all its burdens.

Although indentures exclude principal and interest obligations from the matters subject to modification with the consent of given proportions of bondholders, a corporation can still go to its bondholders with proposals affecting these obligations. Corporations in financial difficulties often propose to their bondholders the reduction or deferment of interest payments, the extension of maturities, and even reductions in the principal amounts of their obligations. But seeking the help of bondholders in these directions pertains to the management of outstanding bond issues,

---

[1] Another exception is that the proportion of bondholders' assents required for modifications cannot itself be modified. Thus, holders of, say, 66⅔ per cent of outstanding bonds cannot approve an indenture amendment making the consent of holders of only 51 per cent of the bonds sufficient for further adjustments in terms.

to be taken up in Chapter 30,[2] rather than to the reservation of rights in indentures, as discussed here.

SPECIAL FEATURES TO PROMOTE SALE

Just as convertibility and warrant features are added to some issues of preferred stock to increase their attractiveness to investors, so also are such features given to some bond issues for the same objective. As with preferred stocks, too, common stock is almost always the security for which convertible bonds may be exchanged or for which warrants attached to bonds may be exercised. Occasionally, bond issues are made convertible into preferred stock and short-term issues into longer-term ones, but these occasional departures from the general rule only emphasize the preeminent role of common stock as the thing offered. Making bonds convertible into common stock is a practice of considerable popularity; on the other hand, attaching to bonds warrants to buy common stock, like the similar practice with respect to preferred stocks, appears to have far less appeal.

In relation to the discussion of convertibility which follows immediately, Table 28–2 describes a variety of conversion features found in the indentures of several bond issues at present outstanding.

Convertibility

Although "promotion of sale" is the objective of convertibility features in bond issues, circumstances differ among corporations as to why such a promotional device is needed. Corporations of weak credit standing can hardly expect to attract the more conservative classes of bond buyers regardless of what they offer, but they may hope to reach successfully less conservative classes that may be impressed by the speculative interest that convertibility provides. They may or may not want conversion to take place, but they are extremely anxious to borrow, and they can offer convertibility without apparent immediate cost. They may have little or nothing to pledge as security for their bond issues—as is evidenced by the fact that most convertible bonds are debentures—and the only other alternative might be the offering of an extremely high interest rate, something that might threaten solvency.

But corporations of strong financial position also offer convertible bonds. Sometimes they do so when the supply of long-term loan funds in the market is tight but the common stock market is quite strong, as in times when business is "booming." The tightness in the bond market means that long-term interest rates are high, but these corporations expect to be able to shade their rates downward materially by offering the conversion privilege—the buoyancy in the common stock market in-

---

[2] See below, pp. 752–61.

TABLE 28–2
Convertibility Features of Some Bond Issues

Corporation and Bond Description	Year Issued	Amount Outstanding[a]	Offered to Common Stockholders	Period of Convertibility	Conversion Prices (Dollars)
American Machine & Foundry Company, convertible subordinated debenture 4¼s, due 1981............	1961	$39,910,300	Yes	Unlimited	59.63 to 3/1/71 64.56 to 3/1/81
Ashland Oil & Refining Company, convertible subordinated debenture 3⅞s, due 1993.........	1963	35,000,000	No	Unlimited	31
Boeing Airplane Company, convertible subordinated debenture 4⅛s, due 1980............	1958	30,531,000	Yes	Unlimited	50
J. I. Case Company, convertible subordinated debenture 5½s, due 1983............	1958	20,130,100	Yes	First 10 years	22.75
Celotex Corporation, convertible subordinated debenture 4⅛s, due 1976............	1956	10,000,000	No	Unlimited	46.23
Textron, Inc., convertible subordinated debenture 5s, due 1971............	1956	5,626,900	No	Unlimited	31.77 to 12/31/63 38.58 to 12/31/67 45.39 to 12/31/70
United Aircraft Corporation, convertible subordinated debenture 4⅛s, due 1988............	1963	42,884,700	Yes	First 10 years	50

[a] On December 31, 1962, except for 1963 issues of Ashland Oil and United Aircraft.

SOURCE: Moody's Investors Service, *Manuals*.

dicates that investors will rush to get access to new stock issues of good quality even if indirectly through conversion machinery. These corporations do not want to issue additional common stock—they want to trade on the equity—and they may offer the conversion privilege in the expectation that the common stock market will break before its exercise would be advantageous to the bond buyers.

Nevertheless, most convertible issues of strong corporations are offered at times when the supply of funds in the bond market is relatively large but stock prices are not nearly so buoyant as the corporate managements think they should be. The managers decide that projects for which they need long-term funds cannot conveniently be postponed, and they would prefer to sell additional shares of common stock to raise these funds, yet they conclude that sales at current prices would unreasonably dilute the ownership interests of existing stockholders. Confident that the market prices of their common stocks will soon begin a spirited advance, they now sell convertible bonds, setting the conversion terms at levels to insure conversion when this advance has taken place. In August, 1963, for example, the United Aircraft Corporation offered for sale a $42,884,700 issue of its subordinated convertible debenture 4½s at a price of 100. Slated to mature in 1988, the bonds were made convertible into common stock at a price of $50 on or before August 15, 1973. The closing market price of the corporation's common stock on the day before the offering was 45. If, then, all the bonds are converted into common stock before the expiration of the conversion privilege in 1973, the result will be much the same as if United Aircraft, back in 1963, had sold the stock at $50 a share—when, in fact, the market price was only 45. For the 857,694 shares into which the bonds will have been converted, United Aircraft will have got $42,884,700, instead of the $38,596,230 it would have received had it sold that number of shares in 1963 at 45.[3]

Conversion Provisions. In setting conversion terms, some corporations use *ratios* and others use *prices*. The distinction is of no great importance, as either kind of designation can be readily translated into the other. For example, a stipulation that $100 of bonds is convertible into two shares of common stock means that the conversion price is $50 a share; likewise, a stipulation that the conversion price is $33⅓ a share means that the conversion ratio is 3—that three shares of stock will be given for $100 of bonds.

In almost all instances, the conversion price, as stated or as translated from a stated ratio, is set well above the market price of the common

---

[3] This statement disregards two factors that doubtless added weight to the attractiveness of the bond issue from the corporation's standpoint, namely, a comparison of the actual flotation costs of the bond issue (not deducted in the figures for proceeds mentioned) with the higher probable flotation costs of a stock issue, and the probability that the offering price of a stock issue would have been less than 45. As the bonds were offered to the common stockholders on a rights basis, a stock issue would presumably have been offered by the same route but at a "bargain price."

stock prevailing at the time the bonds are sold. Such an arrangement is logical for the corporation that does not want conversion to take place—one that offers convertibility, as one might say, purely as a sales attraction. But it is also logical for the corporation that has every wish to replace the bond issue with common stock. Since such a corporation issues bonds only because the common stock market is temporarily unfavorable, it would be defeating its purpose were it to set the conversion price close to the existing market price of the common stock.

A second common practice is to establish scales of conversion prices graduated upward for successive time periods (or, alternatively, scales of conversion ratios graduated downward), as in the American Machine & Foundry and Textron entries in Table 28–2. Again, such a provision appears to be logical whatever the long-range financing objectives of corporations may be. The corporation that wants to have its bonds remain outstanding hardly expects the market price of its common stock to reach the level of the first conversion price in the first period, and all the less to the levels of the higher conversion prices of the later periods. On the other hand, the corporation that favors conversion expects it to be *forced* near the end of the first period or, if not then, near the end of a subsequent period. Had the market price of the common stock of Textron, Inc., been, say, $35, near the end of 1963, the holder of one of its $1,000 convertible bonds could have exchanged it for approximately 31½ shares of common stock that he could have sold for approximately $1,100. But had he waited till January, 1964, no such opportunity would have remained because of the jump in the conversion price to $38.58. Shortly before December 31, 1967, again, there would be pressure on the bondholder to convert if the market price of Textron's common stock were, say, 44. In converting a $1,000 bond, the bondholder would get approximately 26 shares salable at about $1,140. Again, however, the opportunity would slip by if he waited till after the turn of the year, because of the further jump in the conversion price to $45.39.

As is also indicated in Table 28–2, some corporations, in issuing convertible bonds, limit the duration of the conversion privilege. In the 25-year issues of the J. I. Case Company and the United Aircraft Corporation, the right of the bondholder to convert expires at the end of the tenth year. Such a limitation appears advisable for a corporation that adds the convertibility feature as a sales attraction without wanting conversion to take place; however, it can obviously err by making the conversion period too brief, thus losing the force of the sales attraction. A limitation of this kind also appears to be advisable for a corporation that hopes for conversion, provided that it is fully confident that the market price of its common stock will rise well above the conversion price during the limited period. While a rising scale of conversion prices tends to force conversion before the ends of successive periods, some bondholders may hold off more or less indefinitely; but nobody who is wise in the ways of investment will fail to convert if it would be profitable to do so and if the conversion privilege is just about to expire.

Indentures for convertible bonds almost invariably provide that if the bonds are called for redemption, their owners may still convert to common stock up to the date of redemption or up to a date a few days earlier. Much of the attractiveness of the privilege of converting would be lost if it were possible for corporations to nullify it by calls for redemption. Issuing calls for redemption is, indeed, a third important means of forcing conversion—in addition, that is, to rising scales of conversion prices and time limits upon the conversion privilege. If a corporation's common stock is selling in the market at a price at least moderately above the conversion price, almost all the bondholders, upon receiving a redemption call, can be expected to convert rather than to permit their bonds simply to be paid off at the call price. In May, 1959, Flying Tiger Line, Inc., called for redemption all its convertible subordinated debenture 5½s due in 1967, publishing a newspaper notice to that effect as reproduced in Figure 28–4. At the time of this call, Flying Tiger's common stock was selling in the market in the vicinity of $16 a share, while the conversion price of the bonds was $8.50 a share.

FIGURE 28–4
Notice of Redemption of Convertible Bonds

THE FLYING TIGER LINE INC.

Notice of Redemption and Termination of Conversion Privilege

To the Holders of The Flying Tiger Line Inc.
5½% Debentures Due 1967 (Subordinate) due July 1, 1967

NOTICE IS HEREBY GIVEN that, pursuant to the provisions of the Indenture dated as of July 1, 1952, between The Flying Tiger Line Inc. and Bankers Trust Company, Trustee, the Company has elected to redeem on July 1, 1959 all of its then outstanding 5½% Debentures Due 1967 (Subordinate) due July 1, 1967 at the redemption price of 102% of the principal amount thereof together with interest accrued thereon to the redemption date.

Accordingly, on or after July 1, 1959, unless the Debentures are previously converted into shares of Common Stock of the Company, the redemption price of such Debentures will become due and payable and will be paid at the office of Bankers Trust Company, Corporate Trust Division, 16 Wall Street, New York 15, New York, upon presentation and surrender of such Debentures, accompanied by all coupons appertaining thereto maturing on and after January 1, 1960. Coupons maturing on July 1, 1959 should be detached by the holders of Debentures to be redeemed and presented for payment in the usual manner. Interest on the Debentures will cease to accrue on and after July 1, 1959.

The Debentures are presently convertible into shares of Common Stock of the Company at the conversion price of $8.50 principal amount of Debentures for each share of Common Stock. The Indenture provides, however, that such right to convert shall terminate and expire at the close of business on the third full business day prior to the date fixed for redemption. Accordingly, the right to convert Debentures into Common Stock will terminate at the close of business on June 26, 1959.

Debentures to be converted accompanied by all coupons appertaining thereto maturing on or after July 1, 1959 should be surrendered, on or before June 26, 1959, at the office of Bankers Trust Company, Corporate Trust Division, 16 Wall Street, New York 15, New York, accompanied by a written notice of election to convert such Debentures.

May 29, 1959.

THE FLYING TIGER LINE INC.
By BANKERS TRUST COMPANY, *Trustee*

Finally, indenture provisions concerning the convertibility feature usually include "antidilution clauses" for investor protection. Like the similar provisions found in the contracts for convertible preferred stocks, these clauses require adjustments to be made in conversion prices and ratios when corporations effect split-ups in their common stocks or distribute stock dividends to their common stockholders. In August, 1958, for example, the Union Oil Company of California, after having declared a stock dividend of 2 per cent on its common stock, announced new conversion prices for its convertible subordinated debenture 3¼s due in 1981. The original and revised conversion prices were as follows:

Conversion Periods	Original Prices	Revised Prices
To April 1, 1961...................	$70	$68.63
To April 1, 1966...................	75	73.53
To April 1, 1971...................	80	78.43

In a similar way, the Lockheed Aircraft Corporation, after splitting its common stock on a 4 for 3 basis in June, 1963, announced a reduction in the conversion price applicable to its convertible subordinated debenture 3¾s due in 1980 from $24.27 to $18.20.

Attractiveness of Convertibility. The reason why the privilege of conversion is attractive to bond buyers is that it gives them possibilities of substantial gains while detracting not at all from the relative safety of their positions as creditors.

If during the life of a bond issue the market price of the corporation's common stock never goes appreciably above the conversion price, the bondholders may still be fairly well satisfied as they collect interest semiannually and the principal as the bonds are called or as paid off at the final maturity. They may feel, however, that they have lost something—not only the "substantial gains" that failed to show up, but also a differential in interest income if they accepted a lower rate of interest than they would have demanded had the bonds not been convertible. But even with the market price of common remaining at or below the conversion price, gains may be possible. Should the interest rate on the bonds be 4 per cent and should the corporation pay dividends of 5 per cent on its common stock, the bondholders might convert to get the advantage of the higher rate of return. They might wait for two or three years to be sure that the common dividend rate had become "regular," and they would surely weigh the prospects of its continuance, but their judgment of the corporation's outlook might lead them to give up the relative safety of their position as bondholders for the more speculative one as stockholders.

If, moreover, the market price of a common stock goes well above the conversion price, the bondholder finds himself under no immediate pressure to convert. He may be satisfied to continue to earn interest at the established rate in his relatively safe position as a creditor, while expecting to supplement the interest by a handsome capital gain by selling the bonds some months or years later. Suppose, for example, that a corporation's dividend rate on its common stock is the same as the interest rate on its convertible bonds, but that its prospects are so good that many people are buying the common stock, thereby driving up its price. Assume that the conversion price is $50 and that the market price of the common stock goes to 80. This should cause the market price of the bonds to go to approximately 160.[4] Thus, the bondholder may plan to sell out when satisfied that the price of the common stock is unlikely to rise further, or when, indeed, he expects it to fall. Or he may plan to sell before an increase in the subscription price occurs, as scheduled by a provision in the indenture as described earlier. At any rate, he would be unlikely to see any advantage in converting and thereby assuming the risks of common stock ownership without getting any increase in the rate of return. Nor would he have to convert to get his capital gain, as by obtaining the common stock and immediately selling it, since, as indicated, he could get it by selling the bond directly. If, on the other hand, the corporation were to step up its dividend rate to, say, 6 per cent, he might convert to take advantage of the higher rate of return. In surrendering his bond, he would be in the pleasant position of being able to buy, as it were, at $50 a share, while other investors simultaneously would be paying $80 in the market.

But a word of caution: The bondholder may be extremely disappointed, not only because the conversion privilege may prove to be of no value, but also because the corporation defaults in interest or principal payments somewhere along the way. A convertibility feature does not guarantee a corporation's continued solvency. When, indeed, convertibility is offered by corporations of weaker financial positions to attract investors who would not otherwise be attracted, the investors must realize that incurring dangers of defaults is the price they pay for the added privilege.

Use of Stock-Purchase Warrants

As a rule, a corporation can make an offer of stock-purchase warrants about as attractive to bond buyers as an offer of convertibility. If a conversion ratio of 20 shares of common stock for a $1,000 bond would be attractive in a given instance, the attachment of warrants to buy 20 shares of common at $50 a share should have about equal investment appeal. Should the market price of the common go to 80, and should the warrants be *nondetachable* (exercisable, therefore, only by the bondholder himself), the market price of the bond should go to approximately

---

[4] Why this is so was explained earlier in an analysis of the relationship between the market prices of common stocks and of convertible preferreds. See pp. 542, 544. A recent spectacular example may be cited. On May 31, 1963, the closing market price of the common stock of the Consolidated Edison Company was 86½, and on the same day, the closing price of its convertible 3s—with a conversion price of $25, but with the conversion privilege just about to expire—was 343!

160. At this level the bondholder might sell the bond with attached warrants to take his capital gain; he might hold for a bigger gain expected to result from a further rise in the stock price; or he might surrender the warrants with $1,000 in cash to buy the 20 shares to which he is entitled. Should he take the last-named step, he would have further choices: to take the capital gain by selling the stock, or to hold it for a further rise. And, of course, he would have to make an additional decision whether to keep the bond, now bereft of its speculative feature, or to sell it. Should the warrants be *detachable*—as they are often made to be—they themselves should have a market value close to $600, so that the bondholder could sell them for his capital gain, keeping the bond as a continuing investment or selling it, too, should he wish to pull out completely.

Nevertheless, corporations look with much less favor upon the warrant device than upon convertibility. It has advantages for those corporations that expect to have a continual need of additional funds and that are content to draw them from whatever sources may be available—they get the proceeds of their bond issues in lump sum and then additional cash inflows if and when the warrants are exercised. But most corporations that put out bond issues want to raise specific sums of money for specific projects; they are not interested in setting the stage for further inflows that may occur within a relatively short period of time, that may be delayed for many years, or that may not take place at all—inflows that may occur in driblets or in great spurts, all this depending upon the uncertain time when, if at all, bondholders (or the buyers of detachable warrants) will decide that the common stock is a good "buy" at the warrant price. Through the exercise of warrants, new money might flow in when it could not be used economically; this would mean a dilution in the claims to earnings of the existing common stock. In a word, the issuance of stock-purchase warrants attached to bonds tends to introduce an important element of uncertainty in long-range financial planning.

Indenture provisions governing the use of warrants parallel those pertaining to convertibility. Subscription prices are almost always set well above the market prices of common stock at the time the bonds are issued; there is frequently a rising scale of subscription prices for successive periods; often the period in which warrants may be exercised is limited; and the protection of antidilution clauses is provided. For illustration, the indenture provisions of a recent issue of bonds with warrants may be cited. In its $3,500,000 issue of 6½ per cent subordinated debenture bonds, issued in January, 1963, and maturing in 1978, the Tandy Corporation attached to each $100 of bonds one warrant entitling the holder to buy seven shares of the corporation's common stock at $7.50 a share in the period from January 1, 1965, through December 31, 1967, and at $9.00 a share from January 1, 1968, through December 31, 1969. The warrants were protected by antidilution clauses. The range of closing prices for Tandy's common stock on the New York Stock Exchange in January, 1963, when the warrants were issue was $6\frac{3}{4}$–$7\frac{3}{4}$.

Questions

1. Is it not contradictory for people to invest in a corporation's long-term bonds while insisting that it set up a sinking fund for periodic bond redemption? Discuss.

2. Why does the attitude of industrial corporations toward sinking funds for bond redemption generally differ from that of public utilities?

3. What support is there for the proposition that the size of sinking fund contributions should increase from time to time during the life of a bond issue? that it should fall?

4. What merit is there in basing the size of sinking fund contributions on the amount of the corporation's profits?

5. Distinguish between the older and the modern theories of sinking fund management.

6. What choices does the typical corporation have in disposing of the cash that it is required by its indenture to allocate to a sinking fund?

7. Why are corporations moving away from the older practice of setting sinking fund call prices at levels above par value? Are they substituting anything for the premiums formerly paid? Explain.

8. What kinds of restrictions upon payments of cash dividends are commonly found in bond indentures? upon other kinds of cash payments?

9. What are the varieties of "events of default" on account of which trustees and bondholders can take action to protect the latters' interests? What are "days of grace"? What connection is there between events of default and days of grace?

10. What kinds of actions can trustees take to protect bondholders' interests following events of default? What can the bondholders themselves do?

11. What is "acceleration"? What bearing does it have upon the protection of bondholders' interests?

12. Why do corporations generally want rights to call bonds for redemption beyond what are needed for sinking fund calls? What is the usual scope of such additional call privileges?

13. If the holders of a large proportion of a corporation's bonds, such as 75 per cent, approve changes in the indenture, are nonvoting and dissenting bondholders bound by these changes? Explain.

14. Why can both strong and weak corporations benefit from adding convertibility features and stock-purchase warrants in their bond issues?

15. Under what circumstances can holders of convertible bonds be "forced" to exercise their conversion privileges? Why might a corporation want to exert force in this direction?

Problems

1. The bond issues of five corporations, designated below by the letters A to E, are convertible into the respective common stocks at the ratios and prices indicated. All the common stocks are affected by split-ups or distributions of stock dividends, so that, in accordance with antidilution provisions in the bond indentures, the conversion ratios and prices must be changed. What would be the new levels of the ratios or prices for the five bond issues?

Corporation	Conversion Price	Conversion Ratio	Change in Common Stock
A	$40		3 per cent stock dividend
B	28		3 for 2 split-up
C		3 shares	10 per cent stock dividend
D		4 shares	2 for 1 split-up
E	32		100 per cent stock dividend

2. The bonds of a certain corporation are convertible into its common stock at a conversion price of $25. What, if anything, would be indicated about the probable level of the market price of the common stock if the bonds were selling in the market at 96? 100? 104? 150?

chapter 29

THE SALE OF BOND ISSUES

Offerings to the general public, offerings to the existing security holders, and sales in bulk to institutional investors (private placements) are the three principal channels for the selling of bond issues. How the first two of these combined compare in importance with the third is indicated in Table 29–1 where SEC data of public offerings and private placements

TABLE 29–1
Corporate Bonds Publicly Offered and Privately Placed, 1946–62[a]
(Estimated gross proceeds in millions of dollars)

Year	Publicly Offered	Privately Placed	Private Placements as Percentage of Total
1946	$3,019	$1,863	38.2
1947	2,889	2,147	42.6
1948	2,965	3,008	50.4
1949	2,437	2,453	50.2
1950	2,360	2,560	52.0
1951	2,364	3,326	58.4
1952	3,645	3,957	52.1
1953	3,856	3,228	45.6
1954	4,003	3,484	46.5
1955	4,119	3,301	44.5
1956	4,225	3,777	47.2
1957	6,118	3,839	38.6
1958	6,332	3,320	34.4
1959	3,557	3,632	50.5
1960	4,806	3,275	40.5
1961	4,706	4,720	50.1
1962	4,487	4,529	50.2

[a] Substantially all new issues of bonds offered for cash sale in the United States in amounts over $100,000 and with terms to maturity of more than one year.

SOURCE: Securities and Exchange Commission, *Annual Report*, 1962, p. 185; and *Statistical Bulletin*, April, 1963, p. 11.

for the period 1946–62 are presented. The race is close. In some years, private placements slightly or moderately exceed public offerings, and in others fall short by somewhat wider margins. Offerings to existing security holders are for the most part the tendering of new issues of convertible bonds to common stockholders; however, bondholders are occasionally offered new bonds in exchange for their present holdings.

Related to sales of bonds in some respects is the "assumption" of bond issues in mergers and consolidations. It is a common practice for the surviving corporation in a merger or the new corporation in a consolidation to take full responsibility for the outstanding bond issues of the corporation or corporations it is absorbing, carrying them thereafter as its own liabilities. While this is not a sale of new bonds, it is an important means by which corporations gain the ownership of operating assets—often great volumes of assets of large values. Accordingly, the "assumption" of bond issues deserves to be discussed in this chapter as a means of financing with bonds.

SALES TO THE GENERAL PUBLIC

In offering new bond issues to the general public, corporations in almost all instances use the services of investment bankers—a fact indicated by SEC data of registered corporate securities flotations in the year 1962. Of a total of $4,172,651,000 of bond issues registered for immediate offering for cash for the accounts of the issuing corporations, $4,050,806,000 was underwritten by investment bankers, $55,656,000 was handled by the bankers on an agency basis, and only $66,189,000 was sold by the corporations direct. While these sales included offerings to existing security holders and "other special groups," as well as offerings to the general public, other SEC figures clearly show that underwritten sales of bonds were chiefly offerings to the general public. Of total effective registrations of corporate bonds *and stocks* for immediate cash sale for the accounts of the issuers totaling $5,821,325,000 in 1962, only $787,054,000 was offered to existing security holders and only $24,188,000 to "other special groups." Since the offering of new stock issues by rights to existing stockholders is a much more common practice than the offering of bonds to any class of existing security holders, it is a reasonable conclusion, moreover, that most of the $787,054,000 of issues just referred to consisted of stock offerings.[1]

When corporations want to have the assistance of investment bankers in floating bond issues, they make their approach to the bankers in either of two ways: (1) by direct negotiation with single houses, or (2) by broadside invitations to many banking houses to submit bids for the issues. The procedure of direct negotiation was described at length in Chapter 17 in the discussion of common stock flotations; as the procedure is much the same for bond flotations, little needs to be added here. On the other hand, "competitive bidding," because it was passed over earlier, deserves a more extended examination at this time.

Direct Negotiation

The typical corporate management prefers to take its proposition for a bond flotation to the single investment banking house of its choice, just as it so chooses when planning to bring out additional issues of

---
[1] See Securities and Exchange Commission, *Statistical Bulletin*, July, 1963, p. 16.

common or preferred stock. It it is turned down by the first house approached, it may go to a second and then to a third—but always to each house individually, without attempting to offer its bonds broadside to many houses simultaneously. This preference is surely indicated by the fact that the procedure of "competitive bidding" is little used outside the areas wherein it has been promoted by government regulation. It is also demonstrated by the fact that public utility and railroad corporations that are subject to competitive bidding rules often use the direct negotiation approach when it is possible to do so on account of exceptions to or special exemptions from the competitive bidding rules. However, offers of bond issues for competitive bids are often made by utilities that are not subject to competitive bidding requirements imposed by government regulation.

In direct negotiation with the single investment banking house of its choice, a corporation usually seeks an underwriting commitment. The bankers make a preliminary investigation and, if things look promising, follow this up with a detailed investigation. If that, too, comes out satisfactorily, they are likely to agree to make the underwriting commitment. They then help the corporation to prepare the registration statement and the related prospectus for filing with the SEC as well as documents necessary for qualifying the bonds for sale in various states according to the terms of their blue-sky laws. This kind of preparatory work is more complex for a bond issue than for a stock issue, made so by the necessity of drawing up the bond indenture which is itself, as we have had occasion to note, a long and complex document. A trustee must be selected, and the details of the indenture worked out in meticulous detail. If the bonds are to be offered in interstate commerce, the indenture must meet the requirements of the federal Trust Indenture Act,[2] and copies must be filed with the registration statement. Further work falls to the originating investment banking house when it decides to form an underwriting syndicate with other houses and a selling group of securities dealers—as it is most likely to decide for any issue of substantial size.

In some instances, investment bankers refuse to underwrite but agree to assist with the sale of bond issues on a best-efforts basis. As a rule, however, best-efforts selling is much less common in the flotation of bond issues than in the flotation of stock issues. Most investment bankers doubtless conclude that if underwritten bonds would be difficult to sell, the bonds must be so unsafe or otherwise lacking in investment qualities as to make it unwise for them, on any basis, to urge their customers to buy. Because stocks are by nature speculative, they are likely to have fewer qualms in offering on a best-efforts basis issues thought to be too risky for underwriting.

---

[2] See above, pp. 629–30.

Competitive Bidding

Although competitive bidding rules imposed by governmental agencies are applicable to the stock issues as well as to the bond issues of regulated corporations, competitive bidding for bond issues has been much more significant than for stock issues. For one thing, the regulated corporations have issued much greater volumes of bonds than of stocks since the rules were imposed; and for another, exemptions from the rules have been and are granted much more often for stock issues than for bond issues. Accordingly, except for a footnote, the matter of competitive bidding was ignored in the earlier discussion of stock selling, being deferred to this chapter where it most importantly applies.

Scope of Competitive Bidding. Although governmental bodies had long offered some or all their debt issues for competitive bids, it was not until 1926 that a significant requirement in this direction was imposed on business corporations. This was the rule of the Interstate Commerce Commission requiring railroads subject to its juridiction to offer their equipment-trust certificates on a competitive bidding basis. The next important step in the same direction was taken by the SEC by virtue of its powers under the Public Utility Holding Company Act of 1935; it prescribed, effective May 7, 1941, that registered public utility holding companies and their operating subsidiaries use the competitive bidding procedure for most of their new issues, as well as for sales of securities from the portfolios of the holding companies. Next came, in 1944, a broadening of the rule of the Interstate Commerce Commission making it applicable to all issues of securities of interstate railroads having proceeds of more than $1 million; and this was followed up in 1950 by the imposition of a competitive bidding rule by the Federal Power Commission, applicable to public utilities operating in interstate commerce but not subject to the jurisdiction of the SEC. Meanwhile, some of the state public service commissions, by exercising powers already held or on the basis of new grants of power by the legislatures, imposed competitive bidding rules on utilities and railroads coming under their regulatory jurisdiction.

The competitive bidding rules are generally subject to certain exceptions set forth in the laws or regulations. For issues under the SEC's jurisdiction, for example, exceptions are granted for those with proceeds of less than $1 million, for private borrowings from financial institutions with maturities of ten years or less, and for nonunderwritten rights offerings to existing security holders. Moreover, the regulatory agencies are empowered to grant specific exemptions for given flotations, as when they are persuaded that better prices can be obtained by direct negotiation. In some instances, regulated corporations offer issues for competitive bids only to receive none, and then receive permission to proceed with direct negotiation.

The extent to which competitive bidding requirements are applicable, as well as the significance of exemptions, is indicated by the record of offerings of public utility holding companies and subsidiaries that are subject to the supervisory authority of the SEC. In the period from May 7, 1941, through June 30, 1962, these companies sold by the competitive bidding route 839 issues of securities, chiefly bonds, with an aggregate sales value of $12,300 million; while 231 issues having a total sales value of $2,371 million were sold by other procedures allowed as exceptions to the SEC's competitive bidding rules.[3]

Competitive bidding procedures are available, of course, to any corporation even though it is not required by government regulation to take that route. As was stated earlier, many public utility corporations do offer their securities for competitive bids even when not required to do so. On the other hand, the offering of securities by the competitive bidding route has made very little progress among the mass of industrial corporations.

Procedure. A corporation that plans to offer a bond issue for competitive bids must largely go it alone in preparing the issue for the market. It may ask an investment banking house for advice, but it can hardly expect to get a great amount of detailed assistance from it, as in direct-negotiation procedures. No matter how great might be its desire to underwrite the issue, the investment banking house would hardly want to go to much expense in helping, knowing that its bid might prove not to be the best one. The corporation might ask the bankers for help by promising them a fee for their services; but, under the rules of the regulatory commissions, the acceptance of a fee in this connection generally precludes the submission of a bid. Thus, bankers willing to provide help for a fee would have to have no interest in submitting a bid.

With preparations completed and legal requirements as to registration, if applicable, satisfied, the corporation publishes a notice in which it invites bids for the whole issue, as in Figure 29–1. In this notice, the bonds are described briefly, the place where all documents can be examined is named, how copies of the prospectus and the statement setting forth the rules for the bidding can be obtained is indicated, and the day and hour by which bids must be submitted are stated. Usually, also, the notice sets a time and place for a meeting at which corporation officials will be on hand to explain whatever details of the proposed issue prospective bidders want to inquire about. The meeting is usually set for a time several days before that on which the bids are to be submitted.

Several prominent investment banking houses that often serve as originators of new security issues may be interested in submitting bids for the proposed bond issue. Such a house will line up other houses tentatively for an underwriting syndicate. Conferences will be held with the repre-

---

[3] Securities and Exchange Commission, *Annual Report*, 1962, p. 89.

FIGURE 29-1

Advertisement for Competitive Bids for a Bond Issue

BROCKTON EDISON COMPANY

Public Invitation for Bids for the Purchase of
$5,000,000 Principal Amount of First Mortgage and
Collateral Trust Bonds, _____% Series due 1989

BROCKTON EDISON COMPANY hereby invites bids for the purchase from it of $5,000,000 principal amount of First Mortgage and Collateral Trust Bonds, ...% Series due 1989. Such bids will be received by the Company at 49 Federal Street (8th Floor), Boston, Massachusetts, up to 11:00 A. M., Boston Time, on Tuesday, June 23, 1959, or such later date as may be fixed by the Company as provided in the Terms and Conditions for Bids for the Purchase of such Bonds dated June 16, 1959. Copies of such Terms and Conditions for Bids, the Registration Statement and Prospectus and other related documents are available and may be examined at 49 Federal Street (8th Floor), Boston, Massachusetts, or 90 Broad Street (21st Floor), New York, N. Y. Bids need be considered only from persons who shall have furnished to the Company certain information on the questionnaire referred to in said Terms and Conditions for Bids before 11:00 A. M., Boston Time, on Friday, June 19, 1959, and who have received copies of such Prospectus, and only if made in accordance with and subject to the Terms and Conditions for Bids.

Officers and representatives of the Company, counsel for the Company, representatives of Messrs. Patterson, Teele & Dennis, independent public accountants, and Messrs. Ropes, Gray, Best, Coolidge & Rugg, counsel for the prospective Purchasers of the above-mentioned securities, will be available at 49 Federal Street (8th Floor), Boston, Massachusetts, on Friday, June 19, 1959 at 11:00 A. M., Boston Time, to meet with prospective bidders for the purpose of reviewing with them the information with respect to the Company contained in the Registration Statement and Prospectus and for the purpose of considering matters referred to in the Terms and Conditions for Bids. All prospective bidders are invited to be present at such meeting.

BROCKTON EDISON COMPANY
By PAUL E. MILSTEAD, *President.*

June 16, 1959.

sentatives of these houses, with particular attention to the level of the bid to be submitted, but usually the final decision is deferred until a meeting on the morning of the day upon which the bids are to be submitted. When a bid has been accepted, the originator signs the underwriting agreement with the corporation, the syndicate agreement is signed by all the underwriting houses, and arrangements are completed for the setting up of a selling group if one has been decided upon, as is most likely.

It is possible, of course, that no investment banking house will be sufficiently interested in a proposed bond issue to submit a bid for itself or for itself and the other houses of a tentative syndicate. A goodly number of invitations for bids meet such negative responses. Moreover, the offering corporations invariably reserve the right to reject all bids, so that offerings may fail, at least on the first round, because all bids are thought to be too low.

Bids. In offering a bond issue for competitive bids, the corporation usually names neither the price at which it will sell the bonds nor the interest rate that the bonds will carry. It is left to the bidders to name both price and interest rate. One group of houses may offer 102.61 for the bonds stipulating that the interest rate shall be 4¾ per cent; and another may offer 100.66 stipulating that the interest rate shall be fixed at 4½ per cent. The corporation will accept the better bid, unless it chooses to reject both. But, assuming that the bonds are to have a 20-year maturity, which of these is the better bid? The first will give the corporation $1,026.10 for each $1,000 bond of its issue, it will have to pay back only $1,000 at maturity, and, in the meantime, it will be paying interest at 4¾ per cent on only the par value. The second bid will give the corporation only $1,006.60 for each $1,000 bond, it will have to pay back $1,000 at maturity, but, in the meantime, it will get by with a slightly lower rate of interest on the par value. The answer to the question, therefore, must be in terms of *effective* rates of interest. Bond tables reveal that the effective rate on a 20-year 4¾ per cent bond sold at 102.61 is 4.55 per cent, and that on a 20-year 4½ per cent bond sold at 100.66 it is 4.45 per cent. The bid at 100.66 with a 4½ per cent interest rate proves to be the more favorable one.

In practice, bids are often much closer than in the foregoing illustration, only a slight effective-rate differential separating one from another. For example, the American Telephone and Telegraph Company, in offering in May, 1963, a debenture issue of $250 million to be due in 1999, received a bid of 100.171 "for a 4⅜ per cent coupon" from a 138-member underwriting group headed by Morgan Stanley & Company, and a second bid of 102.11 with a prescription for an interest rate of 4½ per cent from a group of approximately 250 investment banking houses headed jointly by the First Boston Corporation and Halsey, Stuart & Co., Inc. The Morgan Stanley group won the privilege of underwriting because its bid meant an annual interest cost to A.T. & T. of 4.37 per cent, whereas acceptance of the second bid would have meant an annual interest cost of 4.38 per cent! Similarly, in April, 1962, the Northern Indiana Public Service Company received seven close bids in offering $20 million of its first-mortgage bonds, Series L, to be due in 1992. All bidders designated a "4⅜ per cent coupon," and a group of bankers headed by Halsey, Stuart won the contest with a bid of 100.82. The other bids from prospective managers of other syndicates were as follows:

White, Weld & Co.	100.651
Eastman Dillon, Union Securities & Co., Lehman Brothers, and Bear, Stearns & Co., jointly	100.611
Equitable Securities Corporation	100.611
Dean, Witter & Co., Blyth & Co., Inc., and Merrill Lynch, Pierce, Fenner & Smith, Inc., jointly	100.61
First Boston Corporation	100.567
Kuhn, Loeb & Co.	100.54

In naming a price in its bid, an investment banking house, needless to say, expects that it, the other underwriters, and the dealers of the selling group will be able to resell to their customers at a higher price. And, of course, the bankers must agree among themselves how the expected spread is to be shared among the manager of the syndicate, the syndicate members, and the members of the selling group.

Pros and Cons of Competitive Bidding. There has been a long debate about the merits and drawbacks of competitive bidding. With some exceptions, the investment bankers have been critical, but the government regulatory agencies appear to be satisfied with the results of their competitive bidding rules. The corporations that are subject to these rules seem, too, to be generally satisfied, but it is noteworthy that most unregulated corporations, especially industrials, do not take the competitive bidding route although free to do so.

Since the development of competitive bidding has been largely the result of government regulation, most of the arguments in favor have been focused upon the promotion of the general welfare, rather than upon the advancement of the interests of particular groups, whether corporations, bankers, or investors. From this standpoint, it is argued that competitive bidding enables corporations to get long-term funds more cheaply—that competing bankers will bid up the prices of (or, alternatively, bid down the rates of interest upon) the security issues they are anxious to underwrite; that they will have much less influence upon the policies of corporations whose securities they underwrite; and that a few large houses will be prevented from getting the lion's share of underwritings.

The gist of the first of these arguments is that a lower cost of funds to public utilities and railroads should enable them to supply their services to the public at lower rates. The second argument is predicated upon the proposition that investment bankers have often tried to dominate the affairs of corporations whose securities they have underwritten on a direct-negotiation basis, and especially that such domination, if effective simultaneously over many corporations, leads to many kinds of restraints of trade. The third argument grows out of allegations that, in a system of direct negotiation, large corporations, in particular, limit their proposals of security flotations to a handful of large investment banking houses of national reputation and that these houses, in forming syndicates, repeatedly invite given groups of houses and repeatedly ignore many others than could function just as effectively. The argument is, therefore, that underwriting by direct negotiation leads toward monopoly in the investment banking industry itself. Obviously, the three arguments are closely related. If a small group of large houses dominate the affairs of many corporations, the corporations will undoubtedly go to this group with their flotations, and, at the same time, the dominating bankers will surely dictate the allocation of handsome underwriting spreads for themselves.

The opponents of competitive bidding—a class largely made up of investment bankers, although by no means including all such bankers[4]—have some difficulty in advancing their position on the grounds of general welfare; they are more inclined to argue that direct negotiation is

---

[4] Among the strong supporters of competitive bidding practices is Halsey, Stuart & Co., Inc., one of the largest of our investment banking houses.

beneficial for corporate issuers of securities and for investors, although they often carry their arguments further to say that benefits to corporations and investors also contribute to the general welfare. In the first place, the bankers find it imperative to deny that they try to dominate the corporations whose securities they underwrite by direct negotiation. They often admit that attempts at domination were common in the past, but they claim that this aspect of "finance capitalism" is now obsolete. Corporate managements, they say, welcome them to their boards of directors to gain the benefits of their broad knowledge of financial markets and security management, just as they welcome "outside" directors from other walks of life to get the benefits of knowledge and experience of other kinds. An investment banking house to which a corporation always takes its long-term financing will have a continuing interest in its welfare—and all the more so if a member of the house sits on the corporation's board of directors where he can keep an eye on developments. In times of difficulty, investment bankers in this position can be expected to do everything possible to aid the corporation— something that should be of benefit to all its employees, to all the people who own its securities, and probably to its customers as well. It is argued that such devotion can hardly be expected of bankers who win a corporation's security issue by a low bid; such bankers know that future business with the corporation will depend, not upon what help they may thereafter give to it, but simply on how the bids turn out the next time it offers a security issue.

In answer to the argument that competitive bidding enables corporations to obtain long-term funds more cheaply—evidenced by the fact that underwriting spreads on competitive bidding deals are generally substantially less than upon negotiated deals—the opponents of competitive bidding argue that the corporations pay less because they get fewer services. The competitive bidder, it is argued, incurs no expense in helping the corporation to prepare its security issue for the market; it does not even offer advice on the character and terms of the issue; and it accepts no responsibility for continued interest in the corporation and its securities in the future. Services that the corporation does not pay for and does not get are likely to be the very ones that would be of most benefit to the investing public. An investment banking house that bids for a security issue thereby signifies its willingness to take it as the corporation designed it; but if it had worked out the details on a negotiated basis, it might have insisted upon a much stronger array of protective provisions in the interests of its customers, the security buyers.

It is more difficult for the opponents of competitive bidding to explain away the fact that underwriting spreads for all issuers, both those that sell by direct negotiation and those that sell by the competitive bidding route, are nowadays generally much less than they used to be. Because this is true, it can hardly be explained away. But to preclude giving too much credit to competitive bidding for this development, opponents of that practice often argue that the rapid growth of private placements has been the more important reason for the decline in the size of underwriting spreads. Such an argument, however, only indicates that there may be more than one reason why investment bankers are now willing to work harder for a given reward than they were formerly.

SALES TO EXISTING SECURITY HOLDERS

The sale of bonds by corporations to their existing security holders is very largely the sale of convertible issues to common stockholders. Whether or not the preemptive right obtains, such offerings are made chiefly because of convictions of corporate managers that the common stockholders are the most likely buyers—not for reason of their interests in bond investment as such, but for reason of their interests in eventually getting additional common shares by way of the conversion route. In some instances, corporations offer new bonds to existing bondholders in exchange for their holdings, but a discussion of this kind of operation can best be deferred to the next chapter which is devoted to the management of outstanding bond issues.

Corporations that offer convertible bonds to their common stockholders are generally of the class that would prefer to be issuing common stock in the first place. They want conversion to take place, and they anticipate that the common stockholders will actually convert when the market prices of their common stocks improve. In other words, these corporations issue convertible bonds because the market for bonds is generally favorable, while that for their common stocks is not as strong as they think it should be. Their managers may fear that the depressive effect on the market prices of their stocks would be too great were they to offer at once the same number of shares as that into which the bonds are made convertible. But their expectation is that, when the market for their stocks has gained strength, the bonds will flow back for conversion, perhaps gradually, or perhaps in bulk especially near the times when the conversion prices are scheduled to rise.

No corporation could hope to rival the record of the American Telephone and Telegraph Company as a large-scale offerer of convertible bonds to its stockholders. From 1946 to 1958, it made eight offers, the largest—for approximately $718 million—coming in 1958, and all eight totaling a little over $3,967 million. (To keep things humming in one of the off years, 1956, it made a rights offering of 5,726,000 shares of common stock, and later, in 1961, another offering of common stock, this time 11,191,112 shares.) But many other corporations have offered convertible bonds to their common stockholders, some once, and some repeatedly. Though not up to A.T. & T. standards for size, some have been relatively large, as, for example, General Telephone and Electronics Corporation's issue of $46,630,400 in 1956, Boeing Airplane Company's sale of $30,597,600 in 1958, the issue of Pan American World Airways of $46,971,000 in 1959, that of Trans World Airlines of approximately $107 million in 1961, one of Air Reduction Company of $45 million in 1962, and United Aircraft Corporation's issue of approximately $43 million in 1963.

Procedure

The procedure of making a rights offering of convertible bonds is much the same as for additional issues of common stock, as described at length in Chapter 18; hence, only a brief description is necessary here. The directors adopt a resolution setting forth the terms of the offering, establishing a record date as of which the names of the stockholders to whom the offering will be made are to be determined, and setting a later date and hour at which the subscription books will be closed. As soon as possible after the record date, the secretary of the corporation or the stock-transfer agent sends a subscription warrant to each stockholder whose name appeared on the books at the close of business on that day. The stockholder then may subscribe by filling in the warrant and submitting it to the corporation or its subscription agent with his payment (or with the first instalment of his payment, if payment in instalments has been authorized); he may endorse the warrant and sell it to somebody else or give it away; or, of course, he may do nothing.

A rights offering for convertible bonds, like one for additional common stock, is made on a pro rata basis. Each stockholder is given the right to subscribe in the proportion of the number of his shares to the total outstanding. Suppose, for example, that a corporation having 500,000 shares of common stock outstanding is making a rights offering of $5 million of convertible bonds. The subscription warrants that it issues represent 500,000 rights, and 100 rights and cash equal to the subscription price are required for the purchase of a $1,000 bond. The owner of 400 shares gets 400 rights; and, with the requisite amount of cash, he may buy bonds of a par value of $4,000.

Transactions in Rights

As in a rights offering for new common stock, a corporation that offers bonds by the rights procedure expects most of its stockholders to subscribe, but, if there are hundreds or thousands of stockholders, it hardly anticipates a perfect response. Because it wants to sell all the bonds offered, it hopes, therefore, that nonsubscribing stockholders will pass on their warrants to other investors who will enter subscriptions. It does more than hope for this—it strongly encourages it by offering the bonds at a price somewhat below what it would expect to set were it making an offering to the general public. As the subscription price in rights offerings of convertible bonds is set at 100 in a great majority of cases, this means that the interest rate designated for the bonds is set slightly higher than would be needed for a sale to the public at 100. If the corporation's estimation proves to be reasonably accurate, the rights will have a market value determined by the difference between the offering price and what investors think the bonds will be worth when they have been issued. With a rights value established, stockholders who do not want to exercise their rights will surely have every reason to sell them.

Let us assume that the corporation of the foregoing illustration offers its bonds to the stockholders at the customary subscription price of 100. This is a "bargain" price—the corporate managers intend it to be that—but outsiders also recognize it as such. The latter, accordingly, begin to bid prices higher than 100 for bonds to be delivered to them "when issued." They want to enter into contracts at once at, say, 101 or 102 for future delivery, for they expect to be able to resell at, say, 103 or 104 when delivery is made after the end of the subscription period. They hope to make a nice profit on a speculation of quite short term. But their spirited bidding may drive up the price of bonds "when issued" to, say, 103. Stockholders who do not want to buy and hold the new bonds to which they are entitled may be quite willing to enter into contracts for future sales at 103. A pleasant prospect, indeed, do they have of buying from the corporation at 100 and then quickly selling at 103. Speculators who do not think that the market price will reach 103 may sell short for future delivery, expecting to make a profit equal to the difference between that selling price and the lower price at which they hope to be able to buy later to make delivery. At any rate, bids and offers from sources such as these establish a market value for the not-yet-issued bonds, and if this value is in excess of the subscription price, the stockholders' rights to subscribe also have a market value. In terms of the illustration, a market price for bonds "when issued" of 103 should give each right a market value of close to 30 cents, as determined by the following formula:

$$\frac{\text{Market value of bond} - \text{Subscription price}}{\text{Number of rights required to buy one bond}} = \text{Value of a right}$$

Substituting, we get:

$$\frac{\$1,030 - \$1,000}{100} = 30 \text{ cents}$$

Thus, the stockholder who does not want to buy and hold bonds may sell for future delivery as many bonds as he is entitled to buy from the corporation, with assurances of a gain of $30 on each, or, for a gain of equal amount, he may simply sell each 100 of his rights. In either transaction, the objective of the corporation to dispose of the bond issue is served. In the first alternative, the stockholder actually subscribes for his allotment of the bonds, although he does not hold them for long;

in the second, whoever buys his rights in the market, or, anyway, whoever holds them near the end of the subscription period will presumably subscribe.

In the Pan American World Airways rights offering of $46,971,000 of its convertible subordinated debentures in the summer of 1959, for example, the subscription price was set at 100, and 140 rights were required for the purchase of each $1,000 bond. Early in the subscription period, bonds sold on a "when issued" basis at prices as high as 112½! Accordingly, rights sold in the market at prices as high as 87.5 cents.

Question of Dilution

The "gain" derived by a stockholder who sells his rights to subscribe to convertible bonds, or who subscribes and then immediately sells the bonds, is not necessarily all "frosting on the cake." It will prove so to be if no subsequent conversion of bonds into common stock takes place; in that circumstance, the stockholder suffers no dilution in his rights to earnings, assets, and voting power. The amount of common stock outstanding remains the same, and his proportionate interests are as before. But if subsequent conversions do take place, dilution results, so that the "gain" turns out to be, in part at least, the proceeds of the sale of some of the stockholder's ownership interests.

Stockholders' Attitudes

As in the disposal of rights to subscribe directly to additional shares of common stock, the attitudes of stockholders toward subscriptions to convertible bonds differ. All who are interested in control will be strongly inclined to exercise their rights to subscribe. Hardly less attracted will be the stockholders who choose to accumulate wealth in the form of corporate assets, as well as those who are "loyal" to the corporation in appreciation of its dividend policies. Some may subscribe to bonds, though they would not subscribe direct for additional stock, because they want to balance their investment portfolios. But many, particularly smaller stockholders, are likely to look upon the rights as a "dividend" and to hurry to sell them in the market. Nor may we fail to mention those who, not understanding what is going on, can be depended upon to deposit their subscription warrants in the wastebasket. In the 1958 offering of A.T. & T. convertible bonds, for example, holders of rights permitting subscriptions to $1,915,000 of the bonds (out of the total offering of $718,313,000) neither exercised nor sold their rights.

Registration and the Bankers

When rights to subscribe to convertible bonds are to be offered in interstate commerce to many stockholders, registration with the SEC is required no less than when rights offerings of common stock are made. For such offerings, too, the bond indentures must satisfy the requirements of the federal Trust Indenture Act. Also applicable are the qualification requirements of many of the state blue-sky laws.

In a study of securities flotations in the years 1951, 1953, and 1955, the SEC found that corporations collectively handle a much larger proportion of their direct offerings of bonds to their own security holders without the assistance of investment bankers than with that assistance, the ratio in the three years having been almost 3 to 1.[5] However, this ratio was heavily weighted by rights offerings of A.T. & T. in each of the three years made without banker participation. When the bankers do participate in financing of this kind, they usually serve on a basis of standby underwriting. Best-efforts dealer-manager arrangements are much less popular in rights offerings of bonds than in stock offerings by the rights procedure.

PRIVATE PLACEMENTS

Although the private placement of common and preferred stocks was briefly treated in Chapters 19 and 23, private placement occurs much more frequently in the sale of bond issues. The important role of this means of selling bonds in the period since 1946 was indicated earlier in this chapter in Table 29–1 on page 715. There we saw that private placements have been averaging annually pretty close to half of the total volume of bond sales.

Presumably the private placement of bond issues would have accounted for an even larger proportion of total bond sales in the postwar years were it not for the competitive bidding rules applicable to most public utility and railroad issues, as discussed earlier. The life insurance companies and other institutional buyers of bonds privately placed rarely submit bids for bonds (or other securities) offered by the competitive bidding route. Although as free to submit bids as are other classes of investors, they choose to buy bonds in bulk on a more certain basis than the hit-or-miss basis of competitive bidding. For this reason, bonds sold by competitive bidding are almost always "public offerings" and very rarely do they become "private placements."

The influence of competitive bidding rules can be seen in the data of Table 29–2 in which bond sales figures for 1953 and 1955 are classified according to the fields of enterprise of the issuers. Leaving corporations in the communications industry out of consideration momentarily, one immediately notices that the largest proportions of public offerings, and the smallest, accordingly, of private placements, were those of railroads and electric, gas, and water companies—precisely the enterprises that are most extensively subject to the competitive bidding rules. The sharp contrast between the selling channels used by railroads, subject to competitive bidding rules, and other transportation companies, not so subject,

---

[5] Securities and Exchange Commission, *Volume and Nature of Corporate Securities Offerings,* mimeographed release, July, 1957, p. 15.

TABLE 29–2
Corporate Bonds Publicly Offered and Privately Placed,
by Industry of Issuer, 1953 and 1955
(Dollar amounts in millions)

INDUSTRY	TOTAL OFFERINGS[a]	PERCENTAGES	
		Publicly Offered	Privately Placed
Manufacturing.....................	$ 4,047	45.4	54.6
Electric, gas, and water............	3,575	65.6	34.4
Communication...................	1,780	90.7	9.3
Mining..........................	329	12.0	88.0
Railroad.........................	844	97.4	2.6
Other transportation...............	566	5.3	94.7
Finance and real estate............	2,743	40.5	59.5
Commercial and miscellaneous.......	619	28.0	72.0
Total........................	$14,503	55.0	45.0

[a] Estimated proceeds.

SOURCE: Securities and Exchange Commission, *Volume and Nature of Corporate Securities Offerings,* mimeographed release, July, 1957, p. 13.

is especially noteworthy. Likewise of note is the fact that all classes of issuers, except railroads, the utilities, and the communications companies, sold substantially more bonds by private placement than by public offerings. Since the communications companies are not subject to competitive bidding rules, their selection of sales channels looks peculiar until one recalls the dominant position of A.T. & T. and its subsidiaries among these companies. In the two years of the table, A.T. & T. issued more than $1,600 million of convertible debenture bonds by way of rights offerings to its common stockholders, thus putting these issues in the public offerings category.

Private Buyers

Institutional investors buy bonds for their own long-term investment; unlike investment bankers, they do not buy for resale. But what classes of institutions have so much money that they can, at a stroke, so to say, buy entire bond issues? The answer is largely in the singular: life insurance companies. Commercial banks, casulty insurance companies, philanthropic foundations, religious, educational, and charitable institutions (for the investment of their endowment funds), and the trustees of pension and retirement funds are also significant as outlets for private placements, but the combined acquisitions of privately placed bonds by all these classes of institutions are dwarfed by the acquisitions of life insurance companies. This is shown in Table 29–3.

The dominant role of life insurance companies on the buying end of private placements is also suggested by their total holdings of corporate bonds and the growth of these holdings over the years, as shown in Table 29–4. One must not infer, however, that the total bond holdings of life insurance companies are acquired by the private placement route.

TABLE 29-3
Purchasers of Bonds Privately Placed, 1947–55
(Percentages of total amounts)

	1947	1950	1953	1955
Life insurance companies	93.0	83.4	87.0	85.0
Other insurance companies	.1	.7	.1	.3
Banks	2.7	12.1	5.7	5.8
Eleemosynary institutions	2.5	.5	.4	1.2
Others[a]	.4	2.5	5.5	6.0
Unknown	1.3	.8	1.3	1.7
Total	100.0	100.0	100.0	100.0

[a] "Includes other corporations, pension and retirement funds, partnerships and individuals. This is probably a minimum figure for the group as such sales are not always publicized or reported to the S.E.C."

Source: Securities and Exchange Commission, *Volume and Nature of Corporate Securities Offerings*, mimeographed release, July, 1957, p. 6.

Like any other class of investors, they can buy bonds in the market. For the larger companies, nevertheless, so great is the pressure of funds demanding prompt investment that bulk purchases must be emphasized. Even here, however, there is one alternative to acquisitions by private placement, namely, buying in large lots from investment bankers who are underwriting public offerings. In an earlier chapter, it was mentioned that the originating investment banking house, as manager of the underwriting syndicate, may reserve a portion of the issue being underwritten for sale to institutional investors.[6]

TABLE 29-4
Corporate Bondholdings of Life Insurance Companies,
Selected Years, 1917–62
(In millions of dollars)

Year	Railroad	Public Utility	Industrial and Miscellaneous	Total
1917	$1,813	$ 113	$ 49	$ 1,975
1920	1,775	125	49	1,949
1925	2,238	687	97	3,022
1930	2,931	1,631	367	4,929
1935	2,625	2,114	575	5,314
1940	2,830	4,273	1,542	8,645
1945	2,948	5,212	1,900	10,060
1950	3,187	10,587	9,526	23,300
1955	3,912	13,968	18,179	36,059
1960	3,668	16,719	26,728	47,115
1961	3,594	16,999	28,690	49,283
1962	3,496	17,330	30,718	51,544

Source: Institute of Life Insurance, *Life Insurance Fact Book*, 1963, p. 64.

Cost Factors in Private Placements

At first glance, one might conclude that any corporation planning to sell a bond issue should first offer it to life insurance companies or to

[6] See above, p. 407.

other institutional investors. The flotation costs ought to be much less in a private placement than for a public offering. Some of the economies come readily to mind: no underwriting commissions to investment bankers; no expenses for the preparation of a registration statement and prospectus and for qualifying under blue-sky laws; no need, probably, to hire a trustee. Moreover, the institutional investor might be willing to take notes rather than bonds, thereby eliminating engraving expenses and avoiding the federal issuance tax which applies to bonds but not to notes. Even further, the legal staff of the institutional investor—especially that of a life insurance company—ought to be willing to bear most of the burdens of preparing the indenture; since the institution would want to have a hand in working out every detail of the indenture, it would probably be happy to have its own people take major responsibility for the preparation of the document.

All such economies—or many of them, in the individual case—are quite real in private placements.[7] But this does not necessarily mean that the *total cost of borrowing* to the corporation—flotation costs plus interest burdens during the life of an issue—will be less in a private placement than in a public offering. The investment officers of life insurance companies and other institutional investors are shrewd bargainers. Fully aware of the economies of private placements, they will surely insist that their institutions share in these benefits, demanding interest rates somewhat higher than would be designated were the bonds being offered publicly. Especially will they want an upward adjustment of interest rates to compensate for expenses incurred by their institutions in the acquisition of bonds on a private placement basis, as when their legal staffs do most of the work of preparing the indentures. Another adverse cost factor may arise in the retirement of the indebtedness. Privately placed bonds are always redeemable at the full contract price; whereas corporations that sell bonds by public offerings may at times be able to buy them in the market for retirement at prices substantially below the call prices.

Other Pros and Cons of Private Placements

Closely related to economies is the typical institutional investor's willingness to buy a corporation's bond issue in instalments over a period of months or years. The institutional investor's "takedowns" can be scheduled to match the corporation's spending plans. If a corporation is launching a three-year building program, for example, it can arrange to have portions of the bonds taken from time to time as money is needed to pay the building contractor, and it begins to incur interest

---

[7] As an example, the Brooklyn Union Gas Company estimated that about $36,000 of expenses were avoided when, in April, 1963, it sold $19.2 million of 4⅜ per cent first-mortgage bonds by private placement rather than by competitive bidding. *The Wall Street Journal*, April 26, 1963, p. 21.

obligations on the bonds only when they have thus been taken by the institutional investor. On the other hand, successive public offerings of groups of bonds in a relatively short period such as three years would multiply flotation costs, while a single public offering of the full issue at the beginning of the construction period would require the temporary investment of much of the proceeds pending their eventual spending for the building program. In the latter alternative, because of the high degree of safety that would doubtless be wanted, the rate of interest earned on the temporary investments would surely be less than that being paid on the bonds themselves.

Another comparable advantage of private placements is gained when institutional investors make commitments to take bonds to be issued at some time in the future. The financial managers of a corporation may know that their expansion program will require a very large outlay of cash in 10 to 12 months, and they may want to finance this with a bond issue. Investment bankers would hardly be willing to make an immediate underwriting commitment for a public offering subject to such a lengthy delay; but institutional investors often find that advance commitments tie in most conveniently with their own financial planning. The institutional investor may have already selected investment outlets for currently inflowing funds, but as it expects the inflow to continue indefinitely, it finds imperative a constant lining up of outlets for future inflows.

If a corporation that has sold a bond issue to an institutional investor by private placement gets into financial difficulties, it has, so far as the bonds go, only one creditor to deal with. This could be advantageous. To arrange deferments of obligations to pay interest or principal, temporary reductions in the interest rate, or other modifications of the corporation's obligations should be an easier task than getting the approval of a large majority of hundreds or thousands of individual bondholders. Moreover, the institutional investor may be willing to advance additional funds to save the corporation from a perilous situation, whereas thousands of individual bondholders would doubtless be unwilling to pay in assessments for a purpose of this sort.[8] Likewise, when indenture terms prove to be too restrictive, getting the consent of a single institutional investor to modifications should be much easier than getting the approval of the widely scattered holders of two thirds or three fourths of bonds sold by a public offering.

But having only one bondholding creditor to deal with can be a source of disadvantages. It is often claimed so to be. Indentures drawn for private placements often contain more restrictive provisions and tighter ones than do those for public offerings. The institutional investor may not want to enforce rigorously all the restrictive provisions,

---

[8] What corporations can try to do to meet difficulties in fulfilling their obligations on bond issues is discussed further in Chapter 30. See pp. 752–61.

but at least it must be consulted by the corporate managers should they want permission to do something that the indenture forbids or limits. In short, the institutional investor expects to have a much more decisive influence upon the financial policies of the corporation whose bonds it buys in bulk than is expected or wanted by the trustee of a publicly offered bond issue.

Size of Private Placements

The bulk of private placements of bonds comprises issues of less than $5 million, while the bulk of public offerings through investment bankers are issues of at least $5 million. The SEC data of Table 29–5 show

TABLE 29–5
Registered Public Offerings and Private Placements of Bonds,
by Size of Issue, 1951, 1953, and 1955
(Percentages of total number of issues)

Size of Issue (In millions of dollars)	Registered Public Offerings	Private Placements
Under 0.5	. . .	20.6
0.5– 0.9	1.9	18.3
1.0– 1.9	5.7	21.2
2.0– 4.9	10.9	19.1
5.0– 9.9	16.6	8.5
10.0–19.9	27.2	5.8
20.0–49.9	29.8	4.2
50.0 and over	7.9	2.3
Total	100.0	100.0

SOURCE: Securities and Exchange Commission, *Volume and Nature of Corporate Securities Offerings,* mimeographed release, July, 1957, p. 9.

that 79.2 per cent of the number of private placements in the years 1951, 1953, and 1955 were issues of less than $5 million, while issues of $5 million or more accounted for 81.5 per cent of the number of registered issues sold through investment bankers.

As these figures suggest, many bond issues of smaller corporations not well known to the investing public tend to gravitate toward the institutional investors. The investment bankers are likely to be only mildly interested, if interested at all, in proposed bond issues of corporations of moderate size that have never made public offerings of either stocks or bonds. But, though not well known in the investment community, such a corporation may have a financial position that is quite sound; hence, it may have no great difficulty in arousing the interest of one or more institutional investors. Because they do not expect to resell, the institutional investors are not much concerned about the marketability of the bonds they buy; if, therefore, they are satisfied as to the safety of proposed bond issues, they will surely be inclined to buy. For the issuing corporation, a disadvantageous aspect of depending upon the ready-made interest of institutional investors is that it still fails to promote wide public interest in its securities.

To show, however, that the institutional investors are also interested in large bond issues of prominent corporations, some large private placements of the early months of 1963 may be mentioned: $16.5 million of "promissory notes" of the Oxford Paper Company due July 1, 1983 (with the institutional investors committed to buy an additional $15 million by October 29, 1964); $50 million of first-mortgage bonds of Dayton Power and Light Company, 4.45 per cent series, due in 1993; $18 million of 4¾ per cent first-mortgage bonds of Portland General Electric Company, also due in 1993; $50 million of "promissory notes" of Litton Industries, Inc., due in 1984; $60 million of 4⅜ per cent "notes" of the Aluminum Company of America maturing in 1988; and $60 million of 4½ per cent "notes" of American Metal Climax, Inc., due in 1988. It was also announced that a group of insurance companies had made commitments through Kuhn, Loeb & Company and the First Boston Corporation to buy in instalments up to December 31, 1964, $105 million of the first-mortgage bonds of Wheeling Steel Corporation, as well as to accept, if offered, an additional $15 million up to December 31, 1965.

Investment Bankers as Finders

Although corporations that place their bonds privately with institutional investors need no underwriting by investment bankers, they often employ the bankers as "finders." They are willing to pay the bankers a "finder's fee" in the belief that the bankers will be able to find institutional buyers even though they themselves could not, or that the bankers will be able to get for them better terms than they themselves could hope to get by a direct approach. To call attention to their services as finders, investment bankers often insert advertisements of successful placements in prominent newspapers and financial publications. Such an advertisement is reproduced as Figure 29–2.

In its studies on security flotations in the years 1951, 1953, and 1955, the SEC found that investment bankers and other agents served as finders in placing 57 per cent of the amount of debt issues privately placed in those years. Fees paid for this service varied from 1.86 per cent of the proceeds of the smallest issues to .22 per cent of the proceeds of the largest, with the median for all size groups amounting to .83 per cent.[9]

THE ASSUMPTION OF BOND ISSUES

In numerous instances, corporations use bonds for financing asset acquisitions in what might be called an indirect fashion. This is the procedure of "assuming" the bond liabilities of other corporations, a com-

---

[9] Securities and Exchange Commission, *Cost of Flotation of Corporate Securities, 1951–1955*, June, 1957, pp. 26, 27.

FIGURE 29–2
Newspaper Notice of a Private Placement

The undersigned represented the Company in negotiating an agreement.
for the purchase of these Notes by certain institutions.

$15,000,000

United Artists Corporation

6% Participating Promissory Notes

An agreement has been executed which permits the Company to sell $10,000,000 of the above amount on or before
July 2, 1959, and the balance on or before July 1, 1961.

F. EBERSTADT & CO.

May 7, 1959

---

mon practice in mergers and consolidations. Corporation A sells a bond
issue by a public offering or a private placement and uses the proceeds to
acquire a given array of assets. Then along comes Corporation B with
a merger proposition that the stockholders of A find irresistible. The
merger is effected, and B now owns the assets that A had acquired with
its bond issue; but, at the same time, B becomes fully responsible for
meeting all the obligations and covenants of A's bond indenture. It
alone remains with this responsibility, for A ceases to exist as a separate
entity if the merger is carried through as a "statutory fusion" in the
manner provided for in state corporation laws, as would be most likely.

Choice of the Surviving Corporation

Now it is clear that the surviving corporation of a merger or the new
corporation of a consolidation could choose to sell its own bond issue to
raise cash to retire the outstanding bonds of the corporation to be absorbed. The merger agreement could provide that the cash be paid
over so that the bonds of the corporation to be absorbed could be called
for redemption before the effective date of the merger. The surviving
corporation would then acquire the assets of the other without any
need of assumption.

However, the prime movers in many mergers and consolidations want
to carry them through with minimum outlays of cash. Common stock-

holders of the corporation to be absorbed are offered common stock of the surviving corporation. Similarly, if the former has preferred stock outstanding, an exchange offering of preferred stock in the surviving corporation is ordinarily made. If, then, it is also possible to take over the bonds (and other liabilities) of the corporation to be absorbed just as they stand, a very important further economy in the use of cash results. Indeed, very little cash may be needed if most of the stockholders agree to accept the exchange offers and if all, or almost all, the liabilities are assumed—very little cash for the acquisition of assets of many kinds and substantial values.

Position of the Bondholders

A curious thing about assumptions of bond issues is that the owners of the bonds themselves ordinarily having nothing to say about the matter. The corporation that issued the bonds passes out of existence, as Corporation A in the illustration, and its bondholders simply become creditors of the surviving corporation. The bondholders or their trustee, it is true, can take legal proceedings to stop a proposed merger on the grounds that its results would be fraudulent; but, if fraud is not intended, the promoters of the merger can usually satisfy the court that the safety of the bondholders' position would not be impaired. Sometimes, moreover, indentures have restrictions upon mergers and consolidations—in some instances, outright prohibitions, and, in others, requirements for the consent of the holders of two thirds or three fourths of the outstanding bonds. Nevertheless, the more common practice is for indentures to reserve to the corporation the right to merge or consolidate with others, provided only that, should it be absorbed, the successor corporation will accept full liability for the bonds.

Such an acceptance of liability—the specific "assumption" of the bonds—is usually set forth in a "supplementary indenture" entered into between the surviving corporation and the original trustee or a successor trustee. The supplementary indenture, needless to say, cannot change the interest rate, maturity, sinking fund requirements, or any of the other terms of the original indenture. Nor can it distrub any of the liens held by the bonds being assumed. If, however, the original was an open-end indenture, the supplementary indenture may close the issue, should the surviving corporation so wish. Likewise, it is generally understood that an after-acquired property clause in the assumed bonds no longer will have effect, unless the original indenture specifically prescribed how it should continue to apply after merger or consolidation. Finally, a supplementary indenture must usually provide adjusted conversion prices or ratios for assumed bonds whose conversion rights are to continue after the merger or consolidation.

Even if agreements for merger or consolidation say nothing about the disposition of outstanding bonds and other debts of corporations beir.g absorbed, and even if supplementary indentures binding the surviving corporations are not drawn up, there is no question as to their liability for these debts. It is a well-settled principle of law that, if no provision is made in a merger settlement for the paying off of such debts, the surviving corporation necessarily accepts responsibility for them. Provisions in the state corporation codes are generally quite clear and unequivocal on this score. For example, the Delaware law puts it this way:

. . . but all rights of creditors and all liens upon any property of any of said constituent corporations shall be preserved unimpaired, and all debts, liabilities and duties of the respective constituent corporations shall thenceforth attach to said resulting or surviving corporation, and may be enforced against it to the same extent as if said debts, liabilities and duties had been incurred or contracted by it. [10]

Questions

1. Compare the volume of bonds offered to the general public with the volume sold by private placement in the period since 1946.

2. To what extent, if at all, do the registration requirements of the federal Securities Act apply to sales of bonds (*a*) to the general public, (*b*) to corporations' own common stockholders, and (*c*) to institutional investors as private placements?

3. To what extent, if at all, are the services of investment bankers employed when bonds are sold in each of the three channels mentioned in Question 2? Distinguish between the services of the bankers as underwriters and as "finders."

4. Describe the steps in selling a bond issue by the competitive bidding procedure.

5. What classes of corporations are required to offer their bond issues for competitive bids? Why are they so required?

6. For what reasons are investment bankers generally critical of the competitive bidding procedure for selling new bond issues?

7. What is the significance of the fact that investment bankers name both a price and an interest rate when submitting competitive bids for a new bond issue?

8. Under what circumstances is an offering of convertible bonds to a corporation's existing common stockholders likely to be successful?

9. Do stockholders' rights to subscribe to new issues of convertible bonds always have a market value? Why or why not?

10. Why is it said that a stockholder's ownership interests may or may not be diluted if he fails to subscribe to his allotment of convertible bonds offered by the rights procedure?

11. Why is the private placement of bonds much more voluminous than the private placement of common and preferred stocks?

12. In view of the economies of private placements, why do not all corporations dispose of their bond issues in this way?

13. What are the principal institutional buyers of privately placed bonds? Why do these institutions strongly favor buying by private placement?

---

[10] State of Delaware, *General Corporation Law*, sec. 259(a).

14. What is meant by the assumption of a bond issue? In what kinds of transactions are assumptions quite common? Why is this procedure favored by assuming corporations?

15. Can a corporation that assumes a bond issue subsequently repudiate its obligation on the grounds that it was not the issuer of the bonds? Explain.

Problem

Orley & Jackman, Inc., has outstanding four million shares of common stock of $5.00 par value, and it is now bringing out an $8 million issue of 5 per cent convertible debenture bonds which it offers to its common stockholders at par. The present market value of the common stock is 35, and the conversion price for the new bonds is set at 40. John Doe is the owner of 5,000 shares of the common stock, but he does not want to buy any of the bonds. Noticing that the proposed bonds are selling in the market on a "when issued" basis at 104, he decides to sell his subscription rights.

a) Leaving brokerage commissions out of account, how much approximately should Doe realize on the sale of these rights?

b) By selling his rights, does he suffer an immediate dilution in his ownership interests? Why or why not?

c) As related to this sale of his rights, what later circumstances might cause him to suffer a dilution in his ownership interests or a further dilution, as the case might be?

chapter 30

THE MANAGEMENT OF
OUTSTANDING BOND ISSUES

Once a corporation has sold or assumed a bond issue, its principal problems related to the management of the issue are those of fulfilling the obligations it has undertaken. It must find the means to pay interest at the designated rate as the semiannual payment dates come around, to make such sinking fund contributions annually or semiannually as the indenture prescribes, and to pay off the principal of whatever bonds remain at the final maturity date. (For a serial issue, of course, the sinking fund requirement is generally absent, but, in its place, is the even more pressing requirement for the direct retirement of portions of the issue as they mature periodically.) In addition, the corporation must be ever on guard to fulfill the other convenants of the indenture—those having to do with the prompt payment of its taxes, the keeping of its properties in a good state of repair, of providing adequate insurance protection, and so on. The corporation's financial managers can hardly afford to lose sight of the probable grave consequences of defaults that are not or cannot be quickly corrected.

For many bond-issuing corporations, nevertheless, problems of management of the kinds mentioned are not at all difficult to cope with. They remain comfortably solvent throughout the lives of their bond issues, in good times and bad, and rarely is there question as to their capacity to do all the things promised in their indentures. Such corporations, however, face certain managerial problems of a different kind, two of which deserve consideration in this chapter: whether bond retirement should be pushed at a pace beyond that prescribed by the mandatory sinking fund provisions of the indenture, and whether, somewhere along the way, the whole issue, or what remains of it, should be replaced by a new one. The answer to the first question will generally depend upon the original attitude of the corporation toward bond financing, while the answer to the second will generally be based upon a variety of circumstances.

But a goodly number of corporations encounter much more pressing problems in the management of their bond issues. They do not remain comfortably solvent during the lives of these issues; sooner or later, they come to the rather scary realization that they face a default. It may be that cash is not available, and cannot be made available, to meet an interest or sinking fund payment. It may be that, though the corporation scrapes together enough cash to meet current interest and sinking fund obligations, it is unable to get enough in addition to pay some of its maturing taxes or to repair its operating properties. It may be that all goes well till the approach of the final maturity when comes the realization that cash cannot possibly be supplied for the redemption of the bonds still outstanding. In circumstances such as these, what can the corporate managers do?

SOLVENT CORPORATIONS—THEIR PROBLEM OF SPEED OF RETIREMENT

A corporation whose bond issue was a second or third choice in the order of its financing preferences is likely to want to eliminate it from its financial structure as quickly as possible. If it wanted to issue common or preferred stock but chose bonds because the bond market was buoyant while that for stocks was in the doldrums, a rapid retirement of the bonds would appear to be in order. On the other hand, a corporation that issues or assumes bonds because it wants to trade on the equity will probably want to slow down the process of retirement as far as that may be possible.

Corporations Choosing Rapid Retirement

A corporation that puts out a bond issue reluctantly because it would prefer stock financing may change its attitude, of course, while the bonds are outstanding. Because of unstable earnings, its managers may have feared the dangers of trading on the equity, but they encounter no difficulty in making interest and sinking fund payments, and they are most pleased to see the rate of earnings on the common stock expand as a result of the bond financing. Perhaps earnings prove to be less unstable than they used to be, or perhaps it is found to be much less difficult than was expected to manage the cash account in such manner that a sufficiency is available for bond requirements even in years when earnings are small or negative.

Assuming, however, that there is no such change in attitude, what can the corporation do to speed bond retirement? In the indenture itself, it will surely have set the stage for speedy retirement. In the first place, it will probably have trimmed the maturity as closely as safety would seem to permit—making it, for example, 15 years, even though investors would have been as willing to buy, say, 20- or 25-year maturities. Secondly, it will probably have obligated itself to make sinking fund contributions sufficient to retire the entire issue by approximately equal instalments during its life. Thirdly, it will surely have reserved the right to call any amount of bonds for redemption beyond the amounts required for the sinking fund. And, finally, it may have made the bonds convertible into common stock at the option of the holder, while limiting the duration of the conversion privilege or setting a scale of rising conversion prices for successive periods to exert pressure toward early conversion.

If, then, the cash throw-off from depreciation and profits after taxes is only sufficient to meet the stipulated sinking fund requirements, after allowance for the replacement of depreciating assets, for expansion, and for the payment of reasonable dividends, the corporation must be satisfied with a pace of retirement no greater than that envisaged in the sinking fund provisions—unless, perhaps, conversion becomes advantageous for the bondholders, so that bonds are retired by that route. If, however, the cash throw-off is well in excess of what is needed for the sinking fund, dividends, the replacement of assets, and expansion, the corporation will be able to use the excess for further retirements by buying up bonds in the market or by exercising the call privilege. Moreover, substantial increases in the market price of the corporation's common stock would probably go hand in hand with the development of excess cash throw-offs, so that conversion would be likely to proceed rapidly.

In either of the situations just described, the corporation is not likely to have any problems of special difficulty at the time the bond issue matures. If redemption has taken place only at the sinking fund pace, the final instalment to be retired will be no greater or not much greater than earlier ones, and if these earlier instalments have been met without strain the final one should likewise be no great burden. If additional redemptions have taken place by calls beyond sinking fund requirements and by conversions, it may be that very few or none of the bonds will still be outstanding at the final maturity.

Corporations Choosing to Continue Trading on the Equity

Corporations that issue bonds with the intention of keeping bonded debt in their financial structures indefinitely to gain the advantages of trading on the equity may also have a change in attitude while the bonds are outstanding. Perhaps earnings that had been stable begin to develop a pattern of considerable instability, or perhaps the margin of earnings available for bond interest falls considerably below the level anticipated, even though having a pattern of stability at the lower level.

Indenture Provisions. But again assuming no such change in attitude, what can a corporation do to slow the pace of bond retirement—to continue, as far as feasible, the program of trading on the equity? In its indenture, it would probably have given the bonds a remote date of maturity; nevertheless, it may not have been able to go beyond 25 or 30 years for lack of investor interest in still longer maturities. Moreover, were it issuing bonds at a time of upsweeping yield curves, it would have had economy in interest charges as a strong incentive for keeping the life of the issue down to a moderate length. It might have wanted to avoid mandatory sinking fund provisions, but, here again, investors would probably have insisted upon some provision for periodic retirement. At least, they would have been likely to demand sinking fund contributions to keep pace with the depreciation of the assets to be acquired with the proceeds of the bond issue. However, they might have been satisfied to permit the corporation to use much of the sinking fund contributions for additions and improvements to operating properties. Accordingly, the corporation could slow down the pace of bond retirement by scheduling expenditures for expansion in such manner as to use up the sinking fund contributions to the extent permitted. The corporation would surely not have made the bonds convertible into common stock; but, on the other hand, it would probably have reserved the right to call bonds for redemption beyond the amounts provided for in the sinking fund stipulations. The latter power it would hardly expect to use, but it would be convenient to have it available should there be a change of attitude while the bonds were outstanding.

Additional Issues. A corporation that wants to continue to trade on the equity can reach that goal, of course, not only by slowing the pace of redemption of existing bonds, but also by putting out additional bonds from time to time. It will surely have had the foresight to make its indenture an open-end one, so that additional bonds subject to its terms can be issued as additional properties are acquired, provided, of course, that earnings limitations and other protective restrictions in the indenture upon total bonds to be outstanding are not violated. Thus, as some of the bonds of earlier "series" are retired by sinking fund operations, they may be more than replaced by new "series."

Meeting Maturities. But bonds have maturity dates. No matter how reluctant a corporation may have been during the life of a bond issue in providing for some periodic retirement, and no matter how gladly it may have used sinking fund cash for improvements rather than for retirements, it must definitely do something about the bonds at their maturity. By the very circumstances of its management, most of the bonds will be outstanding as the maturity date approaches; and by the circumstances of its objectives, it will have anticipated all along putting out a "refunding" issue to take the place of the maturing one. But it may run into difficulties. The bonds may mature at a time of tight money, and the tightness may be especially severe in the market for long-term funds. That would mean that interest rates for new long-term borrowing would be quite high, perhaps much higher than the rate on the maturing bonds.

Suppose, for example, that a corporation's 25-year bond issue bearing interest at the rate of 4 per cent is coming due at a time when the rate on new borrowings for almost any maturity would be 5½ per cent (the yield curve being, as we would say, flat or horizontal). Were the corporation to refund with a new 25-year issue, it would have the unpleasant prospect of having to pay the much higher rate for that lengthy period—certainly a change in the cost situation that would cloud the advantages of trading on the equity.[1] What to do? Had the corporation's managers foreseen the coming of the tight-money situation and taken prompt action in keeping with that foresight, they might have had an ideal solution to their problem. Assume that, two years before the maturity date, the corporation could have put out a new 25-year bond issue at a rate of 4½ per cent. It might have looked strange to be issuing 4½ per cent bonds and using the proceeds to retire 4 per cent bonds; but the wisdom of the action would be proved if, as assumed above, the rate actually did go to 5½ per cent two years later. The payment of an extra one half of 1 per cent in each of the two years would seem to be a small price to pay for a saving of 1 per cent annually for 23 years.

In the absence of a fortunate anticipation and action of this kind, a possible solution would be the retirement of the maturing bonds out of the proceeds of bank loans. This, too, would be an anticipatory procedure—taken in the expectation of a fall in long-term interest rates in a short period of years. For example, it might be possible to borrow from commercial banks on the basis of a one-year loan, renewable for two additional years at the option of the corporation. Even if the interest rate on the bank loan were somewhat higher than 5½ per cent, it would prove to be cheap should the long-term rate actually fall to a level around 4 or 4½ per cent within the three-year period.

Needless to emphasize is the possibility that a bond maturity can also come at a highly favorable time. If the corporation of the illustration found it possible, at the maturity of its original bonds, to put out a 25-year refunding issue at, say, 3½ per cent, the advantages of trading on the equity would doubtless appear all the more glamorous.

Exchange Offers. When corporations put out refunding bond issues, they sometimes offer them on a direct exchange basis to the holders of the older issues that are slated for replacement. The holder of a maturing bond thus may take cash or a bond of the new issue. If the original bonds were sold by private placement to institutional investors and if these institutions want to take the new issue, the exchange takes place, as it were, at one stroke. But even when the existing bonds were originally sold by public offering and are widely held, exchange offers are usually advantageous for the corporations making them. With respect to public offerings especially, an advantage of the exchange procedure is that it cuts down flotation costs. This is so even though investment bankers are usually called upon to underwrite exchange offers—to agree to buy at a

---

[1] It might be anticipated that long before the expiration of the 25 years, it would be possible to effect another refunding at a lower rate of interest. But refundings are expensive in themselves in flotation costs and call-price premiums on bonds to be replaced.

designated price whatever bonds of the refunding issue are not exchanged. But they fix a moderate commission for the entire issue, and a higher margin only for the bonds that they have to take over. Thus, the more bonds that are exchanged the less proportionately the total underwriting cost will be. (The amount paid by the bankers for bonds taken over is the means, of course, whereby the corporation can pay off in cash the maturing bonds not offered for exchange.)

But whether or not existing bondholders will accept exchange offers is another question—that depends upon what advantage, if any, they see in it for themselves. In terms of the illustration, many of the holders of the 4 per cent bonds would presumably have been highly pleased to have received two years before maturity, an exchange offer of 4½ per cent bonds. Were the corporation of the illustration actually to decide upon a 5½ per cent issue at the time of maturity of the original bonds, it could probably also count upon many exchanges. But were it able to offer a refunding issue at only 3½ per cent, because of easy conditions in the market for long-term funds, exchanges would probably be much fewer.

An interest rate on new bonds apparently advantageous to most holders of existing bonds was designated by the Atlantic Coast Line Railroad Company in an exchange offer made in May, 1963. It offered new 25-year general-mortgage bonds, Series E, bearing interest at 4.95 per cent in exchange, dollar for dollar, for four of its outstanding issues shortly to mature, namely, its own general-mortgage Series A and B bonds, outstanding in the amounts of $32,176,000 and $40,000, and bearing interest at rates of 4½ and 4 per cent respectively, with both maturing on June 1, 1964, and two series of the first consolidated mortgage bonds of the Charleston & Western Carolina Railroad Company that had been assumed by Atlantic Coast Line in a merger. The latter issues were outstanding in the amounts of $2,589,000 and $3,063,000 with interest rates of 5 and 4¼ per cent respectively, and both issues were slated to mature on January 1, 1964. No alternative cash offer was made, as cash payment could be postponed till the maturities of unexchanged bonds. A group of investment bankers were engaged to "solicit acceptance of the offer" but they did not underwrite in the sense of agreeing to buy new bonds not accepted by existing bondholders.

Another recent exchange offer was made in July, 1963 by the Associated Oil & Gas Company. It sold a $6,600,000 issue of 6 per cent convertible subordinated debenture bonds due in 1975 principally to expand its working capital. But it added to the issue another $1 million of bonds which it offered in exchange for its outstanding 6½ per cent convertible subordinated debentures due in 1971. Although the holders of the old bonds were thus asked to give up one half of a percentage point in the interest rate, they had inducements to make the exchange because of a more attractive range of conversion prices and in the extension of maturity.

SOLVENT CORPORATIONS—REFUNDING ALONG THE WAY

Reasons for Early Refundings

Oftentimes corporations that are able to maintain sound financial positions decide upon switches in their bonded debt long before the maturities of bonds already outstanding. The objectives of this kind of action vary; most commonly, they are the following: (1) to get rid of obnoxious indenture restrictions, (2) to "consolidate" several existing issues, (3) to effect a substantial lengthening of maturity, and (4) to reduce the costs of carrying long-term debt.

Getting Rid of Indenture Restrictions. The most direct way to get rid of obnoxious restrictions in a bond indenture is to get rid of the indenture itself; this can be done by calling and paying off all the bonds issued under the indenture. When this has been done, the indenture no longer has any binding force: it is a completed contract.

Very often corporations take steps to get rid of indenture restrictions in connection with plans for new financing. Let us assume that a corporation has outstanding a closed-mortgage bond issue of $8 million. It wants to borrow an additional $5 million but its financial managers realize that, to find buyers, they will have to offer a mortgage lien. With the closed-mortgage issue outstanding, all that they can offer is a second mortgage. Accordingly, they decide to make the new issue $13 million, and they are able to give it a first-lien status by using a sufficient amount of the proceeds to retire the existing bonds. Again, the existing issue might be an open-end one, but with property and earnings limitations so severely drawn that the corporation's additional issue would have to be limited to $3 million. Thus, the drawing up of a new indenture with property and earnings limitations designed to permit an initial new issue of $13 million of bonds would seem to meet the corporation's problem. In each of these instances, of course, the new issue would be only partially a "refunding" one.

Sometimes, however, corporations find indenture restrictions so burdensome that they are willing to go to the bother and expense of refunding without, at the same time, trying to raise "new money." If they can find investors who are willing to buy new issues under indentures not having the obnoxious features, they may decide to go ahead. An original indenture may have provided for sinking fund contributions at a level designed to retire the whole bond issue by equal instalments during the period of its life. But the corporation finds that these contributions are gravely draining its working capital, thereby endangering its solvency. At the same time, the financial managers have every reason to believe that the corporation would have no difficulty refunding a substantial part of the debt if it were left at maturity. Hence, they may decide to refund at once to slow down the rate of sinking fund retirements.

Consolidation of Two or More Issues. Refunding to consolidate existing bond issues most commonly occurs after corporate mergers and consolidations, and usually the raising of new money is a goal as well as the bond consolidation itself. Suppose that Corporation A has absorbed Corporations B and C in a merger. At the time of the merger, each of the three corporations had a bond issue outstanding. As a feature of the merger agreement, A assumed the bond issues of B and C. Therefore, it has three bond issues now outstanding, doubtless with different interest rates, maturities, sinking fund requirements, restrictive provisions, and so on. This might not be too difficult to handle, but now A wants to do some additional long-term borrowing. Will it add a fourth issue to which probably it can give a standing only inferior to that of the existing three? It would seem much better to make the new issue large enough not only to supply the new money desired but also the means to call and pay off the three existing bond issues. Not only would this make for simplicity in the corporation's financial structure—something almost always desirable in itself—but also for ease in complying with contractual obligations. Even more than this, the consolidated issue might be salable with a lower interest rate than the rates of the existing issues. If the merger has been successful in the sense of making A's earning power greater than the former separate earning capacities of itself, B, and C, its bonds ought to be more attractive to investors than had been those of the formerly separate corporations—hence the probability of a lower interest rate.

Extending Maturities.   At times when the bond market is buoyant, corporations may have inducement to refund existing issues to "lengthen" their long-term debt despite the fact that the existing issues still have many years to run. There could be such an inducement even though the interest rates to be paid upon the refunding issues were no lower, or even slightly higher, than those carried on the issues to be replaced. Suppose, for example, that a corporation eight years ago put out a 15-year bond issue bearing interest at the rate of 5 per cent. It strongly favors trading on the equity—it did not favor the 15-year maturity of its present issue, but that was the longest term it was able to get at the time of its flotation. Now, however, the corporate managers are convinced that they could sell a 30-year issue having an interest rate of 5 per cent. To financial managers strongly wedded to a policy of trading on the equity, the immediate replacement of an issue due to mature in seven years by one to mature in 30 years could appear to be highly advantageous.

Reducing the Costs of Long-Term Debt.   By far, however, refundings that are effected long before the scheduled maturities of the issues replaced are chiefly attributable to strivings toward reduced interest costs. A corporation may have had to designate a quite high rate of interest on its bond issue because at the time of its sale its financial position was weak —without the high rate, the bonds would not have been salable at all. But the corporation has been highly successful, and its credit rating is now quite strong. Yet its high-rate bonds have still many years to run till maturity. It could now sell a bond issue of equal size—or of a much larger size, if it so wanted—at a much lower rate of interest. Should it do so? Or, again, a blue-chip corporation, during a period of tight money, may have been hard pressed for cash to complete an expansion program, and it may have put out a bond issue at that time to raise the money. Because of the dearth of loan funds, and despite its blue-chip status, it may have had to set a relatively high interest rate. But now, a few years later, a plentiful supply of long-term funds is available, and corporations comparable to it in prestige are borrowing at much lower rates than it is paying. Should it proceed with a refunding operation?

To the question raised twice in the preceding paragraph, most corporation managements answer with a hearty yes—*after analyses of all the costs involved in refunding* have clearly shown that it would result in substantial savings over the years. They know that a simple comparison of interest rates is not an adequate analysis. Thus, a corporation surely will not save $100,000 annually if it now has outstanding a bond issue of $10 million bearing interest at 5 per cent and if it could sell an issue of equal amount with an interest rate of 4 per cent. Beyond a comparison of interest rates, consideration must be given to the premiums to be paid on the retirement of the outstanding bonds, the flotation costs of the new issue, sinking fund and call-price provisions in both old and new indentures, possibilities that the new bonds would be retired more rapidly than the sinking fund provisions in the new indenture would require, and the income tax effects of the refunding.

Cost Factors—Illustration

For illustration, let us assume that a certain corporation five years ago put out a $12 million issue of 25-year bonds bearing an interest rate of 5 per cent. In conversations with investment bankers near the end of the fifth year, the managers of the corporation learn that they could sell new bonds to the public at par at a rate of 4 per cent. As this sounds like a favorable opportunity for refunding, they decide to explore the matter further. The existing bond indenture has a sinking fund provision requiring the retirement of $500,000 face amount of the bonds annually, the sinking fund call price being par value. So far, then, $2 million of the bonds have been retired, and the fifth year's sinking fund payment will bring this figure up to $2.5 million. The prospective new issue, therefore, would presumably be in the vicinity of $10 million. But not exactly $10 million. For calls outside the scope of the sinking fund, the old bonds have a call price of 103. Thus, it would appear that the corporation would need a new issue of $10.3 million to retire the old bonds. Moreover, the investment bankers estimate that flotation costs of a new issue of between $10 million and $11 million would be about $260,000, so that this would seem to bring the cash needed for refunding to $10,560,000.

But the corporate managers realize that tax savings would become available in connection with the refunding. The premium of $300,000 to be paid upon the retirement of the old bonds could be deducted in the fifth year as an expense for income tax purposes, as could any unamortized costs of flotation upon the old bonds still standing on the books. We may assume that total costs of selling the old bonds amounted to $312,500 and that this has been subject to a straight-line charge-off to expenses annually. After the regular charge of the fifth year, therefore, $250,000 would remain unamortized, but, should the refunding be effected, this amount could likewise be taken at once in lump sum as an income tax deduction. Thus, the total charge-offs incident to the refunding would be $550,000, and, assuming that the corporation always has income high in the 52 per cent bracket of the federal corporation income tax, the tax saving would be 52 per cent of $550,000, or $286,000. Since the corporation's tax liabilities would be reduced by $286,000, this sum could presumably be diverted from operations to be used for the retirement of the old bonds, reducing the needed amount of the refunding issue from $10,560,000 to $10.274,000.

To make it possible to estimate the dollar advantage or disadvantage of refunding as closely as possible, we may assume that the new bonds would closely parallel the old in terms and conditions—that they would have a 20-year maturity (equal, therefore, to the remaining life of the old bonds), that 5 per cent of the face amount would be retirable annually by mandatory sinking fund requirements, and that the sinking fund call price, as in the old bonds, would be the par value. With these assumptions in mind, then, would it be advantageous for the corporation to issue $10,274,000 of new 4 per cent 20-year bonds to take the place of the existing bonds? The existence of an advantage and its size could be demonstrated as follows:

Net Cost of Carrying Old Bonds to Maturity		*Net Cost if Refunding Is Effected*	
Interest at 5 per cent for 20 years on average amount of bonds to be outstanding, that is, $5,250,000[2]......	$5,250,000	Interest at 4 per cent for 20 years on average amount of bonds to be outstanding, that is, $5,393,850[3]......	$4,315,080
Remaining flotation costs to be amortized............	250,000	Flotation costs of new bonds	260,000
	$5,500,000		$4,575,080
Less tax saving at 52 per cent[4]..................	2,860,000	Less tax saving at 52 per cent...................	2,379,042
			$2,196,038
		Add additional debt to be amortized[5].............	274,000
Net cost..................	$2,640,000	Net cost.................	$2,470,038

[2] This is found by adding the amount of bonds to be outstanding at the beginning of the 20-year period and the amount to be outstanding in the twentieth year and dividing by 2. Bonds of a total of $10,000,000 will be outstanding at the beginning

It would appear, therefore, that the refunding would be quite advantageous. Over the period of 20 years, the net saving would be the difference between the net cost of carrying the old bonds of $2,640,000 and that of carrying the new of $2,470,038, or $169,962. While this would be much less than a saving of $100,000 a year that a simple application of a 4 per cent rate as against a 5 per cent rate on $10 million of bonds would produce, it would surely be well worth the taking.

Would the refunding be advantageous if, all other terms and conditions being as described, the rate of interest to be offered on the new bonds had to be 4¼ per cent or 4½ per cent? The best way to answer a question of this kind is to compute a break-even rate for the new bonds—one above which there would be some advantage in refunding, however small, and below which refunding would be clearly disadvantageous. Obviously, the break-even rate is one that would make the cost of carrying the new bonds exactly the same as that of carrying the old, that is, $2,640,000. Letting x stand for the rate we are seeking, our formula, based upon the analysis presented in the table above, would be as follows:[6]

$$.48\,[(5,393,850 \cdot 20x) + 260,000] + 274,000 = 2,640,000$$
$$51,780,960x + 124,800 + 274,000 = 2,640,000$$
$$51,780,960x = 2,241,200$$
$$x = 4.3282\%$$

It is thus clear that the corporation would still be ahead were the new bonds to bear interest at 4¼ per cent, but that the refunding would increase its costs were the rate to be 4½ per cent.

Cost Considerations

When the question of refunding is entirely one of seeking lower overall costs of carrying bonded indebtedness, an analysis such as the foregoing should suffice for a sound decision. However, factors ignored in the illustration or different from those of the illustration could complicate the estimation of savings. If, for example, the sinking fund call

---

of the 20-year period (the sixth year of the original 25-year period, of course) and of $500,000 in the twentieth year. Hence:

$$\frac{\$10,000,000 + \$500,000}{2} = \$5,250,000$$

[3] See the preceding footnote. Here the result works out as follows:

$$\frac{\$10,274,000 + \$513,700}{2} = \$5,393,850$$

[4] As long as interest and amortizable flotation costs can be taken as income tax deductions against income taxable at 52 per cent, the net cost to the corporation is really only the remaining 48 per cent. We assumed that the corporation of the illustration always has income well into the 52 per cent tax bracket. The computation indicates, of course, that the corporation expects to continue to have income at that level and that it anticipates no change in the tax rate in the 20-year period.

[5] The payment of the additional debt would not represent a deductible expense; hence no tax saving is entered with respect to it.

[6] The multiplier .48 is, of course, the net cost to the corporation of its interest and flotation expenses after allowing for the tax saving of 52 per cent.

prices, instead of being par for both old and new issues as in the illustration, were to be higher in the new indenture than in the old, the prospective saving would be somewhat reduced. Likewise, the refunding would appear to be less attractive—perhaps materially so—should there be strong probability that within a few years the corporation would want to reduce its bonded debt by substantial calls beyond sinking fund requirements. Again, the maturity of the new issue might be different from the remaining life of the old. Were the corporate managers to be told by the bankers that the new issue could not carry a maturity of more than 15 years, the attractiveness of the refunding would be materially diminished —it would be necessary to amortize the added debt of $274,000 and to prorate the flotation costs of the new bonds over the shorter period. On the other hand, were the corporate managers to be told that the new issue could be a 25-year one, the refunding project would look all the better, because the annual prorations would be smaller than in the illustration.

Even when the primary interest in refunding is one of eliminating restrictive indenture terms, consolidation of several existing issues, or extending the maturity of bonded debt, cost factors are not likely to be ignored. As was indicated earlier, refunding for these purposes is often combined with projects for raising new funds by the bond route. Thus, the corporation with mortgage bonds already outstanding under a closed indenture might decide to go ahead with a second-mortgage issue were its estimates of the total costs of carrying the two issues less than for a large new issue whose proceeds would be used in part to pay off the closed-mortgage bonds. In a similar way, the surviving corporation in a merger, in consideration of the costs involved in refunding, might decide against the consolidation of bond issues assumed in the merger process. When, however, the elimination of objectionable features in existing indentures seems to corporate managers to be extremely important, and additional financing, if considered at all, to be of secondary importance, cost comparisons tend to break down. The objective becomes primarily qualitative, and though a dollar value can be put upon it when the costs of refunding are considered, this value can be set at almost any level depending upon the intensity of the managers' dissatisfaction with the existing indenture.

Some Recent Refundings

To illustrate the various motives that prompt corporate managements to refund outstanding bond issues "along the way," three recent refunding transactions may be cited.

A simplification of its financial structure and the eliminate of diverse restrictions in separate indentures were apparently the objectives of the Pacific Power and Light Company when, in November, 1962, it offered $64 million of its mortgage bonds in exchange for an equal amount of the first-mortgage bonds of the California Oregon Power Company which it had assumed upon absorbing the latter in a merger. The California Oregon bonds were in seven series bearing interest at rates ranging from 2⅞ to 3⅞ per cent and with maturities ranging from 1974 to 1986, and Pacific offered seven series of its mortgage bonds of identical face amounts and maturities. But, to induce the California Oregon bondholders to make the exchange, it designated for each series of its own bonds a rate of interest one half of a percentage point greater than had been carried by the matching series of California Oregon bonds.

A long-term saving in interest costs was given by the Brooklyn Union Gas Company as the reason for its sale of $19,200,000 of 25-year debenture bonds to a group of institutional investors in April, 1963, and use of the proceeds—with a small amount of additional cash—to redeem $19,600,000 of 25-year debentures sold only two years earlier on the basis of competitive bids. The interest rate on the new bonds was 4⅜ per cent while the rate on the called bonds had been 5⅛ per cent.

In May, 1963, the American Telephone and Telegraph Company sold a $250 million issue of 4⅜ per cent debenture bonds due in 1999 and used the proceeds in calling for redemption a $250 million issue of 5 per cent debentures issued in 1957 and maturing in 1983. Although the "5 per cent coupon" of 1957 had been A.T. & T.'s costliest financing since 1930, investment bankers expressed surprise that the refunding was undertaken on such a narrow margin between the two interest rates—a narrowness emphasized by the fact that while a price of 100.171 was received from the underwriting syndicate for the new bonds, the call price of the 5 per cent bonds was 106.461. Accordingly, the 16-year extension in maturity must have been A.T. & T.'s principal objective in the refunding.

CORPORATIONS IN FINANCIAL DIFFICULTIES

Difficulties in meeting indenture obligations may be encountered by corporations at any time during the lives of their bond issues or they may come to the fore, so to say, only as the bonds approach the final maturity dates. The nature of the difficulties tends to vary somewhat according to the timing of their appearance, although, obviously, temporary solutions for difficulties encountered along the way may only intensify those faced at maturity.

Difficulties along the Way

Nature of Difficulties. It is patent that the inability of a corporation to fulfill the covenants of its indenture as to the payment of interest, the making of sinking fund contributions, the payment of taxes, the keeping of properties in a state of proper repair, and so on, results from a shortage of working capital, and, specifically, of cash. In most instances, this shortage is due in turn to operating losses. Such losses drain working capital. If the drain is heavy or if, though moderate, continued long enough, the capacity of the corporation to maintain normal operations and at the same time to meet all kinds of obligations coming due must be diminished. The cash throw-offs from depreciation charges, if they are covered in part, may be sufficient to save the corporation from embarrassment for a while, or even indefinitely; but it may be that, for the continuance of normal operations, they must be promptly spent for the replacement of fixed assets. And, of course, there may be no cash throw-offs from this source, the operating losses exceeding the amount of the depreciation charges.

The corporate managers face a dilemma. The cash balance and inflowing cash are insufficient to meet all the outlays necessary to keep the corporation operating *and solvent.* If they use cash to fulfill all the covenants of the indenture, they will not have enough left both to meet the claims of creditors other than the bondholders and to carry on operations. If they decide that they must remain solvent at any cost by meeting the claims of other creditors, in addition to those of the bondholders, they probably will succeed only in deferring the day of insolvency. For they would have to cut back upon inventories, credit extensions to customers, and outlays for day-to-day operating expenses, and this policy could hardly result other than in greater operating losses. If they choose to maintain operations by using for that purpose cash that would otherwise be earmarked for the nonbondholding creditors, default occurs at once— and default upon obligations to trade creditors, to banks on their short-term loans, and so on, can have consequences as dire as defaults upon bond obligations. Of course, the choice could be to default upon one or more of the indenture obligations.

Clearing the Way for Short-Term Borrowing. Possibly the corporation can save itself if it is able to get the bondholders to agree to relax some of the restrictive provisions of the indenture. It may have agreed to maintain a working capital ratio of $2\frac{1}{2}$ or 3 to 1, or to limit its total indebtedness to what now appears to be a much too small percentage of its net tangible assets. Banks and other lenders may be quite willing to grant new short-term loans—but not as long as these restrictions stand. Hence, an obvious remedy for the corporation's problem would be to seek the consent of the bondholders to a relaxation of these restrictions to permit the additional borrowing. The corporation will surely have provided in the indenture that the holders of some large proportion of the outstanding bonds, such as $66\frac{2}{3}$ or 75 per cent, could approve indenture modifications *binding upon all the bondholders.* Such a provision, therefore, would seem to open the door for an attempt to apply this remedy.

Clearing the Way for Additional Bonds. Getting bondholders to consent to modifications in the terms of existing indentures may enable corporations to correct working capital deficiencies through new long-term borrowing. For many corporations, this apparently would be an even better solution to financial difficulties than having indentures modified to permit new short-term borrowing. Investors may be willing to buy new bonds—especially, of course, those of corporations whose difficulties are not extreme—if only the corporations can clear the way for their issuance. It is even possible that a corporation could find buyers for a new issue of bonds having claims inferior to those of the existing bonds—as a new debenture issue where the existing one is a mortgage issue, or a new issue of subordinated debentures where the existing one is an ordinary debenture issue—if only it can get the existing bondholders to relax indenture provisions limiting total indebtedness in relation to working capital or to capital stock and surplus. Or it might be able to find buyers of bonds of the same ranking as those already outstanding, whether mortgage bonds or debenture bonds, if it could get the existing bondholders to "open" a closed indenture or to relax the property, earnings, and other restrictions of an open-end indenture.

Should its difficulties be of a greater degree of severity, however, it might be able to find buyers for new bonds only if in a position to give them prior ranking to the existing bonds. Hence, its solution would be to ask the holders of mortgage bonds to yield the priority of their liens to the new issue, or to ask the holders of debenture bonds to permit a new issue of mortgage bonds without securing the debentures "equally and ratably." For all such kinds of consents on the part of bondholders, the typical indenture provides, once again, that approval by the holders of 66⅔ per cent or 75 per cent of the outstanding bonds makes the modifications agreed upon binding upon all the bondholders.

Although not in "financial difficulties" in the sense of facing insolvency, several corporations in recent years have sought and obtained the consent of bondholders to changes in indenture terms to obviate difficulties in borrowing, financing foreign subsidiaries, and meeting other financial problems. In the summer of 1958, Atlas Plywood Corporation (now Atlas General Industries, Inc.) was successful in getting holders of sufficient percentages of its two 5 per cent debenture issues to permit a relaxation in indenture requirements for the maintenance of certain ratios between current assets and current liabilities and between current assets and funded debt, as well as a relaxation in restrictions upon the payment of cash dividends. To get sufficient assents, Atlas offered an increase in the interest rate of one fourth of a percentage point. In January, 1959, the Bristol-Myers Company announced that its bondholders had consented to the elimination of an indenture limitation of $1 million upon the funded debt of certain foreign subsidiaries and to the elimination of provisions that prevented the company and its North American subsidiaries from guaranteeing the debts of certain non-North American subsidiaries. At the same time, the company agreed to a new indenture limitation of $2 million upon guaranties of itself and its North American subsidiaries for debt of the non-North American subsidiaries. In the summer of 1960, holders of the requisite proportions of four series of the collateral-trust bonds of the New England Gas and Electric Association agreed to an indenture modification increasing the long-term borrowing capacity of its subsidiaries from 60 per cent of the par value of their outstanding stock to 60 per cent of this par value plus their earned surplus and cash premiums received in the sale of the stock. The subsidiaries' stock had been pledged as security for the collateral-trust bonds. In March, 1963, the Allied Chemical Corporation announced that holders of more than 66⅔ per cent of its debenture bonds had approved amendments to the indenture modifying restrictions applicable to its foreign subsidiaries in mortgaging properties, incurring and guaranteeing debt, selling additional stock, and effecting mergers; expanding the borrowing capacity of its domestic subsidiaries; and authorizing the creation and assumption of certain liens in connection with its oil and gas production.

Cutting Expenditures for Maintenance. Should the corporation, however, have no prospective suppliers of additional working capital, the relaxation of indenture terms having to do with total indebtedness or working capital ratios would be of no help. Another remedy would have to be sought. Should the shortage of working capital be not especially severe, a decision might be made to remedy it by cutting "to the bone" expenditures for the repair and maintenance of the corporation's properties. Consent might be asked of the bondholders for this departure from the obligations of the indenture—the covenant to keep the properties in a proper state of repair; but the cutback might be effected without the bondholders' consent in the expectation that neither the trustee nor the bondholders would be likely to get excited about it.

Seeking Relaxation of Sinking Fund Requirements. Should the shortage of working capital be of greater severity, a more likely point of attack would be the sinking fund provisions of the indenture. On an outstanding bond issue of $10 million bearing interest at 5 per cent, the corporation's interest cost for the year would be $500,000, but its sinking fund obligation might be an equal amount. Its financial managers might realize that they could meet one of these obligations, together with all other necessary outlays not related to the bond issue, but not both. They would be much more likely to attack the sinking fund provisions than the interest obligation. They would know that holders of, say, 66⅔ per cent of the bonds could authorize a change in the sinking fund requirements binding not only upon themselves but also upon dissenting bondholders. On the other hand, their indenture would surely provide that the right of the *individual* bondholder to interest at the prescribed rate could not be affected without his specific consent. An effort to get the bondholders' consent to a modification of sinking fund requirements could be couched in moderate terms. The bondholders might be asked to waive the whole requirement for only a year or two, to cut the requirement in half for two or three years, or, perhaps, to cut the mandatory requirement to a modest figure, making the rest depend upon the size of earnings.

According to an announcement of Stanrock Uranium Mines, Ltd., in January, 1959, its request for a waiver of its obligation to meet sinking fund payments in January and July, 1959, on its 5¾ per cent bonds due in 1963 had been granted by holders of the requisite proportion of the bonds. The corporation obligated itself to make up the missed payments by substantially equal amounts on the last five sinking fund payment dates and the final maturity date. In this instance, however, the consent of the bondholders did not save the corporation from further financial difficulties. Later in 1959 a receiver was appointed, and in the following year a trustee was named to supervise the corporation's reorganization in bankruptcy under the Canadian law. The trustee eventually paid off the principal of the bonds in instalments and all the defaulted interest, and in 1963 made a final offer of interest on the defaulted interest for the respective periods of default, although there remained a dispute about how payment was to be made—whether in Canadian or United States dollars—and therefore about the proper amount of the payment.

Seeking Relaxation in Interest Obligations. But the sinking fund requirements might already be moderate, or getting the bondholders to consent to their reduction might not be enough to repair the corporation's working capital position. After meeting operating expenses and liabilities unrelated to the bond issue, it still would not have enough money to pay the prescribed interest on the bonds. In this situation, an attack upon the interest obligations themselves would appear to be in order. The financial managers of the corporation might simply ask the bondholders to consent to an extension in the time of payment; such a request would be appropriate should they expect that an early improvement in operating results would enable the corporation to make up the amount deferred as well as to meet further accruals. Were they not so optimistic, however, they might ask that the fixed rate be cut down substantially, the balance of the prescribed rate to be made contingent upon earnings. Or they might ask for such a cut coupled with a deferment of even the reduced rate for one or two or more periods. Knowing that no bondholder would be bound by other bondholders' assenting votes, no matter how large the proportion of assents might be, the corporate managers might look around for something to offer as compensation for votes of approval. Being already in distress, they would hardly seem to be in a position to offer something attractive, but an effort in that direction could be made—perhaps a new convertibility feature, perhaps a more generous sinking fund arrangement *contingent upon earnings*, or even perhaps a more generous rate of interest. As for the last named, were the fixed rate of interest to be cut from, say, 5 per cent to 2 per cent, according to the corporation's proposal, the offer might be an additional 4 per cent *if earned*.

Seeking Exchanges for Other Securities. In some circumstances, the managers of corporations in financial difficulties "along the way" may be able to persuade bondholders that their long-run interests would be best served by giving up their existing absolute claims to principal and interest—possibly including interest already defaulted—for some type of security having contingent claims. In exchange for bonds having "standard" features, for example, they might offer income bonds, subordinated debentures, preferred stock, common stock, or some combination of these. Their ambitions in this direction would be all the stronger should they be able to assure the bondholders that new sources of outside financing would be immediately available upon the yielding of the latters' fixed claims.

In the summer of 1963, Alsco, Inc., a manufacturer of aluminum siding and other aluminum products, was able to persuade the holders of about 70 per cent of its $3,419,000 of 5½ per cent convertible subordinated debentures, due in 1974, to vote changes in the bond indenture to clear the way for a recapitalization program, as well as to surrender their debentures in exchange for common stock. The exchange was made on the basis of 121 shares of common stock for each $1,000 bond. The principal inducements to the bondholders to make the exchange were the following: the exchange ratio itself, since the ratio in the original indenture was approximately 63 shares; a vote of the common stockholders for a reverse split in their holdings of 1 for 10; the corporation's default upon its June 1 interest obligation; and an agreement by Kaiser Aluminum & Chemical Sales, Inc., which was Alsco's principal creditor, to cancel $3 million of its $4.9 million claim in exchange for 386,952 shares of common stock, and to cancel another $1 million in exchange for the assets (with the assumption of the liabilities) of Alsco's Canadian subsidiary. Kaiser had originally stipulated that it would participate in the deal only if holders of 80 per cent of the debentures agreed to make the exchange for stock, but it subsequently consented to go ahead despite the lower level of bondholder acceptance.

Possibility of Reorganization in Bankruptcy. Another remedy that the corporation could select would be to file a petition for its reorganization in bankruptcy. But that could result in such a sweeping change in the corporation's position, including possibly the wiping out of all the interests of the common stockholders, that it would likely be chosen voluntarily only if all other kinds of adjustment proposals proved to be fruitless. This possibility, then, we may ignore beyond its mention since our interest here is in what corporate managements can do to try to weather difficulties in meeting indenture obligations—not what successors to management, such as trustees in bankruptcy, have powers to do under the laws.[7]

---

[7] Some attention to the fate of bonds in corporate reorganizations was given in Chapters 19 and 27. See above, pp. 458–59 and 664–65.

Difficulties at Maturity

Nature of Difficulties. The use of one or more of the remedies just described to meet financial difficulties in managing outstanding bond issues "along the way" may simply postpone the evil day. If, for example, a corporation gets its bondholders to consent to a substantial cutback in periodic sinking fund contributions, it will have all the more of its bonds remaining to be paid off at the final maturity; if substantial redemption periodically was found to be financially impossible, all the more difficult will be a need to redeem a very large proportion of the bond issue at one stroke. On the other hand, difficulties in meeting obligations under bond indentures often originate only as the maturity date approaches. Until close to maturity, a corporation may have been able to pay interest, to meet sinking fund payments, and to fulfill all the other covenants of its indenture with relative ease. But the sinking fund provisions may have been designed for only partial redemption, as the corporation, wishing to continue to trade on the equity, planned for a substantial refunding at maturity. But maturity may come in a period of rather severe depression —the corporation may be operating deep in the red, so that it cannot hope to find buyers for a refunding issue. Nor can the corporation arrange short-term bank loans to pay off the bond issue as a stopgap measure, because the bankers feel that lending to it would be much too risky.

Possible Remedies. Short of filing a petition for reorganization in bankruptcy, or of taking even more drastic steps toward liquidation and dissolution, a corporation finding itself unable to pay off the principal of its bonds at maturity would be most likely to propose to the bondholders an extension of the maturity for a period of years, possible five or ten. Of course, it would agree to pay interest during the additional period, as well as to fulfill other indenture obligations. As a matter of fact, to induce acceptances of its proposal, it might offer a higher rate of interest for the additional period. Alternatively, or in addition, it might offer some other inducement, such as to make the bonds convertible into common stock or to give them a mortgage lien where before they had none. All the more could it hope for the success of its proposal for an extension, whether or not offering a higher interest rate or some other inducement, were it able to effect a partial redemption. For example, bondholders would be more likely to go along with the extension were they offered cash equal to, say, 40 per cent of the principal of their bonds, so that the extension would involve only the remaining 60 per cent of their claims. In deciding what to offer and how to go about making the offer, the corporate managers would have to keep in mind the right of nonassenting bondholders to be paid off in full. This right of the individual bondholder could not be disturbed by fellow bondholders no matter how large their vote to accept the corporation's proposal for an extension. Thus, the acceptance of an offer by holders of, say, 65 per cent of the maturing bonds might still not save the corporation from reorganization in bankruptcy if it still could not provide the cash to pay off the holders of the remaining 35 per cent.

Early in 1963, for example, the Strategic Materials Corporation reported that it had arranged with its creditors for a deferment of interest and an extension of maturities on approximately $2,100,000 of its obligations. After suffering heavy losses in 1961 and 1962, it had found itself "with insufficient cash to support current operations and to service its existing debt." [8] Among the creditors, holders of $1,500,000 of 6 per cent notes due November 1, 1963, agreed to take in exchange subordinated 6 per cent notes of equal face value to mature in 1969. Inducements to these and other creditors included the addition of stock-purchase warrants to the corporation's obligations; commitments by prospective lenders, including the Koppers Company which had a 5 per cent stock interest in Strategic, to advance $2 million of new funds on a long-term basis; and an agreement of the Koppers Company to take over the management of Strategic for two years for a fee of $1.00 a year.

As many things are possible, the corporation could offer the holders of its maturing bonds preferred or common stock in full or partial settlement of its principal obligations. Typically, however, bondholders would not be interested in such an offer unless they were owners individually of large blocks of the bonds and the offer was extremely generous, probably to the extent of giving them a large measure of control. (When the Alsco recapitalization mentioned earlier was declared effective, the original common stockholders held only 88,961 common shares as a result of the 1 for 10 reverse split, while the former bondholders who had exchanged their bonds for stock held more than 300,000 shares and Kaiser held 386,952 shares.)

Small corporations in particular are sometimes able to get by with partial payment of the principal of their bond issues at maturity as final settlement. Such a scaling down in the total obligation would probably be a "composition settlement." The corporate managers would tell the bondholders that the corporation could pay, say, 60 cents per dollar of principal claims, and ask them to accept this and to discharge the corporation from all further liability. Acceptance of the offer by two or more bondholders would make it binding upon them—unless, as would be likely, the corporate managers stipulated that the settlement would be effective only if approved by holders of, perhaps, 80 or 90 per cent or more of the bonds, in which case it would not be binding upon any assenting bondholder until assents had been received from the prescribed proportion. Such a stipulation would be virtually indispensable, since

---

[8] *The Wall Street Journal*, January 21, 1963.

nonassenting bondholders would still have to be paid off in full. A sufficient number of assents might be obtained if most of the bondholders were convinced that an extension would not help—that the corporation would have difficulty paying interest during the period of the extension and the principal at its end—and that a forced liquidation of the corporation's assets would give them less than 60 cents on the dollar. To the corporation, in turn, the settlement would be expected to be advantageous in permitting it to survive and in letting the stockholders retain their ownership interests, though sadly depleted. The offer would presumably permit the corporation to retain some assets to carry on with; indeed, it might have access to new equity or loan funds once the bonds had been eliminated.

Application of Remedies

The manner in which and the extent to which remedies for difficulties in the management of outstanding bond issues can be applied depend very importantly upon who the bondholders are. If they are few in number and are relatives, close friends, or business associates of the managers of the corporations that experience difficulties, as is entirely possible in small corporations, various remedies may be accepted unanimously without much delay, although possibly with a goodly show of anger. The bondholders may readily agree to deferments of interest, sinking fund, and principal payments or to the scaling down of one or more of these types of payments. Even in relatively large corporations, if the bondholders are chiefly stockholders who bought and hold the bonds because they are convertible, ready acceptance of "adjustments" to the corporations' obligations on the bonds can ordinarily be expected. Such owners are unlikely to want the seizure and sale of the corporation's properties for the satisfaction of their claims as bondholders, or to demand reorganization in bankruptcy, since the result would tend to be disastrous to their position as stockholders.

Even when bond issues are large and amounts held by stockholders are inconsequential, who the bondholders are remains important. The application of remedies, if possible at all, necessarily follows different courses if, on the one hand, the bonds are held in bulk by institutional investors or if, on the other, they are widely scattered in the hands of hundreds or thousands of individual investors.

Issues Held by Institutional Investors. The position of a corporation that faces default upon a bond issue sold in bulk to, say, a life insurance company may appear to be not unduly alarming. So far as the bonds go, it has only one creditor to deal with. Moreover, that one creditor is likely to have a lot of money available for helping the corporation to solve its financial problems, if only it chooses to use some of it for this purpose. Much the same can be said if the entire issue was split up between two or three institutional investors. Dealing with two or three creditors should not be particularly difficult, and possibilities of direct financial aid should be no less promising.

It is true that an institutional investor is most unlikely to rush to seize assets to satisfy its claims or to institute legal proceedings for the reorganization or liquidation of a debtor corporation. And it is true that it may advance additional funds to the corporation so that it can pay off the claims of other creditors who might be more inclined to take legal actions that would be crippling to the corporation. Beyond this, it may be willing to advance funds for working capital, so that the debtor corporation can continue normal operations. But there is a price for such forebearance and assistance. The usual price is the surrender of some or many of the ordinary prerogatives of management. The institutional investor, as a condition for its forebearance and assistance, may demand that some of the corporation's operating policies be changed. It may, in effect, order the adoption of certain kinds of new policies. Usually it will demand that all new policies, and especially all proposals for sizable expenditures, be made subject to its veto. It may go further than this: it may demand a comprehensive change in managerial personnel—the resignations of present directors and officers, or some of them, and their replacement by people in whom it has more confidence.

If measures of the kinds demanded by the institutional investor prove successful in the sense that the corporation is able to make up its defaulted payments of interest and principal and to cure other defaults that may have occurred, the institutional investor may be quite satisfied to revert to its former position simply as a creditor, retaining only such rights as were accorded to it as such in the indenture. If the measures prove unsuccessful, or if the corporation refuses to accept its dictates in the first place, it can ordinarily be expected to take legal steps to enforce its claims. In effect, it may ask for either reorganization or liquidation, although the final decision as to which of these procedures will be adopted would be that of the court rather than its own decision.

Bonds Widely Held. The fact that a large bond issue is said to be widely held does not mean that the entire issue is owned in driblets. In almost all cases, there will be at least a few individual and institutional investors who hold blocks of substantial size—perhaps bought in the course of the original flotation or accumulated by purchases from time to time in the market. The combined holdings of the eight or ten largest investors in a given issue might not amount to more than 15 or 20 per cent of the total outstanding, yet an indenture modification proposal would surely be off to a good start if approval of all or most of these large investors were assured. Hence, a corporate management that is in difficulties in meeting indenture obligations will typically "sound out" such investors first. If it gets their assent to a given proposal, it can use this fact as a bit of "advertising" when it takes the proposal to the smaller bondholders; if it does not, it may be able to change its proposal in such manner as to get the large investors to switch their negative votes to affirmative ones. The large investors, in turn, may suggest modifications in proposals that would make them acceptable, or, indeed, recommend quite different approaches to the problem that the corporate management would find not unreasonable. The large investors, at any rate, are much less likely to demand comprehensive changes in managerial policies or in the management itself than an institutional investor or two or three owning the entire issue.

If the corporation's situation is really grave and prospects are that it will continue to deteriorate, the large bondholders may be satisfied with nothing short of reorganization in bankruptcy—they may show interest in no proposal other than this. Should this be their attitude, the corporate managers are unlikely to take their proposal to the mass of small bondholders. With the threat of a negative vote of 15 or 20 per cent of the bonds hanging over, the prospect of getting the approval of 66⅔ or 75 per cent for indenture modifications not involving principal or interest, or of 80 or 90 per cent for adjustments to claims to principal or interest, would obviously be slim.

But if all or most of the large investors in a corporation's bond issue are willing to go along with a proposed adjustment in indenture terms, the prospects are good that a sufficient number of the smaller bondholders will find the proposal reasonable enough to deserve their approval also. In presenting the proposal to the smaller bondholders, the corporate management must set forth its case as clearly as possible— showing the source and nature of the difficulties, trying to demonstrate how helpful the proposed modifications in indenture terms will be toward clearing up the difficulties, and emphasizing that the bondholders' interests will be better protected through the adoption of the proposal than they could be in any other way. The usual procedure is to ask the bondholders to deposit their bonds with a designated bank or trust company as an evidence of their assent; however, the bondholder is ordinarily privileged to withdraw his bond at will if he wants to sell it or if he changes his mind and wants to cancel his assent. Thus, there may be considerable uncertainty from day to day about how many of the bonds placed on deposit will be left there, as it were, for final tabulation. At any rate, if the aggregate of bonds deposited and left reaches the level necessary to put the corporation's proposal into effect, a supplemental indenture is entered into between the corporation and the trustee in which the modifications of the terms of the original indenture are stated. If the modifications include changes in the corporation's interest or principal obligations, a notation of these changes is stamped on each bond before it is returned to the assenting bondholder. For modifications not involving adjustments in interest or principal, however, stamping is ordinarily unnecessary.

Questions

1. What kinds of indenture provisions should be helpful to a corporation that wants to speed up the retirement of its bonds?

2. How can indenture provisions be written to enable a corporation to slow down reductions in the volume of its bonded debt?

3. Why might it be advisable for a corporation to refund an outstanding bond issue a year or two before maturity even though required to set a higher rate of interest on the new issue than that carried on the old?

4. Under what circumstances might a corporation be wise to meet the maturity of a bond issue out of the proceeds of bank loans even though it wants to continue to trade on the equity with long-term debt?

5. How could it be advantageous to a corporation to persuade holders of maturing bonds to exchange them for new bonds, instead of selling the new bonds and using the proceeds to pay off the maturing issue?

6. For what reasons do corporations sometimes float new bond issues and simply use the proceeds to retire outstanding bonds long before their maturities?

7. If a corporate management is tempted to refund an outstanding bond issue to gain the advantage of a lower rate of interest, what kinds of costs should it consider before finally deciding?

8. For decisions about refunding outstanding bond issues, why are federal income tax rates an important consideration?

9. For a corporation in financial difficulties, what kinds of indenture modifications might clear the way for new short-term borrowing? for new bond issues?

10. To what extent are indenture modifications agreed to by given proportions of bondholders binding upon those who do not give their consent?

11. Why is a corporation in financial difficulties more likely to seek bondholders' consent to a modification of its sinking fund obligation than its interest obligation?

12. For the corporation that is unable to pay off its bonds at maturity, what remedies short of reorganization in bankruptcy might be sought? Would not the bondholders be hurting their own interests were they to consent to such remedies?

13. If a corporation is unable to pay off its bonds at maturity, are its chances of survival likely to be better if the bonds are held in bulk by institutional investors or in small amounts by many investors? Discuss.

Problem

The Pindar Corporation has outstanding $12 million of 25-year 5 per cent bonds. The original issue, sold ten years ago, amounted to $20 million but $8 million of the bonds have been retired by sinking fund redemptions of $800,000 a year. The sinking fund call price is the par value. The flotation costs of the bond issue amounted to $420,000, but this amount is being charged off on a straight-line basis of $16,800 a year.

The corporation's directors are considering the refunding of the outstanding bonds as a means of reducing interest costs. They are assured by investment bankers that they would have no difficulty in selling at par new 15-year bonds bearing interest at 4¼ per cent. Flotation costs would amount to about $280,000. The new bonds like the old would have to provide, beginning within a year, equal annual contributions to a sinking fund to retire all bonds by the final maturity. The bankers feel that a sinking fund call price of 100 would be satisfactory.

Would it be financially advantageous for the corporation to proceed with the refunding? What net saving over the 15-year period could be expected? Assume that the call price of the old bonds beyond sinking fund requirements is 103. Assume also that the corporation's income is always well into the 52 per cent bracket of the income tax, so that this rate should be used in any estimation of tax economies.

Part X

FINANCING WITHOUT SECURITIES

chapter 31

CURRENT LIABILITIES AS
SOURCES OF ASSETS

Because of their very great importance as means of acquiring assets, stocks and bonds deserve the many chapters devoted to them in this textbook; nevertheless, securities flotations and the management of outstanding securities issues typically require much less of the time and attention of corporate financial managers than the search for and the administration of asset sources not related to securities issues. Many corporations have only one security flotation during their lifetimes—the common stock issue at the time of their establishment; and this is true even of some corporations that are long-lived. Many never issue preferred stock. Many never sell bonds. And even where corporations "frequently" add to their outstanding securities issues, the frequency for the individual corporation is not likely to be oftener than every few years—unless something routine is done, such as giving the common stockholders a stock dividend every quarter or every six months or selling according to the terms of an employee stock-purchase plan. For the typical corporation, moreover, the management of outstanding securities issues requires relatively little of the time and attention of its financial officers. As long as it remains solvent and reasonably profitable, decisions about its securities issues are required only occasionally: whether to pay the quarterly dividend on the preferred, how much to pay on the common, how much must be turned into the redemption fund for the preferred, whether the common should be split up, what optional contribution, if any, should be made to the bond sinking fund, whether cash should be used to redeem bonds outside the scope of sinking fund operations, and so on.

The asset sources not related to securities are of two kinds: (1) earnings; and (2) debt incurred with trade suppliers, banks and other lenders, employees, sellers of equipment, taxing authorities, and others. As earnings as a source of assets were analyzed at length in Chapters 24 and 25, we shall confine our attention in the present chapter and the two following to the asset sources of the second kind.

SUPERVISION OF DEBT UNRELATED TO SECURITIES

The main reason why obligations to creditors such as trade suppliers and banks, as asset sources, require much time and attention of financial managers is that they are chiefly short-term. A trade supplier may

allow 30 days for payment, but he may permit a discount if payment is
made within ten days; if, therefore, advantage is to be taken of the discount offer, not much delay in finding the means of payment is possible.
The corporation may obtain a loan from a bank repayable in 60 days;
hardly, therefore, does it get the money before it must be thinking about
paying it back—quite a different situation is this from a sale of common
stock, the proceeds of which never have to be paid back. Even when
liabilities of the kinds considered here are intermediate- or long-term,
close and continuous attention to their management is generally necessary. For the most part, such debts are repayable in monthly, quarterly,
or semiannual instalments—quite unlike a bond issue for which the required sinking fund contribution may be payable only annually, and the
total contributions over the life of the issue may be designed to retire
only a portion of it. Thus, if a corporation signs an equipment purchase
contract obligating itself to make payments in equal quarterly instalments
over a three-year period, the debt it incurs is one third short-term and
only the remaining two thirds is intermediate-term.

A second reason why liabilities owing to trade suppliers, banks, and
other creditors of this class require much time and attention is the turnover among credit grantors. Negotiations with prospective new credit
grantors are frequently necessary. The turnover may be the result of
deliberate choices of the corporation, or it may be required, as it were,
by the attitudes and policies of the credit grantors. Though a given
supplier of certain raw materials may be able and willing to sell on
credit all that the corporation needs, it may choose to buy from many
suppliers to promote competition for its business among them as well as
to avoid becoming dependent upon the one. Some suppliers may give
poor service or deliver goods not of the quality contracted for, so that
others must be substituted. Substitution may also be necessary if given
suppliers pass out of the picture through failure. A bank may be unwilling to grant the amount of short-term loans for which the corporation
thinks its financial position qualifies it; accordingly, it must seek a substitute lender or, at least, other lenders that will supply funds over and
above what the bank will advance.

IMPORTANCE OF DEBT UNRELATED TO SECURITIES

A basic fact about debts unrelated to securities issues is that virtually
all corporations, regardless of area of operations, size, and other characteristics, make substantial use of them. By definition, corporations having
simple common stock structures depend upon such liabilities as the only
source of assets beyond the common stock and retained earnings sources
themselves. But substantial dependence upon these sources generally
features also the policy of other corporations even though they may
also depend quite heavily upon preferred stocks or bonds or both as
other sources of assets.

The liabilities unrelated to securities, as indicated above, are chiefly short-term in nature, but some are intermediate- and long-term. For the purposes of this and the following chapter, we may limit our attention to the short-term liabilities. Recent statistics of these are presented in Table 31–1. Here we have a compilation of the current liabilities of corpora-

TABLE 31–1
Current Liabilities of Business Corporations, 1960–61[a]
(Dollar amounts in millions)

Industry	No. of Tax Returns	Accounts Payable	Bonds, Notes, and Mort-gages[b]	Other Current Liabil-ities	Total	Per Cent of Total Assets
Agriculture, forestry, fisheries.............	17,139	$ 299	$ 582	$ 100	$ 981	24.2
Mining and quarrying....	13,017	1,104	746	865	2,715	16.0
Construction............	72,332	4,153	1,516	897	6,566	42.7
Manufacturing..........	165,863	24,158	10,702	16,230	51,091	19.5
Public utilities..........	43,852	4,361	3,246	7,111	14,717	10.2
Transportation........	*33,491*	*2,706*	*1,437*	*1,860*	*6,004*	*12.4*
Communication.......	*5,431*	*381*	*279*	*2,584*	*3,244*	*10.5*
Electric and gas.......	*1,299*	*1,213*	*1,421*	*2,603*	*5,238*	*8.3*
Wholesale trade........	117,437	9,986	4,853	1,956	16,795	39.2
Retail trade............	217,269	6,612	4,744	2,753	14,109	31.0
Services...............	121,024	2,233	2,185	1,081	5,498	27.7
Total..............	767,933	$52,906	$28,574	$30,993	$112,472	20.4
Per cent of total current liabilities............		47.0	25.4	27.6	100.0	

[a] Corporations filing federal income tax returns for fiscal years ending between July 1, 1960, and June 30, 1961, excluding corporations engaged in trade not allocated to wholesale or retail; in finance, insurance, and real estate; and in miscellaneous operations not classified as to industry.

[b] Maturity of less than one year.

SOURCE: U.S. Treasury Department, Internal Revenue Service, *Statistics of Income, 1960–61—Preliminary: Corporation Income Tax Returns* (Washington, D.C.: U.S. Government Printing Office, 1962), pp. 17–18, 20–21, 24. (Percentages supplied by the author.)

tions as found in the balance sheets filed with their federal income tax returns for fiscal years ending between July 1, 1960, and June 30, 1961. All the important industrial areas in which corporations operate are included, except for the fields of financial institutions and real estate operations, these being excluded because of their peculiar asset and liability structures, and, because, in any case, they are ordinarily outside the purview of corporate financial management as our field of study.

On the basis of the data of Table 31–1, and with the assumption that the 1960–61 experience was not significantly out of line with the continuing situation, we conclude that corporations of the included industrial groups obtain collectively about one fifth of their total assets by contracting short-term liabilities unrelated to securities—truly a proportion of no mean importance. The very great dependence of corporations in the construction industry and in wholesale trade upon these short-term sources is especially noteworthy, but hardly less remarkable is their significance to corporations in retail trade and in the service industries.

It is often said that transportation, electric, gas, communications, and other public utility corporations, because of the preponderance of their investment in fixed assets, are much less dependent upon short-term debt than are corporations in other industrial fields; and, of course, the figures of the table bear this out. Nevertheless, the dependence of these corporations upon short-term debt is obviously not inconsequential. Certainly, the use of short-term sources by the public utilities as a group in the amount of more than $14.7 billion could hardly be dismissed as inconsequential.

The bottom line of Table 31–1 indicates that, among the short-term liabilities that serve as sources of corporate assets, those made available by trade suppliers—accounts payable—are by far the most important. The other two sources are shown to be of close to equal weight, with "other current liabilities," including chiefly accrued expenses, having a slight edge over "bonds, notes, and mortgages." The item "bonds, notes, and mortgages"—even with the addition of the footnote in the table: "maturity of less than one year"—is somewhat disturbing. At this stage of our discussion, we are not especially interested in bonds nor, indeed, in mortgage loans which generally are of long term. What the designation means is that the short-term liability for borrowed money includes the principal of bonds and mortgage obligations coming due within one year—whether partial payments due on continuing obligations or payments due because the maturities come within the year—as well as instalment payments on intermediate- and long-term loans not evidenced by bonds or secured by mortgages. But we must be satisfied with the kinds of statistics that are available. In any event, it is reasonable to assume that a very large part of the liability of $28,574 million for "bonds, notes, and mortgages" represents short-term loans—loans of original maturity of not more than one year—the kinds in which we are particularly interested at this juncture. Thus, the Federal Trade Commission and the Securities and Exchange Commission, in their joint report on the finances of manufacturing corporations for the first quarter of 1961, estimated the liability of these corporations (excluding newspaper publishing corporations) upon short-term bank loans at $8,559 million, and that for instalments on longer-term debt coming due within the year at only $2,284 million.[1]

For the discussion of the three kinds of short-term liabilities, as classified in the table, attention will be given in the present chapter to accounts payable and other current liabilities, leaving for the following chapter an examination of the sources of short-term loans. Before getting into this discussion, however, we should find it advantageous to consider the principles of financing by means of short-term debt as they relate to business corporations.

---

[1] Federal Trade Commission–Securities and Exchange Commission, *Quarterly Financial Report for Manufacturing Corporations*, First Quarter, 1961, p. 34.

PRINCIPLES OF FINANCING WITH SHORT-TERM DEBT

The principles that should serve as guides to corporate managements in the use of short-term liabilities as sources of assets are the following: (1) for greatest safety, short-term debt financing should be avoided; (2) there is generally justification for short-term debt financing to provide for seasonal expansion of current assets; (3) if trading on the equity is an appropriate financial policy, either long-term or short-term debt financing of current assets is acceptable; and (4) special circumstances at times justify temporary short-term debt financing beyond what would otherwise be appropriate.

Avoidance of Short-Term Debt

Debt is always a source of danger to solvency, and corporations that avoid it are relieved of many anxieties. They may be unsuccessful, with operating losses consuming their assets, but they can decide to quit business, to liquidate their remaining assets gradually and carefully, and thus to conserve something for the stockholders. On the other hand, unsuccessful corporations that have many debts may be forced by unpaid creditors to reorganize or liquidate at the very times when the stockholders' claims would be most adversely affected. Corporations without debt can often weather severe financial reverses—to make up their losses, as it were, after coming through periods of difficulties; but unpaid creditors are often unwilling to wait to see whether debtor corporations can overcome adversities.

As a rule, short-term debt is more dangerous than long-term debt. It is true that, when short-term debt is contracted, the financial managers of a corporation have only to look a short distance into the future in judging its capacity to make payment, whereas capacity to repay long-term debt is clouded by all the uncertainties about what may happen in a lengthy period of years. But should an optimistic short-term forecast turn out to be a bad one—should cash inflows suddenly fall off sharply because of an unforseen recession in business activity—the corporation might be very quickly in trouble if it has many short-term obligations; hardly would this be true were its debts chiefly long term.

Suppose, for example, that Corporation A has $8 million of current assets, no fixed assets, $4 million of current liabilities, and $4 million of stockholders' equity; and that Corporation B has an identical asset situation, $4 million of bonds, and $4 million of stockholders' equity. Corporation B's bonds have a sinking fund provision requiring the retirement of 5 per cent of the issue annually. Should, then, a business setback occur and cash inflows be greatly reduced for the two corporations, surely Corporation A would have much greater difficulty in paying off $4 million of obligations all maturing within a short period of time, than would Corporation B in meeting its sinking fund requirement of $200,000.

A policy of avoiding short-term debt in the interests of greatest safety can hardly mean, however, an absolute avoidance of such debt. A corporation having such a policy would hardly pay its payroll daily, pay its accruing taxes and other expenses, as for light, power, and water, before their due dates, and insist upon cash payment to trade suppliers who customarily allow, say, 30 days for payment. What the policy means, then, is that the corporation would hold cash or high-quality short-term investments over and above its other requirements to take care of these *unavoidable* short-term debts, as they might be called. Assume that it needs $6 million of current assets for the usual scope of its operations. and that "unavoidable" short-term debts usually run around $1.5 million. Accordingly, it should have $7.5 million of current assets, the additional $1.5 million made up of cash or short-term high-quality investments. Essentially, therefore, it would be financing its normal current asset requirements of $6 million without debt, or, at least, without current debt.

Short-Term Debt Financing for Seasonal Expansion

A policy of avoiding short-term debt can be quite expensive for corporations whose scale of operations fluctuates substantially according to seasonal patterns; the greater the size of the fluctuations, the greater the cost would be likely to be. If short-term debt is avoided, current assets must be supplied from long-term sources, either from the contributions of stockholders or from the proceeds of long-term borrowing. But such assets, once supplied from long-term sources, remain continuously on hand (although, of course, changing in composition more or less constantly). If, then, substantial amounts of these assets are needed only for peak periods, they must remain out of operation for the remainder of the year. It would appear to be quite uneconomical to have stockholders supply on a full-time basis assets subject to only part-time use, or to pay interest to bondholders for 12 months for the use of assets for periods of, perhaps, three or four months.

Accordingly, incurring short-term debt for seasonal current asset requirements is generally regarded in the business community as strongly justified. Although many corporate managers are wedded to the doctrine that debt should generally be avoided as dangerous to solvency, they are often willing to make an exception for the incurring of short-term debt for seasonal purposes. If orders or market prospects justify peak-period operations, debt contracted to finance this expansion ought not to be difficult to pay off—it should not, therefore, be a serious source of danger: this is their defense for the exception. Many commercial bankers, too, emphasize seasonal lending, as when they say that most of their "working capital loans" to business are or should be confined to financing the expanded requirements of peak seasons.

To illustrate the theory of short-term debt financing for peak-season requirements, we may expand upon the example given previously. For its normal operations outside the peak season, the corporation needs $6 million of current assets, but because it has "unavoidable" current liabilities of $1.5 million, it customarily carries an additional $1.5 million in short-term investments. Let us say, therefore, that its ordinary working capital position is somewhat as follows:

Current Assets:		*Current Liabilities:*	
Cash and short-term investments	$2,500,000	Accounts payable, accrued wages, etc.	$1,500,000
Accounts receivable	2,200,000		
Inventories	2,800,000		

For its peak period, the corporation must carry accounts receivable of $4 million and it needs inventories of $6 million; hence, it must expand these two assets by a total of $5 million. Its managers would probably decide that, if incurring short-term debt is justified for seasonal expansion, all the more reasonable would be the use for this purpose of the $1.5 million of short-term investments. That would leave only $3.5 million of the expansion in receivables and inventories to be financed with debt, and the result would show up as follows:

Current Assets:		*Current Liabilities:*	
Cash	$1,000,000	Accounts payable, accrued wages, bank loans, etc.	$5,000,000
Accounts receivable	4,000,000		
Inventories	6,000,000		

Were the trade creditors and the lending bank or banks to insist upon the maintenance of a working capital ratio of, say, 2 to 1, the corporation obviously would easily qualify.

Trading on the Equity

As was just indicated, financing peak-season additions to current assets by way of short-term debt is a means of avoiding the cost of idle assets, whether supplied by stockholders or bondholders. Another way of putting this is to say that it is a means of trading on the equity—of using debt as a lever to raise the rate of earnings upon the common stockholders' investment. If short-term loans can be obtained from commercial banks at a rate of interest of 5 per cent per annum, and if the banks' advances can be employed to yield a return of 10 per cent, the rate of net earnings for the common stockholders is obviously increased. Thus, short-term debt, no less than bonds and other forms of long-term debt, can be employed to give common stock "leverage."

It is obvious, too, that nothing in the nature of short-term debt necessarily limits its use to peak-season requirements. Corporations that have no pronounced seasonal patterns in their operations often depend rather heavily on short-term debt as a source of current assets. Their managers deliberately accept the risks of trading on the equity—of insolvency—in striving toward a higher rate of earnings for the common stock. In many instances, they doubtless conclude that these risks are not great because of the stability of their operations. In any case, they do not expect to go to extremes in incurring short-term obligations; even if they should be so inclined, they would surely be held in restraint by limits imposed by creditors and prospective creditors—limits in terms of working capital ratios and relationships of total debt to equity. Nevertheless, the statistics of business failures always remind us that many corporations do go much too far in incurring short-term debt, and that, accordingly, creditors are not sufficiently careful in setting their limits.

In certain respects, the employment of short-term debt for trading on the equity has advantages over the use of long-term debt for this purpose. Interest always has to be paid on bonds, but there appears to be no charge of this kind on trade debts and on accrued wages, taxes, and other expense items. Even in the matter of loans, interest rates on short-term loans are often lower for the given borrower than on bonds, as is generally true in periods of upsweeping yield curves. In short-term debt financing, there are no flotation costs comparable to those on bond issues. And, finally, short-term creditors are generally much less inclined to impose restrictions upon managerial discretion than are bond buyers, as by "protective provisions" in indentures.

But a price is paid for these advantages—if it is true that short-term debt is a greater danger to solvency than is long-term debt. The comparison of the positions of Corporations A and B on pages 771–72 showed why there usually is greater danger in short maturities. Thus, corporate managers may well decide that the weight of advantage is on the side of long-term debt. They may decide that, having chosen to go after the advantages of trading on the equity, they had better do this by concentrating rather heavily on long maturities. That this is the decision of many corporate managers is indicated, at least roughly, by recent statistics of new financing. As shown in Table 31–2, a substantial proportion of the "new money" raised in recent years through the cash sale of corporate securities was earmarked for working capital—very clearly a use of long-term funds for the acquisition of short-term assets.[2] Even more significant are the figures of Table 31–3 which show that in the years 1960–62 combined, corporations of all industrial groups except public utilities routed to working capital quite large proportions of the new money raised through securities issues offered for cash sale. These indications are "rough" because the reports of the SEC from which the

---

[2] By definition, "new money" is earmarked for the expansion of plant and equipment or for working capital—and not, for example, for the redemption of existing debt.

TABLE 31–2
Securities Issues to Raise Working Capital, 1946–62[a]
(Dollar amounts in millions)

Year	Total Issues for New Money	Issues to Raise Working Capital	Per Cent of Working Capital Issues to Total
1946.....	$ 3,279	$1,164	35.5
1947.....	4,591	1,182	25.7
1948.....	5,929	1,708	28.8
1949.....	4,606	882	19.1
1950.....	4,006	1,041	26.0
1951.....	6,531	1,421	21.8
1952.....	8,180	1,868	22.8
1953.....	7,960	2,313	29.1
1954.....	6,780	1,670	24.6
1955.....	7,957	2,624	32.9
1956.....	9,663	2,954	30.6
1957.....	11,784	2,744	23.3
1958.....	9,907	2,115	21.4
1959.....	8,578	2,494	29.0
1960.....	8,758	3,097	35.4
1961.....	10,829	3,290	30.4
1962.....	8,323	2,622	31.5

[a] Substantially all new issues of securities offered for cash sale in the United States in amounts over $100,000 and with terms to maturity of more than one year, but excluding intercorporate transactions and issues of investment companies.

SOURCE: Securities and Exchange Commission, *Annual Reports* and *Statistical Bulletin*, June, 1963, p. 13. (Percentages supplied by the author.)

data of the two tables were taken do not distinguish between stock and bond issues as sources of the new money, and because we do not know to what extent the corporations issuing securities were simultaneously expanding their short-term debt. On the first of these points, however, we do know on the basis of other SEC statistics that the volume of non-

TABLE 31–3
Securities Issues to Raise Working Capital, by Industry, 1960–62 Combined[a]
(Dollar amounts in millions)

Industry	Total Issues for New Money	Issues to Raise Working Capital	Per Cent of Working Capital Issues to Total
Manufacturing............	$ 6,973	$2,862	41.0
Mining..................	538	287	53.3
Electric, gas, and water....	7,664	85	1.1
Railroad................	522	10	1.9
Other transportation.......	1,270	58	4.6
Communication..........	3,661	21	.6
Finance and real estate....	5,596	4,561	81.5
Commercial and other.....	1,687	1,125	66.6
Total...............	$27,911	$9,009	32.3

[a] Substantially all new issues of securities offered for cash sale in the United States in amounts over $100,000 and with terms to maturity of more than one year, but excluding intercorporate transactions and issues of investment companies.

SOURCE: Derived from Securities and Exchange Commission, *Statistical Bulletin*, February, 1963, p. 18.

refunding bond issues offered for cash sale in the respective periods
covered in the two tables far exceeded the volume of stock issues
similarly offered.

Special Circumstances for Short-Term Debt Financing

One instance of a special circumstance that might justify extraordinary short-term borrowing was mentioned in the preceding chapter: the
maturing of bond issues in times of tight money and high interest rates,
and the temporary use of short-term loans pending later bond issues.
Other occasions for such "interim financing" sometimes arise. As an
example, a corporation might use short-term loan funds to meet the
early costs of constructing a new factory building, planning a later bond
issue both to repay these loans and to meet the remainder of the
construction costs.

Usually there is danger in expanding short-term debt on the grounds
that it is justified by "special circumstances"—not simply the ordinary
danger of short maturities, but, additionally, the temptation to regard
too many kinds of circumstances as "special." Thus, the incurring of
extraordinary amounts of short-term debts to finance the introduction of
new lines of goods or to carry through extraordinary advertising campaigns might be "justified" by the expectation that cash throw-offs from
greatly expanded earnings will easily take care of the additional debt.
But the new lines of merchandise may flop, and the advertising campaigns miscarry, leaving the corporations with very serious problems of
meeting their short maturities. On the other hand, it may be possible
to avoid even the ordinary danger of short-term debt. If, for example,
short-term borrowing is undertaken in anticipation of a later bond issue,
and if the corporation has a commitment from a reputable life insurance
company to buy the issue at the later date, the interim financing would
seem to be an entirely safe procedure.

ACCOUNTS PAYABLE

Scope of Accounts Payable

In Table 31–1, we saw that, for American business corporations collectively, accounts payable represent by far the most important short-
term source of assets; according to corporate balance sheets filed with
federal tax returns for 1960–61 (excluding some classes of corporations
as noted in the table), they amounted to 47 per cent of the total of
short-term sources. But the significance of trade payables differs from
industry to industry, as is revealed by the additional data from the same
source presented in Table 31–4. From these data, we conclude that trade
payables are least significant for manufacturing corporations and most
significant in the construction, wholesale trade, and service industries.
The relative low proportion of trade payables to the current assets of

TABLE 31–4
Accounts Payable in Relation to Total Current Assets,
by Industry, 1960–61[a]
(Dollar amounts in millions)

Industry	Accounts Payable	Current Assets	Per Cent of Accounts Payable to Current Assets
Agriculture, forestry, fisheries......	$ 299	$ 1,367	21.9
Mining and quarrying............	1,104	5,462	20.2
Construction....................	4,153	9,369	44.3
Manufacturing..................	24,158	131,156	18.4
Public utilities.................	4,361	17,912	24.3
Wholesale trade.................	9,986	32,088	31.1
Retail trade....................	6,612	31,235	21.2
Services.......................	2,233	6,894	32.4
Total.....................	$52,906	$235,483	22.5

[a] For corporations filing federal income tax returns for fiscal years ending between July 1, 1960, and June 30, 1961, excluding corporations engaged in trade not allocated to wholesale or retail.

SOURCE: U.S. Treasury Department, Internal Revenue Service, *Statistics of Income, 1960–61—Preliminary: Corporation Income Tax Returns* (Washington, D.C.: U.S. Government Printing Office, 1962) pp. 17–18, 20–21, 24. (Percentages supplied by the author.)

corporations in retail trade is somewhat surprising; but if we look at a breakdown of this area, as in Table 31–5, we see that in one of its divisions, eating and drinking establishments, it is extremely high, and quite high in others, as food stores and apparel and accessories stores.

A further observation is that, in almost all fields of enterprise, trade payables tend to be much more important as a source of assets for small corporations than for large ones. Often large corporations are able to get special price concessions on the goods they buy by agreeing to pay cash on delivery or, indeed, by making advance payments to help their

TABLE 31–5
Accounts Payable in Relation to Total Current Assets
in Retail Trade, 1960–61[a]
(Dollar amounts in millions)

Area	Accounts Payable	Current Assets	Per Cent of Accounts Payable to Current Assets
Food............................	$1,175	$3,143	37.3
General merchandise...............	1,276	8,538	14.9
Apparel and accessories............	828	2,979	27.8
Furniture, home furnishings, and equipment......................	579	2,779	20.8
Automobile dealers and gasoline service stations.................	779	5,879	13.2
Eating and drinking places..........	321	649	49.5
Building materials, hardware, and farm equipment..................	661	3,254	20.3
Other retail stores.................	993	4,014	24.7

[a] For corporations filing federal income tax returns for fiscal years ending between July 1, 1960, and June 30, 1961.

SOURCE: U.S. Treasury Department, Internal Revenue Service, *Statistics of Income, 1960–61—Preliminary: Corporation Income Tax Returns* (Washington, D.C.: U.S. Government Printing Office, 1962), pp. 21–22. (Percentages supplied by the author.)

suppliers to meet their costs of production; while small corporations are rarely in a position to bargain in this way. When, moreover, trade suppliers allow discounts for payment within a few days, the large corporations are much more likely to have cash to take advantage of these discount offers than are small ones. Suppose, for example, that a given corporation buys on terms of 2/10 n/30 and that it gets a shipment of goods every ten days billed at $20,000. If it pays on the tenth day to take advantage of the discount, the average amount of its accounts payable is $20,000; but if it ignores the discount offer and waits till the thirtieth day to make payment, the average amount of its trade payables is $60,000.

Significance of Accounts Payable

In view of earlier discussions in this textbook, little needs to be added here about the significance of accounts payable as a source of assets. In Chapter 6, it was explained that accounts payable constitute a *permanent* source of assets equal to the minimum level to which they fall over the years, and that they constitute a temporary source in amounts by which they rise above this minimum. It was also pointed out that when trade creditors sell goods on account and await payment for some days or weeks after their business customers have resold the goods for cash, they, in effect, supply the latter with cash for general operations.

All of Chapter 9 was devoted to the management of accounts receivable. But, in interbusiness transactions, the accounts receivable of some firms are simply the accounts payable of others. Hence, an attempt to treat accounts payable at length here would require a repetition of most of what was said in that chapter—although, to be sure, with a switch in viewpoint. A few observations, therefore, should suffice.

While retail and service establishments usually have a choice to sell on account or only for cash, the general rule for sales transactions among businesses is that credit will be made available to the buyer *if he qualifies*. Manufacturers are generally willing to sell on account to other manufacturers and to wholesalers and jobbers, and the wholesalers and jobbers, in turn, to sell on account to retailers. But the business buyer must qualify. He must satisfy the seller as to his character, capacity, and capital, the seller's judgment being based upon an analysis of credit information gathered from the sources described in Chapter 9. Although, therefore, the availability of trade credit may be said to be the rule, it may be denied to given firms because of serious weakness in character, capacity, or capital. Nevertheless, trade suppliers are generally more liberal in granting credit to weak firms than are financial institutions in granting loans. It is not unusual for trade suppliers to sell on account to firms already in a bad way, to lengthen the allowed credit period, and to grant other concessions precisely to try to rescue them from their difficulties. Wanting to preserve outlets for their goods in given cities or regions, these trade suppliers are sometimes ready to accept quite serious risks.

Cost of Trade Credit

Sometimes it is said that trade credit is expensive. In the selling price of his goods, the seller-on-account, if he is at least to break even, must cover interest on the cash absorbed in the goods he sells, the expenses of credit administration, and his bad-debt losses. Hence, the buyer who always pays within the allowed credit period, it is said, shares these costs, no less than the delinquent buyer whose very delinquency gives rise to a goodly portion of the costs. But if the seller has only one price at which he will sell either on account or for immediate cash payment, the buyer is hardly in a position to avoid his share of the costs of credit selling. Were he to insist upon making immediate or early cash payment without getting a price concession or a discount, he would simply be adding to his costs—he would have an interest cost in supplying cash before being obliged to do so. Accordingly, buyers usually accept sellers' extensions of credit without a lot of worry about the costs involved.

When, however, sellers allow liberal discounts for early payment, the buyers are given the opportunity, as it were, to avoid all or most of the costs of trade credit. If all buyers from a given seller take the discounts, the latter's costs of credit administration must be quite substantially reduced, so that any buyer's remaining share in these costs must be quite small; if only some of the buyers take the discounts, they presumably shift most of the seller's credit costs to the buyers who do not. Thus, the expensiveness of trade credit should be especially apparent to buyers unable to take advantage of discount allowances. The illustration in Chapter 8 showed that a buyer of goods could, in effect, earn interest for 20 days at the rate of 30.7 per cent per annum by borrowing money at 6 per cent to take advantage of a 2 per cent discount allowed for payment within ten days, the net being due in 30 days.[3] Surely a reduction in the cost of goods of this proportion—$167.33 on a bill of $10,000 in the illustration—would go a long way toward offsetting whatever costs of credit had been included in the seller's original invoice.

OTHER CURRENT LIABILITIES

Corporate short-term liabilities, other than trade payables and liabilities for borrowed money, also make an appreciable contribution to assets. For the corporations surveyed in Table 31-1, this contribution amounted to 27.6 per cent of the total current liability contribution. In relation to the current assets of these corporations, as set out in Table 31-4, it amounted to 13.2 per cent.

---

[3] See above, p. 166.

In compiling the statistics of corporate income and expenses and financial positions, from which the data of Table 31–1 were drawn, the Treasury includes in "other current liabilities" all kinds of accrued expenses payable within a year, such as accruals for wages, taxes, rent, and interest, certain additional liabilities related to payrolls, dividends payable, and other items "not arising from the purchase of goods and services and not evidenced by bonds, notes, or mortgages." [4] For the typical corporation, however, accrued expenses far exceed in size and importance all other items of "other" current liabilities.

Accrued Expenses

Accrued expenses, or at least substantial proportions of them, may be said to be "volunteer" sources of assets. They are, in large part, unavoidable even for corporations that have plenty of current assets supplied from long-term sources. It is accepted practice to pay payrolls every week or every two weeks or, in some cases, monthly; hence, any corporation that continues to operate will have some liability for accrued wages. It will have its assets augmented by the contribution of service made by the employees, and it is hardly likely to insist upon paying wages daily even if it is already well heeled in its cash balance. It is accepted practice for taxing authorities to set tax payment dates beyond the dates of tax accruals, and corporate managers, while in their right minds, can hardly be expected to insist upon advance payments. Thus, their corporations temporarily retain assets equal to the amount of accruing taxes. It is accepted practice for public utilities to supply their power, gas, water, and telephone services on a daily basis but to bill for these services only monthly. Therefore, they contribute to corporate assets as their services are used—a contribution that is measured, at any time, by the amount of accrued expenses for such services.

Corporations that have no need to engage in short-term debt financing are generally pleased to accept contributions to assets by way of accruing expenses. It is a matter of convenience; it would be quite burdensome to them to try to pay their payrolls or their bills for electric power from day to day. But the generality of corporations doubtless accept such contributions with enthusiasm because they are enabled to conserve cash; they are thereby relieved of the necessity of relying more heavily upon other sources of assets—sources that for many in relatively weak financial positions might be difficult to tap. As was explained in Chapter 6, a corporation whose accrued expenses never fall below a certain level has in these accruals a permanent source of assets of that amount, and a temporary source of fluctuating amounts as the accruals rise above the minimum level.

---

[4] U.S. Treasury Department, Internal Revenue Service, *Statistics of Income, 1960–61—Preliminary: Corporation Income Tax Returns* (Washington, D.C.: U.S. Government Printing Office, 1962), p. 13.

An interesting aspect of accrued expenses is that, though largely a "volunteer" source of assets, they are subject to some management. Corporations that are hard pressed financially may be able to ease their difficulties somewhat by increasing, as it were, their dependence upon this source. Any deferment of the payment of accrued expenses would be helpful. If the payroll period is now one week, it might be made two weeks; or if salaries are now paid twice a month, they might be made payable only monthly. A mild degree of slowness in paying utility bills might be tolerated, at least for a time, by the utility companies. Even the nonpayment of taxes on their due dates might be a remedy for short-run financial difficulties—the penalties for delinquencies might not be too great a price to pay for a "breathing spell."

Other Payroll Obligations

For the typical corporation, other payroll obligations are similar to accrued wages in consisting of temporarily unpaid compensation for labor service. Specifically, they are accumulated obligations to make payments into pension funds, union welfare funds, and the like, whether required by collective-bargained contracts or voluntarily provided by corporations to make employment more attractive. While obligations of this kind are accruing in the course of the year, the corporation is able to retain and use in ordinary operations assets of equivalent amount, so that the accruals, entered as liabilities, are recognized as the temporary source of these assets.

Dividends Payable

When cash dividends are declared by the directors of solvent corporations, they become, as we know, obligations to pay; as such, they are carried as current liabilities in corporation balance sheets. Between the date of declaration and the date of payment, however, the corporation continues to have the use of assets equivalent to the amount of the dividends, so that the dividend liability can be said to be the source of these assets. The dividend liability can also be described as a contribution of the stockholders, since dividends are chargeable against the surplus accounts and these accounts constitute a part of the stockholders' equity.

Deferred Items

Many corporations receive cash as income before it is earned. The cash obviously adds to their assets, and it is available for general corporate use, but the fact that goods must be delivered or service provided against the cash already received is indicated by the inclusion of "deferred credits" or "deferred credits to income" among current liabilities in balance sheets.

Transportation companies incur liabilities for services when they sell tickets in advance of voyages, flights, and trips scheduled for later dates, as do theater corporations in selling tickets for later performances—sometimes performances scheduled months ahead as for "hits." In a similar way, retail store corporations, in selling "gift certificates," obligate themselves to deliver goods as selected by the holders of these certificates, and likewise for restaurant corporations in selling "meal tickets."

In producing machinery and equipment according to the specifications of buyers, manufacturing companies sometimes require the buyers to make advance payments; in other cases, large buyers make advance payments to small suppliers on a voluntary basis to help the latter to meet costs of production. The federal government, in buying military equipment and supplies, has been especially generous in making advance payments to producers of these goods. Its advances were especially large during the period of World War II when they supplied numerous firms with the means to produce war materials; but its policy of making advances has been continued, although, of course, on a reduced scale, in the postwar period. At the end of the first quarter of 1963, for example, total advances of the federal government outstanding to manufacturing industries amounted to $2,322 million. Of this total, $1,479 million had been received by manufacturers of aircraft and parts; $532 million by manufacturers of electrical machinery, equipment, and supplies; $38 million by other machinery manufacturers; $32 million by producers of rubber and plastics; and smaller amounts by other producers including instrument manufacturers, manufacturers of motor vehicles and equipment, and producers of primary metals.[5]

Corporations that own facilities that they rent out often receive advance rental payments that are included as "deferred credits" among their current liabilities. Similarly, royalty payments by patent licensees are sometimes made in advance.

Questions

1. Why is the management of debt unrelated to security issues usually much more time consuming than the management of security issues?

2. In relation to total assets, what is the importance of current liabilities as sources? How does this importance differ from industry to industry? Among the current liabilities, what is the relative importance of accounts payable?

3. Why is it proper to speak of some current liabilities as being "unavoidable"? How can the presence of "unavoidable" current liabilities be reconciled with the proposition that, for greatest safety, short-term debt financing should be avoided?

4. Why is it said that avoiding short-term debt can be quite expensive for firms whose operations are subject to wide seasonal fluctuations?

---

[5] Federal Trade Commission—Securities and Exchange Commission, *Quarterly Financial Report for Manufacturing Corporations,* First Quarter, 1963, pp. 34–49.

5. Is there any danger to a corporation's solvency if it confines short-term financing very largely to seasonal requirements? Explain.

6. Aside from seasonal financing, what justification is there for the use of short-term debt financing as a means of trading on the equity?

7. Why is it said that, as a rule, trade payables are a relatively more important source of assets for small corporations than for large ones?

8. Compare the availability of trade credit for business firms with the availability of credit for consumers.

9. Would it not be economical for business firms to pay cash for what they buy, thereby avoiding the costs of trade credit? Discuss.

10. What justification is there for saying that accrued wages, accrued taxes, and other accrued expenses are sources of assets?

11. To what extent are accrued expenses, as a source of assets, subject to management by the individual corporation?

12. Explain how "deferred credits" function as sources of assets.

Problem

In the slack season of the Nolen Manufacturing Corporation, which lasts about six months, its balance sheet generally looks like this:

U.S. government obligations.	$ 6,000,000	Current liabilities.........	$ 2,000,000
Other current assets........	9,000,000	Common stock............	18,000,000
Fixed assets..............	5,000,000		
	$20,000,000		$20,000,000

As the firm gets into the peak season, it liquidates the government securities to expand inventories and accounts receivable. To get better prices, it pays cash for most of its raw materials, so that little of the necessary expansion of current assets is financed by trade payables. However, there is expansion in accrued payroll and other accrued expenses, and this, with some expansion of trade payables, generally amounts to about $1 million. In the peak season of approximately six months, therefore, the corporation's balance sheet generally takes on this appearance:

Current assets............	$16,000,000	Current liabilities.........	$ 3,000,000
Fixed assets..............	5,000,000	Common stock............	18,000,000
	$21,000,000		$21,000,000

The corporation is closely owned by three brothers who draw out all its income as salaries and dividends—this explains the lack of a surplus account in the balance sheets. One of the brothers, John Nolen, is dissatisfied with the corporation's finances. He says that, in effect, a substantial amount of the equity is really being invested in government securities which pay a return averaging only around 3 per cent a year. He wants his brothers to join him in voting to retire $5 million of the stock, and in using the money withdrawn in another corporate venture which promises, in his opinion, a before-tax rate of return of 15 per cent. He has already talked the matter over with a lending officer of a local bank who, after investigation, said that the bank would lend up to $5 million at 6 per cent per annum to take the place of the money to be withdrawn by stock retirement.

Present a numerical analysis of the corporation's situation and John Nolen's proposal either in support of the proposal or in opposition to it.

chapter 32

SHORT-TERM LOANS

Corporations that want to borrow for short-term purposes may seek loans from one or more of several sources. Most corporations, however, go first to the commercial banks: these are the predominant short-term lenders to business. Some borrow from the commercial banks, as it were, indirectly, through the use of letters of credit and bankers' acceptances. Some, though usually depending in part upon commercial bank direct loans, go to the open market and have their promissory notes offered broadside to investors. Others find commercial finance companies especially responsive to their requests for loans on pledges of accounts receivable. And sellers of durable goods on instalment contracts find several classes of institutions willing to grant inventory loans in order to get assignments of the instalment contracts themselves. For the present chapter, then, the objective is an examination of these varied sources of short-term loans.

SHORT-TERM LOANS OF COMMERCIAL BANKS

For most business corporations, the commercial bank is the logical place to turn to if there is a need of current assets over and above what can be supplied from long-term sources and on the basis of trade payables, accrued expenses, and "other" current liabilities. As was pointed out in Chapter 7, commercial banks are distinguished from all other classes of financial institutions in that they receive deposits of the public subject to the obligation to repay on demand on the written order of the depositor. Any bank that provides "checking accounts" to the public is, therefore, a commercial bank.

When businesses must pay cash for the goods they buy, when they need cash to make early payments to trade suppliers to take advantage of discounts, when they get into seasonal periods of expansion, when they run short of cash in paying payrolls and in meeting operating expenses for other than seasonal reasons, when they want to make preliminary payments upon fixed asset acquisitions pending later bond or stock issues, when tax bills come due without sufficient cash to meet them, when rising prices make extraordinary drains upon cash—such are the occasions for seeking short-term loans from the commercial banks.

Commercial banks are readily accessible to business enterprises. Granting loans is their principal source of profits, so that they welcome business borrowers and, one might add, borrowers of many other classes. What is more, there are a great number of these institutions scattered throughout the country, so that every city, town, and village, except for the very smallest, is served by one or more, or, at least, by a branch of an institution whose principal office is located elsewhere. At the end of 1962, 13,427 commercial banks were in operation in the United States, and some of these, in turn, were maintaining branches to the total number of 12,068.[1] Commercial banks vary in size from the Bank of America, located in California, with total assets at the end of 1962 of $13,417 million to quite small institutions in villages and hamlets having assets individually much less than a half million dollars.

From the standpoint of total assets, the commercial banks are our most important class of financial institutions. Their total assets at the end of 1962 amounted to $297,116 million, far in excess of the total assets at that time of $133,169 million reported by life insurance companies which are second in total resources among our financial institutions.[2]

Volume of Short-Term Loans

General Statistics. Although commercial banks are the principal short-term lenders to business, it is impossible at most times to discover precisely what their outstanding volume of loans of this description amounts to. Statistics of their total outstanding "commercial and industrial loans" are published monthly by the Board of Governors of the Federal Reserve System and semiannually by the Federal Deposit Insurance Corporation, but these statistics do not differentiate between short-term loans and so-called "term loans," that is, those with original maturities of more than one year. In their reports of commercial and industrial loans, moreover, the two bank supervisory agencies do not include loans to businesses secured by real estate mortgages, although, to be sure, most real estate loans to business are of the term variety. It is probable, too, that a moderate amount of reported "consumer loans" is actually used for business purposes. However, the figures for commercial and industrial loans remain of great importance in indicating the predominant position of the commercial banks as lenders to business. Even without a breakdown for short-term and term loans, the data of commercial and industrial loans, as presented on an annual basis for the postwar period in Table 32–1, must impress one as to the outstanding role of the commercial banks as contributors to the assets of business enterprise. The absolute level of their outstanding loans in each of the postwar years is impressive, but even more so, of course, is the record of expansion of close to 250 per cent in the period of 17 years covered in the table.

Special Surveys. Specific information about the proportion of short-

---

[1] *Federal Reserve Bulletin,* April, 1963, pp. 551, 552.
[2] *Federal Reserve Bulletin,* June, 1963, pp. 808, 821.

TABLE 32–1
Outstanding Commercial and Industrial Loans of
Insured Commercial Banks, 1946–62[a]
(In millions of dollars)

End of Year	Amount	End of Year	Amount
1946	$14,019	1955	$33,210
1947	18,015	1956	38,707
1948	18,765	1957	40,546
1949	16,939	1958	40,457
1950	21,808	1959	40,195
1951	25,788	1960	43,132
1952	27,816	1961	45,157
1953	27,158	1962	48,668
1954	26,823		

[a] Beginning in 1959, loans by commercial banks to other financial institutions which had previously been included very largely in commercial and industrial loans were placed in a separate category. For June 10, 1959, this change in classification resulted in a reduction in reported commercial and industrial loans of $4,447 million. But the year-end data for 1958 and earlier years, as shown in this table, were not adjusted to conform to the change in classification. Accordingly, the amounts of commercial and industrial loans reported for the period 1959–62 are not closely comparable with the amounts reported for 1946–58.

SOURCE: Federal Deposit Insurance Corporation, *Annual Reports.*

term loans among total commercial bank advances to business enterprises is provided by occasional detailed surveys of the loans of member banks of the Federal Reserve System.[3] In the postwar period, such surveys have been made by the Board of Governors of the System as of November 20, 1946, October 5, 1955, and October 16, 1957. The latest of these surveys revealed that $25,197 million, or 62.3 per cent of total member-bank loans to business of $40,618 million (including loans secured by real estate), had original maturities of one year or less. In number, there were 801,000 short-term loans on the books of the member banks, equal to 62.5 per cent of the 1,281,000 business loans of all maturities.[4]

The survey of October 16, 1957, provided a breakdown of short-term business loans according to the size of borrowers. As presented in Table 32–2, details of this breakdown indicate that the great mass of short-term loans in *number* go to smaller businesses. Because, however, the average of loans granted to smaller enterprises is relatively small itself, the preponderance of the funds advanced go to the larger enterprises. Nevertheless, total loans in the *amount* of $8,600 million granted to borrowers having assets of less than $1 million indicate the availability of commercial bank credit in substantial volumes to smaller businesses. As revealed in

---

[3] Although fewer than half of the commercial banks of the country are members of the Federal Reserve System, the member banks account for around 85 per cent of the loan volume of all commercial banks. Hence any conclusions that can be drawn from member-bank surveys are largely applicable to the whole commercial banking system.

[4] *Financing Small Business: Report to the Committees on Banking and Currency and the Select Committees on Small Business by the Federal Reserve System* (85th Cong., 2d sess.), Parts 1 and 2 (Washington, D.C.: U.S. Government Printing Office, 1958), p. 382. (Percentages supplied by the author.)

TABLE 32–2
Outstanding Short-Term Business Loans of Member Banks,
by Size of Borrower, October 16, 1957

Size of Borrower (Total assets in thousands of dollars)	Amount (In millions)	Number (In thousands)	Average Size of Loans[a]
Less than 50......................	$ 783	295	$ 2,654
50 to 250........................	3,311	326	10,156
250 to 1,000.....................	4,506	108	41,722
1,000 to 5,000...................	4,755	33	144,091
5,000 to 25,000..................	3,600	9	400,000
25,000 to 100,000................	2,562	3	854,000
100,000 or more..................	5,264	4	1,316,000
Not ascertained..................	416	23	18,087
All borrowers...............	$25,197	801	$ 31,457

[a] Computed by the author.

SOURCE: *Financing Small Business: Report to the Committees on Banking and Currency and the Select Committees on Small Business by the Federal Reserve System* (85th Cong., 2d sess.), Parts 1 and 2 (Washington, D.C.: U.S. Government Printing Office, 1958), p. 382.

the table, the spread in the average size of loan, as among borrowers of different size groupings, is especially noteworthy.

From the survey of October 16, 1957, it is also possible to derive figures for business loans classified on the basis of the business of the borrowers. These figures are presented in Table 32–3. They reveal that the principal borrowers from commercial banks are retail establishments, manufacturers of metals and metal products, transportation and other public utility companies, sales finance companies, companies of the petroleum group, real estate firms, and wholesalers. At the same time, they show that substantial differences exist among the various groups in their dependence upon short-term and term loans respectively. While sales finance companies, wholesale and retail trade establishments, and manufacturers of metals and metal products are the leading short-term borrowers, the leaders in term borrowing are the transportation and other public utility companies and the companies of the petroleum group. Especially worthy of note is the extremely heavy proportion of short-term loans in relation to total loans to sales finance companies, commodity dealers, wholesalers, and manufacturers of textiles, apparel, and leather.

A further revelation of interest in the earlier survey of October 5, 1955, is that while corporations were the borrowers on only 28.2 per cent of the number of loans (371,000 of a total of 1,317,000), they had received 77.7 per cent of the total amount of the commercial bank advances ($23,948 million out of a total of $30,820 million.)[5] In this classification, no breakdown was made for short-term loans as against term loans; hence the figures cited refer to loans of all maturities.

---

[5] *Federal Reserve Bulletin,* April, 1956, p. 335.

TABLE 32–3
Outstanding Business Loans of Member Banks, by Business
of Borrower and Maturity, October 16 1957
(Dollar amounts in millions)

Business of Borrower	Total Loans	Short-Term Loans	Per Cent of Total	Term Loans	Per Cent of Total
Manufacturing and mining:					
Food, liquor, and tobacco.......	$ 2,392	$ 1,907	79.7	$ 485	20.3
Textiles, apparel, and leather....	1,685	1,371	81.4	314	18.6
Metals and metal products.....	5,526	3,621	65.5	1,905	34.5
Petroleum, coal, chemicals, and rubber.....................	3,750	987	26.3	2,763	73.7
All other.....................	2,793	1,726	61.8	1,067	38.2
Trade:					
Retail trade..................	4,588	3,201	69.8	1,387	30.2
Wholesale trade..............	2,982	2,382	79.9	600	20.1
Commodity dealers...........	816	728	89.2	88	10.8
Other:					
Sales finance.................	3,095	2,829	91.4	266	8.6
Transportation, communication, and other public utilities.....	4,169	1,330	31.9	2,839	68.1
Construction.................	1,980	1,384	69.9	596	30.1
Real estate..................	2,976	1,669	56.1	1,307	43.9
Service......................	2,262	1,068	47.2	1,194	52.8
All other nonfinancial.........	1,605	994	61.9	611	38.1
All businesses............	$40,618	$25,197	62.0	$15,421	38.0

Note: Items may not add to totals because of rounding.

SOURCE: *Financing Small Business: Report to the Committees on Banking and Currency and the Select Committees on Small Business by the Federal Reserve System* (85th Cong., 2d sess.), Parts 1 and 2 (Washington, D.C.: U.S. Government Printing Office, 1958), pp. 375, 391; and *Federal Reserve Bulletin*, April, 1959, p. 354.

Lines of Credit

When corporations have repeated occasions to borrow from the commercial banks, they generally seek to clear the way for this borrowing in advance by asking for "lines of credit," and banks are usually quite willing to regularize their relationships with their customers by establishing lines of credit for them. A line of credit is a commitment of a bank to grant loans to a given customer up to a specified amount within a given period of time, usually one year. If a corporation has a line-of-credit commitment of $50,000, it can expect to have its requests for loans for any sum up to that total honored without delay. In its financial planning for the year ahead, therefore, it can proceed with confidence that the bank funds will be available when needed.

Features of Lines of Credit. When a line of credit is arranged for, a bank and its business customer usually agree upon the maturity of the loans to be granted, whether or not they are to be secured by pledges of property, the kind and value of the property to be pledged, if any, and, perhaps, the interest rate to be charged. Sometimes, however, the interest rate is set only on a contingent basis—to be actually determined, when the loans are granted, in relation to the bank's "prime rate" at that time (to be discussed later), the discount rate of the Federal Reserve bank of the district, or some open-market rate. For example, it may be stipulated that the rate of interest will be 2 percentage points above the Federal Reserve discount rate in effect at the time the loans are granted. As a rule, lines of credit are "revolving"—this means that if early loans during the designated period are repaid, further loans to the full amount of the credit line may be readily obtained. If a corporation with a $50,000 credit line borrows $30,000 and then repays $15,000 of this loan, it would have further borrowing rights of $35,000.

Sometimes the individual bank receives requests from well-qualified corporations for lines of credit too large, in its judgment, to be granted entirely on its own. In such instances, it is likely to ask other banks in the same city or in other cities to participate with it in providing the line. In its annual report for the year 1962, for example, the Consolidated Edison Company stated that it had available a one-year line of credit of $100 million with 12 New York City banks allowing "complete flexibility" in borrowing and repayment "with interest at the prime commercial rate." It said that this was the seventeenth consecutive year for its line-of-credit arrangements.[6]

As lines of credit are usually "opened" for one year, annual negotiations with banks for the continuation of the lines are generally necessary. This is convenient for the customer in further financial planning; if, for example, he wants to have his line increased, the annual conference with the bank's lending officer is the time to arrange for it. It is also convenient for the bank in planning its own lending and investing policies for the year ahead. Should a situation of tight money be developing, for example, it may find it necessary to scale down all or most of its advance loan commitments.

Qualifications for Lines of Credit. To obtain a line of credit and have it kept open, a corporation must "play ball" with the bank. In the first place, a well-managed bank will surely ask for copies of the corporation's articles of incorporation and bylaws—to determine whether or not these contain any limitations upon its capacities to incur debt and to pledge assets. Secondly, it will ask for a resolution of the corporation's board of directors specifically stating that the designated officers with whom the bank is to deal are authorized to borrow in its behalf and to pledge its property, if the loans are to be secured. And thirdly, it will demand financial statements and other credit information. Indeed, the line of credit will be opened, if at all, only after these data, as well as credit information drawn from other sources, have been thoroughly analyzed to yield a judgment upon character, capacity, and capital. Finally, the corporation will be expected to continue to supply the bank with informa-

---

[6] *Annual Report,* 1962, p. 22.

tion relevant to continuing credit analysis—copies of financial statements, possibly monthly or quarterly, and details about its borrowings from other banks or other lenders, important changes contemplated in its operating policies, new litigation in which it may be involved, and so on. As was pointed out in an earlier chapter, cash budgets are often highly useful in negotiations for bank loans.[7]

Firm Commitments. The ordinary line of credit, as just described, is often said to be a "moral commitment" of the bank. It has no contractual obligation to grant the loans as agreed upon, but, if it is a competently managed institution, it will surely make every effort to honor requests for loans from those having credit lines. Its reputation would suffer severe damage were it to take its "moral commitments" lightly. Only if there is serious deterioration in the financial affairs of corporations and other firms having credit lines—between the times the lines are opened and the loans are requested—are banks held to be justified in refusing credit-line loans.

Sometimes, however, corporations want absolute assurances that loans requested up to given amounts will be granted within designated periods of time regardless of banks' judgments about their financial positions at the time the loans are requested. They, therefore, ask for "firm commitments." In making such a commitment, a bank obligates itself contractually to grant the loans under the credit line when requested to do so. However, it usually asks for compensation for thus binding itself. In ordinary credit-line borrowing, the corporation pays interest only on loans actually taken, but for a firm commitment, it must pay a low-rate fee, perhaps one half or three fourths of 1 per cent per annum, on the whole line for its full duration, whether or not it is used. While having a firm-commitment line of $100,000 for a year and actually borrowing $80,000 for an eight-month period within this year, a corporation would pay the commitment fee on $100,000 for the full year and an additional "regular" interest charge on $80,000 for the eight months.

Multiple Lines of Credit. Many larger corporations seek and obtain lines of credit at several banking institutions simultaneously. An important reason for this is that banking laws limit the amount that a bank can lend to the individual borrower. In the federal law applicable to national banks, for example, the general rule is that loans to the individual borrower cannot exceed an amount equal to 10 per cent of the bank's capital stock and surplus.[8] Exceptions are made for certain kinds of secured and guaranteed (endorsed) loans, but not for loans secured by real estate and equipment or by stocks and bonds other than securities of the federal government itself.

---

[7] See above, p. 258.

[8] Banks, of course, do not lend their capital stock and surplus, since these are simply book accounts representing the equity of their stockholders. Capital stock and surplus, therefore, are referred to only as a measuring device in the application of the "10 per cent rule" as well as other rules for limiting bank loans.

A second reason why corporations obtain multiple lines of credit is to avoid too close dependence on single lending institutions. A corporation that can qualify for total short-term loans of $500,000 may prefer to borrow $100,000 from each of five banks rather than the entire amount from one, even though the one would not be hampered by loan limits in the banking laws. With its credit reputation established at the five banks, the corporation would presumably have no difficulty in getting its lines at three or four of the banks increased should one or two get into tight situations necessitating a curtailment of their lines.

Still another reason for multiple lines is the desire of corporations to continue short-term borrowing the year around. Many banks insist that the individual borrower "clean up" his short-term loans at some time within the year and remain out of debt to them for, say, a month. Short-term loans are supposed to be chiefly for short-term purposes, as for seasonal expansion, so that repayment should be forthcoming when the short-term objective has been accomplished. Banks are pleased to lend to good customers, but they want to have assurance that the customers remain "good" in the sense of having the capacity to repay. The "annual cleanup," therefore, gives them this assurance. But some corporations do not go along with this idea—they want to have short-term bank loans as a continuing source of current assets. By having two or more credit lines, therefore, they can keep each bank happy, cleaning up their loans with it by simply using the lines of credit established elsewhere.

Other Short-Term Lending

The foregoing discussion is not meant to imply that commercial banks lend only to corporations and other businesses that have arranged for lines of credit. Many short-term loans are granted on the basis of immediate negotiations as funds are needed. Some corporations borrow only sporadically; they prefer to wait till shortly before the time funds will be needed to open negotiations. In anticipation of their sporadic borrowings, however, they may be quite willing to submit statements and other credit information to the bank in advance, and to continue to supply data on current developments, so that delays for credit analysis will be avoided when the time for borrowing arrives. Even, indeed, should they be negligent in this matter, the banks in their respective communities would be likely to build up credit files concerning them—from information picked up here and there—so as to be ready for them, as it were, should they come around to borrow.

Size Relationships in Short-Term Lending

As a rule, large corporations gravitate toward large banks for loans, both short-term and longer-term, and small corporations toward smaller banks. Small corporations located in big cities will generally be well received by the lending officers of the big banks of these cities; but as most small corporations are located in small towns and cities, they are likely to turn first to local institutions. On the other hand, large corporations that are located in small towns and cities, knowing the loan limits that apply to the banks of these communities, often go direct to the banks of the big cities. The loan limits apply to these banks, too, but because of their large capital stock and surplus balances, they can grant much larger loans to individual borrowers than can banks of the smaller cities and towns.

Sometimes, nevertheless, relatively large corporations are able to make quite satisfactory arrangements for loans with banks in the smaller communities. Although such banks may not be able to lend as much as their corporate customers might want and can qualify for, the banks themselves may go to the big city banks—their "correspondent banks"—and get them to advance whatever amounts they themselves cannot advance. Such "participations" by big city banks in loans arranged by out-of-town banks are quite common.

On the other hand, sometimes even a big city bank cannot provide as much as a giant corporation wants and can qualify for, or it may not want to make the full loan requested, even if not precluded by legal loan limits, for reasons of avoiding too great a concentration of risk. In such circumstances, banks often call upon other banks in the same cities and in other cities to join them in lending "syndicates." The bank that issues the invitation and the banks that accept it split up the loan among themselves in agreed-upon proportions.

Promissory Notes

The promissory note may be said to be the standard instrument for short-term bank loans. The vast majority of borrowing corporations sign promissory notes as evidence of their obligations to repay. For unsecured loans especially, quite simple note forms are often used, containing only the date of the instrument, the promise to pay "to the order of" the bank, the time of payment—as "on demand" or "60 days after date"—and the signature of the corporation as attested by the signature of its treasurer or other authorized officer or officers. Oftentimes, more elaborate note forms are used with a great number of if's, and's, and whereas's, and some have so many provisos that they resemble bonds in complexity. Of considerable complexity, for example, is the "collateral note" which is generally used when there is a pledge of assets for the security of a loan. Nevertheless, the essential feature of any promissory note is the unconditional promise to pay on demand or at the designated time in the future "a sum certain in money."

In relatively rare instances, corporations obtain short-term bank loans by "discounting" other obligors' promissory notes and accepted drafts. In some lines of business—a very few—buyers on time are required to give the sellers promissory notes promising payment at the expiration of the allowed credit period. Sometimes, too, sellers draw drafts or orders-to-pay on buyers; when these have been "accepted" by the buyers, they become their promises to pay. In borrowing at a bank, then, a corporation having such notes and accepted drafts in its possession may ask the bank to "discount" them in lieu of signing its own promissory note for the amount of the loan. In discounting such instruments, the bank deducts from their maturity value its interest charge for the loan, the remainder thus being the net amount or "proceeds" of the loan. The signers of the promissory notes and the drawees (acceptors) of the drafts are primarily liable on their instruments, but the borrowing corporation, as endorser of the notes and as drawer of the drafts, is secondarily liable. The bank is much more interested in the corporation's secondary liability than in the primary liability of the signers and drawees about whose credit standing it may know nothing; hence, it consents to the discount transaction only when, upon the basis of the usual kind of credit analysis, it has confidence in the corporation's capacity to "make good" on the instruments should the signers and acceptors default.

Interest Rates on Short-Term Bank Loans

Spreads in Interest Rates. Interest rates on short-term bank loans being granted at any time vary rather widely depending upon the size of the loans, the size and location of lending banks, the size and particularly the credit standing of the borrowers, and the purposes of the loans; and they vary from time to time depending upon changes in the lending capacities of the banks and in total demands for short-term funds. Some of these influences are clearly reflected in the data of Table 32–4, taken from the

TABLE 32–4
Interest Rates on Short-Term Business Loans of Member Banks,
by Size of Borrower, 1955 and 1957
(Average rates on loans made between July 1 and survey date)

SIZE OF BORROWER (TOTAL ASSETS IN THOUSANDS OF DOLLARS)	PER CENT PER ANNUM		NET INCREASE
	1955	1957	
Less than 50................................	5.5	6.1	.6
50 to 250...................................	5.0	5.6	.6
250 to 1,000...............................	4.6	5.4	.8
1,000 to 5,000.............................	4.1	5.1	1.0
5,000 to 25,000............................	3.7	4.8	1.1
25,000 to 100,000..........................	3.4	4.6	1.2
100,000 and over...........................	3.2	4.4	1.2
All borrowers[a].............................	4.2	5.0	.8

[a] Including a small amount of loans to borrowers whose size was not ascertained.

SOURCE: *Financing Small Businesses: Report to the Committees on Banking and Currency and the Select Committees on Small Business by the Federal Reserve System* (85th Cong., 2d sess.), Parts 1 and 2 (Washington, D.C.: U.S. Government Printing Office, 1958), p. 388.

member-bank loan surveys of 1955 and 1957. The period 1955–57 was one of increasing credit tightness; hence, all classes of borrowers, by size groupings, were paying higher rates of interest in 1957 than in the earlier year. However, the increase in rates bore more heavily on the larger

borrowers than upon the smaller ones. This emphasizes the fact that interest rates charged by the smaller banks tend to be much more sluggish
than those charged by large banks. As smaller businesses borrow chiefly
from the smaller banks, they do not gain the benefits of declining interest
rate levels so quickly or so broadly as do the larger borrowers; yet, at the
same time, they are not penalized so quickly or so broadly as are the
larger borrowers in periods of rising rate levels. As the table indicates,
nevertheless, larger borrowers are likely at all times to be favored with
interest rate differentials of substantial size.

Prime Rates. The commercial banks of our large cities announce from
time to time what they call their "prime rates" for business loans. In a
given city, when a large bank announces a change in its prime rate upward or downward, the other banks of the city generally quickly fall
into line; thus the prime rate is usually the same at all the banks of the
city. As the prime rate is one to be charged to borrowers of high credit
standing, the typical bank expects a goodly proportion of its business
customers to qualify for this rate. Borrowers of weaker credit standing
must pay rates in excess of the prime rate, the size of the differentials
depending upon the degrees of weakness. Needless to say, however,
many applications for loans are rejected, regardless of the rates of interest
the applicants would be willing to pay. Banks in smaller cities rarely
publicize their prime rates; however, they doubtless have basic rates in
mind as they discuss loan terms with their customers. Moreover, in dealing with larger customers who could go to the big cities for loans, they
must make their own rates competitive with the prime rates prevailing
there.

Discount Procedure. For most of their short-term loans to business
enterprises, commercial banks use the discount procedure in charging interest. On its face, the borrower's promissory note is noninterest bearing,
and the bank advances the face amount as reduced by its interest charge.
This, once again, is the "proceeds" of the loan. Thus, on a loan of
$10,000 for 60 days, the interest charge being 6 per cent per annum, the
borrower would receive $9,900 and would have the obligation to pay
back $10,000 in 60 days. Actually, then, the effective rate of interest
would be slightly more than 6 per cent: interest of $100 on an advance
of $9,900 for 60 days means a rate of approximately 6.383 per cent.
Should this borrower want exactly $10,000 as the proceeds of his loan, he
would have to make the face amount of the note $10,101.01—if the bank
insisted on the last penny.

Security for Short-Term Loans

Volume of Secured Loans. The 1957 survey of member-bank loans
revealed that, by amount, 44 per cent of short-term advances to business
firms were secured by pledges of assets or by endorsements or other
guaranties. Security was provided much more often by small borrowers

than by larger ones. While borrowers having assets of less than $50,000 provided security for 66 per cent of the aggregate amount of their loans, firms having assets of $100 million or more supplied security for only 13 per cent of the amount of their loans. For small borrowers, it is of interest to mention, small banks required security less frequently than did large ones.[9]

Reasons for Security. The principal reason why banks require borrowers to pledge assets is to compensate, as it were, for weaknesses in the latters' capacity or capital or both. If a bank has misgivings about the managerial competence of a loan applicant, or if the applicant wants a larger loan than the bank thinks justified in consideration of his own equity in his business, it is likely to grant the loan only if it itself is protected by a pledge of acceptable assets. To a given applicant, for example, a bank might be willing to lend up to $10,000 on an unsecured basis, but, should he want to borrow $15,000, it would be likely to want security *for the entire amount.* According to typical bank practice, this would mean that the value of the assets pledged would have to be substantially in excess of $15,000. If the bank decided, on the other hand, that the loan applicant was lacking in character—in integrity—it would be likely to conclude that no amount of security would compensate for this deficiency. Most banks avoid loans to people of "shady" reputation if for no other reason than that dealings with such people reflect unfavorably upon their own reputations.

A second reason for pledging assets as security for business loans is to enable the banks to grant larger loans than they otherwise would be legally permitted to grant. It was mentioned earlier that the banking laws set limits to the amounts banks may lend to the individual borrower, and specifically cited was the national bank rule restricting loans to the individual borrower to an amount not exceeding 10 per cent of the lending bank's capital stock and surplus. But the banking laws make exceptions for certain kinds of secured loans. In some cases, the exceptions permit loans of unlimited amount on certain kinds of security; and, in others, they merely raise the loan limit. For example, a national bank may lend to a single borrower an amount up to 50 per cent of its capital stock and surplus if the loan is secured by warehouse receipts covering readily marketable nonperishable staple commodities, provided that the market value of the pledged commodities exceeds the amount of the loan by certain stipulated percentages.

A third reason for secured loans is the unwillingness of loan applicants to reveal as much information about themselves as the banks consider necessary for adequate credit judgments. If the banks are satisfied about the character of these applicants, they may decide that ample collateral will be accepted as compensating for their own lack of information.

---

[9] *Financing Small Business,* p. 384.

In some areas, assets are pledged for the safety of business loans because, as one might say, it is a matter of custom. But it is a custom largely confined to financial institutions. Thus, when commercial banks themselves borrow from other commercial banks, they almost invariably pledge assets.

Kinds of Assets Pledged. Probably the most common reason why business enterprises obtain short-term loans from the commercial banks is to buy raw materials for manufacturing operations and finished goods for resale. Hence, it is no surprise to find that inventories are the assets most commonly pledged upon short-term business loans. If it is possible to store goods in warehouses under the control of licensed and bonded warehousemen, a bank taking a pledge of these goods is assured that the borrower will not be able to sell them and use the proceeds without its knowledge and consent. It will demand warehouse receipts issued by the warehouseman, thus gaining control of the goods: the warehouseman will release the stored goods only upon instructions from the bank as the holder of the receipts. If the loan matures and remains unpaid, and if the bank expects no payment in the ordinary course of business even should it give the borrower more time, it can itself obtain the goods from the warehouseman, sell them, and thus reimburse itself. Loans on warehoused goods, it may be mentioned, are made whether the goods are stored in warehouses owned by the licensed warehouseman or owned by the borrowers but placed under the control of such a warehouseman. Warehouses owned by storers of goods but controlled by licensed warehousemen are known as "field warehouses."

Goods that borrowers must keep in their possession can be pledged by means of other kinds of instruments sanctioned by law. Raw materials to be used in production by manufacturers can be pledged by chattel mortgages, and finished goods held for display and sale, by chattel mortgages or trust receipts. A chattel mortgage represents a lien upon pledged goods, while a trust receipt acknowledges that title to the goods is in the lending bank and that the borrower serves as trustee for the bank in handling and selling the goods. Trust receipts are most commonly used when goods pledged are readily distinguishable from other goods, as when they bear serial numbers or other identifying marks; thus, they are convenient in obtaining loans for carrying automobiles, electrical appliances, typewriters, other kinds of office machines, and similar goods. Should a borrower sell goods held under trust receipts without accounting to the bank for the proceeds, he might be charged not only with breach of contract but also with the crime of "fraudulent conversion" (embezzlement).

Second in importance among types of assets pledged for short-term business loans are stocks and bonds. Stocks and bonds are easily used for pledge purposes. In putting them up as collateral, the borrower authorizes the lending bank to sell them to reimburse itself should there be a default; if he fulfills his obligations, it is a simple matter for the bank to return the pledged securities to him. Corporations not infrequently pledge stocks and bonds owned in subsidiaries and, sometimes, securities held in unrelated corporations. As a rule, however, the pledging of stocks and bonds upon short-term loans is a more likely procedure for proprietorships and partnerships than for corporations. A proprietor may own securities for investment purposes in addition to the assets of his business, and he may pledge some of these if he wants to borrow to expand the assets of his business. But the typical nonfinancial corporation has no stocks and bonds of subsidiaries because it has no subsidiaries, and if it holds other securities as a means of temporarily putting idle funds to work, it is much more likely to sell these when it needs cash than to pledge them as security for loans.

Although accounts receivable rank second to inventories among the current assets of nonfinancial business corporations collectively, they are used much more rarely than inventories as security for short-term bank loans. Until late in the 1930's, most commercial banks showed little interest in "accounts receivable financing." Since then, many have developed interests in and facilities for this kind of financing, but the major role in lending on accounts receivable is held by commercial finance companies. Accordingly, an examination of the procedures of accounts receivable financing may be deferred to a later point in this chapter where the work of the commercial finance companies is discussed.

In some cases, chattel mortgages on equipment and mortgages on real property are provided by borrowers as security for short-term business loans. Many advances so secured, however, probably have only the appearance of short-term loans; in other words, banks may grant them originally on a short-term basis with the understanding that they will be renewed, perhaps repeatedly, for a longer period. Certainly, the mortgaging of real property, which itself is a rather complicated operation, appears to be a cumbersome short-term lending procedure. Even so, if banks insist upon security, and business firms desperately need money, they are unlikely to hesitate long in giving pledges of equipment and real property.

Endorsements and Other Guaranties

When commercial banks are unwilling to grant short-term loans on an unsecured basis, they may be satisfied to go ahead without pledges of assets provided that the would-be borrowers can get endorsements or other guaranties for their notes from third parties whose credit reputations are impressive. A third party who is willing to accept responsibility for the repayment of a borrower's loan can so signify by cosigning the latter's promissory note, by endorsing it, or by signing a "letter of guaranty" addressed to the lending bank. The legal significance of these three procedures is much the same, since the bank is usually accorded the right to proceed directly and immediately against the guarantor to collect payment if the borrower defaults. Naturally, therefore, banks accept guaranties in lieu of pledges of assets only if confident of the guarantors' ability to pay. The very acceptance of a guaranty indicates, indeed, greater confidence in the guarantor than in the borrower.

As for corporate financing, guaranties are most commonly provided by officers and especially principal stockholders of small, close corporations upon loans to these corporations, and by parent companies upon loans to their subsidiaries. To the principal stockholder of a close corporation, a bank might be willing to lend very large sums, but because he has invested only a small part of his wealth in the corporation, it is unwilling to lend to it without special protection. If the corporation does not want to pledge its assets, or if it has no assets that would be acceptable for pledge purposes, a guaranty by the principal stockholder is the logical alternative. In a similar way, a subsidiary of a strong parent corporation may have a weak credit standing, yet, on account of its status as a distinct legal entity, it alone would be responsible for the repayment of any loans it might obtain. But it would quickly become an attractive customer for loans were banks assured by the parent that it would guarantee all advances to it.

Bankers' Acceptances

A peculiar means whereby business concerns obtain short-term bank loans to buy goods for inventory is in the use of commercial letters of credit and bankers' acceptances. The means is peculiar because the banks that advance the funds have no negotiations with the borrowers, and usually, indeed, do not even know who they are or what their credit standing is.

As commercial letters of credit and bankers' acceptances are chiefly used for transactions in international trade, we may take an import transaction to illustrate their use. Suppose that an American firm is negotiating with a British manufacturer for the purchase of a shipment of dinnerware valued at $20,000. The British manufacturer is willing to sell on a 60-day deferred-payment basis but is unwilling to rely upon the unsupported promise to pay of the American firm. He stipulates, therefore, that he will ship the goods if the American firm will get from its bank a commercial letter of credit authorizing him to draw a 60-day draft upon the bank itself. Upon applying to its bank for the letter of credit, the American firm would be subjected to a credit investigation much as if it were applying for a direct loan—unless, of course, the bank already had a complete credit file on the firm kept up to date with its cooperation. Since the bank is being asked to authorize the drawing of a draft which, upon acceptance, will become its own promise to pay, it wants to be sure that the applying firm will be able to provide it with the means to fulfill this promise.

If the bank is satisfied with the credit standing of the importing firm, the latter must sign a contract promising to pay the bank at or shortly before the maturity of the draft (acceptance) an amount of money sufficient to meet it, plus a commission for the bank's services. The bank then issues the letter of credit—it is, indeed, in the form of a letter—addressed to the British manufacturer specifically authorizing him within a given period of time to draw one or more drafts payable in 60 days up to the total of $20,000. In the letter, certain conditions are set out to be satisfied by the manufacturer—stipulations about the kinds and qualities of the merchandise, the method of shipment, insurance upon the shipment, and so on. The failure of the manufacturer to fulfill these conditions would release the bank from its obligation to accept the draft or drafts to be drawn.

With assurances of getting the American bank's promise to pay, the manufacturer ships the goods, draws the draft upon the American bank, and sells it to his own (British) bank for British money, that is, "sterling." Since the draft is noninterest bearing, and since the British bank will not be able to collect the full amount of the draft till its maturity, it pays the manufacturer less than its face value, that is to say, it discounts it. Now the owner of the draft, the British bank sends it to its correspondent bank in the United States, and this bank, in turn, presents it to the bank that issued the letter of credit. If the latter is satisfied that the conditions of its letter have been satisfied, it writes its acceptance on the face of the draft, thus making it specifically its promise to pay. The instrument—now a *banker's acceptance*—is then returned to the correspondent bank.

If the British bank, as owner, decides to have the correspondent bank as its agent hold the acceptance to maturity—enabling it to earn the full amount of the discount charged the manufacturer—it thereby, in effect, grants a loan to the American importer whom it presumably does not know. The importing firm gets its goods and has approximately 60 days to pay, and the British exporter got his money when he sold the draft. It is the British bank, therefore, that is providing the financing. But if the British bank decided that it would like to have dollars at once instead of waiting till the maturity of the acceptance, it would order its correspondent to sell the acceptance to a dealer in such instruments. Like the British bank itself, the dealer would buy on a discount basis, expecting to make a profit by reselling the acceptance at a lower rate of discount (which would mean, of course, a higher price). He would offer the acceptance, with others, to customers who are interested in investing in such instruments. Such customers are chiefly our metropolitan banks. Thus the buying bank would substitute itself, as it were, for the British bank as the lender to the American importing firm—again, we may assume, knowing nothing about it.

The British bank would be willing to buy the draft in reliance upon the obligation to pay of the American bank that issued the letter of credit, and likewise for the acceptance dealer and his customer, in buying the acceptance. Thus, the American bank, though not lending money to the importing firm, would be "lending its good name," as is often said. For this "loan" of its good name, as was mentioned above, it would charge a commission—not, it will be noted, interest.

As a rule, the issuance of commercial letters of credit and the acceptance of drafts drawn under them is pretty closely confined to the large banks of our principal cities. However, almost every commercial bank in the country has "correspondent" relationships with one or more of these institutions, so that, through them, it can arrange financing by means of bankers' acceptances for its business customers.

According to a report of the Federal Reserve authorities, outstanding dollar acceptances of American banks amounted to $2,658 million at the end of April, 1963.[10]

THE SALE OF COMMERCIAL PAPER

Just as a corporation may sell a bond issue in bulk to a syndicate of investment bankers, depending upon them, as it were, to peddle the bonds among their customers, so may it also sell to a commercial-paper dealer a batch of short-term promissory notes, expecting the dealer to resell these notes to his customers. However, financing by selling "open-market commercial paper," or simply "commercial paper," as the notes are called, is far less popular than financing with bond issues. Probably not more than 450 firms are borrowers in the commercial-paper market at any given time.[11]

The principal borrowers in the commercial-paper market, as groups, are sales and consumer finance companies. The larger companies peddle their own notes. They depend upon the market so heavily and so continuously that they save considerable sums on commissions and interest charges by bypassing the dealers. At the end of April, 1963, for example, outstanding commercial paper sold direct by finance companies was estimated at $5,155 million, and that marketed through commercial-paper dealers, also including an undisclosed amount of finance company paper. at only $2,204 million.[12] Aside from the finance companies, borrowers upon commercial paper include corporations scattered through almost all important areas of manufacturing and merchandising.

When a corporation approaches a commercial-paper dealer for the first time, it is subjected to a rigorous credit investigation. Because the dealers buy issues of notes outright, and because they want to resell quickly, they want to be sure that the notes are of such good quality that their customers will readily buy. For the same reasons, corporations that have sold many issues of notes to the dealers must continue to maintain high

---

[10] *Federal Reserve Bulletin*, June, 1963, p. 820.
[11] Federal Reserve Bank of Cleveland, *Monthly Business Review*, October, 1960, p. 4.
[12] *Federal Reserve Bulletin*, June, 1963, p. 820.

credit standings to qualify for still further sales. Defaults upon open-market commercial paper have been exceedingly rare.

Open-market promissory notes sold through dealers are usually made out for round amounts, such as $5,000, $10,000, and $25,000, and sometimes for amounts up to $100,000. As the issuing corporation does not know who the ultimate payees of the notes will be, it makes them payable to the order of itself, and then endorses them; thus they can then pass from hand to hand without further endorsements. The dealer himself does not endorse the notes, nor are they secured by pledges of assets. Accordingly, open-market buyers depend entirely upon the unsupported promises to pay of the issuing corporations. The maturity is usually 90, 120, or 180 days, although in some cases it is as long as 270 days.

Open-market commercial paper sold through dealers usually does not bear any interest rate on its face. The dealer buys the notes on a discount basis, charging a rate of discount that varies with the degree of tightness or ease in the whole market for short-term funds. He ordinarily expects to earn a return by reselling the notes to his customers at a lower rate of discount; nevertheless, the principal source of his profit is a commission charged the issuing corporation. Commissions usually range between one eighth and one fourth of 1 per cent of the face amount of total note issues.

Upon buying issues of short-term notes the dealer quickly offers them to his customers, often selling on an option basis. On this basis, the customer is allowed ten days, or in some instances 14 days, to make his own investigation of the issuing corporations, and to return the notes to the dealer if not satisfied with the results of this investigation. The customers are chiefly commercial banks. But while the banks of our large cities are the chief issuers of commercial letters of credit and investors in bankers' acceptances, banks of smaller cities and towns are most prominent among the buyers of open-market commercial paper. Regardless of the size and location of the buying banks, however, a situation results comparable to that found in the use of bankers' acceptances. The banks that buy commercial paper are grantors of short-term loans to the corporate issuers of the paper; but the loans are made, as it were, indirectly and impersonally, since, obviously, the corporations make no applications for loans to the buying banks.

LOANS OF COMMERCIAL FINANCE COMPANIES

Burden of Carrying Receivables

For many manufacturing and mercantile enterprises, a principal problem of short-term financing is that of carrying large volumes of accounts receivable. All or almost all sales may be made on account, and credit periods, due to custom or sharp competition, may be relatively long. Many buyers on account may be "slow pay"—they may be desirable customers, because they ultimately pay, but they stretch out the credit period by allowing their accounts to go delinquent. The volume of accounts receivable may constitute a very large proportion of total current assets, perhaps exceeding the value of inventories or, at least, not falling far short of that value. Such enterprises may be in a position to borrow limited amounts from the commercial banks on an unsecured basis or by the pledge of inventories, or they may not qualify to borrow on an unsecured basis or their inventories may be of a kind not readily adaptable for pledge purposes. For one reason or another, at any rate, they cannot obtain from the commercial banks as much in short-term advances as they need. As security for loans that would be commensurate with their needs, the best they have to offer are the very accounts receivable that give rise to their problem, but the commercial banks with which they deal may have no enthusiasm for loans on accounts receivable. Where can they go?

Role of Commercial Finance Companies

One answer is that such enterprises can turn to the specialized lenders on accounts receivable, known as commercial finance companies and sometimes as commercial receivables companies. Commercial finance companies differ from sales finance companies in that they are specialists in lending upon *interbusiness* accounts receivable while the sales finance companies are principally buyers of contracts evidencing obligations to pay of *consumers*. Commercial finance companies differ from factors in that the latter buy interbusiness accounts receivable outright whereas the former, as indicated, simply grant loans on the security of such accounts. In Chapter 9, it was pointed out that business enterprises can economize in their investment in accounts receivable by using the services of factors. In using the aid offered by commercial finance companies, on the other hand, they enjoy no such economy—they must still carry their own accounts receivable, but they are helped in doing so.[13]

As indicated, then, the commercial finance companies are interested in granting loans on accounts owned by business concerns but representing the obligations of other business concerns. Such accounts receivable originate, of course, when manufacturers sell on account to other manufacturers and wholesalers, and when wholesalers sell to retailers. It is in these areas that the commercial finance companies concentrate their work: they stand ready to lend to the manufacturers and wholesalers on pledged receivables, provided, as always, that the borrowers can qualify on the basis of character, capacity, and capital.

---

[13] Although a distinction is thus made among the *functions* of commercial finance companies, sales finance companies, and factors, a few large sales finance companies have divisions or subsidiaries providing commercial finance and factoring services; some commercial finance companies also provide factoring services; and some factors have facilities for lending upon business accounts receivable.

Loan Procedures and Terms

After a manufacturer or wholesaler has satisfied a commercial finance company as to its creditworthiness, it usually proceeds to borrow on a day-to-day basis. As sales are made, it turns copies of the invoices over to the finance company, and the latter advances (loans) an agreed-upon percentage of the amount of these invoices, at the same time, of course, getting a lien upon the obligation of the buyers of the invoiced goods. The buyers are not notified of the assignment of their accounts to the finance company; hence, they make payment to the manufacturer or wholesaler in the regular way. But the latter is under contractual obligation to turn all such payments over to the finance company. To the extent that these payments exceed the finance company's loans and charges, they are returned to the borrowing manufacturer or wholesaler. In this way, the amount of a finance company's loans to a given customer changes from day to day, being increased as new invoices are assigned, and being reduced as payments are received from the enterprises whose accounts had previously been assigned.

Depending upon manufacturers' and wholesalers' financial positions, the volume of their credit sales, the quality of the accounts assigned, the size of invoices, and other factors, commercial finance companies vary the amount of their loans between 70 and 90 per cent of the face amount of the assigned accounts, but occasionally going as high as 95 per cent. Advances at 80 per cent are probably most common.[14] The finance company takes no responsibility for bad-debt losses, as does a factor. If accounts turn out to be uncollectible, the borrower must substitute good accounts or repay the loan out of his portion of collections from good accounts or from other sources.

Because the loan balance of each customer of the commercial finance companies is likely to fluctuate quite frequently—for many, indeed, from day to day—they customarily charge interest on the basis of per diem rates. The customer's monthly bill for interest is determined by multiplying the sum of the daily loan balances by the agreed-upon per diem rate. Thus, a charge of one thirtieth of 1 per cent a day would amount to an annual effective rate of approximately 12 per cent on the fluctuating amounts borrowed. Per annum rates, as thus translated, appear to range most commonly between 9.5 and 18.5 per cent.[15] For this reason, receivables financing is often said to be an expensive way to borrow. However, the commercial finance companies defend their charges on the grounds that their administrative costs in taking care of the numerous details of receivables financing are high; that they take greater risks than do, say, the commercial banks in the size of their loans in relation to borrowers'

---

[14] *Financing Small Business,* p. 458.
[15] *Ibid.,* p. 461.

equities and in lending to less creditworthy applicants; and that borrowers pay the charges only on money actually used and precisely for the number of days that it is used.

Other Functions

Although the commercial finance companies do not absorb bad-debt losses on accounts assigned to them, they customarily work closely with the manufacturers and wholesalers that use their services in evaluating the creditworthiness of the latters' customers, as well as in advising upon other matters of financial management. In any case, they find it expedient to keep rather careful watch upon borrowers, chiefly by means of frequent audits of their books. Since the obligors on assigned accounts make their payments to the borrowing firm, it is in a position to defraud the finance company by using these payments for purposes other than meeting its obligations to it. Since this supervisory and advisory work is expensive, it accounts for a goodly part of the administrative costs referred to in the preceding paragraph.

Manufacturers and wholesalers that borrow from the commercial finance companies on assigned accounts receivable are sometimes granted additional loans for extraordinary purposes, as to expand the scope of operations or to take advantage of opportunities to buy large quantities of raw materials or finished goods at favorable prices. These additional loans are almost always secured, usually by pledges of inventories, but occasionally by pledges of other kinds of assets including even real estate.

LOANS FOR INVENTORY TO INSTALMENT SELLERS

In Chapter 9, we saw that the sale or assignment of instalment contracts by dealers in certain kinds of goods to institutions such as sales finance companies enables the dealers to economize their investment in accounts receivable. Instalment buyers of automobiles, electrical appliances for the home, other consumer durable goods, farm machinery, machine tools and other manufacturing equipment, and heavy construction equipment sign contracts—usually conditional sales contracts—in which they obligate themselves to make payments monthly or at other intervals over a period of two or three or more years. If, then, the seller of such durable goods is in need of cash, he may sell these instalment contracts to a sales finance company, a commercial finance company, or a commercial bank.

Often, however, the need of dealers for cash precedes the time of sale: they need cash to acquire the goods to be sold. They want inventory loans, and they expect the subsequent sale of their customers' instalment contracts to provide the funds with which these loans can be repaid. Because, indeed, the purchase of instalment contracts is highly profitable to the financial institutions, the dealers are often in a strong position to demand inventory financing. They agree to sell their customers' instalment contracts to a given financial institution only if it will supply them with funds for the acquisition of inventory.

Accordingly, commercial finance companies grant inventory loans to dealers in manufacturing, construction, and farm machinery and equipment; sales finance companies, to dealers especially in automobiles and other consumer durable goods, but also, some of them, to dealers in industrial and farm equipment; and the commercial banks, to dealers in most lines, but especially to those in consumer durables. Inventory loans for the acquisition of consumer durables are often called "floorplan loans"; others of the kinds described are variously referred to as "wholesale financing," "industrial financing," and "equipment financing."

As a rule, the financial institutions are not at all enthusiastic about granting inventory loans to dealers. Competition is so severe among the different classes of institutions and among those of each class that interest rates are kept at quite moderate levels, and most of the institutions complain that they make no profit on this phase of their business. Supervision is expensive, and in some instances its costs may even exceed interest earnings. Although the loans are usually secured by pledges of the inventories themselves, much policing is necessary to be sure that the dealers properly account for all sales of the pledged goods. It is all too easy for dealers to defraud the lenders if they have a mind to do so. In the absence of constant surveillance, a dishonest dealer can pledge the same goods to two or more lenders, sell the goods for cash without accounting for the proceeds, sell on instalment contracts but assign the contracts to a lender other than the lender on inventory, "strip" pledged goods, selling parts thereof and leaving only shells, as it were, for the lender's security, and so on. Of course, the lenders try to avoid unscrupulous dealers; nevertheless, in their competition for instalment contracts, they are inclined to be less strict in selecting the dealers to whom they will lend than in other phases of their lending operations.

Questions

1. How are commercial banks distinguished from other classes of financial institutions? How important are they as short-term lenders to business enterprises?

2. What is a line of credit as provided by a commercial bank? Why do business firms find it convenient to have lines of credit? Can any business firm get a line of credit if it wants it? Explain.

3. How does a "firm commitment" of a commercial bank differ from a line of credit?

4. Defend or attack this proposition: Most commercial banks charge about 6 per cent a year on their short-term loans to all classes of business borrowers.

5. In short-term lending by commercial banks to business firms, what use is made of each of the following: promissory notes, trust receipts, warehouse receipts, letters of guaranty?

6. For what reasons do commercial banks require some of their business customers to pledge assets as security for short-term loans?

7. It is said that commercial banks usually charge interest on short-term business loans by the "discount procedure." What does this mean?

8. What is a commercial letter of credit as issued by a commercial bank? What is a banker's acceptance? Explain how these instruments are used in inventory financing. Why is this kind of financing often described as being indirect or impersonal?

9. What is open-market commercial paper? What is the procedure in using it as a means of short-term borrowing? Who are the ultimate lenders?

10. What is "accounts receivable financing"? Explain the procedure of commercial finance companies in providing this kind of financing.

11. What rates do commercial finance companies charge for their financing services? How do they justify the relatively high levels of these rates?

12. If the institutions that grant inventory loans to instalment sellers make little or no profit on these loans, as they claim, why do they not simply eliminate this kind of lending?

Problems

1. For the full calendar year 19xx, the Pandora Sales Company, Inc., has a bank line of credit of $800,000 on a firm commitment basis. It is to pay a commitment fee of one half of 1 per cent, and interest at the rate of 5 per cent on the amount of its borrowings. The commitment fee and all interest charges are to be paid at the end of the year, and interest is to be computed for the exact number of days but on a 360-day basis (for example, the time factor on a 25-day loan would be $\frac{25}{360}$). What would Pandora owe the bank at the end of the year for the fee and interest if its borrowings and repayments during the year were as follows:

Date	Borrowed	Repaid
January 18	$350,000	
February 26	200,000	
March 17	220,000	
September 19		$250,000
October 25		180,000
December 12		340,000

2. The Farwell Company has an arrangement with a commercial finance company for continuous borrowing on the security of pledged accounts receivable. The finance company advances 80 per cent of the face amount of assigned invoices, and charges interest on these advances at the rate of $\frac{1}{24}$ of 1 per cent per day. In the month of April, advances made to Farwell and payments received from its customers and turned over to the finance company were as follows:

Date of Assignment	Amount Advanced	Payoff Date
April 2	$36,000	April 20
April 5	45,000	April 27
April 12	25,000	April 30
April 16	50,000	Unpaid
April 22	60,000	Unpaid

a) What would be the finance company's total charge for interest for the month of April?

b) At what annual effective rate of interest is Farwell borrowing?

chapter 33

LONGER-TERM LOANS AND CREDITS

Not only do corporations generally have access to trade credit, short-term loans, and other short-term means of acquiring assets; they often have available to them intermediate- and long-term sources of assets other than stocks, bonds, and the accumulation of retained earnings. The additional intermediate- and long-term sources include term loans of commercial banks, mortgage loans of life insurance companies, equipment credits and loans of sellers and certain classes of financial institutions, and loans of the Small Business Administration, an agency of the federal government.

TERM LOANS OF COMMERCIAL BANKS

Although the commercial banking system long had the tradition of granting to business enterprises only short-term loans for what were said to be "working capital purposes," the tradition began to break down in the decade of the 1930's. The sharp decline in loan demands of all kinds in that decade led the commercial banks to cast about for new loan outlets, and upon finding sound business firms that wanted to borrow for periods longer than one year, they were generally pleased to forget their tradition and to grant the loans. Even before the 1930's, loans that had the complexion of present-day term loans were often granted. The purposes for which loans were granted were often long term, as for the purchase of real property and equipment, even though the maturities were short. There were usually "understandings" between the bankers and the borrowers that the loans, though ostensibly short term as evidenced by the borrowers' promissory notes, would be renewed periodically.

Nowadays, at any rate, most commercial banks grant business loans having original maturities beyond one year as a matter of routine operations. Some continue to camouflage some of their longer-maturity loans by having borrowers sign short-term notes with understandings as to renewals; but most apparently see no good reasons for such juggling of maturities.

Extent of Term Lending

In the special survey of the business loans of member banks of the Federal Reserve System as of October 5, 1955, referred to in the preceding chapter, it was found that term loans totaled $10,441 million, equal to 33.9 per cent of total business loans of $30,820 million.[1] Approximately two years later, in the special survey as of October 16, 1957, it was found that member-bank term loans amounted to $15,421 million, equal to 38 per cent of total business loans of $40,618 million.[2] While short-term loans increased in the two-year period by 23.6 per cent, term loans increased by 47.7 per cent. In 1957, 37.4 per cent of the number of loans were of the term variety.

The data of Table 33–1, taken from the two surveys, indicate that in

TABLE 33–1
Percentages of Term Loans to Total Member-Bank Business Loans,
by Size of Borrower, 1955 and 1957
(Percentages of dollar amounts)

Size of Borrower (Total assets in thousands of dollars)	1955	1957
Less than 50	28.7	46.2
50 to 250	29.9	37.0
250 to 1,000	24.0	28.5
1,000 to 5,000	23.5	29.8
5,000 to 25,000	35.4	39.1
25,000 to 100,000	48.2	47.7
100,000 and over	44.5	40.3
All borrowers[a]	33.9	38.0

[a] Includes a small amount of loans to borrowers whose size was not ascertained.

SOURCE: *Financing Small Business: Report to the Committees on Banking and Currency and the Select Committees on Small Business by the Federal Reserve System* (85th Cong., 2d sess.), Parts 1 and 2 (Washington, D.C.: U.S. Government Printing Office, 1958), p. 383.

both 1955 and 1957 borrowers of the two largest sizes, and in 1957 those of the smallest size, as groups, had larger proportions of term loans to their total loans than did enterprises of the intermediate size groupings. Term borrowing, of course, is not weighted solely according to the size of borrowers. The industrial areas in which borrowers operate represent an important determinant of term borrowing. If we refer to Table 32–3 in the preceding chapter (p. 788), we see that in 1957 term borrowing by companies producing petroleum, coal, chemicals, and rubber and by transportation and other public utility companies was especially high, at 73.7 per cent and 68.1 per cent of the total amounts of their loans respectively; relatively high for service establishment at 52.8 per cent, real estate enterprises at 43.9 per cent, manufacturers of metals and metal products at 34.5 per cent, retail trade establishments at 30.2 per cent, and construction firms at 30.1 per cent; but quite low for sales finance companies at 8.6 per cent, commodity dealers at 10.8 per cent, manu-

[1] *Federal Reserve Bulletin*, April, 1956, p. 334.
[2] *Financing Small Business: Report to the Committees on Banking and Currency and the Select Committees on Small Business by the Federal Reserve System* (85th Cong., 2d sess.), Parts 1 and 2 (Washington, D.C.: U.S. Government Printing Office, 1958), p. 382.

facturers of textiles, apparel, and leather at 18.6 per cent, and wholesale trade establishments at 20.1 per cent. Some cross relationships between size of borrowers and their industrial settings are of interest; for example, the special survey of 1955 revealed that while only 14.6 per cent of the amount of loans to construction firms having assets between $250,000 and $1 million were of the term variety, term loans accounted for 30.1 per cent of the advances to construction firms having assets of less than $50,000, and for 58.5 per cent for loans to construction firms having assets of $100 million or over. Proportions of term borrowings in these size classes among companies of the petroleum group were, respectively, 37.5, 55.7, and 88.4 per cent; among retail trade concerns, 19.8, 39.9, and 61.2 per cent; and among wholesale trade enterprises, 12.5, 20.2, and 36.8 per cent.[3]

Frequently, two or more banks participate in granting term loans to given corporations (much as they often participate in arranging large lines of credit for short-term purposes, as mentioned in the preceding chapter), and sometimes, banks and other classes of lenders, especially life insurance companies, join forces in providing large term loans. When banks participate with life insurance companies and other nonbank lenders, the borrower's instalment repayments in the first few years of the life of the loan usually go to the banks, with the nonbank lenders waiting for the later instalments for their repayment. To illustrate participations of these kinds, some recent transactions may be cited. In November, 1962, Frontier Airlines announced that it had obtained a five-year loan of $3.5 million in which participations were taken by four banks located in Denver, Salt Lake City, Phoenix, and New York City. In July, 1963, Virginia Dare Stores Corporation completed arrangements for a combination of short-term and term loans totaling $7,550,000, with three banks participating, namely, the Irving Trust Company and the Commercial Bank of North America, both of New York City, and the Rhode Island Hospital Trust Company. After making arrangements to increase its outstanding issues of both common and preferred stocks, to meet a condition laid down by three banks and two life insurance companies with which it was trying to arrange a $220 million long-term loan, the Georgia-Pacific Corporation announced in December, 1962, that the loan contract had been negotiated. The Bank of America of California and the Chase Manhattan Bank and the First National City Bank, both of New York City, were the lending banks, and the insurance companies were the Metropolitan and the Prudential.

Purposes of Term Loans

Probably the most common reason why corporations seek term loans from the commercial banks is to acquire equipment. Manufacturers borrow on a term basis to buy machinery and other factory equipment;

---

[3] For other cross relationships between the size of borrowers and their industries, see *Federal Reserve Bulletin*, April, 1956, p. 334.

merchants, to buy or have installed shelves, cabinets, showcases, warehouse equipment, and delivery trucks; hotels and restaurants, furniture, carpet, kitchen equipment, and so on; and transportation companies, airplanes, trucks, busses, taxicabs, and other rolling stock. The acquisition of real property is also an important reason for term borrowing—the buying of land as sites for factory, store, and office buildings, garages, and warehouses, the purchase of existing buildings, and meeting the costs of the construction of new buildings.

Not infrequently term loans represent "interim financing"—a means of defraying the developmental costs of sizable expansion projects over a period of a few years pending later issues of stocks or bonds as the long-term means of financing.

Rather often, too, term loans are granted for working capital purposes, that is, for the acquisition of inventories, the carrying of accounts receivable, and the repayment of various kinds of short-term debt. Although banks are inclined to insist that working capital loans should generally be short term, they are often willing to make exceptions to their own rules. Term loans for working capital appear to be reasonable for firms that are expanding rapidly. Such firms may acquire needed additions to fixed assets by stock and bond issues, but, as they must also expand inventories and receivables substantially and cumulatively over a period of years, they may look to the commercial banks for special help in this direction. Because of the cumulative aspect of the expansion, short-term loans would not be particularly helpful. In other instances, even when expansion is not taking place rapidly, some bankers do not hesitate to provide working capital advances on what might be called a continuous basis—by term rather than by short-term loans. As long as they are confident of the solvency of borrowing firms, why, these bankers ask themselves, should they insist upon "annual cleanups" of working capital loans? If borrowers simply go to other institutions to get funds to "clean up" their loans at a given bank, that bank, in effect, drives profitable business to rival lenders.

Maturities of Term Loans

In its special study of member-bank business loans in 1957, the Board of Governors of the Federal Reserve System found the *amount* of term loans having original maturities from one to five years almost exactly equal to the amount with original maturities in excess of five years. However, the *number* of term loans with maturities of one to five years was almost three times the number with maturities over five years. This relationship indicates, of course, that larger term loans tend to have longer maturities than do the smaller ones, and the probability, therefore, that larger borrowers get maturities nearer to their wishes than do smaller enterprises. Nevertheless, the study also revealed a short-run movement of larger loans into the shorter maturity classification: while the number of loans in each of the two maturity classifications expanded by percentages almost exactly equal between 1955 and 1957 (31.3 per cent and 31.2 per cent respectively), the amount of loans maturing in one to five years expanded by 58 per cent, while those maturing in over five years expanded by only 38.2 per cent.[4]

Of relatively minor importance are term loans having maturities of more than ten years. In the member-bank loan survey of 1957, it was found that only 10 per cent of the amount of term loans and 5.3 per cent of their number had maturities beyond ten years.[5]

The "maturity" of most term loans is simply the date on which a final instalment on the loan is due. Most term loans are repayable in equal instalments periodically, as monthly, quarterly, or semiannually. Thus, a bank can consider as short-term loans one third of a three-year advance and one fifth of a five-year advance. Such a short-term element in term lending has doubtless been a major factor in encouraging banks to expand the volume of their term loans so heavily in the postwar years. It is of major importance, too, for borrowers' financial planning. If a corporation obtains a "five-year" term loan repayable in equal quarterly instalments, one twentieth of the loan is really a three-month loan, another twentieth, a six-month loan, and so on; and, of course, only a final twentieth is truly a five-year loan.

The final instalment on some term loans is a "balloon" payment—it is much larger than the regular instalments up to that time. For example, a corporation might obligate itself to pay off half of the amount of a five-year loan by regular semiannual instalments within 4½ years and the remainder of the loan at the end of the fifth year. Such an arrangement ordinarily indicates either an understanding between the bank and the borrower that the balance of the loan will be extended at the end of the original period, or an expectation of the borrower that he will be able to make the balloon payment from some special source of funds, as from the proceeds of a stock or bond issue.

Interest Rates on Term Loans

By comparison with charges on short-term loans, the pattern of interest rates on term loans is rather confused. In years of upsweeping yield curves for open-market investments, one might expect the commercial banks to graduate their rates upward according to the lengths of maturities. But the surveys of member-bank loans to business of 1955 and 1957—these having been years of upsweeping curves of open-market yields—reveal no such pattern. Table 33–2 shows the range of short-term and term rates charged upon loans obtained by borrowers of different size classifications in the period from July 1 to the survey dates of the two years (October 5 and October 16, respectively). One notices that,

---

[4] *Financing Small Business*, p. 382.
[5] *Federal Reserve Bulletin*, April, 1959, p. 357.

TABLE 33–2
Interest Rates on Member-Bank Loans to Business, by Size of Borrower and Maturity of Loan, 1955 and 1957
(Average rates on loans made between July 1 and survey date; per cent per annum)

SIZE OF BORROWER (TOTAL ASSETS IN THOUSANDS OF DOLLARS)	1955			1957		
	1 Year or Less	1 to 5 Years	Over 5 Years	1 Year or Less	1 to 5 Years	Over 5 Years
Less than 50..........	5.5	7.9	5.2	6.1	8.7	5.8
50 to 250.............	5.0	6.2	5.0	5.6	7.1	5.6
250 to 1,000..........	4.6	5.2	4.8	5.4	6.0	5.4
1,000 to 5,000.........	4.1	4.6	4.3	5.1	5.7	5.1
5,000 to 25,000........	3.7	3.9	4.1	4.8	4.9	4.8
25,000 to 100,000......	3.4	3.9	3.6	4.6	4.6	4.3
100,000 and over......	3.2	3.2	3.6	4.4	4.4	3.9
All borrowers[a].....	4.2	4.9	4.1	5.0	5.7	4.7

[a] Includes a small amount of loans to borrowers whose size was not ascertained.

SOURCE: *Financing Small Business: Report to the Committees on Banking and Currency and the Select Committees on Small Business by the Federal Reserve System* (85th Cong., 2d sess.), Parts 1 and 2 (Washington, D.C.: U.S. Government Printing Office, 1958), p. 388.

for the smaller borrowers, intermediate-term rates were generally materially larger than the short-term rates, but that long-term rates were generally considerably below the intermediate rates, and, for the smallest borrowers, even below the short-term rates. The most probable explanation for the peculiarity of this pattern is that the intermediate-term rates must have been weighted heavily upward by the charging of interest for the full period of equipment-purchase loans even though repayable in instalments,[6] whereas the long-term rates must have been weighted downward somewhat because of the prevalence of real estate security upon the longer-term loans.

The figures of the table reveal quite clearly that, for all maturities,

----

[6] In granting equipment loans, it is a common practice for banks and other lenders to include in the face amount of the borrowers' notes interest for the full periods of the loans. If the borrower then repays this augmented face amount in equal periodical instalments, the effective rate of interest amounts to approximately double the nominal or quoted rate. In other words, he pays interest upon the full amount of the loan for the full period to maturity even though he is periodically reducing the principal by his instalment payments. A popular formula for estimating effective rates in such instalment payment arrangements is the following:

$$i = \frac{2pc}{n+1},$$

where i is the effective rate of interest per annum, p is the number of instalment payments in one year, c is the interest charge as a percentage of the principal of the loan, and n is the total number of instalment payments to be made. For illustration, let us assume that a corporation borrows $10,000 to buy equipment. The nominal rate of interest is 5 per cent, the term of the loan is three years, and the corporation is to repay in equal quarterly instalments within that period. It signs a note for $11,500 (the principal plus interest at 5 per cent for each of the three years or a total of 15 per cent), and each of its instalment payments will therefore amount to $958.33. Substituting in the formula and solving:

$$i = \frac{2 \times 4 \times .15}{12 + 1} = \frac{1.20}{13} = 9.23\%.$$

larger enterprises borrow at rates substantially below those charged the smaller enterprises. But such a revelation is hardly surprising. Somewhat surprising, however, is the disclosure that, in the two years of the surveys, the length of maturity seemed to have no important influence upon the rates paid by the larger borrowers.

Security for Term Loans

Security is provided by borrowers of term loans much more frequently than by short-term borrowers; in the member-bank loan survey of 1957, the proportions were found to be 44 per cent of the amount of short-term business loans and over 60 per cent of the amount of term loans. Nevertheless, as in short-term lending, small borrowers are more often required to provide security on term loans than are the larger ones. For maturities of more than five years, for example, it was found that virtually every loan to borrowers having less than $1 million of assets was secured, while only two thirds of the number and one third of the amount of such loans to larger borrowers were secured.[7]

The mortgaging of real estate is the predominant means of providing security for term loans, especially those with maturities of more than five years. Loans for the purchase or construction of real property are almost always secured by mortgages on the property itself; but, quite often, real property is pledged even when the proceeds of loans are to be used for the acquisition of equipment, for working capital, or for other purposes. For many borrowers, real property is the most valuable asset and, as it were, the most convenient one available for pledge purposes.

Because a great number of term loans are granted for buying and installing equipment, it is understandable that equipment constitutes the second most important kind of asset put up as security for term loans. Equipment is pledged by the use of instruments such as chattel mortgages.

As for other kinds of assets pledged for the safety of term loans, stocks and bonds are of some prominence. But, as was pointed out in the preceding chapter in the discussion of security for commercial bank short-term loans, stocks and bonds are much more likely to be pledged by proprietors and members of partnerships than by corporations. Stocks and bonds held by corporations in subsidiaries may, indeed, be pledged; but the typical corporation, if it held stocks and bonds in unrelated companies simply for investment returns, would sell these to raise money rather than borrow and pledge them.

Term-Loan Agreements

While many term loans are granted upon terms and conditions hardly more elaborately set out than for typical short-term loans, a great num-

---

[7] *Financing Small Business*, p. 384.

ber are governed by the provisions of comprehensive "term-loan agreements" which the borrowers sign. In content, a term-loan agreement resembles a bond indenture, although rarely is it as long and detailed. Term-loan agreements tend to be somewhat more restrictive upon the borrowers' discretion in adopting financial policies than are indentures. On the other hand, no trustee is needed, since the lending bank expects to be able to "police" the borrower and thus look after its own interests.

As signed by a corporate borrower, a term-loan agreement, in the first place, establishes all the features of the loan—the amount, the interest rate, a description of the property pledged, if any, and repayment obligations, as the timing and amount of instalment payments to be made. Almost always there is provision for the "acceleration" of the maturity of the whole obligation, at the discretion of the lending bank, should terms of the agreement be violated by the borrower. In addition, there are "warranties" of the corporate officers who sign for the corporation stating their authority to act in its behalf, assuring the lending bank that the loan is not precluded by any provisions of the corporation's charter or bylaws, and giving assurance, likewise, that financial statements submitted and to be submitted are and will be accurate and complete.

As indicated, the typical term-loan agreement contains various restrictions upon the borrower's financial policy. Consent of the lender must be obtained for borrowing from other sources, pledging the corporation's properties for any purpose, and guaranteeing the obligations of other enterprises or individuals. Usually there are requirements that working capital be not reduced below a stipulated level or that a given working capital ratio be maintained. Usually, too, there are limitations upon the payment of cash dividends, increases in officers' salaries, and the payment of bonuses to them, as well as limitations or absolute prohibitions upon the purchase of treasury stock and the retirement of preferred stock. Fixed assets may ordinarily be sold only with the consent of the lending bank; moreover, the bank is usually privileged to require that the proceeds of such sales be used to pay down the amount of the loan (usually to be applied to the most remote instalments first).

The typical term-loan agreement contains a list of additional "covenants" closely comparable with those contained in bond indentures: that the borrower will pay all its taxes promptly, keep its properties in a good state of repair, provide for adequate insurance protection, maintain adequate accounting records, give the lender access to these records for purposes of verification, and supply financial statements to the lender at stipulated intervals.

MORTGAGE LOANS OF LIFE INSURANCE COMPANIES

As we saw in Chapter 29, life insurance companies are of outstanding importance as buyers of corporation bonds, chiefly by private placements. But these financial institutions are also of major importance as grantors of long-term loans to business borrowers without the formalities of bond issues. Smaller enterprises, in particular, find it highly convenient to be able to borrow without having to work up all the details and to incur the expenses of bond issues. Of total mortgage loans of $46,902 million held by life insurance companies at the end of 1962, more than one third were reported as loans on business properties and apartment developments.[8]

Purposes of Loans

The great majority of loans by life insurance companies to business enterprises are mortgage loans. The reason for this is that most of the loans of this majority are for the purchase of land and for the purchase and construction of buildings. In a special survey of the business loans of 67 life companies (having in total about three fourths of the assets of all life companies) in 1956, the Life Insurance Association of America found that over two fifths of the number of mortgage loans authorized in that year were loans upon retail trade properties, about one seventh on office buildings, and about one ninth on manufacturing plants. Loans on office buildings were substantially larger on the average than those upon retail trade properties and manufacturing plants.[9]

Mortgage loans granted by insurance companies upon manufacturing plants usually go to the enterprises that occupy and use these plants. On the other hand, most of the loans for which office buildings are pledged are granted to investors who plan to rent out space in the buildings. In between are the mortgage loans granted upon retail trade properties: the Federal Reserve authorities, on the basis of interviews, estimate that about half of these loans go to investors and the other half to those occupying and using the properties.[10] Although loans to investors in real estate are not of direct concern to us in our study of corporate financial management, it is to be remembered that the leasing of fixed facilities enables corporations and other business enterprises to "economize" in their investment in assets—in their need of cash. Thus, in lending to real estate investors for the purchase and construction of office buildings and retail trade properties, as in the "shopping centers" that have mushroomed in recent years in many suburban sections of the country, the insurance companies expand opportunities for business enterprises to "economize" in their asset requirements.

The life insurance companies often grant loans for the acquisition of machinery and equipment—chiefly the heavier varieties—as well as, sometimes, for the purchase of inventories and for other working capital purposes. As a rule, however, they still demand real estate mortgages as security for these loans.

---

[8] Institute of Life Insurance, *Life Insurance Fact Book*, 1963, p. 66.

[9] *Financing Small Business*, p. 514.

[10] *Ibid.*, p. 517.

Terms and Conditions

Life insurance companies are basically interested in long-term invest-ment. Because their liabilities are predominantly long term—building up over the years as long, so to say, as the people they insure survive—they like to find outlets for their investment funds that will "stay put" for lengthy periods. While the typical commercial bank hesitates to go beyond ten years in term lending, the typical insurance company is in-clined to think of maturities of less than ten years as much too short. Their mortgage loans to business, accordingly, generally run from 15 to 25 years and sometimes as long as 30 years. But while desiring long-term investment, the insurance companies want to be reasonably sure of payment; hence, their mortgage loan contracts with business bor-rowers usually call for instalment repayment, the instalments most com-monly being made due at semiannual or annual intervals.

Interest rates charged by life insurance companies on mortgage loans to business borrowers tend to run somewhat higher than the interest rates they earn on corporation bonds bought by private placement. Nevertheless, the differentials between their advances of the two types are not wide (sometimes, indeed, running in the opposite direction), as is indicated by interest rate data for 1955 and 1956 compiled by the Life Insurance Association of America and presented in Table 33–3. As

TABLE 33–3
Interest Rates on Bond and Mortgage Advances Made by Life Insurance Companies to Business in 1955 and 1956
(Per cent per annum)

AMOUNT OF ADVANCE (IN THOUSANDS OF DOLLARS)	1955		1956	
	Bonds	Mortgages	Bonds	Mortgages
Under 25..................	} 4.09	5.11	} 5.53	5.29
25 to 50...................		4.88		5.10
50 to 100..................	4.72	4.75	4.99	5.00
100 to 250.................	4.63	4.67	5.27	4.92
250 to 1,000...............	4.67	4.62	5.04	4.88
1,000 to 5,000.............	4.34	4.56	4.77	4.87
5,000 to 10,000............	4.20	4.47	4.55	4.72
10,000 and over............	3.95	4.68	4.36	4.68

SOURCE: *Financing Small Business: Report to the Committees on Banking and Currency and the Select Committees on Small Business by the Federal Reserve System* (85th Cong., 2d sess.), Parts 1 and 2 (Wash-ington, D.C.: U.S. Government Printing Office, 1958), p. 519.

one would expect, the data also reveal differentials in favor of the larger mortgage loans—accounted for chiefly by the lower relative costs of administering the larger loans as well as by the fact that the larger bor-rowers generally have better credit standings than have the smaller ones. However, the differentials appear to be quite moderate.

Lending Facilities

Applications for mortgage loans are customarily accepted by life insurance companies at their head offices and at branch offices. The latter are scattered throughout the country or in various states or regions, depending upon the individual company's geographical expansion. Some companies, such as the Prudential, depend heavily upon their own personnel to find and promote lending opportunities; but most prefer to rely mainly upon "correspondents" to find good mortgage outlets for their funds.

Commercial banks, mutual savings banks, and other classes of financial institutions that are themselves mortgage lenders often serve as correspondents by referring to given insurance companies applications for mortgage loans that they do not want for their own portfolios. But the principal correspondents of the life insurance companies are the individuals, partnerships, and corporations that specialize in the origination and supervision of mortgage loans known as "mortgage bankers." Essentially, the mortgage bankers are middlemen: their very function is to find good loans to be passed on to life insurance companies and other long-term investors. They may grant some loans on their own, but, even when they do, they usually expect to carry the loans only temporarily; in most instances, they will have commitments from life insurance companies and other investors to take these loans off their hands in a few months or in a year or two. A second function of the mortgage bankers is to "service" the loans passed on. In working with a life insurance company, a mortgage banker will agree to collect interest and principal upon the loans he has "originated," at the same time seeing that the borrowers pay their taxes promptly, have their properties adequately insured, keep them in good repair, and so on. The mortgage bankers receive commissions both for originating loans and for servicing them after they have been taken over by the life insurance companies. Since, indeed, the servicing of loans produces annual commissions continuing for many years, whereas the origination of a given loan occurs but once, the mortgage bankers find their servicing function especially profitable.

EQUIPMENT FINANCING BY SELLERS

If it is reasonable for dealers in automobiles and other consumer durable goods to sell on contracts providing for instalment payments over periods of two or three years or more, selling on such a basis would appear to be all the more reasonable for sellers of machinery and other equipment to be used by manufacturers, wholesalers, retailers, and service establishments. Whereas consumer durable goods are not sources of income to the buyers, machinery and equipment sold to businesses are expected to serve very importantly as producers of income, so that the instalment buyers of such productive facilities should be all the more able to meet their instalment obligations.

Many kinds of machinery and equipment are, indeed, available for purchase by business concerns on a deferred-payment basis, and much use is made of this means of financing fixed asset acquisitions. Credit granted by sellers of equipment might be regarded as a kind of trade credit, but trade credit, as we saw in Chapter 31, is regarded as essentially short term in character. Equipment credit, on the other hand, is almost always of intermediate term.

Scope of Equipment Financing

Most equipment credit originates in direct sales of machinery and other operating facilities to the ultimate business users; hence, manufacturers of the equipment are the chief suppliers of the credit. To accelerate sales, and especially to "push" their products competitively, manufacturers often allow liberal periods of payment. Distributors of and dealers in industrial equipment also often provide intermediate-term credit to their business customers, as, for example, dealers in automobiles, in providing credit to taxicab and other transportation companies; dealers in refrigeration equipment, for installations in hotels, restaurants, and grocery stores; and dealers in many lines of store and office equipment. The manufacturers of equipment of these kinds often extend credit to the dealers and distributors, but these extensions of credit are generally of short term. The dealers and distributors are expected to have relatively rapid turnovers; it is, therefore, the ultimate buyer who wants a longer time for payment.

In numerous instances, too, manufacturers provide their business customers with credit to acquire facilities which they themselves do not produce. An outstanding example of this kind of financing is the assistance given by oil companies to service station operators in buying tanks, pumps, and other facilities. Other examples are the assistance given by grain companies to millers in acquiring grain storage facilities and that given by dairies to grocery stores to acquire dairy product refrigeration equipment.

Terms in Equipment Financing

The business enterprise that buys equipment on the instalment plan is usually required to make a down payment ranging from 20 to 33⅓ per cent of the cost of the equipment. Interest at 5 or 6 per cent per annum is then added to the balance of the purchase price, and the balance as thus augmented is apportioned over the credit period. If, in a given transaction, the balance after the down payment amounted to $20,000, the interest rate, 5 per cent, and the credit period, three years, the debtor would have a total obligation of $23,000. Assuming a provision for monthly instalments, his payments would be approximately $640. (Since the monthly payments would be constantly reducing the principal of the obligation, while the interest had been computed on the entire amount of the principal for the full period of three years, the effective rate of interest, it should be noted, would be close to 10 per cent a year.[11]) Monthly instalments are usually provided for, and the credit period customarily does not exceed three years except for sales of heavy industrial machinery for which it may be as long as five years or even longer.

The seller usually retains title to, or obtains a lien upon, equipment sold on the instalment plan. The buyer may sign a conditional sales contract with the title retained by the seller until final payment is made, or the title may go to the buyer with the seller getting a lien by means of a chattel mortgage.

Sellers' Position in Equipment Financing

In selling equipment on the instalment plan to business customers, some manufacturing companies hold the buyers' contracts to maturity. Strongly financed themselves, they have ample funds not only to carry inventories and meet current operating expenses, but also, as it were, to invest heavily in intermediate-term receivables. In this way, they gain the profits of both manufacturing and financing—the latter by earning the interest charged on their customers' instalment contracts. In quite a few instances, manufacturing companies want to enjoy the profits of instalment financing but prefer to separate their manufacturing and customer-financing operations; accordingly, they establish subsidiaries to buy and hold their customers' contracts. Thus, we find in operation the General Electric Credit Corporation, the Westinghouse Credit Corporation, the Allis-Chalmers Credit Corporation, the International Harvester Credit Corporation, and many others. Still other manufacturers, not so well heeled and preferring, therefore, to "get their money out of" customers' contracts at once, sell them to commercial finance companies or to the commercial finance subsidiaries or divisions of sales finance companies.

Unlike manufacturers, equipment distributors and dealers rarely carry the "paper" of customers who buy on the instalment plan. They establish continuing relationships with commercial finance and sales finance companies, turning over to them the instalment contracts as soon as signed by their customers.

LOANS OF THE SMALL BUSINESS ADMINISTRATION

If smaller corporations and other "small" business enterprises are unable to obtain adequate intermediate-term loans on "reasonable" terms from commercial banks and other private lending institutions, they may be able to obtain them from the Small Business Administration (SBA). This agency of the federal government was set up in 1953 precisely for the purpose of promoting the interests of small businesses. The SBA's

---

[11] See footnote 6 on page 812.

functions include lending, assisting small enterprises to get a fair share of government procurement contracts, and helping them to solve managerial problems. In addition, the SBA is authorized to grant loans to businesses and homeowners for rehabilitation following storms, floods, and other natural disasters and to businesses in areas declared by the President or the Secretary of Agriculture to be "disaster areas" on account of drouths.

Qualifications for SBA Business Loans

To qualify for an SBA business loan (other than a "disaster loan") a firm must be "small" according to the criteria established in the legislation. This means that, as a rule, it must have not more than 250 employees, if a manufacturing concern; less than $5 million of annual sales, if a wholesaler; and less than $1 million of annual sales, if a retailer or a service establishment. Other criteria of smallness are set up for other lines of business, as for construction and transportation companies. However, the SBA is permitted to make exceptions in applying these criteria. In manufacturing, for example, firms having more than 1,000 employees are definitely classified as large, but those having between 250 and 1,000 employees may be designated small or large depending upon the type of manufacturing activity.

Besides qualifying as to its smallness, a business firm that applies for an SBA loan must be able to show that it has made reasonable efforts to obtain loans from private sources and that the private lenders have turned down its application or have agreed to lend only on terms regarded by it as unduly onerous.

A third qualification for borrowing for business purposes from the SBA is that the applying firm must be able to provide adequate collateral for its loan. Although the law says that the loans of the SBA "shall be of sound value or so secured as reasonably to assure payment," and although this prescription would permit unsecured loans to borrowers of good credit standing, the SBA has consistently insisted upon pledges of assets for security. Many loan requests have been rejected because the applicants could not provide what the SBA would regard as adequate security.

Scope of the SBA's Lending Authority

For the individual borrower, loans of the SBA for business purposes are limited to $350,000 and to maturities of not more than ten years. Although the maturity stipulation permits short-term loans, only a few of the SBA's advances have had maturities of one year or less. The most common maturity appears to be five years, but a goodly proportion of the loans have maturities over five years with a significant concentration at the maximum maturity of ten years. A much smaller proportion have maturities of less than five years, chiefly in the range between three and five years.

The SBA's total lending capacity for ordinary business purposes and for reason of "disasters" is limited to $1,325 million. This sum serves as a "revolving fund" in the sense that, as loans are repaid, new loans up to the maximum may be granted.

Lending Procedures and Terms

Unlike its predecessor, the Reconstruction Finance Corporation, the SBA has not been an enthusiastic lender. In the early period of its operations, it was widely criticized as being extremely restrictive in its loan policies. Although it has "opened up" somewhat since then, it continues to be quite cautious in approving loans. It recently described its procedure as follows:

> In counseling a businessman, SBA financial specialists first pinpoint his problems, then recommend possible solutions. Often, problems are resolved without need of borrowing. However, if borrowing appears to be the answer, SBA helps the businessman seek financing from private lending institutions. When necessary, SBA will consider participating in a loan with private sources. If none of the needed funds can be obtained from private sources, SBA will consider making a direct Government loan to the small business.
> The agency's program of financial assistance is designated to supplement the lending activities of commercial banks, not compete with them. Therefore, SBA always strives for bank participation, and one of its principal objectives is increased cooperation with banks in meeting the term-credit needs of small business.[12]

Even when the SBA decides that applicants are deserving of its financial aid on the grounds both of creditworthiness and inability to obtain adequate funds on reasonable terms from private sources, it prefers to have commercial banks and other private lenders participate in granting the loans—to take responsibility for some portion of each loan, but not less than 10 per cent. It prefers what are called "deferred participations." By this arrangement, the private lender grants the entire amount of the loan originally, but the SBA stands ready to take off its hands the portion that represents its own commitment should the borrower default. For example, an SBA deferred participation commitment of 75 per cent on a $10,000 loan would mean that the private lender, upon the borrower's default, could demand $7,500 from the SBA, remaining, therefore, as the lender of only the balance of $2,500, but having the full risk of nonpayment of this amount.[13] When the SBA cannot get private lenders to agree to deferred participations, it asks them for immediate participations by which it and they at once advance funds to borrowers according to

---

[12] Small Business Administration, *Annual Report*, 1962, p. 16.

[13] On deferred participations arranged for before July 1, 1963, the SBA is committed to take over its portion of loans whenever the participating private lenders so request; but, beginning with that date, defaults of borrowers were made a condition for such take-overs. To soften the effects of this change in policy, however, the SBA agreed to make "liquidity advances" to participating private lenders for not more than 90 days in any year at a rate of interest of 4½ per cent. Such advances are really loans to help the private institutions to take care of peak-season loan demands of their regular customers.

their respective commitments. In terms of the illustration just given, the SBA would immediately advance $7,500 of the $10,000 loan, and the private lender the remaining $2,500. For immediate participations, as for deferred ones, private lenders must be willing to take responsibility for at least 10 per cent of the amount of each loan—in other words, the SBA's own participation never goes beyond 90 per cent. If, however, the private lender is willing to take a participation of at least 50 per cent of a loan for at least half of the period that it is to be outstanding, the SBA is willing to give it priority in repayment. By this arrangement, as adopted in 1962, the earlier instalment payments of the borrower go to the private lender until it is fully paid off, so that the SBA depends upon the later instalments for the repayment of its own participation.

The final alternative open to the SBA—and the least desirable one from the standpoint of its general policy—is to grant loans without the cooperation of commercial banks and other private lenders. Upon such "direct loans," it advances all the funds, has the sole responsibility for supervision, and absorbs all losses on defaults.

On its direct loans and on its advances in participation with private lending institutions, the SBA charges interest at a uniform rate of 5½ per cent per annum. However, the private institutions are permitted to charge higher rates on their portions of the participation loans.

Volume of Operations

The SBA reports that in the whole period of its operations to the end of 1962, it approved 35,072 business loans (aside from "disaster loans") for a total of $1,737 million, and that its operations reached their highest level in 1961 with 13,680 applications received and 6,836 approved for total advances of $369.4 million.[14] Details of its operations in the period 1960–62 are presented in Table 33–4.

TABLE 33–4
Loans Approved by the SBA, 1960–62
(Dollar amounts in millions)

TYPE OF LOAN	1960		1961		1962	
	Number	Amount	Number	Amount	Number	Amount
Direct....................	1,530	$ 59.6	2,733	$110.5	2,043	$ 72.0
Immediate participation....	2,144	122.6	3,553	231.8	3,283	208.8
Deferred participation......	338	13.0	550	27.1	627	35.2
Total................	4,012	$195.2	6,836	$369.4	5,953	$316.0

SOURCE: Small Business Administration, *Annual Report*, 1962, p. 18.

Questions

1. How does the volume of term lending by commercial banks compare with the volume of their short-term business lending?

---

[14] *Ibid.*, pp. 16, 18.

2. For what kinds of operations do business firms generally prefer bank term loans to short-term advances?

3. What kinds of "participations" do banks sometimes arrange when requested to grant term loans of very large amounts?

4. What is the usual range of the maturities of term loans? What requirements are there, if any, for instalment repayment? What is a "balloon" payment? Why is such a payment provided for?

5. How do the rates of interest charged on term loans compare with rates charged on short-term business loans?

6. What is the distinction between nominal and effective rates of interest as charged on term loans? How is it possible for these two kinds of rates to differ as they apply to a given loan?

7. Give several examples of "protective provisions" for lending banks contained in term-loan agreements.

8. For what purposes do life insurance companies grant mortgage loans to business firms? For what maturities? On what basis of repayment?

9. What is the function of firms such as the General Electric Credit Company and the International Harvester Credit Company?

10. What role is played by commercial finance companies in "equipment financing"? How are instalment contracts used in financing of this kind?

11. What qualifications must business firms have to borrow from the Small Business Administration? For what purpose does the SBA grant loans? For what maturities?

12. How does the SBA "participate" with private financial institutions in granting loans on an immediate basis? on a deferred basis? Who bears the loss upon defaults of participation loans?

Problem

In each of the following instances, using the formula of footnote 6 on page 812, determine what effective rate of interest the buyer would be paying for the financing of equipment purchases on an instalment basis. Assume in all cases that interest at the nominal rate for the full period of financing is added to the original unpaid balance. In (a), for example, interest at 22½ per cent is to be added to the original balance of $50,000, and this sum is then to be paid off in 20 equal quarterly instalments.

	Original Balance	Period of Financing	Nominal Rate of Interest	Timing of Payments
a)	$ 50,000	5 years	4½	Quarterly
b)	80,000	4 years	5	Quarterly
c)	80,000	4 years	5	Monthly
d)	100,000	3 years	6	Monthly
e)	100,000	3 years	6	Semiannually

INDEX

INDEX

This book has been set on the Linotype in 10 point Janson, leaded 2 points, and 9 point Janson, leaded 1 point. Part and chapter numbers and titles are in Futura Demibold. The size of the type page is 27 by 47 picas.